HANDBOOKS

Y0-CAW-060

BRAZIL

MICHAEL SOMMERS

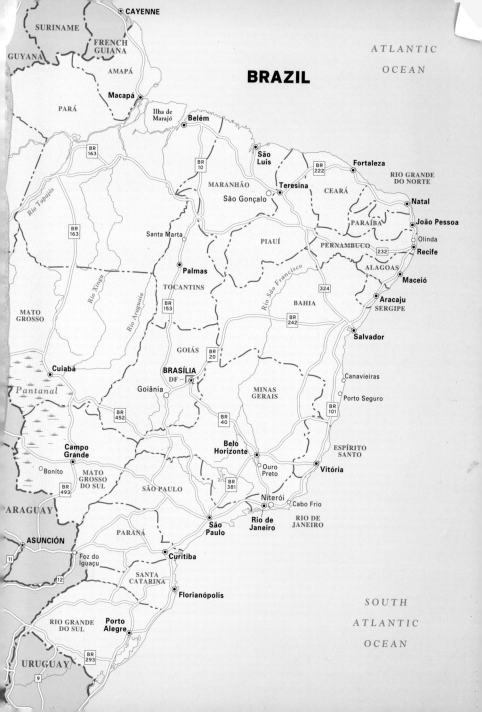

Contents

▶ **Discover Brazil** **6**
Planning Your Trip 8
Explore Brazil. 13
· The 21-Day Best of Brazil 13
· Best Beaches 14
· Carnaval and Other *Festas*. 17
· *Cidades Maravilhosas:*
   The Best of Rio de Janeiro
   and São Paulo 19
· *Feijoada, Churrasco,*
   and *Cachaça:* A Regional
   Food and Drink Tour 21
· Two Weeks Along the Amazon . . 23

▶ **Rio de Janeiro** **25**
Rio de Janeiro City 29
Vicinity of Rio de Janeiro City . . . 91
Inland from Rio de Janeiro City . . 93
Costa do Sol 101
Costa Verde 108

▶ **São Paulo** **118**
São Paulo City 121
Vicinity of São Paulo City 164
Serra da Mantiqueira 166
Serra do Mar. 170
Litoral Norte. 175

▶ **The South** **186**
Paraná. 190
Santa Catarina. 211
Rio Grande do Sul 231

▶ **Minas Gerais** **245**
Belo Horizonte. 249
Sabará. 265
Ouro Preto 267
Mariana. 277
Congonhas 279
São João del Rei 281
Tiradentes 287
Diamantina. 293

▶ **Bahia** **300**
Salvador 305
North of Salvador 345
The Recôncavo 351
Chapada Diamantina 355
The Southern Coast 362

▶ **Brasília and the Pantanal** . . . **386**
Brasília 392
Goiás 409
The Pantanal 417

▶ **Pernambuco and Alagoas... 441**
  Pernambuco.................. 445
  Alagoas..................... 477

▶ **The Northeast Coast....... 495**
  Natal and Rio Grande do Norte .. 500
  Fortaleza and Ceará........... 515
  Maranhão.................... 533

▶ **The Amazon................ 547**
  Pará........................ 554
  Amazonas................... 583

▶ **Background................ 604**
  The Land.................... 604
  Flora and Fauna.............. 609
  History..................... 613
  Government................. 624
  Economy.................... 626
  People and Culture........... 628
  Art and Architecture......... 633

▶ **Essentials 643**
  Getting There................ 643
  Getting Around 645
  Visas and Officialdom 647
  Sports and Recreation........ 649
  Accommodations 652
  Food....................... 654
  Conduct and Customs 662
  Tips for Travelers 663
  Health and Safety 666
  Information and Services 671

▶ **Resources 677**
  Glossary 677
  Portuguese Phrasebook 680
  Suggested Reading........... 688
  Internet Resources.......... 690

▶ **Index....................... 692**

▶ **List of Maps 716**

Discover **Brazil**

When most people hear the word Brazil, they immediately envision themselves lying on a white-sand beach lapped by warm turquoise waters, while sipping a lime *caipirinha*. Indeed, Brazil's 7,400 kilometers (4,600 miles) of stunningly varied coastline are sheer bliss for surfers and divers, not to mention dog paddlers and sun worshippers. Yet, Brazil is also home to the desert-like Sertão, lush coastal mountainscapes, the dense Amazon rainforest, and the Pantanal, a wetland ecosystem teeming with exotic flora and fauna.

Just as varied as the country's geography are Brazilians themselves. While the rest of South America was conquered by Spain, Brazil was colonized by Portugal, which explains the adoption of Portuguese as the national language as well as a predilection for grandiose baroque architecture and *bolinhos de bacalhau* (crunchy codfish balls). However, in northern Brazil, more than 20 percent of the Amazon is controlled by the region's indigenous peoples. And in Bahia's picturesque capital of Salvador, 85 percent of the population is of African descent, and numerous festivals are linked to the Afro-Brazilian Candomblé religion. Meanwhile, in São Paulo, large Italian, Japanese, and Lebanese immigrant communities mean that pizza, sushi, and *kibes* are as commonplace as *feijoada,* the succulent national stew of beans flavored with salted beef and pork.

In Brazil the past and the future are constantly colliding. The gleaming modernist capital of Brasília coexists with the spectacular 12,000-year-old cave paintings in the hills surrounding the Amazonian river town of Monte Alegre. And there's no escaping the glaring discrepancies between rich and poor. Just climb to the lush summits of Corcovado and gaze down at the luxury condos squeezed between beautiful beaches and Rio's sprawling slums.

Despite difficult economic and social circumstances, Brazilians are champions at the art of enjoying themselves. The Carnaval festival is merely one example. *Festas* (festivals) abound in Brazil and are almost always accompanied by the pulsating beat of samba, *forró, chorinho,* and *maracatu.*

Rivaling Brazil's musical richness is the contagious *alegria* (joyfulness) of its inhabitants. You'll be hard-pressed to find a people that exhibit the good humor and warmth of Brazilians. Life flows to a different rhythm here and the *alegria* you'll find will leave you wanting more.

Planning Your Trip

▶ WHERE TO GO

Rio de Janeiro

Squeezed between lush mountains and the Atlantic Ocean, Rio de Janeiro is one of the world's most visually stunning cities. Historically and culturally rich, its iconic sights include Pão de Açúcar, Corcovado, and the beaches of Copacabana and Ipanema. Its glorious architecture and terrific museums are complemented by a relaxing vibe and infamous nightlife. The small state of Rio de Janeiro has numerous getaways from the urban bustle, ranging from cool mountain retreats and virgin Atlantic rainforests to beautiful sandy beaches.

São Paulo

The city of São Paulo, Brazil's economic and cultural powerhouse, is often overlooked by foreign tourists, but this mega-metropolis offers a wealth of artistic, gastronomic, nightlife, and shopping options. Its electric hustle-bustle can be felt on the main drag of Avenida Paulista, but urban oases, such as Parque do Ibirapuera, also abound. The interior of São Paulo state possesses Alpine-style resorts and unspoiled swaths of forest. The Litoral Norte features a string of trendy beach resort towns whose gorgeous sands are framed by mountains.

The South

Known as O Sul (The South), the trio of narrow states running south from São Paulo is very different from the rest of Brazil. The area was settled largely by 19th-century immigrants from Germany, Poland, Ukraine, and

Avenida Paulista with Museu de Arte de São Paulo in the foreground, São Paulo

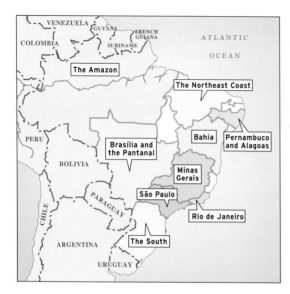

Minas Gerais

Despite important mining and metal industries and the sophisticated capital of Belo Horizonte, this inland state has a rural character enhanced by its rugged mountains, robust cuisine, and bracing *cachaças*. Minas Gerais is also steeped in history: You'll find extravagant baroque churches lined with pure gold, along with 17th-century colonial mining towns such as Ouro Preto, Mariana, São João del Rei, Tiradentes, and Diamantina. Collectively known as the *cidades históricas,* each one has its own flavor, but all showcase splendid Brazilian colonial architecture.

Italy, and European influence remains strong. Compelling natural attractions include the rugged beaches of Santa Catarina, the spectacular Serra Gaúcha mountain range of Rio Grande do Sul, and the breathtaking spectacle of Iguaçu Falls.

Brasília and the Pantanal

Brazil's space-age capital, Brasília, sits in a flat plateau region known as the Planalto. The city symbolically marks the heart of Brazil and offers a unique mélange of utopian modernist architecture. Brasília is the gateway to the state of Goiás, which features colonial towns and the savannah-like Cerrado riddled with waterfalls. Farther west, Mato Grosso and Mato Grosso do Sul constitute a vast Wild West region with a frontier feel. Both states share the world's largest wetlands, the Pantanal, a region teeming with wildlife.

Bahia

Salvador da Bahia was Brazil's first capital, a legacy that has left it with a splendid historical center and one of Brazil's richest and most vibrant traditional cultures. A strong African influence colors everything here, from religious celebrations and *festas* to music, dance, and cuisine. Bahia boasts Brazil's longest coastline and some of its most captivating tropical

Praia da Galheta, Florianópolis, Santa Catarina

IF YOU HAVE . . .

tuiuiús in the Pantanal

- **ONE WEEK:** Visit Rio de Janeiro and/ or Salvador in Bahia with side trips to beaches.
- **TWO WEEKS:** From Bahia, add a trip to the Chapada Diamantina, Alagoas, or Pernambuco. From Rio de Janeiro, add a trip down the coast to São Paulo, or to the *cidades históricas* of Minas Gerais.
- **THREE WEEKS:** Add a trip to the Pantanal, the Amazon, and Iguaçu Falls or the Northeast coast of Ceará and Rio Grande do Norte.
- **FOUR WEEKS:** Add a trip to Florianópolis or to São Luís and the Lençóis Maranhenses.

beaches, stretching north to Sergipe and south to Bahia's frontier with Espírito Santo. Inland, the Chapada Diamantina is a lush oasis of mountains and waterfalls, speckled with colonial diamond mining towns.

Pernambuco and Alagoas

Pernambuco's coastal capital of Recife is steeped in a vibrant local culture, while Olinda is one of Brazil's most spellbinding colonial towns, with baroque churches perched on palmy hills and a thriving artists' scene. Inland, the rich culture of the Sertão offers a feast of *forró,* sun-dried beef, and unique artisanal traditions. Heading south, the coast is lined with drop-dead gorgeous beaches. The snorkeling is superb along the coast of Alagoas, a tiny state to the south, anchored by the laid-back capital of Maceió.

The Northeast Coast

The beachscapes in this region, which extend, uninterrupted, from Rio Grande do Norte across the state of Ceará and into Maranhão, vary from Saharan dunes navigable by buggy, sandboard, or dromedary to sweeping white beaches backed by crumbling red cliffs. Bustling and touristy capital cities of Natal and Fortaleza offer rustic resorts, such as the famously secluded Jericoacoara. Maranhão provides a transition between the arid Northeast and the lush, wet Amazon. Its island capital of São Luís is a heavily atmospheric city with a striking colonial center.

The Amazon

The vast forested region bisected by the Amazon River and its thousands of tributaries is referred to as O Norte (The North). Its two largest states, Amazonas and Pará, are sparsely populated, and the river continues to be the major source of life and transportation. The rainforest is best explored from trips out of Amazonas's buzzing capital of Manaus and the town of Santarém, where you can also bask on white-sand river beaches. At the Amazon's mouth is the fascinating colonial city of Belém and the Switzerland-sized Ilha de Marajó.

Ilha de Marajó in the Amazon

▶ WHEN TO GO

Most of Brazil boasts a tropical climate, which means that you'll encounter warm temperatures year-round, particularly in the Northeast and the Amazon. Bahia, Alagoas, and Pernambuco each have rainy seasons (May–August). Wet seasons (May–December) in the Amazon and Pantanal last for six months. The South is the only region that has a real "winter," which you'd probably rather avoid unless you're in the mood for fondue and fireplaces. Summers can be sweltering, particularly in Rio and São Paulo. Ultimately, the best times to visit the Southeast and South are March–June and September–November.

The other main consideration is high-season vs. off-season. During the summer Brazilians take long holiday weekends and inevitably head to the closest beach. The biggest exodus takes place from late December through Carnaval, and there's another in July. During these times, all beaches, mountain resorts, and eco-destinations fill up. Accommodation prices can rise by up to 50 percent, and plane tickets need to be purchased in advance. Summer means heat, crowds, and higher prices, but it's also when Brazil kicks into high gear with intense party scenes and multiple *festas*. If you prefer tranquility and like your beaches and mountains remote and secluded, then plan your trip to coincide with off-season. You'll discover Brazilians in a less revved-up state, and in otherwise touristy areas, the diminished hustle and hassle can be very welcome.

▶ BEFORE YOU GO

Passports and Visas

If your country requires Brazilians to have travel visas, you will have to get a visa from the nearest Brazilian consulate before entering Brazil. To date, citizens of Canada, the United States, and Australia require visas.

Citizens of the United Kingdom (and other European Union countries) and New Zealand don't need visas, but do need a passport that is valid for six months and a return ticket. Upon arrival, you'll be given a 90-day tourist visa.

All visitors who arrive in Brazil and go

through customs will receive an entry form, which you should *not* lose. You'll need to hand it back to the Polícia Federal when leaving the country. Should you want to extend your stay, you can renew your visa, 15 days before it expires, at the visa section of the Polícia Federal headquarters in any major city. The fee for renewal is the equivalent of US$10. If you exceed the 180-day limit, you won't be deported, but you will pay a fine.

Vaccinations

The one vaccination that is required for Brazil is yellow fever. This is absolutely essential for visiting the Amazon region, but there have been isolated, yet recent, occurrences in the Pantanal, Brasília, and even Minas Gerais and Bahia. Be sure to bring an international certificate of vaccination since Brazilian authorities will sometimes ask for proof of vaccination for travelers going to and from the Amazon. If you've been in any other South American country (with the exception of Chile and Argentina) 90 days prior to coming to Brazil (as well as some African ones) you will also need proof of yellow fever vaccination. Since it takes 10 days for the vaccine to take effect, you can either have it at home or, if you're going to spend time in a big city or the coast before heading to the Amazon, you can easily get the vaccine in Brazil at any public *posto de saúde* (health clinic)—ask at any pharmacy for the nearest location—where it will be administered free of charge. Other recommended vaccines include hepatitis A, hepatitis B, typhoid, and rabies shots.

Getting There

The two main gateways are Rio de Janeiro's Tom Jobim airport and São Paulo's Guarulhos airport. From Europe, Portugal's national airline, TAP, offers flights to northeastern capitals such as Salvador, Recife, Natal, and Fortaleza (with connections in Lisbon). If you're going to Manaus, TAM and United operate direct flights from Miami that are much more convenient than flying all the way to São Paulo for a connecting flight. American is also set to begin direct flights to Salvador from Miami.

If you're planning to travel around to far-flung regions in Brazil, you should purchase a Brazil Airpass (sold by TAM), which can only be purchased abroad along with your international ticket.

Getting Around

Flying is an ideal way to get from one region to another in record time, but with the exception of the Amazon, you can also get anywhere you want to go by bus. Due to lack of passable roads, the Amazon is a region where flying is a must (unless you want to spend days on a boat). Although there are many regional *aerotaxis,* it's safest to stick to the main domestic operators.

For shorter bus trips, advance purchase isn't necessary, but for interstate travel, especially during high-season or holiday periods, it's recommended you purchase your bus ticket in advance. Although major companies sell tickets via travel agents, often your best (and only) option is to purchase them at the *rodoviária* (bus station). When purchasing a ticket, specify you want it *sem seguro* (without insurance), an added fee that bequeaths a small sum of money to your loved ones should you be involved in a fatal bus crash.

For visiting natural attractions around big cities and beach hopping, having a rental car gives you much more freedom to hit off-the-beaten-track places where buses don't go. If you do rent a car, try to avoid driving at night. An international driver's license is more widely recognized than a foreign license, but the latter is valid for up to six months.

Explore Brazil

▶ THE 21-DAY BEST OF BRAZIL

Three weeks is probably the minimum amount of time required to get a quick sampling of some of Brazil's most noteworthy attractions, landscapes, and cultures. Considering the country's sheer size and diversity, and the distances and travel time involved, this itinerary is very selective. After all, the goal is to enjoy your time, not to exhaust yourself, and many of Brazil's destinations involve some sort of relaxation. This itinerary involves lots of air travel (the most efficient but not always the cheapest way to get around the country).

Day 1

After landing in Rio de Janeiro, go straight to your hotel, dump your bags, lather up with sunscreen, and recover from the long flight with a refreshing coconut water and a nap on Copacabana or Ipanema beach. Take refuge from the noonday sun at one of the healthy per kilo restaurants in Ipanema or Leblon and maybe do some boutique browsing. In the late afternoon, taxi to Cosme Velho. Check out the Museu Internacional de Arte Naïf do Brasil and then ride up to Corcovado for a view of Guanabara Bay (Baía de Guanabara) as the city lights come on. After dinner, go bar- or club-hopping in the Zona Sul.

Day 2

Head to the Centro to visit a museum or two as well as historic sights in the area. Highlights include Cinelândia, the Museu Nacional de Belas Artes, Igreja da Ordem Terceira de São Francisco da Penitência, Confeitaria Colombo, Paço Imperial, and Centro Cultural Banco do Brasil. Have a late lunch in Centro at the Bistrô do Paço,

and then take the *bonde* (trolley) up to Santa Teresa to wander the cobblestoned streets and check out the Museu Chácara do Céu. Linger in a traditional *botequim* (neighborhood bar) or relax at your hotel before heading to Lapa to experience its famous bohemian nightlife.

Day 3

Hop an early morning bus or flight from Rio to São João del Rei in Minas Gerais. Spend the rest of the day exploring the historic center's baroque treasures, including the splendid rococo Igreja de São Francisco de Assis. In the evening, take a bus (or a cab) to neighboring Tiradentes, which is full of fine Mineiro restaurants and charming *pousadas*.

Day 4

Spend the day soaking up Tiradentes's charms, wandering its cobblestoned streets,

BEST BEACHES

Brazil boasts close to 8,000 kilometers (5,000 miles) of beautiful Atlantic beaches. Whatever your mood or budget, there is a beach to suit everyone.

BEST URBAN BEACHES

Known as a "crab culture" because 70 percent of the population lives on the coast, city life is often synonymous with beach life. These beaches are not tranquil, but they are both visually stunning and overflowing with life.

- **Copacabana and Ipanema in Rio de Janeiro**
- **Porto da Barra in Salvador in Bahia**
- **Ponta Verde in Maceió**
- **Ponta Negra in Natal**
- **Praia do Futuro in Fortaleza**

Praia da Pipa, Rio Grande do Norte

BEST ISLAND PARADISES

There is always something deliciously castaway-like about fleeing to an idyllic tropical island. The following beaches fit the bill.

- **Ilha Grande in Rio de Janeiro**
- **Ilhabela in São Paulo**
- **Ilha de Boipeba in Bahia**
- **Fernando de Noronha in Pernambuco**
- **Ilha de Marajó in Pará**

BEST PARTY BEACHES

Take ample amounts of sun, sand, and surf, shake them up with Brazilians' chronic *alegria* or joyfulness (fueled by music and *caipifrutas*), and you get the following permanently festive beach scenes.

- **Búzios in Rio de Janeiro**
- **Maresias in São Paulo**
- **Praia da Joaquina in Santa Catarina**
- **Morro de São Paulo in Bahia**
- **Praia da Pipa in Rio Grande do Norte**

HIPPEST BEACHES

Many of Brazil's hippest beaches were once tiny fishing towns until they were discovered in the 1970s by hippies in search of paradise. Over time, they've succeeded in becoming quite cosmopolitan, without having lost their laid-back groove or eco-friendly vibe. To mellow out in style head to the following beaches.

- **Praia do Rosa in Santa Catarina**
- **Trancoso in Bahia**
- **São Miguel dos Milagres in Alagoas**
- **Canoa Quebrada in Ceará**

BEST TOTAL GETAWAYS

For those fed up with civilization and who long to return to a more primitive, natural state, the following beaches (and their surroundings) are not only secluded and unspoiled, but hypnotically beautiful.

- **Lagoinha do Leste in Santa Catarina**
- **Caraíva in Bahia**
- **Praia do Carro Quebrado in Alagoas**
- **Praia dos Carneiros in Pernambuco**
- **Jericoacoara in Ceará**
- **Lençóis Maranhenses in Maranhão**
- **Alter do Chão in Pará**

Igreja de São Francisco de Assis, Ouro Preto

and exploring baroque jewels such as the Igreja Matriz de Santo Antônio. In the afternoon, return to São João del Rei in time to catch a bus bound for the most resplendent of Minas Gerais's historic gold-mining cities, Ouro Preto. After checking into a centuries-old *pousada,* such as the Pouso do Chico Rey, dine on Mineiro fare at the Casa dos Contos Restaurante and then sample the town's lively nightlife, on and around Rua Direita.

Day 5

After a lavish Mineiro breakfast at your hotel, put on serious hiking shoes and take to Ouro Preto's steep cobblestoned streets. Be prepared to overdose on sumptuous baroque churches slathered in gold leaf. Not to be missed are the Igreja Matriz de Nossa Senhora do Pilar and the Igreja de São Francisco de Assis, the masterpiece of baroque sculptor extraordinaire Aleijadinho. If you can see only one museum, make it the Museu do Oratório. In the evening, sample artisanal *cachaças* at local student bars, such as Bardobeco.

Days 6-8

Take an early morning bus to Belo Horizonte and hop a flight to either Campo Grande in Mato Grosso do Sul or Cuiabá in Mato Grosso. Both of these cities are prime gateways for discovering the Pantanal wetlands, teeming with exotic flora and fauna. From either city, travel to a *fazenda* lodge within the wetlands. Spend the next three days horseback riding, canoeing, and hiking through unspoiled landscapes in search of capybaras, giant otters, elusive jaguars, and brilliant-colored macaws.

Day 9

Return from your *fazenda* lodge to Campo Grande or Cuiabá and fly to Brasília. Spend the day marveling at Oscar Niemeyer's space-age architecture. After watching the sunset from the Torre de Televisão, welcome yourself back to civilization by splurging for dinner at one of the capital's sophisticated restaurants, such as the unusual Patú Anu. Take in a film or concert or head to a local bar, such as the classic Bar Beirute, before turning in.

Day 10

Fly to Salvador in Bahia and check into a hotel in the beach neighborhood of Barra or the colonial districts of Pelourinho or Santo Antônio. Stroll around these neighborhoods and then have drinks at a bar overlooking the sea before dinner. The Solar do Unhão, a former sugar plantation that houses the Museu de Arte Moderna, is a good choice.

Day 11

Spend the morning wandering through the steep cobblestoned streets of the Pelourinho, or "Pelô." Among this historic neighborhood's most exceptional treasures are the resplendent baroque Igreja e Convento de São Francisco and the interesting Museu Afro-Brasileiro, which offers a good overview of Bahia's Candomblé religion. After a languorous Bahian lunch in the Pelô, head to Porto da Barra to check out the beach scene. In the evening, check with the municipal tourist office to see if there are any Candomblé *festas* being held at traditional *terreiros*. Otherwise, head to Rio Vermelho to feast on *acarajés* (crunchy bean fritters) and discover the city's bohemian *bairro* (neighborhood).

Days 12-14

Treat yourself to a couple of days of relaxation on a beautiful Bahian beach. Although

Porto da Barra, Salvador, Bahia

there are hundreds of beaches to choose from, select a destination within 2–3 hours of Salvador. The easiest getaway is to hop a bus north along the Linha Verde and shack up in Praia do Forte (somewhat chic and touristy), Imbassaí (tranquil with a cosmopolitan edge), or Diogo (utterly primitive). Alternatively, you can hop a fast launch to Morro de São Paulo (party central), or a bus and boat to Boipeba (secluded) or Barra Grande (a bit of both), all of which lie south of Salvador.

Praia do Forte, Bahia

CARNAVAL AND OTHER *FESTAS*

Brazilians' fame for merrymaking is not an exaggeration. Although Carnaval is the most spectacular example, the year is filled with fantastic events, many of which mingle centuries-old religious traditions with celebrations that are distinctly profane.

REVEILLON

Fireworks, cheap champagne, and revelers clad in white wade into the sea with flowers for the Afro-Brazilian sea goddess, Iemanjá. The biggest bash is in Rio (January 1).

FESTA DO BONFIM

Bahianas lead a procession through Salvador's Cidade Baixa for the ritual washing of the steps of the Igreja do Bonfim with perfume (second Thursday in January).

CARNAVAL

Five days of throbbing music and unbridled hedonism. The biggest and most spectacular festivities are in Rio de Janeiro, Salvador, Recife, and Olinda, but many other cities, towns, and villages join in the fun (February–March).

giant *bonecos* from Olinda's Carnaval

AS CAVALHADAS

A haunting re-creation of a medieval battle between Christians and Moors is sumptuously dramatized in the colonial town of Pirenópolis in Goiás (May).

PARADA GAY

Avenida Paulista shuts down for São Paulo's Gay Pride Parade, one of the world's largest and most exuberant (May).

FESTAS JUNINAS

In the northeastern Sertão, June is devoted to bonfires, *forró* dancing, drinking fruit liqueurs, and eating delicacies made from corn in celebration of Santo Antônio, São João, and São Pedro. One of the biggest events is the Festa de São João in Caruru, Pernambuco (mid-late June).

BUMBA-MEU-BOI

In São Luís, Maranhão, splendid costumes, pounding drums, and whirling dancers characterize this popular *festa*, which combines African, Indian, and Portuguese influences to re-create the story of a strict master, a wily slave, and a prize bull (end of June).

CÍRIO DE NAZARÉ

The highlight of the Amazon's most important religious festival is the pageantry that accompanies the procession of Pará's patron saint, Nossa Senhora de Nazaré, through the streets of Belém (second weekend of October).

Day 15

Return to Salvador and fly to Manaus, capital of Amazonas. Take a tour of the extravagantly ornate Teatro Amazonas or take in a concert or dance performance there and visit the riverside market and a museum or two. If you have time, inspect the Meeting of the Waters, in which the milky brown Rio Solimões merges with the dark Rio Negro from the Rio Amazonas. Feast on local river fish, ice cream in

Ponta Negra, Manaus, Amazonas

exotic flavors, and *caboclinho* sandwiches (a vegetarian offering made with a baguette and slices of a yellow Amazonian fruit known as *tucumã*). Depending on what time you arrive, you might stay overnight in Manaus or head right into the rainforest to a jungle lodge. If you stick around, spend the evening keeping cool at a bar in Ponta Negra overlooking the Rio Negro, such as the perpetually lively Laranjinha.

Days 16-17

To experience the pristine Amazon of your dreams, you'll have to head out of Manaus and up the Rio Negro or Rio Solimões. A minimum of two nights at a jungle lodge in the heart of the forest, such as the Pousada Uacari in the midst of the Reserva Mamirauá, including all meals, guided excursions, and activities (such as piranha fishing and swimming with river dolphins), should satiate your eco-urges.

Day 18

Return from the jungle to the "civilization" of Manaus. Get on a plane to Rio de Janeiro, where you can treat yourself to a night on the town with dinner at a contemporary Zona Sul eatery, such as Carlota, followed by bar-hopping in Lapa.

Day 19

If you've fallen in love with Rio, stick around for the final days of your stay. Otherwise, hop a bus to Paraty. Check into one of the charming *pousadas* in the colonial center. After a seafood lunch at Banana da Terra spend the afternoon wandering around the town and poking into the quartet of colonial churches. Relax at your hotel, and then have a gourmet dinner at the elegant Merlin o Mago, followed by a nightcap at a breezy outside bar, such as the Margarida Café.

Day 20

After a quick stroll around town, take a bus to Trindade and spend your last full day in Brazil sprawled in the sand, munching on giant shrimp. If you're feeling active, you can take a hike through the Atlantic rainforest past the beaches of Praia Cachadaço, Praia do Sono, and Praia do Antigo. At the end of the day, return to Paraty.

Day 21

Return to Rio. If you leave early in the morning, you'll probably have time for a farewell lunch in the Centro before heading to the airport.

▶ *CIDADES MARAVILHOSAS:* THE BEST OF RIO DE JANEIRO AND SÃO PAULO

Brazil's two "marvelous cities," Rio and São Paulo, are only five hours apart by bus or car. To get from one metropolis to the other, there are two possibilities: an inland route that goes meandering through the lush mountains of the Serra do Mar and a coastal route of stunning mainland and island beaches and trendy resort towns. Why not do them both? The distances are very manageable, and a round-trip gives you the best of both worlds in two weeks or less. This flexible day-by-day itinerary offers highlights of both cities, with the rest of the time dedicated to enjoying the countryside and taking ample time out to relax as you make your way from one city to the other. The journey below is designed to be done by car. Distances are short, roads are well-maintained, and driving allows you to visit attractions off the beaten track, such as remote beaches and coffee plantations. You can also easily do this journey by bus, but you'll need to cut out some stops along the way to accommodate increased travel time.

Day 1

Since most international flights land in São Paulo, "Sampa" is a good place to begin this itinerary (although for an initial impression of Brazil, nothing beats Rio de Janeiro). After checking into your hotel, head for lunch in Centro or Jardins. Spend the afternoon poking around Centro's mishmash of architecture and monuments. Stroll around Jardins, checking out boutiques as the light fades. Jardins is a fine place for cocktails in a fashionable bar, such as Skye, with its fabulous city views, followed by dinner at D.O.M. for fantastic contemporary Brazilian cuisine.

Day 2

Take a half day to visit either Museu de Arte de São Paulo (MASP) and Avenida Paulista; the Museu Afro Brasil and/or MAM (Museu de Arte Moderna) at Parque do Ibirapuera; or the Pinacoteca do Estado and/or Museu da Língua Portuguesa at the Estação da Luz. If you really like museums, combine the two separate destinations and make a full day of it. Otherwise, take time to go browsing through hip Vila Madalena, which, along with neighboring Pinheiros, is a fun place to dine, drink, and hear live music.

Days 3-4

Pick up a rental car in the morning and drive from São Paulo to Bananal. On the way, stop for breakfast and walk around the pretty little colonial town of São José do

Pinacoteca do Estado, São Paulo

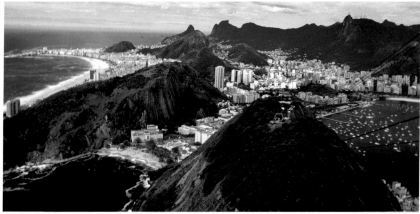

aerial view of Rio de Janeiro from Pão de Açúcar

Barreiro. Arrive in Bananal in time for a late lunch, then spend the afternoon leisurely exploring the town. Spend the night in town or at a *pousada* in a converted coffee plantation manor nearby. The next morning, visit a coffee plantation, such as Fazenda dos Coqueiros, before heading to the Recanto da Cachoeira, where you can while the rest of the day away being doused by cascades.

Day 5

Get up early and head to Rio de Janeiro. Check into a hotel and then go for lunch in the Zona Sul. Hit the beaches of Copacabana and Ipanema for some fun in the sun. Have dinner in a restaurant in Ipanema or Leblon, followed by a *chope* (draft beer) at a *botequim* (neighborhood-style bar).

Day 6

Explore the historical sights of Centro, which include Cinelândia, Paço Imperial, and the Igreja do Mosteiro de São Bento. Among the area's many museums, standouts include the Museu Nacional de Belas Artes, the Museu de Arte Moderna. and the Centro Cultural Banco do Brasil. After lunch in Centro at the Brasserie Rosário take the

bonde (trolley) up to atmospheric Santa Teresa, where you can visit the Museu Chácara do Céu. In the evening, put on your dancing shoes and visit the lively bars and dance halls of bohemian Lapa.

Day 7

Avoid the crowds and take advantage of the morning light by heading out early to Cosme Velho for a ride up to Corcovado. Drop by the Museu Internacional de Arte Naïf do Brasil and then walk down towards Botafogo to the Parque and Palácio do Catete. After lunch, head to the Jardim Botânico for a stroll beneath the imperial palms. Spend the sunset hours along the beaches of Ipanema and Leblon before dinner—try Roberta Sudbrack for inventive Brazilian fare—and a night of live music (check the daily paper *O Globo* for listings).

Day 8

Pick up a rental car and head down the Costa Verde to Angra dos Reis. Stash your car, and then take the boat across to Ilha Grande. After checking into a *pousada* in or around Vila Abraão, have lunch and explore the pretty village. If time permits, take a boat trip

FEIJOADA, CHURRASCO, AND CACHAÇA: A REGIONAL FOOD AND DRINK TOUR

tacacá, a broth with dried shrimp and *jamba* leaves from Belém in the Amazon

If Brazilian cuisine is not well known outside of Brazil, it's because – aside from the classic combo of *feijoada* and *caipirinhas* – Brazilian cooking is all about the sum of its regions. Were you to be led by your taste buds on a trip throughout Brazil, you would need to make stops in the following culinary havens.

RIO DE JANEIRO AND SÃO PAULO

Although neither Rio nor São Paulo has a distinctive cuisine of its own, like all cosmopolitan metropolises they have sophisticated dining scenes. They also serve as laboratories for a new breed of contemporary chefs who are revisiting regional traditions and ingredients in astonishingly delicious ways. At the same time, they rival each other in the preparation of Brazil's classic dish: *feijoada.*

RIO GRANDE DO SUL

While tending the cattle herds of the southern plains, the Gaúcho cowboys of Rio Grande do Sul popularized the art of **churrasco** – rubbing chunks of beef in rock salt and slow-grilling them over charcoal. While waiting for the meat to cook, they would sip **chimarão,** a pungent brew made from the *erva maté* plant. Today, both *churrasco* and *chimarão* are ubiquitous throughout Rio Grande do Sul.

MINAS GERAIS

Like its rugged landscapes, Mineiro cooking is robust and flavorful. Savory pork and chicken dishes, **tutu à mineiro** (a velvety bean puree), creamy white cheeses, and a wide range of delicious desserts made from local Cerrado fruits, not to mention the finest **cachaças** in the country, make Minas a diner's and drinker's dream. The historic cities of **Ouro Preto** and **Tiradentes** have wonderful restaurants serving regional cuisine from wood-burning stoves.

BAHIA

With its rich African legacy, Bahian food is legendary throughout Brazil, and Salvador is its culinary capital. Coconut milk, cilantro, dried shrimp, crushed cashews, hot peppers, and limes are some of the main ingredients that go into specialties such as **moqueca** (an aromatic fish and/or seafood stew cooked in palm oil and coconut milk). Many traditional dishes, such as **vatapá, caruru,** and **abará,** are associated with Candomblé rituals. **Acarajés,** crunchy bean fritters stuffed with a variety of fillings, are sold in squares and on street corners by Bahianas wearing traditional white turbans and hoop skirts.

PARÁ

Fruit from the rainforest and fish from the mighty Amazon and its tributaries characterize the cooking of Pará. The Tupi names themselves are exotic – *cupuaçu, bacuri, açai, pupunha, pirarucu,* and *tucunaré* – but wait until you see them colorfully displayed at the **Mercado Ver-o-Peso** or taste them at one of **Belém**'s excellent restaurants. Don't leave town without sampling **tacacá,** a local broth featuring dried shrimp and *jambu* leaves, or **pato no tucupi,** an aromatic duck stew.

to one of the island's most splendid beaches, Saco do Céu.

Day 9

Get up early to take the full-day boat excursion that will take you to the island's most secluded and stunning beaches. You'll visit around eight of them, with stops for swimming and snorkeling. Back in Vila Abraão, satisfy your hunger by devouring fresh seafood or fish. If you'd like to stay in one spot, hike (or take a taxi-boat) to Praia Lopes Mendes, considered the loveliest beach on the island. Swim, snorkel, and soak in the sun all day. If you're feeling more botanically inclined, take a trekking tour through the jungle instead.

Day 10

Return to Angra dos Reis and drive south to Paraty, where you'll be spending the night at one of many centuries-old *pousadas* sprinkled throughout the historic center. For lunch, Banana da Terra is a fine place to sample local fare. In the afternoon, poke around town or head to the nearby beach of Paraty-Mirim. In the evening, splurge for a gourmet dinner at Merlin o Mago.

Day 11

Spend the day exploring the beaches around Paraty. At the nearby beach of Trindade you can lie out in the sun or hike through the Atlantic rainforest to more deserted beaches, such as Praia Cachadaço, which is good for snorkeling. Paraty Tours offers half-day diving, kayaking, and schooner trips tours as well as treks into the surrounding Atlantic rainforest. At the end of the day, return to Paraty.

Day 12

Leave Paraty early, heading south. Stop for a swim at a deserted beach, such as Praia do Prumirim or Praia de Puruba. Have lunch in Ubatuba, and then continue south to Praia do Lázaro. Check into a *pousada* and then walk to the adjacent beach of Domingas

Paraty, Rio de Janeiro

Dias for a dip and some sun. Dine on seafood in Praia do Lázaro at the charming Solar das Águas Cantantes.

Day 13

Drive south past São Sebastião. Stop at Praia Toque-Toque for a quick dip. Then continue south to the beaches of Camburi and Camburizinho, where you can have lunch at one of the many fine restaurants. After dessert and coffee, soak up your final rays of sun. Depending on what time your flight leaves the next day, you could stay overnight in Camburi or Camburizinho or else return to São Paulo and spend the night in the city.

Day 14

If you spent the night on the coast, return to São Paulo in time to hand in your car and catch your flight. If you spent the night in São Paulo, you could visit a museum or go shopping in Jardins and have a leisurely farewell lunch at Brasil a Gosto before heading to the airport.

▶ TWO WEEKS ALONG THE AMAZON

Spend 14 days exploring the world's largest, most diverse, and most mysterious rainforest. Screeching birds, snapping piranhas, caimans with glow-in-the-dark eyes, and frolicking river dolphins are banalities in these parts. For bases use the jungle capital of Manaus, located at the point at which the Rio Solimões and Rio Negro form the Rio Amazonas, and Belém, a striking colonial city at the mouth of the Amazon with rich culinary and cultural traditions. Midway between both cities is Santarém, a lazy river outpost that offers an authentic taste of life along the Amazon as well as the pristine white-sand river beaches of Alter do Chão.

Day 1

Arrive in Manaus. If you're flying directly via Miami, you'll arrive in the morning and check into a hotel. If you're flying via São Paulo, you'll arrive late in the afternoon. The two major sights you'll definitely want to see are the sumptuous Teatro Amazonas and the spectacle of the Rio Negro merging with the Rio Solimões to form the mighty Amazon, known as the Meeting of the Waters. Extra time can be spent exploring the market and a museum or two near Centro. Sample local river fish and *caboclinho* sandwiches. In the evening, catch a performance at the Teatro Amazonas (if you didn't visit during the day) or taxi to a riverside bar in Ponta Negra, overlooking the Rio Negro.

Days 2-4

Leave Manaus and head up the Rio Negro or Rio Solimões to a jungle lodge, such as the Anavilhanas Jungle Lodge amid the 400 islands of the Anavilhanas Archipelago, where you can experience the unspoiled Amazon (transportation from Manaus is usually included in the rate). A minimum of two nights at a jungle lodge in the heart of the forest is an ideal Amazonian baptism. Meals, guided excursions, and most activities, such as piranha fishing and swimming with river dolphins, are included.

Day 5

Return to Manaus and fly to Santarém on the shores of Rio Tapajós. Check into a *pousada* and wander around this riverside town, watching boats come and go. Sample local fish at Peixaria Piracatú, and later on, have drinks overlooking the river at O Mascote, a popular gathering place.

Day 6

Take a day excursion from Santarém to the Floresta Nacional do Tapajós, where you can hike through the rainforest and observe rubber tappers at work.

an *igapó* (flooded rainforest) in the Amazon

Day 7

Take an early bus to Alter do Chão, known as "the Caribbean of the Amazon" because of its pristine river beaches. Check into a *pousada* and then spend the day taking canoe trips along the river.

Day 8

Spend the morning on the beach before returning to Santarém and flying to Belém. Wander around the colonial district of Cidade Velha, where you can poke into churches and rubber barons' palaces. Feast on Amazonian cuisine at one of Belém's fine restaurants, such as the reputed Lá em Casa. Afterwards, head to Estação das Docas for a nightcap and some live music.

Day 9

Begin the morning by wandering through the exotic wares at the Mercado Ver-o-Peso. Following lunch, head to the Mangal das Garças to check out exotic birds and butterflies, and the Pólo Joalheiro to see (and purchase) precious gemstones.

Day 10

Take an early boat trip along the Ilha do Papagaio to observe the island's parrots waking up. Return to Belém and make sure to visit the glorious Basílica de Nossa Senhora de Nazaré and the Museu Paraense Emílio Goeldi, a chunk of Amazonian forest that is reputed for its vast collection of Amazonian flora and fauna. If you missed the early morning boat trip, take a sunset cruise along the Rio Guamá. Don't leave town without having savored an exotic fruit ice cream at Cairu.

Days 11-13

Take a boat to Ilha de Marajó and check into a *fazenda* lodge on a working water buffalo farm. For the next two days, canoe through mangroves, sprawl on deserted beaches, and visit the pretty towns of Soure and Salvaterra. Try buffalo steaks as well as cheese and desserts made with buffalo milk.

Day 14

Return to Belém, where you can catch a flight to São Paulo or Manaus.

RIO DE JANEIRO

Rio de Janeiro is one of those rare cities—like Paris, Venice, and New York—that is so legendary you think you know it. Even if you've never been there, it's easy to hear "Rio" and automatically conjure up its postcard sights: Pão de Açúcar, the statue of Christ the Redeemer atop lush Corcovado, and the sweeping white crescent of Copacabana beach. When you do finally arrive, you receive a shock because—although you've seen them in countless films and photographs—these landmarks are even more impressive in real life. Better yet, even if you return to Rio a second, third, fourth...time—and you inevitably will—that initial shock will never wear off. After all, this is the city that Cariocas (residents of Rio) refer to proudly as the Cidade Maravilhosa (Marvelous City). As you get to know it, you will discover that they are not exaggerating.

Like many a modern tourist, Brazil's imperial family enjoyed Rio to the hilt, but when they couldn't stand the heat (40 degrees Celsius anyone?), they literally took to the hills. In fact, Emperor Pedro II went so far as to build an ornate pink summer palace (now a fascinating museum) in the mountains. Other members of the court soon followed suit, giving rise to the imperial town of Petrópolis. Only an hour away from Rio—but usually 5–10 degrees cooler—Petrópolis, Teresópolis, and other neighboring towns continue to offer refuge to vacationers who can take advantage of sophisticated amenities while surrounded by majestic scenery. When nature beckons, the national parks of Serra dos Órgãos and Itatiaia are close

© CHRISTIAN KNEPPER/EMBRATUR

HIGHLIGHTS

◖ Corcovado: Crowned by the all-embracing statue of Christ the Redeemer, "Hunchback" mountain was recently voted one of the Seven Modern Wonders of the World (page 40).

◖ Pão de Açúcar: One of Rio's most instantly recognizable icons is this monumental chunk of sugar loaf-shaped granite rising out of the Baía de Guanabara (page 43).

◖ Copacabana Beach: Urban beaches don't get any more dazzling than this gorgeous arc of sugary fine sand that is a microcosm unto itself (page 45).

◖ Ipanema and Leblon: More than just fabulous beaches, these two adjacent neighborhoods are the eternal epitome of Carioca cool, with shady streets, bars, boutiques, restaurants, and a bossa nova vibe (page 48).

◖ Carnaval: Samba the day and night away for five days at Rio's spectacularly hedonistic *festa* to end all *festas* (page 56).

◖ Floresta da Tijuca: Brazil's largest urban park, Floresta da Tijuca, is a lush green oasis of native Atlantic forest that is perfect for a refreshing getaway (page 70).

◖ Museu Imperial: The former summer residence of Dom Pedro II, located in Petrópolis, offers a glimpse into the life of an emperor in the tropics (page 94).

◖ Búzios: Brazil's version of St. Tropez is a tropical chic playground with sophisticated amenities, a celebrated nightlife, and beaches for every taste under the sun (page 104).

◖ Ilha Grande: The largest of the many islands in the Bay of Angra dos Reis, Ilha Grande is an island paradise that captures the essence and ethos of "back-to-nature" (page 109).

◖ Paraty: One of the most charming and best preserved Portuguese colonial towns in Brazil is surrounded by breathtaking mountains and idyllic beaches (page 111).

LOOK FOR ◖ TO FIND RECOMMENDED SIGHTS, ACTIVITIES, DINING, AND LODGING.

by with their orchid-laced hiking trails winding through native Atlantic forest.

Natural attractions are also in abundance along the coasts of Rio de Janeiro state. East of the city are the pulsating, upscale resort towns of Cabo Frio and Búzios, which offer beautiful sandy beaches, with calm pools for snorkeling fans and big waves for surfers. Búzios is particularly charming with its cobblestoned streets and shades of St. Tropez: It was actually a bikini-clad Brigitte Bardot who, in the '60s, put this fishing village on the map. Meanwhile, those in search of more tranquil options can head south along the Costa Verde (Green Coast), named for the verdant mountains that provide a striking backdrop to the unspoiled beaches. Highlights along this coast include Angra dos Reis, which serves as the departure point for the island paradise of Ilha Grande, and the beautifully preserved colonial town of Paraty.

PLANNING YOUR TIME

Anything less than three days in Rio is sheer absurdity. A week will give you time to explore museums and historic sights, shop, and lounge on the city's famous beaches as well as take a day trip or two to the surrounding beaches or mountains of Rio de Janeiro state.

Despite the great variety of its attractions, Rio de Janeiro state is extremely compact in size. Whether you're headed to the mountains or the sea, most sights are usually only two or three hours away. While some of these destinations (such as Petrópolis and Teresópolis) can be visited as day trips from Rio, it would be a crime to rush when faced with such intense natural beauty and such utterly relaxing environs. Two or three days reserved for the mountains surrounding Petrópolis and Itatiaia and another couple (at least) for the beautiful beaches of Búzios and Arraial do Cabo (north of Rio) or Ilha Grande and Paraty (south of Rio) will give you adequate time to unwind and explore.

Tourists visit Rio all year-long, but there are several factors to consider when planning a trip here. In summer (December to early March)

Rio sizzles—both figuratively (festivities and nightlife are at their zenith) and literally (with temperatures hovering around 40°C/104°F and lots of sticky humidity). If you can't stand the heat, make sure you have an air-conditioned hotel, or head for the (much cooler) hills. Another option is to visit in the winter (June to September), which is a lovely time. The sun is less intense and the beaches won't be quite so crowded (at least during the week). Moreover, nights are comfortably cool (around 15–20°C, 60–70°F). The cold fronts that come up from Argentina, bringing cool winds and rain that can last for two or three days, are the only thing to look out for. Rio enjoys a considerable amount of precipitation (all that lushness wouldn't exist otherwise) throughout the year. Between March and May, rains are particularly frequent, as well as in December. If you want to take part in either of Rio's most famous and fabulous festivities—Reveillon (New Year's Eve) and Carnaval—be prepared to, first of all, have deep pockets and, secondly, make flight and hotel bookings many months in advance.

HISTORY

The virgin Atlantic rainforests of Rio de Janeiro were inhabited by the Tamoio Indians when a Portuguese expedition led by navigator Gaspar de Lemos entered the picturesque Baía de Guanabara in January 1502. Thinking that the bay was the mouth of a river, Lemos baptized it Rio de Janeiro (River of January), and despite his mistake, the name stuck.

It was the colony-hungry French who originally settled the region in the 1550s. After only a decade, they were driven away the Portuguese in 1667, who took control of the region and of the Tamoio as well. Over the next century, the Tamoio were enslaved, rounded up and sent to live in Jesuit reservations, or (most frequently) killed in battle. By the 17th century, the small fortified town on the bay had become Brazil's third major settlement after the colonial capital of Salvador and the northeastern towns of Recife and Olinda. Prompted by the booming sugar-trading industry in these regions, Portuguese settlers in Rio also invested in sugarcane plantations—and in the African slaves necessary for their operation. As a result, by the 18th century, the majority of Rio's inhabitants were of African origin. Despite their servile status, they mingled somewhat freely (and intimately) with their European masters, thus creating a mixed-race society. African religious and cultural customs seeped into the fabric of daily life. They remain strongly present to this day.

In the early 1700s, Rio got a boost when gold was discovered in the neighboring state of Minas Gerais; its port subsequently became the taxation and transportation center from which all Brazil's wealth was shipped off to Europe. As a result of its growing strategic importance, the colonial capital was transferred from Salvador to Rio in 1763. But despite its growing political and economic prominence, the city remained a muddy backwater until the early 19th century.

In 1808, Napoleon Bonaparte's army invaded Portugal. Forced into flight, Portugal's king, Dom João VI, sought refuge in Rio—along with some 10,000 nobles, ministers, and royal hangers-on. The tropics agreed so well with the king and his court that even after Napoleon's defeat at Waterloo, in 1815, they were loath to go home. Consequently, the king invented the United Kingdom of Portugal, Brazil, the Algarves, and the Guinea Coast of Africa, and proclaimed Rio de Janeiro as its capital. As the seat of the empire, Rio thrived. Royal patronage favored the development of the arts and sciences. Around the court, a sophisticated and cultured Brazilian elite flourished. Befitting its new status, the city itself—at least the wealthy neighborhoods—finally got a much-needed overhaul. Grand palaces sprang up and the city's streets were paved and illuminated.

Even though the wealth from sugar and gold was dwindling—creating a large class of poor, unemployed slaves that migrated to the city's mushrooming slums—new fortunes were being made from the coffee plantations that now covered the surrounding hills.

With the arrival of the 20th century, Rio continued to grow and expand. The center acquired a splendid belle epoque makeover with elegant squares, avenues, theaters, and palaces inspired by Baron Haussman's Paris. Meanwhile, a tunnel blasted through the mountains opened up access to what would become the world-famous beach *bairros* of Copacabana, Ipanema, and Leblon. By the 1940s, aided in part by the Good Neighbor Policy propaganda of Hollywood films such as *Flying Down to Rio* and anything starring homegrown phenomenon Carmen Miranda, Rio had garnered a reputation as a tropical Paris. Its curvaceous deco nightclubs, glamorous casinos, and plush hotels (the most famous being the Copacabana Palace) lured the international jet set. Meanwhile, the old colonial Centro, with the exception of its magnificent churches, was razed and replaced by high-rise office buildings. As the city grew the lush hillsides filled up with slums known as *favelas,* where Rio's poor (mostly black) population built sprawling neighborhoods out of wood and cement blocks.

When the nation's capital moved to the newly constructed city of Brasília in 1960, Rio didn't miss a beat. Nor did it bat much of an eyelid as the nation's economic power became consolidated in São Paulo in the 1970s and '80s. And even today, in spite of increasing urban violence and the escalating drug wars that pit police against armies of traffickers, through it all, Rio manages to remain a truly marvelous city with an indomitable spirit and an irresistible beauty.

Rio de Janeiro City

Rio's setting is incomparable: The city is squeezed between the Baía de Guanabara and dramatic mountains covered in native Atlantic forest. Although this tropical metropolis of eight million is both urban and urbane, every street you walk on seems to end in an explosion of towering green or a soothing slice of blue. Swimming, surfing, hang-gliding, and hiking through the Floresta da Tijuca are some of the most obvious ways of taking advantage of Rio's natural splendors. Meanwhile, this 500-year-old city is hardly lacking in impressive architecture. Rio was not only the capital of the Brazilian Empire, but, until 1960, of its republic as well. As a result, its downtown is a treasure trove of baroque churches, imperial palaces (many of which have been converted into cultural centers), and monumental buildings and squares.

History of a more recent variety is present in the Zona Sul neighborhoods of Copacabana, Ipanema, and Leblon; all three are famed for the stunning white-sand beaches that serve as playgrounds for Cariocas and tourists from all walks of life. It was here that bossa nova was born and the bikini made its mark. Despite all the beautiful people, Zona Sul retains a relaxed casualness that is typical of Rio. Sip a fresh tropical nectar at a juice bar or enjoy an icy beer at one of many rustic bars known as *botequins,* and watch as barefoot surfer boys and bikini girls in Havaianas stroll through the streets lined with designer boutiques and art deco apartments.

While daytime in Rio is languid, nighttime sizzles with possibilities. For dinner, choose from a profusion of world-class restaurants. Then either chill at a swanky Zona Sul lounge, dance, drink, and flirt at a nightclub, or join the pulsating throngs in the historic *bairros* of Lapa and Santa Teresa who flock to listen to live *chorinho, forró,* and, of course, samba. Speaking of samba, it's impossible to mention Rio without alluding to the world-famous extravaganza known as Carnaval. It

doesn't matter whether you take in the parades at the Sambódromo, dance through the streets with a traditional neighborhood *bloco* (Carnaval group), or merely make it to one of the *escola de samba* (samba school) rehearsals held throughout the year. The Carnaval spirit is highly contagious. Like Rio itself, it will leave you wanting more.

SIGHTS

What's left of Rio's colonial past and most of its churches and museums are concentrated in its old downtown core, known as Centro. However, beaches, shopping, restaurants, nightlife, and most hotels—as well as access to the Floresta da Tijuca—are in the more upscale Zona Sul neighborhoods. The area north of Centro is known as the Zona Norte. This vast urban zone is home to Rio's lower-class neighborhoods and encompasses the Rodoviária Novo Rio (bus station), Aeroporto Internacional Tom Jobim (Galeão), and Maracanã soccer stadium. Despite Rio's sprawl, getting around the Centro and Zona Sul neighborhoods, in particular, is fairly easy. The excellent Metrô subway service links the Zona Norte, Centro, Flamengo, Botafogo, Copacabana, and Ipanema. Throughout the city, numerous buses run at all hours of the day (safe) and night (unsafe).

Centro

The Centro refers to Rio's historic downtown commercial district. Narrow cobblestoned alleys, grand baroque churches, turn-of-the-20th-century Parisian-inspired avenues and architecture, and the ubiquitous high-rises and urban chaos of a 21st-century megalopolis make up a bewildering if often fascinating patchwork. Although some areas are sorely neglected, as part of an effort to revitalize the area over the last few years many museums and cultural centers have opened or have been revamped. Meanwhile, stylish bistros have joined some of the city's most traditional bars

RIO DE JANEIRO

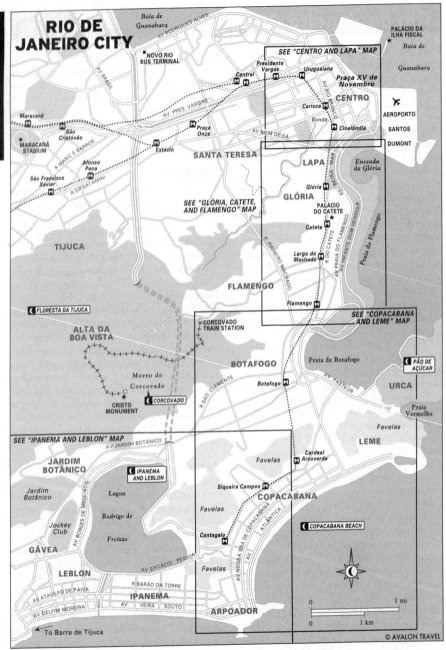

and cafés. As an antidote to the upscale beach culture of Zona Sul, pockets of the Centro are quite interesting, particularly if you want to get a sense of Rio's rich past.

Despite the traffic, navigating the area is quite easy on foot. Centro is also well-served by buses from Zona Sul and Zona Norte (take anything marked "Centro," "Praça XV," or "Praça Mauá") and by Metrô (the most convenient stations are Cinelândia, Carioca, Urugaiana, Presidente Vargas, and Praça Onze). Although during the day and into the early evening Centro is usually jam-packed, at night and on weekends the area is as quiet as a ghost town and quite unsafe to stroll around. If you're thinking of taking in an exhibition or performance during these times, it's best to take a taxi.

PRAÇA XV

Historically, Praça XV comprised the symbolic heart of Centro, and since most buses pass by this large plaza, it's a practical point from which to begin exploring the area. Its full name, Praça XV de Novembro, refers to November 15, 1899, the day when Brazil's first president, Manuel Deodoro de Fonseca, stood and declared Brazil to be a republic. Many significant historical events have taken place here—among them the crowning of Brazil's two emperors, Pedro I and Pedro II, and the abolition of slavery in 1888. On Thursdays and Fridays, a colorful street market fills the square with vendors hawking everything from food and handicrafts to antique stamps and coins.

PAÇO IMPERIAL

Praça XV's original name was Largo do Paço because it served as a large public patio to the stately Paço (i.e., Palácio) Imperial (Praça XV de Novembro 48, Centro, tel. 21/2533-4491, www.pacoimperial.com.br, noon–6 P.M. Tues.–Sun., free). Built in 1743, the palace was a residence for Portugal's colonial governors. It then housed the Portuguese court itself when Dom João VI fled Napoleon's forces in 1808. When the royal palace moved to the Palácio da Quinta da Boa Vista (today the Museu Nacional), the

Paço Imperial continued to host receptions and events. Today, it houses interesting temporary exhibits of contemporary art. Overlooking the internal courtyard is a lovely café and restaurant, the Bistrô do Paço, as well as a book and CD store and a small cinema that shows independent and repertory films.

IGREJA NOSSA SENHORA DE CARMO DA ANTIGA SÉ

Across Rua 1 de Março from Praça XV is the Igreja Nossa Senhora de Carmo da Antiga Sé (Rua Sete de Setembro 15, Centro, tel. 21/2242-4828, 8 A.M.–5 P.M. Mon.–Fri., free). Constructed in 1761, it served as Rio's principal cathedral until 1980. Many of the city's major religious commemorations—including Emperor Pedro I's coronation and the baptisms and marriages of Emperor Pedro II—were celebrated here. Although the exterior retains little of its original facade, the interior is a rococo feast with altars richly decorated in silver and a splendid panel of Nossa Senhora do Carmo.

ARCO DO TELES

Directly across Praça XV from the Paço Imperial, you'll notice an impressive arch that leads down the Beco de Telles, a cobblestoned alley lined with rather elegant 19th-century buildings. Wandering down this street and the equally narrow and atmospheric Travessa do Comércio, Rua Visconde de Itaboraí, and Rua Ouvidor allows you to get a sense of what Rio was like in the 18th and 19th centuries. Today, these twisting streets are home to a vibrant collection of restaurants and bars where workers from the neighborhood congregate for a quick lunch or an after-work beer or *caipirinha*.

CULTURAL CENTERS

As you walk along Rua Visconde de Itaboraí, you'll encounter several particularly impressive buildings. These former administrative palaces underwent inspired renovations in recent times and now operate as dynamic cultural centers. Most of the (usually very engaging) art exhibitions are free, as are many of the musical events. Built in 1922, the **Centro Cultural**

dos Correios (Rua Visconde de Itaboraí 20, Centro, tel. 21/2253-1580, noon–7 P.M. Tues.–Sun.) was formerly the headquarters of Rio's postal service, and there is still a small post office should you have the urge to send a postcard. A great café overlooks the adjacent Praça dos Correios, where live musical performances frequently take place.

Dating from 1816, the **Casa França-Brasil** (Rua Visconde de Itaboraí 78, Centro, tel. 21/2253-5366, www.fcfb.rj.gov.br, 10 A.M.–8 P.M. Tues.–Sun.) was Rio's first neoclassical construction and originally served as the city's main customs building. Aside from temporary art exhibits, there is a small cinema and a charming French bistro.

The **Centro Cultural Banco do Brasil (CCBB)** (Rua 1 de Março 66, Centro, tel. 21/3808-2000, noon–8 P.M. Tues.–Sun., www.bb.com.br/cultura) is a splendid neoclassical building. Since the 1920s it has served as the headquarters for Banco do Brasil (which explains the convenient presence of ATMs in the foyer). Banco do Brasil is a major patron of the arts, and the CCBB's magnificent interior welcomes most major national and international art exhibits as well as musical and theatrical performances that travel to and throughout Brazil. With a bookstore, café, and decidedly regal tea salon, it is also a favorite meeting point for Cariocas to browse, nibble, sip, and simply hang out.

IGREJA NOSSA SENHORA DA CANDELÁRIA

Across Rua 1 de Março from the CCBB you can't miss the monumental Igreja Nossa Senhora da Candelária (Praça Pio X, Centro, tel. 21/2233-2324, 7:30 A.M.–4 P.M. Mon.–Fri., 9 A.M.–noon Sat., 9 A.M.–1:30 P.M. Sun., free), located on the site of Rio's first church. Begun in 1775, the present church took over 100 years to complete, which accounts for its eclectic mixture of baroque and Renaissance elements. The interior is filled with a splendid and multihued array of marble, along with decorative elements such as doors made from finely wrought bronze. Ceiling panels recount

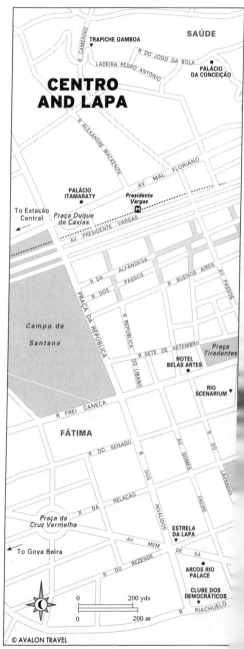

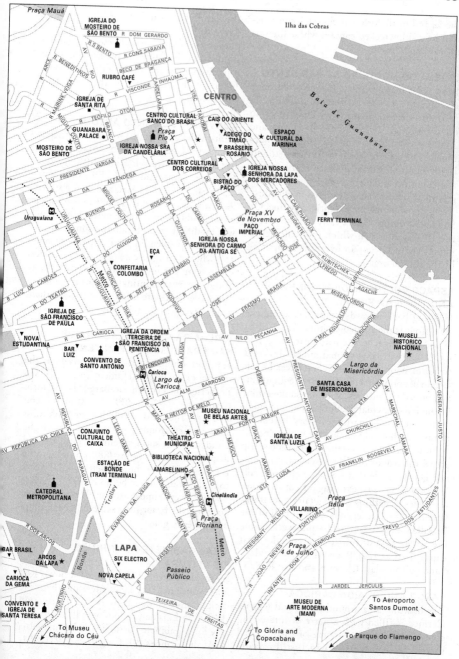

the legend of the original church's construction by a shipwrecked captain whose life was miraculously saved.

IGREJA DO MOSTEIRO DE SÃO BENTO

Rio's most magnificent example of baroque architecture is the 17th-century Igreja do Mosteiro de São Bento (Rua Dom Geraldo 68, Centro, tel. 21/2291-7122, 8–11 A.M. and 2:30–6 P.M. daily, R$7 guided visit), near Praça Mauá. The austere facade masks a startlingly lavish interior featuring delicately carved naves and columns, and altars embellished with angels and cherubs that are covered in gold dust. The painted panels are exceptionally fine. On Sunday mornings, arrive early to take part in the 10 A.M. mass, in which the Benedictine monks chant Gregorian hymns accompanied by the church organ.

ESPAÇO CULTURAL DA MARINHA AND THE ILHA FISCAL

Heading back towards Praça XV, along the waterfront is the Espaço Cultural da Marinha (Av. Alfred Agache, Centro, near Praça XV, tel. 21/2233-9165, www.mar.mil.br/sdm/ecm/ ecm.htm, noon–5 P.M. Tues.–Sun., free). Its collection of antique maps, navigating equipment, and buried treasure rescued from sunken ships in the Baía de Guanabara offers an engaging glimpse at Brazil's maritime history. Part of the exhibits are housed in a floating submarine.

From here, you can take a guided boat trip across the bay to the Ilha Fiscal, the site of a neo-gothic castle that housed a customs collection center. The extravagant construction resembles something out of a fairy tale: It was here that the last legendary royal ball of the Brazilian empire was held—one week before the declaration of Brazil as a republic. Boat trips depart at 1, 2:30, and 4 P.M. Thursday–Sunday. Tours last 1.5 hours and cost R$8.

LARGO AND RUA DA CARIOCA

The bustling area around Largo and Rua da Carioca is filled with a maze of interesting cobblestoned streets—some of them closed to vehicles—pockets of which still capture the flavor of 19th and early 20th century Rio. Largo da Carioca itself is usually packed with outdoor vendors. From this square, you will immediately be impressed by the monumental hillside complex consisting of the Igreja de São Francisco da Penitência and the Convento de Santo Antônio.

CONVENTO DE SANTO ANTÔNIO

Built in the early 1600s to house Franciscan monks, the Convento de Santo Antônio (Largo da Carioca, Centro, tel. 21/2262-0129, 8 A.M.–6:30 P.M. Mon. and Wed.–Fri., 6:30 A.M.–7:30 P.M. Tues., 8–11 A.M. and 4–6 P.M. Sat., 9–11 A.M. Sun., free) is one of Rio's oldest surviving buildings. Although most of the church was modified, you can admire some baroque works and a splendid sacristy panel of blue-and-white Portuguese *azulejos* (ceramic tiles) illustrating the life of Santo Antônio. Many of the convent's paintings, sculptures, and ceramic tiles work are original, but to see them you'll have to make an appointment.

IGREJA DA ORDEM TERCEIRA DE SÃO FRANCISCO DA PENITÊNCIA

Far more impressive than the *convento* is the interior of the Igreja da Ordem Terceira de São Francisco da Penitência (Largo da Carioca, Centro, tel. 21/2262-0197, 9 A.M.–noon and 1–4 P.M. Tues.–Fri., R$2), one of Rio's most sumptuous baroque jewels. You're sure to be blinded by the sheer amount of pure gold on display—400 kilograms (880 pounds) to be precise. While the church itself took 115 years to build (construction began in 1657), the last 30 years were almost exclusively dedicated to covering the beautifully sculpted cedar altars and naves in gold.

REAL GABINETE PORTUGUÊS DE LEITURA

From the Largo da Carioca, walk down Rua da Carioca to Praça Tiradentes, and then take a right on Avenida Passos. At the intersection with Rua Luís de Camões, you'll come upon the Real Gabinete Português de Leitura (Rua Luís de Camões 30, Centro, tel. 21/2221-

3138, www.realgabinete.com.br, 9 A.M.–6 P.M. Mon.–Fri., free). The unusual facade with its stylized sailors' knots, seashells, and Moorish motifs is typical of Manueline style, which was popular in Portugal during the reign of Manuel I (1495–1521). Inside is one of the largest libraries of works in the Portuguese language. It's worth taking a peek at the stunning reading room with its mile-high ceilings, jacaranda tables, and seemingly endless polished wood bookshelves reminiscent of a medieval library.

CENTRO DE ARTE HÉLIO OITICICA

A block away from the Real Gabinete, an imposing neoclassical building houses the Centro de Arte Hélio Oiticica (Rua Luís de Camões 68, Centro, tel. 21/2232-4213, 11 A.M.–5 P.M. Tues.–Fri., 11 A.M.–5 P.M. Sat.–Sun.). The building is devoted to one of Brazil's most avant-garde and influential contemporary artists: Hélio Oiticica (1937–1980). Born into a Carioca family of leftist intellectuals (among other things, his father was a math teacher, an experimental photographer, and an entomologist), Oiticica grew up surrounded by radical ideas. In his short life, the innovative Carioca artist produced an important body of work ranging from his initial abstract compositions exploring space and color (slightly similar to the modern works of Klee and Mondrian) to his later and highly imaginative "anti-art" sculptural objects and "habitable paintings." The most famous of these were hybrid banners-tents-capes (known as *parangolés*) designed to be worn while swaying to samba rhythms. Aside from a permanent collection that focuses more on Oiticica's earlier works, the center also hosts temporary exhibitions of contemporary art.

CINELÂNDIA

Walking south from Largo de Carioca along Rua Uruguaiana, your path will intersect with **Avenida Rio Branco,** one of Centro's major thoroughfares. Early 20th-century photos reveal it to be a grand European-style avenue flanked with imposing neoclassical buildings and shaded by a canopy of trees. It was here that the city's artists, intellectuals, and fashionable elite came to promenade. Originally called Avenida Central, it cut a swath of modernity through the labyrinth of crumbling mansions, flophouses, and brothels that had dominated the district since colonial times.

Although most of this traffic-laden avenue has been disfigured by ugly modern high-rises, the stretch that opens up onto the monumental **Praça Floriano** has retained many of its magnificent buildings, among them the Theatro Municipal, the Biblioteca Nacional, and the Museu Nacional de Belas Artes. It gives an impression of how grand Rio must have been in the early 20th century.

The area encompassing Praça Floriano is known as Cinelândia: In the 1930s, ambitious plans existed to turn this elegant plaza into a Carioca version of Broadway—only instead of theaters, movie palaces were built, including Rio's first cinemas. Only one of these glamorous deco palaces is still intact—the Cine Odeon BR—while the rest were snatched up by churches, such as the Igreja Universal de Deus (Universal Kingdom of God). The many cafés scattered around Praça Floriano still draw an eclectic mixture of Cariocas who drop by during happy hour.

THEATRO MUNICIPAL

If when you first set eyes upon the Theatro Municipal (Praça Floriano, Centro, tel. 21/2299-1677, www.theatromunicipal.rj.gov .br), you immediately think of Paris, it's probably because this splendid theater was modeled after Paris's Opéra Garnier. Since 1909, Brazil's premier theater has played host to some of the world's most prestigious orchestras and opera, dance, and theater companies. The interior is a sumptuous feast of marble, bronze, and gold with ample glitter provided by gilded mirrors and crystal chandeliers. Onyx banisters line the grand marble staircase, and there are some wonderful mosaic frescoes and stained-glass windows. If you're without the time or inclination to take in a performance, take a guided tour (R$10), offered hourly 1–5 P.M. during the week.

BIBLIOTECA NACIONAL

The largest library in Latin America, and the eighth largest in the world, Rio's Biblioteca Nacional (Av. Rio Branco 219, Centro, tel. 21/3095-3879 or 3095-3811, www.bn.br, 9 A.M.–8 P.M. Mon.–Fri., 9 A.M.–3 P.M. Sat.) boasts some 13 million tomes—the first of which were brought to Brazil by Dom João VI in 1808. Completed in 1910, the building is an eclectic fusion of neoclassical and art nouveau styles. You don't have to be a serious bibliophile to opt for a guided tour (R$2) of the grandiose interior (tours begin at 11 A.M., 1 P.M., and 3 P.M. on weekdays).

MUSEU NACIONAL DE BELAS ARTES

Adjacent to the *biblioteca* is yet another imposing neoclassical temple—this one devoted to art. The Museu Nacional de Belas Artes (Av. Rio Branco 199, Centro, tel. 21/2240-0068, www.mnba.gov.br, 10 A.M.–6 P.M. Tues.–Fri., 1–6 P.M. Sat., R$4) housed Rio's national school of fine arts before being converted into a somewhat somber museum. It has a modest collection of European works, but you should really focus your attention on the national collection, which provides an excellent overview of 19th- and 20th-century Brazilian painting. Displayed chronologically, highlights include early- to mid-20th-century painters who, departing from European influences, experimented with new and distinctly Brazilian styles and subject matter. Among those represented are Anita Malfatti, Cândido Portinari, Lasar Segall, and Afredo Volpi. An interesting gallery displays Brazilian folk art. The museum hosts traveling exhibitions as well.

MUSEU HISTÓRICO NACIONAL

A 10–15-minute walk east of Praça Floriano will bring you to the Museu Histórico Nacional (Praça Marechal Âncora, Centro, tel. 21/2550-9260, www.museuhistoriconacional.com.br, 10 A.M.–5:30 P.M. Tues.–Fri., 2–6 P.M. Sat.–Sun., R$6). This sprawling museum occupies three historic buildings: the 17th-century Forte de Santiago, an 18th-century arsenal, and an ammunitions depot. As such, there is ample space to showcase the 250,000 artifacts on display, ranging from carriages to canyons. Among this vast collection are some truly precious objects—like the pen that Princesa Isabel used in 1888 to sign the Lei Áurea, which abolished slavery. There are also marvelous glass vials and medicine bottles from the imperial pharmacy, Emperor Dom Pedro II's throne, and the largest coin collection in Latin America. The recently reorganized and spruced up collection does a fine job of illustrating Brazil's rich history, dating from the arrival of the first Europeans in 1500 to the declaration of the republic in 1889. If you're looking for an introduction to Brazil's past, a visit to this museum is highly recommended.

Lapa

One of Rio's most traditional and notorious neighborhoods, Lapa has had many incarnations. It was originally a beach (known as the "Spanish Sands") before being paved over and made into a rather posh 19th-century residential neighborhood. The **Passeio Público** (Rua do Passeio Público, Lapa, 7:30 A.M.–9 P.M. daily) evokes what Lapa must have been like when it was still a swank *bairro* where well-to-do families strolled beneath the shady trees of this elegant park.

By the turn of the 20th century, Lapa's fortunes had declined. Middle-class families migrated south, and a colorful collection of gangsters, tricksters, low-lifes, prostitutes, bohemians, and sambistas started moving in. They created a wildly bohemian underground scene that become the stuff of Carioca legend. During the 1930s, Lapa was not unlike New York's Harlem. However, as the century wore on, buildings became increasingly dilapidated and disreputable, and crime escalated. Until a decade ago, the neighborhood was very down and out.

Then, unexpectedly, a renaissance began to take hold of Lapa. Nightly samba jams were held beneath the arches of Lapa's colonial aqueduct. A row of antiques stores opened along the Rua do Lavradio. Inspired by Barcelona's Gaudí, a Chilean artist named Selarón began

bonde (tram) traveling on top of the Arcos da Lapa

covering a steep 215-step staircase to the neighborhood of Santa Teresa with a bright mosaic of ceramic plate fragments (many sent to him from all four corners of the globe). But most of all, Lapa became famous for its intensely vibrant nightlife, where Cariocas from all walks of life congregate to eat, drink, and dance the night away.

Although Lapa's fortunes have recently taken a turn for the better, it is still somewhat seedy around the edges. During the day, it's quiet, and even a bit deserted in places. At night, although its main streets are teeming with people, it's potentially dodgy if you don't take care (and cabs). Nonetheless, it's a wonderfully atmospheric slice of old Rio that shouldn't be missed.

Lapa's most iconic landmark is the **Arcos da Lapa.** Originally known as the Aqueduto da Carioca, this distinctly Roman 42-arch aqueduct was built in 1750 to supply fresh water from the Rio da Carioca to the residents of Centro. In 1896, it got a new lease on life as a viaduct over which *bondes* (trams) transported passengers to the elegant hillside neighborhood of Santa Teresa.

Close to the Arcos de Lapa is the **Catedral Metropolitana** (Av. República de Chile 245, Lapa, tel. 21/2240-2669, 7:30 A.M.–5:30 P.M. daily, free), a cone-shaped modernist cathedral that was built between 1964 and 1979. Inside, the sense of spaciousness (it holds 20,000 people!) coupled with pared-down minimalism is conducive to contemplation. If you visit on a sunny day, you'll be bewitched by the psychedelic patterns of gold, green, blue, and yellow that are refracted through the four immense stained-glass windows. A small Museu de Arte Sacra (R$2) includes objects such as the baptismal fonts used to christen the emperors' offspring and the gold roses Princesa Isabel received from Pope Leo XII after abolishing slavery.

Santa Teresa

It would be a shame to come to Rio de Janeiro and not visit the utterly charming, bucolic hilltop neighborhood of Santa Teresa, one of the city's oldest residential *bairros*. In the 19th century, wealthy Cariocas built gracious villas along its narrow winding streets, with terraces and balconies overlooking the lush green mountains and blue waters of the Baía de Guanabara. The views are still alluring, as is the neighborhood, which is why after a long period of decline, many artists began to move in, snatching up the dilapidated villas for a song and transforming them into ateliers and galleries. After an initial revival in the '60s and '70s, a second revitalization has recently begun to take place, resulting in the trickling in of boutique hotels and fashionable bistros as well as improved security (surrounded by *favelas,* Santa Teresa has traditionally had a somewhat dodgy reputation, particularly at night).

Spearheaded by the neighborhood artists' efforts, Santa Teresa has gradually evolved into a vibrant community. On a regular basis, many small-scale artistic and musical events take place in "Santa." Among the most popular is an event known as **Portas Abertas** (www.vivas-anta.com.br). Held twice a year, on weekends in May and November, Santa Teresa's "Open Doors" event involves over 100 resident artists, who literally open the doors to their homes and studios so you can view their work (and their often fantastic living spaces).

The easiest and, by far, most diverting way to get to Santa Teresa is to hop aboard the old-fashioned *bonde* (trolley) that clangs its way up the hills from Centro. *Bondes* leave from the **Estação Carioca** (Rua Professor Lélio Gama, Centro, tel. 21/2240-5709, departures every 20 minutes 6 A.M.–10 P.M. daily, R$1), located near the Carioca Metrô station. The ride itself is wonderfully scenic since the *bonde* tracks pass over the Arcos de Lapa before climbing up the steep hills of Santa Teresa, until the *bonde* finally clatters to a halt at the charming **Largo das Guimarães.** Although security on the open-sided *bondes* has been beefed up due to numerous thefts, you'll want to keep visible valuables to a minimum.

MUSEU CHÁCARA DO CÉU

The Museu Chácara do Céu (Rua Murtinho Nobre 93, tel. 21/2507-1932, www.museuscas-tromaya.com.br, noon–5 P.M. Wed.–Sun., R$2, free Wed.) is among Rio's most lovely museums. Surrounded by a beautiful hilltop garden

designed by noted landscaper Roberto Burle Marx, the museum is located in an attractive modernist house built in 1957 by Raimundo Castro Maia, a wealthy business magnate with a great eye for art. His impressive private collection includes the works of some fine Brazilian masters, such as Alberto Guignard, Emiliano Di Cavalcanti, and Cândido Portinari. Also exhibited are sketches and paintings of Brazil created by visiting Europeans, most notably Jean-Baptiste Debret, a French painter whose watercolors portray 19th-century Cariocas from all walks of life. The international collection took a serious hit during Carnaval of 2006, when thieves entered the museum and made off with a Monet, a Picasso, a Matisse, and a Dali in broad daylight.

Adjacent to the museum is the **Parque das Ruínas** (Rua Murtinho Nobre 169, tel. 21/2252-1039, 8 A.M.–8 P.M. Tues.–Sun.), a small but leafy park built around the atmospheric ruins of a palace that belonged to Laurinda Santos Lobo, a wealthy Carioca who was a generous patron of the arts during the early 1900s. Today, its renovated remains house a cultural center that features art exhibits. A small café offers magnificent views of Pão de Açúcar and Corcovado.

Glória and Catete

In the mid-19th century, the neighborhoods of Glória and Catete were considered outskirts of Rio. Their proximity to Centro and the Baía de Guanabara lured Rio's burgeoning upper-middle class, and they remained fashionable addresses until the mid-20th century. Since then, the area has lost some of its luster; however, Catete in particular is quite lively with lots of local bars and restaurants as well as a handful of interesting sights.

IGREJA NOSSA SENHORA DA GLÓRIA DO OUTEIRO

The *bairro* Glória is named after the dazzling white Igreja Nossa Senhora da Glória do Outeiro (Praça Nossa Senhora da Glória, tel. 21/2225-2869, 9 A.M.–noon and 1–5 P.M. Mon.–Fri., 8 A.M.–noon Sat.–Sun., free),

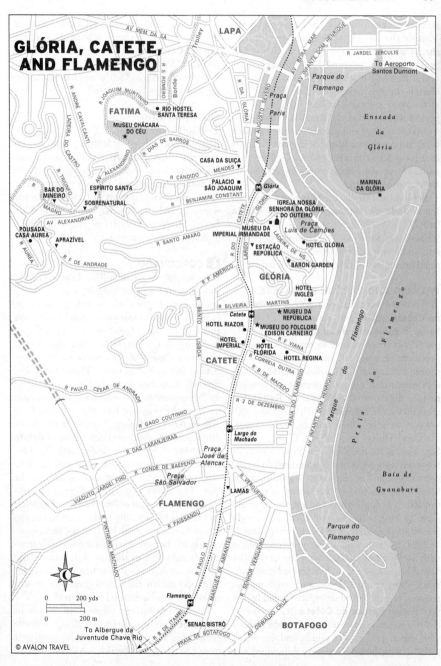

GLÓRIA, CATETE, AND FLAMENGO

AV. MEM. DA SÁ

LAPA

Trolley

Bonde

R. S. ROMERO

R JARDEL JERCULIS

To Aeroporto
Santos Dumont

AV. BEIRA MAR

AV. INFANTE DOM HENRIQUE

Parque do
Flamengo

Enseada
da
Glória

R. JOAQUIM MURTINHO

FATIMA

RIO HOSTEL
SANTA TERESA

MUSEU CHÁCARA
DO CÉU

R. ANDRÉ CAVALCANTI

LADEIRA DO CASTRO

R. DIAS DE BARROS

Praça
Paris

AV. AUGUSTO SEVERO

AV. DA GLÓRIA

R. DA GLÓRIA

CASA DA SUIÇA

MENDES

MARINA
DA GLÓRIA

R. ALEXANDRINO

R. CÂNDIDO

PALACIO
SÃO JOAQUIM

Glória

BENJAMIM CONSTANT

IGREJA NOSSA
SENHORA DA GLÓRIA
DO OUTEIRO

R. TRIUNFO

BAR DO
MINEIRO

ESPIRITO SANTA

SOBRENATURAL

MAGNO

AV. ALEXANDRINO

R. SANTO AMARO

MUSEU DA
IMPERIAL IRMANDADE

Praça
Luís de Camões

LADEIRA DE NS

HOTEL GLÓRIA

POUSADA
CASA AUREA

R. AUREA

APRAZÍVEL

R. F. DE ANDRADE

R. DO CATETE

LARGO DA GLÓRIA

ESTAÇÃO
REPÚBLICA

BARON GARDEN

R. P. AMÉRICO

GLÓRIA

HOTEL
INGLÊS

R. BENTO

R. LISBOA

R. SILVEIRA

MARTINS

Catete

MUSEU DA
REPÚBLICA

HOTEL RIAZOR

MUSEU DO FOLCLORE
EDISON CARNEIRO

HOTEL
IMPERIAL

HOTEL
FLÓRIDA

R. F. VIANA

CATETE

R. CORREIA DUTRA

HOTEL REGINA

R. B. DE MACEDO

PRAIA DO FLAMENGO

AV. INFANTE DOM HENRIQUE

Parque do Flamengo

Praia
do
Flamengo

R. PAULO CÉSAR DE ANDRADE

R. 2 DE DEZEMBRO

R. GAGO COUTINHO

R. DAS LARANJEIRAS

Largo do
Machado

Praça
José de
Alencar

R. CONDE DE BAEPENDI

Praça
São Salvador

R. VERGUEIRO

LAMAS

Baía de
Guanabara

VIADUTO JARDEL FIHO

FLAMENGO

R. PAISSANDÚ

R. PINHEIRO MACHADO

Parque do
Flamengo

R. PAULO VI

R. MARQUÊS DE ABRANTES

R. SENHOR VERGUEIRO

0   200 yds
0   200 m

Flamengo

SENAC BISTRÔ

BOTAFOGO

To Albergue da
Juventude Chave Rio

R. B. DE ITAMBI

PRAIA DE BOTAFOGO

AV. OSWALDO CRUZ

© AVALON TRAVEL

perched dramatically atop the Morro da Glória. Visiting the church involves a steep climb up the Ladeira da Glória or a less exhausting ride up the recently restored 1940 funicular (access at Rua do Russell 300). This early baroque church (built between 1714 and 1739) is one of the most stunning in Rio. In fact, it was a personal favorite of the Brazilian royal family (many princes and princesses were baptized here). Boasting an unusual octagonal shape, its interior is adorned with marvelous blue-and-white Portuguese *azulejo* panels by reputed artist Mestre Valentim.

Behind the church, the **Museu da Imperial Irmandade de Nossa Senhora da Glória** (tel. 21/2225-2869, 9 A.M.–5 P.M. Mon.–Fri., 9 A.M.–1 P.M. Sat.–Sun., R$2) houses a small museum with religious art, ex-votos and some personal belongings of Empress Teresa Cristina.

PALÁCIO AND PARQUE DO CATETE

When Brazil was declared a republic, the **Palácio do Catete,** the former mansion of a German baron, became the official residence of Brazil's presidents. It remained so until 1960, when president number 18, Juscelino Kubitschek, moved the capital to Brasília. Kubitschek was also responsible for transforming his opulent former digs into the **Museu da República** (Rua do Catete 153, Catete, tel. 21/2558-6350, www.museudarepublica.org.br, noon–5 P.M. Tues. and Thurs.–Fri., 2–5 P.M. Wed., 2–6 P.M. Sat.–Sun., R$6, free Wed. and Sun.). A more or less interesting collection of presidential photos, documents, and objects as well as sumptuous furnishings conjure up the history of republican Rio. The highlight is the apartment where Getúlio Vargas lived—and died. Seemingly frozen in time from the day he shot himself in 1954, it features the smoking revolver along with his bloodied pajamas with the fatal bullet hole. The palace itself, with its stained-glass windows, shiny parquet floors, and lavish marble fixtures, is quite grand. It is surrounded by the very elegant **Parque do Catete** (9 A.M.–6 P.M. daily), a welcome green oasis of green decked out with imperial palms, fish ponds, and serpentine paths. The grounds include an exhibition space,

a theater, a small cinema, and a café. Adjacent to the *palácio* is the small **Museu de Folclore Edison Carneiro** (Rua do Catete 181, Catete, tel. 21/2285-0441, 11 A.M.–6 P.M. Tues.–Fri., 3–6 P.M. Sat.–Sun., R$2), which has an interesting collection of Brazilian folk art.

Cosme Velho

Tranquil Cosme Velho is a pretty residential neighborhood that winds its way up the hills towards Corcovado. At the Estação Cosme Velho, hordes of tourists line up to catch the mini-train that whisks them up the mountain to the outstretched arms of Cristo Redentor, which in 2007 was elected as one of the New Seven Modern Wonders of the World by a global jury of cybervoters.

◖ CORCOVADO

Even before you arrive in Rio, the word will be rolling around on your tongue: "Corcovado"—and not just because it's the title of one of the best-known and most languorous bossa nova tunes of all times (penned by João Gilberto and sung, in English, by his then wife, Astrud Gilberto). One of Rio's most instantly recognizable and oft-visited icons, "Hunchback" (the English translation lacks the lyrical sonority of its Portuguese name) mountain rises straight up from the center of Rio to a lofty height of 700 meters (2,300 feet). Equally iconic is the 30-meter (100-foot) art deco statue of **Cristo Redentor** (Christ the Redeemer), his outstretched arms enveloping the surrounding city, that crowns Corcovado's sheer granite face. The statue, a gift from France to commemorate 100 years of Brazilian independence in 1921, didn't actually make it up to the top of the mountain until 1931. Since then, however, it has become a true beacon, visible from almost anywhere in the city. It is particularly striking at night when, due to a powerful illumination system, the Cristo glows like an otherworldly angel against the darkened sky.

Needless to say, the views from the top of Corcovado are utterly breathtaking. They're even more impressive than those proffered from Pão de Açúcar (which is half the size).

© TONY GALVEZ

statue of Cristo Redentor perched atop Corcovado

The most scenic—and most fun—way to get to the top of Corcovado is by taking the 19th-century cog-wheel train from the **Estação Cosme Velho** (Rua Cosme Velho 513, Cosme Velho, tel. 21/2558-1329, www.corcovado.com.br, R$36 round-trip fare including R$5 entrance fee). Trains depart every 30 minutes 8:30 A.M.–6:30 P.M. daily. The crazily steep ride takes 20 minutes and treats you to stunning views of the beaches of Zona Sul and the Lagoa Rodrigo de Freitas. Once you get off the train, you reach the Cristo by walking up a flight of 220 steep steps. If you're feeling a little lazy, choose between the recently installed escalator or the panoramic elevator. From Cosme Velho station, you can also get a taxi to the top, which costs R$5, with an additional R$5 per passenger. Avoid weekends, when the road becomes clogged with traffic and the lines for the trains are quite long. If possible, it's best to beat the crowds by leaving early on a weekday morning when you'll have the added privilege of seeing Rio bathed in golden light. It goes without saying that you should choose a clear day for your visit.

MUSEU INTERNACIONAL DE ARTE NAÏF DO BRASIL

A five-minute walk uphill from the Estação Cosme Velho, the Museu Internacional de Arte Naïf do Brasil (Rua Cosme Velho 561, Cosme Velho, tel. 21/2205-8612, www.museunaif.com.br, 10 A.M.–6 P.M. Tues.–Fri., noon–6 P.M. Sat.–Sun., R$8) lays claim to having the world's largest collection of *arte naïf,* or naive art. The delightfully expressive and colorful paintings in this colonial mansion portray many elements of popular Brazilian culture, including *futebol,* Carnaval, and scenes from daily life. Although most of the works exhibited (spanning five centuries) are by self-taught Brazilian artists, there are international works from over 100 countries. A small boutique sells *naïf* art from contemporary artists.

A little farther uphill from the museum, on the opposite side of the street, is the **Largo de Boticário** (Rua Cosme Velho 822). Named after the imperial family's *boticário* (apothecary), who was a resident, this enchanting 19th-century square resembles a period film set with its colorfully painted villas offset by tropical foliage.

Flamengo and Botafogo

Stretching along the Baía de Guanabara from Centro to the tunnel that leads to Copacabana are the sprawling and attractive *bairros* of Flamengo and Botafogo. In the 19th century, both were posh residential neighborhoods. Many of the wide avenues and tree-lined side streets still conserve an impressive number of elegant apartment buildings and gracious mansions, some of which formerly housed foreign embassies back in the day when Rio was still Brazil's capital. In the mid-20th century, Rio's rich and fashionable elite began to abandon the area for the newly minted glamor of the Zona Sul. In their heyday, the lovely white beaches of Flamengo and Botafogo were the equivalent of Copacabana and Ipanema today. Although they remain lovely from an aesthetic viewpoint (and serve as very scenic soccer fields), the pollution factor is such that nobody would dream of swimming in their waters these days.

While you'll undoubtedly glimpse snatches of Flamengo and Botafogo as you're careening back and forth between Centro and the Zona Sul, if you have some time to spare it's worthwhile to wander the area's streets. Less chaotic than Centro and far less touristy than the Zona Sul, these neighborhoods offer an appealing and colorful slice of Carioca life. Apart from numerous traditional bars and restaurants, the area has a few sights that are worth checking out.

PARQUE DO FLAMENGO

In 1960, much of Flamengo's beach disappeared beneath tons of earth. This radical landfill was part of an ambitious project to create a vast public park on prime oceanfront real estate that would come to be known as Parque do Flamengo (Av. Infante Dom Henrique). A formidable woman named Maria Carlota de Macedo Soares was in charge of this massive undertaking. A vanguard intellectual from one of Rio's most traditional families, "Lota" was the lover of American poet Elizabeth Bishop (who, at the time, lived in Rio with her). A great fan of modernism, Lota sought out the talents of leading landscape designer Roberto Burle Marx and architect Affonso Eduardo

Reidy. Battling bureaucracy and machismo (her all-male crew and colleagues balked at taking orders from a woman), she was able to carry out most (though not all) of the original project. Today, this sweeping ribbon of green is Rio's most popular playground. It contains running, cycling, and skateboard paths, various playing fields, a children's park, a puppet theater, and an area reserved for model planes. It is also home to two museums: the Museu de Arte Moderna and the Museu Carmen Miranda. On Sundays and holidays, part of Avenida Infante Dom Henrique is closed to traffic and Cariocas descend in droves upon the park. On weekends, in the evenings, outdoor concerts featuring top names in Brazilian music are often held here.

MUSEU DE ARTE MODERNA

Housed in a stunning modernist steel and glass creation, designed by Affonso Eduardo Reidy and overlooking the Baía de Guanabara, the Museu de Arte Moderna (MAM, Av. Infante Dom Henrique 85, Flamengo, tel. 21/2240-4944, www.mamrio.com.br, noon–6 P.M. Tues.–Fri., noon–7 P.M. Sat.–Sun., R$5) boasts one of Brazil's most interesting and important collections of 20th-century art. A sampling of international artists commingles with key works by leading national figures such as Anita Malfatti, Tarsila do Amaral, Lasar Segal, Emiliano Di Cavalcanti, Cândido Portinari, Ivan Serpa, and Antônio Dias. Aside from hosting some quality temporary exhibits, the museum has a cinema that screens art films and a bright and attractive café with a great collection of international magazines.

MUSEU CARMEN MIRANDA

Although Carmen Miranda died tragically in 1955, at the age of 46, the legend of the "Lady in the Tutti Frutti Hat" lives on. A small, weirdly bunker-like complex houses the Museu Carmen Miranda (Av. Rui Barbosa in front of 560, Flamengo, tel. 21/2299-5586, www.funarj.rj.gov.br, 11 A.M.–5 P.M. Tues.–Fri., 1–5 P.M. Sat.–Sun., free). Drag queens and fans of Golden Age Hollywood

© CHRISTIAN KNEPPER/ANIMA/EMBRATUR

view of Pão de Açúcar from Praia do Flamengo

will adore this gloriously kitschy shrine featuring Carmen memorabilia. Highlights include her infamous sky-high platform shoes (Miranda was a tiny 1.52 meters/5 feet), outrageous gowns, gaudy costume jewelry, and of course, the inimitable headdresses topped with tropical fruit.

MUSEU DO ÍNDIO
Occupying a handsome 19th-century mansion in Botafogo, the Museu do Índio (Rua das Palmeiras 55, Botafogo, tel. 21/2286-8899, www.museodoindio.org.br, 9 A.M.–5:30 P.M. Tues.–Fri., 1–5 P.M. Sat.–Sun., R$3, free Sun.) possesses an extremely important collection of artifacts reflecting Brazil's diverse indigenous groups. Among the objects on display are hunting and cooking implements, traditional costumes, musical instruments, and religious talismans. These are accompanied by interesting multimedia displays that provide a good introduction to the social, religious, and economic life of various tribes. The museum shop sells an attractive (and decently priced) array of authentic handicrafts.

Urca
Squeezed onto a promontory facing Botafogo and sheltering Pão de Açúcar—one of Rio's most celebrated landmarks—the tiny residential neighborhood of Urca has resisted much of the urban mayhem characteristic of Rio's other beachside *bairros*. Neglected by tourists, unmarred by developers, and ignored by *assaltantes* (thieves), it is a lovely place to stroll around, take in the view, and watch local anglers cast their lines off the scenic cove of Praia Vermelha.

◖ PÃO DE AÇÚCAR
Rio's equivalent of Paris's Eiffel Tower and New York's Statue of Liberty is the monumental chunk of granite known as Pão de Açúcar, which guards the entrance to the Baía de Guanabara. No matter how many times you contemplate this rugged natural sculpture, the sensation is one that will definitely take your breath away. Rio's original inhabitants, the Tupi, referred to it as *pau-nh-acugua* (high, pointed mountain), which is something of an understatement. When the Portuguese arrived on the scene, both the Tupi term and the

mountain itself reminded them of a *pão de açúcar* (sugar loaf): a conical mound of sugar made by pouring liquid cane juice into a rounded mold that was then left to harden. The name stuck and today Pão de Açúcar is one of Rio's most recognized icons.

As can be imagined, the panoramic views of Rio and the Baía da Guanabara glimpsed from the top of Pão de Açúcar are quite stupendous. You can reach the summit by taking a glass-sided cable car up the mountain—an unforgettably scenic journey with two stops. The first is at **Morro da Urca,** a 210-meter (690-foot) mountain where there is a restaurant and some small shops. The second stop is at the actual 396-meter (1,300-foot) summit of Pão de Açúcar. From here trails lead through the lush forest with its tiny *mico* monkeys and rare wild orchids. **Cable cars** depart every 30 minutes from Praia Vermelha (Av. Pasteur 520, Urca, tel. 21/2461-2700, www.bondinho.com.br, 8 A.M.–10 P.M. daily, R$35). To avoid long lines, steer clear of weekends, holidays, and peak hours (10 A.M.–3 P.M.), and make sure the day is a clear one. If you're in a romantic frame of mind—or would like to be put in one—make the trip in the late afternoon. The sunset and twilight, with the lights of Rio glittering in the dusk against the mountain silhouettes, are truly bewitching.

Zona Norte

When traveling from the Tom Jobim international airport to Centro or Zona Sul you'll get your first sight of Rio's sprawling Zona Norte district. For the most part, there is no reason to see more of it than the glimpse afforded from your bus or taxi window. The area is largely residential with working class and poor neighborhoods alongside vast *favelas.* Poverty and drug-related violence has made large pockets extremely unsafe. The exception is the Quinta da Boa Vista (which is fairly close to Centro and easily accessible by Metrô), a vast park with some interesting sights, among them the Museu Nacional. If you have some extra time to kill while in Rio, you can combine its attractions into a day trip.

QUINTA DA BOA VISTA AND MUSEU NACIONAL

A former sugar plantation, the Quinta da Boa Vista (Av. Pedro II between Rua Almirante Baltazar and Rua Dom Meinrado, São Cristovão, 10 A.M.–4 P.M. Tues.–Sun.) was where Brazil's imperial family took up residence between 1822 to 1889. Befitting royalty, the expansive grounds feature lots of parkland, tree-lined walkways, statues, flower gardens, grottoes, lakes, and even a zoo.

The emperors themselves lived in the stately neoclassical Palácio de São Cristovão, which is home to the Museu Nacional (tel. 21/2568-8262, www.acd.ufrj.br/museu, 10 A.M.–4 P.M. Tues.–Sun., R$3). Brazil's oldest scientific museum, the enormous and somewhat eclectic collection was started by Dom João VI. The archaeological section focuses on prehistoric Latin American peoples, while the ethnological collection has some interesting artifacts related to Brazil's indigenous cultures. Among the highlights in the mineral section is the Bendigo Meteorite, which landed in the state of Bahia in 1888 and is the heaviest metallic mass known to have crashed through the planet's atmosphere. To get to the Quinta da Boa Vista, take the Metrô to São Cristovão. If you're in search of peace and tranquility, avoid weekends.

FEIRA DE SÃO CRISTOVÃO

Near the Quinta da Boa Vista is the traditional Feira de São Cristovão (Pavilhão de São Cristovão, São Cristovão, tel. 21/2580-5335, www.feiradesaocristovao.org.br, 10 A.M.–4 P.M. Mon.–Thurs., from 10 A.M. Fri. to 10 P.M. Sun., R$1). Also known as the Feira Nordestina, this massive outdoor market reunites people, produce, and music from Brazil's northeastern states, many of whom migrated to Rio for work but still get homesick for the food, drink, and sheer animation of their home states. The *feira* has 700 *barracas,* where vendors hawk typical products ranging from hand-woven hammocks from Ceará and leather hats and sandals from the sun-baked Sertão to jars of herb-infused *cachaças,* hot peppers, and amber-colored *dendê* (palm) oil from Bahia. The place is especially lively on the weekends (the *barracas* stay open around the clock), when Rio's Northeast expats congregate here to listen to performances of *forró* (country-like music featuring fiddle, accordion, and percussion) and *repentistas* (musical preachers). To get to the *feira*, take any bus marked "São Cristovão" leaving from the Zona Sul.

Copacabana and Leme

Although its glamour days are long gone, Copacabana still manages to live up to its legend as the world's most famous strip of white sand. Originally a tiny fishing village, it didn't gain neighborhood status until the 1891 dynamiting of the Túnel Velho through the mountains opened up the deserted beaches of the Zona Sul to the beginnings of urbanization. With the construction of the Mediterranean-style luxury hotel Copacabana Palace in 1923, the wealthy and fabulous came flocking. A slew of gorgeous deco apartment buildings soon rose up along the beachfront's Avenida Atlântica. Before long "Copa" was not just *the* place to live but *the* place to party. Tycoons, movie stars, royalty, and the international jet set transformed its sweeping carpet of sand into their personal playground.

A Copa address became so coveted that by '60s and '70s, the long but narrow neighborhood (hemmed in by mountains) was the most densely populated urban area in the world. To this day, Copa is not unlike a tropical Manhattan: People fork out absurd amounts of money to live in one of the thousands of closet-sized apartments located in the ugly high-rises that have mushroomed in the streets behind the oceanfront. The most populous of them all is the Edifício Richard, located Rua Barata Ribeiro 194, which has 507 apartments (45 per floor).

While many of Rio's rich and fashionable have since moved on to the more chic neighborhoods of Ipanema and Leblon, Copa has become—for better or for worse—one of Rio's most eclectic, vibrant, and democratic neighborhoods, a place where street kids and

millionaires, models and muscle men, doormen and nannies from the Northeast of Brazil and American tourists from the deepest, darkest Midwest all rub shoulders. While during the day senior citizens swarm the beaches and the dozens of bakeries along the main drag of Avenida Nossa Senhora de Copacabana, by night the stretch of Avenida Atlântica towards Ipanema is a hot spot for prostitutes and for the (many foreign) johns who travel to Copa in search of more piquant forms of R&R. There is also the complication of four major *favelas* covering the steep hills behind the middle-class condos. Shoot-outs between drug traffickers and police mean that it's not uncommon for shots to ring out (and stray bullets to fly).

Although Copa is not the safest place in the world, the oceanfront is well-policed, and if you're aware and don't flash your valuables, you will be fine. It's best to stick to well-populated areas, particularly at night, and it is also advisable to take a taxi unless you're strolling beneath the well-lit hotel exteriors on Avenida Atlântica. Despite its darker and seedier sides, Copacabana is full of a vibrancy and diversity that is unrivaled by any other Rio neighborhood. Although its glamor has definitely faded, it's hard to resist the charm of the local restaurants and traditional bars that coexist alongside the multitude of 24-hour gyms and juice bars. Copa may be a little decadent and tacky in places, but it is also, quite simply, fun. And whatever you may think of the *bairro* itself, there is no denying the allure of its beach, the magnificent crescent-shaped sweep of sand that is a world unto itself.

◖ COPACABANA BEACH
Urban beaches don't get any more dazzling than this 4.5-kilometer (2.8-mile) strip that stretches in a gorgeous arc from Pão de Açúcar to the Forte de Copacabana. The sand is sugary fine and white and is a striking contrast to the blue of the open Atlantic and the hypnotically wavy, white-and-black mosaic promenade that separates it from busy Avenida Atlântica. More than just affording a great view or acting as an outdoor tanning salon, the *praia* of

BEACH DOS AND DON'TS

In Rio, the beach is a fundamental part of life and lifestyle. Although it all appears incredibly laid-back, in truth, Cariocas have developed a very sophisticated *cultura de praia* with habits and codes that it's worth taking note of if you want to blend in.

· **Don't** wear a bathing suit from home. Chances are you're going to be hopelessly out of style. Rio's cutting-edge bikini and *sunga* (the male version of a bikini) styles are always light years ahead of the rest of the world, and since prices are generally affordable, you should purchase one (or several) on location.

· If you're female, **do** know that Cariocas are not at all shy about revealing a lot of flesh, although the days of the *fio dental* (dental floss) thong have mercifully passed. However, you **don't** want to take your top off. Aside from a brief headline-making phase on Ipanema a few summers ago – when a few women going topless led to the police enforcing decades-old decency laws – topless sunbathing is a no-no. Moreover, Cariocas are very proud of their tan lines.

Arraial do Cabo, Costa do Sol, Rio de Janeiro

· If you're male, **don't** don a Speedo-style bathing suit – these are for Olympic swimmers. For the last couple of years, stylish *sungas* have been modeled on men's full briefs. **Do** know that surfing shorts are for surfing or for wearing over your bathing suit as you go to and from the beach, but definitely not for lounging around on the sand or swimming.

· On the way to and from the beach, **do** wear flip-flips (Havaiianas are the coolest) and **don't** wear shoes. Females should cover up (lightly) with a lightweight top and micro shorts or skirts. Walking to and from the beach, males can flaunt their bare chests but otherwise should wear a T-shirt.

· **Don't** take any valuables to the beach and don't leave your possessions unguarded. Take a beach bag instead of a purse. If you're alone, ask a respectable-looking neighbor to keep an eye on your stuff while you take a dip.

· **Don't** bring a towel to the beach (even if you're staying in a swanky hotel with very plush ones). *Kangas* are lighter and de rigueur. They are sold all over the beaches. If you want more comfort, rent a chair.

· **Don't** schlep food or drinks to the beach. Rio's beaches are terrifically well serviced with vendors who sell all sorts of drinks and snacks (both healthy and unhealthy).

· Rio's beaches have strong currents in places. **Don't** go swimming if a red flag is flying. Only go in the water in areas where locals are already swimming.

· **Don't** get a sunburn. Not only will you suffer on your vacation and contribute to possible skin cancer, but the red lobster look is definitely uncool and will brand you as a foolish gringo.

© TONY GALVEZ

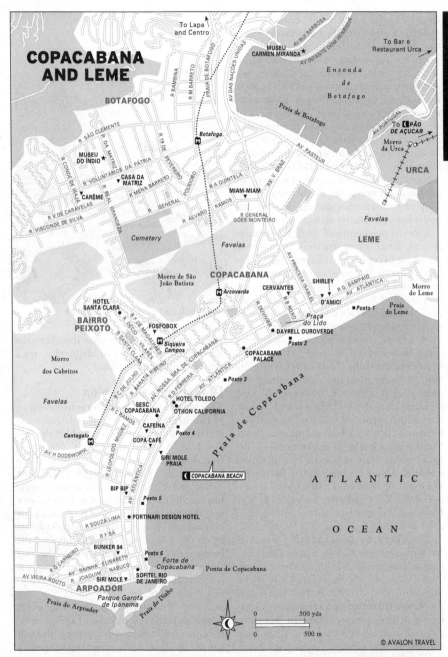

COPACABANA AND LEME

To Lapa and Centro

AV RUI BARBOSA

To Bar e Restaurant Urca

MUSEU CARMEN MIRANDA ★

AV INFANTE DOM HENRIQUE

Enseada de Botafogo

BOTAFOGO

R BAMBINA
R M BARRETO
PRAIA DE BOTAFOGO
PRAIA DE BOTAFOGO

Praia de Botafogo

AV DAS NAÇÕES UNIDAS

AV PORTUGAL

To PÃO DE AÇÚCAR

R SÃO CLEMENTE

Botafogo

Morro da Urca

AV PASTEUR

R DA MATRIZ
R 19 DE FEVEREIRO

URCA

R CONDE DE IRAJÁ
R VOLUNTÁRIOS DA PÁTRIA

MUSEU DO ÍNDIO ★

CASA DA MATRIZ

AV V. BRAZ

R A QUINTELA

CARÊME

R REAL GRANDEZA

R MENA BARRETO

MIAM-MIAM ▼

R V DE CARAVELAS
R VISCONDE DE SILVA

R GENERAL RAMOS

R ALVARO RAMOS

R GENERAL GÓES MONTEIRO

Favelas

LEME

Cemetery

Favelas

AV PRINCESA ISABEL

Morro do Leme

Morro de São João Batista

COPACABANA

Arcoverde

CERVANTES

SHIRLEY

R G. SAMPAIO

AV. ATLANTICA

Praia do Leme

HOTEL SANTA CLARA

D'AMICI

● Posto 1

BAIRRO PEIXOTO

R DECIO VILARES
R F DE MAGALHÃES

FOSFOBOX

R DUVIVIER
R B BROXO

Praça do Lido

Morro dos Cabritos

R SANTA CLARA

Siqueira Campos

● DAYRELL OUROVERDE

● Posto 2

R C DE JULHO
R BARATA RIBEIRO
AV NOSSA SRA DE COPACABANA

COPACABANA PALACE

Favelas

R D FERREIRA

AV. ATLANTICA

● Posto 3

R LEOPOLDO MIGUEZ
R RAMOS

SESC COPACABANA

HOTEL TOLEDO

OTHON CALIFORNIA

Praia de Copacabana

ATLANTIC

CAFEÍNA

● Posto 4

Cantagalo

COPA CAFÉ

AV H DODSWORTH

SIRI MOLE PRAIA

◀ COPACABANA BEACH

OCEAN

BIP BIP
AV. ATLANTICA

● Posto 5

R SOUZA LIMA

● PORTINARI DESIGN HOTEL

R F SÁ

BUNKER 94

● Posto 6

R G CARNEIRO
AV. RAINHA ELISABETH
R JOAQUIM NABUCO

SIRI MOLE ▼

Forte de Copacabana

SOFITEL RIO DE JANEIRO

Ponta de Copacabana

AV VIEIRA SOUTO

ARPOADOR

Parque Garota de Ipanema

Praia do Arpoador

Praia do Diabo

0   500 yds

0   500 m

© AVALON TRAVEL

Copacabana is a way of life. From dawn to dusk there is always something happening on Copa's beach—whether it's an early-morning yoga class for seniors, a *Vogue* photo shoot, an early evening volleyball practice for pre-teen girls, or midnight hookers on the prowl for foreign tourists. The beach is also meeting spot and a pickup place. You can get a tan or a tattoo, drink a *caipirinha* at a fancy *barraca* or an icy *água de coco* sold by one of many hundreds of *ambulantes,* who hawk everything from strangely addictive bags of *Globo* biscuits to transistor radios. Of course, in a pinch, you can go swimming—the chilly temperatures coupled with an undercurrent demand caution—but you can also do so much more.

Like the neighborhood itself, Copacabana beach is actually very stratified, and different points are occupied by different "tribes." The one-kilometer (0.6-mile) stretch closest to the tunnel that leads to Botafogo—between Morro do Leme and Avenida Princesa Isabel—is actually known as **Praia do Leme** (the small attractive residential *bairro* behind it is known as Leme as well). Leme is popular with families and older residents. The stretch of Copacabana in front of the Copacabana Palace is fashionable with gay men and transvestites. The patch near Rua Santa Clara is popular with jocks, particularly fans of *futebol* and *futevolei* (a Brazilian version of volleyball in which no hands are allowed). Closer to Ipanema, Postos 5 and 6 (which refer to the beacon-like lifeguard posts) draw an eclectic mix of seniors and *favela* kids. At the very end, in front of the Forte de Copacabana, is a fishermen's colony, one of the oldest and most traditional in Rio. Here, you can watch *pescadores* haul in their catch and mend their nets.

The **Forte de Copacabana** (corner of Av. Atlântica and Rua Francisco Otáviano, Copacabana, tel. 21/2521-1032, 10 A.M.–4 P.M. Tues.–Thurs., 10 A.M.–noon Fri., 9 A.M.–1 P.M. Sat.–Sun., R$4) was built in 1912 and houses the **Museu Histórico do Exército,** with a collection of army paraphernalia that will probably only interest military buffs. Much more enticing are the views of Copacabana beach

volleyball game on Ipanema beach

© MICHAEL SOMMERS

and the bay. You can gaze upon them from the Confeitaria Colombo—an idyllic place for a late-afternoon drink or snack.

Ipanema and Leblon

The most coveted—and expensive—slice of beachfront property in Rio de Janeiro is without a doubt the area from which the first chords of "A Garota de Ipanema" ("The Girl from Ipanema") were set down by two bohemian poets. The year was 1962, and Tom Jobim and Vinícius de Morais were enjoying ice-cold *chope* (draft beer) at their favorite neighborhood bar when one of many enticingly bronzed and bikinied young Cariocas sashayed by on the way to the beach and inspired the languorously cool bossa nova jewel. The song that seduced the world also summed up the seductive charm of what had become Rio's hippest, most happening beach *bairro*. Since the swinging '60s, Ipanema has been a magnet for a cosmopolitan yet funky mix of artists, musicians, and leftist intellectuals, along with a rich and trendy crowd who consistently fall prey to

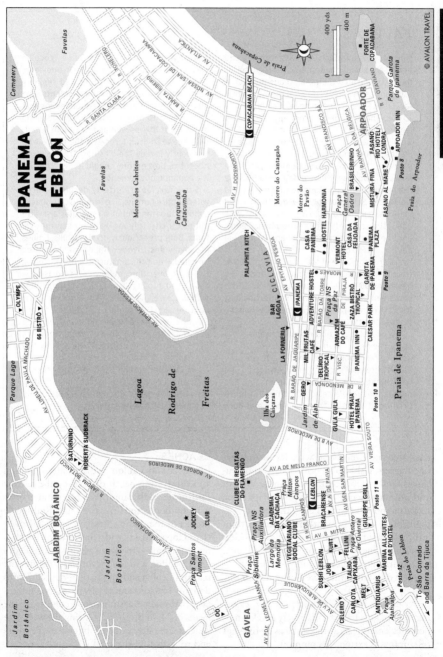

IPANEMA
AND
LEBLON

© AVALON TRAVEL

FAVELAS

One of Rio's and Brazil's most complex and pervasive social phenomena, *favelas* are far more complicated than their inadequate English translation "slums" would suggest. The first *favelas* in Rio de Janeiro developed in the late 1890s. The federal government had offered land to demobilized soldiers from northeastern Brazil so that they could settle on Rio's vacant slopes. When the government went back on its word, the soldiers occupied the promised land and baptized it Morro da Favela – *favela* is a tough thorny plant native to the semi-arid Northeast. Subsequent *"favelados"* were freed slaves who immigrated to Rio in search of work and settled on the hillsides surrounding Centro and the wealthier commercial and residential *bairros*. As Rio grew, so did its *favelas*, as poor Brazilians from all over the country migrated to the city in the hopes of finding work. Today, Rio has over 600 *favelas*, which are home to 20-25 percent of the city's population. Unfortunately, they are growing at a much faster rate than the rest of the city.

Rio's *favelas* are notorious for several reasons. The first is their proximity to Rio's most upscale neighborhoods. The largest ones are almost literally perched right on top of the wealthiest Zona Sul *bairros* (ironically, this means that *favela* residents enjoy far more privileged views than their rich neighbors below). Also, most are controlled by cocaine cartels. The results are twofold. On one hand, the drug lords maintain order and security within the *favela* in return for residents' loyalty. However, other consequences include easy access to drug use and to drug dealing as a way of life, as well as the violent shootouts between drug lords and the police who frequently invade the hillsides. Tragically, innocent victims getting caught in the crossfire is a common phenomenon.

Some *favelas* are utterly desolate places where entire families live in minuscule shacks cobbled together out of scrap materials, without electricity, running water, or sewage systems. Built precariously on steep hills, homes are easily destroyed – and residents injured or killed – due to rainstorms and landslides. However, over time, quite a few *favelas* have developed into highly organized communities with day care, medical clinics, and even Internet cafés and DVD rentals. Rio's largest *favela*, Rocinha, even has a McDonald's. Residents are not all destitute. Many have (low-paying) jobs in the surrounding neighborhoods. They live in concrete or cinder-block houses (some of them 2-3 stories high) with fridges, stoves, TVs, and air-conditioners. More importantly, they enjoy a sense of community spirit and engage in grassroots activism.

the lovely neighborhood with its shady tree-lined streets, fashionable bistros, bars, and boutiques, and magnificent white sands. Vibrant and animated both day and night, Ipanema retains a more bohemian edge than neighboring Leblon, which is slightly more sedate, tranquil, and residential (and richer), but no less appealing. Due to the importance of the beach, both Ipanema and Leblon carry off the impressive feat of being both incredibly chic and disarmingly casual. To wit: The sight of tattooed surfer boys, barefoot and dripping wet, carrying their boards past the discreetly jeweled millionaires ensconced at the terraces of five-star restaurants is extremely common.

BEACHES

Ipanema and Leblon is essentially one long and captivating beach divided by the narrow Jardim de Alah canal, which separates both neighborhoods and links the Lagoa Rodrigo de Freitas to the ocean. Straighter and narrower than Copacabana's wide crescent, the beach is no less scenic—Ipanema begins at the Pedra do Arpoador, a dramatic rock jutting into the sea, and Leblon ends at the twin-headed Morro de Dois Irmãos, a fantastically shaped mountain that really does poetically conjure up the heads of "Two Brothers." During the week, the beaches are fairly tranquil, but when the weekend rolls around the sand is a sea of bronzed,

Historically, the government treated *favelas* as blighted areas (they weren't even indicated on maps), and the elite and middle class guiltily ignored them (while employing many *favela* dwellers as nannies, cooks, and housekeepers). However, in the last two decades, with the realization that *favelas* won't go away, this thinking has shifted significantly. Projects such as Favela Bairro have been instrumental in helping to begin integration of these communities into the city's urban fabric. *Favelas* are increasingly included on city maps, and *favelados* are being given legal titles to their property.

More recently, *favelas* have started attracting tourists, who are curious to see firsthand how Brazil's very significant other half lives. While it's dangerous to wander alone into a *favela*, tours are available with guides who know the lay of the land. Several companies have jumped on the *favela* tour bandwagon, but the most experienced and knowledgeable is **Favela Tours** (tel. 21/3322-2727 or 21/9772-1133, www.favelatour.com.br, R$65), run by Carioca Marcelo Armstrong. Armstrong speaks fluent English and offers perceptive and insightful commentary as he leads groups on three-hour walking tours of the *favelas* of Rocinha and Vila Canoas. Part of the tour fee is donated to community projects. Although some might be scared of

potential danger or leery of the voyeuristic aspects of touring a poor neighborhood, Armstrong is well known within the communities. He vouches for both visitors' safety and the fact that residents appreciate foreigners getting a firsthand glimpse at a neighborhood that is about much more than the reductionist clichés of drugs, violence, and poverty. Furthermore, aside from pumping some money into the local community, if *favelas* become more of a tourist destination, police will be forced to diminish their often aggressive behavior towards their residents.

Indeed, *favela* tourism seems to be on the rise. In addition to offering trips into Rocinha with local English-speaking *motoboys* (delivery boys on motorcycles), **Be a Local** (tel. 21/9643-0366, www.bealocal.com, half-day trip R$65) also takes visitors to *favela* parties where they can dance the night away to the pounding strains of local funk. And in early 2005, the first *favela* hotel opened on the Morro Pereira da Silva, above Catete. **Pousada Favelinha** (Rua Antonio Joaquim Batista casa 13, Laranjeiras, no phone, www.favelinha.com, R$75 d) offers five double and dormitory rooms, all with balconies offering spectacular views. Guests who show up with toys for the local children's project receive two free *caipirinhas*, sippable on the rooftop terrace.

bikinied bodies, engaging in activities as varied as playing *futevolei* and smoking illicit joints. On Sundays, the main oceanfront drags of Avenida Viera Souto (Ipanema) and Avenida Delfim Moreira (Leblon) are closed to traffic, and the whole area becomes a massive outdoor recreational scene where, between sips of *água de coco* and ice-cold beer, you can inspect the latest styles in flip-flops and beachwear.

Like Copa, Ipanema and Leblon are divided into tribal territories. With its big waves, Praia do Arpoador (the edge of Ipanema closest to Copa) is a surfers' mecca. The area around Posto 8 (off Rua Farme de Amoedo) is a magnet for gay men to show off their *sungas*, while Posto

9 (the area off of Rua Vinícius de Morais) has long been the territory of artists and intellectuals who would rather flaunt their leftist viewpoints. Posto 10 is pretty much a family affair, and the end of Leblon is where young couples congregate with their tots on account of the playground and diaper-changing facilities.

Lagoa

If you go strolling along the shady streets of Ipanema and Leblon, you'll approach a vast lagoon ringed by luxury villas and apartment buildings set against the backdrop of mountains, including the famed and fabulous Corcovado. The **Lagoa Rodrigo de**

Freitas—or quite simply "Lagoa"—is a saltwater lagoon around which already svelte Cariocas get sportily dressed to the nines and power-walk, jog, and cycle until they break a sheen. The less athletically inclined (but still nicely decked out) prefer to sip an *água de coco* or *caipirinha* at one of the many kiosks around the lagoon, all of which serve food and drink. Also surrounding the Lagoa are posh private clubs, skating parks, tennis courts, and a heliport. In the evening, live music is often played at the kiosks (the best of which are near the Parque dos Patins and the Corte do Cangalo).

Jardim Botânico

On the far side of the Lagoa (across from Ipanema) is the lush upscale neighborhood of Jardim Botânico. While wealthy residents may lack sea views, they are handsomely rewarded by being in between the jungly slopes of Corcovado and the exotic flora of one of the world's best botanical gardens. Aside from possessing some of the city's chicest restaurants and bars, Jardim Botânico is where the Globo television network has its Rio headquarters, ensuring the presence of lots of celebs (and paparazzi).

A 138-hectare (340-acre) urban oasis (it's been scientifically proven that the temperature is always a bit cooler here than elsewhere in this often humid city), Rio's botanical garden, also called **Jardim Botânico** (Rua Jardim Botânico 1008, Jardim Botânico, tel. 21/3874-1808, www.jbrj.gov.br, 8 A.M.–5 P.M. daily, R$4), offers an unparalleled green mix of native Atlantic forest, lagoons covered with giant lily pads, and over 8,000 plant species. Many of them—pineapples, cinnamon, and tea among them—were introduced here prior to their cultivation in the rest of Brazil. Created by Dom João I, who planted the park's signature double row of imperial palms, the Jardim Botânico is a wonderfully tranquil refuge during the week (on weekends, it fills up with Cariocas and their kids). Highlights include the scent garden, the cactus garden, and the fabulous *orquidário,* featuring over 1,000 species of wild orchids. Kids

(and adults) with a fondness for the mildly gruesome will enjoy the carnivorous plant collection. Near the entrance is a pretty café and a great gift shop with lots of eco-souvenirs.

Adjacent to the Jardim Botânico is the **Parque Lage** (Rua Jardim Botânico 414, Jardim Botânico, tel. 21/2527-2397, 8 A.M.–5 P.M. daily, free), designed by 19th-century English landscaper John Tyndale. Its winding paths snake around small ponds and through the lush tropical landscape that covers the lower slopes of Corcovado.

Gávea

Although less hip and happening than Ipanema and neighboring Leblon, Gávea is an attractive, well-to-do neighborhood with lots of pretty tree-lined streets, easy access to the Lagoa, and quite a lively bar scene.

JOQUEI CLUBE

If you've ever dreamed about a day (or night) at the races, then you should head to Rio's Joquei Clube, also known as the Hipódromo da Gávea (Praça Santos Dumont 131, tel. 21/2259-1596). You've likely never seen a racetrack with such stupendous surroundings (the Cristo Redentor hovers directly above the bleachers). Built in 1926, the rather grand complex was featured in the 1946 Hitchcock film *Notorious,* in which Cary Grant (as a U.S. government agent) and Ingrid Bergman (as a former Nazi spy) took some time out from espionage and romance to bet on the horses. Even if you don't want to gamble (race days are Monday, Friday, Saturday, and Sunday), the club itself is a fun place to grab a drink (no shorts allowed). If you prefer shopping to racing, come on the weekend for the **Babilônia Feira Hype** (2–10 P.M. every second Sat.–Sun., R$5), a large combination flea/fashion market.

INSTITUTO MOREIRA SALLES

Located halfway up a steep hill full of striking villas, the Instituto Moreira Salles (IMS, Rua Marquês de São Vicente 476, Gávea, tel. 21/3284-7400, www.ims.com.br, 1–8 P.M. Tues.–Sun.) is one of the city's loveliest privately owned cultural centers. One of Rio's most prominent families, the Moreira Salles (owners of Unibanco, one of the country's major banks) commissioned architect Olavo Redig de Campos to build this house in 1951, and the result is Brazilian modernism at its most streamlined and alluring. The equally enticing gardens were landscaped by Roberto Burle Marx. The Moreira Salles family has always had a strong commitment to the arts (yes, Walter Salles Jr.—the director of the films *Central Station* and *The Motorcycle Diaries*—is a member of the clan), and part of their important collection of historical photographs (many depicting 19th- and 20th-century Rio de Janeiro) can be viewed, along with temporary exhibitions. There is also a cinema, a boutique, and an inviting café that serves a lavish (though extravagantly priced) afternoon tea.

São Conrado, Barra, and Recreio

After Leblon, Rio's coastal road, Avenida Niemeyer, goes through a long tunnel that burrows beneath the Morro de Dois Irmãos, whose slopes are home to one of Rio's largest *favelas,* Vidigal. Although from a socio-economic perspective, the successive beach neighborhoods are considered extensions of the Zona Sul, geographically, they are part of the Zona Oeste, since they are situated west of Copacabana, Ipanema, and Leblon. These sprawling neighborhoods are much more recent and lack the history and charm of the Zona Sul. While their beaches are attractive and unspoiled, the neighborhoods themselves offer little aside from a collection of soulless restaurants, bars, and gigantic shopping malls where the middle class Cariocas and *novo ricos* (nouveau riche) hang out. None of these neighborhoods were laid out with pedestrians in mind. Cars rule, but the coastline is also well-served by buses from the Zona Sul with destinations marked "Barra" and "Recreio."

São Conrado is a small and very posh neighborhood full of luxury high-rise condominiums and a fancy shopping mall. In a disarming contrast, these chic edifices gaze directly onto Rio's biggest and most notorious *favela:* **Rocinha,** home to over 200,000 Brazilians, whose brick and cement dwellings cover the otherwise jungle-carpeted Morro de Dois Irmãos. Although Rio is all about glaring contradictions and brutal extremes, nowhere else is the divide between rich and poor so prominently, fascinatingly, and perversely apparent. São Conrado's main draw is the small and spectacular **Praia do Pepino** (Cucumber Beach), where hang gliders burn off their adrenaline after taking off from the neighboring peaks of Pedra da Gávea and Pedra Bonita.

Another long tunnel brings you to the mega-developed, super-suburban, Miami-like *bairro* of **Barra da Tijuca** (known simply as "Barra"). A decade ago, this 16-kilometer (10-mile) stretch of coastline was little more than a long wild sweep of white sand with a few *barracas.* Now it is the playground for Rio's middle classes, who alternate days spent on the beaches and at the many *shoppings* with nights at the *bairro*'s many bars, clubs, and *shoppings.* Barra's one saving grace is its beach, which remains amazingly unspoiled, particularly during the week. On weekends, however, the sands sizzle with lots of young tanned and toned bodies in a partying frame of mind. The trendiest strip, at the beginning of the Barra (between Postos 1 and 2), is known as **Praia do Pepê** (access from Av. do Pepê). Although the surf is rough, you can swim here. You can also engage in all varieties of sports in the water and on the sand.

Barra da Tijuca becomes more deserted the farther west you travel. Eventually it turns into the 11-kilometer (7-mile) long beach known as **Recreio dos Bandeirantes**, whose untamed surroundings and rough waves are a magnet for Rio's surfing crowd. Particularly attractive is the small and secluded **Prainha** beach, at the end of Recreio. The spectacular waves and presence of several renowned surfing academies make it a mecca for surfers. Even more deserted is **Grumari,** whose reddish sands are framed by spectacular mountains covered in lush native Atlantic forest. Both Prainha and Grumari are located in protected nature reserves. Despite the fact they can't be reached by bus, they can fill up on the weekends with Cariocas seeking a quick back-to-nature fix.

MUSEU CASA DO PONTAL

Inland from the far end of Recreio dos Bandeirantes is the Museu Casa do Pontal (Estrada do Pontal 3295, tel. 21/2490-3278, www.popular.art.br/museucasadopontal, 9:30 A.M.–5 P.M. Tues.–Sun., R$5). Although it takes a while to get there (buses run from the Zona Sul), the final destination is worth it. Back in the late '40s, French designer and art collector Jacques Van de Beuque began traveling throughout Brazil (especially the Northeast), where he discovered a fantastically rich artisanal tradition that nobody—not even Brazilians—was aware of. To preserve and promote these works, he built a vast house surrounded by tranquil gardens. Today, it shelters the largest collection of Brazilian folk art in the country, with over 5,000 works ranging from wonderful clay figures of popular Northeast characters to the extravagant costumes worn by celebrants of traditional Bumba-Meu-Boi *festas.*

SÍTIO ROBERTO BURLE MARX

The idyllic Sítio Roberto Burle Marx (Estrada da Barra de Guaratiba 2019, tel. 21/2410-1412, tours by appointment only, 9:30 A.M. and 1:30 P.M. Tues.–Sun., R$5) is another attraction worth the time and effort to get to. Between 1949 and 1994, this bucolic country estate was the primary residence of renowned landscape architect Roberto Burle Marx, whose most famous projects in Rio include the Parque do Flamengo and Copacabana's iconic black-and-white mosaic "wave" promenade. The surrounding nursery/gardens—featuring more than 3,500 plant species collected from Brazil and around the world—were designed with great flair. Indeed, it was said about Marx—who was also a painter—that he used plants as other artists used paint. The colonial house (originally part of a coffee plantation) and adjoining atelier have been transformed into a museum where you can admire the artist's works, possessions, and rich collection of Brazilian folk art. If you don't have a car, take the bus marked "Marambaia-Passeio" that passes through the Zona Sul.

ENTERTAINMENT AND EVENTS

Rio boasts an impressive and dynamic arts scene with a multitude of events held at venues that are often quite striking. For information about what's going on (in Portuguese) check out the arts sections of the two daily papers, *Jornal do Brasil* and *O Globo,* or purchase *Veja Rio,* which comes with *Veja* magazine and offers comprehensive listings of everything going on in the city. For upcoming events in English as well as Portuguese, log on to www.riodejaneiro-turismo.com.br. Tickets (which are generally quite affordable) can be purchased directly at theaters and concert spaces.

Performing Arts

Rio most prestigious—and extravagantly ornate—performing arts space is the **Theatro Municipal** (Praça Floriano, Centro, tel. 21/2299-1677, www.theatromunicipal.rj.gov.br), which hosts the biggest national and international names in music, dance, opera, and theater. The Theatro Municipal has its own renowned symphony orchestra, opera company, and ballet troupe.

The historic **Sala Cecília Meireles** (Largo da Lapa 47, Lapa, tel. 21/2224-4291, www.funarj.rj.gov.br), built in 1926, was a grand hotel and a cinema before being transformed into a music hall featuring classical music performances. Located inside the grandiose former headquarters of the Banco do Brasil, the **Centro Cultural Banco do Brasil (CCBB)** (Rua 1 de Março 66, Centro, tel. 21/3808-2000, www.bb.com.br/cultura, noon–8 P.M. Tues.–Sun.) offers a consistently excellent selection of some of Rio's—and Brazil's—finest contemporary theater, dance, film, and music. Many events are free.

One of Rio's oldest and most distinguished theaters, **Teatro João Caetano** (Praça Tiradentes, Centro, tel. 21/2221-0305) features a diverse range of musical and dance as well as theatrical performances.

Concert Halls

Rio's most legendary concert hall is the

Canecão (Av. Venceslau Brás 215, Botafogo, tel. 21/2105-2000, www.canecao.com.br). Upon releasing new CDs, Brazil's major artists often kick off their national tours at this giant supper club next to Shopping Rio Sul.

Rio's biggest concert hall is the gigantic, state-of-the-art **Citibank Hall** (Av. Ayrton Senna 3000, Shopping Via Parque, Barra da Tijuca, tel. 21/2156-7300, www.citibankhall.com.br), where major national and international musical, theatrical, and dance events take place. Located beneath the Arcos de Lapa, **Circo Voador** (Flying Circus, Rua dos Arcos, Lapa, tel. 21/2533-5873, www.circovoador.com.br) has been one of the city's most vanguard outdoor musical venues since the 1980s. It continues to host big national stars as well as alternative local bands and theatrical groups.

Cinema

Rio is one of the Latin America's most important film markets, and you can see everything from Hollywood blockbusters to national, European, independent, and art films. Apart from the ubiquitous multiplexes in the city's shopping areas, Rio boasts numerous small art house cinemas, the largest concentrations of which are located in Botafogo, Ipanema, and Leblon. One of the city's biggest cinephile hangouts is the **Unibanco Arteplex** (Praia de Botafogo 35, Botafogo, tel. 21/2559-8750, www.ims.com.br). Along with six state-of-the art screens, it has a café, bistro, and great bookstore. Nearby are the **Espaço Cinema** (Rua Voluntários da Pátria 35, Botafogo, tel. 21/2226-1986) and the **Estação Botafogo** (Rua Voluntários da Pátria 88, Botafogo, tel. 21/2226-1988), which belong to the Grupo Estação (www.estacaovirtual.com.br), a group of cinemas that show a mixture of national and international independent and art films. Estação also has two cinemas in Ipanema: **Estação Laura Alvim** (Av. Vieira Souto 176, Ipanema, tel. 21/2267-4307), which has three small theaters in a cultural center overlooking the beach, and **Estação Ipanema** (Rua Visconde de Pirajá 605, Ipanema, tel. 21/2279-4603).

Although Rio was once home to an impressive number of glamorous movie palaces, the only survivor that still screens films is the **Cine Odeon BR** (Praça Mahatma Gandhi 5, Centro, tel. 21/2240-1093), a handsomely restored deco gem in Cinelândia that often hosts star-studded premiers. For two weeks in late September/early October, Rio hosts a topnotch international film festival, the **Festival do Rio** (www.festivaldorio.com.br), which always features an engaging array of movies.

Festivals and Events

There is always something going on in Rio, but the biggest, most popular, and most characteristically Carioca extravaganzas are, without a doubt, Reveillon and Carnaval.

REVEILLON

Ringing in the New Year on Copacabana Beach is one of the most magical and mystical New Year experiences—at least in the Western Hemisphere. Rio's Reveillon is second only to Carnaval in terms of pure spectacle. As night falls, millions of people clad in white congregate on the beach of Copacabana. The white symbolizes the purity of the new year and is also the color associated with Iemanjá, an immensely popular Afro-Brazilian religious deity ("*orixá*") whose title is Queen of the Seas. As legend has it, Iemanjá is a vain woman who loves beautiful things. Accordingly, revelers arrive at the beach bearing her favorite gifts: roses, perfumes, jewelry, and champagne. At the stroke of midnight, they wade into the ocean and toss their offerings into the dark Atlantic. If Iemanjá accepts their gifts, they are ensured a happy year. If the waves sweep them back to shore, better luck next time.

Midnight also signals the start of a gigantic fireworks display (touted as the world's biggest) and a series of open-air live music shows that take place at stages erected at various points along the beach. Then it's dancing and drinking the night away under the stars until morning, when everyone rings in the first day of the year (and rinses off the night's excesses) with a dip in the ocean.

BIRTH OF RIO'S CARNAVAL

The precursors to Rio's Carnaval were the *festas de entrudo*. Beginning in the late 1700s, these street celebrations allowed the masses to challenge the status quo – most famously by hurling flour and *limões de cheiro* ("scented lemons," which were actually wax balls filled with cheap perfume) in the streets and at the homes of the ruling elite. By the mid-19th century, Rio's upper classes decided they deserved some fun of their own. Inspired by the masquerade balls of Paris and Venice, they held fancy *bailes* (costume balls). In the tradition of Roman Carnavals of yore, they organized processions featuring carriages that were decorated according to allegorical themes.

Although Rio's lower classes were prohibited from joining in the parades, they watched from the sidelines (and gleefully tossed *limões de cheiro* at the bourgeoisie). Discontent with their exclusion, they also began to form lively *blocos* (groups) and *bandas* (bands) that marched in parades and danced the night away in Rio's streets. Many of these musical groups were organized by Rio's significant black population, who retained a strong African heritage.

Featuring groups playing string and woodwind instruments, drummers, and costumed dancers, they were the precursors of Rio's *escolas de samba* (samba schools). Over time, the tensions that existed between Rio's upper and lower classes melted away under the shared heat given off by the increasingly popular *festas*. While the masses adopted the flamboyant costumes and floats of Rio's upper castes, the elite were lured by the multitudes' intoxicating samba rhythms and percussion instruments. The result was a completely original hybrid celebration.

By the turn of the century, music was written specifically for Carnaval. In the early decades of the 20th century, some of Rio's most talented lyricists and musicians composed tunes that took the city by storm. Carnaval sambas were recorded on vinyl, and when radio came along, they were broadcast throughout Brazil. Each *escola de samba* enlisted composers to write words and melodies, which inspired the choreography of an elaborate procession. In 1932, the first Carnaval competition between *escolas de samba* was held, and the tradition has remained pretty much unchanged.

◖ CARNAVAL

Why is it that whenever people hear the word "Carnaval," Rio de Janeiro automatically springs to mind? Rio isn't the only city to host this Bacchanalian celebration, but its signature parades, balls, and *escolas de sambas* combined with the nonstop merrymaking have made it the most spectacular of Brazil's—not to mention the planet's—Carnavals. To experience Rio's hedonistic five-day *festa* in all its butt-swaying, ear-blasting, eye-popping, mind-blowing glory, make sure to book your accommodations *far* in advance.

Sambódromo: The Sambódromo is the most famous Carnaval event. It consists of the *desfiles* (parades) of the top *escolas de samba* (known as the Grupo Especial, or Special Group). These take place in a massive concrete stadium called the **Sambódromo** (Rua Marquês de Sapucaí, Praça Onze, Cidade Nova). Designed by Oscar Niemeyer, it can seat 90,000 people. *Desfiles* are held on the Sunday and Monday nights of Carnaval and involve 14 *escolas de samba* that compete against each other.

On each night (starting at 9 P.M. and going on until the morning of the next day), the *escolas* have between 85 and 95 minutes to strut their stuff for a table of judges who award points for various aspects of their performances, among them choreography, costumes, floats, decorations, *samba de enredo* (theme song), and percussion. Every year, the *escolas* invest incredible amounts of money, time, hard work, and talent in an attempt to outdo one another and be crowned champion. The final results are absolutely spectacular: a kaleidoscope of whirling and twirling sequins, feathers, and gaudy, flamboyant color. If you miss the competition itself, on the following Saturday you can catch the eight top schools performing in the championship parade, which also takes place at the Sambódromo. In fact, tickets to this "best of" compilation event are much cheaper than those for the *desfiles.*

Getting inexpensive **tickets** to the Sambódromo is a tricky affair since most of them are sold long before the event itself (they usually go on sale in January). Lineups are enormous and savvy scalpers and travel agents often snatch up the best seats. Two good sources of information about Carnaval in general and ticket outlets are the **Rio Carnival Guide** (www.rio-carnival.net) and **Riotur** (www.riodejaneiro-turismo.com.br), the municipal tourist secretariat. The latter sells (expensive) tickets (R$500) in private boxes for tourists, which are much more comfortable than the regular bleachers. Tickets for other sections range R$10–290. Try to sit in the central sections, which offer the best views and the most animation. You can also purchase tickets online at www.rio-carnival.net, or in person at Rio travel agencies (which usually charge a commission). If you find yourself without tickets at the last minute, head straight for the Sambódromo and look around for scalpers (they'll be looking around for you). If you're willing to miss the first couple of schools and arrive fashionably late (like most Cariocas), you can usually get some good bargains.

Although you can get to the Sambódromo by bus, these are usually packed, rowdy, and full of pickpockets. You're much better off taking a taxi or the Metrô (which runs 24 hours during Carnaval) to Praça Onze (if you're seated in an even-numbered sector) or Central (for an odd-numbered sector).

Street Carnaval: In recent years there has been a revival of the many neighborhood and resident association *blocos* and *bandas* that traditionally took to the streets and let loose in an explosion of music and merrymaking that some swear is way more fun than sitting around in the Sambódromo. Although the costumes of the *blocos* aren't as ornate as those of the *escolas de samba,* some are highly inventive and downright hilarious. Many men—both gay and straight—dress in drag. If you want to join in the fun, all you have to do is appear at a *bloco*'s headquarters on the day and time of its parades (Riotur provides this info). Check to see if you're expected to don the *bloco*'s traditional colors or to purchase a T-shirt (sold on the spot). Festivities usually kick off in the afternoon and last far into the night.

Blocos **and** *Bandas:* Centro is home to some of the city's most traditional *blocos.* Among the most popular are **Bafo de Onça, Bloco Cacique de Ramos,** and **Cordão do Bola Preta,** whose followers sport lots of *bolas pretas* (black polka dots). Santa Teresa features the **Carmelitas de Santa Teresa,** Glória has the **Banda da Glória,** and Botafogo boasts several lively traditional *blocos,* among them **Barbas, Bloco de Segunda,** and **Dois Pra Lá, Dois Prá Cá.** Copa's most famous *bloco* is **Bip Bip,** many of whose members are professional musicians, while bohemian Ipanema has some of the most wildly alternative groups, among them **Banda Ipanema, Símpatia É Quase Amor,** and the highly popular **Banda Carmen Miranda,** in which men of all sexual persuasions don platform shoes and tutti-frutti turbans to pay their respects to the Brazilian bombshell.

The city of Rio also organizes outdoor shows and festivities throughout the city. The two biggest events, however, are **Rio Folia** and the **Bailes da Cinelândia.** Rio Folia takes place around the Arcos da Lapa and features an eclectic and alternative mixture of various Brazilian musical tendencies. Cinelândia's outdoor *bailes* make an effort to revive Rio's traditional Carnaval balls of yore with a roster of top name singers and samba bands animating the crowds.

Carnaval Balls: The extravagant Carnaval balls of yesteryear are alive and well at Rio's clubs and hotels. Live samba bands supply the rhythms, and costumes (many of them quite spectacular) are de rigueur. Despite air-conditioning, the atmosphere is guaranteed to get hot and steamy as the night wears on. The

OFF-SEASON CARNAVAL ACTIVITIES

If you can't get to Rio for Carnaval, you can still experience an authentic slice of the action by taking part in the *ensaios* (rehearsals) every weekend by Rio's various *escolas de samba*. Aside from getting a behind-the-scenes glimpse at the makings of a successful *desfile* (parade), you'll get to soak up some authentic neighborhood atmosphere while listening to terrific samba. Since most schools are in the Zona Norte, sometimes close to *favelas*, you're best off taking a tour or a taxi. Below are a few of the most traditional samba schools. Mangueira and Salgueiro are the most popular for tourists, with the best infrastructure. They are also the closest to the Centro.

- **Beija Flor** (Praçinha Wallace Paes Leme 1025, Nilópolis, tel. 21/2791-2866, www.beija-flor.com.br)

- **Grande Rio** (Rua Almirante Barroso 5-6, Duque de Caixias, tel. 21/2771-2331, www.academicosdograderio.com.br)

- **Império Serrano** (Av. Ministro Edgar Romero 114, Madureira, tel. 21/2489-8722, www.imperioserrano.com)

- **Mangueira** (Rua Visconde de Niterói 1072, Mangueira, 3872-6878, www.mangueira.com.br)

- **Portela** (Rua Clara Nunes 81, Madureira, tel. 21/2489-6440, www.gre-portela.com.br)

- **Salgueiro** (Rua Silva Teles 104, Andaraí, tel. 21/2253-7608, www.salgueiro.com.br)

- **Unidos da Tijuca** (Clube dos Portuários, Rua Francisco Bicalho 47, Cidade Nova, tel. 21/2516-4053, www.unidosdatijuca.com.br)

As Carnaval approaches, the *escolas de samba* hold dress rehearsals at the Sambódromo, which are open to the public. You can also catch them at the newly opened **Cidade de Samba** (Rua Rivadávia Correia 60, Gamboa, tel. 24/2213-2503, www.cidadedosambarj.globo.com, 10 A.M.–5 P.M. Tues.–Sat., R$10), a vast complex created out of Rio's abandoned dockside warehouses. Here the *Grupo Especial escolas* have ample space to store materials, sew costumes, build allegorical floats, and display their talents to the public – usually on Thursday nights, when a combined show and buffet costs R$150. Since this area is only starting to be revitalized, make sure you take a taxi here.

For more information about *escolas de samba* and *ensaios*, contact the **Liga das Escolas de Samba** (tel. 21/3213-5151, www.liesa.globo.com).

---

most famous and fabulous event (costumes or formal wear required) is the **Magic Ball** held at the Copacabana Palace (Av. Atlântica 1702, Copacabana, tel. 21/2445-8790) on Saturday night, which attracts an international throng of rich and gorgeous people, for whom R$1,500 (the average price of a ticket) is chump change. Tickets to most other balls, however, are in a much more affordable range of R$30–50. Those held at the **Scala** club (Av. Afrânio de Melo Franco 292, Leblon, tel. 21/2239-4448), on every night during Carnaval, are some of the wildest and most spectacular, culminating on the last night with the immensely popular **Gala Gay.** Many other clubs also organize

bailes in which gay men can go all out in terms of their cross-dressing fantasies. Among the most legendary are those held nightly at Copacabana's famous gay club **Le Boy** (Rua Raul Pompéia 102, Copacabana, tel. 21/2513-4993). Since the one thing Cariocas don't take lightly is Carnaval, no matter where you go, you'll be expected to show up in a seriously extravagant costume.

For up-to-date information about Carnaval, check out Riotur's website, www.riodejaneiro-turismo.com.br, and the Rio Carnaval Guide website, www.rio-carnival.net, both of which have complete and updated information in English.

BOTEQUINS

Rio is legendary throughout Brazil for its *botequins*, informal bars that function as neighborhood headquarters for residents from all walks of life. Whether considered *pé sujo* ("dirty foot") – i.e., mildly mangy holes-in-the-wall – or *pé limpo* ("clean foot") – somewhat more refined and up-scale – the simple *botequim* is first and foremost a democratic enclave where Cariocas get together (usually after work or the beach) to talk about *futebol*, politics, or their sex lives for hours at a time.

The drink of choice is an ice-cold *chope* (draft) served in traditional glasses that come in three sizes: the *tulipa* ("tulip"), the *garotinho* ("little boy"), and the mug-sized *caldeireta* (rarely seen since Cariocas subscribe to the belief that the larger the glass, the warmer and more undrinkable the beer gets). To nibble, there are always plenty of mouthwatering *petiscos* (bar snacks), the most common being *bolinhos de bacalhau* (deep-fried codfish balls), *carne seca desfiada* (shredded sun-dried beef), and velvety thick *caldo de feijão* (black bean broth), traditionally served with chopped cilantro, *torresmos* (pork rinds), lime, and *pimenta* (hot pepper).

NIGHTLIFE

As laid-back and relaxing as Rio can be by day, at night it becomes a buzzing hive of activity. As soon as happy hour rolls around, Rio's traditional casual bars—*botequins*—are flooded with Cariocas downing ice-cold *chopes* (draft beer) and trading quips and *fofocas* (gossip). While some tuck in for the night, for others these neighborhood bars are merely warm-up zones. Rio is one of the most musical cities you'll ever encounter, and there is no shortage of bars, clubs, dance halls, and open air venues featuring live performances of Brazil's myriad musical styles. Since Cariocas rarely listen to music without succumbing to the urge to move their bodies, most of these places feature dancing as well. For those who prefer a more

globalized beat, the city has its share of nightclubs and discos, although they are blander and more mimetic than one might expect (in terms of contemporary sounds, São Paulo definitely has the advantage). Although most of Centro shuts down after happy hour, more traditional bohemian *barros* of Santa Teresa and Lapa have been reclaimed by new bohos who flock to hear samba, *chorinho*, *forró*, and other home-grown melodies. Meanwhile, the swankier watering holes and night spots of the Zona Sul offer more internationally urban brands of fun, albeit with a decidedly bossa nova twist.

Centro

Centro doesn't have much of a nightlife to speak of (yet). However, amid its narrow old streets are some of the city's oldest and most atmospheric *botequins*, which fill up with the Rio's working crowd when happy hour rolls around.

BARS

Adega do Timão (Rua Visconde de Itaboaraí 10, Centro, tel. 21/2224-9616, 4 p.m.–midnight Tues.–Sun.) is a small, charming little bar decorated with nautical gear and a fancy crystal chandelier thrown in for good measure. Its proximity to the Centro Cultural Banco do Brasil and Espaço Cultura dos Correios has made it a beer stop *obligé* for the culture crowd.

Founded in 1887, **Bar Luiz** (Rua da Carioca 39, Centro, tel. 21/2262-6900, www.barluiz.com.br, 11 a.m.–11 p.m. Mon.–Sat.) is a classic old Carioca *botequim* with a German accent—and menu, including a famous potato salad with homemade mayo, as well as various grilled sausages and schnitzels. Whatever you choose, it will invariably go nicely with the creamy *chope* on tap, considered one of the best in town.

Both for people-watching and monument-gazing, its hard to beat **Amarelinho** (Praça Floriano 55-B, Cinelândia, tel. 21/2240-8434, www.amarelinho.com.br). Cinelândia's most famous yellow-tiled outdoor bar offers views of the Theatro Municipal and Biblioteca Nacional and hundreds of Cariocas parading back and forth. The *frango a passarinho*

GAY RIO

With a reputation as the "Marvelous City," one would expect Rio to have more of a gay scene. While the vibe is gay friendly, there is not really a gay area to speak of, and fewer specifically gay and lesbian venues than there are in São Paulo. Actually, lesbian venues are pretty nonexistent. As in many other cities in Brazil, instead of a gay neighborhood, GLS (a Brazilian slang term for *gay, lesbica, e simpatisante;* i.e., gay friendly) spaces rule, with gays, lesbians, and heteros mixing socially.

The closest thing Rio has to a gay hood is a high-profile strip of Ipanema beach stretching from Posto 8 to Posto 9. If you're walking along Avenida Vieira Souto, you'll see beach *barracas* flying rainbow flags and the toned outlines of well-oiled muscles. The street perpendicular to the beach, **Rua Farme de Amoedo,** also attracts a gay crowd. **A Bofetada** (Rua Farme de Amoedo 87-A, Ipanema, tel. 21/2227-1675, 8 A.M.-close daily, no cover) is a laid-back and friendly bar that draws a mixed GLS crowd and offers great views of the action.

Nearby, the **Dama de Ferro** (Rua de Vinícius de Morais 288, Ipanema, tel. 21/2247-2330, www.damadeferro.com.br, 11 P.M.-close Wed.-Sat., R$15 cover) is a funky lounge/disco/art gallery operated by artist Adriana Lima. The inspired furnishings in the industrial chic lounge are by Lima and are for sale. Upstairs, local and international DJs make sure that everyone's taken care of on the musical front. The bathrooms, which open right onto the dance floor, are tiny galleries unto themselves. To say the menu is unusual is an understatement when faced with the likes of chicken sorbet with warm tomato topping.

On the street parallel to Rua Farme de Amoedo, **Rua Teixeira de Melo,** there are a few other gay spots, including the intimate **Galeria Café** (Rua Teixeira de Melo 31, Ipanema, tel. 21/2523-8350, www.galeriacafe.com.br, 10:30 P.M.-close Wed.-Sat., noon-8 P.M. Sun., R$15 cover), another hip hybrid space sheltering a café and art gallery. Come night, it holds sizzling *festas* with soul and drum-bossa music that reels in a trendy crowd. Sundays are reserved for the clothing and design bazaar, where you can check out local designers' creations while getting your groove on.

Copacabana also has a few gay spots. As in Ipanema, the gay crowd has conquered a prize strip of beach – directly in front of the Copacabana Palace – where the *barracas* **Quiosque 35** (open 24 hours) and **Rainbow** are located. Meanwhile, at night the most eclectic group of homegrown and international gays (among them Calvin Klein, a Carioca convert) line up to enter the notorious temple of gaydom, **Le Boy** (Rua Raul Pompéia 102, tel. 21/2513-4993, www.leboy.com.br, 11 P.M.-close Tues.-Sun., R$10-15 cover, free before midnight). Aside from dancing galore, this enormous club offers debauchery in the form of go-go boys and a *quarto escuro* (dark room). Upstairs, its sister club, **La Girl** (Rua Raul Pompeia 102, Copacabana, tel. 21/2513-4993, www.lagirl.com.br, 11 P.M.-close daily, R$10-15 cover, free before midnight) attracts a rather glam following of girls who just wanna have fun.

In Lapa, **Fundição Progresso** (Rua dos Arcos 24, tel. 21/2220-5070, 9 P.M.-close daily, R$70 cover for *festas*) is popular for its frequent GLS *festas*, whereas **Cabaret Casanova** (Rua Mem de Sá 25, tel. 21/2221-6555, Fri.-Sun., R$5-10 cover) is Rio's oldest gay bar, dating back to 1929. It attracts a refreshingly non-trendy (downwardly mobile) crowd who cheer on good old-fashioned drag queens. Another alternative to the Zona Sul's upscale muscle boy scene are the wild parties held at Centro's **Cine Ideal** (Rua da Carioca 62, Centro, tel. 21/2221-1984, www.idealparty.com.br, 11:30 P.M.-close Fri.-Sat., R$18-28 cover). Housed in an ingeniously renovated belle epoque building that was formerly one of Rio's most glamorous cinemas, this massive disco – featuring various bars and a fabulous open-air rooftop lounge – is a current hot spot. For more info about Rio's gay scene, check out www.riogaylife.com.

(chicken nuggets doused in sautéed garlic) is a happy-hour favorite. Close by, **Villarino** (Av. Calógeras 6, Loja B, Centro, tel. 21/2240-1627, noon–10 P.M. Mon.–Fri.) doesn't serve *chope* at all, but whiskey. It was a favorite haunt of a midcentury bohemian crowd that included Tom Jobim and Vinícius de Morais, who used it as their private clubhouse. Today the retro *uisqueria* (whiskey bar) with its scarlet banquettes and elegant marble tables attracts a suit and tie crowd who alternate whiskey shots with bites of delicious prosciutto and brie sandwiches.

LIVE MUSIC

In 2004, **Trapiche Gamboa** (Rua Sacadura Cabral 155, Gamboa, tel. 21/2516-0868, www.trapichegamboa.com.br, 6:30 P.M.–1 A.M. Tues.–Thurs., 6:30 P.M.–3:30 A.M. Fri., 8:30 P.M.–3:30 A.M. Sat., cover R$12–20) was a pioneer when it opened its doors in the otherwise louche and deserted port zone of Centro. But when it started offering some of the best live samba performances in town, music lovers took notice—as did other risk-taking entrepreneurs who, feeling that trendy Lapa has become saturated, slowly began moving into the neighborhood. As a result, it's home to a progressive and hip scene. For a change from the classic lime *caipirinhas,* try one made with fragrant red *pitangas.*

Gafieiras were originally ballrooms where Rio's working classes came to dance the night away. They began springing up in Centro during the 1920s, and a few have survived. The oldest and most famous is **Nova Estudantina** (Praça Tiradentes 79, Centro, tel. 21/2232-1149, 8 P.M.–1 A.M. Thurs., 10 P.M.–4 A.M. Fri.–Sat., cover R$15–25), whose decor conjures up its beginnings in 1928. Aside from live orchestras playing traditional ballroom ditties, live bands play *forró,* soul, and rock. The crowd is very mixed with people of all ages, and because there's room for 1,500 dancing fools, you certainly won't feel claustrophobic. On Wednesday and Friday evenings master *sambistas* and their bands perform outdoors (behind the MAM)

at the **Clube Santa Luzia** (Av. Almirante de Noronho 300, Centro, tel. 21/9426-6456, 8 P.M., cover R$8). In terms of the enchantment factor, it's hard to surpass samba-ing in front of a moonlit Pão de Açúcar.

Lapa

After long decades of being down and (very) out, Rio's former bohemian quarter par excellence got a new lease on life by retransforming itself into the city's undisputed hot spot to listen and dance to live music. From Thursdays onwards, its many bars, clubs, and narrow streets (particularly Rua Joaquim Silva) pulse with a variety of rhythms, revelers from every Carioca *bairro,* and an increasing number of tourists. Although not quite as edgy as it used to be, Lapa still rules Rio's musical roost.

BARS

Like Centro, Lapa has some wonderful old *botequins* that have survived from its heyday, whose walls, if they could talk, would surely have a lot of stories to tell. **Bar Brasil** (Av. Mem de Sá 90, Lapa, tel. 21/2509-5943, 11:30 A.M.–11 P.M. Mon.–Fri., 11:30 A.M.–4 P.M. Sat.) is a neighborhood institution, serving German food such as *eisbein, kassler,* and sauerkraut—perfect between sips of frothy beer. The canvases on the walls are by Chilean artist Selarón, who is responsible for the mosaic-covered staircase that leads up to Santa Teresa. Dating from 1903, **Nova Capela** (Av. Mem de Sá, Lapa, tel. 21/2252-6228, 11 A.M.–5 A.M. daily) is the only one of Lapa's old-time *botequins* that stays open into the wee hours. If you're feeling hungry, try the house specialty: *cabrito com arroz-de-brocolis* (roasted goat kid with broccoli rice).

LIVE MUSIC AND NIGHTCLUBS

In Lapa's streets and renovated old buildings you'll encounter an astonishing diversity of music, and as revitalization of this *bairro* continues unabated, new bars and clubs are opening all the time. The majority are on Rua do Lavradio and Rua Mem de Sá. For listings and schedules of all performances and events in Lapa, check out www.lanalapa.com.br.

Rio Scenarium (Rua do Lavradio 20, Lapa, tel. 21/3147-9005, www.rioscenarium.com.br, 6 P.M.–2:30 A.M. Tues., 6:30 P.M.–2:30 A.M. Wed.–Thurs., 7 P.M.–2:30 A.M. Fri., 8 P.M.–2:30 A.M. Sat., cover R$12–25) is one of the city's most enchanting and original bars. If it's lost some of its cachet (lots of gringos trying to samba), it's retained its unique charm. Located on Lapa's antiques row, Rio Scenarium's three floors are chock-full of antiques, which are rented out to film and TV productions—you can sit, sprawl, and lounge upon certain pieces while others are merely eye candy. On most nights, top names in samba, *choro,* and *forró* perform, inciting the mixed public to take to the dance floor. Arrive early (before 8 P.M.) or reserve a table because the place gets packed.

Carioca da Gema (Rua Mem de Sá 79, Lapa, tel. 21/2221-0043, www.barcariocadagema.com.br, 6 P.M.–close Mon.–Fri., 8 P.M.–close Sat., cover R$15–20) is a classic spot to listen to top quality samba and *choro* performed by big names and rising stars. The ambiance is warm and rustic and there is a copious menu. More sophisticated and upscale (and consequently pricy) than its neighbors, **Estrela da Lapa** (Av. Mem de Sá 130, Lapa, tel. 21/2509-7602, 6 P.M.–close Mon.–Fri., 7 P.M.–close Sat., www.estreladalapa.com.br, cover R$20–25) is undeniably charming with its wooden fixtures, art nouveau wrought-iron balconies, and romantic lighting. Music runs the gamut from samba and *choro* to MPB and rock. On weekends, DJs often host *festas.*

Clube dos Democráticos (Rua do Riachuelo 91, Lapa, tel. 21/2252-4611, www.clubedosdemocraticos.com.br, Wed.–Sat. 9:30 P.M.–2 A.M., cover R$7–15) has been around since 1867. Started by three friends who bought it with winnings from a lottery ticket, the Clube served as headquarters for one of Rio's most high-society Carnaval clubs. Members were a forward-thinking republican and abolitionist bunch (which didn't stop Emperor Pedro II from partying here) whose bashes were legendary well into the 1940s. Then gradually the animation faded as the house sank into dilapidation. In 2004, a young historian who fell in love with the facade organized a *baile* that became such a cult hit that dance soirées are now held regularly in the vast ballroom. Music ranges from samba to *choro* and the crowd is young and eager to strut their stuff. Also located in a renovated old house, **Six Electro** (Rua das Marrecas 38, Lapa, tel. 21/2510-3230, www.clubsix.com.br, 11 P.M.–close Fri.–Sat., cover R$20–40) features three floors where you can mellow out to the post-modern likes of trance, drum 'n' bass, hip-hop, and electronica. The decor mingles medieval and industrial flourishes. Five bars and a pizzeria ensure you'll have enough to eat and drink.

Santa Teresa
BARS
The unpretentious bars of "Santa" are increasingly luring an alternative crowd charmed by the laid-back vibe of this boho *bairro*. Inspired by the typically rustic bars of Minas Gerais, **Bar do Mineiro** (Rua Paschoal Carlos Magno 99, Santa Teresa, tel. 21/2221-9227, 11 A.M.–2 A.M. Tues.–Sat., 11 A.M.–midnight Sun.) is a charmingly old-fashioned *botequim,* accessorized with black-and-white photos and miniature wooden *bondes*. Aside from its delicious homemade *pastéis* stuffed with fillings such as *feijão mineiro* and *carne seca com abóbora* (sun-dried beef with pumpkin), the bar is noted for its *feijoadas.* While mellow during the week, on weekends it gets quite crowded.

Equally picturesque is **Goya Beira** (Largo das Neves 13, Santa Teresa, tel. 21/2232-5751, 5:30 P.M.–midnight Sun.–Thurs., 5:30 P.M.–2 A.M. Fri.–Sat.), a simple but welcoming bar looking out onto Praça Neves and the rumbling *bondes.* Aside from icy beer, try the *cachaças* infused with orange or ginger. The homemade pizza is quite tasty.

Flamengo and Botafogo
Both Flamengo and Botafogo are home to some of the city's most traditional watering holes, where you can eat and drink well while soaking up some authentic Carioca atmosphere.

BARS

A Flamengo favorite, **Belmonte** (Praia do Flamengo 300, Flamengo, tel. 21/2552-3349, 10 A.M.–4 A.M. daily) is a little more refined (*pé limpo*) than your average Carioca *botequim*—which perhaps explains its popularity. It gets so busy in the late afternoons that customers stand and balance their cups on barrels of beer. The *empadas*—with a variety of fillings—complement the icy *chope*. Although others have opened throughout the city, this original bar is the most atmospheric.

NIGHTCLUBS

Located in an attractive old house, **Casa da Matriz** (Rua Henrique Novaes 107, Botafogo, tel. 21/2266-1014, www.casadamatriz.com.br, 11 P.M.–close Mon. and Wed.–Sat., cover R$10–25) hosts some of the most happening dance parties in town, courtesy of an eclectic roster of house DJs and a styling, alternative crowd with a proclivity for contemporary sounds. Monday's A Maldita ("The Damned") *festas* promise that you'll begin the week feeling trashed. If you need a breather, check out the rotating photo exhibits or flake out in the lounge.

LIVE MUSIC

If you want to listen to live *choro* played outdoors in attractive surroundings, head to the pretty residential *bairro* of Laranjeiras, adjacent to Flamengo. On Saturdays, from 11 A.M.–close, the group Choro na Feira plays in the tree-shaded Praça da Rua General Glicério, where a colorful *feira* (open-air market) is held. To satiate your hunger and thirst, have a deep-fried *pastel* (a type of turnover) and an icy beer. On Sundays, starting at 11 A.M., it's the turn of students from the Escola Portátil de Música to play in the attractive Praça São Salvador, also in Laranjeiras.

Urca

One of this neighborhood's few bars, **Bar e Restaurante Urca** (Rua Cândido Gaffré 205, Urca, tel. 21/2295-8744, 11 A.M.–11 P.M. Mon.–Sat., 11 A.M.–6:30 P.M. Sun.) is among the most scenic *botequins* in Rio. A recent renovation restored its 1930s facade and spruced up the interior. Fortunately, the view over the Baía de Guanabara remains bewitching. On Saturdays, a traditional *feijoada* is served.

Copacabana and Leme

Copa throbs at night, but more as a result of red-light district action on Avenida Atlântica and the oceanfront restaurants and bars crammed with international tourists. Nonetheless, there are a few exceptional enclaves.

BARS

Cervantes (Rua Barata Ribeiro 7-B, Copacabana, tel. 21/2275-6147, www.restaurantecervantes.com.br, noon–4 A.M. Sun. and Tues.–Thurs., noon–6 A.M. Fri.–Sat.) is one of Copa's favorite *botequins,* especially after a night of carousing. The house specialties are the delicious and impossibly thick sandwiches—most of which feature *abacaxi,* a native species of pineapple. Try the *Cervantes especial—abacaxi* with filet mignon and paté.

Bip Bip (Rua Almirante Gonçalves 50, Loja D, Copacabana, tel. 21/2267-9696, 7 P.M.–1 A.M. daily) is a tiny hole-in-the-wall *botequim* with two saving graces: its location on a quiet Copa street, which allows tables and chairs to be arranged outside, and terrific musical jams by top Carioca samba, *choro,* and bossa nova performers. Utterly unpretentious, "Bip" is a welcome antidote to Copa's touristy oceanfront bars.

NIGHTCLUBS

Bunker 94 (Rua Raul Pompéia 94, Copacabana, tel. 21/2521-0367, 11:30 P.M.–close Thurs.–Sat., cover R$10–20) is a classic Copa hot spot that reels in a mixed local and international public. The diverse tunes at this trilevel joint—including rock, funk, hiphop, and soul—are spun by some of the city's top DJs. A more recent upstart on Copa's club scene is **Fosfobox** (Rua Siqueira Campos 143, 22-A, Copacabana, tel. 21/2548-7498, www.fosfobox.com.br, 11 P.M.–close Wed.–Sun., R$15–20), an underground basement club that shares space with an antiques gallery. Depending on your spatial sensibilities "Fosfo's" dance floor is either intimate or claustrophobic, but the upstairs Fosfobar is definitely conducive to mellowing out. The DJ-spun soundtrack ranges from rock to techno and the scene is Copa cool with a definite alternative edge.

Ipanema and Leblon

Both Ipanema and Leblon possess a vibrant nightlife that runs the gamut from laid-back, beloved sidewalk *botequins* to stylish bars, lounges, and a few nightclubs that attract an eternally fashionable crowd.

BARS

Garota de Ipanema (Rua Vinícius de Morais 49-A, Ipanema, tel. 21/2523-3837, 11 A.M.–2 A.M. Sun.–Thurs., 11 A.M.–4 A.M. Fri.–Sat.) is the famous bar (originally called Bar do Veloso) where Vinícius de Morais and Tom Jobim were inspired to write "The Girl from Ipanema" after being mutually seduced by said girl (named Helô Pinheiro), who was passing by on her way to the beach. This event alone has made the bar somewhat of a *ponto turístico,* but since this is Ipanema and the *chope* is nice and cold, you could do a lot worse.

Jobi (Rua Ataulfo de Paiva 1166-B, Leblon, tel. 21/2274-0547, 8 A.M.–4 A.M. daily) is a classic Leblon address and a classic Carioca *botequim,* long frequented by artists, journalists and intellectuals (for this reason, passing pedestrians always shoot surreptitious glances at the outdoor tables in search of celebs). It's perennially chosen as one of the city's top bars due to the quality of its *chope* and flavorful *petiscos*—such as *carne seca desfiada* (shredded sun-dried beef), *bolinhos de bacalhau,* and velvety *caldo de feijão*—you'll need to arrive early if you want a table.

Close by, on a shady side street, **Bracarense** (Rua José Linhares 85, Leblon, tel. 21/2294-3549, 7 A.M.–midnight Mon.–Sat., 9 A.M.–10 P.M. Sun.) is quite tiny, but as this laid-back neighborhood bar fills up with locals on the way home from work or the beach, the surrounding sidewalk quickly overflows with tables and stools. The *petiscos* here are justly celebrated: The house specialty, *bolinho de aipim com camarão* is a crisp ball of deep-fried pureed manioc filled with shrimp and creamy Catupiry cheese.

If you're feeling beer weary, head to the **Academia da Cachaça** (Rua Conde da Bernadote 26, Loja G, Leblon, tel. 21/2239-1542, www.academiadacachaca.com.br, noon onwards daily) to savor one of the city's most famous *caipirinhas.* Lured by the hundreds of bottles of Brazil's national liquor on display (and available for purchase), you might also want to sample some of the finer *pingas* (*pinga* means "drop"—slang for *cachaça*) on the menu, which rival the smoothest whiskies. Once you've whetted your appetite, dig into the famous *feijoada* or try the *escondidinho,* sun-dried beef hidden (*escondido*) beneath a creamy blanket of pureed manioc.

If you can't afford to splurge on a room or even a meal at Rio's brand-new design hotel of the moment, Hotel Fasano, the next best thing is a cocktail in its supremely sophisticated bar/ lounge, **Londra** (Av. Vieira Souto 80, Ipanema, tel. 21/3202-8000, www.hotelfasano.com.br, 7 P.M.–1 A.M. Mon.–Wed., 7 P.M.–2:30 A.M. Thurs.–Sat.) designed by Philippe Starck. With minutes of this hotel's opening in August 2007, the bar had been anointed as *the* place to see and be seen in the Zona Sul. Trendiness aside, the warm brick walls, inviting leather sofas, elegant service, and a mean apple martini will have you mellow in no time.

Leblon's best bar with a view is the always-stylish and very romantic **Bar d'Hotel,** on the second floor of the Hotel Marina All-Suites (Av. Delfim Moreira 696, Leblon, tel. 21/2172-1100, www.marinaallsuites.com.br, 6 P.M.–2 A.M. daily). Aside from its tasteful decor—a mix of modern design and antiques—the stunning views of Ipanema and Leblon beaches make it a favorite cocktail haunt for Carioca lovebirds (both gay and straight). The selection of cocktails is quite creative and includes *caipiruby* (a vodka *caipirinha* made with red fruits) and the royal (vodka, cointreau, lime, ginger, and pomegranate juice). Snacks range from mini lamb burgers with foie gras to delicious Nutella crêpes (no sharing allowed, or you'll have to pay extra). If you want a coveted window table, reserve in advance.

LIVE MUSIC AND NIGHTCLUBS

One of Rio's swankiest musical clubs, **Mistura Fina** (Av. Rainha Elisabeth 769, Ipanema, tel. 21/8212-3883, www.misturafina.com.br, noon onwards daily, cover R$20–60) just moved to renovated space on the second floor of Barril 1800 with magnificent ocean views. Although its main fare is jazz, this anthological piano bar also hosts a variety of national and international performers that play MPB, blues, and samba. In keeping with the prices and refined ambiance, the clientele is older and more upscale. If you feel the urge to nosh, there is an extensive and excellent menu.

Melt (Rua Rita Ludolf 47, Leblon, tel. 21/2249-9309, cover R$10–20) is utterly Leblon: sleek, chic, and oh so fashionable, just like the toned and tanned crowd that turns up to work up a glow on the dance floor. The musical selection—ranging from samba-rock to hiphop—is courtesy of a rotating handful of DJs. Creative dishes are served in the candlelit downstairs lounge.

Lagoa and Jardim Botânico

QUIOSQUES

With its laid-back environs and stunning views of Corcovado and Lagoa Rodrigo de Freitas, the Lagoa has become quite a scene with its many *quiosques* (kiosks; some are quite sophisticated). The unusually named **Palaphita Kitch** (Av. Epitácio Pessoa, Kiosk 20, Parque do Cantagalo, Lagoa, tel. 21/2227-0837, www.palaphita-kitch.com.br, 6 P.M.–3 A.M. daily) is by far the most imaginative and seductive of these kiosk bars. Zona Sul cool meets the Amazon rainforest with lounge furniture made from reforested wood and plenty of lush foliage as a decorative flourish. At night, the place is lit up by torches. As soothing music lulls you, sip on exotic fruit drinks and feast on appetizers made with Amazonian ingredients such as wild passion fruit and *jacaré* (cayman).

BARS

Also overlooking the Lagoa, **Bar Lagoa** (Av. Epitácio Pessoa 1674, Lagoa, tel. 21/2523-1135, 6 P.M.–2 A.M. Mon., noon–2 A.M. Tues.–Sun.)

is a beloved *botequim* whose art deco interior hasn't changed much since the 1930s. It was originally named Bar Berlin; the owner strategically changed its name during World War II, but the kitchen continues to serve hearty yet simple German fare that goes nicely with an icy *chope*.

Upscale Jardim Botânico also has a thriving bar scene, frequented by a young and stylish crowd. Both worldly and relaxed (if a little preppy), **Caroline Café** (Rua J.J. Seabra 10, Jardim Botânico, tel. 21/2540-0705, www.carolinecafe.com.br, noon–2 A.M. Mon.–Wed., noon–4 A.M. Thurs.–Fri., 7 P.M.–4 A.M. Sat.) is one of those rare places that, despite having been around for years, has never gone out of fashion. Sporting two floors and a romantic terrace, it offers various ambiances to choose from, including a lounge with DJ-spun tunes. The imported beers are a big draw, as are the delicious burgers and fries.

Much more recent, but already a major neighborhood hit is **Saturnino** (Rua Saturnino de Brito 50, Jardim Botânico, tel. 21/3874-0064, www.saturnino.com.br, 6 P.M.–close daily). While the interior is stylish, the most coveted tables are outside beneath an enormous fig tree (if it rains, there's a retractable roof). The ridiculously long drink menu boasts over 200 offerings—if you're feeling indecisive go for the mixed *caipivodca* kit, with a sampling of six different *caipis* ranging from pineapple with mint to mango with *pimenta*.

Gávea

The area known as Baixa Gávea has been a nocturnal hot spot for years, luring beautiful young Zona Sulistas to the lively bars fanning out from Praça Santos Dumont.

BARS

Braseira da Gávea (Praça Santos Dumont 116, tel. 21/2239-7494, 11:30 A.M.–1 A.M. Mon.–Thurs., 11:30 A.M.–3 A.M. Fri.–Sat., 11:30 A.M.–1 A.M. Sun.) is one of the most traditional *botequins* on the scene. It serves up a delicious charcoal-grilled chicken with fries that satisfies late-night hunger pangs.

NIGHTCLUBS

Gávea is also home to one of the Zona Sul's trendiest nightclubs, **OO** (Av. Padre Leonal França 240, Gávea, tel. 21/2540-8041, www.00site.com.br, 8:30 A.M.–3:30 A.M. Thurs.–Sun., cover R$20–50), which is located inside Rio's planetarium. Star-gazing also occurs inside this sleek and chic hybrid bar/disco/restaurant with the likes Mick Jagger and Javier Bardem appearing among the usual bevy of wealthy young Zona Sulistas, models, and TV celebs. To keep clients on their well-pedicured toes, the tunes are extremely eclectic and vary from house to '80s and '90s memorabilia, with guest DJs taking charge of frequent *festas.*

SHOPPING

Like any big, cosmopolitan city, Rio is a great place for shopping, with something for most tastes and budgets. The best things to buy in Rio (as opposed to elsewhere) are Brazilian beach fashions and surfwear, antiques, and CDs. Precious and semiprecious stones are a classic purchase. You can also find traditional arts and crafts from all over the country.

Shopping Malls

Rio's *shoppings* are more than just malls: They are microcosms where Cariocas can shop 'til they drop, and also wander around, gossip, flirt, read, eat, drink, check out a movie or play, and even go skating. Depending on the neighborhood, the clientele, shops, and ambiance vary vastly.

Shopping Rio Sul (Rua Lauro Müller 116, Botafogo, tel. 21/3527-7200, www.riosul.com.br, 10 A.M.–10 P.M. Mon.–Sat., 3–9 P.M. Sun.) is one of the oldest and most popular *shoppings.* Its convenient location in Botafogo, close to the tunnel entrance to Copacabana, means that every single bus under the sun passes right in front of its doors. In 2007, it emerged from a makeover looking considerably refreshed.

Until recently, the chicest *shopping* in town was the appropriately named **São Conrado Fashion Mall** (Estrada da Gávea 899, São Conrado, tel. 21/2111-4444, www.scfashionmall.com.br, 10 A.M.–10 P.M. Mon.–Sat.,

3–9 P.M. Sun.), a small but decidedly sleek mall accessorized with plenty of tropical foliage and skylights. The boutiques are all *"feshun"* (Carioca speak for "fashion"), i.e., tasteful and pricy. Most of the food court offerings follow suit.

Giving São Conrado a serious run for its *reais* is the newest *shopping* on the block, **Shopping Leblon** (Av. Afrânio Melo Franco 290, Leblon, tel. 21/3138-8000, www.shoppingleblon.com.br, 10 A.M.–10 P.M. Mon.–Sat., 3–9 P.M. Sun.), which opened its glittering doors at the end of 2006. Befitting its Leblon address, it is a beautiful place for beautiful people. Aside from 200 stylish stores, cinemas, and a cultural center, its food court boasts stunning views of Lagoa Rodrigo de Freitas and Corcovado.

In a sprawling suburban neighborhood filled with massive malls (and parking lots) **Barra Shopping** (Av. das Américas 4666, Barra da Tijuca, tel. 21/4003-4131, www.barrashopping.com.br) is the most massive of Rio's malls, with over 500 stores, an indoor amusement park suggestively dubbed "The Hot Zone," and the most "modern" bowling alley in all of Latin America.

Carioca Fashion

If *shoppings* leave you feeling cold (a literal possibility, given the way they blast the air-conditioning), take your "buysies" to Ipanema, whose tree-lined streets are stuffed with boutiques selling the latest creations from Brazilian and Carioca designers. The largest concentration of stores can be found on Rua Barão da Torre, Rua Gárcia d'Avila, Rua Anibal de Mendonça, and Rua Visconde de Pirajá, where many *galerias* (similar to micro malls) offer hidden treasures that you'd never guess existed. Two of the biggest and most posh are **Galeria Forum Ipanema** (Rua Visconde de Pirajá 351, Ipanema, tel. 21/2523-2140, www.forumipanema.com.br, 9 A.M.–8 P.M. Mon.–Fri., 9 A.M.–6 P.M. Sat.) and **Galeria Ipanema 2000** (Rua Visconde de Pirajá 547, Ipanema, tel. 21/2512-4224, www.ipanema2000.com.br, 9 A.M.–9 P.M. Mon.–Sat.).

Rio fashion is all about beachwear—it's a great place to buy the cutting-edge bikini or *sunga* (male version of bikini), guaranteed to transform you into the queen or king of your neighborhood or health club swimming pool back home. Men can indulge in surfwear and some summery streetwear (jeans and T-shirts), but otherwise Carioca designers cater more to women, in general with clingy, sexy lines and designs in bright colors and featuring interesting details. Women will find lots of great shoes—the more high-heeled, the better—while both sexes will delight in the variety of funky flip-flips available.

Blue Man (www.blueman.com.br), **Lenny** (www.lenny.com.br), **Bum Bum** (www.bumbum.com.br), **Salinas** (www.salinasswimwear.com), and **Rosa Chá** (www.rosacha.com.br) are all very cool Carioca labels whose eternally fashionable *sungas* and bikinis are sold at their various brand-name boutiques around town. Catering to younger women, Salinas and Bum Bum's styles are showy, daring, and revealing, while Lenny and Rosa Chá's designs are geared towards a more discreet, older and upscale female clientele. Blue Man has the widest array of masculine gear. In Ipanema, Blue Man, Lenny, and Bum Bum have stores in Forum Ipanema, while Salinas is in Galeria Ipanema 2000. Rosa Chá is at the São Conrado Fashion Mall.

If you're male (and young), you'll make out better at **Galeria River** (Rua Francisco Otaviano 67, Arpoador, tel. 21/2522-1967, www.galeriariver.com.br/river.html, 9 A.M.–8 P.M. Mon.–Sat.), an alternative enclave whose tiny but well-stocked stores are devoted entirely to the art, lifestyle, and fashion of surf. Aside from surf gear and surf wear, this is a great place to get a surfer's haircut, a tattoo (or three), or to energize yourself with a super-healthy *vitamina,* chock-full of fruit juices and medicinal herbs.

Landlubbers who crave a more urban style (but with latent beach possibilities) should check out streetwear brands with a distinctly Carioca flavor, such as **Totem** (www.totempraia.com.br), featuring bright hues and tropical prints (they have a store in Galeria Ipanema 2000), and the sleekly casual, outdoorsy designs of **Osklen** (www.osklen.com), with stores in both São Conrado Fashion Mall and Shopping Rio Sul. Just for men, **Complexo B** (www.complexob.com.br) carries unique, often whimsical, well-cut pieces, many of which incorporate the designer's patron saint, São Jorge. The original store is in Galeria River. Meanwhile, women will appreciate the sophisticated yet contemporary designs of **Maria Bonita** (www.mariabonita.com)—available at boutiques in São Conrado Fashion Mall and on Rua Vinícius de Moraes 149, in Ipanema. For distinctly Carioca bags of all sizes, for both sexes and for all purposes, **Gilson Martins** (www.gilsonmartins.com.br) designs ingenious models in comic-book colors that are as sculptural (some are shaped as Pão de Açúcar and the Cristo Redentor, for example) as they are functional. His largest store, on Rua Visconde de Pirajá 462, also has a gallery displaying art works, jewelry, design pieces, and accessories.

For a change of pace—and price—head to a cluster of pedestrian-only streets in Centro, known as **Saara** (www.saararioo.com.br), which is Portuguese for Sahara. The name is not accidental; it conjures up the bazaar-like atmosphere of bustling shops (many owned by Lebanese immigrants) where working-class Cariocas head for bargains. Along with discount clothing, all types of articles and accessories for making Carnaval costumes are sold: from ribbons, spangles, and sequins to gaudy kitsch worthy of Carmen Miranda. Aside from it being a great place to pick up dirt cheap Carioca souvenirs (there are lots of R$1.99 stores), you'll enjoy simply wandering around and soaking up the colorful atmosphere. The most interesting streets include Rua da Alfândega, Rua Buenos Aires, Rua Senhor dos Passos, and Rua das Andradas. The closest Metrô stops are Uruguaiana and Presidente Vargas.

Jewelry

Rio's equivalent of Tiffany's is **H. Stern** (Rua Visconde de Pirajá 490, Ipanema, tel. 21/2274-3447, www.hstern.com.br, 10 A.M.–7 P.M.

Mon.–Fri., 10 A.M.–3 P.M. Sat.). If you haven't already heard of Brazil's most famous miner and maker of jewels, you will. Its PR team sends flyers to basically every hotel in Rio offering to pick you up, take you to the Ipanema headquarters for an interesting tour of their ateliers, and bring you back home again (hopefully with a small bag full of pricy rocks). Specialists in Brazil's dazzling array of precious and semiprecious stones, H. Stern's jewelers create some very innovative contemporary designs as well as more classic, conservative bling.

Antonio Bernardo (Rua Gárcia d'Avila 121, Ipanema, tel. 21/2512-7204, www.antoniobernardo.com.br, 10 A.M.–8 P.M. Mon.–Fri., 10 A.M.–4 P.M. Sat.) is a goldsmith, artist, and orchid lover (he adopted the Jardim Botânico's *orquidário*) who designs beautifully wrought contemporary jewelry with great attentiveness to color, form and texture.

Books and Music

Like most places in Rio, *livrarias* aren't just for reading or browsing, but for seeing and being seen. This explains why they fill up on weekends and at night (many are open until midnight) with real and pretend intellectuals who spill into the delightful cafés and bistros that coexist with the stacks of books and magazines. Aside from author readings, many offer intimate live musical performances of jazz, samba, *chorinho,* and bossa nova—all of which only enhance the romance factor. The best *livrarias* are in Ipanema and Leblon, where aside from a wide assortment of English-language books and media, you'll be seduced by the excellent array of art and coffee table books. These are also great places to buy maps and guidebooks.

The main branch of **Livraria da Travessa** (Rua Visconde de Pirajá 572, Ipanema, tel. 21/3205-9002, www.livrariadatravessa.com.br, 9 A.M.–midnight Mon.–Sat., 11 A.M.–midnight Sun.) has an extensive collection of books about Rio (some in English), as well as lots of CDs and DVDs. Its sleek mezzanine bistro, **B!,** has delicious things to nibble on.

The main branch of **Letras & Expressões**

(Rua Visconde de Pirajá 276, Ipanema, tel. 21/2521-6110, www.letraseexpressoes.com.br, 8 A.M.–midnight Mon.–Thurs., 8 A.M.–2 A.M. Fri.–Sat., 8 A.M.–midnight Sun.) is a favorite hangout for intellos and insomniacs, who end up staying up even later after ordering the cappuccino in **Café Ubaldo,** reportedly the best in the city. The collection of international magazines is enormous, and you can buy all types of fancy cigars (including Cuban) at its tobacco shop.

In Leblon, you'll find smaller branches of Livraria da Travessa and Letras & Expressões, along with the tiny but charming **Beco dos Virtudes** (Av. Ataúlfo de Paiva 1174, Loja 3, Leblon, tel. 21/2249-9525), a combination gallery and secondhand bookstore that sells contemporary artworks by local artists as well as new, imported, rare, and used books devoted to art, architecture, design, and cinema.

Many *livrarias* have good CD sections devoted to Brazilian music. However, if you're a serious aficionado, equally seduced by golden oldies and the latest trends, all roads lead to **Modern Sound** (Rua Barata Ribeiro 502, Copacabana, www.modernsound.com.br, 9 A.M.–9 P.M. Mon.–Fri., 9 A.M.–8 P.M. Sat.). In existence since 1966, this megastore has an amazing variety of CDs and very friendly, helpful staff. In the evenings, its Allegro Bistro Musical hosts great shows featuring diverse performers from all over Brazil.

Bossa nova fans should head to the **Espaço Cultural Toca do Vinícius** (Rua Vinícius de Morais 129, Ipanema, tel. 21/2247-5227, www.tocadovinicius.com.br), a CD store/shrine to the poet, diplomat, and beloved Carioca composer who penned "A Garota da Ipanema" (on this very street) along with Tom Jobim. Aside from personal mementos and original music by Vinícius, this is a good place to pick up bossa nova, *chorinho,* samba, and MPB CDs and vinyl. On Sundays, out front there are frequently free shows—often with a piano on the sidewalk.

Antiques

As the former imperial and republican capital of Brazil, Rio had a lot of luxury going for it, not to mention scores of aristocratic families used to high living—until their luck or money ran out and they needed to hock their goods. Consequently, there are some interesting knickknacks floating around if you have the eye and patience to find them. In Copacabana avoid the posh antiques stores at the touristy Shopping Center Cassino Atlântico and instead head off the beaten track to the **Shopping dos Antiquários** (Rua Siqueira Campos 143, Copacabana, tel. 21/2255-3461, 10 A.M.–7 P.M. Mon.–Sat.). Located in a slightly beat-up, weirdly futuristic shopping center—Rio's first—dating from the 1960s, this *shopping* boasts over 70 antiques stores, specializing in everything from colonial furniture, baroque sacred art, and antique dolls to deco dishware and Bakelite jewelry. Along with the serious stuff, there are some fun junk stores with surprising treasures.

Rio's other antiques mecca is Lapa's **Rua do Lavradio,** one of Rio's oldest residential streets. Alongside classic antiques stores and secondhand shops, new boutiques specializing in early- to mid-20th-century Brazilian designs and furnishings have been cropping up, among them **Ateliê e Movelaria Belmonte** (Rua do Lavradio 34, tel. 21/2507-6873, 9 A.M.–6 P.M. Mon.–Fri., 11 A.M.–2 P.M. Sat.) and **Mercado Moderno** (Rua do Lavradio 130, tel. 21/2508-6083, 9 A.M.–6 P.M. Mon.–Fri., 9 A.M.–3 P.M. Sat.). On the first Saturday afternoon of every month, the local merchants' association organizes the **Feira do Rio Antigo,** in which all the stores on Rua Lavradio join together with other antiques dealers for an open-air market, which also features live music and dance performances.

Arts and Crafts

Neither Rio de Janeiro nor the surrounding state has much to boast of in terms of folk art or traditional crafts. However, if you won't be traveling to other parts of Brazil, there are a few recommended boutiques where you can pick up some authentic artifacts and objets d'art. For indigenous art and objects, there's nowhere better than **Artíndia,** within the Museu do Índio (Rua das Palmeiras 55, Botafogo, tel. 21/2286-8899, www.museodoindio.org.br, 9:30 A.M.–5:30 P.M. Tues.–Fri., 1–5 P.M. Sat.–Sun.). It carries an enticing variety of items made by various groups, ranging from jewelry and ceramics to musical instruments. Prices are quite reasonable, and proceeds are reverted to the indigenous communities.

With its wares decorating a lovely house on Largo dos Guimarães, **La Vereda** (Rua Almirante Alexandrino 428, Santa Teresa, tel. 21/2507-0317, 10 A.M.–8 P.M. daily) offers a terrific selection of traditional art and handicrafts from all over Brazil as well as contemporary works by neighborhood artists.

Markets

Rio has some lively outdoor markets, most of which are held on the weekends. The most famous is Ipanema's **Feira Hippie** (Praça General Osório, Ipanema, 9 A.M.–6 P.M. Sun.). It features a crowded but lively hit-and-miss jumble sale atmosphere that attracts an awful lot of tourists (and pickpockets) and is somewhat overrated. If you happen to be in the otherwise deserted Centro on Saturday between 9 A.M. and 5 P.M., you might enjoy browsing through the cornucopia of antiques and bric-a-brac on display at Praça XV's **Feira de Antiguïdades.** On Sunday, the same goods migrate to Gávea's Praça Santos Dumont.

For more contemporary wares, head to the **Babilônia Feira Hype,** which takes place on alternate weekends at Gávea's Joquei Clube (Praça Santos Dumont 131, 2–11 P.M. every second Sat.–Sun., R$5). This large combination flea/fashion market has an interesting assortment of clothing, jewelry, and design pieces by up-and-coming Rio designers as well as various outdoor eateries with views of the nearby racetrack.

SPORTS AND RECREATION

Blessed with so many natural attractions, it is unsurprising that Cariocas are a pretty sporty bunch. Beach activities—everything from walking, jogging, and yoga to surfing, soccer, and volleyball—are very popular, as are radical sports, especially those that take advantage of the city's mountain peaks. Meanwhile, the exuberantly green Floresta da Tijuca offers an oasis for athletes who want to commune with nature.

Parks

◖ FLORESTA DA TIJUCA

Although the dense tropical forest that covers Rio's jagged mountains possesses a distinctly primeval quality, the truth is that by the 19th century, the original Atlantic forest that had existed for thousands of years had been almost completely cleared away to make way for sugar and coffee plantations. The deforestation was so dire that by the mid-1800s, Rio was facing an ecological disaster that menaced the city's water supply. Fortunately, inspired Emperor Dom Pedro II had a green conscience. In 1861 he ordered that 3,300 hectares be replanted with native foliage—the first example of government-mandated reforestation in Brazil's history. Over time, the forest returned to its original state, and today this urban jungle boasts an astounding variety of exotic trees and animals ranging from jewel-colored hummingbirds to monkeys, squirrels, and armadillos.

Within the Floresta lies the largest urban park in Brazil, the **Parque Nacional da Tijuca** (tel. 21/2492-2253, 8 A.M.–5 P.M. daily). A veritable oasis in the midst of the city, it is particularly refreshing during the dog days of summer. The park has various walking trails—many of them quite easy—waterfalls where you can stop for a drink (or a dip), grottoes, and many lookout points that offer stunning views of the city. The most spectacular of these are the **Mesa do Imperador** (Emperor's Table)—where Dom Pedro II liked to picnic with members of his court—and the **Vista Chinesa.** Another highlight is the charming **Capela Mayrink,** with panels painted by the talented modernist artist Cândido Portinari.

The easiest way to explore the park is by car. If you don't have access to one, take a taxi: You can usually negotiate with drivers to drop you off and pick you up for a reasonable rate. You can also take a guided Jeep tour with a company such as **Jeep Tour** (tel. 21/2589-0883, www.jeeptour.com.br) or **Trilhas do Rio Ecoturismo & Aventura** (tel. 21/2425-8441, www.trilhasdorio.com.br). If you want to venture in on your own, take the Mêtro to Saens Pena and then a bus going to Barra da Tijuca that stops at Alta da Boa Vista. For an organized hiking tour, see the *Hiking, Climbing, and Adventure Sports* listings. The park entrance is at Praça Alfonso Viseu, and a few hundred meters inside is a visitors center where you can buy a map (although trails are well marked). Robberies are increasingly common, so be careful not to venture too far off the beaten track, and don't go alone. It's safer to visit on weekends, when the park is more crowded. Near the entrance, there are three restaurants and a café. Or if you want, bring along food for a picnic.

Within the Floresta da Tijuca, the **Museu do Açude** (Estrada do Açude 764, Alto da Boa Vista, tel. 21/2492-2119, 11 A.M.–5 P.M. Thurs.–Sun., R$2, free Thurs.) occupies the former house of wealthy industrialist Raymundo Ottoni de Castro Maya. Beautifully decorated with antiques and Portuguese *azulejo* panels, the neoclassical villa, completely engulfed by jungle, exhibits Castro Maya's impressive art collection, which runs the gamut from ancient Oriental ceramics to works by contemporary Brazilian artists.

Cycling

Rio has a considerable number of bike paths. Those in search of a languorous outing can take to the paths that line the beaches (stretching from Flamengo to Leblon and then along Barra) and ring the Lagoa Rodrigo de Freitas. Meanwhile, hard-core jocks can take on the steep trails leading into the Floresta da Tijuca. You can rent bikes in many places along the Zona Sul beaches and around the Lagoa. A particularly wide range of models are available at **Special Bike** (www.specialbike.com.br) in both Botafogo (Rua São João Batista 21-A, tel. 21/2539-0693) and Ipanema (Rua Visconde de Pirajá 135-B, tel. 21/2267-7778) for around R$60 a day.

Hiking, Climbing, and Adventure Sports

Rio possesses an enormous number of options for hiking and climbing within and around the city. **Rio Hiking** (tel. 21/2552-9204, www.rio-hiking.com.br) is highly recommended. This mother-son outfit also offers more radical sport outings including rappelling, climbing, cycling, trekking, kayaking, and scuba diving.

Trilhas do Rio Ecoturismo & Aventura (tel. 21/2425-8441, www.trilhasdorio.com.br) has expert guides who are highly knowledgeable about Rio's natural surroundings. They lead hiking, biking, horseback riding, climbing, and trekking tours in and around the city. There is even a yoga tour. A four-hour hike up Pão de Açúcar costs R$130, while a six-hour hike up and around Pedra da Gávea is R$160. Other half- and full-day adventure sports excursions range from R$130–250 depending on the activities included.

Trilharte Ecoturismo (tel. 21/2245-5626, www.trilharte.com.br) also offers many interesting eco-trips—all of which are slanted towards adventurers with cameras. Photographic safaris to a wide range of photogenic destinations involve hiking, horseback riding, climbing, and rafting. The only drawback is that tours are in Portuguese. Trip prices vary depending on the length of time and activities involved. They range from R$35 for a light hike up the Pão de Açúcar to R$180 (including lunch) for a full-day guided excursion into the Mata Atlântica.

Meanwhile, if you have ever dreamed of scaling Pão de Açúcar or Corcovado, **Companhia da Escalada** (tel. 21/2567-7105, www.guiadaurca.com/companhia, R$100–160 pp) organizes rock-climbing classes and excursions for beginners and experts.

Sailing and Boating

Better than gazing at the Baía da Guanabara is to actually get out upon its blue waters. **Saveiro's Tour** (Av. Infante Dom Henrique, Marina da Glória, Glória, tel. 21/2225-6064, www.saveiros.com.br) rents out all types of sea-worthy vessels as well as water-skis. Those

interested in a mini cruise yacht that will take you coast to destinations suc Grande, Angra dos Reis, hour tour around the Baía R$30 per person.

Hang Gliding

The popularity of hang gliding in Rio—second only to surfing—is unsurprising viewing the spectacular surroundings involved. The classic (and most breathtaking) trip is to jump off Pedra Bonita (in the Parque Nacional da Tijuca) and glide down to the Praia do Pepino in São Conrado. Both **Just Fly** (tel. 21/2268-0565, www.justfly.com.br) and **HiltonFlyRio** (tel. 21/2278-3779, www.hiltonflyrio.com) charge between R$240 and R$280 for the thrill, including transportation to and from your hotel.

Surfing

Rio is a surfers' haven, luring wave junkies from around the world to the beaches of Arpoador, Barra, Recreio, Prainha, and Grumari. If you want to hone your technique, **Escola de Surf Rico de Souza** (tel. 21/2438-1821, www.ricosurf.globo.com) offers daily lessons at its headquarters (in front of Posto 4 at Barra) and at Prainha. Private lessons (including equipment) cost R$60 per person for one hour. The school has lots of information about surfing conditions, events, and equipment rental. It even operates a special surfer bus service (R$2), with buses departing daily from Largo de Machado in Botafogo and stopping off at all the best surf spots between Copacabana and Prainha. To buy or rent surf equipment, check out the stores at **Galeria River** in Arpoador (Rua Francisco Otaviano, 67).

Soccer

Brazil's favorite sport is also Rio's, and you'll see everyone from women to *favela* kids to beer-bellied seniors dribbling, passing, shooting, and scoring, particularly on the beaches. However, if you want to see the real deal, head to the largest and most famous *futebol* stadium

world: **Maracanã** (Rua Profesor Eurico
lo, Maracaná, tel. 21/2229-2941, tickets
15–40). Built in 1950 to host the World Cup,
the stadium seats close to 200,000 people. Even
if soccer itself leaves you cold, it's worth taking
in a game for the sheer theatrics of the crowd as
they toot whistles, beat drums, unfurl gigantic
banners, and wield smoke bombs in team colors.
When things aren't going well, fans shed tears,
implore saints, and hurl death threats (as well
as cups of urine—for this reason, consider seats
in the lower levels, which are sheltered by a protective canopy). However, when victory rears its
head, it's like a collective mini Carnaval.

Rio's four biggest and most traditional
teams are Flamengo, Fluminense, Botafogo,
and Vasco da Gama. Each has its diehard followers, but the most toxic rivalry of all is the
legendary Flamengo-Fluminense ("Fla-Flu")
match-up. Games are played throughout the
week and throughout the year. When going to
a game, avoid rabid fans on the bus and take
the Metrô or a taxi. During the day, Maracaná
is open for guided tours (9 A.M.–5 P.M. daily,
8–11 A.M. on game days, R$14).

ACCOMMODATIONS

As one of the world's most beautiful cities—
and Brazil's number one tourist destination—
Rio's hotels feel entitled to charge a lot for the
(undisputed) pleasure of staying in the Cidade
Maravilhosa. For the most part, however, the
choices are underwhelming. Centro offers few
options, and at any rate, it is dead and unsafe
at night. The well-located—albeit beachless—
neighborhoods of Botafogo and Flamengo
offer an assortment of affordable options. Santa
Teresa, a hilly bohemian neighborhood, has
been experiencing a major transformation, with
more and more intimate bed-and-breakfasts
and boutique hotels popping up. If you want
to be where all the action is—night and day—
that would be the Zona Sul neighborhoods of
Copacabana, Ipanema, and Leblon. Copa is
mostly full of mammoth overpriced chains,
which, aside from the high-end luxury hotels,
offer fairly standard rooms in various states of
decay. More tranquil and tony Ipanema and

Leblon have a few sophisticated options and a
sprinkling of more reasonable alternatives.

Centro

Usually, Centro appeals more to business travelers than to sun worshippers, who might find
it frustrating to be so far from the glittering
sands of Copacabana and Ipanema. However,
staying in Centro gives you the advantage of
proximity to Rio's historic landmarks and
many of its museums. It's well served by Metrô
and bus, so you can get anywhere you want
fast, and prices here are far less expensive than
those in Zona Sul. On the downside, the place
clears out at night and on weekends. Lack of
action means it's also not very safe, so be prepared to spend a lot on cab fare.

R$50-100

Hotel Belas Artes (Av. Visconde do Rio
Branco 52, Centro, tel. 21/2252-6336, www.ho-
telbelasartes.com.br, R$78–87 d), in a hand-
some historic building in the heart of Centro,
is a well-regarded hotel that offers simply furnished but spotless rooms with high ceilings and
wooden floors—all for an unbeatable price.

R$200-300

Operated by the Windsor chain (which
owns several handfuls of hotels in Rio), the
Guanabara Palace (Av. Presidente Vargas 392,
tel. 21/2195-6000, www.windsorhoteis.com,
R$255–280 d) is Centro's toniest accommoda-
tion option. While modern and comfortable—
it's a favorite with business execs—it won't win
any style awards. Lack of charm is compensated for by the rooftop pool and terrace featuring stunning 360-degree views of the city
and Guanabara Bay.

Lapa

Following Lapa's transformation from seedy
red-light district to nocturnal hot spot, a couple
of its former crash pads have been upgraded.

R$100-200

The formerly down-and-out **Arcos Rio Palace**
(Av. Mem de Sá 117, Lapa, tel. 21/2242-8116,

www.arcosriopalacehotel.com.br, R$160–175 d) is now a safe and comfortable hotel with amenities such as a swimming pool, sauna, and cyber café. Aside from the nice price, the real bonus is direct access to Lapa's vibrant nightlife.

Santa Teresa

With its new lease on life and increased safety, bucolic and bohemian "Santa" provides a wonderful antidote to the Zona Sul beach scene. Taking advantage of the abundance of atmospheric belle epoque villas, a handful of visionary entrepreneurs are going the restoration route and opening up guesthouses that meet the requirements of every pocketbook.

R$50-100

Rio Hostel Santa Teresa (Rua Joaquim Murtinho 361, Santa Teresa, tel. 21/3852-0827, www.riohostel.com, R$35 pp, R$100–120 d) offers tidy, welcoming dorm rooms and minimally decorated double rooms with magnificent views (reserve in advance) for impossibly low prices. The lounge and pool areas are a definite bonus, as is the prime location along the *bonde* line, which offers access to Santa Teresa's charms and Lapa's nocturnal offerings. Very popular with the international backpacking set.

R$100-200

An equally boho vibe is at work at **Pousada Casa Aurea** (Rua Aurea 8, tel. 21/2242-5830, www.casaaurea.com.br, R$110–140 d), a renovated villa featuring rustic rooms and a leafy garden and patio area with lots of hammocks to swing in.

Meanwhile, to experience life with the locals, a wonderful option is staying as a guest in a private home. **Cama e Café** (Rua Progresso 67, Santa Teresa, tel. 21/2221-7635, www.camaecafe.com.br) is a B&B network that links travelers and (often very interesting) residents. In Santa Teresa, you can choose from more than 50 offerings based on factors such as cost, comfort, and common interests. Many of the hosts are artists and liberal professionals, with at least a smattering of English and an impressive knowledge of the city. While

budget and break-the-bank options exist, the majority of offerings are nicely priced within the R$100–180 range.

OVER R$300

Since 2006, several luxury guesthouses have opened in Santa Teresa that offer welcome alternatives to the megahotels of Copacabana and Ipanema. **Solar de Santa** (Ladeira dos Meirelles 32, tel. 21/2221-2117, www.solardesanta.com.br, R$335–490) is a very enticing example of this new trend. Owned by one of the founders of the world-renowned Cirque du Soleil, this sprawling 19th-century villa is ensconced in a tropical garden that feels miles away from urban chaos. Light-flooded rooms are beautifully decorated with works by local artists (many of which can be purchased). In fact, billing itself as a purveyor of "creative tourism," the hotel offers guests original services such as custom-designed tours of the city (focusing on fashion, architecture, photography, and gastronomy) and visits to the artists' studios in Santa Teresa.

More refined, but no less seductive, is **Mama Ruisa** (Rua Santa Cristina 132, Santa Teresa, tel. 21/2242-1281, www.mamaruisa.com, R$500 d). Originally from Paris, the owner ceaselessly combed antiques stores with the goal of creating an elegant and vaguely retro ambiance for this gleaming mansion's seven spacious guest rooms, terraces, and salons. Having succeeded magnificently, he then added beautifully landscaped gardens punctuated by an inviting blue pool. The fabulous city views glimpsed through the trees are the only indication you're in Rio. Aside from the usual creature comforts, spa services (manicures, pedicures, massages) and chauffeured city tours are available.

Glória and Catete

Since the 1920s, Glória's name has become synonymous with the grand Hotel Glória (which closed indefinitely in 2008) overlooking the Baía de Guanabara. Working-class Catete is somewhat frayed around the edges, but lively and convenient. The *bairro* offers some very good deals if you're not too picky.

R$50-100
Hotel Riazor (Rua do Catete 160, tel. 21/2225-0121, www.hotelriazor.com.br, R$70) is clean and vaguely funky if you're in the right mood, but also kind of shabby. Nonetheless it's only a block from the Catete Metrô and the price is very right.

R$100-200
The Hotel Inglês (Rua Silveira Martins, Catete, tel. 21/2558-3052, www.hotelingles.com.br, R$125 d) bills itself as the only high-quality two-star hotel in town, and thanks to a recent facelift, this claim is pretty accurate. Modern, no-nonsense rooms with all the basics and lots of space to move around make this business execs' favorite a good choice for anyone who wants some bang for their buck.

Occupying an impressive old building across the street from the Palácio Catete, the **Imperial Hotel** (Rua do Catete 186, tel. 21/2556-5212, www.imperialhotel.com.br, R$125–150 d) has been modernized to the point of blandness. However, the rooms are spacious and spotless, the location is great, and the price very reasonable.

If you check into the **Baron Garden** (Rua Barão de Guaratiba 195, Glória, tel. 21/2245-9929, www.barongarden.com, R$90–R$110 d), an unusually located hybrid guesthouse/hostel, you definitely won't run the risk of running into any other tourists. One of Glória's very few accommodations options, this handsome old manor at the top of a steep hill (the arduous climb is compensated by the stunning views) offers only 16 beds, including private doubles and an eight-bed dorm room (R$45 per person). While the trappings are hardly luxe, the house has plenty of character and a homey vibe, which is actively cultivated by the friendly owners. The opportunities to rustle up a meal in the Baron's gleaming tiled kitchen or chill out in a hammock by the scenic pool adds to the home-away-from-home sensation.

Flamengo and Botafogo
Located between Centro and the Zona Sul, Flamengo and Botafogo are well served by buses and Metrô. Both *bairros* possess a faded grandeur coupled with a lively neighborhood atmosphere that makes them appealing—and significantly more affordable—untouristy alternatives to the Zona Sul beach scene.

R$50-100
One of Rio's most popular hostels is **Albergue de Juventude Chave do Rio** (Rua General Dionísio 63, Botafogo, tel. 21/2286-0303, www.riohostel.com.br, R$30–40 pp). Located in an attractively renovated old house, its dormitory rooms are outfitted with bright blue bunks that can sleep up to 70 backpackers. The surrounding area has a great selection of bars and nightlife options.

R$100-200
When the **Hotel Regina** (Rua Ferreira Viana 29, Flamengo, tel. 21/3289-9999, www.hotelregina.com.br, R$154 d) opened in the mid-1920s, around the corner from the Palácio do Catete, it quickly became the hotel of choice for government diplomats and ministers. Although a few architectural remnants allude to its history, the Regina is hardly as grand as it once was. However, its small rooms are bright and comfortable, and it is well located on a quiet street half a block from the Parque de Flamengo.

R$200-300
Hotel Flórida (Rua Ferreira Viana 81, Flamengo, tel. 21/2195-6800, www.windsorhoteis.com.br, R$250–310 d) is a tried-and-true Flamengo favorite, owned by the Windsor hotel chain. Rooms are sizable and discreetly decorated. The most attractive ones overlook the gardens of the Palácio do Catete. Free Internet service, a rooftop pool, and the option of breakfast in bed are welcome extras.

Urca
R$50-100
The **Carioca Easy Hostel** (Rua Marechal Cantuaria 168, Urca, tel. 21/2295-7805, www.cariocahostel.com.br, R$35–40 pp, R$110 d) is a well-maintained hostel that allows guests the rare privilege of staying in

© TONY GALVEZ

Copacabana's iconic mosaic walkway

residential Urca. Although the dorm rooms are small, the hostel itself—housed in a pink villa whose immediate backdrop is Pão de Açúcar's rocky facade—has polished wood floors, a small pool, and a pleasant garden.

Copacabana and Leme
R$50-100
Only a block from the beach, **☾ SESC Copacabana** (Rua Domingos Ferreira 160, Copacabana, tel. 21/2548-1088, www.sescrj.com.br, R$89–135 d) is not only the best deal in Copa, but you have the bonus of staying in an architectural landmark designed by Oscar Niemeyer. The bargain prices are due to SESC being a type of union for tradespeople that offers cultural, recreational, and vacation facilities for both members and (at higher, but still unbeatable costs) nonmembers. Rooms are coolly minimalist, and those above the 10th floor offer terrific views of Corcovado.

R$100-200
Hotel Santa Clara (Rua Décio Villares 316, Copacabana, tel. 21/2256-2650, www.hotel-santaclara.com.br, R$153–168 d) occupies a pretty, whitewashed house with blue shutters that feels more like a home than a hotel. Try for a room on the top floor, which are the brightest and breeziest. Although five blocks from the beach, it is also nicely removed from Copa's bustle.

Another quiet and affordable alternative to Copa's mega chains is the **Hotel Toledo** (Rua Domingos Ferreira 71, Copacabana, tel. 21/2257-1990, www.hoteltoledo.com.br, R$165 d), located on an attractive leafy street only a block from the beach. Rooms are small, but clean and fairly pleasant. This is one of Copa's best bargains.

R$200-300
For those Eagles fans who've always dreamed of living it up at the Hotel California, your fantasy can come true when you check into the **Othon California** (Av. Atlântica 2616, Copacabana, tel. 21/2132-1900, R$210 d). Well sort of. The original trappings of the once-grand 1940s hotel are on splendid display in the lobby and dining areas and barely

apparent in the comfortable though nonde-script rooms.

The **Dayrell Ouroverde** (Av. Atlântica 1456, Copacabana, tel. 21/2543-4123, www.dayrell.com .br, R$250–310 d) has been a favorite with Brazilians ever since it opened its doors in 1950. Both public and private rooms are classy and un-derstated with elegant original furnishings and an airy spaciousness enhanced by views of the Atlantic. Rooms at the back provide glimpses of Corcovado.

Opened in 2003, the **Portinari Design Hotel** (Rua Francisco Sá 17, Copacabana, tel. 21/3222-8800, www.portinaridesignho-tel.com.br, R$270 d) had the guts to be dar-ing by inviting a handful of leading Brazilian architects and decorators to design each of the hotel's 11 floors. The overall results are mostly inspired—although there are some misses along with the hits. For this reason, you should check out the photos on the hotel website to select a room whose colors and accessories mesh with your personal preferences. Aesthetics aside, all rooms are very well outfitted, with amenities ranging from broadband and flatscreen TVs to complimentary flip-flops. The fitness center includes a spa with a sauna and whirlpool. The hotel is only half a block from the beach.

OVER R$300

One of the most legendary hotels in the world and a national landmark, the ◖ **Copacabana Palace** (Av. Atlântica 1702, Copacabana, tel. 21/2548-7070, www.copacabanapalace.com.br, R$820–1,230 d) is as famous as the beach it sits upon. In fact, when this dazzling white wed-ding cake of a hotel was constructed in 1923, Copacabana was little more than an unspoiled strip of sand surrounded by mountains. A de-cade later, the Palace played a prominent role in the RKO classic *Flying Down to Rio,* the first film to pair Fred Astaire and Ginger Rogers. Since then, it has attracted a nonstop cavalcade of international stars, jet-setters, heads-of-state, and royalty. When not holed up in the luxury of their poshly furnished rooms, they can often be spotted lounging around the Olympic-sized turquoise pool, playing a few sets on the

rooftop tennis court, or dining in one of the two highly reputed restaurants, **Cipriani** and **Pergula**. The hotel recently added a full-ser-vice spa to its long list of pampering services.

The Copacabana Palace's most serious rival is the **Sofitel Rio de Janeiro** (Av. Atlântica 4240, Copacabana, tel. 21/2525-1232, www.sofitel.com.br, R$900–1,250 d). What this ultramodern, somewhat overpriced hotel lacks in terms of charm and pedigree, it tries to make up for with a dazzling array of enticing extras. The swanky rooms are outfitted with plasma TVs, extra large and comfortable beds, and balconies from which you can eat break-fast or sip cocktails while staring at the entire length of Copacabana beach. Moreover, there are *two* rooftop pools (the better with which to catch both the sun's morning and afternoon rays). The hotel restaurant, **Le Pré Catalan,** is considered one of Rio's top French restaurants. The location—on the frontier between Copa and Ipanema—is unbeatable.

Ipanema and Leblon
R$50-100

To stay cheaply in Ipanema, hostels are the only way to go. Fortunately, there are several fairly nice options available. **Hostel Harmonia** (Rua Barão da Torre 175, Casa 18, Ipanema, tel. 21/2423-4905, www.hostelharmonia.com, R$45 pp) offers clean but basic hostel accom-modations in a restored villa with dorm and double rooms. Equally simple, but much smaller, is its neighbor, **Casa 6 Ipanema** (Rua Barão da Torre 175, Casa 6, Ipanema, tel. 21/2247-1384, www.casa6ipanema.com, R$40 pp, R$120 d). In fact, it only has two dormi-tory rooms and a double. However, its very size and a welcoming atmosphere conspire to make guests feel at home. Both of these hostels are located on a tranquil and leafy side street.

R$100-200

At the **Adventure Hostel** (Rua Vinícius de Moraes 174, Ipanema, tel. 21/3813-2726, www.adventurehostel.com.br, R$50–60 pp, R$130–160 d), bunking accommodations are spotless, if spartan, but the common rooms are cheery and welcoming. The hostel offers a fantastic range of services, including airport and bus station pickups, bike and surfboard rentals, and the organization of urban "adventures" ranging from paragliding to *favela* tours.

In terms of low price and great location, it's hard to beat the **Vermont Hotel** (Rua Viconde de Pirajá 254, Ipanema, tel. 21/2522-0055, R$140–185 d), situated on Ipanema's bustling main shopping drag. However, you get what you pay for: Rooms are somewhat cramped and noisy, and the decor is not what one would call uplifting.

R$200-300

A good-value pick is the unassuming **Ipanema Inn** (Rua Maria Quiteria 27, Ipanema, tel. 21/2523-6093, R$170–250). It has a terrific location only half a block from the beach, yet that half-block difference makes a world of difference in terms of price. The spotless rooms, with nice wooden accents, are bright and modern, and service is good.

The **Arpoador Inn** (Rua Francisco Otaviano 177, Ipanema, tel. 21/2523-0060, R$175–230 d) is not only the most affordable beachfront hotel in Ipanema, but it is also within spitting distance of Copacabana. Actually, it looks onto Praia do Arpoador, whose giant waves make this stretch of beach a surfers' mecca. The rooms themselves are functional, if a little torn and frayed around the edges (especially the cheaper standard ones, which are a little on the sad side). If you want a sea view, you'll have to pay a lot extra (R$350) for it.

OVER R$300

Luxury accommodations are much easier to come by in Ipanema and Leblon than budget options. Straddling both neighborhoods, the **Hotel Praia Ipanema** (Av. Vieira Souto 706, Ipanema, tel. 21/2141-4949, www.praiaipanema.com, R$500–540 d) allows you to live it up in posh Zona Sul style without maxing out your credit card. Tastefully minimalist rooms all have private balconies with sea views (which increase in magnificence the higher up the room), as does the rooftop pool. There is also a spa.

Owned by the Dutch chain Golden Tulip, the **Ipanema Plaza** (Rua Farme de Amoedo 34, Ipanema, tel. 21/3687-2000, www.ipanemaplazahotel.com, R$405–550 d) is sleek with just the right level of sophistication. Its spacious rooms are awash in neutral tones with blond wood furnishings. Really chic—and not much more expensive—are the boutique-style master suites on the newly inaugurated "Ipanema floor"—trappings include Italian-designed furniture, fine linens, and Jacuzzis. The rooftop pool and bar offers views of the beach and Corcovado that will mesmerize by day or night. The hotel has a notoriously gay-friendly reputation.

Caesar Park (Av. Vieira Souto 460, Ipanema, tel. 21/2525-2525, www.caesarpark-rio.com, R$820–1,110) is a tried-and-true luxury favorite of celebrities, dignitaries, and Madonna, none of whom can resist the topnotch service, multiple amenities (including a great health club), and a coveted location right across the street from the beach. Captains of industry swear by its state-of-the-art business center and the executive lunches served in its acclaimed contemporary restaurant, **Galani**—on Saturday, one of the city's most sought-after *feijoadas* is served. Only deluxe rooms offer views of the beach, but once you're out on the sands, you'll be duly pampered (with towels, lounge chairs, fresh fruit and drinks) and protected (by the hotel lifeguards and security staff).

Caesar Park's hold on the front line of Ipanema's luxury hotel market came to an end in August 2007 with the much-awaited opening of the **◖ Fasano Rio Hotel** (Av. Vieira Souto 80, Ipanema, tel. 21/3202-4000, www.fasano.com.br, R$945–1,020 d). For their Carioca debut, the Fasano family—which owns some of São Paulo's most celebrated high-class hotels and restaurants—procured the talents of French design guru Philippe Starck. Working with a team of local Brazilian artists, Starck's design references the glamor of 1950s Rio, when the city was a favored port of call for the international jet set. Retro furnishings merge with lots of glass, wood, and marble, not to mention the blue Atlantic, which is prominently on display from the sumptuous rooms as well as the rooftop pool, fitness center, spa, and restaurant, **Al Mare.**

Ruling the luxury roost of Leblon is Rio's "other" boutique hotel: the **Marina All-Suites** (Av. Delfim Moreira 696, Leblon, tel. 21/2172-1100, www.marinaallsuites.com.br, R$695–1,108 d). It's less cool and sleek than the Fasano; the designers dared to inject some color into the decorative equation. The result is top-of-the-line comfort that is elegant but home-like, which is probably why homegirl Gisele Bündchen and recent Brazilian transplant Calvin Klein are both devoted guests (Gisele prefers the Diamante suite). Other model types can be seen hanging around the penthouse pool, taking in a film at the in-house movie theater, or downing *caipirinhas* at the **Bar D'Hotel.**

FOOD

In keeping with a city of its size, sophistication, and diversity, Rio has an impressive restaurant scene featuring the best of so-called *alta* and *baixa culinária* ("high" and "low" cuisine). In terms of the former, Rio has really taken off in the last decade. In particular, the neighborhoods of Ipanema and Leblon, Jardim Botânico, and Centro have seen a rise in stylish eateries owned and operated by some of the most vanguard chefs in the country. While some focus on international cuisine, others innovatively marry traditional European cooking techniques with distinctive Brazilian ingredients, creating a *nouvelle cuisine tropicale.*

Simultaneously, many traditional neighborhood *churrascarias* and *botequins* offer up tasty *comida caseira* (home-cooking) ranging from hearty *caldos* (soups), robust sandwiches, barbecued chicken and beef to the classic Saturday *feijoada,* in which the famed Brazilian stew of beans, pork, and sausages is garnished with sautéed *couve* (kale), *farofa* (crunchy manioc flour), and orange slices. The obligatory libation is, of course, the *caipirinha,* made with *cachaça,* sugar, crushed ice, and lime.

Although carnivores fare well in Rio, fish and seafood lovers will be equally spoiled. In keeping with Cariocas' fame as a body-conscious bunch, there are also numerous vegetarian, organic, and all-round healthy eateries—many of them self-service per-kilo buffets where diners can control their weight down to the last gram—particularly in the Zona Sul. Propitiously located between the beaches and seemingly endless number of gyms are juice bars serving up dozens of varieties of fresh fruit juices, vitamin drinks, and healthy *sanduíches naturais.*

Aside from restaurants, bars and *botequins* (see *Bars*) are also great places to eat. Menus invariably feature a satisfying array of *petiscos* (appetizers) that, depending on your willpower, will either tide you over between meals or leave you contentedly stuffed. In recent times, a new crop of charming cafés has sprung up, many of them located in the city's cultural centers, cinemas, and *livrarias* (bookstores). Aside from serving gourmet coffee and delicious bistro-style meals, they tend to have quite fabulous desserts. As you'll witness everywhere from the street *barracas* in Lapa to the *padarias* (bakeries) in Copa, Cariocas have a pronounced sweet tooth, and satisfying sugar cravings is absurdly easy.

Although Rio's top restaurants are not at all cheap, the prices are quite decent when compared to the equivalents in major North American and European cities. As such, it's definitely worth your while to splurge once or twice. You can then atone for your sins by seeking out more reasonably priced culinary experiences at the city's beach *barracas,* bars, bakeries, and bookstores.

Centro

Rio's commercial hub has scads of eating options, especially during the weekdays, when downtown bustles with activity. You'll find a wide range of choices: from speedy self-service buffets and bars serving *prato feitos* or "PFs"—simple home-cooked specials of the day, usually consisting of the basic meat, beans, rice triumvirate—to contemporary bistros (many located within the area's museums and cultural centers) and an increasing number of top-end gourmet restaurants.

CAFÉS AND SNACKS

🄲 **Confeitaria Colombo** (Rua Gonçalves Dias 32, Centro, tel. 21/2232-2300, www

.confeitariacolombo.com.br, Mon.–Sat.) is an exceptionally elegant belle epoque café and one of the few vestiges of how grand life must have been if you were an aristocrat in turn-of-the-20th-century Rio. Stepping off the gritty narrow street and into the dazzling interior provides a living definition of the word "contrast." The interior—outfitted with French stained glass, Portuguese *azulejos,* and immense Belgian mirrors with jacaranda frames—resonates with Old World charm. More than a century later, Colombo is still a Rio institution: While working Cariocas cluster around the bar chasing pastries with *cafezinhos,* slack-jawed tourists can take *chá da tarde* (high tea) in the salon or indulge in the Saturday afternoon *feijoada,* accompanied by live samba and choro.

Ideally located in the foyer of the Centro do Comércio do Café (the 100-year-old regulating body of Brazil's prize crop) **Rubro Café** (Rua da Quitanda 191, Centro, tel. 21/2516-0610, www.rubrocafe.com.br, 7:30 A.M.–8 P.M. Mon.–Fri.) is where the people who really *know* about coffee go to get their caffeine fix. More than 20 gourmet coffee drinks are served in this airy, modern space, as well as breakfast fare, sandwiches, salads, and desserts. Rubro is the name of the delicious house blend, which you can also buy to take home with you.

CONTEMPORARY
You have to walk past a lot of bling to get to **Eça** (Av. Rio Branco 128, Centro, tel. 21/2524-2401, www.hstern.com.br/eca/, noon–4 P.M. Mon.–Fri., R$45–55). Located in the basement of H. Stern jewelers, this elegant restaurant is single-handedly responsible for the arrival of contemporary cuisine in Rio's business district. Celebrated Belgian chef Frédéric de Maeyer brings a Gallic sensibility and sense of inventiveness to the kitchen. The results—tuna with goat cheese sorbet and arugula or fresh fish in a pistachio crust with leek risotto—are sophisticated and surprising. For dessert, Maeyer gets (understandably) nationalistic and resorts to Belgian chocolate for the preparation of airy soufflés and tortes.

Ambiance is everything at **Cais do Oriente** (Rua Visconde de Itaboraí 8, Centro, tel. 21/2233-2531, www.caisdooriente.com.br, Tues.–Sat. noon–midnight, Sun.–Mon. noon–4 P.M., R$40–50), located in a stunningly renovated 19th-century warehouse. Actually there are several ambiances to choose from: the palmy open-air patio, the mezzanine lounge with a stage for live music performances, and the main salon that is sumptuously decorated with antiques, Oriental carpets, and gigantic mirrors. The menu, as varied as the surroundings, offers a mishmash of Asian and Mediterranean dishes prepared with a contemporary twist. The overall sensation is otherworldly.

VARIED
Looking out onto a whitewashed courtyard inside the Paço Imperial, **Bistrô do Paço** (Praça XV 48, Centro, tel. 21/2262-3613, www.bistro.com.br, 11:30 A.M.–7:30 P.M. Mon.–Fri., noon–7 P.M. Sat.–Sun., R$12–18) offers a tranquil oasis from the surrounding noise, heat, and traffic of Centro. Lunch is a rapid but tasteful affair with delicious salads, sandwiches, and daily specials. At around 1 P.M., it gets quite crowded with hungry execs.

Brasserie Rosário (Rua do Rosário 34, Centro, tel. 21/2518-3033, www.brasserierosario.com.br, 11 A.M.–10 P.M. Mon.–Fri., 11 A.M.–7 P.M. Sat., R$20–30) is a gourmet café, delicatessen, bakery, wine cellar and bistro all rolled into one very attractive, high-ceilinged, stone-walled building dating from the 1860s. Light eaters can choose from myriad antipasti, salads, and unusual sandwiches made with freshly baked breads, while those with serious hunger pangs can attack the likes of artichoke herb risotto or grilled bass served with couscous and topped with a basil froth.

Santa Teresa
Santa Teresa is known for its handful of typical bars and charming restaurants, many of which are located in atmospheric old houses and often boast bewitching views of the city below.

BRAZILIAN

The delicious fish and seafood served at **Sobrenatural** (Rua Almirante Alexandrino 432, Santa Teresa, tel. 21/2224-1003, noon onwards daily, R$25–40) are caught daily and inspire the preparation of simple home-style Brazilian dishes such as fish *moqueca* (a Bahian stew that uses coconut milk, tomatoes, cilantro, and lime) with shrimp sauce. The generous portions are enough to feed two or three.

Aprazível (Rua Aprazível 62, Santa Teresa, tel. 21/2508-9174, www.aprazivel .com.br, noon–1 A.M. Thurs.–Sat., 1–6 P.M. Sun., R$35–50)—which is Portuguese for "delightful"—is the perfect name for this restaurant occupying a bucolic villa. Rustic jacaranda tables fill the warm honey-colored interior and spill out onto the veranda and lush tropical garden, both of which offer panoramic views of the Baía de Guanabara. The cuisine riffs on the traditional fare of Minas Gerais, yielding dishes such as *galinhada caipira* (organic chicken seasoned with sausage and garnished with braised kale and banana) and *rainha do baião* (tilapia bathed in cilantro-scented olive oil served with a mixture of okra and tangy *coalho* cheese). The wine menu, designed by American expat and indie filmmaker Jonathan Nossiter (who made the excellent wine documentary *Mondovino*) focuses on unsung local vintages. Since the restaurant gets full on weekends, reservations are recommended.

There's no need to journey to the Amazon to savor exotic ingredients such as piranha, mozzarella made from the Ilha de Marajó's buffalo herds, and fruits such as *jambu, taperabá,* and *cupuaçu*. Amazonian chef Natacha Fink uses these and many other delicacies at **Espírito Santa** (Rua Almirante Alexandrino 264, Santa Teresa, tel. 21/2508-7095, www.es-piritosanta.com.br, 11:30 A.M.–6 P.M. Mon.–Wed., 11:30 A.M.–midnight Thurs.–Sat., 11:30 A.M.–7 P.M. Sun., R$25–35). This innovative restaurant is housed in a coral-colored 1930s villa that is surrounded by a lovely terrace. Start off with crab claws served with *jambu* vinaigrette and then move on to sole stuffed with shrimp in a *taperabá* sauce, accompanied by hearts of palm. Save room for desserts such as crisp fritters filled with guava, cashews and *cupuaçu*. Exotic *caipirinhas* are made with artisanal *cachaças*.

Glória and Catete

If you happen to be visiting museums in Catete, there are a few nicely priced and pleasant eating options.

SWISS

Casa da Suíça (Rua Cândido Mendes 157, Glória, tel. 21/2252-5182, www.casadasuica .com.br, noon–3 P.M. and 7 P.M.–midnight Mon.–Fri., 7P.M.–1 A.M. Sat., noon–4 P.M. and 7P.M.–11 P.M. Sun.), a decades-old Swiss restaurant housed on the ground floor of the Swiss Consulate, is one of the more unexpected culinary presences in Rio. Although the chef is actually Austrian, he has had his work cut out for him trying to convince Cariocas that there is more to Swiss cuisine than the quintessential fondue. His attempts to prove otherwise result in dishes such as pork stuffed with ham and emmenthal cheese and filet mignon with oysters. However, in spite of the tropical heat and humidty, the fondues—particularly the classic cheese with herb version served with chunks of fresh pears and mushrooms—are in high demand. While the restaurant's cozy dining salons ooze Old World charm, on "winter" Sundays the delightful back garden is *the* place to stuff yourself on raclette.

VARIED

Estação República (Rua do Catete 104, Catete, tel. 21/2225-2650, 11 A.M.–midnight Mon.–Sat., 11 A.M.–11 P.M. Sun.) is a cheery and spacious per kilo restaurant with an enormous range of offerings. To boot, its extended hours are quite rare for a self-service place. Carnivores will appreciate the *churrascaria* featuring juicy barbecued meats, while more diet-conscious souls can take refuge in salads and sushi.

Flamengo and Botafogo

Aside from traditional *botequins* and *churrascarias,* Flamengo and Botafogo have an increasing number of hip little cafés and some very fine bistros. Prices are generally lower than those in the fashionable Zona Sul, and you won't find yourself rubbing elbows with tourists.

CONTEMPORARY

Part of the Senac restaurant school, **(Senac Bistrô** (Rua Marques do Abrantes 99, Flamengo, tel. 21/3138-1540, www.senacbistro.com.br, noon–4 P.M. and 7 P.M.–midnight Tues.–Sat., noon–5 P.M. Sun., R$30–40) is located in a splendid early-20th-century domed mansion constructed by a Czech tycoon. At very affordable prices, this model restaurant serves up (very) carefully prepared contemporary bistro fare with Brazilian accents—cashew-crusted stone bass with banana puree and raisin chutney is just one example. During the week, the *executivo* lunch menu features an entrée and main course for R$25.

(Miam-Miam (Rua General Góes Monteiro 34, Botafogo, tel. 21/2244-0125, www.miammiam.com.br, 7:30 P.M.–12:30 A.M. Tues.–Fri., 8 P.M.–1:30 A.M. Sat., R$25–35) is a tiny but very cozy and romantic café/bar, owned and operated by Roberta Ciasca out of her grandmother's early-20th-century house. A decade ago, 21-year-old Ciasca went backpacking through Europe and ended up at the Cordon Bleu cooking school in Paris. When she opened Miam-Miam in 2006, her creative comfort food—arugula rolls stuffed with roast beef and parmesan, and chicken pancakes with asparagus, mushrooms, Emmenthal, and tarragon—quickly seduced the city's gourmets.

BRAZILIAN

Lamas (Rua Marquês de Abrantes 18, Flamengo, tel. 21/2556-0799, www.cafelamas.com.br, 9:30 A.M.–3 A.M., R$25–35) has been around since 1874, and though it has since changed addresses, everything about the place—from the food and suave bow-tied waiters to the retro ambiance—is suffused with an aura of Rio's dining past. The front is a *botequim* where you can enjoy an icy *chope*, while the restaurant is at the back. The house specialties are the succulent filets mignons, served with lots of trimmings.

Meat is the *raison d'être* of **Porcão Rio's** (Av.

Infante Dom Henrique, Aterro de Flamengo, tel. 21/3389-8989, www.porcao.com.br, 11 A.M.–midnight Sun.–Thurs., 11 A.M.–1 A.M. Fri.–Sat., R$68 pp). Its *rodízio de carne* (rotation of meat) is an ingenious—not to mention fattening—Brazilian culinary tradition: Waiters circulate the dining room, brandishing various just-grilled cuts of meat, and clients pick and choose what they want. Started by two Gaúcho brothers from Brazil's most carnivorous state, Rio Grande do Sul, Porcão has become an institution, as well as a popular (and fairly pricy) chain. Growth, however, hasn't spoiled the quality of the food or service. In fact, aside from mouthwatering cuts of beef, the price includes unlimited trips to the fabulous buffet, which includes everything from salads and seafood to sushi. Due to its privileged seaside location right in front of Pão de Açúcar, Flamengo's immense Porcão is the best of the bunch.

INTERNATIONAL

Flávia Quaresma is one of Brazil's most renowned chefs, and if you want to see what all the fuss is about head to her latest eatery, **Carême** (Rua Visconde de Caravelas 113, Botafogo, tel. 21/2537-2274, R$45–55), a cozy little Parisian-style bistro with a small number of daily specials written on a blackboard (along with the weather conditions in Paris). Classics such as a filet mignon in red wine sauce served with golden potatoes, mushrooms, bacon, and onions share menu space with more unusual recipes such as roasted lamb in a cocoa pepper sauce served on polenta.

Copacabana and Leme

Although the views from the tourist-flooded restaurants along Avenida Atlântica are incomparable, the food is usually overpriced and lackluster. Otherwise, Copa's most interesting edible options are divided between the five-star kitchens of its most luxurious hotels and a few traditional restaurants and *botequins*.

CAFÉ AND SNACKS

Located on a small yet animated street between Avenida Atlântica and Avenida Nossa Senhora da Copacabana, **Cafeína** (Rua Constante Ramos 44, Copacabana, tel. 21/2547-8561, www.cafeina.biz, 8:30 A.M.–11:30 P.M. Tues.–Sat., 9 A.M.–8:30 P.M. Sun.–Mon., R$10–20) is a lively little café with sidewalk tables that make excellent perches for people-watching. Even if you have breakfast in your hotel, the pastries and coffee are so good you might want seconds. For light meals, there are salads and daily specials.

CONTEMPORARY

The intimate ◖ **Copa Café** (Av. Atlântica 3056, Loja B, Copacabana, tel. 21/2235-2947, 7 P.M.–2 A.M., R$35–45) has brought a welcome touch of hipness to Avenida Atlântica. In the downstairs bar/lounge, an alternative GLS crowd sips cocktails, nibbles on gourmet burgers, and warms up for the night's adventures with sultry DJ-spun tunes. Meanwhile, upstairs is given over to contemporary dining, with refined dishes such as duck cooked in vanilla-steeped port with Moroccan couscous, and langoustine risotto with curried apples and ginger.

BRAZILIAN

To truly savor Bahian cuisine—with its emphasis on seafood and fish—there's nowhere better than the beach. With this in mind, head to the recently opened **Siri Mole Praia** (Av. Atlântica, Quiosque 32 in front of Rua Bolivar, Copacabana, tel. 21/3684-6671, 3 P.M.–midnight Mon., 9 A.M.–midnight Tues.–Sun., R$60–80). For a snack, order the crunchy *acarajés*, Afro-Brazilian bean fritters fried to a crisp in *dendê* (palm) oil and stuffed with dried shrimp, *caruru* (seasoned okra), and *vatapá* (a puree featuring shrimp, cashews, *dendê*, and coconut milk). For a light bite choose from the refreshing seafood starters and salads, or else go whole hog and order a famous *moqueca*: a succulent fish or seafood stew cooked with tomatoes, coconut milk, cilantro, lime, and *dendê*. The most popular are made with either *siri mole* (soft-shelled crab), lobster, or shrimp.

INTERNATIONAL

Shirley (Rua Gustavo Sampaio 610, Loja A, Leme, tel. 21/2542-1003, noon–1 A.M. daily, R$18–30) is a small and modest neighborhood haunt on a shady street in Leme. Since 1952, it has been serving up tasty and generous portions of Spanish seafood dishes such as paella and *zarzuela*. Try to avoid it during peak weekend hours—when the kitchen gets harried and, as a result, the food isn't always up to par.

Also in Leme is one of the city's best-kept Italian secrets. Refined and discreet **D'Amici** (Rua Antônio Vieira 18, Leme, tel. 21/2541-4477, noon–1 A.M. daily, R$55–70) is a favorite lunch spot for execs and politicians, not to mention socialites who swear by the robust portions and eclectic menu. Specialties run the gamut from simple classics (melt-in-your-mouth osso buco and lasagna Bolognese) to more sophisticated and daring dishes such as ostrich carpaccio and wild boar roasted with herbs in a wine sauce. The sommelier is one of Rio's finest. Although it's not listed on the menu, the *petit gâteau de goiabada* (guava jelly) served with a white cheese sorbet is pretty sublime.

Ipanema and Leblon

Between the two of them, eternally fashionable Ipanema and Leblon reign supreme over Rio's dining scene. By day, svelte and sun-kissed residents haunt healthy vegetarian restaurants and sleek per kilo eateries that serve up salads galore and continuously rehydrate themselves at juice bars. In the evening, however, they dress up (casually chic) and go all out at international and contemporary restaurants where the decor is as tasteful as the fare on the (usually pricy) menus. For lighter, more affordable fare, head to the neighborhoods' *botequins,* cafés, and bistros in the area's many bookstores.

CAFÉS AND SNACKS

Armazém do Café (Rua Maria Quitéria 77, Ipanema, tel. 21/2522-5039, 8 A.M.–8 P.M. Mon.–Fri., 8 A.M.–6 P.M. Sat.), a chain of gourmet cafés, currently has eight locations around Rio, including four in Ipanema. Since Brazil is the land of coffee, Armazém, which takes its beans quite seriously, is a great place to learn about and savor different homegrown blends. One of the most popular is *frevo,* made with an organic bean from the state of Pernambuco. For noshing, there are sandwiches as well as sweet and savory pastries.

Located on the mezzanine of Ipanema's Livraria da Travessa, there's nothing at all bookish about **B!** (Rua Visconde de Pirajá 572, Ipanema, tel. 21/2249-4977, www.livrariada-travessa.com.br, 9 A.M.–11 P.M. Mon.–Sat., 1–11 P.M. Sun.). B! serves breakfast, creative sandwiches, and bistro-style meals along with desserts, coffee, and drinks, and is an appealing place to hang out at any time of the day.

Talho Capixaba (Av. Ataulfa da Paiva 1022, Leblon, Loja A/B, tel. 21/2512-8750, www.talhocapixaba.com.br, 7 A.M.–10 P.M. Mon.–Sat., 8 A.M.–9 P.M. Sun.) originally opened as a neighborhood butcher shop in the 1950s. Over the years, it kept expanding, adding a fine food delicatessen, cheese shop, and one of the best bakeries in town. Choose from more than 20 types of bread and then design the sandwich of your dreams.

For the most divine pastries in town, head to nearby **Kurt** (Rua General Urquiza 117, Loja B, Leblon, tel. 21/2294-0599, www.confeitariakurt.com.br, 8 A.M.–7 P.M. Mon.–Fri., 8 A.M.–5 P.M. Sat.). Rio's oldest pastry shop opened in the 1940s when Kurt Deichmann fled to Rio from Nazi Germany, armed with recipes for French mousses, Austrian and Hungarian tortes, and other sweet delights. Particularly sought-after is the *picada de abelha* ("bee sting"): a torte filled with vanilla cream and topped with a coating of honey, walnuts, and crunchy caramel. Since this is body-conscious Leblon, there are sugarless diet tortes as well.

If you have a sweet tooth, you won't be able to resist **Mil Frutas Café** (Rua Gárcia d'Avila 134, Ipanema, tel. 21/2521-1384, www.milfrutas.com.br, 10:30 A.M.–12:30 A.M. Mon.–Fri., 9:30 A.M.–1:30 A.M. Sat.–Sun.). Nostalgic for the exotic fruits of her youth in northeastern Brazil, Renata Saboya abandoned her journalism career to make all-natural gourmet sorbets from the exotic likes of *açai, bacuri, cupuaçu, jabuticaba, mangaba,* and *pitanga*. The results—icy bursts of pure distilled flavor—were an immediate success. Since then several Mil Frutas Cafés have opened around town, and though there are not yet *mil* (a thousand) flavors, there are close to 200, including the decidedly nonfruity white chocolate with *pimenta,* absinthe, and jasmine. Ipanema's Mil Frutas Café also serves snacks and light meals.

VEGETARIAN

◖ **Celeiro** (Rua Dias Ferreira 199, Leblon, tel. 21/2274-7843, www.celeiroculinaria.com.br, 10 A.M.–6 P.M. Mon.–Sat., R$20–30) is a classic vegetarian eatery that is an institution for Leblon's body-conscious residents. It all started in the early '80s when the Herz sisters couldn't keep up with the demand for their carrot cake, which they sold at a São Conrado beach *barraca*. Teaming up with their mother, they opened their own restaurant. Aside from healthy baked goods, they began concocting salads—such as chicken and cashew, and white bean and sun-dried tomato—made with organic products supplied from regional farms. Today, on any given day, there are over 50 fantastic salads, served on a per kilo basis, along with soups, snacks, and desserts.

Equally appetizing are the organic offerings at the tiny **Vegetariano Social Clube** (Rua Conde de Bernardote 26, Loja L, tel. 21/2294-5200, www.vegetarianosocialclube.com.br, noon–midnight Mon.–Sat., noon–6 P.M. Sun., R$15–20), which opened when a group of health-conscious pals from Leblon decided to do something about the lack of hard-core vegan restaurants in the hood. Choose from buffet or à la carte options, which include pizzas and tofulettes (eggless omelettes). To drink, there are lots of organic juices and even *caipirinhas* made with organic *cachaça* or sake. Saturday's tofu *feijoadas* have a large vegetarian following.

BRAZILIAN

Although Rio's most traditional dish—*feijoada*—is characteristically eaten on Saturday, for years now **Casa da Feijoada** (Rua Prudent de Moraes 10, Ipanema, tel. 21/2247-2476, www.cozinhatipica.com.br, noon–midnight daily, R$35–50) has been serving up a mouthwatering version for those who get cravings on any day of the week. Since gringos frequent the place, the house breaks with convention by letting customers select their own pieces of meat (thus allowing the more squeamish to avoid ears, tails, and feet). Along with the classic accompaniments of braised *couve* (kale), *torresmos* (pork rinds), fried *aipim* (manioc), and *farofa,* the somewhat steep all-you-can-eat price of R$47 includes *caldo de feijão,* a *caipirinha,* and homemade desserts. For those who aren't in a bean-ish frame of mind, there are other classic Brazilian options. Or you could head to **Brasileirinho** (Rua Jangadeiros 10, Loja A, Ipanema, tel. 21/2513-5184, www.cozinhatipica.com.br, noon–midnight daily, R$20–30). Despite the same ownership, this rustically decorated *boteco* is smaller and simpler (not to mention cheaper). Although you can take advantage of the same delicious *feijoada* (for a more modest R$32), the focus here is the succulent regional fare of Minas Gerais. Among the most popular Mineiro offerings are *carne seca com abóbora* (sun-dried beef with pumpkin) and *tutu à mineira,* a hearty stew of pork and pureed beans.

CONTEMPORARY

Zaza Bistrô Tropical (Rua Joana Angélica 40, Ipanema, tel. 21/2247-9101, www.zazabistro.com.br, 7:30 P.M.–12:30 A.M. Sun.–Thurs., 7:30 P.M.–1:30 A.M. Fri.–Sat., R$35–45) is a funky hippie chic eatery where tropicality—Asian, African, and American—rules. Typical main dishes on the inventive, organic menu include lamb *shishbarak* served on truffles and Arabian ravioli with yogurt mint sauce and almonds. The colorful, whimsical decor, including red velvet flowers hanging from the ceiling, silk pillows scattered around the floor, and lots of candlelight—is conducive to romance and relaxation. Customers are encouraged to take off their shoes and sprawl for a while.

◖**Carlota** (Rua Dias Ferreira 64, Lojas B-C, Leblon, tel. 21/2540-6821, www.carlota.com.br, 7:30 P.M.–midnight Tues.–Sat., 1–5 P.M. Sat., 1–11 P.M. Sun., R$40–50) is owned and operated by one of Brazil's top contemporary chefs, Carla Pernambuco, who is known for her unusual multicultural combinations of flavors and textures. Her most recent forays into Iberian culinary traditions have yielded specialties such as crunchy shrimp with smoked ham risotto and *bacalhau* (cod) ravioli in a truffle mascarpone sauce. Among her legendary desserts is a guava soufflé bathed in a creamy sauce of Catupiry cheese. Due to the size of this intimate Leblon bistro—dominated by soothing whites and natural woods—reservations are recommended.

INTERNATIONAL

It's a Carioca cliché that only tourists eat at Rio's usually lackluster seaside restaurants, but when the much-awaited Hotel Fasano, designed by Philippe Starck, opened in August 2007, Rio's rich and hungry were forced to make an exception for **Fasano Al Mare** (Av. Vieira Souto 80, Ipanema, tel. 21/3202-4000, www.fasano.com.br, 6:30–10:30 A.M., noon–4 P.M. and 7 P.M.–1 A.M. daily with extended weekend hours, R$80–100). In fact, this gorgeous restaurant is all about the ocean. Aside from bewitching views of Ipanema beach, the inspired maritime decor includes polished sea shells and Murano glass lamps that resemble octopus tentacles. Then there is the menu, offering seafood delights prepared by Luca Gozzani, a three-star Michelin chef imported from Italy. São Paulo's Rogério Fasano, hotelier and restaurateur extraordinaire, is also the man behind the Carioca version of **Gero** (Rua Anibal de Mendonça 157, Ipanema, tel. 21/2239-8158, www.fasano.com.br/gerorio, noon–4 P.M. and 7 P.M.–1 A.M. Mon.–Fri., noon–2 A.M. Sat., noon–midnight Sun., R$60–80), routinely considered the one of the top Italian restaurants in the city. The simple decor—skylights, blond wood floors, and exposed brick walls hung with black and white photos—belies the fact that even Rio's rich and trendy sometimes find themselves on the waiting list to dine here. Avoid the crush and high prices and come for a three-course R$70 lunch during the week, when you can partake of delicious Italian classics such as an impeccable ravioli stuffed with mozzarella in a basic tomato sauce as well as the more refined likes of quail stuffed with foie gras and saffron risotto.

For simpler Italian fare, head to **La Forneria**

(Rua Maria Quitéria 136, Ipanema, tel. 21/2287-0335, www.laforneria.com.br, noon–1 A.M. Sun.–Thurs., noon–2 A.M. Fri.–Sat., R$28–38). This pleasantly rustic house with a privileged view of Lagoa Rodrigo de Freitas serves up more than 30 types of delicious thin crust pizza baked in a wood-burning oven. Try the del Contadino, which is topped with buffalo mozzarella, cambert, fresh figs, and prosciutto.

The sushi chefs at **Sushi Leblon** (Rua Dias Ferreira 256, Leblon, tel. 21/2512-7830, noon–4 P.M. and 7 P.M.–1:30 A.M. Mon.–Fri., noon–1:30 A.M. Sat., 1:30 P.M.–midnight Sun., R$45–55) are actually from the northeastern coastal state of Ceará, a region with a strong fishing tradition. Once they acquired Japanese preparation techniques, there was no stopping them. As a result, this sophisticated address has attracted a loyal following. Both visually striking and appetizing, the sushi prepared always includes startling innovations such as eel sushi with quail's eggs and truffle oil. Non-sushi fare is equally creative: Try the sea urchin ceviche seasoned with ginger, *pimenta,* and Sicilian limes.

(**Antiquarius** (Rua Aristides Espinola 19, Leblon, tel. 21/2294-1049, www.antiquarius.com.br, noon–2 A.M. Mon.–Sat., noon–midnight Sun., R$70–90) is indisputably one of Rio's finest restaurants. When it opened in 1977, Brazilians were amazed to discover that Portuguese cuisine went far beyond its signature specialty of *bacalhau* (salted cod). This elegant eatery offers up this classic—neophytes should try the simplest version, roasted in the finest olive oil with onions, garlic, and olives. Diners can also sample lesser-known regional delicacies, such as duck risotto with olives and *paio* sausage, or lobster with lemon rice and *couve,* as well as some truly delectable desserts. Rounding out the experience are antique furnishings, fresh flowers, and fine English porcelain along with impeccable service.

VARIED

Gula Gula (Rua Henrique Dumont 57, Ipanema, tel. 21/2259-3084, www.gulagula.com.br, noon–midnight Sun.–Thurs., noon–1 A.M. Fri.–Sat., R$15–25) is one of the best, least expensive, and typically Carioca eateries in town. The laid-back, casual vibe and simple, no-nonsense but appetizing quiches, salads, pastas, and grilled meats have proved to be a winning formula, spawning 12 restaurants throughout the Centro and Zona Sul. The most attractive is this Ipanema location, which is situated in an spacious two-story house replete with art deco fixtures and furnishings.

A mere block from Ipanema beach, **Delírio Tropical** (Rua Gárcia d'Ávila 48, Ipanema, www.deliriotropical.com.br, tel. 21/3208-2977, 9 A.M.–10 P.M. Mon.–Sat., 9 A.M.–9 P.M. Sun., R$12–17) is a great place for a healthy meal after soaking up the sun. Choose from an array of colorful and unusual salads along with hot daily specials, then take a seat in the upstairs dining area, which is tropically accessorized with hanging ferns and climbing vines. The glass walls afford a tree-house like view of the comings and goings of beach bums below.

In the heart of Leblon, **Fellini** (Rua General Urquiza 101, Leblon, tel. 21/2511-3600, www.fellini.com.br, R$20–30) offers one of Rio's most extensive and refined per kilo self-service buffets. There's no need to splurge at a five-star restaurant when you can savor the likes of foie gras ravioli, honey-lacquered duck, lobster, escargots, and even caviar. Aside from more mundane (but no less delicious) options, there are dishes for vegetarians and diabetics. On weekends, avoid prime time or you'll have to stand in line.

For years **Giuseppe Grill** (Av. Bartolomeu Mitre, Leblon, tel. 21/2249-3055, noon–4 P.M. and 7 P.M.–midnight Mon.–Thurs., noon–1 A.M. Fri.–Sat., 11 A.M.–11 P.M. Sun., R$30–40) was the carefully guarded secret of meat-loving business execs who worked in Centro (the original restaurant is at Rua Sete de Setembro 65, tel. 21/2509-7215). But when, in 2007, a more upscale version opened in Leblon, the rest of the city suddenly discovered the succulent joys of some of the finest cuts of beef this side of the Pampas. All meats—red meat abstainers can opt for chicken or fish—are slowly grilled, roasted, or barbecued over charcoal and served with *caseiro* (home-cooking) style garnishes such as cream of spinach, potato soufflé, and *farofa* with raisins. A special prix fixe menu offers an entrée, main course, and dessert for R$49. The impressive wine cellar boasts over 450 labels.

Lagoa and Jardim Botânico

The dozen sophisticated kiosks scattered around the Lagoa Rodrigo de Freitas offer a wide range of delicious fare (ranging from Arabian dishes to sushi) both day and night. Meanwhile, the reserved, upscale residential neighborhood of Jardim Botânico is second only to Ipanema and Leblon when it comes to gourmet eating experiences

CONTEMPORARY

Roberta Sudbrack (Av. Lineu de Paula Machado 916, Jardim Botânico, tel. 21/3847-0139, 7:30 A.M.–midnight Tues.–Sat., noon–3 P.M. Thurs.–Fri., www.robertasu-brack.com.br, R$85–100) is considered one of Brazil's most inventive contemporary chefs, whose culinary creations are a feast for the senses. Self-taught, Sudbrack went from operating a hot dog stand in Brasília to becoming presidential chef during the tenure of Fernando Henrique Cardoso. Her casually tasteful Jardim Botânico restaurant features two floors; the upstairs is dominated by a single, long 18-person dining table where strangers can bond over innovative concoctions such as langoustine with pistachio milk and roasted pork with potato chantilly. In order to take advantage of the freshest ingredients, the menu changes daily.

INTERNATIONAL

With the opening of **Bráz** (Rua Maria Angélica 129, Jardim Botânico, tel. 21/2535-0687, www.casabraz.com.br, 6:30 P.M.–12:30 A.M. Sun.–Thurs., 6:30 P.M.–1:30 A.M. Fri.–Sat., R$30–40), 2007 became known as the year that São Paulo pizza (deemed the best in Brazil) finally invaded Rio. Topped with the freshest ingredients, these fine-crust pizzas—touted as "paintings you can eat"—taste as great as they look. The house specialty, the *caprese,* comes adorned with artisanal buffalo mozzarella, tomatoes, giant basil leaves, and white olive pesto.

One of Brazil's most stellar chefs, Claude Troisgros migrated from Paris to Rio 25 years ago and started a (culinary) revolution by marrying sophisticated French cooking techniques with the unusual textures, flavors, and colorful fresh produce distinctive to Brazil. You can savor Troisgros's surprisingly original and visually striking creations at **Olympe** (Rua Custódio Serrão 62, Jardim Botânico, tel. 21/2539-4542, www.claudetroisgros.com.br, 7:30 P.M.–12:30 A.M. Mon.–Sat., noon–4 P.M. Fri., R$80–90), situated in a lovely house that is both as unpretentious and refined as the menus themselves (Troisgros offers several). The "Epecialidades" menu features classic creations such as quail stuffed with *farofa,* raisins, and pearl onions, and bathed in a sauce of *jabuticabas* (a purplish native fruit not unlike a blackcurrant). The "Criatividade" menu allows you to taste test the chef's current experiments: recent results include grilled Amazonian fish in a creamy sorrel sauce with asparagus. Finally, truly adventurous souls can splurge on the R$168 "Confiance" menu, a four-dish tasting feast that Troisgros dreams up daily according to the ingredients at hand and whatever inspires him. Foodies eager to sample Troisgros's culinary wizardry but without the deep pockets necessary for Olympe needn't despair—Troisgros has opened the more affordable **66 Bistrô** (Av. Alexandre Ferreira 66, Jardim Botânico, tel. 21/2266-0838, www.66bistro.com.br, noon–4 P.M., 7:30 P.M.–12:30 A.M. Tues.–Sun., R$25–40). With his son, Thomas, in charge of the kitchen, this charming Parisian-style bistro is already *the* place to lunch—apparently not even celebrities can resist a weekday "executive" menu whose buffet of antipasti, salads, and several main dishes costs a mere R$28 (R$34 if you succumb to the desserts). Evenings and weekends, the menu is à la carte. A favorite house specialty is the chicken roasted in Dijon mustard.

INFORMATION AND SERVICES
Tourist and Travel Information

Riotur (www.riotur.com.br) is the city travel association. You can pick up maps and brochures at its tourist centers. The main branch is in Centro (Praça Pio X 119, 9th floor, 9 A.M.–6 P.M. Mon.–Fri., tel. 21/2271-7000), but there are also branches in Copacabana (Av. Princesa Isabel 183, tel. 21/2541-7522, 9 A.M.–6 P.M. daily) as well as at the Aeroporto Internacional Tom Jobim (6 A.M.–midnight daily) and the Rodoviária Novo Rio (8 A.M.–8 P.M. daily). For up-to-date information or listings in English, you can make a free call to Riotur's tourist hotline, **Alô Rio** (tel. 0800/285-0555, 9 A.M.–6 P.M. daily).

For (scant) information about the rest of Rio de Janeiro state, you can visit **TurisRio** (www.turisrio.rj.gov.br), with offices at the Aeroporto Internacional Tom Jobim (10 A.M.–9 P.M. daily) and in Centro (Rua México 125, tel. 0800/282-2007, 9 A.M.–6 P.M. Mon.–Fri.).

Banks

The most advantageous place to exchange currency is at major branches of **Banco do Brasil**. There is a branch at Aeroporto Internacional Tom Jobim as well as in Centro (Rua Senador Dantas 105, tel. 21/3808-2689) and Copacabana (Av. Nossa Senhora da Copacabana 1292, tel. 21/2523-1441). There is an **American Express** at the Copacabana Palace (Av. Atlântica, 1702B, Copacabana, tel. 21/2548-2148 or 0800/702-0777). Otherwise, it is easy to take out money at the city's many ATMs. Banco do Brasil, HSBC, Bradesco, and Citibank all accept international bank cards. The largest concentrations of banks are on Avenida Rio Branco (Centro), Avenida Nossa Senhora da Copacabana (Copacabana), and Avenida Visconde de Pirajá (Ipanema).

Communications

The main post office is in Centro (Rua 1 de Março 64, tel. 21/2219-5315), but there are numerous agencies throughout the city, including one at Aeroporto Internacional Tom Jobim (open 24 hours) and branches in Copacabana (Av. Nossa Senhora de Copacabana 540) and Ipanema (Rua Visconde de Pirajá 452). Hours are 8 A.M.–6 P.M. Monday–Friday, 8 A.M.–noon Saturday.

For international telephone calls, Rio has quite

a few international calling centers, which also have Internet access. **Central Fone** (www.centralfone.com.br) has many locations throughout the city, including Centro (Av. Rio Branco 156, 9 A.M.–9 P.M. Mon.–Fri., 10 A.M.–4 P.M. Sat.) and Ipanema (Rua Vinícius de Moraes 129, 9:30 A.M.–8 P.M. Mon.–Fri., 11 A.M.–6 P.M. Sat.–Sun.). There are many call centers/cyber cafés in Copacabana, among them **Locutório** (Rua Francisco Sá 26, 8 A.M.–2 A.M. daily) and **Telerede** (Av. Nossa Senhora da Copacabana 209, 8 A.M.–midnight daily).

These days, most hotels—whether you're staying in a five-star or a hostel—offer Internet access for guests. Many bookstores—such as **Letras & Expressões** (Rua Visconde de Pirajá 276, Ipanema, tel. 21/2521-6110, www.letraseexpressoes.com.br, 8 A.M.–midnight Mon.–Thurs., 8 A.M.–2 A.M. Fri.–Sat., 8 A.M.–midnight Sun.) and **Café com Letras** (Rua Bartolomeu Mitre 297, Loja C, Leblon, tel. 21/2249-3079, 8 A.M.–midnight Mon.–Sat., 10 A.M.–8 P.M. Sun.)—have Internet cafés. If you happen to be traveling with a laptop, most *shoppings* have free wireless connections (but be very careful when carting around your computer due to risk of theft).

Emergency Services

In the event of a medical emergency, dial **193** for Pronto Socorro (First Aid). If you need to visit a hospital in Copacabana, **Clínica Galdino Campos** (Av. Nossa Senhora de Copacabana, Copacabana, tel. 21/2548-9966, www.galdinocampos.com.br) is a private clinic that has a tradition of treating foreigners. It is open 24 hours and has English-speaking staff. In Ipanema, **Hospital Ipanema** (Rua Antônio Parreiras 67, tel. 21/2287-2322) is a public hospital with emergency services. For nonemergencies, contact the **Rio Health Collective** (Av. das Américas 4430, Barra de Tijuca, tel. 21/3325-9300). By phone, they can provide you with names of qualified specialists who speak English.

Rio is filled with pharmacies, many of which take turns staying open for 24 hours. Two locations of **Drogaria Pacheco** that never close are in Copacabana (Av. Nossa Senhora de Copacabana 534 A/B, tel. 21/2548-1525) and Catete (Rua do Catete 248, tel. 21/2556-6792).

In the event of a crime, call **190** to reach the police. There is a special **Delegacia Especial de Atendimento ao Turista** (Tourist Police) unit whose Leblon headquarters (Av. Afrânio de Melo Franco 159, tel. 21/3399-7170) is open 24 hours a day. Agents are generally helpful and speak English.

Consulate services can also advise you with respect to police and medical problems: **Australia** (Av. Presidente Wilson 231, 23rd Floor, Centro, tel. 21/3824-4624), **Canada** (Av. Atlântica 1130, 5th Floor, Copacabana, tel. 21/2543-3004), **United Kingdom** (Praia do Flamengo 284, 2nd Floor, Flamengo, tel. 21/2555-9600), **United States** (Av. Presidente Wilson 147, Centro, tel. 21/3823-3000).

Laundry Services

For both washing and dry-cleaning services in the Zona Sul, try **Lavakilo** (Rua Almirante Gonçalves 50, Copacabana, 7:30 A.M.–7:30 P.M. Mon.–Fri., 8 A.M.–5 P.M. Sat.) and **Lavanderia Ipanema** (Rua Farme de Amoedo 55, Ipanema, 7:30 A.M.–9 P.M. Mon.–Sat.).

GETTING THERE

Most international travelers arrive in Rio by air, although if you're traveling from another city in Brazil, you'll arrive by bus or car.

Air

Rio has two airports. International flights and the majority of domestic flights arrive and depart from the **Aeroporto Internacional Tom Jobim** (Av. 20 de Janeiro, Ilha do Governador, tel. 21/3398-4527), also known as Galeão, situated in the Zona Norte, around 20 minutes from Centro and 45–60 minutes from the Zona Sul. Right in Centro, adjacent to the Parque de Flamengo, is Rio's oldest airport, **Aeroporto Santos Dumont** (Praça Senador Salgado Filho, Centro, tel. 21/3814-7070), where flights are basically limited to the Rio–São Paulo air shuttle.

Both airports have kiosks for special airport taxis, where you pay your fare in advance based on the distance of your destination. These are often more expensive than just hailing one of the white *rádio taxis* available at the taxi stands. Two major taxi companies are **Coopertramo** (tel. 21/2560-2022) and **Transcoopass** (tel. 21/2590-6891). Always make sure you use a bona fide taxi company. Taxi fare from Galeão is around R$60 to Flamengo, R$70 to Copacabana, and R$80 to Leblon.

From Galeão the **Real** (tel. 21/2560-7041 or 0800-24-0850) bus company offers regular *executivo* service for R$6 to Rio. Buses cut through Centro (along Av. Rio Branco) and then stop at Aeroporto Santos Dumont before continuing along the oceanfront *avenidas* of Flamengo (Av. Beira Mar), Copacabana (Av. Atlântica), Ipanema (Av. Vieira Souto), and Leblon (Av. Delfim Moreira), including stops at all the major hotels along the way. For hotels that are inland, just ask the driver in advance to let you off at the nearest cross street (*"Por favor, pode me deixar na Rua. . . ?"*). Buses leave the airports daily, at 30-minute intervals between 5:20 A.M. and 11 P.M. To get to the airport, you can grab the same bus (on the reverse route) or ask your hotel to call you a cab and settle on a fixed rate in advance.

Bus

Rio's main bus station, **Rodoviária Novo Rio** (Av. Francisco Bicalho 1, São Cristovão, tel. 21/3213-1800), is a major transportation hub. Buses arrive from and depart to all points of Brazil and to other South American countries. It is located in a run-down dockside area of Centro on the edge of the Zona Norte. Despite its importance, the station itself is also pretty run-down, which is why a (long overdue) major renovation is underway to transform it into a spankingly modern station filled with shops, restaurants, bookstores, and cafés.

Getting to and from the *rodoviária* from anywhere in the city is very easy. Just hop on any bus with "Rodoviária" posted as its destination on the front. A taxi will set you back around R$20 to Centro and R$40 to Copacabana.

GETTING AROUND

Rio has a very extensive and inexpensive public transportation system consisting of a limited but efficient Metrô and a far-reaching, if slightly more confusing, bus system. For everywhere else—and nighttime—there are taxis.

Metrô

Rio's Metrô subway system (www.metrorio.com.br, tel. 21/3211-6300) is clean, efficient, and safe (not to mention gloriously air-conditioned). The only problem is its size. To date, there are only two lines. Parts of the Zona Norte (Maracaná for instance) are well serviced, as is Centro. In terms of the Zona Sul, however, Linha 1 (to date) only goes as far as Cantagalo station in Copacabana. To get to Ipanema from Copacabana, Integração Expressa shuttle buses ferry passengers to Praça General Osório from Siqueira Campos station. Tickets can be purchased in the stations as *unitários* (singles, R$2.40), *duplos* (two-way, R$4.80) or *múltiplos* (10 trips for R$24). If you're going to be taking a bus at your final Metrô stop, you can save money by purchasing a combined *integrado* ticket, which is less expensive than paying for two separate voyages. The Metrô runs 5 A.M.–midnight Monday–Saturday, 7 A.M.–11 P.M. Sunday.

Bus

Buses go everywhere in Rio. Except when they're mired in rush-hour traffic (usually 7–9 A.M. and 5–7 P.M.), they tend to go very, very fast, which, depending on your thrill factor, can prove either exhilarating or hair-raising. The other drawback to Rio's municipal buses is that they're not the safest form of locomotion going due to pickpockets and occasional armed holdups. That said, if you leave your valuables at the hotel and limit yourself to daytime trips between points in the Centro, Zona Sul, and the western beaches of Barra and Recreio, you'll be fine. Do take care to have your change already counted out beforehand, and always keep bags (including knapsacks) or other belongings closed (with a zipper or button) and close to your chest, especially when it's crowded. By day, buses run with great frequency. By night, you can risk taking buses between main stops in Flamengo, Botafogo, Copacabana, Ipanema, and Leblon, which are usually quite busy until around 9 or 10 P.M. Otherwise, however, stick to taxis.

Final destinations are written on the front of the bus and along the side you will have the main stops along the routes. Make sure you check this out. From the Centro, for example, there are buses whose final destination is Leblon that careen along the coast through Copacabana and Ipanema, while others go inland via Botafogo and Jardim Botânico. After paying your fare (R$2) to the *cobrador* at the back of the bus, make your way to the front, so you can make an easy exit when you get to your stop. If a bus stop is not clearly marked, look for a clump of people waiting. You can signal for a bus to stop by sticking out your arm.

Taxis

Taxis are often the best way to get around Rio. Taxi service is reasonably priced, and for specific trips you can often bargain a fixed price with your driver (if language is a problem ask someone at your hotel or hostel for help as well as approximate prices). There are two kinds of taxis in Rio. Yellow cabs with blue stripes are the most common. They can be hailed in the street and are cheaper. Large, white, air-conditioned radio cabs are usually ordered by phone and are more expensive. Two reliable companies are **Centro de Taxis** (tel. 21/2593-2598) and **Coopacarioca** (tel. 21/2518-1818). Most Carioca cab drivers are friendly and honest (although very few speak English), but there are a few who specialize in scamming gringo tourists. Unless you've agreed on a set fare, check to make sure the meter is always running. During the daytime until 8 P.M. the "Bandeira 1" rate is cheaper than at night, holidays, and weekends when the rate is "Bandeira 2."

Car Rental

Quite frankly, unless you're a daredevil with a lot of patience, driving in Rio de Janeiro itself is not exactly recommended. It's not that

Cariocas are poor drivers, but they tend to forget they're not at the Indy 500. Then there are the rush-hour traffic jams, which aren't only stressful, but also stiflingly hot with the tropical sun beating down. One-way streets, poorly marked turnoffs, and holdups—at stoplights and when you're parked—are further dissuading factors. In truth, renting a car only makes sense if you're going to be doing lots of day trips in and around the state of Rio de Janeiro. Major companies include **Avis** (www.avis.com.br) in Copacabana (Av. Princesa Isabel 350, tel. 21/2543-8481); **Hertz** (www.hertz.com.br) with agencies at Galeão (tel. 21/3398-4339), Santos Dumont (tel. 21/2262-0612), and Copacabana (Av. Princesa Isabel 334, tel. 21/2275-7248); and **Localiza Rent a Car** (www.localiza.com.br), with agencies at Galeão (tel. 21/3398-5445), Santos Dumont (tel. 21/2240-9181), and in Copacabana (Av. Princesa Isabel 214, tel. 21/2275-3440).

City Tours

An increasing number of organized tours allow you to explore Rio's diverse neighborhoods and natural attractions and to experience different aspects of Carioca life and culture.

Carlos Roquette (tel. 21/9911-3829, www.culturalrio.com.br) is a former judge with an art history degree and a great command of English (and French) who has been leading historic and cultural tours of Rio for over 25 years. Aside from the dozens that already exist—ranging from the conventional ("Baroque Rio," "Belle Epoque Rio," and "Art Deco Rio") to the more unusual ("Esoteric Rio," "Lesbian Rio," "People Watching," and "Historic Barbershops")—Roquette can also custom-design tours for individuals and groups of all sizes. Customized private tours average around R$50 per hour (discounts are available).

Private Tours (tel. 21/2232-9710, www.privatetours.com.br, four-hour city tour R$50–60), run by Carioca Pedro Novak, offers various Jeep tours around Rio as well as to historic towns, beaches, and natural attractions throughout Rio de Janeiro state. The highly personalized tours are tailored to groups of up to four people.

Be a Local (tel. 21/9643-0366, www.bealocal.com.br) matches foreign visitors with English-speaking locals in an attempt to show them aspects of Carioca life—a funk party in a Rio *favela*, a soccer game at Maracanã—that they could otherwise never experience. A half-day trip with a *moto-boy* to a *favela* costs R$65. **Ika Poran** (tel. 21/3852-2916, www.ikoporan.org) runs tours to cultural and social development projects located within Rio's poorer communities and *favelas* in an attempt to show foreigners that social problems have solutions. Visitors get to interact with residents, and most of the tour fee goes to specific projects. A full-day tour including lunch and transportation costs R$145 per person. A half-day tour costs US$53. Trips are organized through the Triple M travel agency (tel. 21/2224-0202).

Perhaps the most spectacularly scenic tour you could ever take in Rio is by helicopter. **Helisight** (tel. 21/2511-2141 or 2542-7895, www.helisight.com.br) offers various breathtaking forays into Rio's blue skies that last 6–60 minutes (with prices ranging from a hefty R$150 to a stratospheric R$875 and a required minimum of three people).

Vicinity of Rio de Janeiro City

ILHA DE PAQUETÁ

Located in the Baía de Guanabara, the small Ilha de Paquetá has been a favorite Carioca getaway since Dom João VI began coming here in the early 19th-century. He was responsible for building the Capela de São Roque, around which the lively five-day **Festival de São Roque** takes place in August. On most weekends and holidays, the island is routinely packed with families from the Zona Norte who crowd the (polluted) beaches and seaside bars. During the week though, the island makes for a relaxing day trip. Tranquility reigns and the slightly dilapidated colonial buildings retain their allure—albeit slightly faded. The trip in itself is worthwhile for the splendid views of Rio and the bay.

Getting There and Around

Ferries leave at two-hour intervals 7 A.M.–11 P.M. daily, from the **Estação das Barcas** (tel. 21/2533-7524, R$4.50 Mon.–Fri., R$9.50 Sat.–Sun.) at Praça XV de Novembro. The trip takes a little over an hour. If you're in a hurry, hydrofoils (tel. 21/2533-4343) will get you there in half the time at double the price, with several departures and returns a day. Although no vehicles are allowed on the island, you can easily (and cheaply) rent a bike and pedal around.

NITERÓI

Only 17 kilometers (10.5 miles) across Baía de Guanabara, the well-to-do, suburb-like city of Niterói makes a great day trip. Aside from its long white-sand beaches and space-age Niemeyer buildings—including the iconic, Star Trek–worthy Museu de Arte Contemporânea (MAC)—you get to view Rio in all its dazzling beauty from the other side of the bay.

Sights

By far, the most compelling attraction in Niterói is the **Museu de Arte Contemporánea (MAC)** (Mirante da Boa Viagem, tel. 21/2620-4000, 11 A.M.–6 P.M. Tues.–Sun., R$4). Designed by Oscar Niemeyer and inaugurated in 1996, this fantastic UFO-shaped construction sits upon a slender cylindrical base whose diameter is only 9 meters (30 feet). Since the museum is perched upon an outcrop overlooking the Baía de Guanabara, the 360-degree views are spectacular, often rivaling the museum's hit-and-miss art exhibits. To reach the museum from Niterói's ferry terminal, as you leave the terminal take a right and walk 50 meters (164 feet) and then catch the 47B minibus.

The MAC was the first construction of what will eventually constitute the Caminho Niemeyer (Niemeyer Route). Other projects include the striking Teatro Popular (completed in mid-2007), the Catedral Metropolitano de Niterói, and the Fundação Oscar Niemeyer, which will house the architect's works and private art collection as well as an art school. When completed, Niterói will be second only to Brasília as a showcase for the vanguard architect's constructions.

For a taste of history (and more spectacular views), hop the 33 bus (or take a 15-minute cab ride) to Jurujuba to admire the **Fortaleza de Santa Cruz** (Estrada General Eurico Gaspar Dutra, tel. 21/2711-0462, 9 A.M.–5 P.M. daily, R$4). Erected in 1555 out of granite and whale oil, this was the first fortress to be built overlooking the Baía de Guanabara. The fortified complex shelters the early-17th-century Capela de Santa Bárbara as well as a sun clock, a prison, and a firing wall still riddled with bullet holes.

Beaches

The beaches close to Niterói's center are polluted, but if you take a bus due south—from the ferry terminal, take any bus marked "Itacoatiara"—you will encounter some surprisingly unspoiled and very attractive beaches, among them **Piratininga, Camboinhas, Itaipu,** and the most spectacular of them all, **Itacoatiara** (about 45 minutes from Niterói's center), which is framed by lushly forested hills. From here,

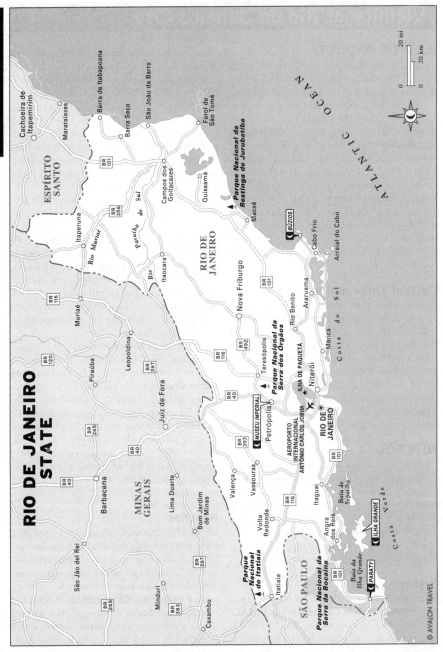

RIO DE JANEIRO STATE

© AVALON TRAVEL

© CHRISTIAN KNEPPER/EMBRATUR

Museu de Arte Contemporánea in Niterói, designed by Oscar Niemeyer

you have unrivaled views of Pão de Açúcar and Corcovado across the bay. All of these beaches are well equipped with *barracas* where you can feast on fresh fish and seafood.

Getting There

The most scenic way of getting to Niterói is by taking the ferry that leaves from the Estação das Barcas at Praça XV de Novembro. Boats operated by Conerj (tel. 21/2533-6661)—often jammed with commuters during rush hour—leave at 15–30 minute intervals 7:30 A.M.–midnight and at 60-minute intervals midnight–6 A.M. Ferry rides cost R$2.30. Quicker and more comfortable, Transtur hydrofoils (tel. 21/2533-4343, R$5) leave at 15-minute intervals, from 6:30 A.M.–9 P.M. Monday–Friday.

Inland from Rio de Janeiro City

When the going gets hot, Cariocas have historically headed for the cool, forest-clad mountains surrounding Rio, and the charmingly rustic resort towns that conjure up a tropical version of the Alps.

PETRÓPOLIS

Only an hour's drive north from Rio, the summer getaway of the Brazilian emperor and his family still provides a welcome refuge, offering—aside from imperial trappings—cool respite, fine food, and mountain scenery. Upon visiting this idyllic region, Dom Pedro I was so enchanted by the majestic landscapes and moderate temperatures that he drew up plans for a villa. However, it fell to his son, Pedro II—who founded Petrópolis (named after his imperialness) in 1843—to actually build his dream house, which (in keeping with the emperor's lofty ambitions) ended up as a full-fledged royal palace. Not wanting to be out of the loop, barons, counts, and marquis came flocking to construct elegant mansions. The town's alpine climes also attracted numerous German immigrants, which explains the Bohemian influence present in the architecture as well as the hearty German food and pastries available at local bars and bistros. If you're seeking tranquility, you'll find more of it during the week, since weekends (particularly in the summertime) fill up with Cariocas. Exploring Petrópolis by foot is easy, but you can also hire a horse-drawn carriage, available in front of the Museu Imperial.

Sights

Most of historic Petrópolis lies beyond the somewhat congested commercial center, concentrated in a bucolic cluster of streets lined with 19th-century mansions and laced with tree-shaded canals. Many of the most splendid *casas* are on the main street of Avenida Koeler.

◖ MUSEU IMPERIAL

Surrounded by beautifully landscaped gardens, the elegant neoclassical pink edifice that functioned as Dom Pedro II's summer digs now houses the Museu Imperial (Rua da Imperatriz 220, tel. 24/2237-8000, www.museuimperial.com.br, 11 A.M.–6 P.M. Tues.–Sun., R$8). After replacing your shoes with soft-soled slippers, you can glide around the gleaming parquet floors and inspect the myriad regal trappings whose highlights include Dom Pedro I's golden scepter and Dom Pedro II's fairy tale–like crown encrusted with 639 diamonds and 77 pearls. From the ceremonial throne room and the ornate dining room—where the elaborately set table makes you feel as if hungry royals could show up at any minute—to the stables and even the royal commode, the palace gives you a rare day-in-the-life glimpse of an emperor in the tropics. At night (8 P.M. Thurs.–Sat., R$28), a sound-and-light show illuminates the palace facade. Even if you don't understand the Portuguese narration, the music and setting create a beguiling atmosphere.

CATEDRAL DE SÃO PEDRO DE ALCÂNTARA

The imposing French neo-gothic Catedral de São Pedro de Alcântara (Rua São Pedro de Alcântara 60, tel. 24/2242-4300, 8 A.M.–6 P.M. daily), with its 70-meter (230-foot) tower, wasn't completed until 1939. Aside from its somber aura and lovely stained-glass windows—depicting scenes from poems written by the multitalented Dom Pedro II—its main attraction is the marble, bronze, and onyx Imperial Mausoleum housing the mortal remains of Dom Pedro II, his wife, Dona Teresa Cristina, and their daughter, Princesa Isabel.

PALÁCIO DE CRISTAL

The Palácio de Cristal (Rua Alfredo Pachá, tel. 24/2247-3721, 9 A.M.–5:30 P.M. Tues.–Sun.) is a striking iron-structured glass palace that was made in France and assembled in Brazil for Princesa Isabel. The princess held fashionable balls and parties here, the most memorable of which occurred in 1888, when she gave out letters of liberation to slaves before signing the Lei Áurea, which officially ended slavery in Brazil. Isabel's husband, the Conde d'Eu, used the palace as a hothouse, where he cultivated orchids. In modern times, it is used as a stage for theatrical and musical events.

CASA DE SANTOS DUMONT

Brazilians have long snubbed their noses at the Wright Brothers. As far as they're concerned, the first human being to take to the skies in a plane was Alberto Santos Dumont, who in 1906 completed the first nonassisted flight in his plane, which he baptized *14-Bis*. Flying machines aside, Santos Dumont was an avid builder and inventor. He designed the gracious house known as Casa de Santos Dumont (Rua do Encanto 22, tel. 24/2247-3158, 9:30 A.M.–5 P.M. Tues.–Sun., R$3). Aside from his personal effects, the house displays various other inventions, among them an alcohol-heated shower and a bed that can be transformed into a desk.

PALÁCIO QUITANDINHA

Slightly outside of the center (more easily reached by car or taxi), the Palácio Quitandinha (Av. Joaquim Rola 2, tel.

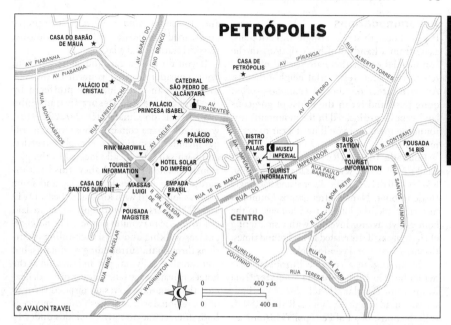

24/2237-1012, 9 a.m.–5 p.m. Tues.–Sun., R$5) is an impressive if slightly jarring Norman-style palace that was built in the 1940s to house the largest and most glamorous hotel/casino in all of Latin America. While it attracted the likes of Marlene Dietrich, Orson Welles, and Lana Turner, its days as a luxury gaming den were short-lived; in 1946 gambling was outlawed in Brazil and the casino was transformed into a posh apartment complex. Today, it functions as an events center. You can explore its surprisingly vibrant interior—the work of famed American decorator and Hollywood set designer Dorothy Draper, who irreverently colored the walls in tones of shocking pink, scarlet, and turquoise, reminiscent of a Technicolor movie. Note that the lagoon out front is shaped like Brazil.

CASA DE PETRÓPOLIS

The former home of José Tavares Guerra, nephew of the Barão de Mauá, the Casa de Petrópolis (Rua Ipiranga 716, tel. 24/2231-

6197, 1:30–6:30 p.m. Thurs.–Tues., R$3) is a Victorian mansion whose architecture was inspired by Guerra's early years spent living and studying in England. Guided tours are offered of the sumptuous interior with its crystal chandeliers, brocade covered walls, marble fireplaces, and polished jacaranda furniture. The lovely gardens were a favorite strolling spot of Dom Pedro II.

Other Petrópolis palaces of note aren't open for visitation, but their exteriors are worth a look. These include the pretty pink **Palácio Princesa Isabel** (Av. Koeler, 42), home of the imperial princess, and the grand **Palácio Rio Negro** (Av. Koeler, 255), built by the Barão do Rio Negro, a rich coffee planter. After he sold it, the house became the official summer residence of Brazil's presidents. The **Casa do Barão de Mauá** (Praça da Confluência 3) was home to the Barão de Mauá—one Brazil's most famous entrepreneurs, he founded the Banco do Brasil and was the man behind the construction of the nation's first railroad (linking Rio and Petrópolis).

Accommodations

If you choose to stay overnight in Petrópolis, aside from a handful of basic options in the commercial center there are several nice hotels in the older, residential neighborhoods. An even larger number of *pousadas*—often quite posh and set in the midst of gorgeous landscapes—are located in the mountains surrounding town, but you'll need a car to get to reach them.

Pousada 14 Bis (Rua Buenos Aires 192, tel. 24/2231-0946, www.pousada14bis.com.br, R$130–180 d) is centrally situated and fetchingly rustic to boot. Named after Santos Dumont's historic plane, the lounge pays homage to the homegrown aviator/inventor with a smattering of engaging artifacts related to his life and times. Rooms are cozy and comfortable.

Occupying an attractive European-style manor built in 1814, **Pousada Magister** (Rua Monsenhor Bacelar 71, tel. 24/2242-1054, www.pousadamagister.com.br, R$165–180 d) is in the midst of all of Petrópolis's historic attractions. The comfortable rooms lack much of a decorative scheme—giving undue attention to the somewhat twee floral bedspreads (rooms are named after flowers)—but all boast soaring ceilings, immense windows, and polished wood floors.

Despite a steep uphill walk from the center of town, the **Pousada Monte Imperial** (Rua José de Alencar 27, tel. 24/2237-1664, www.pousadamonteimperial.com.br, R$195 d) is worth the physical exertion. With friendly service and small but cozy rooms offering views of the town below, this *pousada* is a lovely rural retreat within spitting distance of Petrópolis proper.

Surrounded by mansions that once belonged to barons and counts, **❰ Hotel Solar do Império** (Av. Koeler 376, tel. 24/2103-3000, www.solardoimperio.com.br, R$343–500 d) will make you feel quite regal. In fact, this ornate 1875 mansion provided refuge for Princesa Isabel while her own *palácio* down the street was undergoing renovation. The stately rooms are decorated with period furniture, while offering all modern conveniences. Amenities include a swimming pool and spa,

and the **Leopoldina** restaurant. The pretty landscaped grounds are filled with flowers, classical statues, and a lagoon.

If you do have a car, and some bucks to boot, consider treating yourself to the natural and man-made luxuries proffered by the **Tankamana Eco Resort** (Estrada Júlio Capua, Vale do Cuiabá, tel. 24/2222-9181, www.tankamana.com.br), whose welcome ritual includes fresh flowers, chocolate truffles, and bath salts. Idyllically located in the gloriously isolated Cuiabá Valley, this back-to-nature resort features spacious log and stone cabins—outfitted with king-sized beds, DVD and CD players, and whirlpools—that are laid out to ensure maximum privacy. The hotel organizes walking and horseback-riding excursions through the surrounding mountains, but you can also easily stay put and unwind at the hotel's private waterfall. Among other delicacies, the restaurant serves up inspired versions of the regional specialty: fresh trout. Service is both discreet and attentive, and kids under 14 are not permitted. The resort is 37 kilometers (23 miles) from Petrópolis—take the Estrada Aldo Gelli—near the town of Itaipava.

Food

Petrópolis has become somewhat of a gourmet destination, but like the region's best accommodations, many of the finest restaurants are located far from the city center, requiring a car to get to them. In the center itself, **Rink Marowil** (Praça da Liberdade 27, tel. 24/2243-0743, 11 A.M.–4 P.M. and 6–9 P.M. daily, R$15–25) has a nicely priced per kilo self-service buffet with a wide choice of dishes as well as an à la carte menu at night.

Occupying a lovely old house with vaulted ceilings, **Massas Luigi** (Praça da Liberdade 185, tel. 24/2244-4444, www.massasluigi.com.br, 11 A.M.–midnight daily, R$20–30) is a fine place to go for tasty homemade pasta and pizza. Try the cannelloni with *carne seca* (sun-dried beef) in a creamy Catupiry cheese sauce.

A great option for a light meal or a lavish high tea (complete with croissants and madeleines) in imperial surroundings is the Museu Imperial's

Bistro Petit Palais (Av. Imperatriz 220, tel. 24/2237-8000, noon–7 P.M. Tues.–Wed., noon–8 P.M. Thurs., noon–midnight Fri.–Sat., noon–7 P.M. Sun., R$15–25). Aside from main entrées, there are quiches, salads, and sandwiches. **Empada Brasil** (Rua Dr. Nelson de Sá Earp 234, tel. 24/2237-7979) makes some of the most tasty *empadas* around. Fillings range from heart of palm to leek with crab meat.

If you want to venture out of town for an unforgettable meal in an unforgettable setting, one of the closest and most delicious options is the ◖ **Pousada da Alcobaça** (Rua Agostinho Goulão 298, tel. 24/2221-1240, www.pousadadaalcobaca.com.br, 1:30–10 P.M. daily, R$45–55). Located in the bucolic region of Correas (11 kilometers/7 miles) from the center of Petrópolis), this beautiful *pousada* occupies an early-20th-century Norman country house surrounded by fragrant herb and vegetable gardens that supply the produce for the excellent breakfasts, lunches, and teas prepared by owner and chef Laura Góes. What Góes doesn't grow or raise herself she purchases from neighbors who do. Specialties include trout in delicate sauces, roast veal and duck, and a highly reputed *feijoada* that is served on Saturdays. Reservations are a must.

Information

Tourist information (tel. 24/2246-9377 or 0800-24156) is available at several kiosks throughout town, including at the *rodoviária* (8 A.M.–8 P.M. daily) and at the Praça dos Expedicionários, next to the Museu Imperial (9 A.M.–6 P.M. Mon.–Sat., 9 A.M.–5 P.M. Sun.). You can also log on to www.petropolis.rj.gov.br, which offers information in both Portuguese and English.

Getting There

From Rio, **Única** (tel. 21/2263-8792) provides bus service to Petrópolis's spanking new bus station (1.5-hours from Rio), the **Rodoviária de Petrópolis** (tel. 24/2249-9858). Buses leave approximately every 15 minutes. By car from Rio, take the BR-040, which offers a splendid if hair-raising hour-long drive through the mountains (beware of rain and crowded weekend rush hours).

PARQUE NACIONAL DA SERRA DOS ÓRGÃOS

Created in 1939, this national park owes its name to early Portuguese explorers, who thought that its strangely shaped rocky peaks bore an uncanny resemblance to a church pipe organ. Stretching between Petrópolis and Teresópolis, the park comprises 12,000 hectares (30,000 acres) of exuberant Atlantic forest with waterfalls, hiking trails, and the postcardworthy **Dedo de Deus** (Finger of God), rising 1,692 meters (5,551 feet) above sea level. Higher, but less dramatic, is the **Pedra do Sino** (Bell Rock, 2,263 meters/7,425 feet). There are plenty of other peaks to marvel at and even scale—a fact that has made the park one of Brazil's most popular climbing, trekking, and radical sport destinations. From the park's uppermost summits, on a clear day you can see all the way to Rio de Janeiro and the Baía de Guanabara.

Hiking

The park has numerous trails, ranging from easy 30-minute strolls to the very taxing but spectacular three-day, 42-kilometer (26-mile) venture from Petrópolis to Teresópolis. However, since most trails are unmarked, you should hire a guide if you're thinking of doing more than a short hike. Information about guides is available at the park's main entrance and headquarters (Av. Rotariana, tel. 21/2152-1100, www.ibama.gov.br/parnaso, 8 A.M.–5 P.M. Tues.–Sun., R$3 pp, R$5 per vehicle). For longer, more strenuous hikes and radical sports excursions such as rappelling and canyoneering you can contact **Trekking Petrópolis** (tel. 24/2235-7607, www.rioserra.com.br/trekking). May–October is the best time for trekking, while November–February is more conducive to bathing in the park's many icy streams and waterfalls.

Getting There

The park is 5 kilometers (3 miles) from the

© EDITORA PEIXES/EMBRATUR

Dedo de Deus (Finger of God) in the Parque Nacional da Serra dos Órgãos

center of Teresópolis on the BR-116 leading to Rio. The entrance close to Petrópolis is 16 kilometers (10 miles) from the center of town on the Estrada União-Indústria.

TERESÓPOLIS

Nowhere near as charming nor as imperial as Petrópolis, Teresópolis is a bustling, modern, upscale alpine resort nestled in the Serra dos Órgãos mountain range. The town's name pays homage to Empress Teresa Cristina, wife of Dom Pedro II, who was taken by the area's magnificent mountain scenery and refreshing climate. The highest town in Rio de Janeiro state, Teresópolis's main interest lies in its proximity to the Parque Nacional da Serra dos Órgãos.

Accommodations and Food

Most of Teresópolis's more interesting accommodations are amid the lush mountains surrounding the town itself. The best is the utterly charming **Hotel Rosa dos Ventos** (tel. 21/2644-9900, www.hotelrosadosventos.com.br, R$370–410 d). Located some 20

kilometers (12 miles) outside of town on the RJ-130 road to Nova Friburgo, it is Brazil's only hotel in the exclusive international Relais & Chateau hotel chain. Accommodations are handsomely rustic yet luxuriously accessorized alpine chalets with fireplaces and balconies that keep you in constant contact with nature. In fact, nature lovers need never leave the hotel complex, which includes 10 kilometers (6 miles) of nature trails for walking and mountain biking, two swimming pools, a lake for kayaking, and stables for horseback riding. Also on the premises are four gourmet restaurants and three bars.

For a more central and much cheaper option, try the **Várzea Palace Hotel** (Rua Prefeito Sebastião Teixeira 41, tel. 21/2742-0878, R$75 d). Although its elegance has faded, this formerly grand hotel (dating from 1916) offers clean and comfortable rooms in a retro setting.

If overexposure to fresh mountain air sends your appetite into overdrive, head to one of Brazil's finest Russian restaurants, **Dona Irene** (Rua Tenente Luís Meireles 1800, tel. 21/2742-2901, noon–midnight Wed.–Sat., noon–6 P.M. Sun., R$60), for a feast fit for a czar. After starting off with a shot of house vodka, dig into the likes of borscht, marinated herring, chicken Kiev, stroganoffs, and *varenikes* stuffed with filet mignon. Reservations are required.

Manjeiricão (Rua Flávio Bortoluzzi de Sousa 314, tel. 21/2642-4242, 6–11 P.M. Thurs.–Fri., noon–midnight Sat., noon–11 P.M. Sun., R$25–35) serves up delicious thin-crust pizza baked to perfection in a wood-burning oven. The light and airy crust is the result of the dough being made with mineral water. All herbs and vegetables come from the restaurant's own garden. One of most requested pizzas features basil, walnuts, garlic, cream, and parmesan.

Information

For maps and information about the surrounding area, head to the centrally located **tourist office** (Praça Olímpica, tel. 21/2742-9149, 8 A.M.–6 P.M. daily) or log on to www.teresopolison.com.br (in Portuguese).

RIO DE JANEIRO

Getting There

Viação Teresópolis (tel. 21/2742-2676) offers bus service every 30 minutes between Teresópolis and Rio de Janeiro (two-hour trip) and every hour between Teresópolis and Petrópolis (1.5 hour trip). To reach Teresópolis directly from Rio by car (1.5 hour trip), take the BR-040 and the BR-116. The driving time by car between Petrópolis and Teresópolis is about 45 minutes.

NOVA FRIBURGO

If this attractive mountain town causes you to conjure up images of Julie Andrews crooning "Edelweiss," you're not delirious, but merely in one of Brazil's oldest and only Swiss colonies. Although it's hard to imagine, in the early 1800s, Switzerland was so (temporarily) poor that 100 Swiss families up and left their hometown of Fribourg to settle in these mountainous climes. This explains the prevalence of wooden chalets and chocolate shops and the profusion of restaurants serving cheese fondue and raclette. What it doesn't explain is that Nova Friburgo is the Brazilian capital of lingerie. In the downtown *bairros* of Olaria and Ponte da Saudade (near the bus station) are dozens of fine lingerie manufacturers that export nationally and throughout the world, and where discriminating shoppers can pick up some fancy panties, slips, or bustiers for a song.

In the summertime, Cariocas descend upon Friburgo in hordes, and who can blame them? The climate is cool, the pretty architecture is framed by a blaze of brightly colored flowers in permanent bloom, and the surrounding woods are filled with hiking trails and cooling waterfalls. To survey the surrounding countryside, take a ride from the center of town on a cable car that ascends 1,450 meters (4,750 feet) up to **Morro da Cruz** (Praça dos Suspiros, tel. 22/2522-4834, 9:30 A.M.–5 P.M. Tues.–Sun., R$20). You can also take a steep but gratifying 6-kilometer (3.5-mile) hike up to the 2,310-meter (7,579-foot) summit of **Pico da Caledônia;** the top provides equally breathtaking views and also serves as a launching pad for hang gliders.

Accommodations and Food

The majority of the most appealing hotels and restaurants in the region are located in the countryside surrounding Friburgo, meaning that in most cases you'll need a car to get to them. In town, a simple and comfortable option is the **Hotel São Paulo** (Rua Monsenhor Miranda 41, tel. 22/2522-9135, www.hotelsaopaulo.com.br, R$90 d), located in a pastel-colored old house. Despite the abundance of natural wood fixtures, the decor is somewhat somber and spartan. Amenities include wireless Internet access and a small pool.

If you want to be surrounded by mountain greenery galore, there are multiple options in the surrounding area. By far one of the nicest is **Akaskay** (Estrada Norge Hamburgo, Mury, access at Km 71 off RJ-116, tel. 22/2542-1163, www.akaskay.com, R$240–280 d), some 9 kilometers (6 miles) from Friburgo. Its comfortable Swiss chalet–style lodgings are entirely outfitted with cedar wood and feature stone fireplaces (unfortunately, electric). The surrounding area is equally alpine with stunning mountains crisscrossed by babbling brooks. A natural spring-water pool, a Jacuzzi, and a temple where Saturday morning yoga classes are held are all conducive to unwinding.

One of Friburgo's finest and most centrally located restaurants, the small and charming **C Crescente Gastronomia** (Rua General Osório 21, tel. 22/2523-4616, 11:30 A.M.–11 P.M. Mon.–Tues. and Thurs.–Sat., 11:30 A.M.–5 P.M. Sun., R$30–40) has an eclectic menu that runs the gamut from steaks and chicken to duck, rabbit, and local trout. Sauces and side dishes change according to the season, and the wine menu is nicely varied.

Information

The **tourist office** (Praça Doutro Demervel B. Moreira, tel. 22/2523-8000, 8 A.M.–8 P.M. daily) has maps and hotel listings as well as information about hikes and walks. You can also log on to www.novofriburgotur.com.br.

Getting There

There is regular bus service with **Viação**

1001 (tel. 0300/313-1001, www.autovia-cao1001.com.br, 5 A.M.–9 P.M. daily) from Rio's Rodoviária Novo to Nova Friburgo, via Niterói. Although the trip takes three hours, the scenery is breathtaking. Buses arrive at the Rodoviária Sul (Ponte de Saudade), 4 kilometers (2.5 miles) south of the center of town. If you're coming from Teresópolis, you'll arrive at the Rodoviária Norte (Praça Feliano Costa) around 2 kilometers (1.2 miles) north from the center. If you're driving from Rio, you'll need to head across the Rio-Niterói bridge and then follow the BR-101, BR-104, and BR-116.

PARQUE NACIONAL DO ITATIAIA

With rocky mountain peaks to climb and dense tropical forest to hike through, Brazil's oldest national park (founded in 1937) spans the state frontiers of Rio de Janeiro, São Paulo, and Minas Gerais. The easily accessible lower regions are covered with lush native Atlantic forest, wild orchids and begonias, and spectacular waterfalls such as **Itaporani, Véu de Noiva** and **Maromba,** all of which are easy to reach and boast beckoning (if chilly) pools for bathing. Its numerous easy hiking trails can be easily explored by families, without a guide, and are easily accessible from the pretty mountain towns of **Itatiaia** and **Penedo.** The upper part of the park—dominated by a stark and imposing landscape of sculpted rocks—also has its attractions, among them the dramatic peaks of **Agulhas Negras** (2,548 meters/8,360 feet) and **Prateleira** (2,791 meters/9,157 feet). To scale them, you'll have to be in superb shape and be accompanied by a guide.

The entrance to the lower portion of the park is easily reached by following the 2-km (1.2-mile) stretch of BR-116 that links the town of Itatiaia to the entrance of the **Parque Nacional do Itatiaia** (tel. 24/3352-1461, 8 A.M.–5 P.M. daily, R$3 pp, R$5 per vehicle). This is where you'll find the Centro de Visitantes, which offers information and maps. The best time to visit the lower parts of the park are from January to February and October to December. For climbing Agulhas Negras and Prateleira,

May through August is best due to low rainfall (although temperatures can get chilly).

Accommodations and Food

Nestled in the mountains, the town of **Itatiaia** is the best and most convenient base for visiting the park. It has many hotels located right on the BR-116 (known as the Via Dutra), which leads to the park's entrance, as well as several actually in the park. **Chalés Terra Nova** (Estrada Parque Nacional, Km 4.5, tel. 24/3352-1458, www.chalesterranova.com.br, R$160–190 d, full board) is one of the latter—located right in the midst of lush Atlantic forest. The basic but comfortable accommodations are split between a main house and individual chalets, which are ideal for groups or families. Aside from a sauna and swimming pool, there is a small lake for trout fishing, a treetop walking course, and access to mountain bikes.

The oldest and one of the finest hotels of the region, the **Hotel Donati** (Estrada Parque Nacional, Km 9.5, tel. 24/3352-1110, www.hoteldonati.com.br, R$185–280), is also located within the park, in an area surrounded by bromeliads and fragrant pines. Since 1931, its charming chalets have sheltered nature lovers from composer and poet Vinícius de Morais to modernist painter Alberto Guignard (who was inspired to paint the doors and windows of the main cabin). Some of the chalets have Jacuzzis, while all have fireplaces. Among the restaurant's many offerings are fresh trout and fondues.

Another option is to stay in the town of **Penedo,** 14 kilometers (9 miles) away and easily accessible by bus. Penedo was founded in 1920 by a Finnish immigrants. Part of a master plan in which forward-thinking Finns set up a handful of self-sufficient, back-to-nature communities throughout South America, the Penedo group was soon forced to deal with the unhappy fact that the mountains in which they settled weren't fertile for agriculture. While the majority returned to Scandinavia, an optimistic few remained to develop Penedo as a pseudo-Nordic tourist resort. As a result, the town is often overrun with weekenders from Rio and São Paulo who come to purchase local jams and chocolates and visit the Parque de Itatiaia. Aside from Saturday polka night at the **Clube Finlândia** (Av. das Mangueiras 2601, tel. 24/3351-1374), which houses a small museum tracing the history and handicrafts of the region's Finns, the most prevalent Finnish legacy in Penedo is the many Finnish saunas (a feature of most of the hotels).

One of the most inviting hotels in town is the **Pousada Serra da Índia** (Estrada Vale do Ermitão, tel. 24/3351-1185, www.serradaindia.com.br, R$150–240 d), which involves a precipitous 2-kilometer (1.2-mile) climb from the center. Perched upon a mountain slope (ensuring atmospheric misty mornings), the delightful Swiss-style chalets offer quite spectacular views. Rooms are cozy and comfortably outfitted with king-sized beds and fireplaces. Aside from the requisite sauna, there is a pool and a spa. Breakfasts include homemade yogurts, compotes, and strudels.

Curiously, in terms of culinary legacies, Swedish food is much more in vogue than Finnish fare in Itatiaia. **Restaurante Skandinavia** (Av. das Mangueiras 2631, tel. 24/3351-1529, 6–11 P.M., R$10–20) is a delicious inexpensive option for Swedish-style open-faced sandwiches. Meanwhile, one of the only Finnish restaurants in the country is **Koskenorva** (Estrada das Três Cachoeiras 3955, tel. 24/3351-24532, noon–midnight daily, R$30–40), surrounded by a pretty garden decorated with the artist/owner's sculptures. Specialties include wild mushroom soup, fresh and marinated trout, and a Finnish version of smorgasbord, with diverse meats, fish, and potatoes.

Information

For information about Itatiaia, visit the **tourist office** (Praça Mariana Leão Rocha 20, tel. 24/3352-6777, www.itatiaia.rj.gov.br, 10 A.M.–6 P.M. daily, closed off-season). Penedo also has a tourist office (tel. 24/3351-1704, 1–6 P.M. Mon.–Fri., 10 A.M.–6 P.M. Sat.–Sun.), or you can log on to www.penedo.org and www.penedo.com.

Getting There

Cidade do Aço (tel. 0800/703-4022, www.cidadedoaco.com.br) operates regular bus service from Rio to both towns. By bus, the trip from Rio takes approximately three hours. By car, from Rio, take the BR-116.

Costa do Sol

Running east from Rio, the Costa do Sol lives up to its name by offering over 100 kilometers (60 miles) of gorgeous coastline that seduces Carioca and international sunseekers in droves. Come summertime, the main towns of Cabo Frio, Arraial do Cabo, and Búzios in particular buzz with activity.

CABO FRIO

A quick two-hour drive east along the coast from Rio, "Cabo" is a favorite summer and weekend retreat for middle-class Cariocas and other sunseeking getaway artists. They are lured by its sugary white dunes, limpid green waters, and deliciously cool breezes (which is where the *frio* comes in), as well as a party hearty atmosphere. Founded in 1615 by the Portuguese, it was from Cabo that the new colony's precious brazilwood (which gave the country its name) set sail for Europe. Two centuries later, having depleted supplies of this precious wood, the region turned to fishing. More recently, it has invested in the manufacture of salt and in tourism.

In terms of the latter, Cabo has met with success—perhaps too much for some tastes. Despite a relaxed vibe and a reputation as "Brazil's cleanest city," the town itself is quite overdeveloped and unattractive. In the summer, the population multiplies tenfold, mostly with families and their teenage kids. When not chilling in the region's sand dunes or nibbling on seafood in the many *barracas* and bars, vacationers are strutting (and purchasing) their stuff on the "Rua dos Biquinis," where over 100 boutiques sell beach togs of every brand, style, and price range imaginable under the sun.

Beaches

Cabo Frio's main draw is its beaches. The closest to town and most famous is **Praia do Forte**. Its white sands are guarded by **Forte São Mateus** (Praia do Forte, 10 A.M.–4 P.M. Tues.–Sun., free), a stone fortress built in 1616 as protection against the region's many pirates. In summer, the adjective "crowded" is an understatement: You'll be challenged to see a patch of sand through the wall-to-wall bodies. And although the blue water is picturesque, the surface is a traffic jam of sailboats and windsurfers. For a bit of privacy, head north a few kilometers to **Praia Brava,** whose rough waves attract surfers (and nudists), followed by **Praia das Conchas,** with its calmer waters and beach kiosks.

Praia do Peró boasts impressively wild dunes and a more urbanized stretch of beach with lots of kiosks where you can pig out on small local shrimp sautéed with garlic and lime along with other fresh seafood. Although Cabo's dunes are truly alluring, it's not always safe to go wandering through them; check beforehand with the tourist office or locals to get the lay of the land.

Accommodations and Food

Arraial do Cabo to the south and Búzios to the north are much more attractive places to stay than Cabo. And since they're both so close (Arraial is only 6 kilometers/4 miles away), you're better off staying there and day-tripping to Cabo Frio. Cabo Frio's forte is seafood, and unsurprisingly, there are many places to indulge in the ocean's bounty. **Hippocampus** (Rua Marechal Floriano 283, tel. 22/2645-5757, 11 A.M.–midnight daily, R$20–30), with tables overlooking the lively Canal Boulevard, is a great place for people-watching while digging into grilled fish and seafood. On the same street, but slightly more upscale, is the traditional **Picolino** (Rua Marechal Floriano 319,

tel. 22/2643-2436, noon–7 P.M. Sun.–Mon., noon–midnight Tues.–Sat., R$30–40), located in an attractive 100-year-old house and reputed for its tasty fish dishes. As a warm-up, diners receive a platter of squid and mussels bathed in a mustard sauce that is justly famous.

Information

There is a **tourist office** on Praia do Forte (Av. do Contorno, tel. 22/2647-1689, 9 A.M.–6 P.M. daily). There is also lots of information (in Portuguese) at www.cabofrioturismo.rj.gov.br.

Getting There

There are numerous direct daily buses from Rio de Janeiro to Cabo Frio operated by Viação 1000 (tel. 0300/313-1001, www.autoviacao1001.com.br). The **Terminal Rodoviária de Cabo Frio** (tel. 22/2643-1521) is a 3-km (2-mile) walk from the center. If you're driving from Rio, take the BR-101, followed by the RJ-124 and RJ-140. It's a quick two-hour drive.

ARRAIAL DO CABO

Arraial do Cabo is only 6 kilometers (4 miles) south of Cabo Frio, but it is much less built up and more tranquil than either Cabo or Búzios to the south. Nonetheless, come summertime, its stunning white beaches and limpid blue waters draw their share of sand-and-sea worshippers. Not only are the crystalline waters off Arraial considered a diver's paradise, but Praia de Farol, on nearby Ilha de Cabo Frio, is considered one of the most beautiful beaches in all of Brazil.

Beaches

Closest to town is **Praia dos Anjos,** an attractive strip of sand with enticing turquoise waters whose only flaw is that it can get a little packed with water-sports enthusiasts. If you're after seclusion, it's only a short walk to the beaches of **Prainha** (north of town) and the sweeping stretch of **Praia Grande** (to the west)— equipped with *barracas* serving fresh fish and seafood—that extends all the way up to the Brazilian surfers' paradise of Saquarema. You can also follow a steep 1-kilometer (0.6-mile) trail from Praia dos Anjos (or take a boat) to the lovely and deserted **Praia do Forno,** where you can snorkel and then relax on a floating restaurant/bar.

The most fantastic beach of all, **Praia do Farol** is on Ilha do Farol, a small island paradise fringed with fine white sand and sculpted dunes, whose 390-meter (1,280-foot) peak offers magnificent views. You can get a boat to the *ilha* from Praia dos Anjos. To spend the day on the beach on your own, you'll have to get authorization from the local *marinha* (naval base) in town. Otherwise, you can go on an excursion.

Sports and Recreation

DIVING
Arraial is considered one of the best spots for recreational diving in Brazil. Aside from its transparent blue waters, it is the only place where the ocean currents—which usually flow north–south along the Brazilian coast—flow east–west, provoking a phenomenon whereby the deep, cold currents from Antarctica rise to the surface. While this means that water temperatures are always quite cold, it also results in the presence of many nutrients, which in turn attract an unusually rich variety of marine life. Add to this more than 30 sunken galleons—the consequence of heavy pirate activity off the coast during the 17th and 18th centuries—and you're in for an underwater treat.

Daily diving excursions usually cost around R$120. For more information, contact **Mr. Diver** (Rua Dom Pedro I 50, tel. 22/2622-1945, www.mrdiver.com.br) or **Deep Trip** (Av. Getúlio Vargas 93, tel. 22/2622-1800).

BOAT TRIPS
A wonderful way to explore Arraial's marine splendors is by boat. **Frôr Turismo** (Rua Santa Cruz 7, Loja 4, Praia dos Anjos, tel. 22/7834-0340, www.fror.com.br) offers four-hour excursions for R$30, with stops in the Prainhas do Atalaia and Ilha do Farol. On the island, aside from lounging on Praia do Farol, you can visit Gruta Azul, an underwater cavern that turns blue when illuminated by the sun.

Accommodations and Food
For cheap digs, it's hard to beat the pleasant **Hostel Marina dos Anjos** (Rua Bernardo Lens 145, Praia dos Anjos, tel. 22/2622-4060, www.marinadosanjos.com.br, R$30–46 pp). Affiliated with the International Youth Hostel Association, it offers basic but cheerily spotless dormitory and double rooms in a house with hammock-slung verandas. The friendly staff can provide you with lots of information about the region. You can also rent bikes and diving equipment.

More upscale is the breezy **Capitão n'Area Pousada** (Rua Santa Cruz 7, Praia dos Anjos, tel. 22/2622-2720, www.capitaopousada.com, R$125–175 d). Outfitted in soothing maritime whites and blues, it possesses amenities such as a pool, fitness center, and a terrace bar with lovely views of Praia dos Anjos. Its charming restaurant, **Porto das Delícias,** serves up some of the tastiest fare in town.

If you're searching for something more secluded, **Estalagem dos Corais** (tel. 22/2262-2182, www.estalagemdoscorais.com.br, R$100–110) on Prainha offers pleasant, comfortable accommodations along with a sauna and an attractive pool. **Saint Tropez** (Praça Daniel Barretto 2, Praia dos Anjos, tel. 22/2262-1222, 6 P.M.–midnight Mon.–Tues., noon–midnight Wed.–Sun., R$20–30) takes advantage of the local daily catch to serve up simple but succulent dishes incorporating fresh fish, shrimp, squid, and mussels.

Information
Located at the entrance to town, the **tourist office** (tel. 22/2622-1650, 9 A.M.–6 P.M. daily) has information about excursions as well as diving and boating trips. You can also log on to www.arraialdocabo-rj.com.br.

Getting There
There are numerous direct daily buses from Rio de Janeiro to Arraial operated by **Viação 1001** (tel. 0300/313-1001, www.autoviacao1001.com.br). From Cabo Frio, buses leave every 20 minutes. For more information call the *rodoviária* (tel. 22/2622-1488).

◖ BÚZIOS

Búzios is the Gisele Bündchen of Brazilian beach resorts: both naturally beautiful and sophisticatedly chic, it is internationally renowned and capable of commanding high prices. Before it became Brazil's most perennially stylish beach getaway, Armação de Búzios was a tiny fishing village perched on the tip of a peninsula, 190 kilometers (118 miles) east of Rio de Janeiro. All of that changed when, in 1964, sultry French starlet Brigitte Bardot happened upon it with her Brazilian boyfriend of the moment. Aided by the international paparazzi, the bikinied "B. B." singlehandedly put the place on the map. Before long, she had moved on to other boys and other beaches, but idyllic Búzios—the name by which both the village of Armação and the entire peninsula came to be known—quickly become a favorite stop on the global jet-setters' paradise party circuit.

The other beach resort that Bardot made famous in the '60s was St. Tropez, and it is interesting to note that both destinations have far more in common than this coincidence. Búzios's narrow cobblestoned streets, yacht-infested waters, cafés and bistros, and softly illuminated landscapes are decidedly Mediterranean, so much so that the endless comparisons to St. Tropez that it garners are not at all far-fetched. Moreover, as the little town has grown, both the permanent population and the tourists who flock here every summer are increasingly international and monied. In the last 20 years, designer boutiques, chic restaurants, and posh hotels have mushroomed, and it's often hard to recognize the little fishing village that was. Although the cachet of its Bardot days is long gone, those prepared to fork out big bucks for sophisticated lodgings, food, and nightlife will also gain a very considerable bonus: unlimited access to some of Brazil's most enchanting beaches. And if you time your visit to avoid the hustle and bustle of the summer months, not only will you find a more pleasantly placid Búzios, but a considerably more affordable one as well.

The peninsula of Búzios has three main settlements. Closest to the mainland, on the isthmus is **Manguinhos,** which is the most commercial of the trio. A road paved with hotels leads the way to the charming main village of **Armação.** Most of the chicest boutiques, hotels, restaurants, and bars are concentrated here, clustered near and along the celebrated main drag of **Rua das Pedras** and its extension, the **Orla Bardot.** A 15-minute walk north along the coast from Armação will bring you to the peninsula's oldest settlement, **Ossos,** with its pretty harbor, yacht club, and sprinkling of hotels.

Beaches

Visitors to Búzios can either take or leave its cosmopolitan trappings, but no one can resist its beaches. There are close to 30 of them, ranging in size from tiny isolated coves to mile-long sweeps of sand, and each flaunting its own distinctive attributes and personality. The beaches closest to the northern part of the isthmus at Manguinhos are **Praia de Manguinhos** and **Praia Rasa,** where high winds and low waves attract windsurfers and sailboats as well as families with kids. Going towards Armação, **Praia dos Amores** and **Praia das Virgens** are unspoiled, quite deserted, and framed by lush vegetation. **Praia da Tartaruga**'s limpid blue waters are the warmest on the peninsula and ideal for snorkeling.

While the beaches in Armação—**Praia do Canto** and **Praia da Armação**—are pretty to contemplate, they are too polluted for swimming. Picturesque **Praia dos Ossos,** with the 18th-century Igreja de Sant'Ana gazing out over its calm seas, attracts sailors and windsurfers but also isn't recommended for bathing. Farther north, the pristine beaches of **Azeda** and **Azedinha** are framed by exuberant foliage and famed for their unofficial topless sunbathing. The clear blue waters are good for snorkeling, as are those of neighboring **João Fernandes** and **João Fernandinho.** The beach at João Fernandes is wide and also quite trendy, with numerous beach bars (many run by Argentineans) that serve fresh lobster and seafood. João Fernandinho is smaller and

© TONY GALVEZ

the surf scene in Búzios

less crowded, with enticing natural pools for bathing.

On the easternmost tip of the peninsula are the more isolated beaches of **Praia Brava,** a wide beach whose rough waves attract surfers; **Praia Olho de Boi,** a pretty little beach favored by nudists; and **Praia do Forno,** a tranquil beach with cool but calm waters and natural pools whose lack of crowds is ensured by its difficult access. On the southern end of the peninsula, going towards the mainland, **Praia da Ferradura** is more built up, but its calm waters in a sheltered cove are ideal for families with young children as well as fans of sailing and windsurfing. Also pretty, and more isolated, is **Praia da Ferradurinha,** which is good for diving.

Closest to the mainland, **Praia de Geribá** is a long sweeping beach that is beautiful but also quite urbanized. It's popular with surfer boys and partying twenty-somethings. However, if you feel like being pampered to the hilt, with everything from giant parasols to fancy drinks, this is the place to come. Much more rustic and unspoiled are **Praia**

dos Tucuns, Praia José Gonçalves, and **Praia das Caravelas.** You can get to most of Búzios's beaches easily by walking, or else by taking a minivan or a taxi.

Sports and Recreation

Búzios offers an enormous diversity of beach activities and water sports.

DIVING
The limpid blue waters off the peninsula offer ideal conditions for diving. **Casamar** (Rua das Pedras 242, Armação, tel. 22/2623-2441, www.casamar.com) organizes daily excursions (including snacks and drinks) for divers of all levels (as well as lessons) to the islands of Âncora and Gravatá, where you can see bright coral and fish, sea turtles, and, if you're lucky, dolphins. A five-hour excursion costs R$150.

SAILING, WINDSURFING, AND KITESURFING
The wind conditions at many of Búzios's beaches are excellent for sailing and windsurfing. **Búzios Vela Clube** (Praia de Manguinhos,

tel. 22/2623-0508) offers lessons for novices as well as equipment rental for pros. Eight hours of windsurfing and sailing lessons range from R$270–300 per person. Equipment rentals costs R$25 (sailboats) and R$50 (windsurf board) per hour. Praia da Rasa has become a mecca for aficionados of kitesurfing. **Búzios Kitesurf School** (tel. 22/9956-0668) offers lessons and rents equipment as well. A basic course (8–10 hours) costs R$600.

BOAT EXCURSIONS

Sampling Búzios's many beaches by boat is a delicious option. **Interbúzios** (Rua Manuel Turíbia de Farias 203, tel. 22/2623-6454, www.interbuzios.com.br) offers daily three-hour schooner trips, with various departure times, that stop at 12 beaches and three islands for R$40. More rapid (and reserved) are the daily catamaran excursions offered by **Tour Shop** (Av. José Bento Ribeiro Dantas 550, tel. 22/2623-4733, www.tourshop.com.br), which hit 15 beaches and four islands for R$60 and provide snorkels and masks as well as drinks. Both schooners and catamarans depart from the pier at Praia de Armação.

Nightlife

Aside from its beaches, Búzios is famous for its nightlife, most of which is concentrated along Armação's Rua das Pedras and its extension, Avenida José Bento Ribeiro Dantas, also known as the Orla Bardot. Búzios's nocturnal scene sizzles all year-round, but during the summer months it boils over. Things don't get going until around 11 P.M., and the partying (which entails a lot of eating, drinking, and checking people out) is so intense that most of the area's hotels serve breakfast until noon and most boutiques don't open their doors until the afternoon. The *creperia* **Chez Michou** (see *Food*) is a perennial hot spot, as is **Pátio Havana** (Rua das Pedras 101, tel. 22/2623-2169, www.patiohavana.com.br, 6 P.M.–close, no cover), a sophisticated place with various spaces including a wine cellar, whiskey club, bistro, tobacco shop, and a stage that hosts live jazz, blues, and MPB performers.

Anexo (Av. José Bento Ribeiro Dantas 392, tel. 22/2623-6837, 6 P.M.–close, no cover) is a popular lounge-bar/bistro with sofas gazing out towards the sea and a dance floor. Serious dance-aholics can get their fix at **Privilège** (Av. José Bento Ribeiro Dantas 550, tel. 22/2623-0288, www.privilegenet.com.br, 10 P.M.–close, R$40–70 cover), where three resident DJs serve up an eclectic mix of rhythms to a crowd of international beauties. Having worked up a sweat, you can chill out on the terrace, or at any of the five bars, one of which serves sushi.

Accommodations

Where you choose to stay in Búzios depends on your personality (as well as your financial situation). If you want to be near all the action, you'll want to stay in Armação or Geribá. However, if you prize tranquility and seclusion, consider accommodations at the peninsula's other beaches (see *Beaches*). In terms of price, Búzios is definitely not a bargain, especially in high season, when reservations are a must. However, if you choose to come during the off-season (anytime other than July and December–March) and during the week, you can often take advantage of discounts of 30–40 percent. In general, the lower-priced options are small but homey *pousadas* in and around Armação and Ossos. Prices listed here are for off-season.

By far the best deal in Búzios is the **Búzios Central Hostel** (Av. José Bento Ribeiro Dantas 1475, Praia da Armação, tel. 22/2623-2329, www.buzioscentral.com.br, R$32–46 pp). The dormitory and double rooms are cheery, if a little claustrophobic. However, the common spaces—a TV room, lush gardens, and a small pool—more than compensate, as does the excellent location close to Rua das Pedras. Bedding and breakfast are extra.

Located between Armaçao and Praia Geribá, **Pousada El Riconcito** (Av. Geribá 142, Praia Geribá, tel. 22/2623-1712, www.buziosonline.com.br/rinconcito, R$90–140 d) offers good value with a Mexican twist. The coral-colored bungalows resemble a hacienda, while the tropically hued rooms conjure up a Frida Kahlo painting. The short distance from the sea is offset by the nicely landscaped gardens.

◖ **Pousada Janellas do Mar** (Rua Bela Vista 8, Praia João Fernandes, tel. 22/2623-9698, www.pousadajanellasdomar.com.br, R$160–178) is an extremely fetching hilltop eco-*pousada* designed and operated by green Gaúcho architect Helena Oestreich. It was constructed entirely from demolition materials—including furniture, doors, and windows—and painted with artisanally produced organic paints. Rooms are simple but original, and feature private verandas with sea views.

Just off Praia Geribá, **Pousada Casa da Praia** (Rua Papagaio 16, Praia Geribá, tel. 22/2623-6830, www.casadapraia.tur.br, R$160–190 d) is ideal for families and groups. Consisting of several attractive *casas* constructed of (light-colored) brick and surrounded by a pool and gardens, it offers double, triple, and quadruple rooms and flats, all of which are bright and comfortable.

Casas Brancas Boutique Hotel & Spa (Alto do Humaitá 10, Praia de Armação, tel. 22/2623-1458, www.casasbrancas.com.br, R$405–689 d) has been around since 1973, long before the term "boutique hotel" had ever been uttered. Perhaps for this reason, the Andalusian-like white hilltop casas overlooking Praia de Armação possess none of the contrived sleekness of more contemporary design hotels. The spacious, luminous rooms are soothing refuges featuring lots of whites and natural woods that harmonize with the surroundings. Indeed, health and serenity are the hotel's forte. In addition to yoga classes and various feel-good treatments at the newly-minted spa, its delightful terrace restaurant serves up tasty "light" Brazilian-Mediterranean fare.

Those in search of all-out luxury will find it in spades at **Pérola** (Av. José Bento Ribeiro Dantas, Praia de Armação 222, tel. 22/2620-8507, www.thepearl.com.br, R$370–1,055 d), where upon arriving, guests are greeted with champagne. Lounging around the pool, you'll be treated to fresh fruit and *refrigerated* towels, and when you want to go hit the beach, you'll be shuttled to the Espaço Perola: the hotel's very own sophisticated beach lounge on unspoiled Praia Rasa, where you can stretch out in suspended sofas and drowse off to a soundtrack of rising tides and DJ-spun bossa nova. The hotel's spacious minimalist accommodations come in various sizes. Mezzanine lofts are ideal for families, while couples can get cozy in rooms with their own private garden Jacuzzis.

Food

It's impossible to go hungry in Búzios, particularly in Armação, which is home to dozens of sophisticated and highly reputed eateries. One of the town's top restaurants, ◖ **Satyricon** (Av. José Bento Ribeiro Dantas 478, Praia da Armação, tel. 22/2623-2691, www.satyricon.com.br, 5 P.M.–2 A.M. daily in low season, R$65–80) became so famous after it opened that it spawned a second (equally famous) restaurant in Ipanema. The Búzios original has the advantage of a wide terrace with seductive ocean views, which prove conducive to the savoring of the freshly caught fish and lobsters (those aquariums aren't just for decoration) prepared with Italian seasonings and flair.

Rivaling Satyricon in terms of refinement and price is **Sawasdee** (Av. José Bento Ribeiro Dantas 422, Praia da Armação, tel. 22/2623-4644, www.sawasdee.com.br, 6 P.M.–close Thurs.–Tues., R$50–65), which specializes in creative Thai-influenced cuisine. Two of the most popular dishes are stir-fried shrimp in oyster sauce with slivers of mango and cashews, and grilled marinated duck in tamarind sauce with sautéed algae.

Capricciosa (Av. José Bento Ribeiro Dantas 500, Praia da Armação, tel. 22/2623-1595, www.capricciosa.com.br, 5 P.M.–midnight Sun. and Tues.–Thurs., 6 P.M.–2 A.M. Fri.–Sat., R$25–35) is another successful Búzios gourmet endeavor that proved so popular that Cariocas demanded outlets in Rio as well. You will understand why when you bite into the astonishingly crisp and light crust pizzas with toppings that range from traditional (bacon, ham, tomatoes, mushroom, and eggs—the restaurant's signature pie) to unlikely (goat cheese, poached pears, orange, and walnuts).

Bananaland (Rua Manuel Turíbia de Farias 50, Praia de Armação, tel. 22/2623-2666, 11 A.M.–midnight daily, R$12–20) is a self-service per kilo restaurant that offers one of Armação's most affordable and varied eating options.

Chez Michou (Rua das Pedras 90, Praia de Armação, tel. 22/2623-2169, www.chezmichou.com.br, 1 P.M.–close daily, R$10–15) is a Búzios institution famous for its mouthwatering crêpes. The crêpes (you can choose from more than 40 sweet and savory fillings) are quite sublime. At night, it becomes one of Búzios's major hot spots for tanned twentysomethings. For sweet sustenance of a more tropical variety, head to **Mil Frutas** (Av. José Bento Ribeiro Dantas 362, Praia da Armação, tel. 22/2623-6436), Rio's finest *sorveteria*, where succulent flavors range from the most exotic Amazonian fruits to cocktail-worthy concoctions featuring sake and *cachaça*.

Serious beach bums can avoid the congestion of Armação and hop from *barraca* to *barraca* on the peninsula's many beaches. João Fernandes, Brava, Ferradura, and Geribá have lots of idyllic palm-thatched bars that serve up grilled fish and seafood at reasonable prices. At Manguinhos, you can watch the local fisherfolk haul in the daily catch and then join them at the **Bar dos Pescadores** (Av. José Bento Ribeiro Dantas 85, Box 7, Associação dos Pescadores de Manguinhos, Praia de Manguinhos, tel. 22/2623-7437, 10 A.M.–6 P.M. daily, R$20–30). Shaded by a giant almond tree, this appealingly modest hangout serves up fish and seafood dishes that are especially good. It's an ideal vantage point for watching the sunset.

Information

The **tourist office** (tel. 0800/249-999, 8 A.M.–midnight daily) is at the entrance to town. A good source of online information is the bilingual website www.buziosonline.com.

Getting There

Búzios is a little over two hours by bus from Rio. There are numerous daily buses operated by **Viação 1001** (0300 313-1001, www.autoviacao1001.com.br). By car, take the BR-101 from Rio to Rio Bonito, and then follow the RJ-124, RJ-106, and RJ-102 to Búzios.

Costa Verde

Stretching south from Rio de Janeiro to the state of São Paulo is one of southern Brazil's most captivating and (for the time being) unspoiled coastlines. Costa Verde (Green Coast) is an apt name: Not only do the clear Atlantic waters sparkle in hues of turquoise and jade, but the sugary white-sand beaches are invariably backed by verdant jungle-covered mountains.

ANGRA DOS REIS

While the green mountainscape surrounding Angra dos Reis (Bay of the Kings) is dropdead gorgeous, the modern, industrialized town itself is anything but. The proximity of a Petrobras oil refinery means that tankers often clog the port, and the looming presence of Brazil's most important nuclear reactors, Angra-1 and Angra-2, casts a pall on the environment. However, though the town itself is on the unattractive side, the surrounding area—where Rio's crème-de-la-crème spend weekends in their beach mansions and private yachts (not to mention private islands)—boasts some sophisticated resorts and seductive *pousadas*. Featuring their own private *praias*, many are destinations in themselves. Most of all, Angra is the primary point of departure for discovering the 365 islands—and over 2,000 beaches—dotted throughout the bay.

Angra's main attraction is its magnificent

bay, and the best way to explore it is by boat. **Mar de Angra** (Av. Júlio Maria 16, tel. 24/3365-3321, www.mardeangra.com.br) offers six-hour schooner trips for R$25. One popular route visits the islands of Catagueses, Botinas, and Gipóia, stopping at the latter's idyllic Praia das Flechas for swimming and lunch. Another visits Ilha Grande, taking time out for diving in Lagoa Azul. A simpler, less crowded possibility is to hire a boat at the **Associação dos Barqueiros** (Av. Júlio Maria, tel. 24/3365-3165).

Angra's limpid green waters offer great visibility (especially in the winter months) and lots to see, ranging from sunken ships to marine life that includes colorful fish, turtles, and seahorses. **Frade Diver** (Rua do Porto 1, tel. 24/3369-2816, www.fradediver.com.br) provides gear rental and offers excursions as well as lessons for divers of all levels. For a three-hour outing, experienced divers pay R$170, while beginners pay R$220. A basic two-day course that includes two outings costs R$550 per person.

◖ Ilha Grande

The largest of the many beautiful islands in the Bay of Angra, Ilha Grande boasts more than 100 pristine white-sand beaches, many of which—like the stunning *praias* of **Lopes Mendes, Cachadaço, Saco do Céu, Aventureiro,** and **Parnaioca**—are considered among the most beautiful in all of Brazil. A 90-minute boat ride away from Angra, Ilha Grande's 192 square kilometers (74 square miles) of Atlantic forest are entirely preserved, and no motorized vehicles are allowed on the island. There are, however, abundant walking trails, a wide range of accommodation possibilities, and, of course, beach after beach after beach.

Before becoming one of Brazilians' preferred back-to-Eden retreats from civilization, Ilha Grande went through phases as a pirate hangout and a leper colony. Until recently, it also housed two penitentiaries reserved for some of Brazil's most hardened and violent criminals (some of whom, from time to time, escaped, thus scaring the daylights

out of the island's community of fisherfolk). Although the second prison was demolished in 1994—opening the door to tourism—the not-yet-overgrown ruins of the original jail still cast a slightly haunting spell.

Ferries and launches from Angra dos Reis all dock at the main village of **Vila do Abraão,** a picturesque and palmy beachfront settlement clustered around a gleaming white colonial church and backed by mountains. Although there's not much of anything to do here, Vila Abraão provides the main base for exploration—on foot or by boat—of the island's natural attractions.

SPORTS AND RECREATION

The best way to discover Ilha Grande's beaches, coves, and grottoes is by boat; many sites are otherwise inaccessible due to the dense and tangled jungle surrounding them. **Sudoeste SW Turismo** (Vila Abraão, tel. 24/3361-5516, www.sudoestesw.com.br) offers eight-hour day trips on schooners and on motorized launches (for up to 20 people), which can circle the island. Trips usually include visits to seven or eight beaches with stops for snorkeling, diving, basking in the sun, and lunch. The eight-hour-long trip costs R$70 per person (on a fishing schooner) and R$150 (on a private launch for small groups of up to 10). You can also target individual beaches by hiring a boat at the **Associação dos Barqueiros de Ilha Grande** (tel. 24/3361-5046). Depending on the destination and the number of people traveling, prices can range from R$25–50 per person.

To concentrate specifically on Ilha Grande's spectacular underwater treasures, take advantage of the diving and snorkeling opportunities. **Elite Dive Center** (tel. 24/3361-5501, www.elitedivecenter.com.br) offers lessons, equipment rental, and excursions to the most scenic aquatic spots around the island. A six-hour outing (including a snack and drinks) costs R$145. A four-day basic course for beginners (with six diving excursions) costs R$850.

Jungle enthusiasts can tap into their inner Tarzan and Jane by tackling the numerous hiking trails that weave through the spectacularly lush Atlantic forest that carpets the island. The rainforest is home to wildlife that includes monkeys, parrots, hummingbirds, and (unfortunately) many mosquitos (for your sanity, repellent is a *must*). Most trails are well signed, but it's best to take a few precautions, such as informing your *pousada* of your route and equipping yourself with water, snacks, and sun protector. Also carry a flashlight since night can fall quickly. For serious treks into the interior, such as the five-hour hike across the island to **Praia da Parnaioca** or the three-hour climb up to the summit of **Bico do Pagagaio** (Parrot's Beak), it's wise to hire a guide. **Sudoeste SW Turismo** organizes day trips as well as overnight camping and hiking excursions (R$150 per person) to these and other destinations for individuals and small groups, led by knowledgeable bilingual guides.

ACCOMMODATIONS

Most accommodations in Ilha Grande are located in or around Vila Abraão, although some more exclusive *pousadas* are hidden away in secluded natural settings. Aside from camping sites (which abound), *pousadas* tend to be fairly simple, although not always that cheap. Less expensive than many beach *pousadas* and more tranquil due to its luxuriant hillside setting, (**Pousada Naturália** (Rua da Praia 149, Vila Abraão, tel. 24/3361-5198, www.pousadanaturalia.net, R$100–200) is an enticing option. Double, triple, and quadruple suites are handsomely finished with lots of polished natural wood and wide terraces where you can settle into a hammock and gaze out to sea.

Also welcoming is the cozy **Pousada Mara e Claude** (Rua da Praia 333, Vila Abraão, tel. 24/3361-5922, ilhamara@ilhagrande.org, R$120–180 d). The friendly proprietors, Mara and Claude (a former sausage-maker from the south of France), have decorated the modest rooms with homey touches that will make you feel like a house guest.

For complete Edenic isolation, with lots of comfort and shades of Zen, it's hard not to succumb to the spell cast by **Sankay Pousada** (Enseada do Bananal, tel. 24/3365-4065, www.pousadasankay.com.br, R$270–370 d full board, reservations essential, closed in June). Located on the northeastern shore of the island, the only way to get here is by boat (pickup and return from Angra dos Reis is included in the price). A dozen individually decorated chalets (for double, triple, or quadruple occupancy) overlook a very private beach, making this enchanting *pousada* ideal for small groups and families as well as couples. A multilingual library, a swimming pool, and sauna complement the natural relaxants offered by waterfalls and a crystalline sea full of brightly colored fish.

FOOD

Unsurprisingly, fresh fish and seafood constitute the main culinary fare on Ilha Grande. Vila Abraão has lots of simple, rustic bar/restaurants to choose from. **Lua e Mar** (Rua da Praia 297, Vila Abraão, tel. 24/3361-5113, 11 A.M.–11 P.M. Tues.–Sun., R$20–30), with its tables and chairs spread out beneath a giant tree overlooking the beach, is reputed for serving up the island's most succulent fish and seafood *moquecas*.

Located in the beachfront *pousada* of the same name, **O Pescador** (Rua da Praia, Vila Abraão, tel. 24/3361-5113, 5–11 P.M. daily, R$30–40) offers tasty dishes with an Italian influence, accompanied by a small but well-chosen wine menu.

INFORMATION

Ilha Grande's **tourist office** (tel. 24/3361-5508, variable hours) is close to where the ferries dock. Ilha Grande doesn't have any bank machines. Make sure you come equipped with cash (although some tonier places accept credit cards).

GETTING THERE

Barcas S.A. (tel. 24/3365-6426, R$7 Mon.–Fri., R$15 Sat.–Sun.) offers daily ferry service during the week to Ilha Grande. Boats leave from Angra (departing at 3:30 P.M. during the week and at 1:30 P.M. on weekends) and from the nearby town of Mangatariba (8 A.M. daily).

Return boats from Vila Abraão leave daily for Angra at 10 A.M. and for Mangatariba at 5:30 P.M. If you miss the ferry, you can wait around for a motorized launch to fill up and leave from Angra's pier (this is more likely to happen quickly during the summer).

Ilha Gipóia

The second largest island in Angra's bay, Ilha Gipóia is also the most visited. Not only is it only a quick 30-minute boat ride away from Angra's pier, but its waters are ideal for snorkeling and diving and its beaches are spectacular. The most popular, **Praia do Dentista**, is famous for its floating bars, where (stranded on the waves) you can feast on fresh grilled fish, lobster, and even sushi, all of which are delivered by boat. There is even a *sorveteria* that sells ice cream out of a canoe. Those in search of more privacy can take a boat to the deserted beaches of **Juruba** or **Praia do Norte**.

ACCOMMODATIONS

If you want to stay on the island, check into the **Pousada Canto do Hibisco** (Praia do Vitorino, tel. 24/9991-6605, www.ilhadagipoia.com.br, R$330–520 d for full board), which offers six attractive and secluded beach bungalows surrounded by tropical forest.

INFORMATION

Angra's **tourist office** (Largo do Lapa, tel. 24/3367-7855, 8 A.M.–6 P.M. daily) is conveniently located across the street from the bus station and the Cais de Santa Luzia—from where boats and schooners leave. For information about Angra, Ilha Grande, and the surrounding area, www.angra-dos-reis.com is a useful bilingual site.

GETTING THERE

Viação Costa Verde (tel. 21/2233-3809, www.costaverdetransportes.com.br) offers hourly bus service between Rio and the Angra *rodoviária* (tel. 24/3365-2041). The 160-km (100-mile) journey takes 2.5–3 hours. By car, from Rio, take the BR-101 Rio–Santos highway, but beware of traffic on weekends and holidays.

◖ PARATY

Midway between Rio and São Paulo, set amidst blue ocean and steep, jagged, green mountains, Paraty is one of the most charismatic colonial towns you'll ever encounter. Paraty first emerged as a tiny port town in the early 1700s as a consequence of the gold boom in neighboring Minas Gerais. An ancient Guianá Indian trail was widened into a route used to transport extravagant quantities of gold through the Serra do Mar mountains and down to Paraty, from where it was shipped to Portugal. Over the next century, Paraty grew into a modest, yet stately town. Its cobblestoned streets filled up with single-story whitewashed mansions—with colorfully painted windows and doors—and austere but lovely churches. However, over time, numerous bandit raids and pirate attacks led to the building of a new gold route linking Minas directly with the city of Rio. As a consequence, Paraty's importance declined.

Over the next two centuries, the town slowly fell into oblivion, its lovely architecture faded and frozen in time. In fact, until 1954, the only way to reach Paraty was by boat. In 1960, the town was connected to both Rio de Janeiro and São Paulo by the BR-101 (Rio–Santos) highway, and in 1966, its historical center was declared a national monument. However, it wasn't until the 1970s that Paraty began to attract a small trickle of hippies and artists, who were drawn to this perfectly preserved colonial jewel. In subsequent years, the town blossomed into a cosmopolitan place. Artists and entrepreneurs from around the globe transformed its 18th- and 19th-century houses into private homes and ateliers, boutiques, cafés, restaurants, and hotels, which in turn lured a steady stream of weekenders from Rio and São Paulo, as well as international tourists and, more recently, an alternative GLS crowd.

As a result, Paraty boasts a particularly vibrant cultural and gastronomic scene. Although during the summer Paraty can get quite busy, it has managed to stave off the mass hysteria and upscale trendiness of other resort towns such as heels. During high tide, the sea actually swallows up some of the streets closest to the port, temporarily transforming them into tropically Venetian canals. While tides and rainwater can leave the streets slippery, they also keep them clean.

The best way to explore Paraty is by wandering around at random. Among the town's most handsome *sobrados* (mansions) is the **Casa de Cultura** (Rua Dona Geralda 177, tel. 24/3371-2325, 10 A.M.–6:30 P.M. Wed.–Mon., R$5). Built in 1758, it hosts cultural events and has a permanent exhibition tracing Paraty's history.

Several baroque churches are also particularly interesting. The town's oldest church, **Igreja de Santa Rita dos Pardos Libertos** (Largo de Santa Rita, tel. 24/3371-1620, 9 A.M.–noon and 2–5 P.M. Wed.–Sun.) dates from 1722. Built by freed slaves, its interior houses a small collection of religious artifacts. Constructed a few years later, **Igreja Nossa Senhora do Rosário** (Rua do Comércio, 9 A.M.–noon and 1:30–5 P.M. Wed.–Sun.) was built by and for Paraty's slave population. Despite its simplicity, it is the only church in town with gold decoration on its altars (added in the 20th century).

Paraty's principal and most grandiose church, **Igreja Matriz de Nossa Senhora de Remédios** (Praça da Matriz, 9 A.M.–5 P.M. daily) was where the bourgeoisie worshipped. Outside, on the Praça Matriz, there is a small daily crafts market selling local handicrafts. Meanwhile, the town's aristocrats held their services in the late-18th-century **Igreja Nossa Senhora das Dores** (Rua Fresca, 1–5 P.M. daily), with a privileged view of the sea (and access to cooling breezes).

Beyond the *centro histórico,* take a 15-minute walk past Praia do Pontal to the **Forte Defensor Perpétuo** (9 A.M.–noon and 2–5 P.M. Tues.–Sun., R$1). Crowning the Morro da Vila Velha, this fortress was built in 1703 to protect Paraty's gold from being hijacked by pirates. Restored in 1822, it houses a small museum with a display of local artisanal objects as well as a store selling handicrafts.

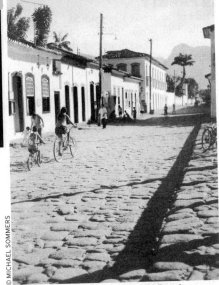

cobblestoned street in colonial Paraty

© MICHAEL SOMMERS

Búzios. During off-season, the town is sleepier without being dull, and it is easier to soak up its seductive atmosphere. Urban charms aside, the surrounding region holds numerous natural attractions. Close by are dozens of gorgeously primitive beaches and deserted islands as well as the majestic Serra do Mar mountain range, its unspoiled tropical forest punctuated with refreshing waterfalls.

Sights

Paraty's compact *centro histórico* is considered by UNESCO to be one of the world's most outstanding examples of Portuguese colonial architecture. Although the streets are laid out on a grid plan, the uniformity of the bleached houses coupled with streets' multiple names can make it somewhat of a challenge to find your bearings. The crazily paved streets—constructed by slaves out of large irregular stones known as *pés-de-moleque* ("street kids' feet")—mean that vehicles can't circulate, but also makes getting around treacherous for those with disabilities or sporting high

Beaches

Paraty is rich in beaches: More than 200 can be found along the surrounding coastline and among some 65 islands. Most of the island beaches can be visited by boats leaving from Paraty's Cais de Porto. Those up and down the coastline can be reached by car or bus. Although the town has its own beaches, they aren't that attractive. The closest, **Praia do Pontal,** is a 10-minute walk from the *centro histórico.* While its beach *barraca* scene is lively, swimming isn't recommended. Cleaner and more deserted are **Praia do Forte** and **Praia do Jabaquara.**

Some of the finest and most easily accessible beaches are at **Trindade,** a fishing village and former hippie hangout, 25 kilometers (16 miles) south of Paraty along the Rio–Santos highway. The stunningly wild beaches of **Cepilho** and **Brava** are ideal for surfing, while **Praia do Meio** and **Praia Cachadaço** (which is also good for snorkeling) are prized for their calm waters and natural swimming pools. You can get to Cachadaço by a 20-minute hike through the forest or by boat from Praia do Meio. Trindade's most far-flung beaches—**Praia do Sono** and **Praia do Antigo**—are gloriously unspoiled. Reaching them entails a 2–3-hour hike.

Also close by—18 kilometers (11 miles) southwest of Paraty (8 kilometers/5 miles of which are on an unpaved road)–is **Paraty-Mirim,** with a lovely bay, invitingly calm waters, and beach *barracas.* You can reach it by municipal bus or by boat. From here, you can catch a boat to the beautiful beaches of **Saco do Mamanguá, Cajaíba,** and **Grande da Deserta.** These beaches are all backed by lush jungle and boast waterfalls in close proximity.

Sports and Recreation

By sea or by land, there are lots of natural attractions to explore in the area surrounding Paraty.

BOAT EXCURSIONS AND DIVING

Various schooners offer five-hour trips around Paraty's bay with stops at islands such as Ilha Comprida (known for its diving) as well as otherwise inaccessible beaches such as Praia da Lula and Praia Vermelha. Lunch is included, as are *caipirinhas* (and sometimes rambunctious live music that might grate on those who imagined a more bucolic outing). For more information contact **Paraty Tours** (Av. Roberto Silveira 11, tel. 24/3371-1327, www.paraty-tours.com.br), which also organizes diving, kayaking, horseback riding, and hiking trips. A five-hour tour with Paraty Tours costs R$20 per person. Individuals and small groups can also charter boats at an hourly rate from the *barqueiros* at Cais de Porto.

TREKKING

At the **Associação de Guias de Turismo de Parati** (tel. 24/3371-1783), individuals and small groups can hire guides to take them up and down the forested coastline to secluded beaches, with stops for bathing in bays and waterfalls. Another enticing journey is to follow the **Caminho do Ouro,** the route along which gold was transported over the mountains from Minas to Paraty during colonial times. The historical hike along a 2-km (1.2-mile) stretch of irregular cobblestones can be done in the company of a guide from the **Centro de Informações Turísticas Caminho do Ouro** (Estrada Paraty-Cunha, tel. 24/3371-1783, 9 A.M.–noon and 2–5 P.M. Wed.–Sun., R$20). Ascending into the Serra do Mar, you are treated to breathtaking views of Paraty and the ocean.

Entertainment and Events

Considering its size, Paraty has a vibrant and cosmopolitan nightlife and cultural scene, although most of the action takes place during the summer and on weekends.

NIGHTLIFE

Charming bars with live music aren't hard to find in Paraty. **Margarida Café** (Praça do Chafariz, tel. 24/3371-2441, www.margaridacafe.com.br) is an appealingly atmospheric restaurant/bar serving innovative cuisine and pizza and featuring live music every night. **Bar do Lúcio** (Praça da Matriz 3, tel. 24/3371-8663, www.luciocruzz.com.br/bar)

has a mellow bohemian vibe. MPB, jazz, and bossa nova keep things cool, and there are frequent exhibits of works by local artists. **Paraty 33** (Rua da Lapa 357, tel. 24/3371-7311, www.paraty.com.br) has a low-key tavern atmosphere and lures a younger, more animated crowd intent on partying the night away.

You don't have to understand Portuguese to be enchanted by the plays performed by the Contadores de Estórias at the **Teatro de Bonecos** (Rua Dona Geralda 327, tel. 24/3371-1575, 9 P.M. Wed., Fri., and Sat., R$40). This talented, world-renowned troupe of actors manipulates a disarmingly lifelike cast of doll-like puppets (*bonecos*) who mutely act out poignant and hilarious dramatic sketches. Leave the kids (under 14) at home, since these puppet shows are for adults only.

FESTIVALS

Aside from **Carnaval,** Paraty comes alive in the winter months (May–August) for several popular *festas.* The **Festa do Divino** takes place 40 days after Easter and lasts for two weeks. This colorful religious festival originated in the Portuguese islands of Madeira and the Açores. Religious parades and celebrations are held along with theatrical, dance, and musical performances that take place in the street. During the third weekend in August, *cachaça* lovers from far and wide descend upon the town for the **Festival da Pinga,** at which time the streets are flooded with the local liquor.

Not just for bookworms, the **Festa Literária Internacional** (www.flip.org.br), which takes place for five days in August, lures more visitors to Paraty than Carnaval. Aside from readings and debates attended by the likes of Paul Auster, Salman Rushdie, Margaret Atwood, and Ian McEwan, the town comes alive with cultural and culinary happenings.

Shopping

Paraty is famous for its *cachaças,* produced by traditional alembics in the surrounding region. The varieties available range from "white" and aged to those suffused with honey (great for a sore throat), cinnamon, and numerous herbs, spices, and fruits. One of the most potent brands is Corisco, while Paratiana and Maria Izabel are smoother and more discreet. Specialized *cachaça* boutiques—where you can sample the wares, even if you don't want to purchase—include the **Armazém da Cachaça** (Rua do Comércio, tel. 24/3371-7519) and **Empório da Cachaça** (Rua Dr. Samuel da Costa 22, tel. 24/3371-6329).

Accommodations

Paraty has no shortage of enticing places to stay; the *centro histórico* has numerous *pousadas* housed in colonial mansions, ranging from cozy and affordable to refined and luxurious. In the summertime and during holidays, finding a room can be tricky, so make sure you reserve in advance. You might have more luck outside the *centro histórico,* but the charm factor will be less. During off-season, particularly during the week, you can often negotiate rates reduced up to 30 or 40 percent.

One of the most attractive and affordable hotels in the *centro histórico* is the **Solar do Gerânios** (Praça da Matriz, tel. 24/3371-1550, www.paraty.com.br/geranio, R$100 d). Located in a rambling *sobrado,* its homey atmosphere is enhanced by the friendly owner and her cats. Rooms are small, but spotless and cheery. The best ones have small balconies overlooking the square.

Pousada do Príncipe (Av. Roberto Silveira 69, tel. 24/3371-2266, www.pousadadoprincipe.com.br, R$115–179) has rooms fit for a *príncipe* (prince) or *princesa,* but with prices that a plebeian can afford. In fact, this sprawling *pousada* is owned by Dom João de Orleans e Bragança, great-great-grandson of Brazilian emperor Dom Pedro II. It was transformed into a handsome guesthouse by architect/princess Stela Orleans de Bragança. The rooms aren't exactly regal, but they are bright and comfortable with views of a courtyard garden and swimming pool. Common spaces are slightly more palatial, and the portraits of the imperial family add an intimate monarchist touch.

Lacking in historic character, yet somewhat quaint, **Pousada Flor do Mar** (Rua Fresca 257, tel. 24/3371-1674, www.pousadaflordomar.com.br, R$100–120 d) offers clean and colorfully painted rooms for a nice price.

Pousada do Ouro (Rua da Praia 145, tel. 24/3371-2033, www.pousadadoouro.com.br, R$230–290 d) is a highly attractive guesthouse with tastefully furnished colonial-style rooms in a beautiful 18th-century *sobrado* (and a less impressive annex). Small touches—such as vases of wild orchids by the bedside—are abundant. A sauna, fitness room, and pool round out the amenities.

Those in search of luxury at affordable prices will find it in spades at C **Pousada da Marquesa** (Rua Dona Geralda 99, tel. 24/3371-1261, www.pousadadamarquesa.com.br, R$300–400 d). Rooms (those in the main house are nicer) are beautifully furnished with local antiques and artwork that capture the refined yet rustic ambiance of a tropical colonial home. Verandas and comfortable salons abound and the shady garden boasts a large pool where guests can sprawl on chaise lounges veiled by billowy white curtains.

Upon arriving at the **Pousada de Arte Urquijo** (Rua Dona Geralda 79, tel. 24/3371-1362, www.urquijo.com.br, R$290–330 d, no children under 12), guests are invited to remove their shoes and don comfortable Japanese slippers in which they can glide around the polished wood floors of this originally renovated 18th-century *sobrado*. Painter/proprietor Luz Urquijo has an artist's eye for detail, reflected in the unusual furnishings, bright, bold canvases on the walls (many by Luz and her daughter), and charming touches such as incense, wafting music, plush towels, and over-sized robes.

One of Paraty's oldest guesthouses, **Pousada Pardieiro** (Rua do Comércio 74, tel. 24/3371-1370, www.pousadapardiero.com.br. R$310–364 d, no children under 15) effortlessly captures the rustic charm and simplicity of Paraty. The cluster of 18th-century houses converted into atmospheric apartments resembles a private colonial village. Rooms are impeccably furnished with antiques. They face a pool and tranquil gardens whose trees are filled with monkeys. Service is attentive.

Food

The majority of Paraty's restaurants—as well as the most expensive—occupy charming *sobrados* in the *centro histórico*. In recent years, Paraty has attained quite a gastronomic reputation, with many restaurants taking advantage of the abundance of fresh fish and seafood to create innovative fare. Caiçara is the name given to local specialties that draw on fish, game, fruits, and vegetables traditionally used by the Costa Verde's indigenous peoples. One of the most popular recipes is a dish called *camarão casadinha* ("married shrimp"). This aptly named treat consists of two jumbo shrimp, tied together and fried after having being stuffed with a filling of tiny shrimp and *farofa*. You can savor this speciality at **Hiltinho** (Rua Marechal Deodoro 233, tel. 24/3371-1725, 10 A.M.–midnight daily, R$50–60), a traditional eatery famed for its *camarões*, both "married" and in other delicious arrangements. Aside from its main location in the *centro histórico*, there is also a Hiltinho (tel. 24/9276-5291, noon–6 P.M. daily in summer) on the Ilha de Algodão (an hour's boat ride away) in Paraty's bay.

C **Banana da Terra** (Rua Dr. Samuel Costa 198, tel. 24/3371-1725, noon–midnight Wed.–Sun., R$40–45) serves up Caiçara fare with a touch of refinement, prepared by Ana Bueno, considered one of Brazil's top chefs. True to the restaurant's name, various varieties of bananas make frequent appearances on the menu—in guises both savory (banana-and-cheese-stuffed squid gratinéed with shrimp) and sweet (warm banana tart with cinnamon ice cream).

The colorful interior at **Brik a Brak** (Rua Dr. Samuel Costa 267, tel. 24/3371-1445, noon–midnight daily, R$15–25), with its exposed stone walls displaying vibrant works by local artists, is as creative as the original dishes dreamed up in the kitchen. Abundant salads, sandwiches, quiches, and appetizers make this an ideal spot for a light bite. Other appealing

COOKING AND OTHER PLEASURES

For an informative – and mouthwatering – introduction to Brazil's regional cuisines, treat yourself to a night of cooking and eating at the **Academia de Cozinha e Outros Prazeres** in Paraty (Rua Dona Geralda 288, tel. 24/3371-6468, www.chefbrazil.com, lessons begin at 7 P.M., R$170). The "Academy of Cooking and Other Pleasures" is run by Yara Costa Roberts, a professional chef, whose fluent English is a result of years she spent in the U.S. spreading the word about Brazilian cooking. Several nights a week, Yara offers small groups of 10 a chance to learn – hands-on – how to prepare dishes from Bahia, the Amazon, the Cerrado region (in the Central-West), and her own home state of Minas Gerais. Once the lesson is over, sous-chefs get to sit down at Yara's table and dig into the delicious results of their travails.

features are the pretty courtyard garden and live music in the evenings.

The location of **Sabor da Terra** (Av. Roberto Silveira 180, tel. 24/3371-2384, 11 A.M.–10 P.M. daily, R$10–16), just outside the *centro histórico,* may justify the low-wattage decor and equally low prices. However, this per kilo restaurant earns high marks in terms of the variety, freshness, and tastiness of its buffet offerings, including grilled fish and *churrasco* as well as salads and seafood dishes.

Another inexpensive option is **Le Castellet** (Rua Dona Geralda, tel. 24/3371-7461, noon–11 P.M. Wed.–Mon., R$10–20). Chef Yves Lapide has outfitted this cozy little crêperie with attractive decorative touches from his native Provence, but the delicious sweet and savory crêpes are his real forté, along with other French fare such as seafood bouillabaisse and *tarte tatin.*

Considered one of Brazil's finest restaurants, (**Merlin o Mago** (Rua do Comércio 376, tel. 24/3371-2157, www.paraty.com.br/merlin, 7 P.M.–1 A.M. Thurs.–Tues., R$65–80) is owned and operated by German Hado Steinbracher, a former photojournalist and restaurant critic turned immensely creative chef. At his refined and romantic candlelit restaurant, Steinbracher turns out dishes based on French cuisine and laden with strong Asian and Brazilian influences. One of his best-loved dishes is *filé masqué,* in which a filet of *robalo* fish is "masked" in a delicate crêpe and bathed in a sauce mixing oranges, saffron, almonds and caviar.

If the idea of lunching in style on a deserted tropical island—taking time out for a dip in warm waters in between gourmet courses—appeals to you, Paraty has a handful of idyllic options. Aside from the island outlet of Hiltinho, **Kontiki** (tel. 24/3371-1666, 10 A.M.–5 P.M. daily in summer, R$50–60) is a sophisticated restaurant, perched on the tiny Ilha Duas Irmãs (10 minutes from Paraty), that is famous for its copious seafood paellas. The restaurant provides masks, fins, and kayaks as well as a complimentary boat that whisks diners/snorkelers to and from Paraty's Cais de Porto. More rustic, yet no less enchanting is **El Lahô** (tel. 24/3371-2253, noon onwards daily, R$30–40), located on tiny Ilha Catimbau, where the seafood is scrumptious but if you lean back too far in your chair you could end up in the water.

Information

The **Centro de Informações Turísticas** (Praça Macedo Sorares, tel. 24/3371-1897, 8 A.M.–7 P.M. daily), at the entrance to the *centro histórico,* has maps, bus schedules for other beaches, and other information. Two useful bilingual sites with lots of information are www.paraty.com.br and www.paraty.tur.br.

Getting There

Viação Costa Verde (tel. 24/3371-1326,

www.costaverdetransportes.com.br) offers bus service between Rio and Paraty, with 8–9 buses daily. The 236-kilometer (147-mile) journey takes four hours. **Viação Reunidas** (tel. 24/3371-2090, www.reunidas.com.br) offers bus service between São Paulo and Paraty, with four buses daily. The 330-kilometer (205-mile) journey takes six hours. The **bus station** (*rodoviária* is 500 meters from the *centro histórico*.

By car from Rio, simply follow the BR-101, the Rio–Santos highway.

SÃO PAULO

When most people think of São Paulo, they immediately conjure up the smog-horizoned, high-rise infested, megalopolis of 20 million for which the expression "concrete jungle" is an understatement. Teeming with noise, activity, and a certain degree of urban chaos, São Paulo is bewildering for those unfamiliar or unenamored with cities its size—and enchanting for those who are. Brazil's economic and cultural powerhouse (having long supplanted Rio on both fronts) is overflowing with banks and mega corporations as well as an astounding number of world-class museums, cultural centers, theaters, concert halls, and cinemas. Rife with contrasts and contradictions, São Paulo mingles First World sophistication with *favelas*. Haute couture and haute cuisine coexist alongside *camelôs* (illegal sidewalk vendors) hawking pirated Armani shades and makeshift vans selling deliciously messy hot dogs for R$1. While the working rich rely on the world's largest fleet of private helicopters to commute from posh suburbs to glittery office buildings, the less fortunate—and far more numerous—working poor spend hours snarled in kilometrical traffic jams caused by the world's largest fleet of municipal buses. If you're looking for Brazil's quintessential tropical paradise, you won't find it here. However, you will encounter a unique and fascinating fusion of elements from all over the country—and the world.

The surrounding state of São Paulo is as diverse as its capital. The wealthiest and most populous of Brazil's states—as well as the most developed in terms of industry and agriculture—São Paulo is also rich in impressive

© CHRISTIAN KNEPPER/EMBRATUR

HIGHLIGHTS

◖ **Avenida Paulista:** Raw, vital, messy, and fascinatingly diverse, São Paulo's mega main drag constitutes the city's vibrant nerve center (page 130).

◖ **Museu de Arte de São Paulo (MASP):** One of Latin America's finest art museums is housed in an iconic modernist building that is an attraction in itself (page 131).

◖ **Parque do Ibirapuera:** São Paulo's version of Central Park, this vast green urban oasis is filled with some of the city's finest museums (page 133).

◖ **Campos do Jordão:** With hiking trails, Swiss chalets, and abundant fondue and chocolate, Paulistanos' favorite mountain getaway evokes a tropical version of the Alps (page 166).

◖ **Bananal:** In the 19th century, this colonial gem of a town was the center of the biggest coffee-growing region in the world. The surrounding plantations of the coffee barons are still intact and worth a visit (page 172).

◖ **Ilhabela:** Brazil's biggest off-coast island is a nature lover's dream replete with virgin rainforests and unspoiled beaches (page 178).

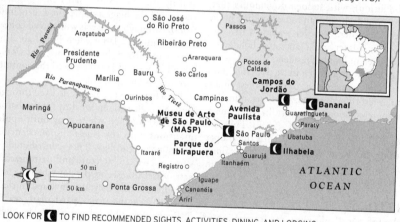

LOOK FOR ◖ TO FIND RECOMMENDED SIGHTS, ACTIVITIES, DINING, AND LODGING.

natural attractions. The coastline leading north from the historic city of Santos up to Rio de Janeiro is lined with stunning white-sand beaches backed by native Atlantic forest. São Sebastião is a teeming hot spot with every kind of water sport imaginable and nonstop nightlife. Meanwhile, north of Ubatuba and on the island of Ilhabela you'll find primitive beaches that you can have all to yourself. Traveling inland offers similar contrasts: While the mountain resort of Campos do Jordão attracts a fur-clad crowd with a penchant for fondues and fireplaces, the tiny colonial towns and century-old coffee plantations of the Serra da Mantiqueira range remain largely unknown even by many native Paulistanos (natives of São Paulo). Well-maintained highways and an extensive and efficient bus system mean that most attractions are easy to get to: All it takes is a 2–3-hour drive from the city and you're in another world.

PLANNING YOUR TIME

Most international travelers only spend enough time in São Paulo to change planes at its busy airport. However, despite its vast size, beachlessness, and—some would say—lack of visual appeal, the city of São Paulo is one of the world's most vibrant, diverse, and often surprising metropolises. For a dose of sophisticated urban living—with all the culture, fine dining, and shopping that entails—it is definitely worth spending a couple of days here. If you're a true urban soul, stick around for a whole week in order to explore the city's many neighborhoods and take advantage of its fantastic nightlife. In a pinch, you can always make a quick day trip or overnight getaway to the coast or mountains.

When planning a trip to São Paulo, there are several things to keep in mind. In terms of the weather, summer months are often unbearably hot and sticky in the capital (a fact made worse by pollution), with sudden downpours that, due to poor drainage, can cause flooding in the streets. Summer, however—along with long weekends, "winter break," and other holidays—is also when millions of residents hightail it out of the city (transforming it into a pleasant "ghost town") and migrate to the coast. At these times, popular resorts get very crowded, meaning that advance reservations are a must. In winter, temperatures can plunge to 10°C (50°F). This isn't a big deal if you're equipped with the proper clothing, but be aware that many places don't have heating. The mountains, in particular, can get very chilly.

HISTORY

Although São Paulo gives the impression of being a relatively new city, it was actually founded over 450 years ago. Older still is the port of Santos (originally known as São Vicente). Brazil's second-oldest settlement, it dates back to 1507. While São Vicente was an important port for the Portuguese, São Paulo dos Campos de Piratininga was a tiny Jesuit outpost, settled in 1554 by priests intent on converting the local Tupi-Guarani Indian population to Catholicism. Perched atop a plateau, on the banks of the Rio Tietê, close to the Paraná and Prata Rivers, its strategic location ensured residents protection from attacks as well as fluvial transportation. In fact, it was from here that, in the 1600s, gangs of Portuguese settlers set off to discover Brazil's

uncharted hinterlands. Known as *bandeirantes* because they carried Portugal's *bandeira* (flag), these rugged adventurers were motivated by the promise of finding diamonds and gold and enslaving Indians. Along the way, they opened up much of Brazil's interior.

However, it wasn't until the mid-19th century that São Paulo's fortunes really took off. Spurred by the arrival of Confederate refugees who fled the American South following the U.S. Civil War, local planters had unsuccessfully dabbled in cotton plantations before deciding to switch over to coffee. With this new crop, they struck gold: The fertile red soil of the hills provided ideal growing conditions, and by the late 1800s, São Paulo state was the one of the biggest coffee producers in the world. Although there was widespread concern about plantation labor when Brazil abolished slavery in 1889, a flood of immigrant workers from Europe and Japan ensured the continuation of this lucrative crop.

For a few decades, São Paulo lived through a veritable coffee boom. Wealthy "coffee barons" moved to the city, where they built opulent mansions with the finest imported materials money could buy. They contributed vast sums to civic architecture and patronized the arts. Wisely foreseeing the day when the boom would fizzle out, they also invested in the region's nascent industries, particularly textiles.

By the early 20th century, São Paulo—which for 300 years had remained a sleepy, provincial town—was becoming a bustling and somewhat grand metropolis with elegant parks and wide European-inspired boulevards. British, German, and French companies flocked to invest in the city's infrastructure while immigrants from the rest of Europe, the Middle East, and Asia came in droves to work in the factories that sprang up in and around the city. As the population multiplied exponentially, commerce flourished and skyscrapers sprang up. The nation's automobile industry started in São Paulo, and by the 1940s the country was experiencing its first traffic jams. To clear space for the six-lane *avenidas* and viaducts necessary to (attempt to) ease the eternal congestion of vehicles, buildings were knocked down with amazing speed—and, unfortunately, complete disdain for historical or architectural preservation. By the 1950s, São Paulo was the largest industrial center in Latin America. In the 1970s, it had become the driving force of Brazil's "Economic Miracle," a period of exponential economic growth that attracted a vast new wave of immigrants from Brazil's poor northeastern states to the city (and its suburban *favelas*).

Today, São Paulo state still concentrates much of the nation's industrial activities, while the increasingly globalized city of São Paulo reigns supreme as the most important commercial, financial, technological, and service center in Latin America. Currently, São Paulo state boasts a population of 40 million and an economy that accounts for 34 percent of Brazil's GNP. Despite its relative wealth and pockets of extremely sophisticated First Worldliness, the same extreme social and economic inequalities—as well as severe problems ranging from pollution to urban violence—that plague the rest of Brazil are rampant. The only difference between São Paulo and a city like Rio is that, to a visitor's eye, these socio-economic extremes may be less immediately visible.

São Paulo City

In Brazil, they say that Rio is all play while São Paulo is all about work. Indeed, the world's fifth-largest city is an economic force that generates a significant portion of Brazil's wealth. And yes, the majority of travelers who check into São Paulo's ultramodern hotels and dine at its internationally renowned restaurants are in town for business, not pleasure. It's also true that when you climb to the 35th floor of the landmark Banespa building and glimpse what appears to be an endless concrete jungle that extends a full 360 degrees, you might wonder what the appeal could possibly be.

Few vestiges remain of São Paulo's early days as a Jesuit missionary settlement, or as a thriving 19th-century trade center where coffee barons lived it up in grand style. However, its bustling downtown nonetheless offers a vibrant mishmash of history and architectural styles, ranging from surviving colonial churches to belle epoque and art deco apartment buildings. The clean lines of Brazilian modernism are on display in the elegant residences of the neighborhood of Higienópolis, and the city's version of the Champs-Elysées, Avenida Paulista, offers a daunting collection of '70s, '80s, and '90s skyscrapers that if not beautiful are undeniably impressive.

Just as varied as the city itself are its residents (known as Paulistanos). Aside from Portuguese, São Paulo boasts particularly large Italian, Japanese, and Lebanese communities. Working class and "popular" *bairros* exist alongside heavily guarded, posh residential areas. The aptly named Jardins (Gardens) neighborhood is home to the city's rich and powerful, as well as some of the most luxurious boutiques, galleries, and bistros on the planet. Indeed, "Sampa"—as it is lovingly referred to by residents—is all about highs and lows: If you're after foie gras, you'll find it, but you can just as easily enjoy a cheese-filled *pastel* washed down with sugarcane "juice" at a street market. This mixture is reflected in unparalleled eating opportunities, as well as cultural offerings that rival those of New York and London. A vibrant arts scene, great museums, and an intense and varied nightlife ensure that Paulistanos play harder than anyone else in Brazil. And when they tire of both work and play, there is always Parque do Ibirapuera, a vast oasis of green that is the perfect place to recharge one's batteries.

SIGHTS

As a mega-metropolis that has grown at a breakneck pace with plenty of real estate booms and busts, São Paolo can seem a bit overwhelming in terms of its immense size. It's best to think of

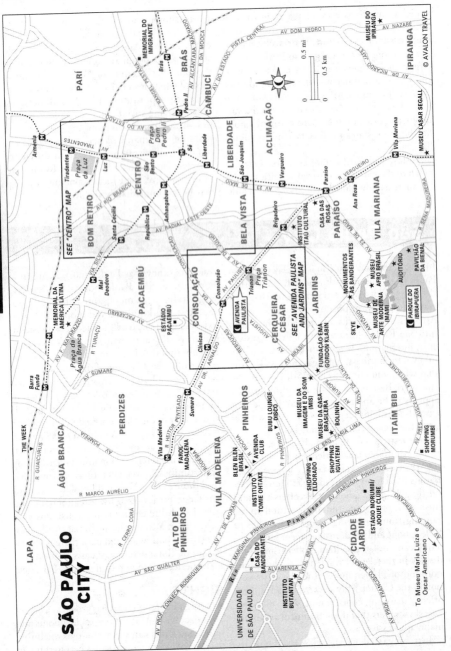

SÃO PAULO CITY

© AVALON TRAVEL

it as an ensemble of villages, each of which can be explored individually. Fortunately, the vast majority of attractions are located within the central core and are easily reached by Metrô, bus, or foot.

Centro

São Paulo has undergone immense transformations since its foundation in 1554. However, hidden away in its original downtown core are a few interesting vestiges of the city's colonial past, which are all the more striking for being hemmed in by a forest of skyscrapers. Although you should always be on the alert for pickpocket types, wandering around Centro during the day is a fairly safe, if mildly chaotic, experience. At night, however, much of the area clears out, making taxis necessary.

The geographic, historic, and symbolic center of São Paulo is **Praça da Sé.** By day, this vast plaza is filled with thousands of Paulistanos hurrying to and from somewhere, along with *camelôs* (illegal sidewalk vendors) hawking cheap wares and small clusters of street kids. It is here that many protests and demonstrations have been held—one of the most famous occurred in 1984 when 300,000 citizens demanded direct democratic elections following two decades of military rule.

CATEDRAL DA SÉ

Dominating the Praça da Sé is the Catedral da Sé (Praça da Sé, Centro, tel. 11/3107-6832, 8 A.M.–7 P.M. Mon.–Fri., 8–5, Sat., 8 A.M.–1 P.M. and 3–6 P.M. Sun., free, crypt R$4). The city's main cathedral, this imposing mid-20th-century neo-gothic building is large enough to hold 8,000 people. Architecturally, the church is not very compelling. However, the sculpted columns inside are unusual in that, along with the usual saints and angels, they feature tropical elements such as coffee beans, exotic fruits, toucans, and armadillos.

EDIFÍCIO SÉ

Directly across from the cathedral, at the far side of the *praça,* the magnificently brooding art deco Edifício Sé (Praça da Sé 111, Centro, tel. 11/3321-4400, www.caixacultural.com.br, 9 A.M.–9 P.M. Tues.–Sun., free) dates from the 1930s and serves as the São Paulo headquarters of Brazil's federal bank, the Caixa Econômica Federal. The grandiose, marble-lined main floor and mezzanine have been renovated into a cultural center with interesting temporary exhibits. It's really worthwhile to check out the bank's offices and coffers. The wooden office furniture—gorgeously streamlined and made in Brazil—will delight design aficionados.

SOLAR DA MARQUESA DOS SANTOS

Just around the corner from the Edifício Sé is the pretty pink Solar da Marquesa dos Santos (Rua Roberto Simonsen 136, Centro, tel. 11/3105-2030, www.prodam.sp.gov.br/dph/museus/solar, 9 A.M.–5 P.M. Tues.–Sun., free). São Paulo's oldest residential dwelling, this 18th-century mansion's former occupants included the Marquesa de Santos, who was the (most famous) mistress of Emperor Dom Pedro II. Today, it houses a small museum with temporary art exhibits devoted to different aspects of the city.

PÁTIO DO COLÉGIO

Around the corner from Rua Roberto Simonsen, you'll find the Pátio do Colégio (Pátio do Colégio 2, Centro, tel. 11/3105-6899, www.pateo collegio.com.br, 9 A.M.–5 P.M. Tues.–Sun., R$5). This whitewashed Portuguese colonial edifice is actually a replica of the original 16th-century Jesuit college that was the first building in São Paulo. Founded by José de Anchieta and Manuel da Nóbrega, two priests who were bent on catechizing the region's indigenous population, the college's construction marked the beginning of the city's history.

In the garden, where there is a pleasant café, you can see one of the college's original walls, fashioned out of clay, leaves, and cattle blood. Part of the Pátio do Colégio, the small and rather modest **Museu Padre Anchieta** contains a few relics—such as the original 16th-century granite baptismal font—and documents that recount the history of São Paulo's early years.

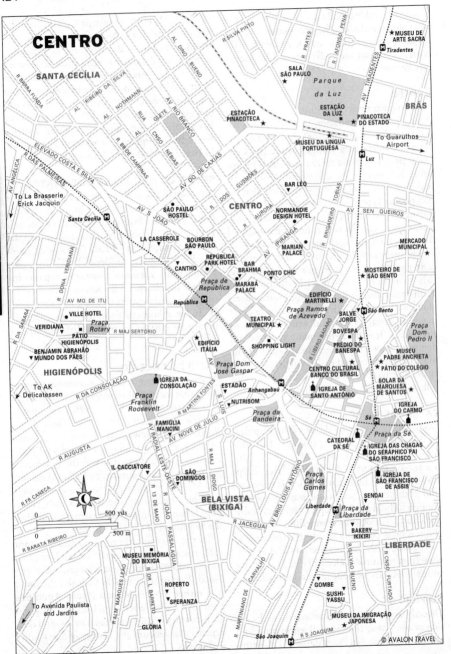

CENTRO

SANTA CECÍLIA

R BARRA FUNDA
AL RIBEIRO DA SILVA
AL NOTHMANN
R NOTHMANN
RUA GLETE
AV BA DE CAMPINAS
AV RIO BRANCO
AL DINO BUENO
R SILVA PINTO
R PRATES
R JAFONSI PENA

★ MUSEU DE
ARTE SACRA
🅼 Tiradentes

SALA
SÃO PAULO
★

*Parque
da Luz*

ESTAÇÃO
PINACOTECA ★

ESTAÇÃO
DA LUZ 🅼

PINACOTECA
★ DO ESTADO

BRÁS

To Guarulhos
Airport

AV ANGÉLICA
R DAS PALMEIRAS
ELEVADO COSTA E SILVA

To La Brasserie
Erick Jacquin

Santa Cecília 🅼

AV DO CAXIAS
AV S JOÃO
R DOS GUSMÕES
CENTRO
R AURORA

MUSEU DA LINGUA
PORTUGUESA ★

🅼 Luz

BAR LÉO ▼

SÃO PAULO
HOSTEL ▼

NORMANDIE
DESIGN HOTEL ▼

R BRIGADEIRO TOBIAS
AV SEN QUEIROS

MERCADO
MUNICIPAL
★

LA CASSEROLE ▼

BOURBON
SÃO PAULO ●

R DONA VERIDIANA

CANTHO ▼

REPÚBLICA
PARK HOTEL ●

BAR
BRAHMA ▼

AV PIRANGA
MARIAN
PALACE ▼

PONTO CHIC ▼

MOSTEIRO DE
★ SÃO BENTO

AV MQ DE ITU

*Praça de
República*

MARABÁ
PALACE ▼

República 🅼

EDIFÍCIO
MARTINELLI ★

🅼 São Bento

R DA SABARÁ
VERIDIANA
VILLE HOTEL ▼

*Praça
Rotary*

R MAJ SERTORIO

TEATRO
MUNICIPAL ★

*Praça Ramos
de Azevedo*

SALVE
JORGE ▼

BOVESPA ■

*Praça
Dom
Pedro II*

PÁTIO
HIGIENÓPOLIS ■
BENJAMIN ABRAHÃO ▼
MUNDO DOS PÃES ▼

HIGIENÓPOLIS

EDIFÍCIO
ITÁLIA ▲

SHOPPING LIGHT ■

R LIBERO BADARÓ

PRÉDIO DO
BANESPA ■

MUSEU
PADRE ANCHIETA ★
★ PÁTIO DO COLÉGIO

To AK
Delicatessen

R DA CONSOLAÇÃO

IGREJA DA
CONSOLAÇÃO ⛪

*Praça
Franklin
Roosevelt*

R MARTINS FONTES
S LUIS
AV RADIAL LESTE-OESTE

ESTADÃO ▼

*Praça Dom
José Gaspar*

Anhangabaú 🅼

CENTRO CULTURAL
BANCO DO BRASIL ★

SOLAR DA
MARQUESA
DE SANTOS ★

NUTRISOM ▼

*Praça da
Bandeira*

IGREJA DE
SANTO ANTÔNIO ⛪

IGREJA
DO CARMO ⛪

FAMIGLIA
MANCINI ▼

AV NOVE DE JULHO
R AUGUSTA

R MAJ DIOGO

Sé 🅼

IL CACCIATORE ▼

SÃO
DOMINGOS ▼

R 13 DE MAIO
R JOÃO

*Praça
Carlos
Gomes*

Praça da Sé

CATEDRAL
DA SÉ ⛪

IGREJA DAS CHAGAS
DO SERÁPHICO PAI
SÃO FRANCISCO ⛪

R FR CANECA

BELA VISTA
(BIXIGA)

AV BRIG LOUIS ANTÔNIO
PASSALAGUA

Liberdade 🅼

*Praça da
Liberdade*

IGREJA DE
SÃO FRANCISCO
DE ASSIS ⛪

SENDAI ▼

R BARATA RIBEIRO

R JACEGUAI

BAKERY
IKIKIRI ▼

LIBERDADE

R GALVAO BUENO
R CNSO FURTADO

0 _____ 500 yds
0 _____ 500 m

MUSEU MEMÓRIA
DO BIXIGA ■

R DR L BARRETO

ROPERTO ▼
SPERANZA ▼

R MARTINIANO DE CARVALHO

GOMBE ▼
SUSHI-
YASSU ▼

To Avenida Paulista
and Jardins

R ALM MARQUES LEÃO

GLÓRIA ▼

São Joaquim 🅼

R S JOAQUIM

MUSEU DA IMIGRAÇÃO
JAPONESA ★

© AVALON TRAVEL

SÃO PAULO

MOSTEIRO DE SÃO BENTO AND VICINITY

Continuing along Rua Boa Vista from the Pátio do Colégio brings you to Largo de São Bento. Amid a cluster of high-rise financial buildings is the Mosteiro de São Bento (Largo de São Bento, Centro, tel. 11/3328-8799, www.mosteiro.org, 6 A.M.–6:30 P.M. Mon.–Fri., 6 A.M.–noon and 4–6 P.M. Sat.–Sun., free). Though it dates back over 400 years, the Benedictine monastery has received numerous facelifts over the centuries. Its basilica was built in 1912. Compared with the sober facade, the interior is more ornate. An interestingly subversive pagan touch is the painting of a red sun (representing God) with beams radiating the 12 signs of the zodiac. Most of the monastery is off-limits to visitors since its quarters are home to the Benedictine monks, who not only sing divinely (Gregorian chants are performed at 7 A.M. Mon.–Fri., 6 A.M. Sat., 10 A.M. Sun.), but also bake well: Try the *pão de mandioquinha* (a type of sweet potato bread) and the *bolo Santa Ecolástica,* a cake made with apples and walnuts, which are sold on the premises.

Near the monastery is a trio of more modern, but equally striking landmarks. Built in 1901 to house the Banco do Brasil's city headquarters, the **Centro Cultural Banco do Brasil (CCBB)** (Rua Álvares Penteado 112, Centro, tel. 11/3113-3651, www.bb.com.br/cultura/, 10 A.M.–9 P.M. Tues.–Sun.) is an opulent beaux arts building decked out with mosaic murals and crystal chandeliers that hosts a wide variety of cultural and artistic events. Close by, the **Prédio do Banespa** (Rua João Bricola 24, Centro, tel. 11/3249-7180, 10 A.M.–5 P.M. Mon.–Fri.) was São Paulo's answer to the New York's Empire State Building. Inaugurated in 1947, this grand skyscraper—headquarters of the Banespa bank—remains one of Sampa's tallest buildings. From the panoramic deck on the 35th floor, you are treated to impressive views of the city. Prior to the Banespa building, Sampa's tallest building was the elegant **Edifício Martinelli** (Rua Libero Badaró 504, Centro, www.prediomartinelli.com.br), completed in 1929.

VIADUTO DO CHÁ

Going left down Rua Libero Badaró from the Edifício Martinelli brings you to the Vale do Anhangabaú, a narrow valley festooned with fountains and swaying palms and straddled by the **Viaduto do Chá.** Designed by 19th-century French architect Jules Martin, the Viaduto de Chá was the first of São Paulo's many overhead passes. Its original purpose was to facilitate transport between the coffee plantations that occupied the valley. In more recent times, viaducts have mushroomed throughout the city in an attempt to ease Sampa's crazy traffic flow.

From the Viaduto de Chá, you can get a sense of Sampa's intense activity as well as a great view of two of the city's most prestigious buildings. Inaugurated in 1939, the **Palácio Anhangabaú** (Viaduto do Chá 15) functions as São Paulo's city hall. The shrubbery sprouting from the rooftop is actually a garden featuring over 400 native plants, among them coffee bushes, sugarcane, and even a mango tree.

More dazzling is the **Teatro Municipal** (Praça Ramos de Azevedo, Centro, tel. 11/3223-3022, www.prefeitura.sp.gov.br/cidade/secretarias/cultura/teatromunicipal/). Built at the turn of the 20th century at the behest of São Paulo's coffee aristocracy, the theater reflects the opulence of the era (not to mention the art nouveau style of Paris's Opéra Garnier). Venetian mosaics, Florentine sculptures, Italian marble, gold leaf fixtures, and a chandelier with 7,000 crystals from Belgium are a few of the splendid trappings on display. Free guided tours are available (1 P.M. Tues. and Thurs., 10 A.M. Sat.).

LARGO DE SÃO FRANCISCO

Returning to Rua Libero Badaró from the *viaduto* and continuing west, a short walk will bring you to the Largo de São Francisco. Crowning this square is one of São Paulo's oldest churches, the **Igreja das Chagas do Seráphico Pai São Francisco** (Largo de São Francisco 173, Centro, tel. 11/3106-5297, 7 A.M.–5 P.M. Mon.–Fri., free). It is one of the city's finest examples of baroque architecture;

construction began in 1676 and lasted for well over a century. The well-preserved interior features plenty of gold-leaf paneling, which adds shimmers of light to this otherwise dimly lit church.

Also on the Largo is São Paulo's highly reputed Faculade de Direito (Law Faculty) and the **Igreja de São Francisco de Assis** (Largo de São Francisco 133, Centro, tel. 11/3291-2400, 7 A.M.–7 P.M. Mon.–Sun., free). Though it has suffered many alterations over the centuries, this church retains its original adobe walls from the 17th century.

MERCADO MUNICIPAL

Within easy walking distance from Pátio do Colégio and the São Bento Metrô stop is São Paulo's Mercado Municipal (Rua da Cantareira 306, Centro, tel. 11/3228-9332, www.mercadomunicipal.com.br, 6 A.M.–6 P.M. Mon.–Sat., 8 A.M.–4 P.M. Sun.), known affectionately by Paulistanos as the **"Mercadão"** (Big Market). Built in 1932, this vast neoclassical-style food hall featuring stained-glass windows with images of agricultural activities is a major mecca for the city's restaurateurs and foodies. Each day, over 1,000 tons of fresh produce and delicacies imported from all over Brazil and the world are purchased from its 300 stalls. If you don't feel like food shopping, simply feasting your eyes, nose, and taste buds on the variety of colors, aromas, and flavors is satisfying.

Should all the goods on display incite hunger pangs, head to the **Hocca Bar** (Rua G, Box 7), where you'll have to line up in order to savor the *pastéis de bacalhau* (deep-fried pastries filled with salted cod) that have been a favorite snack since 1952. Other traditional snacks can be found at the market's bars and *lanchonetes,* and at the recently renovated mezzanine, where a handful of restaurants offer a refreshing new slant on the food court concept.

PRAÇA DA REPÚBLICA

At the tail end of the 19th century, Praça da República was hardly very republican—instead it was a posh downtown square around which São Paulo's coffee barons built lavish city dwellings. However, as commerce—and its attendant trappings of noise, traffic, and riffraff—swept the city's center, the barons decamped to a new and more bucolic neighborhood that came to be known as Higienópolis. Their former downtown mansions were quickly (and lamentably) destroyed, giving way to modernist buildings, some of them still quite lovely, others sadly run-down. Today, Praça da República is a vibrant but somewhat forsaken square in need of a good renovation. On Sundays, it is the site of a colorful crafts and antiques market.

Two of the standout modernist buildings off of Praça da República have become Paulistano icons. Constructed between 1956 and 1965, **Edifício Itália** (Av. Ipiranga 344, Centro, tel. 11/2189-2929, www.terracoitalia.com.br) was built with the mission of surpassing the reigning Banespa building in height. And indeed, for a long time, it proudly held the title as tallest building, not only in town, but in all of Latin America. Today, it is still top-ranked among the city's skyscrapers. To take in the glorious view, ride the elevator up to the swank **Terraço Itália** restaurant, on the 42nd floor. If you don't want to splurge for a mediocre meal or pay a cover charge at the bar, during the week between 3 and 4 P.M. visits are free. Quite striking from the outside is the **Edifício Copan** (Av. Ipiranga 200), a curling S-shaped building that could only have been dreamed up by Oscar Niemeyer. The building is as famous as a living space as it is for its design—boasting over 1,160 apartments and close to 6,000 residents, it is rare the Paulistano who hasn't known someone who has lived here at some point in time.

Luz

Until the early 20th century, Luz wore its name—"Light"—well: It was one of São Paulo's more resplendent neighborhoods, with handsome buildings surrounding a bucolic park. In subsequent decades, it fell into disrepute and disrepair, with areas given over to prostitution and drugs. However, in the last decade, there has been a successful effort to revitalize the area. After dark, Luz is still quite sketchy and not a place to go wandering around, but during the day its growing roster of topnotch museums, many housed in renovated historical buildings, have given a new shine to the *bairro*. All attractions in the area are easily reached by taking the Metrô to Luz station.

ESTAÇÃO DA LUZ

The crowning landmark of the neighborhood, Estaçáo da Luz is a very grand, rosy red-brick train station that looks deliciously out of place plunked down in the middle of São Paulo's urban sprawl. It was designed by British architect Charles Henry Driver, and the materials used for its construction were shipped directly from England. Renovated in 2004, a portion houses the Museu da Língua Portuguesa, while the rest continues to function as a busy station linking the capital to towns in the surrounding region.

MUSEU DA LÍNGUA PORTUGUESA

Even if you don't read or speak Portuguese, you'll likely enjoy the Museu da Língua Portuguesa (Praça da Luz, tel. 11/3326-0775, www.museudalinguaportuguesa.org.br, 10 A.M.–6 P.M. Tues.–Sun., R$4, free Sat.). Fittingly located in the largest Portuguese-speaking city in the world, this original and imaginative museum relies on engaging interactive games and innovative multimedia to trace the fascinating history of the Portuguese language in Brazil.

PINACOTECA DO ESTADO

São Paulo's oldest art museum, the **Pinacoteca do Estado** (Praça da Luz 2, Luz, tel. 11/3229-9844, www.pinacoteca.sp.gov.br, 10 A.M.–6 P.M. Tues.–Sun., R$5, free Sat.) has been around since 1905. Back then, its collection consisted of a mere 26 paintings. Today, it has swollen to an impressive 7,000 works, most of them representing major Brazilian painters and sculptors of the 19th and 20th centuries. Aside from the permanent collection, the Pinacoteca hosts some of São Paulo's most compelling temporary exhibitions, featuring both national and international

artists who work in all media. The building itself—a neoclassical palace made of honey-colored brick that received an inspired renovation in the late 1990s—is spacious and showcases the art splendidly.

Downstairs a charming café serves pastries and light meals. Although the service is notoriously shoddy, sitting at an outside table facing the sculptures in the Parque da Luz more than compensates. Purchasing a ticket to the Pinacoteca also gives you access to its nearby sister gallery, the **Estação Pinacoteca** (Largo General Osório 86, Luz, tel. 11/3337-0185, 10 A.M.–6 P.M. Tues.–Sun.). Built in 1914 as a railroad warehouse, during the military dictatorship it was converted into the headquarters of the DOPS (Department of Political and Social Order), a repressive organ that specialized in torturing political prisoners. Following a renovation in 2003, it reopened as an extension of the Pinacoteca with a permanent collection of works by Brazilian modernists such as Tarsila do Amaral and Emiliano Di Cavalcanti as well as Picasso, Chagall, and Léger. Part of

Pinacoteca do Estado

© MICHAEL SOMMERS

SÃO PAULO

the building houses the Museu da Liberdade, where you can learn about Brazil's military dictatorship, view photos of political prisoners, and even (rather morbidly) step into the cells in which they were held.

SALA SÃO PAULO

Of the four best concert halls in the world from the point of view of impeccable acoustics, only one occupies a train station. The Sala São Paulo (Praça Júlio Prestes, Luz, tel. 11/3223-3966, www.salasaopaulo.art.br) is inside the grand hall of the restored Estação Júlio Prestes, an 1920s-era station whose interior, designed in Louis XVI-style, is both sober and grandiose. The auditorium roof is made from wooden panels that can be positioned to enhance the quality of whatever type of music is being played. The *sala* is the headquarters of OSESP (São Paulo State Symphony Orchestra). If you can't catch a performance, guided visits are available (tel. 11/3367-9573, 1 and 4 P.M. Mon.–Fri., 1:30 P.M. Sat., 2 P.M. Sun., R$5, free Sat.).

PARQUE DA LUZ

Adjacent to the Pinacoteca do Estado and directly across the street from the Estação da Luz, the Parque da Luz (Praça da Luz, Luz, tel. 11/3227-3545, 9 A.M.–6 P.M. Tues.–Sun.) is São Paulo's oldest public garden. Upon its completion in 1825, the park quickly became the favorite playground of the city's elite, who enjoyed strolling among its ponds, bandstands, and fig trees, eucalyptus, and imperial palms. In more recent times, the park was taken over by homeless people, junkies, and prostitutes. After a recent restoration—which included the introduction of a sculpture garden and beefed-up security—a few prostitutes still discreetly show off their wares, but the park is also popular with families, couples in love, and those seeking some bucolic respite.

MUSEU DE ARTE SACRA

Although the best of Brazilian religious art is in Minas Gerais and Bahia, São Paulo's Museu de Arte Sacra (Av. Tiradentes 676, Luz, tel. 11/3326-1373, http://artesacra

.sarasa.com.br, 11 A.M.–7 P.M. Tues.–Sun., R$4) does an admirable job of showcasing works culled from the churches of these two states as well as other Brazilian regions. The impressive 5,000-piece collection, which provides a wonderful overview of Brazilian baroque and rococo styles, includes sculptures and sacred artifacts fashioned out of wood, terra-cotta, silver, and gold. The museum is housed in the Mosteiro da Luz, a carefully conserved 18th-century monastery still inhabited by cloistered nuns.

Liberdade

In June 1908, a Japanese ship carrying 800 passengers docked at the port of Santos. Most of the immigrants on board made their way to the booming capital and settled in a central neighborhood known as Liberdade (Liberty). Lured by job opportunities, more Japanese followed and by the end of World War II, the *bairro* had consolidated its reputation as the city's Little Japan. Although the first generation of immigrants worked on coffee plantations, later generations became successful business people and politicians. Today, São Paulo boasts the largest Japanese population outside of Japan. More recently, Chinese and Korean immigrants have moved into Liberdade, but the heart and soul of the neighborhood—not to mention most of the stores and restaurants—are still Japanese. To get to Liberdade, take the Metrô to Liberdade station.

More exotic than attractive, Liberdade's core is concentrated around the red-lantern-lined streets of Rua Galvão Bueno, Rua dos Estudantes, and Rua da Glória. Here you'll find scores of great restaurants and supermarkets, along with emporiums displaying a wide range of wares from semiprecious stones, Buddhist oratories, and silk kimonos to Hello Kitty paraphernalia. On weekends, during the day, the Praça da Liberdade is animated by the **Feira da Liberdade** (www.feirada liberdade.com.br). The stands at this open-air market sell everything from Japanese medicinal herbs to cheap and delicious bowls of stir-fried *yakissoba,* a mixture of noodles, meat, and vegetables that has become a Paulistano staple, second only to sushi.

IMMIGRATION

São Paulo's history and identity are indissociably linked to immigration. One of the most multicultural cities on the planet, the city was built by immigrants, who arrived from all over Brazil and the world, lured by the endless opportunities available. As a result, Paulistanos are an incredibly diverse people who live, work, and mingle together in harmony, without the ethnic conflicts that affect some other major metropolises. Among the ethnic groups who have left their mark most deeply on the city are Italians (approximately 60 percent of the people boast at least one Italian ancestor), Spanish, Germans, Japanese, Lebanese, and Syrians.

For an in-depth look at the history of immigration and its impact on the fabric of city, visit the **Memorial do Imigrante** (Rua Visconde de Parnaiba 1316, Moóca, tel. 11/6669-1866, www.memorialdoimigrante.sp.gov.br, 10 A.M.–5 P.M. Tues.-Sun., R$4). The museum hosts temporary exhibits and an interesting permanent collection of photographs, documents, and artifacts, such as household objects and clothing. Even more compelling is the neoclassical architectural ensemble that shelters the museum. Known as the Hospedaria dos Imigrantes, these buildings lodged newly arrived immigrants – up to 10,000 of them at a time. Upon docking at the port in Santos, the new arrivals were herded onto trains bound for the Hospedaria (which had its own train station), where they then waited for coffee plantation and factory owners to come with offers of work. While in limbo – they couldn't leave without a signed contract – immigrants lived in immense dormitory rooms and were under constant surveillance by armed guards so they wouldn't run away. Between 1888 and 1978, over three million immigrants passed through the Hospedaria.

Although the memorial is a quick five-minute walk from Brás and Bresser Metrô stations, the neighborhood is a bit dodgy, so take a cab from the station. On weekends, for R$4, you can take advantage of an antique tram that runs from the museum entrance to Bresser Metrô as well as an old-fashioned steam train that connects the complex with both Brás and Moóca Metrô stations.

SÃO PAULO

Those with a more lingering interest in the history of Japanese immigrants in Brazil can check out the **Museu da Imigração Japonesa** (Rua São Joaquim 381, Liberdade, 7th-9th floors, tel. 11/3209-9565, www.nihonsite.com/muse/index.cfm, 1:30–5:30 P.M. Tues.–Sun., R$5). Aside from some interesting documentation, there is also a pleasant Japanese-style garden on the rooftop.

Higienópolis

Lying west of Praça da República, the lovely residential *bairro* of Higienópolis developed during the late 1890s. Relative to the increasingly congested and commercialized Centro, the elevated heights of this region offered a "hygienic" alternative to the frequent floods and epidemics that put an increasing damper on life in the city's downtown. By 1900, Sampa's wealthiest families were flocking to Higienópolis in droves. The opulent mansions they built in the early 1900s gave way to seductively streamlined deco and modernist apartment buildings of the '30s, '40s, and '50s. Although only a few of the houses remain, many of the apartment buildings are still standing.

Higienópolis remains one of São Paulo's most traditional and wealthiest residential *bairros,* with a who's who of famous dwellers ranging from former president Fernando Henrique Cardoso to iconic rocker Rita Lee. It also has a significant (both secular and orthodox) Jewish population, which accounts for the many kosher products available in the neighborhood's numerous delicatessens. Although there aren't many sights, there are quite a few pleasant little restaurants and cafés, and simply wandering around—scoping out people and apartment buildings—is an agreeable way to spend a low-key afternoon. Architecture buffs take note—among the most striking modernist buildings (in order of walkability) are the following: **Edifício Piauí** (Rua Piauí 428, at the corner of Rua Sabará), **Edifício Cinderela** (Rua Maranhão 163, at the corner of Rua Sabará), **Edifício Lausanne** (Av. Higienópolis 101), **Edifício Prudência** (Av. Higienópolis 265), **Edifício Parque das Hortênsias** (Av. Angélica 1106), **Edifício Bretagne** (Av. Higienópolis 938), **Edifício Louveira** (Rua Piauí 1081), and **Edifício Arper** (Rua Pernambuco 15). Close to Edifício Cinderela is the very charming **Praça Villaboim,** a tiny jewel of a park surrounded by restaurants, bars, and boutiques.

(Avenida Paulista

While Paris has the Champs-Elysées, and New York boasts Fifth Avenue, São Paulo wouldn't be São Paulo without Avenida Paulista (www.avenidapaulista.com.br). In comparison to these other two famous main drags, Avenida Paulista is more varied, vital, messy, and raw. In fact, the first time you lay eyes upon *a Paulista* (as residents refer to it), you'll be in for somewhat of a shock. The multilane thoroughfare resembles a freeway, and the roughly hewn, unpolished concrete skyscrapers that line it really do resemble a "concrete jungle." It's hard to imagine that a little over a century ago, this 2.8-kilometer (1.7-mile) *mega-avenida* was a mere country road. In the late 1800s, it was widened into a European-style grand avenue by coffee barons and industrial magnates who chose to live along the *avenida* in sumptuous mansions that were built in wildly diverging architectural styles. Shortly after, Avenida Paulista was the first of São Paulo's streets to be paved (with asphalt imported from Germany). It was also the first to go completely vertical in the 1940s, as São Paulo's industrial economy grew at rates of up to 60 percent a year. By the 1970s, the avenue had been widened to keep up with escalating traffic, and almost all of its beautiful mansions had been replaced by skyscrapers (one of the very few survivors is now a McDonald's) housing banks and multinational companies.

In recent years, corporate headquarters have moved south to the spanking new *bairros* of Brooklin and Berrini. However, Avenida Paulista still remains the city's symbol and vibrant nerve center: a place where commerce and culture thrive (the *avenida* concentrates numerous cultural centers and large-screen cinemas) amid urban hustle and bustle. Strolling along its wide black-and-white mosaic sidewalks may not be the most relaxing experience in the world, but nowhere else in the city comes close to capturing and condensing the city's energy and adrenaline. This is especially the case whenever the city is in the throes of a major protest or celebration (particularly political or sports victories); inevitably, traffic comes to a standstill and *a Paulista* explodes into partying mode.

CONJUNTO NACIONAL

The elegant Conjunto Nacional (Av. Paulista 2073, Cerqueira Cesár, tel. 11/3179-0000, www.ccn.com.br, 9 A.M.–10 P.M. Mon.–Fri., 10 A.M.–9:30 P.M. Sat., 2–8 P.M. Sun.) was Latin America's first shopping center. Inaugurated in 1956, by the 1960s it had become Sampa's most glamorous address. Those who lived in the coveted modernist apartments were treated to stunning views (the skyscrapers were yet to come) and could camp out at the swanky Restaurante Fasano, where the likes of Marlene Dietrich and Nat King Cole entertained other international luminaries such as Ginger Rogers, David Niven, President Eisenhower, and Fidel Castro (the latter two on separate occasions). After falling into decay and suffering damage from a fire in the late 1970s, it wasn't until the late '90s that a restored Conjunto recaptured some of its former glory. Today, it is a great place to have a *cafezinho,* take in a movie, or browse through the fantastic range of books at the Livraria Cultura.

PARQUE TRIANON

Back in the day when Avenida Paulista was the domain of the coffee aristocracy, Parque Trianon (Rua Peixoto Gomide 949, Cerqueira César, tel. 11/3289-2160, 6 A.M.–6 P.M. daily), less grandly known as Parque Tenente Siqueira Campos, was *the* place to go strolling.

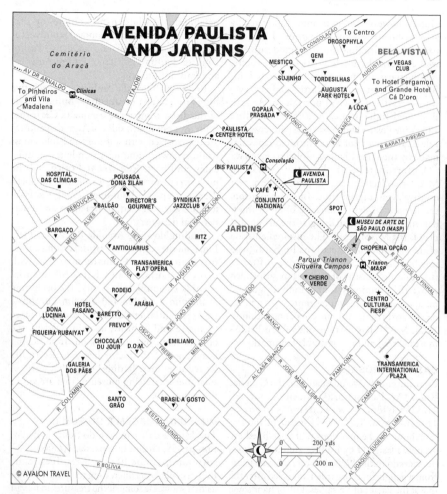

AVENIDA PAULISTA AND JARDINS

Originally designed in 1892 by French landscaper Paul Villon, the park received a more tropical makeover in 1968 by Roberto Burle Marx, who played up the exuberant textures and colors of the native Atlantic forest. Today, this small but surprisingly lush oasis, punctuated with benches, sculptures, and fountains, provides a welcome contrast to the congested avenue. By day, the park attracts a colorful mixture of visitors—from bookworms to lunching tycoons. Its more jungly depths are legendary as a gay cruising area.

◖ MUSEU DE ARTE DE SÃO PAULO

Paulistanos are justifiably proud of the Museu de Arte de São Paulo (MASP, Av. Paulista 1578, Cerqueira César, São Paulo, tel. 11/3251-5644, www.masp.art.br, 11 A.M.–6 P.M. Tues.–Sun., till 8 P.M. Thurs., R$15, free Tues.), considered one of Latin America's finest art museums. The top floor boasts Brazil's most important collection of European art, including multiple works by Flemish, Italian Renaissance, and French Impressionist painters along with some wonderful Degas sculptures in bronze. Foreign visitors, however, might be more captivated by artists who are less known outside of Brazil—paintings by leading Brazilian modernists as well as works by foreign artists/adventurers. Among the most interesting of these were Jean-Baptiste Debret, a French artist and engraver who specialized in vivid portraits of African slaves and Indians in early 19th-century Rio, and Franz Post, a Dutch baroque painter whose Edenic renderings of Brazil inspired tapestries made by the famed French Gobelins factory.

Unfortunately, of the 7,000 works in MASP's collection, only around 500 are ever on display at a given time. In compensation, the temporary exhibitions are often of international caliber. As striking as the art on display is the MASP itself. The inspired creation of the vanguard architect Lina Bo Bardi (who was born in Italy and naturalized in Brazil), the building consists of a giant box suspended above the ground by four spindly bright red pillars. The effect is quite impressive, and it's hardly surprising that since its completion in 1968, MASP has become one of São Paulo's most beloved and recognizable landmarks.

CASA DAS ROSAS

Near the end of Avenida Paulista, the Casa das Rosas (Av. Paulista 37, Cerqueira César, tel. 11/3285-6986, www.casadasrosas.sp.gov.br, 11 A.M.–9 P.M. Tues.–Sun.) is one of the few remaining of the mansions that once lined the avenue. Designed by leading architect Ramos de Azevedo in the 1920s, the *casa* takes its name from a delightful rose garden, modeled after the one at the Palace of Versailles. Full of handsome wooden furnishings and stained-glass windows, the house itself is devoted to poetry—aside from frequent readings and events, the library boasts over 30,000 volumes of verse.

Jardins

Avenida Paulista is the final frontier of Sampa's downtown area. Lying to the southwest is the leafy sprawl appropriately known as Jardins (Gardens). Modeled after the British garden suburbs of the early 20th century, Jardins is a wealthy and perennially fashionable residential neighborhood whose name conjures up lifestyles of Brazil's rich and famous. Jardins actually embraces four separate "gardens": Jardim Paulista, Jardim Paulistano, Jardim América, and Jardim Europa.

Bordering Avenida Paulista, the exclusive high-rise condos of **Jardim Paulista** (part of the district known as Cerqueira César that spills over onto both sides of Avenida Paulista) are interspersed with some of São Paulo's most world-renowned and über-trendy restaurants, cafés, and bars. **Rua Oscar Freire** and the posh streets surrounding it contain a shopper's dream of upscale boutiques selling the fashionable wares of leading Brazilian and international designers.

Leading down to Avenida Brigadeiro Faria Lima, on the edge of Pinheiros, Jardim Paulista turns into **Jardim Paulistano,** an area with many restaurants and bars. Meanwhile, Avenida Estados Unidos marks the beginning of **Jardim América** and **Jardim Europa**—two residential enclaves that are even more exclusive and wealthy, as evidenced by the opulent mansions that peek out from behind heavily guarded, thickly hedged, electrically fenced-in estates. Jardim Europa has a trio of small but interesting museums that are worth dropping into.

MUSEU DA IMAGEM E DO SOM (MIS)

The Museu da Imagem e do Som (MIS, Av. Europa 158, Jardim Europa, tel. 11/3062-9197, www.mis.sp.gov.br, 10 A.M.–6 P.M. Tues.–Sun., R$3) usually hosts interesting temporary exhibits that showcase some of the treasures in its vast archive of historic and contemporary Brazilian photographs. On weekends, international shorts and art films are screened in the theater.

FUNDAÇÃO CULTURAL EMA GORDON KLABIN

Close to the Museu da Imagem e do Som, the Fundação Cultural Ema Gordon Klabin (Rua Portugal, Jardim Europa, tel. 11/3062-5245, www.fcegk.org.br, 2–6 P.M. Tues., Thurs., Fri., R$10) is located in a fabulous mansion inspired by Berlin's Palace of Sanssouci. This private home was built in the 1950s by wealthy philanthropist and paper and cellulose heiress Ema Gordon Klabin. Klabin was so concerned with showcasing her constantly growing international and Brazilian art collection that she had the ceilings built to heights of 5 meters (16 feet). As you wander from room to room, you'll encounter everything from 6th-century B.C. Greek vases to paintings by Marc Chagall and Chaim Soutine. A highlight of the beautiful garden is the orchid hothouse.

MUSEU DA CASA BRASILEIRA
Housed inside a 1930s saffron-colored villa, the Museu da Casa Brasileira (Av. Brigadeiro Faria Lima 2705, Jardim Europa, tel. 11/3032-3727, www.mcb.sp.gov.br, R$4, free Sun.) displays an eclectic permanent collection of Brazilian and international furniture dating from the 17th century to the present. It also displays temporary exhibits focusing on various aspects of furniture and design. A delightful place for lunch or afternoon tea is the **Quinta do Museu** restaurant (www.quintadomuseu.com.br), where tables are scattered around the villa's original kitchen and throughout the adjacent garden.

Pinheiros and Vila Madalena
The major thoroughfare of Avenida Brigadeiro Faria Lima marks the southwestern frontier of Jardins. South lies the upscale commercial neighborhood of **Itaim Bibi,** where some of the city's achingly trendy restaurants and bars open and close with impressive velocity. North are the adjacent *bairros* of Pinheiros and Vila Madalena. Pinheiros mixes a forest of commercial high-rises with some interesting boutiques, galleries, restaurants, and a lively nightlife scene.

North of Pinheiros, Vila Madalena is Sampa's bohemian *bairro* par excellence. Originally, the area was a blue collar neighborhood where workers lived in small bungalows surrounded by gardens where they raised livestock and vegetables. In the 1970s, students and professors from the nearby University of São Paulo—along with artists, musicians, and hippies—began to migrate here for the affordable housing combined with a relaxed, bucolic setting. Many have never left, which explains the lingering intellectual/artist vibe tinged with vestiges of hippiedom and accounts for street names such as Rua da Harmonia (Harmony), Rua da Simpatia (Sympathy), and Rua do Girassol (Sunflower). By day, Vila Madalena is a wonderfully laid-back place to wander around. Rua Aspiculta and surrounding streets such as Rua Fradique Coutinho and Rua Fidalga are lined with funky boutiques, second-hand stores, and numerous art galleries where you can spend hours browsing. At night, the *bairro* buzzes with activity as its restaurants, bars, and clubs fill up with a mixed and alternative crowd.

INSTITUTO TOMIE OHTAKE
The Pinheiros neighborhood's most compelling attraction is the Instituto Tomie Ohtake (Av. Brigadeiro Faria Lima 201, tel. 11/2245-1900, www.institutotomieohtake.org.br, 11 A.M.–8 P.M. Tues.–Sun.), which occupies the first two floors of a wildly flamboyant office tower whose curving facade is painted in tones of magenta and violet. The building showcases the signature style of one of Brazil's most daring architects, Ruy Ohtake (responsible for the design of two of Sampa's chicest hotels: the Unique and the Renaissance, both located in Jardim Paulista). Meanwhile, the institute pays homage to Ruy's mother, Japanese-Brazilian artist Tomie Ohtake. Her paintings and engravings that are on display, ranging from early landscapes to later abstractions, all incorporate Japanese artistic elements, most notably traditional brushstroke techniques. Other galleries also display temporary exhibits of contemporary art. In the Grand Hall, the **IT** store sells an enticing array of objects, jewelry, and T-shirts by innovative Brazilian artists and designers. There is also a sleekly attractive restaurant/café, specializing in Pan-Asian-Brazilian creations, that is a hot spot for Sunday brunch.

Parque do Ibirapuera
Paulistanos' equivalent of Central Park is Parque do Ibirapuera (entrances on Av. Pedro

Alvares Cabral, Av. República do Libano, and Av. IV Centenario, tel. 11/5574-5177, 5 A.M.– midnight daily, free), a sweeping 160-hectare (395-acre) expanse of green that Paulistanos unironically refer to as their *"praia"* (beach). Indeed, on any given sunny, summer weekend its tree-shaded lawns are so blanketed by sprawlers, tanners, readers, and picnickers that the comparison is not far-fetched. Created in the 1950s to commemorate Sampa's 400th anniversary, the park project was headed by two stellar talents of the day: Oscar Niemeyer and Roberto Burle Marx. Various curvy, concrete, well-illuminated Niemeyer pavilions today house a handful of topnotch museums, earning the area the nickname of "Museulândia." Contrasting with the futuristic buildings, Burle Marx's inspired landscaping mingles sweeping lawns with ponds, wooded areas, and bursts of flowers and tropical foliage. There is also a planetarium, a Japanese pavilion modeled after the Katsura Imperial Palace in Kyoto, and a Bosque de Leitura (Reading Woods), where on Sundays you can borrow books from a portable library and take to the trees for some reading. Music lovers can rock out at the free open-air concerts often held at a Roman-style amphitheater or enjoy more erudite melodies at the Niemeyer-designed **Auditório Ibirapuera.** The athletically inclined can rent bikes, or go jogging, skateboarding, or rollerblading along scenic trails, but be aware that they can become congested with toned and trim locals.

The easiest way to get to the park is to take the Metrô to Brigadeiro station. Then take one of many buses or walk (around 30 minutes) down Avenida Brigadeiro Luís Antônio until you reach Portão 9, one of numerous entrances to the park. Dominating the Praça General Estilac Leal is the dramatic **Monumento às Bandeirantes.** The work of renowned modernist sculptor Victor Brecheret, this imposing granite landmark pays homage to the intrepid 16th- and 17th- century adventurers of Portuguese origin (the *bandeirantes*) who opened up much of Brazil's interior.

PAVILHÃO DA BIENAL DE ARTE

Designed by Oscar Niemeyer, the Pavilhão da Bienal de Arte is a vast rectangular building with glass windows and sky-high ceilings. It opened in 1957 to house the **São Paulo Bienal de Arte,** one of the world's largest and most important art biennials. Held in even-numbered years, during the months of October and November, this event reunites more than 12,000 works by national and international artists. There are usually plenty of misses along with the hits, but since it is free (and arguing about the quality of the art in a bar afterwards is a spirited Paulistano ritual) you can wander around to your heart's content, focusing on the provocative stuff and ignoring the drivel. Many other events take place at the Pavilhão, among them the Bienal de Arquitetura (held in even-numbered years) and Brazil's twice-yearly biggest fashion event, São Paulo Fashion Week.

On the third floor is a small branch of the **Museu de Arte Contemporânea (MAC)** (Pavilhão da Bienal, 3rd Fl., Ibirapuera, tel. 11/5573-5255, www.mac.usp.br, 10 A.M.–7 P.M. Tues.–Sun., free). Although its permanent collection is modest, interesting temporary exhibitions of contemporary art are held here. To view the much more impressive main collection— considered one of Brazil's finest collections of contemporary art—you'll have to visit the MAC at the University of São Paulo (USP, Rua da Reitoria 160, Cidade Universitaria, tel. 11/3091-3039, 10 A.M.–6 P.M. Tues.–Fri., 10 A.M.–4 P.M. Sat.–Sun., free). Plans are in the works to reunite the entire MAC collection within the park's Detran building, hopefully by 2009.

MUSEU DE ARTE MODERNA

The first modern art museum to be founded in Latin America, the Museu de Arte Moderna (MAM, Av. Pedro Alvares Cabral, Portão 3, Ibirapuera, tel. 11/5549-9688, www.mam.org.br, 10 A.M.–6 P.M. Tues.–Sun., R$5.50, free Sun.) actually focuses more on Brazilian contemporary works than modern art per se (this due to the confusing fact that in 1963, the MAM's director donated the modern collection to MAC—as a result, when the

the Museu de Arte Moderna with the reflection of Parque do Ibirapuera

museum began rebuilding its collection, its focus was on contemporary pieces). A trio of temporary exhibits showcase works from the permanent collection along with visiting national and international exhibitions. The curving glass and concrete building was designed by Oscar Niemeyer and then renovated by Lina Bo Bardi in the 1970s. Aside from a museum shop, there is a lovely minimalist restaurant, serving contemporary fare, that looks out onto the sculpture garden and the **Oca,** a spacey dome-shaped Niemeyer pavilion—its name, "Oca," comes from its resemblance to similarly shaped indigenous dwellings—where temporary art exhibits and other events are held.

MUSEU AFRO BRASIL

Niemeyer also designed the pavilion that houses the Museu Afro Brasil (Pavilhão Padre Manoel da Nóbrega, Portão 10, Ibirapuera, tel. 11/5579-0593, www.museuafrobrasil.com.br, 10 A.M.–5 P.M. Wed.–Mon.). This is a museum you shouldn't miss: Its three floors offer a compelling look at the rich historical, cultural, and artistic legacies of Brazil's Afro-Descendentes population, dating from the 16th century to the present day. Highlights include finely crafted African artifacts along with objects and clothing used in Afro-Brazilian celebrations and rituals. Particularly harrowing is a room devoted to the slave ships that brought so many Africans—literally packed side-by-side like sardines—to the New World. Insightful temporary exhibits by black artists from Brazil and overseas offer more contemporary visions of the African diaspora.

Greater São Paulo City

If you have some extra time, São Paulo has several other interesting attractions that are worth visiting, despite being slightly more far-flung.

MUSEU LASAR SEGALL

Although not well known outside of Brazil, Lasar Segall is one of the country's most singular modernist artists. A large portion of his paintings, drawings, and engravings can be seen at the Museu Lasar Segall (Rua Berta 111, Vila Mariana, tel. 11/5574-7322, 2–7 P.M. Tues.–Sat., 2–6 P.M. Sun., free), where he lived and worked from 1932 until his death in 1957. Born in Lithuania, Segall delved into German expressionism before immigrating to São Paulo, where he was seduced by the color palette and textures of his tropical surroundings. This lovely museum provides a great introduction to his colorful universe. To get to the museum, take the Metrô to Vila Mariana.

MUSEU DO IPIRANGA

History buffs will enjoy a visit to the Museu do Ipiranga (Parque da Independência, Ipiranga, tel. 11/6165-8000, www.mp.usp.br, 9 A.M.–5 P.M. Tues.–Sun., R$2), also known as the Museu Paulista. It occupies a grand, Renaissance-style palace built in 1890 to commemorate Brazilian independence (which took place in 1822; it took a few decades for the final project to be approved). The museum is chock-full of paintings, furnishings, household objects, and other artifacts that conjure up 19th- and early-20th-century Brazilian society. Fans of things royal can delight in the many knickknacks belonging to the Brazilian imperial family. The surrounding Parque do Ipiranga is also called Parque da Independência because it was here that Dom Pedro I proclaimed Brazil's independence. In fact, the spot where he dramatically cried out: "Independence or Death!" is marked by a monument beneath which lies the tomb of Dom Pedro I and his wife, Empress Leopoldina. Many buses pass by the park, departing from Praça da Sé (4113), Praça da República (4205, 4631), and Vila Mariana (4706) Metrô station.

INSTITUTO BUTANTAN

Adults and kids with a fondness for reptiles will be in heaven at the Instituto Butantan (Av. Vital Brasil 1500, Butantã, tel. 11/3726-7222, www.butantan.gov.br, 9 A.M.–5 P.M. Tues.–Sun., R$5). The institute is one of the world's foremost research centers of poisonous snakes and insects, with the aim of creating antivenin serums. Located on the University of São Paulo's sprawling campus, it is home to some 54,000 slithering creatures, ranging from common Brazilian anacondas and boa constrictors to exotic imports such as the Indian python, which can measure up to a spooky 6 meters (20 feet) in length. There is also a colorful collection of iguanas, scorpions, frogs, and lethal spiders. Also on the premises is the Museu de Microbiologia, where you can gaze through microscopes at everything from fleas and fungi to human blood samples. To get to the *instituto,* take the Metrô to Cidade Universitária and then a quick taxi ride (finding your way by foot is tricky).

FUNDAÇÃO MARIA LUIZA E OSCAR AMERICANO

Located in the chic and wealthy suburban *bairro* of Morumbi, the Fundação Maria Luiza e Oscar Americano (Av. Morumbi 4077, www.fundacaooscaramericano.org.br, 11 A.M.–5 P.M. Tues.–Fri., 10 A.M.–5 P.M. Sat.–Sun., R$8) occupies an elegant streamlined house, reminiscent of a Frank Lloyd Wright design. It was built in 1952 as a residence for wealthy engineer Oscar Americano and his wife, who were avid collectors of Brazilian art. The interior displays an impressive ensemble of paintings, furnishings, and religious art as well as some objects belonging to Brazil's imperial family, such as Princesa Isabel's furniture and Princesa Leopoldina's fine porcelain. After checking out the art, take a leisurely stroll through the beautifully landscaped gardens, whose wooded areas are home to over 50 types of birds. If you come in the afternoon, treat yourself to the lavish high tea (R$40), which includes brioches, croissants, tarts, and cakes.

MEMORIAL DA AMÉRICA LÁTINA

Niemeyer fans will either love or disdain this late '80s ensemble of nine concrete buildings that comprise the Memorial da América Látina (Av. Auro Soares de Moura Andrade 664, Barra Funda, tel. 11/3823-4600, www.memorial.org.br, 9 A.M.–6 P.M. Tues.–Sun., free). The absence of greenery accentuates the barrenness of the architecture. Of more interest is what's inside the buildings themselves. The Pavilhão da Criatividade contains an enticing permanent exhibition of traditional arts and crafts from all over Latin America, while the Salão de Atos houses Portinari's giant 1949 masterpiece, *Tiradentes,* painted to honor the 19th-century Mineiro freedom fighter. Contemporary art exhibits as well as dance, theater, and film events frequently take place. To get here, take the Metrô to Barra Funda.

NIGHTLIFE

Sampa has one of the hippest, most happening, and varied culture and nightlife scenes this hemisphere has ever seen. In terms of performing arts, aside from its own home-grown talent, São Paulo lures the best Brazil—and the world—has to offer. Meanwhile, there are cafés, bars, lounges, and clubs that cater to every walk of life. Unlike other Brazilian cities, whose coastlines and tropical climes create nocturnal options that tend to be outdoors, Sampa's indoor night spots invest heavily in decor, ambiance, and vibe—the result is something for every urban *"tribo"* (tribe) under the moon.

Centro

Vast portions of Centro are deserted after dark. However, a nascent revitalization, coupled with the presence of some of the city's most traditional happy hour bars, means that the area has some authentic watering holes that are worth checking out (as long as you take a taxi).

BARS

Salve Jorge (Praça Antônio Prado 17, Centro, tel. 11/3107-0123, www.barsalve jorge.com.br, 11 A.M.–11 P.M. Mon.–Fri., noon–7 P.M. Sat.), is the offspring of a favorite Vila Madalena bar and restaurant. Its recent arrival in the heart of São Paulo has signaled the hopeful beginnings of Centro's renewal. Upon entering, your eyes will definitely be drawn to the gorgeous crystal chandeliers and 4,000 bottles suspended from the sky-high ceiling. However, the bankers, lawyers, and stock traders (the Stock Exchange is across the street) who pour in after the work day is done are just thankful that they finally got a happy hour haven in their very own neighborhood.

Bar Léo (Rua Aurora 100, Centro, tel.

11/3221-0247, www.barleo.com.br, 11 A.M.–8:30 P.M. Mon.–Fri., 11 A.M.–6 P.M. Sat.) is a small, simple, and beloved old-style *boteco* that has been serving up the city's iciest, frothiest, most delicious draft since the early '60s (the bar itself dates back to 1940). You'll be hard pressed to find sitting space during weekday happy hours and Saturday afternoons. However, the beer, bonhomie, and home cooking are worth standing for. Aside from daily lunch specials, tasty *petiscos* include *bolinhos de bacalhau* (salted cod balls) and a mean roast beef sandwich, known as the *sanduíche polaco.*

Part of the fame of **Bar Brahma**'s (Av. São João 677, Centro, tel. 11/3333-0855, www.barbrahmasp.com, 11:30 A.M.–1 A.M. Mon.–Wed., 11:30 A.M.–2 A.M. Thurs.–Fri., 11:30 A.M.–3 A.M. Sat., 11:30 A.M.–midnight Sun., cover R$5–45) is due to its location at the corner of São João and Ipiranga avenues. This famous crossroads—a symbol of Paulistano glamor days—was eternalized by singer/composer Caetano Veloso in his paean "Sampa." Although the handsomely restored bar (which opened in 1948 and then was closed for most of the '90s) has lost some of its former bohemian cachet, it continues to be a classic address that you should visit at least once. Old-guard singers perform standards from yesteryear, and the draft beer (Brahma, of course) is always perfectly chilled.

The **Estadão** (Viaduto 9 de Julho 193, Centro, tel. 11/3257-7121, www.estadaolanches .com.br, open 24 hours daily) earned its name from the fact that São Paulo's first ever 24-hour bar and luncheonette was conveniently located next to the offices of the *Estado de São Paulo* newspaper. When it first opened in the 1960s, it was a favorite haunt of journalists. They still frequent the place all night long, as do taxi drivers, politicians, office boys, rockers, and revelers of all stripes. Little has changed about the white-tiled, fruit-festooned bar since then—including customers' predilection for its famously gargantuan *pernil* (pork) sandwich, a Sampa classic. The beer is always icy, but fresh fruit juice can be whipped up at a moment's notice.

GAY SAMPA

Although Rio's more exhibitionistic/hedonistic gay scene is more legendary, Sampa's gay offerings are much more diverse and eclectic, and often more underground. In Centro, the area between Praça da República and Largo do Arouche shows few signs of gayness during the day, aside from a smattering of funky clothing boutiques catering specifically to gay boys who want to make an indelible impression. After dark, however, the area attracts a fantastically mixed (but definitely not fashionable nor yuppie) gay crowd of all ages as well as trannies and hookers. Most bars are on the once-elegant Avenida Vieira de Carvalho. The scene is kind of seedy, but very vibrant. Gringos are actually better off going in the company of a Brazilian pal or two.

In terms of clubs, **Cantho** (Largo do Arouche 32, Centro, tel. 11/3362-1295, www.cantho.com. br, 11 P.M.-5 A.M. Wed. and Fri.-Sat., 9 P.M.-5 A.M. Sun., R$15-20) reels in a 35-and-over clientele with '70s and '80s tunes, glittery globes, and lots of Cher and Madonna videos as well as strategically placed sofas in dark corners.

Just off Avenida Paulista – in the Consolação district – the bars and clubs on Rua Augusta and Rua Frei Caneca (nicknamed Rua Gay Caneca) attract a younger, more alternative GLS (*gay, lesbica, e simpatisante;* i.e., gay-friendly) public. Although very eclectic, **A Lôca** attracts a big gay and lesbian crowd, especially on Sundays, as does the **Vegas Club** in Consolação.

On the other side of *a Paulista,* Jardins is the playground of upwardly mobile and fashionable gays and lesbians, who frequent sophisticated cafés, bistros, and bars such as the **Ritz**. More geared to males is **Director's Gourmet** (Alameda Franca 1552, Cerqueira César, tel. 11/3064-7958, www.gourmetbar. com.br, 10 P.M.-3 A.M. Tues.-Sat., 9 P.M.-3 A.M. Sun.), a small and dusky bar that pays homage to the seventh art with a director's chair suspended from the ceiling, classic movie posters

plastering the walls, and a menu of gourmet sandwiches named after famous directors. Entertainment is provided by DJs spinning seductive mixes of pop, electric, and house music.

One of Vila Madalena's few GLS bars, **Farol Madalena** (Rua Jericó 179, Vila Madalena, tel. 11/3032-6470, www.farolmadalena.com.br, 7 P.M.-1 A.M. Tues.-Sat., 5 P.M.-midnight Sun., cover R$5-7) is a buzzing lesbian hot spot where girls let off steam while listening to live MPB and rock. The innovative bar menu includes *petiscos* such as sautéed shimeji mushrooms and chicken wings with banana sauce.

Meanwhile the biggest and trendiest club (gay or otherwise) in town is **The Week** (Rua Guaicurus 324, Lapa, tel. 11/3872-9966, www.theweek.com.br, 10 P.M.-close Fri.-Sat., R$30-40). Within its impressive 6,000 square meters (65,000 square feet) are two dance floors, three lounges, six bars, and a deck with a swimming pool. Saturday nights' "Babylon" parties are legendary. Homegrown and international DJs spin electronic and techno tunes with such verve that the public often ends up quite literally baring their chests.

Several gay and lesbian happenings have become major city events. For two weeks every November, hundreds of short and long features from all over the world – all dealing with themes of sexual diversity – invade various cinemas and cultural centers during the **Mix Brasil Festival** (www.mixbrasil.com.br). And in July, São Paulo hosts one of the planet's biggest and most festive gay pride parades. The **Parada de Orgulho GLBT** (www.paradasp. org.br) offers millions of people an excuse to take to Avenida Paulista, which is flooded with *trio elétricos* blasting party music. For an in-depth guide to gay Sampa (in Portuguese), pick up *Guia GLS São Paulo* by Sérgio Ripardi (Publifolha, 2007), a talented and openly gay journalist who writes for the city's main newspaper, *Folha de São Paulo.*

Avenida Paulista

Although there are few nightlife options right on Avenida Paulista, behind it—in the districts known as Consolação (adjacent to Rua de Consolação) and Bela Vista (which includes Bixiga)—bars and clubs run the gamut from sleazy dives, go-go clubs, and 24-hour fluorescent sidewalk bars to cutting-edge hot spots that attract a younger and extremely eclectic crowd.

BARS

Funky, offbeat, and laid-back, **Drosophyla** (Rua Pedro Taques 80, Consolação, www.drosophyla.com.br, 8 P.M.–1:30 A.M. Mon.–Wed., 8 P.M.–2 A.M. Thurs.–Sat.) occupies a lovely 1940s house that features a back yard filled with lime, pear, and *jabuticaba* trees. An arty crowd regularly gathers to converse amid the mellow tunes and visual kitsch that includes lamps made from macaroni and aquariums filled with dead cell phones. The imaginative menu's culinary influences range from Mineiro (empanadas filled with Minas cheese) to Polynesian (marinated raw tuna in coconut milk). The

Avenida Paulista

caipirinhas—mango with *pimenta rosa* and *carambola* (star fruit) with basil—are delicious.

Choperia Opção (Rua Carlos Comenale 97, Bela Vista, tel. 11/3288-7823, 4 P.M.–close daily) is a good *opção* for a cool drink within spitting distance of Avenida Paulista. Hidden conveniently behind the MASP, its plastic tables and chairs are shaded by two enormous rubber trees. The clientele veers towards preppy. The *chope* isn't that great for a *choperia*, but the *caipiroskas*—vodka mixed with kiwis, passion fruit, and strawberries—pack a wallop.

NIGHTCLUBS

A Lôca (Rua Frei Caneca 916, Bela Vista, tel. 11/3159-8889, www.aloca.com.br, midnight–6 A.M. Thurs., midnight–10 A.M. Fri.–Sat., 7 P.M.–6 A.M. Sun., cover R$20) is one of Sampa's most legendary underground *"infern-inhos"* (little hells). Its dark caverlike innards attract a colorfully vanguard mix of gays, lesbians, drag queens, rockers, and alternatives of all types and stripes itching to dance the night away to rock and electronica. Theme nights abound, so check the listings in advance.

Gloria (Rua 13 de Maio 830, Bela Vista, tel. 11/3287-3700, www.clubegloria.com.br, 11 P.M.–close Fri.–Sat., cover R$25–35) was formerly a church (in the 19th century) and an underground theater (in the late 20th century) before its recent transformation into a nightclub. Vestiges of its former lives have been integrated into its present incarnation as a temple where the funky and fashionable worship. The space features an '80s style-lounge decked out in gold leather futons, a mirrored dance floor, and four bars, one of which serves only drinks made with champagne. Twice a month, bad boy stylist Alexandre Herchcovitch and his inseparable pal, Johnny Luxo, freelance as DJs. Tunes tend towards house and electro.

Among the scores of divier, grungier night spots lining Rua Augusta, **Vegas Club** (Rua Augusta 765, Consolação, tel. 11/3231-3705, www.vegasclub.com.br, 11:30 P.M.–5 A.M. Tues.–Thurs., 11 P.M.–7 A.M. Fri., 11 P.M.–11 A.M. Sat., 10 P.M.–close Sun., cover

SÃO PAULO

R$15–30) makes a statement with its glam aura lifted from '50s-era Las Vegas. The resulting prevalence of neon and red velvet appears to strike a chord with the hip and happening crowd of playboys, gay boys, and *moderninhos*. The music varies from techno and hiphop to funk and rock.

LIVE MUSIC

Geni (Rua Bela Cintra 539, Jardim Paulista, tel. 11/3129-9638, www.geniclub.com.br, 6 P.M.–1 A.M. Tues.–Sun., cover R$10–20) was the name of the madame whose brothel once occupied this imposing villa. Restored and decorated in a retro boudoir style that mixes plush red sofas and easy chairs with modern art works, each room has its own unique ambiance. One salon outfitted with a small stage functions as a micro club, where rock, jazz, and soul shows take place. The crowd tends towards trendy twenty-somethings. There is an extensive menu of *petiscos* to nibble on.

Jardins

Sleek, chic, often intimate, and always super-fashionable, the bars and lounges of Jardins generally attract an older, more sophisticated and moneyed crowd as well as a significant international and gay and lesbian public.

BARS

Located in the ultra-sophisticated Fasano Hotel, **Baretto** (Rua Vitório Fasano 88, Jardim Paulista, tel. 11/3896-4000, www.fasano.com.br, 6 P.M.–3 A.M. Mon.–Fri., 8 P.M.–3 A.M. Sat., cover R$30 after 9:30 P.M.) is hands-down the classiest bar in town. Refined and elegant, its subtle lighting, rustic wood floors, leather sofas, and velvet paneled walls cast a romantic spell. The mood is further enhanced by the outstanding nightly performances of jazz and bossa nova on the bar's intimate stage. The cocktails, if not overly imaginative, are impeccably mixed.

Balcão (Rua Melo Alves 150, Jardim Paulista, tel. 11/3063-6091, 6 P.M.–2 A.M. Mon.–Sat., 6 A.M.–1 A.M. Sun.) is an apt name for this ingeniously original bar whose 25-meter (82-foot) *balcão* (counter) curves and zigzags throughout the interior. The placement of barstools on both sides creates an atmosphere that is particularly conducive to conversing as well as neighbor gazing. The public is an older crowd (30s–50s) who sip wine and *caipirinhas* and tuck into sandwiches on ciabatta bread, while casting the odd gaze towards the original Roy Lichtenstein that dominates one wall.

Located on the rooftop of the Hotel Unique, **Skye** (Av. Brigadeiro Luís Antônio 4700, Jardim Paulista, tel. 11/3055-4702, www.skye.com.br, noon–3 P.M. Mon.–Fri., noon–4 P.M. Sat.–Sun., 6 P.M.–1 A.M. Sun.–Thurs., 6 P.M.–2 A.M. Fri.–Sat.) is one hell of sexy hotel bar. Tables spill onto a wooden deck with lounge chairs, a cool blue pool, and stunning views of the emerald expanse of Parque do Ibirapuera backed by skyscrapers. At night, the pool is lit up in red, the distant skyscrapers glow like fireflies, and DJs spinning electronic bossa nova and house music turn the rooftop into an achingly hip lounge. The indoor restaurant serves innovative Brazilian fusion cuisine.

LIVE MUSIC

Syndikat Jazzclub (Rua Moacir Piza 64, Bela Vista, tel. 11/3375-9185, www.syndikat.com.br, 8 P.M.–2:30 A.M. Tues.–Fri., 9 P.M.–2:30 A.M. Sat., cover R$7–15) is an intimate and mellow little club whose jazz shows take place in a smoky basement with pillows scattered around the floor. The more spacious main floor is a fine place to relax and indulge in imported beer and crepe-like *panquecas*.

Pinheiros and Vila Madalena

After dark, these two adjoining *bairros* are always hopping. Offering some of the city's biggest array of nightlife options, their bars and clubs attract an mixed public.

BARS

With a relaxed vibe and a classic '50s bar atmosphere **Astor** (Rua Delfina 163, Vila Madalena, tel. 11/3815-1364, www.barastor.com.br, 5 P.M.–3 A.M. Mon.–Thurs., noon–4 A.M.

Fri.–Sat., noon–midnight Sun.) is one of Vila Madalena's most popular watering holes. The beer is icy and there is an extensive wine list. However, you'll be hard-pressed to find customers merely drinking—the long list of *petiscos* includes mouthwatering fare such as gorgonzola and Italian sausage *madeleines* and spicy meatballs cooked in Stella Artois beer.

A wonderful place for a drink or a bite under the stars is **Pé de Manga** (Rua Arapiraca 152, Vila Madalena, tel. 11/3032-6068, www.pedemanga.com.br, 6 P.M.–2 A.M. Mon.–Thurs., 6 P.M.–4 A.M. Fri., noon–4 A.M. Sat., noon–10 P.M.). Surrounding the lovely main house is an enormous patio sheltered by a trio of century-old mango trees. Unsurprisingly, the house cocktail is a simple but perfect mixture of vodka and frozen mango.

Sharing the premises of the Centro Brasileiro Britânico, **Drake's Bar and Deck** (Rua Tacambira 163, Pinheiros, tel. 11/3812-4477, www.drakesbar.com, noon–1 A.M. Mon.–Sat., noon–11 P.M. Sun.–Mon., cover R$8) features a happy commingling of Britain and Brazil. While the interior is as warm and pubby as any bar in England (attracting Brits who drown their homesickness with Old Speckled Hen on tap), the garden is pure tropical jungle festooned with *ipê* trees and bromeliads. The drink menu features more than 100 imported beers.

NIGHTCLUBS

Laid-back and not trying too hard, **Blen Blen Brasil** (Rua Inácio Pereira da Rocha 520, Pinheiros, tel. 11/3815-4999, www.blenblen.com.br, 8 P.M.–3 A.M. Mon.–Sat., cover R$35) nonetheless impresses with the range of the musical bands that perform here. Mondays are reserved for jazz, Fridays for *gafieira* (ballroom samba), and Saturdays the dance floor heats up with "Blen Blen Black," a night devoted to soul, funk, samba-rock and other funky Afro beats. **Avenida Club** (Av. Pedroso de Moraes 1036, Pinheiros, tel. 11/3814-7383, www.avenidaclub.com.br, 9 P.M.–close Wed., 8:30 P.M.–close Thurs., 10 P.M.–close Sat., 7 P.M.–close Sun., cover R$15–25) is another refreshingly untrendy spot. This hybrid space

features a café, a bar, and a vast ballroom with a shiny wooden floor where couples can trip the light fantastic to live and recorded samba, rumba, bolero, tango, and *forró*.

For something (a lot more) fashionable, **Bubu Lounge Disco** (Rua dos Pinheiros 791, Pinheiros, tel. 11/3081-9546, www.bubulounge.com, 11:30 P.M.–close Wed. and Fri.–Sat., 7 P.M.–close Sun., cover R$15–40) attracts an eclectic GLS crowd who lounge, flirt, drink, and dance in this sleekly modern multiambiance club, whose decorative highlight includes a mega aquarium. The house DJs and live bands are as diverse as the public, with a predilection for MPB, electronica, and lots of musical flashbacks to the '70s, '80s, and '90s.

LIVE MUSIC

Occupying a beautifully preserved old house, **Piratininga** (Rua Wisard 149, Vila Madalena, tel. 11/3032-9775, www.piratiningabar.com.br, 6 P.M.–2 A.M. Mon.–Thurs., 6 P.M.–close Fri.–Sat., 3 P.M.–1 A.M. Sun., cover R$8) is a classic Vila Mada *boteco* frequented by a laid-back clientele. The warm, softly lit interior gives off a romantic vibe, aided by the strains of live jazz and bossa nova that waft down from the mezzanine stage. The refreshing house cocktail, *caipi pira,* mixes vodka and Persian limes.

Decorated with photos of famous *sambistas* and *escola de samba* costumes, **Samba** (Rua Fidalga 308, Vila Madalena, tel. 11/3819-4619, 7 P.M.–midnight Wed., 7 P.M.–1 A.M. Thurs., 7 P.M.–2 A.M. Fri., 1 P.M.–2 A.M. Sat., 6 P.M.–midnight Sun., cover R$10–20) lives up to its name by serving as an informal temple devoted to the best of Carioca and Paulistano samba rhythms. Informal and authentic, it is a great place to hear some top names and cut a rug. On Saturday afternoons a tasty *feijoada* is served.

Grazie a Dio! (Rua Girassol 67, Vila Madalena, tel. 11/3031-6568, 8 P.M.–1:30 A.M. Mon.–Thurs., 8 P.M.–2 A.M. Fri.–Sat., 8 P.M.–midnight Sun., cover R$15–20) started off as a Mediterranean bistro. The rear dining area continues to serve up eclectic fare whose influences range from Italian to Moroccan. Meanwhile, the dance floor at the front of the house is always packed with youths grooving to live performances of pop, samba-rock, and salsa. Shows begin at 10 P.M. Afterwards, DJs keep the momentum going until closing.

ENTERTAINMENT AND EVENTS

São Paulo boasts the most vibrant and varied cultural scene in Brazil. Surpassing even Rio (after all, Cariocas have the beach for entertainment), the city reunites the best of Brazil and a fantastic array of offerings from the rest of the world. Irrespective of whether they were born or migrated here, Paulistanos are notoriously innovative, and the city pulses with creative energy that spills over into all the arts. Moreover, Sampa is blessed with an incredible number of topnotch cultural centers, cinemas, theaters, and concert halls, giving those in need of diversion endless options.

For information about what's going on (in Portuguese) consult the arts sections of the leading paper, *A Folha de São Paulo* (which publishes a terrific cultural guide on Fridays featuring listings for the upcoming week). Also pick up a copy of the weekly guide *Veja São Paulo*, which comes with *Veja* magazine and offers comprehensive listings of everything going on in the city. For upcoming events in English as well as Portuguese, log on to www.guiasp.com.br. Tickets for concerts, shows, and other events can be purchased directly at theaters and concert halls (some of which will deliver tickets to your hotel for an extra fee) or at **Show Tickets** at Shopping Iguatemi (Av. Brigadeiro Faria Lima 1191, 3rd Fl., Jardim Paulistano, 10 A.M.–10 P.M. Mon.–Sat., 2–8 P.M. Sun.). **Ticketmaster** (tel. 11/6846-6000, www.ticketmaster.com.br) sells tickets over the phone or by Internet.

Performing Arts

The splendid turn-of-the-20th-century **Teatro Municipal** (Praça Ramos de Azevedo, Centro, tel. 11/3222-8698, www.prefeitura.sp.gov.br/cidade/secretarias/cultura/teatromunicipal/) is home to the highly reputed **Orquestra Sinfônica Municipal** and the city's classical

---

THE SESC SYSTEM

Serviço Social do Comércio (SESC, tel. 0/800-118-220, www.sescsp.org.br) was created in 1940 to benefit workers from the trade and service industry. SESC cultural and recreational centers are all over Brazil. However, in São Paulo they're inextricably linked to the city's cultural life. Without SESC, Paulistanos would be cultural orphans – over 300,000 people a week turn out to see performances by top names in music, theater, and dance. They can afford to do so because SESC events are very reasonably priced or free. The city boasts 14 SESC centers, most of them occupying creatively renovated abandoned buildings or boldly modern constructions that have become architectural landmarks. The state-of-the-art theaters and concert halls share space with cafés, bars, galleries, and libraries.

Four of the larger, most interesting, and most accessible SESC centers are: **SESC Paulista** (Av. Paulista 119, Paraíso, tel. 11/3179-3700), **SESC Vila Mariana** (Rua Pelotas 141, Vila Mariana, tel. 11/5080-3000), **SESC Pinheiros** (Rua Paes Leme 195, Pinheiros, tel. 11/3095-9400), and **SESC Pompéia** (Rua Clélia 93, Pompéia, tel. 11/3871-7700), which has a terrific bar.

---

ballet company, **Balé da Cidade**. It also features high-quality classical music, dance, and opera performances. The Estação Júlio Prestes, a renovated train station, houses the **Sala São Paulo** (Praça Júlio Prestes, Luz, tel. 11/3223-3966, www.salasaopaulo.art.br), whose impeccable acoustics are enhanced by the auditorium's unique roof featuring adjustable wooden panels. Home to the acclaimed **Orquestra Sinfônica do Estado de São Paulo** (OSESP), it also hosts other orchestras.

The futuristic **Auditório Ibirapuera** (Parque do Ibirapuera, Portão 2, tel. 11/6846-6040, www.auditorioibirapuera.com.br) could only have been designed by Oscar Niemeyer.

During performances of erudite music, the enormous red tongue-shaped door behind the stage often opens, allowing you to meditate upon the greenery of Ibirapuera park.

The state-of-the-art **Teatro Alfa** (Rua Bento Branco de Andrade Filho 722, Santo Amaro, tel. 11/5693-4000, www.teatroalfa.com.br) and the more traditional **Teatro Cultura Artística** (Rua Nestor Pestana 196, Cerqueira César, tel. 11/3258-3344, www.culturaartistica.com.br) are both top venues for concerts, theater, and dance. Two leading contemporary dance companies that you should catch if you have a chance are **Ballet Stagium** (www.stagium.com.br) and **Cisne Negro** (www.cisnenegro.com.br). Meanwhile, even if your Portuguese is shaky, it's worth checking out the interactive offerings of vanguard dramaturge José Celso (Zé Celso) Martinez Corrêa, who operates the historical **Teatro Oficina** (Rua Jaceguai 520, Bela Vista, tel. 11/3104-0676, www.teatro oficina.com.br). Planned by architect Lina Bo Bardi, the landmark theater was designed to break down boundaries between actors and audience. Although performances of playwrights such as Euripedes, Shakespeare, and Genet last for hours, the fact that audience members are encouraged to walk in and out of the narrative action ensures you won't be bored.

Concert Halls

São Paulo has two mega-capacity, ultramodern concert halls where major entertainment events take place. With seating for 5,000, **Credicard Hall** (Av. das Nacoes Unidas 17955, Santo Amaro, tel. 11/6846-6010, www.credicard hall.com.br) is where the biggest national and international popular music stars play when they come to town. **Citibank Hall** (Av. dos Jamaris 213, Moema, tel. 11/6846-6040, www.citibankhall.com.br) attracts its share of big name pop performers as well as events ranging from awards ceremonies to auctions.

Cultural Centers

Along Avenida Paulista, several other cultural centers are housed in interesting buildings, all of which host free art exhibitions.

The FIESP (Federation of Industries of São Paulo State) building is easily recognizable by its wildly sloping ultramodern facade. It is home to the **Centro Cultural FIESP** (Av. Paulista 1313, Cerqueira César, tel. 11/3146-7405, www.sesisp.org.br/home/2006/centro cultural, 8 A.M.–5 P.M. Mon.–Fri.), which has an art gallery, a theater, and a cinema. Another major cultural center where something interesting is always going on is the **Instituto Itaú Cultural** (Av. Paulista 179, Cerqueira César, tel. 11/2168-1700, www.itaucultural.org.br, 10 A.M.–9 P.M. Tues.–Fri., 10 A.M.–7 P.M. Sat.–Sun.), which is owned by the Itaú bank.

Cinema

Paulistanos adore a *cineminha*. In fact, during weekends and holidays, lineups are enormous and prime time screenings are often sold out. Aside from *shopping* multiplexes, the majority of the city's biggest and best theaters are conveniently concentrated on or around Avenida Paulista. Outfitted with a small bookstore and a cool café/restaurant that looks onto Avenida Paulista, the **Reserva Cultural** (Av. Paulista 900, Cerqueira César, tel. 11/3287-3529, www.reservacultural.com.br) shows high-minded commercial films on four large screens. Devoted cinephiles consistently flock to the **Espaço Unibanco** (Rua Augusta 1470/1475, Consolação, tel. 11/3288-6780), a complex of five theaters that screen first-run Brazilian, international, and art films and host film festivals. The café is habitually stuffed with celluloid junkies downing expresso. Nearby on the third floor of Shopping Frei Caneca, the **Unibanco Arteplex** (Rua Frei Caneca 569, Consolação, tel. 11/3472-2365, www.unibancoarteplex.com.br) adds prestigious Hollywood pictures to its roster of indie and international films. **CineSesc** (Rua Augusta 2075, tel. 11/3082-0213, Jardim Paulista, www.sesc.org.br) functions as a cinematheque with an enormous screen and low ticket prices that organizes retrospectives and screens repertory films. A bar at the back of the theater allows you to sip cocktails while watching movies.

SÃO PAULO

Festivals and Events

CARNAVAL

Most people are surprised to discover that São Paulo has a Carnaval. Somehow the very notion seems at odds with the city's hardcore urban image. Yet, just like Rio, the city has its own traditional neighborhood *escolas de samba,* who spend all year rehearsing for the day in which their members dress up, mount extravagant floats, and parade through their very own Oscar Niemeyer-designed **Sambódromo** (Av. Olavo Fontoura 1209, Parque Anhembi, Santana, tel. 11/6226-0400), located near the Tietê bus terminal. The results (televised on national TV) are less showy and spectacular than Rio de Janeiro's *desfiles.* However, it's also much easier and somewhat cheaper to get tickets for the festivities. If you're in the mood for samba, you'll be richly rewarded. Depending on how far away (high up in the stands) or close you are to the action—and how much pampering you demand—prices range from R$15 to R$1,000. You can purchase tickets at travel agents or Ticketmaster (tel. 11/6846-6000, www.ticketmaster.com.br). Even if you miss Carnaval itself, you can sit in on rehearsals at the neighborhood *escolas.* Schools worth checking out include **Vai Vai** (Rua São Vicente 276, Bela Vista, tel. 11/3105-8725, www.vaivai.com.br), **Rosa de Ouro** (Av. Colonel Euclides Machado 1066, Freguesia do Ó, tel. 11/3931-4555, www.sociedade rosasdeouro.com.br), and **Mocidade Alegre** (Av. Casa Verde 3498, Limão, tel. 11/3857-7525, www.mocidadealegre.com.br). For more information contact the **União de Escolas de Samba Paulistanas (UESP)** (Rua Rui Barbosa 588, Bela Vista, tel. 11/3171-3713, www.uesp.com.br).

FILM FESTIVALS

São Paulo hosts some terrific and extremely well-organized film festivals. **E Tudo Verdade (It's All True)** (www.itsalltrue.com.br) is an international documentary film festival held in late March/early April. **Anima Mundi** (www.animamundi.com.br), held in late July, is Latin America's biggest animated film festival, featuring creative short and long features along with television cartoons, commercials, and cyber creations. The **Mostra Internacional de Cinema de São Paulo** (www.mostra.uol.com.br) has become one of the world's foremost film festivals, with screenings of more than 600 long features and 60 shorts from all over the world. It takes place in late October.

SHOPPING

São Paulo is a shopper's paradise. In a country that takes great pride in its malls—affectionately known as *shoppings*—Sampa's are by far the biggest and glitziest—and a *very* far cry from suburban strip malls in America. Meanwhile, unlike many other Brazilian cities, São Paulo also has a large selection of boutiques, particularly concentrated in Jardins (a Brazilian version of Rodeo Drive) and Vila Madalena (more funky, alternative fare and lots of art).

Twice a year, the Pavilhão da Bienal das Artes in Parque do Iberapuera hosts **São Paulo Fashion Week** (www.spfw.com.br), an increasingly important industry event that showcases the latest trends from consecrated national designers and lures international media, buyers, and screaming fashion groupies hoping to catch sight of Gisele Bündchen. As Brazilian fashion has taken off, Sampa has come into its own as a *capital da moda,* where home-grown and international designers display and sell their wares in glitzy showrooms and flagship stores. Meanwhile, if cheap buys are what you're after, secondhand stores and the vibrant bazaar-like atmospheres of Bom Retiro and Rua 25 de Maio are full of surprising bargains.

Shopping Malls

Aside from designer boutiques, Sampa's sleekly alluring *shoppings* unite fantastic food courts, mega book-and-CD stores, trendy cafés, movie theaters, and much more. Hours are generally 10 A.M.–10 P.M. Monday–Saturday, 2–8 P.M. Sunday.

Inaugurated in 1966, **Shopping Iguatemi** (Av. Brigadeiro Faria Lima 2232, Jardim

Paulistano, tel. 11/3816-6116, www.iguatemi saopaolo.com.br) has been São Paulo's most sophisticated *shopping* for decades. Apart from 360 chic boutiques (with an enormous international presence ranging from Burberry to Tiffany's), it possesses several movie theaters, gourmet cafés and restaurants, and a gigantic Saraiva bookstore.

The discreetly hidden **Shopping Pátio Higienópolis** (Av. Higienópolis 618, Higienópolis, tel. 11/3823-2300, www.patio higienopolis.com.br) is spacious and airy with a great mix of stores, eating options, and a cinema. Just off Avenida Paulista, the super-trendy **Shopping Frei Caneca** (Rua Frei Caneca 569, Consolação, tel. 11/3472-2000, www.freicaneca shopping.com.br) is nicknamed "Shopping Gay Caneca" due to its popularity with fashion-forward gays and lesbians. Aside from boutiques (which are skewed to a younger, more alternative clientele), it has a food court, a gourmet supermarket, a great cinema—the Unibanco Arteplex—and two theaters.

Paulistano Fashion

For an introduction to São Paulo fashion, head to Jardins, where the majority of local designers have their showrooms. São Paulo's **Rua Oscar Freire** boasts nine blocks of unadulterated luxury shopping with over 100 (heavily guarded) boutiques representing Brazilian designers along with international brands ranging from Diesel to Armani. Even if you're not in the mood to buy, many of the stores are creatively designed and the window shopping is fantastic. While Oscar Freire is the main fashion drag, the surrounding streets of Rua Augusta, Alameda Lorena, Rua Dr. Melo Alves, Rua Bela Cintra, Rua Haddock Lobo, and Rua da Consolação are also teeming with interesting stores.

STREET AND CASUAL WEAR

In terms of the coolest in Brazilian casual and streetwear—including the extraordinarily comfortable and super stylish Brazilian jeans that have taken the world by storm—Paulistano designers have long been in the vanguard.

Although the following labels can be found in the most upscale shoppings around town (and around the country), you'll find the flagship stores in Jardins. **Fórum** (Rua Oscar Freire 918, tel. 11/3085-9310, www.forum.com.br) singlehandedly put Brazilian jeans on the map with high-quality, form-fitting jeans that have become a closet staple for celebs from Jennifer Lopez to Meg Ryan.

Responsible for introducing stone-washed jeans to Brazil, **Ellus** (Rua Oscar Freire 990, tel. 11/3082-3120, www.ellus.com.br) has since evolved considerably into one of Brazil's most sexy and adventurous casual wear labels. It scored a recent coup with its ad campaign featuring New York indie actress/fashionista Chloe Sevigny. The sultry, colorful, and youthful designs of **Zoomp** (Rua Oscar Freire 995, tel. 11/3064-1556, www.zoomp.com.br) are extremely popular with hip young things who proudly flaunt the brand's yellow lightning bolt logo. **M. Officer** (Rua Oscar Freire 944, tel. 11/3085-6866, www.carlosmiele.com) showcases the flawlessly cut and original casual clothing line of Paulistano designer Carlos Miele, a darling of the international fashion press whose flagship ready-to-wear Carlos Miele store in New York's Meatpacking District put him on the map. **Iódice** (Rua Oscar Freire 940, tel. 11/3085-9310, www.iodice.com.br) is another homegrown label for both men and women, featuring pared-down, casual designs with refined details.

For cutting-edge alternative streetwear head to **Galeria Ouro Fino** (Rua Augusta 2690, tel. 11/3082-7860), where more than 100 boutiques have something for urban hipsters of every type. Aside from clothing and shoes by up-and-coming designers, you can get tattoos, body piercings, or a radical new haircut. Because it is popular with DJs and musicians—there are a few great vinyl stores—the place is littered with flyers announcing shows, *festas,* and other nocturnal events.

PRÊT-À-PORTER

Jardins is also a great place to check out the ready-to-wear collections of Brazil's most renowned designers. The son of a Lebanese gar-ment merchant, **Fause Haten** (Rua Oscar Freire 1102, tel. 11/3081-8685, www.fausehauten .com.br) originally began making clothes as a way to make money to travel. Over the years, his sensual and often extravagant designs—along with his shell-shaped jewelry fashioned out of white and yellow gold—have earned him acco-lades as one of Brazil's most original designers.

Brazil's bad boy of design, **Alexandre Herchcovitch** (Rua Haddock Lobo 1151, tel. 11/3063-2888, www.herchcovitch.uol.com.br), grew up in São Paulo's Orthodox Jewish com-munity, where his mother, a lingerie seamstress, taught him the basics of sewing. At age 16, he made his first organza dress, and by his early 20s, he was designing his own edgy collection. Mixing elements from sources as diverse as punk rock, Judaism, Disney, and drag, his clothes have gone from seducing denizens of Sampa's under-ground scene to luring international jet-setters. Today, Herchcovitch—a DJ and famous fixture on the local club scene—shows collections in Paris and New York as well as São Paulo.

Gloria Coelho (Rua Bela Cintra 2173, tel. 11/3085-6671, www.gloriacoelho.com.br) has built an acclaimed career by fusing the most disparate references into clean, modern, smart designs with a futuristic edge. Her former assis-tant and present husband, **Reinaldo Lourenço** (Rua Bela Cintra 2167, tel. 11/3085-8151, www.reinaldolourenco.com.br) is known as the "poet" of Brazilian fashion due to the lyri-cal sensibility that informs his contemporary clothing. **Adriana Barra** (Rua Peixoto Gomide 1801, Casa 5, tel. 11/3064-3691, www.adriana barra.com.br) is one of the most promising stars on the fashion circuit. Her fluid, feminine designs recapture the glamor and romance of earlier times while remaining firmly grounded in modern times.

SHOES

Back in the days when Americans were wearing "jelly shoes," Brazilians were wedging their feet into "Melissas," the original "jelly" invented in Brazil in 1979. After 30 years on the mar-ket, these humble plastic shoes got a major revamping with the opening of the **Galeria Melissa** (Rua Oscar Freire 827, tel. 11/3083-3612, www.galeriamelissa.com.br). This wildly inventive design gallery/shoe temple sells cut-ting-edge versions of this surprisingly flexible and comfortable classic, reimagined by design gurus such as Alexandre Herchcovitch, the Campana brothers, and Karim Rashid.

The shoes at **Fernando Pires** (Rua Consolação 3534, tel. 11/3068-8177, www .fernandopires.com.br) are definitely not for conservative feet. With the goal of transform-ing women into "Greek goddesses," Pires specializes in flamboyant footwear such as high-heeled tie-up sandals encrusted in jew-els and thigh-high metallic leather boots in Carnaval colors. Women in search of their inner drag queen will be in heaven. Men's shoes are slightly more discreet.

Cheap Buys

Shopping in São Paulo doesn't have to be syn-onymous with shelling out wads of cash. There are some amazing bargains to found, particu-larly in two areas of Centro. **Rua 25 de Março** (www.portal25.com.br) is not unlike a modern-day souk. On a slow day, an average 400,000 shoppers cram the 400 stores lining the street and hidden within small *galerias,* which hawk everything from housewares, toys, fabrics, and Carnaval paraphernalia to clothing, jewelry, and shoes. The prices are stupendously cheap (which accounts for the crowds), but part of the fun is bargaining for even further discounts. Shopping on 25 de Março—and the surround-ing streets of Rua Comendador Abdo Schain, Rua Barão de Duprat and Rua Cavalheiro Basílio Jafret—can be a lively and interesting experience, but also a chaotic and exhausting one. Avoid Saturdays and holidays (when the number of shoppers can hit the one million mark) and don't bring small kids. Easiest ac-cess is via São Bento Metrô. Also be aware that many designer goods are fake.

Great deals are also to be found in the *bairro* of **Bom Retiro** (www.omelhordobom retiro.com.br), adjacent to Luz (take the Metrô to Luz station). Sampa's traditional garment

DASLU AND DASPU

Brazil's socio-economic extremes are glaringly apparent in two of the country's most head-line-grabbing fashion phenomenons: Daslu and Daspu. **Daslu** (Av. Chedid Jafet 131, Vila Olímpia, tel. 11/3841-4000, www.daslu.com.br, 10 A.M.–8 P.M. Mon. and Wed.–Sat., 10 A.M.–10 P.M. Tues.) is Brazil's largest, chicest, and perhaps most controversial luxury megastore. As the exclusive purveyor of many international couture names, including Chanel, Valentino, and Louis Vuitton, it attracts a steady stream of millionaires, socialites, and soccer stars who drive up in limousines or land their helicopters on the roof. The over-the-top decorative scheme includes marble staircases and crystal chandeliers that shriek opulence while the airbrushed staff consists largely of Paulistana debutantes. Services include a spa and hair salon as well as champagne and sushi bars. Although you likely can't afford to buy anything, as a sociological experience – that will leave you alternately fascinated and/or repulsed – it makes for an interesting visit. Underlining its status as one of Brazil's most unapologetic symbols of flagrant inequality, the store is located right next to Coliseu, one of São Paulo's many *favelas*.

A wonderfully subversive counterpoint to Daslu is **Daspu** (tel. 21/2224-3532, www.daspu. com.br). Whereas the name Daslu pays homage to its well-bred founder, Lucia (Lu) Piva de Albuquerqe Tranchesi, Daspu – short for *das putas* (from the whores) – is a fashion label founded by a former Rio prostitute, Gabriela Leite. The hip and very affordable Carioca street fashions sold in selected stores as well as on its online *"putique"* (international orders are accepted) are all designed, sewn, and modeled on the runway by members of the world's oldest profession. However, these talented women are interested in making more than just clothes: Daspu is involved in promoting safe sex, defending prostitutes' rights, and attempting to change the public's attitudes towards the profession.

district was originally inhabited by Jewish immigrants. Today, it is largely Korean and boasts hundreds of wholesale stores selling clothing and accessories that are up to 40 percent cheaper than they would be in shopping centers. Less hectic and more organized than Rua 25 de Março, Bom Retiro also has the advantage of an abundance of great, inexpensive Korean restaurants (open for lunch only).

Books and Music

São Paulo has many bookstores, but the best of all is the newly renovated **Livraria Cultura** (Av. Paulista 2073, Cerqueira César, tel. 11/3170-4033, 9 A.M.–10 P.M. Mon.–Sat., noon–8 P.M. Sun.). Located in the Conjunto Nacional building, this sprawling bookshop has a terrific selection covering all subjects (as well as a considerable number of English-language titles) along with national and international magazines, CDs, and DVDs. This is a great place to pick up art books as well as travel guides and maps.

Among the several branches of the French chain FNAC, the largest is **FNAC Centro Cultural** (Praça das Omaguas 32, Pinheiros, tel. 11/3579-2000, www.fnac.com.br, 10 A.M.–10 P.M. daily). Spread over three massive floors, along with a gallery and cyber café, are over 100,000 books (including many in English) as well as CDs, DVDs, and photography and computer equipment.

Although the megastores carry impressive musical selections, collectors with a specific penchant for rare and alternative Brazilian music should head to **Baratos Afins** (Rua 24 de Maio 62, Lojas 314-318, Centro, tel. 11/3223-3629, www.baratosafins.com.br). This record and CD store is also an important indie label. It was founded by Arnaldo Baptista, the guitarist of the '60s rock group Os Mutantes, which has been a major influence on artists as diverse as Kurt Cobain and Beck. Over the years, BA has recorded and rereleased an impressive number of Brazilian underground and alternative artists—you'll find these and other treasures in this fantastic store.

SÃO PAULO

Antiques

Jardins is home to numerous antiques stores. One of the city's oldest and most respected dealers is **Nóbrega** (Rua Padre João Miguel 1231, Jardim Paulista, tel. 11/3068-9388, www.nobrega1935.com.br, 9:30 A.M.–7 P.M. Mon.–Fri., 10 A.M.–2 P.M. Sat.). Aside from an impressive antiques collection, a gallery space displays modern and contemporary Brazilian art. A classic Sunday afternoon activity is to browse through the small but colorful selection of antiques and collectibles on display at the **Feira de Antiguidades do MASP** (Av. Paulista 1578, Cerqueira César, 10 A.M.–5 P.M. Sun.), which takes place beneath the museum's suspended structure. Also lots of fun is the **Feira de Antiguidades e Artes** (Praça Benedito Calixto, Pinheiros, www.pracabeneditocalixto.com.br, 9 A.M.–7 P.M. Sat.). where you'll find a colorful collection of bric-a-brac of varying quality. Held in a pretty square, the market itself—with lots of food and drink kiosks—is a gathering place for a young and alternative crowd.

Arts and Crafts

The proprietors of **Amoa Konoya** (Rua João Moura 1002, Jardim América, tel. 11/3061-0639, www.amoakonoya.com.br, 9 A.M.–7 P.M. Mon.–Fri., 9 A.M.–6 P.M. Sat.) travel throughout Brazil, visiting remote indigenous communities whose artisans create the pottery, basketry, art works, musical instruments, carvings, and ornaments sold in this charming boutique. **Galeria Brasiliana** (Rua Artur de Azevedo 520, Jardim América, tel. 11/3086-4273, www.galeriabrasiliana.com.br, 10 A.M.–6 P.M. Mon.–Fri., 10 A.M.–5 P.M. Sat.) is widely reputed for its impressive collection of contemporary Brazilian folk art. Among its wares are sculptures, paintings, engravings, toys, masks, and other objects made by artisans from all over the country. Although these aren't cheap trinkets, the quality is exceptional.

More affordable and funky are the exclusive artistic and design objects at **O Design Animado** (Rua Fidalga 182, Vila Madalena, tel. 11/3815-6841, www.odesignanimado.com.br, 10 A.M.–7 P.M. Mon.–Fri., 10 A.M.–6 P.M. Sat.).

While some of the works are signed by consecrated art world names, others are made by discovered talents such as Jonas, a street kid responsible for the inspired airplanes, cars, and Afro-Brazilian *orixás* fashioned out of recycled aluminum cans.

São Paulo has the most important art gallery scene in Brazil. Galleries are concentrated in Jardins and Vila Madalena, and as you're strolling around you're bound to stumble upon at least a handful. **Galeria Luisa Strina** (Rua Oscar Freire 502, Jardim Paulista, tel. 11/3088-2471, www.galerialuisastrina.com.br, 10 A.M.–7 P.M. Mon.–Fri., 10 A.M.–5 P.M. Sat.) is a São Paulo pioneer on the gallery circuit. Strina's daring and distinguished collection features important Brazilian contemporary artists working in a wide range of mediums. Reputed as a champion of up-and-coming Brazilian artists is **Galeria Fortes Vilaça** (Rua Fradique Coutinho 1500, Vila Madalena, tel. 11/3032-7066, www.fortesvilaca.com.br, 10 A.M.–7 P.M. Tues.–Fri., 10 A.M.–5 P.M. Sat.), who also represents major names such as Vik Muniz and Beatriz Milhazes. Photography fans should check out **Espaço Ophicina** (Rua Aspicuelta 329, Vila Madalena, tel. 11/3813-8466, www.espaco-ophicina.com.br, 9 A.M.–6 P.M. Mon.–Fri., 11 A.M.–3 P.M. Sat.), which exhibits and sells intriguing works by São Paulo photographers.

SPORTS AND RECREATION
Parks

Despite its reputation for being a concrete jungle, São Paulo offers quite a few welcoming green oases in and around the city. Although the most famous and centrally located is **Parque do Ibirapuera** (see *Sights*), near the southern outskirts of the city is the **Parque do Estado,** a vast expanse of native Atlantic rainforest with walking trails and picnic areas as well as a botanical garden and zoo. The easiest way to get to the park is to take the Metrô to Jabaquara—from the station it's only a quick taxi ride to the entrance.

JARDIM BOTÂNICO

One of the highlights of Parque do Estado

is the Jardim Botânico (Av. Miguel Stéfano 3031, Água Funda, tel. 11/5073-6300, www.ibot.sp.gov.br, 9 A.M.–5 P.M. Wed.– Sun., R$3), which specializes in the study and preservation of native plant and tree species. A large lagoon festooned with lily pads and other aquatic plants splices the park in two, separating shady woods from a tunnel of bamboo. Among the gardens' many scenic paths is a suspended treetop walking trail that cuts through native Atlantic foliage where you can catch sight of sloths, monkeys, and brightly colored toucans.

JARDIM ZOOLÓGICO
The other big draw at the Parque do Estado is the Jardim Zoológico (Av. Miguel Stéfano 4241, Água Funda, tel. 11/5073-0811, www.zoologico.sp.gov.br, 9 A.M.–5 P.M. Tues.– Sun., R$12). São Paulo's very popular menagerie has over 3,500 beasts and birds from all over the globe, including some extremely rare animals such as a white rhino and a Siberian tiger (currently the largest feline in existence). Since the zoo is quite spread out, spring for the minibus (R$5) that will drive you around to visit all the animals.

Soccer
Paulistanos take their soccer very seriously. The two major rivals are São Paulo and Corinthians, and when they butt heads sparks fly. Games are played either at São Paulo's home stadium of **Morumbi** (Praça Roberto Gomes Pedrosa, Morumbi, tel. 11/3749-8000, www.saopaulo.fc.net) or at the Corinthians' unofficial home stadium of **Pacaembu** (Praça Charles Miller, Pacaembu, tel. 11/6846-6000). Try to avoid finals—not only will the stadiums be sold out, but the fans' testosterone levels get dangerously high. Otherwise, catching a game is a heady experience. The well-funded teams boast some of the nation's top players, and the atmosphere among fans is an intoxicating mixture of gripping suspense and over-the-top melodrama. Indeed, it is recommended to spring for covered seats that will protect you from the projectiles lobbed in anger by

frustrated fans. Tickets can be purchased at the stadiums themselves or online at www .ingressofacil.com.br.

ACCOMMODATIONS
São Paulo attracts many more business travelers than tourists. So, many of its hotels are multinational and local chains that, while big on amenities such as work stations and wireless Internet, are often short on charm. A good number of them are located in far-flung but up-and-coming business hoods such as Brooklin and Berrini, which are convenient for getting to and from airports and meetings, but not so useful if you want to explore the city. You'll also find accommodations around Avenida Paulista (much better for your purposes) and adjacent Jardins. The city boasts a surprising array of world-class, decadently luxurious hotels (even more than Rio) that are great for living it up. Meanwhile, cheaper lodgings are available in Centro, which is slowly undergoing renovations and beginning to offer more interesting options, but at night the area can be rather dangerous. Many of the fancier hotels offer great discounts. Ironically, rates are often cheaper in summer months of December–February (high season everywhere else in Brazil) since this is when Paulistanos head to the beaches. You can also get impressive discounts on weekends— when business travelers are scarce. In fact, in an attempt to fill rooms, many hotels offer weekend "honeymoon" specials that seduce couples both married and otherwise.

Centro
Staying in Centro—around Praça da República—has the advantages of being cheaper and more convenient than other parts of São Paulo. The downside is that come nighttime, much of this area shuts down. To ensure your safety, rely on taxis.

R$50-100
For budget travelers, the clean and cheery **São Paulo Hostel** (Rua Barão de Campinas 94, Centro, tel. 11/3333-0844, www.hostel.com.br, R$64–78 d), right around the corner from

charming Largo do Arouche, is a great find. The double rooms are larger and more comfortable than your average hotel room. If you're really cash-strapped, you can bunk in a dorm room for R$29–36. The hostel offers laundry and Internet services and is a great place to meet other travelers.

One of São Paulo's first high-rise apartments buildings, the **Marian Palace** (Av. Cásper Líbero 65, Centro, tel. 11/3228-8443, www.marian.com.br, R$75–168 d) was built by a Polish princess in the 1940s and then transformed into a hotel in the 1950s. Although its glamor is somewhat faded, its art deco flourishes are well preserved. Aside from original lamps, chairs, and bathroom fixtures, the building's curves result in some interesting spatial configurations. Rooms are spacious (except for the cramped singles). A bonus is the rooftop swimming pool. Also good value is the **República Park Hotel** (Av. Vieira de Carvalho 32, Centro, tel. 11/3331-5595, www.republica parkhotel.com, R$90–100 d), which is situated on a formerly chic and now very gay, but always comfortingly lively, street adjacent to Praça da República. Although the formerly posh hotel no longer merits any style awards, the rooms are comfortable (those high up offer great views) and the staff is friendly.

R$100-200

A harbinger of the revitalization poised to transform Centro is the **Marabá Palace** (Av. Ipiranga 757, Centro, tel. 11/2137-9500, R$160–256 d), which opened in 2007 atop a splendid old cinema. Bringing some much needed glamor back to Centro, the hotel has nonetheless opted for contemporary sophistication over nostalgic retro. Amenities such as a fitness room and sauna as well as soundproof rooms and impeccable service add to the comfort factor.

When the **Normandie Design Hotel** (Av. Ipiranga 1187, Centro, tel. 11/3311-9855, www.normandiedesign.com.br, R$180–210 d) decided to upgrade and modernize, it took the "design" in its name very seriously. While the lobby is immaculately white, the "design

apartments" resemble chessboards. Black curtains, black furniture, and even black bedding contrast with light walls and ceiling tones, creating an effect that is ultra smooth and cool though perhaps overly minimalist for some (and downright stark for others).

R$200-300

Occupying an elegant old building on Sampa's main gay drag, the **Bourbon São Paulo** (Av. Vieira de Carvalho 99, Centro, tel. 11/3337-2000, www.bourbon.com.br, R$200–250 d) is a traditional business traveler's hotel with spacious, handsomely outfitted guest and common rooms, along with the added amenities of free wireless Internet, a fitness center, and sauna.

Avenida Paulista

Although hardly ultra-cheap, there are some bargains to be had in the generally large and modern hotels surrounding Avenida Paulista. Though the surroundings are less than bucolic, you have the advantage of being smack dab in the middle of all the urban action. Ideally located in terms of bus and Metrô service, you are in walking distance of a fair number of neighborhoods and attractions, which means less time-consuming, stress-inducing exposure to infamous Paulistano traffic jams.

R$100-200

Part of the budget Ibis chain owned by Accor hotels, the **Ibis Avenida Paulista** (Av. Paulista 2355, Cerqueira César, tel. 11/3523-3000, www.accorhotels.com.br, R$129 d) offers fantastic prices for the privilege of staying right on Avenida Paulista (and the edge of Jardins). If the rooms are a little on the bland and impersonal side, they are also modern, spotless, and well-cared for.

Another good bargain only five minutes from Avenida Paulista is the **Augusta Park Hotel** (Rua Augusta 922, Cerqueira César, tel. 11/3124-4000, www.augustapark.com.br, R$98–122 d). Though the apartments are pretty basic and a little cramped, they have the advantage of living rooms and kitchenettes. Opt for one in the rear of the building to avoid the noise of passing cars and weekend party-ers. The rooftop boasts a swimming pool and gym and the staff is quite helpful. While some stretches of lively Rua Augusta are seedy—with all-night peep shows and prostitutes—the area is more tawdry than dangerous.

R$200-300

◖ Hotel Pergamon (Rua Frei Caneca 80, Consolação, tel. 11/3123-2021, www.perga-mon.com.br, R$250–280 d) brags that it was the first hotel in Brazil to introduce the concept of "Chic & Cheap," back in 1999. Its pioneer-ing efforts have met with success, and this early boutique hotel is the darling of increasingly hip Rua "Gay" Caneca. The ultracontemporary, minimalist decor resists being too cool by the occasional splash of tropical color, warm natural woods, and works by Brazilian artists. Rooms on the upper floors offer terrific panoramic views.

Equally comfortable but much more traditional is the **Grande Hotel Cá d'Oro** (Rua Augusta 129, Consolação, tel. 11/3236-4300, www.cardoro.com.br, R$215–260 d), which hasn't changed much since it opened in 1953 as the city's first five-star hotel. Owned and operated by multiple generations of an Italian family, the hotel oozes Old World style. Rooms are large and refreshingly non-designer, while the lobby and living rooms are warm and welcoming with leather armchairs, Persian carpets, and a fire-place. Service is old school as well.

Jardins

Befitting the swankiness of the neighbor-hood, Jardins is where the *crème de la crème* of Sampa's luxury hotels are clustered—if you want to live it up in style, and are prepared to spend big, this is the *bairro* for you. Low rollers need not despair: Although more modest digs are harder to come by, a handful of midrange options do exist.

R$100-200

◖ Pousada Dona Ziláh (Alameda França 1621, Jardim Paulista, tel. 11/3062-1444, www.zilah.com, R$150–160 d) is a rar-ity in São Paulo, let alone in the heart of chic Jardins; a welcoming B&B located in a charming old house. If the rooms are a little spartan and amenities scarce, the cozy home-like atmosphere, great location, and affordable prices more than compensate.

More impersonal, but equally affordable, is the **Paulista Center Hotel** (Rua Consolação 2567, tel. 11/3852-0733, www.paulistacenter hotel.com.br, R$110–120 d) a nondescript but very adequate hotel perched on the edge of Jardins, just off Avenida Paulista. Attracting mostly business travelers, the no-nonsense rooms are sizable and quite comfortable.

R$200-300

São Paulo is full of apartment hotels known as *flats*. Catering largely to business travelers who crave some semblance of a home away from home, such as living rooms and kitchenettes, many can be found in Jardins. **Transamerica America Flats** (www.transamericaflats.com.br) has several comfortable and relatively afford-able options around São Paulo. In Jardins, both the **Transamerica Flat Opera** (Alameda Lorena 1748, Jardim Paulista, tel. 11/3062-2666, R$185–205) and the **Transamerica International Plaza** (Alameda Santos 981, Cerqueira César, tel. 11/3146-5966, R$218–375) have large and modern, if slightly neutral suites, with kitchens and access to swimming pools, gyms, and saunas. If you don't feel like cooking, room service is available. The former is in the heart of Jardins's most swanky shop-ping district, while the latter is only a block away from MASP and Avenida Paulista.

OVER R$300

Alternately described as bearing an uncanny re-semblance to an ark or a watermelon, **◖ Hotel Unique** (Av. Brigadeiro Luís Antônio 4700, Cerqueira César, tel. 11/3055-4700, www.hote-lunique.com.br, R$1,040–1,245) definitely lives up to its name. Designed by hot local architect Ruy Ohtake, the hipper-than-thou hotel doesn't even have its name advertised on its space-age exterior. What it does have, however, are impec-cably designed white-on-white rooms that are equally high-comfort and high-tech. From your digitally controlled hydro-massage bath you can flip through the endless channels on your plasma TV, dim the lighting, and adjust the view by angling the electronic wooden blinds that cover the porthole windows. The rooftop **Skye** bar is (justifiably) one of the hippest places in town, not least because of its swimming pool, which, at night, glows with red lights and throbs with soothing underwater DJ tunes.

Another favorite of jet-setters and models—who often fly in directly by helicopter and land on the hotel's private heliport—is **Emiliano** (Rua Oscar Freire 384, Cerqueira César, tel. 11/3069-4369, www.emiliano.com.br, R$956–1,739 d). The most exclusive—and most expensive—of Sampa's designer hotels, Emiliano is reputed for its stellar service, which begins the minute you arrive and receive a welcome massage. A butler to pack and unpack your luggage, complimentary glasses of wine, and toiletries customized to your skin type are just a few of the pampering details that will leave you feeling utterly spoiled. There are also the rooms themselves: airy, modern, and steeped in creature comforts ranging from ultrasoft Egyptian bed linens to gleaming marble bathroom/spas.

Famous throughout São Paulo for their highly reputed gourmet restaurants, the enterprising Fasano family added world-class hoteliers to their impressive résumé when they opened **Fasano** (Rua Vitório Fasano 88, Cerqueira César, tel. 11/3896-4000, www.fasano .com.br, R$714–834 d), which is discreet and clubby with a streamlined 1930s edge. This sophisticated hotel is appealingly understated in comparison with most of the city's five-star options. Polished wood and supple leather in warm tones of caramel and chocolate abound. Service is outstanding. As an added bonus, you don't have to step outside for a bite. Within the hotel itself you'll find **Fasano,** considered one of the finest restaurants in Brazil; **Nonno Ruggero,** a second multi-starred restaurant, where breakfast is served; and **Baretto,** a refined jewel of a bar featuring live music.

Higienópolis

Most tourists (and guidebooks) mysteriously overlook the elegant residential neighborhood of Higienópolis when it comes to hotel listings. Although accommodations here are sparse, there are some good bargains, and the *bairro* itself is not only attractive, tranquil, and safe, but centrally located.

R$100-200

The modern, nondescript rooms at **Ville Hotel** (Rua Dona Viridiana 643, Higienópolis, tel. 11/3257-5288, www.hotelville.com.br, R$110 d) are not very stylish, but they are fairly spacious. Furthermore, the price and the location (only a short walk from Santa Cecilia Mêtro) are quite unbeatable. More attractive are the impressively large condo-style accommodations at **Tryp Higienópolis** (Rua Maranhão 371, Higienópolis, tel. 11/3665-8200, www.solmelia .com, R$155–220 d), a hotel that is part of the Spanish Meliá chain. Light, bright, and warmly accessorized, the rooms are a terrific bargain, particularly when you factor in the sundeck and swimming pool.

FOOD

São Paulo is a food-lovers' haven that few other cities in the world can rival. Paulistanos love to eat out and the city has a fantastically diverse restaurant scene with something for every palate and wallet. At the high-end of the scale are world-class kitchens ruled over by innovative chefs that offer both traditional and contemporary cuisine at prices more affordable than the equivalent eating experiences would cost in London, Paris, or New York. Even so, if your purse strings are tight, many top restaurants offer weekday lunchtime *executivo* menus that allow you to sample toned-down versions of master chefs' creations at a fraction of the price. At the other end of the price spectrum, numerous bakeries, cafés, and bars offer bites, snacks, sandwiches, and other forms of sustenance for every occasion and appetite. Due to its diverse immigrant population, the city is also rich in international cuisine, with special mention going to Lebanese, Japanese, and Italian. In terms of the latter, Sampa's *ristorantes,* cantinas, and pizzerias offer some of the best *cocina*

LITTLE ITALY

Between Avenida Paulista and Centro, in a cluster of hilly streets known officially as **Bela Vista** – and popularly as **"Bixiga"** – is where you'll find São Paulo's "Little Italy." In the early 20th century Italian immigrants (primarily from Calabria) flocked to this *bairro*. Many were stonemasons, and it was with leftovers from construction sites that they built their own houses, many of which are still standing. Although today Bixiga is more ethnically varied (and more run-down), Italian traditions are still strong, especially when it comes to food. A large number of decades-old bakeries and cantinas line Rua 13 de Maio and surrounding streets. Unfortunately, many are geared to tourism and feature mediocre, all-you-can-eat Italian banquets along with kitschy decorative schemes and hokey performers singing Italian lounge standards. However, there are also a few simpler (and calmer) traditional *ristorantes* where you can savor tasty authentic fare in charmingly rustic surroundings.

São Domingos (Rua Santo Domingos 330, Bela Vista, tel. 11/3104-7600, 7 A.M.-8 P.M. Mon.-Sat., 7 A.M.-3 P.M. Sun.) is a *traditionalíssimo* Italian neighborhood bakery/emporium that has been around for close to a century. Aside from freshly baked bread, there is everything you could ever want for an antipasto – from cheese and olives to prosciutto and pancetta. On weekends fresh focaccia and *empadas* emerge with regularity from the oven. The cannolis and *pastiera de grano* are divine.

After more than 60 years in operation, **Roperto** (Rua Treze de Maio 634, Bela Vista, tel.

11/3288-2573, www.cantinoroperto.com.br, 11:30 A.M.-midnight Sun.-Thurs., 11:30 A.M.-1 A.M. Fri.-Sat., R$35-40) is still considered one of the best and most authentic of Bixiga's cantinas. The forte is honest southern Italian fare. In the warmly rustic dining room, you can choose from an array of homemade pastas (portions are large enough for two) ranging from a standard yet scrumptious lasagna Bolognese to gnocchi served with a pesto sauce that includes walnuts, almonds, and peanuts. The house specialty – tenderly roasted kid with potatoes and broccoli – is enough to feed three.

The family-owned **Il Cacciatore** (Rua Santo Antônio 855, Bela Vista, tel. 11/3110-5119, noon-3 P.M. and 6:30 P.M.-midnight Tues.-Fri., 6:30 P.M.-1 A.M. Sat., noon-5 P.M. Sun., R$35-45) has been serving robust specialties from Lombardy since the early 1950s. Entrées include the mouthwatering likes of pappardelle with wild boar sauce and rabbit cooked in red wine with creamy polenta. Try the ravioli stuffed with pumpkin and raisins, swimming in a rosé wine sauce and dusted with crushed amaretto biscuits. One portion easily feeds two people.

If you're in the mood for pizza, head to **Speranza** (Rua Treze de Maio 1004, Bela Vista, tel. 11/3288-3512, www.pizzaria.com.br, 6 P.M.-1:30 A.M. Mon.-Fri., 6 P.M.-2 A.M. Sat., 6 P.M.-1 A.M. Sun., R$20-30). Since 1958, this warm and animated restaurant has been seducing pizza lovers with a secret Neapolitan recipe for crunchy medium-crust pies covered with toppings both traditional (pepperoni and mozzarella) and trendy (shiitake mushrooms).

italiana this side of the Atlantic. In fact, in São Paulo, pizza is as much a staple as *feijoada*, and many claim you can get a better pizza here than in Italy.

Centro
CAFÉS AND SNACKS
Ponto Chic (Largo do Paissandu 27, Centro, tel. 11/3222-6528, www.pontochic.com.br, 8 A.M.–midnight Mon.–Sat.) earned its name from the fact that when this now famous

luncheonette first opened in 1922, it immediately became the "chic point" for the city's intellectuals, artists, and soccer stars to meet. Then, as now, the most popular item on the menu was the *sanduíche Bauru*, a hefty sandwich of roast beef with tomato, cucumber, and a deliciously gooey melted mixture of four cheeses, all served on French bread. Invented here, it has since gone on to become a São Paulo culinary icon. A side order of crisp fries is the perfect accompaniment.

SÃO PAULO

SÃO PAULO

VEGETARIAN

Hidden away on the second floor of a nonde-script office building, **⊂ Nutrisom** (Viaduto 9 de Julho 160, 11 A.M.–3 P.M. Mon.–Fri., 11:30 A.M.–4:30 P.M. Sun., R$14–16 pp) is light, bright, and a little spartan—the better with which to showcase the extensive vegetar-ian buffet of hot and cold dishes that attracts a diverse array of veggie lovers. Included in the all-you-can-eat price are fresh fruit juices and dessert.

INTERNATIONAL

More than just an Italian cantina of the red-checkered tablecloth variety, **Famiglia Mancini** (Rua Avanhandava 81, Centro, tel. 11/3256-4320, www.famigliamancini .com.br, 11:30 A.M.–1 A.M. Sun.–Wed., 11:30 A.M.–2 A.M. Thurs., 11:30 A.M.–3 A.M. Fri.–Sat., R$40–60) is a phenomenon that keeps both Paulistanos and tourists lining up at the door year after year. Instead of *alta cocina* what you get is heaping portions (enough to feed two very hungry people) of every kind of pasta and sauce you can imagine. You could just as easily satiate your hunger at the ban-quet-like buffet of *antipasti*.

⊂ La Casserole (Largo do Arouche 346, Centro, tel. 11/3331-6283, www.lacasserole .com.br, noon–3 P.M. Tues.–Fri., 7 P.M.–midnight Tues.–Thurs., 7 P.M.–1 A.M. Fri.–Sat., noon–4 P.M. Sun., R$35–45) has hardly changed at all since it first opened in 1954. A quintessential Parisian bistro, its retro charm and bonhomie has long made it a favorite for discreet VIPs in search of classic French fare such as onion soup, duck à l'orange, and steak frîtes, prepared to per-fection and served with flair by the atten-tive *garçons*. If you come for lunch during the week, take advantage of the R$35 three-course *menu executivo*.

Liberdade

Although Liberdade has an increasing number of Chinese and Korean eateries, the stand-outs remain the neighborhood's traditional Japanese restaurants.

JAPANESE

Bakery Ikikiri (Rua dos Estudantes 24, Liberdade, tel. 11/3277-4939, 8 A.M.–7 P.M. daily) is a Chinese bakery that offers fragrant steamed buns and other Asian goodies as well as Japanese bubble tea.

Gombe (Rua Tomás Gonzaga 22, Liberdade, tel. 11/3209-8499, 11:30 A.M.–2 P.M. and 6:30–11:30 P.M. Mon.–Sat., R$15–30) is an old-time favorite that specializes in *robata*—a traditional cooking style of northern Japan in which the daily catch is grilled over small fires. The most coveted seats in this restau-rant are those surrounding the grill where you can watch the chefs sear skewers of squid and fish. The menu also boasts a large variety of Japanese noodles.

Another favorite address is **Sendai** (Rua da Glória 148, Liberdade, tel. 11/3241-1129, 11:30 A.M.–2:30 P.M. and 6:30–10:30 P.M. Mon.–Fri., noon–3 P.M. and 6–10:30 P.M. Sat., R$25–35). The long, narrow, unadorned din-ing area is divided into low tables on one side and a sushi bar on the other. Aside from sushi and sashimi, there are plenty of grilled special-ties as well as *sugaki,* a refreshing oyster salad with cucumber.

Sushi-Yassu (Rua Tomas Gonzaga 98, Liberdade, tel. 11/3209-6622, R$35–45) is one of the most traditional Japanese restau-rants in Liberdade. The extensive menu boasts over 100 offerings—most of which focus on classic recipes such as stir-fried Japanese spin-ach with smoked fish shavings and cold wheat noodles with lightly battered shrimp. For pri-vacy, there are seven screened-off rooms with tatami mats.

Higienópolis
CAFÉS AND SNACKS

Benjamin Abrahão Mundo dos Pães (Rua Maranhão 220, Higienópolis, tel. 11/3258-1855, www.benjaminabrahão.com.br, 6 A.M.–8:30 P.M. daily) is considered one of the best *padarias* (bakeries) in town. Delicious baked goods and over 50 varieties of bread emerge from its ovens daily. Their freshly made sand-wiches are very tasty, as are the *chipas*—golf-ball-size baked dough stuffed with fillings such as guava jelly and white cheese with herbs.

CONTEMPORARY

Housed in a creamy brick mansion with a pretty veranda and a warmly furnished lounge, **Carlota** (Rua Sergipe 753, Higienópolis, tel. 11/3661-8670, www.carlota .com.br, noon–4 P.M. Tues.–Fri., 7 P.M.–midnight Mon.–Thurs., 7 P.M.–1 A.M. Fri., noon–1 A.M. Sat., noon–6 P.M. Sun., R$50–60) is owned and operated by one of Brazil's most innovative contemporary chefs, Carla Pernambuco. Although she hails from *churrasco*-famous Rio Grande do Sul, Pernambuco's trademark dishes feature unusual multicultural combinations of flavors and textures, such as grilled jumbo shrimp with fresh asparagus, shiitake mushrooms, and cashew rice. Her eponymous dessert is a warm *petit gâteau* of bananas served with cinnamon ice cream.

PIZZA

Veridiana (Rua Dona Veridiana 661, Higienópolis, tel. 11/3120-5050, www.veridiana .com.br, 7 P.M.–12:30 A.M. Sun.–Thurs., 7 P.M.–1:30 A.M. Fri.–Sat., R$30–40) is named after Dona Veridiana, a baron's daughter and early feminist who scandalized late 19th-century Sampa when she divorced her husband and turned her palatial mansion into a famous literary salon (where she also entertained her lovers). Today the cathedral-like interior is home to the city's most sumptuous pizzeria. Exposed brick walls lit by candlelight cast a warm glow on the tables, often filled by celebs who swear by the medium-crust pizzas topped with delicacies such as escarole, imported anchovies, and wild boar.

INTERNATIONAL

In the charming old manor occupied by **AK Delicatessen** (Rua Mato Grosso 450, Higienópolis, tel. 11/3231-4497, noon–3 P.M. and 8 P.M.–midnight Tues.–Sat., noon–4 P.M. Sun., R$25–40), rising young chef Andrea Kaufman breathes new life into European and Middle Eastern Jewish culinary classics.

Help yourself to the likes of marinated sardine tartare and sweet and sour cucumbers at the salad bar downstairs, where you can also order a crunchy falafel sandwich. Upstairs, in an intimate dining area whose walls are swathed in colored fabrics, try the veal goulash topped with sour cream and the pastrami-stuffed beef with gratinéed brie, served with delicate potato latkes. *Arroz-doce* brûlé perfumed with cardamom and rose water is a wonderful update of a Jewish grandmother's rice pudding.

Born and bred in the Loire Valley, but naturalized as a Brazilian citizen, chef and *grand gourmand* Erick Jacquin is considered one of the best French chefs in the city. At his elegantly modern ◖ **La Brasserie Erick Jacquin** (Rua Bahia 683, Higienópolis, tel. 11/3826-5409, www.brasserie.com.br, R$50–70), he treats diners to dishes such as roast duck in black pepper sauce and lamb with Provençal vegetables, prepared with understated flair. Jacquin's great specialty is his homemade foie gras, which comes in many guises including a surprisingly sublime version bathed in guava cream. The desserts, particularly the *petit gâteau*, are irresistible, and the wine list is outstanding.

Avenida Paulista
CAFÉS AND SNACKS

Located inside the Conjunto Nacional's gigantic, new Livraria Cultura, **V. Café** (Av. Paulista 2073, tel. 11/3170-4033, 9 A.M.–10 P.M. Mon.–Sat., noon–8 P.M. Sun.) has immediately become the city's most sought-after literary café. Flaking out in a cushiony chair and leafing through piles of books and magazines in the company of attractive bookworms and a top-of-the-line espresso is a great way to while away an hour or two. For snacks or light meals, there are inventive sandwiches (try the roast beef with arugula, ginger, thyme, and honey mustard on pumpernickel) and a variety of cakes.

VEGETARIAN

Lactovegetarianism goes Indian at **Gopala Prasada** (Rua Antônio Carlos 413, Consolação, tel. 11/3283-3867, www.gopalaprasasda.com.br, 11:30 A.M.–3 P.M. Mon.–Fri., noon–3 P.M. Sat.,

R$12–20). Incense wafts through the interior, rose petals are scattered on the floor, and the constantly changing daily menu features healthy fare flavored with spices from the Orient. A second adjacent dining room at Rua Antônio Carlos 429 is also open for dinner on Fridays and Saturdays.

BRAZILIAN

After close to half a century of existence, **Sujinho** (Rua da Consolação 2078, Consolação, tel. 11/3231-5207, www.sujinho.com.br, 11:30 A.M.–5 A.M. daily, R$10–20) is still a notorious all-day and after-hours hangout where Paulistanos meet, mingle, and dig in to reasonably priced and deliciously tender barbecued meat. A wide array of side dishes allows you to assemble a meal according to your appetite. Try to nab one of the sidewalk tables so you can observe the people passing by.

A discerning carnivore's paradise, **Baby Beef Rubaiyat** (Alameda Santos 86, Paraíso, tel. 11/3141-1188, www.rubaiyat.com.br) is a family-owned chain famed for its sublimely tender cuts of meat. Quality is ensured because the Iglesias family raises all its own cattle on a ranch in Mato Grosso do Sul, as well as chickens, wild boar, Dorper lambs, and a special breed of pig. An impressive wine list complements the food, and the service is excellent.

CONTEMPORARY

Although it's been around for over a decade, **Spot** (Alameda Ministro Rocha de Alameda 72, Cerqueira César, noon–3 P.M. and 8 P.M.–1 A.M. Mon.–Fri., 1–5 P.M. and 8 P.M.–1 A.M. Sat.–Sun., R$20–30) has never gone out of style—you can tell by the cooler-than-thou crowd who squeeze into this sleek glass box surrounded by the skyscrapers of Avenida Paulista. While it can get a little noisy, the people-watching is great fun. The varied if not overly inspiring menu offerings—an attractive array of appetizers and salads, pastas, and grilled meats—are ideal for a snack or a full-fledged meal.

Mestiço (Rua Fernando de Albuquerque 277, Cerqueira César, tel. 11/3256-3165, www.mestico.com.br, 11:45 A.M.–midnight Sun.–Mon., 11:45 A.M.–1 A.M. Tues.–Thurs., 11:45 A.M.–2 A.M. Fri.–Sat., R$20–30) usually refers to a person of mixed ethnicity. It's an appropriate name for this perpetually hip, but down-to-earth eatery that traffics in culinary influences as diverse as Bahia (home state of the owner/chef) and Thailand. As colorful as the creatively presented food is the spacious interior, whose pastel-hued walls are covered with a constantly changing selection of art.

PIZZA

For the last few years **Bráz** has consistently been crowned as one of the city's best pizzerias. The most recent and inviting of its several locations is **Quintal do Bráz** (Rua Gandavo 447, Vila Mariana 5082-3800, www.quintaldobraz.com.br, 6:30 P.M.–12:30 A.M. Sun.–Thurs., 6:30 P.M.–1:30 A.M. Fri.–Sat., R$30–40), where tables are scattered throughout a relaxing green *quintal* (garden). Aside from the truly outstanding pizzas, this location offers a wonderful selection of antipasti and the recently invented *pizza carola,* a hybrid that is part calzone and part pizza.

INTERNATIONAL

The dishes on the menu at **Shin Zushi** (Rua Afonso de Freitas 269, Paraíso, tel. 11/3889-8700, 11:30 A.M.–2 P.M. and 6–10:30 P.M. Tues.–Sat., 6–10 P.M. Sun., R$25–35) are so tradition-bound that this is the only place outside of Japan you're likely to find them. Could this be why most of the clientele are Japanese? Noteworthy are the sushi, sashimi, and melt-in-your-mouth shrimp and vegetable tempura.

Tenda do Nilo (Rua Coronel Porto 638, Paraíso, tel. 11/3885-0460, noon–3:30 P.M. Mon.–Fri., 12:30–4 P.M. Sat., R$16–25) is one of the tiniest and least expensive Middle Eastern restaurants in São Paulo. It is also one of the best. The simple yet mouthwatering Lebanese dishes are prepared according to recipes passed down by the cook's mother. Try the *fatte:* toasted Syrian bread topped with beef, chickpeas, and creamy white cheese steeped in garlic. Then cleanse your palate with "1001

Nights," a moist cake of semolina bathed in a pistachio cream.

Jardins
CAFÉS AND SNACKS

Situated in deepest, darkest Jardins, **Galeria dos Pães** (Rua Estados Unidos 1645, Jardim América, tel. 11/3064-5900, www.galeria dospaes.com.br, 24 hours daily) is a mélange of bakery, delicatessen, wine shop, and café. Though it never closes, this *superpadaria* is always packed, though the clientele changes hourly. The breakfast buffets, featuring more than 50 items, are a great start to any day, while creative sandwiches (named for famous painters) make for practical lunches. After a night out on the town, revelers often stop by and ward off potential hangovers by downing bowls of nourishing broth from the late-night soup buffet.

Chocoholics will go cocoa *louco* at **Chocolat du Jour** (Rua Haddock Lobo 1672, Jardim Paulista, tel. 11/3062-3857, www.chocolat dujour.com.br, 10 A.M.–8 P.M. Mon.–Fri., 10 A.M.–6 P.M. Sat.). The interior of this celebrated Paulistano chocolatier resembles a swanky jewelry shop, except that the coveted bling on display in glass cases is edible. The outstanding truffles are made with a secret mixture of Belgian and Brazilian chocolate. Kids will love the chocopop (chocolate-covered popcorn). A small café serves espresso and hot chocolate.

If São Paulo had an equivalent to the infamous Deux Magots in Paris, it would be **Santo Grão** (Rua Oscar Freire 413, Jardim Paulista, Sao Paulo, tel. 11/3082-9969, www.santo grao.com.br, 9 A.M.–1 A.M. Mon.–Thurs., 9 A.M.–2 A.M. Fri.–Sat., 9 A.M.–midnight Sun.), except that this clubby, modern café is frequented by a hipper, less touristy public than its Left Bank doppelgänger. Nonetheless, as a people-watching scene, it is unparalleled. The extensive variety of gourmet *cafés* (including an aromatic house-grown blend) are prepared and served with the utmost care. Salads, sandwiches, and light gourmet meals are available, as is breakfast. However, nothing goes better

with a freshly pulled *demi-tasse* than a Nutella crepe topped with cream *sorvete*. A second smaller café is nearby (Av. Alameda Santos 1940, tel. 11/3285-5922).

A charmingly retro diner/luncheonette, **Frevo** (Rua Oscar Freire 603, Jardim Paulista, tel. 11/3082-3434, www.frevinho.com.br, 10:30 A.M.–1 A.M. Sun.–Wed., 10:30 A.M.–2 A.M. Thurs.–Fri., 10:30 A.M.–3 A.M. Sat., R$10–20) has been serving up snacks, sandwiches, and decadent sundaes since 1956. The *pièce de résistance* is the legendary *beirute* sandwich. The traditional version combines cheese, tomatoes, oregano, and a hearty slab of roast beef.

VEGETARIAN

One of the best vegetarian restaurants in the city, **Cheiro Verde** (Rua Peixoto Gomide 1078, Jardim Paulista, tel. 11/3289-6853, www.cheiro verderestaurante.com.br, 11:30 A.M.–3 P.M. Mon.–Fri., noon–4:30 P.M. Sat.–Sun., R$10–15) serves fresh, creative, and inexpensive ovolactovegetarian salads, tarts, pastas, and pizzas in a relaxing environment.

BRAZILIAN

One of the brightest rising stars in Sampa's gastronomic firmament is Ana Luiz Trajano, the chef at **◖ Brasil a Gosto** (Rua Professor Azevedo do Amaral 70, Jardim Paulista, tel. 11/3086-3565, www.brasilagosto.com.br, R$35–50). Having steeped herself in culinary traditions from all over Brazil, Trajano revisits classic recipes, revitalizing them with unpredictable and delightfully contemporary twists. Shrimp with heart of palm in orange vinaigrette and *badejo* fish, encrusted with *baru* (a rare type of cashew), and served with a creamy *banana da terra* puree are examples of the inspired fare served in the tastefully appointed and relaxed dining room.

Another inspired female chef devoted to the cause of Brazilian cuisine is Mara Salles of **Tordesilhas** (Rua Bela Cintra 465, Consolação, tel. 11/3107-7444, www.tordesilhas .com, noon–3 P.M. and 7 P.M.–midnight Tues.–Fri., noon–5 P.M. and 7 P.M.–midnight Sat., noon–5 P.M. Sun., R$25–40). While Salles—a former secretary who couldn't ignore her passion for cooking—tackles traditional regional dishes with gusto, she also goes out on creative limbs with the unusual likes of carpaccio of *carne-de-sol* (sun-dried beef) and pork ribs with *mulato* risotto. If you want a sampling of the best of Brazilian cuisine, come for the Sunday buffet, which offers a cornucopia of regional dishes.

If you can't make it to Bahia and want to sample its fragrant Afro-inspired cuisine, head to **Bargaço** (Rua Oscar Freire 1189, Jardim Paulista, tel. 11/3085-5058, www.restaurante bargaco.com.br, noon–3 P.M. and 6:30 P.M.– midnight Mon.–Fri., noon–1 A.M. Sat., noon– 11 P.M. Sun., R$40–65). Try one of various types of *moqueca,* a succulent seafood stew cooked in a heady concoction of coconut milk, *dendê* (palm) oil, tomatoes, cilantro, and lime. Despite the upscale address and ambiance, prices are surprisingly decent.

In 1946, Afonso Paulillo (nicknamed "Bolinha") decided to stop driving taxis for a living and open up a small hole-in-the-wall serving his—and most other Brazilians'— favorite dish: *feijoada.* Little did he know that **Bolinha** (Av. Cidade Jardim 53, Jardim Europa, tel. 11/3061-2010, www.bolinha.com.br, R$59–69 pp) would become a local institution, renowned for serving the city's most celebrated version of Brazil's national dish. Although this isn't the cheapest *feijoada* in town, couples can take advantage of a chivalrous rule whereby women get to eat for free after 7 P.M.

Rodeio (Rua Haddock Lobo 1498, Jardim Paulista, tel. 11/3474-1333, www.churra scariarodeio.com.br, 11:30 A.M.–3:30 P.M. and 6:30 P.M.–1 A.M. Mon.–Thurs., 11:30 A.M.–1 A.M. Fri.–Sat., 11:30 A.M.–midnight Sun., R$50–70) is a traditional *churrascaria* where the entrepreneurial and artistic classes head to get their red meat fix. The house specialty—*picanha* (rump steak) cooked to perfection on a mini grill at your table—is melt-in-your-mouth divine. However, there are plenty of other meats to choose from, including pork tenderloin and even ostrich. Side dishes range from fried bananas to grilled hearts of palm.

CONTEMPORARY

Internationally celebrated chef Alex Atala has garnered extraordinary success with **D.O.M.** (Rua Barão de Capanema 549, Jardim Paulista, tel. 11/3088-0761, www.dom restaurante.com.br, noon–3 P.M. and 7 P.M.– midnight Mon.–Thurs., noon–3 P.M. and 7 P.M.–1 A.M. Fri., 7 P.M.–1 A.M. Sat., R$65– 75). Atala's forte is applying classic cooking techniques to unusual ingredients and culinary traditions (he has a predilection for those from the Brazilian Amazon). The resulting creations are all about contrasting textures (scallops marinated in coconut milk with mango *croquante*) and inspired flavors (filet mignon braised in bitter chocolate and watercress) that challenge the most jaded taste buds. Showcasing the food to maximum effect is the seductively modernist dining space designed by noted architect Ruy Ohtake. It includes an open kitchen where you can see the master chef at work. Reservations are essential.

INTERNATIONAL

Located inside the elegant Hotel Fasano, **Fasano** (Rua Vitorio Fasano 88, Jardim Paulista, tel. 11/3062-4000, www.fasano.com.br, 7:30 P.M.–1 A.M. Mon.–Sat., R$85–100) is São Paulo's undisputed temple of Italian *alta cocina.* Within its glossy dark interior (the walls are black Italian marble) wealthy and fashionable foodies of the world unite to partake of refined versions of classic Italian dishes such as partridge roasted in white wine with creamy polenta and an aromatic *risoto del contadino* with Tuscan sausage, white beans, and red wine. If you're in the mood to really splurge, indulge in the R$260 *menus de degustação*—veritable mini banquets created according to specific themes and regions. Reservations are essential.

Before **Antiquarius** (Alameda Lorena 1884, Jardim Paulista, tel. 11/3082-3015, noon–3 P.M. Tues.–Sat., noon–5 P.M. Sun., 7 P.M.–1 A.M. Mon.–Thurs., 7 P.M.–2 A.M. Fri.–Sat., R$90– 100) came along (the original is in Rio), most Brazilians thought Portuguese cuisine was limited to various ways of preparing *bacalhau* (salted cod). The chefs at this elegant—if overbearingly formal—restaurant serve inspired versions of this classic. However, they also have a way with seafood, as witnessed by the *arroz de polvo* (octopus risotto) and *açorda de frutos de mar,* a robust stew featuring shrimp, squid, and octopus. Although the prices are steep, the food is outstanding. The divine desserts are based on centuries-old recipes prepared by the nuns of Portugal's convents.

Considered Sampa's finest Middle Eastern restaurant, **Arábia** (Rua Haddock Lobo 1397, Cerqueira César, Sao Paulo, tel. 11/3061-2203, www.arabia.com.br, R$25–35) serves delicately prepared traditional specialties such as charcoal grilled lamb *mechoui* and banquet-worthy *mezzes*—a sampling of 18 items ranging from taboule and hummus to Syrian sausage that can easily feed up to five people. The Moroccan couscous served on Saturdays has quite a following.

VARIED

Sporting scarlet leather banquettes and a casually urbane New York–like vibe, the **Ritz** (Alameda França 1088, Cerqueira César, tel. 11/3062-5830, noon–3 P.M. and 8 P.M.–1 A.M. Mon.–Fri., 1 P.M.–1 A.M. Sat.–Sun., R$15–25) has long been a favorite haunt of Sampa's art, fashion, and gay and lesbian crowd, who swear by its gourmet diner fare. Aside from inventive salads and pastas, the star of the menu is the hamburger (charbroiled over volcanic rocks) served with rice balls and garnished with horseradish, hollandaise, and spicy tamarind sauces.

◖ **Figueira Rubaiyat** (Rua Haddock Lobo 1738, Jardim Paulista, tel. 11/3063-3888, www.rubaiyat.com.br, noon–3:30 P.M. and 7 P.M.–12:30 A.M. Mon.–Fri., noon–12:30 A.M. Sat.–Sun., R$45–85) is owned by the Rubaiyat restaurant chain, which is renowned for its succulent cuts of fine beef. The *figueira* refers to the immense 80-year-old fig tree that spreads its great limbs throughout much of this beautiful restaurant. Such a bewitching setting would seem to be a hard act to follow, but the food doesn't disappoint. Although the menu features all the delectable

meats of its Rubaiyat siblings, the specialty here is fish and seafood. The signature dish is the *caixote marinho:* a reimagined paella cooked in a custom-made brick oven.

Pinheiros and Vila Madalena
CAFÉS AND SNACKS

At **DeliParis** (Rua Harmonia 484, Vila Madalena, tel. 11/3816-5911, www.deliparis.com.br, 7 A.M.–10:30 P.M. Mon.–Sat., 8 A.M.–10:30 P.M. Sun.), Vila Mada meets Montmartre. At this *boulangerie*/bistro you can savor light French fare such as quiches, croissants *au chocolat,* and *tarte tatin* at the sidewalk tables, which conjure up a Parisian café. On the weekends, the scrumptious all-you-can-eat *petit déjeuner* draws famished folk from all over the neighborhood.

A favorite neighborhood hang-out, **Empanadas Bar** (Rua Wisard 489, Vila Madalena, tel. 11/3032-2116, www.empanadasbar.com.br, 5 P.M.–2 A.M. Mon.–Thurs., 5 P.M.–3 A.M. Fri., 2 P.M.–3 A.M. Sat., 2 P.M.–2 A.M. Sun.) keeps expanding, both in size (it currently takes up an entire block) and in the number of delicious oven-baked empanadas it serves (between 25,000 and 30,000 a month!). Whether you opt for a classic filling such as spicy ground beef or the more unorthodox likes of heart of palm, roquefort, and guava with cheese, you'll find it impossible to eat just one.

BRAZILIAN

At **Feijoada da Lana** (Rua Aspicuelta 421, Vila Madalena, tel. 11/3814-9191, noon–3:30 P.M. Mon.–Fri., 12:30–5:30 P.M.), *feijoada* is the *plat de résistance.* Lana prepares hers using velvety black beans that are kept steaming hot in an immense clay cauldron. The rest of the classic fixings—sun-dried meat, sausages, and pork—are served separately (meaning you don't have to eat ears, tails, or snouts). During the week, all-you-can-eat *feijoada* is R$22. On the weekends, the price doubles to R$44, but you also get *caipirinhas* and dessert.

If you can't get to Minas to try its much-vaunted regional cuisine, a popular Paulistano alternative is **Consulado Mineiro** (Praça

Benedito Calixto 74, Pinheiros, tel. 11/3064-3882, www.consuladomineiro.com.br, noon–1 A.M. Tues.–Sat., noon–midnight Sun., R$35–45). Dishes are hearty, tasty, no-nonsense affairs such as *galinhada,* a risotto made with saffron, rice, chicken, and vegetables and served with *tutu,* a rich puree of beans with pork. The equally requested *mexidão* is a stew whose "mishmash" of ingredients include sundried beef, pork, beans, kale, pork rinds, egg, and fried bananas. The generous portions easily feed two.

PIZZA
Oficina de Pizzas (Rua Inácio Pereira da Rocha 15, Vila Madalena, tel. 11/3813-8389, www.oficinadepizzas.com.br, 7 P.M.–midnight Sun.–Thurs., 7 P.M.–1:30 A.M. Fri.–Sat., R$30–40) serves delicious, medium-crust pizzas in a relaxing ambiance enhanced by exposed brick walls and Gaudi-inspired mosaics. The wine list is very decent. A second location is also in Vila Madalena (Rua Purpurina 517, tel. 11/3816-3749).

INTERNATIONAL
Allez Allez (Rua Wisard 288, Vila Madalena, tel. 11/3032-3325, www.allezallez.com.br, noon–3 P.M. Tues.–Fri., 1–3 P.M. Sat., 8 P.M.–midnight Mon.–Sat., R$40–50) is a charming but unfortunately too small bistro that gets mobbed by foodies who line up to sample the culinary talents of chef Luiz Emanuel Cerqueira. French classics are prepared with original twists—try the tongue roasted in black truffle oil and frogs legs tempura *à Provençal.* To avoid claustrophobia, arrive early.

Jun Sakamoto (Rua Lisboa 55, Pinheiros, tel. 11/3088-6019, 7 P.M.–12:30 A.M. Mon.–Thurs., 7 P.M.–1 A.M. Fri.–Sat., R$30–40) is indisputably Brazil's most talented vanguard sushi chef. However, if you want the rare privilege of sitting at his individual bar—reservations are essential since he only accepts eight guests a night—you'll have to play by his rules. You'll also have to pay a high price (R$175), since Sakamoto uses refined ingredients, including foie gras and flakes of pure gold. This means

letting the maestro choose what you're going to eat—and how (for instance, Sakamoto decides exactly how much of his homemade soya sauce he'll allow you to douse on your spectacular sushi). A less structured alternative is to eat at a table, where you're free to try other menu offerings, such as squid salad with bamboo shoots and cubes of sole fried in sesame oil.

INFORMATION AND SERVICES
A highly efficient and organized city, São Paulo is better equipped than many places in Brazil to deal with foreign visitors, even though the city receives more business travelers than tourists. Staff at airports, bus stations, and major hotels are quite informative and usually speak at least a little bit of English. Banks that accept foreign ATM cards are easy to find, especially on Avenida Paulista.

Tourist and Travel Information
São Paulo Turismo (tel. 11/6226-0400, www.cidadedesaopaulo.com) is the city travel association. It has over a dozen tourist information kiosks scattered at convenient points around the city where you can pick up (very general) maps and get information. For a really detailed city map, pick up one published by Quatro Rodas, available at larger newspaper and magazine stands or bookstores. Most tourist information kiosks are open daily 9 A.M.–6 P.M. Among the most central locations are Praça da República (at Rua 7 de Abril) in Centro; on Avenida Paulista (in front of the Parque Trianon and right across the street from MASP), and on Avenida Brigadeiro Faria Lima (outside Shopping Iguatemi) in Jardim Paulista. There are also branches at the Tietê bus station, and at both Congonhas and Guarulhos airports.

Information on São Paulo state is trickier to find. The Secretaria Estadual de Turismo do Estado de São Paulo has an information center at the international arrivals floor of Guarulhos as well as a website (www.turismo.sp.com.br). Other useful bilingual websites to consult include www.spturis.com (for the city) and www.saopaulo.sp.gov.br/ingles/saopaulo/turismo (for the entire state).

Banks and Currency Exchange

You can exchange foreign currency without having to pay a fee at **Action** (tel. 11/4002-1818, www.actioncambio.com.br), an agency affiliated with Brazil's Central Bank. It has various offices throughout the city, including Congonhas (7 A.M.–11 P.M. Mon.–Fri.) and Guarulhos airports (9 A.M.–5 P.M. Mon.–Fri.) as well as a location in the Hotel Renaissance (Alameda Santos 2233, Cerqueira César, tel. 11/3069-2265, 7 A.M.–10 P.M. Mon.–Fri., 10 A.M.–8 P.M. Sat.–Sun.), just off Avenida Paulista in Jardins. You can exchange money at major branches of Banco do Brasil in Centro (Rua São Bento 465) and on Avenida Paulista (Av. Paulista 2163). Other major banks such as Citibank, Bank Boston, HSBC, Bradesco, and Santander Banespa all accept international cards with Visa/Plus and/or MasterCard/Cirrus logos. You'll find branches of these banks concentrated around Avenida Paulista, Avenida Brigadeiro Faria Lima in Jardins, and Rua 15 de Novembro in Centro. Banks are open during the week 10 A.M.–4 P.M. ATMs are open daily 6 A.M.–10 P.M. (and closed during the night for security reasons).

Communications

The main **Correios** (post office) is at Rua Líbero Badaró 595, in Centro (8 A.M.–10 P.M. Mon.–Fri.). There are another 300 or so agencies throughout the city including several along Avenida Paulista.

Finding an Internet connection is very easy in São Paulo. The vast majority of hotels offer Internet access to guests. Moreover, if you have your own laptop (which you should always carry with great discretion), an increasing number of place have wireless. You'll find Wi-Fi hot spots, free-of-charge, in most of the more upscale *shoppings*—including Shopping Iguatemi and Shopping Frei Caneca—as well as at popular café chains such as **Fran's** (www.franscorp.com.br) and **Cafeera** (www.cafeera.com.br). Many bookstores, such as **Livraria Cultura** and **FNAC** (see *Shopping*), have cyber cafés. **Cyber Games and Internet** (www.cyberlan.com.br) is a chain of cyber cafés that is open 24 hours—one of the most convenient is at Rua Augusta 2346, Cerqueira César, tel. 11/3511-2580.

Emergency Services

In the event of a medical emergency, dial **192** for an ambulance. Two of the most distinguished private hospitals in the country are **Hospital Albert Einstein** (Av. Albert Einstein 627, Morumbi, tel. 11/3747-1233, www.einstein.com.br) and **Hospital Sírio Libanês** (Rua Dona Adma Jafe 91, Bela Vista, tel. 11/3155-0200, www.hsl.org.br). São Paulo has three major pharmacy chains, each with numerous locations that are open 24 hours; here is a sampling of locations: **Droga Raia** (Rua José Maria Lisboa 645, Jardim Paulistano, tel. 11/3884-8235, www.drogaraia.com.br), **Drogaria São Paulo** (Av. Angélica 1465, Higienópolis, tel. 11/3667-6291, www.drogariasaopaul.com.br), and **Drogasil** (Av. Brigadeiro Faria Lima 2726, Cidade Jardim, tel. 11/3812-6276, www.drogasil.com.br).

In the event of a crime, you can contact the police by dialing **190.** There is a special **Delegácia de Turismo** (Av. São Luís 91, Centro, tel. 11/3214-0209, 8 A.M.–8 P.M. Mon.–Fri.) police unit that deals specifically with crimes involving foreign tourists. Its 24-hour hotline has English-speaking operators.

GETTING THERE
Air

São Paulo has two airports. **Guarulhos International Airport** (tel. 11/6455-2945), also known as Cumbica, is 30 kilometers (20 miles) northeast of the center of the city. The larger of the two airports, it is used for all international flights and a large portion of domestic flights. The majority of international flights land in Guarulhos before continuing on to other major cities—this usually involves a connecting flight. Much closer to the center is the older and smaller **Congonhas Airport** (tel. 11/5090-9000). Limited to domestic flights, it also operates frequent air shuttles that connect São Paulo with Rio de Janeiro (a speedy 30-minute jaunt). For a long time, Congonhas had a reputation for being very congested. This situation came to a head in July 2007, when—as an indirect consequence of months of chaos caused by increased air traffic and a lack of air traffic controllers—a TAM airliner crashed on the runway. All passengers aboard were killed, making it the worst aviation disaster in Brazilian history. As a result, the airport has been undergoing renovations, and many national flights that passed through Congonhas have been rerouted to other airports, including Guarulhos.

At both airports, you will find kiosks for taxis that can take you into the city for a fixed price, calculated according to your final destination. Expect to pay around R$75–85 from Guarulhos and R$30–40 from Congonhas. A much cheaper alternative is to take an *executivo* bus. **Airport Bus Service** (www.airport busservice.com.br, tel. 11/6221-0244, R$28) offers regular service from Guarulhos to Praça da República, the major hotels around Avenida Paulista, the Tietê and Barra Funda bus stations, and Congonhas. Buses leave daily at 30-minute intervals 6 A.M.–11 P.M., with less frequent service throughout the night.

Bus

São Paulo has three major bus terminals. All are conveniently connected to Metrô stations (which bear the same names as the bus terminals) and can be easily reached by numerous municipal buses. To the north, **Rodoviária Tietê** (Av. Cruzeiro du Sul, Santana, tel. 11/3235-0322) is the second-largest bus terminal in the world. From here, you can catch a bus for anywhere in Brazil as well as Argentina, Chile, Uruguay, and Paraguay. You can also take express buses to Rio, which leave at 10-minute intervals during the day and at 30-minute intervals at night. The terminal recently underwent an all-out renovation and is now a bright and extremely well-organized transportation hub well-equipped with restaurants, bookstores, and other amenities.

Near the Memorial da América Látina, **Rodoviária Barra Funda** (Rua Maria de Andrade 664, Barra Funda, tel. 11/3235-0322) has buses that service the interior of

São Paulo state and the state of Paraná (including Iguaçu Falls).

Close to Congonhas airport, **Rodoviária Jabaquara** (Rua dos Jequitibás, Jabaquara, tel. 11/3235-0322) is the departure point for buses to the region surrounding Santos and the southern coast of São Paulo state.

Socicam (tel. 11/3235-0322, www.socicam .com.br) is a private company that operates all of São Paulo's bus terminals. Its website lists all bus companies, routes, and schedules. You can buy bus tickets at the terminals themselves or at travel agents throughout the city. It's advisable to purchase tickets in advance during weekends and holidays.

GETTING AROUND

São Paulo has a very extensive and inexpensive public transportation system consisting of a relatively limited but efficient Metrô and a far-reaching, if slightly more confusing, bus system. There is also no shortage of taxis, which come in especially handy at night.

Metrô

São Paulo's Metrô system (tel. 11/3286-0111, www.metro.sp.gov.br, 5 A.M.–midnight daily) is clean, efficient, and safe. The only problem is its small size, although its four principal lines are slowly being extended and others are under construction. However, you will find the Metrô convenient for zipping around Centro, going up and down Avenida Paulista, getting to the museums around Estação da Luz, and for exploring the *bairro* of Liberdade. It is especially useful during morning and afternoon rush hour, when taxis and buses come to a standstill. During these times, the Metrô runs smoothly, although the crowds can be daunting. Fortunately, Paulistanos have been trained to line up when getting on and off trains. Tickets are sold in the station, although for security reasons kiosks are only open 6 A.M.–10 P.M. Lineups to purchase a ticket can also be pretty long (making purchasing multiples a good idea). A single trip costs R$2.40. If you plan to take a Metrô and bus (or vice versa), it is cheaper to buy a *bilhete de integração* at a Metrô station or on a bus, which allows you to transfer from one to the other for R$4.10. For updated prices and a map of lines, check out the Metrô's bilingual website.

Bus

Buses go everywhere in São Paulo—except when they're stuck in rush-hour traffic (usually worst 7–9 A.M. and 5–7 P.M.). Despite a fleet of over 10,000 vehicles, buses can get very crowded. Moreover, figuring out which bus goes where is a bit confusing, especially if you don't speak Portuguese. Final destinations are marked on the front of the bus, while major stops are listed along the side. Although bus stops themselves are clearly visible, buses will only stop if you flag them down with your arm. After clambering aboard at the front of the bus, you pay the *cobrador* (collector) in the middle and go through the turnstile. The exit is at the rear. You can pay for your fare in cash (R$2.40)—exact change isn't necessary, but the *cobrador* won't have change for large bills over R$10. An alternative is to purchase an electronic ticket known as a *bilhete único*. Sold and rechargeable at SPTransportes kiosks at bus terminals and at lottery agencies, these cards allow you to make three separate bus trips in two hours for a single fare. For information about itineraries, **Transporte Público de São Paulo** (www.sptrans.com.br) offers a free number to call (156). For security reasons, be careful to keep your belongings close to you at all times, and separate your fare beforehand to avoid needlessly flashing wads of cash.

Taxis

Easy to find, taxis are the best and safest way of navigating São Paulo by night. By day, they can be useful for getting to specific destinations off the Metrô or main bus lines, although like other vehicles, they can get stuck in traffic during rush hour. Moreover, considering São Paulo's immensity, if you start shuttling back and forth across the city, you will rack up a small fortune in cab fares. *Taxis comuns* are

the least expensive taxis. You can either hail one in the street (unless it's raining) or find one at a *posto* (taxi stand). *Rádio taxis* are a bit larger and a bit more expensive. Major companies include **Coopertaxi** (tel. 11/6941-2555), **Ligue Taxi** (tel. 11/3866-3030), and **Delta** (tel. 11/5572-6611), which has some English-speaking dispatchers. Check to make sure the meter is always running. Valid during the daytime until 8 P.M., the "Bandeira 1" rate is cheaper than the night, holiday, and weekend rate, or "Bandeira 2."

Car Rental

Although São Paulo is definitely a city in which cars rule, you'll have to possess vast amounts of patience (and a certain degree of insanity) to consider renting a car here. Traffic is a nightmare, parking is a nightmare, and rainstorms (when streets are instantly inundated due to poor drainage) create nightmarish flooding. Add carjackings, the exhaust fumes of thousands of idling buses, and the hundreds of daredevil *"motoboys"* who weave in and out of traffic on scooters, and you'll really appreciate sidewalks.

The only instance in which renting a car makes sense is if you want to explore the coast or mountains of São Paulo state, particularly small towns or isolated beaches that are hard to reach by bus. Major companies include **Avis** (Rua da Consolação 335, Centro, tel. 11/3259-6868, www.avis.com.br), **Hertz** (Rua da Consolação 439, Centro, tel. 11/3258-9384, www.hertz.com.br), and **Localiza** (Rua da Consolação 419, Centro, tel. 11/3231-3055 or 0800-99-2000).

City Tours

Odyssey South America (Largo do Arouche 63, Centro, tel. 11/3331-0278, www.odyssey southamerica.com.br) is a travel agency that operates bilingual walking tours of the city to the historic parts of Centro, Avenida Paulista, and the Mercado Municipal. It also offers excursions to attractions in São Paulo state. **Graffit** (tel. 11/5549-0528, www.graffit .com.br) offers a wide range of interesting city tours organized around diverse themes such as religion and art, gastronomy, ethnic neighborhoods, and gay and lesbian attractions. **Go In São Paulo** (tel. 11/3289-3814, www.goinsaopaulo.com.br) runs custom-made city tours designed for individuals and small groups that are led by English-speaking guides. Excursions around the state—to north coast beaches or coffee plantations—are also available.

Vicinity of São Paulo City

Paulistanos love the city of São Paulo, but with the greater metropolitan area possessing close to 20 million inhabitants, the urge can be strong to trade urban stress for the respite of the surrounding countryside. Fortunately, the state of São Paulo offers a great variety of getaway options. Just make sure you avoid long weekends and holidays when literally millions choose to escape. Not only will destinations be more crowded—and prices higher—but you'll inevitably get stuck in the infamous traffic jams that can stretch for miles.

EMBU

The quickest, easiest, and most interesting day trip you can take from São Paulo is to the small colonial town of Embu, 27 kilometers (17 miles) west of the city. Founded in 1554, many of its historic whitewashed houses and churches have been preserved. Make sure to visit the **Igreja Nossa Senhora do Rosário** (Largo dos Jesuítas 67, tel. 11/4704-2654, 9 A.M.–5 P.M. Tues.–Sun., R$2), an impressive late-17th-century baroque church. Inside the adjacent monastery, the **Museu de Arte Sacra dos Jesuítas** houses a collection of sacred art that includes intricately carved saints and an 18th-century organ made by local Indians.

Shopping

Embu is famous (perhaps overly so) for its many artisans' studios—specializing in wood and stone carving, leather work, furniture-making, and decorative arts—as well as its numerous antiques stores. On weekends, the small town hosts an antiques fair and handicraft market that lures day-trippers and bargain-hunters from the city (to avoid the crowds, arrive early). You could easily spend all day browsing. Note that in terms of antiques, many are not originals, but replicas.

Malyla's Artes e Antiguidades (Rua Nossa Senhora de Rosário 116, tel. 11/4704-3984) specializes in original certified antiques from the 18th, 19th, and 20th centuries, while **Em Jericó** (Rua Nossa Senhora do Rosário 112, tel. 11/4241-9384) has a stock of over 2,000 original antiques. **Empório King** (Rua Joaquim Santana 41, tel. 11/4704-3469) sells works crafted out of wood, ceramic, and iron from Minas Gerais and the Northeast. At **Guarani Artesanatos** (Largo dos Jesuitas 153, tel. 11/4704-3200), you'll find sculptures fashioned out of precious *pau brasil* (brazilwood) and carvings made from soapstone and semi-precious stones. All stores are open daily, usually 9 A.M.–6 P.M.

Food

Hidden away in a charming little alley off Rua Siqueira Campos, **Empório São Pedro** (Viela das Lavadeiras 28, tel. 11/4781-2797, noon–5 P.M. Wed.–Sun., 8 P.M.–1 A.M. Fri.–Sat., R$30–40) occupies an antiques store, where you can browse while feasting on dishes such as asparagus tortellini and roast lamb with sun-dried tomato risotto.

Information

The **tourist office** (Largo 21 de Abril, tel. 11/4704-6565, www.embu.gov.sp.br, 9 A.M.–6 P.M. daily) is right in the center of town.

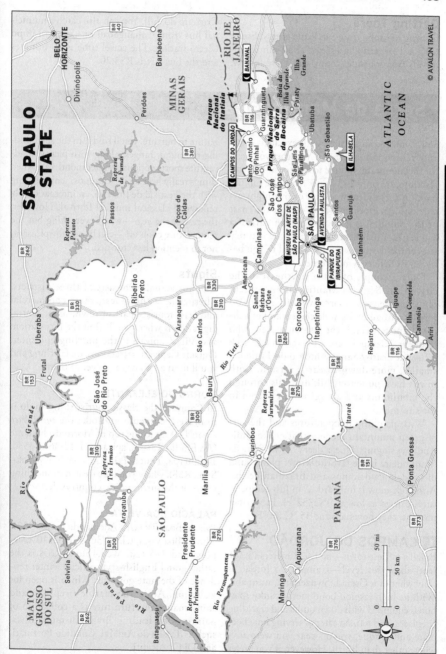

SÃO PAULO

© AVALON TRAVEL

Getting There

Getting to Embu from São Paulo is easy. Embu Cultural *executivo* buses leave at 30-minute intervals from outside Rodoviária Tietê (on Av. Cruzeiro do Sul). You can also catch a municipal bus from Anhangabaú or Campo Limpo Metrô station. The travel time is 30 minutes and the bus fare is R$3.20.

Serra da Mantiqueira

São Paulo is a small state with excellent roads and transportation systems. Whether you head for the mountains or take to the coast, most attractions are only 2–3 hours from the capital, making them ideal weekend or overnight excursions. An excellent way to explore the coast or the mountains is to make them part of a Sao Paulo–Rio itinerary, in which you leisurely stop at the destinations that appeal to you between Brazil's two mega cities.

Only a couple of hours northeast of the city, in the Serra da Mantiqueira mountain range, is the tony resort town of Campos do Jordão, with its Swiss-style chalets and matching alpine scenery. If the fashion mavens who frequent "Campos" are a bit too much, seek refuge at nearby Santo Antônio do Pinhal, a smaller, more down-to-earth version. Both towns have numerous hiking trails through the mountains and are refreshingly cool in the summer.

With its chilly temperatures and the sort of green mountain scenery that evokes Julie Andrews singing "Doe, a deer . . ." the Serra da Mantiqueira is the favorite winter playground of upscale Paulistanos and Brazilian celebs. Although snow is unheard of, in July temperatures can go as low as 0°C (32°F). In warmer months, they hover around 15 °C (60°F).

◖ CAMPOS DO JORDÃO

Brazil's loftiest town—at 1,628 meters (5,341 feet) above sea level—Campos do Jordão is somewhat of a Gstaad, Switzerland, wannabe. With its high fashion boutiques, swanky spas, hotels equipped with down quilts and crackling fireplaces, and refined eateries serving hot chocolate and fondue, you'd swear you were anywhere other than Brazil. However, if you prefer nature to nurture, you'll find it in the surrounding mountain ranges, along with plenty of adventure sports options. Winter months are when things really heat up in "Campos," culminating with the Festival de Inverno, an internationally renowned classical musical festival. However, the rest of the year—when everything but the temperature cools off—can be equally pleasant, not to mention less crowded.

Sights

Campos actually consists of three districts: Abernéssia is the oldest, most commercial and least touristy part of town; more central Jaguaribe is where you'll find the bus station; and Vila Capivari is the bustling epicenter. Outside Capivari, attractions are far-flung and you'll need a taxi or car to get to them.

MORRO DO ELEFANTE

In Capivari, the classic tourist thing to do is to brave the lineups and take the *miniférico* (chair lift) up to the top of Morro do Elefante (Av. Emílio Ribas, Capivari, tel. 12/3663-1530, 1–4:30 P.M. Thurs.–Fri., 9 A.M.–5:30 P.M. Sat.–Sun., R$8), where you'll be treated to smashing views of the surrounding countryside.

PALÁCIO BOA VISTA

Palácio Boa Vista (Av. Ademar de Barros 3001, Alto da Boa Vista, tel. 12/3663-3762, 10 A.M.–noon and 2–5 P.M. Wed.–Sun., R$5) is the rather grand English-style official winter residence of the state governor, which is open for visitation. Amid the marble fireplaces and shiny mahogany furniture is a collection of paintings by leading Brazilian modernists, such as Tarsila do Amaral, Cândido Portinari, and Di Cavalcanti.

CASA DA XILOGRAVURA

Those with a penchant for printmaking will enjoy the woodcuts and engravings exhibited at the Casa da Xilogravura (Av. Eduardo Moreira da Cruz 295, Jaguaribe, tel. 12/3662-1832, 9 A.M.–noon and 2–5 P.M. Thurs.–Mon., R$2).

HORTO FLORESTAL

Horto Florestal (Av. Pedro Paulo, tel. 12/3663-3762, 8 A.M.–5 P.M. daily, R$4) is a state park 12 kilometers (7.5 miles) east from Capivari, with easy hiking trails that wind through one of the state's few remaining forests of striking *araucária* pines. Waterfalls, a river brimming with trout, and the presence of squirrels, parrots, butterflies, and chattering *macacos-prego* ("nail" monkeys) round out the natural attractions.

PEDRA DO BAÚ

For a rigorous physical challenge, tackle the rocky peak of Pedra do Baú (Estrada São Bento do Sapucaí, tel. 12/3662-1106, 8 A.M.–6 P.M. Wed.–Sun., R$5). Rising to an altitude of 1,950 meters (6,400 feet), Pedra do Baú is situated within a park 25 kilometers (16 miles) north of Campos that can be explored on horseback or foot. To climb the peaks, it's recommended that you hire a guide. **Altus Turismo** (Av. Brasil 108, Loja 8, Capivari, tel. 12/3663-4122, www.altustur.tur.br) offers hiking and mountain biking tours to Pedra do Baú as well as the surrounding Serra da Mantiqueira. Depending on the length of the tour and the destination, expect to pay R$35 to $85 per outing. (The popular hiking tour to Pedra do Baú costs R$65).

Entertainment and Events

NIGHTLIFE

In June and July, Vila Capivari's bars are stuffed to the gills, particularly those on Avenida Macedo Soares and Rua Djalma Fojaz (also known as Boulevard Geneve). **Baden Baden** (Rua Djalma Fojaz 93, tel. 12/3663-3659, www.badenbaden.com.br, 11 A.M.–11 P.M. Sun.–Thurs., 11 A.M.–2 A.M. Fri.–Sat.), is *the* spot to see and be seen while quaffing the delicious

house-brewed beer and munching on large portions of sauerkraut with German sausage.

After 10 P.M., roving twenty- and thirty-somethings take to the dance floor at hot spots such as **Winter Lounge** (Rua José Oliveira Damas 500, Capivari, tel. 12/8187-8905, 11 P.M.–close Fri.–Sun., R$40–50). One of the town's more grown-up *danceterias,* its signature sound is "psytrance"—electronic music with a psychedelic edge that combines heavy guitar riffs with sounds from nature (e.g., wailing winds and crashing waves).

FESTIVALS AND EVENTS

One of Brazil's premier festivals of erudite music, the **Festival de Inverno** (www.festivaldeinverno.gov.sp.br) is the high point of Campos's calendar. Each July, renowned musicians, choirs, symphonies, and chamber music groups from all over the world come and perform in churches, auditoriums, and the Praça da Vila Capivari.

Accommodations

Hotel prices are not that cheap in Campos, and during the winter months of June and July they really skyrocket. Advance reservations are essential. In general, the more nights you stay, the cheaper the rate, but during July there is often a minimum stay of three days required. Inaugurated in 2007, **Pousada Santha Serra** (Rua Escolástica M. Da Fonseca 358, Vila Capivari, tel. 12/3663-1633, www.pousadasanthaserra.com.br, R$128–160 d) is a clean, modern, and attractive hotel that is a 10-minute walk from Praça Capivari. Rooms are simply furnished, but comfortable (and equipped with heaters), and possess panoramic mountain views.

You'll need to take a taxi to get to the **Pousada Alto da Boa Vista** (Rua da Hortências 605, tel. 12/3262-4900, R$160–180 d). Located in the posh neighborhood of Alto da Boa Vista, the *pousada* is set in a picturesque wooded area with walking paths. Accommodations for groups and families as well as couples are in cozy chalets with warm wood accents, roaring fireplaces, and in some cases, Jacuzzis. A playground, pool, game room, home movie theater and barbecue area make this an ideal choice for those with kids.

Nestled in rolling hills 4 kilometers (2.5 miles) south of Abernéssia, **(Hotel Toriba** (Av. Ernesto Diedricksen 2962, tel. 12/3262-1566, www.toriba.com.br, R$294–470 d) is one of Campos's most traditional hotels. Inaugurated in 1943, the stylish guest rooms in this Alpine-style villa are suffused with a rustic elegance. Amenities range from a fitness spa, a golf course, and even ice skating to a small farm for children. Three on-site gourmet restaurants—including one that serves the best fondue in town—mean you never have to leave the premises (in fact, full board is available).

Campos's first boutique hotel, the **Hotel Frontenac** (Av. Dr. Paulo Ribas 295, Capivari, tel. 12/3669-1000, www.frontenac.com.br, R$372–620 d) is a refined and utterly charming European-style lodge. Multiple creature comforts, a highly reputed international restaurant, a relaxing piano bar, and outstanding service make it a favorite for those in search of an idyllic getaway.

Food

Among Campos's local culinary specialties are fresh rainbow trout and *pinhões* (pine nuts), which turn up in everything from cakes and cookies to savory dishes. In keeping with the climate and the recurring allusions to things Swiss, you'll also find an abundance of fondue and chocolates. **Só Queijo** (Av. Macedo Soares 642, Capivari, tel. 12/3663-7585, www.soqueijo.com.br, noon–1 A.M. Thurs.–Sun. off-season, noon–1 A.M. Mon.–Sun. Jan. and May–July, R$40–60) is a romantic faux-Swiss eatery with red tablecloths, candlelight, and roaring fireplaces where you can feast on trout, cheese raclette, and a variety of fondues. A word of warning: The homemade pâtés served as starters are addictive enough to ruin your appetite for the main course.

Situated on the road leading to the Horto Florestal, **(Harry Pisek** (Av. Pedro Paulo 857, tel. 12/3663-4030, www.harry pisek.com.br, noon–5 P.M. Mon.–Fri., noon–11 P.M. Sat., noon–6 P.M. Sun., R$22–35) is considered one of the finest German restaurants in Brazil. Of Austrian descent, owner Harry Pisek spent five years in Stuttgart studying the art of sausage making. You can put his expertise to the test by ordering the Harry Pisek Wurst, featuring five homemade varieties including sausages with herbs, Emmenthal, and a mixture of beef and pork. Equally renowned is the stuffed pork cheek.

Bia Kaffee (Rua Professora Isola Orsi 12/33, tel. 12/3663-1507, www.biakaffee.com.br, noon–midnight Fri.–Sat. and noon–8 P.M. Sun. off-season, noon–10 P.M. daily in Jan., noon–midnight daily in July, R$12–25) is also a Campos classic. This charming little café/bistro serves hearty German fare as well as scrumptious strudels, tortes, and a fabulous *tarte tatin*.

Il Pezzo (Av. Macedo Soares 193, tel. 12/3663-3468) is ideal for a quick, cheap snack—the crunchy square pizza slices served hot from the oven come in both savory and sweet versions. Also delicious are the paninis.

Chocoholics are in for a treat due to the town's chocolate-making tradition. At **Araucária** (Av. Macedo Soares 135, tel. 12/3663-4306), you can watch (and smell) the chocolates being made. Popular enough to warrant four locations, **Montanhês** (Praça São Benedito 5, Capivari, tel. 12/3663-1979, www.chocolatemontanhes.com.br) is sought after for its (spiked) hot chocolate drinks and 100 varieties of truffles.

Information

Campos do Jordão's **tourist office** (tel. 12/3262-2799, 8 A.M.–8 P.M. daily) is on the main highway, 2 kilometers (1.2 miles) before Abernéssia. For online information, check out www.camposdojordan.com.br.

Getting There

The *rodoviária* (Av. Doutor Januário Miraglia, tel. 12/3262-1996) is between Jaguaribe and Capivari. São Paulo has daily bus service to Campos with **Expresso Mantiqueira** (tel. 0800/999-701, www.expresso

mantiqueira.com.br) from Tietê terminal. Campos do Jordão lies 167 kilometers (104 miles) northwest of São Paulo. By car, take the BR-116, the SP-070, and SP-123. The travel time from São Paulo is roughly two hours.

SANTO ANTÔNIO DO PINHAL

A mere stone's throw (or scenic mountain train ride) from "Campos" is the much quieter and less trendy Santo Antônio do Pinhal, where the emphasis is more on nature and sports than creature comforts. In fact, if you're after R&R without the ballyhoo, you can bypass Campos altogether.

The area surrounding Santo Antônio is an important orchid-producing region. Just outside of town, the **Jardim dos Pinhais** (Rodovia SP-046 1645, tel. 12/3666-2021, 9:30 A.M.–6:30 P.M. daily, R$13) is a botanical garden with a dazzling array of orchids and other exotic plants.

Accessible by car, the **Cachoeira do Lageado** is a 15-meter-high (50-foot-high) waterfall 8 kilometers (5 miles) from town. **Pico Agudo** (1,700 meters/5,577 feet), whose summit offers impressive views of the Pedra do Baú and Paraíba valley, is 9 kilometers (5.5 miles) out of town. Pico Agudo is a popular launching pad for hang gliders and paragliders. To try these adventurous activities, contact **Xénios Ecoturismo** (Rodovia SP-46 2600, tel. 12/3666-1815, www.xeniosecotur.com.br), which also operates tree-trekking, rappelling, and cascading excursions.

Sights

The highest (and one of the most scenic) train journeys in Brazil is the 20-kilometer (7.5-mile) ride between Campos do Jordão and Santo Antônio do Pinhal that winds through forest-covered mountains at altitudes of 1,740 meters (5,710 feet). The railway was inaugurated in 1914 to carry passengers with lung ailments from São Paulo to the healthy mountainous climes. Make sure you sit on the right-hand side from Campos to obtain the most breathtaking views. In Campos, climb aboard at the **Estação Emílio Ribas-Ferrovia de Capivari**

(Av. Emília Ribas, Capivari, tel. 12/3663-1531, www.efcj.com.br, R$35 round-trip). In Santo Antônio, the quaint whitewashed **Estação Eugénio Lefèvre** is in the center of town.

Accommodations and Food

Most accommodations in Santo Antônio are in the countryside, several kilometers from the center of town. One of the closest to the center is the lovely and quite affordable **Pousada Mirante** (Rua José Cândido Machado 128, tel. 12/3666-1443, www.mirantepousada.com.br, R$150–180 d). Surrounded by greenery, the four cozy stone chalets are outfitted with fireplaces, roughhewn wooden furniture, and hand-embroidered sheets and quilts.

Some 5 kilometers (3 miles) from Santo Antônio, along the road leading to Pico Agudo, is the utterly charming **Pousada Quinta dos Pinhais** (tel. 12/3666-2030, www.quinta dospinhais.com.br, R$380–790 d). Its privileged setting offers magnificent views of the Serra da Mantiqueira and the Pedra do Baú. You can contemplate the scenery from virtually anywhere—be it your room's private wooden Jacuzzi, the lounge chairs surrounding the pool, or the estate's rambling gardens and fruit orchards. The exquisitely designed chalets—built with recycled materials and precious Brazilian hardwoods—boast king-sized beds and fireplaces. Extras range from being greeted with wine and chocolates to having breakfast served to you anywhere on the grounds.

An atmospherically rustic restaurant with a thatched roof, **Santa Truta** (Av. Antônio Joaquim de Oliveira 267, tel. 12/3666-2764, noon–10 P.M. Sun.–Thurs., noon–midnight Fri.–Sat., R$20–30) does justice to the region's favorite fish with mouthwatering recipes such as trout in roquefort sauce with sautéed potatoes, and trout with almond risotto in a red grape sauce.

Aside from panoramic views and a soothing soundtrack of live jazz and MPB, **Restaurante Camponesa** (Rua Turmalina 18, tel. 12/3666-1728, 7–11 P.M. Wed.–Thurs., noon–3 P.M. and 6–11 P.M. Fri., noon–1 A.M.

Sat., noon–5 P.M. Sun. regularly; noon–3 P.M. and 6 P.M.–midnight daily in July, R$25–40) seduces with an eclectic seasonal menu. The focus is on fresh regional products such as rainbow trout served with locally grown shiitake mushrooms and exotic game. For dessert, try the torte made from local pine nuts, served with ice cream.

Information

For information about Santo Antônio (in Portuguese), check out www.guiapinhal .com.br.

Getting There

If you don't want to go to Campos first, **Expresso Mantiqueira** (tel. 0800/999-701, www.expressomantiqueira.com.br) operates two direct buses daily from Tietê terminal. By car, take the BR-116, followed by the SP-123 and SP-046. The travel time from São Paulo is roughly two hours.

Serra do Mar

Traveling east in the direction of Rio de Janeiro will bring you to the lush range of mountains known as the Serra do Mar. Covered with increasingly rare native Atlantic forest, it spans the northern coast of São Paulo state and the southern coast of the state of Rio de Janeiro. In the midst of a lush mountainous landscape are the charming towns of São Luís do Paraitinga and Bananal, a colonial gem surrounded by 19th-century coffee plantations. More isolated than the increasingly developed resorts of the coastline, this region is sprinkled with these small historical towns that have remained largely untouched by time, where you can savor simple, regional cooking and witness vibrant cultural manifestations of years gone by. The main draw, however, is the countryside itself—hikers, climbers, rafters, and waterfall junkies will definitely not be disappointed. The Parque Nacional da Serra da Bocaina, a patch of native Atlantic forest replete with numerous waterfalls and hiking trails, is the highlight for outdoor enthusiasts.

SÃO LUÍS DO PARAITINGA

Nestled in the mountains, São Luís is a small colonial town that has preserved its many handsome 18th- and 19th-century mansions and churches as well as the popular traditions of the Vale do Paraíba. This valley was an important passageway for São Paulo's *bandeirantes* as they forged their way north to Minas Gerais. Later, São Luís emerged as an important trading post for *tropeiros*—roving merchants who carried supplies to and from São Paulo and the wild frontier towns of the interior. The crops that supplied sustenance—*feijão,* manioc, corn, and sugar (distilled into fine *cachaças*)—were instrumental in the development of the town as well as the elaboration of a robust *tropeiro* "cuisine," which is still very alive today.

Parque Estadual da Serra do Mar

São Luís do Paraitinga is within the boundaries of the vast Parque Estadual da Serra do Mar, a nature preserve that encompasses 17,000 hectares (42,000 acres) of native Atlantic forest replete with rivers, waterfalls, and natural pools. The **Núcleo Santa Virgínia** (Rodovia Osvaldo Cruz Km 78, tel. 12/3671-9159, 8 A.M.–5 P.M. daily)—located 30 kilometers (19 miles) from São Luís—administers the area of the park around São Luís leading all the way to Ubatuba on the coast and has monitors that can guide you over the handful of hiking trails. Advance reservations are necessary.

Cia de Rafting (Rua Celestino de Campos Coelho 198, tel. 12/3902-7557, www.ciaderafting .com.br) operates rafting and kayaking trips down the Rio Paraibuna as well as hiking and horseback eco-excursions.

© MICHAEL SOMMERS

Serra do Mar, near Bananal

Festivals and Events

São Luís do Paraitinga is famous throughout Brazil for its traditional street **Carnaval.** Instead of the fervent (imported) rhythms of samba and *frevo* (they are banned by official decree), you'll only hear only old-fashioned *marchinhas* (or marching band songs) that recall Carnavals of yesteryear. With gigantic papier-mâchê dolls, festive decorations, and colorfully costumed residents organized into *blocos,* the atmosphere is festive without being out of control.

Held 40 days prior to Easter, the **Festa do Dívino Espírito Santo** includes a weeklong celebration involving traditional music, processions, fireworks, and public feasting that have a distinctly local character. If you're planning on visiting during either of these festivals, you'll need to book a hotel months in advance, or hope that you can rent a local room last minute.

Accommodations and Food

Probably the nicest option in town is the **Pousada Vila Verde** (Rua Benfica 63, tel. 12/3671-1720, www.vilaverdeparaitinga .com.br, R$55–110 d). Rooms occupy a faux-colonial cluster of pastel-painted houses, located five minutes from Praça da Igreja Matriz. Another good option is **Pousada Primavera** (Via de acesso Renato Aguiar 400, tel. 12/3671-1289, www.primaverapousada .com.br, R$95–115). Although the clean rooms of this modern *pousada* are somewhat spare, the bucolic grounds with a pool and great sweeping views more than compensate.

A *tropeiro* legacy, the local culinary specialty is *afogado,* a hearty and none too lean stew of beef and pork cooked over a low flame with cumin, parsley, and onions. It's served with a generous dusting of manioc flour as well as a shot or two of local *cachaça.* You'll find this dish at many restaurants in town, among them the cheery **Cantinho dos Amigos** (Rua Coronel Domingues de Castro 121, tel. 12/3671-1466, www.cantinho dosamigos.com.br, 11 a.m.–4 p.m. Mon.–Thurs. and 11 a.m.–midnight Fri.–Sun. regularly, 11 a.m.–midnight daily Jan. and July, R$12–24), which specializes in home-cooked regional fare as well as pizzas baked in a wood-burning oven.

Tempero da Terra (Rua Coronel Domingues de Castro 178, tel. 12/3671-1574, 11 A.M.–10 P.M. daily, R$15–25) is another typical restaurant known for its appetizing local fare. For cakes, sandwiches, and sweet and savory baked goods, head to **Cafeteria das Artes** (Praça Oswaldo Cruz, tel. 12/3671-2662), located in a charming historic house that also sells handicrafts and exhibits works by local artists.

Information

Paratingo Turismo (tel. 12/3671-2691, www.paratinga.com.br), across the street from the bus station, has information about the town and region as well as maps. You can also check out www.saoluizdoparaitinga.sp.gov.br.

Getting There

São Luís do Paraitinga is 180 kilometers (112 miles) from São Paulo. The **rodoviária** is on Praça Oswaldo Cruz (tel. 12/3671-1127). **Litorânea** (tel. 11/6221-0244, www.litoranea.com.br) offers daily bus service from Tietê terminal. If you're driving, take the BR-116 to Taubaté and then turn off onto Rodovia Dr. Oswaldo Cruz. If you're arriving from the coast, the town is only 42 kilometers (26 miles) inland from Ubatuba. The travel time to São Luís do Paraitinga from São Paulo is roughly two and a half hours by car and three hours by bus.

◖ BANANAL

This terrifically charming colonial town at the foot of the Serra da Bocaina mountain range was a major hub during the coffee boom that swept through São Paulo state in the 19th century. An architectural feast, the elegant squares and *solares* (mansions) are still intact, as are the surrounding plantations of the coffee barons.

Sights
PRAÇA PEDRO RAMOS

Bananal's main square is the charming, tree-shaded Praça Pedro Ramos. Perched upon the square, the early 19th-century **Igreja de Matriz** (tel. 12/3116-5153, 7–11 A.M. and 1–5 P.M. Wed.–Sun.) is simple, but quite lovely. Nearby, the **Pharmácia Popular** (Rua Manuel de Aguiar 156, tel. 12/3116-1218) lays claim to being Brazil's oldest pharmacy still in operation. Inside, little has changed since it was inaugurated in 1830 by a French chemist. The polished pine shelves and cabinets are stuffed with wonderful old porcelain and glass vials containing bromides, remedies, powdered blood, and morphine.

Jarringly out of place is the European-style **Estaçao de Estrada de Ferro** (Praça Dona Domiciana), an abandoned train station that now houses the municipal library. Built in 1889, the mustard-hued steel plates covering the exterior were manufactured in Belgium according to specific instructions given by Bananal's coffee barons. Beside the station is a mildly rusting steam train from the same era.

FAZENDAS

During the 1850s, Bananal was the world's primary producer of coffee, and the hills surrounding the town are still dotted with grand plantation mansions (although the coffee has given way to eucalyptus). Within close proximity to the town, several of these *fazendas* (estates) can be visited, although you should reserve by phone in advance.

Built in 1855, **Fazenda dos Coqueiros** (tel. 12/3116-1358, www.fazendadoscoqueiros.com.br, 9:30 A.M.–6:30 P.M. daily)—named after the swaying coconut palms that lead up to the gracious main house—is 5 kilometers (3 miles) from Bananal along the SP-068. The *fazenda* has been in the family of the friendly Carioca owners for over a century—that they live amidst the original furnishings conspires to bring history to life. And there is a ton of history: from the original furniture and fixtures (including an antique toilet) to more harrowing effects such as the medieval gadgets used to torture slaves and the dungeon-like *senzala* where they were herded at night so that their collective body heat would rise to warm their masters.

The region's most opulent estate is the elegant **Fazenda do Resgate** (tel. 12/3116-1577, 7–11 A.M. Tues., 7–11 A.M. and noon–4 P.M. Wed.–Fri.), 8 kilometers (5 miles) from Bananal along the SP-064. Built in 1818, the interior is quite smashing and features splendid murals painted by noted Spanish painter José Maria Villaronga as well as a chapel. The *fazenda* was the first plantation in São Paulo to cultivate coffee on a large scale. At its most productive, it employed 400 slaves, and the owner, Manual Aguiar Valim, was among the richest men in Brazil.

WATERFALLS

Bananal is nestled amidst the Serra da Bocaina, a largely unspoiled region of mountains covered in dense Atlantic forest that stretches all the way to the southern coast of Rio de Janeiro state. Exploring the region is quite difficult without a car or guided excursion. However, you can still get a small taste of what the area has to offer. From the center of town, you can easily walk through the hills along a 6-kilometer (4-mile) stretch of the Estrada da Turva to the **Recanto da Cachoeira** (tel. 12/3116-5527, R$4). Owned by a local couple, this small patch of tamed wilderness—with the Rio Turva running through it—is open to visitors. After getting a hydromassage in the cascades, you can relax with beer and snacks at a small shaded bar or on a tiny island in the middle of the river.

Two more impressive waterfalls can only be reached by car. The nearby **Cachoeira da Usina** (Rodovia SP-247 Km 9) is on the premises of the Fazenda Cachoeira. More distant, the **Cachoeira do Bracui** (Rodovia SP-247 Km 38) has five separate falls and a magnificent view that stretches as far as the bay of Angra dos Reis.

PARQUE NACIONAL DA SERRA DA BOCAINA

Encompassing much of the Serra da Bocaina, the Parque Nacional da Serra da Bocaina (Estrada da Bocaina Km 27, tel. 12/3117-2183) spans the states of São Paulo and Rio de Janeiro, embracing the coastal towns of Angra, Paraty,

and Ubatuba. Although access is difficult (you need a four-wheel-drive) and infrastructure is virtually nonexistent, this national park offers over 100,000 hectares (250,000 acres) of virgin Atlantic forest brimming with wild orchids, hortensias, and bromeliads, dozens of waterfalls, and the chance of catching a glimpse of rare beasts such as the spotted jaguar and *mono-carvoeiro* monkey. The park's entrance is 27 kilometers (17 miles) from the pretty little colonial town of **São José do Barreiro,** 45 kilometers (28 miles) from Bananal in the direction of São Paulo.

The best way to visit the park is by guided tour. In São José, **MW Trekking** (Praça Coronel Cunha Lana, tel. 12/3117-1220, www.mw trekking.com.br) offers day trips that include hiking, with stops for lunch and bathing in waterfalls. For more intrepid souls, the company offers a three-day trek that follows the **Trilha do Ouro** over the hills to the Praia de Mambucaba, a gorgeous beach located between Paraty and Angra. In the 18th century, slaves laid the massive stones (many of which still exist) of this trail. The route was used by *tropeiros* to carry precious gold, and later coffee, down to the coast, where it could be shipped off to Europe. This R$560 excursion includes food and lodgings supplied by locals who offer rooms in their simple homes (without electricity) as well as home-cooked meals prepared in wood-burning ovens.

Shopping

A 20-minute walk from the center of Bananal will bring you to the **Chácara Santa Inêz** (Av. João Barbosa de Camargo 1494, tel. 12/3116-1591, www.cachacaminuca.com.br), where Engels Maciel, a German chemist, distills some of the most ambrosial *cachaça* in the country. *Cachaça* has a long history in the region; before turning to coffee, 18th-century planters cultivated sugar. Its precious by-product, *cachaça,* was not only tippled by the aristocracy of the day, but was also used to barter for the slaves needed to work the plantations. Using a completely organic process and barrels (for aging) made with precious Brazilian woods, *cachaça de Minuca* (named for Engels's wife) has won

SÃO PAULO

numerous awards. Aside from touring the alembic and sampling the wares, you can also purchase homemade organic vinegars, jams, and jellies made by Minuca from fruits planted on the property.

Accommodations

Overlooking Bananal's main square, **Hotel Brasil** (Praça Pedro Ramos 45, tel. 12/3116-0411, R$40 d) was built in 1847 as the grandiose residence of one of Bananal's richest coffee barons. In 1928, it was transformed into a hotel that has since fallen somewhat into disrepair. Nevertheless, the absolutely palatial rooms are spotless and retain their original features, including terraces overlooking the square.

A handful of coffee *fazendas* around Bananal have been converted into reasonably priced hotels that offer a deliciously authentic bucolic atmosphere for those equipped with cars. Located 12 kilometers (7.5 miles) from Bananal, **Fazenda Boa Vista** (SP-068 Km 327, tel. 12/3116-1539, www.fazenda boavista.com.br, R$170–190 d) lies in a forested conservation area ribboned with walking trails that lead to waterfalls. Constructed in 1780 by the wealthy Barão da Boa Vista, the estate mansion has often been used by TV crews filming period dramas. Rooms in the main house and outlying *casas* are rustic, but cozy. Kitchens equipped with wood-burning stoves offer guests the possibility of playing house.

More elegance is on display at the **Fazenda Independência** (SP-064 Km 329, tel. 12/3116-1100, www.fazendaindependencia.com.br, R$200–300 d), 14 kilometers (9 miles) from Bananal. Dating back to 1822, the main plantation house is awash in dark mahogany furniture, Persian carpets, and comfy upholstered chairs. Wide verandas face onto the pool and sweeping grounds landscaped by Roberto Burle Marx. You can opt for half or full board. It's worth spending the extra *reias* for the posher master suites.

Food

In town, there are several options for honest home-style cooking. **Padaria Paremol** (Rua Manuel de Aguiar 60, tel. 12/3116-1136, daily for lunch, R$5–10) is a retro-style bakery that serves up hearty lunches such as roasted pork with *feijão*, salad, and macaroni. **Restaurante 418** (Praça Pedro Ramos, tel. 12/3116-5418, daily for lunch and dinner, R$10–20) is a cozy combination bar/restaurant where all the locals hang out. It's a perfect spot for tasty sandwiches as well as filet mignon and french fries.

For alfresco dining, head to the **Restaurante Estação** (Av. Rubem de Melo 53, tel. 12/3116-1287, daily for lunch and dinner, R$15–25) facing Bananal's train station. Deliciously grilled local trout is accompanied by an enormous heart of palm salad. For dessert, try the homemade *doces*—preserved fruits such as green papaya and orange served with a slab of creamy white cheese.

Information

For maps and information, visit the small **tourist office** (Rua Manual de Aguiar 38, tel. 12/3116-2007), which isn't always open, or log on to www.bananal.sp.gov.br. If you don't have a car, you can hire taxis to take you to *fazendas* and waterfalls.

Getting There

Bananal is 330 kilometers (205 miles) from São Paulo and 150 kilometers (93 miles) from Rio de Janeiro. By bus from São Paulo's Tietê terminal, **Pássaro Marron** (tel. 11/6221-0244, www.pas-saromarron.com.br) has daily service to Bananal via Guaratinguetá (where you'll need to change buses), with a few direct buses on weekends. In Bananal, the tiny bus station is located on Praça Dona Domiciana. By car, from São Paulo take the BR-116 north to Queluz, then the SP-068 to Bananal. From Rio, take the BR-116 to Barra Mansa and then follow to the SP-064. The travel time to Bananal from São Paulo is roughly three and a half hours by car and five hours by bus.

Litoral Norte

Although few foreigners are aware of it, São Paulo state boasts one of the most attractive, and popular, coastlines in Brazil. Known as the Litoral Norte (North Coast), it extends for more than 250 kilometers (155 miles) from Santos—passing through the resort towns of São Sebastião and Ubatuba—up to the frontier of Rio de Janeiro state. Natural attractions include beckoning white-sand beaches and majestic mountains covered in dense rainforest. In recent years, the urban development of some of the larger resort towns has taking on a frightening aspect, marked by an excess of condos and *shoppings*. Fortunately, there are still many smaller towns and isolated beaches where you can successfully get away from it all. During the summer, long weekends, and holidays, the *litoral* is mobbed by millions of Paulistanos fleeing the city. If you visit off-season or during the week, you'll be treated to tranquility at significantly discounted prices.

The Litoral Norte officially begins at Santos, 70 kilometers (43 miles) from São Paulo. The largest maritime port in Latin America, Santos was founded (as São Vicente) in 1545. During the 19th century, it prospered as a result of São Paulo's coffee boom. Its recently restored historical center may hold some interest for fans of 19th-century architecture. Otherwise, the town itself is somewhat ratty and the beaches are quite unappealing. Equally unimpressive is nearby Guarujá, 15 kilometers (9 miles) away. This terrifically crowded and excessively built-up resort town has long been Paulistanos' favorite getaway despite beaches that are nothing to write home about. In terms of beaches, things only start to get interesting as you make your way north towards the town of São Sebastião, which is only a boat ride away from the snorkeler's and diver's island paradise of Ilhabela.

SÃO SEBASTIÃO

When Paulistanos say they are "going to São Sebastião," they're not actually referring to the busy seaside town with the colonial center located 220 kilometers (137 miles) from São Paulo, but to the 100-kilometer (62-mile) expanse of beaches and resort towns around it (included in the municipality of São Sebastião). In fact, very few people visit São Sebastião itself. Despite a pleasant colonial center, the presence of a large oil refinery and lack of good beaches mean that its primary interest is as an access point to the stunning natural beauty of Ilhabela, only a 15-minute ferry ride away.

More likely, "going to São Sebastião" means traveling to Maresias, Camburi, Juqueí or any of the other couple dozen beaches that precede it along the SP-055 highway linking Santos and Rio de Janeiro. The beaches themselves (most of which have *pousadas* and restaurants) are incredibly varied. You'll find tiny secluded coves as well as kilometrical sweeps of sand lined with fancy vacation homes and stylish bars. While some beaches have calm waters that are ideal for toddlers, others boast awesome waves that seduce surfers. Ultimately, whether you're in search of a family vacation, a flirtation fest, or a relaxing retreat, you'll likely find what you're looking for.

Beaches

Traveling east from Santos and Guarujá along the coast towards São Sebastião, after about 65 kilometers (40 miles) you'll reach **Barra da Una,** the first beach of interest and a major nautical center. From here, you can go sailing, hire a launch to take you diving off nearby islands, or go paddling up the nearby Rio Una in a kayak. Only 3 kilometers (2 miles) west of Barra da Una is the gorgeously secluded **Juréia,** backed by exuberant vegetation and blessed with a bewitchingly green sea. Farther along, **Juqueí**'s wide sandy beaches and calm waters are popular with families, as is the horseshoe-shaped **Praia da Barra do Sai.** The super-trendy, beautiful beaches of **Camburi** and **Camburizinho** are magnets for a toned and tanned crowd who surf (the

SÃO PAULO

Juqueí beach near São Sebastião

waves are rougher here) and sun by day and mellow out at night at the many rustic-chic bars and restaurants.

If you're young, on the loose, and looking for even more action, avoid the excessively overdeveloped **Boiçucanga** and continue east until you hit **Maresias**, a gathering point for movers and groovers from all over the state. Big swells attract surfers, but a dangerous current makes bathing risky (although the blue-green sea is certainly seductive). As wild as the ocean is Maresias's nightlife with its multiple bars and discos. Another 5 kilometers (3 miles) east, **Santiago** is much more tranquil, as are neighboring **Toque-Toque Pequeno,** a quiet little fishing town with a relaxed vibe and a privileged view of the setting sun, and **Toque-Toque Grande.** Both Toque-Toques offer beckoning sands and good snorkeling. Hidden between them is the beautifully wild and quite deserted tiny **Praia de Calhetas.**

Sports and Recreation

To explore the islands off the coast, take a half-day boat schooner trip with **Green Way** (Av. Mãe Bernarda 2332, Juqueí, tel. 12/3891-1075, www.greenway.com.br), an operator specializing in ecotourism. Departing from Barra da Una, trips (R$100–150 pp) include stops for diving and swimming. Equipment and snacks are included. GreenWay offers kayak trips on the Rio Una (R$55 pp) as well as hiking, biking and Jeep excursions into the native Atlantic forest. It also offers surfing classes for kids and adults of all levels of experience.

Nightlife

Sirena (Rua Sirena, Maresias, tel. 12/3077-0020, www.sirena.com.br, 10 P.M.–7 A.M. Fri.–Sat., cover R$25–70) bills itself as the best club in Brazil. Its phenomenal fame reels in beautiful young revelers from all over São Paulo state, who are seduced by the pseudo-Asian decor and casual beach vibe. Aside from electronic music, Sirena regularly features some of the top DJs on the international circuit. The club's most serious rival is **Galeão** (Estrada de Camburi 79, tel. 12/3865-1515, Camburi, www.ogaleao.com.br, 10 P.M.–4 A.M. Fri.–Sat., cover R$20–40), where you'll hear a more eclectic musical mix of soul, funk, and hiphop.

Accommodations

Accommodations along this coast are not exactly cheap, especially in the summer, when prices go up and booking in advance becomes essential. You'll find the greatest concentration of hotels in Juqueí, Camburi, Camburizinho, Boiçucanga, and Maresias, with the latter two offering the widest selection in terms of quality and price. If you're looking for something more affordable, try São Sebastião itself.

Camburi Hostel (Rua Tijucas 2300, Camburi, tel. 12/3863-6880, www.ajcamburi .com.br, R$30 pp, R$65–75 d) is a very appealing hostel run by an eco-friendly couple. Hidden within a patch of Atlantic rainforest (and a fair hike from the beach), it is surrounded by waterfalls and hiking trails. Rooms for couples, families of four, and groups of up to six are available. Amenities include a 24-hour kitchen, a barbecue area, a library full of English-language books, and a vast garden with hammocks and a pool. If you call in advance, the owners will pick you up from the closest bus stop, 2 kilometers (1 mile) away, for R$5. They also offer transportation to and from the beach.

Another great bargain is the simple but charming **Pousada da Ana Doce** (Rua Expedicionário Brasileiro 196, São Sebastião, tel. 12/3892-1615, www.pousadaanadoce .com.br, R$100–120 d), which occupies a lovely old house in São Sebastião's historical center. The owners are welcoming and the small but quaint rooms feature verandas overlooking a pretty internal garden.

Opened in 2007, **Pousada Porto Mare** (Rua Sebastião Romão César 400, Maresias, tel. 12/3865-5272, www.pousadaportomare .com.br, R$220 d) is a welcome new addition to Maresias's sometimes less-than-inspiring choice of hotels. Although it's right in the middle of the *movimento,* the large garden, featuring a pool and sauna, offers respite, as do the modern, tastefully appointed rooms.

On beautiful Praia da Barra do Sai, **Pousada da Foca** (tel. 12/3863-6800, www.pousadada foca.com.br, R$240–270 d) has comfortable, attractively decorated rooms (including a few with mezzanines for families or groups). The bar serves drinks around a lovely pool, overlooking a thick patch of rainforest, as well as on the beach. Playing right into a Hollywood cliché of a secluded hotel in the tropics is ◖ **Pousada Ilha de Toque-Toque** (Toque-Toque Grande, tel. 12/3864-9110, www.ilhadetoquetoque.com.br, R$270–350 d). Perched on a lush hillside overlooking Praia Toque-Toque Grande, and with access to Praia de Calhetas, this rustic-chic *pousada* boasts a gorgeous pool and decks and patios galore. A launch takes small groups snorkeling and diving.

The spa is not the only antistress tonic you'll encounter at the alluring **Villa Bebek** (Rua Zezito 251, Camburizinho, tel. 12/3865-3320, www.villabebek.com.br, R$350–480 d), located on hip Camburizinho beach. The beautifully decorated bungalow rooms—featuring Balinese ornaments and original artworks—are soothing enough, as are the landscaped gardens. However, the real treat is stepping out of your room and into the courtyard swimming pool shaped like a long, curvy river—a distraction so enticing that you'll be hard-pressed to make it to the beach.

Food

The best restaurants along the coast are concentrated in Camburi (sophisticated and pricy) and Juqueí (more casual and beachy). In terms of the latter, there are many fine options along Avenida Mãe Bernarda. At **Chapéu de Sol** (Av. Mãe Bernarda 2001, Juqueí, tel. 12/3863-3028, 11 A.M.–11 P.M. Sun.–Thurs., 11 A.M.–2 A.M. Fri.–Sat., R$40–50) local chef Marisa Ferreira concocts simple and enticing fish and seafood dishes such as grilled *robalo* stuffed with seafood that two people can gorge on before or after hitting the beach.

Dining at ◖ **Manacá** (Rua do Manacá 102, Camburizinho, tel. 12/3865-1566, www .restaurantemanaca.com.br, 6–11 P.M. Thurs., 1–11 P.M. Fri.–Sat., 1–9 P.M. Sun., 1–11 P.M. daily in Jan., R$65–75) involves putting a dent in your budget, but you'll be well rewarded with creatively refined dishes, such as shrimp in a ginger tangerine sauce with wasabi and white cheese mousse crowned with caramelized guava. Equally seductive is the ambiance—built on stilts in the midst of tropical forest, the restaurant resembles an elegant tree house. Advance reservations are a must.

Somewhat surprisingly, Maresias is rather bereft of good eating options. However, for great pizza, head to **A Firma** (Rua Sebastião Romão César 419, Maresias, tel. 12/3865-6142, 7 P.M.–close Thurs.–Mon., R$20–30), where the young and famished stock up on calories prior to a night of partying.

Information and Services

In the town of São Sebastião, the **tourist office** (Av. Dr. Altino Arantes 174, tel. 12/3892-1808, 10 A.M.–8 P.M. daily) offers information on the entire coastline. You can also consult www.saosebastiao.com.br and www.saosebastiao.tur.br.

Getting There

From São Paulo's Tietê terminal, daily bus service is operated by **Litorânea** (tel. 0800/999-701, www.litoranea.com.br). The *rodoviária* (tel. 12/3892-1072) is at Praça da Amizade 10. If you're driving from São Paulo, take the BR-116 or SP-070 to the SP-099, followed by the Rio–Santos highway (BR-101/SP-055), which leads to São Sebastião. You will pass all the other beaches along the way. The travel time from São Paulo to São Sebastião is roughly three hours by car and four hours by bus.

◖ ILHABELA

Brazil's largest off-coast island is only a 15-minute ferry boat ride from São Sebastião. Once you're there, it's utter relaxation all the way (provided you're armed with mosquito repellent—85 percent of the volcanic island is covered in damp, virgin Atlantic forest and, as a result, extremely annoying bloodsuckers called *borrachudos* are usually out in full force). With dozens of beaches, over 300 waterfalls and constant breezes (which makes the surrounding

waters a sailor's and windsurfer's dream), the island is a magnet for every kind of nature enthusiast, ranging from hikers and deep-sea divers to indolent hammock-swinging Robinson Crusoe types. It also draws a fair amount of fancy folk from São Paulo—many of whom have luxurious villas tucked away on beaches, along with private piers and helicopter pads. This explains the high number of eco-chic hotels and gourmet restaurants as well as the somewhat high prices. Things get especially astronomical on holiday weekends and in January, not to mention crowded (with traffic jams on the island's main coastal road). If you're in search of peace and tranquility, avoid these times like the plague.

Vila Ilhabela

The island's main settlement is the pretty little town of Vila Ilhabela. It is located on the sheltered west coast of the island, a 20-minute drive north from the ferry dock at Perequê. Aside from a small (fairly touristy) commercial center, the town has some attractive vestiges of its colonial past, including the charming whitewashed **Igreja Matriz,** perched picturesquely on a hilltop. Several kilometers before the entrance to town, on the way to the ferry, is an impressive 18th-century mansion belonging to the **Fazenda Engenho d'Agua,** one of the most important of Ilhabela's many former sugar plantations. This history of cane cultivation explains the preponderance of fine *cachaças* on the island.

Beaches

Ilhabela has no shortage of stunning beaches. Those on the west coast facing São Sebastião have calmer waters, but they are also smaller and often more crowded. They can be easily reached by car as well as the municipal bus line that goes up and down the main paved road. This road extends along the western coast from **Porto do Frade** in the south to **Ponta das Canas** at the northern tip, where strong breezes attract windsurfers and kitesurfers.

South from Ponta das Canas, among

ILHABELA

Ponta das Canas
Jabaquara
Praia da Fome
Praia do Pinto
Praia do Poço
Praia do Viana   **VIANA**
Ponta Grossa
Praia Saco da Capela
CHEIRO VERDE   ● **MAISON JOLY**
POUSADA HIBISCUS ●   ○ Vila Ilhabela
POUSADA SACO DA CAPELA ●
CURA
Praia Perequê   ▼**DECK**
Cachoeira da Toca
Cachoeira do Gato
Barra Velha
Cachoeira da Agua Branca
POUSADA ECOLÓGICA RECANTO DA CACHOEIRA
ENTRANCE PARQUE ESTADUAL DE ILHABELA
Praia Baía de Castelhanos
Praia Feiticeira
Mansa
Praia do Julião
Vermelha
Praia Grande
Ilhabela
Praia do Curral ● **DPNY BEACH**
Saco do Sombrio
▼ **BARULHO D'AGUA**
Ponta de Sela
Cachoeira da Laje
Enchovas
Borrifos
Bonete
Sepituba
Ponta de Sepituba
0   2 mi
0   2 km
Ponta do Diogo

© AVALON TRAVEL

the nicest beaches are tiny **Praia do Viana, Feiticeira,** and **Praia do Julião,** all of which are relatively tranquil and popular with families. The young and restless tend to congregate on **Praia do Curral,** known for its restaurants, bars, and nightly *festas* where DJs and dancers take to the sand.

The most gorgeous and wild beaches are those on the eastern coast—which also happen to be the most tricky to get to. While some beaches can be reached by following the hiking trails that wind through the jungle, others are only accessible by Jeep, and getting to the most far-flung spots requires a boat. **Praia do Bonete,** a tiny fishing village on the southeast coast, attracts surfers, as does **Praia de Castelhanos,** a magnificent 2-kilometer (1-mile) stretch of beach with a waterfall named after the Castilian pirates that frequented it centuries ago. The macabre name of **Praia do Fome** came from the slaves who arrived from Africa *com fome* ("with hunger") and were taken to this beautiful beach to gain weight before being sold. Relatively more accessible, on the northeastern coast of the island, **Jabaquara** is a lovely beach fed by two streams and a freshwater lagoon.

Sports and Recreation
PARKS
The reason that Ilhabela's nature is so unspoiled (and its eastern coast so inaccessible) is that the majority of the island is preserved within the limits of a 335-square-meter (3,600-square-foot) natural park known as **Parque Estadual de Ilhabela.** Whether you decide to explore the island's treasures by sea or land (there are plenty of hiking trails and several dirt roads), in most cases you'll need to do so with an organized excursion. **Archipelagus** (Av. Pedro Paulo de Morães 713, Pequéa, tel. 12/3896-3086, www.ilhastur.com.br) offers boat, Jeep, and trekking tours around the island for around R$60–70. Among the most popular trips are a bumpy Jeep ride across the park to beautiful Praia de Castelhanos, and trekking to **Cachoeira da Laje,** a spectacular waterfall near Praia do Bonete.

Aside from organizing excursions, **Lokal Adventure** (Av. Princesa Isabel 171, Perequê, tel. 12/3896-5777, www.lokaladventure.com.br) also rents cars, motor scooters, bikes, horses, and canoes for adventurous souls who want to do some exploring on their own. An easy solo outing is the 3-km (2-mile) hike inland from Praia de Feiticeira to **Cachoeira da Toca** (8 A.M.–6 P.M. daily, R$7.50), a waterfall with various cascades and pools.

WATER SPORTS
Ilhabela boasts a fantastic array of water sports. Due to the winds that blow off the northern tip, the island is considered one of the best places for sailing along the Brazilian coast. In July, it hosts Latin America's most prestigious sailing regatta, the **Semana Internacional da Vela.** If you want to take sailing lessons, or rent a sailboat or kayak, contact **Maremar Turismo** (Av. São João 574, Perequê, tel. 12/3896-3679, www.maremar tur.com.br).

With its crystalline waters, particularly off the east coast, Ilhabela boasts excellent diving and snorkeling opportunities. Beginners can get their feet wet at the **Reserva Marinha da Ilha das Cabras,** an island off of Perequê, where you can view coral, anemones, and a parade of colorful fish. Another underwater adventure is exploring the handful of sunken ships. **Colonial Diver** (Av. Brasil 1751, Pedra Miúdas, tel. 12/3894-9459, www.colonial diver.com.br) offers diving lessons, excursions and rents equipment. An hour-long dive for beginners costs R$200.

Accommodations
Ilhabela is one of the most expensive places to stay along the Litoral Norte, especially in the summer (when reservations are essential). Although stylish eco-chic guesthouses are a dime a dozen, budget bungalows are harder to come by. The vast majority of lodgings are in Vila Ilhabela, but there are an increasing number of options along the entire western coast of the island. Of good value in Vila is the charming **Pousada dos Hibiscus** (Av. Pedro de Paula Moraes 720, tel. 12/3896-1375, www.pousadadoshibiscos.com.br, R$135 d), whose jungly internal courtyard features a bar, pool, sauna, and bursts of flowers. Rooms are standard but pleasant whitewashed affairs with dark wood furniture, tile floors, and whirling ceiling fans.

South of Vila, off Saco da Capela beach, **Pousada Saco da Capela** (Rua Itapema 167, tel. 12/3896-8020, www.sacodacapela.com.br, R$169–189 d) offers attractive rooms (the best have polished hardwood floors and private verandas) in bungalows scattered amidst native vegetation. If well-equipped with bug spray, hard-core jungle enthusiasts will adore the **Pousada Ecológica Recanto da Cachoeira** (Rua Benedito Garcêz 164, Água Branca, tel. 12/3896-3098, www.ecoilha.com.br, R$120–150 d), on the edge of the Parque Estadual de Ilhabela (just off the road leading to Praia de Castelhanos). Bird calls provide a constant soundtrack while the backdrop includes views of the Pico do Baepi. Basic but pleasant rooms have verandas and hammocks, and there is a nice pool for cooling off.

The grooviest new hotel on the block is the über-boutiquey **DPNY Beach** (Av. José Pacheco de Nascimento 7668, Praia do Curral, tel. 12/3894-2121, www.dpnybeach.com.br, R$530 including dinner), on trendy Praia do Curral. Almost overly designed, the rooms are drop-dead gorgeous with richly colored walls, zebra motifs, mosaic tiles, and southeast Asian ornaments. The beds are king-sized, TV screens are plasma, and everybody gets an iPod (laptops are available at the bar). The hotel's private beach club doubles as a lounge where house music plays day and night and the contemporary restaurant, **Tróia,** has one of the most inventive kitchens on the island.

It's no exaggeration to say that **◖ Maison Joly** (Rua Antônio Lisboa Alves 278, tel. 12/3896-1201, www.maisonjoly.com.br, R$550–800 d) is fit for royalty. Idyllically perched upon a hilltop overlooking Vila Ilhabela, this exclusive luxury guesthouse has hosted everyone from the Swedish monarchy to the Rolling Stones. The individually furnished rooms are understated, yet refined, and boast beautiful verandas overlooking the sea. A classy piano bar, a "Zen" Space, an Anti-Jet Lag Spa, and a romantic restaurant serving delicious Mediterranean-inspired cuisine make it difficult for you to venture beyond the hotel.

Food

Like hotels, restaurants on Ilhabela are not exactly cheap, although you can always spend the day nibbling away at *barraca* fare on the beaches. Vila Ilhabela has a few *lanchonetes* and some scenic bars along the waterfront where you can fill up on *petiscos* and ice-cold beer. **Cheiro Verde** (Rua da Padroeira 109, tel. 12/3896-3245, noon–11 P.M. Sun.–Fri., noon–11 P.M. Sat., R$10–20) offers honest home-cooking for great prices. The lunchtime PFs (*prato feitos*)—consisting of a choice of fish, shrimp, squid, chicken, or beef with *feijão,* fries, and salad—inspire lineups during high season. For lunch, a decent inexpensive option at Perequê is **Cura** (Rua Princesa Isabel 337,

tel. 12/3896-1341, 11 A.M.–4 P.M. Tues.–Sun., R$10–20), which lays out a tasty and varied self-service buffet.

A little north of Vila Ilhabela, **Deck** is a favorite local hangout (Av. Almirante Tamandaré 805/821, Itaguassu, tel. 12/3896-1489, www.deckrestaurantehotel.com.br, noon–midnight Sun.–Tues. and Thurs., noon–2 A.M. Fri.–Sat., noon–2 A.M. daily in Jan.–Feb., R$25–35), with a relaxing beachfront setting and an oddly eclectic menu reuniting seafood, German specialties, and pizzas.

More upscale, but also popular with the natives, is **Viana** (Av. Leonardo Reale 1560, Praia da Viana, tel. 12/3896-1089, www.viana.com.br, 1–11:30 P.M. Fri.–Sun., 1–11:30 P.M. daily Dec.–Feb. and July, R$40–60), where you can eat inside or right on the sand (while watching the sunset). The menu features fresh fish and seafood cooked with Brazilian seasoning and flair. The main attraction is *camarão,* which comes in versions such as shrimp with mango risotto, and Bahian style *moqueca,* flavored with coconut milk.

For a change of scenery, head to **◖ Barulho d'Agua** (Rua Manual Pombo 250, Praia de Curral, tel. 12/3896-1406, www.barulho dagua.com.br, 8:30 A.M.–1 A.M. daily, R$30–45). The name of this *pousada*/restaurant—Sound of Water—is inspired by the river that runs right by the enchantingly decorated dining area, nestled in a patch of forest. The imaginative cuisine relies on fresh ingredients that result in creations such as artichoke hearts with gratinéed shrimp, and salmon with cashew nuts in a passion fruit sauce. Meanwhile, back in Vila Ilhabela, you can satisfy ice-cream cravings with a cone or *picolé* (popsicle) at **Sorveteria Rocha** (Rua São Benedito 23/31, tel. 12/3896-1793, www.sorveteria rocha.com.br), whose factory in São Sebastião has been churning out ice cream since 1948.

Information

There is a **Posto de Turismo** at the ferry landing at Perequê (Rua Bartolomeo de Gusmão 14, tel. 12/3896-2440, 9 A.M.–6 P.M. Mon.–Fri., 10 A.M.–4 P.M. Sat., 10 A.M.–2 P.M. Sun.),

SÃO PAULO

SÃO PAULO

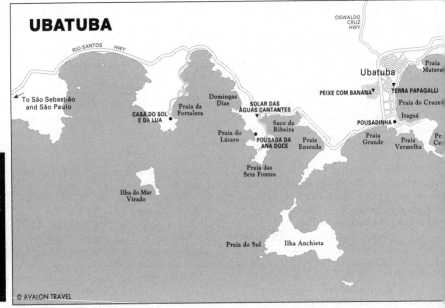

UBATUBA

RIO-SANTOS HWY

OSWALDO CRUZ HWY

To São Sebastião and São Paulo

CASA DO SOL E DA LUA

Praia da Fortaleza

Domingas Dias

SOLAR DAS AGUAS CANTANTES

Saco da Ribeira

Praia do Lázaro

POUSADA DA ANA DOCE

Praia Enseada

Praia das Sete Fontes

Ilha do Mar Virado

Praia do Sul

Ilha Anchieta

Ubatuba

Praia Matara

PEIXE COM BANANA

TERRA PAPAGALLI

Praia do Cruze

POUSADINHA

Itaguá

Praia Grande

Praia Vermelha

Pr Ce

© AVALON TRAVEL

where you can pick up detailed maps of the island. Check out the beaches yourself at photo-laden websites such as www.ilhabela.com.br and www.visitilhabela.com.br. In Vila Ilhabela, **Standby** (Rua da Padroeira 63, tel. 12/3896-6843) is the island's only cyber café—luckily it's open 24 hours.

Getting There
Balsas (ferries) (tel. 12/3896-8286, free for passengers, R$16 for cars) make the 20-minute crossing from São Sebastião to Ilhabela every half hour 6 A.M.–midnight, and hourly thereafter. If you plan to rent a car on the mainland (which will give you great mobility on the island), be aware that traffic lineups are insane on weekends and in summer. Avoid the hassle and call in advance to reserve (tel. 0800/555-510). From Perequê, municipal buses leave regularly for Vila Ilhabela.

UBATUBA
Nearing the state of Rio de Janeiro, Ubatuba and its surrounding coastline offer some of

southern Brazil's most varied and attractive sand beaches, along with a mesmerizing green ocean dotted with islands. Like many towns along this coast, Ubatuba rocks hard during the summer months, when it is invaded by vacationing Paulistanos and Cariocas, and then settles down during the rest of the year.

As is the case with São Sebastião, when Brazilians talk about going to "Ubatuba," they are actually referring less to the town than to the surrounding 90 kilometers (56 miles) of coastline that stretches along the Rio–Santos highway from Praia da Figueira to Camburi.

Aside from some rather uninspired nightlife options, the town of Ubatuba itself holds few attractions other than the local branch of the **Projeto Tamar** (Rua Antônio Athanasio da Silva 273, Itagua, tel. 12/3822-6202, www.tamar.org.br, 10 A.M.–6 P.M. Sun.–Tues. and Thurs., 10 A.M.–8 P.M. Fri.–Sat., 10 A.M.–8 P.M. daily Dec.–Feb. and July, R$5), a refuge and study center for Brazil's endangered species of sea turtles that will especially appeal to curious kids.

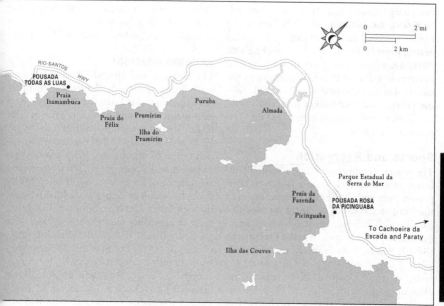

Beaches

While Ubatuba itself has some passable beaches, they pale in comparison to the more unspoiled sheltered coves and sandy expanses you'll find north and south of town. The majority of these are easily accessible by car and municipal buses as well as by boat.

Going south from Ubatuba, the initial stretch of coastline is fairly built up and gets quite crowded in the summer. Things only begin to get more interesting 15 kilometers (9 miles) from town as you arrive at tiny **Praia da Sununga,** whose big waves attract surfers. Here you can also see the legendary **Gruta que Chora,** a cavern where trickling water gives the illusion that the walls are "crying." Adjacent **Praia do Lázaro**'s placid waters are a favorite with families, while the next beach over (accessible on foot), **Domingas Dias,** is a beckoning cove with soft, sugary sand. Fronting a condo complex 24 kilometers (15 miles) south of Ubatuba, **Vermelha do Sul** is a well-preserved beach with reddish sands flanked by exuberant vegetation that is popular with water sports enthusiasts.

Farther south the beaches are even more pristine, although access is more difficult. From Vermelho do Sul, a sinuous road leads to the lovely **Praia da Fortaleza,** where there are only a few hotels, restaurants, and summer homes. A 40-minute walk away is the beautifully deserted **Praia do Cedro,** where the ocean is transparent and you can float in natural pools.

The beaches to the north of Ubatuba are generally less developed—and even more attractive—than those to the south. Some 15 kilometers (9 miles) north of Ubatuba, **Itamambuca** is a surfer's mecca whose *barracas* are always crowded. A more tranquil surfing spot is neighboring **Praia do Félix,** where jungly mountains come right down to the sea. Farther north, **Praia do Prumirim** and **Praia de Puruba** are beautiful beaches where you can bathe in waterfalls and rivers as well as the sea. **Ubatumirim** boasts a long stretch of hardpacked sand that is ideal for walking to the secluded **Praia da Justa.**

Farther north, a scenic 30-minute walk

from busy Praia da Almada brings you to idyllic **Brava da Almada,** which is part of the Parque Estadual da Serra do Mar. The coastal headquarters of the park are at nearby **Praia da Fazenda,** a lovely beach where you can swim in rivers as well as in the sea. Bordering on the state of Rio are **Picinguaba,** a picturesque fishing village, and **Camburi,** a seductively wild beach whose only signs of civilization are a few primitive *barracas.*

Sports and Recreation

The pristine condition of the beaches and rainforest surrounding Ubatuba is due to their preservation within the coastal boundaries of the **Parque Estadual da Serra do Mar** (see *São Luís do Paratinga*). The park's coastal headquarters are located at the **Núcleo Picinguaba** (BR-101 Km 11, Praia da Fazenda, tel. 12/3832-9011, 9 A.M.–5 P.M. daily), 40 kilometers (25 miles) north of Ubatuba. If you want to explore the park—with its myriad cascades, rivers, hummingbirds, and rare orchids—you need to get in touch with the visitors center. The staff can provide you with maps as well as guides that can lead you along the hiking trails that cut through the rainforest. Another option is to contract a guide with the **Associação de Monitores de Ubatuba** (tel. 12/9142-3692, www.ameuubatuba.com.br).

Another compelling feature of Ubatuba's coastline is its many offshore islands. One of the largest, **Ilha Anchieta,** is a short boat ride away from the central beaches of Itaguá and Saco da Ribeira. Before becoming a natural park, the island housed a jail where political prisoners whiled away their days during the Vargas years (the ruins are still visible). The island is crisscrossed by trails leading to various deserted beaches, and its clear waters offer great diving. **Mykonos Turismo** (Rua Flamenguinha 17, Praia Saco da Ribeira, tel. 12/3842-0329, www.mykonos.com.br) organizes excursions to Anchieta (with stops at beaches along the way) and to **Ilha do Prumirim,** north of Ubatuba, for around R$25 per person. **Omnimare** (Rua Guaicurus 30, Itaguá, tel. 12/3832-

2005, www.omnimare.com.br) offers diving courses as well as six-hour diving excursions to Anchieta and other islands (R$120–170).

Accommodations

The hotels in and around Ubatuba are generally more affordable than those in other resorts along the Litoral Norte. For bargain-seekers, **Pousadinha** (Rua Gurani 536, Itaguá, Ubatuba, www.pousadinha.com.br, tel. 12/3832-2136, R$60–90 d) is a convenient option in the center of town. It is close to Praia da Itaguá, which looks pretty, but whose waters are unsuitable for swimming. (Henry Miller fans take note: The Tropic of Capricorn passes through here.) The basic but clean rooms occupy an appealing old villa whose exterior is painted a bright shade of watermelon pink. Groups or families of four can also rent chalets with fully equipped kitchens.

South of town, **Pousada da Ana Doce** (Travessa JK 54, Praia do Lázaro, tel. 12/3842-1336, www.pousadaanadoce.com.br, R$140–160 d) is a pretty, intimate, and comfortable choice with a pool and nine rooms that each house up to four people. The *pousada* has kayaks and sailboats available for guest use. Mere steps away from the sands of tranquil Praia da Fortaleza, **A Casa do Sol e da Lua** (Rua do Refúgio do Corsário 580, Praia da Fortaleza, tel. 12/3848-9412, www.acasadosoledalua.com.br, R$160–240 d) is a casual family-style hotel occupying an adapted family beach house. Meals are served at a collective table, nightly DVD sessions are held in the living room, and there are plenty of decks and hammocks spread around the property where you can disappear with a book or a passion fruit *caipirinha.* The friendly owners love cooking and are constantly making *petiscos* for guests. Getting here involves a 7-kilometer (4.3-mile) drive from the Rio–Santos highway.

North of Ubatuba, nestled in a jungly garden, **Pousada Todas as Luas** (Praia Itamambuca, tel. 12/3845-3129, www.todasasluas.com.br, R$100–150 d) is owned by a couple of surfers, which accounts for the laid-back atmosphere that reigns here. Rooms are simple but soothing, as are the grounds, which feature plenty of hanging hammocks, a playground, and a yoga bungalow.

Pousada Rosa de Picinguaba (Av. Beira Mar 183, Praia de Picinguaba, tel. 12/3836-9119, www.pousadarosapicinguaba.com.br, R$100–160 d) is a charming option for those looking to get off the beaten track. Located in a tiny fishing village, Rosa's B&B/artist's atelier is idyllically surrounded by virgin beaches and the Parque Estadual da Serra do Mar. Accommodations are rustic, but full of beachhouse character, and adorned with Rosa's engaging ceramic pieces.

Food

Aside from beach *barracas,* there are lots of casual restaurants where you can gorge on fresh fish and seafood. The local specialty is a dish called *azul-marinho* ("marine blue"). This evocatively named fish stew mixes fresh fish with *bananas-nanicas* (dwarf bananas), which when cooked in a cast iron pot—together with tomatoes, onions, and cilantro—take on an unusual bluish tinge that is due to oxidization. Served in a clay casserole, the dish is accompanied by *pirão* (a mush of manioc flour mixed with the stew's juices) and pureed banana. In Ubatuba, a good place to sample this and other regional seafood dishes is **Peixe com Banana** (Rua Guarani 255, Praia do Cruzeiro, tel. 12/3832-1712, noon–11 P.M. Wed.–Mon., noon–11 P.M. daily in Jan. and July, R$40–50), a casual eatery where generous portions serve two or three. **Terra Papagalli** (Rua Xavantes 537, Itaguá, tel. 12/3832-1488, 6–11 P.M. Mon. and Wed.–Thurs., noon–midnight Fri.–Sun., R$50–60) also specializes in seafood. The menu changes based on the catch of the day and the chef's mood. The simple but inventive dishes such as *pescada* fish cooked in mint-flavored olive oil and served with grilled tomato and mango are big enough to share.

South of town, one of the region's best restaurants is in the charming **Solar das Águas Cantantes** hotel (Estrada do Saco da Ribeira 253, Praia do Lázaro, tel. 12/3842-0288, www.solardasaguascantantes.com.br, 12:30–4 P.M. and 6–10 P.M. Wed.–Mon., 12:30–10:30 P.M. daily Dec.–Feb., R$40–50). The house specialties are the fabulous *moquecas*—variations of the famous Bahian stew of fish and/or seafood cooked in *dendê* (palm oil) and coconut milk.

Information

The **tourist office** (Av. Iperoig 365, Centro, tel. 12/3833-9123, 8 A.M.–4 P.M. daily) is a good source for maps and info about the region's beaches. Various websites also have tourist information: www.ubatuba.com.br is in Portuguese, but it features photos of all the beaches. Less extensive is the English site www.ubatuba-brazil.com.

Getting There

Ubatuba's **Rodoviária Litorânea** (Rua Maria Vitória Jean 381, tel. 12/3832-3622) in the Centro offers bus service to and from São Paulo, Rio de Janeiro, and Paraty. From São Paulo's Tietê terminal, daily bus service is operated by **Litorânea** (tel. 0800/999-701, www.litoranea.com.br). The town itself is 235 kilometers (146 miles) from São Paulo and is right on the Rio–Santos highway (BR-101/SP-505). The travel time from São Paulo to Ubatuba is roughly four hours by car and five hours by bus.

SÃO PAULO

THE SOUTH

Brazil's "Sul," or "South" consists of three states—Paraná, Santa Catarina, and Rio Grande do Sul—which stretch south from São Paulo towards Brazil's frontier with Uruguay and Argentina. This region is not what most international travelers have in mind when they think of Brazil. The climate and vegetation are more Mediterranean than tropical, and the population—descendants of German, Italian, Polish, and Ukrainian immigrants—is distinctly European (which accounts for so many natural blonds).

Life is much more organized and efficient than in other parts of the country, and because it has Brazil's highest standard of living, you'll see fewer *favelas* and a lot less of the have/have not reality that is so visible in much of the rest of the country. The South may lack the more pungent history and exoticism of the rest of Brazil; however, the pretty, patchwork farming communities of its interior and the attractive capitals of Curitiba, Florianópolis, and Porto Alegre provide pleasant distractions. Moreover, the South boasts some spectacular natural getaways unlike anywhere else in Brazil.

The coastline of Paraná entices with its handful of colonial towns, luxuriantly forested mountains, and the idyllic islands of the Bay of Paranaguá. Meanwhile, backed by native Atlantic jungle, the sweeping coastline of Santa Catarina is one of the most captivating in Brazil. The dozens of beaches that rim the picturesque and increasingly hip island city of "Floripa" have made the Catarinense capital a radical sports mecca for practitioners of surfing, paragliding, windsurfing, and sandboarding.

© CHRISTIAN KNEPPER/EMBRATUR

HIGHLIGHTS

◖ The Serra Verde Express: One of the world's most breathtaking train trips is the adrenaline-charged three-hour journey from Curitiba to the coast, past the cloud-shrouded peaks and deep canyons of the jungle-covered Serra do Mar (page 199).

◖ Ilha do Mel: No vehicles are allowed on this environmentally protected island in the Baía de Paranaguá, reputed for its deserted beaches and rugged, windswept landscapes (page 202).

◖ Iguaçu Falls: One of the most spectacular natural wonders on the planet, these 275 roaring falls are set against an iridescent backdrop of lush Atlantic rainforest (page 204).

◖ East Coast Beaches of Florianópolis: Facing the open Atlantic, Santa Catarina's cool island capital's east coast beaches are the island's longest and most dramatic, attracting a crowd of surfers, sandboarders, and hipsters (page 216).

◖ Reserva Biológica Marinha da Ilha do Arvoredo: Off the coast of the Porto Belo peninsula, the clear azure waters surrounding this island offer the best diving in southern Brazil (page 226).

◖ Praia do Rosa: On most Brazilian travel gurus' top 10 beach lists, this beautifully unspoiled beach, backed by verdant hills and lagoons, is ideal for swimming, surfing, and whale-watching (page 229).

◖ Gramado: Seemingly ripped from an outtake of *The Sound of Music*, charming Gramado is an upscale mountain resort surrounded by majestic landscapes that rival the Alps (page 239).

◖ Parque Nacional de Aparados da Serra: This natural park's hiking trails weave through a series of dramatic canyons – including the spectacular Cânion de Itaimbezinho – as well as lush forests and waterfalls (page 243).

LOOK FOR ◖ TO FIND RECOMMENDED SIGHTS, ACTIVITIES, DINING, AND LODGING.

THE SOUTH

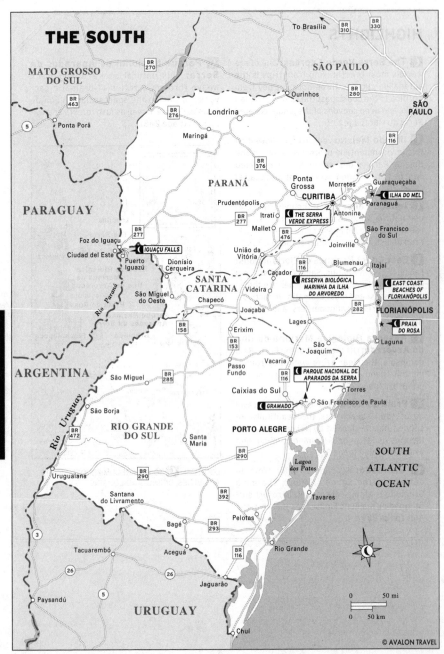

THE SOUTH

MATO GROSSO
DO SUL

SÃO PAULO

To Brasília

BR 310

BR 330

BR 270

BR 280

SÃO PAULO

BR 463

Ponta Porã

5

BR 276

Londrina

Maringá

BR 116

Ourinhos

PARANÁ

BR 376

Ponta Grossa

Morretes

Guaraqueçaba

CURITIBA

ILHA DO MEL

PARAGUAY

Prudentópolis

Antonina

Paranaguá

BR 277

Itratí

THE SERRA VERDE EXPRESS

Mallet

São Francisco do Sul

BR 476

Foz do Iguaçu

IGUAÇU FALLS

Joinville

Ciudad del Este

Puerto Iguazú

Dionísio Cerqueira

União da Vitória

BR 116

Blumenau

Itajaí

SANTA CATARINA

Caçador

RESERVA BIOLÓGICA MARINHA DA ILHA DO ARVOREDO

EAST COAST BEACHES OF FLORIANÓPOLIS

São Miguel do Oeste

Videira

Chapecó

Joaçaba

BR 282

FLORIANÓPOLIS

Lages

BR 158

Erixim

São Joaquim

PRAIA DO ROSA

ARGENTINA

BR 153

Vacaria

Laguna

São Miguel

BR 285

Passo Fundo

BR 116

PARQUE NACIONAL DE APARADOS DA SERRA

São Borja

Caixias do Sul

GRAMADO

Torres

BR 472

São Francisco de Paula

RIO GRANDE DO SUL

Santa Maria

PORTO ALEGRE

Rio Paraná

Rio Uruguay

BR 290

SOUTH ATLANTIC OCEAN

Uruguaiana

BR 290

Lagoa dos Patos

Santana do Livramento

BR 392

Tavares

Bagé

BR 293

Pelotas

Aceguá

BR 116

Rio Grande

Tacuarembó

Paysandú

3

26

5

26

Jaguarão

URUGUAY

Chuí

0   50 mi

0   50 km

© AVALON TRAVEL

As for Rio Grande do Sul, while its coastal pleasures are scant, it more than compensates with the varied attractions of its interior. Its varying landscapes run the gamut from the magnificently rugged Aparados da Serra National Park—a hiker's haven—to the alpine charms of Gramado and Canela, which, in winter, are reminiscent of quaint Swiss villages. Land of the proud Gaúcho, Rio Grande do Sul is also known for its unique cowboy culture. Barbecued beef—the famous *churrasco*—is in abundance and will send carnivores' salivary glands into overdrive. And the local wines are getting as good as some of those made in neighboring Argentina and Chile.

Of course, the number one reason that most tourists visit the South is to glimpse the world's largest and most impressive waterfalls: Iguaçu Falls. Words don't do justice to this natural extravaganza. Iguaçu is not just one big cascade, but a series of 275 falls that rush over a 3-km-wide (2-mile-wide) precipice. In comparison, Niagara Falls is but a piddling stream.

PLANNING YOUR TIME

The South is hardly overflowing with historic and architectural treasures. And you won't encounter much of the African or Indian-influenced cultural heritage that is so strong in other parts of the country. However, if you love nature, outdoor sports and activities, and are curious to see how northern European settlers have adapted to life in the subtropics, it is worth exploring this compact trio of states. The tourist infrastructure is among Brazil's best, and poverty and crime are much less of a problem than in other parts of the country. Moreover, exploring the region's attractions can easily be added on to a trip to neighboring Rio de Janeiro and São Paulo. Indeed, many tourists head directly from Rio or Sampa to spend a day or two in the area's biggest draw: Iguaçu Falls. However, an interesting and easy excursion would be 4–5 days spent in either Curitiba, including side trips to Paranaguá Bay and Ilha do Mel, or in Florianópolis, with its surrounding region beach resorts.

If you have a week or 10 days at your disposal, drive or take a bus down the coast from Curitiba to Porto Alegre, exploring cities and beaches along the way and making side trips into the interior. In the South, the roads are excellent and distances between attractions are relatively small (for Brazil). From Curitiba, you can fit in a side trip—via bus or plane—to Iguaçu Falls.

Note that while summers can be hot, winters are quite chilly, with temperatures plunging to 5–10°C (40–50°F) in coastal regions and to the freezing point in the interior. Autumn (March–May) is quite a nice time in terms of weather.

HISTORY

Compared to much of the rest of coastal Brazil, the South's history is fairly recent. Officially, from 1500 onward, Portugal controlled the Atlantic coastline and interior all the way south to the Rio de la Plata. However, for centuries the area remained largely unsettled by Portuguese colonists. Aside from the presence of Azorean fishing communities along the coasts Paraná and Santa Catarina, the most significant presence during the 17th and early to mid-18th centuries was that of Jesuit missionaries. Bent on converting local Guarani Indians, they established various missionary communities in the interior, particularly near the border with neighboring Argentina and Uruguay. By the time the Portuguese crown expelled the Jesuits from Brazil in 1767, much of the grassy highland plains of Rio Grande do Sul (the famous Pampas) had been given over to vast ranches owned by cattle barons of Spanish origin who employed Gaúchos—cowboys of mixed Spanish, Portuguese, and Indian descent—to care for their vast herds.

Large-scale settlement and development of the South as a whole didn't occur until the mid-19th century, when European immigrants—notably from Germany, Italy, and to a lesser extent Poland and Ukraine—arrived en masse, lured by the promise of fertile land, a temperate climate, and the commercial opportunities provided by burgeoning towns. Armed with advanced farming techniques and industrial know-how, these newcomers quickly transformed the South into a thriving region reputed for its dynamic economy, progressive politics, and clean and efficient cities whose inhabitants enjoy one of Brazil's highest standards of living.

Paraná

The wealthiest of all Brazil's states, Paraná is both an agricultural and industrial powerhouse whose development was spurred on by the many immigrants it lured to its territory during the late 19th and 20th centuries. As a result, European cultural and culinary traditions are quite pronounced, especially in the small, isolated agricultural settlements of the interior.

Although Paraná was part of Portugal's Brazilian colony, aside from a few coastal outposts and the tiny settlement of Curitiba (founded in 1693 as a gold mining camp), the territory was pretty much neglected. A scant population of adventurous Portuguese farmers commingled with the seminomadic population of native Guarani Indians. Things began to change in 1853, when the Paraná separated from the state of São Paulo. At this time, the economy was based on two activities: timber extraction (Paraná was once covered with *araucárias*, an umbrella-shaped pine tree that is now very scarce) and the cultivation of *erva maté* (a bush whose leaves are used to make a pungent tea popular with Gaúchos). However, the new provincial government started a massive campaign to lure immigrants to the region in order to develop the economy and open up the interior. From the late 1800s to the early 1900s, Germans, Italians, and Poles planted coffee and, later, soybeans. The efficiency of their small-scale farms contrasted with the vast slave-driven plantations that were the norm in other parts of Brazil. They also opened up businesses in and around the new capital of Curitiba, which—having emerged from its isolation due to the newly constructed railroad—grew in leaps and bounds. Today, Paraná's prosperity is based on state-of-the-art agro-businesses and highly modern industries, while Curitiba has blossomed into a dynamic and eco-friendly city of 1.7 million that has become a model for other urban centers throughout Latin America.

CURITIBA

When Brazilians from other parts of the country visit Curitiba, they are invariably impressed with the Paranaense capital. Aside from its efficiency, safety, and general air of well-being, it provides an interesting example of enlightened urban planning. Due to city mayor (and later state governor) Jaime Lerner, a visionary architect who first came to power in the 1970s, Curitiba was an environmentalists' dream long before Al Gore came along. Concerned with the traffic pollution that was already afflicting large Latin American cities, Lerner inaugurated a modern, inexpensive, and very extensive municipal bus system and turned much of the small but carefully preserved historic center into an agreeable pedestrian district. Recycling and antipollution programs were adopted, and amidst new high-rises, vast tracts of land were transformed into public green spaces. In fact, this truly emerald city boasts more than 30 municipal parks and wooded areas with plenty of walking and biking trails. Though not fascinating—you can easily see its most interesting sites in a day—Curitiba is definitely refreshing (located high up on a plateau, it is Brazil's coolest state capital) and provides a good base for exploring the rest of Paraná.

Sights

Curitiba's downtown core and historic center are compact and easy to explore on foot. To get to outlying attractions and the majority of the city's parks, you can rely on the terrific municipal bus system. Better yet is the very handy **Linha Turismo** (tel. 41/3352-8000,

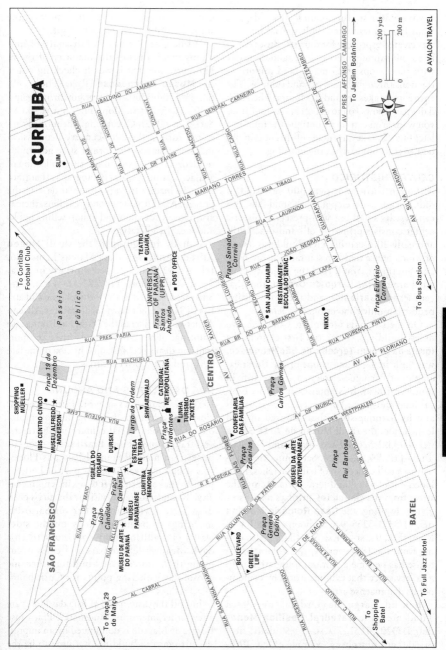

THE SOUTH

CURITIBA

To Coritiba Football Club

To Jardim Botânico →

AV. PRES. AFFONSO CAMARGO →

200 yds
200 m
© AVALON TRAVEL

SLIM

RUA UBALDINO DO AMARAL
RUA AMINTAS DE BARROS
RUA XV DE NOVEMBRO
RUA B. CONSTANT
RUA GENERAL CARNEIRO
AV. SETE DE SETEMBRO
RUA DR DE FAIVRE
RUA MARIANO TORRES
RUA NILO CAIRO
RUA COM. MACEDO
RUA TIBAGI
AV. SILVA JARDIM
RUA C. LAURINDO

Passeio Público

To Coritiba Football Club

TEATRO GUAÍRA
UNIVERSITY OF PARANÁ (UFPR)
POST OFFICE

Praça Santos Andrade

Praça Senador Correia

RUA JOSÉ LOUREIRO
RUA JOSÉ BONIFÁCIO
AV. V. DE GUARAPUAVA
RUA JOÃO NEGRÃO
TR. DE LAPA
RUA ANDRÉ DE BARROS

SAN JUAN CHARM
RESTAURANTE: ESCOLA DO SENAC

NIKKO

Praça Eufrásio Correia

To Bus Station

RUA PRES. FARIA
RUA RIACHUELO

SHOPPING MUELLER
Praça 19 de Dezembro
IBIS CENTRO CÍVICO
MUSEU ALFREDO ANDERSON

RUA MATEUS LEME

Largo da Ordem
SHWARZWALD
CATEDRAL METROPOLITANA

CENTRO

RUA XAVIER
RUA BR
RUA DO RIO
RUA PEDRO IVO
BARANCO
AV. LUÍS
RUA LOURENÇO PINTO
AV. MAL. FLORIANO

DURSKI
ESTRELA DE TERRA
CURITIBA MEMORIAL

Praça Tiradentes
LINHA TURISMO TICKETS
RUA DO ROSÁRIO

CONFEITARIA DAS FAMÍLIAS

Praça Carlos Gomes

AV. DR. MURICY

SÃO FRANCISCO

RUA 13 DE MAIO
RUA KELLERS

Praça João Cândido

IGREJA DO ROSÁRIO
Praça Garibaldi
MUSEU PARANAENSE
MUSEU DE ARTE DO PARANÁ

R. E. PEREIRA

RUA DAS FLORES
Praça Zacarias

MUSEU DA ARTE CONTEMPORÂNEA

RUA DES. WESTPHALEN

Praça Rui Barbosa

RUA DES. PEDROSA

BATEL

To Praça 29 de Março

AL. CABRAL

RUA SALDANHA MARINHO

BOULEVARD
GREEN LIFE

Praça General Osório

RUA VOLUNTÁRIOS DA PÁTRIA

RUA VICENTE MACHADO
RUA C. ARAÚJO
R. V. DE NACAR
RUA 24 HORAS
R. V. DE EMILIANO PERNETA
RUA C. EMILIANO PERNETA

To Shopping Batel

To Full Jazz Hotel

9 A.M.–5:30 P.M. Tues.–Sun.), which departs from Praça Tiradentes. This special bus line was created especially for tourists. Buses circulate at 30-minute intervals throughout the day with short stops at 23 major (and minor) attractions throughout the city and suburbs. The entire tour takes around 2.5 hours. The R$15 daily pass allows you to get off at any four stops you want. You can then continue the tour on a later bus. To take advantage of this option, it's best to start out early in the morning.

CENTRO HISTÓRICO

Although Curitiba is over 300 years old, it didn't begin to develop until the mid-late 19th century. Its small but well-preserved historic center consists primarily of handsome 19th- and early-20th-century civic buildings, many of which house trendy restaurants, cafés, bars, and boutiques. You'll find the majority clustered around the **Largo da Ordem,** the adjacent **Praça Garibaldi,** and the surrounding pedestrian-only cobblestoned streets.

On the Largo da Ordem are Curitiba's two oldest buildings. The city's first church, the **Igreja da Ordem Terceira de São Francisco,** was built in 1737 and is one of the finest examples of Portuguese colonial architecture in southern Brazil. It is noteworthy for its typical blue-and-white Portuguese *azulejo* panels and its baroque-style altars doused in gold leaf. Inside, the small **Museu de Arte Sacra** (tel. 41/3321-3265, 9 A.M.–noon and 1–6 P.M. Tues.–Fri., 9 A.M.–2 P.M. Sat.–Sun., free) displays a small collection of baroque relics, fashioned out of wood and terra-cotta. Across the street from the church is Curitiba's oldest surviving dwelling, the **Casa Romário Martins** (tel. 41/3321-3255, 9 A.M.–noon and 2–6 P.M. Mon.–Fri., 9 A.M.–2 P.M. Sat.–Sun.). Also dating from the 18th century, this colonial-style house has become a cultural foundation with a gallery space that exhibits works by contemporary Paranaense artists.

Behind Largo da Ordem, on Praça Tiradentes, the **Catedral Basílica Menor** (tel. 41/3222-1131, 7 A.M.–9 P.M. daily, free) is a rather uninspiring example of late 19th-century neo-gothic architecture built on the site of Curitiba's first wooden chapel.

While Curitiba has its fair share of museums, you can skip the majority of them. However, one that is worth checking out is the **Museu Paranaense** (Rua Kellers 289, tel. 41/3304-3300, www.pr.gov.br/museupr, 9:30 A.M.–5:30 P.M. Mon.–Fri., 11 A.M.–3 P.M. Sat.–Sun., R$2). Occupying a beautifully restored turn-of-the-20th-century neoclassical mansion that was the former state governor's residence, it houses an interesting collection of artifacts, paintings, and photographs that trace Paraná's history from precolonial days to the present. Aside from temporary exhibits, there is also a lovely tea salon and a shop selling books and local handicrafts.

Equally intriguing is the small **Museu Alfredo Andersen** (Rua Mateus Leme 336, tel. 41/3222-8262, www.pr.gov.br/maa, 9 A.M.–6 P.M. Mon.–Fri., 10 A.M.–4 P.M. Sat.–Sun., free), located in the former home and atelier of Norwegian-born local painter Alfredo Andersen, considered the "father of Paranaense painting." The striking landscapes and portraits on display conjure up Curitiba of the late 19th and early 20th centuries.

RUA DAS FLORES AND AROUND

In 1971, Curitiba's mayor, Jaime Lerner, closed off a section of Rua 15 de Novembro, one of the commercial center's main streets, and transformed it into Brazil's first open-air pedestrian mall. Renamed Rua das Flores, this urban intervention was part of Lerner's plan to make Curitiba into a kinder, greener city. To underscore his vision, the city's children were invited to gather on Saturday mornings to paint and draw on the sidewalks (a tradition that continues to this day). Meanwhile, the bars and cafés occupying the restored pastel buildings became end-of-day gathering points for Curitibanos of all stripes.

Just off the eastern end of Rua das Flores are a few other interesting landmarks. Praça José Borges de Macedo is dominated by an impressive art nouveau building that used to be the city hall. From here, if you head three blocks north along Rua Barão do Rio Branco you'll arrive at the **Passeio Público** (Rua Luiz Leão, tel. 41/3223-6574, 6 A.M.–8 P.M. Tues.–Sun.). Inaugurated in 1886, the city's first park is a peaceful oasis with lakes for boating, walking paths, and shady oak, sycamore, and purple-blossomed *ipê* trees.

CENTRO CÍVICO

Famed Brazilian architect Oscar Niemeyer has had many hits and misses throughout his long career, but the **Museu Oscar Niemeyer** (Rua Marechal Hermes 999, Centro Cívico, tel. 41/3350-4400, www.pr.gov.br/mon, 10 A.M.–5 P.M. Mon.–Fri., 11 A.M.–3 P.M. Sat.–Sun., R$4) has definitely been a hit since its unveiling in 2002. The museum consists of two concrete buildings: a long, gleaming rectangle designed in the '70s and the famous "Olho" ("Eye"), which resembles an enormous eye suspended in the air. Multiple stained-glass windows suffuse the interior with colored light. Aside from a small permanent exhibition documenting Niemeyer's career, various galleries host high-quality temporary exhibits of contemporary art. The museum is in the Centro Cívico, a sprawling modern complex of state government buildings that was built in the 1980s. If you don't want to walk the 3 kilometers (2 miles) from downtown, take the Linha Turismo bus, or any bus marked "Centro Cívico."

PARKS

Curitiba is overflowing with parks and wooded areas. The Museu Oscar Niemeyer overlooks the **Bosque Papa João Paulo** (6 A.M.–6 P.M. daily), a wooded area named in honor of Pope John Paul II's 1980 visit to Curitiba. Among several log cabins built by Polish immigrants in the 1880s is a small museum where you can buy Polish handicrafts. In a pretty wooden house at the park's entrance, **Kawiarnia Krakowiak** (Travessa Wellington de Oliveira Vianna 40, tel. 41/3026-7462, 10 A.M.–9 P.M. daily) serves a "colonial tea" with scrumptious Polish cakes including *kremòwka*, a creamy vanilla *mille-*

feuille that was the favorite of Pope John Paul II when he visited. If the weather is cold, warm up with one of many hearty soups— the "Hungarian" soup is made with wine and ginger while the "Curitibana" soup includes pine nuts.

The popular **Jardim Botânico** (Rua Engenheiro Ostoja Roguski, Jardim Botânico, tel. 31/3364-6694, 6 A.M.–8 P.M. daily, R$3) features winding trails that lead though formal French gardens, shaded by peach trees and *araucárias*, as well as a patch of native Atlantic rainforest. The highlight is the elegant steel and glass hothouse modeled after London's Crystal Palace, featuring a collection of rare Brazilian plants.

The **Parque Tanguá** (Rua Nilo Peçanha, Pilarziho, tel. 41/3352-7607, open 24 hours daily) occupies two former stone quarries linked by a tunnel through the rocks. Aside from a lake, an artificial waterfall, and a panoramic lookout, there are numerous hiking and biking trails through the greenery.

Curitiba's equivalent of New York's Central Park is **Parque Barigüi** (Rodovia do Café/BR-227, Santo Inácio, tel. 41/3339-8975, open 24 hours daily). The city's biggest park by far, it gets packed on weekends. **Parque Tingüi** (Rua Dr. Bemben, Pilarzinho, 41/32401103, 6 A.M.–7 P.M. daily) is a pleasant park that pays homage to Paraná's Ukrainian community with a replica of a 19th-century onion-domed Ukrainian church. Inside, traditional crafts are displayed, including an impressive collection of *pêssankas* (hand-painted Easter eggs).

Bosque Alemão (Rua Niccolo Paganini, Jardim Schaffer, tel. 41/3338-6835, open 24 hours daily) is a wooded parkland that honors Paraná's German population. Classical musical concerts are held at the chapel-like Bach Oratorium, and kids can pretend to get lost by following the "Hansel and Gretel Trail" through the woods. A lookout point offers great panoramic views of the city and the surrounding Serra do Mar.

Parque da Pedreira (Rua João Gava, Abranches, tel. 41/3355-6071, 8 A.M.–10 P.M. Tues.–Sun.) also used to be a rock quarry

THE SOUTH

© CHRISTIAN KNEPPER/EMBRATUR

A highlight of Curitiba's Jardim Botânico is its hothouse full of rare Brazilian plants.

before it was converted into a green space with a lake and two theaters. The outdoor Pedreira Paulo Leminski amphitheater is the stage for large shows and concerts, but the park's true highlight is the **Ópera de Arame**—a superbly designed "wire" opera house designed by local architect Domingos Bongestabs. Its delicate structure of tubular steel and wire mesh features walls of glass that allow you to contemplate the surrounding lakes and woodlands. Even if there are no performances scheduled, the opera house is an architectural marvel and well worth the visit.

Entertainment and Events

Curitiba has a lively arts scene for a city of its size. One of Brazil's premier theaters, **Teatro Guaíra** (Rua 15 de Novembro, Centro, tel. 41/3322-2628) has three auditoriums where you can often see high-caliber theater, dance, and classical music performances. Although the acoustics are less than impressive, in terms of aesthetics, it is worth your while to check out a concert at the **Ópera de Arame** in Parque da Pedreira (see *Parks*).

Shopping

Shopping Estação (Av. Sete de Setembro 2775, Centro, tel. 41/2101-9000, www.shopping estacao.com, 10 A.M.–10 P.M. Mon.–Sat., 2–8 P.M. Sun.) is built around Curitiba's original 19th-century railroad station. Apart from over 100 stores, it has bars, restaurants, movie theaters, and a trio of small museums devoted to the history of Paraná's railways, the Brazilian environment, and perfumes (featuring some great old TV commercials and lots of fragrance testing).

The **Shopping Crystal Plaza** (Rua Comendador Araújo 731, Batel, tel. 41/3332-2744, www.crystalplaza.com.br, 10 A.M.–10 P.M. Mon.–Sat., 2–8 P.M. Sun.) is Curitiba's chic *shopping,* with upscale boutiques as well as restaurants and a cineplex.

Rua 24 Horas (entrance Rua Visconde de Nacar, Centro, tel. 41/3225-1732) is a small gallery of stores off Rua das Flores where a few (but not all) stores are open 24 hours daily. Aside from making purchases, you can get a late night/ early morning bite. It has been abandoned in recent times, but a renovation is pending.

For authentic Paranaense handicrafts, **Arte Nossa** (Alameda Dr. Murici 950, tel. 41/3234-1118, www.artenossa.pr.gov.br, 9 A.M.–6 P.M. Mon.–Fri.) sells everything from local indigenous art to hand-painted Ukrainian eggs. You can also find a good range of local arts and crafts, as well as food, at the animated **Feira de Artesanato,** which takes place in the Largo da Ordem and Praça Garibaldi on Sundays between 9 A.M. and 3 A.M.

Accommodations

Hotels are mostly located in the center as well as in the nearby *bairros* of Centro Cívico and Batel. Although prices are quite affordable, many hotels offer discounts during low season and weekends, and prices are often much lower than those quoted.

The **Curitiba Eco Hostel** (Rua Luís Tramontin 1693, Campo Comprido, tel. 41/3274-7979, www.curitibaecohostel.com.br, R$45–55 d) is much more of a bucolic country retreat than your average urban youth hostel. Attractive wooden lodgings—with dormitory and double rooms—blend harmoniously with the surrounding woods. Rooms (with small balconies) and common spaces are warm and rustic, and there is a large heated pool as well as free Internet and a 24-hour restaurant. The prices are incredible. The only drawback is the location—8 kilometers (5 miles) from the center of town; however, it is easily reached by bus from Praça Rui Barbosa.

The Ibis hotel chain has a slew of good-value bargain hotels in Curitiba. Spotless, efficiently run, although somewhat spartan, the **Ibis Centro Cívico** (Rua Mateus Leme 358, Centro Cívico, tel. 41/3324-0469, www.ibis.com.br, R$89 d) has a little more character than others in the chain because its restaurant and reception area occupy charming old houses. The Paranaense chain Slaviero also has quite a few options in the capital. Centrally located, the low-cost **Slim** (Rua Conselheiro Araújo 435, Alto da XV, tel. 41/3017-1050, www.hotels laviero.com.br, R$140 d) has modern, comfortable rooms whose only drawback is the bland decor. The reception areas and restaurant are reminiscent of an airport lounge, albeit an airy, sleek one. Frills include a fitness room and Internet access.

At the other end of the spectrum is Slaviero's **Full Jazz Hotel** (Rua Silveira Peixoto 1297, Batel, tel. 41/3312-7000, www.hotelfull jazz.com.br, R$264–368 d). One of Curitiba's rare boutique hotels, its minimalist decor jives nicely with the jazz theme that extends from a jazz CD and DVD library to a cool piano bar. The discreetly decorated rooms, outfitted in pleasing neutral tones, are stylish and comfortable.

Located in a historical landmark building where Curitiba's very first hotel opened in 1917, the **San Juan Charm** (Rua Barão do Rio Branco 354, Centro, tel. 41/3219-9900, www.sanjuanhoteis.com.br, R$154–242 d) is all about retro elegance. The palatial-sized luxury suites feature soaring ceilings, polished wooden floors, and antique replicas as well as king-sized beds and swimming pool sized bath tubs. Nearby, **Nikko** (Rua Barão Rio Branco 546, Centro, tel. 41/2105-1808, www.hotelnikko.com.br, R$110–180 d) offers an alternative to Curitiba's more pronounced Polish/German/Ukrainian influences. Hidden behind a 19th-century facade, this refined and modern Japanese hotel offers a soothing atmosphere replete with cool colors, simple geometric forms, vases of flowers, and lots of Oriental touches. Rooms are small, but relaxing, oases. A bamboo garden with a goldfish pond and a sushi bar complete the ode to Japan.

Food
RESTAURANTS

Curitiba has a fairly varied restaurant scene, and it is possible to eat well and quite affordably. European cuisine representing Paraná's major immigrant groups is a strong point—you'll find many options in the center. Contemporary eateries are clustered in the chic *bairro* of Batel.

For delicious inexpensive fare, there are many choices. **Green Life** (Alameda Dr. Carlos de Carvalho 271, Batel, tel. 41/3223-8490, 11 A.M.–3 P.M. daily, R$10–15) serves a varied

THE SOUTH

PARANAENSE COOKING

Athough few people are aware of it, there is such a thing as Paranaense cooking – a fusion of the region's historical and geographical influences that is quite unique. Native Guarani Indians were very fond of the *pinhões* (pine nuts) that were abundant due to the region's *araucária* pine forests. You'll find *pinhões* in everything from traditional *paçoca* (a sweet and crunchy nut brittle) to *pinhão* pancakes, cream soups, and soufflés.

Another Guarani staple was corn, which is present in many recipes in the form of *quirera*, a polenta-like porridge made of white or yellow corn flour. Such foodstuffs, along with sun-dried and salted beef and pork, came in handy for the early *tropeiros*. As they criss-crossed the dense forests of Paraná in seach of riches, they required hearty sustenance that could be stored over long journeys. Among the most famous of these *tropeiro* dishes are *quirera Lapiana*, in which smoked pork ribs are cooked with *quirera*, and *paçoca de charque*, cured beef fried with onions and garlic, and mixed with manioc flour. Perhaps the most distinctive dish of all is *barreado*. Invented by the Azorean fishermen who settled the coastal towns of Antonina and Morretes, this robust stew of beef, bacon, potatoes, and spices is sealed ("*barreado*") with a covering of manioc flour, and then stewed for hours in a clay casserole. It may not be light, but it's certainly tasty.

vegetarian per kilo buffet featuring organic produce grown at the restaurant's own farm outside Curitiba. The **Restaurante-Escola do Senac** (Rua André de Barros 750, 2nd Fl., Centro, tel. 41/3219-4854, 11:30 A.M.–2:30 P.M. Mon.–Sat., R$10–20) is run by the Curitiba branch of the Senac restaurant school. This means that the apprentice chefs are highly motivated and the waitstaff are on their best behavior. Aside from a constantly changing à la carte menu—with a choice of entrée, main course, and dessert—*barreado* is served on Thursdays and *feijoada* on Saturdays.

Located in a historic house, **◖ Estrela da Terra** (Rua Jaime Reis 176, São Francisco, tel. 41/3222-5007, www.estrelada terra.com.br, 11:30 A.M.–2:30 P.M. Mon.–Fri., 11:30 A.M.–4 P.M., R$16–25) is one of the few restaurants in Curitiba that serve typical Paranaense cuisine. Hearty dishes created by the state's earliest settlers—and revealing a marked indigenous influence (creamed corn, manioc, and pine nuts)—are laid out in a lavish and very affordable buffet. Try Paraná's most famous dish, *barreado*. The house specialty, *estrela da terra,* consists of *charque* (cured beef) cooked with creamy Catupiry cheese and served inside a roasted pumpkin.

Leave room for desserts such as orange pudding with grilled fruit.

Slightly removed from the center, **Cantinho do Eisbein** (Av. dos Estados 863, Água Verde, tel. 41/3329-5155, 11:30 A.M.–3 P.M. and 7–11:30 P.M. Tues.–Sat., 11:30 A.M.–3 P.M. Sun., R$20–30) is a highly recommended German restaurant. The owners themselves greet you and serve the generous portions of *eisbein* (pork knees), *kassler* (smoked pork loin), and a delicious stuffed duck, accompanied with garnishes such as apple puree, sweet red cabbage, and white sausage.

Durski (Av. Jaime Reis 254, São Francisco, tel. 41/3225-7893, www.durski.com.br, 11:30 A.M.–2:30 P.M., 7:30 P.M.–midnight Mon.–Fri., 11:30 A.M.–4 P.M. and 7:30 P.M.–midnight Sat., 11:30 A.M.–4 P.M. Sun., R$40–50) is considered the best Ukrainian restaurant in Brazil. If you're feeling hungry, go all out and order the *banquete eslavo* (Slavic banquet)—a feast of Ukrainian, Polish, and Russian dishes ranging from borscht with smoked ham and cream to goulash and potato *varenikes* (dumplings) stuffed with ricotta and topped with mushrooms. The setting is intimate and the wine cellar is impressive.

For some of the finest gourmet creations in

town, Curitibano foodies head to **🅒 Boulevard** (Rua Voluntários da Pátria 539, Centro, tel. 41/3224-8244, noon–2:30 P.M. and 7:30–11:30 P.M. Mon.–Sat., 7:30 P.M.–midnight Sun., R$40–55). Although Chef Celso Freire's culinary roots are French and Italian, he has a fondness for Brazilian ingredients. Marinated *perna-de-moça*, a local fish from Paranaguá Bay, and roast rabbit with mushrooms and cream of corn are two examples of dishes on the recently elaborated Paranaense menu. For dessert, try the irresistible passion fruit consommé with *abacaxi* (white pineapple) ice cream and macaroons. At the bar, *miniaturas gastronômicas*—tapas-sized portions of menu items—are served (6:30–8:30 P.M.) along with wine.

Meanwhile, the traditional 19th-century northern Italian *bairro* of Santa Felicidade (8 km/5 miles northwest of the city center) has become—for better and for worse—a gastronomic circuit for tourists and locals. Along the main drag of Avenida Manoel Ribas you'll find a rather overwhelming number of cantinas and trattorias (with seating capacities of up to 2,000), many dubiously decorated to resemble *castelos* and *palazzos*. Aside from the kitsch factor, the food itself is often mediocre (not to mention the wine, which is made from local grapes). There are, however, exceptions, such as **Famiglia Fadanelli** (Av. Manoel Ribas 5667, Santa Felicidade, tel. 41/3372-1616, 7–11 P.M. Tues.–Fri., noon–3:30 P.M. and 7–11:30 P.M. Sat., and noon–3:30 P.M. Sun., R$20–30), with a more discreetly modern decor, a well-chosen wine list, and a carefully honed menu that ranges from delicious antipasti to specialties such as pork cutlets with crunchy broccoli and cheese-stuffed *agnoletti* pasta in a sauce of grapes and toasted almonds.

CAFÉS AND BARS

In the late 19th and early 20th century, Paraná was a thriving place due to simultaneous booms in coffee and immigration. One of the most delicious consequences is the abundance of European-style cafés and tea salons that opened up on and around Rua das Flores, several of which still draw (largely mature) crowds around

tea time. **Confeitaria das Famílias** (Rua das Flores 374, Centro, tel. 41/3223-0313, 7 A.M.–11 P.M. daily) has been satisfying Curitibanos' sugar cravings since 1945 with a mouthwatering array of pastries. It was here that the legendary *torta Martha Rocha* was invented. A concoction of chocolate and vanilla cake with cream and walnut praline was an attempt by the founder of the *confeitaria* to console his wife, who was devastated when Rocha, a.k.a. Miss Brazil of 1954, lost the Miss Universe crown because of two extra inches on her hips.

The majority of Curitiba's most interesting bars are divided between the historic center and the trendy *bairro* of Batel. Popularly known as the "Bar do Alemão" (German bar), **Schwarzwald** (Rua Dr. Claudino dos Santos 63, Centro, tel. 41/3223-2585, www.bardoalemao curitiba.com.br, 11 A.M.–2 A.M. daily) is a perpetually lively gastronomic (and somewhat touristic) institution famous for its Bohemian ambiance, fine German cuisine, and dependably icy draft beer. Another animated spot is **Jacobina** (Rua Almirante Tamandaré 1365, Juvevê, tel. 41/3016-6111, www.jacobina bar.com.br, 11:30 A.M.–1 A.M. Mon.–Sat.), whose warm, homey vibe is accentuated by the ad-hoc decor of old TVs, typewriters, teapots, and frying pans. The menu features very tasty and inexpensive fare that ranges from classic Brazilian home-cooking to international dishes such as Moroccan couscous and Oriental chicken with ginger. Although it sounds suspect, the *sorvete de queijo* (cheese sorbet) topped with guava sauce is pretty divine. On Saturday afternoons an all-you-can eat *feijoada* is accompanied by live *chorinho*.

For live music, head to **Santa Marta** (Rua Bispo Dom José 2030, Batel, tel. 41/3343-2803, www.santamartabar.com.br, 6 P.M.–2 A.M. Tues.–Sun., noon–4 P.M. Sat., no cover), located in an immense 80-year-old house whose pleasant deck is shaded by an enormous *jabuticaba* tree. Every night at 9 P.M., there are performances running the gamut from MPB and samba-rock to "surf music." Since Santa Marta is the patron saint of cooks, it's not surprising that the food is quite tasty. Saturday afternoons draw a hungry crowd for the all-you-can-eat *barreado* buffet and live *chorinho*.

Information

Like Curitiba itself, the municipal **tourist office** is an efficient place. You'll find information centers with helpful staff and plenty of maps at the Rodoferroviária (Av. Afonso Camargo, 41/330, tel. 41/3320-3121), at Rua 24 Horas (Rua Coronel Mena Barreto, Loja 18, tel. 41/3324-7036), and at the Museu Oscar Niemeyer (Rua Marechal Hermes, Centro Cívico, tel. 41/3350-4466). There is a tourist information hotline (tel. 41/3352-8000) along with a bilingual website, www.viaje .curitiba.pr.gov.br. The state tourist office, **Paraná Turismo** (Rua Deputado Mário de Barros 1290, Centro Cívico, tel. 41/3254-1516, www.pr.gov.br, 9 A.M.–6 P.M. Mon.–Fri.) has lots of information about attractions throughout Paraná including transportation schedules and maps. The website is bilingual.

Services

Main **bank** branches can be found around the commercial hub of Centro near Praça Osório and Rua das Flores. The main **post office** is at Rua XV de Novembro 700, near Praça Santos Andrade. In the event of an emergency, dial **192** for an ambulance, **193** for the fire department, and **190** for the police. **Hospital Universitário Cajuru** (Av. São José 300, Cristo Rei, tel. 41/3360-3000, www.pucpr.br/saude/ alianca/cajuru) is a centrally located hospital.

For Internet access, try **Lig Lig** (Rua Amintas de Barros 144, Loja 1, 8 A.M.–2 A.M. daily), near the Teatro Curitiba.

Getting There

Curitiba is easily reached from all other Brazilian cities by air. There are numerous daily bus connections from Rio, São Paulo, Florianópolis, and Porto Alegre.

AIR

Curitiba's modern **Aeroporto Internacional Afonso Pena** (Av. Rocha Pombo, São José dos Pinhais, tel. 41/3381-1515) is 21 kilometers (13 miles) east of the city's center. To get to the center of town, a taxi will set you back around R$50. A much better bargain is the excellent **Aeroporto Executivo** (tel. 41/3283-4321), a minibus that runs between the airport, the Rodoferroviária, Teatro Guaíra, Shopping Estação, and Rua 24 Horas. It costs R$6 and shuttles leave at 20-minute intervals.

BUS

The main bus station and train station are one and the same, hence the hybrid moniker of **Rodoferroviária** (Av. Presidente Afonso Camargo 41/330, tel. 41/3320-3000). Buses travel to destinations throughout the state and country as well as to Argentina, Paraguay, and Chile. **Itapemirim** (tel. 0800/723-2121, www.itapemirim.com.br) offers service to and from São Paulo (6 hours away). **Pluma** (tel. 0800/646-0300, www.pluma.com.br) heads all the way south to Porto Alegre (12 hours). **Sulamericana** (tel. 41/3373-1000, www.sula.com.br) offers service to Foz do Iguaçu (10 hours). The only passenger trains still in activity run along the scenic line that goes to Paranaguá (tel. 41/3320-4007). Although the Rodoferroviária is an easy walk (around a dozen blocks) from the historic center, you can also grab a minibus that stops near the front entrance.

Getting Around

Getting around town is easy. Although you can walk to most sights, the city's municipal bus system is an urban planner's dream. From the two central municipal bus terminals at Praça Tiradentes and Praça Rui Barbosa, you can get a bus for anywhere in the city, the suburbs, and to nearby towns (the destination is clearly marked on the front). Taxis are also easy to flag down.

In Curitiba, traffic is lighter than in other major Brazilian cities. If you want to rent a car to get around the city and explore the surrounding state, try **Avis** (www.avis.com.br), with locations at the airport (tel. 41/3381-1370) and Centro (Av. Salgado Filho 1491, tel. 41/3296-1889), and **Hertz** (www.hertz.com.br), with locations at the airport (tel. 41/3381-1382) and Centro (Av. Nossa Senhora de Aparecida, 41/3731, tel. 41/3269-8000).

Around Curitiba
PARQUE ESTADUAL DE VILA VELHA
Less than 100 kilometers (62 miles) northwest of Curitiba, in the midst of a rolling green plateau region known as Campos Gerais, the Parque Estadual de Vila Velha (8:30 A.M.–5:30 P.M. Wed.–Mon., tel. 42/3228-1539, R$12) is an easy day trip from Curitiba (or an interesting stop off on your way to Foz do Iguaçu). Aside from small lakes (including a crater lake where you can go swimming), the park's stellar attractions are the two dozen fantastically shaped rock formations hewed out of reddish sandstone. Dating back 300 million years, they are the result of glacial activity combined with subsequent erosion. Their life-like aspect has earned many of these sculptures nicknames, such as "the Boot," "the Sphinx," and "the Camel's Head." You can visit the area on foot, following a clearly marked 2.5-kilometer (1.5-mile) trail or by taking a tractor-pulled wagon. The park itself is very well organized with a visitor center, a restaurant, and food and drink kiosks.

From Curitiba, Vila Velha is a 90-minute bus ride with departures every hour—take a *semi-direito* bus from the Rodoferroviário to the town of Ponta Grossa and ask the driver to let you off at the entrance to the park. Make sure you check the schedule for return buses so you can flag down a bus back to Curitiba in the late afternoon. By car, follow the BR-376.

CURITIBA TO PARANAGUÁ
Between Curitiba and the coastal town of Paranaguá lie 120 kilometers (75 miles) of spectacular mountains carpeted in thick jungle that are part of the Serra do Mar. The height of the peaks and density of the vegetation has ensured the preservation of one of the largest remaining patches of native Atlantic rainforest that once covered the entire Brazilian coast. For centuries, nothing more than a winding cobblestoned road linked Curitiba to the colonial port of Antonina—a grueling two-day

journey by horse-drawn carts. Then in 1885, a railway was built to connect Curitiba with the port of Paranaguá, whose deep waters were better suited for the immense ships required to transport Parana's booming coffee harvest overseas. Today, the railway is one of the few lines in Brazil still active. Although you can drive or take a bus to Paranaguá, neither compares with four hours spent aboard the Serra Verde Express. Stop-off points along the way include the colonial town of Morretes and the Parque Estadual do Marumbi, an unspoiled idyll that draws hikers, rafters, and those hardy enough to climb the 1,500-meter (4,920-foot) rocky Marumbi peak. Paranaguá itself, currently Brazil's second largest port after Santos, offers few attractions aside from a cluster of dilapidated historical buildings—Antonina and Morretes are much more charming. However, it's in Paranaguá that you can catch a boat for the lovely Ilha do Mel.

The Serra Verde Express
Many of Brazil's railways were financed and built by European (mostly British) companies, but the Curitiba–Paranaguá railway line was a 100 percent Brazilian project. A masterful engineering feat, the route features some 67 bridges and viaducts and 13 tunnels. Tracks are sometimes perilously close to sheer cliffs, which makes for an adrenaline-charged journey. However, it's hard to be anxious when surrounded by so much natural beauty. As you plunge from Curitiba's highlands down to the blue Atlantic you'll be treated to visions of cloud-shrouded peaks, deep canyons ribboned with waterfalls, and the vegetation's transformation as it becomes increasingly lush and tropical.

The most breathtaking part of the voyage is the first three hours between Curitiba and the town of Morretes. Make sure when you buy your ticket that you reserve a seat on the left side (and on the right side on the return trip). The Serra Verde Express (tel. 41/3323-4077, www.serraexpress.com.br) operates two types of trains. Passenger trains (*trem convencional*) depart from Curitiba's Rodoferroviária at 8:15 A.M. every day, arriving at Morretes at 11:15 A.M. and at Paranaguá (Sunday only) at 12:15 P.M. The return train leaves from Paranaguá (Sunday only) at 2 P.M. and Morretes at 3 P.M., and arrives back in Curitiba at 6 P.M. More luxurious is the *Litorina,* a tourist train with air-conditioning, panoramic windows, bilingual guides, and snacks and drinks, which makes a scenic stop at the Santuário de Cadeado. It runs daily between Curitiba and Morretes, departing the Rodoferroviária at 9:30 A.M. and returning from Morretes at 2:30 P.M. Ticket prices vary. From Curitiba to Morretes, the *trem convencional* offers three fares: *econômico* (R$28), *turístico* (R$50) and *executivo* (R$78), with the return trip costing R$22, R$34, and R$47, respectively. Morretes to Paranagúa (and vice versa) costs an extra R$11. Tickets for the *Litorina* cost R$118 (and R$90 for the return), and it is recommended that you reserve in advance, especially on weekends, holidays, and in the summer.

BWT Operadora (tel. 41/3323-4077, www.bwtoperadora.com.br), a tour operator that is part of the same group as Serra Verde Express (in fact they share office space in Curitiba's Rodoferroviária), organizes day excursions to attractions in the region between Curitiba and Paranágua. Trips include a train ride to Morretes along with activities such as rafting and hiking in the Parque Estadual do Marumbi and/or historic tours of Morrete and Antonina (punctuated by a typical lunch of *barreado*) with a return by van to Curitiba.

If you're driving from Curitiba to Morretes, follow the **Estrada Graciosa,** a stunning 33-kilometer (21-mile) stretch of road that leads off the BR-116. Although the sinewy route will take you an hour longer than the alternative BR-277 highway, the views of the surrounding landscapes (including the peaks of Marumbi and Paraná) are well worth it. Along the way, you can purchase locally produced honey, *cachaça,* and *balas de banana* (chewy banana candies).

Parque Estadual do Marumbi

Both the railway line and the Estrada da Graciosa pass right through the Parque Estadual do Marumbi (tel. 41/3462-3588, www.cosmo.org.br, 8 A.M.–6 P.M. daily, free). Aside from feasting your eyes upon virgin Atlantic rainforest, you can scale mountains and bathe in waterfalls. The park offers plenty of well-marked hiking trails, many of which were carved out of the wilderness centuries ago by Indians and early settlers. One of the easiest is a 45-minute trail that leads to the hilltop of Rochedinha, with stops for bathing in natural pools created by the Rio Taquara. More adventurous souls can climb to the summit of Monte Olimpo, which at 1,539 meters (5,049 feet) is the highest peak in Paraná.

GETTING THERE
The Serra do Mar Express stops at Marumbi station, which is within the park. At the entrance is a visitors center with maps of the trails and other information. The park is also accessible by bus from nearby Morretes.

Morretes
Straddling the Rio Nhundiaquara, this pretty little colonial town at the foot of the Serra do Mar was founded by Jesuits in 1721. Aside from its cobblestoned streets and colorful old houses, the town is famous for its fine *cachaças* and artisanally produced *balas de banana*—the surrounding area boasts several colonial sugar plantations and *bananeiras* (banana trees) are everywhere. Most visitors just spend enough time to feast on *barreado* and stroll around the historic center. However, its languorous small-town atmosphere (except on busy summer weekends) makes it a nice place to stay if you want a base for exploring the Parque Estadual de Marumbi—local buses go to nearby São João de Graciosa, which is 2 kilometers (1.2 miles) from the entrance to the park—and the nearby town of Antonina, 18 kilometers (11 miles) away.

ACCOMMODATIONS AND FOOD
The nicest hotel within the town itself is the charming **Hotel Nhundiaquara** (Rua General Carneiro 13, tel. 41/3462-1228, www.nundiaquara.com.br, R$200 d) located in

a whitewashed 17th-century mansion perched on a scenic bend in the river. The rooms are fairly simple, but appealing. Reserve in advance so you can get one overlooking the river. The hotel's **Restaurante Nhundiaquara** has been serving up *barreado* along with seafood dishes for over 60 years. Its tables scattered along a veranda offer picturesque views.

A cheaper alternative is to rent one of the six fully equipped chalets at **Pousada Ecocatu** (Estrada da Graciosa 1219, tel. 41/3462-1512, www.netpar.com.br/ecocatu, R$90–100) a 1-kilometer (0.6-mile) walk from town. The raw brick chalets aren't that pretty, but are clean and functional. Aside from a pool, you'll be surrounded by greenery and scenery.

In Morretes, **Armazém Romanus** (Rua Visconde do Rio Branco 141, tel. 41/3642-1500, 11 A.M.–3 P.M. and 7–10 P.M. Mon.–Sun.) serves up a notoriously good traditional *barreado,* albeit a health-conscious one (all the meat's fat is removed prior to cooking), accompanied by grilled local bananas. Other specialties include giant shrimp and fish dishes.

INFORMATION

The **tourist office** (Rua Visconde do Rio Branco 45, tel. 41/3462-1024, www.morretes.pr.gov.br, 8 A.M.–6 P.M. daily) has information about the town and surrounding region, including the Parque Estadual de Marumbi. You can also check out www.morretes.com.br, a great site in Portuguese. **Calango Expedições** (Praça Rocha Pombo, tel. 41/3462-2600, www.calangoexpedicoes.com.br) offers hiking, biking, mountain climbing, and rafting trips into the Parque Estadual de Marumbi and along the coast.

GETTING THERE

You can get to Morretes from Curitiba, 70 kilometers (43 miles) away, by train (see *The Serra Verde Express*) or by frequent bus service with **Viação Graciosa** (tel. 41/3462-1115, www.viacaograciosa.com.br). Two buses a day travel via the Estrada da Graciosa. By car, the fastest route is to the BR-277 and then the PR-408. A slower but far more scenic route is to take the BR-116, followed by the Estrada Graciosa. Frequent buses also pass through Morretes to and from Antonina and Paranaguá.

Antonina

From colonial times to the 1940s, Antonina was Paraná's most important port. Since its role was taken over by Paranaguá, Antonina has slipped into something of a backwater, albeit an appealing one full of preserved but faded 18th- and 19th-century buildings that gaze out over the blue waters of the Baía de Paranaguá. Drowsy Antonina comes to life during Carnaval. As in neighboring Morretes, its charms can be easily soaked up in a couple of hours. However, if you plan on spending more time in the region Antonina makes a pleasant base. At the nearby Rio Cachoeira you can go swimming in waterfalls or rafting down the river.

ACCOMMODATIONS AND FOOD

Sharing space with formerly grand colonial houses on the town's pretty main hilltop square, **Pousada Atlante** (Praça Colonel Macedo 266, tel. 41/3432-1256, www.atlante.com.br, R$75–100 d) offers comfortable lodgings in a beautiful historic house with a small pool. Get a room with a balcony that overlooks the 18th-century Igreja Matriz Nossa Senhora do Pilar and the Baía de Paranaguá. **Caçarola do Joca** (Praça Romildo G. Pereira 42, tel. 41/3432-1286, 11:30 A.M.–2 P.M. Mon.–Wed., 11:30 A.M.–5 P.M. and 7:30–10 P.M. Sat., 11:30 A.M.–6 P.M. Sun., R$20–30) is located in an atmospheric old house whose walls were constructed by the Jesuits who founded the town. The restaurant is acclaimed for its *barreado,* whose traditional preparation involves 20 hours of slow cooking over a low flame. In high season (Dec.–Feb. and July) it is also open Thursday and Friday (11:30 A.M.–2 P.M.).

INFORMATION

The **tourist office** (Praça Carlos Cavalcanti, tel. 41/3432-4520, www.antonina.pr.gov.br, 9 A.M.–5 P.M. Mon.–Fri., 10 A.M.–5 P.M. Sat.–Sun.) is located in the old train station. **Icatu**

Rafting (tel. 41/3433-1010) offers rafting trips down the Rio Cachoeira.

GETTING THERE
Antonina is 86 kilometers (53 miles) from Curitiba and 18 kilometers (11 miles) from Morretes. **Viação Graciosa** (tel. 41/3432-1272, www.viacaograciosa.com.br) offers frequent bus service to Curitiba and Paranaguá via Morretes.

Paranaguá
One of Brazil's oldest urban settlements, Paranaguá was founded in the 1550s on the banks of the lazy Rio Itiberê as it flows into the Baía da Paranágua. The town's importance as a major commercial port has destroyed much of its charm. Nonetheless its small historical center has its share of handsome old houses and Portuguese-style colonial churches. These, together with a low-key atmosphere and some unassuming but very decent seafood restaurants, make it a worthwhile place to kill a few hours while you're waiting for a boat to Ilha do Mel or for the Sunday Serra Express train to Curitiba.

SIGHTS
Among Paranaguá's handful of churches, the oldest and most imposing is the **Igreja Nossa Senhora do Rosário** (Largo Monsenhor Celso, no phone, 8 A.M.–6 P.M. daily), parts of which date back to 1578. Nearby, built by and for the town's slave population, the modest 18th-century **Igreja de São Benedito** (Rua Conselheiro Sinimbu, no phone, 8 A.M.–6 P.M. daily) still retains all its original features. Construction of the imposing stone Colégio dos Jesuítas began in the late 1600s when the city's elite invited Jesuit priests to set up a school for their sons. After later serving as a military barracks and a customs house, it is now occupied by the **Museu de Arqueologia e Etnologia** (Rua General Carneiro 66, tel. 41/3422-2511, 9:30 A.M.–noon and 1–6 P.M. Tues.–Fri., noon–6 P.M. Sat.–Sun., R$3), which has an engaging collection of local Tupi-Guarani artifacts and regional folk art created by Paraná's earliest European settlers.

FOOD
Casa do Barreado (Rua José Antônio da Cruz 78, tel. 41/3423-1830, noon–3 P.M. Sat.–Sun., R$25) has the best food in town combined with a lovely garden setting. The highlight of the prix fixe self-service regional buffet is *barreado,* but there is also *galinha na púcura* (chicken cooked in a clay casserole) and grilled fresh fish. Locally produced *cachaças* and delicious homemade desserts are also included.

Overlooking the river, **Danúbio Azul** (Rua 15 de Novembro 95, tel. 41/3423-3255, 11:30 A.M.–6 P.M. and 7–11 P.M. Mon.–Sat., 11:30 A.M.–4 P.M. Sun., R$15–20) offers both à la carte and buffet service featuring a variety of salads, meat, and seafood dishes. For cheap and tasty seafood, head to the **Mercado Municipal do Café** (Rua General Carneiro, tel. 41/3423-2155, 9 A.M.–6 P.M. Mon.–Sat., 9 A.M.–noon Sun.), a former coffee market where you'll find a string of rustic restaurants and bars as well as stalls selling regional handicrafts.

INFORMATION
The **Estação Ferroviária** (Av. Arthur de Abreu, 124), the grand train station where you can catch the Sunday *Litorina* train to and from Curitiba and Morretes (see *The Serra Verde Express*) has a tourist information center. You'll also find one at the **Estação Nautica** (Rua General Carneiro 258, tel. 41/3425-4542), on the waterfront, where boats leave for islands in the Baía de Paranaguá. Aside from city maps, you can also get bus, train, and boat schedules.

GETTING THERE
Paranaguá is 92 kilometers (57 miles) from Curitiba. **Viação Graciosa** (tel. 41/3423-1215, www.viacaograciosa.com.br) offers frequent bus service to Curitiba and Antonina via Morretes.

Ilha do Mel
Paraná's beaches aren't much to write home about, with the exception of Ilha do Mel, a 10-kilometer-long (6-mile-long) island that is the Baía de Paranaguá's main attraction. A 90-minute boat ride from Paranaguá, its deserted beaches and rugged landscapes are

protected as part of an ecological reserve, which has kept development to a minimum. Consequently, the (well-marked) roads and walking trails that crisscross the island are all sand and no cars are allowed. Accommodations, while comfortable, are fairly basic. Although during the summer months the island's two villages of Encantadas and Nova Brasília fill up with young *surfistas* and eco-hippies, a rule limiting the number of visitors to 5,000 a day ensures peace and tranquility.

BEACHES

Straddling two sheltered bays, **Nova Brasília,** in the middle of the island, is the larger of Ilha do Mel's two settlements and home to most of its 1,000 residents. An easy 40-minute walk north leads to one of the island's most beautiful beaches, the 4-kilometer (2.4-mile) stretch of white sand known as **Praia da Fortaleza.** The *fortaleza* in question is **Fortaleza Nossa Senhora dos Prazeres,** an 18th-century Portuguese fortress that offers wonderful views of the bay along with the islands of Superagüi and Ilha das Peças.

A 15-minute walk south along the coast from Nova Brasília will bring you to the **Farol das Conchas.** Perched on a verdant hilltop straddling the **Praia do Farol** and the sheltered cove of **Praia de Fora,** this 19th-century lighthouse offers wonderful views that are worth the steep climb.

From Praia de Fora, it's a two-hour walk (best undertaken at low tide and not when it's rainy due to slippery rocky patches) along the mountainous southeast coast to **Encantadas,** a pretty little fishing village. Along the way, you'll pass some of the island's most attractive white-sand beaches. **Praia Grande** and **Praia do Miguel** are surfers' paradises backed by rugged mountains and luxuriant vegetation. Closer to Encantadas (and less deserted), **Praia de Fora das Encantadas** is home to the **Gruta das Encantadas,** a cavern set in the cliffs that is a hot spot for mermaids (according to local legend).

SPORTS AND RECREATION

From Nova Brasília and Encantadas, boats can be hired to take you to various beaches as well as to the nearby islands of Ilha das Palmas, Ilha das Peças and Ilha do Superagüi. The latter two compose the **Parque Nacional do Superagüi.** This protected region of mangrove swamps is home to a rich diversity of flora and fauna, including *chauás* (red-faced parrots), and *mico-leões-de-cara-preta* (black-faced lion monkeys). While jaguars are a rare sight, wild orchids are rampant. Ilha do Superagüi also boasts the aptly named 37-kilometer (23-mile) **Praia Deserta.** From Novo Brasília, Superagüi is only a 20-minute trip by high-speed motorboat,. For information about excursions or to hire a boat, contact **Transporte Marítimo Nova Brasília** (tel. 41/3455-1129).

ACCOMMODATIONS AND FOOD

Accommodations in Ilha do Mel mostly fall largely into two categories: rustic and exceedingly rustic. In general, Encantadas's *pousadas* are more modern, while those in Nova Brasília are simpler but more charming. For all-out isolation, try the handful of basic offerings on Praia da Fortaleza. In summer and during holidays, Ilha do Mel's *pousadas* fill up fast and reservations are a must. Often, there is a minimum stay of 2–3 nights. In terms of nourishment, fish and seafood are the culinary mainstay. Although you'll find no shortage of restaurants in both Nova Brasília and Encantadas, the most memorable meals can often be found in *pousadas*.

Just off Nova Brasília's pier, **Pousadinha** (Praia do Farol, tel. 41/3426-8026, www .pousadinha.com.br, R$40–70 d) offers attractive wooden lodgings nestled in a nicely landscaped garden. Two large *"lunar"* rooms can accommodate groups of up to six. The staff is friendly and you can rent surfboards, bikes, and boats. The pretty **Restaurante Pousadinha** (noon–9 P.M. daily, R$15–25) serves tasty local fare for lunch and Italian dishes at dinner. A more romantic option is the **Pousada das Meninas** (Praia do Farol, tel. 41/3426-8023, www.pousadadasmeninas.com.br, R$130–150 d), a collection of charming though somewhat cramped bungalows (housing 2–6 people) ingeniously constructed from organic and re-cycled materials and decorated with whimsical flair. Bikes, surfboards and other water-sports equipment can be rented.

One of the island's newest *pousadas* is **Canto da Figueira** (Praia de Fora, tel. 41/3426-8127, www.cantodafigueira.com.br, R$150 d), named after the large fig tree that dominates the verdant garden. Rooms are quite comfortable with lots of wood, gleaming bathrooms, and stone steps leading up to a mezzanine where there is an extra bed. On deserted Praia Grande, more than just serious wave aficionados will appreciate the **Grajagan Surf Resort** (Praia Grande, tel. 41/3246-8043, www.grajagan.com.br, R$160–320), owned and operated by a die-hard surfer. Accommodations in brick bunga-lows are fairly modest (especially considering the hefty prices). The best (and most expensive) face the sea and boast great verandas that look out over jungle and the beach.

Located on the trail that leads to the Praia de Fora das Encantadas, **Pousada Fim da Trilha** (Encantadas, tel. 41/3426-9017, www.fimda trilah.com.br, R$150–180 d) is one of the nicer options. Surrounded by greenery, rooms offer amenities such as hot running water, air-conditioning, and a DVD player. Its restaurant, the **Restaurante Fim da Trilha** (noon–4 P.M. and 8–10:30 P.M. daily, R$20–35), serves up some of the best seafood on the island. Specialties include lobster *à moda da casa,* calamari with seafood cooked in beer, and a copious paella.

Closer to Novo Brasília, **Restaurante Sol e Mar** (Praia de Fora, tel. 41/3426-8021, 11 A.M.–close daily, R$25–40) is renowned for inventing *moqueca da Ilha do Mel,* a local version of the classic Bahian fish and seafood stew.

INFORMATION

There is a small **tourist information** kiosk at Novo Brasília's pier that is usually open 7:30 A.M.–8 P.M. You can also check out the bilingual website www.ilha-do-mel.com, which offers some good general information, although it hasn't been updated in some time. There are no banks on the island, so make sure you stock up on cash before leaving the

mainland. There is an Internet café, **Ilha do Mel Café** (tel. 41/3426-8065, 9 A.M.–9 P.M. daily), located in a pretty house on the trail between Nova Brasília and the Farol. In addition to purchasing coffee and snacks, you can download digital photos and get information about boat trips.

GETTING THERE

From Paranaguá, several boats make the 90-minute trip (R$21–24) from the Estaçao Nautica, stopping first at Nova Brasília and then at Encantadas. Schedules can change according to tides and weather conditions (avoid making the trip in poor weather). For more information contact **Abaline** (tel. 41/3455-2616), which offers three regular ferry trips a day to and from the island with departures from Paranaguá at 9:30 A.M., 1:30 P.M., and 4:30 P.M. and return trips leaving Encantadas at 8 A.M., 1 P.M., and 4:30 P.M.

◖ IGUAÇU FALLS

The Iguaçu Falls need no introduction; they're quite simply one of the most spectacular natural wonders on the planet. The sheer scale of the falls is so tremendous that no words or photographs can do justice to the experience of actually see-ing them. Set amid a primitive landscape of daz-zlingly green rainforest, Iguaçu Falls consists of 275 80-meter-high (260-foot-high) cataracts that thunder over a 3-km-wide (2-mile-wide) precipice. The sound is deafening and the sight is absolutely unforgettable. Eleanor Roosevelt summed up the spectacular sight of these fa-mous falls when she declared: "Poor Niagara! This makes it look like a kitchen faucet."

The falls straddle Brazil's border with Argentina and are located within the param-eters of Brazil's Parque Nacional do Iguaçu and Argentina's Parque Nacional Iguazú. Both the Brazilian city of **Foz do Iguaçu** and the smaller Argentinean town of **Puerto Iguazú** are about 20 kilometers (12 miles) away from the falls. Also close by is **Ciudad del Este,** a run-down Paraguayan frontier town where Brazilians flock in massive numbers to buy cheap duty-free goods (many of them counterfeit).

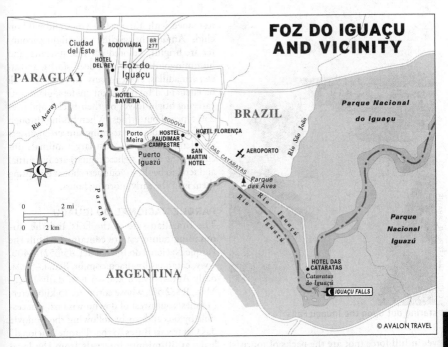

FOZ DO IGUAÇU AND VICINITY

© AVALON TRAVEL

Of the three border towns, Foz do Iguaçu attracts the largest number of tourists. A modern and not very attractive city, "Foz" grew in leaps and bounds during the 1970s and '80s; its unbridled development was propelled by the construction of the monumental and controversial Itaipu Dam. South of town, the meeting of the Iguaçu and Paraná rivers marks the shared frontier between Brazil, Argentina, and Paraguay. The Ponte Presidente Tancredo Neves spans the Rio Iguaçu and connects Foz with Puerto Iguazú, while the Ponte da Amizade, crossing the Rio Paraná, links Foz with Ciudad del Este. Although it's no longer the louche frontier town famed for contraband that it once was, avoid walking around the riverfront at night or crossing the bridge to Paraguay on foot.

If you're not a fan of heat and intense humidity (along with hordes of tourists), avoid visiting the falls during the summer months. Between April and October, it's cooler but rainier (especially September and October). Downpours

not only obstruct scenic views, but can also result in the closing of some walkways due to the Rio Iguaçu's rising waters. While the Brazilian side offers the most stunning panoramic views, 70 percent of the cataracts are in Argentina, which is where you'll need to go if you want to get up close and personal. To take advantage of the surrounding forest, visit sites such as the Itaipu Dam, and indulge in some adventure sports, plan on spending several days.

Sights

The Rio Iguaçu's source is in the coastal mountains near Curitiba. Fed by tributaries, the river winds west for 1,200 kilometers (746 miles), growing wider and increasing in force until it plunges dramatically in the multiple cascades that make up the Iguaçu (Tupi-Guarani for "Great River") Falls. To be treated to their full effect, you really need to see them from both the Brazilian and Argentinean sides. If you can, try to visit the Parque Nacional do Iguaçu in the early morning—the heat is not

staring out upon the Iguaçu Falls

yet in full force (nor are the packs of tourists) and the light is ideal for photographs. For similar reasons, the best time to visit the Parque Nacional Iguazú is in the late afternoon. In theory, you can take organized excursions that will allow you to visit one side in the morning and the other in the afternoon (you need at least half a day to explore each). However, in reality, two days are required to visit the many sights and experience the falls from multiple vantage points. Remember to come armed with raingear and waterproof bags for cameras—the (cold) spray from the falls can leave you drenched, and the aftermath (in an air-conditioned bus) can be unpleasant.

Aside from the falls, the other major natural attraction is the surrounding dense green rainforest. Protected by the Parque Nacional do Iguaçu (in Brazil) and Parque Nacional Iguazú (in Argentina), most of the forest is off-limits to visitors. However, even the trails leading to the falls allow you to experience this unique ecosystem whose lushness extends from the giant ferns covering the forest floor to the treetop canopies festooned with Tarzan-like vines and wild orchids. Among the wildlife you might encounter are brightly colored parrots, toucans, and hummingbirds, monkeys, deer, sloths, anteaters, armadillos, and caimans. Insect lovers will be enchanted by iridescent spiders, giant ants carrying bright leaves on their backs, and over 250 types of butterflies. When hiking through the forest, make sure to bring sunscreen, insect repellent, and water. Most larger animals (including the rarely sighted jaguar) are nocturnal and tend to be shy—your best shot at glimpsing them is in the early morning hours.

PARQUE NACIONAL DO IGUAÇU

The Brazilian side of the falls and the surrounding rainforest are contained within the Parque Nacional do Iguaçu (tel. 45/3521-4400, www.cataratasdoiguacu.com.br, 8 A.M.–5 P.M. daily Apr.–Nov., 8 A.M.–6 P.M. daily Dec.–Mar., R$12.50), whose entrance, 15 kilometers (9 miles) southwest of downtown Foz, is accessible by bus and car by following the Rodovia das Cataratas. Buses to the "Parque Nacional" leave at 30-minute intervals from the local *rodoviária* (bus station) in downtown Foz. If driving, you'll have to leave your car at the main visitor center. After paying the admission fee, you'll board a free double-decker bus that departs at 15-minute intervals, traveling along an 11-kilometer (7-mile) road that leads to the Hotel das Cataratas. From here a panoramic 1.5-kilometer (1-mile) trail winds through the forest to various lookout points and catwalks that provide stunning views of the falls. At the end of the trail at Porto Canoas, is a smaller visitors center, with a souvenir stand, Internet service, and a snack bar. The **Restaurante Porto Canoa** (tel. 45/3521-4446, noon–4 P.M. daily) serves up a great self-service buffet lunch with terrace tables overlooking the falls.

Many swear that the most breathtaking view of Iguaçu Falls from above. Departing from a heliport next to the Parque das Aves, **Helisul** (Rodovia das Cataratas Km 16.5, tel. 45/3529-7474, 9 A.M.–5:30 P.M. daily) operates 10-minute helicopter tours for R$140 that fly thrillingly close to the falls.

Another alternative is tackling the falls head on from a boat. **Macuco Safari** (Rodovia das Cataratas Km 21, tel. 45/3529-6262, www .macucosafari.com.br, R$150) offers an adrenaline-filled foray into the cataracts themselves. The two-hour adventure begins with a guided tour in an electric Jeep, followed by a short hike through the forest to the Rio Iguaçu. After waterproofing yourself and your belongings, you'll board an inflatable motorboat that sails up the river to the Cachoeira dos Mosqueteiros, where you'll receive an invigorating bath.

The falls also provide a backdrop to various radical sports. Located within the park (near the Hotel das Cataratas) **Cânion Iguaçu** (Rodovia das Cataratas Km 27.5, tel. 45/3529-6040, www.camposdosdesafios.com.br) is an eco-friendly company that organizes outings and provides guides and equipment for adventure sport enthusiasts of all levels and ages. Activities include rock climbing and rappelling, tree-trekking through the forest, and white-water rafting down the Rio Iguaçu.

PARQUE NACIONAL IGUAZÚ

The Argentinean side of the falls and the surrounding rainforest are contained within the Parque Nacional Iguazú (tel. 37/5742-0722, www.iguazuargentina.com, 8 A.M.–6 P.M. daily, 18 *pesos*). Although it receives fewer visitors than its Brazilian counterpart, it boasts a larger number of cataracts as well as more vantage points from which to observe them up close. Make sure to bring a bathing suit as there are pools in the river that are ideal for taking a dip.

If you have a car, getting to the Argentinean park is quick. The distance from Foz to Puerto Iguazú is 23 kilometers (14 miles), then follow Ruta 12 for 5 kilometers (3 miles) to the park entrance. Without a car, it's easy but somewhat time-consuming to get to the park from Foz. If you're pressed for time, you're better off joining a Brazilian excursion organized by some of the travel agencies and hotels in Foz. Alternatively, buses make the 30-minute trip to Puerto Iguazú, leaving at 45-minute intervals from the local *rodoviária* in Foz. From Puerto Iguazú's bus station, hourly buses make the 30-minute trip to the park's entrance. If you don't have Argentinean *pesos*, you can pay for your bus fare and all fees within the park (including food and drinks) with Brazilian *reais* or U.S. dollars.

At the entrance to the park is a visitors center with souvenir shops, a café, a restaurant, and the **Centro de Interpretación de la Natureza,** a natural history museum that provides a good introduction to the region's flora and fauna. From here, at 25-minute intervals, mini trains shuttle you through the forest to the falls. The first stop is the **Estación Cataratas,** point of departure for two easy walking trails. The 900-meter (2,950-foot) Circuito Superior trail is at eye level with the top of the falls—catwalks allow you to actually walk behind some of them. The Circuito Inferior is a 1.5-kilometer (1-mile) circular trail that meanders through the forest and gives you a vision of the falls from below. A highlight is the free boat trip that takes you across the river to the Isla San Martín, where a lookout point offers a terrific view of the Argentinean falls. You'll also find natural pools where you can swim. The second train stop is the **Estación Garganta del Diablo.** From here, a 2-kilometer (1.2-mile) trail follows the Rio Iguaçu upstream to the Garganta del Diablo (Devil's Throat), where you'll be treated to the spectacular vision of 14 separate falls flowing together to form the most powerful waterfall (in terms of volume of water flow per second) on the planet. Although you'll be completely drenched, the sensation is absolutely otherworldly. Aside from spume and spray galore, you'll see multiple rainbows, butterflies, and kamikaze-like swifts making vertical dives from cliffs to snatch insects out of the air.

Located within the park's visitor center, **Iguazú Jungle Explorer** tel. 35/5742-1600, www.iguazujunglexplorer.com) is an ecotourism agency that offers guided hiking tours through the park along with boat trips up the Rio Iguaçu rapids that will bring you thrillingly close to the falls.

PARQUE DAS AVES

Located just before the entrance to Parque Nacional do Iguaçu, the Parque das Aves

(Rodovia das Cataratas Km 17, tel. 45/3529-8282, www.parquedasaves.com.br, 8:30 A.M.–5:30 P.M. daily, R$16) boasts a colorful collection of more than 900 types of tropical birds (most of them from Brazil and many of them quite rare) that are housed in enormous walk-in aviaries within the forest. The vision of so many specimens of parrots, toucans, and parakeets (as well as butterflies) is quite amazing. Many of the birds' feathers appear to have been painted by a color-mad artist, and the accompanying soundtrack is worthy of a Hollywood jungle movie. Parque das Aves has a gift shop and restaurant on the premises.

ITAIPU DAM

Until the full completion of China's Three Gorges Dam (scheduled for 2011), the Usina Hidrelética de Itaipu, or Itaipu Dam (Av. Tancedro Neves Km 11, tel. 0800/645-4645, www.itaipu.gov.br, tours 8 A.M., 9 A.M., 10 A.M., 2 P.M., 3 P.M., and 3:30 P.M. Mon.–Sun., R$13) is still the world's largest hydroelectric power plant. Measuring 8 kilometers (5 miles) in length and 200 meters (657 feet) in height, it currently supplies 25 percent of Brazil's electricity and 78 percent of Paraguay's. An amazing feat of engineering, the dam cost a whopping US$18 billion dollars and used enough concrete to build a two-lane highway from Moscow to Lisbon.

Meanwhile, the damming of the Rio Paraná is as controversial as it is impressive. On one hand, Itaipu has been lauded as a safe and non-polluting energy source that has helped fuel southern Brazil's incredible economic growth. However, the dam's social and environmental impact—the loss of Indian settlements, the displacement of 40,000 families, and the destruction and damage of 700 square kilometers (270 square miles) of rainforest—has been severely criticized, despite efforts of Itaipu Binacional (the Brazilian-Paraguayan company that administers the dam) to fund reforestation and relocate animals. Polemics aside, if you decide to visit Itaipu—located 10 kilometers (6 miles) from Foz—its sheer monumentality is undeniably impressive (although make sure you visit when the spillway is open—otherwise you're wasting your time).

Ninety minute *"panorâmica"* visits begin with a 15-minute video showing the dam's construction followed by an hour-long guided bus tour. Other sights include an ecological museum and a biological nature reserve (guided walking tours to the latter begin at 8 A.M. and 2 P.M.). Friday and Saturday nights at 8:30 P.M., nocturnal tours include a theatrical sound and light show. Hourly buses from the local *rodoviária* take you to the right to the dam's visitors center.

Accommodations

There is no shortage of accommodations in Foz. The more expensive (and often overpriced) tourist-oriented resorts are located along the Rodovia das Cataratas. Surrounded by greenery and recreational areas, they are ideal for families even though many, built in the 1970s, are in sore need of some refurbishing. In Foz itself, you'll find more basic options geared towards business travelers and Brazilian shoppers in search of cheap duty-free goods in Cidade del Este. During off-season, you can get some very big discounts.

Conveniently located in the center of Foz, **Hotel del Rey** (Rua Tarobá 1020, tel. 45/3523-2027, www.hoteldelreyfoz.com.br, R$155 d) is a modern, budget option with sizable, well-kept rooms and a swimming pool, small fitness center, and Internet access. More quaint, but equally affordable, is the German-owned **Hotel Bavieira** (Av. Jorge Schimmelpfeng, tel. 45/3574-3566, www.hotel bavieiraiguassu.com.br, R$116 d). Occupying a pseudo-Bavarian chalet, rooms range from doubles to adjoining suites that can lodge up to six people. They are clean though somewhat spartan. Lots of freshly baked breads and cakes make breakfast something to look forward to.

Of the many options on the Rodovia das Cataratas, the best bargain is the IYHA-affiliated **Hostel Paudimar Campestre** (Rodovia das Cataratas Km 12.5, tel. 45/3529-6061, www.paudimar.com.br, R$21–24 pp). Surrounded by greenery, its cozy wooden cabins can sleep 2–8 people, and there are special suites for families. Rooms are clean, but hostel-like. More impressive are the facilities, including free Internet access, an on-site restaurant, swimming pool, and fitness room. There is even a travel agency where you can change currency and book excursions. Close to the airport (and to the falls), it is easily accessible by municipal bus, and the multilingual staff are helpful.

The **Hotel Florença** (Rodovia das Cataratas Km 13, tel. 45/3529-7755, www.hotelflorenca .com, R$150 d) is a large and laid-back resort that combines great service and amenities—including two pools and a tennis court—with extremely affordable prices. The modern rooms are plainly furnished, but quite spacious. **The San Martin Hotel** (Rodovia das Cataratas Km 21, tel. 45/3521-8881, www.hotelsan martin.com.br, R$176–320 d) is one of the nicer big 1970s-style resorts and the closest to the entrance of the Parque Nacional do Iguaçu. It is also right next to the Parque das Aves. The sizable rooms with white linens and hardwood floors are quite comfortable (the more luxurious suites are attractively minimalist). However, the best feature is the vast expanse of green space: a mixture of landscaped gardens with recreational facilities and untamed jungle through which a walking trail leads to the Rio Iguaçu.

In operation since the 1950s, the **◖ Hotel das Cataratas** (Rodovia das Cataratas Km 24.5, tel. 45/3521-7000, www.tropical hotel.com.br, R$400–900 d) is the oldest hotel in Foz (the pale pink neoclassical main building was actually built close to a century ago). Moreover, it is also the only one actually within the Parque Nacional do Iguaçu, giving you privileged access to the spectacular falls. Only a few rooms—the wildly expensive deluxe ones—actually offer views of the cataracts. Neither these, nor the more basic standard rooms, are luxurious, yet their vintage furniture and polished wooden floors give them an appealing retro charm. A renovation is expected to spruce things up. Aside from a large pool, the hotel is surrounded by forest with walking trails. The **Restaurante Itaipu** serves a delicious lunch buffet.

Food

Nobody really comes to Iguaçu Falls for the food, and although there is no shortage of sustenance, don't count on having any serious gourmet experiences. Seeing as you're in frontier land, *churrasco* is the way to go. **Bufalo Branco Churrascaria** (Rua Engenheiro Rebouças 530, tel. 45/3523-9744, www.bufalobranco.com.br, noon–11:30 P.M. daily, R$35–45) is one of the most popular addresses in town for succulent cuts of barbecued beef (not to mention pork, chicken, lamb, and turkey testicles!?). Non-carnivores can opt for grilled *surubim*, a local fish, as well as the varied buffet of salads and desserts.

The welcoming **Empório da Gula** (Av. Brasil 1441, tel. 45/3574-6191, 11:30 A.M.–midnight Sun.–Fri., 4 P.M.–midnight Sat., R$20–30) is another good, and less expensive, choice for *churrasco*. It also offers a wide variety of other dishes. Nearby, **Barbarela** (Av. Brasil 1119, tel. 45/3028-2251, 9 A.M.–8 P.M. Mon.–Fri., 9 A.M.–6 P.M. Sat., R$5–10) is a great place for a snack or quick and healthy meal. The sandwiches are fresh and thick and there are numerous tropical fruit juices to quench your thirst.

To savor fish from the region's mighty rivers, head to the banks of the Rio Paraná. Located at Foz's somewhat out-of-the-way Cataratas Iate Clube is the **Dourado Restaurante** (Av. Guido Welter 800, tel. 45/3523-6776, www.cataratas iateclube.com.br, 11:30 A.M.–3:30 P.M. and 8–11 P.M. Tues.–Sun., R$20–25). Locals swear by the excellent fresh fish *rodízio* (weekends there is a buffet) with a choice of dishes such as *piapara* vinaigrette or *surubim moqueca* (a stew featuring coconut milk). Fish dishes and river views are equally appetizing at the **Clube Maringá** (Rua Dourado 111, tel. 45/3527-3472, www.restaurantemaringa.com.br, 8 A.M.–11 P.M. Mon.–Sat., 8 A.M.–5 P.M. Sun., R$25–35), a simple cantina-style restaurant with a large buffet. One of the specialties is grilled *dourado*, a large fish known as the "golden salmon," which is particularly abundant in the Rio Paraná's waters around Iguaçu.

Information and Services

There are many **tourist information** centers around Foz. The staffs invariably speak English and you will find lots of information including bus schedules and maps. Aside from the main downtown office at Praça Getúlio Vargas 69 (tel. 45/3521-1461, 7 A.M.–11 P.M. daily), you'll find locations at the airport (tel. 45/3521-4276, 9 A.M.–9 P.M. daily), the international *rodoviária* (tel. 45/3522-1027, 6 A.M.–6 P.M. daily), and the local *rodoviária* (tel. 45/3523-7901, 7:30 A.M.–6 P.M. daily). You can also call the bilingual toll-free tourist hotline, **Teletur** (tel. 0800/451-516, 7 A.M.–11 P.M. daily) or log on to the website (www.iguassu.tur.br).

Avenida Brasil is lined with numerous banks where you can withdraw money with your ATM card or exchange money. Many travel agencies along this avenue also exchange money at decent rates. For Internet access and international phone calls head to **USNet** (Av. Brasil 549, Sala 3, tel. 45/3523-2289, 9 A.M.–10 P.M. Mon.–Sat., 9 A.M.–3 P.M. and 6–10 P.M. Sun.).

BORDER CROSSINGS

To cross the border from Foz do Iguaçu into Argentina or Paraguay, you will need to have a valid passport and—depending on your nationality—a tourist visa if you're going to leave Brazil for any longer than a day trip. For more information contact the **Argentinean Consulate** (Rua Travessa Vice Consûl E.R. Bianchi 26, tel. 45/3574-2969, 10 A.M.–3 P.M. Mon.–Fri.) and/or the **Paraguayan Consulate** (Rua Marechal Deodoro 901, tel. 45/3523-2898, 8:30 A.M.–5:30 P.M. Mon.–Fri.).

Getting There and Around

You can fly to Foz do Iguaçu directly from Curitiba and São Paulo. The **Aeroporto Internacional Foz do Iguaçu** (Rodovia das Cataratas Km 13, tel. 45/3521-4276) is 13 kilometers (8 miles) southeast of downtown Foz. To get to the center of town, a taxi will cost around R$50. Airport buses (5 A.M.–midnight daily) leave at 15-minute intervals (45-minute intervals on Sun.) to the local bus station.

Buses from cities throughout south and southeastern Brazil as well as Buenos Aires and Asunción arrive and depart from the **Rodoviária Internacional** (Av. Costa e Silva, tel. 45/3522-2590), which is 5 kilometers (3 miles) from the center of Foz. The 10-hour trip between Curitiba and Foz is operated by **Sulamericana** (tel. 41/3373-1000 or 45/3522-2515, www.sula.com.br). **Pluma** (tel. 0800/646-0300, www.pluma.com.br) offers service to and from São Paulo—a 16-hour journey. Several municipal buses offer service to the downtown local bus station, or **Terminal Urbano**, on Avenida Juscelino Kubitschek. From here, Parque Nacional buses leave at regular intervals between 8 A.M. and 6 P.M. to the entrance of Parque Nacional do Iguaçu. Regular buses also depart from here for Puerto Iguazú and Ciudad del Este. To get to Foz from Curitiba—a 640-kilometer (398-mile) drive—follow the BR-277.

It is quite easy to get around Foz and to visit surrounding attractions by bus and taxi. However, if you want to do some exploring on your own, you can rent a car at **Avis** (Rodovia das Cataratas Km 16.5, tel. 45/3523-1510, www.avis.com.br) or **Localiza** (Av. Juscelino Kubitschek 2878, tel. 45/3522-1608, www.localiza.com.br).

Santa Catarina

The smallest of Brazil's southern states, Santa Catarina is famed for its beautiful coastline, which draws sun-and-surf seeking tourists from neighboring Argentina and Uruguay as well as Paulistanos and even Cariocas. Since the latter are hardly lacking in beach discernment, you know that Santa Catarina's *praias* have to be something special indeed. Wild and windswept—although increasingly developed due to the rise in tourism—the sugary sands are invariably backed by rolling hills covered in native Atlantic forest. Rough open seas lure surfers from all around the world, but there are also plenty of sheltered coves for soakers and floaters. Some of the best beaches in the South surround the pretty island capital of Florianópolis, a vibrant, youthful, and prosperous city on the Ilha de Santa Catarina, whose umpteen beaches range from highly developed to practically deserted. Base yourself in "Floripa" and then spend two or three days (or even more) beachcombing. On the mainland, highlights north of Florianópolis include the clear turquoise waters of Porto Belo and Bombinhas, whose Reserva Biológica Marinha da Ilha do Arvoredo offers excellent deep-sea diving. Heading south, you'll discover Garopaba, an Azorean fishing village famed for its surfing, its whale-watching, and for Praia do Rosa, which usually makes experts' lists of top 10 Brazilian beaches. Farther on, the pretty little town of Laguna also offers some fine beaches as well as the best-preserved ensemble of colonial architecture in the state.

During colonial times, Santa Catarina marked the frontier between Portuguese and Spanish territories. As a buffer zone without any apparent riches, the region remained undeveloped, with the exception of small villages inhabited by fishermen from the Azores. Having realized the region's strategic importance, in the 1820s Dom Pedro II enticed immigrants from Germany, and later Italy, to settle the fertile hills and valleys of the interior. In contrast to the vast slave-operated plantations of the Northeast, these European immigrants planted small, family-run farms that set the standard for an ethos of efficiency and egalitarianism that has lasted until today. The very visible results of this legacy are an abundance of (real) blonds as well as a general prosperity (in Brazilian terms) that is unknown in the rest of the country. Indeed, Santa Catarina boasts one of the narrowest disparities between rich and poor in Brazil, and Florianópolis's quality of life seduces harried middle-class Brazilians fed up with the stress and crime of cities such as Rio and São Paulo.

Coastal Santa Catarina has a subtropical Mediterranean-like climate that translates into hot humid summers and cool (as in 15°C/60°F) winters. The mountainous interior, however, is a different story, with snow being quite common in the highest areas during June and July. One word of caution: Beware of the southern winds (from down Antarctica way), which make the air temperature seem 10°C cooler. If you're looking for crowds and a party atmosphere (as well as high prices and temperatures), January and February are the best times to enjoy Santa Catarina's beaches. Otherwise, try to visit during the months of November, December, March or April, when prices and temperatures decrease and you'll have the beaches to yourself.

ILHA DE SANTA CATARINA

The capital of the state of Santa Catarina—Florianópolis—is located on the island of Santa Catarina. If you worry that the state and island sharing the same name might have confusing ramifications—don't. More confusing is that when Brazilians refer to "Florianópolis," they aren't just referring to the city, but to the entire 420-square-kilometer (162-square-mile) Ilha de Santa Catarina, all of which lies under the municipal jurisdiction of Florianópolis. That said, the city itself is invariably and affectionately referred to as "Floripa."

THE SOUTH

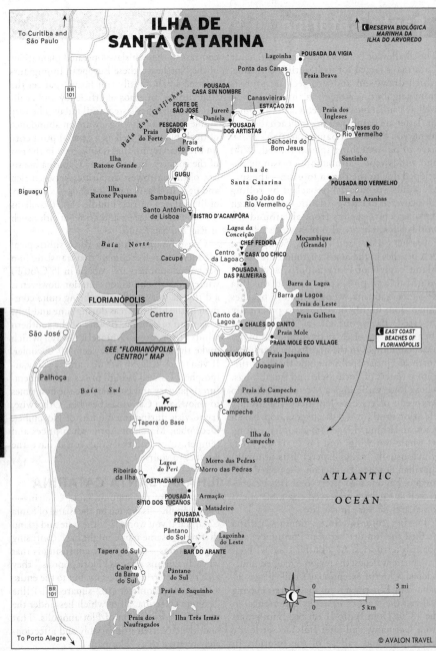

ILHA DE SANTA CATARINA

RESERVA BIOLÓGICA MARINHA DA ILHA DO ARVOREDO

To Curitiba and São Paulo

BR 101

Lagoinha

POUSADA DA VIGIA

Ponta das Canas

Praia Brava

POUSADA CASA SIN NOMBRE

Canasvieiras

ESTAÇÃO 261

Baía dos Golfinhos

FORTE DE SÃO JOSÉ

Jurerê

Daniela

POUSADA DOS ARTISTAS

Praia dos Ingleses

PESCADOR LOBO

Praia do Forte

Praia do Forte

Cachoeira do Bom Jesus

Ingleses do Rio Vermelho

Ilha Ratone Grande

GUGU

Ilha de Santa Catarina

Santinho

Biguaçu

Ilha Ratone Pequena

Sambaqui

São João do Rio Vermelho

POUSADA RIO VERMELHO

Santo Antônio de Lisboa

BISTRO D'ACAMPÔRA

Ilha das Aranhas

Baía Norte

Lagoa da Conceição

CHEF FEDOCA

Moçambique (Grande)

Cacupé

Centro da Lagoa

CASA DO CHICO

POUSADA DAS PALMEIRAS

Barra da Lagoa

Barra da Lagoa

Praia do Leste

FLORIANÓPOLIS

Centro

Canto da Lagoa

CHALÉS DO CANTO

Praia Galheta

São José

SEE "FLORIANÓPOLIS (CENTRO)" MAP

Praia Mole

PRAIA MOLE ECO VILLAGE

EAST COAST BEACHES OF FLORIANÓPOLIS

UNIQUE LOUNGE

Praia Joaquina

Joaquina

Palhoça

Baía Sul

Praia do Campeche

AIRPORT

HOTEL SÃO SEBASTIÃO DA PRAIA

Tapera do Base

Campeche

Ilha do Campeche

Ribeirão da Ilha

Lagoa do Peri

Morro das Pedras

Morro das Pedras

ATLANTIC

OCEAN

OSTRADAMUS

POUSADA SÍTIO DOS TUCANOS

Armação

Matadeiro

POUSADA PÉNAREIA

Pântano do Sol

Lagoinha do Leste

Tapera do Sul

BAR DO ARANTE

Caieria da Barra do Sul

Pântano do Sul

Praia do Saquinho

BR 101

Praia dos Naufragados

Ilha Três Irmãs

To Porto Alegre

0   5 mi

0   5 km

© AVALON TRAVEL

IMMIGRANTS FROM EUROPE

In the 19th century, southern Brazil was a magnet for immigrants from Europe: Italy, Poland, Ukraine, and, most notoriously, Germany and Austria. In fact, Dona Leopoldina, the Austrian-born first wife of Brazilian emperor Dom Pedro I, must have been rather homesick when she embarked on a mission to lure her countrymen to the unfarmed territories of subtropical southern Brazil. Accordingly, agents were sent to central Europe to hype the fertile fields (actually tangled Atlantic forests home to indigenous peoples) to adventurous farmers, who subsequently showed up in droves and settled regions of central and eastern Rio Grande do Sul and eastern Santa Catarina.

To this day there is a surprising number of fair-skinned people in the region – Gisele Bündchen is only the most famous – along with a Viennese café culture, folk dances reminiscent of the polka, a significant number of Lutheran churches, and a fondness for draft beer, potato salad, sauerkraut, and, of course, pork sausages. If you're in the vicinity of traditional German towns such as Blumenau and Joinville (Santa Catarina) or Novo Hamburgo, Gramado, and Santa Cruz do Sul (Rio Grande do Sul), you're sure to encounter more than a little bit of Bavaria. Blumenau and Santa Cruz do Sul hold traditional German Oktoberfests.

Nomenclature aside, the island is a microcosm unto itself, and an extremely attractive and varied one at that. Over 40 percent of the island consists of rolling hills covered with lush Atlantic forest and punctuated by two lagoons. However, the main attraction is the incredible array of stunning beaches. Officially, the island boasts 42 *praias,* but when the tides are low, there are closer to 100. Contrasting with Floripa's modern urban bustle are centuries-old Azorean fishing villages, lined with pastel houses, where you can watch *pescadores* haul in the day's fresh catch and then savor the fruits of their labor while seated at *barracas* overlooking the sea.

Roads on the island are in top shape, and municipal bus service is quite extensive. However, since the island is big—54 kilometers (34 miles) from the northern tip to the south—exploring its many beaches in a short time can involve an inordinate amount of traveling (particularly if you don't have a car). If you're intent on doing a lot of beach-hopping and want urban amenities, you're best off basing yourself in Floripa's Centro. If, however, you're after R&R, choose a beach on the prettiest coasts—north or east—and leave the hard-core exploring for another time.

Florianópolis

Founded in 1726 and settled largely by Portuguese immigrants from the Azores, Florianópolis was a little more than a small fishing town until the early 19th century when, having benefited enormously from the region's thriving whaling trade, it became the capital of Santa Catarina. Most of the Centro's charming pastel-hued buildings—those that remain—are from this era. Yet despite Floripa's modern skyline and dynamic growth, this city of close to 400,000 still manages to retain a laid-back, small town flavor that is very appealing. Due to its compact size and relative lack of history, Florianópolis's urban attractions are limited and can be easily seen in half a day.

SIGHTS

Although most of Floripa—the historic and commercial center, the upscale neighborhood of Beira Mar, the airport, bus stations, and most hotels and restaurants—sits upon the western coast of the island, other *bairros* (many of them industrial) are located on the mainland. The island is linked to the mainland by two bridges—the Ponte Colombo Machado Salles and the Ponte Hercílio Luz. One of the world's largest suspension bridges, the **Ponte Hercílio Luz** bridge was inaugurated in 1926.

THE SOUTH

a view of Florianópolis and the Ponte Hercílio Luz

It has since become the city's most recognizable landmark. The sight of this Golden Gate rival illuminated at night is quite enchanting.

Floripa's few attractions are concentrated in the historic center. Across from the main bus station (site of the former port), a gracious building with a saffron facade houses the **Mercado Público** (Av. Paulo Fontes, 7 A.M.–7 P.M. Mon.–Fri., 7 A.M.–1 P.M. Sat.) that dates back to the 1890s. Amidst the market's colorful stalls and lively atmosphere are numerous patio bars and restaurants. Featuring live music and serving beer and shrimp, they serve as a favorite meeting point for Floripanos. A pedestrian-only zone surrounds the market and the nearby **Casa da Alfândega** (Rua Conselheiro Mafra 141, tel. 48/3028-8102, 9 A.M.–6:30 P.M. Mon.–Fri., 9 A.M.–2 P.M. Sat.), a handsome biscuit-colored neoclassical building from 1875 that used to be the city's customs house. Today, it lodges a local artisans' association where you can purchase traditional Azorean crafts ranging from ceramic bowls to delicate lace.

At the end of Rua Conselheiro Mafra is the city's oldest square, **Praça XV de Novembro,** a lovely tree-shaded plaza whose focal point is a majestic 100-year-old fig tree. Among the restored historic buildings surrounding the square is an 18th-century palace that used to be the governors' residence. Today it houses the **Museu Histórico de Santa Catarina** (Praça 15 de Novembro 227, tel. 48/3028-8091, 10 A.M.–6 P.M. Tues.–Fri., 10 A.M.–4 P.M. Sat.–Sun., R$2) which possesses a rather trivial collection of indigenous and colonial artifacts. However, the ornate interior, with its glossy parquet floors and elegant period furnishings, is worth peeking at.

Sitting at the top of Praça XV is the imposing **Catedral Municipal.** Although it cuts an impressive figure, few of its colonial features remain following a radical overhaul in the 1920s. The best preserved of the city's churches, the **Igreja de Nossa Senhora do Rosário** (Rua Marechal Guilherme 60) is perched a top a rather grand flight of stairs. Leading off Praça XV de Novembro, **Rua Felipe Schmidt** is the main street of a pedestrian zone that makes for pleasant strolling and window gazing.

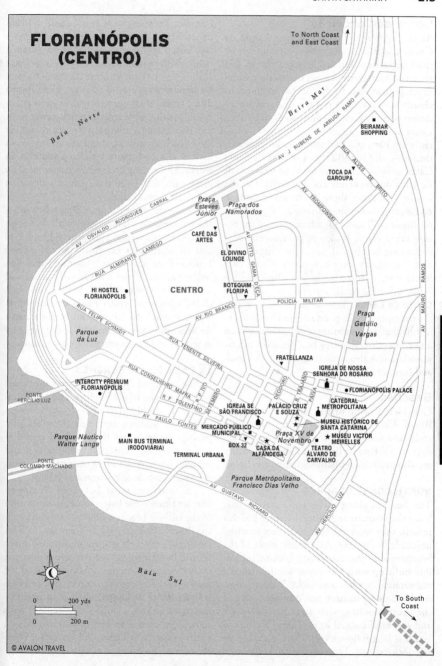

FLORIANÓPOLIS (CENTRO)

To North Coast and East Coast

Baía Norte

Beira Mar

AV J RUBENS DE ARRUDA RAMO

BEIRAMAR SHOPPING

RUA ALVES DE BRITO

TOCA DA GAROUPA

AV TROMPOWSKY

AV OSVALDO RODRIGUES CABRAL

Praça Esteves Júnior

Praça dos Namorados

RUA ALMIRANTE LAMEGO

CAFÉ DAS ARTES

EL DIVINO LOUNGE

AV OTTO GAMA D'EÇA

BOTEQUIM FLORIPA

CENTRO

HI HOSTEL FLORIANÓPOLIS

POLÍCIA MILITAR

AV MAURO RAMOS

Praça Getúlio Vargas

RUA FELIPE SCHMIDT

AV RIO BRANCO

Parque da Luz

RUA TENENTE SILVEIRA

FRATELLANZA

IGREJA DE NOSSA SENHORA DO ROSÁRIO

RUA CONSELHEIRO MAFRA

DEODORO

R TRAJANO

PAIVA

FLORIANÓPOLIS PALACE

INTERCITY PREMIUM FLORIANÓPOLIS

PONTE HERCÍLIO LUZ

R F TOLENTINO

T P TIVO

7 SETEMBRO

IGREJA SÉ SÃO FRANCISCO

PALÁCIO CRUZ E SOUZA

CATEDRAL METROPOLITANA

AV PAULO FONTES

MERCADO PÚBLICO MUNICIPAL

MUSEU HISTÓRICO DE SANTA CATARINA

Parque Náutico Walter Lange

MAIN BUS TERMINAL (RODOVIÁRIA)

BOX 32

CASA DA ALFÂNDEGA

Praça XV de Novembro

TEATRO ÁLVARO DE CARVALHO

MUSEU VICTOR MEIRELLES

PONTE COLOMBO MACHADO

TERMINAL URBANA

Parque Metrópolitano Francisco Dias Velho

AV GUSTAVO RICHARD

AV HERCÍLIO LUZ

To South Coast

Baía Sul

0   200 yds
0   200 m

© AVALON TRAVEL

THE SOUTH

Lagoa da Conceição

At the center of the island, the Lagoa da Conceição is a lovely lagoon surrounded by thick vegetation, situated between Floripa and the trendy east coast beaches of Praia Mole and Praia da Joaquina. By day, its placid and deliciously warm waters draw families and practitioners of every kind of water sport imaginable. Come sundown, an abundance of trendy restaurants, bars, and nightclubs make it *the* gastronomic and nightlife spot of Ilha de Santa Catarina (which accounts for some serious traffic jams on weekends and holidays). On the lagoon's southern shore, the town of **Centro da Lagoa** (known alternatively as "Centrinho" or simply as "Lagoa") is where most of the action takes place. It also possesses some nice swimming beaches. If you crave a little peace and tranquility, you can catch a boat that leaves hourly from the dock (or brave a long 7-km/4.5-mile walk around the shore) to **Canto da Lagoa.** Surrounded by nature, this charming little village on the northwest shore is inhabited by a mixture of fisherfolk, artists, and *alternativos.* Boasting beaches and a nearby waterfall, it is also a relaxing spot to kick back and feast on fresh fish.

Beaches

Considered some of the finest in southern Brazil, Floripa offers beaches for every age, style, and inclination. If you want lots of action, you'll find it, but peace and tranquility are also available without searching too hard.

NORTH COAST BEACHES

The beaches along the island's north coast boast the warmest and calmest waters. For this reason, they were the first to attract tourists, particularly families. As a result, most of the beaches along this coast have become incredibly built up with numerous soulless hotels, restaurants, condos, and tacky T-shirt shops. At the extreme western tip, **Daniela** is one of the nicer beaches, with aquamarine waters and soft sand backed by greenery. Facing the beach is Ilha Ratones with its medieval-looking 18th-century Forte de Santo Antônio de Ratones. Traveling west, you'll come to **Praia de Jurerê.** Although very developed, it has a fine beach and is close to **Praia do Forte,** a fishing village built adjacent to the impressive 18th-century Forte São José da Ponta Grossa. **Canasvieiras** is out of control, while **Ponto das Canas,** at its western end, is more manageable with a wide strip of beach, fewer summer houses, and a privileged westward-looking view that makes for ideal sunset viewing. From here, it is a 20-minute walk to **Lagoinha do Norte,** an enticing little beach surrounded by green hills with calm transparent waters that are ideal for snorkeling.

Facing the open Atlantic, **Praia Brava** attract surfers and hangers-on with its rough seas. Unfortunately, this pretty beach has also attracted some extremely ugly four-story condos. Even worse is neighboring **Praia dos Ingleses,** one of the most heavily urbanized beaches on the *ilha* (island). Surfers also flock to the somewhat wilder **Praia do Santinho,** which is bracketed at one end by the Costão do Santinho mega resort and at the other by deserted sand dunes fringed with vegetation.

█ EAST COAST BEACHES

Facing the open Atlantic, Floripa's east coast beaches are the island's longest and most dramatic. A combination of cold water, rough waves, and undercurrents keeps families (and package tours) at bay but attracts a crowd of surfers and young, tanned singles (both gay and straight) intent on strutting their stuff as well as their ultra-fashionable *sungas* and bikinis.

The northernmost beach of **Praia do Moçambique** is the longest and most primitive of the island's beaches. Due to its inclusion in the Reserva Floresta do Rio Vermelha, its 8 kilometers (5 miles) of gorgeous unspoiled dunes framed by pine forests are complete unmarred by human construction, making it ideal for long walks. The continuation of Moçambique is **Praia Barra da Lagoa,** which is anchored by **Barra da Lagoa,** a small fishing colony with some simple *pousadas* and restaurants located at the entrance to Lagoa da Conceição. From the edge of the village, a rickety wooden bridge crosses a river, and if you follow the path on the other side, you'll arrive at the secluded beach of **Prainha.**

From Barra da Lagoa, another hilly trail leads to the beautifully unspoiled beach of **Praia da Galheta,** whose waters are warmer and more placid than elsewhere along the coast and where nude sunbathing is permitted. From Galheta, another trail leads south to hip and happening **Praia Mole,** whose name (*mole* means soft) derives from the large grains that make this sand so invitingly fluffy. Many of the bronzed young things who frequent this beach are surfers or wish they were. Most are also single, giving Mole a well-deserved reputation for being the flirtiest beach on the island. The stretch of sand nearest to Galheta is a gay and lesbian hot spot. In summer, all roads lead to Mole (creating hour-long traffic jams) and the beach's many bars pulsate day and night.

Also extremely popular—although somewhat overblown—is neighboring **Praia da Joaquina,** which is famed for having the best waves on the island. Major surfing competitions are held here and surfers rule the waters. Although the beach is quite wide, in summer it is invaded by so many beach bars, frescoball games, and sunbathers in various states of preening that you'll be challenged to actually glimpse a patch of sand.

The continuation of Joaquina is the more deserted but equally stunning **Praia do Campeche,** which gazes out towards the **Ilha do Campeche.** From the nearby village of Armação, it's only a 30-minute boat ride (fishing boats will take you for around R$25 pp) to the tiny island, where, when you're not busy snorkeling in emerald waters, you can kick back at one of two beach *barracas* that serve grilled fish and icy beer. Ilha do Campeche's is also famed for its glyphs—mysterious symbols and inscriptions carved into over 160 stones—which date back over 5,000 years. On the island, monitors are available to guide you along four different trails (R$5–10). Between April and November, you'll need to reserve your visit with IPHAN (tel. 48/8417-7102), the federal organization that protects the island's archaeological heritage.

SOUTH COAST BEACHES

The south coast beaches are the wildest and most unspoiled on the island. Some say they are also the most lovely, although be forewarned—the water is *frio!* Tourism has made very few inroads, and even asphalt has yet to reach the most remote strips of sand (in compensation, countless walking trails lead along the coast).

South of Campeche, the quaint fishing village of **Armação** nestles against a rugged backdrop of green hills. Although the waters of **Praia da Armação** are rough and dangerous, signed trails lead to nearby coves and natural pools that offer safer swimming. There's a handful of charming *pousadas,* making this an excellent place to stay.

From Armação, you can walk along a trail to **Praia do Matadeiro,** and then continue on for another three hours through native forest to what many consider the most drop-dead gorgeous beach on the island: **Praia da Lagoinha do Leste.** The turquoise waters and white sand framed by lush mountains are spectacular, and an added bonus is the *lagoinha,* a beautiful freshwater lagoon that sits just behind the beach. The area is preserved within the Parque Municipal da Lagoinha do Leste, and as such you'll find no signs of civilization.

Another shorter, marvelously scenic (and somewhat steep) 90-minute mountain trail leads south from Lagoinha to **Pântano do Sul.** Although it lacks the charm of Armação, Pântano is one of the island's most active fishing villages, and is an ideal place to tuck into the fresh catch of the day or raw oysters. The beach isn't the best along this coast, but swimming conditions in the protected bay are much safer. A far more beautiful beach is **Praia de Solidão,** whose name, "Solitude Beach," is quite fitting for this out-of-the-way spot that can only be reached by a steep 40-minute hike from Praia do Saquinho farther south. At one end, a waterfall cascading into a natural pool offers freshwater bathing. Equally gorgeous and even more off-the-beaten track is **Praia dos Naufragados,** at the southern tip of the island. Although it can only be accessed by boat (25 minutes) or by a challenging hour-long mountain hike from Caieiras da Barra do Sul, your efforts will be amply rewarded by the paradisiacal landscapes and the bewitching views out to sea.

WEST COAST BEACHES

Facing the mainland of Santa Catarina, the beaches north and south of Florianópolis are less spectacular (and far less touristy) than other parts of the island. The main attractions are a trio of the island's oldest and most atmospheric Azorean fishing colonies. Between 1748 and 1756, as a result of natural disasters and overpopulation, more than 6,000 Azorean immigrants crossed the Atlantic and settled on the protected west coast of the Ilha de Santa Catarina, where they survived by fishing, cultivating manioc, and hunting whales (whose blubber and oil was a precious fuel). **Ribeirão da Ilha** (south of Floripa) and **Santo Antônio de Lisboa** and **Sambaqui** (to the north) all possess simple Portuguese colonial churches and typical Azorean whitewashed houses with blue trim. The men still make their living by fishing; in fact Ribeirão and Santo Antônio da Ilha are renowned for the mussels and oysters farmed offshore. Meanwhile, the women continue the centuries old traditions of intricate lace-making, which you can purchase in both villages. Although the beaches are quite small—and appealingly sprinkled with fishing nets and brightly painted wooden boats—the villages themselves are pleasantly languorous. And it goes without saying that the fresh fish and seafood is fantastic—in fact, many people stop by just for lunch.

Sports and Recreation

Ilha de Santa Catarina offers a terrific wealth of outdoor activities on both land and sea.

SURFING

The east coast is legendary for its surfing scene, particularly on the beaches of Joaquina, Mole, and Moçambique. On Praia da Joaquina, near the Cris Hotel, **Easy Surf** (tel. 84/9971-3486, rentals R$20–25) is a surfing school operated by Brazilian surf champ Karina "Kika" Abramov that offers lessons for all ages and levels as well as surfing outings and board rental. During the *tainha* fishing season (April–June), surfing is prohibited on the island.

SANDBOARDING

For those who fear wiping out in the waves, much softer landings are in store when you and your board take to the Saharan-like dunes behind **Praia da Joaquina.** You can rent boards in front of the Dunas bar.

PARAGLIDING

The east coast beaches and Lagoa da Conceição boast ideal wind conditions for paragliding (*parapente*). Based in Centro da Lagoa, **Parapente Sul** (Rua José Antônio da Silveira 201, tel. 48/334-0791, www.parapentesul .com.br, R$100 for a 15-minute flight) is a highly reputed sports outfitter that offers lessons on the dunes of Joaquina before you take to the skies, flying over Praia Mole. If you're raring to go, but without experience, you can also fly tandem (*vôo duplo*) with an instructor for R$120 for 15 minutes.

WINDSURFING AND KITESURFING

Windsurfers and kitesurfers who want the challenge of rough winds and waves can take to the east coast beaches, while calmer souls can stick to the placid waters of the north coast beaches and the lagoon. In Lagoa, **Openwinds** (Av das Rendeiras 1672, tel. 48/3232-5004) offers courses and equipment rental. Their eight-hour basic windsurfing course costs R$380 per person and their basic four-hour kitesurfing course will set you back R$520. Equipment rentals cost R$35–45 per hour.

DIVING

An hour's boat ride from the island's north coast, the waters surrounding Ilha do Arvoredo (see *Reserva Biológica Marinha da Ilha do Arvoredo* in the *Porto Belo* section) offer some of the best diving in the South. In Canasvieiras,

© TONY GALVEZ

sandboarding in the dunes of Praia da Joaquina, Florianópolis

Acquanauta (Rua Antenor Borges 324, tel. 48/3266-1137, www.acquanautafloripa.com.br) rents diving and snorkeling equipment, offers lessons, and runs numerous trips to Arvoredo for R$135 (divers) and R$60 (snorkelers). A diving excursion to the Ilha do Arvoredo costs between R$135–150.

BOATING EXCURSIONS

Two of the most popular boating trips are to islands off the coast of Ilha de Santa Catarina. **Scuna Sul** (Av. Oswaldo Rodrigues Cabral, Centro, tel. 48/3225-1806, www.scuna sul.com.br) operates schooner excursions from Canasvieiras, via the dolphin-inhabited Baía dos Golfinhos to **Ilha de Anhatorim,** where you can visit the region's oldest fort, dating from 1744, the **Forte de Santa Cruz do Anhatorim.** An alternative route from Floripa takes you beneath the Hercílio Luz bridge and stops at the **Ilha de Ratones Grande,** where you can clamber around the 18th-century **Fortaleza de Santo Antônio de Ratones.** Both half-day outings include stops for lunch (not included in the R$25–35 cost).

Nightlife

Floripa's hippest and liveliest nightlife offerings can be found in Lagoa da Conceição. With great lagoon views, **John Bull Pub** (Av. das Rendeiras 1046, tel. 48/3232-8535, www.john-bullpub.com.br, 9 P.M.–4 A.M. Thurs.–Sat., 10 P.M.–4 A.M. daily in summer, cover R$15–20) is a perennially happening place to listen and dance to good live music, especially national and local rock bands. **Confraria das Artes** (Rua João Pacheco da Costa 31, tel. 48/3232-2298, www.confrariadasartes.com.br, 8 P.M.–5 A.M. Tues.–Sun., cover R$10) is an original mixture of nightclub, gourmet restaurant, and antiques and furniture store that attracts foreign DJs, homegrown supermodels (Gisele has been sighted), and beautiful young folk on the prowl.

For something quieter and more intimate, yet no less hybrid, head to **Vecchio Giorgio** (Av. Afonso Delambert Neto 103, Loja 7, tel. 48/3232-0600, www.vecchiogiorgio.com.br, 8 P.M.–close Wed.–Sat., 8 P.M.–onwards Tues.–Sun. in summer), a warm bar/lounge/restaurant/art gallery decorated with eclectic, secondhand furniture, where local filmmakers screen short features, musicians perform new melodies, and customers mellow out and nibble on pseudo-Italian snacks.

In Floripa itself, an appealingly laid-back place for an icy *chopp* is **Botequim Floripa** (Av. Rio Branco 632, tel. 48/3333-1234, www .botequimfloripa.com.br, 5:30 P.M.–2 A.M. Mon.–Fri., 7 P.M.–2 A.M. Sat.). Modeled after a traditional '60s-era *botequim*, the floors are checkerboard tile and the walls are covered with old photos of the city. Thursdays and Fridays can get pretty packed. Meanwhile, the super groovy spot of the moment for dancing the night away is at the plush and funky **El Divino Lounge** (Rua Almirante Lameggo 1147, tel. 48/3225-1266, www.eldivino brasil.com.br, 8 P.M.–close Tues.–Sun., cover R$5–10), where, aside from dance floors and swank lounge areas, you'll find a restaurant, sushi bar, boutique, and cyber café. In Jurerê, the same group owns the super-sophisticated El Divino Club along with El Divino Beach, a very sexy beach lounge that extends right onto the sands.

Entertainment and Events

Floripa's **Carnaval** has become one of the most flocked-to festivals of the South. Even Cariocas abandon Rio to join in the festivities, which feature a significant gay and lesbian contingent. If you want to indulge, make sure you book accommodations far in advance.

Shopping

For regional folk art and handicrafts, particularly ceramics and Azorean lace, check out the **Casa da Alfândega** (see *Sights*) and the **Casa Açoriana** (Rua Cônego Serpa 30, tel. 48/3235-1262, 1–9 P.M. Tues.–Thurs., 1–9 P.M. Fri., 10 A.M.–9 P.M. Sat., 10 A.M.–7 P.M. Sun.; 10 A.M.–11 P.M. daily Dec.–Mar.) in Santo Antônio de Lisboa. For clothing, especially cutting-edge beach- and surfwear, head to the chic **Beira Mar Shopping** (Rua Bocaiúva 2468, tel. 48/3223-6425, 10 A.M.–10 P.M. Mon.–Sat., 2–8 P.M. Sun.), where you'll also find cinemas and a food court.

Accommodations

If you plan to do a lot of exploring, it's best to base yourself in the Floripa's Centro. However, if you just want to flake out, choose accommodations according to the type of beach holiday you're in the mood for. If you want plenty of nightlife to go along with your chilled-out days, try the more touristic (and overdeveloped) Praia Brava or dos Ingleses (north coast) or the more attractive rough surf beaches of Joaquina and Mole (east coast). Less crowded are beaches such as Daniela (north coast), whose calm waters make it a favorite for families, and Campeche and Armação (east coast). For more rustic simplicity and tranquility, check out the traditional Azorean fishing villages of Santo Antônio de Lisboa and Ribeirão da Ilha. Come summertime, prices are high and reservations are essential. Prices listed below are during low and mid-season.

CENTRO

Staying in Floripa itself is advantageous if you don't have a car and want to bus it to many beaches around the island. Good bargains are to be had, and since hotels are primarily geared to business travelers, prices are often lower on weekends. The cheapest option is the cheery, well-kept **HI Hostel Florianópolis** (Rua Duarte Schutel 227, tel. 48/3225-3781, www.floripahostel.com.br, R$25–32 pp, R$60 d). A 10-minute walk from the *rodoviária,* it has spotless dorm rooms as well as private rooms for couples and families. Aside from a kitchen where you can rustle up a meal, there is a pleasant dining area and outdoor terrace.

More sleek and upscale is the **InterCity Premium Florianópolis** (Av. Paulo Fontes 1210, tel. 48/3027-2200, www.intercityhoteis .com.br, R$105–165 d), a gleaming hotel right across from the bus station. Spacious rooms are decorated with modern panache and feature enormous windows that, from high up, afford outstanding views of the bay and mainland. Amenities include an Internet café, a rooftop pool, Jacuzzi, and sauna. The **Florianópolis Palace** (Rua Artista Bittencourt 14, tel. 48/2106-9633, www.floph.com.br, R$130–220

d) is nowhere near as grand as it sounds. Yet for the affordable price, this modern '70s-era hotel geared towards upscale execs is a very comfortable and convenient option. Opt for a room with a panoramic city view. Extras include a pool and sauna.

LAGOA DA CONCEIÇÃO

Despite the fact that Lagoa is the restaurant and nightlife hub of the island, there are actually few places to stay here. If you want to be close to east coast beaches by day and all the action at night, staying in the town of Centro da Lagoa is a good bet. A quick walk from Centrinho, **[** **Pousada das Palmeiras** (Rua Laurindo da Silveira 2720, tel. 48/3232-6227, www.pousadadaspalmeiras.com.br, R$225–370 d) is a beautiful and relaxingly Zen tropical hideaway where each of the five suites and one bungalow (with kitchens and most with Jacuzzis) is named after a defining natural element. To wit, the "palm suite" features soothing pale green walls and plenty of live palm fronds, while the blue "lagoon suite," features a veranda Jacuzzi from which you can gaze out at the equally blue *lagoa*. King-sized beds, fine linens, CD and DVD players, and fabulously healthy breakfast banquets round out the luxuries.

A more rustic yet no less enticing option is to rent one of the charmingly old-fashioned, wooden A-frame bungalows at **Chalés do Canto** (Rua Laurindo da Silveira 2212, tel. 48/3232-0471, www.chalesdocanto.com.br, R$100–160 d). To ensure privacy, the chalets—which sleep up to five—are scattered amidst the woodlands surrounding the pretty fishing village of Canto da Lagoa (3 km/2 miles from Centro da Lagoa). Each unit is equipped with a full kitchen, fireplace, and TV, while hammocks on wooden decks afford beautiful views of the *lagoa*.

NORTH COAST

For those in search of calm seas and tranquility, **Pousada dos Artistas** (Av. das Pitangueiras 1216, Praia da Daniela, tel. 48/3282-5512, www.pousadadosartistas.com.br, R$105 d), on

Praia da Daniela, is a practical and affordable option. The spotless one- and two-bedroom apartments with full kitchens and verandas are bright and modern, if a little lacking in warmth. Amidst the urban development and *movimento* of Praia do Jurerê, **Pousada Casa Sin Nombre** (Rua dos Polvos 58-A, Praia do Jurerê, tel. 48/3282-1379, www.casasin nombre.com.br, R$140–210 d) is a lovely exception. Built and decorated in the style of a whitewashed Mediterranean villa, with dark wood fixtures, wrought iron, and plenty of plants and quaint knickknacks in the common spaces (the rooms are plainer), this cozy guesthouse exudes a home-like warmth.

Located at the absolute northern tip of the island, on what is one of the north coast's most beautiful beaches, the pretty pink **[** **Pousada da Vigia** (Rua Conselheiro Walmor Castro 291, Lagoinha, tel. 48/3284-1789, www.pousadada vigia.com.br, R$230–340 d) is an enchanting and intimate hotel with eight apartments and two luxury suites (with private Jacuzzis and saunas) nestled against a backdrop of Atlantic forest. Although hardly spacious, rooms are breezy and tastefully furnished with fine linens and local handicrafts. The private balconies that offer fantastic ocean views are perhaps the best feature.

EAST COAST

Sitting within a vast green area between the lagoon and the wild, deserted sands of Praia de Moçambique, **Pousada Rio Vermelho** (Rodovia João Gualberto Soares 8479, Praia de Moçambique, tel. 48/3269-7337, www .riovermelhopousada.com.br, R$140–150 d) offers a total getaway. The main lodge is a paragon of rustic chic with hardwood floors, patchwork quilts, throw pillows, and hand-woven carpets. Individual chalets are somewhat more basic, and are equipped with kitchens. There is also a lovely pool.

Set upon a swatch of land that stretches from Praia Mole to the *lagoa*, **Praia Mole Eco Village** (Estrada Geral da Barra da Lagoa 2001, tel. 48/3239-7500, www.praiamole.com.br, R$144–312 d) offers something for everyone with a variety of accommodation options dispersed among orchid-strewn gardens. The smallest and charming Vista Mar building overlooks the beach. The larger Bloco Central is close to the swimming pool, spa, and tennis courts. Meanwhile, rooms in the gracious Solar das Acácias offer captivating views of the lagoon. Ideal for groups and families of up to six are the spacious one- and two-bedroom private bungalows. All rooms are simply, but warmly, decorated with wooden furniture and paintings by local artists. Activities available range from yoga and pilates classes to guided nature walks, horseback riding, and fishing and diving expeditions. Just off the lovely Praia do Campeche, **Hotel São Sebastião da Praia** (Av. Campeche, Praia do Campeche, tel. 48/3338-2070, www.hotel saosebastiao.com.br, R$160–190 d) is a fine option with comfortable, attractively appointed rooms set amid sprawling tropical greenery, along with a nice-sized pool.

SOUTH COAST

Nature lovers will be smitten with the **C Pousada Sítio dos Tucanos** (tel. 48/3237-5084, www.pousadasitiodostucanos.com, R$108 d), which sits on a private nature reserve on the edge of the Parque Municipal da Lagoa do Peri and offers sweeping views of Praia da Armação. The country-style chalet accommodations are simple but cozy. Equally inviting are the living room decorated with folk art and the dining room where homemade breakfasts (dinner is available too) are served at wooden tables that gaze out at the lush hills. The friendly German owner organizes eco-outings of all sorts, from mountain hikes to whale-watching excursions. A few steps away from a secluded stretch of Praia da Armação, **Pousada Pénareia** (Rua Hermes Guedes de Fonseca 207, Praia da Armação, tel. 48/3338-1616, www.pousadapenareia.com.br, R$120–150 d) offers modern and attractively appointed rooms with verandas, sea views, and lots of peace and tranquility (no children under 12 allowed). Guests are pleasantly pampered—the hotel offers everything from beach chairs and volleyballs to inflatable kayaks and bikes.

Food

Florianópolis is a seafood lover's paradise. The island is the biggest producer of oysters in the world, which are served fresh and deliciously raw (accompanied by lime wedges) at many beachside eateries and in the rustic little restaurants in the Azorean fishing villages on the west coast. Also popular are shrimp—both pink and white—which are prepared in many different fashions along with a local fish, *tainha,* whose tender meat melts in your mouth.

CENTRO

By day, the center of Floripa boasts many inexpensive eating options. At night, however, most people head to the chic Beira Mar neighborhood or to Lagoa da Conceição. Downtown, a classic spot to eat and hang out is at the Mercado Municipal (see *Sights*), where you can fill up on fish and seafood while slugging back icy beers. **Box 32** (Mercado Municipal, tel. 48/3244-5588, www.box32.com.br, 10 A.M.– 10 P.M. Mon.–Fri., 10 A.M.–3 P.M. Sat., R$10– 25) is a Floripa institution that draws locals and tourists. The delicious shrimp-stuffed *pásteis* are particularly addictive, as are the *bolinhos de bacalhau*. More substantial fish and seafood entrées are also available (for a heftier price).

Another traditional downtown spot is **Fratellanza** (Rua Trajano 342, tel. 48/3222-1416, www.fratellanza.com.br, 11:30 A.M.– 2:30 P.M. and 5–11:30 P.M. Mon.–Fri., R$20–30), facing the staircase leading up to the Igreja de Nossa Senhora do Rosário. The food is hearty Italian fare—served as a per kilo buffet at lunch and à la carte in the evenings. In the summer, a piano is hauled out onto the stairs, turning the place into one of Floripa's main musical attractions. (In the winter, the piano is moved inside for more intimate shows.)

In Beira Mar, **Café das Artes** (Rua Esteves Junior 734, tel. 48/3322-0690, 11:30 A.M.– 11 P.M. Mon.–Fri., 4–11 P.M. Sat.–Sun., R$10– 20) is a swish, arty little café/gallery. Works by local artists are exhibited on exposed stone walls that reveal the whale oil formerly used for mortar instead of cement. Caffeine fans swear by the aromatic house blend, whose flavor is enhanced by the likes of chocolate-brazil nut torte and blackberry cashew muffins. There are also savory items such as chicken *empadas* as well as tasty light meals.

The finest seafood in town can be had at the **Toca da Garoupa** (Rua Alves de Brito 178, tel. 48/3223-1220, www.tocadagaroupa.com.br, noon–3 P.M. and 7 P.M.–midnight daily, R$50–60). This refined yet unpretentious Beira Mar restaurant was founded by a group of friends whose hobby was deep-sea fishing. Grouper is the main ingredient in the reputed *moquecas*. Other specialties include seafood and *bacalhau* risottos and penne with shrimp and pesto. Leave room for desserts such as walnut "stroganoff."

LAGOA DA CONCEIÇÃO

Lagoa possesses a great variety of restaurants. You'll find many casual places serving fish and seafood as well as the traditional *sequência de camarões,* in which waiters circulate, *rodízio*-style, offering dish after dish of shrimp prepared in a variety of ways, such as steamed, grilled, breaded, stuffed with creamy Catupiry cheese, and *au vinaigrette.* With panoramic views of the lagoon, **Casa do Chico** (Av. das Rendeiras 1620, Lagoa da Conceição, tel. 48/3232-5132, www.casadochico.com, 11:30 A.M.–12:30 A.M. Tues.–Sun., open Mon. in summer, R$20–30) is a simple and much-loved institution. Aside from the *sequência de camarões,* try *torpedo de siri,* a type of crab fritter, as well as grilled *linguado* (sole) swathed in seafood and cream and gratinéed with parmesan.

At the more upscale **Chef Fedoca** (Rua Senador Ivo d'Aquino Neto 133, Lagoa da Conceição, tel. 48/3232-0848, www.chef fedoca.com.br, 11:30 A.M.–3 P.M. and 7:30 P.M.–midnight Tues.–Fri., 11:30 A.M.–midnight Sat., 11:30 A.M.–6 P.M. Sun.; 11:30 A.M.–midnight daily Dec.–Mar., R$40–50), located on the picturesque marina, the star attraction, apart from the *sequência de frutas do mar,* is the famous fish and shrimp *moqueca* invented by Fedoca, a former diver cum chef.

NORTH COAST

As developed as it is, the north coast is not an easy place to find good eating options. A very pleasant exception to the rule is the low-key but sophisticated **Estação 261** (Av. das Raias 261, Praia do Jurerê, tel. 48/3282-9944, 11:30 A.M.–2:30 P.M. daily, 7 P.M.–midnight Tues.–Sat., R$35–45). At lunch, choose from a small per kilo buffet of contemporary dishes, while at dinner, à la carte specials include imaginative and attractively presented salads, seafood, and grilled meats, all of which serve two.

More modest is the family-style **Pescador Lobo** (Rua José Cardoso de Oliveira, Praia do Forte, tel. 48/3282-0631, 9 A.M.–5 P.M. Mon.–Thurs., 9 A.M.–8 P.M. Fri.–Sun., 9 A.M.–midnight daily in summer, R$25–35), overlooking the sea and the Fortaleza de São José da Ponta Grossa. It's owned by a local fisherman whose nickname is Lobo ("Wolf"), and the robust seafood dishes (portions feed two) includes specialties such as gratinéed sole with cream corn and shrimp cooked in a pumpkin.

EAST COAST

On super cool Praia da Joaquina, the **Unique Lounge** (Rua Prefeito Acácio Garibaldi São Thiago, Praia da Joaquina, tel. 48/3232-4088, www.uniquelounge.com.br, 8 P.M.–close Tues.–Sun.; 8 P.M.–close Mon.–Thurs. and 4 P.M.–close Fri.–Sun. in summer, R$20–35) is definitely singular. Surrounded by typical Azorean houses, this hybrid lounge/bar/restaurant occupies a converted manioc flour mill. The exterior is a jungly tangle of trees punctuated with a saltwater aquarium. Inside, things take a turn for the Oriental with a sushi bar, a Buddha statue, and lots of languor-inducing sofas. The restaurant menu offers lots to nibble on (such as manioc chips with salmon paté), but you can also dine on the likes of T-bone lamb steak with pesto or penne with shiitake mushrooms. When you've had your fill, get your groove on in the (acoustically sealed-off) dance floor, where DJs work the tanned and trendy crowd.

SOUTH COAST

◖ Bar do Arante (Rua Abelardo Otacílio Gomes 254, Pântano do Sul, tel. 48/3237-7022, 10 A.M.–close daily, R$25–35) has been around since 1958, when Arante and his wife, Osmarina, opened a little shack in Pantâno do Sul. Originally, they sold market produce and plates of simple, succulent fish and seafood dishes. In the '60s, after relocating to the beach, the bar became headquarters for students who came to camp on the deserted south coast. In those pre-cell phone days, they left written messages to each other—which explains the thousands that are still taped all over the walls and ceiling (if you want to leave one, just ask the waiter for paper and a pen). The sheer number of these notes also attests to the popularity of Osmarina's cooking. Try the *camarão à Dona Osmarina*—shrimp baked with tomatoes, cheese, and mushrooms and served with salad, rice, and french fries. All dishes feed two. On the weekends, a typical island buffet is served with numerous hot and cold specialties for R$23 per person.

WEST COAST

When faced with serious seafood cravings, Floripanos head to the island's traditional Azorean fishing villages of Sambaqui, Ribeirão da Ilha, and Santo Antônio. As a teenager, Daniel de Andrade worked as a cook on fishing boats, before turning landlubber and opening **Gugu** (Rua Antônio Dias Carneiro 147, Sambaqui, tel. 48/3335-0288, 11:30 A.M.–3 P.M. Tues.–Sun., 6–11 P.M. daily, R$25–35), which specializes in seafood. One of the most popular dishes is the seafood risotto with sole, crab, shrimp, squid, and oysters, which, like all the copious entrées, serves two.

(Ostradamus (Rodovia Baldocero Filomeno 7640, Ribeirão da Ilha, tel. 48/3337-5711, www.ostradamus.com.br, noon–11 P.M. daily in summer, noon–11 P.M. Tues.–Sat. and noon–6 P.M. Sun. the rest of the year, R$40–50) is the island's high temple of oysters. In a pretty pumpkin colored colonial house overlooking the sea, oyster junkies gather to savor these freshly farmed jewels, served by the dozen (and carefully prepared—ultraviolet radiation is used to remove impurities). The most popular recipes include gratinéed with cheese,

doused with ginger and lime juice, and balsamic vinegar and orange sauce. Main entrées for two feature dishes such as grilled sole with shrimp and mushrooms.

Widely considered to be the finest gourmet dining experience on the island, **Bistro d'Acampôra** (Rodovia SC-401 Km 10, Santo Antônio de Lisboa, tel. 48/3235-1073, www.dacampora.com.br, 8 P.M.–midnight Tues.–Sun., R$70–80) is located on the highway leading north from Floripa to Santo Antônio, in an unpretentiously warm and welcoming space adjacent to the home of chef Zeca d'Acompora. Only 50 diners a night have the privilege of savoring d'Acompora's contemporary creations, which combine classic French techniques with the chef's Italian-German background and the island's Azorean traditions. Although there is no set menu, past dishes included mango stuffed with fresh crab and grilled shrimp with Moroccan couscous. The wine list is superb. Reservations (which can be made online) are essential.

Information

There are several branches of the **tourist office** around Floripa and the island, including one at Largo da Alfândega (tel. 48/3222-4906, 8 A.M.–6 P.M. daily), the Terminal Rodoviário Rita Maria (Av. Paulo Fontes 1101, tel. 48/3212-3127, 8 A.M.–10 P.M. Mon.–Fri., 8 A.M.–6 P.M. Sat.–Sun.), and Praia da Joaquina (8 A.M.–5 P.M. daily Dec.–Mar.). Also check out the sites www.guiafloripa.com.br and www.pmf.gov.sc.br/turismo (in Portuguese). For information about Santa Catarina, check out the state's bilingual site, www.santacatarina turismo.com.br, as well as www.belasantacatarina .com.br (in Portuguese).

Services

For exchanging currency and withdrawing money from ATMs, head to the banks along Rua Felipe Schmidt and the streets surrounding Praça 15 de Novembro, where you'll also find the main post office. Internet cafés are quite numerous.

In an emergency dial **192** for an ambulance,

190 for the police, and **193** for the fire department. For medical treatment, try the **Hospital Universitário** (Av. Beira-Mar Norte, Trindade, tel. 48/3331-9100, www.hu.ufsc.br).

Getting There and Around

By air, Florianópolis can be reached directly from Rio, São Paulo, Curitiba, and Porto Alegre. The **Aeroporto Internacional Hercílio Luz** (Av. Diomício Freitas, 48/3393, tel. 48/3331-4000) is 12 kilometers (8 miles) south of the city center. Taking a taxi into town will cost around R$40. Regular municipal "Aeroporto" buses take around 45 minutes to get to Centro.

Buses from around the state and country arrive at the modern **Terminal Rodoviário Rita Maria** (Av. Paulo Fontes 1101, tel. 48/3212-3100), located between the Hercílio Luz and Colombo Machado Sales bridges.

Across from the front entrance of the main *rodoviária* is one of several municipal bus stations. From here buses serve Florianópolis and points along the south coast. From another terminal at the corner of Rua José da Costa Moelmann and Avenida Mauro Ramos, buses depart to beaches on the east and north coasts. Regardless of your destination, you can usually choose from simple (often crowded) municipal buses and more expensive, plush, air-conditioned *executivo* minibuses.

Although bus service around the island is extensive and dependable, buses themselves are infrequent and service can be slow. For this reason, if you're going to be moving around a lot or if you want to explore a maximum number of beaches, you're much better off renting a car (but bear in mind that in summer traffic jams to the most popular beaches are quite common). The roads are in top condition and well marked, and drivers are quite courteous. **Hertz** (tel. 48/3224-9955, www.hertz.com.br) has offices at the airport, in Floripa's Centro, and at Praia de Santinho. **Avis** (tel. 48/3225-7777, www.avis.com.br) has offices at the airport and at four locations throughout the island. For competitive rates, try **Yes** (tel. 48/3266-1918), which has offices at the airport, in Floripa's

center, and in Canasvieiras. It will also deliver cars to any hotel on the island. **Tropix Turismo** (tel. 48/3239-2217, www.tropix.com.br) rents both cars and motorcycles, which is an excellent way to explore the island.

PORTO BELO

The coastline running north from Florianópolis is quite spectacular. It is also insanely mobbed in the summertime by tourists from São Paulo, Paraná, and Argentina. Unfortunately, its many natural attractions are marred by the type of unbridled urbanization epitomized by the resort town of Balneário Camboriú. Billed as the South's "Pequena Copacabana," this tourist mecca 80 kilometers (50 miles) north of Florianópolis possesses the Rio neighborhood's high-rises and animation without any of its charm. To date, the area that has best fended off development is the peninsula of Porto Belo, 60 kilometers (37 miles) north of Floripa. Here, you'll find some of the state's loveliest beaches along with emerald waters that are ideal for snorkeling and diving. The small town of Porto Belo is the departure point for exploring the beautiful neighboring beaches of Bombas and Bombinhas, which although crowded by families in the summer still have not been overwhelmed. Close by—accessible only by boat or on foot—a dozen small, deserted coves offer peace and tranquility.

Beaches

Although the central beaches of **Porto Belo** and **Perequê** are nice enough, only a few kilometers east en route to Bombinhas (easily reached by walking) are the more enticing and secluded beaches of **Estaleiro** and **Caixa d'Aço.** For an easy island getaway, hop a boat from the dock in front of the Praça dos Pescadores to the **Ilha de Porto Belo** (tel. 47/3369-4146, www.ilhadeportobelo.com.br) which can be visited 8 A.M.–7:30 P.M. daily October–March and 8 A.M.–5 P.M. daily April–September. The 10-minute trip costs R$8 (return-trip included). Aside from sunning and swimming, you can hike to Pedra da Cruz, a rock with 4,000-year-old inscriptions, or don

THE SOUTH

diving gear to follow seven underwater trails. The **Eco-Museu Univali** (Ilha de Porto Belo, tel. 47/3261-1287, daily Sept.–Mar., R$4) has a few interesting treasures, including some 20,000 year-old fossils.

Only 5 kilometers (3 miles) from Porto Belo are the twin beaches of **Bombas** and **Bombinhas** (separated by a promontory), both of which have become a little too trendy and crowded of late. It's best to visit during off-season when you can take advantage of their alluring natural attributes: a sheltered bay with white-sand beaches backed by rolling green hills. Continuing east from Bombinhas, less crowded but easily accessible beaches include the small, very pretty **Lagoinha** and **Sepultura,** with calm waters that are ideal for swimming and snorkeling. Facing the open sea, **Quatro Ilhas** and **Mariscal** are prized by surfers in search of swells. The continuation of Mariscal is **Canto Grande,** from which a 4-kilometer (2.5-mile) trail (or dirt road) leads to the beautiful and secluded **Praia da Tainha.**

For guided hiking trips to even more far-flung beaches, contact **Casa do Turista** (Av. Governador Celso Ramos 2460, Sala 5, tel. 47/3369-5030, www.casadoturista.com.br) in Porto Belo or **Caminhos e Trilhas** (tel. 47/9973-0584, www.caminhosetrilhas.com.br) in Bombinhas.

◖ Reserva Biológica Marinha da Ilha do Arvoredo

Hands down, the best place for diving in the entire South is in the clear azure Atlantic waters surrounding the Ilha do Arvoredo, a biological reserve accessible from both Bombinhas and Florianópolis. Dive operators in Bombinhas offer half-day diving tours to the coral reefs surrounding the southern part of the island, which are teeming with brightly colored fish, dolphins, and sea turtles. Both **Patadacobra** (Av. Vereador Manoel José dos Santos, tel. 47/3369-2119, www.patadacobra.com.br) and **Acquatrek** (tel. 47/3369-2137, www.acquatrek.com.br) offer diving courses and half-day outings for divers of all levels. Excursion rates are R$100–150.

Accommodations

Stylish *pousadas* are hard to come by around Porto Belo, and even more basic accommodations don't come cheap. Most hotels are situated along the adjacent beaches of Bombas and Bombinhas. **Hotel Cores do Mar** (Rua Martim Pescador 125, Bombas, tel. 47/3369-1435, www.hotelcoresdomar.com.br, R$130–180 d) is a modern hotel close to the beach with simple rooms painted in tropical sherbet hues. All rooms possess small balconies. A swimming pool, Internet café, and surrounding garden are welcome features.

In Porto Belo, the **Pousada Vila Verde** (Rua Domingos Jaques 867, Praia do Perequê, www.pousadavilaverde.tur.br, R$140–275 d) is a bright, sunny, attractive hotel with a pool facing right onto popular Praia do Perequê. Rooms are basic but airy and appealing, with balconies overlooking the sea. One of the few really charming options in the region is the **Pousada Quintal do Mar** (Av. Aroeira da Praia 1641, Praia de Mariscal, tel. 47/3393-4389, www.quintaldomar.com.br, R$179–299 d). Each of the quartet of exquisitely designed and decorated apartments within this pale yellow beachfront villa is like a small but beautiful home. Creature comforts extend from the fine linens and CD players in the rooms to the garden gazebos with hammocks and pillows that are very conducive to lounging. Children under 12 are prohibited.

Food

In Porto Belo, **Ilha de Pirão** (Av. Governador Celso Ramos 2207, tel. 47/3369-4941, 11:30 A.M.–3 P.M. Tues.–Sun., 7–11:30 P.M. Fri.–Sat.; 11 A.M.–11:30 P.M. daily Dec.–Feb., R$25–40) is a relaxed and inviting little restaurant owned by a couple of agronomical engineers who began cooking as a hobby. The menu features dishes such as grilled octopus with vegetables and seafood with Spanish rice (portions feed two people). Start out with a *caipirinha* made from locally produced *cachaça.*

With a wide balcony overlooking Praia de Bombas, **Camarão Peixe e Cia** (Av. Leopoldo Zarling 1045, Praia de Bombas, tel. 47/3369-

2999, 11 A.M.–4 P.M. Sun.–Thurs., 11 A.M.–midnight Fri.–Sat.; 11–midnight daily Dec.–Feb., R$20–35) specializes in regional fish and seafood dishes such as the aromatic *caldeirada de frutos do mar,* a seafood stew for two prepared in a clay casserole. Three can easily feast upon the *sequência de camarão,* an endless parade of shrimp cooked in various manners.

Cantina Lopes (Rua Vereador José Manoel dos Santos 800, Loja 101, tel. 47/3369-0341, noon–midnight daily, R$20–35) serves up tasty Italian fare. Aside from various homemade pastas, the chef has a predilection for seafood. The *plat de résistance* is the *gran piato del mare:* a banquet of delicacies both chilled (raw oysters, marinated squid, octopus, and shrimp) and hot (lobster, salmon, crab) that costs R$140 and feeds at least two people. If you have any room left order the *abacaxi surpresa,* a pineapple filled with neapolitan gelato and topped with a salad of "red" fruits.

Information

In Porto Belo, the **tourist office** (Av. Governador Celso Ramos, tel. 47/3369-5378, 9 A.M.–noon and 2–5 P.M. daily, 8 A.M.–9 P.M. daily Dec.–Feb.) has information about the entire peninsula. You can also log on to www.portobelo.com.br and www.bombinhas.sc.gov.br.

Getting There

Porto Belo is easy to get to from Florianópolis, only 55 kilometers (34 miles) away. **Santo Anjo** (tel. 48/3224-9004, www.santoanjo.com.br) offers frequent bus service. By car, just follow the BR-101 north.

GAROPABA

Located 95 kilometers (59 miles) south of Florianópolis, Garopaba was a tranquil Azorean fishing village until the 1970s, when its beautiful beaches and striking mountain backdrops were discovered by hippies from neighboring Rio Grande do Sul. A decade later the *surfistas* moved in and, to this day, the area remains one of the country's major surfing

---

WHALE-WATCHING

Every year, between June and November, the southern coast of Santa Catarina is transformed into a giant open-air aquarium for watching humpback whales swim north from Patagonia in search of (relatively) warmer waters in which to reproduce and nurture their offspring. For centuries one of the major economic activities along Santa Catarina's coast, whale hunting was finally banned in 1973, and 140 kilometers (85 miles) of coastline was declared an Environmental Protection Area. The ocean off the coast of Garopaba and Praia do Rosa is one of the best places for viewing whales up close. They sometimes come within 50 meters (164 feet) of the beach. However, for surefire sightings, take an organized boat excursion. For information, contact the **Instituto Baleia Franca** (Estrada Geral da Praia do Rosa, Ibirapuera, tel. 48/3355-6111, www.baleiafranca.org.br, R$90 pp Mon.-Fri., R$140 pp Sat.-Sun.), which offers trips accompanied by biologists.

---

meccas during the summer months. Between June and November, it is also the best place on the Brazilian coast for whale-watching.

Beaches

While Garopaba's small beach is pleasant enough, the real attractions are the wilder beaches within close proximity of the village. **Praia Siriú,** 10 kilometers (6 miles) to the north, is a beautiful beach backed by 40-meter-high (131-feet-high) dunes that are excellent for sandboarding. Although the waves are rough, you can swim in the calm waters of the Rio Siriú. Surfers, however, are lured by the beaches to the south, the most famous being **Praia do Silveira,** 3 kilometers (2 miles) from Garopaba. Another 5 kilometers (3 miles) south is the hip and happening **Praia da Ferrugem,** which has bars along the shore that attract visiting young Paulistanos and Gaúchos in the summer. Natural ocean pools offer a calmer

© CHRISTIAN KNEPPER/EMBRATUR

the wild and windswept beaches of Garopaba

alternative to otherwise big waves, but the water here is usually pretty chilly.

Accommodations and Food

Lodgings in Garopaba are generally basic, no-frills affairs, and many are only open in the summer. You can choose between Garopaba, which is more popular with families, and Ferrugem, favored by young *surfistas.* In Garopaba, **Pousada Mares do Sul** (Rua Francisco Pacheco de Sousa 393, Garopaba, tel. 48/3354-3866, www.mares dosulpousada.com.br, R$100–150 d) is a fairly nice option with large rooms and walls painted in bright tropical shades. Perched on a hilltop above Praia de Ferrugem, the relaxed **Pousada do Morro** (Estrada Geral do Capão, Praia da Ferrugem, tel. 48/3254-0098, www.pousadadomorro.com.br, R$110–135) offers a variety of accommodations from double rooms to two-room apartments equipped with kitchens that sleep up to five people. Lots of vegetation and a swimming pool add to the restful atmosphere.

Garopaba and the surrounding beaches

have a fair number of basic fish and seafood restaurants. A little more expensive, although more charming than most is **Armazém do Mar** (Rua Ptolomeu Bitencourt 44, Garopaba, tel. 48/3254-4145, 7–11 P.M. Fri.–Sat. May–Nov., noon–midnight daily Dec.–Apr., R$30–40), located in a fetching house with a great veranda that shares space with a shop selling local handicrafts. The house specialties are *moqueca do armazém,* featuring grouper, shrimp, squid, and octopus, and *peixe do armazém,* in which fresh fish is stuffed with shrimp, cream, heart of palm, and sun-dried tomatoes.

Information

For selective listings and information in Portuguese, as well as some rather overexposed photos, check out www.garobapa.com.br.

Getting There

From Florianópolis's Rodoviária Rita Maria, **Paulotur** (tel. 48/3244-2777, www.paulotur .com.br) operates daily bus service down the coast. If you're driving from Floripa, take the BR-101 south and then turn onto the SC-434.

◖ PRAIA DO ROSA

Just 18 kilometers (11 miles) down the coast from Garopaba, Praia do Rosa is routinely touted as one of the most beautiful beaches in southern Brazil, with its beckoning bay of sugary sand backed by verdant hills and lagoons. Although its big waves draw surfers, in recent years Praia do Rosa has become the most eco-chic resort along the Santa Catarina coast, renowned for its gourmet restaurants and handful of seductively posh *pousadas* tucked away in the hills. Fortunately, despite the sophisticated tourist infrastructure, it retains an unspoiled rustic charm. If you want to avoid the hipster scene altogether, come off-season (although some places close down). May–June is the period for *tainha* fishing, while July–November is whale-watching season. Plan on doing a lot of steep hiking up and down the jungly hills. Nearby lagoons (where windsurfing is the rage), waterfalls, and beaches such as Praia Vermelha and Praia do Luz can only be reached by foot or on horseback.

Accommodations and Food

You'll be tempted to spoil yourself by checking into one of Praia do Rosa's bewitching hilltop eco-chic *pousadas*. ◖ **Pousada Quinta do Bucanero** (Estrada Geral do Rosa, tel. 48/3355-6056, www.bucanero.com.br, R$330 d, closed in June) is a refined and romantic affair (no kids under 14) where the rawness of glass, stone, and natural wood is offset by hand-painted porcelain, plush carpets, and exquisite art works. Beautifully furnished rooms with wooden verandas offer hypnotic views of the jungle-fringed bay below. A little more country, but no less charming, is the equally lofty **Pousada Caminho do Rei** (Caminho do Alto do Morro, tel. 48/3355-6062, www.caminho dorei.com.br, R$200–360 d), whose decor mixes local folk art, hand-woven carpets, patchwork quilts, and jars full of tropical flowers. Each of the eight aerie rooms is individually furnished, and all boast stunning views. Amenities include a pool, sauna, a games and reading room, and a cozy candlelit restaurant serving seafood and Swiss-Italian dishes.

Simple, warm, and welcoming, the **Regina Guest House** (Caminho do Alto do Morro, tel. 48/3355-6066, www.reginagh.com.br, R$95–135 d) has the advantage of being close to the beach. In terms of lodgings, you can choose between individual bungalows nestled in the forest and the main building, a renovated manioc flour mill decorated with colorful local handicrafts. All guests receive a *"kit praia"* that includes a beach chair, towel, and parasol. The restaurant, ◖ **Bistrô Pedra da Vigia** (7 P.M.–12:30 A.M. Thurs.–Sat., 7 P.M.–12:30 A.M. daily Dec.–Feb., R$15–25) serves delicious French-inspired bistro fare with an emphasis on local fish and seafood. The apple torte is divine.

Although you might be surprised to come across pad thai in these parts, **Tigre Asiático** (Estrada Geral do Rosa, tel. 48/3355-7045, www.tigreasiatico.com, 7–11 P.M. daily) is famed for being one of the best Thai restaurants in Brazil. Purists will note that traditional dishes have been adapted slightly for Brazilian palates. Soft lighting and Asian flourishes enhance the mood.

Information

For selective listings and information in Portuguese, log on to www.praiadorosa.tur.br.

Getting There

From Florianópolis **Paulotur** (tel. 48/3244-2777, www.paulotur.com.br) has two buses a day to Praia do Rosa. Local bus service from Garopaba is much more frequent. By car from Garopaba, follow the Estrada Geral do Rosa.

LAGUNA

Some 20 kilometers (12 miles) south of Praia do Rosa, Laguna, founded in 1676, is Santa Catarina's second-oldest town. While few of its churches, mansions, and public buildings date back that far, the well-preserved historic center (facing a lagoon) makes an interesting stop if you're on your way south. Although the modern part of town (gazing out at the open Atlantic) has become a popular seaside resort, Laguna's beaches aren't that spectacular. Its

THE SOUTH

vibrant street Carnaval, however, is quite a festive affair.

Sights

With its cobblestoned streets, faded pastel buildings, and typical Portuguese colonial architecture, Laguna's small historic center is more quaint and atmospheric than stunning. On the main square, **Praça Vidal Ramos,** the late-17th-century **Igreja Santo Antônio dos Anjos** is one of Santa Catarina's oldest surviving baroque churches. The *praça* also shelters the **Casa de Anita** (tel. 48/3646-2542, 8 A.M.–6 P.M. daily, R$1), an early 18th-century house devoted to Anita Garibaldi, the wife of the legendary father of Italian unification, Giuseppe Garibaldi. The two met and fell in love in 1839 when Garibaldi was working as a mercenary during Brazil's Guerra dos Farrapos, a conflict that pitted republicans against monarchists. Anita didn't live in the colonial house—her godparents did—but she was married here. Inside, old photos of Laguna mingle with trivial personal effects such as the revolutionary's hairbrush. Less interesting is the Museu Anita Garibaldi, located in the former city hall and jail.

Beaches

The town's main beach, **Praia do Mar Grossa** is nice enough, but quite urbanized. You're better off taking a 10-minute boat trip followed by a 17-kilometer (10.5-mile) drive along a dirt road (you'll need a car) to the more untamed dunes and beaches around **Farol Santa Marta,** a small town built around a 19th-century lighthouse rumored to be the third highest in the Americas. Although the scenery is impressive, strong currents make swimming in the open sea dangerous.

Accommodations and Food

Most hotels and restaurants—which tend towards basic and nondescript—are located near the beach at Mar Grosso. The shiny, new **Hotel Marina Sul** (Rua Engenheiro Sá Rocha 225, tel. 48/3647-2555, www.marinasulhotel.com.br, R$50–120 d) is modern, spacious, and somewhat reminiscent of a recently inaugurated airport terminal. While lacking in personality, rooms are very large and well appointed, and overall this hotel is a good bargain.

Arrastão (Av. Sen Gallotti 629, tel. 48/3637-0418, 11 A.M.–2 P.M. and 6:30–10 P.M. Mon.-Sat., 11 A.M.–4 P.M. Sun.; 11 A.M.–4 P.M. and 6:30 P.M.–midnight daily Dec.–Feb., R$20–30) is a good place for large portions of unpretentious fish and seafood dishes such as *camarão tropical,* breaded shrimp served with rice, french fries, and salad.

Information

The **tourist office** (Av. Calistrato Müller Salles, tel. 48/3644-2411, 8 A.M.–6 P.M. Mon.-Sat., 8 A.M.–1 P.M. Sun.) is at the entrance to Laguna, 3 kilometers (2 miles) from the center of town. The state website has some information in Portuguese (www.laguna.sc.gov.br).

Getting There

By bus, **Santo Anjo** (tel. 48/3224-9001) provides regular service from Florianópolis. By car, Laguna is 124 kilometers (77 miles) south of Florianópolis along the BR-101.

Rio Grande do Sul

Brazil's southernmost state, bordering Argentina and Uruguay, Rio Grande do Sul is also—along with Bahia and Minas Gerais—one of Brazil's most distinctive regions, with a climate, culture, and regional identity all its own. In fact, it is the only Brazilian state where a separatist movement exists. With some very good restaurants and topnotch cultural venues, the capital of Porto Alegre is a pleasant enough city, but much more interesting is the mountainous Serra Gaúcha region of the interior. Only two hours from Porto Alegre lie the picturesque resort towns of Gramado and Canela, renowned for their alpine landscapes and German immigrant traditions. Those in search of all-out wilderness can take to the hiking trails that crisscross the magnificent Parque Nacional de Aparados da Serra, famed for its series of spectacular canyons covered with lush vegetation and waterfalls. If you're on your way to or from Argentina or exploring all of the South from São Paulo on down, 3–5 days spent in this unique Brazilian region is definitely worth your while.

The fierce independence and distinctiveness of the modern-day Gaúcho (inhabitant of Rio Grande do Sul) dates back to the region's beginnings as a type of Wild West frontier zone between the Spanish and Portuguese colonial empires. As early as the 18th century, cowboys, traveling solo or in small bands, earned their livelihoods driving immense herds of cattle across the high plains of the Pampas. Fearless and ruthless, they also worked as mercenaries for powerful landowners and colonial governments, who were constantly seeking to expand and defend their territories. Products of miscegenation between Indians, Spanish and Portuguese settlers, and African slaves, these "Gaúchos"—a pejorative term of indigenous origin—and their rough and tough lifestyle became the stuff of legends, as synonymous with Rio Grande do Sul as cowboys in Texas.

The term Gaúchos became synonymous with all residents of Rio Grande do Sul during the Guerra dos Farrapos, a failed war of independence that pitted Rio Grande do Sul's free-thinking rebels against imperial forces. Lasting from 1835 to 1845, this series of battles constituted the longest war ever fought in the Americas. During this period, Rio Grande do Sul became a short-lived autonomous republic, and its citizens defiantly adopted the "Gaúcho" moniker that was used as in an insult by monarchists in Rio. Subsequently, the courageous Gaúcho became a symbol of the state as well as a popular hero who would subsequently be idealized in local literature, music, and art.

By the beginning of the 20th century, the Gaúcho way of life began disappearing. In the mid–late 19th century, German and Italian immigrants arrived en masse, establishing efficient farms and bustling towns. As the century wore on, cattle farming became increasingly industrialized and the Pampas was taken over by cash crops such as soybeans. Today, it is only in small towns deep in Rio Grande do Sul's hinterlands that Gaúcho traditions—performing in rodeos, wearing typical *bombachas* (baggy trousers), ponchos, felt hats, and leather boots—still persist. Yet other legacies, such as drinking bitter *erva maté* and eating *churrasco*—the wandering cowboys' staple of slow-cooked, charcoal-grilled cuts of beef seasoned with rock salt—are now part of the proud lifestyle of all Gaúchos.

PORTO ALEGRE

Stretched out along the eastern shore of the Rio Guaíba, the prosperous Gaúcho capital of 1.5 million resembles a somewhat generic European or North American city. Although it has a reputed gastronomic scene (particularly if you're a card-carrying carnivore) and a very dynamic cultural life for a Brazilian city its size, in terms of attractions, Porto Alegre is not really worth going out of your way to visit. However, as a departure point for excursions into the Serra Gaúcha, or as a stopover on a Brazil–Argentina journey, there is definitely a

THE SOUTH

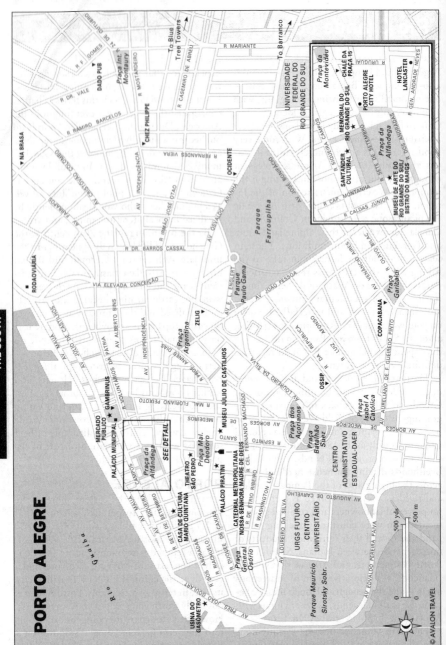

THE SOUTH

PORTO ALEGRE

Rio Guaíba

USINA DO GASÔMETRO ★

MERCADO PÚBLICO ★
GAMBRINUS ★
PALÁCIO MUNICIPAL ★
Praça da Alfândega
SEE DETAIL

CASA DE CULTURA MARIO QUINTANA ★
THEATRO SÃO PEDRO ★
Praça Mal. Deodoro
PALÁCIO PIRATINI ★
CATEDRAL METROPOLITANA NOSSA SENHORA MADRE DE DEUS ★
Praça General Osório

MEDEIROS
MUSEU JULIO DE CASTILHOS ★
Praça Argentine
ZELIG ▶
Parque Paulo Gama

DADO PUB ★
Praça Int. Montauny
CHEZ PHILIPPE ★
OCIDENTE
NA BRASA ▶
RODOVIÁRIA ■

Parque Farroupilha

OSSIP ★
Praça Isabel A Católica
Praça dos Açorianos
Praça Batalhão Suez
CENTRO ADMINISTRATIVO ESTADUAL-DAER

COPACABANA
Praça Garibaldi

URGS FUTURO CENTRO UNIVERSITÁRIO

Parque Maurício Sirotsky Sobr.

UNIVERSIDADE FEDERAL DO RIO GRANDE DO SUL

To Blue Tree Towers
To Barranco

R MARIANTE
R E GOMES DE OUTUBRO
R DR. VALE
R RAMIRO BARCELOS
AV FARROUPILHA
R CRISTOVÃO COLOMBO
AV INDEPENDÊNCIA
R CASEMIRO DE ABREU
R MOSTARDEIRO
R FERNANDES VIERA
AV JOSÉ BONIFÁCIO
AV OSVALDO ARANHA
R IRMÃO JOSÉ OTÃO
R DR. BARROS CASSAL
VIA ELEVADA CONCEIÇÃO
AV ALBERTO BINS
AV INDEPENDÊNCIA
R VOLUNTÁRIOS DA PÁTRIA
R PROF. ANNES DIAS
R MAL. FLORIANO PEIXOTO
SANTO
DE
R BORGES
R ESPIRITO
AV LOUREIRO DA SILVA
AV JOÃO PESSOA
AV E L ENGLERT
AV VENÂNCIO AIRES
R JOÃO BLAC
R GEN. LIMA E SILVA
R LUIZ AFONSO
R DA REPÚBLICA
AV AURELIANO DE F GUEIREDO PINTO
DE MEDEIROS
R CEL. FERNANDO MACHADO
R DE ETHIO RIBEIRO
R WASHINGTON LUIZ
AV AUGUSTO DE CARVELHO
AV EDVALDO PEREIRA PAIVA
R PRES. JOÃO GOULART
R DOS ANDRADAS
R RIACHUELO
R DUQUE DE CAXIAS
AV SIQUEIRA
AV SETE DE SETEMBRO
AV MAUÁ
AV JOÃO DE CASTILHOS
AV JOÃO DE CASTILHOS
AV MAUÁ
CAMPOS

0   500 m
0   500 yds

SEE DETAIL

Praça da Montevidéu
CHALÉ DA PRAÇA 15
MEMORIAL DO RIO GRANDE DO SUL ★
SANTANDER CULTURAL ★
MUSEU DE ARTE DO RIO GRANDE DO SUL/ BISTRO DO MARGS ★
Praça da Alfândega
PORTO ALEGRE CITY HOTEL ●
HOTEL LANCASTER ★

R URUGUAI
R GEN. ANDRADE NEVES
R SIQUEIRA CAMPOS
R CAP. MONTANHA
R CALDAS JUNIOR
R DOS ANDRADAS
R SETE DE SETEMBRO

© AVALON TRAVEL

day's worth of sights and activities to keep you agreeably occupied.

Founded in 1755, "Porto"—as it is fondly referred to by its inhabitants—began life as a Portuguese outpost whose mission was to defend the Brazilian colony from its Spanish rivals to the south. It wasn't until the 19th century, when the commercialization of Rio Grande do Sul's vast cattle herds became a serious business, that the city began to thrive. Soaring demand in exports led to the development of a port on the giant Lagoa dos Patos, a deep freshwater lagoon fed by the Rio Guaíba. Throughout the 20th century, the city grew at breakneck pace, becoming the largest and the most economically important of Brazil's southern capitals. More recently, as host of events such as the controversial World Social Forum—which has provided a counterpoint to the First World elitism of the World Economic Forum—and the distinguished Bienal de Artes do Mercosul, Porto Alegre has proved itself to be a progressive and cosmopolitan place.

Sights

Most of Porto Alegre's most interesting attractions are located within the old city center (Centro) next to the river, a compact region easily explored on foot. Although a late-20th-century building boom resulted in a sea of nondescript office towers and busy thoroughfares, a significant number of grand neoclassical buildings happily survived the wrecking ball. Walking around the Centro is safe enough during the day, but be careful at night (take a cab) when businesses close and the area becomes more deserted.

MERCADO PÚBLICO

The city's geographic and symbolic heart is the Mercado Público (Praça XV de Novembro, Centro, tel. 51/3289-1756, www.portoalegre.rs.gov.br/mercadopublico, 8:30 A.M.–7 P.M. Mon.–Fri., 8:30 A.M.–6 P.M. Sat.). Completed in 1869, this rather grand, biscuit-colored neoclassical building has an interesting (and very well-organized) array of stalls proffering everything from food, wine,

cookware, and herbs to handicrafts from all over the state. Be sure to check out the stalls selling religious objects used in Afro-Brazilian Umbanda rituals as well as the umpteen varieties of Gaúchos' bitter and beloved *erva maté*. For refreshments, do like the locals and stop for an icy *chopp* at **Naval** or an icy *suco* or *sorvete* at **Banca 40,** which has been selling homemade ice creams for over 50 years. The Café do Mercado (Loja 103, tel. 51/3029-2490) serves up one of the best espressos in the city. The market is a favorite gathering place during happy hour (bars and restaurants stay open later than the markets' stalls).

PRAÇA DA ALFÂNDEGA

From the market and Praça XV, a labyrinth of pedestrian streets running parallel to Rua Sete de Setembro lead uphill towards the Praça da Alfândega, where you'll immediately notice a trio of very handsome neoclassical buildings. Built in the late 1920s, **Santander Cultural** (Rua Sete de Setembro 1028, tel. 51/3287-5500, www.santandercultural.com.br, 10 A.M.–7 P.M. Mon.–Fri., 11 A.M.–7 P.M. Sat.–Sun.) is a former bank headquarters that was purchased by the Spanish Banco de Santander and converted into a great cultural center. Aside from a main-floor gallery that hosts important exhibits of national art and features a cinema, the Café do Cofre is a charming café located inside the former safe.

The palatial turn-of-the-20th-century Correios (post office) building now houses the **Memorial do Rio Grande do Sul** (Rua Sete de Setembro 1020, Centro, tel. 51/3225-8490, www.memorial.rs.gov.br, 10 A.M.–6 P.M. Tues.–Sun., free). If you want to bone up on Rio Grande do Sul's history, this is the place to peruse illustrated timelines and learn about famous Gaúchos (among them President Getúlio Vargas and beloved diva Elis Regina) via videos, photos, and documents. Occupying the former customs house is the **Museu de Arte do Rio Grande do Sul (MARGS)** (Av. Sete de Setembro 1010, Centro, tel. 51/3227-2311, www.margs.org.br, 10 A.M.–7 P.M. Tues.–Sun., free), with a mildly interesting collection of works by Brazilian and Gaúcho artists as well as frequent temporary exhibits and a rooftop café with great views of the city.

PRAÇA MARECHAL DEODORO

Heading south from Praça da Alfândega, uphill along Rua General Câmara, you'll come to the Praça Marechal Deodoro (also known as Praça da Matriz), which is also surrounded by several elegant buildings. On one corner is the city's prestigious **Theatro São Pedro** (Praça Marechal Deodoro, tel. 51/3227-5100, www.teatrosaopedro.com.br, noon–6 P.M. Mon.–Fri.). Hiding behind its neoclassical facade is an enchanting baroque interior that can only be visited by reservation, unless you're attending a performance. However, the lovely Café do Theatro is open to the public 4–9 P.M. (Wed.–Fri.) and 6–9 P.M. (Sat.–Sun.).

Flanked by Roman columns, the rather imperious **Palácio Piratini** (Praça Marechal Deodoro, tel. 51/3227-4100, 9–11 A.M. and 2–5 P.M. Mon.–Fri.) is home to the state governor's palace. At half-hour intervals guided tours are given. Quite intriguing are the painted panels illustrating a local folk tale whose protagonists include a slave, his sadistic master, and the Virgin Mary. The two statues guarding the main doors (representing Industry and Agriculture), are by Paul Landowski, the French sculptor responsible for Rio de Janeiro's iconic statue of Cristo Redentor.

Despite its Italian Renaissance facade, the **Catedral Metropolitana Nossa Senhora Madre de Deus** (Rua Duque de Caxias, 1047, Centro, tel. 51/3228-6001, 7 A.M.–noon and 2–7 P.M. daily) is a strictly 20th-century affair. On the same street, in an attractive 19th-century private residence, the **Museu Júlio de Castilhos** (Rua Duque de Caxias, 1231, Centro, 10 A.M.–7 P.M. Tues.–Fri., 2–5 P.M. Sat.–Sun., R$4) showcases an eccentric collection of historical paraphernalia. Highlights range from a quintet of cannons used by Garibaldi's troops during the Guerra dos Farrapos to the size 16 boots of a local giant who measured 2.18 meters (7.2 feet) who was a circus attraction in the 1920s.

Entertainment and Events
NIGHTLIFE

The most happening neighborhood in terms of nightlife is Moinhos de Vento, where there are lots of hot spots on Rua Fernando Gomes and Rua Padre Chagas. Younger, artier student types frequent the more alternative bars in Cidade Baixa—surrounding the Parque Farroupilha—where you can often hear live music being played. The city's progressive politics have spilled over into the arts and music scene, making Porto a surprisingly vanguard place. There is a fairly active gay and lesbian community—for listings of events or *festas,* log on to www.nuances.com.br.

The eternally fashionable **Dado Pub** (Rua Fernando Gomes 80, Moinhos do Vento 3395, www.dadobier.com.br, 11:30 A.M.– 2:30 P.M. and 6 P.M.–close Mon.–Fri., 11:30 A.M.–4 P.M. and 6 P.M.–close Sat.–Sun.) began life as a riff on an Irish pub, but became so popular that it expanded into a bar/restaurant with a vast menu that accompanies the home-brewed ale. Although its location ensures an upscale clientele, the bar's pubby flavor keeps it down-to-earth.

Extremely eclectic **Ocidente** (Av. Osvaldo Aranha 960, Bom Fim, tel. 51/3312-1347, www.ocidente.com.br, noon–2:30 P.M. Mon., noon–2:30 P.M. and 9 P.M.–3 A.M. Tues.–Thurs., noon–2:30 P.M. and 9:30 P.M.–6 A.M. Fri., noon–3:30 P.M. and 10 P.M.–6 A.M. Sat., cover R$10–20) is a nocturnal institution. During the week, performances here range from indie rock bands to "electronic" literary salons. On weekends, things get groovy as DJs take charge of thematic *festas* such as the Best and Worst of the '80s. Friday attracts a gay and lesbian crowd. Meanwhile, vegetarians can drop by for the lactovegetarian lunch buffet served during the week.

Tiny **Ossip** (Rua da República 666, Cidade Baixa, tel. 51/3224-2422, 7 P.M.–close daily, no cover) is a favorite haunt of Alegrenses from all walks of life who meet to chat late into the night. For nibbling, there are appetizing *petiscos* and sandwiches on ciabatta bread that go down nicely with local beers such as Polar and La Brunette. Nearby, **Zelig** (Rua Sarmento Leite 1086, Cidade Baixa, tel. 51/3286-5612, www.zelig.com.br, 7:30 onwards Tues.–Sat., cover R$5–7) is another favorite laid-back hangout. It's famed for having the best *chopp* in town, Coruja. For something to nosh, try the spinach yogurt pancakes or the open-faced sandwiches on dark rye with toppings such as German sausage, quails' egg, eggplant caviar, and cherry tomatoes. On weekends, there's a varied mix of live music and DJ-spun tunes.

CULTURAL CENTERS

Before being transformed into one the city's foremost cultural centers, the elegant pale pink **Casa de Cultura Mario Quintana** (Rua dos Andradas 736, Centro, tel. 51/3221-7147, www.ccmq.rs.gov.br, 9 A.M.–9 P.M. Tues.–Fri., noon–9 P.M. Sat.–Sun.) was the formerly grand, belle epoque Hotel Majestic, where renowned local poet Mario Quintana resided for some time (his room is now a museum). Today, the building houses various art exhibition spaces along with a bookshop, candy store, theater, three arthouse cinemas, and—for fans of MPB—the recently opened Elis Regina gallery with photos and recordings of this great singer.

In the ground floor courtyard, the lovely **Café Catavento** serves snacks and light meals. At 7 P.M. Wednesday–Friday, there are always free musical performances. Meanwhile, on the 7th floor, the **Café Concerto Mario Quintana** offers sweeping views over the Rio Guaíba as well as lunch, brunch, afternoon tea, and happy hour specials accompanied by live jazz and classical music.

Porto Alegre's other major cultural hub is the **Usina do Gasômetro** (Av. Presidente João Goulart 551, tel. 51/3212-5979, www.porto alegre.rs.gov.br/smc, 9 A.M.–9 P.M. Tues.–Sun.). Built in the 1920s, on the banks of the Rio Guaíba, the towering 110-meter (350-foot) red-brick smokestack of this former coal-fire power plant has become a city landmark. The renovated interior has various galleries, a cinema, theater, and bookstore, along with a café featuring one of the finest views of Porto's legendary sunsets over the river.

FESTIVALS AND EVENTS

From mid-January to mid-February, Porto Alegre sizzles during **Porto Verão Alegre** (www.portoveraoalegre.com.br), a summer festival of dance, music, and theatrical performance held throughout the city for next-to-nothing prices. In late September, **Semana Farroupilha** commemorates September 20, 1835, which marked the beginning of the Revolução Farroupilha. This popular uprising led to the declaration of the short-lived Republic of Rio Grande do Sul as well as a 10-year war of independence (the Guerra dos Farrapos) against imperial troops. The weeklong festivities include parades, traditional Gaúcho music and dancing and, of course, lots of food.

Shopping

At the **Mercado Público** (see *Sights*) you'll find regional wines, *erva maté* (as well as *cuias* and *bombas*), and local handicrafts. On Sunday, 9 A.M.–5 P.M., head to the centrally located **Parque Farroupilha** (also known as Redenção) for the very lively **Brique de Redenção,** a Sunday flea market featuring a great mix of art, antiques, and regional handicrafts. For sophisticated shopping, check out the fashionable boutiques in Porto's chicest mall, **Moinhos Shopping** (Rua Olavo Barreto 36, Moinhos do Vento, tel. 51/3346-6013, www.moinhos shopping.com.br, 10 A.M.–10 P.M. Mon.–Sat., 3–8 P.M. Sun.), which also boasts a fancy food court and a cineplex.

Accommodations

There is no shortage of decent budget accommodations options in Centro (which tends to be a bit abandoned at night). Posher options can be found in upscale Moinhos de Vento, home to the city's fashionable restaurant and bar scene. Since Porto attracts far more business travelers than actual tourists, hotels offer weekend discounts. The quasi Continental climate ensures that most hotels have heating in the winter and air-conditioning in the summer.

After viewing the gleaming art deco exterior of the **Hotel Lancaster** (Travessa Engenheiro

THE SOUTH

Acelino de Carvalho 67, tel. 51/3224-4737, www.hotel-lancaster-poa.com.br, R$80–85d), the rather bland modern interior comes as a bit of a letdown. The rooms are pleasant enough, though basic and rather small. Still, the hotel is good value and is well located in the midst of Porto Alegre's commercial hub.

Opened in 1951, the interior of **Porto Alegre City Hotel** (Rua Dr. José Montaury 20, tel. 51/3212-5488, www.cityhotel.com.br, R$185–208 d) hasn't changed that much in half a century. The marble lobby, decked out in dark wood and red plush chairs, exudes a certain retro elegance, as do the wood-paneled fitness room and billiards. The remodeled rooms, while hardly luxurious, retain an old-fashioned aura that is hard to come by in Porto Alegre's mostly modern chain hotels. Speaking of modern chains, if you feel like a little luxury without forking out too many *reais*, the **Blue Tree Towers** (Av. Colonel Lucas de Oliveira 995, tel. 51/3019-8000, www.bluetree.com.br, R$248–286) is a very sleek and attractive high end choice in the pretty residential *bairro* of Bela Vista. Rooms are tastefully appointed and very comfortable. Amenities include an Internet café and access to a high-end local gym.

Food

Vegetarians beware! In Rio Grande do Sul's capital, *churrasco* is an art form and the city's *churrascarias* are temples where carnivores fervently worship the most succulent cuts of red meat on the planet. Although you'll find *churrascarias* and *rodízios* throughout Brazil, the best (not to mention the cheapest) are in Porto Alegre. Although all *churrascarias* serve salads and vegetable dishes on the side, if meat really isn't your thing, there are also some fine eateries representing Rio Grande do Sul's major immigrant groups: Italians, Germans, and Poles. Centro has many options during the day, but at night, when the area closes down, you'll have to search for sustenance in surrounding regions such as swanky Moinhos de Vento.

CAFÉS AND SNACKS

Located in the Museu de Arte do Rio Grande

ERVA MATÉ

Throughout Rio Grande do Sul, you'll notice the common sight of locals using a silver straw to sip what appears to be a hot potion from a rather primitive-looking polished gourd. The straw is known as a *bomba*, the gourd is a *cuia*, and the bitter, pungent, and ultimately quite addictive drink that is enjoyed solo or passed around among companions is a strong tea known as *chimarrão*, made from the ground-up leaves of a small local evergreen tree known as *erva maté*. Guarani Indians were the first to partake of this medicinal drink – whose benefits are similar to those proffered by Japanese green tea – and it subsequently caught on with roving Gaúchos on the Pampas.

Both in rural areas and in cities, today Gaúchos of all ages and backgrounds regularly indulge in this favorite beverage, in which leaves are brewed in hot (not boiling) water, in the *cuia* itself, and then passed around communally until the empty *cuia* needs to be refilled by the last slurper. This communal ritual continues – slowly, so that the tea and accompanying conversation and/or meditation can be richly savored – until there is no flavor left in the leaves. Etiquette requires the person who prepares the *erva maté* to take the first sip (usually a bit more bitter) and then pass it around until all the *chimarrão* has been consumed. Adding sugar or sweetener is definitely against the rules.

do Sul (MARGS), the **Bistrô do Margs** (Praça da Alfândega, tel. 51/3018-1380, 11 A.M.–9 P.M. Mon.–Fri., 11 A.M.–7 P.M. Sat.–Sun., R$15–25) is conveniently situated if you're sightseeing. You can choose to sit in the warmly minimalist dining room or on the outside terrace, which is ideal for people-watching. The nicely priced menu offers simple but creatively prepared salads, fish, and meat dishes as well as enticing desserts. This is a popular happy hour meeting point, especially on Thursday and Friday when live music is played.

CHURRASCO

Coming to Porto Alegre and not indulging in the sublime melt-in-your-mouth cuts of Pampas-raised beef is akin to traveling to Japan and never partaking in sushi. Flaunting the convention of swank *superchurrascarias* with their vast cavernous dining rooms, **Portoalegrense** (Av. Pará 913, São Geraldo, tel. 51/3343-2767, www.churrascariaportoalegrense.com.br, 11:30 A.M.–2 P.M. and 7:30–11 P.M. Mon.–Sat., closed in Feb., R$12–20) is a simple, traditional family-run restaurant in a large, rustically furnished house where the focus is all on the meat. Delicious *picanha* (rump cut), *costelas* (spare ribs), and *costeletas de carneiro* (lamb chops) are particularly reputed.

Equally traditional is **(Barranco** (Av. Protásio Alves 1578, Petrópolis, tel. 51/3331-6172, www.churrascariabarranco.com.br, 11 A.M.–2 A.M. daily, R$20–30). In a given month, some 15,000 local carnivores devour 8,000 tons of prime cuts of beef, pork, and lamb. The best seats are those scattered beneath a shady canopy of jacarandas that is particularly alluring during the city's scorching summer months. For dessert, try the delicious *pudim de laranja* (orange pudding). Those craving variety should head to **Na Brasa** (Rua Ramiro Barcelos 389, Floresta, tel. 51/3225-2205, 11:30 A.M.–3 P.M. and 7 P.M.–midnight Mon.–Fri., 11:30 A.M.–midnight Sat.–Sun., R$35 pp), where both classic and more exotic cuts—ostrich, quail, and *javali* (wild boar)—are served *rodízio* style. The salad buffet features a range of fine cheeses, sun-dried tomatoes, and artichoke hearts along with traditional regional side dishes.

TRADITIONAL

Located in the Mercado Público, **Gambrinus** (Av. Borges de Medeiros 85, tel. 51/3226-6914, www.mercadopublico.com.br, 11 A.M.–9 P.M. Mon.–Fri., 11 A.M.–4 P.M. Sat., 11 A.M.–3 P.M. Sun., R$20–35) has been around for 120 years—making it the oldest restaurant in the city and a culinary and cultural institution. The tavern-like decor with its tiled walls, soaring ceilings, and old-fashioned wooden tables is simple and welcoming. The forte is fish and seafood, and daily specials range from *bacalhau* (salted cod) to grilled eel with shrimp sauce. Since there is no dessert, head across to Banca 40 for *sorvete*. Another restaurant with a charming setting is **Chalé da Praça XV** (Praça XV de Novembro, tel. 51/3225-2667, 11 A.M.–midnight Mon.–Fri., 11 A.M.–10 P.M. Sat.–Sun., R$15–30), located in a historic art nouveau-ish building whose steel structure was sent over in pieces from England. This is a good place to try regional specialties or for a happy hour drink and snack.

INTERNATIONAL

Occupying a very attractive early-20th-century house, **(Chez Philippe** (Av. Independência 1005, Independência, tel. 51/3312-5333, www.chezphilippe.com.br, 7:30–11:30 P.M. Mon.–Sat., R$35–55) is owned and operated by one of Brazil's foremost French chefs. Hailing from Provence, Philippe Remondeau has cooking in his DNA—most of his family have been cooks and pâtissiers, and he does them proud with daring inventions that draw on local ingredients and flavors. Foie gras in a pastry shell with watercress, ginger and *jabuticaba* sauce, *namorado* fish with dried mushroom crumble, and passion fruit *mille-feuille* with white chocolate sauce are examples of his unusual creations. If you can't decide on one dish, splurge for the *menu confiança,* a five-course mini banquet for R$100. Reservations are recommended.

Serving authentic southern Italian cuisine, **Copacabana** (Praça Garibaldi 2, Cidade Baixa, tel. 51/3221-4616, www.rest copacabana.com.br, 11:30 A.M.–3 P.M. and 7 P.M.–1 A.M. Tues.–Sun., R$20–35) has been around for three family generations. The faithful diners who clustered around its wooden tables in their student days still swear by the homemade pastas and delicious veal and lamb dishes served in this cozy trattoria.

Information

The **municipal tourist office** (tel. 0800/517-686) has detailed information as well as free

THE SOUTH

city maps. You'll find branches at the airport (7 A.M.–midnight), at the *rodoviária* (7 A.M.–10 P.M. daily), the Mercado Público (9 A.M.–6 P.M. Mon.–Sat.), and the Usina de Gasômetro (10 A.M.–6 P.M. Tues.–Sun.). The municipal website, in Portuguese, is very thorough: www2.portoalegre.rs.gov.br/turismo. For English information, check out the less complete website of the Convention Bureau at www.poaconvention.com.br.

For information about Rio Grande do Sul, the **state tourist office** (tel. 51/3228-7377, www.turismo.rs.gov.br) also has branches at the airport (7 A.M.–7 P.M. daily) and the bus station (7 A.M.–7 P.M. daily).

Services

For money changing and ATMs, the greatest concentration of banks is in Centro, around along Rua dos Andreada and Avenida Senador Salgado Filho near Praça da Alfândega. The post office is at Rua Siqueira Campos 1100. For Internet access, you'll find lots of cyber cafés along Rua dos Andradas, or else brave the lineups for the free **Telecenter** in the Mercado Público.

In an emergency dial **192** for an ambulance, **190** for the police, and **193** for the fire department. For medical treatment, try the **Hospital Pronto Socorro** (Av. Osvaldo Aranha, tel. 51/3289-7999). **Farmácia PanVel** is a pharmacy chain that has a 24-hour delivery service (tel. 51/3218-9000).

Getting There and Around

Porto Alegre is directly connected to Rio, São Paulo, Curitiba and Florianópolis by air. There are also flights to Buenos Aires, Santiago, and Montevideo. The swish, ultramodern **Aeroporto Internacional Salgado Filho** (Av. Severo Dulius 90010, tel. 51/3358-2048) is only 8 kilometers (5 miles) northeast of the city center. Taking a prepaid taxi into town will cost around R$30. There is also a *executivo* minibus airport shuttle service for only R$4. An easy alternative (if you don't have much luggage and are staying in Centro) is the Metrô, which will take you to the Mercado Municipal.

Buses from around the state and country arrive at the rather forlorn **Estação Rodoviária de Porto Alegre** (Largo Vespasiano Veppo, tel. 51/3210-0101). For schedules and prices of bus services throughout Rio Grande do Sul, log on to www.rodoviaria-poa.com.br. Although the bus station is within walking distance of the Centro, the fact that it's surrounded by highways and bypasses means it's easier (and safer) to take a taxi, bus, or the Metrô to your destination.

Although getting around central Porto Alegre is easily done on foot, the city also has an extensive municipal bus service as well as a limited one-line **Metrô** (tel. 51/2129-8000, www.trensurb.gov.br, 5 A.M.–11 P.M. daily)—although quite limited, it is a convenient option for travel between the airport, *rodoviária,* and the Mercado Público.

Roads in Porto Alegre and throughout Rio Grande do Sul are well maintained. Should you want to rent a car, **Avis** (www.avis.com.br) has offices at the airport (tel. 51/3371-4514) and at Avenida Ceará 444, Navegantes (tel. 51/3342-0400), and **Hertz** (www.hertz.com.br) is at the airport (tel. 51/3358-2472) and at Avenida Souza Reis 326, São João (tel. 51/3337-7755).

CITY TOURS

For city tours, the **Linha Turismo** (Travessa do Carmo 84, Cidade Baixa, tel. 51/3212-3464, 9 A.M., 10:30 A.M., 1:30 P.M., 3 P.M., and 4:30 P.M. Tues.–Sun., R$8–10) is a double-decker bus that visits 17 tourist sites. To view Porto from the Rio Guaíba, two boats—the **Cisne Branco** (departing from the port at Av. Mauá 1050, tel. 51/3224-5222, www.barcocisne branco.com.br, Tues.–Sun., R$15), and the more rustic **Noiva do Caí** (departing from the Usina do Gasômetro, tel. 51/3211-5222, R$7), offer several outings a day, lasting an hour.

SERRA GAÚCHA

North of Porto Alegre a series of hills begins, which gradually turns into a mountain range known as the Serra Gaúcha. In the 19th century, the region was settled by two waves of immigrants. In the early part of the century, Germans arrived and built farming

gazing out over the Cânion de Itaimbezinho in the Serra Gaúcha

communities in the lower hills. A few decades later, Italians from the wine-growing regions of Veneto and Trento went farther west, where they found the region's climate ideal for vine cultivation. To the east, the mountains rise, acquiring an Alpine allure that has earned comparisons with Switzerland. Indeed, the twin mountain resort towns of chic Gramado and more laid-back Canela seem much more European than Brazilian. With verdant peaks and wildflower-dotted valleys, Bavarian architecture, and restaurants serving fondues and apple strudel, they are a favorite "exotic" travel destination of Brazilian tourists. In summer, moderate temperatures and icy waterfalls offer cool respite from the heat. Meanwhile, if you visit in winter, aside from hot chocolate and crackling fireplaces, you're likely to encounter snow. Although these two periods are considered high season (and are consequently quite crowded), the region is stunning year-round. If you have a little extra time, head even farther north (and off the beaten track) to the **Parque Nacional de Aparados da Serra,** home of the spectacular Cânion de Itaimbezinho.

Gramado

With its rustic stone and wood chalets set against rugged green mountains, Gramado seems ripped from an outtake of *The Sound of Music.* From fondue restaurants and *chocolaterias* to the chic boutiques and luxury lodges that wouldn't be out of place in Gstaad, this Swiss connection is played to the hilt (sometimes to excess—such as during Christmas when the whole town is lit up like a kitschy theme park). You might find this Alpine aspect twee or charming, but it attracts Brazilian tourists in droves (two million of them per year at last count), making it somewhat of a mob scene. For this reason, avoid the winter (when artificial snowstorms are the rage) and summer, and try to visit in the spring (Oct.–Nov.), when tourism is down and massive clumps of hydrangeas are in full bloom.

SIGHTS

Aside from the pretty town itself, Gramado has a few natural attractions. At the end of Rua Bela Vista, the quaint little **Parque Knorr** (9 a.m.–6 p.m. daily) offers magnificent views of the Vale do Quilombo, a dramatic valley that runs along the road between Gramado and Canela. Around 1.5 kilometers (1 mile) from the center of town, in the midst of a wooden park, the **Lago Negro** is a pretty artificial lake ringed by hydrangeas where you can pedal around in swan-shaped boats. Exploring the mountains on your own from Gramado is difficult without a car. However, if you want to take a guided walking tour, contact the **Refúgio Família Sperry** (tel. 54/3504-1649, www.refugiosperry.com.br), an organic farm surrounded by native forest and waterfalls, located in the Vale de Quilombo. The knowledgeable English-speaking owner takes individuals and small groups on nature walks (advance reservations necessary). A three-hour guided walk costs R$35 per person. **Black Bear Adventure** (Rua Bruno Ernesto Riegel 713, tel. 54/3286-1497, www.blackbear adventure.com.br) offers easy hikes and horseback excursions as well as more radical sports activities such as rafting and rappelling. Rappelling and rafting half-day outings cost R$65 and half-day multi-activity, adventure excursions cost R$90.

ENTERTAINMENT AND EVENTS

During the second week in August, Gramado takes on an air of Sundance or Cannes as celebs, paparazzi, and cinephiles flock to the **Festival de Cinema** (www.festivaldegramado.net), one of the oldest and most prestigious film festivals in Latin America.

ACCOMMODATIONS

Gramado tends to be on the pricy side, especially during high season (summer and winter), although off-season, and during the week, you can find some good discounts. Prices below are for low- to mid-season.

Located in a leafy, upscale neighborhood only slightly removed the bustling center, **Recanto da Lua** (Rua Antônio Accorsi 322, Bavária, tel. 54/3286-2463, www.pousadare cantodalua.com.br, R$90–150 d) is a very good bargain. The rooms inside the large A-frame lodge are pleasant and cozy (standard rooms

are in the attic with sloping ceilings) with lots of wood and farmhouse accents. Breakfasts are copious, and the living room has a roaring fireplace. In the same neighborhood, **Pousada Vovó Carolina** (Av. das Hortências 677, Bavária, tel. 54/3286-2679, www.vovo carolina.com.br, R$165–216 d) is slightly more plush. Except for the master suites, the sedately decorated rooms are a bit small, but possess a nice retro flavor. The lounge has an enormous fireplace and there is also a thermally heated pool. The breakfasts are very copious with lots of home-baked goodies.

Perched graciously on the shore of Lago Negro, the **C Estalagem St. Hubertus** (Rua da Carrière 974, Planalto, tel. 54/3286-1273, www.sthubertus.com, R$230–405 d) is a stately white palace of a hotel surrounded by thick forest and splashes of hydrangeas. Old World elegance holds sway in the luxurious apartments featuring floral prints, fine linens, and refined accents. Although standard rooms are a bit cramped, you can definitely stretch your legs out in the fireplace lounge decorated with stuffed pheasants or the glassed-in salon overlooking the lake where afternoon tea is served. Extras range from a thermal pool to swan-shaped boats in which you can pedal around the lake.

Varanda das Bromélias (Rua Alarisch Schulz 158, Planalto, tel. 54/3286-6653, www.varandadasbromelias.com.br, R$440–710 d) boasts a privileged location amidst a private woodland on the town's highest summit. Billing itself as the region's first boutique hotel, it is a sophisticated departure from the faux Alpine chalets that are the norm. Clean lines, natural wood, lots of glass, contemporary art, and warm accents mingle, creating a unique and quite romantic atmosphere. Each of the exquisitely furnished apartments has its own fireplace and veranda. Aside from a glassed-in pool, there is a spa and fitness center. Service is extremely attentive.

FOOD

In Gramado, you'll find no shortage of fondues (beef and cheese), fresh river trout, and chocolates. Although plenty of cheap fondue *rodízios* have sprung up, if you want the real cheesy deal, you'll have to pay for it. Often touted as one of Brazil's finest Swiss restaurants, **Belle du Valais** (Av. das Hortênsias 1432, tel. 54/3295-1146, www.belleduvalais .com.br, R$50–70) is decidedly romantic with lots of dark wood paneling, sparkling crystal, and a glowing fireplace. Aside from the ubiquitous fondues, try the *pierrade* (filet mignon and chicken cooked over volcanic rocks and served with various sauces) and the lamb with mint puree.

You'll find delicious fondues as well as traditional German dishes at **Gasthof Edelweiss** (Rua da Carrière 1119, Lago Negro, tel. 54/3286-1861, www.restauranteedelweiss.com.br, noon–3 P.M. and 7:30–11 P.M. daily, R$45–60), the godfather of Gramado's Alpine eateries. Signature dishes include rabbit in black beer sauce and honey-roasted pheasant. The wine cellar is so vast that it doubles as a dining room. A more unusual dining experience can be had at **La Caceria** (Av. Borges de Medeiros 3166, tel. 54/3295-1305, www.casadamontanha.com.br, 7 P.M.–midnight daily, R$50–70), located in the luxurious (and kitschy) Hotel Casa da Montanha. The dining room decorated with hunting rifles and stuffed animals heads is the perfect setting for tucking into game such as partridge, duck, wild boar, and even capybara. The wine list features an impressive array of regional vintages. Reservations are essential.

For something lighter and more contemporary (and more affordable), head to **○ O Lugar** (Rua Prefeito Waldemar Frederico Weber 1815, Mato Queimado, tel. 54/3295-1305, 7:30 P.M.–midnight Thurs.–Fri., noon–midnight Sat., noon–4 P.M. Sun., R$25–40), an airy and very attractive bistro designed using rough-hewn stone, wood, and glass. The prix fixe menu (an appetizer, main course, and dessert) is prepared daily by chef Carol Heckmann, based on the freshest ingredients at hand.

For snacks, light meals, coffee, or a glass of wine head to the cafés along the Rua Coberta, a covered passageway leading from Avenida Borges de Medeiros and Rua Garibaldi, where you'll find lots of inviting restaurants and cafés, open from morning to midnight, among them **Armazém 31** (tel. 54/3286-6988), **Petit Café** (tel. 54/3286-4793), and **Bistrô Brillat** (tel. 54/3286-6900), where you can get a mean bowl of soup.

INFORMATION

The helpful **tourist office** (Av. Borges de Medeiros 1674, tel. 54/3286-1475, www .gramadosite.com, 9 A.M.–6 P.M. Mon.–Thurs., 9 A.M.–8 P.M. Fri.–Sun.) has maps as well as hotel and restaurant listings.

GETTING THERE

From the *rodoviária* (Av. Borges de Medeiros 2100, tel. 54/3286-1302), frequent buses arrive and depart from Porto Alegre, Caxias do Sul, and Canela. **Citral** (tel. 51/3228-5128, www .citral.tur.br) has bus service from Porto Alegre to Gramado and on to Canela. Gramado is 115 kilometers (72 miles) northeast of Porto Alegre. By car, follow the RS-020 to Taquara before turning onto the RS-115.

Canela

Canela is smaller, lower (in altitude), and less touristy (as well as more down-to-earth) than its ostentatious sister city, Gramado, 10 kilometers (6 miles) away. Although the town itself is not as picturesque as Gramado, it serves as a better base for adventure sports enthusiasts as it is much closer to two natural parks: Parque Ferradura and Parque Estadual do Caracol. If you don't have your own wheels, **Vida Livre** (Av. Oswaldo Aranha 450, tel. 54/3282-1518, www.vidalivreturismo.com.br) offers half-day tours to the parks as well as full-day trips to the magnificent canyons of the Parque Nacional de Aparados da Serra.

PARQUE ESTADUAL DO CARACOL

Canela's main draw is the Parque Estadual do Caracol (Estrada do Caracol Km 9, tel. 54/3278-3035, 8:30 A.M.–5:30 P.M. daily, R$8). Within its borders is the stunning 131-meter (430-foot) Cascata do Caracol, the tallest waterfall in Rio Grande do Sul. You can gaze on this spectacle from a lookout point, or else climb 927 very steep stairs (which takes about 40 minutes and isn't for the faint of heart or breath) to the top of the falls. Less exhausting are the hiking trails that weave through the park's wooded landscape. If you don't have a car, you can get to the park on the "Caracol Circular" bus that leaves from Canela's *rodoviária.*

PARQUE DA FERRADURA AND PARQUE DO PINHEIRO GROSSO

Another 6 kilometers (4 miles) down the road brings you to the Parque da Ferradura (Estrada do Caracol Km 15, tel. 54/9972-8666, 9 A.M.–5 P.M. daily, R$7), a natural park that offers incredible views into the immense *ferradura*-shaped (horseshoe-shaped) canyon formed by the Rio Caí. A challenging 2-kilometer (1-mile) trail leads down to the river.

Closer to town, the small Parque do Pinheiro Grosso (Estrada do Caracol Km 5, 9 A.M.–5 P.M. daily, free) shelters an immense *araucária,* believed to be at least 700 years old.

SPORTS AND RECREATION

Canela has become an eco-adventure destination with plenty of activities for nature lovers with athletic inclinations. **Atitude Ecologia e Turismo** (Av. Osvaldo Aranha 391, Loja 16, tel. 54/3282-6305, www.atitude.tur.br) offers reasonably priced excursions that include trekking and/or rappelling. Half-day outings cost R$40–65 per person depending on the activities involved. Daredevils can get their adrenaline fix indulging in pendulum jumping—i.e., throwing themselves off the 30-meter-high (98-foot-high) Ponte Passo do Infirmo (which spans the Rio Cará waterfall) and swinging wildly in the air.

ACCOMMODATIONS

From basic rooms to luxury suites, accommodations in Canela offer better value for your money than in trendy (often overpriced) Gramado. A block away from the main *praça,* **Pousada Canela** (Rua Ernesto Dorneles 333, tel. 54/3282-8410, http://pousada canela.com.br, R$90) is a spanking new apartment-style *pousada* whose basic, compact rooms

are bright and attractive. Two larger suites are ideal for couples with kids.

Shaded by *araucária* pines and overlooking a small lake, the **Grande Hotel Canela** (Rua Getúlio Vargas 300, tel. 54/3282-1285, www.grandehotel.com.br, R$140–160) dates back to 1916. Although hardly grand, the comfortable yet rather sedate rooms—in the main building or in individual chalets—are enhanced by old-fashioned fixtures. The common areas are more atmospheric. Aside from a coffee bar, fireplace lounge, and piano room, there is a nice pool, a sauna, and Jacuzzi.

Located in a beautiful old summer residence dating back to the 1930s, **(Quinta dos Marques** (Rua Gravataí 200, Santa Teresinha, tel. 54/3282-9812, www.quintadosmarques, R$215–450 d) is one of Canela's most charming accommodation options. Each of the 13 seductively cozy rooms is individually decorated (the more lavish ones include hot tubs and fireplaces). Custom-made bath products, afternoon tea, a pretty pool, and a "Zen space" in the woods where you can meditate in a Japanese hot tub are soothing extras.

FOOD

Le Monde (Av. Oswaldo Aranha 391, Lojas 9–10, Galeria Florida, tel. 54/3031-1300, noon–3 P.M. and 8:30 P.M.–midnight Fri.–Sat., noon–4 P.M. Sun.; 7–midnight Wed., noon–3 P.M. and 7 P.M.–midnight Thurs.–Sat., noon–3 P.M. Sun. in July, R$50–60) is a tiny little bistro with an open kitchen that is always busy. There's no fixed menu; instead the inspired daily specials—partridge-stuffed tortellini or panko crusted sole with Provençal vegetables—are written on the blackboard. Cozy **Café Canela** (Rua Altenor T. de Souza 15, tel. 54/3282-0062, www.cafecanela.com.br, R$20–30) is proud of its exclusive culinary creations: soups and salads served in hollowed-out round loaves of bread as well as pastas and risottos served in carved-out blocks of cheese. There are also crêpes, salads, and steaks.

Canela is famed for its apple strudel. Aside from traditional German cuisine such as *kessler* and sauerkraut, **Strudelhaus** (Rua Baden Powell

246, tel. 54/3282-9562, noon–3 P.M. and 7:30–11 P.M. Tues.–Sat., noon–4 P.M. Sun., R\$15–25) serves up a tasty version with ice cream. One of the finest recipes to be had in the center of town is at **Confeitaria Martha** (Av. Júlio de Castilhos 151, tel. 54/3282-4190), a bakery that also makes good sandwiches. However, the best of all is served at **C Castelinha Caracol** (Estrada do Caracol Km 3, tel. 54/3278-3208, 9 A.M.–1 P.M. and 2:20–5:40 P.M. daily, R\$4). Built by family of German immigrants, this historic early-20th-century house was constructed entirely from native *araucária* pine, without using a single nail. It's the perfect place to savor the family recipe for strudel alongside homemade fruit jams and waffles.

INFORMATION

The **tourist office** (Largo da Fama, tel. 54/3282-2200, 8 A.M.–7 P.M. daily) is in the center of town. You can also log on to these informative sites (in Portuguese): www.canelars.gov.br and www.canelaturismo.com.br.

GETTING THERE

During the day a Canela/Gramado bus circulates between the two towns at regular 20-minute intervals. From Porto Alegre, **Citral** (tel. 51/3228-5128, www.citral.tur.br) operates buses to Canela. By car, from Porto Alegre, follow the RS-020.

C PARQUE NACIONAL DE APARADOS DA SERRA

Some 40 kilometers (25 miles) northeast from Canela, straddling Rio Grande do Sul's frontier with Santa Catarina, lies the Parque Nacional de Aparados da Serra (tel. 54/3251-1277, 9 A.M.–5 P.M. Wed.–Sun., R\$6), a magnificent natural park that encompasses some 60 canyons as well as breathtaking waterfalls, lush subtropical vegetation, and one of the only remaining *araucária* forests in Brazil. By far, the most dramatic highlight of the park is the 6-kilometer-long (4-mile-long) **Cânion de Itaimbezinho,** which plunges to vertiginous depths of 720 meters (2,360 feet) and boasts two waterfalls. From the visitors center at the main park entrance, 18

kilometers (11 miles) along the RS-429 from the town of Cambará do Sul, two trails allow you to explore the canyon. The easiest 30-minute path leads to the canyon's rim. A second, more difficult route, descending into the canyon itself, requires a guide and trekking gear.

A more recent extension of the park's area into Santa Catarina—known as the **Parque Nacional da Serra Geral** (tel. 54/3504-5389, 8 A.M.–6 P.M. daily, free)—features the gigantic **Cânion da Fortaleza** as well as the impressive **Malacara** and **Churriado** canyons. By car—a tricky 22-kilometer (14-mile) drive over the CS-012, a winding dirt road that is a continuation of Cambará do Sul's main avenue—you can get to the park's entrance, close to the edge of Cânion da Fortaleza. From here, a 30-minute trail leads to a lookout point where, on clear days, you can see the Atlantic Ocean in the distance. From Fortaleza, visiting the other two canyons involves an eight-hour, 22-kilometer (14-mile) strenuous hike (there-and-back) through the forest for which a guide (and some physical preparation) is necessary.

The best time to visit the region is during the winter (although temperatures are chilly) when visibility is best due to the lack of mist, or in the spring (Oct.–Nov.) in order to see wild blossoms. The months of April, May, and September can be very rainy. Call Cambará do Sul's tourist office or check its website (see *Information*) for weather conditions. It is prohibited to swim in the park's river and waterfalls. Although the visitors center at Parque Nacional da Serra Geral is equipped with a tourist office, maps, and a restaurant, there are no guides at either of the parks—to hire one, contact the **Associação de Condutores Locais de Eco-Turismo (Acontur)** (tel. 54/3251-1320), whose headquarters is in Cambará do Sul's Centro Cultural.

Accommodations and Food

The best base for visiting the park is the small cattle town of **Cambará do Sul,** surrounded by flat plains that give no hint of the breathtaking topography nearby. Accommodations in Cámbara do Sul are generally basic, but rustically atmospheric. One of the nicer and more central choices is **Pousada Paraíso** (Rua Antônio Raupp 558, tel. 54/3251-1352, www.paraiso pousada.com.br, R$60–80 d), a family-style place with small, well-appointed rooms and delicious home-baked goods for breakfast. Also close to the center, but located on a farm, is **Pousada Fazenda Pindorama** (Rua Padre João Francisco Ritter, tel. 54/3251-1225, www.pousada pindorama.com.br, R$50–60 pp). The somewhat ramshackle rooms (some nicer than others), in a main building and individual chalets, are simple and come equipped with fireplaces.

Well-heeled ecotourists will prefer the luxuries offered by the (**** **Parador Casa da Montanha** (Fazenda Camarinhas Km 9.5, tel. 54/3504-5302, www.paradorcasada montanha.com.br, R$352 d), set amidst a rolling landscape between Cambará and the entrance to the Parque Nacional de Aparados da Serra. Accommodations consist of chic thermal tents engineered to battle the elements and seduce your senses. To keep you warm and relaxed, there are saunas and Jacuzzis. The hotel organizes trips to the park as well as hiking, horseback-riding, and mountain-bike excursions. Prices include all meals at the *pousada*'s charming restaurant, starting off with a hearty *café colonial* at breakfast. Lunch and dinner feature typical regional dishes, such as *carreteiro de charque* (seasoned cured beef with rice), roasted lamb, and *doce de abóbora* (candied pumpkin). On weekends, noon–2:30 P.M., the restaurant serves a delicious regional buffet that can be enjoyed by nonguests. If you stay for more than one night, special packages are available. There is, however, a two-night minimum on weekends and a three-night minimum during holidays and July.

Eating options are pretty basic as well, although you can get some good hearty local cooking. With its rickety wooden structure resembling a set from a Hollywood Western, (**** **Restaurante Galpão Costaneira** (Rua Dona Úrsula 1069, tel. 54/3251-1005, 11:30 A.M.–3 P.M. and 7:30–10 P.M. daily, R$15–25) is heavy on atmosphere. Inside, the walls are decorated with Gaúcho artifacts, and wooden tables are covered with a collage of handwritten notes left by satisfied customers. The home-cooking doesn't disappoint—there's a copious buffet of regional dishes along with sizzling grilled meats served at your table with the traditional accompaniments of melted cheese and sausages. On weekends, Gaúcho music is performed live.

Information

In Cambará, the **tourist office** (Rua Adail Valim 39, Praça São José, tel. 54/3251-1320, www.cambaraonline.com.br, 8 A.M.–6 P.M. daily) is in the center of town in a historic wooden house. Aside from providing maps and information about the town, park, and surrounding region, the staff can help you find guides or join an organized excursion.

Getting There

Since there is no bus service, if you don't have a car, getting to the Parque Nacional de Aparados da Serra or Parque da Serra Geral requires hiring a **taxi** (tel. 54/3251-1320) or minivan to take you to the entrances and pick you up again. **Canyon Turismo** (Av. Getúlio Vargas 1098, tel. 54/3251-1027, www.canyon turismo.com) offers a wide array of hiking and horseback excursions (lasting from half a day to three days) as well as rappelling and quadricycle outings. Several tour companies based in Gramado and Canela also offer full-day excursions to the parks.

Getting to Cambará by bus is not that easy. From Porto Alegre, 193 kilometers (120 miles) away, **Citral** (tel. 51/3228-5128, www .citral.tur.br) has one daily bus that departs at 6 A.M. and takes five hours—due to numerous stops—to get to Cambará's **rodoviária** (Rua Dona Úrsula 840, tel. 54/3251-1567). Otherwise, from Porto Alegre—as well as from Gramado and Canela—you have to go to the town of **São Francisco da Paula**, 60 kilometers (37 miles) from Cambará, and change buses from there.

If you're driving from Porto Alegre, take the BR-166 to Taquara and then follow the RS-020, straight north. Beware that many of the roads around Cambará are not paved and can be particularly difficult to navigate when it rains.

MINAS GERAIS

Locked within steep mountain ranges and with no coast of its own, the vast state of Minas Gerais is a country unto itself. As a result, Mineiros have a different style and rhythm, with distinctive accents, expressions, and *jeitos,* or ways of doing things. They also have their own cuisine—*comida mineira*—with mouthwatering specialties ranging from *tutu à mineira* (thick and velvety bean puree) to *frango com molho pardo,* chicken cooked in a pungent sauce made from its own blood. Just as varied as its main courses are the infinite desserts and more than 4,000 regionally produced *cachaças* (alcohol made from fermented sugarcane)—the best of which rival world class whiskeys.

Minas is a forward-looking place. An economic powerhouse, its dynamic capital, Belo Horizonte, is a cosmopolitan city with an impressively varied cultural scene and a diverse range of restaurants, bars, and nightlife options. "BH," as it is referred to by locals, is also surrounded by some great getaway destinations, including caves with prehistoric paintings, national parks—replete with canyons and waterfalls—and charismatic historical towns.

Minas first gained attention in the 1700s when Portuguese adventurers discovered that its lush mountains were abundantly stocked with precious stones, diamonds, and, especially, gold. It was during the subsequent gold rush that colonial mining towns such as Ouro Preto and Sabará sprung up amid the valleys of central Minas. Although these towns prospered, Portugal profited the most from the tremendous quantity of gold that was mined by African slaves and shipped off to Europe. Of

© MICHAEL SOMMERS

HIGHLIGHTS

◖ Nightlife in Belo Horizonte: With more bars per capita than any other Brazilian city, Belo Horizonte's *boteco* scene is in a class of its own (page 254).

◖ Igreja de São Francisco de Assis: Ouro Preto is stuffed with magnificent churches, but this jewel created by sculptor Aleijadinho and master painter Manuel da Costa Ataíde is Mineiro baroque at its finest (page 271).

◖ Basílica e Santuário do Bom Jesus de Matosinhos: Aleijadinho's final masterpiece, the *12 Prophets*, is the highlight of this monumental 18th-century sanctuary in the *cidade histórica* of Congonhas. It's one of the greatest and most moving examples of baroque art (page 280).

◖ Igreja Matriz de Santo Antônio: Perched upon a steep hill, Tiradentes's main church has a dazzling interior plastered with half a ton of pure gold (page 287).

◖ Caminho de Escravos: This road was cut into the mountains by thousands of African slaves; wandering along it offers striking views of colonial Diamantina and the surrounding peaks and valleys (page 298).

LOOK FOR ◖ TO FIND RECOMMENDED SIGHTS, ACTIVITIES, DINING, AND LODGING.

the gold that remained in Brazil, much was used to fund the building and decoration of a series of stunning baroque churches whose richness is unparalleled in the New World. Today, while firmly rooted in the present, these *cidades históricas* (historic cities)—Sabará, Ouro Preto, Mariana, São João del Rei, Tiradentes, Congonhas, and Diamantina—with their impressively preserved architecture and traditions, continue to have one foot in the past. Claiming some of the most magnificent baroque and colonial architecture in the Americas, all of them offer glimpses into Brazil's rich past as boom-and-bust frontier towns that once possessed the largest deposits of gold and diamonds on the planet. Although some (Ouro Preto, Tiradentes, and Diamantina) have weathered

the centuries more successfully (and with more charm) than others (Sabará, Congonhas, and São João del Rei), all of them offer a wealth of artistic and cultural diversions as well as exposure to authentic Mineiro life. It is this exciting juxtaposition and overlapping of past and present, baroque and modern, that makes Minas Gerais such a fascinating destination.

PLANNING YOUR TIME

With the exception of Diamantina (six hours north of Belo Horizonte), all of Minas's colonial treasures and a good many of its natural attractions are close together in southern Minas, within easy striking distance of Belo Horizonte (2–4 hours by bus or car). São João del Rei and Tiradentes, the *cidades históricas* farthest

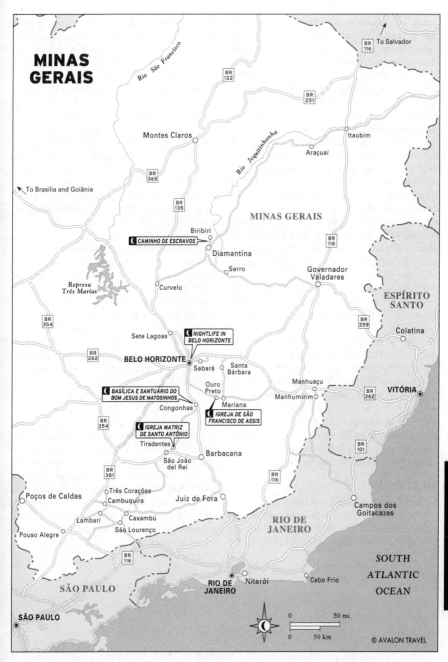

MINAS GERAIS

Rio São Francisco

BR 122

BR 251

To Salvador
BR 116

Montes Claros

Itaobim

Araçuaí

Rio Jequitinhonha

To Brasília and Goiânia

BR 365

MINAS GERAIS

BR 135

Biribiri

CAMINHO DE ESCRAVOS

Diamantina

BR 116

Serro

Governador
Valadares

*Represa
Três Marias*

Curvelo

ESPÍRITO
SANTO

BR 354

Colatina

Sete Lagoas

NIGHTLIFE IN
BELO HORIZONTE

BR 259

BR 262

BELO HORIZONTE

Sabará

Santa
Bárbara

Manhuaçu

VITÓRIA

Ouro
Preto

Manhumirim

BR 262

BASÍLICA E SANTUÁRIO DO
BOM JESUS DE MATOSINHOS

Mariana

Congonhas

IGREJA DE SÃO
FRANCISCO DE ASSIS

BR 354

IGREJA MATRIZ
DE SANTO ANTÔNIO

BR 101

Tiradentes

Barbacana

São João
del Rei

BR 381

BR 116

Três Corações

Poços de Caldas

Cambuquira

Juiz de Fora

Campos dos
Goitacazes

Lambari

Caxambú

São Lourenço

Pouso Alegre

RIO DE
JANEIRO

BR 116

SOUTH

SÃO PAULO

RIO DE
JANEIRO

Niterói

Cabo Frio

ATLANTIC

OCEAN

SÃO PAULO

0   50 mi

0   50 km

© AVALON TRAVEL

MINAS GERAIS

south, are equidistant from Belo Horizonte and Rio de Janeiro. Roads are in top condition and buses run frequently, making traveling between the various destinations easy.

If you have only three days, focus on either Ouro Preto and Mariana (14 kilometers/9 miles apart) or São João del Rei and Tiradentes (12 kilometers/7.5 miles apart): Either of these duos will easily satiate your appetite for colonial history, baroque magnificence, steep cobblestoned hills, and mouthwatering Mineiro cuisine. Five days means you can enjoy all four towns (although you won't have too much time for relaxation), or else choose a pair and then, for a contrast, spend a day or two experiencing the modern pleasures offered by Belo Horizonte. A week to 10 days allows you to hit all of the above cities, with the addition of Congonhas, and—if you're very fast, although it's a shame to rush—Diamantina.

Minas can get hot (not to mention crowded) in the summer months. Although the historic towns tend to be more lively in the summer, accommodations (particularly in Ouro Preto and Tiradentes) fill up quickly and are more expensive, particularly during Carnaval and Semana Santa. July coincides with winter vacation, which means high prices, but also misty mornings, chilly nights, and roaring fireplaces—all of which can be enticing if you bring warm clothing. In August and September, you'll find the climate dry and the historic cities delightfully tranquil. October is usually when the rainy season starts, lasting for four months.

HISTORY

Minas Gerais was an untamed and unexplored region of thickly forested mountains and plains until the early 18th century. At that time, *bandeirantes*—groups of explorers

from São Paulo who journeyed into Brazil's hinterlands in search of precious stones and indigenous people to enslave—ventured into the area north of São Paulo and west of Rio. It wasn't long before they discovered great chunks of glittery rock in the region's riverbeds. In no time at all, one of the world's biggest gold rushes had commenced.

It is estimated that more than half of the world's gold supply—not to mention a serious portion of its diamonds—was hidden in the rivers and hills of the area that came to be known as Minas Gerais. As eager fortune seekers poured in from the rest of Brazil and Portugal, hundreds and thousands of slaves from neighboring Bahia as well as Africa were brought in to work the mines. Over the next century, forests were decimated, hills were hollowed out, and a series of colonial towns sprang up, whose development was spurred on by rampant migration and the wealth derived from of gold and diamonds. Among those looking to get in on the action were a host of religious orders, who settled in these towns and sparked the construction of a series of magnificent churches with interiors lavishly plastered in gold. Their design and decoration was characterized by a unique and highly expressive artistic style that subsequently came to be known as *barroco mineiro,* or Minas baroque.

By the end of the 1800s, the gold rush had petered out, leaving the gold towns more or less preserved in time, whence their monikers as *cidades históricas* (historic cities). New metals, namely iron, steel, and manganese, replaced gold in importance and carried Minas into the industrial age. Today, although gold and diamonds are still to be found, Minas's current prosperity is linked to its manufacturing activities, most notably steel and automobiles.

Belo Horizonte

Although it is one of Brazil's largest (2.6 million people) and most important cities, at first glance, Belo Horizonte—or "BH" (pronounced "BAY ah-GAH")—doesn't seem very alluring. The planned metropolis, with its scores of nondescript high-rises and industrial outskirts that reflect its economic clout, doesn't offer much in the way of history or outright charm. Built in the late 1800s, it was hoped that BH would become a progressive new capital that could replace Ouro Preto, whose fortunes had dwindled after the gold rush. Despite its relative lack of history, Belo Horizonte is nonetheless quite a compelling city with a varied cultural and culinary scene and a sizzling nightlife that easily offers a couple of days' diversion. Although colonial architecture is nonexistent, fans of modernism are in for a treat: the city is replete with interesting houses and buildings from the 1950s (and quite a few deco gems from the preceding decades). Moreover, in the 1940s and early '50s, Belo Horizonte served as a three-dimensional drafting board for an ambitious young architect by the name of Oscar Niemeyer. His earliest and still surprisingly vanguard buildings can be seen in the city center as well as in the well-to-do neighborhood of Pampulha.

Belo Horizonte is also a useful base for exploring the surrounding region. Located in a deep valley ringed by the majestic Serra do Espinhaço mountain range—which explains the name Belo Horizonte (Beautiful Horizon)—the city is close to a wealth of natural attractions that can be visited in under an hour. It is also near three of Minas's most impressive colonial towns: Sabará (only 30 minutes away), Ouro Preto, and Mariana (2 hours), as well as Congonhas (1 hour away), the site of master baroque sculptor Aleijadinho's final—and arguably greatest—works.

SIGHTS

Although BH itself is quite sprawling, almost all of its sights—with the exception of Oscar Niemeyer's Pampulha Complex—are located in either Centro or the leafy upscale neighborhood of Savassi and are easily reached by foot. As a planned city, Belo Horizonte boasts wide streets and avenues lined with a canopy of trees, which make it very agreeable to stroll around. Be warned, however, that it is also quite hilly. Walking around Belo is quite safe by day and even in the early evening. However, at night, be cautious around Centro, especially away from the busier streets.

Centro

Belo Horizonte's bustling Centro features an eclectic mixture of 20th-century architecture. The main drag is tree-lined Avenida Afonso Pena, which begins at the *rodoviária* (main bus station) and cuts straight through the center of the city, passing several interesting sites.

A five-minute walk down Afonso Pena from the bus station brings you to Praça Sete de Setembro. The center of this busy plaza is punctuated by a thrusting obelisk, commemorating Brazilian independence, which locals affectionately refer to as the *pirulito* (lollipop). If you turn left down palm-lined Avenida Amazonas, a five-minute walk will bring you to the Praça Rui Barbosa. Better known as Praça da Estação (Station Plaza), this rather grand square is dominated by a palatial neoclassical train station, built in 1922, that has been painted a rather startling canary yellow.

MUSEU DE ARTES E OFÍCIOS

Located within the handsomely renovated (and still operational) train station is Belo Horizonte's most interesting museum, the Museu de Artes e Ofícios (Estação Central, Centro, tel. 31/3248-8600, www.mao.org.br, noon–7 P.M. Tues. and Thurs.–Fri., noon–9 P.M. Wed., 11 A.M.–5 P.M. Sat.–Sun., R$4, free Sat.). A fascinating array of objects and interactive multimedia displays trace the history of traditional Brazilian trades, crafts, and professions. These include gold and diamond miners, stevedores, street

MINAS GERAIS

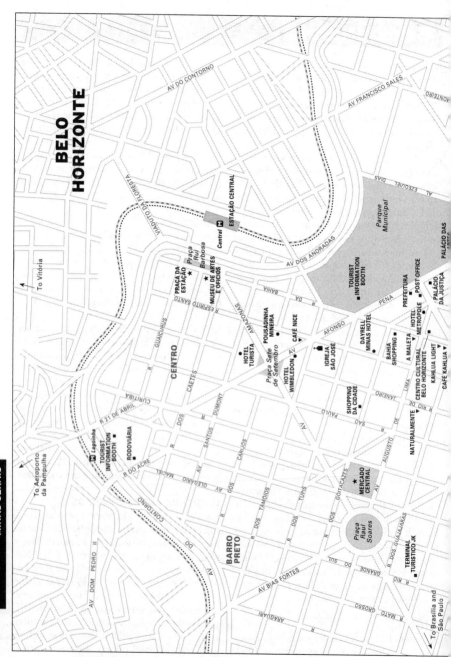

BELO HORIZONTE

MINAS GERAIS

© AVALON TRAVEL

photographers, and a diverse array of vendors, from colonial slave women who sold sweets and fruits from wooden trays perched upon their heads to today's urban hawkers of coffee, sugar-cane juice, and pirated CDs. Although the descriptions accompanying each profession are densely written and a little didactic (English text accompanies the Portuguese), some of the details are quite enlightening. Who knew, for instance, that slaves who worked the gold mines in Minas had it better than their counterparts who toiled in the sugar plantations of the Northeast? This was because the mining bosses gave the slaves a quota of gold they had to mine: any surplus nuggets they found were theirs to keep, and were used to purchase their freedom. Some of the objects on display are also quite astonishing. Particularly shocking is the enormous metal scale that was used to weigh slaves (the slaves were actually placed upon the scale as if they were slabs of meat).

PARQUE MUNICIPAL

Parque Municipal (Avenida Afonso Pena) is a sweeping green oasis that succeeds in conjuring up a mildly tropical version of the *fin de siècle* public parks of Paris upon which it was modeled. Aside from 50 varieties of century-old trees, a lake, fountains, rose gardens and an "orchidarium," this lovely park also shelters Belo Horizonte's most important arts and cultural center: the **Palácio das Artes** (Av. Afonso Pena 1537, Centro, tel. 31/3236-7400, www.palaciodasartes.com.br). Designed by Oscar Niemeyer and inaugurated in 1971, this gleaming white building houses two theaters, a cinema, art galleries, a bookstore, a café, and a large boutique that sells traditional handicrafts from all over Minas.

PRAÇA DA LIBERDADE

From the Palácio das Artes, continue up Rua Sergipe for another five minutes to the Praça da Liberdade. The beautifully landscaped gardens of this large plaza—with its fountains, bandstands, and Greco-Roman sculptures—were modeled after those at the Palace of Versailles, and a distinctly European elegance reigns. At night there are often free theatrical or musical performances. The park is surrounded by impressive buildings that range in style from grand neoclassical palaces (the **Palácio do Governo** and **Secretária de Estado**) to the fluid modernism of the **Biblioteca Pública** and the fantastically curvy **Edifício Niemeyer,** a striking residential building designed by Oscar himself and completed in 1955.

PRAÇA DA SAVASSI

From the Praça da Liberdade, a 10-minute stroll along lively Avenida Cristovão Colombo will bring you to Praça Diogo de Vasconcelos, known by locals as Praça da Savassi. Savassi was the name of a popular bakery that existed here in the 1940s, at a time when the square began attracting BH's high society to its bars and cafés. Today, this vibrant intersection of various avenues continues to attract a sophisticated and eclectic crowd. It is the nerve center for the area known as Savassi that roughly incorporates the neighborhoods of Funcionários, Santo Antônio, and Lourdes: upscale areas with lots of bookstores and funky boutiques, lively bars, and a wide range of varied and highly reputed restaurants.

Beyond the Centro

If you have extra time to spare in Belo Horizonte, there are a couple of worthwhile sights located beyond the limits of Avenida Contorno (which rings the central core of the city).

MUSEU HISTÓRICO ABÍLIO BARRETO

South of Savassi, in the pretty suburban neighborhood of Cidade Jardim, is the Museu Histórico Abílio Barreto (Av. Prudente de Morais 202, Cidade Jardim, tel. 31/3277-8573, www.pbh.gove.br/cultura/museu-abilio-barreto.htm, 10 A.M.–5 P.M. Tues.–Sun., till 9 P.M. Thurs., free). This renovated colonial farmhouse surrounded by greenery is all that's left of the settlement of Arraial Curral del Rey, which preceded the construction of BH. Inside, photographs and artifacts recount the development of the Mineiro capital. The photos in particular—tracing BH's incredible transformation from sleepy mid-19th-century village to the booming early-21st-century commercial hub increasingly full of high-rises—are enlightening. Sunday mornings, there are live music performances, and Tuesday nights feature jazz. The lovely Café Museu serves lunch and dinner as well as coffee and snacks.

PARQUE DAS MANGABEIRAS

For a dose of nature, head to Parque das Mangabeiras (Av. José Patrocínio Pontes, tel. 31/3277-9697, www.pbh.gov.br/mangabeiras, 8 A.M.–6 P.M. Tues.–Sun.), a 230-hectare (570-acre) expanse of native vegetation, only partially tamed by noted Brazilian landscape architect Roberto Burle Marx. Carpeting the steep hills of the Serra do Curral, the park is easily reached by taking the "Aparecida/Mangabeiras" (no. 4103) municipal bus from Avenida Afonso Pena (between Avenidas Amazonas and Tamóios) in Centro. The views of the city are really quite stunning: The best vantage point is from the Mirante da Mata, a lookout that's a 20-minute walk form the entrance. Park maps are available at the visitors kiosk.

Pampulha

In 1940—20 years before he became one of Brazil's most beloved presidents—Juscelino Kubitschek was elected mayor of Belo Horizonte. At the time, Belo was a provincial and conservative town. Kubitschek was a dreamer who believed that mayors shouldn't concern themselves just with "practical matters," but with "beauty" as well. One of his ambitions was to create an entirely new and modern neighborhood with facilities for leisure and recreation, surrounding a lake some 15 kilometers (9 miles) from Centro.

To carry out this task, he called upon the talents of a number of notable vanguard Brazilian artists. Among them were landscaper Roberto Burle Marx, the celebrated modernist painter Cândido Portinari, and a young architect, who had only recently graduated, by the name of Oscar Niemeyer. Excited by the proposal, Niemeyer traveled to Belo Horizonte from Rio to meet with Kubitschek and during dinner sketched plans on a napkin for the modernist constructions that would ultimately become the Pampulha neighborhood.

To get to Pampulha, take the number 2004 "Bandeirantes/Olhos d'Água" bus that leaves from the stop in front of the Hotel Financial, on Avenida Afonso Pena, in Centro. The trip takes about 20 minutes and the bus lets you off right in front of the Igreja de São Francisco de Assis.

IGREJA DE SÃO FRANCISCO DE ASSIS

The highlight of the Niemeyer's contributions to Pampulha is the Igreja de São Francisco de Assis (Av. Otacílio Negrão de Lima, Pampulha, tel. 31/3427-1644, 9 A.M.–5 P.M. Mon.–Sat., 9 A.M.–1 P.M. Sun., R$2). The stunning church with its sensual curves and bold lines was constructed between 1943 and 1945. Its exterior is covered with tiny blue ceramic tiles, the highlight of which is a mural depicting scenes from the life of Saint Francis of Assisi, painted by Portinari. Using tempera (color pigments mixed with egg yolk) Portinari also painted the somewhat Cubist altar panel of Saint Francis. The stray dog beside the patron saint of animals is apparently a veiled reference to Brazil's "mixed race" heritage of indigenous peoples, Africans, and Europeans. Further references to Saint Francis's love for animals are the striking blue-and-white tile mosaics of fish and birds. Portinari's talent is also visible in the 14 canvases decorating the walls that illustrate scenes from the Passion of Christ. The intensely vivid colors of the first paintings in the series contrast with the final canvases, in which pale, washed-out colors reflect the suffering of Christ.

Aside from a striking baptismal font featuring bronze panels with scenes from Genesis, there is also a none-too-private cylindrical confessional. Due to the church's fantastic acoustics, it has never been used. When the church was completed, conservative Belo Horizonte was shocked by its vanguard design and its subversive aesthetic. Many members of the city's elite called for a boycott. Moreover, the clergy refused to recognize this modernist temple because Niemeyer was not only an atheist but also a communist. It wasn't until 1959 that Belo Horizonte's bishop came around and marriages and baptisms could be celebrated in the church.

IATE TÊNIS CLUBE AND CASA DO BAILE

There is a trio of other Niemeyer buildings in Pampulha. Although they are of minor interest, two of them can be visited by taking a pleasant half-hour stroll around the bucolic Lagoa de Pampulha, which is lined with opulent mansions. The Iate Tênis Clube (Av. Otacílio Negrão da Lima 1350, tel. 31/3490-8400) was built in 1943 and is now a favorite hangout of Belo Horizonte's sail-hoisting, racket-swinging elite. Close by is the Casa do Baile (Av. Otacílio Negrão da Lima 750, tel. 31/3277-7433, 9 A.M.–7 P.M. Tues.–Sun.), whose curved lines mirror the outline of the lake. Originally a dance hall where couples could waltz the night away, today it houses a reference center for urban design and architecture.

MUSEU DE ARTE DE PAMPULHA

Hard to get to (if you're already in Pampulha, you'll need to take a car or taxi) due to its location on far shore of the *lagoa* is the Museu de Arte de Pampulha (Av. Otacílio Negrão da Lima 16585, tel. 31/3277-7953, 9 A.M.–7 P.M. Tues.–Sun.). Niemeyer's first Pampulha construction, this modern art museum reveals the strong of influence of his mentor, Le Corbusier. Originally built to be a glamorous casino, it served its original purpose for only three years before being closed down in 1946 when Brazil banned gambling houses. Today its art collection can only be viewed by making an appointment beforehand. The café and surrounding gardens designed by Burle Marx are quite lovely.

ENTERTAINMENT AND EVENTS
◖ Nightlife

In BH, a popular saying is *"não tem mares, tem bares"* ("we don't have beaches, we have bars"), which explains a lot about the way the natives spend their idle hours. At last count, the city boasted more than 8,000 *botecos,* or tavern-like bars. Indeed, Belo Horizontinos love nothing more than bar hopping in the pursuit of beer or *cachaça, petiscos* (delicious bar snacks), and conversation. Lots of no-nonsense inexpensive options exist in Centro, such as the simple sidewalk bars along Avenida Amazonas that stay open until the wee hours. For a bit more atmosphere and a more eclectic, albeit upscale mix of people, head to the happening more sophisticated *bairros* of Savassi, Lourdes, Funcionários, and Santo Antônio. It's also worthwhile to check out the funky residential neighborhood of Santa Tereza, popular with a bohemian crowd.

BARS

A Maleta (Edifício Maleta, Av. Augusto Lima 245, Centro, daily) is a once elegant building in the center of town that, despite being a little worse for wear, has a certain dilapidated charm. While people live on the upper floors, the bars and crowded secondhand bookstores on the main floor and the mezzanine have been a mainstay of BH's left-wing intelligentsia, along with the prerequisite marginals and eccentrics, since the swinging '60s and '70s. From the early afternoon onwards and late into the wee small hours, this is a really fun place to soak up a slice of bohemian BH of yore. Aside from ice-cold beer, there are plenty of cheap nibbles.

The ambiance of stylish **Café Tina** (Av. Cristovão Colombo 336, Savassi, tel. 31/3261-5068, 11:30 A.M.–4 P.M. Mon., 11:30 A.M.–close Tues.–Fri., 4 P.M.–close Sat.–Sun.) is conducive to romance. Tables are sprinkled throughout the intimate rooms of a turn-of-the-20th-century mansion as well as an adjacent courtyard where DJs spin mellow lounge music at night. The whimsical decor, by local artists, changes frequently. During the week, lunch is served. The 2-for-1 draft beer happy hour makes this a popular place to warm up for the night's activities.

Another fun place to kick off the evening is **Bar do Gibi** (Rua Claudio Manoel 329, Funcionários, tel. 31/9737-1290, 6 P.M.–1 A.M. Tues.–Sat.). Gibi, slang for "comic book" in Portuguese, is also the nickname of the owner, who is a major comic book fan. Cartoonish paintings decorate the colorful walls, and flying machines constructed by Gibi himself dangle from the ceilings. The crowd tends towards young and arty types who satisfy their hunger pains with *petiscos* such as grilled steak with sautéed *jiló* (a slightly bitter green vegetable).

One of Belo's most traditional watering holes is **Clube da Esquina** (Rua Sergipe 146, Funcionários, tel. 31/3222-5712, 11 A.M.–3 P.M. Mon., 11 A.M.–3 P.M. and 6 P.M.–2 A.M. Tues.–Fri., 11–2 A.M. Sat., 11 A.M.–11 P.M. Sun.), housed in a belle epoque building that was the site of Minas's first brewery. The place has been around for decades—as have some of its waiters—and is a little more sophisticated than BH's other *botecos*. On weekends, live *chorinho* and MPB (Brazilian popular music) is played. If you want something to nibble on try the *costelinha defumada com mandioca frita* (smoked pork ribs with fried manioc) or the *pasteis de angu,* a type of turnover made from corn flour. At lunchtime, there is a per kilo buffet of Mineiro dishes.

Mercearia Lili (Rua São João Evangelista 696, Santo Antônio, tel. 31/3296-1951, 7 P.M.–midnight Mon.–Fri., 11 A.M.–8 P.M. Sat.) is an actual *mercearia* (general store) that also happens to be a bar. It also happens to have been around since 1949, which means that the clientele is very loyal and the decor is authentically retro. Aside from having a warm neighborhood feel, this bar has a terrific menu with a wide range of hearty *caldos* (soups) and *tira-gostos* (bar snacks). Try the delicious *sacolão* vegetable soup and the justly famous *maça de peito,* melt-in-your-mouth tender chunks of beef grilled and served with sautéed onions and crispy fries.

The arching trees and quaint villas lining Rua Congonhas belie the fact that from Wednesday until the end of the week, this tranquil street becomes Santo Antônio's nocturnal nerve center. Despite a recent change in name from Bar do Lulu to **Butiquim Santo Antônio** (Rua Leopoldina 415, Santo Antônio, tel. 31/3297-3846, www.butiquimsantoantonio.com.br, 6 P.M.–close Tues.–Sat., artistic cover R$6–10), this sprawling bar on the corner of Rua Congonhas is an institution. The rustic house it occupies, considered a historic site, is laid-back and unassuming, obscuring the fact that for years it was a vanguard performance space. These days the diverse clientele comes to hear live rock and samba. Tasty *petiscos* include veal sausage with manioc as well as pizzas baked in a wood-burning oven, and you can sample some fine local *cachaças.*

Half a block away, **Oficina de Ideias** (Rua Congonhas 539, Santo Antônio, tel. 31/3296-5432, 7 P.M.–2 A.M. Mon.–Thurs., 7 P.M.–3 A.M. Fri.–Sat., cover R$5) makes for a nice romantic getaway with candlelit tables and a imaginative decorative scheme with musical instruments mingling with sculptures constructed from recycled materials. A garden offers the welcome presence of leafy mango and avocado trees. On weekends, DJs spin a mellow mix of soul, samba rock, and electronica. Sample the house cocktail, an unusual concoction of tequila, fruit, sorbet, and liqueur made from the native *pequi* fruit. Also in the vicinity is **Salsa Parrilha** (Rua São Domingos do Prata 453, Santo Antônio, tel. 31/3225-7758, 5 P.M.–2 A.M. Mon.–Fri., 11 A.M.–2 A.M. Sat.), a relaxing neighborhood bar with tables that spill out onto the sidewalk. The inviting interior is spacious and features an ever-changing roster of works by local artists. Among the many *petiscos,* try the baked Syrian bread stuffed with four fillings—choices include figs, gruyère, and shredded sun-dried beef. On Saturday afternoons, go for the all-you-can-eat *feijoada* buffet.

NIGHTCLUBS
Andaluz Bar Casa (Rua Congonhas 487, Santo Antônio, tel. 31/3296-5942, www.andaluzbarcasa.com.br, 10 P.M.–4 A.M. Fri.–Sat., cover R$10 before 11 P.M., R$20 after 11 P.M.) is a hip GLS (gay, lesbian, and "sympathizer") hangout with a bar, lounge, terrace, and dance floor animated by some of BH's most inspired DJs (who have a predilection for house). It's located in a rather nondescript villa that contrasts with the contemporary interior and the modern crowd. **A Obra** (Rua Rio Grande do Norte 168, Savassi, tel. 31/3215-8077,

www.aobra.com.br, 10 P.M.–close Wed.–Sat.) is an alternative art/music/dance space that was started by the members of As Meldas, a local rock band, who dreamed of a place where the city's various indie artist tribes could all hang out together. The absence of tables and chairs is conducive to this goal, as is the dance floor where fans of rock and other contemporary rhythms played by local and national bands can boogie on down together. A Obra also hosts performances, art exhibitions, and film screenings.

LIVE MUSIC

Café Com Letras (Rua Antônio de Albuquerque 781, Savassi, tel. 31/3224-9973, www.cafecomletras.com.br, noon–midnight Mon.–Thurs., noon–1 A.M. Fri.–Sat., 5–11 P.M. Sun., cover R$1 Thurs.–Fri., R$7 Sat.–Sun.) is a wonderfully hybrid space; an inspired mixture of bookstore, bar, café, gallery, and live music venue that in its 10-year existence has become a major cultural mecca. Located in a charming old house in the heart of Savassi, the café plays host to national and international musical performers with a predilection for DJs (Thursdays and Fridays) and jazz (weekends). While the 4,000 titles on the shelves might assuage your hunger for knowledge, the imaginative menu—whose daily offerings include the likes of french toast with smoked salmon and pumpkin carpaccio with goat cheese—will take care of your empty stomach.

Located on the second floor of an attractive 1940s villa, **Vinnil Cultura Bar** (Rua Inconfidentes 1068, Savassi, tel. 31/3261-7057, www.vinnil.com.br, 8 P.M.–2 A.M. Tues.–Wed., 9 P.M.–3 A.M. Thurs.–Sat., artistic cover R$5–15) is a combination bar and performance space that offers some of the best and most eclectic live music in the city. Styles range from jazz and blues to *chorinho,* samba, and MPB (Brazilian pop music). Wednesdays are reserved for local bands to unleash their new works. Shows begin at 9 P.M. on Tuesdays and Wednesdays, 10:30 P.M. on Thursdays, and 11 P.M. on the weekends. For a break, head to one of the two verandas, idyllically located at

tree level, and order a portion of *pastéis de angu,* polenta turnovers with a variety of fillings.

Performing Arts

Belo Horizonte has earned itself a reputation as an innovative center in terms of the performing arts, particularly with respect to theater and dance. When you're in town, check to see if any of the following groups are performing: **Grupo Corpo** (www.grupocorpo.com.br) is an internationally renowned troupe that fuses modern dance forms with Brazilian music and cultural influences. **Uakti** (www.uakti.com.br) is a musical group that creates highly original rhythms and melodies by using ingeniously designed instruments. The **Grupo Galpão** (www.grupogalpao.com.br) is a theatrical company that specializes in giving universal classics a new twist by adding elements of street theater. Instead of human actors, **Giramundo** (www.giramundo.org) relies on a company of more than 600 handcrafted puppets (not all of which appear at the same time) in the staging of its own works.

Festivals and Events

In keeping with its innovative arts scene, Belo Horizonte hosts several renowned festivals, including the **Festival Internacional de Teatro** (late July/early August), **Festival Internacional de Dança** (September–October), and the **Festival de Arte Negra** (mid–late November), which celebrates black arts and culture. For programs of events, check out the Belotur tourist office. Foodies and tipplers alike should definitely check out the **Comida di Buteco** festival (April–May, www.comidadibuteco.com), in which the city's top *botecos* compete against each other in an attempt to gauge who is capable of concocting the most lip-smacking *petiscos.* The most delicious part is the fact that the judges consist of the eating public and voting takes place in the bars.

SHOPPING
Shopping Malls

Belo Horizonte has scads of shopping centers. The most central of them all is **Shopping da**

Cidade (Rua Rio de Janeiro 910, Centro, tel. 31/3279-1200, www.shoppingcidade.com.br, 9 A.M.–10 P.M. Mon.–Sat., 10 A.M.–4 P.M. Sun.), with a wide variety of fairly low-priced shopping and eating options as well as a multiplex theater. **Shopping Patio Savassi** (Av. do Contorno 6061, Funcionários, tel. 31/3263-8521, www.patiosavassi.com, 10 A.M.–10 P.M. Mon.–Sat., 2–8 P.M. Sun.) is the most trendy of the city's *shoppings,* with upscale boutiques and eateries and a multiplex—all very tastefully done with lots of wide open spaces and skylights.

Boutiques

The Savassi area is home to most of Belo's funkiest and most avant-garde clothing and jewelry boutiques. In recent years, Belo Horizonte has earned a certain amount of national renown for nourishing the unique talents of a handful of young designers. Among their shared "Mineiro" traits is an appreciation of regional arts and crafts traditions, a tendency to make one-of-a-kind hand-sewn pieces, and an affection for embroidery and unusual pattern cutting. **Ronaldo Fraga** (Rua Raul Pompeia 264, São Pedro, tel. 31/3282-5372, www.ronaldofraga.com.br, 9 A.M.–7 P.M. Mon.–Fri., 10 A.M.–2 P.M. Sat.) is considered on of the most original and imaginative young fashion designers working in Brazil today. His whimsical boutique features a room with clothing from past collections available at discounts of up to 40 percent.

Graça Ottoni worked in business administration before deciding to market the hippie-chic women's clothing she sewed in her spare time. The designs sold at her flagship store, **Graça Ottoni** (Rua Santa Catarina 1471, Lourdes, tel. 31/3335-8366, www.gracaottoni.com.br, 9 A.M.–7 P.M. Mon.–Fri., 10 A.M.–2 P.M. Sat.), rely heavily on appliqué, embroidery, and patchwork. The cool but impeccably cut casual clothes made by designer Zepa for **Ave Maria** (Rua Padre Odorico 98, São Pedro, tel. 31/3281-2564, www.lojaavemaria.com.br, 9 A.M.–7 P.M. Mon.–Fri., 10 A.M.–2 P.M. Sat.) are cult favorites with young urban Brazilians of both sexes.

Markets

The nonprofit **Centro de Artesanato Mineiro** (CEART) is inside the Palácio das Artes (Av. Afonso Pena 1537, Centro, tel. 31/3236-9513, 9 A.M.–7 P.M. Mon.–Fri., 9 A.M.–2 P.M. Sat., 8 A.M.–1 P.M. Sun.) and offers a wide range of traditional Mineiro art and handicrafts from all over the state at surprisingly decent prices. The **Feira de Arte e Artesanato** is a big open-air market that spills out along Avenida Afonso Pena 8 A.M.–2 P.M. every Sunday. Although it purports to sell arts and handicrafts, interesting traditional samples of either are in short supply. More compelling is the people-watching factor.

A much more satisfying market experience can be had at the **Mercado Central** (Av. Augusto de Lima 744, Centro, tel. 31/3274-9434, www.mercadocentral.com.br, 7 A.M.–6 P.M. Mon.–Sat., 7 A.M.–1 P.M. Sun.). Terrifically well-organized, this covered market is the place to stock up on Mineiro foodstuff and cooking ware. Although it will be a challenge to carry them back on the plane, it's hard to resist the copper and soapstone pots and pans available at ridiculously low prices. Foodies will have a field day with the artistically arranged jars of multicolored hot peppers, preserved fruits, bricks of guava jelly and fudge-like *doce de leite,* and, of course, bottle after bottle of fine *cachaça.* **Ronaldo Licores e Cachaças** (Loja 141, tel. 31/3274-9674) is the best place to pick up a bottle. Its shelves stock more than 450 varieties of Mineiro *pinga* ("drop"—slang for *cachaça*), ranging from the most basic brands to the king of *cachaças,* Havana, an aged bottle of which goes for R$480. The staff is knowledgeable and invites you to sample the wares. If you're worried about carrying liquids through customs, opt for the *cachaça* jellies or truffles. After you've scoped out the produce, stop for an icy cold beer at one of the many traditional white tiled bars and sample the local market grub: grilled liver (or beef) accompanied by sautéed *jiló.*

SPORTS AND RECREATION
Soccer

Like most Brazilians, Belo Horizontinos take

their soccer very seriously. Minas's most famous stadium is the **Minerão** (Av. Abraão Carã 1001, Pampulha, tel. 31/3499-1154, www.ademg.mg.gov.br). The two major state rivals are Cruzeiro and Atlético (avoid games in which they face off). To get to the stadium from Centro, take the number 2004 municipal bus that passes in front of the Hotel Financial on Avenida Afonso Pena.

ACCOMMODATIONS

Belo Horizonte itself doesn't attract too many sightseers. It does, however, play host to a large number of business travelers. Consequently, unless there are a few major conventions taking place, accommodations are easy to find and you can negotiate some attractive rates. Although stylish boutique hotels are nonexistent, there are some nicely priced modern options as well as a few plush hotels where you can spoil yourself for far less than you'd be able to in other major Brazilian cities. Most hotels are conveniently situated in Centro or in Savassi.

R$50-100

Pousadinha Mineira (Rua Espírito Santo 604, Centro, tel. 31/3423-4105, R$16 pp) is a classic youth hostel with rock-bottom prices that are impossible to beat. Located in what must have been a somewhat posh old building on the corner of Avenida Afonso Pena, it features male and female dorm rooms and bathroom facilities, each on separate floors. Although everything is spic and span, rooms are also somewhat institutional. The place is a favorite with visiting athletes from all over Brazil. Late sleepers beware: Checkout time is 10 A.M.; breakfast is not included. **Hotel Turista** (Rua Rio de Janeiro 423, Centro, tel. 31/3273.7282, www.hotelturista.com, R$76–80 d) is a great bargain in the busy hub of Belo Horizonte's Centro. Located in a 1950s building that lends it an appealing retro edge, it offers clean and simple rooms with the advantage of some leafy trees peering in through the windows. The only drawback is the urban background noise.

R$100-200

Hotel Metrópole (Rua da Bahia 1023, Centro, tel. 31/3273-1544, www.hotelmetropolebh.com.br, R$125 d) was a little down in the mouth until a recent overhaul spruced up this art deco hotel. From the outside it looks like South Miami, but inside it's all about modern fixtures and comfortable rooms. **Hotel Wimbledon** (Av. Afonso Pena, Centro 772, tel. 31/3222-6160, www.wimbledon.com.br, R$135–190 d) has friendly staff, polished wood floors, and an otherwise pleasant but nondescript decorative scheme. Rooms are comfortable if a little tight, but have sizable bathrooms and cable TV. While quiet at night, during the day a fair amount of noise from the surrounding streets seems to trickle in.

Reminiscent of a 1970s issue of *House & Garden* are the sizable and plush rooms at the **Dayrell Minas Hotel** (Rua Espírito Santo 901, Centro, tel. 31/3248-1903, www.dayrell.com.br, R$168 d), featuring curved modular units and lots of taupe, ivory, and beige. A favorite with business travelers, the Dayrell is one of Belo's most traditional hotels. It is also a terrific bargain. Nice panoramic city views are available from the rooms; even more impressive are those from the small rooftop lounge and pool. **Hotel Caesarea** (Rua Bernardo Guimarães 925, Funcionários, tel. 31/3263-7000, www.boulevardhoteis.com.br, R$150 d) is also a pleasant option that feels more like moving into an apartment building than checking into a hotel. Offering spotless standard rooms, it is located on a quiet tree-shaded street in the Savassi area.

R$200-300

Sleek and modern, the **Royal Savassi Hotel** (Rua Alagoas 699, Savassi, tel. 31/3247-6999, www.royalsavassi.com.br, R$200 d) possesses highly attractive, large rooms with refined contemporary furnishings and mega TVs. Although there isn't a pool and the fitness room is closet-like, being in the heart of Savassi's bar and restaurant scene more than compensates.

The **Ouro Minas Palace Hotel** (Av. Cristiano Machado 4001, Ipiranga, tel. 31/3429-4001, www.ourominas.com.br, R$249 d) is Belo's only five-star option. Since it is 8 kilometers (5 miles) from Centro, in the neighborhood of Ipiranga, there are only two reasons for staying here: (relative) proximity to Confins international airport and the chance to treat yourself to luxury at affordable prices. Opting for a luxury double room will cost you a mere R$289, and splurging for the more decadent executive suites—with king-sized beds, custom-made German wallpaper, and baroque inspired furnishings—will set you back R$500. Other examples of available indulgences include a pillow menu, a swimming pool with a waterfall, special rooms designed for women (featuring beauty products and services), a 24-hour health club, and spa treatments.

FOOD

Belo Horizonte has a thriving restaurant scene and it's possible to eat very well without spending too much. In general, eateries in Centro—often self-service per kilo places that cater to the daily working crowd—tend to be more inexpensive, while options in and around Savassi are more varied, atmospheric, and upmarket.

Cafés and Snacks

Café Nice (Av. Afonso Pena 727, Centro, tel. 31/3222-6924, 7 A.M.–9 P.M. Mon.–Sat., 9 A.M.–1 P.M. Sun.) opened its doors in back in 1939. Step inside and you'll feel as if you've entered one of those coffee shops from an early '40s Warner Brothers film. When he was mayor of Belo Horizonte, Juscelino Kubitschek often scored his caffeine fix here; since then it has become *the* place for campaigning politicos to drop by. Otherwise, it has a faithful clientele who stop in for coffee and *pão de queijo* as well as juices and sandwiches. For a quick, light meal, try the omelettes, especially the *frango com palmito* (chicken with heart of palm).

Café Kahlua (Rua das Guajajaras 416, Centro, tel. 31/3222-5887, www.cafekahlua .com.br, 8 A.M.–9:30 P.M. Mon.–Fri., 9 A.M.–3 P.M. Sat.) is a sleek café with over 60 different kinds of coffee drinks as well as lip-smacking sandwiches and desserts. For a major pick-me-up, try *café bruna;* java mixed with *açaí* and *guaraná* (two natural energy boosters from the Amazon), liqueur, and milk. The crowd who frequents this place is urban and professional with an artsy edge. If you're in need of a bona-fide lunch, try the fresh per kilo buffet served around the corner at **Kahlua Light** (Rua da Bahia 1216, Centro, tel. 31/3214-2648, 11:30 A.M.–3:30 P.M. Mon.–Fri., R$12–17).

Savassi is full of cozy little bookstores with galleries and cafes, but one of the most charming and perennially popular is **Café da Travessa** (Avenida Getúlio Vargas, Rua Pernambuco 1286, tel. 31/3223-8092, www.cafe datravessa.com.br, 8 A.M.–11 P.M. Mon.–Fri., 8 A.M.–6 P.M. Sat., artistic cover R$1.50–10), which serves coffees, drinks, sweet and savory nibbles and executive lunches during the week. On a sunny day, lounging at the outdoor tables shaded by trees will make you feel as if you're on the Parisian Left Bank. The people-watching is just as compelling. There is always something happening at the Livraria da Travessa itself: book launches, poetry readings, and live performances of jazz or bossa nova, making it easy to while away an entire afternoon or evening.

Vegetarian

Mandala (Rua Fernandes Tourinho 390, Funcionários, tel. 31/3261-7056, 11:30 A.M.–5 P.M. Mon.–Fri., noon–5:30 P.M. Sat.–Sun., R$10–15) is a vegetarian fave that occupies a large, attractively decorated villa. Instead of the usual self-service per kilo buffets, the menu features healthy and tasty daily specials that can be savored in the laid-back ambiance. Saturday is the day to try the unorthodox vegetarian version of the classic *feijoada*. **Naturalmente** (Rua Rio de Janeiro 1197, Centro, tel. 31/3213-7029, 11 A.M.–3 P.M. Mon.–Fri., 1:30–3 P.M. Sat.–Sun., R$10–15) offers delicious and nutritious per kilo buffet lunches. Although the choices aren't endless, they are fresh, imaginative, and inexpensive. There are also some 20 fresh juice options. The unassuming yet modern interior is pleasantly soothing.

Contemporary

D'Artagnan (Rua Tomás Gonzaga 607, Lourdes, tel. 31/3295-7878, 7 P.M.–midnight

COMIDA MINEIRA

One of the biggest treats you'll experience in Minas is the local cooking – or *comida mineira*. As one of Brazil's few truly authentic cuisines, it is surprisingly varied and colorful (although not very spicy). Although a predilection for *costelinhas* (pork ribs), *linguiça* (sausage), *torresmos* (fried pork rinds), and a dizzying array of *doces* (sweets) means it is not the lightest or most the most calorie-conscious of cuisines, *comida mineira* is downright delicious.

Traditional Mineiro cooking has its roots in the history of Minas itself. During the gold rush years, African slaves were in charge of preparing meals. Their culinary techniques – the preparation of thick and hearty stews – relied heavily on indigenous ingredients such as yams, manioc, and corn. Traveling miners and *tropeiros* ("troops" of merchants who carried gold and other produce on donkeys' backs) had to eat on the road. Perishable foods were out of the question, so they invented nourishing dishes of *feijão* (beans) cooked with salted pork and sausage, then thickened with manioc flour. Subsequently mashed into a savory puree, this classic dish became known as *tutu à mineira*. Another variation – with the addition of chopped *couve* (kale) and fried egg – is *feijão tropeiro*.

Minas has always had a rich rural culture. With no coastline and cattle raised mainly reserved for dairy products such as Minas's famed creamy white *queijos* (cheeses), meat dishes consisted of *lombo* (pork loin) or *frango* (chicken). In terms of chicken, the most typical recipes are *frango com ora-pro-nobis* (a wild spinach-like leaf), *frango ao molho pardo* (in which the "dark" sauce in question is made from the chicken's own blood), and *frango com quiabo* (okra). The latter, served with *angu* (a heavy cornmeal), was originally used to nourish slaves. Today most Mineiro households savor this classic dish on a regular basis. Since many Mineiro homes have gardens, vegetables such as *couve*, jade-green *chuchu*, and *moranga* (a type of pumpkin) are staples: they usually chopped at the last minute to preserve their freshness and color.

Since the 19th century, southern Minas has been a major producer of coffee beans, and the java served throughout the state is particularly rich and fragrant. Consumed throughout the day, *café* is accompanied by an assortment of cakes, cookies, and biscuits, but most famously by *pão de queijo*: chewy round "cheese bread" the size of a ping-pong ball that is extremely addictive.

No meal would be complete without dessert, and Mineiros take their sweets seriously. Favorite *doces* are regional fruits – such as *goiaba* (guava), *laranja* (orange), and *mamão verde* (green papaya) – preserved in syrup. To offset the sweetness, they are often savored with a slice of creamy white *queijo*. In fact, the marriage of *doce de goiaba* with *queijo* is so popular that it has earned the nickname *Romeu e Julieta*. Another *doce* Mineiros can't seem to live without is *doce de leite*, a rich caramel-like concoction made from boiling sugar and milk. Before tucking into a Mineiro meal, you'll inevitably be expected to *abrir* ("open") your appetite by downing a shot or two of local *cachaça*. The conclusion of a meal involves sampling a *licor* distilled from local fruits such as blackcurrant-like *jabuticaba* and the heavily perfumed *pequi*.

pães de queijo (cheese bread) with a *cafezinho* (espresso-sized coffee)

© MICHAEL SOMMERS

Tues.–Wed., 7 P.M.–1:30 A.M. Thurs.–Sat., R$45–55) is a small and utterly delightful bistro with tables overflowing onto the sidewalk. While the menu is limited, the creativity of dishes—which draw on Brazilian, Asian, and Mediterranean influences and ingredients—is boundless. Despite the elegant surroundings and attentive service, its casual atmosphere makes one feel right at home.

(A Favorita (Rua Santa Catarina 1235, Lourdes, tel. 31/3275-2352, noon–3:30 P.M. and 6:30 P.M.–1 A.M. Tues.–Fri., noon–2 A.M. Sat., noon–midnight Sun., R$50–60) is considered one of the finest and most inventive contemporary restaurants in Belo Horizonte. Its Mineiro chef prides himself on his daring, which results in dishes that mix and match elements of French, Italian, and Thai cuisine such as a creamy mix of portobello, shimeji, and Paris mushrooms with truffle butter and poached egg or the pear tartar in spiced red wine with pistachio cream. Daily specials written on the blackboard are worth taking note of. If you can, grab a table on the coveted enclosed terrace.

Comida Mineira

Belo Horizonte has its share of top addresses where you can savor Mineiro cooking in all its succulent glory. One of the most traditional—and delicious—is **(Dona Lucinha** (Rua Sergipe 811, Savassi, www.dona lucinha.com.br, noon–3 P.M. and 7–11:30 P.M. Mon.–Fri., noon–5 P.M. and 7–11:30 P.M. Sat., noon–5 P.M. Sun.). Dona Lucinha began life cooking delicacies she sold in the market of her hometown, Serro (in northern Minas near Diamantina), and she brought her experience and many recipes with her when she came to the capital. For R$30, you have unlimited access to a mouthwatering buffet of close to 40 dishes—including crisp barbecued pork ribs bathed in caramel and chicken cooked in fragrant *ora-pro-nobis* leaves—which serve as a fine introduction to Mineiro cooking. An equally diverse array of desserts and liqueurs are also included. Both this restaurant and the original in the neighborhood of São Pedro (Rua

Padre Odorico 38, tel. 31/3227-0562) conjure up the warm kitchens of rural Minas.

Another favorite address for Mineiro food is **Cozinha Mineira** (Rua Gonçalves Dias 45, Funcionários, tel. 31/3227-1559, 11 A.M.–1 A.M. Mon.–Sat., 11 A.M.–4 P.M. Sun.), which occupies an airy loft-like space with a back deck, with walls creatively strewn with over 500 painted plates. You can order from an à la carte menu or line up in front of the wood-burning stove and choose from a buffet of close to 50 offerings, most of them regional specialties. From Tuesday to Saturday, groups play live music in the evening.

International

Taste Vin (Rua Curitiba 2105, Lourdes, tel. 31/3292-5423, 7:30 P.M.–midnight Mon.–Fri., R$45–55) is renowned around town for its unpretentious traditional French bistro food served in a pleasantly casual dining room. That the walls are festooned with wine bottles is unsurprising. As a young man, the chef and owner—a former electrical engineer—hated beer and spent his 20s sampling fine vintages while his colleagues quaffed ale. The predilection became a passion and today Taste Vin's temperature-controlled wine cellar is by far the best in the city. The regional French cooking—leg of lamb slowly roasted for seven hours in white wine and, for dessert, a decadent coffee soufflé—are more than worthy of the fine wines that accompany them.

To date, **Amigo do Rei** (Rua Quintiliano Silva 118, Santo Antônio, tel. 31/3296-3881, www.amigodorei.com, 7:30–11:30 P.M. Wed.–Sat., 1–4 P.M. Sun., R$35–45) lays claim to being the only authentic Persian restaurant in Brazil. Exotic dishes include tender beef cooked in a sauce of pomegranates and walnuts, and grilled chicken with *zereshk,* a wild Iranian mountain berry. The restaurant itself is small and simple. Strains of Iranian music enhance the atmosphere.

Dona Derna (Rua Tomé de Souza 1343, 1st Fl., Savassi, tel. 31/3223-6954, www.derna.com.br, 11 A.M.–midnight Mon.–Sat., 11 A.M.–6 P.M. Sun., R$35–45) is a city institution that has been serving up robust regional Italian cuisine since 1960 when Dona Derna got nostalgic for the food of Tuscany, from where she had recently emigrated, and decided to open a restaurant of her own. Today, Derna's son maintains his mother's high standards. Meats, pastas, fish and seafood are all exceptionally flavorful and reminiscent of the kind of fare you'd get in a family-owned trattoria in Italy.

INFORMATION

Belotur is the city travel association, and its staff is very knowledgeable. It publishes a free bilingual monthly guide, *Guia Turística*, with a good city map, distributed throughout the city. Its tourist listings are extensive, even including instructions on what buses to take to different attractions and where to get them. Tourist centers are at Confins airport (tel. 31/3689-2557, 8 A.M.–10 P.M. daily), the *rodoviária* (Praça Rio Branco, Centro, tel. 31/3277-6907, 8 A.M.–10 P.M. daily), and at the Parque Municipal (Av. Afonso Pena 1055, Centro, tel. 31/3277-7666, 8 A.M.–7 P.M. Mon.–Fri., 8 A.M.–3 P.M. Sat.–Sun.). Also consult the website www.belohorizonte.mg.gov.br.

SERVICES

Many major banks accept international cards in Centro. Among them are Banco do Brasil (Rua Rio de Janeiro 750) and Citibank (Rua Espírito Santo 871) next to the Dayrell Minas Hotel. The main post office (Av. Afonso Pena 1270, Centro) is opposite the Parque Municipal.

For Internet service, in Centro, **cominternet.com.br** (64 Rua Goitacazes, 8:30 A.M.–9 P.M. Mon.–Fri., 8:30 A.M.–4 P.M. Sat.) has fast machines and a small café where you can wolf down some *pães de queijo*. In Savassi, **Monkey** (Rua Paraíba 1323, Loja 3, 8 A.M.–midnight daily) is sleek and spacious with big flat screens and comfortable chairs.

In the event of a medical emergency, dial **192** for Pronto Socorro (First Aid). The **Hospital das Clínicas** (Av. Alfredo Badalena 190, Santa Efigênia, tel. 31/3239-7100) is affiliated with UFMG, the federal university. In the event of a crime, call **190** to reach the police.

GETTING THERE
By Air

Most flights arrive at **Tancredo Neves International Airport** (tel. 31/3689-2700). More popularly known as **Confins** (after the suburb where it is located), it is around 40 kilometers (25 miles) from the center of Belo Horizonte. Much closer is the older and smaller **Pampulha Airport** (tel. 31/3490-2001), which is around 15 kilometers (9 miles) from Centro. If you don't want to take a taxi, **Airport Conexão** (tel. 31/3224-1002 or consult www.conexao aeroporto.com.br) offers *executivo* bus service between Confins airport and Centro. Buses arrive at and depart from the entrance to the Belo Horizonte Palace Hotel (Avenida Alvares Cabral 387). Buses run approximately every 30 minutes 5:15 A.M.–11:15 P.M. Regular municipal buses also provide service to both Confins and Pampulha airports from the *rodoviária* at Praça Rio Branco (tel. 31/3271-1335, www .expressounir.com.br). A taxi to Centro or Savassi will set you back around R$70 from Confins and R$30 from Pampulha.

By Bus

The main *rodoviária* (tel. 31/3271-3000, www.pbh.gov.br/rodoviaria) is right in the heart of the city at Praça Rio Branco. From here buses arrive and depart to destinations throughout Minas Gerais and the rest of Brazil.

GETTING AROUND

Because of its many one-way streets, driving a car in Belo Horizonte is tricky. Moreover, the rules of which street goes which way are always changing (even the taxi drivers have trouble keeping up). Since most interesting sights are in Centro, getting around on foot is easy. The bus system is very well organized. There is a subway, but you'll likely never use it since it is more useful for workers getting in and out of the suburbs than for tourists.

Municipal bus service is good and extensive. From Centro and Savassi, it is easy to get anywhere you want to go quickly. Route numbers of the buses are usually listed at bus stops themselves. These numbers and the final destinations are on the front of the bus, and the major stops along the routes are listed on the sides. At night, it's wiser to take a cab. Major taxi companies include **Ligue Táxi BH** (tel. 31/3421-3434 or 0800/301-414) and **Coopertáxi BH** (tel. 31/3421-2424 or 0800/979-2424).

Renting a car can come in very handy for day trips to sites around Belo Horizonte. **Hertz** (www.hertz.com.br) is at both airports and near Praça da Liberdade in Centro (Av. João Pinheiro 195, tel. 31/3224-5166). **Localiza** (www.localiza.com) is also at both airports and in Funcionáiros (Av. Bernardo Monteiro 1567, tel. 31/3247-7956).

AROUND BELO HORIZONTE

Within close proximity of Belo Horizonte are tons of natural attractions ranging from scenic mountains to mysterious caverns. For information about organizing trips to the natural attractions surrounding Belo Horizonte and other parts of Minas, contact **Terra Nossa** (Rua Domingos Vieira 348, Sala 1309, Santa Efigênia, tel. 31/3241-6161, www.terranossa.com). This ecotourism agency is quite centrally located and offers tours throughout Minas and Brazil, with a focus on adventure sports such as climbing, rafting, and canyoneering.

Caverns

Of the supposedly 3,000 grottoes and caverns that exist in Brazil (counting them must have been quite an interesting job), 2,000 are located in Minas and 500 are within striking distance of Belo Horizonte. The most interesting to visit are Rei do Mato, Lapinha, and Maquiné; all make easy day trips, going north from the capital.

GRUTA DA LAPINHA
Located on the outskirts of the town of Lagoa Santa, Gruta da Lapinha (tel. 31/3689-8422, 8:30 A.M.–4:30 P.M., R$10) is famous for its fantastically shaped stalactites and stalagmites and the Véu de Noiva, a crystal formation that resembles a "Bride's Veil." Buses leave from Belo Horizonte's bus station at least once an

hour. By car from BH, take the MG-010, 40 kilometers (25 miles) north.

GRUTA REI DO MATO
Gruta Rei do Mato (tel. 31/3773-0888, 8 A.M.–5 P.M. daily, R$8) earned its name (King of the Bush) from a legend about a fugitive who once lived in this palatially grand cave. Today, this cavern is well illuminated and equipped—but for the tourists who wander through its otherworldly environs decorated with stalactites, stalagmites, and marvelous prehistoric paintings. The cave is 5 kilometers (3 miles) from the turnoff to the town of Sete Lagoas, 70 kilometers (43 miles) north of Belo Horizonte along the BR-040. Buses to Sete Lagoas (which leave around every 30 minutes from Belo Horizonte's *rodoviária*) stop in front of the entrance.

GRUTA DO MAQUINÉ
The entrance to the Gruta do Maquiné (tel. 31/3715-1078, 8 A.M.–5 P.M. daily, R$10) is home to some interesting cave paintings that date back over 6,000 years. As you wander deeper in the cave, you'll encounter seven vast chambers, all of them dripping with stalactites. To experience the magical environs in tranquility, try to avoid the weekend crowds. The cave is 5 kilometers (3 miles) from the town of Cordisburgo along the Via Alberto Ramos. There are several buses a day to Cordisburgo from Belo Horizonte's *rodoviária*. By car, take the BR-040 for 90 kilometers (56 miles) and then the MG-231 for another 20 kilometers (12 miles).

Parque Nacional da Serra do Cipó
Around 100 kilometers (62 miles) northeast of BH, this national park possesses breathtaking scenery, with numerous flowers, waterfalls, and hiking trails that make it a favorite with ecotourists. The most impressive waterfall is the Cachoeira da Farofa. Wildlife you risk running into include monkeys, anteaters, and the poisonous *sapo de pijama* (pajama frog). Only the lower part of the park can be visited without a guide. At the **visitors center** (tel.

MINAS GERAIS

31/3718-7228, www.guaiserradocipo.com.br, 8 A.M.–5 P.M. daily, R$3) at the entrance to the park, you can rent bikes or horses, but there isn't much in the way of food so you should bring a snack or picnic. The best time to visit is during the winter or spring months. Guides and park maps are supplied by the **Associação Comercial da Serra do Cipó** (tel. 31/3718-7017). The park itself can be accessed via the towns of Jaboticatubas and Santana do Riacho, both within its limits. If you're pressed for time, you might be better off driving there (take the MG-010 north from Belo Horizonte) or taking an excursion from Belo Horizonte. **Cipó Aventuras** (tel. 31/3718-7014, www.cipo aventuras.com.br) offers excursions.

Parque Natural do Caraça

Situated 120 kilometers (75 miles) southeast of BH, near the fetching colonial town of **Santa Bárbara,** this private nature reserve is a botanist's dream, replete with an unusual mixture of native Atlantic forest and Cerrado vegetation that carpets the scenic Serra do Espinhaço mountain range. The park's name, Caraça (Big Face), stems from one slope's uncanny resemblance to a giant's head in repose. Within the park's boundaries are lots of lakes, waterfalls, and various hiking trails, along with the **Gruta do Centenário,** one of the world's largest quartzite caves.

Although there are many daily buses from Belo Horizonte to Santa Bárbara, the park entrance is 25 kilometers (16 miles) from town, so you'll have to take a taxi. If driving, take BR 262 from BH to Santa Bárbara and then follow directions. The park is open 7 A.M.–5 P.M. daily and charges an entrance fee of R$10 per vehicle. Walking trails begin right from the entrance and the monks at the Hospedaria do Caraça can supply maps and directions.

Situated near the park's entrance is the **Santuário do Caraça,** a former 18th-century seminary. From the late 1700s to 1911, it housed a school where the sons of Minas's most distinguished families were sent to study (five Brazilian presidents are alumni). After a catastrophic fire in 1968, the building was restored in the 1990s and transformed into a hotel, the **Hospedaria do Caraça** (tel. 31/3837-2698, reservations necessary), which is run by the remaining members of the monastery. Adjacent is the impressive neo-gothic Igreja Nossa Senhora Mão dos Homens, with its French stained-glass windows, grandiose organ, and baroque altars. The symbol of both the sanctuary and the park is the *lobo-guará,* a rare species of wolf. Although it's highly unlikely you'll catch sight of one in the wild, if you stay overnight, you can watch the monks feed a couple of partially tame animals who often come around in the evening in search of a snack.

While the park can be visited all year long, due to the altitude it can get fairly chilly at night and in the winter. Summer's definitely the season to visit if you're intent on plunging into otherwise icy waterfalls and natural pools.

Sabará

Sabará is a mere 20 kilometers (12 miles; a local bus ride) from Belo Horizonte and makes a great day trip. Nestling in a valley where the Rio das Velhas runs into the Rio Sabará, Sabará was one of the first of Minas's gold towns and one of its most important. At the height of Minas's 18th-century gold flush, Sabará produced more gold in one week than the rest of Brazil's gold mining towns in one year. Unsurprisingly, for a while, it was one of the richest cities in the world. Testifying to this fact are the impressive mansions lining its steep cobblestoned streets as well as the handful of baroque churches whose modest exteriors hide a dazzling array of gold-clad treasures. Although centuries of mining have stripped the surrounding hills of their foliage and the town's recent rapid expansion has saddled it with some none too attractive urban sprawl, if you stick to the cobblestones, it's still possible to get the sense that you're stepping back in time. Today you won't find any large chunks of gold in Sabará's rocks, but fortune-seekers continue to pan the rivers in search of precious flakes and slivers (you can see them in action at the tiny Carmo stream running alongside the far end of town going towards Caeté).

SIGHTS

The main square and lovely colonial center of the town is **Praça Santa Rita.** From here, signs point the way to Sabará's main attractions—though it's best to keep in mind that on Monday, almost all sights are closed. Closest to the *praça* is the recently restored **Teatro Imperial** (Rua Dom Pedro II, tel. 31/3672-7690, 8 A.M.–noon and 1–5 P.M. Tues.–Sun.). Built in 1770, it is the second oldest theater in Brazil that is still in operation. The elegant interior boasts not only excellent acoustics, but also beautiful woodwork, crystal chandeliers, and 47 private boxes. Adjacent to Praça Santa Rita, the Praça Melo Viana is dominated by the imposing stone walls of the strikingly simple **Igreja de Nossa Senhora do Rosário dos Pretos** (9–11 A.M.

and 1–5 P.M. Tues.–Sun., R\$1). Construction on this church for Sabará's significant black slave population commenced in 1766 but was never completed. The building still houses the original adobe chapel from 1713.

Sabará has three other churches that are definitely worth seeing. Since they are a bit of a trek from the center, you might want to take a municipal bus to the furthest, Igreja Nossa Senhora do Ó, and then visit the other two as you walk back towards town.

Museu de Ouro

Near Praça Santa Rita, the Museu de Ouro (Rua Intendência, tel. 31/3671-1848, noon–5 P.M. Tues.–Sun., R\$1) is an engaging museum in a sprawling stone house that was the former foundry and deposit for all of Sabará's gold. According to the museum guards, the place is haunted by the ghosts of former slaves who toiled in the rivers and mines. Miners' tools and equipment help you get a sense of the many exacting activities related to the mining and processing of gold. There are some interesting examples of period furniture (many featuring hidden drawers and cabinets used to conceal people's private stashes of gold) as well as domestic and religious objects that conjure up life in colonial Sabará.

Igreja Nossa Senhora do Ó

Three kilometers (1.8 miles) from Praça Santa Rita along the main road to Caeté is the Igreja Nossa Senhora do Ó (Largo Nossa Senhora do Ó, 8 A.M.–5 P.M. Mon.–Fri., 9 A.M.–noon and 2–5 P.M. Sat.–Sun., R\$1). From the outside, it resembles a humble colonial church. In this case, however, appearances are extremely deceiving. The magnificently adorned interior is considered one of the pearls of Minas baroque churches. Such a profusion of burnished gold, rich blues, and scarlet all crammed into such a tiny space is likely to make you gasp, or at least let you out an "Ó"—it was with this exclamation that devotees of the Virgin Mary, in whose

MINAS GERAIS

the Igreja Nossa Senhora do Ó in Sabará

honor the church was constructed, routinely began their prayers. Splendid panels depict scenes from the life of Jesus. Stylistically, much of the imagery—from the painted trees, boats, and birds to the facial features of the Virgin—was inspired by motifs on Chinese porcelain from the Portuguese colony of Macau that were in vogue at the time of the church's construction in 1720.

Igreja Matriz de Nossa Senhora de Conceição

Built between 1700 and 1710, the Igreja Matriz de Nossa Senhora de Conceição (Praça Getúlio Vargas, 9 A.M.–noon and 2–5 P.M. daily, R$2) is Sabará's oldest church. While its exterior is quite plain, the interior offers up a rich feast of intricately sculpted cherubs, flowers, garlands, twists, and tassels, completely bathed in gold. This church also offers more examples of the intriguing mixture of Portuguese baroque and oriental styles. Especially stunning are the doors leading to the sanctuary, which are exquisitely festooned with painted gold and

scarlet pagodas and cranes. Also take note of the fantastically lifelike Christ figure chained and leaning on a column of blue marble.

Igreja da Ordem de Nossa Senhora do Carmo

Constructed in the mid-1700s, the Igreja da Ordem de Nossa Senhora do Carmo (Rua do Carmo, 8 A.M.–noon and 1–5 P.M. Tues.–Sat., 1–5 P.M. Sun., R$2) is the only church in Sabará with works by the great baroque master sculptor Aleijadinho. You can glimpse his expressive genius in certain details of the facade, as well as in the choral, the pulpits, and in the images of São Simão and São João da Cruz that adorn the lateral altars.

FESTIVALS AND EVENTS

Belo Horizontinos flock to two lively festivals that animate Sabará's colonial streets. In May, the **Festival Ora-Pró-Nobis** pays homage to the humble *ora-pró-nobis* leaf that is a favorite ingredient in many savory Mineiro stews made with chicken and pork. Early November (dates depend on the harvest) coincides with the **Festival da Jabuticaba,** in which liqueurs, jellies, sweets, and other delicious drinkables and edibles are inspired by the blackcurrant-like *jabuticaba* fruit, which grows in profusion throughout the region.

SHOPPING

At **Cooperartes** (Praça Santa Rita, tel. 31/3671-4694, www.cooperartes.com.br), the enterprising women of Sabará sell an interesting array of traditional and somewhat whimsical handicrafts as well as mouthwatering local delicacies.

ACCOMMODATIONS AND FOOD

Since all of its sights can be seen in a full day, it isn't necessary to stay overnight in Sabará. There are prettier and more bucolic colonial cities to choose from in Minas. However, if you're looking for a relaxing alternative to the hustle and bustle of Belo Horizonte, it's hard to resist the rustic charms of **Pousada Solar dos Sepúlvedas** (Rua Intendência 371, tel. 31/3671-

2705, www.pousadasolarsepulveda.com.br, R$90 d), situated in a beautiful old colonial mansion next to the Museu de Ouro. All rooms have massive wooden beds that could easily sleep three or four, and are furnished with antiques and colorful ceramic tiles. Most bathrooms claim the luxury of bathtubs with feet (or paws), although if you actually take a (hot) bath you'll be charged extra. Terraces, walkways, and a swimming pool are surrounded by an oasis-like garden of tropical flowers and fruit trees.

For some good home-style cooking, a local favorite is **Cê Qui Sabe** (Rua Mestre Caetano 56, tel. 31/3671-2906, 11 A.M.–11 P.M. daily, R$12–20), whose extensive menu offers both hearty Mineiro dishes such as *lombo* (pork) with *tutu à mineiro,* kale and sausage, as well as more standard fare. At lunch, you can choose from à la carte dishes for two (at least) or a self-service per kilo buffet of Mineiro specialties. Equally good is **314 Sabarabuçu** (Rua Dom Pedro II 279, tel. 31/3671-2313, 11 A.M.–midnight Mon.–Thurs., 11–2 A.M. Fri.–Sat.,

11 A.M.–1 P.M. Sun., R$12–20), which along with a self-service per kilo lunch buffet, offers *churrasco* (barbecued meat). At night, aside from à la carte Mineiro specialties, you can dig into pizzas baked in the restaurant's wood-burning oven.

INFORMATION

The **tourist office** is at the entrance to town. Unless you're coming by car, it's quite a walk to and from the center, and Sabará's sights are so few and well-indicated that you probably don't need a map. A useful website is www.sabara.mg.gov.br.

GETTING THERE

Sabará is practically a suburb of Belo Horizonte. It can be reached easily by municipal buses, which leave around every 15 minutes from Centro. *Executivo* buses also leave frequently from a stop adjacent to the main bus station. If you're driving, take the MG-262 highway leading east out of Belo Horizonte.

Ouro Preto

Minas's first capital, Ouro Preto, is easily the most magnificent of Minas's *cidades históricas.* The picturesque town is hemmed in by the Serra do Espinhaço mountains, which effectively saved the former gold town from the terrors of modern development. Consequently, while Ouro Preto's (very) precipitous cobblestoned streets may induce a certain degree of huffing and puffing, the very steepness of these hills means that most vehicles can't enter the colonial center, making it a pedestrian-only zone, ideal for savoring its architectural gems

Ouro Preto, however, is far from being a living museum. The presence of one of the country's oldest federal universities and a thriving student population ensures a buzzing nightlife and plenty of popular *festas* (most notably Carnaval and the Semana Santa processions). Although it can be visited as a day trip from Belo Horizonte, you need at least two full days

to take in the number of churches (23), museums, and monuments and to simply wander around. Baroque aficionados will feel as if they've died and gone to heaven (with the bonus of great food) when they lay eyes upon the many extraordinary works on display, particularly the creations of a genius sculptor, Aleijadinho, and a master painter, Manuel da Costa Ataíde.

According to legend, Ouro Preto gained its name in the earliest days of Brazil when groups of *bandeirantes* from São Paulo traveled the wild interior in search of riches. On one such expedition made in 1698, a roving *bandeirante* named Antônio Dias de Oliveira came upon some chunks of shiny black metal, which upon close inspection revealed themselves to be gold. As a result, the mining camp that sprang up on the spot came to be known as Ouro Preto (Black Gold).

© MICHAEL SOMMERS

view of Ouro Preto

Although subterfuges were rampant—among them hiding gold dust in one's hair or in religious statues—those who didn't pay taxes were tossed into jail or exiled. Eventually, resentment led to revolt. In 1789, a handful of local malcontents rose up against colonial authorities in a rebellion known as the Inconfidência Mineira. Among the group's leaders was a local poet named Joaquim José da Silva Xavier, known around town as Tiradentes ("Toothpuller") due to his skills as a dentist. When the revolt was quashed, Tiradentes was the only rebel who fessed up to his involvement. As punishment, he was imprisoned for three years before being publicly drawn and quartered in Rio de Janeiro. Most of the other Inconfidentes were exiled to Portugal or its African colonies.

By this time, gold supplies were already dwindling. In 1897, the capital of Minas Gerais moved to Belo Horizonte and Ouro Preto lost both its political and economic clout. Ironically, both "losses" were instrumental in helping to preserve the colonial center, whose status was recognized by UNESCO in 1981 when it was declared a World Heritage site. In recent times, an important aluminum industry has lured migrant workers to the area, creating the growing *favelas* that are mushrooming on the outskirts of town. The town also thrives—for better or for worse—on tourism, which means that it is hardly as placid as Tiradentes or Diamantina, and can get quite crowded, especially on weekends and during holidays.

The surrounding region proved to possess more gold than in any other part of the Western Hemisphere. Eager fortune seekers descended upon the tiny mining town in such droves that there wasn't enough food to feed them all. Tales abounded of (un)lucky souls who keeled over from hunger, their pockets overflowing with shiny nuggets. By the mid-19th century, the population had swelled to over 100,000 (in comparison, the population of Rio de Janeiro was only 20,000). Those who struck it rich set up house in magnificent mansions and imported the finest luxuries money could buy. They also flaunted their wealth by funding the construction of imposing civil buildings and magnificent churches doused in gold, which were decorated by the finest baroque artists of the day.

However, Ouro Preto also experienced outbreaks of disease coupled with high rates of prostitution and crime. Increasingly, residents chafed under the control of the greedy Portuguese crown, which rigidly controlled all mining and transactions and officially demanded one-fifth of all gold that was found.

SIGHTS

Barring the steepness of its streets, Ouro Preto is compact enough that it is easy to get around. However, it's easy to get confused by the street names, of which there are usually two sets, an official name and one used by residents. For instance, the main street of Rua Conde de Bobadela is more frequently known as Rua Direita. What complicates things even further is that generally neither set of names is posted in the streets themselves. So you're often better off aiming for various churches and landmarks

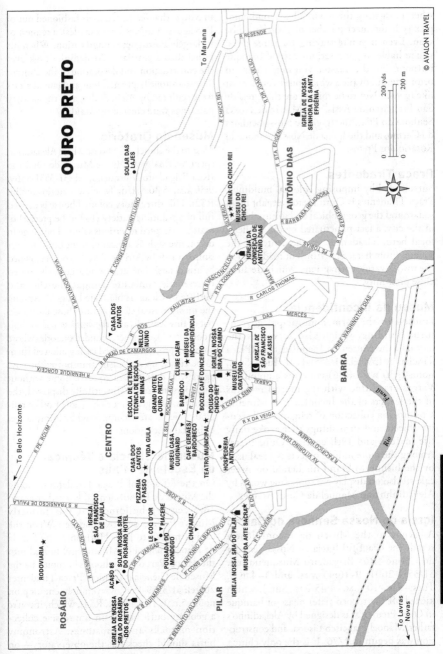

OURO PRETO

To Mariana

To Belo Horizonte

To Lavras Novas

© AVALON TRAVEL

ROSÁRIO

CENTRO

ANTÔNIO DIAS

BARRA

PILAR

IGREJA DE NOSSA SRA DO ROSÁRIO DOS PRETOS

SOLAR NOSSA SRA DO ROSÁRIO HOTEL

ACASO 85

SÃO FRANCISCO DE PAULA

IGREJA SÃO FRANCISCO DE PAULA

LE COQ D'OR

POUSADA DO MONDEGO

PIACERE

CHAFARIZ

PIZZARIA O PASSO

CASA DOS CANTOS

VIDA GULA

GRAND HOTEL OURO PRETO

ESCOLA DE CIÊNCIA E TÉCNICA E ESCOLA DE MINAS

CASA DOS CANTOS

MELLO NUNO

BARROCO

MUSEU CASA GUIGNARD

CAFÉ GERAES/ BARDOBECO

TEATRO MUNICIPAL

HOSPEDERIA ANTIGA

IGREJA NOSSA SRA DO PILAR

MUSEU DA ARTE SACRA

CLUBE CAEM

MUSEU DA INCONFIDÊNCIA

POUSO DO CHICO REY

BOOZE CAFÉ CONCERTO

IGREJA NOSSA SRA DO CARMO

MUSEU DE ORATÓRIO

IGREJA DE SÃO FRANCISCO DE ASSIS

IGREJA DA CONCEIÇÃO DE ANTÔNIO DIAS

MINA DO CHICO REI

MUSEU DO CHICO REI

SOLAR DAS LAJES

IGREJA DE NOSSA SENHORA DA SANTA EFIGÊNIA

RODOVIARIA

R PE. ROLIM

R S FRANCISCO DE PAULA

R HENRIQUE ADEOGLO

R HENRIQUE GORCEIX

R SALVADOR INOFUA

R CONSELHEIRO QUINTILIANO

R BARÃO DE CAMARGOS

R DOS PAULISTAS

R B VASCONCELOS

R DA CONCEIÇÃO

R DR JOÃO VELOSO

R RESENDE

R CHICO REI

R STA EFIGENI

R DR S SILVÉRIO

R CARLOS THOMAZ

R DAS MERCÊS

R PREF WASHINGTON DIAS

R BARBARA HELIODORA

R CEL SERAFIM

R PE TOBIAS

R CABRAL

R COSTA SENA

AV VITORINO DIAS

R PACÍFICO ROMEM

R X DA VEIGA

R DO PILAR

R C OLIVEIRA

R B GUIMARÃES

R BENEDITO VALADARES

R CONS SANT'ANNA

R ANTÔNIO ALBUQUERQUE

R S JOSÉ

R DR G VARGAS

R DIREITA

R SEN ROCHA LAGOA

Rio Funil

200 yds

200 m

MINAS GERAIS

when navigating the town. The second complexity is the sheer number of churches to be seen. Even if you're staying for three days, you're liable to get a serious case of baroque burnout. For this reason, you might want to prioritize in advance which ones you'd most like to visit. Not to be missed are the Igreja de São Francisco de Assis, the Matriz de Nossa Senhora do Pilar, the Igreja de Nossa Senhora do Carmo, and the Igreja de Nossa Senhora do Rosário dos Pretos.

Praça Tiradentes

Surrounded by imposing colonial buildings, Praça Tiradentes is Ouro Preto's elegant main square and the geographical and spiritual heart of the city, a fact punctuated by the statue of local hero, Tiradentes, in the center of the square. From here, a labyrinth of roads lead to the town's various attractions, which are all in close proximity.

Museu da Inconfidência

Housed in the former municipal government building, which also served as the city jail, the Museu da Inconfidência (Praça Tiradentes 139, tel. 31/3551-1121, Tues.–Sun., noon–5:30 P.M., R$6) contains a grandiose Vargas-era shrine with the mortal remains of the leaders of the Inconfidência Mineira. Upstairs is a collection of religious and secular objects and furnishings that evoke daily life in 18th and 19th century Ouro Preto, Among the more unique objects is a seal used by the bishop to brand his herald on sweet cakes. Also on display are some fine works by Aleijadinho and Manuel da Costa Ataíde.

Igreja de Nossa Senhora do Carmo

Adjacent to the Museu da Inconfidência stands the beautiful Igreja de Nossa Senhora do Carmo (Rua Brigadeiro Musqueira, tel. 31/3551-2601, 9–10:45 A.M. and 1–4 P.M. Tues.–Sat., 10 A.M.–4:45 P.M. Sun.), which kicked off the rococo (late) phase of baroque in Ouro Preto. It was designed by Aleijadinho's father, Manoel Francisco Lisboa, and construction was begun in 1776. It is the only church in Minas that features panels fashioned out of Portuguese *azulejos* (ceramic tiles), a request of its largely Portuguese congregation. When his father died a year later, Aleijadinho took over the construction and decoration of the church. The soapstone baptismal font and lateral altars were sculpted by Aleijadinho, and the sacristy paintings were created by Ataíde.

Museu do Oratório

Next to the church, in a house where Aleijadinho spent his final years, is the Museu do Oratório (Rua Brigadeiro Musqueira, tel. 31/3551-5369, 9:30 A.M.–5:30 P.M. daily, www.oratorio.com.br, R$2). This three-story colonial house is packed full of a stunning variety (162 to be precise) of oratories devoted to various saints. The range in decorative style is amazing: from beautiful yet simple (made by African slaves) to ornate (owned by aristocrats). The latter were exquisitely crafted to resemble miniature baroque churches and outfitted with altars blanketed in gold. Among the most unusual examples are those fashioned out of tiny seashells and the *oratório-balas* ("bullet oratories"): compact, rounded oratories whose compact projectile-shaped casing allowed them to be closed up and easily transported by voyagers who didn't want to leave home without their personal saints. Beautifully displayed, the oratories, along with a rich array of other religious objects, are accompanied by informative, bilingual descriptions.

Museu de Ciência e Técnica da Escola de Minas

On the far side of Praça Tiradentes, facing the Museu de Inconfidência, is a rather grand 18th-century building that was formerly Minas's Palácio de Governadores. When the capital moved to Belo Horizonte, the Escola de Minas (School of Mineralogy) moved into the palace. Part of the school is occupied by the Museu de Ciência e Técnica (Praça Tiradentes 20, tel. 31/3559-1597, www.museu.em.ufop.br, noon–5 P.M. Tues.–Sun., R$4), which, if you're a geology buff, boasts an impressive collection of rocks and gemstones. Astronomy buffs should check out the observatory—on

Saturday nights 8–10 P.M., star-gazing is open to the public.

Museu Casa Guignard

Although celebrated Brazilian painter Alberto Veiga de Guignard (1896-1962) was born in Rio and educated in Europe, he spent most of his life in Minas, and during his final years he was in Ouro Preto. Subsequently, the town's landscapes, colors, and textures are all very much present in his vibrant canvases. Aside from his paintings, the Museu Casa Guignard (Rua Direita 110, tel. 31/3551-5155, noon–6 P.M. Tues.–Fri., 9 A.M.–noon and 1–6 P.M. Sat.–Sun., R$2) also has a collection of the artist's photographs, documents, and personal objects.

Teatro Municipal and Casa dos Contos

Built in 1769, Ouro Preto's Teatro Municipal (Rua Brigadeiro Musquete, tel. 31/3559-3224) is not only the oldest theater still in operation in Brazil, but it also boasts some of the finest acoustics. Although this grand old dame wasn't weathering the passage of time very well, a recently finished restoration has revived its former glory. Nearby is the truly impressive Casa dos Contos (Rua São José 12, tel. 31/3551-1444, 2–6 P.M. Mon., 10 A.M.–6 P.M. Tues.–Sat., 10 A.M.–4 P.M. Sun.), whose name—the "House of Accounts"—evokes one of its original functions: as the headquarters of the Intendência do Ouro, the crown entity responsible for the weighing and melting of all gold into bars. In fact, you can still see the immense furnace from which the royal fifth was promptly confiscated. Later, in 1789, this house served as a prison for leaders of the Inconfidência Mineira. The dark and gloomy basement was a *senzala*, in which slaves were kept in far from comfortable conditions. Today it displays some decidedly gruesome instruments of torture. More pleasant are the lovely internal courtyard and the stunning view of the surrounding rooftops from the fourth floor. Along with a small ramshackle collection of colonial furnishings, the *casa* houses a public library and a study center specializing in the gold rush era.

Igreja Matriz de Nossa Senhora do Pilar

One of Ouro Preto's most magnificent churches (along with Igreja de São Francisco de Assis), the Igreja Matriz de Nossa Senhora do Pilar (Praça Monsenhor João Castilho Barbosa, tel. 31/3551-4736, 9–11 A.M. and noon–5 P.M. Tues.–Sun., R$3) is easily the most opulent of Minas's baroque churches. It's almost difficult to take in so much glitter: The angels, seashells, and floral motifs that adorn the altars and pulpits are liberally doused in 400 kilos of pure gold. This was done by covering the wood with a special type of glue which was then coated with the finest gold dust. Even the walls are painted in gold and the effect is of having stepped into someone's jewelry box. Responsible for the exquisite sculptures was talented Francisco Xavier de Brito, an important mentor of Aleijadinho. The basement houses a **Museu de Arte Sacra,** with religious icons and vestments embroidered with silver and gold.

Igreja de Nossa Senhora do Rosário dos Pretos

The modest Igreja Nossa Senhora do Rosário dos Pretos (Largo do Rosário, 9–10:45 A.M. and 1–4:45 P.M. Tues.–Sat., 1:30–5 P.M. Sun., R$4) was built by and for Ouro Preto's significant slave population with profits made from after-hours mining. The simplicity of the interior is supposedly due to the fact that the slaves ran out of gold after spending heavily on the lavish exterior, which is striking with its unusual curved design.

◖ Igreja de São Francisco de Assis

Close to Praça Tiradentes is the Igreja do Pilar's rival for title of Ouro Preto's most magnificent church: the Igreja de São Francisco de Assis (Largo do Coimbra, tel. 31/3551-4661, 8:30 A.M.–noon and 1:30–7 P.M. Tues.–Sun., R$3). This truly stunning edifice is a tour-de-force by Aleijadinho, and his greatest work after the 12 Prophets in Congonhas. Built between 1767 and 1800, it represents the apex of Mineiro baroque. Aleijadinho himself designed the church and supervised its construction. He carved the entire facade, including the marvelous soapstone medallion, and is responsible for most of the exquisite cedar and soapstone carvings on the inside. The splendid ceiling panels that adorn the interior are the work of master painter Manuel da Costa Ataíde and reveal Aleijadinho's frequent collaborator at the height of his powers. The rich colors made from natural pigments have stood the test of time admirably. Note the African features of the Virgin and the many cherubs surrounding her: They were inspired by the painter's *mulata* wife and their many offspring.

Igreja Matriz de Nossa Senhora da Conceição de Antônio Dias and Museu de Aleijadinho

From the outside, the grandiose Igreja Matriz de Nossa Senhora da Conceição de Antônio Dias (Praça Antônio Dias, tel. 31/3551-4661, 8:30 A.M.–noon and 1:30–5 P.M. Tues.–Sat., noon–5 P.M. Sun.), named after Ouro Preto's founder, bears a striking resemblance to the equally flamboyant Igreja Matriz de Nossa Senhor do Pilar. This similarity is hardly surprising: Since its founding, Ouro Preto has been divided into two rival parishes, Pilar and Antônio Dias, each with its own church, which vied to outdo the other in magnificence. To this day, the rivalry is played out during the famous Semana Santa processions, which in even years depart from the Matriz do Pilar and in odd years from the Matriz de Santo Antônio. Inside, however, the similarities end. Much more restrained on the gold, the interior here is nonetheless rich in exquisite details, among them the ornately sculpted altars and the baptismal fonts carved out of soapstone. Antônio Dias died a wealthy man and bequeathed part of his fortune to have the church built on the site of his original mining camp. The church is also famed for being the burial place of Aleijadinho and his

architect father, Manuel Francisco Lisboa, who designed it. In the sacristy the small Museu Aleijadinho (R$5) boasts an interesting collection of baroque and rococo art. It pays homage to the great sculptor with a collection of extraordinary works, among them a quartet of fierce lions—that they resemble mythical monsters more than large felines is due to the fact that Aleijadinho carved them from his imagination.

Mina do Chico Rei

If you continue along Rua Dom Silvério from the Matriz de Antônio Dias, you'll arrive at the Mina do Chico Rei (Rua Dom Silvério 108, tel. 31/3552-2866, 9 A.M.–5 P.M. daily, R$5), one of the oldest of Minas's gold mines that you can visit. According to popular legend, Chico Rei was an African king who was sold into slavery along with most of his tribe in the early 18th century. With the extra nuggets he was allowed to harvest at night and on Sundays, he eventually bought his freedom. Some time later, he acquired his own gold mine and, with its profits, promptly set to work buying the liberty of the other slaves from his tribe. Today you can visit 360 meters (1,200 feet) of underground tunnels that still show the traces of the miners' activities. At the entrance, there is a small collection of original mining tools as well as a café.

Igreja de Nossa Senhora da Santa Efigênia dos Pretos

Chico Rei's mine yielded so much gold that he was able to fund a church of his own, and it was here that Ouro Preto's black population was able to worship. Construction on the Igreja de Nossa Senhora da Santa Efigênia dos Pretos (Rua Santa Efigênia 396, tel. 31/3551-5047, 8:30 A.M.–4:30 P.M. Tues.–Sun., R$1) began in 1733 and continued until 1785. Along the way, many of the slaves who helped build the church contributed financially with gold dust smuggled in their hair. In fact, the soapstone baptismal fonts came in very handy as basins in which donors could rinse the gold out of their hair. Although not much gold was left over for

ALEIJADINHO: A LEADER OF THE BRAZILIAN BAROQUE MOVEMENT

Aleijadinho ("Little Cripple") was a fascinating figure – a genius sculptor and the prolific leading figure in the first authentically national Brazilian artistic movement: Brazilian baroque. He was born in the 1730s in Ouro Preto to a Portuguese carpenter-turned-architect and his mistress/slave, Isabel. Named Antônio Francisco Lisboa, he began sculpting while still a boy. He specialized in carving religious images out of native soapstone and wood that were used to adorn the magnificent churches of his hometown. An architect like his father, he also designed churches.

In his early forties, Lisboa was afflicted with a chronic illness (possibly leprosy or syphilis) that left him increasingly crippled and deformed. Over time, he lost some of his fingers and toes. As his deformities grew more hideous, he stopped going out in public. He would leave for work before sunrise and return home long after dark. At work, he labored behind curtains. In spite of his disabilities and suffering, he continued to sculpt with a passion. Even during his lifetime, Aleijadinho was recognized as one of the finest artists of the rococo (late baroque) style that was then in vogue, and all the *cidades históricas* competed fiercely to have him design and decorate their churches. By the time he was called upon to create the sculptures for the Basílica e Santuário do Bom Jesus de Matosinhos, Aleijadinho was in his seventies and suffering enormously. Not long after completing his oeuvre at Congonhas, he succumbed to his illness and died, penniless, in 1815.

decorative purposes, this understated church—built in honor of a beloved saint of Ethiopian origin to whom the slaves prayed for protection in the mines—boasts some fine art. The altar was sculpted by the Aleijadinho's mentor, Francisco Javier de Brito, and the external figure of Nossa Senhora do Rosário is by the master sculptor himself.

Capela do Padre Faria

Continuing on in the opposite direction from town, Rua Santa Efigênia turns into Rua Padre Faria. Padre João de Faria was among the first *bandeirantes* who settled Ouro Preto and, although getting there is a bit of a walk, it's worthwhile to glimpse this beautifully ornate chapel built in the early 1700s. The oldest religious edifice in town, the Capela do Padre Faria (Rua Nossa Senhora do Parto, 8 A.M.–4:30 P.M. Tues.–Sun.), was erected on the site of the improvised chapel where the *padre* preached the town's first mass. Defying royal decree, its bells were the only ones in Ouro Preto to toll upon receiving news of the execution of Tiradentes in 1792. If you're pressed for time take a municipal bus marked "Capela do Padre Faria."

ENTERTAINMENT AND EVENTS
Nightlife

Due to its large university population, Ouro Preto has quite a vibrant nightlife (except during school holidays, when the students clear out). On weekends, the **Clube CAEM** (Centro Acadêmico da Escola de Minas, Praça Tiradentes, tel. 31/3551-2452, cover and show times vary) hosts live music shows and has a dance floor where mineralogy students and others let loose. Nearby Rua Direita is crammed with bars that are usually very lively during the week. If you want to catch a local band playing jazz or MPB, a good choice is the **Booze Café Concerto** (Rua Direita 42, tel. 31/3551-1482, 11 A.M.–midnight daily), which features live performances on Friday and Saturday nights starting at 9 P.M. The cozy cellar with exposed brick walls has a friendly, mellow vibe.

To sample some of Minas's finest *cachaças,* head to **Bardobeco** (Travessa do Ariera 15, tel. 31/3551-1429, 6 P.M.–close daily, no cover), which has over 60 smooth varieties on its menu, among them the house specialty: Milagre de Minas, a heady mixture flavored with a dozen different herbs and spices. Just as enticing as the *pinga* is the rustic decor of stone floors and wooden ceiling beams. Equally atmospheric is **Acaso 85** (Largo do Rosário 85, tel. 31/3551-2397, www.acaso85.com.br, 8 P.M.–close Tues.–Sun., no cover), with a cavernous interior that attracts late-night drinkers in search of a snack and a *saideira* ("last call").

Festivals and Events

Ouro Preto is famous throughout Brazil for its traditional **Semana Santa** (Holy Week) celebrations, held during Easter. The town takes on a festive air: Windows are hung with white banners and the streets are carpeted with a trail of colored sawdust and flowers that links the two Matriz churches of Antônio Dias and Pilar. Highlights include open-air pageants depicting Christ's last days and splendid religious processions. The town is also known for its **Carnaval,** although the revelry is nowhere near the level of bacchanalia that explodes in Salvador, Recife, and Rio. In late July, when the weather is chilly, things heat up considerably during the **Festival de Inverno,** with a diverse array of artistic, musical and cultural events. If you're planning on spending the night in Ouro Preto during any of these times, be forewarned that the town will be stuffed to the gills and you'll need to book your accommodations in advance to guarantee a room.

SHOPPING

Centuries after the gold rush, Ouro Preto is still a major destination for those in search of jewels and other precious stones. Although there are scores of boutiques selling gems and jewelry, to make sure you're getting the real deal and not a synthetic product, it's better to stick to larger and more traditional addresses with a solid reputation. Stores in Ouro Preto are generally open from 9 A.M.–7 P.M. Monday–Saturday.

One of Ouro Preto's mineral specialties is the imperial topaz, which ranges in hue from pink to apricot. You can find it along with other gorgeous rocks at **Ita Gemas** (Rua Direita 139, tel. 31/3551-4895) and **Luiza Figuiredao Jóias** (Rua Direita 48, tel. 31/3551-2487).

Also recommended is **Brasil Gemas** (Praça Tiradentes 74, tel. 31/3551-2976), where you can visit the jewelers at work in their atelier.

Another specialty of Ouro Preto is soapstone—there are quarries nearby—which accounts for the plethora of carvings and objects ranging from pots to backgammon sets that you'll find around town. In front of the Igreja São Francisco de Assis is a daily handicrafts fair, the **Feira do Largo de Coimbra** (8 A.M.–6 P.M.), which despite its touristy nature carries a lot of soapstone carvings. Meanwhile, if the plethora of saints and oratories in Ouro Preto's churches stirs your cravings for sacred art, you may want to invest in the artifacts sold at **Ciriáco** (Largo do Rosário 41, tel. 31/3551-3375) or **Znelson** (Rua Randolfo Bretas 67, tel. 31/3551-6463).

SPORTS AND RECREATION

It is entirely likely that after a day (or more) of visiting baroque treasures, you might feel as if you've overdosed and want a change of scene. Fortunately, within hiking distance of Ouro Preto's center there are some natural getaways where you can recharge your batteries.

Parque Estadual do Pico do Itacolomi

Back in the late 17th century, the 1,770-meter mountain peak of Itacolomi (a Tupi-Guarani expression for "rock-child") served as a beacon-like landmark for the *bandeirantes* who combed Minas's hills in search of precious stones. Part of the Serra do Espinhaço mountain range, the peak and surrounding region make up the Parque Estadual do Pico do Itacolomi (tel. 31/8835-7260, www.parque doitacolomi.com.br, 8 A.M.–5 P.M. Thurs.–Sun., Tues.–Wed. advance notice only, free). Marking the transition phase between native Atlantic forest and Cerrado ecosystems, the vegetation is quite varied and supports a wide range of wildlife including anteaters, jaguars, and numerous types of hummingbirds. Most of the hiking trails—ranging 8–16 kilometers (5–10 miles)—are quite easy and offer the bonuses of (icy) waterfalls and splendid views. If you're in the mood for a challenge, consider the 20-kilometer (12-mile) climb to the top of Itacolomi peak. The park itself is well-organized with a visitors center, restrooms, and a café. To get there, follow highway MG-356 for 5 kilometers (3 miles) from the center of Ouro Preto.

Maria Fumaça to Mariana

If you want to see the countryside, but without the strenuous physical effort of hiking up and down the hills, a really worthwhile trip—back in time, as well as through the scenic mountain landscapes surrounding Ouro Preto—is to take the train to the colonial town of Mariana, 12 kilometers (8 miles) away. Since 2006, the refurbished turn-of-the-20th-century Maria Fumaça ("Smoking Mary") steam train has been back on track, although only on weekends. The journey lasts an hour. Ouro Preto–Mariana trains leave at 11 A.M. and 4:30 P.M., and Mariana–Ouro Preto trains depart at 9 A.M. and 2:30 P.M. (Praça da Estação Ferroviária, tel. 31/3557-3844, www.tremda vale.com.br, Fri.–Sun., R$18 one way).

ACCOMMODATIONS

Ouro Preto has lots of accommodations options to suit all budgets, many of them in centuries-old dwellings. During holiday periods, take care to reserve in advance.

R$50-100

With a prime location and unbeatable prices, the **Pousada Hospedaria Antiga** (Rua Xavier da Veiga 1, tel. 31/3551-2203, www .antiga.com.br, R$80 d) offers simple yet sizable rooms in the former abode of renowned 19th-century poet and politician Xavier de Veiga. The *pousada* features antique furniture, lofty ceilings, and glistening wooden floors. Hearty breakfasts are served in the stone walled dining room.

You'll have to book in advance if you want one of the six lovely rooms at **Pousada Nello Nuno** (Rua Camilo de Brito 59, tel. 31/3551-3375, www.pousadanellonuno.com.br, R$88 d), two blocks away from Praça Tiradentes.

Owned by a printmaker and engraver whose works—along with those of other local artists—adorn the walls, this intimate *pousada* occupies a historic house with an internal courtyard that exudes unpretentious charm.

R$100-200

Although getting there involves a short but grueling walk up from Praça Tiradentes, **Solar das Lajes** (Rua Conselheiro Quintiliano 604, tel. 31/3551-3388, www.solardaslajes.com.br, R$108–120 d) rewards with outstanding views of church spires, towers, and rooftops ringed by mountains. More than just rooms with views, this friendly and charming *pousada* (owned by a local sculptor) offers tranquility, a verdant garden filled with fruit trees, and excellent prices.

While one can't say that Ouro Preto is short on hotels with history and charm, it's hard to outdo the █ **Pouso do Chico Rei** (Rua Brigadeiro Mosqueira 90, tel. 31/3551-1274, www.pousodochicorei.com.br, R$110–160 d). One of the oldest *pousadas* in town, this palatial 18th-century villa sits next to the Teatro Municipal. The lovely rooms—all featuring rustic antiques, fresh flowers, and privileged views—can accommodate 1–5 people and are named after some of the hotel's most illustrious guests, among them Pablo Neruda, Elizabeth Bishop, and Vinícius de Morais. For a complete contrast with things colonial, check into the **Grande Hotel de Ouro Preto** (Rua das Flores 164, tel. 31/3551-5028, www.hotelouro preto.com.br, R$142–192 d), a jarring modernist block designed by Oscar Niemeyer back in the 1940s. Although its being plunked rather unceremoniously in the midst of the *centro histórico* hasn't endeared it to the locals, the interior is bright, uncluttered, and minimalist. The wide open spaces and ample use of glass offer guests a particularly stunning visual feast of Ouro Preto's baroque treasures—whether from the rooms, multiple terraces, or lovely swimming pool.

R$200 and Over

In Ouro Preto, it's not at all difficult to live (at least for a couple of nights) like someone who just struck gold. Located in a sprawling mid-18th-century mansion, the **Pousada do Mondego** (Largo de Coimbra 38, tel. 31/3551-2040, www.mondego.com.br, R$158–396 d) is both intimate and exquisite, a refined yet relaxed mix of colonial furnishings, rustic accents, and modern Brazilian art works, along with 21st-century amenities such as cable TV and high-speed Internet. Aside from a tea salon where a lavish spread is served daily, there is also a bar, an art gallery, and a boutique selling local crafts. The service is so attentive that you will feel quite spoiled. **【 Hotel Solar Nossa Senhora do Rosário** (Rua Getúlio Vargas 270, tel. 31/3551-5200, www.hotelsolardo rosario.com.br, R$189–498 d) is another top-of-the-line experience with poshly understated, tastefully appointed apartments distributed between a former 19th-century grand hotel and a contemporary annex (where the swankiest rooms are). Aside from a renowned French restaurant, the Coq d'Or, there is an atrium where afternoon tea is served, a scotch bar, a fitness center, sauna, and a hilltop pool with stupendous views. The hotel even has its very own (inactive) gold mine.

FOOD

As befits such a major tourist destination, Ouro Preto is exceptionally well-endowed with a wide variety of food options ranging from simple snack bars to gourmet experiences. Moreover, it is renowned for having some of the finest Mineiro cooking in the state.

There are a fair number of cheap eats along Rua Direita, where cafés and snack bars often fill up with the resident student population. The nicest by far is **Café Geraes** (Rua Direita 122, tel. 31/3551-5097, R$15–25), a welcoming space with tiled floors and lots of wood. Locals flock here to nosh on thick *caldos* (soups) and delicious sandwiches or tuck into the succulent homemade pastries. For those on a tight budget, **Vide Gula** (Rua Senador Rocha Lagoa 79, tel. 31/3551-4493, R$12–20) offers a very reasonable per kilo self-service buffet, with an emphasis on Mineiro specialties.

Near the Casa de Contos, **【 Chafariz** (Rua São José 167, tel. 31/3551-2828, 11 A.M.–4 P.M. Tues.–Sun., R$25) is a rustic eatery that has been around since the 1930s. The reason it has survived so long becomes apparent when you tuck into the banquet of Mineiro specialties, including *doces* and *licores*, that are tantalizingly arranged at a long self-service buffet. Many claim that this is the tastiest Mineiro fare in town. Others swear by the equally delicious offerings at **Casa dos Contos Restaurante** (Rua Camilo de Brito 21, tel. 31/3551-5359, noon–4 P.M. Sun.–Tues., noon–10 P.M. Wed.–Sat., R$20–30), situated in the former *senzala* (slaves' quarters) in an 18th-century mansion. While lunch is a per kilo buffet, dinner is à la carte. Especially good is the *frango ao molho pardo.*

If you can't stand to look at another plate of *tutu à mineira,* **Pizzaria O Passo** (Rua São José 56, tel. 31/3552-5089, www.opasso pizzaria.com.br, 5 P.M.–close daily, R$25–35) offers some culinary respite with its appetizing array of pizzas, pastas, and salads as well as a surprisingly large wine cellar. A spacious outdoor terrace offers alfresco dining with a great view.

There are a handful of upscale eateries in Ouro Preto, all of which are surprisingly affordable. The crème-de-la-crème is **【 Le Coq d'Or** in Hotel Solar Nossa Senhora do Rosário (Rua Getúlio Vargas 270, tel. 31/3551-5200, 7–11 P.M. daily, R$50–70). It is often cited as one of the best restaurants not only in Minas, but in all of Brazil. The Cordon Bleu–trained chef applies French techniques and influences to local ingredients, and the inspired results—pork tenderloin with a *jabuticaba* coulis or salmon in a sauce of green pepper and *pequi*—are sumptuous. The wine menu is excellent and the dining room itself, with its stone walls, pink quartzite floors, and Italian crystal, is discreetly elegant.

Piacere (Rua Getúlio Vargas 241, tel. 31/3551-4297, 7 P.M.–midnight Tues.–Sat., noon–4:30 P.M. Sun., www.restaraunte piacere.com.br, R$35–50) is another top-of-the-line classic. The Italian menu features delicacies such as risotto with fungi and spaghetti with scallops. All the pasta is homemade on the premises. The minimalist decor contrasts nicely with the cavern-like environs of the stone cellar in which the restaurant is housed.

Chocoholics beware: Next to the Igreja Nossa Senhora do Rosário dos Pretos, **Chocolate com Arte** (Rua Getúlio Vargas 66, tel. 31/3551-7330, 9 A.M.–9 P.M. daily) offers serious temptation for chocolate lovers, especially those with a weakness for truffles. Although the best-sellers are those stuffed with a mousse of *maracujá* (passion fruit), there are a wealth of fillings ranging from *abacaxi* (a type of pineapple) to *cachaça*.

INFORMATION AND SERVICES

The main **tourist office** (Praça Tiradentes 41, tel. 31/3559-3269, 8 A.M.–6 P.M. daily) sells detailed maps of the city for R$5. Staff can also organize treks and horseback-riding trips into the surrounding mountains. If you want a guide to accompany you (a wise idea), make sure they are registered with the office. For online information about Ouro Preto, a useful website (in Portuguese) is www.ouro preto.com.br. For info in English check out www.ouropreto.org.br and www.idasbrasil .com.br/oficialouropreto.

Banco do Brasil (Rua São José 195) accepts international bank cards, as does the Bradesco on Praça Tiradentes. For Internet access, **Cyberhouse** (Rua Direita 109, tel. 31/3552-2808, 11 A.M.–8 P.M. daily) offers high-speed access as well as snacks and drinks.

GETTING THERE

There is direct bus service to Ouro Preto from Belo Horizonte, Rio de Janeiro, and São Paulo. **Pássaro Verde** (tel. 31/3559-3252, www .passaroverde.com.br) offers frequent service between Ouro Preto and Belo Horizonte (95 kilometers/59 miles away) with buses leaving between every 1–2 hours every day. The trip takes 1.5–2 hours. The *rodoviária* (Rua Padre Rolim 661, tel. 31/3559-3252) is a 10-minute walk from Praça Tiradentes. If you don't want to deal with the hills, minibus service runs into town. Driving from Belo Horizonte, the journey is very quick. Take the BR-040 in the direction of Rio de Janeiro, and then turn off onto the BR-356, following the signs to Ouro Preto.

Mariana

Only 12 kilometers (8 miles) from Ouro Preto, Mariana is smaller and less ornate—also less touristy—than its neighbor. Founded in 1696 on the site of a major gold deposit and named after King Dom João's wife, Maria Ana of Austria, it proudly claims to be the oldest city in Minas Gerais. Although you can easily discover its attractions in a day trip from Ouro Preto, you might want to stay for a couple of days to fully appreciate its tranquility, scenic mountain backdrop, and pleasant streets lined with elegant colonial homes.

SIGHTS

Mariana's key sites are all clustered together, and thankfully, its streets are much less steep than those of other *cidades históricas*. The most impressive and stately colonial mansions are clustered on or around the principal street of Rua Direita. The main, and surprisingly verdant, colonial square, **Praça Minas Gerais**—at the center of which sits a stirring replica of the original *pelourinho* (whipping post) where slaves were publicly punished—is really quite splendid. It is flanked by two imposing baroque churches, the Igreja de São Francisco de Assis and the Igreja de Nossa Senhora do Carmo, as well as the stately 18th-century Casa de Câmara e Cadeia, the former city hall and jail, which today is the seat of the municipal government.

Churches

Although Mariana possesses fewer churches than Ouro Preto, the handful it does have are

MINAS GERAIS

all quite interesting. In part, this is because Mariana was the headquarters of the bishop of Minas Gerais. Moreover, one of the town's most famous native sons was the master painter Manuel Costa Ataíde, a terrifically expressive artist and superb colorist who often collaborated with the sculptor Aleijadinho on many of Minas's greatest baroque churches.

On Praça Minas Gerais, the lovely **Igreja de São Francisco de Assis** (8 A.M.–noon and 1–5 P.M. Tues.–Sun., R$2), constructed between 1763 and 1794, boasts an ornate medallion above its front door that was sculpted in soapstone by Aleijadinho. Inside, you will find the burial place of Ataíde (look for number 94 on the church floor), who painted the exquisite ceiling panels depicting the life and death of St. Francis of Assisi. Not as impressive, but still quite graceful is the **Igreja de Nossa Senhora de Carmo** (8 A.M.–noon and 1–5 P.M. Tues.–Sun.), completed in 1784, which was recently restored after being partially destroyed by a fire in 1999.

From Praça Minas Gerais, if you walk uphill along the pretty Rua Dom Silvério, you'll reach the **Basílica Menor de São Pedro dos Clérigos** (9 A.M.–noon and 1–4 P.M. Tues.–Sun., R$1). Begun in 1752, it was never entirely finished. More interesting than the actual church are the arresting panoramic views from its palmy hilltop perch. The oldest and most opulent church in town is undoubtedly the **Catedral Basílica de Nossa Senhora de Assunção** (Praça Claudio Manoel, tel. 31/3557-1216, R$1). Built in the early 1700s when the region was still flush with gold, this cathedral is among the most richly ornamented churches in Minas. Both Manoel Francisco Lisboa and his son Aleijadinho (who carved the baptismal font) collaborated on the church as did Ataíde. Aside from the finely carved altars covered in gold, there are chandeliers of Bohemian crystal and a magnificent German organ featuring 969 pipes. Organ concerts are held at 11 A.M. on Fridays and noon on Sundays, for R$12.

Museu Arquidiocesano

Considered one of the finest sacred art museums in Brazil, the Museu Arquidiocesano (Rua Frei Durão, 8:30 A.M.–noon and 1:30–5 P.M. Tues.–Fri., 8:30 A.M.–2 P.M. Sat.–Sun., R$5) has an extensive collection of over 2,000 religious objects, among them works by Aleijadinho and Ataíde, as well as plenty of gold, silver, sculptures, and vestments, most of them dating from the 18th and 19th centuries.

Mina de Ouro da Passagem

Located 5 kilometers (3 miles) outside of Mariana on the road to Ouro Preto, the Mina de Ouro da Passagem (tel. 31/3357-5000, 9 A.M.–5 P.M. daily, R$17) is the largest gold mine in the world currently open to visitors. Between its founding in the early 1700s and its closure in 1985, more than 35 tons of gold were extracted from its dark subterranean tunnels. Today, only a fraction of its labyrinthine passageways are open to visitors, but the experience of wandering through them is deliciously eerie. To begin exploring the underground galleries, you'll have to brave a descent of 120 meters in a creaky cable car. Guided tours provide an interesting history of mining techniques. Bring along a bathing suit to take advantage of the shallow, surprisingly blue (and very icy) underwater lagoon. All buses that run between Mariana and Ouro Preto pass by the *mina;* simply request that the driver let you off in front of the entrance.

ACCOMMODATIONS

Mariana has a number of attractive and affordable *pousadas* within walking distance of Praça Minas Gerais. Located in a very handsome mid-19th century edifice, **Hotel Providência** (Rua Dom Silvério 233, tel. 31/3557-1444, www.hotelprovidencia.com.br, R$50 pp) combines a welcoming ambiance with irresistible prices. Simple but cheery single, double, and triple rooms occupy quarters formerly inhabited by the nuns who still run the adjacent school (guests can use the pool when school's out). For those on a budget, dorm rooms cost R$35 per person. One of the most attractive options in town, the **Pousada Solar dos Côrrea** (Rua Josafa Macedo 70, tel. 31/3557-2080, www.pousadasolardoscorrea.com.br,

R$120 d) offers nicely decorated rooms for up to five people in a beautifully renovated 18th-century manor.

A bit of a walk from the center is the **Pousada Ladim Gamarano** (Rua Raimundo Gamarano 1, tel. 31/3557-1835, R$50–85 d). Perched on Colina São Pedro, it offers attractive views of Mariana and the surrounding mountains. Just as appealing as the backdrop is warm and inviting interior of the *pousada:* Lots of polished wood, a working fireplace, and original furnishings made by owner/artist Ladim Gamarano make guests feel decidedly at home.

FOOD

Mariana's restaurant options are more humble than those in Ouro Preto. For a quick, tasty, and inexpensive lunch, **Lua Cheia** (Rua Dom Viçoso 23, tel. 31/3557-3232, 11 A.M.–3 P.M. daily, 6–10 P.M. Tues.–Sat., R$12–17) is a pleasantly inviting per kilo self-service restaurant with stone walls and wooden floors, which offers scores of salads and hot dishes as well as Mineiro specialties and *churrasco.* Another local favorite, **Dom Silvério** (Praça Gomes Freire 242, tel. 31/3557-2475, 6:30 P.M.–midnight daily, R$20–30) is renowned for serving up the best pizzas in town as well as some very fine lasagnas. Slightly more upscale but still down-to-earth is **Bistrô** (Rua Salomão Ibrahim 61-A, tel. 31/3557-1919, 6 P.M.–midnight Mon.–Sat.,

11:30 A.M.–11 P.M. Sun., R$30–40), a small, cozy restaurant that offers a little bit of everything on its menu, from Mineiro specialties to fish and meat dishes and even sushi.

INFORMATION

There is a helpful **tourist office** (Praça Tancredo Neves, tel. 31/3557-1158, 8 A.M.–5 P.M. daily) where you can get info and purchase a map. You can also consult www.mariana.mg.gov.br (Portuguese only).

GETTING THERE

Local buses from Ouro Preto arrive and depart from Praça Tancredo Neves approximately every 30 minutes. The main bus station (Rodovia dos Inconfidentes, tel. 31/3557-1122) is a 2-kilometer (1.2-mile) hike from town. From here, buses leave and arrive from Belo Horizonte, São João del Rei, and Diamantina.

If you plan to be traveling between Ouro Preto and Mariana on the weekend, forsake buses altogether and take advantage of the **Maria Fumaça steam train** (tel. 31/3557-3844, www.tremdavale.com.br, Fri.–Sun., R$18 one-way), which connects the two towns. The hour-long journey through the mountains is wonderfully scenic. Mariana–Ouro Preto trains depart at 9 A.M. and 2:30 P.M., and Ouro Preto–Mariana trains leave at 11 A.M. and 4:30 P.M. By car, Ouro Preto and Mariana are linked by the BR-356 highway.

Congonhas

Although considered a *cidade histórica,* there is nothing very historical—or attractive for that matter—about Congonhas except for the magnificent Basílica e Santuário do Bom Jesus de Matosinhos; a national treasure that features the last and, according to many art experts, greatest work of Aleijadinho. During the master sculptor's lifetime, Congonhas was a flourishing gold mining town. However, two centuries later, when iron was discovered in the surrounding hills, the resulting industrial activity caused most of the town's colonial architecture to be wiped out and replaced by ugly buildings. Remaining untouched by the wrecking ball was the *basílica,* replete with a magnificent staircase featuring sculptures of the 12 Old Testament prophets and six chapels with carved figures representing scenes from the Passion of Christ. Considered one of the high points of Brazilian baroque, today the sanctuary is recognized as a World Heritage Site by UNESCO.

SIGHTS
◖ Basílica e Santuário do Bom Jesus de Matosinhos

The Basílica e Santuário do Bom Jesus de Matosinhos (Praça da Basílica, 8 A.M.–6 P.M. Tues.–Sun., free) is the only real reason to visit Congonhas—but what a reason! Despite his compromised physical state, Aleijadinho was at the height of his talent when he was summoned to create sculptures for this sanctuary crowning the steep hill known as Morro de Maranhão. The man behind this ambitious project, Feliciano Mendes, was a descendant of the Portuguese royal family. When Mendes was cured from a supposedly fatal disease, he attributed his miraculous recovery to the prayers he had offered up to Good Jesus of Matosinhos (a city in Portugal). As thanks, he vowed to build a magnificent basilica in Christ's honor.

The church itself—modeled after the church of Bom Jesus in Braga, Portugal—is simple on the outside but splendidly ornate on the inside. Construction began in 1757. Although the church was built in four years, it took another 55 years to complete the rest of this vast sanctuary. Aleijadinho himself was only brought on board in 1796. For the next decade, he would work obsessively. Physically, he was so debilitated that his assistants had to strap him to the scaffolding and bind chisels and hammers to his wrists since some of his fingers had fallen off.

Aleijadinho's life-sized statues representing the 12 prophets of the Old Testament are the highlight of any visit to Congonhas. Carved out of native soapstone by Aleijadinho and his disciples, they dominate the majestic stone staircase that leads up to the church. When glimpsed close up, the prophets' faces, ravaged by the elements, are startlingly expressive and often fierce, particularly when viewed against the brooding mountain backdrop.

The other high point of Aleijadinho's oeuvre at Congonhas is the Passion of Christ: seven tableaus he sculpted representing The Last Supper, Calvary, Imprisonment, Flagellation, Coronation, the Carrying of the Cross, and the Crucifixion. The scenes (enclosed behind iron bars for security) are within six small, domed chapels (one of which contains two scenes), designed by Aleijadinho. The chapels—set off by two columns of imperial palms—are strategically placed along a steep hill (symbolizing the ascent towards the cross) that leads up to the 12 Prophets and the church.

In each scene, the carved human figures are rendered even more vivid by the talents of master painter Manuel da Costa Ataíde. Although the Roman soldiers—which were sculpted by Aleijadinho's apprentices—are crudely rendered and resemble rather grotesque, oversized toys, the apostles and Christ are carved in much more detail with veins, furrows, and muscles that almost seem to flex and twitch. The figures of Christ were carved by Aleijadinho himself and are disarmingly lifelike. In the brutally dramatic later scenes contemplating them is harrowing enough to give you goosebumps.

Before leaving the basilica, visit the small sanctuary adjacent to the church. Here, thousands of pilgrims from all over Brazil have left ex-votos, paintings, photographs, and letters to Bom Jesus de Matosinhos, thanking him for miraculous cures and divine intervention in the face of myriad tragedies. Even if you aren't religious and don't read Portuguese, it's difficult not to be moved by such powerful expressions of faith dating back well over two centuries. The oldest ex-voto—from 1722—is from a slave who gave thanks after recovering from a life-threatening fever.

ACCOMMODATIONS AND FOOD

Since Congonhas is so close to Belo Horizonte and the other *cidades históricas,* most tourists spend a couple of hours visiting the *basílica* before hightailing it out of town. However, if you want to check out Aleijadinho's masterpiece lit up by early morning or late afternoon sunlight, not to mention moonlight, consider checking into the **Colonial Hotel** (Praça da Basílica 76, tel. 31/3731-1834, www.hotelcolonial congonhas.com.br, R$85–95 d), right across the street from the sanctuary. This 100-year-old hotel has definitely seen better times, but it has retained a faded air of elegance. The rather stark decor is more than compensated for by the enormously high ceilings, highly polished wood floors, and views of the *basílica*. The hotel's cavernous basement restaurant, **Cova do Daniel** (9 A.M.–8 P.M. Mon.–Thurs., 9 A.M.–10 P.M. Fri.–Sat., 9 A.M.–8 P.M. Sun., R$30–40) is a little on the dim side but serves up reasonably priced fine-tasting Mineiro food for both lunch and dinner.

GETTING THERE

Congonhas is only an hour from Belo Horizonte. The **Sandra bus company** (tel. 31/3201-2927) offers service from Belo Horizonte's *rodoviária* with a stop in Congonhas before continuing on to São Jóao del Rei. There are approximately six buses daily, with fewer running on Saturday and Sunday. There are also daily buses from Ouro Preto, which is two hours away. By car, take the BR-040 south from Belo Horizonte or the BR-265 from São João del Rei until you hit the BR-040 leading north to Congonhas.

São João del Rei

The largest of the *cidades históricas,* São João boasts an impressive colonial center flush with architectural treasures as well as a more developed, commercial area that is less seductive. For better or for worse, it is the only former gold mining town that made the successful transition into modern times. When the gold ran out, São João became a center for commerce and as a result remains quite a lively place. You can see most of São João's sights—a handful of magnificent churches and quite a few elegant old mansions—in a day, although the city is pleasant enough to warrant staying overnight. Otherwise, it is a convenient base for exploring the region, especially if you don't have a car. On the charm scale, however, its smaller neighbor, Tiradentes, only 12 kilometers (8 miles) away, is much prettier and more uniformly colonial.

SIGHTS

All of São João's most interesting attractions are clustered together in the *centro histórico.* Thankfully, there are fewer steep hills to clamber up and down than in Minas's other historic towns. As you walk around, you'll hear a lot of bells ringing: The bells of the city's churches are regulated to chime the hour at slightly different intervals, which creates a symphonic effect.

Igreja de São Francisco de Assis

The Igreja de São Francisco de Assis (Praça Frei Orlando, tel. 32/3372-3110, 8 A.M.–5:40 P.M. Mon.–Sat., 7 A.M.–4 P.M. Sun., R$2) is the most magnificent of São João's attractions, and it is also one of the most splendid examples of late baroque architecture in Minas. The exterior view of the church is quite striking. Monumental in stature, it dominates an elegantly landscaped square surrounded by colonial villas. The main entrance is punctuated by two columns of imperial palms. The original design of the church was one of Aleijadinho's first projects. He also created the sculptures of the Immaculate Virgin and the angels on the building's facade. Inside, Aleijadinho contributed to the main altar and carved the statues of Santo Antônio and São João Evangelista. The church interior is a sublime example of rococo. Much of the sculpted woodwork is without the usual dousing in gold because by the time this church was built, gold was already becoming somewhat scarce in the region. Compensating somewhat for this lack of glitter are the oversized chandeliers fashioned out of Baccarat crystal. On Sundays at 9 A.M. there is a mass at which the traditional Ribeiro Bastos women's choir performs baroque music.

Behind the church, the small cemetery is the final resting place of Tancredo Neves, who, in 1985, following two decades of military

MINAS GERAIS

MINAS GERAIS

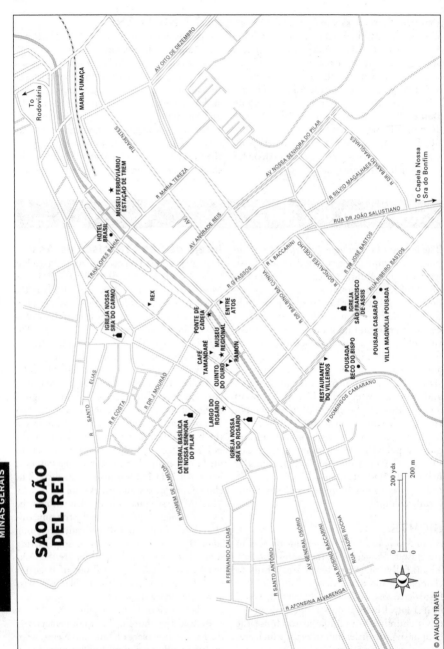

SÃO JOÃO DEL REI

To Rodoviária

MARIA FUMAÇA

AV OITO DE DEZEMBRO

TIRADENTES

MUSEU FERROVIÁRIO/
ESTAÇÃO DE TREM ★

R. MARIA TEREZA

AV NOSSA SENHORA DO PILAR

R SILVIO MAGALHÃES

R DR BASILIO MAGALHÃES

To Capela Nossa
Sra do Bonfim

RUA DR JOÃO SALUSTIANO

HOTEL
BRASIL ●

TRAV LOPES BAHIA

AV ANDRADE REIS

AV

R. GONÇALVES COELHO

R L BACCARINI

R DR JOSÉ BASTOS

REX ▼

R. G. PASSOS

IGREJA NOSSA
SRA DO CARMO ◀

PONTE DE
CADEIA ★

ENTRE
ATOS

R DR BALBINO DA CUNHA

RUA RIBEIRO BASTOS

CAFÉ
TAMANDARÉ ▼

MUSEU
★ REGIONAL

IGREJA
SÃO FRANCISCO
DE ASSIS ◀

POUSADA CASARÃO ●

QUINTO
DO OURO ●

RAMON ★

VILLA MAGNÓLIA POUSADA

R SANTO
ELIAS

R R. COSTA

R DR J. MOURÃO

RESTAURANTE
DO VILLEIROS ▼

POUSADA
BECO DO BISPO ▼

R DOMINGOS CAMARANO

LARGO DO
ROSÁRIO ★

CATEDRAL BASÍLICA
DE NOSSA SENHORA
DO PILAR ◀

IGREJA NOSSA
SRA DO ROSÁRIO ◀

R HOMEM DE ALMEIDA

R FERNANDO CALDAS

R SANTO
ANTÔNIO

AV GENERAL OSÓRIO

RUA ROSINO BACCARINI

RUA PADRE ROCHA

R AFONSINA ALVARENGA

200 yds

200 m

0

0

© AVALON TRAVEL

Igreja de São Francisco de Assis, São João del Rei

dictatorship, was Brazil's first democratically elected president. Tragically, Tancredo died before he could take office, and ever since he has been somewhat of a martyr figure, particularly in São João where he was born and grew up.

Catedral Basílica de Nossa Senhora do Pilar

Built in the 1720s, the Catedral Basílica de Nossa Senhora de Pilar (Rua Getúlio Vargas, tel. 32/3371-2568, 6–10:30 A.M. and 1–7:30 P.M. Tues.–Sun., free) is São João's (and one of Minas's) most sumptuous since gold was in abundance during the time of its construction. The finely sculpted columns and altars are quite dazzling with their gilded angels, flowers, twists, and swirls. The ceiling murals are beautifully painted; their distinctive coloring was achieved by the use of natural pigments. Note the figure of São Miguel, which is encrusted with diamonds and emeralds.

Igreja de Nossa Senhora do Carmo

Perched on a lovely triangular cobblestoned *praça* at the end of Rua Getúlio Vargas, the Igreja de Nossa Senhora do Carmo (Largo do Carmo, tel. 32/3371-7996, 7 A.M.–noon and 4–7 P.M. Mon.–Sat., 7–11 A.M. and 5–7 P.M. Sun., R$1) was designed by Aleijadinho, who also sculpted the frontispiece. Construction on the church began in the 1730s and lasted throughout most of the century, which accounts for the varying styles of baroque. When it came time to decorate the interior, dwindling gold supplies resulted in the exposed white stone whose raw, bleached beauty is offset by angels and flowers painted in frosting-colored pinks and yellows. The unusual sculpture of Christ, unadorned and carved from cedar, was found beneath some rubble when the church was undergoing renovations in the early 20th century. Its origins are a mystery.

Igreja de Nossa Senhora do Rosário

Much simpler than the other churches, Igreja de Nossa Senhora do Rosário (Largo do Rosário, tel. 32/3371-4789, 8–11 A.M. Tues.–Sun.) was built by and for São João's slave population and is the town's oldest church. Located at the

MINAS GERAIS

beginning of Rua Getúlio Vargas, it is adjacent to the elegant Solar dos Neves, the traditional home of the Neves family, where future president Tancredo was born and raised.

Museu Regional

Not far from the cathedral, on Largo Tamandaré is the interesting Museu Regional (Rua Marechal Deodoro 12, tel. 32/3371-7663, 12:30–5:30 P.M. Tues.–Sun., R$1), in a very handsome mansion built in 1859. Spread out among three floors is a collection of furniture (lots of great beds), religious icons, and various domestic items—all of which help illustrate 18th- and 19th-century life in São João.

SHOPPING

As you wander around São João del Rei, you can't help but notice the extraordinary number of boutiques selling finely wrought pewter household and decorative objects. In fact, São João is the pewter capital of Brazil, and this is the place to pick up a decanter, a set of goblets, or a candlestick holder made of this alloy of tin and copper (although they don't come cheap). Interestingly, what may appear to be an age-old artisanal tradition actually only dates back half a century. While doing geological research, an Englishman named John Somers discovered that the hills surrounding São João were rich with tin. As a result, he moved to São João and started his own pewter factory. Over time, his apprentices opened their own ateliers, and today the city is flooded with them (ironically, most of the pewter now comes from the Amazonian state of Rondônia). Situated just behind the bus station, the original **John Somers** factory is still highly reputed. Even if you're not in a purchasing mood, you can visit the small **Museu de Estanho** (Av. Leite de Castro 1150, tel. 32/3371-8000, 9 A.M.–6 P.M. Mon.–Sat., 9 A.M.–4 P.M. Sun.) located on the premises, which features pewter pieces from all over Brazil and Europe.

Other recommended shops to stock up on pewter include **Nolan Pewter** (Praça Frei Orlando 42, tel. 32/3371-7749, www.estanho nolanpewter.com.br), **Ame Arte** (Rua Getúlio Vargas 73, tel. 32/3371-8109, www .amearteestanhos.com.br), and **Imperial Pewter** (Rua da Prata, 132A, tel. 32/3372-3519, www.imperialestanhos.com.br).

ACCOMMODATIONS

São João del Rei has some good options right in the heart of the *centro histórico*. Budget-minded travelers might want to consider basing themselves in São João instead of neighboring Tiradentes, where accommodations are considerably more pricy, especially on the weekends and during holidays. Nonetheless, even in São João take care to book ahead during Carnaval and Semana Santa.

Hotel Brasil (Av. Presidente Tancredo Neves 395, tel. 32/3371-8953, hotel.brasil@ig.com.br, R$20–30 pp) must have been rather grand at one time. Occupying an immense mansion directly across from the old train station, the 100-year-old hotel has definitely seen better times. Rooms are clean but rather bare and a little tired around the edges. Nonetheless, the old fixtures and lofty ceilings imbue the place with a certain retro charm. And there's no beating the location and the price.

Pousada Casarão (Rua Ribeiro Bastos 94, tel. 32/3371-7447, www.pousadacasarao.com, R$130 d) is a great bargain in a spacious historic villa that looks onto the back of the Igreja de São Francisco de Assis. The interior is not as "colonial" as one might expect from the outside, but the hotel itself is welcoming and the rooms are cozy and comfortable. There is a pool as well.

Facing the Igreja de São Francisco de Assis is the **Ⓒ Villa Magnólia Pousada** (Rua Ribeiro Bastos 2, tel. 32/3373-5065, www.pousadavilla magnolia.com.br, R$125–155 d). It too occupies an attractive colonial manse, but here the charm factor is considerably higher with antique furnishings and art work decorating the living and dining areas as well as the rooms themselves. Along with a lovely pool, internal courtyards, terraces, and lots of plants and flowers make the place somewhat of an oasis. Also nearby is the **Pousada Beco do Bispo** (Beco do Bispo 93, tel. 32/3371-8844, www.becodobispo.com.br,

R$150 d). What this lovely *pousada* lacks in history, it makes up for in warmth, comfort, and attention to details. There is a very homey feel to the place, with lots of carefully chosen knick-knacks, polished wood, and a fireplace in the living room. The pool area is quite posh and breakfast is a lavish affair.

The **Villa Buonabitacolo Pousada** (Rua Santo Antôntio 400, Colônia do Marçal, tel. 32/3371-1014, www.buona.com.br, R$130–140 d) is 5 kilometers (3 miles) from São João's historical center, in a bucolic neighborhood surrounded by trees and the low-lying Serra de São José mountain range. Getting here is a bit tricky—you'll need to take a taxi, *moto-taxi*, or have a car—but this ranch-style *pousada* is worthwhile for those in search of respite. While rooms are sizable and comfortable, it's the grounds that are impressively sprawling, with enough space to contain a pool, tennis courts, a movie theater, playground, barbecue area, fitness room, and sauna, not to mention plenty of trees, and a few peacocks to boot. Some apartments have kitchens, making this is an excellent place for groups and families who want to set up house. The friendly owners rent bikes (Tiradentes is only 6 kilometers/4 miles away over the São José mountain range).

FOOD

Locals will tell you that it's much easier and cheaper to pig out in São João than in nearby Tiradentes. **(Restaurante do Villeiros** (Rua da Prata 132A, tel. 32/3372-1034, www.villeiros .com.br, 11:30 A.M.–close daily, R$30–40) is a really charming eatery, with tables sprinkled throughout a prettily decorated colonial mansion and internal courtyard. At lunch, the very reasonably priced per kilo self service buffet features delicious Mineiro specialties as well as a slew of creatively prepared alternatives and plenty of salads. The desserts are really outstanding. There is also an à la carte menu (for both lunch and dinner) with options such as *linguiça com molho de vinho* (pork sausage cooked in wine) and *frango com molho de maracujá* (chicken with passion fruit sauce).

For lunch, another good and inexpensive per kilo restaurant is **Restaurante Rex** (Rua Marechal Deodoro 124, tel. 32/3374-1449, www.restauranterex.com.br, 11 A.M.–3:30 P.M., R$10–15). Its specialty is Mineiro dishes, which can be savored in the casually sophisticated dining room with white tablecloths and pearl pink walls. Reputed to have the best Mineiro food in town is **Quinto do Ouro** (Largo Tamandaré 4, tel. 32/3371-7577, 11 A.M.–10 P.M. Tues.–Sat., 11 A.M.–6 P.M. Sun.–Mon., R$40–50). This charmingly rustic restaurant is justifiably renowned for typical dishes such as *leitão à pururuca, tutu à mineira,* and *frango com quiabo,* as well as its desserts. The presentation is attractive and service is attentive.

Carnivores will appreciate sinking their teeth into the meaty fare at **Churrascaria e Restaurante Ramon** (Largo Tamandaré 52, tel. 32/3371-3540, 10 A.M.–10 P.M. daily, R$30–40), which specializes in substantial portions of prime cuts of barbecued beef as well as chicken. This family-run cantina, featuring long wooden tables and dark blue table cloths, has been in operation for 40 years and is somewhat of an institution.

For something light and contemporary (in terms of both food and ambiance), head to **Entre Atos** (Av. Hermílio Alves 146, tel. 32/3371-9110, 9 A.M.–8 P.M. café, 6 P.M.–close daily for dinner, lunch Sat.–Sun., R$25–40), in a fetching red villa next to the municipal theater. Although locals often drink or dine here before or after a show, during the day it's an inviting place to stop for coffee and snacks (including tempting pastries and organic chocolates). At night, the dinner menu features appetizing selections such as salmon with *molho de maracujá* (passion fruit sauce) and *costelinha ao vapor de laranja* (pork ribs with orange). For café culture of a more traditional variety, head to **Café Tamandaré** (Rua Marechal Deodoro 232, tel. 32/3371-7838, 8 A.M.–5 P.M. Mon.–Fri., 8 A.M.–noon Sat.). The overpowering scent of freshly ground coffee will overwhelm you before you even set foot upon the patterned marble floors of this atmospheric old-fashioned coffee bar. Home-brewed Tamandaré coffee—grown in Minas

Gerais—is ground and packaged in an adjacent room (which accounts for the heady perfume). When you finish getting your caffeine fix, purchase a bag or two to take with you.

INFORMATION

The **tourist office** (Praça Frei Orlando 90, tel. 32/3372-7338, 8:30 A.M.–6 P.M. Mon.–Fri., 8 A.M.–noon Sat.) offers free maps. Two useful websites with listings, information, and maps (both in Portuguese) are www.saojoaodelrei.mg.gov.br. and www.saojoaodelreisite.com.br. For organized tours—by Jeep, mountain bike, or on horseback—throughout the region, as well as information about sports activities such as rappelling and mountain climbing, get in touch with **Lazer e Aventura Turismo** (Rua Antônio Josino de Andrade Reis 232, tel. 32/3371-7956, www.lazereaventura.com).

GETTING THERE AND AROUND

São João is quite easy to get to. **Sandra** (tel. 32/3201-2927 in Belo) company buses run between São João and Belo Horizonte (3.5 hours) with approximately 6–7 buses daily. Service is less frequent on weekends. There are also buses to and from Mariana (with connections to Ouro Preto), Rio de Janeiro, and São Paulo. Buses to Tiradentes (only 12 kilometers/8 miles away) leave at regular intervals throughout the day.

By car from Belo Horizonte, take the BR-040 south and then turn onto the BR-383. São João also has a recently inaugurated airport, 8 kilometers (5 miles) from the center of town, with flights from Pampuha airport in Belo Horizonte and Santos Dumont airport in Rio, operated by **Total** (tel. 0300/789-6464, www.total.com.br).

MARIA FUMAÇA STEAM TRAIN

Today you can count on one hand the number of railroad lines still in operation in Brazil. In most cases one can only imagine what it must have been like to journey over such great distances and be treated to such a variety of magnificent scenery. Fortunately, in the case of the railroad line that connected São João del Rei and Tiradentes, no such imaginings are necessary. The Maria Fumaça (Smoking Mary) is a 19th-century steam train in tiptop condition that makes the 20-kilometer (12-mile) trip between the two historic cities, chugging away on one of the first railroad lines ever built in Brazil. The slow but scenic voyage takes you through the valley of the Serra de São José mountain range, where you can glimpse the vestiges of 18th-century gold-mining activity.

São João del Rei's train station (Avenida Hermílio Alves, tel. 32/3371-8485) features a small museum, where you can gaze at train paraphernalia before purchasing a ticket and jumping aboard the spitting and whistling Mary. The train only operates on Fridays, Saturdays, and Sundays, leaving from São João at 10 A.M. and 3 P.M. and from Tiradentes at 1 P.M. and 5 P.M. A one-way adult ticket costs R$15.

The **rodoviária** (Rua Cristovão Colombo, tel. 32/3373-4700) is about 1.5 kilometers (1 mile) from the *centro histórico*. Unless you don't mind a long hike, catch a local bus out front or a taxi. A much cheaper and more fun way of getting around town is by *moto-taxi*. There is a stand outside the bus station.

Tiradentes

This small, incredibly charming colonial town has a historical center that is splendidly intact and a cinematographic backdrop of rolling green hills that is quite mesmerizing. Its steep cobblestoned streets are lined with gleaming churches and elegant mansions, and bright pink and red tropical flowers blossom in profusion. There are so many perspectives from which to admire the views that you can easily spend hours wandering around, despite the fact that the town itself consists of little more than a dozen streets. Tiradentes's drop-dead beauty and sophisticated cultural and culinary scene make it a favorite refuge for artists and intellectuals as well as upscale visitors from Rio and São Paulo, who descend upon the town on weekends and holidays. In fact, if you want to avoid the crowds, make a point to visit during the week, when you'll have the placid streets and baroque churches to yourself.

SIGHTS

Simply meandering through the town is a main attraction in itself. However, certain sights are worth taking special note of.

Largo das Forras

The main square of Largo das Forras is flanked by the pretty chapel of Bom Jesus da Pobreza and other handsome 18th-century buildings that formerly served as administrative palaces. Today they have become hotels and restaurants, all of which gaze onto a park designed in 1989 by noted landscaper Roberto Burle Marx. At night, when the rest of town falls quiet, this square is where all the action takes place, especially on weekends.

Chafariz de São José

Built in 1749, the striking baroque Chafariz de São José—a well that long supplied the town's fresh water supply—features three faucets protruding from the mouths of a trio of magnificently sculpted heads. Originally, one faucet supplied drinking water, another was used for washing clothes, and the third was reserved for thirsty livestock. Behind the well, a lush woodland area leads to the well's natural water source.

Museu Padre Toledo

The Museu Padre Toledo (Rua Padre Toledo 190, tel. 32/3355-1549, 9–11:30 a.m. and 1–4:30 p.m., R$3) occupies a vast mansion whose sky-high ceilings are covered with frescoes. It belonged to Padre Toledo, a priest, an Inconfidente, and apparently a bon vivant judging by the size and suggested former opulence of his none-too-humble abode. The museum's collection consists of a smattering of religious objects, and domestic furnishings dating from Tiradentes's wealthy gold mining days.

◖ Igreja Matriz de Santo Antônio

It's hard to miss the Igreja Matriz de Santo Antônio (Rua da Câmara, tel. 32/3355-1238, 9 a.m.–5 p.m. daily, R$2), one of the most sumptuous baroque churches in all of Brazil. Perched upon a steep hill, it is visible from myriad points throughout town and you'll certainly waste a lot of film (or digital frames) attempting to get the "perfect" shot (there are several). It's dedicated to Santo Antônio, patron saint of Tiradentes; construction began in 1710, and was only completed some 40 years later. The dazzling interior is plastered with gold—half a ton to be precise—resulting in the resplendence of the seven richly detailed altars and the choir festooned with garlands and flowers. The organ, considered one of the most ornate examples of its kind in the world, was specially made in Portugal. Although the facade was redesigned according to the drawings of Aleijadinho in 1810, the intricate soapstone carvings surrounding the main door were created by one of the master sculptor's pupils. The front patio offers stunning views of the town and the Serra de São José mountains. The sundial sculpted out of native soapstone has become one the city's symbols.

© MICHAEL SOMMERS

a cobblestoned street in Tiradentes

Igreja de Nossa Senhora do Rosário dos Pretos and Other Churches

The town's oldest church (dating from 1708), Igreja de Nossa Senhora do Rosário dos Pretos (Praça Padre Lourival Salvo Rio, tel. 32/3355-1238, 9 A.M.–noon and 2–5 P.M. Tues.–Sun., R$1), on Rua Direita, was where Tiradentes's slave population worshipped, which explains why the altars feature images of black saints. Slaves themselves built it during bright moonlit nights, after having spent days toiling in the mines. The gold flakes they smuggled in their hair and beneath their fingernails were used to adorn the altars.

Tiradentes has some other churches of interest that are worth popping into. If you keep walking up the steep Rua da Santíssima Trindade from the Igreja Matriz de Santo Antônio, you'll come upon the imposing **Igreja de Santíssima Trindade** (8 A.M.–4:30 P.M. daily). Built in 1810, its simple interior features some colorful trompe l'oeil details. From the Largo das Forras, if you

cross the little stone bridge spanning the river and walk up the lovely Largo das Mercês, you'll see the late-18th-century **Igreja de Nossa Senhora das Mercês** (8 A.M.–4 P.M. Sat.–Sun.), with its richly decorated rococo interior. Walking up the Rua São Francisco from the bus station will bring you to the **Igreja de São Francisco de Paula** (5–7 P.M. Sat.). More interesting than the church itself is the spectacular view of the city and surrounding mountains.

FESTIVALS AND EVENTS

Befitting its status as an upscale tourist mecca, Tiradentes boasts an impressive cultural calendar for a town of its size. Apart from a lively music scene, it lures cinephiles to the **Mostra de Cinema** (January), and chefs from all over Brazil and the world—as well as foodies eager to partake in their culinary creations—during the **Festival Internacional de Cultura e Gastronomia** (August). **Carnaval** and **Semana Santa** (Holy Week) festivities are also pretty lively.

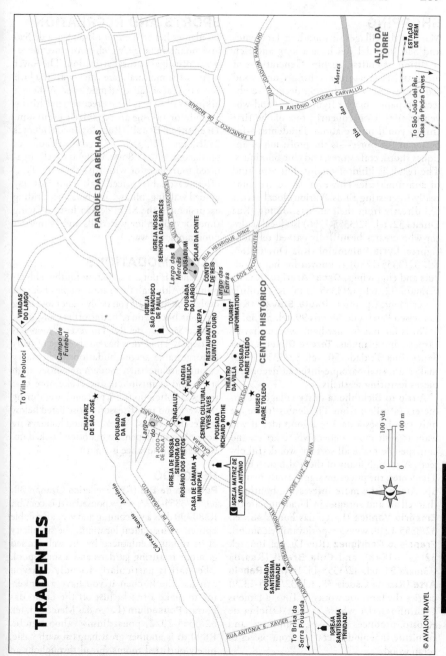

TIRADENTES

To Villa Paolucci

PARQUE DAS ABELHAS

VIRADAS
DO LARGO

Campo de
Futebol

IGREJA NOSSA
SENHORA DAS MERCÊS

IGREJA
SÃO FRANCISCO
DE PAULA

POUSADIUM

SOLAR DA PONTE

Largo das
Mercês

CONTO
DE REIS

POUSADA
DO LARGO

Largo das
Forras

CHAFARIZ
DE SÃO JOSÉ

DONA XEPA

TOURIST
INFORMATION

RESTAURANTE
QUINTO DO OURO

POUSADA DA BIA

Largo
do Ô

CADEIA
PUBLICA

POUSADA
PADRE TOLEDO

CENTRO HISTÓRICO

TRAGALUZ

THEATRO
DA VILLA

CENTRO CULTURAL
YVES ALVES

MUSEO
PADRE TOLEDO

POUSADA
RICHARD ROTHE

IGREJA DE NOSSA
SENHORA DO
ROSARIO DOS PRETOS

CASA DE CAMARA
MUNICIPAL

IGREJA MATRIZ DE
SANTO ANTÔNIO

POUSADA
SANTISSIMA
TRINDADE

IGREJA
SANTISSIMA
TRINDADE

To Brisa da
Serra Pousada

Rio das Mortes

ALTO DA
TORRE

ESTAÇÃO
DE TREM

To São João del Rei;
Casa da Pedra Caves

R ANTÔNIO TEIXEIRA CARVALLIO

R. JOAQUIM RAMALHO

R. FRANCISCO P. DE MORAIS

R. SILVIO DE VASCONCELOS

RUA HENRIQUE DINIZ

R. DOS INCONFIDENTES

R. DIREITA

R. PE. TOLEDO

R. JOSÉ LUIZ DE FAVA

RUA SANTÍSSIMA TRINDADE

LADEIRA SANTÍSSIMA TRINDADE

RUA ANTÔNIA E. XAVIER

Córrego Santo Antônio

RUA DE LIVRAMENTO

R. JOGO DE BOLA

R. DA CHAFARIZ

R. DA CAMARA

100 yds

100 m

© AVALON TRAVEL

MINAS GERAIS

SHOPPING

Many of the villages surrounding Tiradentes and São João del Rei have a long and rich tradition of craftsmanship. Generations of local artists create everything from wood sculptures and wrought-iron decorative objects to papier-mâché figures and hand-woven textiles. Consequently, one of the first things you'll notice about Tiradentes—for better or for worse—is the profusion of antiques shops, craft stores, and chic boutiques. The result is kind of quaint, but also kind of consumeristic. However, there are some really interesting finds. Various local artists sell directly from their ateliers. **Jango** (Rua Direita 32, tel. 32/3355-1756) is a local sculptor who creates beautifully carved religious figures. **Lyria Palombini** (Rua Direita 183, tel. 32/3355-1280) is known for her woodcuts and engravings. **Oscar Araripe** (Rua da Câmara 92, tel. 32/3355-1148) is a prolific experimental painter. **Paula Spivak** (Rua Francisco Pereira de Morais 99, tel. 32/3355-1578) is famous for her hand-woven shawls, carpets, and blankets. **Tereza Oliveira** (Rua Santíssima Tridade 50, tel. 32/3355-1978) makes unusual baroque-inspired decorative pieces featuring seashells.

A trip to Bichinho, a dusty village 7 kilometers (4 miles) from Tiradentes (there are only two buses a day) is a good idea if you want to visit more ateliers where artists and craftspeople make all sorts of wonderful objects. Although many of them also turn up in Tiradentes, the prices are significantly marked up. Among the more interesting boutiques that sell art and antiques in Tiradentes are the **Empório Vanilce** (Largo das Forras 48, tel. 32/3355-1219, www.emporiovanilce.com.br), **Francisco Rodriguez** (Rua Direita 166, tel. 32/3355-1848), and **Cuia Brasil** (Rua da Câmara 83, tel. 32/3355-1521). **Inês Rabelo Arte** (Rua da Cadeia 38, tel. 32/3355-1329) carries the fantastic works of Toto, a famous Bichinho artist whose atelier, Oficina de Agosto, produces canvases, sculptures, and furniture ingeniously crafted from pieces of scrap wood.

SPORTS AND RECREATION

Tiradentes lies at the foot of the Serra de São José mountain range, which constitutes the region's principal natural attraction. The lower parts of the mountain are thick with the lush fauna typical of native Atlantic forest. Although hiking trails exist, locals recommend hiring a guide or taking an organized excursion. **Tiradentes Brasil** (Rua dos Inconfidentes 218B, tel. 32/3355-2477, www.tiradentes brasil.com, 8 A.M.–8 P.M. daily) is a well-organized tour operator with friendly staff. They offer reasonably priced half- and full-day guided walking, biking, and horse-back riding excursions to the Serra de São José, allowing time for dips in icy waterfalls and freshwater pools along the way.

ACCOMMODATIONS

Tiradentes is not a destination for the budget-minded. Although there are a couple of decent deals to be found, if you really want more bang for your buck, you're better off staying in or around São João del Rei. However, if money is no object, Tiradentes has no shortage of truly unforgettable accommodations that marry colonial architecture, modern amenities, high style, and exquisite cuisine. Take note that prices are often up to 50 percent lower during the week and in off-season (those listed below reflect these times). Weekends and holidays are not only more expensive but often booked up. Reserving in advance is a must.

R$50-100

Pousada da Bia (Rua Frederico Ozanan 30, tel. 32/3355-1173, www.pousadadabia.com.br, R$80–90 d) is a welcoming and very affordable option, with an ideal location. The simplicity of its rooms is enhanced by the well-tended grounds featuring gardens and a small pool. The staff is particularly friendly and you can use the kitchen if you have a hankering to make a snack. Just off the Largo das Forras, **Pousadium** (Largo das Mercês 13, tel. 32/3355-2022, pousadium@yahoo.com.br, R$90 d) is another great bargain with basic, nicely outfitted rooms spread throughout an old house. Although it's somewhat lacking in natural light, a homey atmosphere reigns.

R$100-200

The **Pousada do Largo** (Largo das Forras 48-A, tel. 32/3355-1166, www.pousadado largo.com.br, R$180 d) is quite literally a boutique hotel: The vast majority of the regional furnishings, antiques, and handicrafts used to decorate the common rooms of the *pousada* common rooms are for sale (discreet price tags are attached). The soothing whitewashed rooms furnished with dark antiques are a bit small, but the beds are large and comfortable and the bathrooms gleaming. Splurging for a luxury room gets you a Jacuzzi tub with Flintstone-like rock walls. There is also a small swimming pool. Breakfast—served in a wonderful attic mezzanine chock-full of folk art and antiques—is quite lavish, even by Mineiro standards.

Pousada Padre Toledo (Rua Direita 260, tel. 32/3355-2132, www.padretoledo.com.br, R$150 d) boasts a rustic country-style ambiance enhanced by its location in an 18th-century mansion. Some rooms—particularly 1 and 2, which are spacious and have terrific views of the tiled rooftops and mountains—are quite a bit nicer than others (a few are cramped and windowless), so ask to check them out beforehand. Out back is a pool and a stone deck for sunning yourself. The bread served at breakfast is baked fresh from the Padre Toledo bakery around the corner. In the evenings, *caldos* (hearty soups) are served to guests.

For a very decent rate **Pousada Santíssima Trindade** (Rua Santíssima Trindade 140, www.guiatiradentes.com.br, R$130 duplex) offers fully equipped duplex accommodations with kitchens, bedrooms, and living rooms with fireplaces. The seven cottages are quite cozy and have excellent views, overlooking either the mountains or a patch of verdant woodland. This is an ideal choice for families or groups of three or four.

Although it's a bit of a hike from the center of town to **Brisa da Serra Pousada** (Rua Santíssima Trindade 520, tel. 32/3355-1838, www.brisadaserra.com.br, R$190 d), having the impossibly lush and dramatic Serra de São José mountains staring you straight in the face more than compensates. The breathtaking scenery is accentuated by the inspired design featuring multiple gardens and terraces, as well as plenty of natural stone, adobe, wood, and even thousands of dried flowers (which cover the ceiling of the sprawling lounge). Unsurprisingly, the 11 guest chalets are often booked up by honeymooning couples.

R$200-300

❰ **Pousada Richard Rothe** (Rua Padre Toledo 124, tel. 32/3355-1333, www.pousada richardrothe.com.br, R$200–250 d) is an exquisitely stylish *pousada* in a beautifully renovated colonial house. Antiques and an impeccable collection of paintings and objets d'art create a beautifully refined yet extremely comfortable atmosphere. The apartments—each one a different size and featuring distinctive furnishings—are more rustic than the living and dining rooms, which, together with the garden courtyard and turquoise pool, conjure up a Roman villa. Tranquility is ensured by a no-kids-under-12 rule.

Arriving at ❰ **Pousada Villa Paolucci** (Rua do Chafariz, tel. 32/3355-1350, www.villa paolucci.com.br, R$268 d) is like visiting a fabulous film set of a colonial country estate, idyllically ringed by woods and mountains. A 15-minute stroll from the center of town, the main house and surrounding buildings of this former cattle ranch have been converted into luxury lodgings, with a pool and tennis courts, set amidst the expansive grounds. The sumptuous guest rooms are awash with dark shiny wood, antiques, gilt, and deep red velvet, while the immense living and dining pavilions are quite regal. Although it doesn't have its own restaurant, the *pousada* is known for the owner's *leitão de pururca,* a Mineiro specialty of pork roasted to crispy perfection (orders must be made in advance). Unlike some of Tiradentes's other luxury accommodations, Villa Paolucci allows children.

Over R$300

Owned by a British-Brazilian couple, **Solar da Ponte** (Praça das Mercês, tel. 32/3355-1255, www.solardaponte.com.br, R$382–462 d) is a reconstructed colonial villa that is routinely cited as one of the finest hotels in Brazil. Mineiro art and artifacts blend harmoniously with a discreetly English sense of style and comfort, creating a guesthouse that is refined yet unpretentious. The English influence extends to the gorgeously landscaped gardens surrounding the villa, replete with a swimming pool and a lavish afternoon tea. The service is flawless and friendly. If you're in the mood to splurge, the Solar da Ponte is definitely worth it. Children under 12 aren't permitted.

FOOD

Tiradentes is famous for its culinary scene. Although it offers some fine regional Mineiro cooking, in recent years it has become equally renowned as a mecca for haute cuisine. Aside from hosting the Festival Internacional de Cultura e Gastronomia, the town has an impressive number of upscale, romantically lit, critically acclaimed eateries serving experimental contemporary options that seduce foodies from as far away as Rio and São Paulo. The downside is that prices are inflated across the board.

Restaurante Quinta do Ouro (Rua Direita 159, tel. 32/3355-1197, lunch Wed.–Mon., R$12–16) serves a per kilo self service buffet of inexpensive and tasty Mineiro fare, with dishes kept piping hot over a wood-burning stove. This otherwise basic restaurant is nicely located in a high-ceilinged old house looking out onto pretty Rua Direita.

Dona Xepa (Rua Ministro Gabriel Passos 26A, tel. 32/3355-2967, 11 A.M.–9 P.M. Thurs.–Tues., R$25–35) is a warm and welcoming local eatery off the Largo das Forras where you can whet your appetite for hearty Mineiro dishes by sampling one (or several) of the delicious *cachaças* listed on the extensive drink menu. King of the heap is Havana, considered the finest *pinga* on the planet. The house specialty, *Dona Xepa com arroz,* is an aromatic stew of chicken,

corn, and seasonal vegetables. **Conto de Reis** (Largo das Forras 62, tel. 32/3355-1790, daily) is a mellow bar with ample windows that offer a great view of the action taking place on the Largo das Forras. In the evening, tasty and nicely priced sandwiches and light meals can be savored along with a smooth draft, glass of wine, or shot of *cachaça.*

Viradas do Largo (Rua do Moinho 11, tel. 32/3355-1111, noon–10 P.M. Wed.–Mon., R$45–55) is considered, quite unanimously, to be one of the best Mineiro restaurants in the country. The fruits and vegetables that don't come from the restaurant's back garden are purchased fresh from neighboring organic farms. Then they are cooked on a traditional wood-burning stove that has a privileged place in the cozy, country-style dining room. *Viradinha* (a stew featuring beef, beans, kale, pine nuts, and bacon), and *lombo com tutu* (pork with pureed beans) are among the most popular dishes. Since regular portions are big enough to feed three (or even four), you might want to consider a *meia-porção* (half portion).

Tragaluz (Rua Direita 52, tel. 32/3355-1424, www.tragaluz.com.br, 7–10:30 P.M. Wed.–Thurs. and Sun., 7 P.M.–12:30 A.M. Fri.–Sat., R$50–60), another much-touted eatery, specializes in creative adaptations of regional cuisine. The results—such as smoked *surubim* (a freshwater fish) with stuffed zucchini and *banana-da-terra* (a type of plantain) rice, and minced filet with shiitake, yam puree, and kale—are inspired. With lots of burnished wood, candles, and Nina Simone purring in the background, the setting is downright romantic. Leave room for dessert, particularly the fried guava jelly with creamy Catupiry cheese, cashew brittle, and guava sorbet.

Theatro da Villa (Rua Padre Toledo 157, tel. 32/3355-1275, www.theatrodavilla.com.br, 8 P.M.–midnight Tues.–Thurs. and Sun., 8 P.M.–close Fri.–Sat., R$70–80) is Tiradentes's undisputed temple of contemporary cuisine. Culinary pilgrims (with fat wallets) ritually descend upon the elegant restaurant with its winter garden and bewitching mountain views to savor the creative inventions that change in accordance with the seasons. Veal-stuffed partridge in a port reduction with foie gras and filet mignon of wild boar accompanied by wild mushrooms in cocoa sauce are two examples of the mouthwatering fare. Advance reservations are a must.

INFORMATION AND SERVICES

The **tourist office** (Rua Resende Costa 71, tel. 32/3355-1212, 9 A.M.–6 P.M. Mon.–Fri., 9 A.M.–7 P.M. Sat.–Sun.) is right on Largo da Forras. Free detailed maps with listings are available. Online, check out www.tiradentes.mg.gov.br and www.guiatiradentes.com.br (both in Portuguese).

A Bradesco bank (Rua Ministro Gabriel Passos 43) has ATMs that accept international cards. For Internet access, head to **Locadora and Lan House** (Rua dos Inconfidentes 340, tel. 32/3355-2002, 9 A.M.–10:30 P.M.

Mon.–Fri., 9 A.M.–8:30 P.M. Sat., 9 A.M.–10:30 P.M. Sun.).

GETTING THERE

Tiradentes is only a 25-minute bus ride away from São João del Rei. Buses depart at least every hour throughout the daytime. The tiny *rodoviária* (tel. 32/3355-1100) is centrally located, just across the narrow river from Largo das Forras. By car, São João is only 10 minutes away.

If you're traveling Friday, Saturday, Sunday, or on a holiday, you can also take advantage of the Maria Fumaça steam train, which runs between the two towns. Tiradentes's pretty little train station (tel. 32/3371-8485) is a 10-minute walk from the center of town along Rua do Inconfidentes. São João–Tiradentes departures are at 10 A.M. and 3 P.M., and Tiradentes–São João departures are at 1 P.M. and 5 P.M.

Diamantina

Diamantina is the only *cidade histórica* to the north of Belo Horizonte. Unlike Minas's other colonial towns, whose wealth was derived from gold, Diamantina's fortunes were sealed by the astonishing quantity of diamonds waiting to be harvested from the rocky Serra de Espinhaço mountains surrounding the town. Outcrops of these were discovered in the 18th century, and once the word got out, this isolated region was mobbed by fortune seekers. For the next 150 years—until diamonds were found in South Africa—Diamantina was the largest producer of these glittery rocks in the world. What many don't know is that Diamantina is still the largest producer of diamonds in Brazil. Generations of miners, cutters, and jewelers still prosper, and the dream of striking it rich continues to nourish the locals, who were raised on tales of fortunes made and lost. The town is also very proud to be the birthplace of Brazil's eternally loved "bossa nova" president, Juscelino Kubitschek, the man responsible for building Brasília.

Instead of the lush slopes that surround Minas's other colonial gems, Diamantina is set against an arid landscape that is harsh, rocky, and somewhat moon-like. It is also the gateway to the Jequitinhonha Valley, a severely barren and isolated region that is dirt poor but culturally rich, as can be seen by the famous clay sculptures and handicrafts that are sold in Diamantina's boutiques and market. Though its colonial treasures are much less ostentatious, Diamantina—declared a UNESCO World Heritage Site in 1999—is one of the most traditional and best preserved of the *cidades históricas*. While it has no stellar individual attractions, the town and surrounding landscape cast a captivating spell.

SIGHTS

Diamantina's colonial mansions and churches are encrusted into an incredibly precipitous mountain slope paved with enormous stones. Descents are marvelous while ascents will leave you cursing, gasping, and wondering how the

MINAS GERAIS

view of Diamantina, one of the best-preserved *cidades históricas*

locals deal (they walk slowly and rely heavily on cars and motorcycles). However, the core of the town's colonial architecture is quite compact. Do make sure you come equipped with good walking shoes.

Churches

The nucleus of the *centro histórico* is the **Praça Conselheiro Mota,** which is dominated by the **Catedral de Santo Antônio.** Striking from a distance, the mid-20th-century cathedral devoted to the city's patron saint is less inspiring close up. In fact, Diamantina's churches are simpler and less adorned than their glittery baroque counterparts in southern Minas. Their exteriors, with trims outlined in deep blues, ochers, and scarlets are often more striking than the interiors. Despite their lack of grandeur, the churches all charge entrance fees of R$1–2.

Aside from being Diamantina's oldest church (it was built in the 1720s), the **Igreja Nossa Senhora do Rosário** (Largo do Rosário, 8 A.M.–noon and 2–5:30 P.M. Tues.–Sat., 8 A.M.–noon Sun.) is curious for

its slanted walls. The **Igreja São Francisco de Assis** (Rua São Francisco, 8 A.M.–noon and 2–6 P.M. Thurs.–Sat., 8 A.M.–noon Sun.) and the **Capela Imperial do Amparo** (9 A.M.–noon and 2–5 P.M. Tues.–Sat., 9 A.M.–noon Sun.) mix baroque and rococo elements.

The most ornate of the lot is the **Igreja Nossa Senhora do Carmo** (Rua do Carmo, 8 A.M.–noon and 2–6 P.M. Tues.–Sat., 8 A.M.–noon Sun.). Built in the 1760s, it features a gold-leaf-covered organ with 549 pipes.

Casa da Chica da Silva

Chica da Silva, former slave and then mistress of a wealthy diamond contractor named João Fernandes de Oliveira, was one of Brazil's beloved heroines. Between 1763 and 1771 she lived in the handsome mansion João built for her across the street from the Igreja Nossa Senhora do Carmo. Known as Casa da Chica da Silva (Praça Lobo Mesquita, tel. 38/3531-2491, noon–5:30 P.M. Tues.–Sat., 9 A.M.–noon Sun., free), the house disappointingly has few vestiges of its former resident, once the most powerful woman in Diamantina (the belltower of the church was placed at the back so that the ringing bells wouldn't wake her). If you can, see Cacá Diegues's 1976 film *Xica da Silva,* with the incomparable singer/actress Zezé Mota in the title role.

Museu do Diamante

Offering more insight into Diamantina's past, the Museu do Diamante (Rua Direita 14, tel. 38/3531-1382, noon–5:30 P.M. Tues.–Sat., 9 A.M.–noon Sun., R$1), in the former residence of Diamantina's bishop, has a modest but intriguing display of objects ranging from diamond mining tools and some nasty equipment for torturing slaves to colonial furnishings and a room full of beautifully wrought religious altars and saintly icons (some of the latter carved from local stone).

Casa de Juscelino Kubitschek

For a slice of more recent history, brave the steep climb up the Rua São Francisco to the Casa de Juscelino Kubitschek (Rua São

THE ESTRADA REAL

The Estrada Real (Royal Road) was created by the Portuguese crown in the 17th century with the intention of controlling the circulation of Minas's gold and diamonds to the coastal ports of Rio de Janeiro, and from there, to Portugal. The first and most famous route led from Ouro Preto to Paraty – a journey that took three months. A second "shortcut" (it only took 25 days) later connected Ouro Preto directly with the city of Rio. When diamonds were discovered in Diamantina, a third route – actually more of an extension, known as the Rota do Diamante – was built to link Diamantina with Ouro Preto.

Since by law it was prohibited to use any other route, the Estrada Real had an eclectic mixture of traffic: emperors, adventurers, merchants, musicians, miners, slaves, whores, bandits, and intellectuals all traveled the same 1,000 kilometers (620 miles) of winding roads, passing through budding villages and cosmo-politan towns as well as magnificent (and often dangerous) stretches of wilderness. Along with people, animals, and goods, over time ideas also circulated, giving impetus to the transformation of Brazil into an independent republic. It was no coincidence that when the famous Inconfidente rebel, Tiradentes, was tried as a traitor in 1792, his body was drawn and quartered and the parts were exposed at strategic points along the Estrada Real in order to dissuade further republican uprisings.

With industrialization, the old routes fell into disuse and were forgotten. However, the **Instituto Estrada Real** (www.estradareal. org.br), in partnership with the government of Minas Gerais, is currently investing in revitalizing the old gold and diamond roads with the objective of stimulating tourism and preserving both the cultural history and natural beauty of the Estrada.

Francisco 241, tel. 38/3531-3607, 8 A.M.–noon and 2–6 P.M. Tues.–Sat., 8 A.M.–noon Sun., R$2). This humble home is where Brazil's most beloved president (1902–1976) spent his childhood along with his strict but loving mother, Julia, and his older sister (his father died of tuberculosis when Juscelino was only three). It displays original furnishings, including a narrow bed, desk, and the books "Nono" (his childhood nickname) pored over nightly in an attempt to better himself. Photos and some biographical info offer a surprisingly moving glimpse into Kubitschek's early life. Although the museum is fairly basic, it is Diamantina's most visited attraction. Downstairs, in the former basement, stop for a coffee or a dose of local *cachaça* at the appealing Bar do Nono, where souvenirs are on sale.

Passadiço da Glória

One of Diamantina's architectural highlights is the Passadiço da Glória, a striking wooden passageway, painted a rich blue, that spans the steep Rua da Glória. It links two 18th-century buildings known collectively as the Casa da Glória, formerly the residence of diamond supervisors as well as the first bishop of Diamantina.

Mercado Municipal

In the always-lively central square of **Praça Barão de Guaicui,** it's hard to miss the building of the Mercado Municipal. Painted blue and red, the wooden arches of this 19th-century market inspired Oscar Niemeyer's design of the presidential palace in Brasília. On Saturday, the market buzzes with activity. Fresh produce, local handicrafts, homemade baked goods, and *cachaças* are sold here. A local singer is usually on hand to supply a folksy background soundtrack.

FESTIVALS AND EVENTS

Both musical and religious traditions remain strong in Diamantina. Throughout the year, on certain Friday evenings, *serestas* are held, with bands of musicians parading through the *centro histórico* (beginning at Praça Juscelino Kubitschek and ending in front of the Mercado

Municipal). **Vesperatas** (which take place two Saturdays a month between May and October) is another musical event that dates back to the 19th century and attracts tourists from all over Brazil. They reserve tables at the outdoor bars in the Rua da Quitanda, which offer a privileged view of traditionally clad musicians and singers who perform in the windows of the street's mansions while a maestro conducts them from the cobblestones. During Easter, **Semana Santa** festivities and processions are lively events, and in the first weekend in October, the city fills up with revelers who pay homage to **Nossa Senhora do Rosário.**

SHOPPING

As is to be expected, Diamantina is a good place to buy jewels. More interesting—and infinitely more affordable—than diamonds is a local specialty known as *coco e ouro* (coconut and gold). This unusual confection came about as a result of the diamond rage that drew so many jewelers to Diamantina that there weren't enough buyers for their expensive wares. In response, some jewelers went downmarket by cutting coconut husks, polishing them to a lustrous black, and encrusting them with gold, which was a by-product of more lucrative diamond mining. The most traditional place to buy stunning *coco e ouro* earrings and necklaces is at **Padua** (Rua Campos de Carvalho 43, tel. 38/3511-1116, 8 A.M.–6 P.M. Mon.–Fri., 8 A.M.–noon Sat.), a family-owned jewelry store that has been in business since 1888.

As the gateway to the Vale de Jequitinhonha, Diamantina is also an ideal place to purchase the unique and much-celebrated artisanal work made by the craftspeople of this isolated valley region. Enormous ceramic dolls representing brides—most often hand-painted in tones of ocher and cream—are arresting, not only because of their size, but also because of the expressions on the women's faces (said to be self-portraits of their makers). Also prized are ceramic vases, dried flower arrangements and flowers made of straw, and woven *arraiolo* carpets made from lamb's wool. These are beautifully designed with either geometric or floral patterns. **Relíquias do Vale** (Rua Macau do Meio 401, tel. 38/3531-1353, daily) has an extensive selection of local art and handicrafts. In terms of quality, prices, and friendly service, the family-run **Arte do Vale** adjacent to the Mercado Municipal (Praça Barão de Guaicui 135, tel. 38/3531-6482, daily) is also recommended.

ACCOMMODATIONS

Although there are some cheap hotels surrounding the bus station, due to the painfully steep climb from the *centro histórico,* your feet will thank you for forking out a little more money and opting to stay in the colonial thick of things.

Under R$100

Pousada N'há Mocinha (Praça Brasília 36, tel. 38/3531-31000, www.diamantina.net.com.br/nhamocinha, R$30–40 pp) offers one of the best bargains in the center. While a small, not *too* steep hill separates it from the town's main cobblestoned squares, this modern villa is pleasantly located in a somewhat posh residential area. The rooms, ranging from dormitory bunks to doubles, are clean but spartan. The decor features lots of framed saints (the kind that are ripped from calendar pages) and heavy furniture, but excellent views of the town and surrounding mountains compensate. Also a good bargain is the **Pousada dos Cristais** (Rua Jogo da Bola 53, tel. 38/3531-2897, www.diamantina.net.com.br/pousadadoscristais, R$70–80). Whether you choose a room in the main colonial house or one from the more recently constructed "panoramic" wing—which lives up to its name by offering private verandas with stunning views—the atmosphere is appealingly rustic.

For a complete and utter contrast to Diamantina's reigning colonial style, you can't do better than **Hotel Tijuco** (Rua Macau do Meio 211, tel. 38/3531-1022, www.hoteltijuco.com.br, R$90–130). In 1952, Juscelino Kubitschek—then governor of Minas Gerais—invited his friend and future Brasília collaborator, Oscar Niemeyer, to design a hotel for his home town. The result is this spacious, minimalist, and utterly stylish example of Brazilian modernism featuring luminous spaces, lots of natural woods, and original furnishings. When reserving, make sure you get a room with a veranda and a (very impressive) view.

R$100-200

If you want an authentic and truly unforgettable Diamantina experience, reserve a room at the 🅲 **Pousada Relíquias do Tempo** (Rua Macau de Baixo 104, tel. 38/3531-1353, www.pousadareliquiasdotempo.com.br, R$128 d). The owner, Carmen, is the great-granddaughter of a Portuguese goldsmith who immigrated to Diamantina in the 19th century. She grew up in the rambling house that he built and has kept its original furnishings intact while combing the region for antiques and artifacts that pay homage to the city and region she loves. The result is a charming and intimate homestay experience: Guests are invited to peruse her grandfather's leather-bound books in the library and marvel at the fascinating display of diamond mining paraphernalia in the Garimpeiro (miner) museum (both Carmen and her husband's family were "in diamonds"). One of the loveliest features is the open courtyard kitchen with its wood-burning oven and view of the cathedral. At the end of the afternoon, a bell summons guests to tea made from local herbs and leaves, served with homemade biscuits. In the morning, Carmen's mother supervises the preparation of a deliciously hearty breakfast featuring regional specialties such as *jabuticaba* preserves and melt-in-your-mouth cornbread.

A happy—not to mention very comfortable—marriage between past and present can be found at the recently opened **Pouso da Chica** (Rua Macau de Cima 115, tel. 38/3531-6190, www.pousodachica.com.br, R$145-165). The polished wooden floors and exposed adobe walls of the main colonial house create a traditional atmosphere, as does the smoke-scented wood-burning oven upon which cauldrons of hearty homemade soup and toasted

bread greet guests every evening. Rooms, however—whether in the main house or one of seven charming bungalows built in the fruit orchard behind—offer more contemporary creature comforts: 400-thread-count cotton sheets, fluffy oversized towels, marble bathroom counters, and broadband access. Service is very attentive.

FOOD

Diamantina is as good a place as any to sample *comida mineira*. A Mineiro specialty is the use of *ora-pro-nobis*. This spinach-like green leaf was considered a weed until it was discovered that its addition to stews yielded a rich yet delicate flavor. You can sample *frango* (chicken) and *costelas* (pork ribs) *com ora-pro-nobis* along with other Mineiro fare specialties at two modest eateries in front of each other in a tiny alley off the Praça Conselheiro Mota. Favorites with the locals, **Grupiara** (Rua Campos Carvalho 12, tel. 38/3531-3887, lunch Mon., lunch and dinner Tues.–Sun., R$25–30) and **Caipirão** (Rua Caipirão 15, tel. 38/3531-1526, lunch and dinner Mon.–Sat., lunch Sun., R$25–30) offer self-service per kilo buffets with hot and cold dishes as well as à la carte menus that serve hearty portions that feed at least two. Strictly buffet is **Apocalipse** (Praça Barão Guaicuí, 11:30 A.M.–3 P.M. daily, R$12–16), on the second floor of a light-suffused mansion overlooking the marketplace and nearby mountains.

For more of the same, but with a compelling bar ambiance that fuses Diamantina rusticity and religiosity (the stone walls are hung with hand-embroidered banners of saints) with a twist of London pub, try **Recanto do Antônio** (Beco da Tecla 39, tel. 38/3531-1147, www.recantodoantonio.com.br, 11 A.M.–3 P.M. and 6 P.M.–close Tues.–Sun.). If you're in the mood for a light meal or a snack, with the guarantee that you'll be in the midst of all the action, pull up a chair or bar stool at **Café A Baiuca** (Rua da Quitanda 13, tel. 38/3531-3181, www.cafebaiuca.com, 8 A.M.–midnight Mon.–Wed., 8 A.M.–2 A.M. Thurs.–Sat., 9 A.M.–1 P.M. Sun.). Aside from pancakes, omelettes, and sandwiches, the menu features exotic local concoctions such as *linguiça com jiló* and *bolinhos crème de milho com carne seca* (creamed corn and sun-dried beef fritters). To drink, there are delicious beers on tap as well as local *cachaças.*

If you need compelling evidence that *comida mineira* constitutes one Brazil's most flavorful cuisines, you'll find it at **(O Garimpeiro** (Av. da Saudade 265, tel. 38/3531-1044, 6–11 P.M. Mon.–Fri., noon–11 P.M. Sat.–Sun., R$30.) The restaurant belongs to the trying-to-be-posh, but rather lackluster Pousada Garimpeiro and is a bit of walk from the center of town (mercifully, no hills are involved). Although the interior is dark, tables on the veranda offer panoramic views of the city and surrounding mountains. The real highlights are a handful of local dishes prepared with great flair by a local chef, Vandeca, whose grandmother taught him to cook when he was a boy. As an adolescent, he honed his skills by cooking grub for diamond miners up and down the Jequitinhonha Valley. He pays homage to his past in the mines with *bambá do garimpo,* a robust stew of pork, kale, and pureed beans. Another standout is *costelinhas com brotas de samambaia,* in which pork ribs are cooked with delicately pungent giant fern sprouts.

Romantic **Trattoria La Dolce Vita** (Rua Vieira Couto 232, tel. 38/3531-8485, 7–11 P.M. Mon. and Wed.–Sun., noon–3 P.M. Sat.–Sun., R$35–45) occupies a charming house and garden next to Casa Chica da Silva. The creative Italian menu includes focaccias, risottos, pork, and lamb, as well as homemade pastas with sauces ranging from pesto to the more exotic *pequi* and *jabuticaba* (both fragrant local fruits).

INFORMATION

The municipal **tourist office** is on Praça Juscelino Kubitschek (tel. 38/3531-8060, 9 A.M.–6 P.M. Mon.–Sat., 9 A.M.–2 P.M. Sun.), on the first floor of an old mansion that also houses the main police station. You can pick up free city maps and information about

events in Diamantina as well as on how to contact a guide to surrounding attractions. Online resources include www.diamantina .mg.gov.br and www.diamantina.com.br (both in Portuguese).

GETTING THERE

From Belo Horizonte's *rodoviária,* **Pássaro Verde** (tel. 31/3073-7053, www.passaro verde.com.br) offers daily bus service to Diamantina. There are several departures a day and the trip takes around five hours. In Diamantina, the bus station is a (very steep) 15-minute walk (or cab ride) from the center. By car, follow the BR-040 and BR-105 highways north from Belo Horizonte to Curvelo, then take the BR-259 and BR-367, which pass through the town of Gouveia. Diamantina also has a small airport that receives flights from Pampuha airport in Belo Horizonte, operated by **Total** (tel. 0300/789-6464, www.total.com.br).

AROUND DIAMANTINA
(Caminho de Escravos

The dramatic rocky landscape surrounding Diamantina is a fascinating place to explore. The Caminho de Escravos is an old slave road, part of the Estrada Real that was cut into the mountains by thousands of African slaves who were also used to transport loads of diamonds down to Rio de Janeiro and Paraty on the Atlantic coast. Although the road weaves through the mountains for 20 kilometers (12 miles), you need only walk 3–4 kilometers (2–2.5 miles) to take advantage of stunning views of the town and surrounding peaks and valleys. The road begins, in a steep descent, from the Mercado Municipal and is well marked by signposts.

Biribiri

A popular full- or half-day trip—if you don't have a car, you can take a taxi or an organized excursion—is a visit to Biribiri (www.biri biri.com.br). This 19th-century village grew up around a now defunct fabric factory and features an interesting collection of warehouses, workers' residences, a school, and church. Biribiri is 18 kilometers (11 miles) from Diamantina north along the BR-367. Along the way, stop off for a refreshing dip at the **Cachoeira da Sentinela** (9 kilometers/6 miles) and **Cachoeira dos Cristais** (16 kilometers/10 miles), two waterfalls that cascade into (very cold) natural swimming pools.

Garimpo Real

If all the allusions to fortunes found incit. sure-seeking urges, you can do some diam mining of your own with a guide using trad. tional panning techniques. The Garimpo Real is some 25 kilometers (16 miles) from town. Contact **Belmiro** (tel. 38/3531-1557, www .garimporeal.com) for more information.

BAHIA

I can't recall ever meeting anyone who wasn't moved, bowled over, impressed, mesmerized, or inspired in a positive way by São Salvador da Bahia dos Santos. I have seen countless first-time visitors fall head over heels in love with the 500-year-old city, and have never known anyone who left the city indifferent to its heady charms. Brazil's first capital, with its flood of baroque churches and its idyllic setting overlooking the shimmering blue Bay of All Saints, is one of those places where the descriptive cliché "magical" comes in handy. Bahians refers to it as *axé,* or "good energy." But the truth is that in Salvador, life flows to a different rhythm. Time, like the warm Atlantic water that laps its shores, is more liquid here. Although Salvador is a city of 2.6 million, its notoriously good-humored residents are a famously unstressed bunch who work hard but also have the fine art of relaxation down to a T. Of course, Salvador itself is very conducive to languor. Its balmy climate, sea breezes, and enticing beaches are constant companions. Music too is everywhere—from the chants of the beach vendors hawking popsicles and grilled shrimp to the twang of the one-string *berimbaus,* a bow-shaped instrument African origin that accompanies spinning *capoeiristas* as they practice their graceful combination of dance and martial art.

Indeed, its legacy as the jewel in the crown of a Portuguese colonial empire that relied heavily on sugarcane—and slave labor—left Salvador with a large population of African descent. Unsurprisingly, African elements seep into every facet of Bahian culture: from the

HIGHLIGHTS

Pelourinho: The winding streets of Salvador's colonial center are awash in museums, music, magnificent baroque churches, and faded treasures that conjure up its glory days as Brazil's first capital (page 305).

Igreja e Convento de São Francisco and the Igreja da Ordem Terceira de São Francisco: The adjoining church and convent devoted to St. Francis are some of the most glorious examples of baroque art in all Brazil (page 311).

Carnaval: Billed by the *Guinness Book of World Records* as the world's biggest street party, Salvador's mind-blowing Carnaval is also Brazil's longest, lasting a full seven days (page 330).

Mangue Seco: On Bahia's northern coast, Mangue Seco is a deserted paradise of dunes, palms, rivers, and ocean (page 350).

Cachoeira: This sleepy colonial town on the banks of the Rio Paraguaçu preserves some of the African diaspora's oldest religious and musical traditions (page 351).

Parque Nacional da Chapada Diamantina: In the heart of Bahia's arid interior, this lush, mountainous plateau region is filled with hiking trails, waterfalls, and colonial diamond mining towns (page 355).

Barra Grande: Perched on Brazil's third largest bay, the Baía de Camamu, Barra Grande boasts a laid-back vibe and stunning beaches, including the Tahiti-like Taipu de Fora (page 365).

Trancoso: The ultimate in hippie chic, the village of Trancoso is cosmopolitan yet rustic, and blessed with stunning beaches (page 379).

Caraíva: For an idyllic, away-from-it-all beach experience, it's hard to beat the rustic charms of this tiny fishing village surrounded by some of Bahia's most gorgeous and deserted beaches (page 382).

Parque Nacional Marinho dos Abrolhos: This offshore marine reserve is a diver's delight; both Charles Darwin and Jacques Cousteau were impressed by the spectacle of sea life here (page 384).

LOOK FOR ◖ TO FIND RECOMMENDED SIGHTS, ACTIVITIES, DINING, AND LODGING.

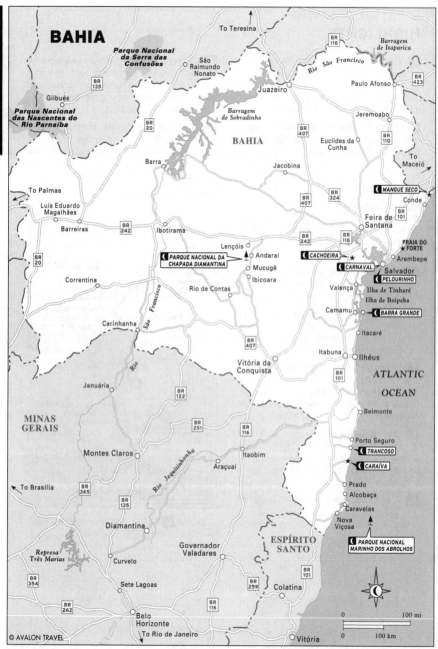

language and music to the popular Candomblé religion and the famous *moquecas* (a fragrant stew of fish or seafood), shrimp *bobós*, and spicy *acarajés* (crunchy deep-fried bean fritters) that have made Salvador a culinary capital. Fused together with Catholic elements, these traditional culinary treats show up in the dozens of popular *festas* that invade the streets in the summer, exuberant celebrations that are equally sacred and profane and which culminate in the world's biggest outdoor party, Carnaval. However, it doesn't matter what time of year you come to Salvador; innovative Soteropolitanos (as the capital's inhabitants are known) are never hard-pressed to find an excuse for a party and are always commemorating something.

It would be a crime to travel to Bahia and not visit Salvador, but it would be pure sin to spend time in Bahia's capital city without exploring a few of the many natural, historic, and cultural attractions within the borders of the largest of Brazil's northeastern states. Although Bahia is vast—roughly the size of France and Spain stuck together—there are many worthy destinations within a couple of hours of Salvador.

The gentle hills and decaying sugarcane plantations of the Recôncavo region that rings the Baía de Todos os Santos is a good place to start. Highlights include the colonial towns of Santo Amaro and Cachoeira, both known for their traditional religious celebrations as well as delicious dishes such as *maniçoba* (a rich stew of shredded beef, ground cashews, and manioc leaves) boiled for three days to ensure the removal of natural toxins. Also close to Salvador is the long string of idyllic beach towns stretching north along the coast. Some, such as Praia do Forte—renowned for its whale-watching and sea turtle reserve—have developed into chic resorts with espresso cafés and sushi bars. Many others, however, such as Diogo and Sítio de Conde, retain the tranquility of small rustic fishing villages.

Blessed with the longest coastline in Brazil, Bahia has no shortage of beaches. Heading south, you can spend days or even weeks migrating from one long unspoiled strip of sand to the next. Two of the biggest draws are the towns of Ilhéus, the historical "cocoa capital," and the ultra-developed Porto Seguro, a famed party capital. Both towns are surrounded by numerous white-sand beaches, but die-hard surf and sand junkies can also venture to dozens of other alluring destinations. Take your pick from the trendy but still Robinson Crusoe–worthy resorts of Ilha de Boipeba, Barra Grande, Itacaré, or Trancoso. Or if you want all-out isolation, consider the area surrounding Caraíva, an unspoiled paradise in the far south of the state. Meanwhile, divers shouldn't miss Abrolhos National Marine Park, an offshore treasure trove of Technicolor coral, fish, and sea birds that was a favorite of both Charles Darwin and Jacques Cousteau.

Natural wonders of another kind await travelers who venture into the Chapada Diamantina region of the Bahian interior. Imagine dramatically sculpted rock formations carpeted in wild orchids and studded with caverns and grottoes. After a day spent hiking, caving, and plunging into waterfalls, unwind at one of many charming eco-resorts situated in centuries-old diamond mining towns such as Lençóis and Mucugê. Although diamonds are in short supply these days, natural riches are in abundance in Bahia.

PLANNING YOUR TIME

For many travelers Salvador is a complete destination in itself. Certainly the city offers all you could want from a Brazilian vacation: a rich local culture, magnificent baroque architecture, tons of museums, a vibrant nightlife with an incredible music scene, a delicious and world-renowned regional cuisine, fantastic beaches, and (in the summertime) some of the most colorful and frenzied popular *festas* in Brazil. To merely get a taste of the place, you'd have to spend at least 3–4 days, but anything less than a week would be somewhat of a crime. Salvador is a notoriously relaxed city with a slower pace of life, so it would be a shame—not to mention downright anti-Bahian—to be forced to spend your time rushing around. Toss in the easily accessible surrounding area,

BAHIA

with its idyllic beaches, the colonial towns of the Recôncavo region, the spectacular natural attractions of the lush waterfall-studded Parque Nacional da Chapada Diamantina, and a pilgrimage to one or several of the famed beaches along Bahia's southern coast, and you could easily spend 2–3 weeks in Bahia, using Salvador as a base.

Bahia can be visited all year-round. The summer months (December to March) are the hottest, with temperatures hovering around 35°C (95°F) and lots of sun. This period is high tourist season, as travelers from throughout Brazil and the world descend upon many of the most popular coastal resorts (Praia do Forte, Morro de São Paulo, Itacaré, Porto Seguro, Arraial d'Ajuda, and Trancoso). The upside is an endless array of festivities. The downside is that prices usually rise along with the temperature. In the summertime Salvador sizzles with its lively ambiance, myriad musical shows and open rehearsals of Carnaval *blocos,* and especially the "season" of popular *festas,* which begin with the traditional Festa de Santa Bárbara (December 4) and culminate in the ever-growing musical madness and mayhem of Carnaval (usually in February or early March). If revelry, combined with relaxation, is what you're looking for, you've come to the right place. With the end of Carnaval comes what Soteropolitanos refer to as the post-Carnaval *ressaca* or "hangover," which means a halt in the partying (until June) and a return to work. Oddly enough, in a show of solidarity, Mother Nature too seems to know that the party is over because the period from April to June is usually very rainy (which doesn't suit Salvador or its coastal regions very well since most of their livelihood revolves around outdoor bars and fabulous beaches). Bahian "winter," which stretches from June through September, is really a lovely time to visit the city and the coastal regions as well as the Chapada. Although short, sudden (and refreshing) downpours are common, the sun shines less intensely and the skies are a deep cerulean blue. Salvador and the Atlantic coast are less touristy and frenzied than in the summer, and except for mid-July through August, which coincides with Brazilian school vacation, the hotels and beaches are much less crowded (many Bahians think it odd to lie on a beach in the "middle of winter").

HISTORY

The history of Brazil began in Bahia. It was on April 22, 1500, that Portuguese navigator Pedro Alvares Cabral accidentally landed on the shores of southern Bahia, after being blown off course on his way to India. The Portuguese disembarked in the harbor known as Porto Seguro (Safe Port) and spent 10 days exploring. Aside from the Tupi Indians, the only thing that sparked their curiosity was a tree with a glossy hard wood that yielded a red dye, known as *pau brasil* (brazilwood). Before setting sail, the Portuguese planted a cross in name of the King Manuel I. With the Tupi in attendance, they celebrated a mass at a spot they baptized Terra da Vera Cruz (Land of the True Cross).

Intrigued by Cabral's discovery, Manuel I sent navigator Amerigo Vespucci back to the new land to explore it further. On November 1, 1501, Vespucci's fleet entered the Baía de Todos os Santos, which he christened with the name of his arrival date (All Saints Day). For a few decades, there was a haphazard attempt to administer the new colony by doling out territories throughout the Northeast (including Bahia) to be administered by wealthy settlers. However, this strategy proved inefficient, and in 1549 the king sent Tomé de Souza to Bahia with the title of first governor general, and the mission of building a settlement on the strategically sheltered bay that would serve as capital for the Brazilian colony. Souza arrived with settlers, builders, merchants, soldiers, and Jesuits. The former set about building the city of São Salvador da Bahia de Todos os Santos (which today has been abbreviated to Salvador), while the latter set about converting and pacifying Bahia's Indian population.

In the beginning, the Portuguese had a rough time of it. The local Caeté Indians killed various troops and feasted upon the Bahia's first bishop (whose appetizing name, Sardinha, is Portuguese for sardine). However, they were soon overcome by the Portuguese. Meanwhile, within decades the Portuguese had exhausted much of the supply of brazilwood and had turned their attentions to sugar, which was being successfully introduced throughout the Northeast. Tomé de Souza incentivized the cultivation of sugar in Bahia. To work the great plantations that sprang up amidst the rolling hills surrounding Salvador, slaves were brought from the coasts of Portugal's African colonies to serve as labor. The entire Northeast grew rich from "white gold" (as sugar was known), and as Brazil's colonial capital, Salvador, with its elegant *praças* and richly adorned baroque churches, became the sparkling jewel in the Portuguese imperial crown. For close to three centuries the city boasted the biggest and most bustling port in the South Atlantic. During this time, Bahia became the biggest importer of African slaves in the New World.

Aside from a lasting legacy of social and economic inequality, the arrival of the African diaspora in Bahia also created a fantastically rich culture that permeated every aspect of society, including religion, music, cuisine,

and language. To this day, Salvador is Brazil's most "African" city, with around 85 percent of the population proudly declaring themselves Afro-Descendentes.

Bahia's fortunes took a turn for the worse in the 19th century. In 1822, with the arrival of the Portuguese crown, Brazil's capital was transferred from Salvador to Rio de Janeiro. Around the same time, São Paulo's coffee boom eclipsed the northeastern sugar trade, which received its final blow with the abolition of slavery. Its baroque grandeur fading fast, Salvador fell into a certain abandon, although it never lost its provincial charms and unique traditions. It wasn't until the 1980s and '90s that oil, industry, and, later, tourism gave Bahia a new lease on life, accompanied by rapid modernization and *favela*-ization (in the last 30 years the population has quintupled to 2.6 million). Today, while many of the treasures of its past are being carefully preserved (while others are shockingly neglected), the city is striving to assert its identity as an increasingly modern city without losing its traditional *jeito baiano* or "Bahian way."

Salvador

SIGHTS

Salvador was originally built around a cliff overlooking the Bay of All Saints, which effectively split the city into two. The Cidade Alta (Upper Town) was home to ornate administrative palaces and churches while the Cidade Baixa (Lower Town) sheltered maritime docks and markets, and later grew into the financial and commercial district. To this day, the two are linked by a series of tortuously steep roads, two funiculars, and one of Salvador's most famous monuments: the art deco Elevador Lacerda.

Over time, the city grew, following the extension of the Cidade Alta's main commercial avenue, Avenida Sete de Setembro, which leads from the Praça do Sé in the colonial Pelourinho district to the main square

of Campo Grande—an area today designated as "Centro." From Campo Grande, Avenida Sete de Setembro continues down to the lively beach neighborhood known as Barra; Barra's iconic black-and-white striped lighthouse marks the point at which the placid Bay of All Saints meets the rougher waters of the Atlantic open sea. At this point, the main coastal road takes over, and continues for 20 kilometers (12.5 miles) to the former fisherman's enclave of Itapuã, whose rustic charms were romanticized in the lyrics of two former residents, Dorival Caymmi and Vinícius de Moraes.

◖ Pelourinho

Most of Salvador's most interesting sights are very conveniently located in the old colonial center of the Cidade Alta known as the Pelourinho

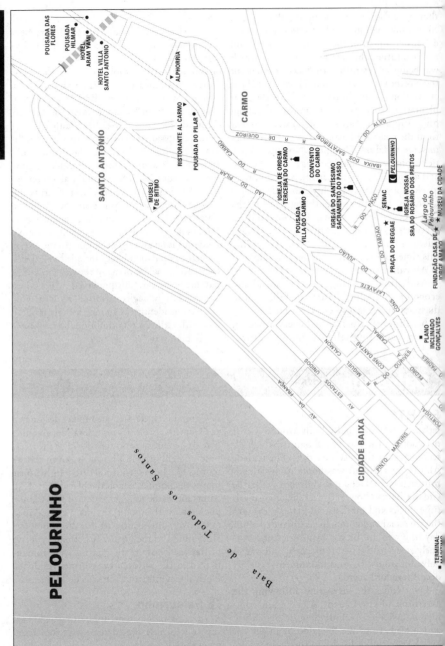

PELOURINHO

Baia de Todos os Santos

CARMO

SANTO ANTÔNIO

CIDADE BAIXA

POUSADA DAS FLORES
POUSADA HILMAR
HOTEL ARAM YAMI
HOTEL VILLA SANTO ANTÔNIO

ALPHORRIA

RISTORANTE AL CARMO
POUSADA DO PILAR

MUSEU DE RITMO

IGREJA DE ORDEM TERCEIRA DO CARMO
CONVENTO DO CARMO

POUSADA VILLA DO CARMO

R. DE QUEIROZ

IBAIXA DOS SAPATEIROSI

PELOURINHO

R. DO ALVO

IGREJA DO SANTÍSSIMO SACRAMENTO DO PASSO

SENAC

IGREJA NOSSA SRA DO ROSÁRIO DOS PRETOS

Largo do Pelourinho

FUNDAÇÃO CASA DE JORGE AMADO

MUSEU DA CIDADE

PRAÇA DO REGGAE

R. DO PAÇO

R. DO TABOÃO

LAD. DO CARMO

R. DO PILAR

R. DO JULIAO

CONS. LAFAYETE

CABRAL

R. CONS DANTAS

R. MIGUEL CALMON

AV. ESTADOS UNIDOS

OURIVES

PEDRO -

- PADRES

PLANO INCLINADO GONÇALVES

PORTUGAL

AV. DA FRANÇA

PINTO - MARTINS

TERMINAL MARÍTIMO

BAHIA

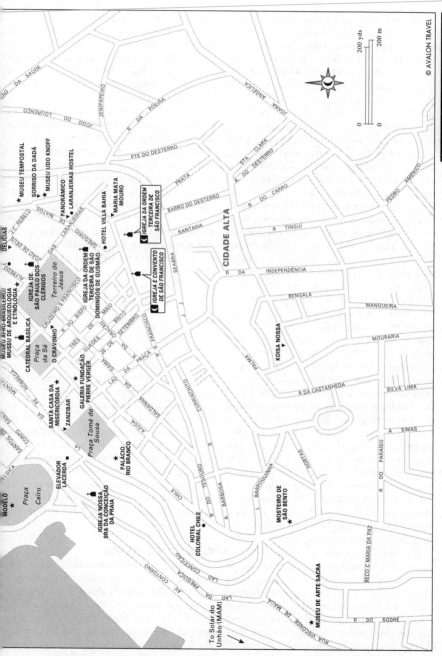

© AVALON TRAVEL

CIDADE ALTA

IGREJA DA ORDEM TERCEIRA DE SÃO FRANCISCO

IGREJA E CONVENTO DE SÃO FRANCISCO

MUSEU TEMPOSTAL
SORRISO DA DADÁ
MUSEU UDO KNOFF
PANORÂMICO
LARANJEIRAS HOSTEL
HOTEL VILLA BAHIA
MARIA MATA MOURO

DELICIAS

MUSEU AFRO-BRASILEIRO/
MUSEU DE ARQUEOLOGIA
E ETNOLOGIA
IGREJA DE
SÃO PAULO DOS
CLÉRIGOS
CATEDRAL BASÍLICA
O CRAVINHO
Praça
da Sé
IGREJA DA ORDEM
TERCEIRA DE SÃO
DOMINGOS DE GUSMÃO
Terreiro de
Jesus

SANTA CASA DA
MISERICÓRDIA
GALERIA FUNDAÇÃO
PIERRE VERGER
ZANZIBAR
Praça Tomé de
Sousa

ELEVADOR
LACERDA
PALÁCIO
RIO BRANCO

MODELO
Praça
Cairu

IGREJA NOSSA
SRA DA CONCEIÇÃO
DA PRAIA

HOTEL
COLONIAL CHILE

MOSTEIRO DE
SÃO BENTO

KOISA NOSSA

MUSEU DE ARTE SACRA

To Solar do
Unhão (MAM)

200 yds
200 m

(a reference to one of the neighborhood's main squares, the Largo do Pelourinho, where slaves were routinely whipped at the *pelourinho*, or "pillory"). Despite its inauspicious past, the "Pelô" provides a feast for architecture buffs, with the largest concentration of baroque architecture in the Americas. Replete with an incredible number of richly adorned churches and convents, its hilly cobblestoned streets also reflect a lot of the vibrancy and color of Bahian life. Only a decade ago, the Pelourinho was a crumbling mess, its buildings dilapidated and its community of pimps, prostitutes, and drug dealers making the neighborhood a definite risk zone. If you're curious as to what the Pelô was like before its overhaul, gaze (from afar!) down some of the neighboring streets behind the Praça da Sé, which have yet to receive their facelifts and which are notoriously dangerous. After being declared a UNESCO World Heritage Site in 1985, the area underwent a massive restoration that saved many of the historic buildings and (somewhat unceremoniously) removed the former inhabitants, replacing them with boutiques, restaurants, bars, and open-air spaces for musical shows. What it lost in terms of gritty authenticity, it made up for in terms of heightened security and animation. Indeed, the Pelô became a vibrant hot spot that attracted both Soteropolitanos and tourists, intent on all forms of merrymaking, whether by day or night.

More recently, however, the Pelô has become somewhat of a tourist showcase that is increasingly forsaken by locals while tourists themselves are increasingly approached by vendors and beggars (thieves tend to keep a low profile due to the heavy police presence). Nonetheless, there is no denying the rich history and sheer magnificence of its gloriously restored edifices, which are consistently impressive, even to the most jaded of Soteropolitanos. While the *bairro* itself can be explored on foot in a couple of hours, in order to take advantage of all the church interiors and interesting museums, boutiques and lovely outdoor bars, you will need a couple of days. The labyrinthine layout of the neighborhood is very conducive to wandering. Just make sure you don't venture off the beaten, police-patrolled track—especially at night. The streets that haven't yet received a facelift are still rife with marginal types and drug dealers, and tourist *assaltos* (muggings) are not unheard of. So if you find yourself on a street that's looking decidedly run-down and in disrepair, turn around.

The best place to start your exploration of the Pelô is at the **Praça Municipal.** Also known as Praça Tomé de Souza—in honor of Salvador's founder and first governor general (a three-ton statue guards the square) this large plaza was the seat of colonial Brazil for over two centuries. Today, most of the square has been converted into a parking lot, which is dominated by the monumental **Palácio do Rio Branco.** Guarded by soaring eagles and topped by an impressive dome, the palace is fondly known by Bahians as the *bolo de noiva* ("the wedding cake"), an appropriate nickname considering its resemblance to a gleaming sugar-coated, multistoried baker's confection. Constructed by Tomé de Souza in 1549 as the governor's palace, over time the building suffered bombardments, partial demolitions, and makeovers—all of which explain its eclectic style, a mixture of neoclassical, Byzantine, and Renaissance elements. Having housed the Portuguese royal family (when they fled Napoleon's troops in 1808) and been a prison, it now houses Bahia's ministry of culture. Step inside and you'll find lots of rococo plasterwork, frescoes, and a small museum with furnishings, as well as artifacts belonging to governors past. that once belonged to the governor. More interesting is the glorious view from the palace's elegant verandas, where you can take in the Cidade Baixa and the Bay of All Saints.

ELEVADOR LACERDA

To the right of the Palácio do Rio Branco, overlooking the ocean, you can't miss Salvador's postcard landmark: the elegantly streamlined, recently restored art deco Elevador Lacerda, which since the 1930s has been shuttling lines of Soteropolitanos up and down from the Cidade Baixa to the Cidade Alta. Open

24 hours a day, it only takes 20 seconds for each of its four elevators to transport its passengers—more than 50,000 of them daily—for a mere 10 centavos. If you want to visit the Mercado Modelo, catch a local bus to Bonfim from Praça Cairu, or grab a boat to Itaparica, the Elevador comes in handy. Otherwise, have a seat at the famous **Sorveteria Cubana** (tel. 71/3322-7000, 9 A.M.–10 P.M.), another 1930s landmark, with comfortable seats overlooking the Bay of All Saints, and indulge in icy treats such as a *coco espumante* (a fizzy old-fashioned coconut ice-cream soda), a banana split, or more tropical flavors such as coco verde and *cupuaçu.* A Bahian joke states that taking a ride on their beloved elevator is the only way to ascend in life.

RUA DA MISERICÓRDIA
Walking down the Rua da Misericórdia, past the new City Hall, you'll pass the **Santa Casa da Misericórdia** (Rua da Misericórida 6, tel. 71/3322-7355, 10 A.M.–5 P.M. Mon.–Fri., 1–5 P.M. Sun., R$5). A religious complex dating from 1549, it was converted into a museum in 2003 as part of an ongoing project to renovate the architectural treasures on this strip. A permanent exhibition of artwork, religious objects, and furniture from the 17th century conjures up Salvador's colonial history, as do its magnificent cloisters, church, and living quarters.

Across the street is the small, but not-to-be-missed **Galeria Fundação Pierre Verger** (Portal da Misericórdia 9, tel. 71/3321-2341, www.pierreverger.org, open daily, free), which shows the unforgettable black-and-white photographs of French photographer, ethnographer, and adopted Bahian, Pierre Verger. Born into a wealthy Parisian milieu in which he never felt at home, in 1932, at the age of 30, Verger turned his back on *la vie mondaine* and took off to explore the world. With a camera in hand to fund his journeys (his pictures were subsequently published in *Life, Paris Match,* and many other major magazines), he traveled throughout Asia, Africa, and the Americas. However, in Bahia he felt an especially strong bond that kept on luring him back for decades until he finally settled there. He ultimately became a professor specializing in the African diaspora as well as a Candomblé initiate. In fact, in the 1940s, Verger was one of the first people permitted to make photographic records of mysterious (and often prohibited) Candomblé rituals. However, his other elegantly composed, yet highly sensual portraits of Salvador's sailors, fishermen, *capoeiristas,* Carnaval merrymakers, circus performers, and other Bahians from all walks of life offer precious and moving glimpses of a past world. In Salvador, the nonprofit Pierre Verger Foundation houses more than 63,000 photographs and negatives. Of these, the gallery exhibits a small, but impressive rotating collection. The small gift store has terrific Verger T-shirts and handbags.

PRAÇA DA SÉ
Rua da Misericórdia opens up onto Praça da Sé. If you're taking a bus from anywhere in the city to the Pelourinho, the bus stop right before the square is the final destination for all buses from Barra, Itapuã, and the airport. This renovated square with its uncomfortable benches and somewhat kitschy fountain was once the site of Salvador's original 16th-century *sé,* or cathedral, which was destroyed in 1933. Excavation sites reveal some of the original cathedral's foundations, but otherwise the square is quite modern. If you stick around too long, you'll quickly discover that the *praça* is a favorite hangout for street performers—ranging from somewhat eery human statues to ubiquitous Michael Jackson impersonators (who endeared himself to Bahians when he filmed his video for "They Don't Care About Us" in the Pelourinho in 1998). Meanwhile, at the far end of the Praça is the entrance to the **Plano Inclinado Gonçalves** (7 A.M.–7 P.M. Mon.–Sat.), a thrillingly steep funicular that whisks 30 passengers at a time between the Cidade Alta and Cidade Baixa.

TERREIRO DE JESUS
Around the corner from Praça da Sé, you'll find yourself in the much more impressive Terreiro de Jesus (officially known as Praça 15

BAHIA

view of Terreiro de Jesus, in the *centro histórico* of Salvador

de Novembro), which marks the beginning of the Pelourinho district. Try to ignore the exaggeratedly made-up, turbaned, and petticoated Bahianas who will encourage you to have your picture taken with them. From this sprawling cobblestoned square you can feast your eyes on four remarkable religious edifices: Catedral Basílica, or Sé; **Igreja da Ordem Terceira de São Domingos de Gusmão** (tel. 71/3242-4185, 9 A.M.–midnight and 2–8 P.M. daily, R$1); the striking rococo **Igreja São Pedro dos Clérigos** (tel. 71/3321-0966, 2–6 P.M. Tues.–Fri.); and farther off, down the Largo de Cruzeiro de São Francisco, the stunning baroque church and convent of São Francisco.

CATEDRAL BASÍLICA

An eclectic mixture of baroque, rococo, and neoclassical styles, the 17th-century Catedral Basílica (Terreiro de Jesus, tel. 71/3321-4573, 8 A.M.–11 A.M. and 3–6 P.M. Tues.–Sat., 10 A.M.–1 P.M. Sun., R$3) was built out of sandstone, shipped in blocks from Portugal, before undergoing reconstruction after an early-20th-century fire. Its recently restored

magnificent interior is a testament to the riches of Portugal's overseas colonies. The 16th-century ceramic tiles in the sacristy hails from Macau, while the delicate ivory and tortoise shell inlay in one altar (third on the right from the entrance) is from Goa. Other precious materials used that adorn the interior include marble, jacaranda, and lots and lots of gold leaf—the altars and ceiling are completely slathered in it.

MUSEU AFRO-BRASILEIRO AND THE MUSEU DE ARQUEOLOGIA E ETNOLOGIA

Adjacent to the cathedral, on the Terreiro de Jesus, these two museums are in the building where Brazil's first school of medicine was created in 1833. The modest Museu de Arqueologia e Etnologia (tel. 71/3321-2013, 9 A.M.–5 P.M. Mon.–Fri., 10 A.M.–5 P.M. Sun., R$1) houses a small collection of archaeological objects—some of them found during the excavations carried out at the Praça da Sé—as well as indigenous tools, weapons, and photos depicting traditional indigenous groups.

Much more interesting is the Museu Afro-Brasileiro (tel. 71/3321-2013, 9 A.M.–6 P.M. Mon.–Fri., 10 A.M.–5 P.M. Sat.–Sun., R$5). Along with maps tracing the trade routes that brought African slaves to Bahia, exhibits of objects and artifacts draw interesting parallels between African and Bahian cultural traditions, including *capoeira* and Candomblé. A highlight is the museum's collection of sacred objects and apparel—as well as photos—related to Candomblé and the cult of individual *orixás*, or divinities, which provide an informative introduction to the Afro-Brazilian religion that is such a strong cultural reference in Bahia. Depicting the *orixás* are the exquisitely carved wooden panels, inlaid with shells and shiny metals, sculpted by one of Bahia's most famous artists, Carybé.

◖ IGREJA E CONVENTO DE SÃO FRANCISCO AND THE IGREJA DA ORDEM TERCEIRA DE SÃO FRANCISCO

Looming magnificently at the far end of the Largo do Cruzeiro de São Francisco is the most magnificent example of baroque architecture on the planet: a religious complex dedicated to Saint Francis of Assisi comprising two churches and a convent. Constructed between 1686 and 1750, the Igreja e Convento de São Francisco (tel. 71/3322-6430, 8:30 A.M.–5 P.M. Mon.–Sat., 8 A.M.–4 P.M. Sun., R$3) takes your breath away before you even enter its main doors, merely by reflection of all the gold leaf paneling—some 800 kilos to be exact—that covers its intricately carved and sumptuously painted ceilings and altars. Little wonder it is famed for being the most richly adorned church in the country. A contrast to so much glitter are the impressive scenes depicting the life of Saint Francis on beautiful blue-and-white Portuguese ceramic tiles, called *azulejos. Azulejos* depicting scenes inspired by Flemish engravings also cover the beautiful convent cloister. On Tuesdays, mass is followed by the distribution of food to the poor, which then—in typical Bahian fashion—morphs into a Pelô-wide celebration

of a more profane nature, known as *terça do Benção* (Tuesday of the Blessing). Except for Tuesday and Sunday, the church is home to a sound and light show (at 11:30 A.M. and 4 P.M., R$7), in which the interior is lit up in all its splendor.

Next door, the Igreja da Ordem Terceira de São Francisco (tel. 71/3321-6989, 8 A.M.–5 P.M., R$3), completed in 1703, is remarkable for its magnificent high-relief facade: a fantastically intricate sandstone tapestry of saints, angels, organic and abstract motifs that you can marvel at for so long, your neck will be stiff. Amazingly, this unique exterior was "hidden" for 150 years until, in 1936, a painter accidentally discovered it when he chipped off a piece of the plaster facade that was covering it up. Inside the church, intricately detailed *azulejo* panels provide a visual narration of the marriage of the king of Portugal's son to an Austrian princess. These fantastically expressive panels provide an important portrait of Lisbon before it was devastated by the Great Earthquake of 1755. The second floor of the church houses a small museum featuring religious art and objects.

MUSEU UDO KNOFF DE AZULEJARIA E CERÂMICA

When you leave the Igreja da Ordem Terceira de São Francisco, you'll be on the cobblestoned Rua Inácio Acciole. Keep walking and take a left on Rua Frei Vicente where you can admire the pastel-colored colonial buildings in hues of sky blue, pale pink, and lime. The carnivalesque color scheme is a modern touch; originally the Pelô's buildings were painted in a more Andalusian white to deflect the heat of the hot tropical sun. The Museu Udo Knoff de Azulejaria e Cerâmica (Rua Frei Vicente 3, tel. 71/3117-6388, 1–6 P.M. Tues.–Sat.) displays a lovely collection of ceramic tiles hailing from Portugal, Spain, Belgium, and Mexico. They are from the personal collection of Horst Udo Knoff, a German expat ceramicist whose own works are featured. Adjacent Rua Gregório de Matos is also filled with striking colonial mansions.

MUSEU TEMPOSTAL

The "artwork" in the engaging Museu Tempostal (Rua Gregório de Matos 33, tel. 71/3117-6383, 1–6 P.M. Tues.–Sat., free) recounts Salvador's surprisingly rapid transformation over the last century. This is achieved with much originality through an exhibition of postcards (the complete collection numbers an impressive 35,000).

MUSEU ABELARDO RODRIGUES

Another attractive 17th-century mansion, the Solar do Ferrão, houses the Museu Abelardo Rodrigues (Rua Gregório de Matos 45, tel. 71/3321-6155, 10 A.M.–6 P.M. Tues.–Sun., R$1). The important collection of over 800 icons of saints, altars, engravings, and other religious objects originally belonged to Pernambucano collector Abelardo Rodrigues, who later sold them to the Bahian state government.

LARGO DO PELOURINHO

Rua Gregório de Matos (and all other major Pelô streets) lead to this impressively sprawling triangular plaza. All the postcard images, guidebook photos, and travel blog shots of the Pelourinho you've ever seen were taken here. When you first set foot in this historic *largo,* you'll likely be overwhelmed by the baroque landscape of church spires and faded pastel mansions, as well as the Cubist-like image of houses rising up and down the Pelô's steep hills. Although its official name is Praça José de Alencar, it is known locally as Largo do Pelourinho due to its dubious past as the site of the *pelourinho* (whipping post). It was here that slaves were publicly flogged (a legal activity in Brazil until 1835) as well as auctioned off to the highest bidder.

Flanked by museums, boutiques, restaurants, and the imposing cerulean blue facade of the famous church of Nossa Senhora do Rosário dos Pretos, these days the steep cobblestoned square buzzes with less nefarious activities. By day, vendors try to hawk *naïf* canvases and coax gringos to put Afro-braids and cornrows in their hair. Meanwhile, nights are often filled with live music and people dancing with enviable poise on the irregular cobblestones.

Housed in an impressive colonial mansion, the **Museu da Cidade** (Largo do Pelourinho 3, tel. 71/3321-1967, 9 A.M.–6 P.M. Mon.–Fri., closed Tues., R$1) offers an eclectic mix of things Soteropolitano. Depictions of Catholic saints and ex-votos mingle with sculptures of *orixás* and other objects related to Candomblé. Meanwhile, more secular offerings include works by local artists and artisans and a room devoted to Castro Alves, one of Brazil's great romantic poets and famously eloquent abolitionists.

Next door, the **Fundação Casa de Jorge Amado** (Largo do Pelourinho 49, tel. 71/3321-0122, 10 A.M.–6 P.M. Mon.–Sat., www.fundacaojorgeamado.com.br) is a small museum/shrine devoted to the life, times, and writing of Jorge Amado, one of Bahia's (and Brazil's) most cherished and internationally renowned writers and *"figuras"* (i.e., a truly memorable human being). It also functions as a center for literary events. With photos, book covers, and other media featuring the author of *Dona Flor and Her Two Husbands* and *Gabriela, Clove and Cinnamon,* the museum provides an overview of Amado's life and career, also touching on that of his lifelong love and companion, Zélia Gattai (a highly renowned writer in her own right). A nice rest stop is the museum's pleasant café (named after Gattai) with its great view of the *largo.*

Halfway down the steep Largo do Pelourinho is one of Bahia's most famous and important churches, the **Igreja Nossa Senhora do Rosário dos Pretos** (tel. 71/3326-9701, 8:30 A.M.–6 P.M. Mon.–Fri., 8:30 A.M.–3 P.M. Sat.–Sun.). This strikingly blue-tinged landmark is a symbol of black pride and resistance. After the king of Portugal gave the site to the Irmandade dos Homens Pretos, a brotherhood of local black men, it took slaves most of the 18th century to construct this church. Built in honor of Our Lady of the Rosary of Black People, it's visually striking with its handsome rococo facade and tiled towers influenced by Indian architecture, a consequence of Portugal's colony in Goa. Services here, in which Catholics hymns merge with traditional African percussion instruments—particularly during the Tuesday mass held at 6 P.M.—reflect Bahia's unique religious syncretism.

At the bottom of the Largo do Pelourinho, lively bars with occupants spilling onto the street are neighbors to the **Casa de Benin** (Rua Baixa dos Sapateiros 7, Pelourinho, tel. 71/3241-5679, 9 A.M.–6 P.M. Mon.–Fri., free). Located in a grand colonial building on the corner, it is worth stopping into for a look at its small collection of traditional artifacts from Benin. This West African country with whom Bahia has maintained cultural ties was the origin of a great many of the slaves who were brought to work on the colonial sugarcane plantations.

IGREJA DA ORDEM TERCEIRA DO CARMO E CONVENTO DO CARMO

From the Casa de Benin rises the very steep Ladeira do Carmo, a climb that will most likely leave you huffing and puffing, but which offers great views of the surrounding Pelô. Around halfway up, to the left, is the majestic Escadas do Carmo staircase, which leads to the imposing though sadly dilapidated Igreja Santíssimo Sacramento do Passo. Both the staircase and the church were immortalized in the first Brazilian film to win the Cannes Festival's Palme d'Or, *O Pagador de Promessas* (1962).

Towering above the Ladeira do Carmo is the dramatic whitewashed complex that houses the Igreja da Ordem Terceira do Carmo and the Convento do Carmo. Constructed in 1636 and rebuilt in 1786 in neoclassical style following after a fire in 1786, the church (tel. 71/3481-4169, 8 A.M.–noon and 2–6 P.M. Mon.–Sat., 8 A.M.–10 A.M. Sun., R$1) could use some major restoration. Nonetheless, the interior—with its tiny, though somewhat disorderly museum of sacred art—is certainly worth a visit. In particular, feast your eyes on the highly expressive cedar carving of Christ, sculpted in 1730 by Francisco Xavier Chagas. A slave nicknamed O Cabra (the Goat), Chagas has been compared to the great *mulato* baroque sculptor of Minas Gerais, Aleijadinho. If the drops of blood on the reclining Christ figure seem to glint and glisten as if they were transparent liquid, it is because they are assembled out of 2,000 encrusted rubies. Chagas is also responsible for the statue of Nossa Senhora do Carmo, whose features were said to be inspired by Isabel, the daughter of Garcia d'Ávila, the largest landowner in the Northeast during colonial times.

Adjacent to the church is the Convento do Carmo, a massive convent built in 1586 that was recently converted into a beautiful luxury hotel. Wander in and examine the stylishly furnished interior, then stop for a drink at the handsome bar-lounge. Situated in the arcaded cloister, the comfortable chairs and sofas of this beguiling spot face the palm-studded oasis in the courtyard.

Santo Antônio

"Santo Antônio" is the name given to the narrow neighborhood that stretches from the plaza in front of the church and convent of Carmo complex down to the vast open square known as Largo do Santo Antônio. The neighborhood's main drag is the Rua Direito de Santo Antônio, an extension of Rua do Carmo. Although bereft of the splendid treasures of the Pelô, for the sheer joy of rambling around a historic *bairro,* Santo Antônio offers a much more enticing—not to mention safer—vibe. Not as old or as reupholstered as the Pelourinho, Santo Antônio offers a much more "authentic" experience of Salvador and hints of what the Pelô could have been had the strategies accompanying its makeover—expulsion of residents and pandering to tourists—not been so brutal. In the last few years, many of its crumbling belle epoque–era mansions have been saved by enterprising hoteliers—many of them gringos—who have opened up restaurants, galleries, and no less than 25 *pousadas.* Luckily, instead of radically transforming the hood, these newcomers spruced it up and then integrated themselves into the fabric of what is still, at heart, a traditional *bairro popular,* with its cozy bakeries, grocery stores, and bars. As you stroll along the uneven cobblestones, admiring the eclectic turn-of-the-20th-century architecture, you can peer into windows and see residents gossiping, watching TV, drinking beer, and attending to the business of their lives. An added bonus of the plethora of newly opened *pousadas* and restaurants is that several are outfitted with panoramic terraces offering splendid views of the Cidade Baixa and the Baía de Todos os Santos. Watching the sun set over the Ilha da Itaparica in the company of amigos and a *bem gelada* (ice-cold beer) is a favorite ritual. As you make your way down the Rua Direito de Santo Antônio, highlights include the **Cruz do Pascoal,** a giant cross planted in the middle of the road, in front of which the faithful used to pray for protection against demons, and the attractive 18th-century **Igreja Nossa Senhora do Boqueirão** (Rua Direito de Santo Antônio 60).

The road eventually opens upon the spacious **Largo de Santo Antônio** square, which is framed at one end by a belvedere overlooking the ocean and at the other by the neoclassical **Igreja de Santo Antônio Além do Carmo.** The church is almost always open due to Santo Antônio's popularity. Not only a protector of the poor, he also intercedes on behalf of lonely hearts and bachelors (as the patron saint of marriage) and specializes in finding lost valuables.

At the far side of the square is **Forte de Santo Antônio Além do Carmo** (Largo de Santo Antônio, tel. 71/3321-7587, 7:30–9:30 P.M. Tues., Thurs., and Sat., and 5:30–7:30 P.M. Sun., free), which was constructed in the 16th century by the Portuguese as a defensive measure against invading Dutch troops. During the years of military dictatorship, the abandoned fort served as a detention center for political prisoners who spoke out against the government. After undergoing renovations, it was reopened in 2006 as a Capoeira Preservation Center, dedicated to preserving this traditional martial art while providing new headquarters for some of the city's oldest *capoeira* schools.

Cidade Baixa

Sadly, the Cidade Baixa, Salvador's port and commercial district, has seen better days. The area is a mélange of decaying historic buildings (some of them formerly quite grandiose), the odd colonial church, warehouses, and decaying 1960s and 1970s high-rises built before Salvador's commercial center moved to the more mod (and characterless) neighborhoods surrounding Shopping Iguatemi. Although there are signs that an urban revitalization could take place here, it will certainly be a while. Today, "Comércio" (as it is known) is fairly bustling during the day, but downright dangerous at night. When you come down from the Cidade Alta to explore its few attractions, take a bus (any one that has "Comércio" written on the side) or the Elevador Lacerda to Praça Visconde de Cairu, or else a taxi. Don't even think about walking up or down the steep roads linking the two *cidades*—they are unsafe, even by day.

MERCADO MODELO

Across the street from Elevador Lacerda, on the far side of Praça Visconde de Cairu, you can't miss this canary yellow 19th-century building that used to be the customs house. In former times, newly arrived slaves were chained in its dank basement until they were auctioned off. After being partially destroyed by arson in 1986, the building was transformed into the Mercado Modelo (Praça Visconde de Cairu 250, tel. 71/3241-2849, 9 A.M.–7 P.M. Mon.–Sat., 9 A.M.–2 P.M. Sun.). This two-story bazaar sells every kind of Bahian handicraft and cliché under the sun. Offerings range from twanging *berimbaus* (a one-string instrument attached to a gourd) and *figas* (good luck charms in the shape of a forearm and fist) to *orixá* refrigerator magnets. If you're in the market for touristy trinkets and are willing to haggle for them, you've come to the right place. Live music and *capoeira* demonstrations are held out back for the benefit of tourists. Although the performances are free, if you decide to take a few snapshots you'll be hit up for a contribution. Upstairs, the traditional restaurants serving typical Bahian food offer magnificent sea views but, like the market itself, have lost their original cachet.

© MICHAEL SOMMERS

Salvador's Cidade Baixa as seen from the Baía de Todos os Santos

FEIRA DE SÃO JOAQUIM

For a more authentic, vibrant, and sensual—albeit chaotic—market experience in Salvador, grab a cab or hop a bus (with the destination "Ribeira" or "Bonfim") from Praça Cairu and head for the city's oldest and biggest outdoor daily market. It's only a short ride away in a neighborhood known as Calçada. São Joaquim is not for the faint of heart. Its labyrinthine lanes are riddled with potholes, puddles, and rotting fruit, and you're always in danger of being run over by a wheelbarrow full of mangoes or smacked in the head with a jackfruit. If you're not a vegetarian, the gory meat section will make you consider the possibility. And if the sight of people tossing live roosters into the trunks of cars surprises those for whom poultry is usually a packaged deal, remember that they're usually for Candomblé rituals. Indeed, São Joaquim is not at all set up for tourism, and for this reason, it's somewhat of an adventure. Pyramids of spices and tropical fruits assault the senses with their fragrant scents and dazzling colors. There are areas where you can buy traditional ceramic pots and vases, and others

selling woven straw hats and mats. However, the most interesting section is where the stalls are devoted to Candomblé artifacts: fistfuls of brightly colored beads associated with different *orixás,* fragrant leaves for sacred baths, and traditional ceramic serving dishes for food and other offerings. Unless you have a strong stomach, it's probably not a great idea to chow down at one of the many *barraca* restaurants serving up dirt-cheap fare. However, do stop for a beer or a shot of *cachaça* and take time to observe and absorb the action.

FORTE SÃO MARCELO

If you walk to the back of the Mercado Modelo, you'll find yourself in front of the Terminal Marítimo. This is where you can catch boats for the Ilha de Itaparica as well as the recently renovated Forte São Marcelo (tel. 71/3321-5286, 9 A.M.–6 A.M. Tues.–Sun., R$10), a circular 17th-century pseudo-medieval fort guarding the entrance to the Bay of All Saints. For R$10, you get whisked across the water to the fort where you can wander amidst digitally simulated galleons and cannons, view exhibits, or simply take advantage of the privileged surroundings in the company of a (somewhat pricy) cocktail. Since January 2007, the fort is home to **Buccaneros** (tel. 71/9617-6933, Tues.–Sun., R$25–45), a nautically themed restaurant boasting contemporary dishes for lunch and dinner.

IGREJA DE NOSSA SENHORA DA CONCEIÇÃO DA PRAIA

Looking back towards the city from the Mercado Modelo or Forte São Marcelo, there's no way to miss the stately baroque Igreja de Nossa Senhora da Conceição da Praia (Rua Conceição da Praia, tel. 71/3242-0545, 7 A.M.–noon and 3–7 P.M. Mon., 7 A.M.–5 P.M. Tues.–Fri., 7–11:30 A.M. Sat.–Sun., free). Built in Portugal in 1736, it was then transported piece by piece to the site of Salvador's first chapel, which overlooks the Bay of All Saints. The patron saint of Salvador, Our Lady of Conception, is also linked to the wildly popular Candomblé *orixá* Iemenjá, goddess of the sea. Accordingly, the saint's feast day on December 8 is the occasion for one of the city's most traditional religious and popular *festas*.

SOLAR DO UNHÃO-MUSEU DE ARTE MODERNA (MAM)

Although you can walk there, it's safer to take a quick taxi ride up the coastal road, past the Igreja de Nossa Senhora de Conceição and Bahia's swanky marina, to one of the city's finest and most beautifully situated museums, the Museu de Arte Moderna. Known by its acronym, "MAM," as well as its original title, the Solar do Unhão, this 17th-century complex hovering over the Bay of All Saints was originally a sugarcane plantation complete with mansion (*solar*), slave quarters, and chapel. In the '60s, the well-preserved ensemble got an inspired refurbishment courtesy of reputed São Paulo modernist architect Lina Bo Bardi. This is when it was transformed into Bahia's Museum of Modern Art. Aside from a permanent collection that boasts token works of major Brazilian modernist painters, the museum showcases temporary exhibitions of contemporary artists from all over Brazil.

Even if the art itself doesn't grab you, the buildings and setting are truly captivating. The adjacent sculpture garden featuring works by local talents such as Carybé and Mario Cravo Jr. winds up and down a shady path overlooking the sea. In the late afternoon, the wooden pier above the ocean is a magical place to have a drink and watch the sun setting behind the Ilha da Itaparica. A small cinema operates, and live music shows often take place on the cobblestoned courtyard, through which tiny *mico* monkeys leap and chatter. If you're in need of serious sustenance, the museum restaurant offers good Bahian food. Be aware that the nightly buffets complete with "typical" musical shows attract plenty of sunburned tourists on packaged tours.

Bonfim

If you hop a bus with the destination "Bonfim" or "Ribeira" from Praça Cairu, Campo Grande, or anywhere else in the city, you will find yourself sailing through the length of the Cidade Baixa, following the 8-kilometer (5-mile) route taken by worshippers and revelers who, on the second Thursday of every January, make their way in a procession to one of Brazil's most famous churches: the Igreja de Nosso Senhor do Bonfim.

IGREJA DE NOSSO SENHOR DO BONFIM

Sacred to Catholics as well as followers of Candomblé (for whom Senhor do Bonfim is equated with both Christ and one of the most important *orixás,* Oxalá), the Igreja de Nosso Senhor do Bonfim is an important pilgrimage site. Morning mass is large, especially on Fridays—Oxalá's day of the week. Even before you arrive at the gleaming church, you'll be able to see it: Splendidly rising up from a hilltop and accessorized by swaying imperial palms, it's an eye-catching example of Portuguese rococo architecture. Upon your arrival at the pretty cobblestoned Largo do Bonfim, you'll likely be accosted by a few vendors plying you with brightly colored *fitas de Bonfim* (Bonfim ribbons). If you choose to follow tradition and tie one around your wrist, make sure you tie three knots and make a wish on each one. Having done so, you'll be stuck wearing it for weeks, months, or even years (for this reason, don't tie it too tight), and when it naturally falls off, your wishes will come true. With the exception of the resplendent panels of blue-and-white Portuguese tiles, the interior of the church is relatively unadorned by Bahian standards. The real interest lies in its importance to Bahians, which becomes clear when you visit the church's small but fascinating **Museu dos Ex-Votos do Senhor do Bonfim** (Largo do Bonfim, tel. 71/3312-4512, 9 A.M.– noon and 2–5 P.M. Tues.–Sat., R$2).

Your visit begins in the Sala dos Milagres (Room of Miracles), whose walls are covered from floor to ceiling with thousands of photographs and handwritten notes accompanied by *fitas*. Whether or not you understand Portuguese, these heart-felt supplications to Senhor do Bonfim—be it pleading for the life of a child, the safe return of a fisherman, or even victory in a soccer championship—are incredibly moving. So are the photos, newspaper clippings, and paintings of miracles: depicting believers being saved from tragedies such as car accidents and fires. Meanwhile, dangling from the ceiling are wooden and plastic heads, limbs, and even organs such as hearts and lungs. These are the offerings of worried patients seeking protection before surgery. The second floor houses older and more precious ex-votos in display cases, including silver heads, arms, hearts, eyes, noses—even livers and intestines offered in thanks by miraculously cured patients. The presence of soccer uniforms indicates that both of Salvador's major teams wouldn't dream of starting *futebol* season without first visiting the church for a blessing.

FORTE DE MONTE SERRAT AND PONTA DE HUMAITÁ

From the Igreja do Bonfim, if you walk uphill from the Largo de Bonfim and take the road that swerves to the left, you'll be treated to some magnificent panoramic views of the entire city. Follow the road for another five minutes, which will lead you downhill to the popular white-sand beach of **Boa Viagem.** A favorite *praia popular*, on weekends it is so packed with residents of surrounding neighborhoods you can barely see the sand. Crowning the beach is the 16th-century **Forte de Monte Serrat,** whose cannons chased off invading Dutch. Today, its functions are decidedly less bellicose—it is a favorite place for smooching couples to get a glimpse of the sunset over the Bay of All Saints. Another great vantage point is the nearby **Ponta de Humaitá,** whose striped lighthouse, tiny 17th-century **Igreja de Nossa Senhora de Monte Serrat,** and sweeping sea views provide a romantic spot for a late afternoon drink.

Centro

Salvador's Centro encompasses a somewhat loosely defined neighborhood that more or less consists of the old "downtown" of the Cidade Alta, which follows Avenida Sete de Setembro (the main drag) from its beginning at Praça Castro Alves to Campo Grande and the sweeping tree-lined Corredor da Vitória. The latter is where Salvador's wealthy live in soaring high-rise apartments overlooking the sea. Chaotic, crowded, and oddly provincial for such a major city, the Centro is nonetheless an interesting place to walk around if you want to get an authentic feel for the city. Filled with museums, churches, shops, markets, and *ambulantes* (street vendors selling every kind of item imaginable), by day it hums with activity, but at night becomes abandoned, and therefore fairly dangerous to stroll around.

From the Praça Municipal, the once elegant **Rua Chile** still displays some grandiose buildings that formerly housed department stores and hotels. Although sadly abandoned, restoration projects are underway in an attempt to regain at least some of its former glory. Rua Chile leads onto the **Praça Castro Alves,** a semicircular plaza where Bahia's famous Romantic poet (Alves) stares out at the Bay of All Saints. Celebrated for his smoldering good looks, passionate prose, abolitionist views, and tragically untimely death at the age of 24, Alves was Bahia's answer to John Keats. Although the square offers little more than magnificent sea views, it plays an important role in municipal life and for years was the traditional meeting point for all the *trio elétricos* (gigantic truck-driven stages) that brought Carnaval to a close on the morning of Ash Wednesday.

MUSEU DE ARTE SACRA DA BAHIA

From the Praça Castro Alves, a fork in the road splits Avenida Sete de Setembro into two. If you take the lower road (Rua Carlos Gomes), the first street on the right will bring you to Ladeira de Santa Teresa. This steep little alley plunges down to the magnificent 17th-century convent of Santa Teresa de Ávila, which was once occupied by the Ordem das Carmelitas Descalços (Barefoot Carmelites Order). Overlooking the sea and surrounded by shady courtyards, its tranquil church, cloisters, and monks' cells are part of the Museu de Arte Sacra da Bahia (Rua do Sodré 276, tel. 71/3243-6511, 11:30 A.M.–5 P.M. Mon.–Fri., R$5). One of the most important, not to mention impressive, museums of sacred religious art in Brazil, its collection of 1,400 pieces includes a wealth of paintings, sculptures, icons, and furniture from Bahia's glorious colonial past.

ALONG AVENIDA SETE DE SETEMBRO

If you take the high road—Avenida Sete—from Praça Castro Alves, within a few meters, you'll find yourself in front of one of the oldest monasteries in all of the Americas, the grandiose **Mosteiro de São Bento** (Largo de São Bento, Centro, tel. 71/2106-5200, 11:30 A.M.–5 P.M. daily), which has undergone numerous renovations since its founding in 1582. It's worth popping in for a quick look at its interior and museum of religious art. If you're a sucker for Gregorian chants, take a cab here on Sunday to hear the monastery's 30 cloistered monks exercise their vocal chords. As you continue along Avenida Sete, you will pass the lively **Praça da Piedade,** where the trees are home to iguanas. The busy square is framed by the impressively domed **Igreja Nossa Senhora da Piedade** and the unusual **Gabinete Português de Leitura,** a library that houses works of Portuguese and Brazilian literature.

CAMPO GRANDE

Another 10 minutes of strolling and you'll reach the elegantly restored Campo Grande, the Centro's most attractive—and verdant— park. It boasts carefully tended flower patches, immense century-old trees, playgrounds, goldfish ponds, and plenty of benches from where you can take it all in. At the center of Campo Grande, the **Monumento ao Dois de Julho,** featuring a statue of a fierce-looking Caboclo (a mythical figure, part Indian, part African, who is a symbol of Bahian independence from the Portuguese), pays homage to July 2, 1823, the date upon which Bahian troops achieved autonomy by expelling Portuguese troops. The monument—and Campo Grande in general—has a strong symbolic significance for Soteropolitanos. Accordingly, a large number of important official and cultural events often take place here. **Teatro Castro Alves,** a gleaming white modernist theater complex directly in front of Campo Grande, is where the city's principal dance, musical, and theatrical events take place.

Corredor da Vitória

From Campo Grande onwards, Avenida Sete de Setembro is known as the Corredor da Vitória. Lined with wonderfully overgrown trees and less wonderful luxury apartment complexes, "Vitória" is where Salvador's elite have traditionally lived. The small but economically important British community that founded this posh hood in the late 19th century and constructed some of its lavish mansions (a few of which still survive) is now home to a handful of small museums and cultural centers.

MUSEU DE ARTE DA BAHIA

Among the more interesting of the museums in this neighborhood is the Museu de Arte da Bahia (Av. Sete de Setembro 2340, tel. 71/3336-9450, 2–7 P.M. Tues.–Fri., 2:30–6:30 P.M. Sat.–Sun., R$5, free Thurs. and Sun.), which houses a hit-and-miss collection of Bahian paintings and furnishings.

MUSEU CARLOS COSTA PINTO

In a gracious private villa that still belongs to Salvador's traditional Costa Pinto family, the Museu Carlos Costa Pinto (Av. Sete de Setembro 2490, tel. 71/3336-6081, 2:30–7 p.m. Wed.–Mon., R$5, free Thurs.) features a rare and magnificent collection of Bahian art and artifacts that offer a glimpse into the grandeur of the Bahian elite during colonial times. Aside from the heavy jacaranda and marble furniture, there's a great collection of delicate Chinese porcelain as well as bric-a-brac fashioned out of precious woods, silver, gold, and ivory. Despite the European finery, you're likely to be most impressed by the fantastic collection of *balangandans:* ornate bracelets with glittery, dangling "charms" ranging from tropical fruits to *figas* (clenched fists symbolizing power). Made of silver and gold, these were gifts given by rich masters to their female slaves, who used them to accessorize their traditional attire of white petticoats and turbans. After feasting your eyes, retire to the lovely courtyard **Balangandan Café** and savor some of the menu's delicious French tarts.

Barra

At the end of Corredor de Vitória—bracketed by a McDonald's on one side and the gleaming white Igreja de Nossa Senhora da Vitória—the descent from Avenida Sete de Setembro begins a steep plunge towards the lively middle-class neighborhood and beach of Barra. This road (known as Ladeira da Barra) offers spectacular sea views that will surely whet your appetite for the beaches awaiting at the foot of the hill. On your way down, you'll pass Bahia's yacht club, with its swan-like array of sail boats, the Cimetério dos Ingleses, where Bahia's Brit expat community encountered a terribly scenic resting place, and, perched upon a verdant hill, the 16th-century Igreja de Santo Antônio da Barra.

PORTO DA BARRA

At the bottom of Ladeira da Barra, you'll find yourself in front of Salvador's most famous beach, Porto da Barra, dramatically framed by two 17th-century Portuguese fortresses: Forte São Diogo and Forte Santa Maria. More than just a small crescent-shaped golden sand beach, "Porto" is an entire microcosm uniting families, gays, tourists, locals, vendors, hustlers, lovers, celebrities, sun worshippers, and volleyball and frescoball aficionados) on one vibrant and colorful strip of sand bathed by the calm and surprisingly clear sea. Indeed, barring the rainy season, no matter how over populated it gets, Porto's waters are always miraculously crystalline.

In the summer, Porto gets so packed it's hard to see the sand, but as a social scene, it is pure fascination. Meanwhile, in the "winter," locals tend to shy away, citing the cold as an excuse (as if anyone could get hypothermia when the thermometer falls to 24°C/75°F), thus leaving the beach deliciously empty. Although Porto has a small-town feel to it—aided by the fact that the only vessels bobbing on its waters are brightly painted wooden fishing boats— it packs a surprisingly urban wallop. While you're hanging out, you'll be bombarded by the songs and chants of passing vendors hawking everything from handmade jewelry (some of it quite inspired) and portable radios to skewered shrimp, grilled cheese (*queijo coalho*) with oregano, fresh fruit popsicles called *picolés* (the best ones are made by a company called Capelinha). You'll also be spoiled—after renting a beach chair and giant parasol (try Nice, located at the second staircase), you'll have your feet regularly refreshed with a watering can and all your drink requests attended to.

Porto da Barra is the classic place to watch the sunset—in fact, applause rings out the moment the glowing orange-red disk descends below the Ilha da Itaparica, bathing both sky and sea in a painterly blaze of colors. Since the beach is lit at night, it is possible to take a moonlight dip. However, be very careful with your valuables (even more so than during the day) since after dark, the area can be kind of hazardous and tourists are often targeted by thieves.

FAROL DA BARRA

Walking along the breezy seaside promenade— past small coves and the increasing number of hotels, gyms, cyber cafés, and bars that are

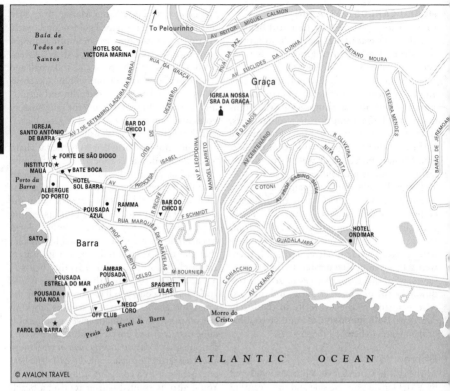

turning Barra into a small-scale Copacabana—you'll soon reach the iconic black-and-white striped Barra lighthouse. Jutting out into the sea at the point where the Bay of All Saints meets the Atlantic, the Farol da Barra is lodged within the 17th-century Forte de Santo Antônio. Although the current lighthouse, constructed of iron, was built in 1836, the original wooden one—dating from 1696—operated using whale oil and was the first lighthouse in all of the Americas. Inside the fort is the mildly interesting **Museu Náutico da Bahia** (tel. 71/3264-3296, 9 A.M.–7 P.M. Tues.–Sun., R$6), with a collection of maps, navigation instruments, model ships, and other seafaring paraphernalia. Just as interesting, if not more, is the secluded bar situated within the lighthouse's sun-bleached walls. During the year, the Farol and surrounding area are the setting for various shows and concerts, the biggest of which occur on New Year's Eve and Day.

BEACHES

Barra is where what Soteropolitanos refer to as the *orla,* or coastline, begins: a long string—roughly 20 kilometers (12.5 miles)—of beaches that stretch north up to Itapuá and the city limits. Aside from Rio Vermelho, the adjoining neighborhoods themselves are of little interest, and if you're looking for good beaches, the ones further away, beginning at Boca do Rio, are the only worthy candidates for bathing. Lots of buses—both municipal and more expensive and air-conditioned *executivos*—leave from the center (Campo Grande and Lapa) or from Barra and speed up and down the coast all the way to Itapuá. On the weekends, particularly in the summer, all of these beaches get really packed.

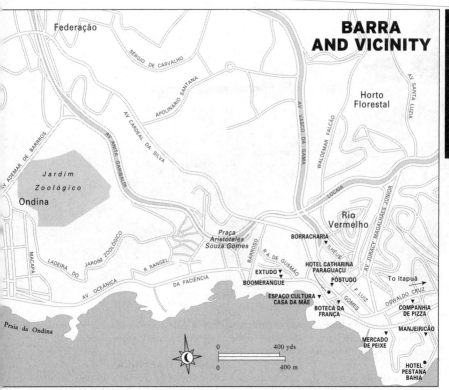

BARRA AND VICINITY

Federação

SÉRGIO DE CARVALHO

APOLINÁRIO SANTANA

AV CARDEAL DA SILVA

AV ANITA GARIBALDI

AV ADEMAR DE BARROS

Horto Florestal

AV SANTA LUZIA

AV VASCO DA GAMA

WALDEMAR FALCÃO

LUCAIA

Jardim Zoológico

Ondina

MACAPA

LADEIRA DO JARDIM ZOOLOGICO

R RANGEL

DA PACIÊNCIA

AV OCEÂNICA

Praça Aristóteles Souza Gomes

BARROSO

R A. DE GUSMÃO

Rio Vermelho

BORRACHARIA

ILHÉUS

AV JURACY MAGALHÃES JÚNIOR

EXTUDO ▼

BOOMERANGUE

HOTEL CATHARINA PARAGUAÇU

POSTUDO ▼

P. LUIZ

To Itapuã

OSWALDO CRUZ

ESPAÇO CULTURA CASA DA MÃE ▼

BOTECA DA FRANÇA

GOMES

COMPANHIA DE PIZZA

Praia da Ondina

MANJEIRICÃO ▼

MERCADO DE PEIXE

HOTEL PESTANA BAHIA

0   400 yds

0   400 m

It's best if you can go early and come back at around 3 P.M. to beat the rush and crush.

Rio Vermelho and Vicinity

After Barra and the middle-class beach neighborhood of Ondina, with its many big chain hotels, comes Rio Vermelho, a bohemian enclave, which is more interesting at night, when its bars, lively squares, and restaurants fill up with the city's artistic and intellectual crowd. Although its beaches aren't good for swimming, it has a pleasant vibe. The neighborhood is enhanced by the always happening Mercado do Peixe and the cobblestoned squares where the city's triumvirate of reigning Bahianas sell their famed *acarajés* and *abarás*.

Rio Vermelho is followed by the rather soulless Pituba, where the city's yuppies live, shop, and party. And from then on, the beaches keep

coming. **Boca do Rio** is a gay mecca whose *barracas,* **Aruba** and **República,** compete for the prettiest and most ripped bikini-clad boys in town. **Jaguaribe** is packed with *barracas,* vendors, surfers, and sun worshippers. Ditto for neighboring **Piatã,** although the waves here are calmer and the beach is framed by coconut palms.

Until only a couple of decades ago, **Itapuã** was but a bucolic palm-fringed fishing village that captivated the imaginations of residents such as Dorival Caymmi and Vinícius de Moraes, both of whom immortalized the beach's idyllic vibe in their unforgettable musical compositions. Today, the neighborhood is somewhat more developed and scruffy and it's not the best beach in town for a swim. Nonetheless, the languorous vibe has somehow survived—as have the fishermen, the swaying palms, and the pretty candy-cane-striped

© MICHAEL SOMMERS

Porto da Barra beach in Salvador

lighthouse, around whose *barracas* congregates a somewhat bohemian crowd who listen to the bossa nova and MPB that are often played live on weekends.

Keep walking beyond the lighthouse and you'll hit the lovely uncrowded white-sand (and rough-watered) beach of **Pedra do Sal,** with some great *barracas,* among them **Aqua Lôca.** More popular with middle-class patrons (who have cars) are the less urban and more un-spoiled beaches that follow: **Stella Maris** and **Flamengo** (municipal buses whose final destination is marked "Praia de Flamengo" depart from Campo Grande or along the *orla*). Aside from offering more shade, water-sports equipment, and natural pools that are ideal for kids, both beaches boast state-of-the-art *barracas* such as **Azul Marinho** and **Biruta Tchê** (Stella Maris), and **Lôro, Cabana Solares, Martim Pescador,** and **Honolulu Tent Beach** (Flamengo).

Baía de Todos os Santos

It's the biggest bay in Brazil—yes, even bigger than Rio's famous Guanabara Bay—and the beckoning blue and always warm waters of the Bay of All Saints are ideal for swimming, sailing, diving, and contemplation.

ILHA DE ITAPARICA

The largest of the bay's 30-plus islands is the 35-kilometer-long (22-mile-long) narrow strip called Itaparica, whose lithe silhouette bisects the sea and the sky for those gazing out over the bay from Salvador. A favorite getaway for Soteropolitanos, Itaparica's many palm-fringed beaches are lined with many weekend and holi-day homes—some quite old and grand, oth-ers resembling *favelas*. In fact, stay away on holiday weekends because getting there and back will mean lining up for hours to catch a boat (make sure you buy your return ticket), and once there, you'll be immersed in a sea of people. However, during the week or in off-season, the *"ilha"* has a laid-back vibe that is conducive to R&R. Although the beaches are inferior to those north of Salvador, soaking in the calm blue water is as relaxing as taking a bath, and the view of the glimmering white city across the bay is quite enchanting. The is-land's major crop is mangos, and you wouldn't

© MICHAEL SOMMERS

the beach at Mar Grande on the Ilha de Itaparica, across the Baía de Todos os Santos

believe there could be such a difference in taste and fragrance, but once you sink your teeth into the real thing (depending on the season, they'll be literally raining down upon you) you will be in mango heaven.

There are two ways of getting from Salvador to Itaparica. The nicest, and simplest, is to grab a boat bound for **Mar Grande** at the **Terminal Turístico Marítimo** (Av. da França, tel. 71/3326-3434, R$3), behind the Mercado Modelo. The scenic trip across the bay takes 45 minutes with departures every 30 minutes between 6:30 A.M. and 7 P.M. (depending on the tides). On the other side, Mar Grande is a lazy beach resort town with some lovely old summer homes and tree-lined streets and lots of seafood restaurants. You can easily explore the beaches by foot or rent a bike. The return trip at the end of the day almost always offers the bonus of a fantastic sunset.

Another way to get to Itaparica is to grab a catamaran or ferry boat from the **Terminal Marítimo de São Joaquim** (Av. Oscar Pontes 1501, tel. 71/3633-1248, R$3), near the Feira de São Joaquim in the Cidade Baixa. Although

you can take a "Ribeira" or "Bonfim"-bound bus, the easiest way to get to the ferry terminal is by taxi. Both ferries and high-speed (and more expensive) catamarans will take you to Itaparica's main bus and boat terminal, aptly named Bom Despacho (Good Send-Off). Ferry crossings take about an hour with departures every hour between 5 A.M. and 11:30 P.M. The speedy catamaran takes about 30 minutes, with boats leaving more or less every 60 to 90 minutes between 7:50 A.M. and 6:20 P.M. The ferry ride to Bom Despacho costs R$3.20 and the catamaran ride to Bom Despacho costs R$6. (Prices are slightly higher on Sat. and Sun.)

From Bom Despacho, buses travel to cities on the Recôncavo as well as southern coast destinations such as Valença, Camamu, Ilhéus, and Porto Seguro. You can also get a *kombi* (collective van service) that delivers locals and beach goers up and down the length of the island to individual beaches. Among the nicer destinations are Praia Ponta de Areia, north of Bom Despacho, and Praia da Penha and Barra Grande, several kilometers south of Bom Despacho. Also inviting is the colonial village of Itaparica, where you'll find a few remaining vestiges of 17th-century buildings.

ILHA DE MARÉ
The tiny Ilha de Maré is completely overlooked by tourists and even many Soteropolitanos. Although it hasn't been that long since the island got electricity, in many ways, taking a boat across the bay to its pristine beaches backed by green hills is like going back in time. The island's settlement consists of a rustic ramshackle of fisherfolk's houses and beachfront bars with an atmospheric colonial church thrown in for good measure. One of the main commercial products is the delicious *doce de banana,* a banana sweet made in wood ovens, then wrapped in banana fiber packages and sold by the dozen by children roaming up and down the sand. On the beaches away from town, *barracas* serve delicious fried fish and *moqueca* as the tide comes in and laps at your legs. To get a boat to Ilha de Maré, you'll need to grab a bus with the destination "Base Naval/São Tomé" (which passes in front of the Teatro Castro Alves, at Campo Grande); ride to the end of the line and then get a boat from the **São Tomé de Paripe terminal** (tel. 71/3307-1447, R$2). The trip takes 20 minutes with departures every 45 minutes between 8 A.M. and 5:30 P.M.

ENTERTAINMENT AND EVENTS
Nightlife
Salvador's nightlife is somewhat of an enigma. Contrary to its fame as a partying place, when the sizzling summer season comes to an end many bars and clubs close early if they don't shut down altogether. Supposedly, the blame falls to the fickleness of Soteropolitanos. However, there is always something happening in Barra and Rio Vermelho, and the Pelô and Centro offer a few old standbys that never go out of style. For listings, check out the entertainment sections of the two daily papers, *A Tarde* and *O Correio da Bahia.* For English tips, check out www.bahia-online.net/happenings.htm—a great website compiled by an American expat living in Salvador who owns a CD store.

LIVE MUSIC
Salvador is justly famous for its music scene. Aside from tons of festivals and shows, there are limitless possibilities for hearing music—often for free. In the summertime especially, the Pelourinho in particular throbs with the beat of drums as the city's Carnaval *blocos* (traditional Carnaval groups associated with organizations or neighborhoods) hold open weekly *ensaios,* or rehearsals, often with special guests in attendance. Usually beginning in November, these *ensaios* are either free or ridiculously expensive (to gouge tourists). Locales change yearly. Taking part will not only ensure you rub shoulders with Salvador's young blood, but will also allow you to witness firsthand how summer musical hits—which eventually captivate all of Bahia and Brazil—are generated. Think of it as a taste of the sheer exuberance and intense musicality of Carnaval, should you not be around for the main event itself. The hottest *ensaios* around include Margareth Menezes and her Os Mascaradas *bloco,* the *tradicionalíssimo* Afro *blocos* Ilê Aiyê (whose rehearsals take place at its headquarters in the *bairro* of Curuzu), Filhos de Gandhy, Olodum, Muzenza, and Cortejo Afro (all of whom perform in the Pelô).

No matter what the season, there is usually always something going on at the Pelourinho's **Praça Tereza Batista** and **Praça Pedro Archango** (both off Rua Gregório de Matos) as well as **Praça Quincas Berro D'Água** (off Rua Frei Vicente). In the summer, these three outdoor areas, surrounded by bars, host musical repertories ranging from samba-reggae to *pagode* that jive with the feverish public's desire to get down, get close, and samba till they drop. In the winter, the tempo slows down, switching to MPB, bossa nova, and *chorinho.* Also not to be missed are the Tuesday night jams on the steep steps of the Igreja do Santíssimo Sacramento do Passo on Rua do Passo, hosted by the terrific homegrown singer and composer Gerónimo. From the top of the stairs the view across the Pelourinho is enchanting, especially if there is a full moon.

A quick cab ride from the Pelô, the newest

musical venue in town has garnered a ton of buzz due to its founder and location. The **Museu do Ritmo** (Av. Jequitaia 1, Comércio) is the brainchild of Carlinhos Brown, composer and leader of the Timbalada *bloco*. This vanguard space was inaugurated during Carnaval of 2007 in the reconstructed ruins of an old marketplace, the Mercado de Ouro. Featuring a big stage and lots of dancing space, when completed this cultural center will also house an art gallery, museum, restaurant, and school.

Up and running since 1958, the beloved **Concha Acústica** (Ladeira da Fonte, Campo Grande, tel. 71/3339-8033), or simply *"a Concha,"* is part of the Teatro Castro Alves complex. Since day one, this massive outdoor amphitheater, which seats 5,000, has hosted the biggest names in Brazilian music and continues to do so, all at affordable prices.

A fairly recent addition to Rio Vermelho's bohemian scene is the **Espaço Cultural Casa da Mãe** (Rua Guedes Cabral 81, Rio Vermelho, tel. 71/9197-9415, 6 p.m.–2 a.m. Thurs.–Sat., 1–11 p.m. Sun., cover R$5). Situated in a cozy whitewashed house with ocean views, this welcoming bar is operated by Roda Bahiana (an NGO based in the Recôncavo town of Santo Amaro) whose mission is to promote the works of local artists and musicians. As a result, you'll often be treated to some very fine and authentic musical performances.

NIGHTCLUBS

Unsurprisingly, when Soteropolitanos want to let their hair down and samba the night away, they tend to favor the breezy, balmy outdoors rather than being cooped up between four walls inside. Because of this, the club scene can be rather uninspiring. Nonetheless, in and around the *centro histórico* there are a few interesting options. The candle-lit **Alphorria** (Rua Direita de Santo Antônio 97, Santo Antônio, tel. 71/3242-3303, 6 p.m.–close Wed.–Sun., cover R$7–10) is in the basement of a colonial mansion where slaves were kept during colonial times (*alforria* means "liberation"). The intact original walls are decorated with antique objects. The musical lineup ranges from afro-

pop and *forró* to salsa and MPB. Should you get hungry, there are great *petiscos* (appetizers), and should you get sweaty, there is a small garden for cooling off. The setting of **Zauber Multicultura** (Ladeira da Misericórdia 11, tel. 71/3326-2964, www.zaubermulticultura.com, 10 p.m.–7 a.m. Thurs.–Sat., cover R$10–15) is also pretty spectacular. Housed in a turn-of-the-20th-century mansion at the end of Ladeira da Misericórdia (it's safer to take a cab there), it reflects the city's interests in revamping the abandoned but terribly atmospheric Comércio neighborhood. The generous sprawl includes a dance floor, stage, lounge, and outdoor terrace with bewitching views of the Cidade Baixa and the Bay of All Saints. Musical attractions are diverse, with an emphasis on electronica as well as local and national alternative bands and DJs. Not only do the barwomen swallow fire, but they mix up a mean *drinque do inferno* (hell cocktail), a combination of vodka, lime, and mint and peach liqueurs, served flambéed.

On a small street off Avenida Sete de Setembro (near Campo Grande), the **Tropical** (Rua Gamboa de Cima 24, Centro, tel. 71/3267-0847, 11 p.m.–6 a.m. Fri.–Sat., cover R$10) is the third and latest incarnation of a gay club called Holmes whose nocturnal happenings were legendary throughout Brazil in the '80s. The decor is festive, gaudy, and heavy on Carmen Miranda tributes. Aside from two bars, a lounge, and the requisite dance floor, there is a stage where local drag queens entertain the mixed, yet largely gay audience. More middle-class and GLS (a Brazilian slang term for "gay, lesbian, and sympathizers") is Barra's **Off Club** (Rua Dias D'Avila 33, Barra, tel. 71/3267-6215, www.off-club.com.br, 11:30 p.m.–3:30 a.m. Thurs. and Sun., 11:30 p.m.–7 a.m. Fri. and Sat., cover R$7–15), just around the corner from the Barra lighthouse. The decor is pretty blasé but with three dance floors (with a bar on each), there's tons of room to rock out to dance and house spun by local DJs.

One of the trendiest clubs of the moment is **Boomerangue** (Rua da Paciência 307, Rio Vermelho, tel. 71/3334-6640, www.boomerangueeventos.com.br, 10 P.M.–close Fri.–Sat., cover R$15), which is aptly named after the multiple boomerangs adorning the walls. The popular dance club features some of Bahia and Brazil's hottest alternative bands and DJs. Nearby is the **Borracharia** (Rua Conselheiro Pedro Luís 101-A, Rio Vermelho, tel. 71/9142-0456, 10 P.M.–close Fri. only, cover R$10). By day it is a tire repair shop, but on Friday nights, Salvador's artists and bohos line up to dance the night away amidst a decor of grease-streaked walls and spare tires. House DJ Roger N'Roll is a legendary emcee with a predilection for soul, samba-rock, and '70s hits. Take note: Be patient when looking for the entrance, which is unmarked.

BARS

Though most of Salvador's bars are at least partially outdoors and pretty basic, what makes them special is their strategic setting: being located in a hidden garden or a colonial mansion, overlooking the ocean, or in a lively cobblestoned *praça* overflowing with Soteropolitanos talking, dancing, laughing, and going about their lives.

The Pelourinho's narrow streets are packed with bars. Though there's no lack of action in the Pelô, some of it—vendors and beggars going after gringos—can be trying. Aside from the ubiquitous bars sprinkled around the Praça Tereza Batista, Praça Pedro Archango, and Praça Quincas Berro D'Água (see *Live Music*), a traditional watering hole with a largely local clientele is **O Cravinho** (Terreiro de Jesus 3, Pelourinho, tel. 71/3322-6759, 11 A.M.–11:30 P.M. daily). *Cravinho,* meaning "little clove," refers to the house specialty of *cachaça* infused with cloves, lime, and honey. This deceptively explosive concoction goes down real nice and costs next to nothing (which is why the bar is always packed). Over 30 such *cachaça* infusions (using herbs, flowers, roots, fruits, and seeds) are left to steep in the great wooden barrels lining the walls.

Just off the nearby Praça da Sé, turn onto the Ladeira da Misericórdia. A few steps down brings you to the **Zanzibar** (Ladeira da Misericórdia 9, Centro, tel. 71/8823-8008, 6 P.M.–close Tues.–Sat., cover R$3–10). The bar's undeniable charm is due to the fact that it was built around the immense trunk of an immense mango tree that's more than a century old. On weekends, the downstairs features local bands who offer up a cool mix of music that ranges from MPB and reggae to soul and jazz. The menu features African-tinged Bahian fare. Upstairs, tables are scattered beneath the leafy mango branches, and the views of the moonlit Bay of All Saints are more intoxicating than even the African-inspired ginger *batida,* which does duty as the house cocktail.

In Santo Antônio, a favorite place to watch the sunset over the Baía de Todos os Santos is the **Bar do Espanhol,** also known as **Bar Cruz do Pascoal** (Rua Joaquim Távora 2, tel. 71/3243-2285, 11 A.M.–close Mon.–Sat.), where any hunger pangs can be assuaged by an *arrumadinho* (bite-sized chunks of sundried beef mixed with black-eyed beans, toasted manioc flour, and diced tomatoes and peppers).

Mouraria is a captivating neighborhood that is completely off the tourist path though it's located just behind the Pelourinho. For years, Thursday has been the customary night to take a seat at one of Mouraria's sidewalk bars clustered around a cobblestoned square and dig into a ceramic pot steaming with *lambretas.* A local clam-like mollusk reputed to be an aphrodisiac (and a great hangover cure), the *lambretas* are steamed with cilantro, onions, salt, and pepper, then served piping hot. Traditionally, the city's "Old Guard" indulges at the square's largest bar, called **Koisa Nossa,** also known as **Os Internacionais** (Travessa Engenheiro Alione 3, Mouraria, tel. 71/3266-4496, 5 P.M.–midnight Tues.–Wed., 5 P.M.–1 A.M. Thurs.–Fri., noon–8 P.M. Sat.), where an estimated 900 dozen are served a week (Tuesdays are two-for-one). Recently, however, a younger crowd has caught *lambreta* fever, and newer bars (with their own two-for-one specials) have opened to keep up with the demand. Although the neighborhood itself is safe, you should come and go by taxi.

Similar to the Mouraria, **Dois de Julho** is another lively old residential neighborhood in the center of town where you can find some authentic watering holes. A perennial favorite is the **Líder** (Largo 2 de Julho 32, Centro, tel. 71/3321-8955, 7 A.M.–1 A.M. Mon.–Sat., 9 A.M.–6 P.M. Sun.), where conversation gets famously animated, often as a result of the running commentary of Zé Carlos, a devoted client whose exuberant complaints about the iciness of the beer and the slowness of the waiters keep things running. Close by, the recently opened **Mocambinho Bar** (Rua Carlos Gomes 135, Centro, 5 P.M. onward. Tues.–Sat.) is a friendly place that draws in a bohemian and alternative crowd and where the home-cooked bar food—sun-dried beef and pumpkin puree, for example—is a few steps above usual bar fare.

In Barra, aside from tourist traps along the ocean, the biggest concentration of nocturnal activity takes place near the residential streets of Rua Belo Horizonte, Rua Florianópolis, and Rua Recife—a neighborhood known as **Jardim Brasil.** Although quiet enough during the week, the place sizzles on weekends. This is when a rather yuppie-ish university-age crowd flocks to roost at the multiple choice of bars and eateries in the area (which close early, at 1:30 A.M.). For a quieter and less collegiate option, you might want to drop by the relatively new **Nego Loro** (Rua Marquês de Leão 183, tel. 71/3264-0250, 5 P.M.–close Mon.–Fri., 10 P.M.–close Sat.–Sun., cover R$5). Here, you can choose between a laid-back sidewalk bar, an indoor lounge with sofas and a snooker table, and a show space where live pop-rock is sometimes played.

Probably the most eclectic nightlife mecca in town takes place in the bohemian *bairro* of **Rio Vermelho.** There is always lots happening here, especially when the weekend rolls around. Unless it's pouring, the outdoor bars on **Largo de Santana** and **Largo de Mariquita** are always packed with long lineups of people waiting to assuage their *dendê* oil cravings with the famed *acarajés* and *abarás* of Dinha, Regina, and Cira (see the sidebar *Acarajé: Salvador's Favorite Snack Food).* As well, the bars and restaurants on **Rua da Paciência** and **Rua de Meio** are always pulsating with activity. Considered one of the best traditional *botecos* (bistro-style bars) in the *bairro,* the always popular, but not too trendy **Boteco da França** (Rua Borges dos Reis 24-A, Rio Vermelho, tel. 71/3335-1529, noon–last client Tues.–Sun.) was opened in 2002 by a former waiter who toiled for many years at two other classic Rio Vermelho haunts—the still thriving **Extudo** (Rua Lídio de Mesquita 4, tel. 71/3334-0671) and **Póstudo** (Rua João Gomes 87, tel. 71/3334-0484). He obviously learned his trade well since aside from attentive service, the Boteco offers an extensive drink menu, including *chope de vinho* (wine on draft), delicious nibbles (try the shredded sun-dried beef with pumpkin puree), and a mellow jazzy-bossa soundtrack that has made it a favorite with intellectuals, artists, and journalists. Meanwhile, if you find yourself in the situation where everything is closing down, the sun is coming up, and you're still raring to go, make a beeline for the **Mercado de Peixe** (Largo de Mariquita). Open 24 hours, this market's many lively bars are a classic "last call" option and they feature plenty of traditional grub—try a thick, chowder-like bean soup, *caldo de feijão,* or *caldo de sururu* (similar to a mussel)—to stave off a hangover.

Performing Arts
Salvador is famed for its rich cultural scene, particularly when it comes to music. Many of the city's most interesting musical happenings are included in the live music venues and bars already mentioned. However, for major musical, dance, and theatrical events—featuring big-name performers from both Brazil and abroad—check out the offerings at Salvador's main theater, **Teatro Castro Alves** (Campo Grande, tel. 71/3339-8000, www.tca.ba.gov.br). As far as dance is concerned, don't miss the nightly performances

LAND OF SAINTS AND *ORIXÁS*

Officially, Brazil is the planet's largest Catholic nation. But despite the abundance of magnificent churches and the number of people wearing religious medallions, when it comes to spiritual matters, the country is a lot more heterogeneous than it might seem. And nowhere is this religious mixture more pronounced than in Salvador. When the hundreds of thousands of African slaves who were shipped across the Atlantic arrived in Bahia, they came armed with the divinities of their homeland. After Portuguese slave masters banned any practices that strayed from Catholicism, many of the slaves slyly pretended to adopt Christian dogmas and rituals, but in reality, their adherence was often only superficial. Instead, they merged Catholic symbols with age-old beliefs preserved from their religious heritages. The result was the syncretic Afro-Brazilian religion known as **Candomblé.**

As Candomblé developed, the *orixás* – traditional African divinities representing various natural forces – became associated with Catholic saints: Oxalá, the Creator, was associated with Jesus Christ; Iemenjá, queen of the seas, was identified as Nossa Senhora da Conceição (Our Lady of Conception); the great warrior and blacksmith, Ogum, was linked to both Santo Antônio and São Jorge; and Iansã, goddess of fire and thunderbolts, was associated with Santa Bárbara. This clever strategy ensured Candomblé's survival for more than four centuries. Nonetheless, during this time, it was often brutally repressed, not only by clerical authorities, but by the ruling elite as well as government and police officials. In fact, until quite recently, there was a lingering prejudice against worshippers, who were known derogatorily as *macumbeiros* (practitioners of *macumba*, or witchcraft).

Candomblé is still very much alive in Salvador. Indeed, its influences and references are woven into the tapestry of daily life. *Terreiros* – the sacred *casas* (houses) and surrounding areas where rituals and celebrations take place – are all over the city, and in many cases the public can attend ceremonies and celebrations presided over by *mães* and *pais de santos* (venerated Candomblé priests and priestesses). Among the most famous and

given by the reputed **Balé Folclórico da Bahia,** held at the Pelourinho's Teatro Miguel Santana (Rua Gregório de Mattos 49, tel. 71/3322-1962, www.balefolcloricodabahia.com.br, 8 P.M. Mon.–Sat., R$20). Although not strictly "folkloric," the graceful and acrobatic choreographies are inspired by *capoeira,* Candomblé, and many other Afro-Bahian traditions, and the dancers themselves are breathtakingly fluid.

Festivals and Events

Brazilians are renowned for their festive disposition, but within Brazil itself, Bahians and, in particular, Soteropolitanos, easily surpass the rest. This is hardly surprising since Salvador has all the prerequisite ingredients for a good party: an idyllic climate, a powerful musical and cultural heritage, the mix of Catholic and Candomblé, and a population that loves an excuse to take to the streets and display their *ginga* (graceful moves). The following are a sampling of the most important and unique *festas.*

FESTA DOIS DE JULHO

While the rest of Brazil celebrates independence on September 7, for Bahians independence is all about July 2, when courageous local forces expelled Portuguese troops from Bahian soil. The festivities begin on the morning of July 2, with a procession from the Igreja of Lapinha through the historic center and the Pelourinho, then finishing up in the afternoon at Campo Grande. Politicians of all parties show up, as do traditional marching bands and baton twirlers, but the quasi-mystical Caboclo figures, effigies of mixed indigenous and European race that are carried through the streets in ornate chariots, are the main draw.

traditional *terreiros* are Gantois, Ilê Axê Opô Afonja, and Casa Branca.

Candomblé rituals vary depending on the *terreiro* and the *orixás*. Although the *casas* are usually very simple, decorations are often quite elaborate, as are the magnificent altars and traditional costumes worn in honor of the *orixás*. You can expect a lot of hypnotic African-inspired drumming and chanting, accompanied by graceful dancing that becomes quite frenzied as initiates "receive" *orixás* and go into a trance-like state in which they may stumble around and fall, literally possessed. Ceremonies often go on for hours at a time before a banquet of traditional food is offered – first to the *orixá*, and then to all those in attendance.

Although (well-behaved) tourists are welcome, Candomblé rituals are sacred events. If you do go, dress simply but formally – long pants and shoes for men, a long skirt and no cleavage for women – and inquire beforehand about using a camera. On no account should you ever join the dance. Most hotels, as well as the Bahiatursa tourism office in the Pelourinho, will be able to provide information about authentic Candomblé festivities. These take place on the specific days associated with various *orixás*. The majority of *terreiros*, including the three listed here, are located in poor suburbs that are best reached by taxi:

- **Gantois** (Rua Alto do Gantois 23, Federação, tel. 71/3331-9231): Founded in 1849. The most important *festa* is held in honor of Oxossi, on June 19.

- **Ilê Axé Opô Afonja** (Rua Direita de São Gonçalo do Retiro 557, Cabula, tel. 71/3384-5229): This traditional *terreiro* houses various *casas*, each devoted to a specific *orixá*. The most important *festas* take place between June and July as well as September and October.

- **Casa Branca** (Avenida Vasco da Gama 463, Vasco da Gama, tel. 71/3335-3100): Brazil's oldest surviving *terreiro* (dating from 1830) is recognized as National Cultural Heritage. The most significant *festas*, held in honor of Oxossi and Xango, take place in May and June.

FESTA DA SANTA BÁRBARA

One of the most moving celebrations is held on December 4 in honor of the patron saint of markets and firefighters, Santa Bárbara. Due to her association with the fiery and feisty Iansã, devotees, in large part women (including many transsexuals), dress in red and white, the symbolic colors of the *orixá*. There's a mass in front of the Igreja de Nossa Senhora do Rosário dos Pretos in the Largo do Pelourinho, then a procession passes through the historic center, stopping at the main fire station and the Mercado de Santa Bárbara, where free *cararu* (made from more than 5,000 pieces okra) is distributed. Throughout the day and into the night, the streets resemble a dancing sea of red.

FESTA SENHOR DOS NAVEGANTES

In Salvador, New Year's Day is synonymous with this beautiful celebration in which the effigy of Nosso Senhor dos Navegantes is transported around the Bay of All Saints by a fleet of decorated boats. Meanwhile, from Praia da Boa Viagem, religious music and lots of samba accompany landlubbers watching the procession.

LAVAGEM DO BONFIM

The most important religious and popular *festa* on the calendar takes place on the second Thursday in January. Dressed in traditional white garb and strings of beads, Bahianas lead an 8-kilometer (5-mile) procession of similarly white-attired and perfumed devotees and partyers from Comércio to the Igreja de Bonfim for the washing (*lavagem*) of the church steps. The *festa* honors Senhor do Bonfim (associated with the important *orixá* Oxalá, whose color is white). After the crowd is doused with

Bahiana in traditional clothing during the Festa da Santa Bárbara, one of Salvador's most authentic *festas populares*

blessed water and perfume, the party really gets going, lasting long into the night.

FESTA DE IEMENJÁ

As the sun rises on February 2, Candomblé worshippers and Bahians from all walks of life begin arriving at the Casa do Peso in Rio Vermelho, where they leave offerings of flowers and perfumes for Iemenjá, the beloved queen of the seas. At the end of the afternoon—when the presents are transported by a fleet of hundreds of decorated fishing boats and tossed into the sea—the streets of Rio Vermelho erupt in major partying.

◖ CARNAVAL

Billed as the biggest street party on the planet (it's listed in *Guinness Book of World Records* as such), Salvador's Carnaval lures an estimated two million local and international revelers to the streets of the Centro, Barra, and Ondina, for madness, mayhem, and plenty of dancing. The merrymaking gets underway timidly (although

in Salvador, "timid" is very relative) on Thursday night when keys to the city are handed over to the Rei Momo (Carnaval King). It then continues (to the yearly dismay of the Catholic Church) until noon on Ash Wednesday, when the leader of the Timbalada *bloco,* Carlinhos Brown, leads a procession of *trio elétricos* full of celebrities such as Daniela Mercury and Ivete Sangalo along Avenida Oceânica. Speaking of *trio elétricos,* these massive stages on wheels outfitted with mega speakers (as well as dressing rooms, lounges, bars, and restrooms) are what propel Carnaval's major musical artists and their guests around the 25 kilometers (16 miles) of closed-off thoroughfares. Each trio belongs to a *bloco,* a type of closed club, which is literally cordoned off from the masses on the sidewalks. For a fee (ranging from R$300 to R$1,500, payable at Central do Carnaval stands), you can join a *bloco* belonging to Gilberto Gil, Daniela Mercury, Ara Ketu, or Timbalada. Aside from a festive costume (known as an *abadá*), you get unlimited beverages, use of the toilet, and protection, courtesy of the *cordeiros,* who are very poorly paid to man the ropes separating *blocos* from the rest of the populace, known as the *pipoca* ("popcorn").

Although being part of a *bloco* allows you to be right in the center of things, to experience Carnaval in all its diversity, leave your valuables at home and take to the streets. This will give you a chance to wander around more freely and fully experience the variety of offerings, from African (such as Olodum, and Ilê Aiyê), indigenous, and even transvestite *blocos* and *afoxés* (such as the 50-year-old Filhos de Gandhy group, whose all-male members dress in long white robes and turbans) to hiphop and reggae groups and DJ-led raves (Britain's Fatboy Slim is a favorite presence).

Carnaval unfolds in three areas, known as "circuits." While the Dôdo Circuito in Barra and Ondina tends to attract the big names associated with *axé* music (Bahia's signature style of throbbing commercial pop), the Osmar Circuito between Campo Grande and Praça Castro Alves features the more traditional and less commercial *blocos.* The Circuito Batatinha in the Pelourinho, with its small samba groups and marching bands, is perfect for children and families.

Whether you indulge for one night or all six, as an unadulterated sensory hedonistic experience Salvador's Carnaval is beyond comparison. If you can't take the heat (not to mention blaring music and chaotic crowds), it's probably best to do like 50 percent of the population and get out of the city. But if you're in the mood to dance, sing, *pular* (jump up and down), and *paquerar* (flirt), from dusk till dawn and back again, you'll be absolutely thrilled.

Note: Considering the possible mayhem when you throw a couple of million drunken people together in 35-degree heat, Carnaval is more or less peaceful thanks to heavy police presence. That said, it's best to use caution. For certain, don't party alone. Pickpockets abound, so be smart and carry photocopied documents and just enough money for snacks, beers, and a cab ride.

For more information about joining a *bloco,* call 71/3535-3000 or log on to www.central-docarnaval.com.br. For information about Carnaval in general, check out www.portal-docarnaval.ba.gov.br.

SHOPPING

Salvador isn't a big shopping mecca. Aside from the main markets, which sell Bahian trinkets and souvenirs, jewelry, and handicrafts **(Mercado Modelo)** as well as authentic Candomblé artifacts and foodstuff **(Feira de São Joaquim),** the most interesting purchases to be made are concentrated in the Pelourinho and Barra. Aside from many tourist traps, the Pelô has an assortment of interesting boutiques and galleries.

Goya Lopes (Rua Gregório de Mattos 20, Pelourinho, tel. 71/3321-9428, www.goyalopes.com.br, 10 A.M.–8 P.M. Mon.–Sat.) is the eponymous boutique of one of Salvador's most interesting clothing and housewares designers. After studying the history of African textiles, Lopes began making clothes for local musicians. Over time, her designs—sold under

the name Didara, which means "good" in Yoruba—have attracted an international following who seek out her bold and colorful, yet refined clothing and housewares inspired by African design motifs.

Another home-grown talent who has made a mark on the national fashion scene is **Márcia Ganem** (Rua das Laranjeiras 10, tel. 71/3322-2423, www.marciaganem.com.br, 10 A.M.–8 P.M. Mon.–Fri., 10 A.M.–6 P.M. Sat.), whose contemporary designs for women are mostly made of polyamide fibers recycled from rubber tires—a surprisingly delicate material that has become her trademark. Equally original is her line of jewelry.

For more casual clothes, check out the terrific tees and other casual clothing at **Loja Axé** (Rua das Laranjeiras 9, tel. 71/3321-7869, www.projetoaxe.org.br), operated by Projeto Axé, the NGO that provides Salvador's street kids with creative outlets to help them overcome the difficulties they face. Although CD stores have pretty much been wiped off the face of the city, **Cana Brava Records** (Rua João de Deus 22, tel. 71/3321-0536, www.canabrava.org, 9 A.M.–close Mon.–Sat.), run by a knowledgeable American expat, is a great place to listen to and purchase Brazilian music. Among its offerings, Cana Brava specializes in traditional music of the Bahian Reconcâvo region.

If you're looking for typical art, housewares, and handicrafts made by artists from all over the state of Bahia, a great source is the **Instituto de Artesanato Visconde de Mauá** (27 Rua Gregório de Mattos, tel. 71/3116-6712, www.maua.ba.gov.br, 9 A.M.–6 P.M. Mon.–Fri., 10 A.M.–1 P.M. Sat.). Although pricy, the quality of the ceramics, woodwork, weaving, and other works is high. There is a second boutique at Porto da Barra (tel. 71/3116-6190, 9 A.M.–6 P.M. Mon.–Sat.), overlooking the sea. Also in Barra is Salvador's largest centrally located shopping mall. Just off the Praia do Farol, **Shopping Barra** (Av. Centenario 2992, Barra, tel. 71/3339-8222, www.shoppingbarra.com, 10 A.M.–10 P.M. Mon.–Sat., 3–9 P.M. Sun.) offers three gloriously air-conditioned levels

BAHIA

featuring Brazilian designer boutiques, a few cafés, food courts, and bookstores, a handicraft market, and a couple of cinemas.

SPORTS AND RECREATION

Unsurprisingly, the vast majority of Salvador's leisure activities revolve around the sand and sea.

Parks

Salvador is not a very green city. The only true area resembling a park is the **Dique de Tororó,** an urban lagoon out of whose calm waters rise gigantic statues of *orixás*. Surrounding the Dique is a walking/jogging path shaded by gigantic trees (and traffic). Kiosks sell *água de coco,* and it's possible to rent a pedalboat and glide around the water. The Dique's shores are flanked by Avenida Presidente Silva e Costa and Avenida Vasco da Gama, and the lagoon itself is on the edge of the *bairros* of Nazaré and Tororó (behind the Lapa bus station).

Boating Excursions

Boats trips around the Bay of All Saints leave from Porto da Barra and from the ferry dock in front of the Mercado Modelo. The full-day excursions stop at the larger islands, including Ilha dos Frades, Itaparica, and Ilha de Maré. Specific information is available at Salvador's largest hotels and at Bahiatursa, or contact a travel operator such as **LR Turismo** (Rua Marquês de Leão 172, Barra, tel. 71/3264-0999), which also runs city tours. **Passeios de Veleiros** (tel. 71/8156-5254) offers short sailboat trips around the bay and even as far as Morro de São Paulo.

Diving

There are about a dozen sunken ships in the Bay of All Saints. If you have the urge to search for buried treasure, the bay's placid waters are very inviting. **Dive Bahia** (Porta da Barra 3809, tel. 71/3264-3820, www.divebahia.com.br) offers diving courses and rents out equipment, as does **Bahia Scuba** (Av. do Contorno 1010, Bahia Marina, tel. 71/3321-0156, www.bahiascuba.com.br).

ACCOMMODATIONS

Where you decide to stay in Salvador depends on your priorities and personal taste. If you want to soak up lots of colonial atmosphere, the Pelourinho and neighboring *bairro* of Santo Antônio offer all sorts of options, from backpacker-filled hostels to sophisticated boutique hotels housed in restored 17th- and 18th-century edifices. Beach bunnies will prefer to be in Barra (still very central) or at the more traditional mega hotel chains in Ondina and Rio Vermelho. Though other options exist farther along Salvador's coast, their distance from the center and lack of neighborhood attractions make them ultimately impractical and not so interesting.

Pelourinho and Santo Antônio

Constantly abuzz, the Pelourinho is where all the action is. As a consequence, it's always humming (or drumming) with activity and rather noisy. In terms of location, however, it's ideal—with lots of transportation options to the Cidade Baixa, Barra, and the other beaches. Off the beaten path—and only reachable by taxi or on foot (factor in a steep climb up the Ladeira do Carmo)—are the many *pousadas* in Santo Antônio, a much more tranquil, residential neighborhood where many foreigners have purchased and stylishly converted 17th- and 18th-century mansions into intimate lodgings.

R$50-100

A cheery and well-run hostel, **Laranjeiras Hostel** (Rua Inácio Accioli 13, tel. 71/3321-1366, www.laranjeirashostel.com.br, R$90–110 d) is situated right in the middle of the Pelô. Housed in a pumpkin-colored colonial mansion (and with its own café/crêperie), this mecca for international backpackers functions as the unofficial headquarters for the young and the sleepless (it's not exactly quiet). Its 17 rooms include singles, doubles, triples, and very affordable male and female dorms (R$20–30 pp), making it the cheapest place to stay in the Pelô. Facilities include a kitchen, washing machines and dryers, and a TV room. Internet access is available. The helpful staff

CAPOEIRA

This uniquely Brazilian activity – a hypnotically graceful but vigorous mix of dance and martial art – has become a popular sport throughout Brazil. However, it is most strongly linked to Bahia, where it originated. In fact, as you wander through the city, it's not at all uncommon to see two men (or women) swinging, kicking, and sparring with each other, within a *roda* (circle) of other *capoeiristas*, who sing and clap to the accompaniment of drums, tambourines, and the twang of a *berimbau* – a traditional one-string instrument.

The *berimbau* is essentially a long piece of wood with a metal wire running along it, whose hypnotic sound is caused by the wire's reverberations. African slaves brought the *berimbau* – and *capoeira* – to Bahia. On plantations, fights sometimes broke out between slaves from different tribes. To avoid severe punishment from plantation owners, the slaves added music and song to the fights and refined the movements so that, when masters suddenly appeared, the air kicks and lunges resembled a dance – which became *capoeira*.

Capoeiristas are so agile they never touch their opponents. Aside from a variety of kicks and lunges, movements include crouches, rolls, spins, and cartwheels. Only a "player's" feet, hands, and head can ever touch the ground. The goal is to develop and demonstrate strength, flexibility, and artistry. Though it's mostly for the benefit of tourists, regular displays of *capoeira* are held at the Mercado Modelo and the Terreiro de Jesus. If it's an authentic experience you're after, head to one of the city's Academias de Capoeira, traditional schools where you can observe classes free of charge. One of the oldest and most famous schools, the Associação de Capoeira Mestre Bimba (in the Pelourinho), offers demonstrations every Tuesday, Friday, and Saturday at 7 P.M. Classes are also available for tourists. At the beginning of 2007, the Forte de Santo Antônio Além do Carmo was transformed into the Centro Esportivo de Capoeira Angola. Here, *capoeira* displays can be seen on Tuesday, Thursday, and Saturday at 7:30 P.M. and on Sunday at 5 P.M. Here are some of the most well-known *capoeira* schools:

- **Associação Brasileira de Capoeira Angola** (Rua Gregório de Matos 38, Pelourinho, tel. 71/9905-3024)

- **Associação de Capoeira Mestre Bimba** (Rua das Laranjeiras 1, Pelourinho, tel. 71/3322-0639, www.capoeiramestrebimba. com.br)

- **Capoeira Angola Irmãos Gêmeos Curió** (Rua Gregório de Matos 9, 2nd Fl., Pelourinho, tel. 71/3321-0396)

- **Escola de Capoeira Mestre Lua Rasta** (Rua Inácio Accioli, Pelourinho, tel. 71/3321-6334)

- **Grupo de Capoeira de Angola Pelourinho** (Forte Santo Antônio Além do Carmo, Largo Santo Antônio Além do Carmo, Santo Antônio, tel. 71/3321-7587)

© TONY GALVEZ

capoeirista

speak English. An added bonus is that being a guest there gets you discounts on everything from *capoeira* and Portuguese lessons to diving excursions in the Bay of All Saints.

Not nearly as charming as its fancier Santo Antônio neighbors, the pretty basic **Pousada Hilmar** (Rua Direita de Santo Antônio 136, tel. 71/3243-4959, www.pousadahilmar.com.br, R$50–65 d) has all the advantages of location (in a colonial mansion overlooking the sea), tranquility, and decidedly more affordable prices.

R$100-200

Though it has one of the most strikingly grandiose exteriors on Rua Direita de Santo Antônio **Pousada Colonial** (Rua Direita de Santo Antônio 368, tel. 71/3243-3329, www.colonialpousada.com, R$90–150 d) is less expensive than its neighbors and more modern in its decor. It is bright, spacious, and impressively vertical, reminding one of an Escher engraving with its many flights of immaculately polished stairs. Large, spotless rooms are available in a variety of prices and sizes. Really marvelous is the top floor's superior suite with its own private balcony and splendid views.

R$200-300

Until recently, accommodations in the Pelourinho itself tended to be geared towards the budget and backpacking crowd, who were crammed into rooms that had been haphazardly constructed out of the colonial buildings' vast—and often rotting—main salons. In the last couple of years, however, this has begun to change. A recent noteworthy example is the delightfully intimate French-owned **Casa do Amarelindo** (Rua das Portas do Carmo 6, tel. 71/3266-8550, www.casadoamarelindo.com, R$200 d). With its great location (near the Terreiro de Jesus), this hotel offers 10 elegant and spacious rooms in a 19th-century mansion. And you won't have to worry about being in the midst of the Pelô's noisy hub since the windows and doors are insulated from the bustle outside (even the ceiling fans

and mini fridges are equipped with silencers). The swimming pool and rooftop lounge, as well as most rooms, boast wonderful views of the surrounding baroque architecture and the Bay of All Saints. As an added feature, a small gym offers morning *capoeira* classes. Meanwhile, with an in-house restaurant featuring innovative dishes that fuse tropical produce with French flair—salmon in *graviola* (a local fruit) and passion fruit sauce and filet mignon with cashew butter—you'll be hard-pressed to eat elsewhere.

On Rua Direita de Santo Antônio, you will find a handful of very attractive, mostly foreign-owned *pousadas* located in colonial mansions. Most of them have been lovingly restored and mix eclectic furnishings with modern conveniences such as cable TV, air-conditioning, and broadband Internet service. Many have verandas, beautiful views of the Baía de Todos Os Santos or the Pelourinho's colonial architecture, and charming bars and lounges that make them idyllic places to stop for a drink, even if you decide not to check in. Owners and staff are invariably multilingual. Be sure to go to them for information about excursions within the city and the surrounding region.

Pousada do Pilar (Rua Direita de Santo Antônio 24, tel. 71/3241-2033, www.pousadadopilar.com, R$230–260 d) is a particularly pleasant option. The 12 renovated rooms are handsomely furnished, immense, and flooded with natural light. Only 7 of them have sea views, but everyone can partake of the lavish breakfast served on the panoramic terrace overlooking the bay.

Opened in 2003 by an English artist with a penchant for red fish (all the wooden furnishings are decorated with bright scarlet fish, painted in *naïf* style, swimming in a sea blue background) **Pousada Colonial** (Rua Direita de Santo Antônio 442, tel. 71/3243-8473, www.hotelredfish.com, R$240 d) inhabits a vast, beautifully renovated colonial building beside the 18th-century Igreja Nossa Senhora de Boqueirão. Both the exterior and interior have been painted in soothing watery shades of green, and rooms—both standard and the luxury suites—are clean, cool, and quite sizable (the largest ones can easily sleep six). Guests can surf the Internet whenever they want and, for an art fix, can feel free to check out whatever's on the walls of the art gallery.

Offering plenty of warmth and charm, the ◖ **Pousada das Flores** (Ladeira do Boqueirão 1, tel. 71/3243-8473, www.pflores.com.br/, R$200–250 d) features nine sprawling rooms that are heavy on atmosphere. Living up to its name, *flores* (flowers) are everywhere: from live bouquets in vases to printed ones on bedspreads and curtains. Efforts to preserve the original 18th-century mansion mean no air-conditioning or TV, and the bathrooms are separated only by floral-themed screens. But minor "discomforts" aside, the rustic-chic furnishings (including modified four poster beds), soft lighting, and the intensely homey aura that engulfs the entire *pousada* will make you seriously consider moving in. Suites 7, 8, and 9 offer lovely private verandas.

OVER R$300

Of all the hotels and *pousadas* in Santo Antônio—and in Salvador—the one that will (*por favor,* excuse the cliché) truly take your breath away is the ◖ **Hotel Aram Yami** (Rua Direita de Santo Antônio 132, tel. 71/3249-4912, www.hotelaramyami.com, R$400–500 d). Bahia meets Bali meets Barcelona in this boutique hotel, whose composite name—which is Tupi for "sun and night"—alludes to the trouble you'll have *not* spending 24 hours a day on the premises. The inspiration of a Brazilian-Spanish couple (both architects) who purchased this colonial mansion as a second home and then decided it was too large to keep to themselves, this seductive hotel offers five roomy apartments. Each suite is a private oasis in which the restored colonial features fuse harmoniously with contemporary furnishings. The decor is equally ingenious: traditional Bahian artifacts mingle with Chinese silk pillows and jewel-hued Japanese lanterns. Two swimming pools (one of them reserved for the lucky guests of the

two-bedroom master suite), a mesmerizingly atmospheric bar with a terrace, and lots of verandas with sea views are further conducive to the utter sense of well-being you'll experience upon checking in. Owner Lola offers discounts depending on the season and number of days you plan to stay.

Although the elegant **Hotel Villa Bahia** (Largo de Cruzeiro São Francisco 16/18, tel. 71/3322-4271, www.lavillabahia.com/, R$340 d) opened in late 2006, the French-owned hotel is all about history. Housed in two 17th-century colonial mansions that look out onto the Largo de Cruzeiro São Francisco, the hotel pays heavy homage to both Brazil's and Portugal's past. Colonial Portuguese antiques abound, meaning lots of baroque details, jacaranda, and Portuguese ceramic tiles. The decor of each of the 17 luxurious rooms is inspired by former colonies ranging from Macau to Madagascar. Inner courtyards and a pool offer respite from the hustle and bustle outside in the Pelô. And be sure to visit the restaurant, where the chef takes fresh local produce and does marvelously French things to it.

When Salvador's first five-star hotel, the ◖ **Convento do Carmo** (Rua do Carmo 1, tel. 71/3327-8400, www.pestana.com, R$820 d) finally opened its enormous wooden doors at the end of 2005, it revolutionized tourism in a city whose idea of luxury accommodations were the sterile and mammoth 300-room beachfront chains located in the middle-class neighborhoods of Ondina and Rio Vermelho. Unsurprisingly, these exude as much charm as modern airport terminals. Owned by Pousadas de Portugal, a hotel group specializing in marrying luxury with history, this magnificent hotel is located in a sprawling 16th-century convent that, aside from some discreet and very handsome trappings of luxury, is remarkably faithful to its religious roots. For solitary confinement (and utter tranquility), cells that once housed Carmelite nuns have been converted into 80 tastefully (if rather neutrally) outfitted rooms with WiFi, LCD TVs, and Egyptian cotton sheets. Arcaded cloisters shelter a bar and restaurant that face onto courtyards anointed with a profusion of tropical plants and a swimming pool. Other highlights include a library, spa, fitness center, home theater, and—of course—a chapel.

Centro

Centro may be a convenient location for visitors but it can be quite dodgy at night (it is, however, lively enough during the day). Inexpensive hotels abound, however, and if you exercise caution and rely on taxis to take you to and from your door, you'll be fine. More tranquil and secure, the Corredor da Vitória, which spans from Campo Grande to Ladeira da Barra, also has several good choices.

R$50-100

Although not as dirt cheap as some of the other centrally located options, in terms of value and comfort, the **Hotel Colonial Chile** (Rua Chile 7, tel. 71/3321-0245, www.chilehotel.com.br, R$70–120 d) is hard to beat. After undergoing a massive renovation, it reopened its doors in early 2006—prior to that, it had been in operation for over a century. The 35 apartments—some of which are lofts and four of which boast terrific sea views—are clean and comfortable, if a little on the starkly minimalist side. More charming are the common dining rooms and living rooms.

R$100-200

From the outside, it looks like just another one of the impersonal high-rise buildings that line the chic and leafy residential neighborhood of Vitória. However, the **Hotel Sol Victoria Marina** (Av. Sete de Setembro, 2068 Corredor da Vitória, tel. 71/3336-7736, www.solbahia.com.br, R$160 d) has some aces up its sleeve. Aside from its terrific location—halfway between Barra beach and the Pelourinho—it is equipped with a refreshing pool and its own private cable car, which whisks you down a jungle-carpeted cliff to an ocean pier outfitted with a restaurant/bar and sundeck. Half of the 215 modern and surprisingly affordable rooms feature terrific views of the Bay of All Saints, and the alfresco breakfast buffet offers an impetus to get out of bed early.

Barra

Barra has tons of accommodations, although you won't find much that's as charming, atmospheric and/or luxurious as the new *pousadas* that have cropped up in the Pelourinho, and especially Santo Antônio. While there are lots of good budget options, some, particularly those facing Porto da Barra, at night can be fairly louche. The more upscale options consist of modern, soulless chain hotels. Nevertheless, a few enterprising souls have begun converting a few of the neighborhood's surviving villas in the tranquil residential streets behind the beach into appealing, if fairly basic, *pousadas.*

R$50-100

If you're up for a hostel experience, the friendly, **Albergue do Porto** (Rua Barão de Sergy 197, tel. 71/3264-6600, www.alberguedoporto.com.br, R$35 d) is a great deal. Located in a lemon-colored villa only a block from Porto da Barra beach, the spartan rooms (named after Brazilian songstresses) are spic and span and the common rooms—including a living room with cable TV, Internet, a shared kitchen, laundry facilities—give off a suitably international hippie vibe with some Bahian accents.

Rua Afonso Celso is one of Barra's pretty tree-lined residential streets that offers tranquility and great beach access. It also has dozens of still-surviving villas, a handful of which have been converted into *pousadas.* Several blocks up from the beach, **Âmbar Pousada** (Rua Afonso Celso 485, tel. 71/3264-6956, www.ambarpousada.com.br, R$90 d, dormitory rooms R$35 pp) is a mixture of *pousada* and hostel that prides itself on its familial atmosphere. Staff are gracious and helpful, and the homey common rooms and verandas are conducive hammock-swinging, journal-writing, web surfing, and checking out the next day's itinerary (or lack thereof) in your guidebook. The rooms (located off the courtyard) are well maintained and feature portable boom boxes for sampling the eclectic CD collection.

Be sure to visit the bar, where you can get a mean *caipirinha*.

R$100-200

On Rua Afonso Celso—and only a block from the beach—is the low-key, attractive, and friendly **Pousada Estrela do Mar** (Rua Afonso Celso 119, tel. 71/3264-4882, www.estreladomarsalvador.com, R$120–140 d). The Scottish owners have transformed two houses into 12 apartments (the upstairs ones are nicer), decorated in maritime-inspired shades of blue and white. Also located in a pretty refurbished villa is the appropriately named (it's painted sky-blue) and very appealing **Pousada Azul** (Rua Doutora Praguer Froes 102, tel. 71/3264-9798, www.pousadaazul.com.br, R$120 d). Three of the eight rooms are lofts with double beds. Internet access and laundry service are available. **☾ Pousada Noa Noa** (Avenida Sete de Setembro 4295, tel. 71/3264-1148, www.pousadanoanoa.com, R$110–130 d) has a privileged beachfront location, in a hibiscus-colored mansion next to Barra's lighthouse. Its 12 rooms—named after 12 European (mostly French) artists—are simple, but very nicely finished and accessorized. If you can't get one with ocean views, toast your "bad" luck by adjourning to the terrace bar, which, libations aside, is an idyllic spot to watch the sunset. Be forewarned that during Carnaval and New Year's, the place will be one big *festa*. The **Hotel Sol Barra** (Avenida Sete de Setembro 3577, tel. 71/3418-7000, www.solbarra.com.br, R$190 d), formerly the Hotel Praiamar, is one of those big conventional hotels with 189 rooms (it's part of the local Sol Express hotel chain). If it lacks personality, it has a few other things going for it, such as a great location facing Porto da Barra beach, excellent security, and modern conveniences (rooms feature cable TV, mini-bars, and wireless Internet). It also has a pool, solarium, and a penchant for odd shades of green as a decorative accent.

Rio Vermelho

Traditionally, Salvador's top-of-the-line, big chain beach hotels were concentrated in the middle-class neighborhoods of Ondina and Rio Vermelho. Rio Vermelho, in particular, is picturesque and full of transportation options, although not as central as Barra. Moreover, the beaches are not good for swimming.

R$100-200

Located in a charming pale pink colonial house—and a more recently built annex—overlooking the sea, the **Hotel Catharina Paraguaçu** (Rua João Gomes 128, Rio Vermelho, tel. 71/3334-0089, www.hotelcatharinaparaguacu.com.br, R$148 d), is a favorite of both Brazilian and foreign travelers (and travel guide writers) who appreciate the homey, intimate atmosphere—unique along Salvador's *orla*. The 32 rooms aren't spacious or stylish, but they are cozy. More alluring are the dining, living room, and reception areas, decorated with local ceramics, lacework, and antiques as well as a whimsical collection of glazed ceramic tiles *azulejos*. Also lovely are the surrounding gardens. The location is perfect for those tempted to indulge in Rio Vermelho's bohemian nightlife.

OVER R$300

If you want to go whole hog and live it up in a classic luxury hotel with all the amenities, then check into the **Hotel Pestana Bahia** (Rua Fonte de Boi 216, Rio Vermelho, tel. 71/2183-8000, www.pestana.com, R$295–310 d), which emerged from a major facelift in 2003 looking much more refreshed and elegant. Its dramatic perch on a hillside allows for stunning views of the Atlantic, which can be viewed from the tastefully furnished rooms as well as two swimming pools. Toss in a sauna, Jacuzzi, fitness room, massage center, 24-room service, cable TV, wireless broadband, babysitting, and a couple of plush restaurants and bars, and you're sitting very pretty.

FOOD

A potent mixture of African and Portuguese influences, along with some indigenous flavors and an emphasis on fish and seafood, Bahian cuisine is justly celebrated, both around Brazil

BAHIA

BAHIAN COOKING

Taking advantage of the ocean's bounty and Africa's rich culinary legacy, Bahian cuisine is a treat for all the senses – though first and foremost are the taste buds. Just consider the key ingredients: coconut milk, *dendê* (palm oil), shrimp (both dried and fresh), cilantro, ginger, spicy malagueta peppers, and lime juice. Among the most emblematic and popular Bahian dishes you're likely to encounter are:

· **bobó de camarão** – a rich stew that combines fresh shrimp and pureed manioc

· **caruru** – diced okra cooked in *dendê*

· **cocada** – a sweet dessert made of coconut and caramelized sugar

· **moqueca** – fish and/or seafood cooked in a mixture of coconut milk, *dendê*, peppers, tomatoes, lime, and cilantro (if you want to avoid the *dendê*, ask for an **ensopada**)

· **vatapá** – a puree of peanuts, cashews, bread, and onions to which *dendê* lends a rich hue

· **xinxim de galinha** – chicken stewed in *dendê*, dried shrimp, and crushed peanuts and cashews

dendê (palm oil), a main ingredient in Bahian cooking

© MICHAEL SOMMERS

and throughout the world, due to its colorful presentations and sophisticated flavors. Palm oil, coconut milk, peppers, cilantro, lime, dried shrimp, and cashews create dishes that are both suave and piquant, and often as fragrant as they are delicious.

Soteropolitanos are famous nibblers. Many meals are enjoyed communally around a bar table (many bars double as restaurants) or on the beach, and delicacies such as *acarajé* and *cocada* are savored in the street. The largest

concentrations of eateries tend to be in tourist areas such as the Pelourinho and Barra, where you'll find lots of good options (both touristy and authentic).

Pelourinho and Santo Antônio

There is no shortage of restaurants in the Pelourinho. For a cheap lunch or dinner with lots of variety, a popular standby for Soteropolitanos who work in the neighborhood as well as tourists is **Panorâmico** (Rua da Laranjeiras 18, Pelourinho, tel. 71/3322-2013, 11 A.M.–4 P.M. and 5–11 P.M. Mon.–Sat., R$12). This pay-by-weight *quilo* restaurant located on the second floor of a colonial house is attractively decorated with woodcuts and offers great views of the Pelô's church domes and red-tiled rooftops. The main draw, of course, is the buffet, which is always fresh and includes plenty of choices for vegetarians, as well as serving up lots of local fare. When leaving, don't forget to cleanse your palate with a shot of complimentary house tea made from an infusion of tropical fruits. More touristy, but a terrific option if you want to sample the diversity of Bahian cuisine, is the **Restaurante do SENAC** (Largo do Pelourinho 13, Pelourinho, tel. 71/3324-4552, 11:30 A.M.–3:30 P.M. and 6:30–10 P.M. Mon.–Sat., R$25), located in a spacious colonial mansion. It's operated by the SENAC restaurant school, so the (somewhat overly formal) service is extremely attentive and the food—an all you-can-eat buffet featuring over 40 regional dishes—is carefully prepared and presented by professors and students.

A little more expensive and a lot more romantic is the appropriately named ◖ **Jardim das Delícias** (Rua João de Deus 12, Pelourinho, tel. 71/3321-1449, noon–1 A.M. daily, R$30–50), housed in a private, leafy courtyard and accessorized by antiques spilling out from the adjacent antiques store. The varied menu has some standard international fare, but the fortes are the typical Bahian *moquecas* (try the rare and exotic version made with *maturi* or green cashew nuts), *mariscadas* (seafood stew), and *bobó de camarão*. There are also dishes from the northeastern interior, such as *carne-de-sol* (sun-dried beef) and *maniçoba,* a stew of beef, cashews, and manioc leaves. Polish off your meal with delicious *cocada de coco verde,* made of fresh slivers of coconut. In the evening, live music—usually bossa nova, *chorinho,* and MPB—ups the romance factor considerably.

Maria Mata Mouro (Rua Inácio Acciole 8, Pelourinho, tel. 71/3321-3929, 11 A.M.–1 A.M. daily, R$50–60) is another much acclaimed restaurant. A favorite with Salvador's elite and visiting VIPs, Mata Mouro's imaginative menu

offers innovative twists on regional and international dishes—all featuring fresh, local ingredients. Take note: The best tables are those in the enchanting inner courtyard. And the wine cellar is noteworthy as well.

An Italian bent characterizes the menu at **Ristorante Al Carmo** (Rua do Carmo 66, Santo Antônio, tel. 71/3242-0283, www.al-carmo.com, 5 P.M.–midnight Mon., 11 A.M.–midnight Thurs.–Fri., 11 A.M.–1 A.M. Fri.–Sat., R$20–30) whose tables are spread amidst a high-ceilinged 18th-century mansion. The pasta and meat dishes are flavorful, and the surroundings warm and romantic. The top-floor terrace features a stupendous view of the Bay of All Saints. At night, soft lighting harmonizes nicely with the mellow strains of live bossa nova and MPB.

Facing onto the Igreja e Convento de São Francisco, French-owned **Le Glacier Laporte** (Largo do Cruzeiro 21, Pelourinho, tel. 71/3266-3649, leglacierlaporte.com, 9 A.M.–8 P.M. daily) serves wonderful sorbet made from local ingredients but that packs a Parisian wallop of distilled flavor.

Cidade Baixa

Almost immediately upon opening in 2005, ◖ **Amado** (Av. do Contorno 660, Comércio, tel. 71/3322-0283, from 11:30 A.M. daily for lunch, from 6 P.M. Mon.–Sat. for dinner, www.amadobahia.com.br, R$50–60) was crowned as Salvador's undisputed king of contemporary cuisine. Self-taught Brazilian wonder-chef Edinho Engel holds court in a spacious modernist warehouse suspended above the Bay of All Saints where the ocean fuses perfectly with the restaurant's wood, glass, and jungle of potted plants. Local ingredients—with an emphasis on seafood and fish—receive daring and sophisticated treatment and the impressive wine cellar features more than 3,000 bottles. If you want to splurge in style, this is the place.

If you visit the Igreja de Bonfim, take advantage of its proximity to the **Recanto da Lua Cheia** (Rua Rio Negro 66, Mont Serrat, tel. 71/3315-1275, 11 A.M.–11 P.M. Wed.–Sat., 11 A.M.–5 P.M. Sun., R$20–30). The ocean

ACARAJÉ: SALVADOR'S FAVORITE SNACK FOOD

When you first begin wandering around Salvador, one of the most distinctive fragrances you'll encounter is the scent of *acarajés* sizzling in cauldrons of amber-colored *dendê* (palm oil). If you've never had the pleasure of biting into one of these round fritters made of pounded black-eyed beans – ideally fluffy on the inside and crunchy on the outside – you certainly will in Salvador. (Go easy though, since *dendê* can play tricks on unaccustomed stomachs.) *Acarajés*, along with *abarás* (in which the bean paste is boiled and then molded with banana leaves), are the city's favorite snack food. From the afternoon into the evening, Bahianas clothed in traditional white turbans and petticoats, and colored beads associated with Candomblé *orixás*, cook and serve up this traditional treat on street corners, squares, and beaches throughout the city. Once the *acarajé* is cut in half, you have the option of several traditional fillings: dried shrimp, *vatapá* (a puree of bread, shrimp, ginger, coconut milk, and cashews), *caruru* (a puree of diced okra), *salada* (usually a mixture of chopped tomatoes and cilantro), and spicy *pimenta*.

Discerning Soteropolitanos all have their own favorite Bahianas, but among the best in the city are **Acarajé da Keka** in Barra (Rua Belo Horizonte, 4-11 P.M. Tues.-Sun.) and **Point do Acarajé,** off Campo Grande (Rua Marechal Floriano 1, tel. 71/3491-1308, 4-11 P.M. Mon.-Sat.). However, the three reigning *acarajé* queens are Dinha, Cira, and Regina – all of whom made tidy fortunes and small empires. Interestingly, the headquarters of all three are in Rio Vermelho: **Dinha** (noon-midnight daily) and **Regina** (3:30-10 P.M. Mon.-Fri., 10 A.M.-10 P.M. Sat.) are across from each other at the lovely square of Largo de Santana, while **Cira** (10 A.M.-11 P.M. daily) is at nearby Largo da Mariquita, although die-hard fans claim the offerings at her original Itapuã location on Rua Aristides Milton (10 A.M.-11 P.M. daily) are more delicious. Unsurprisingly, when McDonald's foolishly attempted to open a franchise in Rio Vermelho during the 1990s, it lasted less than a year. Moreover, recent attempts by evangelical women to compete with Bahianas by making *"bolinhos de Jesus"* (Jesus balls) – essentially an *acarajé* rip-off, but without its supposedly "heathen" references – have been met with disdain and outrage. In fact, in recognition of its cultural importance, in 2004, the *acarajé* received status as nonmaterial cultural patrimony from IPHAN (the Institute for National Artistic and Historical Heritage).

views are just as mesmerizing (if not more so), but the food, ambiance, and clientele are completely different at this typically Soteropolitano restaurant and bar whose tables are shaded by a canopy of tropical fruit trees. The owner began her culinary career by serving *moquecas* out of her garage. As word caught on in the neighborhood, her enterprise grew. Now locals flock to catch the sunset or to while away a Sunday afternoon. At night, there's often live music. The house specialty is the *moqueca de peguari,* made with shellfish from the island of Itaparica, famed for its aphrodisiac qualities. If you come around happy hour, order a fruit *roska* and a *pastel de siri,* a deep-fried pastry stuffed with fresh crab meat. Nearby **Sorveteria da Ribeira** (Praça General Osório 87, Ribeira, tel. 71/3316-5451) is an ice cream parlor in the pretty seaside neighborhood of Ribeira that has been around since 1931. Local tour buses make the trip out here just so out-of-towners can sample a scoop or two of the 50 homemade flavors, including toasted coconut, guava and cream, tapioca, and tamarind.

Centro

There are lots of cheap eats in the bustling Centro, although not so many good ones. And at night, the place all but shuts down. However, several long-standing Soteropolitano institutions—which have been offering up delicious *comida caseira* (home-cooking) for decades—are definitely worth your while if you're looking to lunch like the locals. Close to the

Pelourinho and just off the Praça Castro Alves, **Mini Cacique** (Rua Ruy Barbosa 29, Centro, tel. 71/3243-2419, 11 A.M.–4 P.M. Mon.–Fri., R$15–30) is a favorite lunch destination for business people, particularly those with a liberal bent, which means it can get animated and even a little noisy. The elderly waitresses in pumpkin-colored uniforms are atypically brisk and efficient, so you won't have to wait long to dig into the well-seasoned dishes. The daily specials are the cheapest and often the most succulent. Offerings may include *ensopado de carneiro* (braised lamb stew) or the classic *xinxim de galinha* (braised chicken cooked in palm oil). The owner is of Spanish origin, meaning that classic Bahian cooking shares menu space with some Galician fare such as *tortillas* and *arroz ao polvo* (grilled octopus with rice).

Facing a flower market in the lively neighborhood of Dois de Julho, the small and somewhat claustrophobic **Porto do Moreira** (Largo do Mocambinho 488, Carlos Gomes, Centro, tel. 71/3322-4112, 11 A.M.–4 P.M. Mon.–Sat., 11 A.M.–3 P.M. Sun., R$20–30) is a throwback to Bahia of yesteryear with its tiled walls and oversized whirring fans. If it seems as if the place was ripped from the pages of a Jorge Amado novel, know that Bahia's favorite author was an assiduous fan of the 70-year-old family restaurant's delicious *bacalhaus* (Portuguese salted cod, prepared in various manners) and *moquecas* (including the unusual *moqueca de carne,* made of beef meat seasoned with dried shrimp and palm oil). To ensure a table, arrive a little on the early or late side.

For delicious Bahian food in unpretentious surroundings, grab a bus from Campo Grande labeled "Fazenda Garcia" or hop in a cab and make for the *"fim da linha da Garcia"*—the last stop on the Garcia bus line—which will deposit you in the midst of the lively and popular residential *bairro* of Garcia. You'll need to ask directions to find ◖ **Aconchego da Zuzu** (Rua Quintino Bocaiúva 18, Garcia, tel. 71/3331-5074, noon–4 P.M. Tues., 11:30 A.M.–1 A.M. Wed.–Sat., noon–4 P.M. Sun., R$20–30). It was Zuzu (now over 100

years old) who taught her family to make the Bahian specialties served in this homey backyard restaurant, with tables strewn beneath the shade of a century-old mango tree. Fish and shrimp *moquecas, escabeches,* and *carne-de-sol* (sun-dried beef) are standouts, as are the *feijoadas,* served on Fridays and weekends to the accompaniment of live *chorinho* and samba.

Meanwhile, a practical, affordable, not to mention pleasant option for lunch or dinner is the fresh and varied per kilo buffet at the Teatro Castro Alves's **Café Teatro do TCA** (Rua Leovigildo Figueiras 18, Campo Grande, tel. 71/3328-5818, 11:30 A.M.–3 P.M. daily, 5–11 P.M. performance nights, R$10–15). Local and visiting musicians, dancers, and thespians performing at Salvador's premiere theater eat here, making it a great place for people-watching. Eat light or go for second, third, and fourth helpings—the diverse choice of salads, international, and Bahian main dishes makes it hard not to. After your meal, sink into one of the cushioned wicker chairs on the terrace for coffee or dessert. This is also a good place for a pre- or post-show cocktail.

Barra

If you're too lazy to leave the beach, Barra has its own fair share of eating options aside from the more obvious tourist traps. For a light and wholesome lunch between bronzing sessions, head over to the jasmine-scented **Ramma** (Rua Lord Cochrane 76, Barra, tel. 71/3264-0044, 11 A.M–3 P.M. Sun.–Fri., R$10–15). The owners, a Bahian-Danish couple, have elaborated on a healthy yet appetizing largely vegetarian menu with oriental leanings. Service is *por quilo,* so you can eat as much or as little as you want. It's A favorite with Salvador's upscale yoga and pilates crowd. Another *quilo* favorite that draws a more business-like crowd is **Spaghetti Lilas** (Rua Professor Fernando Luz 75, Barra, tel. 71/3237-9592, 11:30 A.M.–2:30 P.M. Mon.–Fri., noon–4 P.M. Sat.–Sun., R$12–17). The decor is cool and clean and the mouthwatering buffet has plenty of appetizing local and international choices to fill up on.

Two of Barra's most unpretentious and

appealing neighborhood bars are **Bar Chico I** (Rua President Kennedy, 179. Barra, tel. 71/3336-3134, 9 A.M.–last client daily, R$15–30) and **Bar Chico II** (Rua Florianópolis 86, Barra, tel. 71/3267-4386, 11 A.M.–6 P.M. Mon., 11 A.M.–last client Tues.–Sun., R$15–30), which have been watering holes for Barra residents for 30 years. Aside from being owned by the eponymous Chico, both are located on leafy residential streets and offer menus that feature nicely prepared Bahian fare—both as appetizers and full-fledged meals. Great for snacking on with a few friends (and a cold beer) or as a meal in itself are the *arrumadinhos* and *escondidinhos,* which mix your choice of meat (sausage, smoked pork, sun-dried beef, and roasted goat) in an arrangement with beans, salad, and toasted manioc flour (*arrumado* means "tidied up" or "organized") or beneath a layer of pureed manioc (*escondido* means "hidden").

Often overlooked by tourists, but long a favorite with Salvador's artist and intellectual crowd is **Bate Boca** (Rua Alameda Antunes 56, Barra, tel. 71/3264-3821, 11 A.M.–4 P.M. and 6–11 P.M. Mon.–Fri., noon–11 P.M. Sat.–Sun., R$35–45). Entering the cozy interior of this house, only a stone's throw from Porto da Barra, is a pleasantly discombobulating experience; you'll find yourself in the midst of a Marrakesh-inspired decor with Moroccan ceramics vying for wall space with over 500 paintings. The owner's mother, Dona Indaía, inspired local author Jorge Amado to create one of his unforgettable fictional characters, Candoca from *Tieta do Agreste*. In return, the Bahian novelist inspired one of the restaurant's signature dishes, the *filé à Jorge Amado,* consisting of a filet mignon in madeira sauce, served with fried *banana da terra,* crunchy manioc flour, and sautéed potatoes. Other items on the menu are eclectically international. Though portions are generous, try to save space for the excellent homemade desserts.

Being surrounded on all sides by blue ocean might incite cravings for fish and seafood that aren't necessarily fried or bathed in palm oil and coconut milk. When the urge for fresh fish becomes overwhelming, head to trendy

Sato (Av. Sete de Setembro 3959, Barra, tel. 71/3264-6464, www.satorestaurante. com.br, noon–3:30 P.M. Tues.–Fri., 6 P.M.–last client daily, R$35–45) for some sushi as well as original Japanese dishes served in a clean minimalist environment overlooking Porto da Barra. The downstairs contains a sushi bar, grill, and wooden deck, while the sleek upstairs gets downright loungey with a DJ and big plasma TV. Weekday lunch buffets cost R$22.50, while Wednesday evenings and Sundays feature the Festival Tomodachi, a special menu featuring some 60 items, for the price of R$45.

Rio Vermelho

The boho hood of Rio Vermelho comes to life at night with dozens of restaurants where one can drink and even more bars where one can eat (see *Nightlife*). Aside from its beaches, the rest of the *orla* is less interesting, although a few legendary seafood restaurants make great lunch stops after a morning spent lolling on the beaches between Barra and Itapuá.

Catering to Rio Vermelho's significant vegetarian fringe, aside from its diverse and nicely priced healthy *quilo* buffet **Manjeiricão** (Rua Fonte de Boi 3B, Rio Vermelho, tel. 71/3335-5641, noon–3:30 p.m. Mon.–Sat., R$10–15) is a draw because of its oasis-like ambiance, overflowing with tropical fruit trees, flowers, and birds. **Companhia de Pizza** (Praça Brigadeiro Faria Rocha, Rio Vermelho, tel. 71/3334-7443, 5:30 P.M.–1 A.M. Sun.–Thurs., 5:30 P.M.–2 A.M. Fri.–Sat., R$30–40) is Salvador's hippest and arguably best pizzeria. Located in the midst of Rio Vermelho's lively nocturnal scene, the modern, warmly lit restaurant spilling out onto the sidewalk attracts an attractive crowd who swear by the 70 varieties of pizza, not to mention calzones and panzones, all baked in a wood oven. That it's the only pizza palace in town with a nutritionist explains the presence of ingredients such as organic eggs and hydroponic arugula. Other innovations include a "Dessert Laboratory" and a "Waiting *Boteco*"; a bar designed for those without the patience to wait in line for a table.

Orla

If while beach-hopping you're suddenly overcome by with hunger, stop for a seafood banquet at **Yemanjá** (Av. Otávio Mangabeira 4655, Jardim de Armação, tel. 71/3461-9010, www. restauranteyemanja.com.br, 11:30 A.M.–midnight Sun.–Thurs., 11:30 A.M.–1 A.M. Fri.–Sat., R$40–55). Named after the *orixá* of salt waters—and rustically decked out in her signature colors of blue and white—this Bahian fish and seafood temple is one of the city's most popular addresses. *Moquecas*—over 15 varieties—rule supreme, but you can also choose dishes such as grilled lobster and shrimp with creamy Catupiry cheese and cashew nuts. Leave room for the homemade *quindins* (coconut custard) as dessert. The other reigning seafood restaurant along the *orla*, ◖ Mistura (Rua Professor Souza Brito, 41. Itapuã, tel. 71/3375-2623, noon–midnight Sun.–Fri. noon–1 A.M. Sat., R$40–50), lives up to its name (Mixture) by treating fish and seafood to a deliciously innovative mixture of Bahian, Portuguese, African, and Mediterranean (notably Italian) influence. For years, the owners, a Brazilian-Italian couple, ran a beach *barraca* at Itapuã, where the food was so good, they were eventually forced to open a restaurant. These days, the menu features an antipasti buffet as well as seasonal à la carte specialties such a baked *robalo* fish with Sicilian lime risotto and homemade pastas with seafood. All the fish are purchased fresh from Itapuã's local fisherfolk.

INFORMATION

The city's efficient tourist office, **Emtursa,** is located at the Elevador Lacerda (tel. 71/3321-2697, 8:30 A.M.–7:30 P.M. Mon.–Fri., 9 A.M.–5 P.M. Sat.–Sun.). It has a really great bilingual website (www.emtursa.salvador. ba.gov.br), which is loaded with detailed info. The state tourist office, **Bahiatursa** (www.bahiatursa.ba.gov.br) has two locations—one in the Pelourinho (Rua das Laranjeiras 12, tel. 71/3321-2133, 8:30 A.M.–9 P.M. daily) at the airport (tel. 71/3204-1244, 7:30 A.M.–11 P.M. daily). Staff are helpful and friendly. Maps are for sale. Pick up the free pocket guide *BahiaCultural* for monthly events and entertainment listings. Other tourist offices are located at the Rodoviária Central (tel. 71/3450-3871, 7:30 A.M.–9 P.M. daily), the Mercado Modelo (tel. 71/3241-0242, 9 A.M.–6 P.M. Mon.–Sat., 9 A.M.–1:30 P.M. Sun.) and at Shopping Barra (near the SAC, tel. 71/3264-4566, 9 A.M.–7 P.M. Mon.–Fri.). The official Bahian tourism site (www.bahia.com.br) is a great resource for descriptions and listings for Salvador and all of Bahia, but the Portuguese links are more complete than those in English. City maps can be purchased in most main newsstands (the most complete is the published by Geocad and costs around R$6) and in bookshops such as Livraria Siciliana in Shopping Barra.

Gays who want to know more about the local scene should drop by the **Grupo Gay da Bahia** in the Pelourinho (Rua Frei Vicente 24, tel. 71/3321-1848, www.ggb.org.br). Meanwhile all sorts of information—from opening and closing hours to bus schedules—can be had by dialing **Informação Turística** (Tourist Information)—**131,** which includes information in English as well as Portuguese.

SERVICES
Banks

Most major branches of Banco do Brasil and HSBC have at least one ATM that accepts international cards. There is a **Banco do Brasil** (Cruzeiro de São Francisco 11) in the Pelourinho, and others at Shopping Barra, in front of the Mercado Modelo, at Porto da Barra, and at the airport. **HSBC** has a branch in Barra (Avenida Marquês de Caravelas 355). **Citibank** has a branch close to the Farol da Barra (Rua Marques de Leão 71).

Post Offices

You'll find post offices at the airport, as well as in Shopping Barra, at Campo Grande (Rua Visconde de São Lourenço 66), and in Pelourinho (Largo do Cruzeiro de São Francisco 20).

Internet Cafés

Internet cafés have mushroomed around Salvador. If your hotel doesn't have a computer or two, in the Pelourinho you can try the friendly **Bahiacafe.Com** (Praça da Sé, tel. 71/3322-1266, www.bahiasun.com.br, 9 A.M.–11:30 P.M. Mon.–Fri.) or **Internet Café.com** (Rua João de Deus 2, tel. 71/3321-2147, 9 A.M.–9 P.M.). In Barra, there are many options, among them **Aldeia.net & Snack Cyber Café** (Av. Almirante Marquês de Leão 639, Sala 201, tel. 71/3237-2297, 9 A.M.–9 P.M. Mon.–Sat.).

Emergency Services

In the event of a medical emergency, dial **192** for Pronto Socorro (First Aid). In Barra, there are two conveniently located hospitals: the **Hospital Espanhol** (Av. Sete de Setembro 4161, tel. 71/3261-1500) and the **Hospital Português** (Av. Princesa Isabel 914, tel. 71/3203-5555). In the event of a crime, call **190** to reach the police. In terms of crimes involving tourists, you'll have to deal with the special tourist police force. They're the ones you'll see patrolling the Pelourinho wearing "Polícia Turística" armbands. The **Delegacia do Turista** (DELTUR) is on the Largo de Cruzeiro do São Francisco (tel. 71/3116-6817).

GETTING THERE

Most international travelers arrive in Salvador by air, although if you're traveling from another city in Brazil, you'll either arrive by bus or car.

By Air

The **Aeroporto Deputado Luís Eduardo Magalhães (Dois de Julho)** is the city's main airport (tel. 71/3204-1010), and quite a posh one at that. Located inland from Itapuã, it is around 30 kilometers (19 miles) from the city center. A taxi will cost around R$60. There are also *executivo* air-conditioned buses that pass along the coast and head to Praça da Sé, and regular municipal buses, which aren't recommended unless you have very little luggage and an awful lot of time (an hour or more).

By Bus

Salvador's bus station, **Rodoviária Central** (Av. Tancredo Neves, Iguatemi, tel. 71/3460-8300) is across the street from Shopping Iguatemi. From here you can catch buses to all destinations in Bahia and other places in Brazil. In front of the *rodoviária,* you can grab city buses to all destinations or hail a cab (a trip to the Pelourinho or Barra will cost you around R$20).

GETTING AROUND
By Bus

Buses in Salvador are plentiful and go practically everywhere. The main municipal bus station in the Centro is Lapa, but many buses also pass through Campo Grande as well en route to the rest of the city. Regular municipal buses cost R$2 whereas plush, air-conditioned *executivo* buses (which link Praça da Sé, the Atlantic coast, and the airport), are closer to R$5. The final destination is written on the front of the bus and the main stops are listed on the side near the back door. If in doubt, ask the *cobrador* (who takes money at the back of the bus), since some buses have very circuitous routes. As a rule, don't carry a lot of valuables since robberies are common. Don't be surprised, however, if a seated passenger offers to take your bags and hold them safely on his or her lap. This is simply courtesy.

By Taxi

At night, service dwindles and it's often safer to take a cab. Taxi drivers rarely speak English, but in general, they are very friendly. If you want, bargain with them, but at the outset before the meter starts running. Major companies include **Chame Táxi** (tel. 0800/284-7576), **Ligue Táxi** (tel. 71/3357-7777), and **Teletaxi** (tel. 0800/717-111).

By Car

Soteropolitanos are not reputed for their great driving skills. Actually, it isn't that they are poor drivers, but that they have a penchant for not adhering to rules of the road. So be forewarned that driving in Salvador is a challenge. That said, for exploring the surrounding region, especially the beautiful north coast, which stretches all the way up to Bahia's frontier with Sergipe with the advantage of an excellent (privatized) highway, having a car is a big advantage. **Hertz** has an airport office (tel. 71/3377-6554). **Localiza** an airport office (tel. 71/3377-2272) and another in Ondina (Av. Oceânica 3057, tel. 71/3332-1999). **Unidas** has two offices, at the airport (tel. 71/3377-1244) and in Barra (Av. Oceânica 3097, tel. 71/3247-2121). **Business Rent-A-Car** is in Pelourhinho (Rua Direita do Santo Antônio 20, tel. 71/3241-3586).

City Tours
Aside from **LR Turismo** (see *Sports and Recreation*), other operators specializing in city tours include **Tours Bahia** (Largo do Cruzeiro de São Francisco 416, Pelourinho, tel. 71/3322-4383, www.toursbahia), whose excursions are pricy, but varied and professional, and **Privé Tur** (Av. Sete de Setembro 2068, Vitória, tel. 71/3338-1320, www.privetur.com.br), which also organizes schooner trips and trips to beaches.

North of Salvador

ESTRADA DO COCO
The coast going north from Salvador is known as the Estrada do Coco, or the Coconut Road (in honor of the coastline's abundance of swaying coconut palms). Although increasingly subject to the whims of real estate developers, the little villages—and growing number of condo complexes—boast lovely beaches. And the further north you go, the more deserted they become.

Arembepe
Only 50 kilometers (31 miles) north of Salvador, this fishing village was a hippie haven in the '60s. In fact, the actual "hippie village"—consisting of ingeniously constructed palm frond cottages set amidst sand dunes—was so swinging in its heyday that it attracted the likes of Janis Joplin, Mick Jagger, and Roman Polanski. Some hippies still live (without electricity) in the village, making and selling jewelry and macrame and living off shrimp and fish. The placid lagoons attract a mellow crowd intent on smoking reefer in idyllic surroundings. Show up at the end of the afternoon to catch the sunset and moonrise while floating in the warm waters of the Rio Capivara. If you really want that tropical Woodstock experience, come by during the first full moon of January, when the community hosts the **Festival Internacional de Cultura Alternativa,** featuring dance, music, and poetry reading performances. The town of Arembepe attracts weekending and summering

Soteropolitanos and, of late, has been filling up with condos. Despite the recent development, the beaches are attractive enough (especially if you walk far from town itself) and there is a nice unpretentious vibe to the place.

ACCOMMODATIONS AND FOOD
A languid place to while away the hottest hours of the day, **Mar Aberto** (Largo de São Francisco 43, tel. 71/3624-1257, www .marabertorestaurante.com.br, 1:30 A.M.– 10 P.M. Mon.–Thurs., 11:30 A.M.–midnight Fri.–Sat., noon–7 P.M. Sun., R$45–55) is easily the best and prettiest of Arembepe's beachfront restaurants. Although it's a little more upscale and pricy than its neighbors, the extra *reais* are worth it. In fact, day-trippers come all the way from Salvador to dig into the likes of *bacalhau à brasileira* (salted cod cooked in coconut milk), fragrant stews, and *moquecas* featuring seafood, much of which is supplied by Arembepe's local fishermen. For dessert, try *manjar,* a creamy pudding topped with a peppery mango coulis.

Most tourists do Arembepe in a day trip from Salvador or as a stopover on the way up to coast to Praia do Forte and beaches beyond. In truth, there are nicer spots to stay than in Arembepe, but if you do want to spend the night, a good choice is **Hotel Aldeia de Arembepe** (Estrada de Aldeia Hippie, loteamento 9/10, tel. 71/3624-1031, www.aldeia-dearembepe.com.br, R$90–110 d). Here, you'll find rustic faded pink bungalows idyllically situated on a sand dune that straddles an untamed stretch of beach on one side and the hippie village with its palms and lagoons on the other. It is also adjacent to Tamar Arembepe's small sea turtle preservation center, whose headquarters is up the coast in Praia do Forte.

GETTING THERE

Arembepe is easily reached from Salvador via the BA-099 highway. Frequent buses leave from the main Lapa bus station (final destination Monte Gordo) or the Terminal França near the Cidade Baixa's Mercado Modelo. The trip takes about an hour.

Praia do Forte

Ten years ago, Praia do Forte was a simple fishing village with a main street consisting of a soft white-sand path leading from the bus stop to the beach. However, as the site of the country's first eco-resort in the 1980s (long before the prefix "eco" even existed), Praia do Forte began attracting international tourists to its beautiful beaches and surrounding natural attractions: a mixture of native Atlantic forest, lagoons and mangroves. Before you could say "environmental," the main road had become a carefully landscaped and paved thoroughfare flanked by chic bikini-filled boutiques, jewelry shops, pizzerias, *creperias,* cafés, and even a *shopping.* Though all are tastefully designed, the chic commercial strip transformed the flavor of the place. These days, Praia do Forte is lovely and lively with lots to do, but quite touristy—and becoming more and more developed by the day.

SIGHTS

As you're walking around, you're sure to notice the overwhelming amount of turtle imagery on T-shirts, sun hats, and beach towels. That's because Praia do Forte's logo is the sea tortoise; in fact, one of the reason's for the town's success as a thriving eco-resort is the presence of Brazil's acclaimed **Projeto Tamar** (an abbreviation of the Portuguese phrase for sea turtles: *tartaruga marinha*). Founded in 1980 by the

Brazilian Environmental Agency (IBAMA), this nonprofit organization studies and works to preserve the lives of the giant sea turtles living along Brazil's Atlantic coast, which is home to five out of seven of the world's sea turtle species. Until recently, many were facing extinction as a result of rampant overfishing and urbanization that destroyed nesting sites. In Praia do Forte, Projeto Tamar's mission is not only to save the turtles (and their eggs—traditionally a staple food for local fisherfolk), but to actively involve the population in their plight in a sustainable manner. This is done both directly (by patrolling the beach at night to move eggs or hatchlings at risk of being harmed), and indirectly (through increased tourism that the project has brought to the region).

Indeed, eggs, hatchlings, and turtles of all ages find refuge at the **Tamar research station** (tel. 71/3676-1045, www.tamar.com. br, 9 A.M.–7 P.M. daily, R$12), located on the beach just behind the pretty whitewashed Igreja de São Francisco. It's filled with pools and aquariums where you can observe the turtles at various stages of their existence—from utterly cute, tiny hatchlings to gigantic full-grown creatures capable of living up to the ripe old age of 200. The center includes bilingual information and a gift shop selling the infamous turtle-themed paraphernalia (all proceeds go to Projeto Tamar). There's also a shady café and restaurant on the premises.

Praia do Forte is also the headquarters of the recently opened **Instituto Baleia Jubarte** (Av. ACM 51, tel. 71/3676-1463, www.baleiajubarte. com.br), a research station for studying humpbacked whales. Between July and October, these 40-ton mammals trade the frigid waters of Antarctica for warm currents more conducive to reproductive activities. The institute organizes offshore boat trips (R$130 pp) led by resident biologists, which allow you to get a close-up glimpse at these fascinating giants.

Back on land, an important historical landmark is the **Castelo Gárcia d'Ávila** (tel. 71/3676-1073, 9 A.M.–6 P.M. Tues.–Sun., R$3). Originally a lowly clerk for the Portuguese monarchy, the ambitious Gárcia d'Ávila, as a reward for his services to the crown, received the *capitânia* of Bahia (which back in the 16th century embraced a large portion of the Brazilian Northeast stretching up to Maranhão). As a wealthy landowner, d'Ávila based himself in Praia do Forte, where he amassed more wealth by introducing cattle ranching and coconut palm plantations (and by cruelly exploiting slaves). Built between 1551 and 1624 on a strategic hilltop overlooking the sea, his castle—now in ruins—is one of the first stone structures and the only medieval-style fortress in Brazil. The recently renovated **Capela de Nossa Senhora da Conceição** houses a tiny museum. The castle can be reached by walking along a 2.5-kilometer (1.5-mile) stretch of dirt road (known as Rua do Castelo) that branches off from the entrance to Praia do Forte.

SPORTS AND RECREATION

If you choose to stay for a few days, Praia do Forte and the surrounding area offer lots of activities. First and foremost are its palm-fringed beaches, which offer the shelter of crescent-shaped coves and natural pools framed by coral reefs. The clear blue waters of **Praia do Papa-Gente**—a 20-minute walk north—are perfect for snorkeling (masks and fins can be rented at Projeto Tamar). You can also venture into the **Reserva de Preservação Ambiental Sapiranga** (Linha Verde Km 5, tel. 71/3676-0211, 9 A.M.–5 P.M. daily, R$6), an ecological nature reserve consisting of 600 hectares of rivers, lagoons, and virgin Atlantic forest, inhabited by endangered creatures such as the *mico-estrela-de-tufos-brancos* (miniature white tuffed star monkey) and the *preguiça-de-coleira* (a type of sloth). Various trails weave through the brush and there are plenty of opportunities for bathing in the Rio Pojuca. Aside from hiking, you can explore the park by renting a Jeep, bike, a horse, or the ultra-popular quadricycle (built for two). With a canoe, you can paddle around the **Lagoa Timeantube,** a haven for close to 200 exotic bird species. For more information contact **Centrotur** (tel. 71/3676-1091) and **Odara** (tel. 71/3676-1080) located near the beginning of Avenida ACM.

ACCOMMODATIONS

Having become increasingly upscale and Eurocentric, Praia do Forte is not the cheapest place to stay along Bahia's north coast. However, in off-season and during the week, it's possible to find some good discounts.

One of the oldest and most pleasant of Praia do Forte's *pousadas* is the **Pousada Ogum Marinho** (Av. ACM, tel. 71/3676-1165, www.ogummarinho.com.br, R$175–200 d), right off the beach. Rooms are comfortable and feature decent bathrooms as well as small verandas with softly woven hammocks. The restaurant prepares a nice mix of local and international fare. Off the beaten track of Avenida ACM, the **Pousada dos Artistas** (Praça dos Artistas, tel. 71/3676-1147, www.pousadadosartistas.tur.br, R$125 d), with original decoration by its friendly artist owners, provides a quiet refuge surrounded by flowering gardens. Rooms are a little small, but comfortable. For cheap, yet cheery, your best bet is the welcoming **Pousada Balanço do Mar** (Rua da Aurora 25, tel. 71/3676-1059, www.pousadabalancodomar.com.br, R$70–90 d). The most charming place in town is **Pousada Refúgio da Vila** (Lot. Aldeia dos Pescadores, tel. 71/3676-0114, www.refugiodavila.com.br, R$300–550 d), whose lofty living and dining areas are beautifully designed and decorated to take advantage of the light and vivid colors of the surrounding gardens and lovely pool. Rooms are less spectacular, but very well appointed. Too bad some of the balconies overlook more "urbanized" parts of Praia do Forte. The breakfasts are out of this world. Meanwhile, if you feel like splurging, check into the place that put Praia do Forte on the eco-tourist map way back in the 1980s: the **Praia do Forte Eco Resort and Thalasso Spa** (Av. do Farol, tel. 71/3676-4000, tel. 0800/71-8888, www.praiadoforteecoresort.com.br, R$800–1,170 d). Set amidst beautifully groomed gardens well-endowed with swimming pools, bars, and lounge chairs, and overlooking a crescent-shaped beach, this sprawling resort is hardly intimate, yet it definitely makes you feel spoiled and relaxed. All the bright and spacious rooms have ocean views. If the prices seem a bit steep, keep in mind that they include a welcome drink, breakfast and dinner (the spreads are marvelous), sports and leisure equipment, and activities (lots of them) for both adults and children. The thalasso therapy sessions featuring algae and heated seawater are a big bonus.

FOOD

If instead of a serious sit-down lunch, you'd rather spend the hottest hours of the day gorging on a succession of maritime delicacies washed down with icy beer, try any one of the beach *barracas*. Protected by a shady umbrella, you can dig into fresh fried *vermelho* fish or grilled jumbo shrimp in olive oil and garlic while taking time out for dips in the blue sea. For a break from sand and surf, try wandering up and down the main drag of Avenida ACM, where there is no shortage of restaurants. **Sabor da Vila** (tel. 71/3676-1156, lunch and dinner daily, R$25–40) offers a delicious variety of dishes, with some excellent fish and seafood options. If you want a totally Zen experience (not to mention some vegetables) dig into sushi, tempura, and other Japanese fare with a Brazilian bent at **Kasato** (Al. do Linguado, tel. 71/3676-0174, www.kasato.com.br, lunch and dinner Wed.–Sun., R$30–40), a seductive place whose open dining room is surrounded by greenery and romantically lit with paper lanterns.

At night, things heat up along Avenida ACM. If you want to be where the local action is grab a place to sit at **Bar do Souza** (tel. 71/3676-1156), known for its *petiscos* (appetizers), particularly the *bolinhos de peixe* (fish balls). At the other end of the *avenida,* a more international crowd at the **Tango Café** (tel. 71/3676-1367) fights for the tables as well as the empanadas, sandwiches, and delicious desserts. Take note: This is one of the few places in Bahia where you can actually get a real cappuccino.

INFORMATION

For tourist information, stop by the small Bahiatursa office (entrance to Avenida ACM, tel. 71/3676-0283). Also check out www.praia-doforte.com.br. On the main drag, you'll find Internet cafés as well as ATMs. The Banco do Brasil machine accepts international cards.

GETTING THERE

Buses to Praia do Forte leave from Salvador's Rodoviária Central approximately every hour with the **Expresso Linha Verde** (tel. 71/3450-0321) and **Catuense** (tel. 71/3450-4004) bus companies. More comfortable buses run by the **Cacique** (tel. 71/3392-1376) company depart from the Terminal da Calçada in the Cidade Baixa and travel all the way to Porto de Sauípe. The trip takes around two hours, along the BA-099 highway.

LINHA VERDE

Up the coast from Praia do Forte, the Estrada do Coco becomes known as the Linha Verde (Green Line), which stretches all the way up the coast to Bahia's frontier with the state of Sergipe. With the exception of the mega-resort complex of Costa do Sauípe—with its umpteen international hotels surrounded by a fake theme-park likeness of the Pelourinho—the little fishing villages that dot this still unspoiled and beautiful stretch of coast are (for the time being) largely untouched by tourism.

Imbassaí

Only 10 kilometers (6 miles) past Praia do Forte, this seductively low-key village is a welcome antidote to Praia do Forte. It attracts a mix of locals, families, gays, and a few fashionistas (bikini spreads for Brazilian *Vogue* are often shot here). Aside from charmingly rustic *pousadas* and restaurants, the main draws are the beach *barracas* poised along a strip of sand dunes, which straddle Atlantic beaches on one side and the warm, Coca-Cola–colored Rio Imbassaí on the other side. The upshot is that you can spend your day alternating between two utterly relaxing watery worlds (although the river side is more interactive in that you can actually plant your table and chairs in the water and nibble on tiny fried *pititinga* and *agulhinha* fish, while even tinier fish nibble on your toes). If this setup proves too sedentary, you can always go swimming (or crabbing) in

barracas facing the beach in Imbassaí

a nearby lagoon or soak yourself in the waterfall a 30-minute walk away, on the other side of the Linha Verde.

ACCOMMODATIONS AND FOOD

There are quite a range of good *pousadas* and restaurants in Imbassaí. The most charming of lot is the 【 **Eco Pousada Vilangelim** (Al. dos Angelins, tel. 71/3677-1144, www.vilangelim. com.br, R$190–230 d). Although the cozy bungalow rooms are a little snug, you can always hang out in the main dining and lounge areas. Featuring an original decor that blends traditional and contemporary furnishings as well as art from all over Brazil, these common spaces extend to the wooden decks, where a tiled swimming pool is framed by lush foliage. The food (especially the lavish breakfasts) is excellent, and the staff is terrifically attentive. You'll also get a friendly welcome at the simple though lovingly cared for **Pousada Cabanas Cajibá** (Al. das Bromélias, tel. 71/3677-1111, www.pousadacajiba.com.br, R$100–150 d), set amidst a well-tended garden, with a pool, where mico monkeys are frequent visitors. Accommodations are in two-story bungalows. Those on the second floor look out onto a canopy of fruit trees.

For Bahian specialties such as fish, seafood, and *moquecas,* plant yourself beneath the enormous *mangaba* tree that shelters the **Santana Restaurante e Lanchonete** (Rua da Igreja, tel. 71/3677-1237, noon–10 P.M. daily, R$25–40). Aside from the welcome shade, when ripe, the tree's *mangabas* yield a succulent nectar (it will make your lips stick together slightly). Also famed for her *moquecas* is **Vânia** (Al. dos Hibiscos, tel. 71/3677-1040, 11 A.M.–9 P.M. Tues.–Sun., R$25–35), located just off the main drag.

At night, what laid-back action there is unfolds on the main street of Rua das Amendoeiras. **É Massa** (tel. 71/3677-1067, R$15–25) is an Italian restaurant bar owned by an Argentinean expat; it serves tasty salads, empanadas, and homemade pizzas and pastas. Always abuzz with an older crowd is **Nega Fulo** (tel. 71/3677-1019, R$20–30), a romantically lit pizzeria fused with the equally enticing **Jerimum Café,** which has elaborate drinks and mouthwatering desserts.

INFORMATION

For listings, bus schedules, and weather updates visit www.imbassai.info.

GETTING THERE

Imbassaí is only 10 kilometers (6 miles) north of Praia do Forte along the BA-099. Buses leave from Salvador's Rodoviária Central approximately every hour with the **Expresso Linha Verde** bus company (tel. 71/3450-0321). From the Terminal da Calçada **Cacique** buses (tel. 71/3392-1376) bound for Porto de Sauípe also stop at the entrance to town.

Diogo

Even more bucolic and less visited than Imbassaí is Diogo, 4 kilometers (2.5 miles) north. In fact, Diogo is so small that it barely rates as a village. It is reached by turning off the Linha Verde highway and following a mostly sandy track (if you are traveling by bus, this means walking a couple of kilometers). Its most sophisticated accommodation option is the **Pousada Too Cool na Bahia** (tel. 71/9952-2190, www.toocoolnabahia.com, R$90), with eight simple, but comfortable bungalows set in sand dunes and shaded by large fruit trees. You'll have to walk 15 minutes through a stunning white dunescape to reach the beach of Santo Antônio, which—aside from a couple of simple *barracas* serving fresh fish, seafood, and icy beer—is inevitably deserted.

From Diogo onwards, following the BA-099, the unspoiled beaches continue north without interruption. The tiny settlement of **Massarandupió** (115 kilometers/71 miles from Salvador) is famous for its nude beach. **Baixio** (150 kilometers/93 miles) has a lovely crystal blue lagoon as well as wonderful beaches. And **Sítio do Conde** (200 kilometers/124 miles), which is accessible from Conde, on the Linha Verde, is a lazy spot flooded with white sand and coconut palms. From here, you can access the remote beauties of **Siribinha** and **Barra de Itariri** beaches.

◖ Mangue Seco

Another 70 kilometers (43 miles) north from Sítio do Conde, at the end of the Linha Verde, is the ultra-secluded Mangue Seco. Ever since its seductive landscape of palm-studded sand dunes made an unforgettable cameo appearance in *Tieta,* a 1989 *novela* (nightly soap) based on the Jorge Amado's novel *Tieta do Agreste,* Brazilians have been flocking to this slice of paradise in droves. Aside from the rustic little fishing village, you'll find yourself surrounded by coconut plantations, mangroves, rivers, and idyllic white-sand beaches whose big waves attract surfers. Thankfully, despite its fame, Mangue Seco's remoteness keeps the crowds at bay. For those visiting on their own (as opposed to being part of a packaged day trip), getting to the village is a bit tricky. It involves taking a ride in a canoe or motor boat (which can include a long wait in off-season) from Pontal on the Sergipe side of the Rio Real. (Linha Express Verde buses stop in Pontal, and if driving, you can stash your car here). If the tide is high, ask the boatman to take you directly to your *pousada.* If not, you'll have to lug your bags along a sandy trail.

ACCOMMODATIONS AND FOOD

Mangue Seco has a handful of comfortably rustic accommodations, among them **Pousada O Forte** (tel. 75/3455-9039, www.pousadaoforte.com/br, R$80 d), with a picturesque hilltop setting, and the equally appealing **Pousada Fantasias do Agreste** (tel. 75/3455-9011, www.fantasiasdoagreste.com, R$120–160 d). Navigating the 1.5 kilometers (1 mile) of dunes to reach the beach can be done by buggy or on foot. Other dune buggy tours are also available. Unsurprisingly, seafood is in abundance as is the delicious crab-like *aratú,* which are used to make *moquecas.* For deliciously prepared fish and seafood, stop at **Frutos do Mar** (tel. 75/3455-9049, 7 A.M.–9 P.M., R$20–35). A good snack option is *moquequinhas,* tasty slices of cured fish wrapped in palm leaves and sold by local boys on the beach for R$1.

GETTING THERE

There is regular bus service from Salvador's Rodoviária Central all the way up the Linha

Verde to Sítio do Conde on **Expresso Linha Verde** (tel. 71/3450-0321) and **Catuense** (tel. 71/3450-4004). From the Terminal da Calçada in the Cidade Baixa, **Cacique** (tel. 71/3392-1376) buses go as far as Porto de Sauípe (with stops in Imbassaí and Diogo). Check to make sure that the bus actually goes into these village from the Linha Verde. If not, the bus will let you off on the BA-099 highway, near the road leading to the town and village. From there *kombis* (collective vans) regularly shuttle passengers to the coast.

The Recôncavo

Named after the concave-shaped Bay of All Saints, the Recôncavo refers to the former sugarcane region surrounding Salvador. Once the major purveyor of Bahia's great wealth, the colonial cities of Santo Amaro and, particularly, Cachoeira were prosperous regional capitals whose prominence is reflected in the impressive array of baroque churches and gracious mansions that line their sleepy cobblestoned streets and squares. Today, this lush, hilly region is given over to the cultivation of paper (hence the bamboo plantations) as well as fruit and spices such as cloves and peppers. The towns—despite a certain air of dilapidation—retain a distinctive charm. The Recôncavo is also known for its rich cultural traditions, linked to the African heritage of the largely black population descended from the slaves who worked the sugar plantations. Since both towns are within a two-hour drive from Salvador, they can be easily visited in a day trip. However, if you want to soak up the history and distinctive flavor of the Recôncavo, consider staying overnight in Cachoeira.

SANTO AMARO

Only 70 kilometers (43 miles) from Salvador, this typical Recôncavo town—the hometown of Brazilian musical sibling superstars Caetano Veloso and Maria Betânia—is attractive and unpretentious. With elegant squares framed by baroque churches and a couple of ruined plantation manors, it's a pleasant place to wander around for a couple of few hours if you're on your way to or from Cachoeira. Highlights include the attractive colonial buildings around the **Praça da Purificação,** among them the 17th-century **Igreja Matriz de Nossa Senhora da Purificação,** with its Portuguese tiles, and the imposing 18th-century **Convento dos Humildes** (9 A.M.–1 P.M. Tues.–Sun.), at Praça Padre Inácio Teixeira dos S. Araujo, which houses a small museum of religious art. Don't leave without sampling the *sequilhos,* crisp buttery biscuits made by the nuns at the convent.

Festivals and Events

Santo Amaro hosts two of the most interesting *festas populares* in the Recôncavo. On January 6 is the **Festas dos Reis,** during which the town's squares are given over to music and merrymaking. On May 13, **Bembé do Mercado** celebrates the abolition of slavery in Brazil (1888). Offerings are given to the *orixá* Iemanjá, and there are plenty of traditional African-inspired songs and *samba-de-roda* dancing.

CACHOEIRA

Two hours from Salvador, this atmospheric town on the banks of the languid blue Rio Paraguaçu is a treasure trove of arresting colonial architecture, which after years of abandon is slowly being restored. Cachoeira is also a center of Afro-Brazilian culture; there are an extraordinary number of traditional Candomblé *terreiros* as well as the Irmandade da Boa Morte (Sisterhood of Good Death)—a female religious order created by freed slaves over 200 years ago. The order's annual **Festa da Boa Morte** has become a major event, attracting loads of Afro-Descendentes in search of their ancestral roots.

Igreja da Ordem Terceira e Convento do Carmo, Cachoeira, Bahia

During the 17th and 18th centuries, Cachoeira was one of the wealthiest and most populous cities in the Brazilian colony. Its strategic location upriver from the Paraguaçu's entrance into the Bay of All Saints made it an important crossroads for the riches—particularly the gold mined in the Chapada Diamantina—that were being shipped from the interior down to the coast and off to Portugal. Meanwhile, its fertile soil lured Portuguese colonists to cultivate sugarcane in the surrounding hills and led to the importation of thousands of African slaves who worked the plantations. While the slaves toiled, their rich masters poured money into the embellishment of the thriving town, bequeathing a legacy of magnificent baroque churches.

By the early 19th century, colonial rule was being increasingly challenged, and as a hotbed of revolt, Cachoeira achieved national prominence. Cachoeirenses led the battle for independence against Portuguese troops. When Brazil subsequently won its independence, it was in Cachoeira that Dom Pedro I chose to be crowned as Brazil's first emperor.

At the end of the 19th century, sugar prices had diminished and slavery had been abolished. However, Cachoeira and, the neighboring town, São Félix (across the river), still prospered due to the cultivation of tobacco, the quality of which was renowned throughout the world. In recent decades, however, even tobacco's importance has dwindled. Today the glory of former times is but a distant memory preserved in the town's rich architectural and cultural heritage.

Sights

You can discover Cachoeira's treasures in a half-day of pleasant wandering around, which can also include a boat trip along the Rio Paraguaçu. Near the central bus stop is the **Praça Doutor Aristides Milton,** with its baroque fountain and the stately 18th-century **Santa Casa de Misericórdia** (the city's oldest hospital) flanked by a lovely small garden.

PRAÇA DA ACLAMAÇÃO

A much more grand square is the Praça da Aclamação, lined with impressive edifices such as the **Casa da Câmara e Cadeia,** the town's 17th-century jailhouse, which currently functions as its city hall. Also on the *praça,* you can't miss the splendidly baroque **Igreja da Ordem Terceira e Convento do Carmo** (Praça da Aclamação, tel. 75/3425-4853, 9 A.M.–noon and 2–5 P.M. Mon.–Sat., 9 A.M.–1 P.M. Sun.). The church is richly decorated with Portuguese ceramic tiles, an extravagantly ornate gold altar, and an exquisitely paneled ceiling. A side gallery features polychrome Christ figures, produced in the Portuguese colony of Macao, whose gory realism is enhanced by a glittering mixture of bovine blood and rubies. Inside, the **Museu de Arte Sacra do Recôncavo** (R$2) has a collection of religious art and objects. It can be accessed via the cloister of the equally magnificent convent, which operates as a *pousada* with a restaurant.

Housed in a handsome civic building, the **Museu Regional** (Praça da Aclamação 19, tel. 75/3425-1123, 8 A.M.–noon and 2–5 P.M. Mon.–Fri., 8 A.M.–noon Sat.–Sun., R$1) has an unassuming collection of 18th- and 19th-century furniture and decorative objects.

MUSEU HANSEN BAHIA AND VICINITY

Near the Praça da Aclamação is the modest Museu Hansen Bahia (Rua 13 de Maio, 9 A.M.–5 P.M. Tues.–Fri., 9 A.M.–2 P.M. Sat.–Sun., free) devoted to the expressive woodcuts and paintings of Hansen Bahia, a German engraver who fled Nazi Germany for Cachoeira (changing his last name along the way), and never looked back. There is a strong tradition of woodcarving in Cachoeira and as you explore the town you'll come across studios of local artists whose work is characterized by strong African influences. Also on Rua 13 de Maio is the coral-colored building that is the headquarters of the **Irmandade da Boa Morte** (10 A.M.–6 P.M. daily, contributions suggested). Inside, a small museum displays interesting photographs detailing the sisterhood's history and traditions, including the famous Festa da Boa Morte.

From the museum, a steep ascent leads to the **Praça da Ajuda,** where you'll come face-to-face with the **Igreja de Nossa Senhora da Ajuda,** a simple stone church built in the 1590s, which happens to be Cachoeira's oldest (sadly, it can't be visited). Descending an equally steep alley in the other direction will bring you to Rua Ana Nery, where you can visit the 17th-century **Igreja Matriz Nossa Senhora do Rosário,** renowned for its wonderful blue-and-white ceramic tile panels, the largest outside of Portugal.

SÃO FÉLIX

When you're through wandering around Cachoeira, cross the rickety British-built wooden bridge that leads across the river to the town of São Félix. Aside from some attractive pastel-colored riverfront buildings, the main interest of São Félix is the **Centro Cultural Dannemann** (Av. Salvador Pinto 29, tel. 75/3425-2208, www.centroculturaldannemann.com.br, 8 A.M.–noon and 1–4:30 P.M. Tues.–Sat., 1–4 P.M. Sun.), a warehouse that has been converted into a contemporary art center. Aside from interesting temporary shows, the center hosts the prestigious **Bienal do Recôncavo** every second November (in even-numbered years). Famed throughout the world for its fine cigars, Dannemann still produces its heavily perfumed smokes on the premises. To catch a glimpse—and a whiff—of the process, make your way to the rear of the building where women dressed in white sit at ancient wooden tables, rolling cigars as if it were still 1873. Even if you don't inhale yourself, you might want to buy a few to take home as the ultimate gift for the smokers in your life.

Festivals and Events

Without a doubt, the most famous event in Cachoeira is the three-day **Festa de Nossa Senhora da Boa Morte** (see the sidebar *Sisterhood of Good Death*). Held every year in August, it lures visitors from all over Brazil and the world, and for this reason, if you want to stay in Cachoeira, you'd better reserve a hotel *months* in advance. Should you miss this unforgettable celebration, try to make the **Festa**

SISTERHOOD OF GOOD DEATH

The **Irmandade da Boa Morte** (Sisterhood of Good Death) is one of the oldest examples of the survival of African rituals in the New World. The religious order was founded in the early 19th century by elderly black women of Cachoeira, whose official mission was to pray for the dead and provide decent funerals for members. Less official was their commitment to the preservation of African traditions and to the liberation of slaves, by helping them escape or raise money to purchase their freedom. Although it's ostensibly a Catholic order that worships the Virgin Mary, most of the women have roots in Cachoeira's Candomblé *terreiros*, and many of their rites feature allusions to *orixás* and include elements of African religious rituals. These days, the sisterhood has become a symbol of Brazilians' black heritage and culture, and both the Bahian government and Afro-American tourists have contributed to help the otherwise poor women maintain the sisterhood's headquarters and activities. Although there were once more than 300 sisters, today there are only around 20. Rules dictate that to become a member, women must be black and at least 60 years old. Currently, the oldest *irmã* is over 100.

The most important festival in Cachoeira's calendar is the three-day **Festa de Nossa Senhora da Boa Morte,** held every year August 13-15 in honor of the Virgin Mary. On the first night, the sisters – dressed in their traditional white ruffled blouses and petticoats, turbans, shawls, and layers of necklaces fashioned out of gold, cowrie shells, and multicolored beads signifying *orixás* – carry a magnificently decorated figure of the Virgin throughout the streets of Cachoeira. Following a mass in their chapel, they serve a ritual white meal – fish, rice, onions, potatoes, and wine – to guests. The second night's proceedings are more solemn as the sisters commemorate the death of the Virgin by parading through the streets in black skirts and shawls and without jewels. The third day – the Feast of the Assumption – is the most festive day of all. The sisters, dazzling in red skirts and shawls, jewels in full array, honor a new statue of the Virgin at an altar awash in fragrant flowers. Following a final mass, another procession, and a banquet, the proceedings take a turn for the more jubilant (and African) as the sisters gather in a circle in front of the Boa Morte headquarters to perform *samba-de-roda*, dancing to the accompaniment of drums and guitars. Once the rest of the population joins in, the festivities continue until the break of dawn.

de Nossa Senhora da Ajuda, which is held around the middle of November and features the washing of the steps of the Capela de Ajuda as well as plenty of traditional *samba-de-roda* music and dancing.

Accommodations and Food

Hands down, the most comfortable and atmospheric (and really quite affordable) place to stay in town is the **Pousada Convento do Carmo** (Praça da Aclamação, tel. 75/3425-1716, R$60–90), with 26 rooms that are distributed amongst the town's 18th-century Carmelite convent. Ceilings are cathedral-high, dark wood is in abundance, and the plain decor is bereft of worldly goods. Slightly more hedonistic are the

outdoor pool and an elegant restaurant. It serves a mean *maniçoba*, a heady local stew invented by slaves, the main ingredients of which include sun-dried beef and pork as well as stewed manioc leaves that must be boiled for three days beforehand to expel their natural toxins. If you're cash-strapped, try the simpler **Pousada La Barca** (Rua Inocêncio Boaventura 37, tel. 75/3425-1070, R$50). Just past the convent, its basic, but clean rooms offer nice views over the town. Also on the Praça de Aclamação, **Galeria Pouso da Palavra** (tel. 75/3425-1604) is a welcoming little café/gallery owned by a local poet/journalist. It sells CDs, artwork, and delicious desserts and snacks, which you can eat in the pretty back garden.

Information

There is a **Bahiatursa office** (tel. 75/3245-1214) at Praça da Aclamação where you can get a basic map and information.

Getting There

Santana (tel. 71/3450-4951) provides bus service between Cachoeira from Salvador. Buses, all of which pass through Santo Amaro, leave hourly from Salvador's Rodoviária Central as well as from the Santana office in Rua Lauro de Freitas in Cachoeira. If you're driving, take the BR-324 from Salvador for 60 kilometers (37 miles) until it meets the BA-026 near Santo Amaro. From Santo Amaro follow the BA-026 for 38 kilometers (24 miles) to Cachoeira.

Chapada Diamantina

Traveling due west from Salvador, after a few hours the dry and dusty landscape of the northeastern Sertão region begins to change. Mountains and strange rock formations appear and the vegetation turns surprisingly lush, with an abundance of orchids and bromeliads. The transformation signals the beginning of the Chapada Diamantina (Diamand Plateau), a vast and very ancient geological region filled with canyons and gorges, and crisscrossed by rivers and waterfalls. Much of this unique and spectacular area is preserved as a national park. If you find yourself in Salvador with three days or more to spare, visiting the Chapada Diamantina is an adventure you won't regret.

◖ PARQUE NACIONAL DA CHAPADA DIAMANTINA

The Parque Nacional da Chapada Diamantina is bigger than some countries (Holland, for example) and is one of the most fascinating, not to mention drop-dead gorgeous natural regions in Brazil. Within its borders is the Cachoeira da Fumaça, the highest waterfall (380 meters/1,247 feet) in Brazil (and the fifth highest in the world) as well as Pico dos Barbados (2,000 meters/6,562 feet), the highest peak in Bahia. Grottoes hide lagoons whose waters turn to piercing blue when touched by the sun's fingers. The striking vegetation ranges from giant ferns to the rarest of orchids. And there is always the chance of stumbling upon a tiny chunk of diamond or gold.

Only one paved road cuts through the 152-square-kilometer (59-square-mile) park. There are, however, plenty of trails of varying difficulty—best traveled with a guide or on an excursion—many of which were carved out of the landscape by slaves and gold and diamond miners in the 19th century. One of the main bases for exploring the area is charming Lençóis, a former diamond mining town, which is now a lively mix of locals and ecotourists. Other equally enticing diamond towns and their surrounding areas are also worth exploring, namely Mucugê and Andaraí—both of which offer their own access to several of the park's breathtaking natural attractions. The Chapada can be visited all year long, but in the summer, though the sun can be scorchingly hot, periods of rain (sometimes lasting for several days) can put a serious damper on hiking plans. A better time to come is during the winter, when cooler temperatures (which can become downright chilly at night), coincide with the "dry season" that lasts from March to October.

LENÇÓIS

Lençóis means "sheets" in Portuguese. The name alludes to the town's early 19th-century origins as an itinerant camp for hundreds of avid diamond and gold miners who slept beneath makeshift tents of white cotton fabric after long days spent combing the region's river in search of precious stones. Although many struck it rich, by the end of the 19th century most of the big rocks had been found. Over the next 100 years, the former boom town was abandoned and its population shrank significantly. Lençóis's fortunes only revived in 1985;

CHAPADA DIAMANTINA

Gruta Azul

Gruta da Torrinha

Poço do Diabo

Lapa Doce

MORRO DO PAI INÁCIO

BR 24

To Salvador

Tanquinho

Gruta do Lapão

Cachoeira Primavera   Lençóis

Palmeiras

RA 142

Cachoeira da Fumaça

Rio Santo Antônio

Rio São José

Cachoeira do Sossego

Caeté Açu

Vale do Capão

Barra

Rio Roncador

Marimbus Wetlands

Parque Nacional da Chapada Diamantina

Rio Baiano

Cachoeira do Ramalho

Guiné

Rio Preto

Andaraí   Poço Azul

Igatu

Mucugê   Poço Encantado

SCALE NOT AVAILABLE

© AVALON TRAVEL

a river running through the mountainous landscape of the Parque Nacional da Chapada Diamantina

© MICHAEL SOMMERS

with the creation of the Chapada Diamantina National Park, it quickly became a cultural and touristic hub.

Tourism was a catalyst for the (still ongoing) renovation of Lençóis's more than 200 superb colonial homes and civic buildings. Among the most splendid traces of its former grandeur are the **Igreja Nossa Senhora do Rosário,** the wealthy home of the Sá family, which later became the **Prefeitura** (city hall), and the **Subconsulado Francês,** the former French consulate building. Despite its size and relative isolation, Lençóis possesses a surprisingly cosmopolitan flavor due to the collection of nature lovers, adventure sports enthusiasts, New Age groupies and Chapada-holics who linger and loiter in its cobblestoned streets, buoyed by the fact that the entire Chapada Diamantina is at their feet.

Sights and Recreation

Lençóis is close to many of the Chapada Diamantina's most popular draws. One great walk is to follow the Rio Lençóis. After 15 minutes you'll find yourself at the **Poço Serrano,** a series of freshwater pools where you can dip your toes or entire body and enjoy a panoramic view of the town. Another 15 minutes brings you to the **Salão de Areias Coloridas,** an area with caves carpeted in multicolored sands sought after by local artists who layer them in bottles and sell them to tourists. Hire a local youth as a guide (your hotel can reserve one for you) to take you to these attractions and to the nearby **Cachoeirinha** and **Cachoeira da Primavera,** two small waterfalls where you can swim.

Heading out of town to the southwest (follow the signs), a marked 4-kilometer (2.5-mile) trail leads to the **Escorregadeira,** a natural rock waterslide that sends you careening down into swimming pools (wear shorts to avoid scraping the skin off your bottom).

© MICHAEL SOMMERS

A wild bromeliad is a common sight in the Chapada Diamantina.

If you keep going (with a guide since access is tricky), the trail gets more difficult and involves serious rock climbing. After 8 kilometers (5 miles), however, you'll reach the impressive **Cachoeira do Sossego** waterfall, with rock ledges from which you can dive into a deep pool.

Another challenging 5-kilometer (3-mile) trek (guide recommended) north from Lençóis brings you to the fantastic **Gruta do Lapão,** considered to be the largest sandstone cave in South America.

A car or being part of an organized excursion is necessary to discover some of the more far-flung and dramatic natural highlights of the Chapada. The **Poço do Diabo** (Devil's Well), 20 kilometers (12.5 miles) from Lençóis, consists of a series of swimming pools crowned by a majestic 25-meter (82-foot) waterfall. Only 30 kilometers (19 miles) away is **Morro do Pai Inácio,** a 300-meter-high (984-foot-high) mesa formation that's one of the most striking geological formations you'll lay eyes upon. From its cacti-covered summit, you are treated to amazing 360-degree views of the countryside. According to local legend, Inácio was a fugitive slave who scaled the great rock in search of refuge. When cornered by his pursuers, he jumped from the top. Miraculously, he was saved from a fatal fall by the umbrella he opened in midflight.

Near the town of Iraquara, 80 kilometers (50 miles) from Lençóis, are a number of fascinating caverns, including **Gruta da Torrinha** (Estrada da Bandeira, km 64, one–two-hour guided tours R$20 pp), **Gruta Azul** (Estrada da Bandeira, km 75, R$10 pp), **Lapa Doce** (Estrada da Bandeira, km 68, 45-min. guided tour R$14 pp), and **Gruta da Pratinha** (Estrada da Bandeira, km 75, R$10 pp), all clustered fairly close together. Torrinha and Lapa Doce boast a stunning collection of stalactites and stalagmites. The Gruta Azul (Blue Cavern) more than lives up to its name: When lit up directly by the sun, its waters turn to an unearthly azure. At adjacent Gruta da Pratinha, you can rent gear and flashlights and go snorkeling in an underwater lagoon for R$15.

One of the indisputable highlights of this region is the impressive **Cachoeira da Fumaça,** a waterfall so high that most of its water evaporates to mist before hitting the ground (hence its name of Smoke Waterfall). Looking down upon the Cachoeira da Fumaça from above involves a long 6-kilometer (3.5-mile) hike. Getting right beneath it is even more arduous, involving a three-day trek (with a guide, supplies, and camping gear) through the breathtakingly beautiful **Vale do Capão.**

For further information about any of these sights, check with the tour operators in Lençóis or in Ibama (tel.75/3332-2420), which operates the Parque Nacional da Chapada Diamantina.

Festivals and Events

The two biggest events in Lençóis take place in the winter. Throughout most of mid–late June, the town gets into the swing of things with the typically northeastern **Festas Juninas,** the feverish high point of which is the **Festa de São João** on June 23 and 24. Expect lots of corn-based delicacies, homemade fruit liqueurs, smoking bonfires, processions, and *forró* music. In August, the town resembles a latter-day Woodstock when it hosts the **Festival de Inverno de Lençóis,** a musical festival that lures some of the biggest names in Brazilian popular music.

Accommodations

Lençóis has a wide variety of accommodations to choose from. Given its backpacking ethos, there is no shortage of cheap lodgings. Simple, and downright affordable, the small but quaint **Hostel Chapada** (Rua Boavista 121, tel. 75/3334-1497, www.hostelchapada.com. br, R$35 d), located in a 19th-century house, has only seven rooms and 27 beds, but lots of greenery, swinging hammocks, and laundry facilities—everything a backpacker dreams of. Budget travelers will also feel at home at the welcoming **Pousada dos Duendes** (Rua do Pires, tel. 75/3334-1229, www.pousada-dosduendes.com.br, R$60–70 d). Perched on a hilltop, it offers private and dorm rooms as well as a shady garden for hammock slinging and camping. Vegetarian and vegan meals and lunch boxes are available upon request. Since

the British owner also runs a travel agency, she can help arrange guides and excursions. Also very attractive is **Alcino Atelier Hostalage** (Rua Tomba Surrão 139, tel. 75/3334-1171, www.alcinoestalagem.com, R$60–90 d), located in a lovingly restored colonial house whose exterior is painted a creamy buttermilk color. Although part of the hotel is his atelier, owner and artist Alcino Caetano makes guests feel right at home with cozy rooms carefully decorated with antiques, glazed tiles, and shards of ceramic painted by local artists. Verandas with hammocks, a garden replete with fruit trees, and lavish homemade breakfasts complete the picture.

If you spend your days roughing it in the wilds, come sundown you might feel entitled to some pampering. **Portal Lençóis** (Rua Altina Alves 33, tel. 75/3334-1233, www.portalhoteis. tur.br) is a five-star hotel dedicated to spoiling guests with lots of creature comforts including a pool, sauna, and massage therapy. Its apartments (R$320 d) and chalets (R$480 d) are sophisticatedly rustic (or vice-versa) with lots of wood and stonework that blend into the surrounding vegetation. Its privileged hilltop location involves a bit of a climb, but the result is magnificent views.

Also ingeniously integrated into its natural surroundings is the ◖ **Canto das Águas** (Av. Senhor dos Passos 1, tel. 75/3334-1154, www. lencois.com.br, R$205–325 d). A river literally runs right through it, providing the gardens, pool, and restaurant (breakfast is out of this world) with a constantly soothing soundtrack of cascading water. More intimate and affordable, not to mention holistic and harmonious, is the lovely **Pousada Vila Serrano Pousada** (Alto do Bomfim 8, tel. 75/3334-1486, www. vilaserrano.com.br, R$150). Its nine apartments, designed according to the rules of feng shui, emphasize soothing colors, natural textures, soft lighting, and a fusion between indoor and outdoor environments.

Food

Considering the global tribes that pass through and settle down in Lençóis, the astonishing mix of (good) eating options is hardly surprising. The traditional **Neco's Bar** (Praça Clarim Pacheco 15, tel. 75/3334-1179, noon–10 P.M. daily, R$12–18) is reputed for regional specialties such as roasted goat, *godó* (a stew of green bananas and sun-dried beef), *cortado de palma* (diced cactus with ground beef), and a salad of *batata-da-serra,* a local potato found only in the Chapada. Reserving your meal in advance is necessary. To stock up on proteins, head for the lively **Picanha na Praça** (Praça Otaviano Alves 62, tel. 75/3334-1080, 11 A.M.–10 P.M. daily, R$15–20), where the prime cuts of beef and chicken served on sizzling grills will satisfy the most carnivorous urges. Vegetarians also have several options, among them **Gaia Lanchonete Natural** (Praça Horácio de Mattos 114, open daily, R$6–12), which is great for invigorating juices, copious sandwiches, and *"kit lanches";* highly nutritious box lunches that will give you an energy boost when you're out on the trail.

The menu at **O Beco da Coruja** (Rua do Rosário 172, tel. 75/3334-1652, lunch and dinner daily, R$12–18) includes delicious Argentinean tortillas, vegetable tarts, and salads. Another light option is a crisp and flavorful pizza prepared at **Pizza na Pedra** (Av. Senhor dos Passos, tel. 75/3334-1475, dinner only, R$15–25). Toppings include Chilean mushrooms, palma (cactus), and semi-sun-dried tomatoes. Also renowned for Italian specialties is **Os Artistas da Massa** (Rua da Baderna 49, tel. 75/3334-1886, lunch and dinner daily, R$18–30). The fresh, homemade pastas, gnocchis, and lasagnas are as addictive as the cozy ambiance, with jazz wafting through the air. More eclectic is **Cozinha Aberta** (Rua da Baderna 111, tel. 75/3334-1066, 1–10:30 P.M. daily, R$18–30), where an open kitchen allows diners to watch the preparation of colorful dishes that draw on Thai, Indian, and Mediterranean cuisines. To satisfy more refined cravings, such as hankerings for filet mignon in roquefort sauce with black-eyed beans, head to the recently opened **La Pergola** (Praça do Rosário 70, tel. 75/3334-1241, noon–4 P.M. and 6–11 P.M. daily, R$20–35), a French restaurant with tables set amidst a beautiful garden.

Information and Services

There is a tourist information center in the old market on Praça dos Nagôs (tel. 75/3334-1112), and you can also visit the **Associação dos Condutores de Visitantes de Lençóis** (Rua 10 de Dezembro 22, tel. 75/3334-1425, 7:30 A.M.–10 P.M. daily) for information and hiring guides. You can also check out www.guialencois.com, a website in Portuguese with up-to-date events and listings, as well as www.guiachapadadiamantina.com.br, also in Portuguese, which offers information about the entire Chapada region.

Lençóis is brimming with ecotourism agencies that organize excursions and hire out guides. **Adrenalina** (Rua das Pedras 121, tel. 75/3334-1689) specializes in activities such as canyoneering, mountain climbing, cave jumping, rappelling, and trekking. **Marimbus Ecoturismo** (Praça Otaviano Alves, tel. 75/3334-1292, www.marimbus.com) and **Lentur** (Av. Sete de Setembro 10, tel. 75/3334-1271, www.lentur.com.br) are two ecotourism agencies with solid reputations and plenty of excursions and activities. If you want to hire an independent guide, a great source is American expat Roy Funch, founder of the **Fundação Chapada Diamantina** (Rua Pé de Ladeira 212, tel. 75/3334-1305), who knows the area like the back of his hand.

To rent mountain bikes, obtain biking routes, or take a biking excursion, consult **Rony Aleixo Cicloturismo** (Rua do Lagedo 68, tel. 75/334-1700, www.ronybikes.com.).

There's a **Banco do Brasil** at Praça Horácio de Mattos with ATMs that accept international cards. In the same square, Café.com has Internet access.

Getting There and Around

From Salvador, you can fly to **Aeroporto Coronel Horácio de Matos** (tel. 75/3625-8100), 20 kilometers (12.5 miles) from Lençóis. From Salvador's Rodoviária Central, two daily buses depart regularly at 7:30 A.M. and 11:30 P.M. with the **Real Expresso** (tel. 071/3246-8355, www.realexpresso.com.br) bus company (a six-hour trip). Extra buses

BAHIA

are added during high season. If you're driving take the BR-324 until Feira de Santana, then you can choose between taking the BR-116 until it meets the BR-242 or taking the BA-052 until Ipirá, following the BA-488 until Itaberaba. From this point on, both ways follow the BR-242. Whichever route you choose, driving to Lençóis is not for the faint of heart. The roads are often full of potholes and slow-moving trucks.

MUCUGÊ

Smaller and less touristy than Lençóis, Mucugê (named after a native fruit used to make a terrific local liqueur) is another attractive colonial diamond mining town with its share of nearby natural attractions. Aside from pretty 19th-century buildings such as the **Prefeitura** (city hall) and the **Igreja de Santa Isabel,** it possesses the extremely unusual **Cimitério Bizantino.** Built in 1855, following an outbreak of cholera, the haunting ensemble of snow-white gravestones and monuments of this windswept hillside cemetery does indeed bear a striking resemblance to Byzantine architecture.

Sights and Recreation

Situated right in the heart of the Chapada, Mucugê is at close proximity to numerous natural attractions. Only 5 kilometers (3 miles) away is the **Parque Municipal do Mucugê** (access via BA-142, direction Andaraí, tel. 75/3338-2156, 8:30 A.M.–5:30 P.M. daily, R$3), a research and cultivation center that doubles as a wildlife reserve. Relatively short and easy trails lead to the waterfalls of Piabinhas, Tiburtino, and Andorinhas (the furthest away at an hour), all with natural pools for bathing. Also within 15 kilometers (9 miles) of Mucugê are more waterfalls—Cardoso, Córrego de Pedra (which only flows during the rainy season), Sibéria, and Martinha—all worthy of whiling away a few hours.

Festivals and Events

Mucugê is reputed for its vibrant **Festa de São João** (June 23–24) festivities, which include smoky bonfires in the streets, neighbors serving homemade fruit liqueurs from their homes, lots of *forró* music, and dancing from dusk till dawn. Book accommodations in advance and bundle up since the longest night of the year can get chilly.

Accommodations and Food

The nicest place to stay in Mucugê is the **Pousada Mucugê** (Rua Dr. Rodrigues Lima 30, tel. 75/3338-2210, www.pousadamucuge. com.br, R$95 d). Well-equipped rooms occupy a restored 19th-century mansion in the center of town. The reputed restaurant serves local specialties such as *godó,* a stew made with green bananas and sun-dried beef and *cortado de palma,* in which ground beef is mixed with chunks of steamed cactus. Cheaper and more rustic with lots of original stonework is the **Pousada Pé de Serra** (Rua José Alves Campos 33, tel. 75/3338-2066, R$50–80). For delicious home-cooking and regional specialties, try **Dona Nena** (Rua Direita 140, tel. 75/3338-2143, 11:30 A.M.–8:30 P.M. daily, R$10–18) and **Pé de Salsa** (Rua Cel. Propércio, tel. 75/3338-2290, 11:30 A.M.–2:30 P.M. and 6–10:30 P.M. daily, R$8–15).

Information and Services

To book tour guides visit the **Associação dos Condutores de Visitantes de Mucugê** (Rua Cel. Douca Medrado 71, tel. 75/3338-2414, 8 A.M.–noon and 2–9 P.M. daily), whose building also houses the tourist information center (tel. 75/3338-2255). **Km Viagens e Turismo** (Rua Cel. Douca Medrado 126, tel. 75/3338-2152, 8 A.M.–8 P.M. daily) offers guides as well as taxis and rental cars and motorcycles. **Terra Chapada** (Rua Doutor Rodrigues Lima, tel. 75/3338-2284, www.terrachapada.com.br, 8 A.M.–noon and 3–9 P.M. daily) is a travel agent that can put you in touch with guides and arrange excursions.

Getting There and Around

From Salvador, **Águia Branca** (tel. 71/4004-1010, www.aguiabranca.com.br) provides bus service to Mucugê, passing through Andaraí. The trip takes about eight hours. Driving from

Salvador, take the BR-324 to Feira de Santana, then the BR-242 to the town of Itaberaba, where the BA-142 leads to Andaraí and then continues another 50 kilometers (31 miles) to Mucugê.

ANDARAÍ

Between Lençóis and Mucugê, pastel-hued Andaraí is scruffier and more dilapidated than the other two diamond towns, but it is surrounded by its share of fantastic natural sights and is the easiest way to get to Xique Xique de Igatú, a formerly grandiose diamond mining town now reduced to a tiny, but terribly charming mountain village, only 5 kilometers (3 miles) away.

Sights and Recreation

Andaraí is a great point of departure for many of the Chapada Diamantina's star attractions. On the eastern edge of the Sincorá mountain chain, it is perfectly situated for those who want to go trekking through the **Vale do Paty.** It is also less than 10 kilometers from **Marimbus,** a swamp-like ecosystem created by the Rio Santo Antônio, brimming with exotic birds and wildlife such as anteaters, pacas, and giant *sucuri* snakes that measure up to 10 meters (33 feet). The best way to get around the area is by hiring a guide with a canoe and then gliding through the waters adorned with oversized *Victoria amazonica* lily pads and giant water ferns. A few kilometers outside of town is the **Cachoeira de Ramalho** (a medium-to-difficult trek along an ancient miner's trail), surrounded by natural pools. Further afield (20 kilometers/12.5 miles) is the **Cachoeira do Roncador,** featuring pools sculpted out of rose quartz (reached after an easy hike). Meanwhile, 40 kilometers (25 miles) from Andaraí, the not-to-be missed **Poço Encantado** is a subterranean lake, which when illuminated by sunlight (in the morning) lives up to its name by being truly "enchanting."

Accommodations and Food

The **Pousada Sincorá** (Av. Paraguassu 120, tel. 75/3335-2210, www.sincora.com.br, R$80 d) is a warm and appealingly decorated old house that is rightly proud of its hearty "colonial" breakfasts. For light food and especially the delicious homemade ice-cream, visit the **Sorveteria Apollo** (Praça Raul Dantas 1, tel. 75/3335-2256).

Information

For guides and tourist information, contact the **Associação dos Condutores de Visitantes de Andaraí** (Rua Dr. José Gonçalves Cincorá, tel. 75/3335-2225, 8 A.M.–noon and 2–5 P.M. daily).

Getting There

Andaraí is about 100 kilometers (62 miles) from Lençóis (to the north, via the BR-242 and BA-142) and around 50 kilometers (31 miles) from Mucugê (to the south along the BR-142). From Salvador's Rodoviária Central, **Águia Branca** (tel. 71/4004-1010, www.aguiabranca.com.br) provides bus service to Andaraí. The trip takes about seven hours. Driving from Salvador, take the BR-324 to Feira de Santana, then the BR-242 to the town of Itaberaba, where the BA-142 leads to Andaraí.

IGATU

During the 19th-century diamond rush, thriving Igatu had a population in the thousands. These days it's a small village of 350 where Flintstone-like stone houses alternate with pretty pastel villas, all of which are surrounded by the lush fruit and vegetable gardens that supply much of the local produce. As for the splendor of its past, it has been reduced to a bewitchingly haunted area of ruined stone mansions overgrown with mango trees and wild orchids, where from time to time, an uncovered shard of fine European china evokes the grandeur that was Igatu in its heyday.

Sights

The **Galeria Arte & Memória** (Rua Luís dos Santos, tel. 75/3335-2510, 10 A.M.–6 P.M. daily) exhibits found objects as well as contemporary art work by regional artists inside a beautiful space, built upon the ruins of a stone house. As for the town's diamond legacy, you can tour the nearby **Mina Brejo-Verruga** (7 A.M.–7 P.M. daily, R$3), the biggest mine in the region, where, helmeted and armed with a flashlight, you can snake your way through a hand-dug tunnel stretching 400 meters into the side of a mountain. The return to daylight will be a shock, which you can alleviate by a swim in the **Poço do Brejo.**

Accommodations and Food

If you decide to stay overnight in Igatu, the best *pousada* is the lovely and very comfortable **Pousada Pedras de Igatu** (Rua São Sebastião, tel. 75/3335-2281, R$80–100), which has a swimming pool and terrific views of the surrounding countryside. However, if you want a really authentic experience, ask around for rooms to rent with locals, many of whom will also cook local specialties for you on their wood stoves, using the produce grown in their gardens.

Getting There

Igatu can only be reached by a rocky trail that turns off the BA-142 from Mucugê or from Andaraí. In either case, you'll need a four-wheel-drive or the stamina required for a couple hours of uphill hiking. However, when you arrive at this remote town suspended in the mountains, you'll be more than compensated for the hardships of the journey.

The Southern Coast

The Bahian coast leading south from Salvador to the border of the state of Espírito Santo is the longest coastline—and one of the most downright beautiful—in Brazil. Beaches, beaches, and more beaches are the big draw. Whether you like them hip and happening, remote and Robinson Crusoe-worthy, or somewhere in between, you will not be disappointed. From the party scenes of Porto Seguro and Morro de São Paulo, passing through the drowsy colonial charms of Ilhéus and Caravelas, to the utter sensation of being *Lost* in Paradise provoked by the likes of Caraíva, reserve a week (or two), stock up on SPF60, and start exploring.

MORRO DE SÃO PAULO

For over 20 years, this tiny fishing village on the Ilha de Tinharé has been the most popular destination along the Dendê Coast—named after the *dendê* palm, whose fruit produces the amber-colored oil used in traditional Bahian cooking—which stretches from Valença south to Itacaré. During the summer, in particular, it is mobbed by sand and sun worshippers from all over the planet. At these times, "Morro" (as it is called) is party central—a crush of tanned young bodies frolic all day and night among the bars and beaches of the tiny colonial settlement. Fortunately, if this isn't your scene, you don't have to completely give up on Morro de São Paulo. In off-season, especially during the week, it's possible to surrender to the simpler pleasures offered by swaths of native Atlantic forest, coral reefs, and warm turquoise ocean pools. The fact that no cars are present (the primary source of transportation is the wheelbarrow) is a big plus.

Beaches

Aside from the village itself, with its atmospheric 17th-century ruined fortress and 19th-century lighthouse, "Morro" consists of a quartet of nameless but utterly distinctive numbered beaches. Think of **Primeira Praia** (First Beach)—where most of the locals hang out—as a warm-up beach to whet your appetite for what's to come. **Segunda Praia** (Second Beach), packed with *pousadas,* restaurants, clubs, and beach bars is downright urban, but it also has the best swimming and snorkeling. By day, it's full of hip young things knocking around soccer balls, volleyballs, and frescoballs, whereas when night falls, the raves and luaus begin. **Terceira Praia** (Third Beach) is somewhat more tranquil and has some of the best water for diving. Last, but certainly not least, **Quarta**

Praia (Fourth Beach) is the best preserved (and most gorgeous) of them all. Consequently, it's a little more secluded and upscale, with posh but private resorts and restaurants.

Sports and Recreation

From Morro de São Paulo, you can take boat trips around Tinharé island, with stops at the offshore reefs of **Garapuá** and **Moreré,** the beaches of **Tassimirim** and **Cueira,** and the villages of **Boipeba** and **Cairu.** All destinations offer ample opportunities for swimming, snorkeling and then refueling with fresh seafood. An easy hike leads to the pretty village of **Gamboa,** from where you can easily reach the **Fonte do Ceu** waterfall. The trail passes by cliffs of colored clay where you can give yourself a purifying facial—or rather, "clacial." Another highlight is diving in the clear shallow waters off Primeira and Terceira Praias, which you can do by day or night. For more information, contact **Companhia de Mergulho** (Primeira Praia, tel. 75/3652-1200, www.ciadomergulho.com.br) and **Tinharé Dive Club** (Terceira Praia, tel. 75/3652-1573).

Accommodations

Though there's no shortage of accommodations on Morro de São Paulo, be aware that high-season prices are much steeper than off-season. Rates listed are for the off-season. Although Morro is famed for its beaches, you'd be forgiven for trading an ocean view for one of the fetching rooms at **Pousada O Casarão** (Praça Aureliano Lima 190, tel. 75/3652-1022, www.ocasarao.net), located in the village. Choose from one of six rooms (R$170 d) in the early-17th-century main house (where Emperor Dom Pedro II reputedly stayed) or from one of the ten exotically decorated bungalows (R$200 d) set amidst a lush green garden with a swimming pool. **Pousada Aquarela** (Rua Porto de Cima, tel. 75/3652-1202, www.pousadadoaquarela.com.br, R$80–130 d) is simpler, but the rooms are brighter and breezier. Built upon a verdant hillside, it offers guests the luxury of panoramic views from their verandas. If you want to be right in the middle of all the action

on Segunda Praia, **Pousada Villa das Pedras** (tel. 75/3652-1075, www.villadaspedras.com.br, R$160–220 d) is surrounded by boutiques and bars. Its rooms are well equipped and comfortable, though fairly minimalist. The more expensive ones boast sea views. On Terceira Praia, it's hard not to be seduced by the laid-back vibe given off by **Hotel Fazenda Vila Guaiamu** (tel. 75/3652-1035, www.vilaguaiamu.com.br, R$210–240 d, closed in May and June). Seven whitewashed chalets scattered amidst rustling coconut palms are home to 22 light-filled rooms. The conspiracy to relax includes a massage and yoga room on the premises.

The most secluded and upscale hotels are on the 2-kilometer-long (1.2-mile-long) Quarta Praia, among them **Porto do Zimbo Small Resort** (tel. 75/3652-2030, www.hotelportodozimbo.com.br, R$350–590 d). Though neither luxurious nor terribly stylish, this 16-room hotel in the midst of a former coconut plantation—and right in front of inviting natural ocean pools—offers lots of creature comforts at a very affordable price. Moreover, its eco-policies—recycling all materials (with profits going to the staff)—are admirable. For an even more remote locale, walk another few kilometers to **Praia do Encanto,** where the **❰ Anima Hotel** (tel. 75/3652-2077, www.animahotel.com, R$210–240 d) was the first hotel to be built, in 2005, on this utterly dreamy "Fifth Beach." Its nine seductive and fully equipped eco-chalets are the epitome of back-to-nature chic. The only drawback is you might get to feeling a little isolated. On the upside, the hotel offers snorkel masks and binoculars so that you can commune with the exotic fish and birds sharing your ecosystem.

Food

During the day, food options, aside from hotel offerings, are mostly geared towards classic Bahian beach fare, such as the fried fish, crab, shrimp, and *moquecas* that are served at the many *barracas*. For some of the best fish and seafood dishes around, on trendy Segunda Praia try **Club do Balanço** (10 A.M.–7 P.M.

daily, 10 A.M.–midnight daily Jan., Feb., and July, R$8–15). Meanwhile, fans of Quarta Praia swear by **Bar das Piscinas** (9 A.M.–10 P.M.) and **Pimenta Rosa** (10 A.M.–6 P.M. daily, closed June).

At night, culinary pleasures are taken more seriously. For both lunch and dinner, **Sabor da Terra** (tel. 75/3652-1156), on the town's main drag, the Caminho da Praia, beckons with its wide veranda perfect for people-watching. Both Sabor and neighboring **Restaurante Tinharé** (tel. 75/3652-1161) serve well-seasoned Bahian fish and seafood dishes such as *moqueca* and *bobó de camarão*. The wafting scent of freshly baked pizza emerging from a wood oven will lure you to **Restaurante e Pizzaria Bianco e Nero** (Caminho da Paraia, tel. 075/3652-1097, open daily for lunch and dinner, closed Mon. for lunch). For the perfect finishing touch, stop by **Dona Bárbara's** sweet stand (in front of Sabor da Terra), and stock up on homemade goodies such as *brigadeiro, cocadas,* and *quejadinhas.*

Information
There is a **tourist office** at Praça Aureliano Lima (tel. 75/3652-1104, www.morrosp.com. br). You can also check out the bilingual website www.morrodesaopaulobrasil.com.br. Although there are no banks, many places accept credit cards.

Getting There and Around
There are many options for getting to Morro de São Paulo. Both catamarans (3–4 hours) and *lanchas rápidas* (speedboats, which take 2 hours but are more expensive) leave daily from Salvador's Terminal Marítimo in front of the Mercado Modelo. The trip is very scenic, but the ocean can be quite choppy: contact **Catamarã Biotur** (tel. 75/3641-3327 or Salvador tel. 71/3326-7674), **Catamarã Gamboa do Morro** (tel. 75/3641-3327 or Salvador tel. 71/3326-7674), or the Terminal Marítimo (tel. 71/3319-2890). From Salvador, you can also take a small eight-seater plane. Flights take 20 minutes. Contact **Addey Taxi Aéreo** (tel. 75/3652-1242 or Salvador tel. 71/3772-2451), **Aerostar**

Táxi Aéreo (tel. 75/3652-1312), or the Salvador airport (tel. 71/3204-1010) for more information. **Águia Branca** (tel. 71/4004-1010, www. aguiabranca.com.br) and **São Geraldo** (tel. 0800/311-312, www.saogeraldo.com.br) both provide bus service from Salvador to the nearby town of Valença, where many boats make the 20-minute trip.

ILHA DE BOIPEBA
Although only the Rio do Inferno (River of Hell) separates Ilha de Boipeba from the Ilha do Tinharé, where Morro de São Paulo is located, Boipeba is Morro de São Paulo as it was 20 years ago before an influx of tourism blew everything out of proportion. Its beautiful unspoiled beaches are framed by lush jungle and crisscrossed by warm rivers that are ideal for bathing. Although Boipeba is becoming a hip beach resort for those in the know, it has managed to retain a bucolic tranquility along with some 20 kilometers (12 miles) of stunning white-sand beaches protected by coral reefs. The most "developed"—which, thankfully, isn't saying much—is **Boca da Barra.** Here you'll find lots of *barracas* where you can dig into fresh fish and seafood. A half-hour walk brings you to the dazzling white sands of **Tassimirim,** followed by the blissfully deserted **Praia de Cueira**—both of which are ideal for snorkeling. From here, you can keep going for another three hours of the same maritime nirvana to **Ponta dos Castelhanos,** a great diving destination.

Festivals and Events
In early June, the **Festa do Glorioso Divino Espírito Santo** marks three days of celebrations in honor of the island's patron saint. If the idea of *forró* in paradise appeals to you, make a point to show up.

Accommodations and Food
The charming settlement of **Velha Boipeba,** whose epicenter is the 17th- century Igreja do Divino Espírito Santo, offers both simple and more sophisticated accommodations for visitors, as does **Moreré,** a tiny fishing village an

hour away. One of the nicest options in Velha Boipeba is the inviting ◖ **Pousada Santa Clara** (tel. 75/3653-6085, www.santaclara-boipeba.com, R$100–150 d). Owned by two American brothers, it offers 11 bright, minimalist rooms set amidst a lush tropical garden. One of the brothers, Mark, is the culinary genius behind the enticing **Restaurante Santa Clara.** He plans each day's dinner options based on the fresh catch (lobster, shrimp, fish) available and his internationally inspired creative urges.

The spell cast by the **Pousada Vila Sereia** (tel. 75/3653-6045, www.amabo.org.br/br/vilasereia.html, R$190–250) is conducive to romance. Its four private, yet roomy palm-thatched bungalows, situated right on Boca da Barra beach, make for an idyllic getaway. The attentive service includes breakfasts served on your balcony—manioc couscous with coconut milk, homemade jams, and fresh fruits. Although Boipeba is already pretty remote, for complete isolation, nothing beats staying on your own island with a private beach. This is what's in store for guests of the **Pousada Maliale** (tel. 75/3653-6134, www.pousada-maliale.com.br, R$130–180, closed in May). Its 16 spacious and well-equipped rooms are located on São Miguel, a small island in the middle of the Rio do Inferno, a mere five-minute boat ride from Boca da Barra beach. Cheaper and more basic *pousadas* are located in Moreré, as is the ◖ **Restaurante Mar e Coco** (tel. 75/3653-6013, 10 A.M.–5 P.M. daily, call in advance in off-season), which is famed for menu items such as succulent shrimp *moquecas* served with *banana-da-terra* and baked lobster with pesto, as well as for its inviting hammocks, where you can indulge in a post-luncheon siesta.

Information

Many hotels can organize guides or trips for you, including activities such as canoeing, horseback riding, taking nature walks through the Atlantic forest, or snorkeling in the tidal pools. For more information, consult the local **Association of Residents and Friends of Boipeba** (Rua Comendador Madureira, www.amabo.org.br).

Getting There

Difficult access to Boipeba has helped keep the tourist crush at bay. From Valença you can take a boat directly (3.5 hours) or take a bus to the town of Torrinhas and then board a ferry for Boipeba (1.5 hours), which stops in the colonial town of Cairu. From Morro de São Paulo, tour operators can organize trips by boat or Jeep to Boipeba.

PENÍNSULA DE MARAÚ

This peninsula, squeezed between the Bay of Camamu and the open Atlantic, is a region of great natural beauty composed of beaches, islands, rivers, lagoons, dunes, and mangrove swamps. The easiest way to explore the area is by traveling to the mainland city of Camamu, 330 kilometers (205 miles) south of Salvador, and then taking a boat across the Bay of Camamu to the fishing village and main resort town of Barra Grande.

◖ Barra Grande

Despite the increase of *pousadas*, restaurants, and trendy young vacationers from Rio, São Paulo, and Minas Gerais who flock here in the summer for some hippie-flavored R&R, this utterly relaxing fishing village, with its main drag of soft sand leading down to the fluffy sand beaches, is still deliciously unspoiled. Barra Grande is a great place to unwind as well as explore Brazil's third largest bay (after Salvador's Baía de Todos os Santos and Rio's Guanabara). From the town, you can wander endlessly along the coast—enjoying the bay's calm beaches backed by thick mangroves and bisected by lazy rivers as well as the palm-shaded white sands that embrace the open sea.

Sports and Recreation

There are two ways to explore the Baía de Camamu: by land or sea. In the absence of paved roads, the former involves walking or catching a ride with a dune buggy or four-wheel-drive open truck. Highlights include **Praia de Taipu de Fora,** a stunning beach where you can snorkel in pools of vivid blue water, **Morro do Farol de Taipu,** a lush hilltop with panoramic views and terrific sunset-watching, and **Lagoa de Cassange,** a freshwater lake in the midst of Sahara-like dunes. An equally unforgettable experience is taking a boat trip around the bay with stops at many islands. Excursions usually leave early in the morning.

Accommodations

In Barra Grande, there are many choices for lodgings. For a great location with access to the beach and the village, try **Pousada Tubarão** (tel. 73/3258-6006, pousadadotubarao@bol.com.br, R$75–150 d), which is simple and friendly. Its casual restaurant offers delicious fare such as grilled fish and shrimp and lobster risotto. An added bonus is the possibility of savoring them at a table in the tropical garden or on the sandy beach. Around 100 meters (330 feet) from town, as you walk left along the beach from the pier, is the fairly primitive **Pousada Camping Lagosta Azul** (tel. 73/3258-6144, R$35–75, camping R$5–10 per night). Completely immersed in soft sand and tropical foliage, it offers nine basic rooms and a big sandy garden where you're free to pitch a tent. Its restaurant does justice to its name by serving up lobster (*lagosta*) as well as other seafood.

For total luxury—and seclusion to boot—it's hard to one-up the understated tropical chic of **Kiaroa Eco-Luxury Resort** (tel. 73/3258-6212, www.kiaroa.com.br, R$988 d per apartment), which is definitely worth the splurge. Prices include three gourmet meals a day and nonalcoholic drinks (that's a lot of fresh fruit juice and coconut water). If you stay for five days, your transportation to and from Salvador is provided via micro plane to the resort's private airfield. The resort is on Praia de Bombaça, a gorgeously deserted stretch of beach between Barra Grande and Taipus de Fora; you might feel a little isolated, but then again, with creature comforts ranging from saunas and whirlpools to a 24-hour gourmet kitchen, you won't suffer too much.

Food

Near the main square, **A Tapera** (tel. 75/3258-6119, 1–10 P.M. daily Sept.–Feb., 1–10 P.M. Wed.–Mon. Mar.–Oct., closed May) is a favorite for fish and a delicious squid *moqueca*. Scrumptious pizza and other freshly made Italian dishes are served at **Pinocchio** (Praça do Tamarindo, tel. 73/3258-6258, dinner), whose outdoor candlelit tables are spread beneath an enormous tamarind tree. At Taipu de Fora beach, the **Bar do Francês** (open daily, 7 A.M.–midnight in summer, 7 A.M.–5 P.M. in winter) beckons with mats of woven palm fibers and pillows upon which you can curl up under the shade of a palm tree. Thus protected from the noonday sun, nibble at tasty appetizers and down cocktails to your heart's content.

Information

For information in English, www.barra-grande.net is a great site with lots of listings and maps.

Getting There

The easiest, but longest, way to get to Barra Grande is to take one of the frequent ferries or catamarans from Salvador's Terminal Marítimo de São Joaquim (Av. Oscar Pontes 105, Calçada, tel. 71/3254-1020) to Bom Despacho on the Ilha da Itaparica. Right where the ferry docks, there is a bus station where companies such as **Águia Branca** (tel. 71/4004-1010, www.aguiabranca.com.br) have several buses a day to Camamu (3 hours). Upon arrival in Camamu, there are a few options. You can take the rapid and more expensive *lanchas* (speedboats that take roughly 40 minutes) or regular motor boats that make the scenic trip across Baía de Camamu to Barra Grande in 90 minutes. It is also possible to reach Barra Grande by land, going north along a dirt road from Itacaré. This requires chartering a Jeep or other four-wheel-drive vehicle, which is expensive, not to mention slow-going.

ITACARÉ

Until 1998, when a paved highway opened up access to Itacaré from Ilhéus, 70 kilometers (43 miles) to the south, Itacaré was a remote fishing village straddling the mouth of the Rio de Contas. Its stunning beaches backed by native Atlantic forest were a well-guarded secret known to only a few hardcore surfers and getaway artists. Since then, the secret has gotten out and Itacaré has become one of the biggest "It" beaches on the Bahian coast—it draws nature lovers, adventure sports enthusiasts, and revelers from all over Brazil and the globe.

Beaches

Unlike other parts of the Bahian coast, Itacaré's 15 pristine beaches are set off by dramatic hillsides carpeted in lush green vegetation. Many—such as the "urban" beaches of **Resende, Tiririca,** and **do Costa**—are only a few hundred meters walk from Itacaré's center. Those closest to town—especially the nerve center that is **Praia da Concha**—can get pretty crowded in the summer, littered as they are with *pousadas* and bars playing trance-inducing electronic music. However, the further away you get, the more wonderfully deserted the beaches become. In fact, hiking—often up and downhill through virgin forest—to the best of the these *praias de fora* (outer beaches) is part of the unique Itacaré experience. In a few cases, the trails leading to the loveliest beaches pass through private property and you'll be charged a small access fee.

Itacaré has some of the finest waves in the Brazilian Northeast. Surfers will go gaga over **Prainha** (3 kilometers/2 miles) and its neighbors, **Praia São José** (6 kilometers/3.5 miles) and **Praia Jeribucaçu,** as well as the particularly beautiful **Praia Havaizinho** and **Praia de Engenhoca** (roughly 12 kilometers/7.5 miles) from town. If you don't want complete seclusion, **Itacarezinho,**15 kilometers (9 miles) away, and accessible by bus, has a sprinkling of beach *barracas* where you can kick back with a *caipirinha* and refresh yourself in the sparkling freshwater pool formed by the Tijuípe waterfall.

Sports and Recreation

Landlubbers will appreciate Itacaré as much as water rats. Aside from rafting down the Rio de Contas, you can also go canyoneering and tree-trekking, and practice rappelling at the Noré waterfall. Less adventurous souls can rent a canoe and go paddling through the coastal mangrove swamps. You can also explore the area by horseback or mountain bike. Many hotels organize excursions and ecotourism agencies abound, among them: **Ativa Rafting** (Rua Pé da Pancada, tel. 73/3696-2219, www.ativarafting.com.br), **Itacaré Ecoturismo** (Rua Lodônio Almeida 117, tel. 73/3251-3666, www.itacare-ecotour.com.br) and **Caminho da Terra** (Praça Santos Dumont 51, tel. 73/3251-3053, www.caminhodaterra.com.br).

Accommodations

Since the paved highway opened, Itacaré has been flooded with *pousadas*—with everything ranging from backpackers' refuges to tropically chic eco-resorts. In the summertime, price increases are the norm and it's wise to reserve in advance. Prices listed are for the off-season. Some of the most inexpensive options—and also those closest to the action—are near Praia da Concha. **Pousada Jardim Zen** (Condomínio Conchas do Mar, Rua C 15, tel. 73/3251-2109, www.pousadajardimzen.blogspot.com, R$60 d) offers a motel-like strip of seven basic, but tidy rooms with ceiling fans and hammocks, in a tranquil garden setting that's only a quick walk from the beach. Although it's also close to the beach, you'll feel more like Tarzan or Jane of the jungle if you check into **Pousada da Lua** (tel. 73/3251-2209, www.pousadadalua.com, R$100–150 d). Appealingly rustic bungalow apartments and individual chalets are set amidst a dense tangle of fragrant native Atlantic forest, offering ample tranquility (aside from the atmospheric bird calls and monkey cries). Breakfasts are Zen affairs accompanied by mood music and burning incense.

Around 2 kilometers (1.2 miles) from town, a favorite with the international crowd is **(Pousada Sage Point** (tel. 73/3251-2030, www.pousadasagepoint.com.br, R$229–339 d). On a jungly hilltop overlooking beautiful Praia de Tiririca, precious woods dominate the architecture of the 17 tastefully decorated rooms, which integrate harmoniously with the exuberant natural surroundings. Lavish tropical breakfasts are served on your private veranda or at the beachfront restaurant. If you want to live it up and wind down at the same time, you won't do better than the luxurious (**Txai Resort** (tel. 73/2101-5000, www.txai. com.br, R$875–1,050 d). Located 16 kilometers (10 miles) from Itacaré, in the direction of Ilhéus, the rambling palmy grounds of this former cocoa plantation gaze onto the white sands of Itacarezinho beach. Its 40 spacious bungalows and creatively decorated main lounges merge traditional architecture and organic materials with understated luxury whose soothing effects should be immediate. For relaxation reinforcement, yoga classes, massages, and alternative healing therapies are available.

Food

There's lots of fish and seafood to be had at Itacaré's restaurants. **O Restaurante** (Rua Pedro Longo 170, tel. 73/3251-2012, 11 A.M.–midnight daily, R$15–25) is a good pick for Bahian specialties in a colorful setting. Standouts include traditional fish *moqueca* with *banana da terra,* octopus risotto, and more unconventional dishes such as fish with grilled eggplant in cream sauce. For a more contemporary twist on local fare, with Asian influences, savor the likes of grilled jumbo shrimp caramelized with ginger and lime at the warmly inviting **Casa Sapucaia** (Rua Lodônia Almeida 84, tel. 73/3251-3091, 7–11:30 P.M. Mon.–Sat., R$15–25). Daring culinary creativity is the norm at (**Dedo de Moça** (3372, 4 P.M.–midnight high season, 7–11 P.M., low season, open daily, closed in May, R$18–28). Chef Vagner Aguiar experiments with Brazilian ingredients and spices such as cloves and cinnamon to whip up dishes such as grilled fresh fish with pineapple-mango compote or a version of shrimp bobó with coconut rice, served in a pared-down yet welcoming ambiance. Ever popular, especially with the young backpacker/surfer crowd, is **Boca de Forno** (Rua Lodônia Almeida 108, tel. 73/3251-3121, 5 P.M.–midnight Mon.–Thurs., 5 P.M.–1 A.M. Fri.–Sun., R$12–22) whose crispy, thin-crust pizzas are irresistible. Try the namesake house specialty,

with toppings that include heart of palm, sausage, sun-dried tomato, and roasted garlic.

Information

Itacaré has no tourist office, but it does have a terrific bilingual English/Portuguese website, www.itacare.com.

Getting There

Itacaré is 70 kilometers (43 miles) north of Ilhéus along the BA-001 highway. Ilhéus's airport receives daily flights from Salvador, Porto Seguro, and São Paulo. Numerous buses connect the two towns on a daily basis. The trip takes roughly 90 minutes and the *rodoviária* (bus station, tel. 73/3251-2200) is only a short distance from the center. It's also possible to reach Itacaré from Barra Grande, 55 kilometers (34 miles) to the north, via the BA-654. However, to date, this dirt road is in precarious condition and can only be navigated by four-wheel-drive. During high season, tourist agencies in both Itacaré and Barra Grande operate excursions between the two towns.

ILHÉUS

The lazy, welcoming town of Ilhéus is the main city along what is known as Brazil's "Cocoa Coast." The town itself dates back to the early 1500s. During colonial times, it thrived due to the sugarcane trade. However, its true boom came in the late 19th-century with the introduction of *cacau* (cocoa). Plummeting world prices and the abolition of slavery caused the sugar plantations to go into decline. However, cocoa—which earned the nickname *ouro branco* (white gold)—drew freed slaves and entrepreneurs to the lush hills surrounding Ilhéus, all of them seized by the desire to strike it rich (or at least earn a decent living). A handful of "cocoa barons" (known as *coronéis* or "colonels"), with vast plantations, did indeed become immensely wealthy and powerful. They basically ruled over their workers, and the region as a whole, until the 1980s, when a disease known as *vassoura de bruxa* ("witch's broom") decimated the cocoa trees and left the region's economy in ruins, from which it's only

JORGE AMADO

The son of a cocoa farmer, Jorge Amado (1912–2001) was born and raised in Bahia's cocoa-growing capital of Ilhéus, a six-hour ride south of Salvador. Although a number of his novels – including the celebrated *Gabriela, Clove and Cinnamon* – were set in Ilhéus, as a young man Amado moved to Salvador, where he became intrinsically associated with the vibrant and often magical city that would ultimately play a major role in much of his fiction.

As a young man Amado was a card-carrying communist, and the themes of his early books often reflected his social concerns. After leaving the Communist Party in 1956, he started writing more picaresque novels. The most famous, *Dona Flor and Her Two Husbands*, sealed his literary reputation. The 1974 movie adaptation, starring a young and very sensual Sonia Braga, was filmed on location in Salvador. The bold and sexually liberated heroines and the candor of these books initially scandalized Brazil's conservative elite of the time (1950s). In fact, his "morally irresponsible" depiction of his hometown's damsels led to his receiving threats in Ilhéus. Meanwhile, Amado's colorful (some say simplistically folkloric) portraits of Salvador and its inhabitants – sensual *mulatas*, wily *malandros* (tricksters), simple fishermen, and Candomblé priestesses – put Salvador on the cultural map and seduced readers – and tourists – from all over the globe.

recently begun to recuperate. Today, traces of the legacy of the "colonels" can be glimpsed by wandering among the grandiose mansions and civic buildings of Ilhéus's small historical center. You can also read about their exploits in the novels (particularly *The Violent Land*) of famous Brazilian author Jorge Amado, Ilhéus's most illustrious son; many of his books are set in his hometown. Meanwhile, the loss in revenue from cocoa has been somewhat offset by the development of the tourism industry. Ilhéus is surrounded by native Atlantic forest and, to the north and south, boasts some attractive white-sand beaches—all of which make it well worth exploring.

Sights

Ilhéus's tiny historical center makes for a pleasant morning or afternoon stroll. Many of its landmarks have become renowned throughout Brazil due to their presence in Jorge Amado's novels. On Praça Luiz Viana Fialho, the **Teatro Municipal** built in 1932 was formerly a cinema where an adolescent Amado frequently went to watch movies. On a corner of the square, the **Casa de Cultura Jorge Amado** (Rua Jorge Amado 21, tel. 73/3634-8986, 9 A.M.–noon and 2–6 P.M. Mon.–Fri., 9 A.M.–noon

Sat., R$1) is housed in the family mansion, built by the author's father in 1920 after he struck it rich with a winning lottery ticket. Guided tours show you portraits of the artist as a young man as well as personal objects and the room in which he slept. Nearby, the **Praça J.J. Seabra, Praça Rui Barbosa,** and **Rua Antônio Lavigne** all contain early-20th-century homes and palaces that attest to the wealth of the "cocoa barons." Built in 1534, the **Igreja de São Jorge** on Praça Rui Barbosa is Ilhéus's oldest church, while the towering mid-20th-century **Catedral de São Sebastião,** on Praça Dom Eduado, displays an unusual blend of architectural styles.

Despite the catastrophe of the *vassoura de bruxa,* there are still cocoa plantations in operation near Ilhéus. Since cocoa trees require shade to grow, farms preserve many taller tree specimens of native Atlantic forest, which makes a stroll through these estates a pleasurable outing. Aside from watching the entire cultivation and production process, visitors can taste the cocoa and sample the succulent nectar made from its fruit. **Fazenda Yrerê** (tel. 73/3656-5054, R$15) is 11 kilometers (7 miles) from town, on the BR-415 highway that links Ilhéus to Itabuna. Another 9 kilometers (6 miles) out of Ilhéus on the same road is **Fazenda Primavera** (tel. 73/3613-7817, R$12). Advance reservations are necessary. Trips can also be organized through local travel agencies.

Beaches

The beaches within Ilhéus itself are neither very clean nor appealing. Most locals prefer to head north towards Itacaré or to the beaches south of the city. In terms of the latter, after **Praia do Sul,** one of the closest and most popular is **Praia dos Milionários.** Only 7 kilometers (4.5 miles) from the center of town, its name alludes to its past as the favored beach of Ilhéus's wealthy cocoa barons. You don't have to be rich to sit at the many *barracas* along this coconut-shaded beach. Subsequent beaches, such as **Praia de Cururupe** along with **Back Door** and **Batuba**—both in the vicinity of **Olivença,** 16 kilometers (10 miles) from Ilhéus—are wilder and more enticing. Large waves make swimming dangerous, though they attract surfers. Municipal buses from Ilhéus provide frequent

Olivença beach, south of Ilhéus

service to all these beaches from the center or the municipal *rodoviária.*

Accommodations

While hotels in the center of Ilhéus are usually good bargains, they tend to be older and not really in mint condition. On the upside, a handful retain some interesting historical character. The **Ilhéus Hotel** (Rua Eustáquio Bastos 144, tel. 73/3634-4242, www.ilheushotel.com.br, R$50–60 d) is a case in point. Inaugurated in 1930, the block-long hotel was the brainchild of one of richest cocoa barons, who dreamed of building the most modern and luxurious hotel in all of Bahia. At the time, his architectural plans consisted of such novelties as separate bathrooms for men and women, as well as the state's first elevator (still in operation today). Long since overhauled, the rooms are more modern and modest. However, affordability and some stylish remnants of its glory days compensate. More numerous and expensive are the many beachfront options along the stretch of coastal road leading south to Olivença. Of particularly good value is the attractive **Hotel Praia do Sol** (Praia do Sul, tel. 73/3234-7000, www.praiadosol.com.br, R$180 d). Only 5 kilometers (3 miles) away from the center of Ilhéus, this beachfront hotel is surrounded by abundant greenery and offers colorfully decorated, roomy apartments.

Although it's further afield, for luxurious natural and man-made surroundings, it's hard to do better than the recently opened **(Hotel Fazenda da Lagoa** (tel. 73/3236-6137, www.fazendadalagoa.com.br, R$880–1,150 d), located 45 kilometers (28 miles) south of Ilhéus. The 14 sprawling bungalows on this former coconut and *dendê* palm plantation are nestled in a burst of greenery situated between a secluded beach and the Rio Aliança (near the Ecoparque de Una nature reserve). The inspired interior decor mixes colonial antiques with fresh and whimsical pieces by contemporary Brazilian artists. A gourmet restaurant serves a contemporary blend of Bahian and international dishes, while the spa offers relaxing treatments including stone massages and rainforest mud masks. Rates include transportation to and from Ilhéus's airport.

Food

On Praia dos Milionários, **Cabana Gabriela** (tel. 73/3632-1836, 8 A.M.–8 P.M. daily, R$15–25) and **Armação** (tel. 73/3632-1817, 11 A.M.–5 P.M. daily, R$15–25) both offer delicious fish and seafood. In town, an Ilhéus classic is **Bar Vesúvio** (Praça Dom Eduardo 190, tel. 73/3634-2164, www.barvesuvio.com.br, 11 A.M.–2 A.M., R$25–40). Built in 1919, it has appeared in several of Jorge Amado's novels and is a local institution. The menu is a mix of Arab and Bahian specialties. Even if you're not hungry, take a seat at one of the sidewalk tables, order a beer, and engage in some people-watching. Live music is played nightly. Both Arab and Bahian dishes are also available (along with other international fare) at **Sheik** (Oiteiro de São Sebastião, tel. 73/3634-2679, 6 P.M.–last client Mon.–Sat.), considered to be the finest restaurant in the center of town. Perched on top of a hill, it also possesses an unforgettable view. There is often live music at night.

Information and Services

Tourist information is available at the *rodoviária* and the airport. **Bahiatursa** (Rua Estáquio Bastos 308, tel. 73/3231-2679, 7:30 A.M.–5 P.M. Mon.–Fri.) and **Ilhéustur** (Av. Soares Lopes 1741, tel. 73/3634-3510, 9 A.M.–6 P.M. Mon.–Sat.) are both located in the historic center. A good Portuguese/English website is www.brasilheus.com.br. **NV Turismo** (Rua General Câmara 27, tel. 73/3634-4101, www.nvturismo.com.br) specializes in ecotourism and other excursions. A convenient Banco do Brasil ATM that accepts international cards is near the cathedral (Rua Marquês de Paranagua 112).

Getting There and Around

The **Aeroporto Jorge Amado** (tel. 73/3234-4000) is 4 kilometers (2.5 miles) south from the center of town, and close to the beaches south of the city. There are daily flights to Ilhéus from Salvador, Porto Seguro, Rio de Janeiro, and São Paulo. The long-distance *rodoviária* (tel. 73/3634-4121), in Pontal, is also only 4 kilometers (2.5 miles) west from the center of town and easily accessible by taxi or municipal bus. **Águia Branca** (www.aguiabranca.com.br) operates buses from Salvador (6 hours) and Porto Seguro (5 hours), while **São Geraldo** (www.saogeraldo.com.br) operates buses to Rio de Janeiro (23 hours) and São Paulo (28 hours). Driving to Ilhéus from either the north or south, you need to take the BR-101 to Itabuna, and then take the coastal BR-415 for 40 kilometers (25 miles) to Ilhéus.

Around Ilhéus
ECOPARQUE DO UNA

This 380-hectare natural park, 50 kilometers (31 miles) south of Ilhéus along the BA-101 coastal highway, preserves exuberant vegetation and centuries-old trees that are typical of the native Atlantic forest that once covered all of coastal Brazil. Guides will lead you on a short hiking trail (involving some tree-trekking) through the park, allowing you the chance to glimpse the likes of deer, armadillos, and the rare but unforgettable *mico-leão-de-cara-dourada* (golden-faced lion monkey). Other highlights include a demonstration of how latex is extracted from rubber trees and a chance to take a refreshing plunge in a freshwater lagoon. Advance reservations are required. For more information call 73/3633-1121 or consult with Ilhéus travel agencies.

PORTO SEGURO

When you arrive in Porto Seguro, you'll be greeted by banners touting the fact that this is where Brazil "began." Indeed, "Porto's" claim to fame as the nation's "first city" stems from the fact that it was here that, in 1500, Brazil's "discoverer," Pedro Alves Cabral, planted his wooden cross in the name of the Portuguese crown. Half a millennium later, Porto Seguro is better known as the birthplace of the 1980s dance craze known as the *lambada* and as being one of the biggest and ballyhooed beach resorts in all of Brazil. Indeed, despite a few colonial

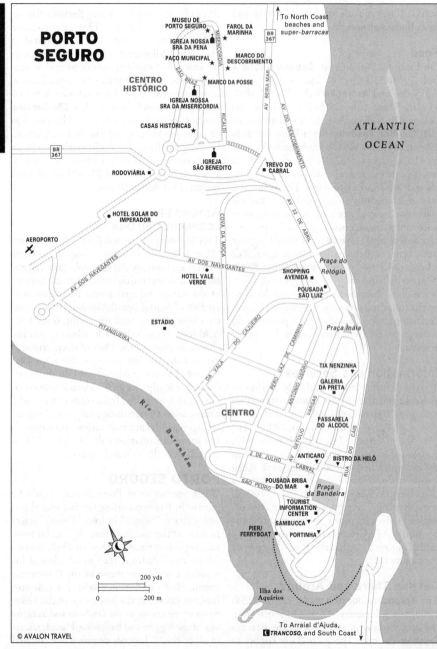

PORTO SEGURO

CENTRO HISTÓRICO

- MUSEU DE PORTO SEGURO
- FAROL DA MARINHA
- IGREJA NOSSA SRA DA PENA
- PAÇO MUNICIPAL
- MARCO DO DESCOBRIMENTO
- MARCO DA POSSE
- IGREJA NOSSA SRA DA MISERICORDIA
- CASAS HISTÓRICAS

MISERICÓRDIA
SÃO BRAZ
RICALDI

AV BEIRA MAR
AV DO DESCOBRIMENTO

ATLANTIC OCEAN

BR 367

RODOVIÁRIA
IGREJA SÃO BENEDITO
TREVO DO CABRAL

To North Coast beaches and super-*barracas*

BR 367

HOTEL SOLAR DO IMPERADOR

AV 22 DE ABRIL

AEROPORTO

COVA DA MOÇA

AV DOS NAVEGANTES

Praça do Relógio

HOTEL VALE VERDE

SHOPPING AVENIDA

POUSADA SÃO LUIZ

AV DOS NAVEGANTES

PITANGUEIRA

ESTÁDIO

DO CAJUEIRO

Praça Indía

DA VALA

PERO VAZ DE CAMINHA

TIA NENZINHA

GALERIA DA PRETA

ANTONIO OSÓRIO

VARGAS

Rio Buranhém

CENTRO

PASSARELA DO ALCOOL

AV GETÚLIO

2 DE JULHO

ANTICARO

CABRAL

BISTRO DA HELÓ

RUA DO CAIS

SÃO PEDRO

POUSADA BRISA DO MAR

Praça da Bandeira

TOURIST INFORMATION CENTER

PIER/ FERRYBOAT

SAMBUCCA

PORTINHA

0   200 yds
0   200 m

Ilha dos Aquários

To Arraial d'Ajuda, TRANCOSO, and South Coast

© AVALON TRAVEL

vestiges and some attractive beaches, Porto Seguro is all about packing in the tourists. Synonymous with two words, "package tour," in the summertime, the place is downright Floridian in its touristic fervor as Brazilian families check into condos and crowds of young party animals crash in fleabag hotels after drinking and dancing the night away. As a party capital, Porto is known for two merry-making institutions: the Passarela do Álcool, or "Alcohol Catwalk," a seaside promenade filled with stands hawking near-explosive fruit cocktails, and sprawling, sophisticated beach bars known as "mega *barracas*"—by day, they function like fully equipped adult playgrounds, while at night they metamorphose into raucous clubs that are home to luaus and raves. Although Porto's heyday has passed, leaving the place a little beat-up and seedy around the edges, if you want to party hearty—and then nurse your hangover on some fine beaches—this is the place to be. Be advised, however, that Porto is neither tranquil nor unspoiled. Those seeking something with more natural beauty and charm are best advised to take a quick look around and then head south to Arraial d'Ajuda, Trancoso, and lovelier points further south.

Sights

Perched strategically on a verdant bluff overlooking the ocean, the handful of colonial buildings that compose Porto Seguro's Centro Histórico mark the beginning of Brazil's official history. A five-minute walk from the *rodoviária* or a fast but steep climb up a staircase from the main traffic circle at the end of Avenida 22 de Abril is all it takes to rewind time a few centuries. A couple of hours can be easily spent—with or without the guidance of the eager (and expensive) local guides—wandering among the pastel-painted houses and gleaming churches. Arrive early in the morning when the light is golden (and before the tourist groups come) and you'll be thankful to have this remarkable ensemble all to yourself. Begin at the foot of Brazil's oldest monument, the **Marco da Posse.** Brought over from Portugal in 1503, this marble column, worshipfully

encased in glass, is tattooed with the insignia of the Portuguese crown and the cross of the Order of Christ.

In the lovely Praça Pero de Campos Tourinho is the simple **Igreja de Nossa Senhora da Penha** (tel. 73/3288-6363, 9 A.M.–noon and 2–5 P.M. daily). Dating back to 1535, it boasts an impressive icon of São Francisco de Assis. In the same green square is the **Casa de Câmara e Cadeia,** the former town hall and Brazil's first public jail. Today, its polished interior houses the small **Museu de Porto Seguro** (tel. 73/3288-5182, 9 A.M.–5 P.M. daily, R$3), with a collection of maps and indigenous artifacts. Nearby, in the Praça da Misericórdia, stands the **Igreja de Nossa Senhora da Misericórdia.** Built in 1526, it is the oldest church in Brazil. Among the treasures inside its modest **Museu de Arte Sacra** (tel. 73/3288-0828, 9:30 A.M.–1:30 P.M. and 2:30–5 P.M. Sat.–Thurs.) are a ruby-encrusted statue of Senhor dos Passos and a life-sized Christ on the crucifix, both dating from the late 16th century. More understated is the tiny whitewashed **Igreja São Benedito** (1549), which now lies in atmospheric ruins.

Beaches

Porto Seguro's beach culture is concentrated on the 20 kilometers (12.5 miles) of low scrub and palm-flanked coastline that spread north from the city center. As far as urban beaches go, you could do a lot worse. The sand is sugary and white and the water, protected by reefs, is not only child-friendly but comes in unreal shades of jade and aqua. **Curuípe, Itacimirim, Mundaí, Taperapuã, Ponta Grande,** and **Mutá** are the names of the beaches that reach up from Porto to Coroa Vermelha, 13 kilometers (8 miles) to the north. The first few are packed with *barracas,* including the famous super-*barracas,* that are total entertainment complexes. By day, these offer *lambada* and *"lambaérobica"* classes, water sports, and Internet access as well as food and drink. By night, their multiple stages host musical performers and DJs that whip the crowd into a sweat to the throbbing strains of *axé, forró,* pop, and techno. The biggest, loudest, and hippest of these are **Tôa-Tôa** (at Praia

THE PATAXÓ

When the Portuguese first arrived in Porto Seguro, they responded to the friendly welcome given to them by members of the local Tupinambá people by enslaving them and appropriating their land. More resistant were inland groups such as the Pataxó, who waged war on the Portuguese on several occasions. Today, the remaining Pataxó still live in the region, most of them on reserves or in villages designated as indigenous territory by the federal government. Their "noble savage" image is used as a marketing logo meant to underscore to those visiting the "Discovery Coast" that this is where Brazil began, but the reality – as evidenced by the many Pataxó women and little kids who march up and down the beaches selling handmade seed jewelry to tourists – is a little sadder.

Along the coast, 13 kilometers (8 miles) north of Porto Seguro lies the pretty beach of **Coroa Vermelha**. Aside from sun and surf, you can see the spot where, after planting a wooden cross in the name of the Portuguese crown, on April 26, 1500, the Portuguese invited the indigenous population to celebrate their first mass on Brazilian territory. You can also view firsthand a Pataxó village, featuring a small, rather dusty museum of indigenous artifacts and a long stretch of craft stands, where the Pataxó sell wooden bowls and feather earrings, and allow you to have your picture taken (you supply the camera) in "traditional" garb. If you're feeling camera shy, you can also take pictures of the Pataxó themselves (usually cute kids), who get up at the crack of dawn to get dressed and gathered.

Closer to Porto is the **Reserva Indígena de Jaqueira** (off Praia de Mutá, 8:30 A.M.–4:30 P.M. Mon.-Sat.), accessible by taxi or through an organized excursion, where Pataxó clothed in traditional costumes show off their bow-and-arrow skills and lead visitors through the Atlantic forest to demonstrate medicinal and sacred plant lore. Visitors who go to Caraíva can visit the nearby reservation at **Barra Velha,** inside the Parque Nacional Monte Pascoal. As a glimpse into how Brazil's indigenous people – at least in this part of the country – are faring 500 years after being "discovered," such options offer much food for thought.

Mundaí), **Axé Moi,** and the granddaddy of them all, **Barramares,** at Praia de Taperapuã. More sedate is the relatively distant beach of Mutá. From the traffic circle in the center of town, numerous municipal buses go north along to coast to the sleepy town of Santa Cruz de Cabrália. At night, you're better off taking a cab than waiting around in the dark.

Nightlife

Porto Seguro is famed for its sizzling nightlife, which begins along the legendary Passarela do Alcool in town, and then keeps going all night long at the many nightclubs and mega-*barracas* along the beaches going north. The **Passarela do Alcool** is an ultra-touristy and pretty garish seaside promenade of bars, restaurants, and hundreds of stands hawking tacky tees, "indigenous" trinkets, and the potent local cocktail, *capeta*. This is both an energizing and intoxicating potion made from pure cocoa powder, the Amazonian jolt-providing *guaraná* powder, vodka, sugar, and ice. As a final touch, sweet condensed milk is added to make the medicine go down nice and easy. The many drink stands along the Passarela—most of them more flamboyantly decked out than a Carmen Miranda tutti-frutti hat—also serve up everything from *caipirinhas* to *batidas* mixed with *cachaça* and fresh fruit.

The Passarela serves as a warm-up station for the nightly extravaganzas held at the mega-*barracas* and theme nightclubs such as **Alcatraz** (BR-367, km 68, 10 P.M.–4 A.M. daily) and **Transylvania** (BR-367, Praia de Mundaí, 10 P.M.–4 A.M. daily) along the beaches of Mundaí and Taperapuã as well as the hippest of them all, the **Ilha dos Aquários** (Ilha do Pacuico, access from Praça do Pataxó, 10 P.M.–4 A.M. daily), located on a private island in the Rio Buranhém, among whose attractions are various immense aquariums filled with glitzy fish. Each *barraca* (some of which operate during normal business hours) has its own *festa* night (widely advertised by fliers along the Passarela). In general, the weekday action is more exciting than on the weekends. Free buses usually head up and down the coast from the traffic circle off Avenida 22 de Abril. The cover for most shows costs between R$30–40. The organization Portonight operates all the *festas*. For more information and listings check out www.portonight.com.br.

Festivals and Events

Porto Seguro's summer festivities come to a head during **Carnaval.** Although much smaller than Salvador's celebration, the *axé*-throbbing merrymaking lasts for a lot longer—until the Saturday following Ash Wednesday. This gives Salvador's mega-stars a chance to migrate south and whip the party into full swing.

A more traditional celebration is the **Festa de São Benedito,** held between December 25 and 27 in the *centro histórico,* in which traditional African music and dances are performed.

Accommodations

With a supposed 37,000 available beds, there is certainly no shortage of accommodations in Porto Seguro. Options range from very basic closet-sized rooms to mega-resorts dripping with amenities, and there is definitely something for every purse string. In off-season, there is lots of availability and discounts galore. Be aware, however, that as early as October things starting going up and by December even the prices of fleabags will have doubled. During New Year's and Carnaval, prices are astronomical, and throughout the summer, it's best to make reservations. Prices below are for off-season.

If you really want to cut corners and are happy with the simple combination of a bed and clean digs, there are many choices, although these same budget *pousadas* are also very tiny, often dark and a bit musty, not to mention totally devoid of any decorative attempts. One of the nicer inexpensive options

is **Pousada São Luíz** (Av. 22 de Abril 329, tel. 73/3288-2238, www.pousadasaoluiz@uol .com.br, R$70 d). The small but spartan white-washed rooms with marine blue accents have basic amenities such as TV and air-conditioning and are clustered around a garden with a swimming pool. Its prime location is close to all the action (and to a McDonald's). Another good pick is the **Hotel Vale Verde** (Av. dos Navegantes 679, tel. 73/3288-2255, www.hotel valeverde.tur.br, R$40) with clean and comfortable rooms and amenities such as Internet access and a swimming pool and sauna. Also inexpensive—albeit quite cramped and dark (at least on the first floor)—is the **Pousada Brisa do Mar** (Praça Dr. Manoel Ribeiro Coelho 188, tel. 73/3288-2943, www.brisadomarpousada. com.br, R$40). What this *pousada* does have going for it is friendly service, and a strategic location on a small square overlooking the sea, a mere block from the *balsa* to Arraial d'Ajuda as well as the Passarela de Alcool.

Not too expensive, and a beguiling example of tropical kitsch, is the **Hotel Solar do Imperador** (Av. do Aeroporto 3117, tel. 73/3288-1581, www.solardoimperador.com.br, R$80). You've never seen an airport hotel quite like this family favorite. Nestled within flamboyantly tropical gardens are 100 (smallish) apartments as well as games rooms, a pool hall, a sauna, and a stone and wood "medieval" wine cellar, all named for princes, lords, and other figures that conjure up imperial stature. The heavy wooden architecture definitely makes an impression, as does the swimming pool with a stunning view of Porto Seguro, the ocean, and acres of lush green landscape. Free vans can take you to beaches and the Passarela de Alcool.

If you prefer something far from the madding crowd, a good upscale option favored by international tourists is the **Villaggio la Torre** (Av. Beira Mar 9999, Praia de Mutá, tel. 73/2105-1700, www.hotellatorre.com.br, R$200–230 d). At 12 kilometers (7.5 miles) from Porto, it's somewhat in the middle of nowhere, but that can be a good thing if the "nowhere" in question happens to be the pristine sands of relatively deserted Mutá beach.

Although no style maven, the all-inclusive hotel has spacious, soothingly neutral rooms and two pools, a sauna, and its own juice bar and pizzeria. It also has a private beach area with cushy lounge chairs.

Food

On Mutá beach (in front of Hotel da Torre) is the reputed **Recanto de Sossego** (tel. 73/3677-1266, 8:30 a.m.–7 p.m. daily, R$35–50). Since the owner hails from Livorno, Italy, it is unsurprising that this restaurant's pasta and seafood—in combinations such as pesto with giant shrimp—are the forte of this eatery. On weekends, be prepared to brave lineups. Back in town, seafood is also the main event at **Bistrô da Helô** (Travessa Assis Chateaubriand, tel. 73/3288-3940, 6:30 p.m.–midnight Mon.–Sat., R$40–50), considered one of Porto's best restaurants. Since the place is small (and rather romantic), reservations are a must if you want to sample creative dishes such as fresh fish bathed in a passion fruit emulsion or grilled shrimp with eggplant and brie risotto.

For Bahian fare, the simple yet traditional **Tia Nenzinha** (Av. Portugal 170, tel. 73/3288-1846, 11 a.m.–midnight daily, R$30–40), located right on the Passarela do Alcool, serves up well-seasoned specialties such as fish *moqueca* with shrimp. More eclectic is the Portuguese-owned **Anticaro** (Travessa Assis Chateaubriand 26, tel. 73/3288-2683, 1–4 p.m. high season only and 6 p.m.–midnight daily, R$35–45), both in terms of its wacky decorative scheme of second-hand store antiques and its menu, which offers such dishes as succulent lobster, fish steamed in champagne, and shrimp with *abacaxi* (a type of pineapple). If you're in the mood for pizza, the best in town is located in a pretty coral-colored house with a cozy white interior called **Sambucca** (Praça dos Pataxós 216, Coelho 188, tel. 73/3288-2366, 6 p.m.–midnight daily, R$20–30), located right beside the pier. For cheap, fast, and delicious *comida por quilo,* head to the nearby **Portinha** (Rua Saldanha Marinha 43, tel. 73/3288-2943, www.brisadomarpousada.com.br, R$10–15). Here you can pick and choose from a buffet of fresh salads and hot dishes warmed over a wood oven before savoring your meal at the wooden picnic tables planted in a leafy garden or out on the cobblestoned street.

Information and Services

There are *tourist offices* at the *rodoviária* and at Praça Manoel Ribeiro Coelho 10 (on the Passarela do Alcool, tel. 73/3268-1390, 9 a.m.–11 p.m. Mon.–Sat.). For information about boat trips and regional excursions, contact **Porto Mondo Adventure** (Passarela do Alcool 344, Loja 101, tel. 73/3288-0040, www.porto-mondo.com) or **Pataxó Turismo** (Rua Oscar Oliveira, tel. 73/3288-1256, www.pataxoturismo.com.br). International bank cards are accepted at the Banco do Brasil and HSBC ATMs in the center of town. In terms of Internet access, there are tons of quite inexpensive options throughout the center, usually charging only R$2–3 for an hour of use.

Getting There

Due to its status as a tourist mecca, there are usually numerous, and often inexpensive (if booked in advance and during off-season) flights available to Porto Seguro from Rio, São Paulo, and Salvador. The international **airport** (tel. 73/3288-1877) is very close to town. After just a 5-minute taxi ride, you'll be in the city center.

Buses from all over Brazil also serve Porto. **São Geraldo** (www.saogeraldo.com.br) has daily service to São Paulo (26 hours), Rio (19 hours), and Belo Horizonte (18 hours), while **Águia Branca** (www.aguiabranca.com.br), whose night bus has reclining sleepers, offers service north to Ilhéus (5 hours) and Salvador (11 hours). The *rodoviária* is a 5-minute taxi or bus ride to the center of town.

If you're traveling by car, you'll need to turn off the BR-101 at Eunápolis and take the Porto Seguro turnoff (the BR-367) for roughly 70 kilometers (43 miles).

Around Porto Seguro

Going north along the coast from Porto Seguro the beaches become more deserted and unspoiled. From Santa Cruz de Cabrália (25 kilometers/16 miles north), a boat trip across the Rio João de Tiba (ferries leave every half hour from the port) brings you to the rustic and surprisingly under-visited fishing settlement of **Santo André.** Its kilometer-long coastline of empty beaches and swaying palms is quite compelling and makes a nice antidote to Porto's urban beach scene. Even further north, you'll hit the surfer's paradise of **Guaiú** and **Mojiquiçaba.**

ARRAIAL D'AJUDA

Despite being only a 10-minute boat ride across the Rio Buranhém from Porto Seguro, Arraial is another world. A major tourist destination in its own right, the town is much more charming than Porto. Aside from its splendid beaches, Arraial's winding streets shaded by lofty trees and overflowing with atmospheric bars and restaurants give off a pleasurable vibe that proves quite addictive. While Arraial boasts a Central Park and its main downtown drag is known as **Rua da Broadway** (or "Bróduei" as it's spelled locally), much more in keeping with NYC is the town's cosmopolitan air and edible fare. Both can be sampled on the **Estrada do Mucugê,** a bustling artery lined with boutiques, bars, and restaurants that magically spring to life come sundown. Proof of how international this thoroughfare has become is in the number of multilingual menus and the 24-hour Internet cafés touting Hebrew keyboards. Indeed, in the summer, Arraial can get as packed as Porto, although the crowd is more alternative and upscale, as are the parties. Most of these all-night affairs are luaus or raves that take place at the sophisticated *barracas* and in the surrounding white sands of Mucugê and Parracho beaches. During off-season, however, the town is deliciously tranquil. Although it was founded in the early 16th-century, aside from the pretty **Igreja Matriz de Nossa Senhora de Ajuda,** built on a cliff and offering stunning views of the beaches below, there are few remnants of its colonial past. However, the present is certainly inviting.

Beaches

A quick and steep descent down the Rua do Mucugê will bring you right onto the soft white sands of Arraial's closest beach, **Praia do Mucugê.** If you turn left, you will pass the more populated beaches of **Apaga-Fogo** and **Araçaipe,** lined with *pousadas,* from which you can rent equipment for water sports activities such as kayaking and windsurfing. Turning right will take you past the trendy **Praia do Parracho,** with its many *barracas,* to the startlingly beautiful **Praia da Pitinga,** whose sugary sands are backed by jagged red and white stone cliffs. Continuing onwards, you'll reach the equally beautiful and deserted **Praia de Taipe,** where sunbathing in the nude is de rigueur. During low tide you can continue on to Trancoso (a 12-kilometer/7.5-mile stroll) and then take a bus back.

Although the coral reefs make for safe swimming on most of these beaches, adults with and without kids find it hard to resist the aquatic options offered at **Arraial d'Ajuda Eco Parque** (tel. 73/3575-8600, www.arraialecoparque. com.br, hours of operation vary according to season, adults R$49, children R$25), located not far from Praia do Mucugê on Praia dos Coqueiros. Supposedly the biggest water park in Latin America, its attractions include a wave pool, twisting water slides, and rappelling and tree-climbing in the native Atlantic forest.

Accommodations

There are an awful lot of accommodation options in Arraial, and the vast majority are quite enticing. Prices are quite reasonable in the off-season, but come summertime, they can double and you'll also need to reserve in advance. Rates listed are for off-season.

One of Arraial's nicest affordable options is the **Tubarão Pousada** (Rua Bela Vista 210, tel. 73/3575-1086, www.tubarao.arraialdajuda. com, R$60–80 d). On a pretty cobblestoned cul-de-sac, facing a cliffside with stupendous beach views, the hotel offers pleasant, homey rooms, all of which open onto a shady oasis with a pool. Also a good bargain is the attractive **Hotel Pousada Saudosa Maloca**

(Alameda da Eugênias 31, tel. 73/2105-1200, www.saudosamaloca.tur.br, R$135 d). Located on a tranquil sandy street, its modern, comfortable rooms with verandas and swinging hammocks overlook a garden with a pool and a cheery breakfast area. In the same price range and with a terrific location, only two minutes from Mucugê beach, is the **Pousada Bucaneiros** (Estrada do Mucugê 590, tel. 73/3575-1105, www.pousadabucaneiros.com. br, R$85 d). Although tightly packed within a garden complex, the simple rooms are enhanced with nice decorative touches. The friendly owners are able to organize walking trips and excursions. Ideal for families or big groups of friends are the three bungalows that come with fully equipped kitchens. For sublime sea views, go across the street, where the massive windows and generous verandas of the tropically swank **Hotel Paraíso do Morro** (Estrada do Mucugê 471, tel. 73/3575-2423, www.paraisodomorro.com, R$220–280 d) will leave you gasping in awe. Recently, when a nightly soap opera called *Paraíso Tropical* wanted to grab the attention of the viewing public during its first few episodes, it did so by filming on location at this colorfully decorated hotel. Although not as close to the beach (but right off the Estrada do Mucugê), the panoramic view from the pool at the **Hotel Pousada Vila do Beco** (Beco do Jegue 173, tel. 73/3575-1230, www.viladobeco.com. br, R$120–220 d) is also pretty hypnotic. The rooms are soothing, as are the grounds planted with tropical fruit trees.

If you want to be right on the beach, you can't do any better than the downright enchanting **C Pousada Pitinga** (Praia de Pitinga, tel. 73/3575-1067, www.pousadapit-inga.com.br, R$324 d, no children under 12), which belongs to the exclusive Roteiros de Charme group of stylish luxury hotels. Set in a lush jungle area that spills right onto the sand, the term "tropical chic" barely does justice to the beautiful rooms that rely on raw and polished natural materials to lull you into a state of total harmony with nature. Discounts are offered in the off-season, but you'll need to book months in advance for the pleasure of such lodgings in the summer.

Food

Even if you don't check into the Pousada Pitinga, the hotel has a wonderful beachfront restaurant, the **Cauim Restaurante,** that offers a varied menu. Main dishes range from contemporized versions of classic Bahian dishes such as *bobó de camarão* to more inventive creations such as the Coroa Vermelha, a type of omelette that mixes rice, seafood, and fresh tomatoes. The service is excellent and the prices surprisingly affordable. Other *barracas* along Parracho and Mucugê beaches also offer all sorts of fish, seafood, and other beach-worthy delicacies that can assuage hunger pains of all sizes throughout the day.

In Arraial itself, most restaurant kitchens, like most of the action, don't get going until the end of the day. However, when they do, the options are very eclectic. In fact, Bahian food is the exception among the sushi bars, Italian cantinas, Argentinean steak houses, and other international eateries—the vast majority of which are concentrated on the vibrant Estrada do Mucugê. When you can't take anymore fish or seafood, **Boi nos Aires** (Estrada do Mucugê 200, tel. 73/3575-2554, www. boinosaires.arraialdajuda.com, 5 P.M.–midnight daily, R$25–45) will have you back in carnivore heaven with its prime cuts of beef flown in from Buenos Aires (although it does grill fish as well). **Manguti** (Estrada do Mucugê 99, tel. 73/3575-2270, www.manguti.com.br, 2 P.M.–midnight daily, R$35–50) is another local favorite that serves up meat, fish, pasta, and its famous gnocchi in a variety of sauces including *manguti* (made from an intriguing mixture of asparagus, mushrooms, peas, and fresh cream). The setting in a cozy little house that is slightly removed from Estrada do Mucugê's buzz is quite romantic. Speaking of romantic, you've never seen a food court quite as fetching as the **Beco das Cores,** an open-air galleria that groups together a series of bewitchingly lit boutiques, bars, and restaurants serving everything from crêpes and pizza to sushi. An alluring ambiance is also one of the attractions of (**Rosa dos Ventos** (Alameda dos Flamboyants 24, tel. 73/3575-1271, 4 P.M.– midnight Mon.–Sat., 1–10 P.M. Sun., R$50– 60), located in a gracious house lit by candles and surrounded by tropical foliage. Another attraction is the surprising menu, which pairs tropical dishes such as fish baked in banana leaves and shrimp and pineapple-like *abacaxi* with wonderfully rich Viennese desserts.

For lighter and less expensive sustenance away from the bustle of Estrada do Mucugê, order one of the delicious homemade shrimp, bean, or vegetable *caldos* (thick soups) at **Nativa** (Praça São Brás, tel. 73/3575-3698, noon–midnight daily, R$10), an unassuming local bar in the main square, which provides a great vantage point for watching the locals hanging out and the hippies selling their wares at the nightly craft market. Also off the beaten track, in a chalet-style house looking onto "Central Park," **Portinha** (Rua do Campo, tel. 73/3575-1289, www.portinha. com.br, noon–10 P.M. daily, R$10–15) is the original *comida por quilo* restaurant that has revolutionized self-service dining along the Costa de Descobrimento. Like its siblings in Porto Seguro and Trancoso, the buffets feature a tasty assortment of varied salads and main dishes kept hot over a wood oven.

If you have a sweet tooth, you'll be in for a treat once you step into the charming Praça Brigadeiro Eduardo Gomes, the square that leads up to the Igreja de Nossa Senhora de Ajuda. **Léo Chocolates** uses pure cocoa from the nearby cocoa-producing region of Ilhéus to make the scrumptious chocolates sold in this tiny store. The truffles are pretty divine, as are the chocolates filled with the slightly tangy Amazonian fruit *cupuaçu*. Tropical flavors are also for the licking a few doors down at the **Uai Sorveteria**, where the seating consists of strangely twisting polished slabs of wood, but the homemade ice cream is ambrosial.

Information

Many hotels have tourist information about Arraial, as does the tourist office in Porto Seguro (Praça Manoel Ribeiro Coelho, tel. 73/3268-1390, 9 A.M.–11 P.M. Mon.–Sat.). You can also check out the website www.arraialdajuda.com.

In Arraial itself, there are many tour agencies that can arrange excursions and provide dune buggies, cars, or motorbikes for rental. Among the options are **Brasil 2000 Turismo** (Estrada do Mucugê 165, tel. 73/3575-1815, www.brasil-2000turismo.com.br) and **Arco-Iris Turismo** (Rua Broadway, tel. 73/3575-1672). The local Bradesco ATM on the Praça São Braz accepts international cards, and 24-hour Internet access is available on the Estrada do Mucugê.

Getting There

Boats, known as *balsas*, leave from Porto Seguro to Arraial at half hour intervals throughout the day. After midnight, they leave at hourly intervals. Round-trip fare is R$2. The *balsas*—some of which allow cars, while others are strictly for passengers—leave from Praça dos Pataxós in Porto Seguro. Tickets can be purchased at **Rio Buranhém Navegação** (tel. 73/3288-2516). Once you arrive at the other side of the river, buses, vans, and *moto-taxis* transport you along the 6-kilometer (3.5-mile) coastal road to the center of Arraial d'Ajuda.

(TRANCOSO

Only 12 kilometers (7.5 miles) south of Arraial is lovely Trancoso. This rather upscale, yet still not too developed former hippie haven is favored by Brazilian and international celebs ranging from MPB diva Gal Costa (whose former digs are now a luxury *pousada*) to none other than raging bull Robert de Niro. Instead of the hardcore partying that goes on at neighboring Porto Seguro and Arraial d'Ajuda, pilgrims to Trancoso often prefer an evening of fine dining followed by drinks at the candlelit alfresco restaurants sprinkled around the Quadrado. (Although the surrounding beaches offer their share of hedonistic nocturnal activities, particularly when the moon is full.)

The **Quadrado** (Square), an immense open-air plaza carpeted in thick grass and framed by luxuriously shady trees, is the rather dreamlike historical, spiritual, and nerve center of Trancoso. On three sides, it is surrounded by colonial homes painted in vibrant colors, many of which now house stylish boutiques, *pousadas* and restaurants. On the fare side is the incandescent **Igreja de São João Batista,** built in the 18th century on the ruins of a Jesuit convent. As you approach the church, you also near the edge of the cliff behind it, which plummets down to an green mass of native Atlantic forest, a long strip of endless white beach, and a great sweep of Atlantic in shades of bright turquoise-green.

Beaches

Only a five-minute descent from the Quadrado is a series of gorgeous unspoiled beaches, fed by rivers and bordered by mangrove swamps and jungle carpeted cliffs. At strategic intervals are sprawling *barracas* where you can catch the sun's rays while bossa nova and lounge music wafts through the air. Closest to Trancoso itself is **Praias dos Nativos,** the more secluded deserted stretches of which attract the odd nudist. With calmer seas are the ultra trendy **Praia dos Coqueiros** and **Praia do Rio Verde,** ideal for bathing. By horseback, buggy, or on foot you can continue south along these primitive beaches, which stretch all the way down to Caraíva.

Sports and Recreation

Among the many recreational activities offered in and around Trancoso are guided cycling tours. Operated by **Natural Ecobike e Aventura** (tel. 73/3668-1955, www.naturalecobike.com), excursions—which take place during the day and night—allow riders to explore both the beaches and Atlantic forest. Meanwhile, golfers are in for a treat if they choose to play the stunning 18-hole **Terravista Gold Course** (tel. 73/2105-2104, 8 A.M.–6 P.M. Mon.–Sat.), located 18 kilometers (11 miles) from Trancoso on a cliffside overlooking the Praia de Taípe.

Entertainment and Events

The nightlife of the town itself is less than wild, particularly in the off-season. However, there is usually a group playing live *forró,* samba, or rock music in the main square off the Quadrado or along the bars that lead down Avenida Principal. In the summertime, things heat up on the beaches of Praia dos Coqueiros and Praia do Rio Verde with parties, luaus, and even raves that last for three days and draw a young, beautiful crowd.

Festa de São Sebastião on January 20 is the most traditional *festa* in the city, complete with processions, fireworks, and the raising of the two decorated masts that can be viewed in front of the church of São João Batista.

Shopping

Aside from the various Brazilian designer labels that wouldn't be out of place in a swank São Paulo shopping mall, the Quadrado has a few unique boutiques worth checking out. Most stores open their doors late, usually at 2 P.M., but they often will stay open until about 11 P.M.

Cobras e Lagartos (tel. 73/3668-1962, www.cobraselagartos.com) uses recycled fabric and a traditional embroidery technique known colloquially as *"frufru"* to make playful pillows, carpets, and other home furnishings as well as cuddly toys, featuring bright colors and interesting textures. Just as original are the wares on display at **Marcenaria Trancoso** (tel. 73/3668-1023, www.marcenariatrancoso.com.br). Incorporating native woods and natural fibers, the polished yet organic wooden objects and decorative accessories sold here combine a tropical aesthetic with contemporary sensibility that is distinctly Brazilian. Around town, you'll notice many of artist Laila Assaf's inspired floral lamps and accessories fashioned out of intricately assembled recycled plastic bottles. To purchase these and other creations, drop into her boutique/atelier **Cheia de Graça** (tel. 73/3668-1492).

Accommodations

Trancoso's charming hotels tend to be on the pricy side, although some affordable options are available. During the summer, prices double and reservations are a must. Prices listed are for off-season.

If you want to be on the Quadrado, a really lovely option is the **C Pousada Porto Bananas** (Quadrado 234, tel. 73/3668-1017, www.portobananas.com.br, R$130–210 d). Various bungalows are spread throughout a jungly garden that will make you feel as if you just checked into Eden. The tastefully simple rooms are decorated with harmonious colors and textures, all of which are very conducive to respite. Equally irresistible, although a little more refined (and expensive) is the **Hotel da Praça** (Quadrado 1, tel. 73/3668-2121, www.hoteldapraca.com.br, R$180–240 d). Trancoso's first hotel opened back in the days when Trancoso was merely hippie without chic. In late 2006, the owners of Porto Bananas got their talented hands on it and hired local artists and architects to give the place an inspired facelift. The result is quite enchanting with unique art works and furnishings that also adorn the hotel's restaurant. Christened **Japaiano,** it has already garnered a reputation for intriguing culinary creations that draw on both Japanese and Bahian cuisine, such as *moqueca* sushi and *bobó de camarão* with wasabi.

You might find it hard to believe that there's anything but luxury on the Quadrado, but those on a budget can take refuge at the **Albergue Café Esmeralda** (Quadrado, tel. 73/3668-1527, cafeesmeralda@terra.com.br, R$30–60 d). Although rooms are dark and cramped, they are clean, Internet service is available, and the owners are terribly friendly. A little off the beaten track, but also of great value is the **Pousada Encantada** (Rua João Vieira de Jesus, tel. 73/3668-2024, www.pousadaencantada.com.br, R$60 d). Although the bungalows are in close proximity and the garden is more residential backyard than tropical paradise, the rooms themselves are in mint condition and the staff makes you feel at home. Another fine choice, only 150 meters (500 feet) from the Quadrado, is the **Pousada Mundo Verde** (Rua João Vieira de Jesus, tel. 73/3668-2024, www.pousadamundoverde.com.br, R$130–150 d). The comfortable rooms aren't stylish, but the verdant surroundings are bucolic. From the pool at the edge of a bluff,

you'll be treated to captivating views of the forest and beaches below.

If prime beach access is what you're searching for, **Pousada Le Refuge** (tel. 73/3668-1150, www.pousadaencantada.com.br, R$50 d), on the trail leading from the Quadrado to Praia de Coqueiros, is the perfect candidate. Clean, unaffected, and definitely affordable, the only drawback (for some) is the hotel's brick structure, which is a bit overbearing. For complete beachfront isolation, **Pousada Bahia Bonita** (tel. 73/3668-1565, www.bahiabonita.com.br, R$300 d without sea views and R$500 d with sea views), located on beautiful Praia do Rio Verde, will answer all your prayers (at a cost). Built and accessorized with lots of precious wood, coconut fibers, and other natural materials, the bungalows are not unlike luxury treehouses. If you have a lot of luggage, you'll need to grab a cab in Trancoso. The alternative is a 30-minute walk through native forest or along the beach.

Food

Just as sophisticated as its accommodations are Trancoso's range of culinary choices. During the day, you might want to take advantage of the fare served at the beach *barracas.* One of the nicest is the Italian-owned **C Cabana de Andrea** on Praia de Coqueiros. The Italian salads and pizzas are flavorful as are the more tropical selections, including shrimp cooked in coconut milk served in a coconut, and grilled shrimp and squid with mango chutney. Aside from beach chairs and hammocks galore, the service is attentive and the mellow soundtrack will put you in a sweet trance. Further down on Praia do Rio Verde, another favorite is **Pé na Praia,** where you can get delicious grilled fish and hefty *caipirinhas.*

Back in town, the restaurant scene doesn't get hopping until sundown. However, as in Porto Seguro and Arraial d'Ajuda, one of the best options, day or night, is the daily self-service per kilo buffet at **Portinha** (Quadrado, tel. 73/3668-1054, open daily for lunch and dinner, R$10–15). The deliciously fresh salads and hot dishes kept sizzling over a wood oven can be savored at wooden picnic tables right on a tree-shaded patch of the Quadrado. Come sundown, if you don't want to repeat the experience, try another Quadrado favorite: **Silvana & Cia** (Quadrado, tel. 73/3668-1122, 1–10 P.M. daily, R$40–50). Beneath a giant almond tree magically lit up with lanterns and candles, Trancoso-born Silvana prepares typical Bahian dishes such as grilled fish, shrimp *bobós*, and *moquecas*. It's nicely priced by Trancoso standards; locals often dine here.

Natives of both Italy and São Paulo (where pizza is king) swear by the crunchy pies prepared in the large open kitchen of **Maritaka** (Rua do Telégrafo, tel. 73/3668-1702, 7 P.M.–close Thurs.–Tues., R$25–35). The ambiance is casual, but toppings include the more refined likes of asparagus and brie. While romantic settings are a dime a dozen in Trancoso, you'd be hard-pressed to compete with that of **El Gordo** (Quadrado 7, tel. 73/3668-1193, www.elgordo.com.br, 1 P.M.–midnight daily, R$40–55). The light cast by Japanese lanterns echoes the lights twinkling along the coastline below this terrace restaurant. Happily, the reputed dishes are as appealing as the view. Cosmopolitan offerings range from exotic sushis and lobster curries to Portuguese salted cod (the owner is Portuguese) prepared in a variety of styles.

Information and Services

Tourist information and reservations for excursions are available at **Trancoso Receptivo** (Rua Carlos Alberto Parracho off the Quadrado, tel. 73/3688-1333, www.trancosoreceptivo.com, 9 A.M.–11 P.M. daily in high season, 9 A.M.–7:30 P.M. Mon.–Fri. and 9 A.M.–1 P.M. Sat. in low season).

Also on Rua Carlos Alberto Parracho is a Bradesco ATM that accepts international cards. In front is a taxi stand with service to surrounding destinations. Meanwhile, if you want to do laundry, check your email, buy some second-hand threads, grab a snack, and chill out to some tunes, all you need to do is head for the **Bacia de Todos as Santas** (Av. Principal, tel. 73/3668-2289, 9 A.M.–10 P.M.).

At this very groovy multipurpose space, you can do all of the above and much more.

Getting There

If you don't have to much luggage, you can reach Trancoso by walking south along the stunning beaches (and wading across a couple of rivers) from Arraial d'Ajuda (12 kilometers/7.5 miles). Otherwise, there is frequent **Brasileiro** bus service from the *balsa* going to Porto Seguro and from Arraial. The trip takes around 40 minutes (most of it through papaya plantations).

◖ CARAÍVA

Off the beaten track—which has left it gloriously intact from developers' radar—Caraíva is most people's fantasy of an idyllic tropical getaway. On the banks of the Rio Caraíva, this tiny fishing village is surrounded by the thick vegetation of mangroves as well as wonderfully deserted white beaches that extend for kilometers in both directions. Its few roads are paved with silky sand instead of asphalt, which hardly matters since no cars exist. If you want to get around, you can hire a donkey-driven wooden chariot or jump into a dugout canoe. Meanwhile, after a 10-year battle with the national energy company, Caraíva finally received electricity in July 2007. However, since residents are used to lanterns and candles, you'll still be able to wander around at night with little more than moonlight and starlight to guide you. There isn't much to do in Caraíva. But if all you want to do is completely relax, in idyllic natural surroundings, it is incomparable.

Beaches

Caraíva boasts some of the most unspoiled and downright beautiful beaches along the Bahian coast. You can walk for hours and there is barely any construction in sight to break the brilliant green of native Atlantic forest and swaying coconut palms. Going south from the **Praia da Caraíva,** the beaches will take you past the **Parque Nacional Monte Pascoal,** a nature preserve which is also partially occupied by the **Barra Velha** Pataxó reservation (excursions can be organized from Caraíva), all the way down to the splendidly isolated beaches of **Barra do Cai** and **Ponta do Corumbau,** where there is wonderful diving.

Once you take a canoe across the Rio Caraíva, you can also make your way north along the coast. A 4-kilometer (2.5-mile) walk brings you to the **Praia de Satu.** Cutting into the red cliffs crowned with jungle are freshwater lagoons where you can swim. Continuing on, these cliffs become increasingly dramatic until you reach **Praia de Espelho** and **Praia de Curuípe,** 9 kilometers (6 miles) and 12 kilometers (7.5 miles), respectively, from Caraíva. Among Brazilian travel writers and hardcore beach aficionados, Praia de Espelho ranks at the top of the "Best Beaches" lists that are frequently compiled. This means that frequent boatloads of tourists show up from Porto Seguro and Arraial d'Ajuda. However, given Caraíva's proximity, you can beat the crowds and enjoy the sheer beauty of the place in splendid isolation. For more information about boat and diving excursions to any of these nearby beaches, contact **Navegação Caraíva** (tel. 73/9985-0241) or Pará at the **Boteco do Pará** (tel. 73/9991-9804), both on the Rua Beira-Rio.

Accommodations and Food

Like everything in Caraíva, hotels are pretty rustic, although they range from very basic to atmospheric. The most attractive of them all is the **Pousada da Lagoa** (tel. 73/9985-6862, www.lagoacaraiva.com.br, R$90–160 d). Brightly painted cabins are nestled among abundant foliage, in the middle of which is a small lagoon. In spite of the recent arrival of electricity, candles are still provided in all the bedrooms and bathrooms. The restaurant serves up nicely prepared fine meals (the breakfasts are delicious) and on summer nights, it serves as bohemian headquarters to the mellow crowd that congregates to listen to great canned and live music. For immediate beach access, a fairly nice option is the **Pousada Cores do Mar** (tel. 73/3668-5090, www.caraiva.com.br, R$90 d). Also beachfront—and riverfront as well—are the pumpkin-colored

bungalows belonging to the **Pousada da Barra** (tel. 73/9885-4302, www.caraiva.com.br, R$70 d). Rooms are simple but airy, and stepping outside means literally stepping into soft sand.

For food, two riverside eateries serve up delicious fare while offering mesmerizing views of the lazy Rio Caraíva and the emerald green vegetation along its banks. Pará, the owner of **Boteco do Pará** (Rua Beiro-Rio, tel. 73/9991-9804, open daily 11 A.M.–last client high season, 11 A.M.–10 P.M. Tues.–Sun. low season, R$20–35) has his own fishing boat, which guarantees the freshness of the fish and *moquecas* at this traditional eatery. Tables are shaded by an immense almond tree and adjacent to the Ponto dos Mentirosos (Liars' Spot), where fishermen traditionally congregate to tell tall tales. Further down, candle- and lantern-lit **Bar do Porto** (Rua Beira Rio, 7 P.M.–last client) serves drinks as well as tasty pizzas baked in its wood-burning oven.

Getting There

Two daily buses operated by **Viação Águia Azul** (tel. 73/3668-1110) connect Arraial d'Ajuda and Trancoso to Caraíva along a dirt road that's hard to navigate during the rainy season. From Trancoso, the journey takes about 90 minutes. There is also boat service from Porto Seguro with **Cia do Mar** (tel. 73/3288-2107).

CARAVELAS

Depending on which direction you're coming from, the last (or first) resort town of consequence in Bahia's extreme south is Caravelas. A decidedly low-key place to unwind for a couple of days, the lovely colonial town—which spans the Rio Caravelas—and its beaches, sum up the best of what Bahia has to offer. Caravelas is also the most convenient place from which to visit the fantastic Parque Nacional Marinho de Abrolhos. Located 70 kilometers (43 miles) offshore, this marine reserve encompasses an archipelago of five islands whose crystalline waters and coral reefs make up one of the world's best diving spots.

Sights

Caravelas has some appealing colonial architecture, the most striking examples of which—including the **Igreja de Santo Antônio**—are clustered around the handsome **Praça de Santo Antônio.** The **Instituto Baleia Jubarte** (Rua Barão do Rio Branco 26, tel. 73/3297-1240, 8 A.M.–noon and 2–6 P.M. Mon.–Fri., 8:30 A.M.–noon Sat.) is a whale research station.

◖ PARQUE NACIONAL MARINHO DOS ABROLHOS

The main draw for most visitors to Caravelas is to view the incredible array of rare and colorful tropical fish that thrive in the transparent blue coastal waters. Abrolhos comes from the Portuguese command *abre os olhos* ("open your eyes"), and visitors to the archipelago will feel guilty if they so much as take time out to blink. Both Charles Darwin and Jacques Cousteau were impressed by the sheer diversity of fish, coral, sea tortoises and marine birds that make their home in this live aquarium. From May to September, when visibility is at its best, it's possible to see to depths of 20 meters. Between July and November, an added bonus is watching the spectacle of humpbacked whales—16 meters (33 feet) in length and 40 tons in weight—who mate and give birth in the warm waters. September and October are the best months to see them in action. July and August can be tricky since rainy weather can result in excursions being cancelled.

From Caravelas, it takes a little over two hours to reach the Abrolhos archipelago by speedboat, and 3.5 hours by catamaran. Full-day excursions, with a minimum of eight people, are offered by two main companies in Caravelas: **Abrolhos Turismo** (Praça Dr. Imbassaí, tel. 73/3297-1149) and **Abrolhos Embarcações** (Av. das Palmeiras 2, tel. 73/3297-1172), for around R$220 a day. If you have time to spare (and money to spend), both companies also offer overnight trips with accommodations on schooners. Diving and snorkeling equipment can be rented for an extra fee. Advance reservations are advised.

Beaches

If you're in search of beaches, you'll have to travel by bus, car, or boat to reach them. To the north, **Praia do Grauça** (10 kilometers/6 miles) and **Praia Iemanjá** (20 kilometers/12.5 miles) are good for swimming, although the waters are murky due to the proximity of the Rio Caravelas. Boat trips can be also organized to small islands off the coast, such as **Coroa Vermelha,** where it's possible to snorkel.

Accommodations and Food

In Caravelas itself, two low-key and attractive options are the **Pousada Canto do Atobá** (Av. Adalício Nogueira 515, tel. 73/3297-1009, www.geocities.com/pousadacantodoatoba, R$60–90), which has pleasant if simple rooms and a pool, and **Pousada Liberdade** (Av. Adalício Nogueira 1551, tel. 73/3297-2067, www.pousadaliberdade.com.br, R$110), with bright and airy chalets spread in a garden amply shaded by palm, mango, and cashew trees. More upscale and with a privileged beach location is the **Hotel Marina Porto Abrolhos** (Rua da Baleia 333, Praia de Grauça, tel. 73/3674-1082, www.marinaportoabrolhos.com.br, R$175–195 d). The breezy rooms are in individual bungalows crowned by palm thatching and surrounded by plenty of swaying trees.

In terms of food, take advantage of the abundance of fresh fish and seafood and head to the **Encontro dos Amigos** (Rua das Palmeiras 370, tel. 73/3297-1600, 11:30 A.M.–11 P.M. daily, R$10–20). Considered the best seafood restaurant in town, it serves up classic Bahian shrimp and fish *moquecas* as well as octopus risottos. Also good for seafood is the rustic **Carenagem** (Rua das Palmeiras 210, tel. 73/3297-1280, 10:30 A.M.–last client, daily, R$10–20), whose copious signature dish, called *sinfonia de peixe* ("fish symphony"), includes not only fish, but oysters, crab, and shrimp.

Getting There

Águia Branca (www.aguiabranca.com.br) offers bus service to Caravelas from Salvador (15 hours) and Porto Seguro (4 hours) via the town of Teixeira de Freitas, as does **São Geraldo** (www.saogeraldo.com.br) from Rio de Janeiro (15 hours). By car, after turning off the BR-101 highway at Teixeira de Freitas, you'll continue along the BA-290 for around 70 kilometers (44 miles) until reaching the coast.

BRASÍLIA AND THE PANTANAL

It was barely 50 years ago that Juscelino Kubitschek was elected Brazil's president, largely as a result of his wildly ambitious plans to construct a capital from scratch right in the middle of Brazil (i.e., in the middle of nowhere). To carry out this endeavor, he hired two young talents: architect Oscar Niemeyer and an urban planner named Lúcio Costa. Construction began in 1957, and three years later, the world's most famous and controversial planned city was unveiled. Although the Royal Institute of British Architects referred to its gleaming space-age geometric palaces, monuments, and "sectors" as "the Moon's Backside" over the years, Brasília's unearthly charms have seduced architecture buffs from around the globe.

Architecture aside, one of Brasília's *raisons d'être* was to facilitate the opening up of the vast and isolated interior of Brazil's Central-West, a region of elevated plains whose unique landscape, the Cerrado, conjures up the muted colors and scrubby foliage of East Africa's savannahs. As a result, the city is an ideal departure point for exploring natural and cultural treasures located in the surrounding state of Goiás. Highlights include the Chapada de Veadeiros, whose surreal rock formations, bathed by numerous waterfalls, are a hiker's paradise, as well as the charming colonial towns of Pirenópolis and Goiás Velho, which are largely overlooked by foreign tourists.

Beyond Goiás, straddling the Wild West frontier states of Mato Grosso and Mato Grosso do Sul, lies one of the most fantastically diverse ecosystems on the planet. Larger than Great

© EDITORA PEIXES/EMBRATUR

HIGHLIGHTS

《 Esplanada dos Ministérios and the Praça dos Três Poderes: The futuristic complex of government palaces designed by Oscar Niemeyer in Brasília comprises gleaming masterpieces of modernist architecture (page 397).

《 Parque Nacional da Chapada dos Veadeiros: Fantastic rock outcrops, myriad waterfalls, and lots of positive energy emanating from quartz crystals make this national park an invigorating eco-retreat (page 412).

《 *Centro Histórico* of Goiás Velho: The former gold mining town and first capital of Goiás is one of the best preserved and most atmospheric colonial towns in Brazil (page 415).

《 Parque Nacional da Chapada dos Guimarães: This park offers a natural grandeur similar to that of the Grand Canyon in Arizona, with scores of waterfalls, tropical foliage, and a wealth of colorful birdlife (page 423).

《 The Pantanal's *Fazenda* Lodges: The best way of getting up close to the amazing wildlife that inhabits the planet's largest wetlands is to check into the cattle ranch/eco-resorts within its depths (pages 426, 432, and 433).

《 *Flutuação* in Bonito: The highlight of this eco-hotspot is donning snorkel gear and "floating" down rivers so clear and crammed with fish that you'd swear you'd fallen into an aquarium (page 438).

LOOK FOR **《** TO FIND RECOMMENDED SIGHTS, ACTIVITIES, DINING, AND LODGING.

Britain, the Pantanal—which literally means "swamp"—is an ecotourist's dream come to life. Alligators, jaguars, anacondas, capybaras (the world's largest rodents), and brilliantly hued exotic birds of every size imaginable are just a few of the most popular forms of fauna you're likely to meet up with. The more than 200 species of fish that live in the Pantanal's rivers make it one of the best places in the world for freshwater fishing—and for eating (make sure to try the piranha soup). Rivaling the flocks of birds and schools of fish are the great herds of cattle that use the wetlands as their pasture. Their presence accounts for vast ranches, some of which,

nestled deep within the Pantanal, double as wildlife reserves and eco-resorts.

The region has other natural treasures as well. Close to Mato Grosso's capital of Cuiabá lies the Chapada dos Guimarães, a magnificent series of cliffs, gorges, and waterfalls that offers great hiking. Located on one of the planet's oldest tectonic plates, it resembles the Grand Canyon gone tropical. And not far from Mato Grosso do Sul's capital of Campo Grande, the unspoiled nature surrounding the town of Bonito constitutes Brazil's most successful example of sustainable ecotourism. Aside from unspoiled tropical landscapes, Bonito's main draw is its

BRASÍLIA AND THE PANTANAL

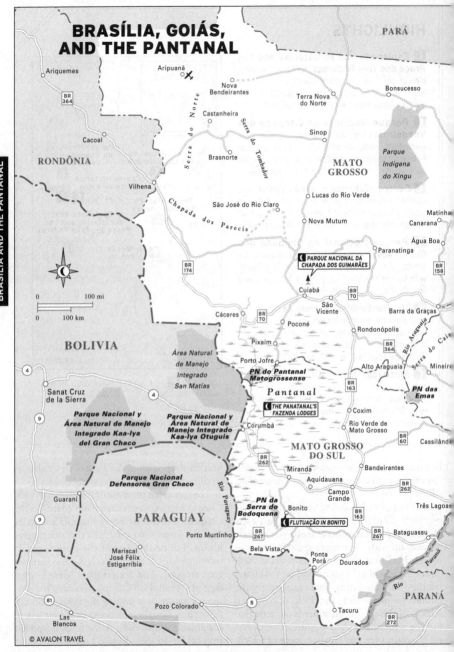

many rivers. Their pure, crystalline waters have given rise to *flutuaçâo,* a sport that involves donning a snorkel, mask, and lifejacket, and then letting the current carry you downriver while you rub shoulders with a dazzlingly colorful array of tropical fish. Although many of these attractions are quite literally off the proverbial beaten track, getting to and traveling through these unique regions is an adventure in itself.

PLANNING YOUR TIME

Brasília was built in the middle of nowhere, and despite the fact that this region is growing faster than any other in Brazil, geographically it continues to be the middle of nowhere. Roads linking major cities are actually in decent shape, but distances are enormous. Although Brasília is easily reached by plane from all other cities, flights to the more remote cities of Mato Grosso and Mato Grosso do Sul (Cuiabá, Campo Grande, and Corumbá) are quite expensive. That said, outside of Brasília and nearby attractions such as Pirenópolis and the Chapada dos Veadeiros— all of which you could comfortably fit into a 5–6-day trip (unless you're a die-hard fan of modernist architecture, you can see most of Brasília's top attractions in one very full day), you'll need to have substantial time at your disposal. For instance, it's well worth spending 3–4 days in Goiás Velho, one of the loveliest of Brazil's historic towns—not only because of its distance, but also to soak up its languid colonial atmosphere and immerse yourself in its unspoiled landscapes. Reserve 5–7 days for Mato Grosso, where you can spend a day or two in the Chapada dos Guimarães and then the remaining time exploring the northern Pantanal. Similarly, a week is recommended for Mato Grosso do Sul, where aside from the southern Pantanal, you might want to explore Bonito, whose natural attractions deserve at least 2–3 days. In terms of the Pantanal, the ideal way to experience the wetlands is to book a package at a *fazenda* lodge. These all-inclusive guesthouses offer a wealth of eco-activities, but also usually stipulate a minimum stay of at least three days.

BUILDING BRASÍLIA

Determined to complete Brasília within the four-year limit of his presidential term, Juscelino Kubitschek lost no time in this monumental – and to many, completely insane – undertaking. Indeed, building a modern capital in the middle of a dusty red plain was no mean feat. The construction site was 125 kilometers (78 miles) from the nearest railroad line, 190 kilometers (118 miles) from the nearest airport, and 600 kilometers (373 miles) from the nearest paved road. An airfield was quickly built and everything – supplies, materials, and over 3,000 workers (many of them poor unskilled laborers from the Northeast) – were flown in while waiting for roads to arrive. Funds for this massive project were raised through vast loans from international banks (which subsequently plunged Brazil into massive debt and was a major source of the crazy rates of inflation that plagued the nation during subsequent decades).

Despite the many obstacles and nay-sayers, particularly politicians in Rio who were definitely not pleased at having to trade their idyllic Carioca lifestyle for a dry dustbowl far from civilization, Kubitschek and his collaborators persevered. Three years after work commenced, on April 21, 1960, more than 5,000 curious VIPs from Brazil and all over the globe flew in for the inauguration of the new city. Following a mass at the still-unfinished Catedral Metropolitano and a brilliant fireworks display – in which Kubitschek's name blazed in enormous letters – Brasília was officially declared Brazil's "capital of the future."

Of course, fanfare aside, there was still a lot of construction left to be done. Aside from most government buildings, many residential and commercial blocks were unfinished, as were certain thoroughfares. To this day, Niemeyer – who turned 101 years old in 2008 and is still hard at work – remains the city's master architect. In fact, in 2006, he completed work on the last two projects originally planned for the city: the **Biblioteca Nacional** (National Library) and the **Museu Nacional.** Meanwhile, over the years, Brasília has grown in leaps and bounds, surpassing the original limits of the Plano Piloto (Pilot Plan) and far exceeding original demographic predictions that estimated a 2000 population of 500,000 residents (today's population is 2.5 million). The result has been *cidades satelites* (satellite cities), consisting of more chaotically organized surrounding suburbs where, as in most major Brazilian cities, the poor live in *favelas*, coming into the city only to take care of the needs of the nation's power elite.

Brasília and Goiás are best visited during the dry season, which lasts from March to October. During this time, skies are impossibly blue and temperatures tend to be comfortable—22°C (75°F), and even cooler in the mountains. From April to June, the blooming wildflowers turn the normally scrubby, dun-colored Cerrado into a patchwork of color. From August to October things heat up, with temperature easily hitting 38°C (100°F), although nights are usually cooler. In Brasília, the Saharan heat and dryness can become quite unbearable, and even the locals complain of parched throats and nosebleeds. Make sure to stock up on mineral water and sunscreen. As for the Pantanal, the rainy season (November to March) turns the wetlands into a lush landscape of green, but makes both wildlife observation and transportation more difficult. For this reason, the dry season (April to October) is usually preferred for travel.

HISTORY

Brazil's Central-West was first explored in the early 17th century by Spanish and Portuguese colonists whose initial efforts were rebuffed by a combination of inhospitable landscapes and fierce Indian attacks from local groups such as the Bororo, Kaiapó, and Paiaguá. It wasn't until a century later when, having struck gold in neighboring Minas Gerais, intrepid Paulistano *bandeirantes* began sending expeditions into the region, propelled by dreams of making fortunes. In 1682, a *bandeirante* by the name of Bartolomeu Bueno da Silva encountered some Goiaz Indians adorned with accessories made from pure gold. According to local legend, when the Indians refused to tell him the source of the precious metal, Silva promptly set a vessel of water (in reality *cachaça*) aflame and threatened to do the same to all the region's rivers if they didn't show him to the gold.

Within a decade, a new gold rush was on. *Bandeirantes,* followed by Portuguese settlers and soldiers, and hundreds of African slaves descended upon the outposts that grew into the towns subsequently known as Goiás Velho (Goiás) and Cuiabá (Mato Grosso). Although some fabulous fortunes were made, many more adventurers died due to disease, poverty (the price of imported goods was astronomical), and the hardships of the months-long journey through the wilderness from São Paulo. Meanwhile, despite some brave shows of resistance, most of the region's Indians were no match for the combination of gunpowder and viruses that the white intruders carried with them (although to this day, some surviving communities—most notably the Terena and Bororo of Mato Grosso and Mato Grosso do Sul—continue to live much as their ancestors did). By the end of the 18th century, many Indians had been decimated and much of the gold had dried up. However, an abundance of fertile land fed by rivers lured cattle ranchers from São Paulo and the South to settle Goiás and Mato Grosso. The herds thrived, in particular, amid the otherwise deserted wetlands of the Pantanal.

Until well into the 20th century, the Central-West remained a sparsely populated wilderness whose urban outposts were quite isolated from the bustling capitals of coastal Brazil. The region's fortunes changed radically, however, with the concretization of the long-held dream of building a new Brazilian capital in the heart of the country. Under the bold and visionary leadership of Juscelino Kubitschek, who became president in 1956, an area known as the Distrito Federal (Federal District) was carved out of the highland plains of Goiás, and within four years, a shiny brand-new capital had risen out of the deep red earth of the Planalto.

While Brasília has its ardent supporters and critics, there is no denying that the city led to the opening up of the entire Central-West, connecting it to the rest of Brazil and ushering in a period of thriving agro-industry that has continued to this day. Currently Goiás, Mato Grosso, and Mato Grosso do Sul (which was created out of the formerly immense state of Mato Grosso in the late 1970s) are Brazil's fastest-growing regions and the leading national producers of lucrative cash crops such as sugarcane, soybeans, rice, cotton, and corn along with beef. Increasingly, vast high-tech farms vie for space with nature reserves, the largest of which, the immense Parque Nacional do Pantanal Matogrossense, has managed (for now) to protect many of the natural treasures enclosed within the watery borders of the Pantanal. Indeed, at the beginning of the 21st century, the biggest issue in the region is one of sustainable development; how to balance continued economic growth with preservation of the region's unique, yet increasingly threatened ecosystems.

Brasília

Some people go gaga over Brasília, while others find it arid and alienating. Of course, how could the world's most famous planned city and undisputed mecca of modernism leave anyone indifferent? Indisputably, Brasília concentrates the most stunning ensemble of modernist architecture on the planet, a fact that earned it recognition as a UNESCO World Heritage Site in 1987. If you have any interest whatsoever in 20th-century architecture, a pilgrimage to this meticulously planned space-age city with its rational lines tempered by graceful curves is an absolute must. And even if you don't, the surreal experience of being plunked down in a futuristic cityscape—where the "future" is seen through a decidedly retro 1950s and '60s version of utopia—is definitely unique. Architecture aside, however, Brasília does hold other attractions. The presence of the nation's political elite, along with international diplomats and visiting dignitaries, has transformed Brasília into a cosmopolitan place. Its sophisticated gastronomic scene is only surpassed by Rio's and São Paulo's, and its cultural offerings—from music to cinema—are world class. Aside from the astounding number of parks and green "sectors" within the city itself, the surrounding Cerrado beckons with its singular vegetation, unusual rock formations, and countless waterfalls.

The idea of a new Brazilian capital located in the heart of the country is as old as the Brazilian republic itself, and was being bandied about as early as the dawn of the 19th century. In the 1890s, Congress once again resurrected the plan. It went so far as to send an expedition into the Planalto (high plains) of Goiás which, at the time, consisted of little more than decaying gold-mining towns, cattle ranches, and Indian territory. It wasn't until the 1950s that Juscelino Kubitschek, former mayor of Belo Horizonte and governor of Minas Gerais, made the new capital a central tenet of his 1955 campaign platform to get elected as Brazil's president. When the victorious Kubitschek took power in early 1956,

he lost no time in getting to work. Through aerial surveys, a site was quickly chosen. An international competition yielded a winning plan submitted by Lúcio Costa, a young urban designer. Working alongside Costa were two long-time collaborators of Kubitschek's who had contributed to daring projects in Belo Horizonte. Landscaper Roberto Burle Marx was responsible for Copacabana's famous mosaic walkway, and architect Oscar Niemeyer was a former pupil of Le Corbusier, the brilliant French modernist who was an advocate of geometrically planned cities.

Lúcio Costa's plan for Brasília followed Le Corbusier's precepts of rectilinear order while playing up the element of space—low buildings, wide boulevards, and vast green expanses. His goal was to emphasize the Planalto's endless horizon, drawing the eye to the point at which the red earth meets the luminous blue skies. Costa once commented: "The sky is the sea of Brasília." Indeed, what makes the city so striking is the contrast of gleaming white buildings set against green lawns and azure skies. As for Niemeyer, although he adhered to Le Corbusier's principles, he also subverted (and improved) them by adding sinuous and sensuous circles, arcs, spirals, and curves to otherwise linear buildings. Softening what could have otherwise taken on shades of totalitarian uniformity, he imbued his buildings with an organic, even playful sensibility more in keeping with a tropical aesthetic and with the Brazilian personality as a whole.

Brasília's urban design is as futuristic as its architecture. If you arrive by plane (and most people do), you'll be treated to an eagle's eye view of the city's layout in the shape of an airplane or a bird with outstretched wings. Lúcio Costa referred to this as the Plano Piloto (Pilot Plan). Once you're on the ground, no matter how confusing Brasília might seem, it helps if you keep in mind this organization of the city into the bird or plane's head, body, and tail.

The body, known as the **Eixo Monumental**

(Monumental Axis), is an 8-kilometer (5-mile) strip of multi-lane boulevards that runs east–west from the **Praça do Cruzeiro** (the plane's tail) to **Praça dos Três Poderes** (the head, or cockpit). Running north–south, and intersecting with the Eixo Monumental, the **Eixo Rodoviário** (known as the "Eixão") is a curving artery that forms the wings of the bird/plane. At the intersection of the two Eixos is the city's transportation hub: the municipal **Rodoviária de Brasília,** from which local buses come and go.

Another signature feature of Brasília is its organization into zones. For instance, the Eixo Monumental is lined with government buildings, monuments, and museums, but is also divided into specific **setores** (**S**) that concentrate clusters of banks (Setor Bancário), hotels (Setor Hoteleiro), and commercial areas (Setor Comércio). Sectors themselves are further subdivided into **blocos** (**Bl.**), which are large buildings; **conjuntos** (**Cj.**), which are building subdivisions; **lojas** (**Lj.**), or stores; and **lotes** (**Lt.**), or lots.

The two "wings" of the bird or plane that branch off either side of the Eixo Monumental are actually referred to as wings: curving south is the Asa Sul (South Wing) and swinging north is the Asa Norte (North Wing). Both of these sweeping districts are largely residential with numbered apartment blocks, known as **quadras** (**Q**) and **superquadras** (**SQ**). Instead of names, roads are numbered according to their distance from the main Eixo and whether they are north (**N**) or south (**S**) of the Eixo Monumental and east (**L**) or west (**W**) of the Eixo Rodoviário.

Despite this precision, for all its rational geometry and its division into sectors and quads, Brasília can be both easy and incredibly confusing to navigate. The problem isn't so much the uniformity of the buildings, but trying to decipher the addresses.

SIGHTS

It will take you a full day (minimum) to visit Brasília's architectural marvels. Although most are located along the Eixo Monumental,

its length, coupled with the inevitably scalding sun, means you'll have to combine walking with buses and taxis to get from one end to the other. Even so, wear sunscreen, carry mineral water, and dress lightly (although not skimpily—no flip-flops, shorts, tank tops—since many of the sights you'll be visiting are government buildings with dress codes).

Eixo Monumental

It's best to start at the tail end of the Eixo Monumental. From the lofty height of Praça do Cruzeiro, you are treated to an impressive view down the Eixo towards the Esplanada dos Ministérios. Surveying the scene is a monumental bronze statue of Juscelino Kubitschek (JK) inside a curving half shell.

MEMORIAL JK

An appropriate beginning to your exploration of Brasília is to pay homage to its founder at Niemeyer's Memorial JK (Praça do Cruzeiro, Eixo Monumental, tel. 61/3225-9451, www.memorialjk.com.br, 9 A.M.–6 P.M. Tues.–Sun., R$4). Constructed out of white marble, its resemblances to an Egyptian pyramid are hardly coincidental. This reverent museum/shrine was inaugurated in 1981, five years after Kubitschek's untimely death in a car accident. Upon entering, your eyes alight upon the gold Rolex and identity documents found on the former president's person when his body was removed the crash. Aside from his library, you can inspect Kubitschek's personal objects, clothing (JK was a notorious dandy), and a mint-condition 1973 Galaxie he tooled around in. A rich collection of photographs, portraying the president's life and the construction of his dream capital, provides an excellent overview of the city's foundation and early years. Upstairs, the mortuary chamber, where Kubitschek's body rests in a black marble sarcophagus, is illuminated by colorful beams filtered through a roof of stained glass. This striking piece was designed by artist Marianne Peretti, who contributed many works to Brasília. Particularly moving is the simple epitaph engraved on JK's tomb: "O Fundador" (The Founder).

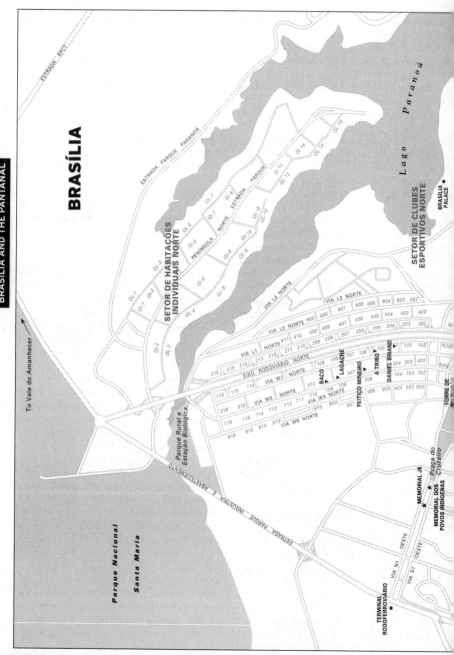

BRASÍLIA

BRASÍLIA AND THE PANTANAL

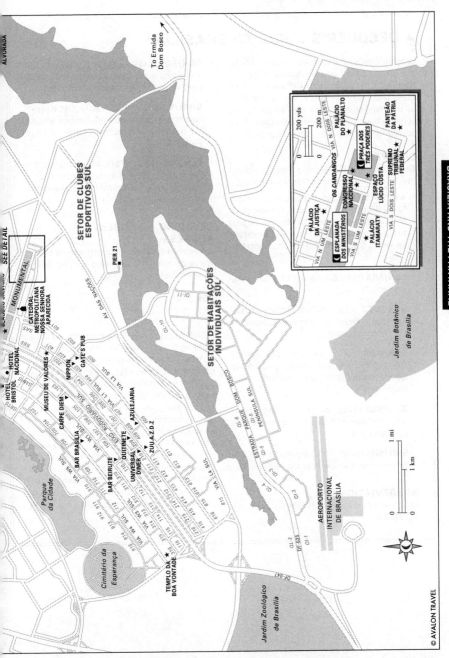

© AVALON TRAVEL

A DECODER'S GUIDE TO BRASÍLIA

Brasília's division into axes, sectors, blocks, and buildings may seem incredibly logical, but translating the coded abbreviations into an address that makes sense can be as confusing as traveling to a country where only cyrillic script is used. The following are some of the acronyms that will come in most handy.

SETORES

The following refer to the *setores* (sectors) that line both sides of the Eixo Monumental.

- **Asa Norte/Asa Sul** The two *asas* (wings), Norte (North) and Sul (South), curving off of the Eixo Monumental and running parallel to the Eixo Rodoviário. The **N** and **S** indicate on which side of the Eixo Monumental an address is.

- **SBN/SBS** (Setor Bancário Norte/Sul) banking sectors

- **SCN/SCS** (Setor Comercial Norte/ Sul) commercial office areas (adjacent to the shopping centers)

- **SDN/SDS** (Setor de Diversões Norte/ Sul) the two shopping centers (Conjunto Nacional and CONIC) on either side of the Rodoviária

- **SEN/SES** (Setor de Embaixadas Norte/ Sul) the two embassy sectors (east of the bank sectors)

- **SHN/SHS** (Setor Hoteleiro Norte/Sul) the two hotel sectors (west of the Rodoviária)

ABBREVIATIONS

Abbreviations in the main residential areas are as follows:

- **SQN/SQS** (Superquadras Norte/Sul) the individual *superquadras* in the main residential wings of Asa Norte and Asa Sul

- **SHIN/SHIS** (Setor de Habitações Individuais Norte/Sul) residential zones around the northern and southern banks of Lago Paranoá

- **CLN/CLS** or **SCLN/SCLS** (Setor Comércio Local Norte/Sul) the commercial blocks (stores, bars, restaurants) set amid the residential *superquadras*

DECODING A RESIDENTIAL ADDRESS

Decoding a residential address can be tricky. We've decoded the following address below as an example.

SQN 204
Bl. B-303

SQN refers to *superquadra* north, no. 204, building B, apartment 303. The *superquadra* number provides the location: The first digit (2) is the position east or west of the Eixo Rodoviário (odd numbers are to the west, even numbers to the east, increasing the farther away you get from the center). The last two digits (04) are the position north or south of the Eixo Monumental. So in the case of 204, you know that the *superquadra* you're looking for is 4 blocks north of the Eixo Monumental and 1 block west of the Eixo Rodoviário. If none of this makes sense, simply write out the address on a piece of paper and let a cab driver take care of the decoding for you.

MEMORIAL DOS POVOS INDÍGENAS

Niemeyer's cylindrical Memorial dos Povos Indígenas (Praça do Buriti, Eixo Monumental, tel. 61/3226-5206, 9 A.M.–5 P.M. Tues.–Fri., 10 A.M.–5 P.M. Sat.–Sun.) imitates the traditional round dwellings of the Bororo Indians. The curving interior shelters an impressive collection of indigenous art—baskets, jewelry, weapons, hammocks, and feather headdresses—the majority made by groups from the surrounding Planalto region, especially around the Rio Xingu. Particularly striking are the ceramic vessel made by the Warao people, intricately decorated with bird and animal motifs. Near the museum café, you'll encounter some authentic and very attractive pieces for sale by local Indians.

TORRE DE TELEVISÃO

From the Memorial dos Povos Indígenas, you'll need to grab a bus or taxi down the Eixo Monumental to get to the Torre de Televisão (Eixo Monumental, tel. 61/3323-7944, 9 A.M.–noon and 2–6 P.M. Mon.–Fri., 11 A.M.–6 P.M. Sat.–Sun., free). From the viewing deck, a third of the way up Lúcio Costa's 224-meter (735 feet) television tower, you're treated to incredible 360-degree views of the city, which are particularly bewitching around sunset. On the main floor, a small crafts market, open from Thursday to Sunday, is a good place to pick up regional handicrafts.

TEATRO NACIONAL CLÁUDIO SANTORO

Cross the Eixo Rodoviário, and on the north side of the *rodoviária* you'll come face to face with another Niemeyer pyramid, housing Brasília's prestigious Teatro Nacional Cláudio Santoro (Eixo Monumental/W3 Norte, tel. 61/3325-2216, 8 A.M.–6 P.M. Mon.–Fri.). Dazzling from the outside, its glass-covered surface permits natural light to suffuse the lobby, where art exhibitions are displayed. The lateral facades embossed with a sea of white cubes and rectangles are the work of Athos Bulcão, while the surrounding gardens featuring native plants are by Roberto Burle Marx. In the foyer, the lyrical bronze statue *O*

Contorcionista (*The Contortionist*) is by noted sculptor Alfredo Ceschiatti. Three separate auditoriums host theatrical productions as well as concerts, dance, and ballet performances. During the week, guided tours are available.

MUSEU DE VALORES

An easy walk south from the *rodoviária,* you can't miss the towering skyscrapers of concrete and dark glass that house the Edifício-Sede do Banco Central. At the rear of the Central Bank building, the Museu de Valores (SBSl, Qd. 3, Bl. B, tel. 61/3414-2093, www.bcb.gov.br/museu, 10 A.M.–5:40 P.M. Tues.–Fri., 2–6 P.M. Sat.) traces Brazilian history via its many monies: from the first coins minted in Portugal to the remarkably stable (and increasingly valorized) *real* of today. The most fascinating section is devoted to a history of gold in different forms, ranging from the ingots featuring the emperor's official stamp to the largest gold nugget ever found in the world, a 61-kilo (135-pound) chunk that was uncovered in the Amazon region.

◖ ESPLANADA DOS MINISTÉRIOS AND THE PRAÇA DOS TRÊS PODERES

Approaching the Praça do Três Poderes along the Eixo Monumental, you'll first be confronted with the Esplanada dos Ministérios, an enormous corridor of 17 identical government buildings facing each other from opposite sides of the street. At the very beginning of the Esplanada, you'll find two of Niemeyer's most recent works, the **Biblioteca Nacional** (National Library) and the **Museu Nacional** (Esplanada dos Ministérios, tel. 61/3325-5220, 9 A.M.–6 P.M. daily). Completed in 2006, both buildings constitute the last of the architectural complexes that were part of Niemeyer's original plans. To date, the gleaming dome-shaped museum, whose cavernous interior features the architect's signature swirling ramps, is only open for temporary art exhibitions.

CATEDRAL METROPOLITANA DE NOSSA SENHORA DA APARECIDA

One of Niemeyer's undisputed masterpieces is the Catedral Metropolitana de Nossa Senhora

Brasília's Catedral Metropolitana de Nossa Senhora da Aparecida is one of Oscar Niemeyer's masterpieces.

da Aparecida (Eixo Monumental, tel. 61/3224-4073, 8 A.M.–5 P.M. Mon., 8 A.M.–6 P.M. Tues.–Sun.). Built on the spot where Brasília was inaugurated, the cathedral's graceful hourglass structure consists of 16 reinforced concrete columns whose thorny tips thrust skywards. The columns provide support for the immense panes of stained glass designed by Marianne Peretti that make the subterranean church seem bathed in heavenly light. The cathedral seems small from the outside. However, once inside you'll be amazed by the soaring spaciousness enhanced by the clean lines and use of white marble. Paintings by Athos Bulcão and a panel depicting the Way of the Cross by modernist painter Emiliano Di Cavalcanti are on display, but the most striking contribution is the three floating angels suspended in the air. They are the work of Alfredo Ceschiatti, who also designed the statues of the four apostles near the entrance. Try to contain any oohs and ahs—the acoustics are such that a word muttered in a low voice can be clearly heard from 25 meters (82 feet) away.

PALÁCIO ITAMARATY

At the end of the Esplanada do Ministérios lie two of Niemeyer's most famous works: the Palácio Itamaraty and the Palácio de Justiça. Housing the Ministry of Foreign Affairs, the Palácio Itamaraty (Esplanada dos Ministérios, tel. 61/3411-8051, www.mre.gov.br, free guided visits daily) is a disarmingly elegant fusion of classicism and modernism. The exterior is impressive enough: its raw concrete arcades sheltering a glittering glass box are reflected in pools of water that surround the construction like a moat. The island gardens featuring Amazonian plants were designed by Burle Marx, while the stunning abstract sculpture *O Meteoro* (*The Meteor*), whose interlocking pieces represent the Earth's continents, was carved by Bruno Giorgi from four tons of Carrara marble. Don't neglect to take a tour inside. The sprawling, open interior with its garden courtyards is a veritable who's who of 20th-century Brazilian artists. Sculptures by Ceschiatti, Victor Brecheret, and Lasar Segall and paintings by Cândido Portinari and Alfredo Volpi are a few of the works that decorate the vast salons furnished with plush Persian carpets and exquisite antiques. Guided visits are 40 minutes long and need to be reserved in advance.

PALÁCIO DA JUSTIÇA

Facing the Palácio Itamaraty, the Palácio da Justiça (Esplanada dos Ministérios, tel. 61/3429-3216, 10 A.M. and 3 P.M. Mon.–Fri.) is similar in style, but less impressively grand than its counterpart. Housing the Ministry of Justice, its architectural highlight is six waterfalls pouring down from the building's facade into a surrounding pool.

PRAÇA DOS TRÊS PODERES

At the western end of the Eixo Monumental, the Praça dos Três Poderes corresponds to the head of the bird (or cockpit of the airplane) as laid out in the Plano Piloto. The nexus of government power is concentrated around the vast plaza itself in the buildings housing the *três poderes* (three powers)—the executive (Palácio Planalto), legislative (Congresso Nacional), and judicial (Supremo Tribunal Federal) branches. The fantastic Niemeyer constructions in which they are housed are widely considered to be the most splendid examples of modernist architecture in the world.

Before exploring them, take a quick glance at the **Espaço Lúcio Costa** (tel. 61/3321-9843, 9 A.M.–6 P.M. daily), which pays tribute to Brasília's mastermind. On display are the original plans (in Portuguese and English) that won him the commission, along with a gigantic maquette of the city that gives a great overview of the Plano Piloto. Also interesting is the **Panteão da Pátria** (tel. 61/3325-6244, 9 A.M.–6 P.M. Tues.–Sun.), which honors national heroes in a building shaped to conjure up a dove.

CONGRESSO NACIONAL

Between the Esplanada dos Ministérios and the Praça dos Três Poderes lies Brasília's most instantly recognizable symbol: the 28-story twin towers flanked by two giant bowl-shaped cupolas that make up the Congresso Nacional (Praça dos Três Poderes, tel. 61/3216-1771, www.camara.gov.br, 9:30 A.M.–5 P.M. daily). The convex (right side up) bowl is where the 500-member Câmara de Deputados (House of Representatives) convenes, while the concave (upside-down) bowl houses the 80 members of the Senado (Senate). Both were originally designed so that the public could hang out on top of them (these days only the Polícia Militar have this privilege). You can, however, take an hour-long tour of the sweeping marble and granite salons decorated with tile panels by Athos Bulcão and paintings by Di Cavalcanti. If the chambers are in session, you can check out the senators and deputies in action.

SUPREMO TRIBUNAL FEDERAL

On the southern side of the Praça dos Três Poderes, the elegant Supremo Tribunal Federal (tel. 61/3217-4037, www.stf.gov.br, 10 A.M.–5:30 P.M. Sat.–Sun.) houses the Brazilian Supreme Court. Guarding the entrance is the striking granite sculpture *A Justiça* (*The Justice*) by Ceschiatti.

The Congresso Nacional building houses the Senate and House of Representatives.

BRASÍLIA AND THE PANTANAL

The dove-shaped Panteão da Pátria sits upon the Praça dos Três Poderes.

PALÁCIO DO PLANALTO

On the northern side of the Praça, the Palácio do Planalto (tel. 61/3411-2042, www.presidencia.com.br, 9:30 A.M.–2:30 P.M. Sun.) is where the president works, which is why you can only visit the interior (including his office) on Sundays, during 30-minute free guided tours. The majestic exterior is notable for its mingling of straight and curving lines and for the ramp leading up the entrance, by which newly inaugurated presidents literally ascend to power (on a day-to-day basis they enter through a back door). During the week, you can observe the changing of the guard at 8:30 A.M. and 6 P.M. Right across from the *palácio,* Bruno Giorgi's famous bronze sculpture, **Os Candangos,** has become a symbol of the city. *Candango* was an expression that referred to the thousands of poor workers, mostly from the Northeast, who were hired to build Brasília and who subsequently settled in the *favela*-like suburbs that surround the city. Originally, it was a derogatory term that African slaves applied to the Portuguese during colonial times. However,

over the years, the pejorative connotation has evaporated and today all native residents of Brasília are called Candangos.

To see where the president lives, visit the **Palácio da Alvorada** (SHTN, tel. 61/3411-2317, www.presidencia.gov.br, 3–5 P.M. Wed.), a quick 15-minute cab ride north (you can also take the 104 bus from the *rodoviária*) from the Praça dos Três Poderes. It sits along the northern shore of Lago Paranoá. The name (*alvorada* means dawn) was supplied by Kubitschek himself, who often referred to Brasília as a "new dawn in Brazil's history." The first of Niemeyer's Brasília buildings to be completed (in 1958), the president's official residence is also one of the most beautiful: the harmonious fusion of glass, white marble, and mirror-like pools is offset by expansive green gardens and an immaculate soccer field (added at the request of President Lula). Tours (around the outside verandas) are only available on Wednesdays. Otherwise, you'll have to be content to gaze at the ensemble from behind the guarded gates.

Beyond the Plano Piloto

Should you have more time at your disposal, there are several interesting attractions located off the main axes of the Plano Piloto. They are linked to Brasília's notorious mystical element, which adds an interesting counterpoint to its culture of political wheeling and dealing. The city's mysticism stems from the vision that came to an Italian priest named Dom João Bosco, in 1883, of a new civilization that would rise up around a lake situated between the 15th and 20th parallels. Kubitschek was a big Bosco devotee, and when his gleaming city of the future rose up (somewhat miraculously) on the shores of an artificial lake, it wasn't long before various cults and New Age groups claimed the area as their utopia.

SANTUÁRIO DOM BOSCO

Often eclipsed by the Catedral Metropolitano, the Santuário Dom Bosco (W-3 Sul, ad. 702, Bl. B, tel. 61/3223-6542, www.santuariodombosco.com.br, 7 A.M.–7 P.M. Mon.–Sat., 7 A.M.–noon and 2–8 P.M. Sun.) is equally splendid. The slender concrete columns of its box-like shell function as frames for the immense floor-to-ceiling stained glass windows whose intricate mosaic motifs are rendered in 12 tones of blue. During the day, the effects of the sun's rays shining through the azure glass are quite dazzling. At night, an equally impressive spectacle is provided by the gargantuan central chandelier fashioned out of 7,400 individual crystals of Murano glass.

TEMPLO DA BOA VONTADE

Located 8 kilometers (5 miles) south of the Eixo Monumental, the Templo da Boa Vontade (SGAS, 915, Lt. 75/6, tel. 61/3245-1070, www.tbv.com.br, temple open 24 hours daily, Egyptian room and gallery open 10 A.M.–6 P.M. daily) is a pyramid topped with an enormous 21-kilogram (46-pound) crystal. Aside from its visual splendor, it is reputed to be the largest crystal rock in the world capable of attracting pure energy. Created by the Legião da Boa Vontade (Goodwill Legion) with the objective of promoting peace and unity among "Earthly and Celestial Beings of all races, philosophies, religious and political creeds, and even atheists and materialists," the temple includes a meditation space, an art gallery, a sumptuously outfitted Egyptian Room, and a sacred fountain whose healing natural waters receive the energies of the giant crystal. To get here, take the 105 or 107 bus from the *rodoviária*.

ENTERTAINMENT AND EVENTS
Nightlife

Although hardly wild, Brasília has a fairly varied nightlife. Many of the best options are concentrated in and around the Asa Sul. Some of Brasília's restaurants also have bars and even host live music performances. Among the more classic watering holes, **Bar Beirute** (Comércio Local Sul, Qd. 109, Bl. A, Lj. 2–4, tel. 61/3244-1717, 11 A.M.–2 A.M. daily) is a local institution that has barely changed since it first opened its doors in 1966. Over the years, major political and cultural figures have engaged in often heated discussions at the tables scattered beneath a canopy of trees. A happy-hour favorite during the week, on Saturday nights it draws a gay and lesbian crowd. As a nod to the original Lebanese owners, the kitchen continues to prepare tasty *petiscos* such as *quibe* and lamb kebabs. **Bar Brasília** (CLS, Qd. 506, Lj. 15, tel. 61/3443-4323, 5:30 P.M.–close Mon.–Thurs., 11:30 A.M.–close Fri.–Sun.) is a popular old-style *boteco* where you can get the best *chope* in town. The draft is served in specially made crystal glasses, at exactly 3°C (37.4°F), and with a 3-centimeter (1.2-inch) head of froth. Snacks include *bolinhos de bacalhau* and *pastéis* stuffed with beef and *pequi* (a Cerrado fruit). Art deco light fixtures and a handsome wooden bar salvaged from a 1950s pharmacy add to the retro atmosphere.

Azulejaria (CLS, Qd. 408, Bl. D. Lj. 1, tel. 61/3443-0698, noon–3 P.M. and 6 P.M.–2 A.M. Mon.–Sat.) got its name from the many hand-painted *azulejos* (ceramic tiles) that decorate this artists' atelier that, over the years, has morphed into an enticing bar/lounge with a wine shop in the basement and tables spilling into the garden. Attracting a more upscale, fashionable crowd, the place is thronged on Thursdays when the tables are removed to make way for DJs spinning dance tunes. In the '80s and early '90s Brasília was known nationwide as a hotbed for Brazilian rock—from which emerged groups such as Legião Urbana, Capital Inicial, and Os Raimundos. Although the rocker scene isn't what it used to be, at the dim, dusky, and vaguely Brit-like **Gate's Pub** (CLS, Qd. 403, Bl. B, Lj. 34, tel. 61/3244-0222, www.gatespub.com.br, 9 P.M.–close Tues.–Sun., artistic cover R$3–20) you can catch some live bands and then continue dancing the night away to DJ-spun music.

Performing Arts

Due to its status as the nation's capital, Brasília receives the best of national and international musicians, theatrical productions, and dance companies. Aside from the **Teatro Nacional Cláudio Santoro** (Eixo Monumental/W3 Norte, tel. 61/3325-2216), other major performing venues include the Academia de Tênis's swanky **Americel Hall** (Setor de Clubes Sul, Lt. 1B, tel. 61/3316-6261) and the **Centro Cultural Banco do Brasil** (SCES, trecho 2, Lt. 22, tel. 61/3310-7087, 9 A.M.–9 P.M., www.bb.com.br), a Niemeyer-designed cultural center that also hosts art exhibitions and screens films. For more information, check out the cultural listings in the daily *Correio Brasiliense* newspaper.

Cinema

Brasília is a surprisingly fertile place for cinephiles. It hosts two major film festivals: the **Festival Internacional de Cinema** (www.ficbrasilia.com.br), in early December, and the **Festival de Brasília de Cinema Brasileiro** (www.sc.df.gov.br), in November. Films are screened at the **Cine Academia** (Setor de Clubes Sul, Lt. 1B, tel. 61/3316-6374, www.cineacademia.com.br), a fantastic complex at the Academia de Tênis with 12 screens devoted to independent and art films, along with a charming restaurant and

bar. **Cine Brasília** (EQ Sul, 106-107, tel. 61/3244-1660, www.sc.df.gov.br/agenda) is a government-operated cinematheque that screens art and repertory films at subsidized prices. Designed by Niemeyer and inaugurated in 1960, it boasts a big screen, a modernist lobby, and very comfy seating.

SHOPPING

Shopping malls reign supreme in Brasília. The oldest and most central *shopping* is the **Conjunto Nacional** (SDN, tel. 61/3316-9733, www.cnbshopping.com.br, 10 A.M.–10 P.M. Mon.–Sat., noon–8 P.M. Sun.). A massive hulk of concrete on the north side of the Rodoviária, it's more democratic than your average Brazilian malls, which are usually either chic or "popular." This one is both. Aside from stores and a supermarket, it has a wide range of eating options. The Siciliano bookstore has English-language books and magazines. More upscale and glossy, with fancier boutiques and food options and cineplexes, are **Brasília Shopping** (SCN, Qd. 5, Bl. A, tel. 61/3328-2122, www.brasiliashopping.com.br, 10 A.M.–10 P.M. Mon.–Sat., 2–10 P.M. Sun.), and **Pátio Brasil Shopping** (SCS, Qd. 7, Bl. A, tel. 61/3314-7400, www.patiobrasil.com.br, 10 A.M.–10:30 P.M. Mon.–Sat., 2–8 P.M. Sun.), which is conveniently close to the hotel sectors.

For indigenous art and objects, aside from those sold at the Memorial dos Povos Indígenas (see *Sights*), try the improvised market held on the patio of the FUNAI building (SEP, Qd. 702, Bl. A)—FUNAI is the federal agency that governs Indian affairs. Indians from near and far come to FUNAI in an attempt to settle conflicts, and they often bring baskets, pottery, and other artifacts to sell (at very reasonable prices) during the week. The FUNAI building is close to the main entrance to the Parque da Cidade.

SPORTS AND RECREATION
Parks

Despite popular perception of Brasília as an arid city where concrete, glass, and asphalt rule, once you get off the beaten Plano Piloto, you'll find a surprisingly vast number of parks that make the capital one of the greenest cities in Brazil. The most central and easiest to get to is the **Parque da Cidade** (Eixo Monumental Sul, tel. 61/3325-1092, 5 A.M.–midnight daily). Officially known as the Parque Sarah Kubitschek, this sprawling park features wooded areas and a large artificial lake. Locals routinely take advantage of its biking, jogging, and walking trails as well as its bars and food kiosks. Another favorite recreational destination is the **Lago Paranoá,** an immense artificial lake surrounded by parkland, walking trails, sports clubs, and restaurants and bars. Most attractions are around the Lago Sul (southern part of the lake), including the **Ermida Dom Bosco** (Estrada Parque Dom Bosco, Lago Sul, Setor de Mansões Dom Bosco, Cj. 12, tel. 61/3367-4505, daily), a sanctuary devoted to Dom Bosco along with a futuristic monastery and gardens designed by Burle Marx that offer panoramic views of the Plano Piloto. From the *rodoviária*, both the 123 and 125 buses circle around the southern shore.

The Cerrado

In only a few decades, rampant urban development and the clearing of surrounding land for the planting of lucrative cash crops such as soy beans has led to the destruction of the majority of the native Cerrado vegetation that once covered the Planalto. Despite this tragic devastation—of roughly 10,000 Cerrado plant species only 44 percent exist elsewhere in the world—several parks preserve this unique mixture of grassland, dry forest, and buriti palms. In Brasília itself, you can follow various hiking trails through a preserved swatch of typical Cerrado vegetation at the well-organized **Jardim Botânico** (Setor de Mansões D. Bosco, Cj. 12, Lago Sul, tel. 61/3366-2141, 9 A.M.–5 P.M. Tues.–Sun., R$2), located along the southern shores of Lago Paranoá. To get here, take the 147 bus from the *rodoviária*. Farther away, along the city's northern fringes, is the vast **Parque Nacional de Brasília** (BR-040 Km 9, Setor Militar Urbano, tel. 61/3465-2013, 8 A.M.–4 P.M. daily, R$3), known popularly as "Água Mineral" due to its abundant freshwater springs and natural pools in which you can take a dip. Several walking

trails lead through preserved Cerrado vegetation including trees bearing *pequi* and *mangaba* fruits and *ipês* sprayed with yellow and violet blossoms. During the week, when the park receives fewer visitors, your chances of glimpsing armadillos, monkeys, and capybaras are higher. To get here, take a cab or the W3 Norte Circular bus, which passes along W3 and can let you off near the park entrance.

Within an hour or two from the city limits, you can venture even more deeply into the Cerrado, although in most cases you'll need a car. For a quick getaway, **Cachoeira da Saia Velha** (BR-040 Km 35 south of Brasília, tel. 61/3627-0000, 8 A.M.–4 P.M. daily, R$7–10) is an ecological reserve with a waterfall and a handful of refreshing natural pools. Also close to Brasília is **Poço Azul** (DF-001 Km 105, tel. 61/9648-1559, 5 A.M.–7 P.M. daily, R$15 per car), a park with waterfalls and brilliant turquoise pools where you can go swimming and diving and also practice rappelling. Bring food and drink for a picnic since there are no restaurants. To get here take the DF-001 from the Eixo Norte towards Lago Oeste for 20 kilometers (12 miles) to the end of the highway, before following a signed dirt road for 9 kilometers (6 miles).

Two hours northeast of the city, the town of Formosa is the base for visiting the **Salto de Itiquira** (tel. 61/3503-5108, 8 A.M.–4 P.M. daily, R$10), a spectacular 170-meter-high (558-foot-high) waterfall, surrounded by a park filled with lush tropical vegetation and natural swimming pools. Although you can take a bus from the *rodoferroviária* (long-distance bus station) to Formosa, getting a ride to the falls (40 kilometers/25 miles away) is tricky and expensive (if you have to depend on a taxi from the bus station). If you have a car, just follow the BR-020 and BR-030 to Formosa and then follow GO-44 along to Itiquira.

Other nearby waterfalls, pools, caves, and gorges can't be reached easily, even by car. Instead they require hiking on trails that weave through striking, unmarred landscapes. For guided day trips, contact **Bluepoint** (SCLN, 310, Bl. D, Lj. 71, tel. 61/3274-033, www.bluepoint.com.br).

ACCOMMODATIONS

From Monday to Thursday—when Congress is in full swing—hotel rooms fill up, prices rise, and reservations are a must. Meanwhile, on weekends, when deputies return to their home states and the city clears out, you can get discounts of up to 50 percent. Since business execs and politicos are much more common than backpackers, no-frills budget accommodations are harder to come by. The cheapest *pousadas* in town—on and around Via W3 Sul—are usually fairly down-and-out and not very safe, not to mention inconvenient. Simplifying matters substantially, hotels in Brasília are concentrated in the central Hotel Sector.

R$100-200

Sporting a cool '70s vibe and lots of glossy marble (walls, floors, and bathrooms), the **Hotel Bristol** (SHS, Qd. 4, Bl. F, tel. 61/3962-6162, www.bristolhotel.com.br, R$160–200 d) is a friendly and well-appointed hotel near the Pátio Brasil *shopping* and five minutes from the Congresso Nacional. A rooftop swimming pool, piano bar, and appealing restaurant add to the already good value. Well situated near the Eixo Monumental, another nicely priced option is the smaller and more basic, but welcoming **Casablanca** (SHN, Qd. 5, Bl. A, tel. 61/3228-8586, www.casablancabrasilia.com.br, R$165 d). Rooms are clean and comfortable (although the artwork includes the likes of Charlie Chaplin posters) and there is a decent restaurant that serves local dishes.

Recently reopened after 30 years of inactivity following a devastating fire, the 🄲 **Brasília Palace** (Setor de Hotéis e Turismo Norte, trecho 1, Lt. 1, tel. 61/3306-9100, R$100–200 d) is Brasília's first hotel. Truth be told, it was inaugurated in 1958—two years before the city even existed. A modernist box designed entirely by Niemeyer (down to the furniture) and decorated with beautiful tile murals by Athão Bulcão, the Brasília Palace was built in an incredible eight months. The enormous pool was an afterthought—when asked on an Easter Sunday what shape it would have, Niemeyer replied "egg-shaped." Upon its completion,

Brazil's "Waldorf Astoria" served as President Kubitschek's private clubhouse. From here he entertained VIPs from far and wide, who flew into the dusty middle of nowhere to watch as the space-age capital rose to life before their eyes. The first visiting dignitary to check in was Paraguayan dictator Alfredo Stroessner, followed by Indira Gandhi, Fidel Castro, Ché Guevara, and Dwight Eisenhower. Sartre and Simone de Beauvoir also showed up and soundly dissed the plans for the new capital. However, when the city was inaugurated in 1960, the Palace was so overpacked that hotel tycoon Conrad Hilton had to bunk in the barber shop. Until Brasília's embassies were built, heads of state were lodged and fêted in the hotel's streamlined rooms on the banks of the recently completed Lago Paranoá. Today, this architectural gem has once again become a hot spot, not only as a hotel, but as place to gather and listen to live jazz, performed Wednesday through Friday, at the swanky restaurant/piano bar, Oscar Jazz and Cucina.

R$200-300

Built in 1961, for decades the **Hotel Nacional** (SHS, Qd. 1, Bl. A, tel. 61/3321-7575, www.hotelnacional.com.br, R$310–390 d) was Brasília's most prestigious hotel, welcoming political bigwigs and international celebrities. In fact, charmed by the throwback '60s decor, excellent service, and cavernous rooms—not to mention a luxurious new spa—many still haunt the place, making reservations essential. Weekend rates are half price. For something more up-to-date, try the high-quality spankingly modern **Meliá Brasil 21** (SHS, Qd. 6, Bl. D, tel. 61/3218-4700, www.solmelia.com, R$220–315 d). For comfort, location, service, and amenities—a full-business center with Internet, a heated rooftop pool, and access to one of the best gyms in town (for R$28 a day)—this hotel is hard to beat. A nice eco-touch is the decorative use of reforested native wood.

FOOD

With all the government officials and foreign diplomats and dignitaries milling around, it is not surprising that Brasília has one of Brazil's most varied and sophisticated dining scenes.

Cafés and Snacks

In his native France, pastry chef Daniel Briand's croissants were deemed so good that he was invited to teach a cooking course in Paris. After falling in love with a Brazilian student, he followed her home to Brasília and opened **Daniel Briand Pâtissier & Chocolatier** (CLN, Qd. 104, Bl. A, Lj. 28, tel. 61/3326-1135, 11 A.M.–10 P.M. Tues.–Fri., 9 A.M.–10 P.M. Sat.–Sun.), a Parisian-style café that serves the finest pastries (and croissants) in town. Aside from his mouthwatering sweets, you can indulge in savory snacks, weekend breakfasts, and light bistro fare such as smoked salmon crèpes with lime and cream. About as hybrid as a food emporium can get, **Quitinete** (CLS, Qd. 209, Lj. 5, tel. 61/3242-0506, 7 A.M.–1 A.M. daily) is a delicious mixture of gourmet delicatessen, bakery, café, restaurant, and cookware boutique. For a mellow and heavily aromatic caffeine fix, try the house blend, whose beans are cultivated exclusively on a São Paulo farm. The charming upstairs restaurant has views of the street and of the bakery below (through a glass roof), where you can enjoy light meals, such as shrimp and vegetable curry, as well as imaginative (if pricy) sandwiches.

Contemporary

Operated by Brasília's super-chef extraordinaire, Mara Alcamin (who is also the creative force behind Quitenete and Universal Diner), **Ⓒ Zuu a.Z.d.Z** (CLS, Qd. 210, Bl. C, Lj. 38, tel. 61/3244-1039, noon–3 P.M. and 8 P.M.–midnight Mon.–Fri., 8 P.M.–1 A.M. Sat., R$55–70) represents the Brazilian capital's introduction to "slow food." Indeed, the exotically mod setting—lofty ceilings, plush sofas scattered with Indian pillows, and hypnotic lounge music—is certainly conducive to hours spent savoring creations such as foie gras flambéed in *cachaça* with grilled *coalho* cheese and a sugarcane reduction. Equally hard to resist is the black sesame crusted tuna on a bed of shimeji mushrooms topped with tamarind coulis, and accompanied by wasabi chantilly, caramelized figs, and pureed manioc. For dessert, try the *suflê de doce de leite,* a decadent butterscotch soufflé.

Brazilian

The *saudade* (nostalgia) of the owner of **Feitiço Mineiro** (CLN, Qd. 306, Bl. 6, Lj. 45–51, tel. 61/3272-3032, noon–3 P.M. and 5:30 onwards Mon.–Fri., and 6 P.M.–close Sat., and noon–5 P.M. Sun., R$20–30) for his home state of Minas Gerais ensures the authenticity of both the homelike decor and the traditional Mineiro fare prepared under the watchful eye of his mother. The lunchtime buffet, displayed upon a wood-burning stove, offers a banquet of typical dishes. In the evenings, à la carte options include specialties such as *costelinha ao velho chico* (pork cutlets served with braised kale, manioc, and the thick bean puree known as *tutu*) and *frango ao molho pardo* (chicken cooked in a fragrant sauce made from its own blood). At night, the restaurant is one of the hottest tickets in town to catch great live music performances while nibbling on an all-you-can-eat buffet of appetizers.

With a bewitching view of Lago Paranoá, the villa that houses **Ⓒ Patú Anu** (Setor de Mansões de Lago Norte, ML 12, Cj. 1, Casa 7, tel. 61/3369-2788, www.patuanu.com.br, 8:30 P.M.–1 A.M. Tues.–Sat., 1:30–6 P.M. Sun.) mixes indigenous and Afro-Brazilian artifacts with elegant table settings, candelabras, and displays of tropical flowers. The menu offers a colorful and textured fusion of dishes with significant Amazonian influences and a predilection for exotic game such as *javalí* (wild boar), *jacaré* (alligator), and cabybara (the world's largest—and most delicious—rodent). On Friday and Saturday nights, live MPB, jazz and blues is performed. If you don't want a full meal, relax in the lounge or on a veranda and nibble on skewers of *jacaré* with tangy *coalho* cheese and *pimenta* (hot pepper) jelly.

International

Lagash (CLN, Qd. 308-309, Bl. B, Lj. 11/17, tel. 61/3273-0098, www.lagash.com.br, noon–4 P.M. and 7 P.M.–midnight Mon.–Sat., noon–6 P.M. Sun., R$30–40) is renowned for its refined and immaculately prepared Moroccan, Lebanese, and Syrian fare. Particularly popular are the succulent lamb dishes such as shredded Moroccan lamb with walnuts and rice, and roasted leg of lamb with dried pears in pomegranate sauce. For a medley of flavors, try the tasting menu, which offers a sampling of 12 dishes for R$36.

At **Nippon** (CLS, Qd. 403, Bl. A, Lj. 28, tel. 61/3224-0430, noon–2:30 P.M. and 7–11 P.M. Mon.–Fri., noon–3 P.M. and 7 P.M.–midnight Sat., noon–4:30 P.M. Sun., R$30–40) chef Jun Ito makes Japanese food as authentic as that you'd be served in Tokyo. Proof of his success is in the rave reviews from the Japanese diplomats and dignitaries who have dined here. However, Ito also has an inventive streak, which explains offerings such as salmon rolls stuffed with shimeji mushrooms and shrimp tempura with shiitake sauce. Although there are more than 150 à la carte choices on the menu, most fans opt for the all-you-can-eat *rodízio* of 50 dishes served Monday to Thursday nights and Sunday at lunch (R$42 pp). There is also a daily lunch buffet.

For mouthwatering pizza, head to **Baco** (CLN, Qd, 309, Bl. A, Lj. 30, tel. 61/3274-8600, 6 P.M.–1 A.M. daily, R$20–30). Crusts come in three varieties: *napolitana* (soft and thick), *romana* (thin and crunchy) and *integral* (whole wheat). Toppings are divided between classic Italian recipes and experimental creations such as the popular shimeji with leeks and gorgonzola with pears. From Sunday to Tuesday, sample all of them at the R$22 per person *rodízio*. There is another location in the Comércio Local Sul (Qd. 408, Bl. C. Lj. 30, tel. 61/3244-2292).

Varied

Operated by superchef Mara Alcamin, **Universal Diner** (CLS, Qd. 210, Bl. B, Lj. 30, tel. 61/3443-2089, 7 P.M.–midnight Mon., noon–3 P.M. and 7 P.M.–midnight Tues.–Sat., noon–4 P.M. Sun., R$35–50) is one of the capital's most offbeat restaurants, whose clientele mixes alternative types with suits and ties. The whimsical decor is a definite draw—oddities include dangling stuffed animals and a chair designed by B. B. King. Then there is the outstanding food, which ranges from the simplicity of a well-cooked filet mignon to "sexy shrimp," (shrimp in a sauce of brie, champagne, and caviar served with strawberry risotto). Although fairly pricy, during the week there are R$30 *pratos executivos* served at lunch. On Friday nights, dance music erupts from the lower level bar.

Brasilienses can't get enough of **Carpe Diem** (CLS, Qd. 104, Bl. D, Lj. 1, tel. 61/3325-5301, noon–1 A.M. daily), which is why there are currently six of these high-quality "rapid" food restaurants scattered around town, each with its own personality. Harried execs prefer the branch in Shopping In Brasília, which specializes in grilled meats and fast service, while cinephiles frequent the Casa Park location before and after film screenings, and families flock to dine at the Terraço Shopping restaurant. The all-round favorite, however, is the original at 104 Sul, which offers a terrific lunch buffet of salads and hot dishes for R$30 as well as à la carte options. The *feijoadas* (R$30 pp) served on Saturdays are legendary.

For a tasty all-natural lunch at a nice price, head to **A Tribo** (CLN, Qd. 105, Bl. B, Lj. 52–59, tel. 61/3039-6430, 11:30 A.M.–3 P.M. Tues.–Fri., noon–4 P.M. Sun., R$12–20), a laid-back and rustic retreat that offers an organic spread of salads and hot dishes prepared on a wood-burning stove. To quench your thirst there are over a dozen natural fruit juices (try the *"bomba"*—a serious pick-me-up that mixes *guaraná*, lime juice, spinach, and mint). The restaurant also opens Thursday nights, offering soups, crêpes, and pizzas as well as live music. The same owners (originally from Angola) also opened the harder to get to, but very enchanting ◖ **Oca da Tribo** (Setor de Clubes Esportivos Sul, Trecho 2, tel. 61/3226-9880, noon–3 P.M. Mon., noon–3 P.M. and 7 P.M.–midnight Tues.–Sat., noon–4 P.M. Sun.). The restaurant is housed in an immense *oca* (a traditional Indian dwelling) with wooden tables, woven reed chairs, and decorative objects made by the Planalto's Xingu group. The slightly more expensive menu offers organic fare as well as sophisticated à la carte options featuring wild game such as boar, buffalo, and ostrich. Weekend buffets are more lavish. Friday and Saturday evenings are animated by live music and romantic torch lighting. To get here, you'll need to take a taxi.

INFORMATION

There are **tourist offices** at the airport (tel. 61/3033-9488, www.sedtur.df.gov.br, 7:30 A.M.–10:30 P.M. daily) and in the Conjunto Nacional shopping mall (tel. 61/3326-7387, 10 A.M.–10 P.M. daily) as well as a kiosk at the Praça dos Três Poderes. Also check out www.aboutbrasilia.com, which has tons of photos and lots of interesting and arcane facts, and www.infobrasilia.com.br, which gives a well-written overview of the city's history. In Portuguese, a good site with listings of what's going on is www.candango.com.

SERVICES

You can exchange and withdraw cash at **Banco do Brasil,** which has 24-hour ATMs at the airport and on the second floor of the Conjunto Nacional shopping center. There is also a **Citibank** (SCS, q. 6, Bl. A, Lj. 186). There is a **post office** at SBN, q. 06, Bl. A, Suite 1A).

In the event of an emergency, dial **192** for an ambulance, **193** for the fire department, and **190** for the police. Hospitals are all in the hospital sector (SHLS and SHLN). **Hospital Santa Lucia** (SHLS, Qd. 76, Conj. C, tel. 61/3445-0000, www.santalucia.com.br) is recommended. A convenient 24-hour pharmacy is **Drogaria Rosário** (SHC 102, Bl. C, Lj. 05, tel. 61/3323-5901, tel. 61/3323-1818 for deliveries). You'll also find pharmacies in the Conjunto Nacional, as well as Internet access at **Cyber Point** (tel. 61/3036-14955, 8 A.M.–10 P.M. Mon.–Sat., noon–6 P.M. Sun.).

GETTING THERE
Air

Due its distance from the coast, most travelers arrive in Brasília by air. There is no shortage of flights from most state capitals, including numerous flights from Rio and São Paulo. Make sure to request a window seat since the view of the Plano Piloto from above is truly unforgettable. The **Aeroporto Internacional de Brasília-Presidente Juscelino Kubitschek** (tel. 61/3364-9000) is a high-tech and futuristic place, located 10 kilometers (6 miles) west of the Eixo Monumental. A taxi from the airport to the hotel sectors costs about R$30–40. You can also take a municipal bus to the *rodoviária,* but then you'll need to get another bus (or a cab) to your hotel.

Bus

Buses from all corners of Brazil arrive and depart at the long-distance **rodoferroviária** (tel. 61/3363-2281), at the western edge of the Eixo Monumental. Aside from destinations in neighboring Goiás, traveling anywhere else involves an exhaustingly long haul: Brasília is 930 kilometers (577 miles) from Rio, 870 kilometers (539 miles) from São Paulo, and 1,000 kilometers (620 miles) from Salvador (20 hours). **Real** (tel. 61/3361-4555, www.viacaoreal.com.br) operates buses to São Paulo (14 hours), **Itapemirim** (tel. 61/3361-4505, www.itapemirim.com.br) services Rio (17 hours), and **Real Expresso** (tel. 61/2106-5100, www.realexpresso.com.br) offers service to Salvador (20 hours).

Car

Although it's possible to drive to Brasília from other Brazilian regions, once again, the distances are enormous and you'll waste a lot of time on the road. The BR-050 connects Brasília with São Paulo. The BR-060 goes west to the Pantanal where it intersects with the BR-153, which stretches north to the Amazon and Belém. Running east to the coast, the BR-020 cuts through the Sertão of Bahia all the way to Salvador.

GETTING AROUND

At first Brasília, with its many Eixos and sectors, seems like an urban planner's trick to confuse a foreign traveler. However, once you get a hang of the "sectors," you will see how orderly it all is. Roads are numbered instead of named.

Digits represent positions and distances north or south of the Eixo Monumental and east or west of the Eixo Rodoviário. Each sector has its own acronym. The central Rodoviária de Brasília—the main urban bus station—is also the city's nucleus. The Eixo Rodoviário crosses over the *rodoviária,* while the Eixo Monumental passes around it.

Brasília is a sprawling city custom-made for cars (and buses), so forget about wandering around town unless you're in a strolling zone (such as a park). The most convenient buses run along the major axes of the Eixo Rodoviário and the Eixo Monumental, all of them stopping at the central *rodoviária,* located at the crossroads of the two.

Bus

The "Plano Piloto Circular" buses are particularly useful, stopping at most monuments, hotels, and *shoppings* along the Eixo Monumental. Bus fare is R$1.80. Otherwise, you're best off taking a taxi.

Taxis

Taxis are usually easy to hail and if you can't make sense of Brasília's sometimes confusing system of *setores* and *quadras,* your cab driver can. You can also call a taxi—**Rádio Táxi Alvorada** (tel. 61/3322-3030) or **Brasília Rádio Taxi** (tel. 61/3344-3060).

Driving

Originally, Brasília's thoroughfares were designed to make traffic lights unnecessary through the use of roundabouts at intersections. Although some traffic lights do exist, roundabouts rule—if you're driving, remember that the car that's already in the roundabout has the right of way. Otherwise, driving here is smoother than in other large Brazilian cities and renting a car is useful if you want to visit the Cerrado around Brasília. **Avis** (tel. 61/3365-2782, www.avis.com.br) and **Hertz** (3365-4040, www.hertz.com.br) both have agencies at the airport. Renting a car in the city can be cheaper—try **Via Rent A Car** (SHS, Qd. 6, Conj. A, Bl. F, Lj. 50, tel. 61/3322-3181).

City Tours

Most hotels offer information about city tours. However, **Bluepoint** (SCLN, 310, Bl. D, Lj. 71, tel. 61/3274-0033, www.bluepoint.com.br), which also offers trips to the surrounding Cerrado, is known for interesting thematic half-day city tours, which range from classical architectural tours to "mystical" tours that offer a glimpse into the pronounced esoteric side of Brasília's personality. Other less traditional but striking views of the city can be gleaned from the water and air. **Tôa Tôa** (tel. 61/9982-1161, www.navegatour.com.br) operates two-hour boat trips around the Lago Paranoá, by day and at night, departing from the ASBAC yacht club, for R$25 per person. And if you're willing to fork out close to R$100, you can get a splendid bird's-eye perspective of Brasília during a 10-minute helicopter ride with **Esat Aerotaxi** (Eixo Monumental at the Torre de TV, tel. 61/3364-9933, www.esataerotaxi.com.br, 8 A.M.–8 P.M. daily).

Goiás

Surrounding Brasília and the Distrito Federal is the state of Goiás. Brazil's "heartland," this state is often overlooked by foreign, and even many Brazilian, tourists, which is both a blessing and a shame since it has some unique attractions. Much of the rolling highlands of Goiás is covered in Cerrado, whose dry yet striking grassland vegetation resembles that of the East African savannahs. Numerous rivers add pockets of lushness while waterfalls and natural springs offer ample opportunities to cool off while tramping over the region's many hiking trails. One of the most spectacular destinations is the Parque Nacional da Chapada dos Veadeiros, which lies in the mountainous region north of Brasília (and is a popular getaway for Brasilienses). This vast natural park offers landscapes you're unlikely to see anywhere else in Brazil, with outcrops of coppery red rock, plunging canyons, myriad waterfalls, and an impressive array of flora and fauna.

The gradual development of ecotourism in Goiás has brought focus on the need to preserve the Cerrado. Sadly, it is estimated that close to 70 percent of this unique ecosystem has already been devastated—compared to 15 percent of the much more lamented Amazon rainforest—to make way for big agro-business such as cattle raising and cultivation of cash crops, which has made Goiás an increasingly wealthy place. Such prosperity is apparent in the state's two major cities, Goiânia (the state capital) and Anápolis, both thriving modern boom towns that nonetheless hold little interest for travelers.

However, Goiás does have its historical attractions. Long before the region struck it rich with agriculture, it experienced a gold boom similar to, but more timid, than that of its neighbor, Minas Gerais. In the late 1600s, the fortune-hunting *bandeirantes,* who ventured inland from São Paulo and into Minas, also began exploring the hinterlands of Goiás. Their early encounters with the region's Goyaz Indians led them to discover that the region's hills were riddled with gold. The subsequent gold rush that lasted until the early 1800s saw the birth of Goiás Velho and Pirenópolis, two prosperous mining towns whose charming colonial architecture and rich cultural and culinary traditions have been carefully preserved to this day.

Goiás has a fairly decent highway system and most attractions are easily reached by bus or car from Brásilia, although distances are considerable. The climate is fairly hot year-round, although the winter months tend to be dry, and rain is frequent in the summer months.

PIRENÓPOLIS

This charming historic town dates back to 1727, when gold was discovered in the riverbed of the Rio das Almas, at the foot of the Serra dos Pireneus. Named for the surrounding mountains, Pirenópolis thrived for a century and then turned into a ghost town when the source of its wealth dried up. In the 1980s, enchanted with its preserved colonial buildings and the abundance of natural crystals and waterfalls in the surrounding region, latter-day hippies, New Agers, and artists arrived to set up alternative communities, open organic restaurants, and begin producing jewelry and handicrafts. After it was declared a National Heritage Site in 1989, the town was discovered by Brasilienses (residents of Brasília) and became a favorite getaway where the nation's powerbrokers could unwind. Although weekends can actually get quite busy, during the week, "Piri" is deliciously tranquil and bucolic.

Sights

Exploring the historical center is easily done on foot. If you notice a glint in the cobblestones it is because they contain quartzite from the surrounding hills. Particularly charming is Rua Direita (or Main Street), which is lined with whitewashed 18th-century mansions, trimmed with green and blue, along with a fetching art deco cinema whose powder blue facade dates

© NICOLAU EL MOOR/EMBRATUR

the pageantry of As Cavalhadas in Pirenópolis

back to 1936. At Praça da Matriz, the **Igreja Matriz de Nossa Senhora do Rosário** (7–11 A.M. and 1–5 P.M. Thurs.–Mon., R$1) is Goiás's oldest church dating back to the early 1730s. Although it was severely damaged as the result of a 2002 fire, it is being restored to its former glory. Dating back to 1750, the nearby hilltop **Igreja de Nosso Senhor do Bonfim** (Rua Bonfim da Serra dos Pireneus) is the town's only church whose original interior has survived. Inside, the sculpted altars showcase a cedar statue of the Senhor do Bonfim that was transported from Bahia by 260 African slaves.

Pirenópolis is famed for having one of the most original and spectacular religious pageants in Brazil: **As Cavalhadas** features horsemen, dressed to represent medieval Moors and Christians, who re-create a battle fought by Charlemagne during the Crusades. The elaborate costumes are astonishingly sumptuous— the Christian *cavalheiros* (knights) wear scarlet, the Moors blue, and a third, more surreal group of characters, the Mascarados, wear fantastic masks fashioned out of papier-mâché. The pageantry lasts for three days and includes parades,

tournaments, and a mock battle in which the Moors (of course) are vanquished and later converted to Christianity. Of Portuguese origin, dating back to the Middle Ages, Cavalhadas have been played out in Pirenópolis since 1826 as part of a larger popular and religious festival, the **Festa do Divino Espírito Santo,** which begins 50 days after Easter. Leading up to the Cavalhadas are numerous celebrations ranging from parades and masked balls to fireworks displays. If you miss the main event, you can at least get a dose of the festivities by visiting the **Museu das Cavalhadas** (Rua Direita 39, tel. 62/3331-1166, 10 A.M.–noon and 2–5 P.M. daily, R$2), which has a splendid collection of costumes, accessories, and photographs.

Engulfed by Cerrado, the countryside surrounding Pirenópolis boasts a considerable number of cascades and waterfalls that can be reached by nature trails that weave through the hills. Only 4 kilometers (2.5 miles) north of town (on a continuation of Rua do Carmo), the **Cachoeiras de Bonsucesso** (tel. 62/3321-1217, 8 A.M.–6 P.M. daily, R$10) are the closest—and most crowded—place to take a cool plunge, with six falls dispersed along a 1.5-kilometer (0.9-mile) trail. The visitors center sells snacks and drinks. Another 2 kilometers (1.2 miles) north along Rua do Carmo will bring you to the **Santuário de Vida Silvestre Vagafogo** (tel. 62/3335-8515, 8:30 A.M.–5 P.M. daily, R$10), an ecological reserve with short hiking trails and tree-trekking platforms that wind through a magnificent patch of Cerrado forest teeming with black howler and brown capuchin monkeys, armadillos, deers, and various birds. There is a waterfall with a refreshing pool as well as beckoning hammocks near the visitors center. The café serves a delicious weekend brunch featuring preserves made from native Cerrado fruits. Both of these attractions can be reached on foot, or by hiring one of the *moto-taxis* that provide transport around town.

If you have a car, there are plenty of other attractions in the vicinity. Taking a guided tour or organized excursion is also a good alternative. **Drena** (Rua Aurora 21, tel. 62/3331-3336, www.drenatur.tur.br) offers a wide array of ecotours throughout the region as well as cultural and history-themed outings and adventure sports such as rappelling, canyoneering, and white-water rafting. **Haras Cavalos de Luz** (Estrada do Bonsucesso Km 2, tel. 62/3331-1807) organizes guided excursions on horseback, including nocturnal outings when the moon is full.

Accommodations

Considering its popularity with weekenders from Brasília, there are lots of good hotel options in Pirenópolis. Not only are they reasonably priced (particularly during the week), but many are located in colonial homes. On weekends and during the Festa do Divino Espírito Santo and Carnaval reservations are necessary. You can also easily rent a room in a local home. A laid-back, welcoming atmosphere reigns at the **Pouso do Sô Vigário** (Rua Nova 25, tel. 62/3331-1206, www.pousadaspirenopolis.com.br, R$80–150 d), which occupies the town's 18th-century vicarage. Rooms are cozy with a mixture of country-style furnishings and framed prints by the likes of Cézanne

and Van Gogh. An oasis-like inner courtyard contains a pool around which copious home-cooked breakfasts are served. The same owners operate the **Pouso do Frade** (Rua do Bonfim 37/39, tel. 62/3331-1046, www.pousadaspirenopolis.com.br, R$100–140 d), with similarly inviting rooms distributed amidst a trio of colonial dwellings, all of which look onto a leafy garden with a pool.

❰ Pousada O Casarão (Rua Direita 79, tel. 62/3331-2662, www.ocasarao.pirenopolis.tur.br, R$130–150 d) is another lovely option located in a renovated 19th-century house. The sizable rooms feature ceramic tile floors and rustic period furnishings. The living and dining areas are simultaneously homey and refined and there is an outdoor pool surrounded by hundred-year-old fruit trees. The most upscale lodgings in town can be found across the river at the **Pousada dos Pireneus Resort** (Chácara Mata do Sobrado 80, tel. 62/3331-1028, www.pousadadospireneus.com.br, R$225–356 d). A prized retreat of Brasília's politicos, this tasteful and tranquil resort is also ideal for families, with a host of kid-friendly amenities ranging from bicycles and donkey rides to a small aquatic park located in the vast garden. Adults can take advantage of a pool, sauna, and fitness and meditation rooms or merely sink into a hammock on the verandas of the attractive rooms. Dinner is included in the rate.

Food

Many of the town's restaurants and bars can be found along Rua do Rosário (also known as Rua do Lazer). Be aware that some only open on weekends. **Restaurante Pireneus** (Praça da Matriz 31, tel. 62/3331-1577, www.pireneusrestaurante.com.br, noon–5 P.M. daily, R$20) is a simple but inviting place that serves up an appetizing banquet featuring Goiana specialties such as *empadão* (a torte-like *empada*), *galinha caipira* (country-style chicken), and *almôndegas* (meat balls) as well as succulently barbecued beef, pork, and chorizo sausage. There are also salads and homemade *doces* galore. Also known for its tasty regional fare is the **Restaurante Pensão Padre Rosa** (Rua

Aurora 14, tel. 62/3331-3577, noon–6 P.M. Tues.–Sun., noon–midnight in Jan. and July, R$10–20), a local favorite occupying a rustic stone house that's been in business since 1952. The copious lunch buffet includes specialties such as *carne ao molho de café* (beef in a coffee sauce), *paçoca de pilão* (sun-dried meat with manioc flour), and *javali assado* (roasted boar) as well as plenty of salads. Leave room for dessert—there are over 40 types of homemade *doces*.

For a bucolic setting, head to **◖ Restaurante Dona Cida** (Rua do Carmo 22, tel. 62/3331-1567, 11 A.M.–5 P.M. daily, R$20–30), where wooden tables are spread amidst a wide veranda and garden filled with the chatter of birds and monkeys. Dona Cida herself oversees the preparation of hearty traditional dishes such as *galinha cabidela* (chicken cooked in its own blood) and *arroz com pequi* (rice cooked with the aromatic *pequi* fruit). Live music is performed on weekends.

Vegetarians will appreciate the healthy fare prepared by Edna Lucena, the town's pioneering hippie-mystic, who first opened **Aravinda Bar e Restaurante** (Rua do Rosário 25, tel. 62/3331-2409, noon onwards daily, R$10–20) in the early '80s as a boutique that sold East Indian garb. On weekends, this beloved and very mellow hangout features live music.

Information

Pirenópolis's **Centro do Atendimento ao Turista** (Rua Bonfim 14, tel. 62/3331-2633, www.pirenopolis.go.gov.br, 8 A.M.–8 P.M. Mon.–Sat.) has information about the region and can put you in touch with local guides. You'll find a Banco do Brasil and Bradesco on Rua Direito. In Portuguese, two useful sites with plenty of photos are www.pirenopolis.com.br and www.pirenopolis.tur.br.

Getting There

Pirenópolis is 160 kilometers (99 miles) away from Brasília. Both **Viação Goianésia** (tel. 61/3233-7891, www.viacaogoainesia.com.br) and **Transportes Santo Antônio** (tel. 61/3234-3997, www.grupoamaral.com.br) offer daily

service from Brasília. In Pirenópolis the **rodoviária** (Rua Neco Mendonça, tel. 62/3331-1080) is a five-minute walk from the center of town. If you're driving from Brasília, take the BR-070, followed by the BR-414 and BR-225.

CHAPADA DOS VEADEIROS

Situated in the northern part of Goiás, the Parque Nacional da Chapada dos Veadeiros and its environs constitute one of the most beautiful and unusual natural eco-systems in South America, replete with exotic flora and fauna, weird rock formations, and plenty of caves, grottoes, and waterfalls. Access to the park is via two towns. Alto Paraíso de Goiás, a magnet for mystics and alternative communities, is 38 kilometers (24 miles) from the park, while right next to the park's entrance, the small village of São Jorge is renowned for its fantastic scenery and hiking trails.

◖ Parque Nacional da Chapada dos Veadeiros

The Parque Nacional da Chapada dos Veadeiros (tel. 62/3455-1116, 8 A.M.–5 P.M. Tues.–Sun., R$5) is situated on what is geographically considered to be one of the oldest parts of the American continent. According to NASA, when observed from outer space, the Chapada's high plateaus are the most luminous point visible on Earth. Although the region's esoteric pilgrims chalk it up to a variety of supernatural forces, the scientific explanation is the vast quantity of quartz crystals embedded in the soil and fantastic outcrops of rock that make hiking through the park such a breathtaking experience. Add to the mixture plunging canyons, crystal-clear streams and cascades, Cerrado vegetation, and wildlife such as giant armadillos, anteaters, deer, extremely rare maned wolves, ostrich-like rheas, and green beaked toucans, and you're in for an eco-treat.

The park's two 10-kilometer (6-mile) long trails can only be explored in the company of a guide. You can hire one easily in Alto Paraíso de Goiás or São Jorge or at the park's entrance. In Alto Paraíso, there are also many eco-tourism outfits that run full-day excursions into the park and offer adventure sports outings. Make sure your guide has been officially registered with IBAMA, the federal environmental protection agency. Also make sure to bring plenty of sunscreen, water, and food. The park can be visited year-round, although the period from May to October coincides with the dry season (heavy rains can make hiking slippery and even dangerous) and also with the blooming of the delicate Cerrado flowers.

Alto Paraíso de Goiás

The Chapada dos Veadeiros's capital of ecotourism and esoterism, Alto Paraíso de Goiás is a trippy, incense-scented place haunted by a surprisingly international collection of astrologists, mystics, and latter-day hippies drawn by the abundance of sublime landscapes, natural crystals, and reports of frequent UFO and extraterrestrial sightings. Many buildings are pyramid-shaped, the better to capture the energies in circulation. Meanwhile, one of the classic pastimes is to hang out at the Aeroporto de UFO, 4 kilometers (2.5 miles) north of town. This deactivated airstrip was supposedly built by a wealthy mystic as a welcoming gesture to receive any UFOs that wanted to land. These days it is the stage for meditation sessions, New Age rituals, and live music concerts, and is especially popular when the moon is full. *Esoturismo* aside, the immediate surrounding area has lots of striking natural features and many waterfalls that you can easily hike to.

ACCOMMODATIONS AND FOOD

Although the alternative atmosphere can get a little tedious, the town offers a wide range of accommodations, mostly concentrated around the main drag of Avenida Ary Valadão. To take advantage of Alto Paraíso's holistic vibes check into **Pousada Alfa e Ômega** (Rua Joaquim de Almeida 15, tel. 62/3446-1225, www.veadeiros.com.br, R$80–130 d). Although the rooms' dark brick walls are hardly conducive to levitation, East Indian ornaments, a meditation room, sauna, and surrounding gardens have more mellowing influences. Ayurvedic massages and alternative therapies are also available. Set amidst a bucolic farm filled with fruit orchards and flowers, the **Casa Rosa Pousada das Cerejeiras** (Rua Gumercindo Barboas 233, tel. 62/3446-1319, www.pousadacasarosa.com.br, R$95–140 d) is a pleasantly tranquil haven. Choose from spacious rooms in the renovated pale pink main *casa* or surrounding chalets with verandas overlooking the Vale do Moinho.

For creative vegetarian fare—salads (lunch is a self-service buffet), sandwiches, and pizzas—head to the lively **Oca Lila** (Av. João Bernardes Rabelo 449, tel. 62/3446-1006, noon–4 P.M. and 6 P.M.–midnight Wed.–Sun., R$10–20), a popular hangout for healthy youth, who flock to the place on weekends when live music is played.

INFORMATION

Located near the *rodoviária,* the **Centro de Atendimento ao Turista** (Av. Ary Valadão 1100, tel. 62/3446-1159, 8 A.M.–noon and 1–5 P.M. daily) is quite helpful. Aside from picking up park maps, you can inquire about guides and excursions. On the Internet, check out www.altoparaiso.com and www.chapada.com, both of which feature bilingual content.

Excursions are recommended, particularly if you're short on time or without a car. **Travessia Ecoturismo** (Av. Ary Valadão 9799, tel. 62/3446-1595, www.travessia.tur.br) and **Alternativas Ecoturismo** (Av. Ary Valadão 1331, tel. 62/3446-1000, www.alternativas.tur.br) offer numerous hiking, mountain biking, and horseback riding trips as well as canyoneering and rappelling. Aside from a wide variety of eco-excursions, **Ecorotas** (Rua das Nascentes 129, tel. 62/3446-1820, www.altoparaiso.com) also organizes alternative therapy and bird-watching outings.

GETTING THERE

Alto Paraíso de Goiás is 220 kilometers (137 miles) from Brasília. **Real Expresso** (tel. 61/3234-8774, www.realexpresso.com.br) and **Santo Antônio** (tel. 61/2106-7199) offer daily bus service from Brasília's *rodoferroviária* (long-distance bus station). If you're driving from Brasília, follow the BR-020 in the direction of Sobradinho and turn onto the GO-118, which leads to Alto Paraíso.

São Jorge

Much smaller and quite a bit prettier than Alto do Paraíso, the village of São Jorge is a former quartz mining town that has given itself over to ecotourism. Despite the influx of nature-loving Brazilian youth in high season, it has managed to retain its small-town flavor. Apart from the advantage of being only 2 kilometers (1.2 miles) from the entrance to the Parque Nacional da Chapada dos Veadeiros, São Jorge boasts a wealth of other natural attractions within close proximity that involve easier hikes than those in the park. The most spectacular is the appropriately named Vale da Lua (Moon Valley), 4 kilometers (2.5 miles) east towards Alto do Paraíso, where the Rio São Miguel has sculpted a canyon out of a lunar landscape of granite.

ACCOMMODATIONS AND FOOD

While São Jorge has fewer hotel options than Alto do Paraíso, the village's *pousadas* have considerably more charm. **Pousada Trilha Violeta** (Rua 12, Qd. 7, Lote 5, tel. 62/3455-1088, www.trilhavioleta.com.br, R$68–98 d) is a case in point. The simple rooms are housed in attractive bungalows painted pale violet (the owners are staunch believers in chromotherapy), with verandas gazing out onto a tranquil garden and a "Zona Zen" for meditation. The friendly staff can help you with guides and excursions. A little more upscale is the enchanting **Pousada Bambu Brasil** (Rua 1, Qd. 1, Lt. 8, tel. 62/3455-1044, www.bambubrasil.com.br, R$98–148 d), whose comfortable rooms, housed in chalets painted in rich mango and pumpkin hues, are offset by exuberant greenery. Natural woods, including bamboo, abound, as do hammocks and lounge chairs, and there is an inviting pool. The Bambu Café serves up delicious snacks, desserts, and light meals. Children under 14 aren't permitted.

Also charming with a pronounced esoteric edge is **Pousada Casa das Flores** (Rua 10, Qd. 2, Lt. 14, tel. 62/3455-1055, www.pousadacasadasflores.com.br, R$158–287 d), where you can indulge in Ayurvedic massages, tarot card and astrology readings, and a dip in the pool or Jacuzzi. Lighting is courtesy of candles or romantic gas lanterns, and breakfast is served on the verandas of the cozy rooms. A very attractive restaurant (open to the public) serves a buffet lunch and à la carte dishes at dinner (you can opt for half- or full-board), and prepares snack boxes for hikers.

For a mixture of local and international fare, head to **Papalua** (Rua 12, Qd. 7, Lt. 8, tel. 62/3455-1085, 5–11 P.M. Fri.–Wed., R$10–20), celebrated for its homemade pasta and crêpes as well as its tasty "trail kit" lunch boxes. **Restaurante da Nenzinha** (Rua 6, Qd. 11, Lt. 2, tel. 62/9669-1004, daily, R$8–15) operates out of the humble home of a former quartz miner, Dona Nenzinha. The home-cooked local dishes served for breakfast and the buffet lunch are simple but delicious. Much of the fresh produce is harvested from Nenzinha's own garden.

INFORMATION

Located at the entrance to town, the **tourist office** (9 A.M.–6 P.M. Mon.–Sat.) is quite helpful. Aside from acquiring park maps, you can inquire about hiring local guides. For information in Portuguese, check out www.portaldesaojorge.com.br. São Jorge has no banks, so make sure you stock up on cash (credit cards are not usually accepted).

GETTING THERE

From Alto Paraíso to São Jorge, **Santo Antônio** (tel. 61/3234-3997) operates only one daily bus that leaves at 3:30 P.M. (and returns at 8:30 A.M.). By car, follow the GO-239 for 36 kilometers (22 miles).

GOIÁS VELHO

A well-kept secret, Goiás Velho (a UNESCO World Heritage Site) is quite simply one of the most attractive and best preserved colonial towns in Brazil. Founded in 1726 by fortune-hunting *bandeirantes* who struck gold in the surrounding hills, over the next century Vila Boa (or "Good Town" as it was originally known) evolved from a rugged mining town into gracious state capital. With the end of the gold rush and subsequent transfer of the capital to Goiânia, Goiás Velho reverted to a certain languor that still envelops the town and makes it so appealing and restful. Aside from the its architectural treasures (almost completely restored after a devastating 2001 flood), the surrounding countryside beckons with its many waterfalls and trails meandering through the Cerrado. Although the town is small, you could easily spend a few days here just soaking up the tranquil atmosphere.

Goiás Velho is surrounded by the Serra Dourada, a region of hills and forests sprinkled with waterfalls and natural pools. The falls closest to town are **Cachoeira Grande,** 7 kilometers (4.5 miles) to the east, and the more spectacular **Cachoeira das Andorinhas,** 1 kilometer (0.6 mile) further. You can easily get to them by hiring a *moto-taxi.*

Sights

€ *CENTRO HISTÓRICO*

Goiás Velho grew in a hurly-burly manner reflected in the crookedness of its cobblestones and the haphazard meandering of its streets. If this lack of urban planning wreaks havoc on today's traffic, it also adds considerably to the town's charms and makes wandering a pleasure. For a fine panoramic view of the ensemble, climb up to the threshold of the Igreja de Santa Bárbara. This adobe and soapstone church is one of the more modest of Goiás Velho's seven colonial churches. The most impressive is the **Igreja de São Francisco de Paula** (Praça Zaqueu Alves de Castro, 9:30–11 A.M. and 1–5 P.M. Mon.–Fri., 9:30 A.M.–noon Sat.–Sun.). Dating back to 1760, it features some lovely murals depicting the life of São Francisco.

Another church, the Igreja de Nossa Senhora da Boa Morte, now houses the **Museu de Arte Sacra da Boa Morte** (Rua Luiz do Couto, tel. 62/3371-1207, 8 A.M.–5 P.M. Tues.–Fri.,

9 A.M.–5 P.M. Sat., 9 A.M.–1 P.M. Sun., R$2). The expressive cedar sculptures carved by Jose Joaquim de Veiga Valle are the pride of its small collection. Veiga Valle was a local baroque artist whose talent earned him comparisons to the legendary Mineiro sculptor Aleijadinho.

Among the town's most interesting secular buildings is the **Palácio Conde d'Arcos** (Praça Dr. Tasso de Camargo 1, tel. 62/3371-1200, 9 A.M.–5 P.M. Tues.–Sat., 9 A.M.–1 P.M. Sun., R$2), seat of the state government before the capital moved to Goiânia in 1937. Currently, the building functions as a cultural center, with a permanent exhibit of furniture dating back to the 18th century. More impressive is the former city hall/municipal jail, which now houses the **Museu das Bandeiras** (Praça Brasil Ramos Caiado, tel. 62/3371-1087, 9–11 A.M. and 1–5 P.M. Tues.–Sat., 9 A.M.–1 P.M. Sun., R$2). This museum traces the history of the region's gold rush via artifacts ranging from slave chains and mining implements to the fancy Portuguese porcelain with which the town's nouveau riche flaunted their wealth.

For many Brazilians, Goiás Velho's most popular—and moving—attraction is the **Casa de Cora Coralina** (Rua Dom Cândido Penso 20, tel. 62/3371-1990, 9 A.M.–5 P.M. Tues.–Sat., 9 A.M.–3:30 P.M. Sun., R$3). One of Goiás's—and Brazil's—most beloved poets, Cora Coralina (1889–1985) grew up in the same house in which her mother and grandmother had been raised. Although she had to drop out of school in her early adolescence, Cora loved to read and began composing her first poems at 14. At 22, she left Goiás for São Paulo and only returned following the death of her husband. By then she was 66. To survive, she made and sold crystallized fruits, but she never stopped writing. At the age of 75, Cora published her first book of poetry—minute observations of Goiás and the rhythms of its daily life—and completed two more books before she died at the age of 95. Built in the 1770s, along the banks of the Rio Vermelho, her house is one of the oldest in town. In the bedroom, kitchen, and room where Cora wrote, her possessions are arranged exactly as she left them.

Also of interest is the **Espaço Cultural Goiandira do Couto** (Rua Joaquim Bonifácio 19, tel. 62/3371-1303, www.goiandirado-couto.com.br, 9 A.M.–noon and 1–5 P.M. Mon.–Sat., 9 A.M.–1 P.M. Sun., R$2). An original character, Goiandira do Couto is a local artist who paints portraits of the town using colored sands from the surrounding Serra Dourada. To date, she has discovered 550 different tonalities.

Festivals and Events

Every year during Easter, Goiás Velho is the stage for one of Brazil's most traditional and haunting religious events, the **Procissão de Fogaréu.** At midnight on Ash Wednesday, all the lights in town are extinguished and pounding drums and blazing torches accompany a procession of 40 robed and hooded figures, as they set off from the Igreja da Boa Morte. While chorales sing Latin hymns and residents brandish candles, these *farricocos* parade around town with the mission of finding and crucifying Christ. The scene is quite medieval and attracts thousands of spectators. Another big draw, although in a completely different vein, is the **Festival Internacional de Cinema Ambiental** (www.fica.art.br), held in early June, which brings together environmentally themed films and videos from all over the world.

Accommodations

Ensconced in a bucolic setting, the eight charming rooms of **Pousada Dona Sinhá** (Rua Padre Arnaldo 13, tel. 62/3371-1667, www.pousadadonasinha.com.br, R$55–85 d) are spread throughout a 200-year-old farm house, whose historic countenance is enhanced by the lovely 18th-century furnishings. Right in the heart of town, **Pousada do Ipê** (Rua do Forum 22, tel. 62/3371-2065, www.pousadadoipegoias.com.br, R$93–120) is a welcoming choice with cozy accommodations. Simpler rooms face onto an inner courtyard, while newer, more spacious ones gaze onto a pretty garden with a pool. **Hotel Casa da Ponte** (Rua Moretti Foggia, tel. 62/3371-4467,

R$60–100 d) is another very affordable choice located in a baby blue 1950s building overlooking the river. The fairly basic rooms are clean and the staff is welcoming. For a room with a view, try the swinging '70s-era **Hotel Vila Boa** (Av. Dr. Deusdete Ferreira de Moura, www.hotelvilaboa.com.br, R$110–165 d). Perched atop the Morro Chapéu do Padre, this somewhat standard hotel has a terrific pool and attentive service.

Food

Goiás Velho is an ideal place to savor traditional Goiana cooking. Although most restaurants are simple (operating out of colonial homes), the home-cooked fare—usually prepared over wood-burning stoves—is rife with colors and textures. Portions are inevitably whopping. The town is especially famed for its *empadãos;* tortes made with a robust filling of pork, chicken, sausage, cheese, and *guariroba,* a local fruit that resembles a slightly bitter heart of palm. Among other Cerrado fruits you'll encounter, the most ubiquitous is the pungently perfumed *pequi,* which accompanies rice and chicken dishes, but also turns up in sweets. Warning: Don't ever bite into a whole *pequi*—the inner nut is protected by a layer of tiny thorns that will leave you feeling as if you bit into a porcupine). The more exotic likes of *murici, mangaba, cagaita, aracá,* and buriti all make appearances in preserves, liqueurs, *sorvetes,* and the *doces* and crystallized fruits sold by women out of their homes (and displayed on windowsills).

One of the best places for local cuisine is **Flor do Îpe** (Rua Boa Vista 32-A, tel. 62/3372-1133, noon–3 P.M. and 7:30 P.M.–midnight Tues.–Sat., noon–4 P.M. Sun., R$10–20), whose tables are scattered round a relaxing tree-shaded garden. Among the house specialties are *galinhada,* a country-style chicken stewed with saffron and rice, and *peixe na telha,* local fish baked on an orange roof tile. While lunch features a buffet, the à la carte dinner entrées are big enough for two. **Dalí Sabor & Arte** (Rua 13 de Maio 26, tel. 62/3372-1640, 11:30 A.M.–11:30 P.M. Tues.–Sun., R$10–20) is a charming restaurant where you can try *empadão, moqueca de peixe* (a Goiana take on the Bahian fish stew), and lots of typical sweets including *pastelinho*, a cake made with caramel-like *doce de leite* and cinnamon.

A little more swank and contemporary is **Goiás Ponto Com** (Praça do Coreto 19, tel. 62/3371-1691, 11 A.M.–3 P.M. Sun.–Tues., 11 A.M.–3 P.M. and 7:30 P.M.–midnight Thurs.–Sat., R$15–25), where entrées include roasted pork with slices of tucum palm, bathed in citrus sauce, and filet of sole smothered in a garden herb pesto and accompanied by a sweet potato mousseline. At lunch, there are only three main-course options, but after sundown the menu expands and the atmosphere gets more romantic courtesy of candlelight.

Information

There is no tourist office in Goaís Velho. For selective information in Portuguese and photos of the town, log on to www.vilaboadegoias.com.br and www.cidadeshistoricas.art.br/goias.

Getting There

Goiás is 320 kilometers (200 miles) from Brasília. However, the city with easiest access is Goiânia, 140 kilometers (87 miles) away. If you're driving, follow the BR-070 from Brasília to Goiânia, and then take the GO-070. Frequent buses make the 2.5-hour journey from Brasília to Goiânia with **Viação Goiania** (tel. 62/3242-4400, www.viacaogoiania.com.br). **Moreira** (tel. 62/3297-1444, www.empresamoreira.com.br) offers service from Goiânia to Goiás Velho.

The Pantanal

The Amazon rainforest may get all the media attention, but it is Brazil's Pantanal region (which spills over into neighboring Bolivia and Paraguay) that has all the wildlife. This unique ecosystem of lakes, rivers, grasslands, and forests is overwhelmingly vast (the size of Great Britain) and amazingly unspoiled. The largest wetlands on the planet, the Pantanal (*pantano* is Portuguese for swamp) is actually not a marsh, but a floodplain that lives in function of the ebb and flow of the giant Rio Paraguai and its tributaries. The fact that most of its area is underwater for six months of the year means there is little human encroachment aside from traditional cattle *fazendas* (farms). As a result, native fauna have the run of the 130,000-square-kilometer (50,000-square-mile) territory. *Jacarés* (caimans), for instance, far outnumber both human beings and cattle, but there are also 30 frog, 500 butterfly, 400 fish, 650 bird, and 75 mammal species—all in fantastic abundance and largely unfazed by human presence.

The creatures you'll come across often seem to have emerged from a mythological menagerie. Aside from giant anteaters, giant armadillos, and giant river otters, you'll also encounter the world's largest rodent (the Alice in Wonderland–worthy capybara, which can weigh up to 45 kilograms/100 pounds); largest stork (the red-necked jaribu); largest flightless bird (the greater rhea, an American cousin of the ostrich whose eggs alone are things of wonder); and the largest snake (the infamous anaconda—which, although it grows to lengths of 9 meters/30 feet, defies its Hollywood reputation by being somewhat of a shy loner). Rarely seen but avidly sought after are the spotted jaguar and jewel-like hyacinth macaw, which can measure up to a 1 meter (3 feet) from tail to beak. The bird's size and stunning cobalt blue and banana yellow plumage have earned it the going rate of tens of thousands of dollars on the black market as well as endangered status.

Spanning the states of Mato Grosso and Mato Grosso do Sul, the Pantanal is a difficult region to travel through. Distances are enormous and roads are scarce. Although the highways linking the major towns are in reasonable shape and have ample bus service, the

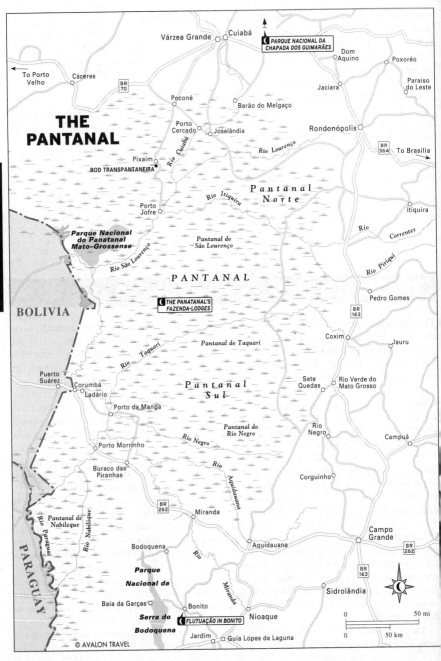

© AVALON TRAVEL

dirt tracks that approach (but don't enter) the Pantanal itself are often only navigable by four-wheel-drive vehicles—in the dry season. "Doing" the Pantanal on your own is only for the very brave and Tarzanic. The best option is to organize an eco-safari—either individually (more expensive) or as a group (cheaper) out of one of the major access towns: Cuiabá and Cáceres (Mato Grosso) or Campo Grande and Corumbá (Mato Grosso do Sul). Although you can explore some regions by Jeep, truck, and horseback, to go deep into the Pantanal requires taking to the rivers in small boats or canoes, which can be hired in outposts such as Porto Jofre. Most tours include accommodations at *fazenda* lodges. These working cattle farms, located deep within the Pantanal, offer accommodations ranging from simple to luxurious along with guided tours and activities such as boating, horseback riding, and fishing. Another option is to book yourself into a *fazenda* lodge in advance (often a cheaper alternative) and then let the hotel take care of all your needs. Those with extra time and money can indulge in the eco-tours offered by "luxury" houseboats, which is the best way to see more elusive larger mammals such as jaguars.

Since the Pantanal can be both wet and downright inundated, when you show up makes a significant difference. During the rainy season (November–March), river levels can rise by up to 3 meters (10 feet), transforming the area into a vast lagoon interspersed with islands of green vegetation where the local fauna takes shelter. Throughout this period, boats are the only means of access. In contrast, during the dry season (April–October), the water recedes, revealing grasslands and dry forests in coppery earth tones. Although the vegetation is less exuberant, it is easier to spot wildlife as the fish trapped in disappearing pools provide banquets for birds and animals who gather in vast numbers. No matter which season you choose to visit, mosquitos are rampant, so bring plenty of repellent as well as long-sleeved shirts and pants made of lightweight material. You'll need them, even though the daily temperature is hot year-round (nights can be cooler). Although malaria isn't a problem, you do need to get a yellow fever shot. Since the Pantanal is a remote region, make sure you come equipped with sunscreen, any medication you might need, and a good pair of binoculars.

Fishing enthusiasts be warned that the Pantanal is one of the best places in the world to go fishing (the season lasts from March to October). To this day new species are being discovered. In terms of traditional favorites, trying sinking your hooks (and teeth) into the highly prized *piraputunga* and *dourado,* as well as *pacu, pintado,* and *surubim.* The most classic catch, of course, is the infamous (and surprisingly delicious) piranha, which can be easily lured by baiting a hook with a chunk of raw steak.

Culturally, the Pantanal is an interesting place, as are the states of Mato Grosso and Mato Grosso do Sul, which retain a rugged Wild West flavor. Although many of the Indian groups that originally occupied the area were largely wiped out by colonists, descendants survive on reservations and their cultural and culinary influence is quite pronounced. Other notable influences include those of the intrepid Paulistano *bandeirantes* who first explored the area, the ranch owners of Spanish and Portuguese descent, and the Gaúchos who emigrated from the South to take care of their herds. Although these days cattle ranching is increasingly mechanized, the cowboy is still a strong presence despite the fact that an increasing number of *fazenda* owners are finding ecotourism to be more profitable (and sustainable) than ranching.

NORTHERN PANTANAL (MATO GROSSO)

Located in Mato Grosso, the northern Pantanal is accessed via the state capital of Cuiabá. Although Cuiabá is some distance from the Pantanal proper, two paved highways lead to the settlements of Poconé, Porto Jofre, and Cáceres on the edge of the wetlands. From here, you can get a quick taste of the Pantanal or venture by boat into its depths.

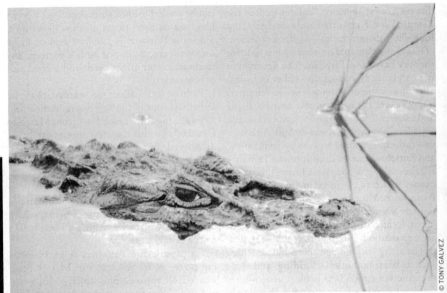

a lurking *jacaré* (caiman)

© TONY GALVEZ

Cuiabá

A thriving commercial center, Cuiabá is the only city of note in the vast state of Mato Grosso. Visually, it is a somewhat jarring mélange of colonial vestiges and mushrooming high-rises, but there is enough to keep you occupied here for a day or two. With the only airport connected to the rest of the country, Cuiabá is also Mato Grosso's most obvious gateway for trips to the northern Pantanal as well as to the nearby Chapada dos Guimarães, a spectacular region of mountains, canyons, and waterfalls that rises up suddenly out of the otherwise flat Cerrado.

Cuiabá was founded in 1719 when a Paulistano *bandeirante* stumbled upon gold deposits along the banks of the Rio Cuiabá. Fortune seekers immediately set out in search of instant wealth, although the 3,000-kilometer (1,864-mile) journey from São Paulo proved so long and treacherous that many never arrived, let alone struck it rich. When gold petered out at the end of the 1700s, the small town remained an isolated outpost in the middle of Indian territory. Throughout the 19th and early 20th centuries, Cuiabá's economy depended upon the region's vast cattle ranches. A link to "civilization" only came in the 1890s when an enterprising Brazilian army officer named Cândido Rondon built a telegraph system from Goiás Velho to Cuiabá and then south to Corumbá. (Rondon's subsequent forays north into the Amazon inspired the western Amazonian state's name of Rondônia). However, it wasn't until the 20th century that trains, planes, and, finally, paved highways connected Cuiabá to São Paulo in the south, Brasília and Goiás to the west, and the Amazon to the north, transforming the city into a major crossroads. Although cattle ranching has dwindled in recent years, economic growth has been spurred on by the cultivation of corn, rice, fruit, and soybeans along with the development of the burgeoning ecotourism industry. As a result, Cuiabá is a lively place with a frontier feel to it. While it is one of Brazil's fastest growing cities, it is also its hottest. Be forewarned that average temperatures are 27°C (81°F) and can hit highs of 45°C (113°F).

SIGHTS

The two parts of the city—Cuiabá itself and Várzea Grande (where the airport is located)—are separated by the Rio Cuiabá. The town's main square is the vibrant **Praça da República,** which is surrounded by federal university buildings, a weird-looking pale pink concrete 1960s cathedral, and one of the town's most attractive old mansions, the Palácio da Instrução. The latter houses the **Museu de História Natural e Antropologia** (Praça da República 151, tel. 65/3321-3391, 8:30 A.M.–4:30 P.M. Mon.–Fri., R$1), which has a little something for everyone. The history section displays interesting old photographs that trace Cuiabá's colorful past while the natural history section will please taxidermists with its collection of stuffed exotic beasts from the surrounding region. Most interesting is the impressive collection of indigenous artifacts, including clubs, arrows, and some really splendid feather headdresses.

A few blocks north, you'll have fun at the **Museu de Pedras Ramis Bucais** (Rua Galdino Pimentel 155, 8:30 A.M.–5:30 P.M. Mon.–Fri., R$5), which features the personal rock collection of a local man named Ramis Bucair. The small, deliciously nutty ensemble includes fossils, gemstones, and Stone Age artifacts, along with a meteorite and a fossilized bone belonging to a local *Tyrannosaurus rex,* both of whose authenticity is suspect. It's also worth checking out the renovated west bank of the Rio Cuiabá. Along the waterfront, the **Museu do Rio Cuiabá** and **Aquário Municipal** (Av. Beira Rio, tel. 65/3623-1440, 9 A.M.–6 P.M. Tues.–Sun.) display maps and exhibits about the river as well as aquariums featuring some of its scaly inhabitants.

NIGHTLIFE

The city's bar scene is concentrated in the center, around Avenida Getúlio Vargas and Avenida Mato Grosso. Most bars serve food and you can count on them for dinner as well as drinks. **Choppão** (Praça 8 de Abril, Goaibeiras, tel. 65/3623-9101, www.choppao.com.br, 10 A.M.–close daily) is a classic hangout that's been around since 1974.

Aside from the cavernous restaurant-bar with its wood-beamed ceiling, there is an outdoor patio that's great for people-watching. The menu is extensive (a mixture of regional specialties and more standard fare), the portions are enormous, and the *chopp* is famously icy. More upscale is **Haus Bier** (Av. Mato Grosso 1000, tel. 65/3027-2000, www.hausbiercuiaba.com.br, 5 P.M.–close Mon.–Fri., 11 A.M.–close Sat.–Sun.), a fashionable restaurant-bar frequented by a youngish crowed. Aside from the tasty local and international fare, this is a comfortable place to kick back with a house-brewed beer and listen to live music.

SHOPPING

Not far from the Museu do Rio Cuiabá, the **Casa do Artesão** (Rua 13 de Junho 315, tel. 65/3322-2047, 9 A.M.–6 P.M. Tues.–Fri., 9 A.M.–2 P.M. Sat.) is an early 20th-century mansion where you can purchase art and handicrafts from all over Mato Grosso, including ceramics, hand-woven articles, homemade liqueurs, and *doces.* For indigenous art and objects head to the FUNAI-sponsored **Loja Artíndia** (Rua Pedro Celestino 301, tel. 65/3623-1675, 8–11:30 A.M. and 1:30–5:30 P.M. Mon.–Fri.). Mato Grossense groups such as the Xavante, Karajá, and Xingú are all well represented with jewelry, baskets, wooden carvings, and musical instruments. Since this is cowboy country, if you want to invest in some authentic *vaqueiro* gear, head to **Selaria e Sapataria Centro Oeste** (Av. Tenente Colonel Duarte 318, tel. 65/3622-1584), where you'll find quality boots, hats, jeans, and chaps.

ACCOMMODATIONS AND FOOD

There are several good choices near the center of town. One of the best budget options is the **Pousada Ecoverde** (Rua Pedro Celestino 391, tel. 65/3624-1386, www.ecoverdetours.com, R$25 pp). Operated by local English-speaking eco-guide, Joel Souza (see *Getting Around*), the simple rooms (two with shared bathrooms) are located in a charming old house belonging to Souza's family. You can borrow books from the library and retire to a

FEASTING ON FISH

*Pintados, pacus, pirapputangas...*and even piranhas. The Pantanal has a cuisine of its own, and unsurprisingly, its main feature is the myriad varieties of fish that can be found swimming in its rivers. Renowned for its rich flavor and meaty texture, *pintado* is the star attraction of any *pantaneiro* menu. You'll find it prepared in many manners – grilled on skewers, *à urucum* (in which it is pan-fried along with cream, coconut milk, tomatoes, and mozzarella), and as the main ingredient of a hearty stew known as *mojica de pintado* (in which it is cut into cubes and cooked with manioc, tomatoes, and herbs). The *pirapputanga* and golden-scaled *dourado* are grilled slowly in order to ease the removal of its many bones, while the fried ribs of the *pacu* are a great delicacy. During the fishes' breeding season (Nov.–Feb.), known as *piracema,* fishing is prohibited and most restaurants will serve frozen fish or those raised in tanks. Meanwhile, piranhas and *jacarés* are a dime a dozen and are frequently featured on menus throughout the region. Grilled *jacaré* steak is surprisingly tender and succulent, while piranha, considered an aphrodisiac, is commonly used to make soups or chowders.

hammock in the gardens shaded by fruit trees. Laundry and cooking facilities are available. More upscale and comfortable is the **Amazon Plaza** (Av. Getúlio Vargas 600, tel. 65/2121-2000, www.hotelamazon.com.br, R$132–168), one of the nicer modern hotels in the center. Although the large, nondescript rooms are blessedly air-conditioned, you can also cool off in the small pool, surrounded by a jungly garden. The restaurant features great breakfasts as well as regional fare.

Cuiabá has a good range of restaurants, most of them very affordable. One of the favorite local traditions is to eat at a *peixaria,* a typical eatery that serves fresh river fish such as *piraputanga, pintado,* and *pacu.* **Peixaria Popular** (Av. São Sebastião 2324, tel. 65/3322-5471, 11 A.M.–3 P.M. and 7 P.M.–midnight Mon.–Sat., 11 A.M.–5 P.M. Sun., R$12–25) is a perennial favorite, where you can try the Mato Grossense specialty known as *mojica de pintado.* The generous portions easily feed two. Further from the center in the *bairro* of Araés is [(**Biba's Peixaria** (Rua General João Severiano da Fonseca 508, tel. 65/3322-3174, 11 A.M.–3 P.M. and 7–10:30 P.M. Mon.–Fri., 11 A.M.–4 P.M. Sat.–Sun., R$20–35). Tucked away in a little hidden street, Biba's is the place to get fresh Pantanal fish. Choose from à la carte specialties such as *pacu* accompanied by *farofa* (toasted manioc flour) with banana, rice, and salad, or indulge in the *rodízio,* which will allow you to sample a little bit of everything. For dessert, try the *rapadura de leite,* a fudge-like *doce* that is typically Cuiabana. Another good place for local cuisine is **O Regionalíssimo** (Av. Beira Rio, tel. 65/3623-6881, 11 A.M.–2:30 P.M. Tues.–Sun.). Located next to the Museu do Rio, this self-service buffet specializes in local fare. Although fish is the mainstay, there are also meat and vegetable dishes. Afterwards, head to **Alaska** (Av. Isaac Póvoas 1100, tel. 65/3028-2723), a local *sorveteria* chain, for some sweet respite from the heat.

INFORMATION AND SERVICES

The state **tourist office** (Rua Voluntários da Pátria 118, tel. 65/3613-9313, www.sedtur.mt.gov.br, 8 A.M.–noon and 2–6 P.M. Mon.–Fri.) is centrally located and supplies information and maps. For changing money or using your ATM card, major banks such as Banco do Brasil and HSBC are on Avenida Getúlio Vargas as well as at the airport. The main post office is at Praça da República.

GETTING THERE

Cuiabá is linked by air to Brasília, Rio, and São Paulo. The **Aeroporto Marechal Rondon** is 7 kilometers (4.5 miles) south from the city center, in Várzea Grande. A taxi to the center will cost around R$25. If you booked a tour to a *fazenda* lodge in the Pantanal, airport transfers may be included. The modern **rodoviária** (Av. Marechal Deodoro, tel. 65/3621-2429) is 3 kilometers (2 miles) north of the city center. If you don't want to take a cab, there are various municipal buses.

Although the landscape is interesting and roads are not bad, Cuiabá is *very* far from everywhere by bus—Brasília, for instance, is 1,100 kilometers (682 miles) away. Campo Grande, gateway to the southern Pantanal, is 10 hours by bus. **Motta** (tel. 65/3621-2514, www.motta.com.br) and **Andorinha** (tel. 65/3621-3422, www.andorinha.com.br) run several buses a day. Renting a car is not that useful unless you want to drive to the Chapada das Guimarães. **Localiza** (Av. Dom Bosco 965, tel. 65/3624-7979, www.localiza.com) and **Unidas** (Praça do Aeroporto, tel. 65/3682-4052, www.unidas.com.br) are two options.

GETTING AROUND

Cuiabá is full of tour operators that can organize trips and offer excursions into the northern Pantanal as well as to the nearby Chapada dos Guimarães. For the Pantanal, operators offer different itineraries that include transportation to a *fazenda* lodge combined with guided excursions into the wetlands. Tour operators usually work with specific lodges, but in terms of the itineraries there is flexibility to customize depending on your budget, interests, and the amount of time available. Prices vary widely, but generally begin at around R$200 a day per person, including all food, lodgings, transportation, guide, and excursion costs. An average price is around R$300. **Pantanal Explorer** (Av. Governador Ponce de Arruda 670, Várzea Grande, tel. 065/3682-2800, www.pantanalexplorer.com.br) is a highly recommended operator that offers a range of interesting Pantanal excursions led by bilingual guides that include canoe and horseback riding excursions as well as hiking. It also offers trips to the Chapada dos Guimarães, the Cerrado, and the southern portion of the Amazon rainforest. **Anaconda Turismo** (Av. Isaac Póvoas, tel. 65/3028-5990, www.anacondapantanal.com.br) is

a travel agency that also works with a wide array of *fazenda* lodges and *pousadas* in the Pantanal. It sells packages to the Chapada das Guimarães and Bonito (in Mato Grosso do Sul), organizes fishing trips to the Pantanal, and also offers individual and group city tours of Cuiabá. Aside from running the Pousada Ecoverde, Joel Souza, a friendly and impressively multilingual local wildlife ecologist, operates **Ecoverde Tours** (tel. 65/3624-1386, www.ecoverdetours.com), another highly regarded outfit with an office at the *pousada* as well as at Avenida Getúlio Vargas 155-A. Avian aficionados should check out the bird-watching excursions offered by **Boute Expeditions** (tel. 65/3686-2231, www.boute-expeditions.com), whose knowledgeable guides are all professional birders.

Chapada dos Guimarães

Only an hour from Cuiabá, the Chapada dos Guimarães is a stunningly beautiful mountainous region situated upon one of the planet's oldest tectonic plates. While the tiny eponymous town is pretty—and the nexus for Brazilian "New Age" types—the surrounding region with its rugged cliffs, plunging canyons, and abundant waterfalls is the real draw. Arid scrubland and coppery red rock formations reminiscent of the Grand Canyon alternate with lush patches of tropical foliage that sprout around the many rivers and natural pools. Much of the area is preserved within the Parque Nacional da Chapada dos Guimarães, a park with breathtakingly scenic (though often unmarked) hiking trails and numerous waterfalls that you can swim in. Take note that in the winter months of July and August, temperatures can go down to freezing. Summer months are better for bathing and for taking advantage of the marvelous vistas (in the winter mist is common), but there are also more crowds.

◖ PARQUE NACIONAL DA CHAPADA DOS GUIMARÃES

Coming from Cuiabá, the entrance to the Parque Nacional da Chapada dos Guimarães (tel. 65/3301-1133, 8 A.M.–5 P.M. daily) is on

MT-251 about 15 kilometers (9 miles) before the town of Chapada dos Guimarães. The park's visitors center is about 8 kilometers (5 miles) past the park entrance, and is equipped with a restaurant, snack bar, store selling *artesenato,* and lots of photos and maps of the park. From here, it's only a five-minute walk to a lookout point where you'll come face-to-face with the park's star attraction: the **Cachoeira Véu da Noiva,** the 86-meter (282-foot) "Bride's Veil" waterfall that goes plunging straight over a sandstone cliff into a pool. If you want to venture down to see the falls from underneath (and take a dip in the pool), you'll require a guide from town. Other popular trails include the **Circuito das Cachoeiras,** a four-hour hike that passes numerous waterfalls, and the strenuous full-day trek that leads to the **Morro de São Jerónimo,** the highest point of the region, from whose summit the views are astounding. You'll also need a guide to visit the **Cidade de Pedra,** a series of monumental quartz and sandstone rock formations that resemble rough-hewn towers of a primitive city. It's 25 kilometers (16 miles) north of town (much of the road is dirt); try to visit in the late afternoon when the sun intensifies the stone's natural red hues and you'll catch glimpses of the magnificent red macaws that circle around the cliffs.

Beyond the park's boundaries are some other worthy attractions. The **Caverna Aroe Jari** is an enormous 1,400-meter-long (4,593-foot-long) sandstone cavern 40 kilometers (25 miles) northeast of town (getting there involves driving along a dirt road and then hiking several kilometers—a guided tour is essential) whose walls are decorated with primitive paintings dating back 8,000 years. An adjacent cave shelters the **Lagoa Azul,** whose crystalline waters turn brilliant blue when hit by the midday rays of the sun. Easier to visit is the **Mirante da Geodésia,** 8 kilometers (5 miles) from town (on an extension of the Rua Cipriano Curvo), which marks the geodesic center of the South American continent (the equidistant point between the Atlantic and Pacific oceans). The *mirante* (lookout) itself is at the edge of a

canyon and offers spectacular sweeping views that include the distant towers of Cuiabá.

CHAPADA DOS GUIMARÃES TOWN

The Chapada's geodesic centrality and the positive energies associated with this fact are partially responsible for the mystical, neo-hippie aura that permeates the small town of Chapada dos Guimarães. Aside from the excess of shops selling crystals, alternative remedies, and health food, the village is attractive. The pretty main square, Praça Dom Wunibaldo, conserves the baroque **Igreja de Nossa Senhora de Santana do Sacramento,** Mato Grosso's oldest church dating back to 1779. If you visit in late June/early July, take advantage of the **Festival de Inverno,** a lively arts and music festival with an interesting alternative edge. The town is also a good place to pick up locally produced art and handicrafts. Several good shops are located on Praça Dom Wunibaldo; among them are **Arte da Terra** (tel. 65/3301-2016, 10 A.M.–7 P.M. Mon.–Sat.), specializing in decorative objects made from native plants of the Cerrado, and **Xingú Artesenato Indígena** (tel. 65/3664-1266, 10 A.M.–7 P.M. Mon.–Sat.), which carries a diverse array of indigenous art and objects such as jewelry and baskets.

ACCOMMODATIONS AND FOOD

You'll find a fair range of places to stay, both in town and in the surrounding countryside. During the summer months and on weekends, it's advisable to make advance reservations. By far the most charming option in town is the ◀ **Pousada Solar do Inglês** (Rua Cipriano Curvo 142, tel. 65/3301-1389, www.chapada-dosguimaraes.com.br/solardoingles, R$190–240 d), a cozy country-style lodge with refined European touches. The latter stem from the fact that the hospitable owner—who claims to treat all guests as "lords" and "ladies"—is an Englishman who lived for years in the Pantanal. As such, one of the bonuses is a smashing (and punctually served) English tea at 5 P.M. A pool, sauna, and lovely garden round out the amenities. Only 2 kilometers (1 mile) from the center of town, the **Pousada**

Villa Guimarães (Estrada de Cima do Jamacá Km 2.5, tel. 65/3301-1366, www.pousadavillaguimaraes.com.br, R$100–180 d) is nestled in the midst of a small ecological reserve. The comfortable rooms, which house up to four, are furnished in soothing tones. Lovely wooden verandas are hung with hammocks that gaze out over greenery. There is a pool and 24-hour Internet access.

For the most part, eating options revolve around simple home-cooked regional fare. You'll find several restaurants and bars on and around Praça Dom Wunibaldo. For lunch, **Nivo's Fogão Regional** (Praça Dom Wunibaldo 63, 10:30 A.M.–3:30 P.M. Tues.–Sun., R$10–20) is an attractive old house decorated with Portuguese *azulejos* that serves up a wide variety of delicious regional fish and meat dishes. Traditional accompaniments include *pirão* and *farofa de banana*. **O Mestrinho** (Rua Quinco Caldas 119, tel. 65/3791-1181, 11 A.M.–3 P.M. and 6:30–10 P.M. Wed.–Mon., R$12–25) is an another classic spot with copious portions of *chapadense* fare as well as an all-you-can-eat churrasco *rodízio* on the weekends.

More expensive and out-of-the-way, but definitely worthwhile is **◖ Morro dos Ventos** (Estrada do Mirante Km 1, tel. 65/3301-1030, www.morrodosventos.com.br, 8 A.M.–5 P.M. daily, R$20–30), whose tables are clustered beneath a thatched-roofed indigenous-style *oca* overlooking a cliff. The views are absolutely stunning. The cuisine follows suit with well-prepared Mato Grossense dishes including *galinha caipira com quiabo* (a stew of country chicken with okra) and *maria-isabel* (a local version of risotto made with sun-dried beef, rice, and herbs). The restaurant is located within a private condominium complex.

INFORMATION

The **tourist office** (Rua Quinco Caldas, tel. 65/3301-2045, www.chapadadosguimaraes.mt.gov.br, 9 A.M.–6 P.M. Mon.–Sat.) has maps of the park and Chapada along with a list of guides. You can also log on to www.chapadadosguimaraes.com.br, an informative site (in Portuguese with a shaky English

translation) with lots of photos. It is operated by **Ecoturismo Cultural** (Praça Dom Wunibaldo 464, tel. 65/3301-1393), a reputed tour operator that organizes guided day trips as well as longer itineraries. Aside from guided excursions, **Atmã** (Rua Quinco Caldas 164, tel. 65/3301-3391, www.chapadaatma.com.br) specializes in a wide range of adventure sports such as rappelling and canyoneering. You can also organize day and overnight trips from Cuiabá.

GETTING THERE

Chapada dos Guimarães is 74 kilometers (46 miles) north of Cuiabá. **Viação Rubi** (tel. 65/3624-9044) buses leave several times a day from the *rodoviária*. The scenic trip takes about one hour. By car, follow the MT-251.

Poconé and Porto Jofre: The Rodovia Transpantaneira

The easiest way to enter the Pantanal from Cuiabá is via the town of Poconé, 100 kilometers (62 miles) to the south. The Pantanal itself begins as you continue south from Poconé along the Rodovia Transpantaneira. Back in the 1970s when mega projects were in vogue throughout Brazil, the plan was to build a highway that plowed all the way through the Pantanal from Poconé to Corumbá. Fortunately, neither human beings nor human technology were any match for this aquatic ecosystem—the project was aborted after 145 kilometers (90 miles), at Porto Jofre, a fishing village on the shores of Rio Cuiabá. Over the years, the former highway has metamorphosed into a decidedly bumpy road connected by 126 wooden bridges in varying states of disrepair. However, despite the fact that it is quite overgrown in spots, it is still the only road that actually leads into the Pantanal. Moreover, the earth that was cleared away for the highway's construction left holes that have become ponds, canals, and lagoons. These watering holes attract a wealth of wildlife, making the journey along the Transpantaneira into a fantastic safari (although one that can only be undertaken in the dry season).

The first stretch of the Transpantaneira, between Poconé and the Rio Pixaim, is lined with numerous *fazenda* lodges (cattle are often driven along the actual *rodovia*). Even if you don't check in as an overnight guest, you can visit these ranch-hotels during the day and partake of the facilities and activities they offer. The second stretch leading to Porto Jofre is much wilder and, in some spots, the road is overgrown with tangled vegetation. Make sure you leave Poconé with a full tank of gas and drive slowly—not only due to the precariousness of the road, but to avoid running over any *jacarés,* deer, or capybaras that may be crossing.

From Porto Jofre, you can venture further into the Pantanal by boat, either by sailing up the Cuiabá and Piquiri Rivers or, if you're feeling very adventurous and have lots of time on your hands, by catching one of the infrequent cargo boats that cut all the way through the Pantanal to the town of Corumbá, in Mato Grosso de Sul (which could take anywhere between two and five days).

(*FAZENDA* LODGES

Although there are several small and very basic hotels in both Poconé and Porto Jofre, you're better off staying at one of the numerous, more comfortable (and more expensive) *fazenda* lodges located in the surrounding region. Aside from full-board accommodations, they offer recreational activities and a variety of guided excursions into the wilder regions of the Pantanal. Prices below are per person.

One of the least expensive Transpantaneira options is the **Pousada do Pixaim** (Rodovia Transpantaneira Km 62, tel. 65/9968-2269, www.pousadapixaim.com, R$150–210), which sits on the banks of the Rio Pixaim and whose typical *pantaneiro* whitewashed buildings are on wooden stilts. Accommodations are basic (although there is air-conditioning), but offer great river views as does the restaurant where tasty regional fish dishes are prepared. Although guided hikes are included in the rate, canoe, boat, and horseback excursions are extra. Close to Poconé, **Pousada Piuval** (Rodovia Transpantaneira Km 10, tel. 65/3345-1338, www.pousadapiuval.com.br, R$195–210) is an appealing place located on a sprawling ranch with lakes and

patches of forest. Rooms are a little tight but inviting and there is a large pool. Included in the daily rate is a guided hike and the choice of an excursion by boat or horseback.

The (**Pousada Araras Eco Lodge** (Rodovia Transpantaneira Km 29, tel. 65/9603-0529, www.araraslodge.com.br, R$350–440) is one of the Pantanal's eco-pioneers, and the owner's conservationist efforts ensure that there is plenty of wildlife in close proximity. Bilingual nature guides offer myriad excursions (all included in the daily rate) on horseback and in canoes (by day and night) as well as photo safaris, piranha fishing, and overnight trips. The lodge is stylishly rustic and makes creative use of organic materials. There is a lovely pool and wooden walkways lead across the lagoons to lofty wildlife observation decks. Reflecting regional culinary traditions, the menu relies on local fish, meats, and organically grown fruits and vegetables. Minimum stay is two days and its international reputation means you'll need to reserve in advance.

Some 40 kilometers (25 miles) from Poconé along the road to Porto Cerrado, the (**Hotel SESC Porto Cercado** (tel. 65/3688-2021, www.sescpantanal.com.br, R$165–198) is within a private eco-reserve, along the banks of the Rio Cuiabá. The sprawling infrastructure offers the comfort of a sizable resort (both standard and luxury rooms are well-appointed) at great value. Amenities include multiple restaurants, swimming pools, squash and tennis courts, as well as Internet access and even a butterfly zoo. Activities and excursions—and there are many of them—are extra, but very affordable and include a variety of river outings.

INFORMATION AND SERVICES

In Poconé, try the **Secretaria de Turismo e Meio Ambiente** (Praça da Matriz, tel. 65/3445-1952, 7 A.M.–1 P.M. Mon.–Fri.) for tourist information. For cash withdrawals, you'll find a Banco do Brasil at Rua Campos Sales 449.

GETTING THERE

From Cuiabá's *rodoviária,* **Tut** (tel. 65/3321-4326, www.tut.com.br) has various daily departures to Poconé. Travel time is 2.5 hours. If you're driving, follow the BR-070 towards Cáceres.

Cáceres

The other access point into the northern Pantanal is via Cáceres, a drowsy little town 220 kilometers (137 miles) west of Cuiabá on the banks of the Rio Paraguai. Although further than Poconé, it offers another alternative for exploring the Pantanal via the river (one that is generally cheaper than the Rodovia Transpantaneira). Lots of boat excursions (including infrequent and inexpensive cargo boats to Corumbá) depart from here. Between March and October, the fishing is fantastic—in September the town plays host to the **Festival Internacional de Pesca,** the biggest freshwater fishing competition in the world. During mating and hatching season (November to February), fishing is prohibited and many *hotéis de pesca* (geared specifically to anglers) close for the season.

ACCOMMODATIONS AND FOOD

Cáceres has several simple and inexpensive hotels that offer a great base for exploring the Pantanal. Although it's somewhat removed from the center of town (close to the BR-070), **Hotel Porto Bello** (Av. São Luís 1888, Jardim Cidade Nova, tel. 65/3224-1437, R$50–90 d) is one of the most comfortable accommodation options in town. Access—by car or bus—is at Km 7 of the BR-365. Fishing enthusiasts should try one of the region's *hotéis de pesca*. Only 8 kilometers (5 miles) from Cáceres (access from the BR-070 Km 728), the **Pousada Fordinha** (Rua dos Quidas 950, www.pousadafordinha.com.br, closed Nov.– Feb., R$125–250) offers fairly basic, but well maintained lodgings right on the banks of the Rio Paraguai. Expert fishing guides will take you out on the river so you can land yourself a whopper, while other boats are available for eco-tours. The restaurant serves typical Mato Grossense fare, taking full advantage of the daily catch. In terms of food, one of the best eating experiences in town is aboard the **Kaskata Flutuante** (end of Rua Colonel José Dulce, tel. 65/3223-2916, 11 A.M.–11 P.M. daily, R$20–30), a floating restaurant on the river. Prepared in various manners, *pintado* is the aquatic star of the menu, but there is beef, chicken, and succulent *jacaré* as well. Don't show up for dinner without dousing yourself in insect repellent.

If your pockets are deep enough, the ideal way for anglers and ecotourists to take advantage of the region's bounty is to book a passage on an exclusive *"barco-hotel"* (also known as *"botels"*). These generally feature 5–10 cabins and range in comfort from standard to fairly luxurious. Although everything (excluding gear)—from meals and liquor to bait and small boat excursions into the wilds—is included in the price, the price itself is usually hefty, ranging R$1,500–5,000 per person for a weeklong trip (usually the minimum). Advance reservations are a must. **Leié** (tel. 65/3223-4907, barcoieie.com.br, R$350–700) is one of the newer *botels* with eight air-conditioned bunk-bed cabins and private bathrooms on two decks. It offers both fishing and ecotourism excursions up and down the Rio Paraguai.

INFORMATION

The local **tourist office** (Rua Riachuelo, tel. 65/3222-3455) has information on hiring boats and finding accommodations. **Leão Tour** (Rua Colonel José Dulce 304, tel. 65/3223-7357, www.visitecaceres.com.br) can help with transportation needs and also runs shorter 2–3-day eco-trips up and down the river.

GETTING THERE

Cáceres is 220 kilometers (137 miles) from Cuiabá. **Andorinha** (tel. 65/3621-3422, www.andorinha.com.br) offers bus service with several departures a day. The journey takes 3–4 hours. By car, follow the BR-174, generally in fairly good condition.

SOUTHERN PANTANAL (MATO GROSSO DO SUL)

The southern Pantanal lies within the state of Mato Grosso do Sul. From the rest of Brazil, the main access city is the modern capital of Campo Grande. While Campo Grande is some distance from the wetlands, the well-paved BR-262 leads to the smaller towns of Aquidauana and Miranda, where many of the southern Pantanal's *fazenda* lodges—some of them extremely sophisticated—are located. It then continues on to the colonial city of Corumbá, close to the Bolivian border, which is actually located within the wetlands. Due to widespread cattle ranching, the Pantanal's untamed regions are more difficult to access from the south than from Mato Grosso in the north. In fact, some of the best *fazenda* lodges are tricky to get to. During the rainy season, you can only reach them by chartering a small airplane, which can be very costly (upwards of R$2,000 for a round-trip, hour-long flight).

Campo Grande

The prosperous and sprawling capital of Mato Grosso do Sul is an agreeable (albeit often sweltering) city, with lots of tree-lined streets, that warrants a day's exploration. Owing to its proximity to Paraguay and Argentina, it is suffused with a distinct Gaúcho flavor reflected in customs such as drinking *tereré* (iced *maté*) and eating *sopa paraguaia* (actually not a soup at all, but an omelette-like torte made with eggs, corn, smoky cheese, and onion). With the state's only airport connected to the rest of the country, Campo Grande is also Mato Grosso do Sul's most obvious gateway for trips to the southern Pantanal as well as the pristine rivers and lush landscapes surrounding the eco-mecca of Bonito.

Founded in 1889, Campo Grande is a fairly new city that only became state capital in 1978. Until quite recently, it was little more than a market center for the region's vast cattle ranches. Despite many brash new high rises, its rural past hasn't entirely rubbed off, and cowboy culture still lingers. Increasingly, however, the crops cultivated in Mato Grosso do Sul's rich red earth have become as important, and profitable, as cattle. Indeed, farmland was what originally drew many immigrants from São Paulo and southern Brazil. With the inauguration, in 1914, of a railroad that stretched from São Paulo to the frontiers of Bolivia and Paraguay, Campo Grande became an important crossroads and thriving boom town that drew immigrants from far and wide, including a surprising number of Arabs and Japanese, most of whom started small businesses in the bustling town and whose presence is still felt today.

SIGHTS

There is enough in Campo Grande to keep you pleasantly occupied for a day. The city center is quite compact and can easily be explored by foot. Taxis are plentiful and cheap. The most useful bus route goes along the main street of Avenida Afonso Pena "Via Shopping Campo Grande," the city's principal *shopping*.

Adjacent to the leafy main square of **Praça da República** in a building belonging to the university, the **Museu Dom Bosco** (Rua Barão do Rio Branco 1843, tel. 67/3312-6491, www.museu.ucdb.br, R$3) is a fascinating museum. The geology section has fossils of everything from gigantic sand dollars to prehistoric fish as well as some multicolored quartz specimens. It's hard not to be knocked out by the two rooms lined floor-to-ceiling with display cases of thousands of gorgeously iridescent butterflies (and creepy crawly insects). The lifelike dioramas starring an expertly stuffed cast of Mato Grosso's most exotic birds and animals (including giant rheas and anacondas) are also quite compelling. Meanwhile, the ethnology section features a splendid collection of artifacts made and used by regional indigenous groups such as the Bororo, Xavante, and Carajá. A new and much larger museum is currently under construction.

For further exposure to local indigenous culture, head to the **Memorial da Cultura Indígena** (Rua Terena, tel. 67/3314-3544, 8 a.m.–6 p.m. daily, R$2). The memorial is composed of two giant *ocas* (circular indigenous dwellings) made from giant bamboo and *bacuri* fibers. One functions as a craft workshop and visitor center, while the other sells authentic *artesanato* such as ceramics and weavings. The complex is situated within Brazil's first urban

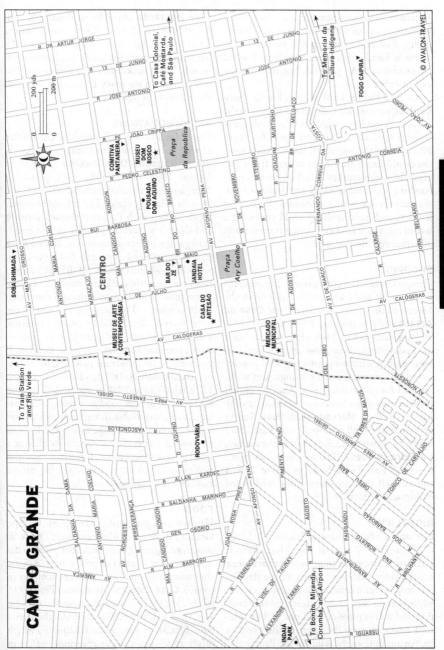

BRASÍLIA AND THE PANTANAL

CAMPO GRANDE

CENTRO

© AVALON TRAVEL

To Train Station and Rio Verde

SOBA SHIMADA ▼

To Casa Colonial, Café Mostarda, and São Paulo

To Memorial da Cultura Indígena

FOGO CAIPIRA ▼

COMITIVA PANTANEIRA ★

MUSEU DOM BOSCO ★

Praça da República

POUSADA DOM AQUINO ●

BAR DO ZÉ ▼

JANDAIA HOTEL ■

CASA DO ARTESÃO ★

Praça Ary Coelho

MUSEU DE ARTE CONTEMPORÂNEA ★

MERCADO MUNICIPAL ★

RODOVIÁRIA ■

INDAIÁ PARK ●

To Bonito, Miranda, Corumbá, and Airport

R DR ARTUR JORGE
R 13 DE JUNHO
R JOSÉ ANTONIO
R PE JOÃO CRIPPA
R PEDRO CELESTINO
R RUI BARBOSA
R 13 DE MAIO
R 14 DE JULHO
AV CALÓGERAS
AV AMÉRICA
R SALDANHA DA GAMA
R MARIA ANTONIO
R ANTONIO MARIA COELHO
AV NOROESTE
R PERSEVERANÇA
R MAL CANDIDO RONDON
R GEN OSÓRIO
R ALLAN KARDEC
R SALDANHA MARINHO
R VASCONCELOS
AV PRES ERNESTO GEISEL
R MARACAJU
R CANDIDO MAL
R D DE AQUINO
R DO RIO BRANCO
AV AFONSO PENA
AV CALÓGERAS
R JOÃO PEDRO
AV ALM BARROSO
R VISC DE TAUNAY
R ALEXANDRE FARAH
R DR JOÃO ROSA PIRES
AV AFONSO PENA
AV MATO GROSSO
R 13 DE JUNHO
R JOSÉ ANTONIO
DE JUNHO
R 15 DE NOVEMBRO
R 7 DE SETEMBRO
R JOAQUIM MURTINHO
R BR DE MELGAÇO
AV FERNANDO CORREIA DA COSTA
R ANTONIO CORREIA
R CALARGE
R BELISARIO
R JORN
AV JOÃO PEDRO
AV 31 DE MARÇO
AV CALÓGERAS
R 26 DE AGOSTO
R JOEL DIBO
AV NOROESTE
R PIMENTA BUENO
AV PRES ERNESTO GEISEL
R FR PIRES DE MATOS
AV TICO CARVALHO
R 26 DE AGOSTO
R ORFEU BAIS
R PAISSANDU
R DOS BARBOSAS
AV BANDEIRANTES
R ROBERTO BRILHANTE
R ENG
R IGUASSU

200 yds
200 m
0
0

Indian reservation, home to the over 9,000 Indians, many of whom belong to the Terena group. East of downtown, it is located in the *bairro* of Tiradentes and accessed from BR-262 (an extension of Av. Joaquim Murtinho) at the exit to Três Lagoas.

To get a feel for local culture, hit the **Feira Central,** on Avenida Calógeras adjacent to the Estação Ferroviária, which is held Wednesday from 5 P.M. to 2 A.M. and Saturday from 10 A.M. into the wee small hours. Aside from the exotic scents and colors of local fruits and vegetables, the market is full of Paraguayans hawking toys and trinkets and Indians from the countryside selling medicinal plants, seed jewelry, and handicrafts. Should you want a bite to eat, you'll find everything from skewers of barbecued meat to *sobá*.

SHOPPING

Campo Grande is a great place to purchase indigenous art and handicrafts. Aside from the Memorial da Cultura Indígena, the **Casa de Artesão** (Av. Calogeras 2050, tel. 67/3383-2633, 8 A.M.–6 P.M. Mon.–Fri., 8 A.M.–noon Sat.) possesses an impressive array of works by local groups with some enticing seed jewelry as well as ceramics, wood carvings, and weavings, all for reasonable prices. Another option for souvenirs (from homemade *doces* to cowboy hats) is the lively **Mercado Municipal** (Rua 15 de Novembro, 6:30 A.M.–6:30 P.M. Mon.–Sat., 6:30 A.M.–noon Sun.). Across from the market, the **Feira Indígena** (Praça Oshiro Takemori, 8 A.M.–5 P.M. Tues.–Sun.) is where Terena Indians sell local produce along with some handmade artifacts.

NIGHTLIFE

Bar do Zé (Barão do Rio Branco 1213, tel. 67/3324-4169, 7 A.M.–6 P.M. Mon.–Sat.) is a classic Campo Grande *boteco* that's been around since the 1940s. Early in the day, locals stop by for a *cafezinho* and savory snacks, while later on they come in search of conversation and a *bem gelada* ("cold one"). The sidewalk tables are great for watching the world go by. An antidote to the wilds of the Pantanal is

Café Mostarda (Av. Afonso Pena 3952, tel. 67/3026-8469, 5 P.M.–1 A.M. Sun.–Thurs., 5 P.M.–3 A.M. Sat.–Sun.), a trendy urban café/bar with sleek metallic furniture, Internet terminals, fancy cocktails, and a sprawling patio where you can sip fancy fruit *caipirinhas* and share *petiscos* or light meals.

ACCOMMODATIONS

There are lots of hotels near the bus station as well as in the modern Centro. The nicely priced **Pousada Dom Aquino** (Rua Dom Aquino 1806, tel. 67/3382-9373, pousada_dom_aquino@hotmail.com, R$60–80d) is a friendly relaxing place. The attractive rooms are decorated with Pantanal-themed artwork and there is a pleasant living area and courtyard garden to lounge around in. **Indaiá Park** (Av. Afonso Pena 354, tel. 67/2106-1000, www.indaia-hotel.com.br, R$105–145 d) gets raves for the orthopedic mattresses and goose down pillows in its sizable though somewhat soulless rooms. The decor in the rest of the hotel features lots of oddly colored tilework and '80s furniture, but amenities are good—with a pool and Internet—as is the location. If you want to treat yourself to a little bit of luxury, the **Jandaia Hotel** (Rua Barão Rio Branco 1271, tel. 67/3316-7700, www.jandaia.com.br, R$240–320 d) is as good as it gets. Rooms are large and comfortable though somewhat lacking in character, while the lobby and lounges are posh if rather dated. Amenities include a small pool, a fitness room, Internet access, and two quite swanky restaurants serving decent local and international fare.

FOOD

History and geography have given Campo Grande a distinctive culinary culture. Due to its cow town legacy, it is an excellent place to dig into succulent chunks of grilled beef. Among the many high-quality carnivore temples in town is **Casa Colonial** (Av. Afonso Pena 3997, tel. 67/3383-3207, www.casacolonial.com.br, 11 A.M.–2 P.M. and 6:30 P.M.–midnight Tues.–Sat., 11 A.M.–4 P.M. Sun., R$20–30), which offers an all-you-can-eat *churrasco rodízio* in lovely atmospheric surroundings. Due to the city's significant Japanese community, decent sushi isn't hard to come by. More popular is *sobá,* a tasty soup of wheat noodles, shredded omelette, and cilantro. Traditionally eaten on New Year's Eve to ensure prosperity in the coming year, *sobá* has become a local staple, spawning *sobarias* where grilled meats, ginger cream, and lots of soya sauce are added to the original recipe. **Soba Shimada** (Av. Mato Grosso 621, tel. 67/3321-5475, 6–11 P.M. daily, R$10–20) is good place to dig into this broth as well as other Japanese specialties, including the equally popular dry version with vegetables, called *yakissoba.*

To indulge in Mato Grossense specialties head to the highly reputed (**Fogo Caipira** (Rua José Antônio 145, tel. 67/3324-1641, 11 A.M.–2 P.M. and 7–11 P.M. Thurs.–Fri., 11 A.M.–midnight Sat., 11 A.M.–4 P.M. Sun., R$20–30). While locals swear by the juicy *picanhas* (rump steaks), out-of-towners can't help but be seduced by more exotic Pantaneira specialties such as *moqueca de jacaré* and *pintado* with *banana-da-terra* and *urucum* (a reddish herb traditionally used by Brazilian Indians) that draw on the wetlands' fantastic array of fish (and caimans). Portions are enormous and easily satisfy two or three. The house dessert, *bolinho de rapadura* (a cake made from caramelized sugarcane) is accompanied by *sorvete de cachaça.* **Comitiva Pantaneira** (Rua Dom Aquino 2221, tel. 67/3383-8799, www.comitivapantaneira.com.br, 11 A.M.–2:30 P.M. daily) is another good place to savor local farm-style cooking in colorful ranch surroundings. The enormous self-service buffet—featuring umpteen beef, pork, chicken, and bean dishes—allows you to try a little bit of everything.

INFORMATION AND SERVICES

The main **tourist office** (Av. Noroeste 5140, tel. 67/3324-5830, 8 A.M.–7 P.M. Tues.–Sat., 9 A.M.–noon Sun.) is very helpful with good maps and lots of information about *fazenda* lodges as well as packages to the Pantanal and Bonito. Banks with ATMs are plentiful at the airport and in the center of town along Avenida

Afonso Pena. You'll find a Banco do Brasil (Av. Afonso Pena 2202) and an HSBC (Av. Afonso Pena 2440). There is a post office right across the street from the *rodoviária* on Rua Barão do Rio Branco.

GETTING THERE

By air, Campo Grande has regular flights to São Paulo and Rio, as well as to Cuiabá and Corumbá. The **Aeroporto Internacional** (Av. Duque de Caxias, tel. 67/3368-6000) is 7 kilometers (4.5 miles) west of the center. A taxi is the easiest way to get downtown and will cost R$25–30.

The long-distance *rodoviária* (Rua Joaquim Nabuco 200, tel. 67/3383-1678) is close to the center, and one block off the main drag of Avenida Afonso Pena. **Andorinha** (tel. 67/3382-3710, www.andorinha.com) has daily service to São Paulo (16 hours) and frequent buses to Campo Grande (10 hours), Corumbá (7 hours), and other major towns in Mato Grosso do Sul. **Cruzeiro do Sul** (tel. 67/3312-9700, www.cruzeirodosulms.com.br) offers bus service to Bonito. If you want to rent a car, try **Avis** (tel. 67/3325-0072, www.avis.com.br) or **Unidas** (tel. 67/3363-2145, www.unidas.com.br).

GETTING AROUND

The Pantanal is too far from Campo Grande to be explored in a day trip. However, it's possible to organize 3–5-day **ecotours** with city-based operators. **Ecological Expeditions** (Rua Joaquim Nabuco 185, tel. 67/3042-0508, www.pantanaltrekking.com)—whose office (across from the bus station) is located within a youth hostel run by the owner—offers very decently priced excursions into the Pantanal (for around R$100–150 pp per day), including horseback riding, boat trips, piranha fishing, and nocturnal hikes. Accommodations are at their own lodge or campsite (where you get to sleep, Indian-style, in hammocks under thatched roofs). They also run tours to Bonito, where they have a hostel as well.

Impacto Turismo (Rua Padre João Crippa 686, tel. 67/3325-1333, www.impactotur.com.br) has an enormous variety of packages to choose from to the Pantanal and Bonito along with a staff of knowledgeable and bilingual eco-guides. They are experts at tailoring trips to a diverse range of interests, and can meet the needs of clients ranging from biologists, bird-watchers, and anglers to families, elderly tourists, and gay and lesbian travelers. They can also arrange transportation and accommodations in *fazenda* lodges and *pesca-hotéis*.

Aquidauana and Vicinity

Heading west from Campo Grande to Corumbá, the BR-262 passes through the towns of Aquidauana and Miranda, both of which serve as a gateways to the southern Pantanal and its many *fazenda* lodges. The sleepy town of Aquidauana is a popular fishing destination with a few sandy beaches, but it's not really worth staying over here. Instead check into the *fazenda* lodges (cattle ranch/eco-resorts) in the vicinity of Aquidauana.

FOOD

If you have a few hours to kill in Aquidauana, you could do far worse than tucking into a hearty meal at **O Casarão** (Rua Manuel A. Paes de Barros 533, tel. 67/3241-2219, 11 A.M.–2 P.M. and 6–11 P.M. Tues.–Sun., R$10–20). Although the specialty is pintado, you can also savor *pacu* and *jacaré*.

GETTING THERE AND AROUND

Aquidauana is 148 kilometers (92 miles) from Campo Grande (a two-hour bus ride). The neighboring town of Anastácio, on the other side of the Rio Aquidauana, is a regional transport hub with bus service to Bonito, Miranda, and Corumbá.

◀ *FAZENDA* LODGES

At **Fazenda Pequi** (BR-262 Km 497.5, tel. 67/3245-0949, www.pousadapequi.com.br, R$140–240), get a privileged behind-the-scenes insight into life on a family-owned *pantaneiro* cattle ranch that dates back to 1850. Guests stay in fairly basic, comfortable rooms in the main house (groups of five or six can

also rent bungalows). Other permanent residents of the property include *jacarés*, capybaras, and various bird species. The wide range of activities includes piranha fishing, night forays, and horseback riding. Only 48 kilometers (30 miles) from Aquidauana, this *fazenda* is less expensive and easier to get to than most in the southern Pantanal.

Fazenda Rio Negro (tel. 67/3326-0002, www.fazendarionegro.com.br, R$350–450) can only be reached by taking an aero taxi (a round-trip flight from Aquidauana will set you back around R$600 pp). The subsequent price is pretty hefty, but this *fazenda* is a once-in-a-lifetime experience. On the banks of the Rio Negro, the vast wetlands are an ecological reserve maintained by a Washington, D.C.-based NGO, Conservation International. The abundance of flora and fauna attracts professional birders, conservationists, and researchers from around the world. Tours by bilingual guides—by horseback, Jeep, or canoe along the Rio Negro—are topnotch. Aside from two VIP rooms, accommodations are fairly modest, but atmospheric—you can choose between a rustic lodge and the picturesque late 19th-century main house featuring polished wood and sweeping verandas.

Miranda and Vicinity

Around 70 kilometers (43 miles) west of Aquidauana, the small town of Miranda is a good base for exploring the Pantanal or Bonito (130 kilometers/81 miles south). Nestled in the foothills of the Serra da Bodoquena, the surrounding region is the traditional territory of the Terena Indians. Considered one of the best "integrated" of Brazil's indigenous groups, many still live in the area and you'll encounter a lot of traditional handicrafts, particularly at the **Centro Referencial da Cultura Terena,** on the BR-262 at the entrance to town.

In recent years, Miranda has given itself over to ecotourism. The Miranda, Salobra, and Agachi Rivers offer excellent fishing and are favorite refuges of shy, magnificent, and increasingly hard-to-glimpse jaguars.

a rare spotted jaguar

ACCOMMODATIONS

An alternative to expensive *fazenda* lodges is staying in town and taking tours to surrounding farms and into the Pantanal. The **Pousada Águas do Pantanal** (Av. Afonso Pena 367, tel. 67/3242-1242, www.aguasdop-antanal.com.br, R$100–140 d) is a lovely budget choice located in a historic house. Bright, air-conditioned rooms are warmly furnished and the ambiance is very welcoming. There is also a pool. The friendly owner operates an ecotourism agency that can organize sports activities and fishing excursions, day visits to *fazendas,* and outings into the Pantanal and to Bonito.

FOOD

For an interesting eating experience, visit **Zéro Hora** (BR-262 Km 55, tel. 67/3242-1330, 11 A.M.–4 P.M. and 6–11 P.M. daily, R$10–20), a restaurant/bar with a varied menu ranging from *pintada belle meunière* to cream of piranha, where you can also buy *pantaneiro* souvenirs.

INFORMATION

For tourist information, your best bet is to consult with the knowledgeable and bilingual staff at the **Águas do Pantanal Tour** agency (Av. Afonso Pena 367, tel. 67/3242-1242, www.aguasdopantanal.com.br). Aside from providing information about Miranda and the Pantanal, they can arrange all sorts of excursions—from eco-outings and day trips to *fazendas* and *fazenda* lodges to packages to the Pantanal and nearby Bonito.

GETTING THERE

Miranda is 210 kilometers (131 miles) from Campo Grande and 200 kilometers (124 miles) from Corumbá along the BR-262. **Andorinha** (tel. 67/3382-3710, www.andorinha.com) offers daily bus service to and from both towns. Miranda is also only 120 kilometers (75 miles) from Bonito. If you're driving, take the paved road to Bodoquena for 70 kilometers (43 miles), followed by a dirt road that leads to Bonito.

◖ *FAZENDA* LODGES

The location of **Refúgio da Ilha** (tel. 67/3384-3270, www.refugiodailha.com.br, R$335–460) is really exceptional: on an island in the Rio Salobra completely surrounded by water and dense greenery. Although fishing is prohibited, masks and snorkels are de rigueur. Bilingual guides share all sorts of fish lore and lead Jeep, canoe, and horseback excursions to spots where it's possible to catch sight of the elusive jaguar. Accommodations are simple, but comfortable, and there are plenty of areas for relaxation and reflection. There is three-day minimum June–October and a two-day minimum December–May. Access is at Km 573 of the BR-262 between Miranda and Corumbá.

One of the Pantanal's most established, most luxurious (and most expensive) *fazenda* lodges, ◖ **Refúgio Ecológico Caiman** (tel. 67/3242-1450, São Paulo tel. 11/3706-8000, www.caiman.com.br, R$420–500) is reputed for its outings, led by excellent bilingual guides and local *pantaneiros,* who know the wetlands inside-out. Despite the fact that Caiman isn't deep into the Pantanal, and its landscapes have been somewhat tamed by intensive cattle farming (guests are encouraged to take part in ranch activities), there is a wealth of wildlife. Accommodations are quite plush—you can choose from rooms inside the original main house or in two outlying *pousadas*. All three are beautifully furnished and equipped with swimming pools. The meals are also quite outstanding and include a traditional outdoor *churrasco pantaneiro* featuring beef raised on the ranch. Canoe, bike and horseback trips, photo safaris, and night outings are all included and there is a three-day minimum. The *fazenda* is 37 kilometers (23 miles) from Miranda, on the road to Agachi. Transfers are available.

Estrada Parque do Pantanal

Before the construction of the BR-262, there was only one land route that connected Campo Grande with Corumbá: a dirt road winding through the southern edge of the Pantanal that was laid by the intrepid Cândido Rondon in the early 1900s, as part of his mission to extend telegraph lines all the way to Brazil's border with Paraguay. With the inauguration of the highway, Rondon's route was abandoned and forgotten until nascent ecotourism brought it back to life, rebaptized as the Estrada Parque do Pantanal. The Estrada consists of 120 kilometers (75 miles) of dirt road linked by 87 precarious wooden bridges that cut through a wild and beautiful patch of the wetlands teeming with wildlife.

ACCOMMODATIONS

On the shores of the Rio Miranda, **Passo do Lontra Parque Hotel** (tel. 67/3231-6569, www.passodolontra.com.br, R$140–240) offers a quintessential Pantanal experience. A multitude of wooden walkways stretched over the marshes and bogs make you feel as if you're walking on water, and the accommodations themselves, in wooden chalets, are all on stilts. The budget prices make this the definitive backpackers' choice—aside from the main bungalows, an apart-hotel complex offers more basic rooms that can house up to six. For those who don't mind roughing it, there

is a *redário* (where you can crash in a rented hammock) on a nearby farm along with camping facilities. There are activities and packages geared both towards ecotourism and fishing here. This hotel is 120 kilometers (75 miles) from Corumbá (access is from Km 8 of Estrada Parque via Buraco das Piranhas). There is also a landing strip for planes.

Serious birders will have a field day at the **Pousada Arara Azul** (tel. 67/9987-1430, São Paulo tel. 11/3865-5131, www.fazendaara-raazul.com.br, R$230–350), which is flooded with feathered creatures including the hotel's namesake, the brilliant blue hyacinth macaw. Other mammals—including rarely seen wolves and jaguars—can also be spotted. Located deep in the Pantanal between two bays, in a region known as Nhecolândia, this is an ideal place to see wildlife—which you can do on foot, horseback, or by boat with guides. Accommodations, while simple, are pleasant—all apartments feature wonderful views—and the home-cooked regional food served buffet style is notoriously good. This *pousada* is 148 kilometers from Corumbá (access is from Km 35 of the Estrada Parque via Buraco das Piranhas).

GETTING THERE

The Estrada Parque do Pantanal extends from Buraco das Piranhas, a settlement located at Km 664 of the BR-262 (100 kilometers/62 miles northwest of Miranda), to Porto da Manga, a fishing village on the banks of the Rio Paraguai (where a raft transports vehicles daily at 6 A.M. and 6 P.M.), which is close to Corumbá. Although a four-wheel-drive is essential during the rainy season (and even so, you should always check weather conditions beforehand), the Estrada Parque is the only portion of the southern Pantanal that you can explore on your own. Along the route, there are various *pousadas* and some of the best *fazenda* lodges in the southern Pantanal.

Corumbá

Although getting to Corumbá involves quite a journey, once you're here, as you can see from the heights of the city's upper town, the

Pantanal is literally at your feet. Subsequently, exploring the wetlands involves less traveling and can be done more inexpensively. Languid and incredibly humid, Corumbá is only 20 kilometers (12.5 miles) from the Bolivian border and 400 kilometers (248 miles) west of Campo Grande (a seven-hour bus ride), Founded in 1776, by the mid-1800s remote Corumbá surprisingly held the title as the largest river port in the *world*. Ships from the Atlantic would sail up the Rio de la Plata to the Rio Paraná and then continue along the Rio Paraguai to what was, at the time, a thriving city. However, by the early 20th century, spurred on by the arrival of the São Paulo–Paraguay railroad, the town's fortunes had declined. Only recently, with the development of ecotourism and sports fishing (the region is considered one of the best freshwater fishing destinations in Brazil), has it gained a new lease on life.

SIGHTS

Although its setting is fairly exotic, there's really not that much to see or do in Corumbá. The oldest and most colorful part of town is the port area, which is lined with some handsome 19th-century colonial buildings. Other sights are a few blocks up from the riverfront. The shady **Praça da Independência** is an elegant square that offers welcome respite from the heat. A block away, the **Museu do Pantanal** (Rua Delamare 939, tel. 67/3231-6574, noon–5 P.M. Mon.–Fri., free) displays taxidermied animals from the Pantanal, artifacts made and used by local Indian groups, and temporary art exhibits.

In a restored old house, the **Estação Natureza Pantanal** (Ladeira José Bonifácio 111, tel. 67/3231-9100, 8 A.M.–noon and 2–6 P.M. Tues.–Fri., 2–6 P.M. Sat., R$3) is operated by O Boticário, one of Brazil's largest and most environmentally engaged cosmetic and beauty products companies (you'll see stores throughout the country). The company is renowned for its research into and sustainable use of products from the Amazon and the Pantanal. This museum features engaging interactive exhibits that highlight the richness of the region's ecosystem.

SHOPPING

For an interesting selection of locally made art and handicrafts visit the **Casa do Artesão** (Rua Dom Aquino 405, tel. 67/3231-2715, 9 A.M.–6 P.M. Tues.–Fri., 9 A.M.–2 P.M. Sat.), located in a former prison, where each cell showcases the work of an individual artist. Common materials you'll come across include fish skin and palm fibers. **Casa de Massabarro** (Rua da Cacimba, tel. 67/3231-2994, 8 A.M.–11:30 A.M. and 1:30–5 P.M. Mon.–Fri., 8 A.M.–noon Sat.) sells clay figures representing the flora and fauna of the Pantanal.

ACCOMMODATIONS AND FOOD

Although there's no real reason to stay in Corumbá itself (it's more of a convenient base than a destination in itself), the town has a large number of hotels, particularly cheap budget choices, most of which are located near the bustling (and sometimes noisy) port. Other options include the more "luxurious" houseboats that travel up and down the Rio Paraguai regions and the *fazenda* lodges of the surrounding region (particularly along the Estrada Parque do Pantanal).

A decent budget place in town is the tranquil **Hotel Santa Rita** (Rua Dom Aquino Corrêa 860, tel. 67/3231-5453, R$90 d). Double, triple, and quadruple rooms are simple but well-cared for and have air-conditioning. Breakfasts are quite copious. The bright and spacious **Santa Mônica Palace Hotel** (Rua Antônio Maria Coelho 345, tel. 67/3231-3001, www.hsantamonica.com.br, R$80–115 d) is fairly dated (late '50s), but is one of the most comfortable hotels in town. Air-conditioned rooms are uninspiring, but big. Amenities include a sizable rooftop pool with a garden patio and free Internet access.

As for food, "when in the Pantanal . . ." eat fish. **Peixaria do Lulu** (Rua Dom Aquino Corrêa 700, tel. 67/3231-5081, 11 A.M.–3 P.M. and 6 P.M.–midnight Mon.–Sat., R$10–20) may be modest in appearance, but in a town where fish rules, this friendly, family-run eatery serves up some of the best grilled *pacu* and *pintado* in town. At **Ceará** (Rua Albuquerque

516, tel. 67/3231-1930, 11 A.M.–2:30 P.M. and 6 P.M.–midnight Tues.–Sun., R$10–20), *pintado* reigns and comes in many guises (some lighter than others)—try the classic *pintado à urucum* or fried *à pantaneira,* which comes accompanied with bananas and manioc.

Sportfishing enthusiasts with money to spare can take to the river on an all-inclusive *barco-hotel* (or *"hotel"*), which vary in size and degree of luxury. Guides, bait, and small-boat excursions (but not always gear) are included in the price, which averages R$300–600 a day per person, and usually there's a five-day minimum. Advance reservations are a must. **Arara Tur** (Rua Manoel Cavassa 47, tel. 67/3231-4851, www.araratur.com.br, R$340–600) operates two comfortable boats, the *Albatroz* (18 cabins) and *Arara Pantaneira* (12 cabins), both outfitted with polished wooden fixtures, air-conditioned quarters, and sundecks. If you want a little more luxury and don't mind a mini-cruise atmosphere, the *Kalypso* (tel. 67/3231-1460, www.peroladopantanal.com.br, R$320–640) is a sprawling three-level ship with 28 air-conditioned cabins as well as a rooftop pool, a sauna, and a wood-paneled restaurant with self-service buffets. There is a six-day minimum.

INFORMATION AND SERVICES

Located on the waterfront, the **tourist office** (Rua Manuel Cavassa 275, tel. 67/3231-5221, 1:30–6 P.M. Mon., 8:30–11:30 A.M. and 1:30–6 P.M. Tues.–Fri.) is a good place for information about accommodations, tour companies, and boat trips. Close by, you'll find most of the fishing and tour operators. You can also check out www.corumba.com.br, a site in Portuguese. **Banco do Brasil** (Rua 13 de Junho, 914) is the only place in town where you can exchange money or get a cash advance on your Visa card (ATMs won't accept foreign cards).

Corumbá is awash with **tour operators** (and some rather aggressive representatives who will approach you in the street) offering fishing excursions, boat trips, and Jeep trips that range from budget to super luxurious, and last from half a day to a week. **Joice Pesca**

e Tur (Rua Manuel Cavassa 1, tel. 67/3232-4048, www.joicetur.com.br) specializes in fishing excursions on a wide variety of vessels and *barco*-hotels. **Canaã Viagens e Turismo** (Rua Colombo 245, 3231-3667, www.pantanalcanaa.com.br) organizes both fishing trips and ecotourism packages into the Pantanal.

GETTING THERE

Corumbá's **Aeroporto Internacional** (Rua Santos Dumont, tel. 67/3231-3322) has regular flights to Campo Grande and is also connected to Rio, São Paulo, and Brasília. It also operates small planes that go into the Pantanal. The airport is 5 kilometers (3 miles) north from the center of town and a taxi will cost around R$20–25. The long-distance **rodoviária** (Rua Porto Carrero, tel. 67/3231-2033) is around 3 kilometers (2 miles) west from the center of town. Numerous daily buses operated by **Andorinha** (tel. 67/3231-2023, www.andorinha.com) link Corumbá with Campo Grande (7 hours), via Aquidabuana and Miranda (3 hours). **Cruzeiro do Sul** (tel. 67/3231-9318, www.cruzeirodosulms.com.br) offers service to Bonito (6 hours). Municipal buses connect the *rodoviária* with the local bus station in the center of town. Alternatively, you can take a taxi or *moto-taxi.*

BONITO

In Portuguese, *bonito* means beautiful and the name is certainly an apt one for this patch of paradise on the southern fringe of the Pantanal. One of Brazil's hippest ecotourist destinations, the small town and surrounding area of Bonito offer visitors a stunning range of natural attractions including caverns, waterfalls, and crystalline blue rivers that are ideal for snorkeling, along with hiking trails that wind through the verdant forests of the Serra da Bodoquena.

Until a few years ago, off-the-beaten track Bonito was completely unknown. Then, along came TV Manchete, which featured the region in one of its lushly shot series, and overnight the place was mobbed by young Carioca and Paulistano ecotourists. Luckily, the summer crowds have done nothing to mar this unspoiled spot. Bonito is one of Brazil's most shining examples of sustainable tourism. The region's attractions are situated on privately owned land that is accessible by car or van. In order to preserve nature, rules abound: Nobody can set foot on any trail or enter any river without making a reservation, paying an eco-charge, and hiring a guide. Moreover, each attraction has a limit of tourists that can visit at any given time. Paradise doesn't come cheap—guides and entrance fees will cost you upwards of R$150 a day—and the further-flung attractions such as Rio da Prata and Buraco das Araras involve spending a frustrating amount of time on the road. However, most admit that the distances and costs involved are a small price to pay for experiencing Bonito's natural marvels. In terms of when to travel, winter (with the exception of July) is recommended—not only will you avoid the summer crowds (and obtain low-season discounts), but reduced rainfall means increased visibility in the region's rivers. The downside is that bathing in the waterfalls is an icy experience.

Sights

Bonito is surrounded by grottos, forests, rivers, and wildlife sanctuaries, most located on private *fazendas,* but which can be visited by guided tours from Bonito. Most are half-day or full-day trips. Besides hiking, sports include horseback riding, climbing, rappelling, white-water rafting, and the activity that is synonymous with Bonito: "floating." Independent-minded adventure-sports enthusiasts will probably chafe at all the rules and the guidance of monitors; however, for kids, elderly travelers, and more reticent or unathletic types, Bonito provides an ideal and safe environment to indulge in such diversions.

GRUTA DO LAGO AZUL

One of Bonito's most popular "must-see" attractions, the Gruta do Lago Azul (Rodovia Três Morros Km 20, R$25) is a deep cavern (accessed by precarious stairs) adorned with stalactites and stalagmites at the bottom of which is an impossibly blue lagoon. It turns a piercing turquoise when hit by the sun's rays, which happens December–January 8:30–9:30 A.M. Although the whole tour takes an hour, you only get to gaze at the lake itself for 15 minutes before the next group of tourists arrives, sending you back up to the surface.

BURACO DAS ARARAS

When a cattle farmer purchased the Fazenda Alegre, he wasn't pleased to find a giant *buraco* (hole) sitting in the midst of his pasture. The hole, with a lake at the bottom, has a diameter of 500 meters (1,640 feet) and a depth of 100 meters (328 feet). However, he soon cheered up upon discovering that the Buraco das Araras (BR-267 Km 58, tel. 67/9995-2586, 7:30 A.M.–5 P.M. daily) was a favorite roosting spot for over 40 exotic bird species, among them the gaudily colored red macaw. Now an ecological refuge, the Buraco can be visited with an excursion (the tour lasts 40 minutes).

Recreation
HIKING

There are wonderful opportunities for hiking in the Serra da Bodoquena, with the bonus of abundant waterfalls and natural pools. The **Parque das Cachoeiras** (Estrada Aquidauna, 18 kilometers from Bonito) boasts six lovely cascades as well as small grottoes and refreshing springs that are ideal for bathing. The **Estância Mimosa** (Estrada Bodoquena, 26 kilometers from Bonito) is a neighboring farm that shares the same six falls and throws in a seventh for good measure. A delicious home-cooked lunch is served at the *fazenda* house. Equally popular are the two trails that weave through native foliage and past numerous cascades to the **Cachoeiras do Rio do Peixe** (Estrada Bodoquena, 35 kilometers from Bonito), located on the Fazenda Água Viva. After taking a dip in the cool water and lounging in the sun, return to the farmhouse of the loquacious owner, Seu Moacir. Following a hearty lunch cooked over a wood-burning stove, and homemade *doces,* you can veg out in a hammock. Guided excursions to all of these attractions range in price R$70–100 and include lunch.

RAPPELLING

There are several places you can rappel in Bonito (including the Buraco das Araras and the Boca da Onça), but the most breathtaking option is to go to the **Abismo Anhumas** (Estrada Campo dos Índios, Fazenda Anhumas, 22 kilometers from Bonito). If you've never rappelled before, this is the perfect initiation. After monitors teach you the ropes, you'll get geared up and then plunge 72 meters (236 feet) into an abyss studded with stalactites and stalagmites. At the bottom is a lagoon the size of a soccer field where you can snorkel. Rappelling and snorkeling costs R$360. Reserve in advance.

RAFTING

Rafting on the Rio Formoso is more about relaxation than thrills and spills. For this reason, it is ideal for kids and families. The 2.5-hour, 7-kilometer (4-mile) journey down the river in rubber rafts involves few rapids, but lots of gorgeous scenery. The voyage ends at the Ilha do Padre, a nature reserve, with lots of foliage and birdlife, where you can bask in the sun, bathe in pools and waterfalls, and have a bite at the restaurant. It's 12 kilometers from Bonito (take the Estrada Ilha do Padre); you can enter the reserve without a guide. The rafting trip costs R$50.

◀ FLUTUAÇÃO

The activity for which Bonito is most famous is *flutuação*, which consists of donning a mask, snorkel, neoprene wetsuit, and life jacket and letting yourself be carried down Bonito's rivers, whose unearthly transparency allows you astonishing close-up interaction with over 80 varieties of fish. The sensation is akin to being let loose within a giant tropical aquarium (for this reason don't show up without an underwater camera). The fantastic visibility (which extends to 50 meters/164 feet) is due to the water's high limestone content, which acts as a natural filter, leaving the rivers exceptionally pure. You don't need to have any diving experience to "float": After a few practice sessions with monitors, just let yourself quite literally go

with the flow. Among the colorful fish you'll find yourself rubbing up against are *piraputangas, dourados,* and *curimbatás*—rest assured that piranhas prefer other aquatic pastures.

One of Bonito's most popular attractions, the **Aquário Natural** (7 km/4 miles from Bonito) is a wildlife sanctuary whose crystalline rivers can be explored with snorkeling equipment or glass-bottomed boats. Recommended for beginners (there is a training session before you hit the river itself), this 0.5-kilometer (0.3-mile) underwater excursion is dazzling, but all-too-brief—its popularity limits your floating time to one hour. The price, R$125, includes lunch and access to hiking trails. Longer and equally stunning (not to mention less expensive) floating experiences can be had on the **Rio Formoso** (Rodovia Guia Lopes, 6 km/3.5 miles from Bonito), **Rio Baía Bonita** (BR-267 to Jardim, 7 km/4 miles from Bonito), the **Rio Sucuri** (Estrada São Geraldo, 17 km/10.5 miles from Bonito), and **Rio da Prata** (BR-267 Km 518, 50 km/31 miles from Bonito). Rio Sucuri is particularly spectacular. The excursion begins at the river's source and then continues for 1.5 kilometers (0.9 mile) along a river bed that is lined with a swaying jungle of aquatic plants. Equipment rental and guides are available at all the *fazendas* through which these rivers flow. Equally fantastic is Rio da Prata—the clear waters are always teeming with fish, and the 2-kilometer (1.2-mile) route itself (preceded by a 40-minute hike through the forest) is Bonito's longest. It is also possible to go scuba diving in the Rio Formoso, Rio da Prata, and the Abismo Anhumas. **Bonito Scuba** (Rua Colonel Pilad Rebuá 1853, tel. 67/3255-2040, www.bonitoscuba.com.br) organizes diving trips and offers lessons.

Nightlife

Taboa Bar (Rua Colonel Pilad Rebuá 1837, tel. 67/3255-1862, www.taboa.com.br, 5 P.M.–2 A.M. daily) is Bonito's big nocturnal hangout. Locals and tourists alike fill the tables inside and on the sidewalk to converse over a beer or *cachaça*—try the house concoction sweetened with honey and cinnamon and given an energetic twist of *guaraná* powder. *Petiscos* of grilled fish and meat can easily serve as a light meal.

Accommodations

Even in high season, there are always lots of places to stay in Bonito. For the backpacking crowd, you can't beat **Pousada Muito Bonito** (Rua Colonel Pilad Rebuá 1448, tel. 67/3255-1645, www.muitobonito.com.br, R$80 d), a welcoming place with farmhouse flourishes and a friendly multilingual staff. Bright, spotless rooms range from single to quadruple. The *pousada* has its own on-site ecotourism agency. Perched on a hill overlooking town, the **Chale do Bosque** (Rua Lício Borralho 100, tel. 67/3255-3213, www.chaledobosque.com.br, R$100–150 d) is an idyllic getaway. Six stone bungalows are decked out in rough-hewn, unpolished wood and sport verandas with panoramic views. High notes go to the comfy beds outfitted with goose feather pillows and patchwork quilts.

More centrally located is the **Pirá Miúna** (Rua Luís da Costa Leite 1792, tel. 67/3244-1058, www.piramiunahotel.com.br, R$120–220 d), an attractively modern lodge constructed out of "eco bricks," with sizable, nicely appointed accommodations and inviting common areas, including a deck, pool, living area, and barbecue patio. On the northwest edge of town, some 3 kilometers (2 miles) from the center, the **Pousada Olho d'Agua** (Rodovia Três Morros, tel. 67/3255-1430, www.pousadaolhodagua.com.br, R$134–197) offers a deliciously tranquil retreat. The lodge—also constructed out of "eco bricks"—is set in the midst of a lush wooded estate dotted with ponds and a lovely pool. The simple, appealing rooms are ensconced in bungalows, as are the main dining and living areas and the inviting bar. Service is high quality and you can take advantage of an in-house tour operator.

Bonito also has its share of *fazenda* hotels in the countryside. The advantage is that many have private access to rivers. The downside is their isolation from town (although some may see this as a plus). The most charming of them all, the **Santa Esmeralda** (Estrada Guia Lopes Km 17, tel. 67/3255-2833, www.hotelsantaesmeralda.com.br, R$215–275 d) is a stellar example of eco-chic—from the spacious private bungalows (accommodating up to six people) with living rooms and verandas to the extremely enticing restaurant, bars, and lounge areas. However, the real attraction is the estate itself: a vast area of verdant rolling hills with nature trails, natural pools, and access to the Rio Formoso (the hotel provides *flutuação* gear as well as kayaks). Prices include dinner as well as breakfast.

Food

It's impossible to go hungry in Bonito. Located in an atmospheric wooden house, **Cantinho do Peixe** (Rua 31 de Março 1918, tel. 67/3255-3381, 11 A.M.–3 P.M. and 6–11 P.M. Mon.–Sat., 11 A.M.–3 P.M. Sun., R$12–20) is a traditional favorite, serving up hearty portions of *pantaneiro* fish dishes. The fresh piranha soup is a nice starter. As a main course, the *pintado ao urucum* is especially good and serves two. The varied menu at **Castellabate** (Rua Colonel Pilad Rebuá 2168, tel. 67/3255-1713, 11:30 A.M.–3 P.M. and 6–11 P.M. daily, closed on Wed. Mar.–June and Aug.–Sept., R$12–22) includes pizzas, pastas, and regional dishes. More daring souls won't be able to resist the *jacaré* steaks (served with fries) and *javonteiro* (a cross between a boar and a wild pig).

Although fish is the common thread running through the menu at **Sale e Pepe** (Rua 29 de Maio 971, tel. 67/3255-1822, 6–11 P.M. Tues.–Sun., daily Dec.–Jan. and July, R$15–30), recipes run the gamut from *pantaneiro* to Japanese and Chinese. In the mood for *dourado* sushi and piranha sashimi? This is the place to come. **Vício da Gula** (Rua 29 de Maio, tel. 67/3255-2041, noon–10 P.M. Tues.–Sun., R$8–18) is a great place for a snack or light meal. The sandwiches and hamburgers are fresh and tasty, and the desserts are quite addictive. For late-night sweet cravings head to the **Palácio dos Sorvetes** (Rua Coronel Pilad Rebuá 1915, daily until midnight off-seasons and until 4 A.M. in summer). Its 45 flavors of ice cream range from classics such as chocolate to the utterly exotic *guavíra* and *bocaiúva,* two of the sweetest and most succulent fruits of the Cerrado.

Information and Services

The **tourist office** (Rua Colonel Pilad Rebuá 1780, tel. 67/3255-1850, www.bonito-ms.com.br, 9 A.M.–5 P.M. daily) is quite helpful. In Portuguese, a useful site is www.portalbonito.com.br. You'll find a **Banco do Brasil** at Rua Luiz da Costa 2279 (tel. 67/3255-1121). A downside to Bonito is that, unless you're on a package, on-site tours of natural attractions don't include transportation, and there is no bus service. One alternative is to share costs of the vans operated by local tourist agencies (around R$35 per day pp). The only disadvantage is you'll have to adhere the vans' schedules. Another option is to take a taxi. While there is no shortage of cabs, they have all made a pact to charge the same rather extravagant rates (upwards of R$130 a day). You might find it more economical to rent a car in Campo Grande (there are no car rental agencies in Bonito).

ECOTOURS

For better or for worse, Bonito's tourism is highly organized. Many of the larger hotels have their own tour companies or can organize guides and/or excursions. However, there is no lack of tour agencies in town. Don't waste your time shopping around—all excursions and activities in Bonito have set prices (although they can be lower across-the-board during off-season). Among recommended agencies are: **Agência Ar** (Rua Colonel Pilad Rebuá 1184, tel. 67/3255-1008, www.agenciaar.com.br) which can put you in touch with tour guides if you have your own form of transportation; **Ygarapé Tour** (Rua Colonel Pilad Rebuá 1956, tel. 67/3255-1733, www.ygarape.com.br), which, aside from excursions and guides, also offers scuba diving for beginners; and **Natura Tour** (Rua 29 de Maio 1000, tel. 65/3255-1544, www.naturatour.com.br). During December, January, and June, it's recommended that you make reservations at least three months in advance.

Getting There

Cruzeiro do Sul (tel. 67/3255-1606 in Bonito, www.cruzeirodosulms.com.br) runs several buses a day between Campo Grande and Bonito. The trip takes around five hours. If you're driving, from Campo Grande take the BR-060 and then the MS-382, both of which are paved.

PERNAMBUCO AND ALAGOAS

In size, the northeastern state of Pernambuco is fairly small. However, in terms of cultural and historical importance, it is a giant. Its capital city, Recife, and the adjacent town of Olinda possess an impressive array of colonial architecture and also lay claim to some of the richest artistic and musical traditions in Brazil. Come summertime, both cities host exuberant, highly colorful street Carnavals that attract revelers from all over the world.

Founded by the Dutch in the 1500s, Recife is known as Brazil's Amsterdam due to the fact that its historical center is dissected by a series of canals flowing into the sea. The similarities, however, end there. Recife is humid, somewhat ramshackle, and quite poor. Yet, it is also a subtly alluring place with numerous historical buildings, a Copacabana-worthy strip of white

sand, and a distinctive cultural scene. Close by is Pernambuco's original capital, Olinda. Its hilltop churches, cobblestoned streets, and lovely squares make it one of the most beautiful examples of colonial architecture in the Americas. No mere ode to the glorious past, Olinda is also home to a thriving artist community, which accounts for its numerous ateliers, galleries, and boutiques.

North and south of Recife, Pernambuco's coast is lined with magnificent white-sand beaches, including those surrounding the famous resort of Porto de Galinhas. Traveling inland, the landscape gives way to the dry, rugged desert-like Sertão, known for its blazing blue skies, red earth, thorn trees, and cattle. Many towns of this vast region are reputed for their traditional crafts such as ceramics and

© CHRISTIAN KNEPPER/ANIMA/EMBRATUR

HIGHLIGHTS

◖ Olinda: Although most are lured by its wealth of splendid baroque churches, Pernambuco's first capital is no living museum, but a vibrant colonial town pulsing with art and life (page 459).

◖ Caruaru: Host of the biggest open-air market in the Northeast, together with the surrounding villages of Alto do Moura and Bezerros, Caruaru provides an unforgettable taste of the Sertão's rich artistic, musical, and culinary culture (page 466).

◖ Porto de Galinhas: Sugary sands and endless palms make Porto de Galinhas one of Brazil's most attractive destinations for the sun, sand, and snorkeling set (page 469).

◖ Fernando de Noronha: The archetype of everyone's fantasy tropical island, carefully preserved Fernando de Noronha is a paradise for divers, surfers, dolphin-lovers, and escapists (page 472).

◖ Barra de São Miguel: The star attraction of this stretch of coast is drop-dead gorgeous Praia do Gunga, whose impossibly white sands are bathed by a turquoise sea and freshwater lagoon (page 487).

◖ Penedo: This picturesque colonial town perched above the Rio São Francisco offers a captivating glimpse of life along Brazil's largest national river (page 488).

◖ São Miguel dos Milagres: Simultaneously unspoiled and exclusive, the idyllic palm-lined beaches and coral-protected waters surrounding this charming fishing village provide the ultimate getaway (page 490).

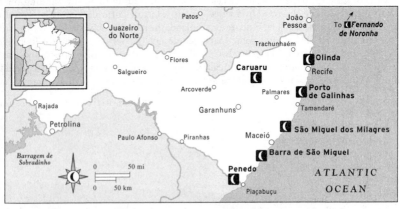

LOOK FOR ◖ TO FIND RECOMMENDED SIGHTS, ACTIVITIES, DINING, AND LODGING.

woodcuts. The most famous of these inland towns, Caruaru, has the largest and one of the most colorful, outdoor markets in Brazil.

Wedged between Pernambuco and Bahia, Brazil's smallest states, Alagoas and Sergipe, are often overlooked by travelers to the Northeast. However, the coast of Alagoas, both north and south of its pretty seaside capital of Maceió, lays claim to some of the most drop-dead gorgeous tropical beaches in Brazil. Clear, turquoise-green lagoons and coral reefs are ideal for snorkeling and diving, or simply floating around. Meanwhile, on Alagoas's border with Sergipe, the charming colonial town of Penedo overlooks the mighty Rio São Francisco, Brazil's longest national river.

Despite the beauty of Pernambuco's and Alagoas's beaches, none of them compare with those you'll encounter if you fly to the island archipelago of Fernando de Noronha, 550 kilometers (342 miles) off the coast of Pernambuco. Aside from pristine beaches, considered to be the most sublime in Brazil, this carefully preserved island ecosystem offers spectacular snorkeling and diving along with a chance to glimpse a fantastic array of exotic flora and fauna. Fernando de Noronha is living proof that you needn't die to get to Paradise.

PLANNING YOUR TIME

Despite its small size, Pernambuco is jam-packed with treasures of every type: from baroque churches and stunning beaches to distinctive regional culture that can easily keep you engaged for days, if not weeks. That said, to soak up some local flavor and see the sights of Recife and Olinda you need a minimum of three days. For some fun in the sun, the beaches of both Pernambuco and neighboring Alagoas are in very close proximity (Recife and Maceió are only four hours apart by car or bus). Many can be enjoyed as day trips from either capital. If you have more time, spend 2–3 days (or more) traveling from one city to the other, stopping overnight at such places as Cabo de Santo Agostinho, Porto de Galinhas, and Tamandaré (southern Pernambuco) or Maragogi, São Miguel dos Milagres, and

Barra de Santo Antônio (northern Alagoas). A trip inland to Penedo from Maceió merits a couple of days, as does a pilgrimage to the market town of Caruaru. Meanwhile, if you're prepared to splurge on a trip to the island paradise of Fernando de Noronha, set aside at least 4–5 days as you'll want to wallow in the sheer idyllic beauty of the place.

Both Recife and Maceió are easily reached by plane and bus from cities around the country. Along the coast, main highways are generally in good shape, and due to the relatively short distances involved, you can easily explore other parts of the Northeast from either state. Temperatures are consistently tropical, and there is lots of sun to go around, although rains can be intense April–July. In summer months, beaches tend to fill up with vacationing Brazilians. The sun is also hottest at this time and temperatures are routinely in the 30s°C (90s°F). If you're venturing into the Sertão, days can be furnace-like in the summer, while nights can cool down (becoming quite cold in June and July).

HISTORY

Along with Bahia to the south, Pernambuco (for a long time Alagoas was part of the colonial province of Pernambuco) was one of the first regions to be colonized by the Portuguese, who founded the small town of Olinda in the 1530s. The gently rolling hills of the coastline proved ideal for the cultivation of sugarcane. After the quick subjugation of the local Indian tribes and importation of shiploads of slaves from Africa, the region was soon covered in vast plantations that transformed Pernambuco and Alagoas into one of the biggest producers of cane in the world. The fabulous riches derived from sugar led to the birth of a wealthy class of aristocrats. Upon Olinda's hills, they built lavish homes and sumptuous churches looking out to sea. All was well until 1630, when Dutch troops arrived, desirous of a tropical sugarcane empire of their own. Having failed to invade Salvador in 1824, the Dutch were resolute about seizing Pernambuco, and in 1630 laid siege to Olinda, burning most of its fine buildings to the ground. Being expert navigators, the Dutch abandoned Olinda. They decided to build a new capital on the marshy islands crisscrossed by rivers, 6 kilometers (4 miles) to the south, which had the advantage of an excellent natural harbor protected by offshore reefs. Versed in the ways of dikes and canals, they set about draining the area and constructing a city christened Mauritzstad after the Johann Mauritz van Nassau, leader of Dutch forces and governor of Dutch Pernambuco. Sugar flowed out while slaves flowed in, and the fortified Dutch outpost rapidly grew into a thriving commercial center. Although by 1640 the Dutch controlled much of Pernambuco and Alagoas, the Catholic plantation owners were loath to accept the Protestant Dutch. Numerous skirmishes and rebellions ensued, and by 1654, Portuguese forces had sent the Dutch packing.

Olinda was rebuilt. In keeping with the architectural style of the day, its numerous churches received sumptuous baroque overhauls. However, despite its political importance as the seat of the plantation aristocrats, Recife was overtaking it as a thriving port city whose bustling commerce was energized by an enterprising class of newly arrived Portuguese merchants. Throughout the 18th century, competition between the two cities was fierce, and even bloody. Ultimately, dynamic Recife (the name comes from *arrecife,* the Portuguese word for reef) won the upper hand while Olinda's fortunes faded, bottoming out in the 19th century with the demise of the sugar trade and the abolition of slavery that affected all of Pernambuco and Alagoas (which had become an independent state in 1817). To this day, sugarcane fields still dominate portions of both states (and Pernambucano *cachaça* is some of the finest in the country). The second largest city in the Northeast, Recife has become an important industrial and commercial center. Meanwhile, decades of restoration and recognition by UNESCO as a World Heritage Site have transformed Olinda into one of Brazil's most stunning architectural gems, attracting legions of artists and tourists. Tourism is also big business along the southern coast of Pernambuco and throughout Alagoas, which are blessed with some of Brazil's most dreamy beaches.

Pernambuco

Along with Bahia, the state of Pernambuco is the other economic, demographic, and cultural powerhouse of the Northeast. With a rich history all its own, it boasts some of Brazil's most unique and fascinating cultural events and traditions, particularly in the realms of art and music. Highlights include the historic cities of Recife and Olinda, along with a beautiful coastline of beaches and the parched rugged landscape of the Sertão, where the poverty of the soil contrasts with the richness of the popular culture.

RECIFE

Although its river canals and bridges sometimes (rather optimistically) earn it the nickname "Amsterdam of the Northeast" (more deluded souls have compared it to Venice), not much of a colonial Dutch legacy remains in Pernambuco's capital. Aside from the recently revamped colonial center, known as Recife Antigo, and a handful of impressive 17th- and 18th-century churches tucked away in the otherwise built-up downtown neighborhoods of Santo Antônio, São José, and Boa Vista, there is not much of a colonial Portuguese legacy either. For baroque treasures, visit the state's first capital of Olinda, across the bay. In fact, many visitors prefer to stay in Olinda, which is smaller and certainly prettier.

However, beyond the sprawling chaos, humidity, and mishmash of architectural styles, Recife is a city that grows on you, with a rhythm and flavor all its own. By day, there is lots to see and do, and if you get a sudden urge to be horizontal on a white-sand beach

PERNAMBUCO AND ALAGOAS

PERNAMBUCO AND ALAGOAS

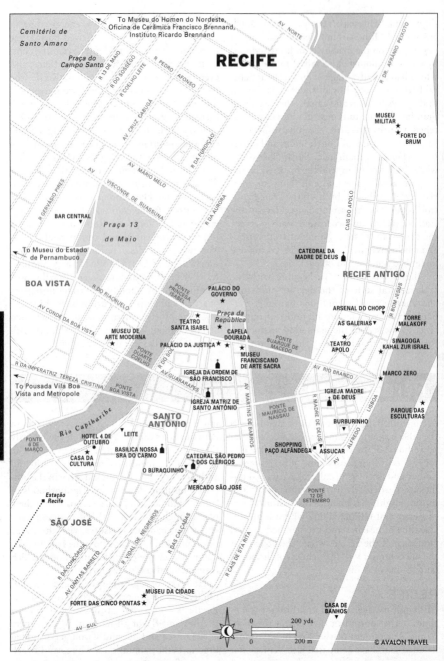

To Museu do Homen do Nordeste,
Oficina de Cerâmica Francisco Brennand,
Instituto Ricardo Brennand

RECIFE

Cemitério de
Santo Amaro

Praça do
Campo Santo

AV NORTE

R DR. AFRÂNIO PEIXOTO

MUSEU
MILITAR
FORTE DO
BRUM

R 13 DE MAIO
R DO SOSSEGO
R COELHO LEITE
R PEDRO AFONSO
R DA FUNDIÇÃO
AV CRUZ CABUGÁ
AV MÁRIO MELO
VISCONDE DE SUASSUNA
R DA AURORA

AV GERVÁSIO PIRES

BAR CENTRAL

Praça 13
de Maio

CAIS DO APOLO

To Museu do Estado
de Pernambuco

CATEDRAL DA
MADRE DE DEUS

BOA VISTA

R DO RIACHUELO

RECIFE ANTIGO

AV CONDE DA BOA VISTA

PONTE
PRINCESA
ISABEL

PALÁCIO DO
GOVERNO

ARSENAL DO CHOPP

AS GALERIAS

TORRE
MALAKOFF

R BOM JESUS

TEATRO
SANTA ISABEL

Praça da
República

MUSEU DE
ARTE MODERNA

CAPELA
DOURADA

TEATRO
APOLO

SINAGOGA
KAHAL ZUR ISRAEL

R DA IMPERATRIZ TEREZA CRISTINA

PONTE
DUARTE
COELHO

PALÁCIO DA JUSTIÇA

R DO SOL

MUSEU
FRANCISCANO
DE ARTE SACRA

PONTE
BUARQUE DE
MACEDO

AV RIO BRANCO

MARCO ZERO

To Pousada Vila Boa
Vista and Metropole

PONTE
BOA VISTA

AV GUARARAPES

IGREJA DA ORDEM DE
SÃO FRANCISCO

R MADRE DE DEUS

IGREJA MADRE
DE DEUS

LISBOA

Rio Capibaribe

PONTE
6 DE
MARÇO

HOTEL 4 DE
OUTUBRO

**SANTO
ANTÔNIO**

LEITE

IGREJA MATRIZ DE
SANTO ANTÔNIO

R MARTINS DE BARROS

PONTE
MAURÍCIO DE
NASSAU

BURBURINHO

PARQUE DAS
ESCULTURAS

CASA DA
CULTURA

BASÍLICA NOSSA
SRA DO CARMO

CATEDRAL SÃO PEDRO
DOS CLÉRIGOS

SHOPPING
PAÇO ALFÂNDEGA

ASSUCAR

R ALFREDO LISBOA

O BURAQUINHO

MERCADO SÃO JOSÉ

PONTE
12 DE
SETEMBRO

Estação
Recife

SÃO JOSÉ

R DA CONCÓRDIA

R DANTAS BARRETO

R VIDAL DE NEGREIROS

R DAS CALÇADAS

R CAIS DE STA RITA

MUSEU DA CIDADE

FORTE DAS CINCO PONTAS

CASA DE
BANHOS

AV SUL

0   200 yds
0   200 m

© AVALON TRAVEL

with a cooling *caipirinha,* you can make for Boa Viagem, the longest urban beach in Brazil. Recife has a surprisingly good restaurant scene and a varied nightlife, spurred on by one of the most singular and creative music scenes in Brazil, responsible for the birth of rhythms such as *frevo, maracatu,* and *mangue beat.*

Recife has a lot of poverty and, unfortunately, is renowned for having a high incidence of violent crime. For this reason, stay clear from the Centro at night and weekends when it's ghostlike. If you go to Recife Antigo or bars in the area take a taxi. In fact, at night, taxis are a must.

Sights

With its winding river canals and twisting old streets, crowded sidewalks cluttered with vendors and indistinguishable modern high-rises, Recife's downtown is somewhat of a puzzle to navigate. Fortunately, most of its historical attractions are within walking distance of each other. Spread out between three small islands that comprise the *bairros* of Recife Antigo (also called Bairro do Recife), Santo Antônio, and Boa Vista, the center is connected to the mainland by numerous bridges that cross the Beberibe and Capibaribe Rivers. You can see most of these sights easily in a day or less, although you should add a second day for the fantastic museums in the outlying suburbs, and a third if you want to flake out on Boa Viagem's beach.

RECIFE ANTIGO (BAIRRO DO RECIFE)

The historic core of Recife, or Recife Antigo, is the oldest part of town, founded by the Dutch in the 1630s. For years, its glorious edifices were left in a tragically dilapidated state, until, spurred on by Salvador's sprucing up of the Pelourinho, Recife's authorities decided to restore and revitalize its historic quarter. Although the makeover itself is a little garish (the paint on those buildings is *very* bright), these efforts succeeded in breathing new life into an area that was once avoided like the plague. At night and on weekends, its many bars and cobblestoned squares teem with Recifenses and tourists alike

who gather to drink and check out live music performances. Lately, a decrease in both cultural events and police has made the area a bit sketchier at night. Exercise caution.

The heart of Recife Antigo is at the Praça Barão do Rio Branco, more commonly known as **Marco Zero.** From here you can look out across the ocean and see the coral reef that inspired the city's name. Jutting up from the reef itself are a series of intriguing phallic sculptures by renowned local ceramicist and artist Francisco Brennand. Should you have the urge to gaze at them up close, you can hop a boat for the **Parque das Esculturas,** leaving from in front of the *praça* (R$2).

One block behind the square, lively **Rua do Bom Jesus,** now filled with bars and boutiques, was one of the main streets of Recife Antigo. For a short while, it was also the center of a small but thriving Jewish community. Although the first Jews had arrived in Olinda in 1537, under Dutch occupation the community flourished. Unlike the Portuguese, who persecuted Jews, the Dutch tolerated Judaism. It was during this period that the first synagogue in the Americas—the **Sinagoga Kahal Zur Israel** (Rua do Bom Jesus 197, Recife Antigo, tel. 81/3224-2128, www.arquivojudaicope.org.br, 9 A.M.–4:30 P.M. Tues.–Fri., 3–6:30 P.M. Sat.–Sun., R$4) was constructed on what was then known as Rua dos Judeus. When the Portuguese finally routed the Dutch from Recife in 1654, most of Pernambuco's Jews fled to New Amsterdam, where they founded what would become the future New York's first Jewish community (others remained in Brazil under the guise of "New Christians"). The synagogue was abandoned and forgotten until excavations in the 1990s uncovered the *mikve,* a ritual fountain used for purification. After major renovations, it reopened as a synagogue, containing a very good museum that traces the history of Jews in Pernambuco. On the ground floor, you can still see vestiges of the original synagogue, including the floor of Dutch tiles and parts of the walls. On the third floor, an excellent video (with English subtitles) describes the Jewish experience in Brazil.

Wandering around, you'll see plenty of handsome old buildings. Of particular note is the **Teatro Apolo** (Rua do Apolo 121), a rather grand mid-19th-century theater constructed out of Portuguese limestone that now houses a cinema, theater, and concert hall. Overlooking the Rio Capibaribe, the **Shopping Paço Alfândega** (Rua da Alfândega 65, Recife Antigo, tel. 81/3419-7620, 10 A.M.–10 P.M. Mon.–Sat., noon–8 P.M. Sun.) is a former convent and customs house that now houses a designer shopping center filled with cool boutiques, cafés, and restaurants. Close by, one of Recife's oldest churches, the **Igreja Madre de Deus** (Rua Madre de Deus, Recife Antigo, tel. 81/3224-5587, 8 A.M.–noon and 2–5 P.M. Tues.–Fri., 8–11 A.M. Sat., 8 A.M.–noon Sun.) is remarkable for its facade featuring stone sculptures carved out of local coral.

SANTO ANTÔNIO, SÃO JOSÉ, AND BOA VISTA

Across the river from Recife Antigo, the *bairro* of Santo Antônio was also originally settled by the Dutch. A block from the Ponte Buarque de Macedo sits the lovely green **Praça da República,** surrounded by grand 19th- and early 20th-century buildings such as the pale pink Teatro Santa Isabel, the Palácio da Justiça, and the Palácio do Governo, seat of the state government. The park was originally the site of Dutch governor Mauritz van Nassau's estate, and its current design—by a 19th-century French landscaper with later embellishments by Roberto Burle Marx—has maintained an air of bucolic languor, thanks to a fountain, myriad palms, and a gigantic African baobob whose origin is a mystery.

A block away from Praça da República lies the most impressive baroque architectural ensemble in Recife. Built in 1606, the **Igreja da Ordem Terceira de São Francisco** (Rua do Imperador Dom Pedro II 206, Santo Antônio, tel. 81/3224-0530, 8–11:30 A.M. and 2–5 P.M. Mon.–Fri., 8–11:30 A.M. Sat., R$2) is distinctive for its cupola lined with Dutch ceramic tiles and blue-and-white Portuguese *azulejo* panels. Next door, a small sacred art museum

displays silver and gold religious artifacts and intricately painted wooden saints. The small cloister of **Convento Franciscano** is ornamented with more *azulejos* depicting Old Testament scenes. Even more impressive is the **Capela Dourada,** an early baroque extravaganza of dazzling gold. Gold leaf covers the sculpted cedar altars and columns, and frames the religious paintings that adorn the walls and ceilings. You are left with the impression of having walked into a jewel box.

Avenida Dantas Barreto leads from Praça da República through the maze of bustling shop-lined streets that stretches from Santo Antônio to the adjacent *bairro* of São José. A few blocks south along Dantas Barreto brings you to the **Catedral de São Pedro dos Clérigos** (Pátio de São Pedro, Santo Antônio, tel. 81/3224-2954, 8 A.M.–noon Mon.–Fri.), one of Recife's most striking churches. Dating back to 1728, the facade is modeled after the church of Santa Maria Maggiore in Rome. Inside, the lack of gold comes as a relief—you are free to admire the beautifully detailed woodwork, including likenesses of the 12 apostles set against a splendid trompe l'oeil background on the ceiling. The church dominates the **Pátio de São Pedro,** a charming rectangular plaza surrounded by restored and brightly painted 18th- and 19th-century houses, many of which are now restaurants, bars and boutiques. A traditional bohemian hangout—in the '80s, the artists and intellectuals who gathered here to read poems and play music were referred to as the "Pátio Generation"—it's a great place to have a drink and hang out. Tuesday nights the Pátio becomes a stage for Terça Negra, featuring music and dance performances related to Pernambuco's African heritage.

Three blocks east of Pátio de São Pedro, in a labyrinth of streets filled with interesting local shops, is the **Mercado São José** (Praça Dom Vital, São José, tel. 81/3424-2322, 6 A.M.–5 P.M. Mon.–Sat., 6 A.M.–noon Sun.). Recife is teeming with markets, but São José, located in an elegant 19th-century cast iron structure imported from France, is the oldest and most traditional. The market is a wonderful place to soak up the local atmosphere and check out wares ranging from *carne-de-sol* and herb-infused *cachaça* to handmade leather goods, ceramics, and *literatura de cordel*. Named after the *cordas* (cords) on which they are displayed in markets, these epic, moral, and historic tales are printed on cheap folio paper and illustrated with wonderfully expressive woodcuts. For a long time, *literatura de cordel* was the most popular and widely diffused form of literature in the Northeast. Even if you don't speak Portuguese, you might want to buy a few booklets as an inspired example of local art.

Also in São José is the impressive **Forte das Cinco Pontas** (Praça das Cinco Pontas, São José, tel. 81/3224-8492, 9 A.M.–6 P.M. Tues.–Fri., 1–5 P.M. Sat.–Sun., R$1), whose name alludes to the original five-pointed adobe fort erected by the Dutch. Although the Portuguese razed it and then rebuilt a more traditional four-pointed fortification out of stone, the name stuck. Inside, a rather musty (and not at all essential) **Museu da Cidade** traces Recife's history through a series of engravings and paintings.

Back towards Santo Antônio along Avenida Dantas Barreto are three more colonial churches. The **Basílica e Convento de Nossa Senhora do Carmo** (Praça do Carmo, Santo Antônio, tel. 81/3224-3341, 7 A.M.–7 P.M. Mon.–Fri., 7 A.M.–noon Sat., 8 A.M.–noon and 6–9 P.M. Sun.) offers another shining example of baroque with the requisite intricate carvings, gold-covered altars, and *azulejo* panels depicting Biblical scenes. The mid- to late-18th-century **Igreja Matriz de Santo Antônio** (Praça da Independência, Santo Antônio, tel. 81/3224-9494, 7 A.M.–noon and 2–6 P.M. daily) features a mixture of styles. That the interior is a little worse for wear gives it a melancholy Old World air. Although the simple facade of **Igreja Nossa Senhora da Conceição dos Militares** (Rua Nova 309, Santo Antônio, tel. 81/3224-3106, 8 A.M.–4 P.M. Mon.–Fri., 8 A.M.–1 P.M. Sat.–Sun.) doesn't register much, if you step inside you'll be startled by exuberantly sculpted columns and altars covered in gold leaf, along with a ceiling fresco depicting a pregnant Virgin Mary.

By now, you're only a block from the river. If you take a left onto Rua do Sol, which runs along the waterfront, a short walk will bring you to the **Casa da Cultura** (Rua Floriano Peixoto, Santo Antônio, tel. 81/3224-2850, 9 A.M.–7 P.M. Mon.–Sat., 9 A.M.–1 P.M. Sun.), which occupies a prison that dates back to the 1860s. While one of the cells gives you an impression of a 19th-century life behind bars, the others have been converted into shops selling art and handicrafts from all over the state of Pernambuco.

If you retrace your steps along Rua do Sol, you'll eventually come to the pretty Ponte Duarte Coelho, Recife's oldest remaining Dutch-built bridge. On the other side of the river, in the *bairro* of Boa Vista, is **Rua Aurora.** Its brightly painted neoclassical buildings, radiant when lit by the early morning sun, are reflected in the waters of the Rio Capibaribe. At number 175, Cine São Luiz, the oldest and grandest cinema in town, dates back to 1952. It's worth dropping by the **Museu de Arte Moderna** (Rua da Aurora 256, noon–6 P.M. Tues.–Sun., R$1) to check out the temporary exhibits of modern Brazilian and Pernambucano art.

BOA VIAGEM

Flanked by gleaming, yet rather dauntingly massive apartment buildings, Boa Viagem as a neighborhood is certainly nowhere near as interesting as Copacabana, to which it is often compared. Aside from hotels, and some good restaurants and bars (mostly centered around the northern stretch known as Pina), the only attraction is the very urban—albeit very attractive—white-sand beach. Although on weekends it can get mobbed, Boa Viagem is otherwise relaxing (and very well-equipped, with vendors hawking everything from grilled shrimp to icy beer). The waters are calm and warm for bathing (there is an offshore reef visible at low tide). However, do *not* venture out far since Boa Viagem is the Brazilian capital of shark attacks. Over the last decade, there have been various instances of careless bathers going out too far and being injured or even killed. If you stay close to shore, there's no reason to worry.

ARREDORES (OUTLYING NEIGHBORHOODS)

A quick bus or taxi ride from the center, the leafy, residential neighborhoods of Graças, Casa Forte, Casas Amarelas, and Várzea are situated on land formerly occupied by sugar plantations. Although out of the way, these *bairros* offer a glimpse at another, more tranquil side of Recife and contain several unusual and very interesting museums.

Located in a gracious neoclassical villa, the **Museu do Estado de Pernambuco** (Av. Rui Barbosa 960, Graças, tel. 81/3427-9322, 10 A.M.–5 P.M. Tues.–Fri., 2–5 P.M. Sat.–Sun., R$1) displays an engaging collection of fine colonial furniture along with engravings and paintings of Recife from the 17th century to 20th century. For an excellent overview of Pernambucano culture, head to the **Museu do Homen do Nordeste** (Av. 17 de Agosto 2187, Casa Forte, tel. 81/3073-6332, 8 A.M.–5 P.M. Tues.–Sun.). Extremely well-organized, the museum relies on objects to depict the rich singularity of traditional life in the Brazilian Northeast. Sugarcane cultivation, Sertanejo cattle culture, Catholicism, Candomblé, and Carnaval are only a few of the themes touched upon. Although it's all highly compelling stuff, the most striking section is devoted to popular art forms of the interior, where there is a strong tradition of making clay figurines illustrating scenes from daily life. One of the greatest practitioners of this art form was Mestre Vitalino, a poor farmer from the village of Alto do Moura, who, in the 1920s, began sculpting highly expressive vignettes—often doused with humor—of the changing rural world around him.

Recife's two most fascinating and original museums both bear the name of Brennand. The renowned artist and ceramicist Francisco Brennand transformed the old brick, tile, and ceramic factory that made his family millionaires into the **Oficina de Cerâmica Francisco Brennand** (Av. Caxangá, Várzea, tel. 81/3271-2466, 8 A.M.–5 P.M. Mon.–Fri., R$3). In this atelier/museum, Brennand, a white-bearded Biblical-looking personage, exhibits his fantastic, often monumental sculptures, along with paintings, drawings, and engravings. Inspired by mythical, historical, and literary figures, many of his sculptures have a surreal flavor, not to mention a distinct erotic charge. The atelier is surrounded by exuberant gardens designed by Burle Marx, which contain lagoons and spouting fountains. There is also a café and boutique. Instead of making art, Fernando's no less colorful cousin, Ricardo, collects it. In 2002, he opened the nearby **Instituto Ricardo Brennand** (Alameda Antônio Brennand, Várzea, tel. 81/2121-0352, 1–7 P.M. Tues.–Sun., R$4, free Tues.) in order to share his eclectic finds with the public. A stately alley of imperial palms leads through a sculpture garden and up to a complex of buildings dominated by a crazily out-of-place medieval castle. The highlights of Brennand's art collection are the paintings by European artists who traveled to Brazil between the 16th and 20th centuries. You'll find it very rewarding to see Brazil through the eyes of these early tourists. Particularly well represented is talented Dutch painter Franz Post (1612–1680), who was officially commissioned to depict the otherworldly tropical landscapes, fauna, and inhabitants of Pernambuco. Precious maps, manuscripts, and money from the Dutch occupation can also be seen. Despite the oddity of finding them in the middle of the tropics, the 3,000 pieces of medieval armor and weaponry (located in the castle) are another other high point of Brennand's collection. Before leaving, stop for a drink at the on-site café.

Nightlife

Compared to the bustle of the day, much of the city—including the center and Boa Viagem—shuts down at night. This shouldn't fool you, however, since there are definitely urban pockets where Recifenses gather to have fun until the wee hours. Indeed, of the northeastern cities, Recife's nightlife is one of the most eclectic, although its nocturnal pleasures aren't always obvious (especially for foreigners). Contributing to Recife's singularity is the diversity of homegrown music styles—ranging from traditional *forró* and *maracatu* to the post-modern strains

FORRÓ

One of the most popular musical traditions throughout the Northeast is *forró,* a lively form of country-style dance music mixed with a bit of rumba, whose resulting swing is very infectious. The origin of the word *forró* has two possible sources. One is as a shortening of *forrobodó,* a term used by Brazilian elitists to refer (rather condescendingly) to the unruly but joyous street dances held by northeastern peasants. The other stems from the mid-19th century, when British engineers came to build railroads throughout Pernambuco. To foster good worker relations, the Brit bosses sometimes held balls to which locals knew they were invited by the "For All" sign posted at the entrance.

Regardless of which version is more accurate, *forró* came to be associated with the dances (a two-step with swing) and the music (a wilder version of the *baião*), played by a trio of accordion, triangle, and *zabumba* drum that swept the Northeast and was given a major boost by the late great *forró* pioneer and poet, **Luiz Gonzaga** (1912–1989). Throughout the 20th century, *forró* evolved, taking on new repertoires and admitting new instruments such as the *pifano* (wooden flute) and

rabeca (a Brazilian fiddle). In recent years, it has caught on in hip pockets of urban centers such as Rio and São Paulo, where the addition of electronic keyboards has endeared it to DJs and clubbers.

Recife has many traditional *casas de forró,* which really get hopping on Friday and Saturday nights (more so after midnight). Most are in *arredores* (outlying neighborhoods), easily reachable by taxi. If you're in the mood to cut a rug in Recife, visit the **Sala de Reboco** (Rua Gregório Junior 264, Cordeiro, tel. 81/3228-7052, www.saladereboco.com.br, 10 P.M.–close Thurs.–Sat.), a very atmospheric dance hall/bar that works hard to capture the flavor of the northeastern interior with authentic decorative details and food. The stage attracts the biggest national names in *forró* as well as up-and-coming local talents. Also not to be missed is a chance to see blind singer and accordionist **Arlindo dos Oito Baixos,** a living *forró* legend, who spent 25 years playing with Luiz Gonzaga. On weekends, he opens his house and backyard (Av. Hildebrando de Vasconcelos 29000, Dois Unidos, tel. 81/3443-9147, R\$5–10) to *forró* performers from far and wide.

of *mangue beat*—that provide the soundtrack to its bars, clubs, and dance halls.

RECIFE ANTIGO

Since the colonial center underwent its facelift, Recife Antigo has become a major nocturnal haunt for Recife's youth. Come sunset, the place starts to buzz, although recent security issues have put a bit of a damper on proceedings. You'll find lots of bars in Rua do Apolo, Rua do Bom Jesus, and Praça Arsenal da Marinha. A favorite is the **Arsenal do Chopp** (Praça Artur Oscar 59, Recife Antigo, tel. 81/3224-6259, 11 A.M.–3 P.M. Mon.–Fri., 4–10 P.M.–close Sat.–Sun.), where the *chopp* comes in three colors: gold (plain), green (with mint liqueur), and red (with red currant liqueur). The sidewalk tables are great for checking out the flow of revelers. A little more removed from

the main sizzle is laid-back **Burburinho** (Rua Tomazina 106, tel. 81/3224-5854, 6 P.M.–close Mon.–Sat.), which draws an eclectic crowd of students, journalists, and artists of all ages to its sidewalk tables with the fetching Igreja de Madre de Deus as a backdrop. Inside, a small stage often hosts local rock and blues bands.

SANTO ANTÔNIO, SÃO JOSÉ, AND BOA VISTA

For the most part, this area is pretty dead (and spooky) at night, the exception being the classic bohemian bars, such as **O Buraquinho** (see *Food*), surrounding the charming **Pátio São Pedro,** where live music is often performed in the evenings. Come Tuesday nights for Terça Negra, an event featuring performances of Afro-Brazilian music such as *afoxé, maracatu,* samba, and reggae. The Pátio gets a lot of happy hour traffic, as does the generically named **Bar Central** (Rua Mamede Simões 144, Boa Vista, tel. 81/3222-7622, noon–2 A.M. Mon.–Fri., 8 P.M.–2 A.M. Sat.), which lures an attractive and eclectic mix of artists, musicians and ad execs, who mellow out to the customized soundtrack or watch the world go by from sidewalk tables. The menu offers an usual mixture of appetizers that draw on Indian, Jewish, Middle Eastern and local recipes. The samosas with *abacaxi* (white pineapple) chutney are particularly irresistible.

Boa Vista is also where you'll find most of Recife's gay offerings. **Metrópole** (Rua da Ninfas 125, Boa Vista, tel. 81/3423-0123, www.metropoledance.com.br, 10 P.M.–close Fri.–Sat.) is Recife's temple of gaydom, a mega club whose fabulous decor changes seasonally. Aside from the large dance floor, there are two bars, one paying homage to Carmen Miranda and another on the roof with a telescope for star gazing. Other gaze-worthy items include the go-go boys and the drag queens.

PINA

Boa Viagem's northern strip of Pina (also known as Polo Pina) was the city's happening nocturnal circuit back in the '90s. After falling out of favor in the new millennium, it has lately crept back in style with a vengeance. Hipster HQ is **Galeria Joana Darc**, in Avenida Herculano Bandeira, a cluster of bars, restaurants and vintage clothing boutiques haunted by a youngish, alternative, GLS crowd. Aside from **Anjo Solto** (see *Food*), check out **Boratcho** (Av. Herculano, Bandeira 513, Pina, tel. 81/3327-1168, www.boratcho.com.br, 7 P.M.–close, Tues.–Sun.), which brings a little bit of Mexico to Recife with its bright Frida Kahlo colors and menu featuring tacos and *tequiroskas* (tequila cocktails made with crushed local fruits such *siriguela* and *umbu-cajá*). This creative bar—owned by a tattoo artist—is also known for its eclectic musical tastes. These run the gamut from *chorinho,* jazz, and samba rock to events such as Thursday's *"sem noção"* (without notion) nights, in which a DJ gets the arty crowd dancing till dawn.

Two popular northeastern bar snacks are *caldinhos,* hearty chowders, and *guaiamuns,* blue-shelled crabs that live in mangroves. Both delicacies reel in customers at the laid-back **Socaldinho Guaiamum** (Av. Conselheiro Auguiar 112, Pina, tel. 81/3326-3766, 5 P.M.–close Mon.–Fri., noon onwards Sat.–Sun.). A special chef watches over the cauldrons of seven bubbling *caldinhos,* ranging from classic black bean to *mocotó* (calves' hoofs), also popularly known as "viagra." Tucked away on a street only footsteps away from the sand, **Biruta Bar** (Rua Bem-Te-Vi 15, Pina, tel. 81/3326-5151, www.biruta.com.br, 11 A.M.–close daily) resembles a rustic beach house. With soft MPB playing in the background and moonlight reflecting on the water, it's a pretty romantic one at that. In keeping with the maritime ambiance, the extensive menu offers plenty of sea fare. The classic request is the seafood "bucket": shrimp, octopus, and fish flambéed in cognac.

BOA VIAGEM

Boa Viagem's main attraction is its beach. After dark, this modern stretch of high-rise condos and hotels is far less inviting. One friendly watering hole is **Entre Amigos–O Bode** (Rua Marquês de Valença 50, Boa Viagem, tel. 81/3466-2023, www.entreamigo-sobode.com.br, 11:30 A.M.–2 A.M. Sun.–Thurs., 11:30 A.M.–4 A.M. Fri.–Sat.), where groups of *amigos* get together to hang out, drink beer, and nibble on a Northeast favorite: roasted *bode* (goat). Imported from the Sertão of Paraíba, it is the most requested dish on the menu (try the version cooked in wine sauce accompanied by cashew rice and sweet potato). During weekdays, there is a nicely priced self-service per kilo buffet for lunch.

UK Pub (Rua Francisco da Cunha 165, Boa Viagem, tel. 81/3465-1088, 6 P.M.–close Tues.–Sun., cover R$5–15) is a sophisticated pub that attracts an upscale crowd of dressed-to-kill 20- to 40-somethings. Aside from the flirt fest, the two main draws are the extensive drink menu featuring more than 50 types of beer and the great live music, which tends towards rock and samba-rock. Although there's no dance floor, you can writhe and shimmy between the tables and in front of the stage. The hottest club in town these days is **Nox** (Av. Engenheiro Domingos Ferreira 2422, Boa Viagem, tel. 81/3326-8836, www.club-nox.com.br, 10:30 P.M.–6 A.M. Thurs.–Sat., cover R$20–30), a high-tech, über designed affair that comes off as more Berlin than Recife. The interior is an avant-garde "membrane" of curvy, computer-controlled panels that can be programmed to light up in 64,000 color variations. With an electronic soundtrack pumped out by top DJs, the results are pretty trippy. Fortunately, there is a rooftop lounge with tatami mats and soothing shrubbery to bring you back down to earth.

Entertainment and Events
PERFORMING ARTS
The elegant **Teatro Princesa Isabel** (Praça da República, tel. 81/3224-1020) is the city's premier venue for theater, dance, and musical performances. In Recife Antigo, the **Cinema Apolo** (Rua do Apolo 121, tel. 81/3232-2820) is a swell old art house cinema occupying the renovated Teatro Apolo. Screenings cost only R$4. For schedules of what's going on, stop by the Casa da Cultura (see *Sights*), and pick up *Agenda Cultural,* a free monthly calendar of events. You can also log on to www.pernambuco.com, which has cultural listings.

FESTIVALS AND EVENTS
Recife's **Carnaval** is one of the big triumvirate of Brazilian Carnavals. While Rio is legendary for its parades and samba schools, and Salvador pulses with *axé* music blasted from the tops of gigantic *trio elétricos,* Recife's frenetic street Carnaval draws on Pernambuco's rich multiplicity of rhythms. The classic soundtrack to Recife's Carnaval is the pulsing *frevo.* Quite appropriately, the word itself is said to be a derivation of *ferver*—meaning "to boil." An unlikely but characteristically inventive mixture of African *capoeira* and Portuguese marches, *frevo* has been around since the 19th century. It is accompanied by dervish-like dancers who twirl around with multicolored parasols, creating an intoxicating aural and visual kaleidoscope that has become Recife's trademark. To see the best *frevo* performances, plant yourself at the Pólo de Todos os Frevos, on Avenida Guararapes, where you'll have the privilege of seeing the Orquestra Spok Frevo do Recife, along with dozens of other traditional groups. Otherwise, *freviocas*—trucks with electric *frevo* groups on board—also ride around the center inciting the multitudes to get their groove on.

However, in an attempt to diversify its Carnavalesque attractions and rescue musical traditions, other local (Afro-influenced) rhythms such as *maracatu, ciranda, afoxé,* samba, *caboclinho, coco-de-roda,* and even rock and techno are increasingly given space during the festivities. Check out the Pólo Mangue, on Avenida Caís da Alfândega, where you can rock out to mangue beat, a musical movement that emerged in Recife in the '90s, when vanguard bands such as Chico Science & Nação Zumbi and Mundo Livre began creatively fusing regional musical traditions with pop, rock, rap, and electronica.

Two groups that are especially remarkable are the *maracatu* and *caboclinhos. Maracatu* groups originally consisted of *nações* (nations) of slaves, whose leaders were crowned as symbolic kings and queens. Descendants of these nations, many with links to Afro-Brazilian religion, still perform the ritual crowning in groups of sumptuously costumed singers, dancers, and percussionists that often number up to 100 people. Meanwhile, *caboclinho* groups date back to early colonial times, when Indians presented elaborate dances to the Portuguese during official ceremonies. Today's *caboclinho* dancers dress up as Indian warriors complete with feather headdresses, loin cloths, bows, and arrows, and dance to the haunting music played with flutes, drums, and rattles.

Recife's Carnaval kicks off Friday night, and over the next five days the entire Centro shuts down to traffic and becomes one enormous *festa.* The party gets started early on Saturday morning with the parade of the Recife's largest *bloco* (Carnaval group), the

Galo da Madrugada, flooding the center with one million dancing souls. Another highlight is Sunday night, when the Pátio do Terço is invaded by the Noite dos Tambores Silenciosos (Night of the Silent Drums). Beginning at 11 P.M., traditional *maracatu* nations pay homage to Pernambuco's population of African slaves (you can imagine the shock when the 300-plus drummers suddenly stop for a minute of silence). Of course, if you're in town at this time, you get the bonus of experiencing two Carnavals at once: only 7 kilometers (4.5 miles) away is Olinda's smaller but equally famous street celebration (see *Olinda*). For Carnaval dates, information, and attractions log on to www.recife.pe.gov.br/especiais/carnaval. If you're already in town, the tourist office can supply you with detailed info and maps.

Shopping

Recife is a great place to load up on local *artesanato*, ranging from *literatura de cordel* and ceramics to leatherwork, embroidery, and lace. The **Casa da Cultura** has a wide selection, but prices are inflated. The **Mercado São José** (see *Sights*) and the shops in the surrounding labyrinth of streets have wonderful finds if you don't mind the fun of hunting around a bit. You can also check out the lively outdoor **Feira de Artesanato** (2–8 P.M. Sun.) held on Rua do Bom Jesus, in Recife Antigo.

For funky designer duds concocted by both local and national designers (such as Alexandre Herchcovitch and Fause Hauten), head to the **Shopping Paço Alfândega** (Rua da Alfândega 65, Recife Antigo, tel. 81/3419-7620, www.pacoalfandega.com.br, 10 A.M.–10 P.M. Mon.–Sat., noon–8 P.M. Sun.). In Boa Viagem, **Shopping Center Recife** (Rua Padre Carapuceiro 777, Boa Viagem, tel. 81/3644-6000, www.shoppingrecife.com.br) is a glitzy, mercifully air-conditioned mall frequented by local fashionistas, where you can buy a bikini or take in a movie at the cineplex.

Accommodations

Visitors to Recife have three options: staying in the Centro (cheap and well-located, but fairly dodgy at night), Boa Viagem (safer, more chic, and with beach access, but you'll pay a price), or (if you want immerse yourself in colonial atmosphere and charm) across the bay in lovely Olinda.

R$50-100

Hotels in Centro tend to be geared more towards not-so-well-heeled business travelers than tourists. Some are a little down and out while others are sorely lacking in style. Most are concentrated in Boa Vista, which is where you'll find one of the nicer bets, the **Pousada Vila Boa Vista** (Rua Miguel Couto 81, Boa Vista, tel. 81/3223-0666, www.pousadavilla-boavista.com.br, R$108–125 d). Although it bills itself as having "colonial" decor, most of the colonial trappings are pretty faux. Rooms are standard but clean and fairly cheery, and the management livens things up by plastering verse by local poets on the brightly colored walls. Inner courtyard gardens and house plants also prettify the proceedings.

In Boa Viagem, **Pousada Casuarinas** (Rua Antônio Pedro Figueiredo 151, Boa Viagem, tel. 81/3325-7048, www.pousadacasuarinas.com.br, R$99–108 d) is a homey guesthouse set back from the beach. Basic, no-nonsense rooms (with or without verandas) are fairly pleasant, while the rest of the *pousada* is quite homelike with a pool, shady courtyard, and hammocks. Internet access and laundry services are available. Cheaper still is the **Hostel Boa Viagem** (Rua Aviador Severiano Lins 455, Boa Viagem, www.hostelboaviagem.com.br, R$70–95). Definitely the nicer of Boa Viagem's two hostels, this backpacker's mecca has small double, triple, and dorm rooms—bunking collectively will cost you R$30–37—which are offset by a garden, pool, and area reserved for hammock swinging. A friendly, laid-back vibe reigns.

R$100-200

Several blocks off the beach, the **Hotel Aconchego** (Rua Félix de Brito e Melo 382, Boa Viagem, tel. 81/3464-2989, www.hotelaconchego.com.br, R$125 d) is a great value option in a sprawling low-slung complex with a large pool and welcome splashes of greenery. Rooms are spotless even though some of the color schemes are iffy. The restaurant has a very decent menu with French flourishes.

R$200-300

Hotel Jangadeiro (Av. Boa Viagem 3114, Boa Viagem, tel. 81/3086-5050, www.jangadeirohotel.com.br, R$226–292) is one of Boa Viagem's nicest affordable beachfront options, especially since a recent renovation upgraded the large and comfy rooms, all of which have full or at least partial sea views (although it's worth dropping the extra *reais* for the rooms overlooking the beach, which have balconies). Amenities include Internet and a small rooftop pool. One of the most styling hotels on the beach, **☾ Beach Class Suites** (Av. Boa Viagem 1906, Boa Viagem, tel. 81/2121-2626, www.atlanticahotels.com.br, R$234–264 d) is an exercise in ultramodernity. Perched on a prized stretch of Boa Viagem, this shiny tower is awash with light, from the sleekly polished lobby to the cool white rooms. Sterility is avoided by the profusion of vibrantly colored artworks. There is wireless Internet in all rooms, and some have microwaves and coffeemakers to boot. A pool, fitness room, and restaurant round out the amenities.

Food

Typical Pernambucano cuisine is an intoxicating mixture of indigenous, African, and European (mainly Portuguese and Spanish) influences. Along the coast, dishes such as *peixada* and *moqueca* feature fish and seafood in stews that are seasoned with cilantro, lime, and coconut milk. From the rugged interior come robust dishes such as *carne-de-sol* (sundried beef) and *bode assado* (roasted goat), cooked with *macaxeira* (manioc) and beans. Ubiquitous throughout Pernambuco are *frango a cabidela* (chicken cooked in a fragrant sauce of its own blood) and *feijoada pernambucana,* which distinguishes itself from *feijoadas* in the rest of Brazil by the rare appearance of vegetables among the obligatory beans and meat. And then there are the desserts; simple, but inspired creations such as tangy *coalho* cheese

dripping with *mel de engenho* (sugarcane molasses) and *cartola,* in which a fried banana is topped with creamy Sertanejo cheese and a dusting of sugar and cinnamon. You can savor all of these specialties in Recife, along with a fine sampling of international fare and some outstanding contemporary cuisine dreamed up by a few of the most daring young chefs on the Brazilian restaurant scene.

RECIFE ANTIGO

You can't get more Recifense than having lunch or a late afternoon drink on the actual reef that inspired the city's name. This is possible if you take the boat from Marco Zero (or get a cab to take you via the *bairro* of Brasília Teimosa) to the **Casa de Banhos** (Arrecifes do Porto do Recife, tel. 81/3075-8776, noon–5 P.M. Wed.–Thurs., noon–7 P.M. Fri.–Sat., R$20–30) a former bath house where Pernambuco's sugar barons came to take the waters, considered medicinal in the late 19th century. Today it is a restaurant/bar with exceptional views of Recife and a small seafood menu of dishes such as *peixada* and shrimp in mango sauce. If you come in late afternoon, try one of the *caldinhos,* chowders made with *sururu* or seafood.

Despite the fact that it's on the fourth (and top floor) of a shopping mall, **☾ Assucar** (Rua da Alfândega 35, Recife Antigo, tel. 81/3419-7582, noon–10 P.M. Mon.–Tues., noon–midnight Wed.–Sat., noon–6 P.M. Sun., R$20–35) can still lay claim to being one of Recife's most captivating restaurants since the mall in question (the Shopping Paço Alfândega) is a former 18th-century convent and customs house featuring panoramic city views. The rustic-chic decor goes nicely with the menu, which takes inventive liberties with classic regional recipes. Crunchy *pescada-amarela* fish is served with a banana-potato-ginger puree while *carne-de-sol* is gratinéed with tangy *coalho* cheese and fried manioc. On weekends, live jazz and MPB are played. It's wise to reserve in advance.

Sentimental Recifenses love **As Galerias** (Rua do Bom Jesus 35, Recife Antigo, 6 A.M.–10 P.M. daily)—a fixture since 1928—as much as first-time tourists do. While gringos are bedazzled by the variety of juices made from exotic fruits such as *graviola* and *acerola*, locals swear by a frothy concoction known as the *maltado*, a revisited American milkshake that, along with baked goods such as peanut and cashew cake, tastes of childhood. Old photos on the wall up the nostalgia factor. On weekends, the place functions as a bar.

SANTO ANTÔNIO, SÃO JOSÉ, AND BOA VISTA

The oldest restaurant in operation in Brazil, **Leite** (Praça Joaquim Nabuco 147, Santo Antônio, tel. 81/3324-7997, 11 A.M.–4 P.M. Sun.–Fri., R$45–55) has been around since 1882. Although the service is old-school impeccable and the decor is classically refined (with an emphasis on polished jacaranda, mirrors, and marble), such staying power is ultimately explained by the food: international fare with a strong Portuguese influence that results in specialties such as *frutas do mar gratinadas* (shrimp, langoustine, octopus, and fish bathed in olive oil, white wine, and herbs) and various forms of *bacalhau* (salted cod). The most famous dessert is the *cartola*, considered to be the best in town. Following in the footsteps of Juscelino Kubitschek and Jean-Paul Sartre, this is a favorite pilgrimage of politicos, business execs, and visiting celebs.

Situated on the lively Pátio de São Pedro, **O Buraquinho** (Pátio de São Pedro 28, Santo Antônio, tel. 81/3224-3765, 11 A.M.–midnight Mon.–Sat., R$7–15), or "Little Hole," is a traditional favorite for inexpensive home-cooked "popular" dishes such as *feijoada, frango à cabidela*, pork tripe, and *carne-de-sol* served with manioc puree, beans, rice, and fresh corn. For dessert try the papaya *doce* with coconut. At night, live music from the patio provides the soundtrack.

PINA

This tiny beach neighborhood wedged between the Centro and Boa Viagem concentrates a wide assortment of restaurants and bars, and it really comes to life at night.

Considered the finest Italian restaurant in town, **Pomodoro Café** (Rua Capitão Rebelinho 418, Pina, tel. 81/3326-6023, www.pomodorocafe.com.br, 7 P.M.–midnight Sun.–Wed., 7 P.M.–1 A.M. Thurs.–Sat., R$22–32) is a charmingly unpretentious trattoria. It's presided over by hot local chef Duca Lapenda, who has a knack for creatively revisiting classic cantina dishes. The homemade pastas are particularly outstanding. Try the cheese-stuffed ravioli with butter and sage or the shrimp flambéed in herb-flavored olive oil with fresh tomatoes, basil, capers, and broccoli. Seating is also available in the garden.

Severino Reis worked his way up from dishwasher to owner of **Pra Vocês** (Av. Herculano Bandeira 115, Pina, tel. 81/3326-3168, 11 A.M.–midnight Sun.–Thurs., 11–2 A.M. Fri.–Sat., R$20–30), one of the most traditional seafood restaurant/bars in the city. The menu is quite varied and ranges from simple fare such as fried *agulinhas* (sardine-sized swordfish) to lobster thermidor. The outside tables are great for icy beer and snacks.

One of the perennially popular gay, lesbian, and hipster hangouts in town, **Anjo Solto** (Av. Herculano Bandeira 513, Loja 14-A, Galeria Joana D'Arc, Pina, tel. 81/3325-0826, www.anjosolto.com.br, 5:30 P.M.–close daily, R$15–20) seduces not just with its intimate quintet of discreetly lit spaces (which include a wine bar), but with its outstanding crêpes. The menu features close to 100 of them—all named after friends and faithful clients—in versions both sweet and savory. The Paulo Carvalho, for example, is filled with garlicky shrimp, cream cheese doused in Sicilian lime, tomato, arugula, and grilled eggplant. There are also terrific salads and some wildly inventive house cocktails.

BOA VIAGEM

Boa Viagem has the most varied and cosmopolitan eating options, but due to the flashiness of the hood, the prices tend to be higher as well.

Refined and unpretentiously elegant, the deliciously affordable **Wiella Bistrô** (Av. Domingos Ferreira 1274, Lojas 14–16, Boa Viagem, tel. 81/3463-3108, www.wiellabistro.com, noon–midnight Tues.–Sat., noon–5 P.M. Sun.,

R$35–45) specializes in meticulously prepared contemporary dishes that lean towards, but are not exclusively French. Seafood *cassoulet* and *magret de canard* with wine-perfumed risotto in sweet and sour sauce are just two examples. An irresistible follow-up is the poached pear served with *graviola* sorbet and topped with a *cachaça* coulis.

In Portuguese "é" means "is," but in Tupi-Guarani it can be translated into "delicious," "hot," and "spicy." The hottest contemporary eatery in town, **É** (Rua do Atlântico 147, Boa Viagem, tel. 81/3325-9323, 8 P.M.–1:30 A.M. Tues.–Sat., www.egastronomia.com.br, R$50–65) stays true to its name by serving up visually arresting contemporary creations in a sultry scarlet lounge lit by candles. Dishes involve a mixture of culinary influences ranging from French and Italian to Japanese, Thai, and Vietnamese and rely on rarefied ingredients such as rose petals, worm salt, and candied foie gras. Sugar-savvy chef Douglas Van der Ley takes his desserts seriously, and there are daily "surprises," such as grilled brioche with vanilla butter, flambéed strawberries and crème anglaise served with white chocolate ice cream, macadamia splinters, and a honey lemon gel.

If you don't have time to travel into Pernambuco's interior, you can get a taste of it at **Parraxaxá** (Av. Rua Baltazar Pereira 32, Boa Viagem, tel. 81/3463-7874, www.parraxaxa.com.br, 11:30 A.M.–10 P.M. Mon.–Fri., 6 A.M.–11 P.M. Sat.–Sun.), whose dining area is decked out to look like a typical country house from the Sertão. The decor is appealing (if a little overdone—and the waiters dressed like Lampião are a tad goofy), but the real attraction is the per kilo buffet that allows you to sample every type of Sertanejo dish under the blazing sun—from grilled *bode* and *carne-de-sol* to *baião-de-dois* (a mixture of beans and *coalho* cheese), and fried, pureed, and boiled manioc (although there are more conventional offerings and salads too). Drop by in the evening for *ceia regional,* the traditional northeastern "supper" that includes favorites such as *pamonha* (a dense corn pudding), *canjica* (cream of white corn with grated coconut and cinnamon) and lots of homemade cakes. And don't miss the weekend breakfast buffet with *tapiocas,* umpteen loaves and cakes, and *café* with *leite* from a nearby farm.

Those with a fondness for sweets will be sorely tempted by Pernambuco's sugary specialties. Two particular favorites are *bolo Sousa Leão,* a delicious cake made with manioc flour, eggs, and coconut milk, topped with a warm sugar syrup, and *bolo-de-rolo,* a tender roly-poly in which spiraled layers of soft cake are lined with creamy guava paste. The best place to sink your teeth into these and many other delicacies is at **Casa dos Frios** (Av. Domingos Ferreira 1920, Boa Viagem, tel. 81/3327-0612, www.casadosfrios.com.br, noon–11 P.M. Mon.–Wed., noon–midnight Thurs.–Sat.). Recife's most traditional (and most swanky) delicatessen has been around since 1957 (the original deli is in the *bairro* of Graças). All of the homemade sweet and savory baked goods are scrumptious and there is also a small (and rather pricy) restaurant. Its state-of-the-art wine cellar is the best in the city. You can buy a bottle and then drink it at one of the tables in the cellar itself. If the climate-controlled atmosphere gives you goosebumps, the waiter will cover you with a woolen wrap. A more healthy way to beat the heat is to head to **Sucão** (Rua Carlos Pereira Falcão, Loja 1, Boa Viagem, tel. 81/3325-2326, noon–10:30 P.M. Mon.–Sat., 4–10:30 P.M. Sun.). Boa Viagem's favorite juice bar serves up more than 100 varieties of *suco* made from fruit delivered fresh every day. The most popular requests are *abacaxi* (white pineapple) with mint, and coconut water with grapes. Less orthodox concoctions such as persimmon mixed with passion fruit, or *graviola* with *cajá* (two delicious northeastern fruits) are equally refreshing. All juices are prepared with or without milk. If you want some instant energy, go for the *vitamina* made from bananas and avocados. For extra sustenance, there are healthy salads and sandwiches.

Information

The main **tourist office** in Boa Viagem (Praça

Boa Viagem, tel. 81/3463-3621, 8 A.M.–8 P.M. daily) has helpful staff and a good free map of the city. There is also a branch at the airport (tel. 081/3462-4960, 8 A.M.–6 P.M. daily) as well as at the Casa da Cultura in Santo Antônio (tel. 81/3224-2850) and in Recife Antigo (Praça do Arsenal, tel. 81/3224-2361). Online, www.recifeguide.com is an English-language guide to the city while www.pernambuco.com/turismo is a good source of information in Portuguese.

Services

There are plenty of **banks** with ATMs—including Banco do Brasil branches in Santo Antônio (Av. Dantas Barreto, 451), in Boa Vista (Rua Sete de Setembro), and in Boa Viagem (Rua Barão de Souza Leão 440). Also try the main *shoppings*. The main **post office** is in Santo Antônio (Av. Guararapes, 250). For Internet access, in Recife Antigo try **NGS** (Shopping Paço Alfândega, tel. 81/3424-8923, 10 A.M.–10 P.M. Mon.–Sat., noon–8 P.M. Sun.).

In the event of an emergency, dial **193** for an ambulance or the fire department, or **190** for the police. There is a special tourist police (tel. 81/3303-7217) unit at the airport. For medical treatment try the **Centro Hospitalar Albert Sabin** (Rua Senador José Henrique 141, Ilha do Leite, tel. 81/3421-5411, www.hospitalalbertsabin.com.br).

Getting There

Recife's **Aeroporto Internacional dos Guararapes** (Praça Ministro Salgado Filho, Boa Viagem, tel. 81/3464-4188) is at the far end of Boa Viagem—conveniently close to beach hotels—and about 12 kilometers (7.5 miles) south of the city center and just a few kilometers from the beachside hotels in Boa Viagem. A taxi to Boa Viagem will cost R$20–25, while one to Olinda will set you back around R$60. Municipal buses also go from the airport straight through Boa Viagem (one block behind the beach) on their way to Avenida Dantas Barreto in the center of town.

Buses from all over Brazil arrive at the **Terminal Integrado de Passageiros (TIP)** (Rodovia BR-232 Km 15, Curado, tel. 81/3452-1999), which is pretty far—14 kilometers (8.5 miles)—from the center. Fortunately, the otherwise useless (for tourists) Metrô links the bus station with Recife's local bus station, **Estação Central.**

Getting Around

Getting around Recife is somewhat tricky since there are many one-way streets and bridges. The urban layout is rather haphazard, and it is hard to identify streets in the center. The bus system is complicated, and routes change frequently. When in doubt, take a taxi—especially at night. By day, taking buses between Santo Antônio and Boa Viagem, and from both of these neighborhoods to Olinda, is fairly straightforward. From Santo Antônio (most stops are on Avenida Dantas Barreto) to Boa Viagem, take any bus marked "Boa Viagem," "Aeroporto," or "Iguatemi"—from Boa Viagem (with stops on Avenida Engenheiro Domingos Ferreira) to the center, grab any bus marked "Dantas Barreto." Bus fare is R$2.30.

Taxis are a great idea, especially at night. You can flag them down easily in the street. Otherwise call **Tele-Taxi** (tel. 081/3429-4242) or **Ligue-Taxi** (tel. 81/3428-6830). Renting a car is not such a great idea in the city due to traffic and security. If you want to rent one to hit the beaches north or south of town, try **Avis** (tel. 81/3462-5069, www.avis.com.br) or **Hertz** (tel. 81/3341-2082, www.localiza.com), both with offices at the airport.

CITY TOURS

Luck Viagens (Rua Jornalista Paulo Bittencourt, Derby, tel. 81/3464-4800, www.luckviagens.com.br) offers a variety of bus tours of both Recife and Olinda, with pickups at your hotel. A half-day tour of both costs R$30 per person. Full-day excursions (R$70) further afield allow you to soak up sun along the beautiful coastlines north of the city, at Ilha de Itamaracá, or south, at the snorkeling haven of Porto de Galinhas. To take advantage of Recife's scenic waterways, consider a tour along its rivers. **Catamaran Tours** (tel.

81/3424-2845, www.catamarantours.com.br) runs both day and night outings on comfortable catamarans, for R$22–35, that drift by the city's major historic attractions. Departures are from the quays at Cinco Pontas.

◖ OLINDA

Pernambuco's mesmerizingly beautiful original capital is a baroque treasure and one of the highlights of the Northeast. Perched on a series of green hills overlooking the sea (and the disparately modern sprawl of Recife), the colonial town is an appealing mixture of nuns and monks, artists and expats, bohemians, and (understandably) a steady stream of tourists. While the lower, modern "Novo Olinda" has grown into a none-too-attractive (and unsafe) extension of Recife, the historic center—declared a World Cultural Heritage Site by UNESCO—offers a captivating mix of baroque churches, artists' ateliers, boutiques, bars, and restaurants.

Sights

Olinda's main attractions are clustered together in its *centro histórico*. Although the area is compact, visiting them involves climbing some fairly steep, but very picturesque cobblestoned streets (the payoff is in the views gleaned from the summits). In part, due to the community involvement of its large artist population, Olinda's historic quarter has escaped the fate of some other colonial centers in Brazil—that of an open-air museum for tourists, restored to look like the backdrop for a movie set. Instead it is an authentic neighborhood where locals work, play, and contribute to the city's rich cultural life. The only annoying feature is the persistence with which local guides will insist on taking you around to see the sights—you can really manage without them. Historic Olinda's main artery is the charming **Rua do Amparo,** where aside from restaurants, bars, and hotels, you'll find many artists' studios.

CHURCHES

The star attraction of Olinda is its stunning collection of baroque churches. There are 18 of them in total, scattered among several steep hills. Although many were originally constructed in the 1500s, when the Dutch invaded Olinda in 1630, most were torched to the ground. Those you see today are the results of reconstructions undertaken by the Portuguese in the 17th and 18th centuries. Opening hours are notoriously unstable, so take the hours listed below with a grain of salt.

You can survey most of these churches from the loftiest *praça* in the city, the **Alto da Sé,** which offers bewitching views of white towers and red tiled roofs nestled in a tangle of palms, and set against a backdrop of blue-green ocean and Recife's glimmering skyline. Alto da Sé itself is a lively place with a daily and somewhat touristy arts and crafts market. The square is dominated by Olinda's main church, the **Catedral da Sé** (Alto da Sé, 8 A.M.–noon and 2–5 P.M. daily). The original church, built in 1540 out of wood and palm thatching, was the first ever constructed in Brazil. What you see today is the reconstructed version from the 17th century. Less ornate than some of the town's other churches, it possesses some attractive *azulejo* decorative panels. Its most striking feature is the postcard-perfect views of Olinda's other churches from the patio.

One of the churches that is sure to (justifiably) catch your eye is the spectacular **Convento de São Francisco** (Rua de São Francisco 280, tel. 81/3429-0517, 7 A.M.–noon and 2–5 P.M. Mon.–Fri., 7 A.M.–noon Sat., R$2), Brazil's oldest Franciscan convent, dating back to 1577. The buildings (only partially destroyed by the Dutch) are awash in beautiful *azulejo* murals. Those paneling the cloisters, portraying the life and death of Saint Francis in tones of blue, yellow, and red, are particularly striking. Other highlights include the ornately carved jacaranda furnishings in the sacristy and the exquisitely painted ceiling frescoes in the church. The cross in front of the convent is made of pulverized coral from local reefs. Equally splendid is the **Igreja e Mosteiro de São Bento** (Rua de São Bento, tel. 81/3429-3288, 8–11 A.M. and 2–5 P.M. daily, R$1), which dates back to 1582. From the outside,

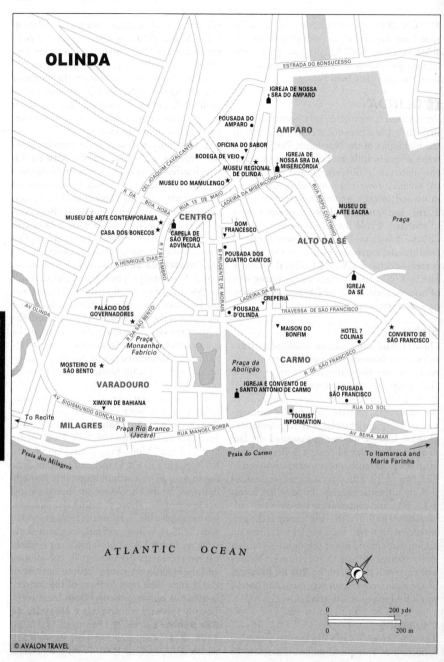

PERNAMBUCO AND ALAGOAS

OLINDA

ESTRADA DO BONSUCESSO

IGREJA DE NOSSA
SRA DO AMPARO

POUSADA DO
AMPARO

AMPARO

OFICINA DO SABOR
BODEGA DE VEIO

IGREJA DE
NOSSA SRA DA
MISERICÓRDIA

MUSEU REGIONAL
DE OLINDA

MUSEU DO MAMULENGO

R. DA BOA HORA
CEL JOAQUIM CAVALCANTE
RUA 13 DE MAIO
LADEIRA DA MISERICÓRDIA
RUA BISPO COUTINHO

MUSEU DE
ARTE SACRA

Praça

MUSEU DE ARTE CONTEMPORÂNEA
CENTRO

DOM
FRANCESCO

ALTO DA SÉ

CASA DOS BONECOS
CAPELA DE
SÃO PEDRO
ADVÍNCULA

POUSADA DOS
QUATRO CANTOS

R. 7 SETEMBRO
R. PRUDENTE DE MORAIS

R. HENRIQUE DIAS

IGREJA
DA SÉ

LADEIRA DA SÉ

CREPERIA

TRAVESSA DE SÃO FRANCISCO

AV. OLINDA

POUSADA
D'OLINDA

PALÁCIO DOS
GOVERNADORES

MAISON DO
BONFIM

HOTEL 7
COLINAS

CONVENTO DE
SÃO FRANCISCO

R. DA SÃO BENTO

Praça
Monsenhor
Fabrício

Praça da
Abolição

CARMO

R. DE SÃO FRANCISCO

MOSTEIRO DE
SÃO BENTO

Praça
Rio Branco
(Jacaré)

VARADOURO

XIMXIN DE BAHIANA

IGREJA E CONVENTO DE
SANTO ANTÔNIO DE CARMO

POUSADA
SÃO FRANCISCO

RUA DO SOL

AV. SIGISMUNDO GONÇALVES

To Recife

MILAGRES

RUA MANOEL BORBA

TOURIST
INFORMATION

AV. BEIRA MAR

To Itamaracá and
Maria Farinha

Praia dos Milagres

Praia do Carmo

ATLANTIC OCEAN

0   200 yds
0   200 m

© AVALON TRAVEL

Convento de São Francisco, Olinda

the monastery is striking with swaying palms adding tropical flourishes to the more austere bleached baroque facade. The main altar is a feast of exquisitely carved cedar doused in gold, and the sacristy is richly outfitted with gold leaf, crystal mirrors, and panels depicting the life of Saint Benedict. If you can, try to show up at 7 A.M. Monday–Saturday or 10 A.M.–noon on Sunday, to hear Gregorian chants.

A particularly steep climb will bring you to the **Igreja de Nossa Senhora da Misericórdia** (Largo da Misericórdia, tel. 81/3494-9100, 5:45–7 A.M., noon–12:30 P.M., and 6–6:30 P.M. daily), whose delicately sculpted altars, ornamented in gold leaf, and clever trompe l'oeil paintings, are particularly sumptuous examples of Brazilian rococo. Visiting hours coincide with prayers of the Benedictine nuns, making silence a must. The captivating **Igreja de Nossa Senhora do Amparo** (Largo do Amparo, tel. 81/3429-7339, 9:15–11 A.M. Sun.) was originally built as a place of worship for single men and musicians in the 1550s, which explains the painted panels to the right of the main altar, depicting the life of Saint Cecilia, patron saint of

musicians. The twisting gold-doused columns, ornate altars, religious paintings, and French and Portuguese tile work are all superb.

Less splendid, but also noteworthy, are the atmospheric **Igreja de Nossa Senhora do Carmo** (Praça do Carmo, 10 A.M.–11 A.M. Sun.), the oldest Carmelite church in Brazil, and the **Igreja de Nossa Senhora do Monte** (Praça Nossa Senhora do Monte, tel. 81/3429-0317, 8:30–11 A.M. and 2:30–5 P.M. daily). Built in 1540, the latter survived the Dutch invasion largely intact. Its simple, austere architecture offers a contrast with the extravagance of baroque. It's been a refuge for Benedictine monks since the 16th century, and 30 monks still reside here. You can hear them singing daily at 5 P.M. They also sell homemade biscuits.

MUSEUMS

Housed in a 17th-century building that formerly served as a bishop's palace, a nunnery, and city hall, the **Museu de Arte Sacra de Pernambuco** (Rua Bispo Coutinho 726, tel. 81/3429-0032, 9 A.M.–1 P.M. Mon.–Fri., R$1) shelters a fine collection of religious art from throughout the state, dating from the 16th to the 20th century. Particularly fascinating is the collection of regional folk art. Note the manger with baby Jesus asleep in a hammock, Mary and Joseph as *mulatos,* and the presence of local legends such as the outlaw, Lampião. Also noteworthy is the collection of paintings done by Indians, in ateliers operated by Jesuit missionaries throughout South America.

The **Museu Regional de Olinda** (Rua do Amparo 128, tel. 81/3429-0018, 9 A.M.–5 P.M. Tues.–Fri., R$1) offers a glimpse into Olinda's glorious past, mainly via the usual opulent array of jacaranda furniture, imported Baccarat crystal, and English porcelain that attests to the lush life derived from sugarcane cultivation (if you had the luck to be a planter and not a slave).

Pernambuco is famous for *mamulengo,* a form of popular theater in which wonderfully expressive handmade puppets act out traditional folk tales, often based on *literatura de cordel.* Although many of the stories are slapstick, they also have a subversive political edge. They pit a cast of clever Indians, cunning Africans, and trickster peasants, as well as animals and supernatural spirits, against repressive authority figures such as wealthy landowners or repressive military figures. Dramatic and comic moments are punctuated by dance and music (courtesy of *forró* musicians). The puppets themselves, made from wood and cloth, are quite wonderful. They can be viewed at the **Museu do Mamulengo** (Rua de São Bento 344, tel. 81/3429-6214, 10 A.M.–5 P.M. Tues.–sun, R$1), which has a vast collection of over 1,200 puppets as well as a theater, the Espaço Tiridá, where performances are often held.

Nightlife

Olinda has a relaxed bohemian vibe that mixes artists, tourists, and Recifenses. Lots of bars are set up on sidewalks and in the lovely *praças,* and there are many hidden away in private leafy gardens. Aside from Alto da Sé, there is also a good range of bars and musical venues along the beach. Music is literally in the streets, especially homegrown specialties such as *forró*

and *maracatu.* On Sundays, 4–10 P.M., samba rehearsals are held by the *bloco* Grêmio Preto Velho at their Alto da Sé headquarters. Saturday and Sunday evenings you can catch *maracatu* at Praça do Carmo. And on the first Saturday of the month, don't miss the *sambada do coco* performed on the Largo da Igreja de Guadalupe.

Olinda's favorite neighborhood hangout, **Bodega de Veio** (Rua do Amparo 212, tel. 81/3429-0185, 8 A.M.–11 P.M. Mon.–Sat., 8 A.M.–2 P.M. Sun.) is a simple family-run convenience store where locals go to buy their beans, rice, and *carne-de-sol,* and usually end up stopping off for a cool *cerveja.* The beer is cheap and so are the portions of salami and *coalho* cheese. The vibe is laid-back and very friendly. On Thursday and Saturday nights, live *chorinho* is performed and *forró* jams are frequent. **Licoteria Notívagaos** (Rua 13 de Maio, tel. 81/3439-6248, 4–10 P.M. Wed.–Thurs. and Sun., 5 P.M.–midnight Fri.–Sat.) is a fine place to sample addictive homemade *licores* made from ingredients such as ginger or banana. Music is supplied by faithful clients who bring in their CDs or records.

One of the cooler haunts in town, **Xinxím da Baiana** (Av. Sigismundo Gonçalves 742, Carmo, tel. 81/9689-0019, 6 P.M.–close Tues.–Sun.) is owned by a Bahian couple, which explains the presence of *pesticos* such as *acarajé* (bean fritters fried in palm oil) on the menu. From Wednesday through Saturday, live performances of *forró,* soul, and national rock lure an alternative crowd intent on dancing up a storm. Down on the beach, **Marola Bar** (Travessa Dantas Barreto, 66–B, tel. 81/3429-7079, 4 P.M.–midnight Mon., 10 A.M.–2 A.M. Tues.–Sat., 10 A.M.–10 P.M. Sun.) is a romantic place to watch the moonrise accompanied by elaborate seafood *petiscos* such as *camarão do dono,* a shrimp dish with *coalho* cheese, arugula, black olive, mushrooms, and hearts of palm. Live MPB provides the soundtrack, except for Saturdays when *forró* takes over.

Festivals and Events
CARNAVAL
Of all Brazil's major street Carnavals, Olinda's

is the most picturesque and also the most democratic. There are no Sambódromos with costly seats, nor are there cordoned off areas or bleachers that afford privileged access to samba schools and *blocos* while the poorer masses are crushed together on the sidelines. Olinda's highly colorful festivities draw people of all ages, colors, and inclinations together. The mass of merrymakers flood the lavishly decorated *praças* and narrow streets of the historic center to dance and weave among riotous *blocos* that blast the pulsing rhythms of frevo, samba, afoxé, and maracatu. Costumes are whimsical and outrageous, and masks are de rigueur. Gigantic *bonecos* (dolls), representing folk heroes or political figures, are the trademark of Olinda's Carnaval. Made of papier-mâché, and painted in festive colors, they go twirling and dancing through the streets along with the throngs.

Other highlights include the appearances of traditional *blocos* such as Elefante, Lenhadores, and Enquanto Isso na Sala da Justiça; the meeting of the dazzlingly costumed *maracatu*

giant *bonecos* from Olinda's Carnaval

groups in the *bairro* of Cidade Tabajara (on Monday); and the always wildly attired transvestite groups. On the final day of festivities (Mardi Gras), the meeting of all the *bonecos* (some of which have been around since the 1930s) brings the celebrations to a close with much fanfare and *alegria*.

For detailed information about groups and events, check with the tourist office or log on to www.carnavaldeolinda.com.br.

ARTE EM TODA PARTE
For 10 days in late November/early December, Olinda's prolific artists open the doors of their ateliers to the public. Not only does this give you a privileged opportunity to view some (mostly) terrific art, but it also allows a rare glimpse into some wonderful historic houses.

Shopping
Due to the confluence of artists and tourists, Olinda is an excellent place to peruse and purchase both original works by local artists and regional crafts. Located in the former customs house, the **Mercado Eufráio Barbosa** (Rua Sigismundo Gonçalves, tel. 81/3439-1415, 9 A.M.–6 P.M. Mon.–Sat.) has a very good array of local handicrafts. Equally full of enticing wares is the **Mercado da Ribeira** (Rua Bernardo Vieira de Melo, tel. 81/3439-2964, 9 A.M.–6 P.M. daily), which also sells antiques. Around Alto da Sé, you'll find a pair of shops that specialize in quality *artesanato*. **Ecological** (Rua Bispo Coutinho 799, tel. 81/3429-1187, www.ecologicalartesanato.com) has a fine collection of woven and embroidered items and ceramics, along with very cool cotton T-shirts, whose colors are derived from natural pigments. Among the unique items at **Imaginário** (Rua Bispo Coutinho 814, tel. 81/3439-4514) are the wooden objects, intricately adorned with hand-painted scenes by artist Geraldo Andrade.

Accommodations
Although hotels in the modern Novo Olinda are cheaper, the area is soulless, and since you came to Olinda for the history, you're much better off paying a little more and staying in the colonial

center (in off-season, you can get good discounts). If you plan to be here during Carnaval, you'll need to book months in advance.

Although Olinda has a youth hostel, **Pousada d'Olinda** (Rua Prudente de Morais 178, tel. 81/3494-2559, www.pousadadolinda.com.br, R$65–75 d) is far superior. It combines hostel prices (a bed in a dorm room costs an unheard of R$20 pp) with the infrastructure of a very appealing *pousada* in the midst of colonial Olinda. Rooms are simple, but pleasant, and the grounds surrounding the main historic house include a patio, small pool, and restaurant. **Pousada São Francisco** (Rua do Sol 127, tel. 81/3429-2109, www.pousadasaofrancisco.com.br, R$84–149 d) is another great bargain. Although the red tile roofs and pastel hues reflect Olinda's colonial architecture, this hotel—a stone's throw from the Convento de São Francisco—is decidedly modern. The air-conditioned rooms are standard, but the walls are adorned with works by local artists, and many are outfitted with balconies offering sweeping views towards Olinda or the sea. A sense of spaciousness prevails, enhanced by the sprawling tropical gardens and nice-sized pool.

Pousada dos Quatro Cantos (Rua Prudente dos Morais 441, tel. 81/3429-0220, www.pousada4cantos.com.br, R$89–247 d) is located in a vast 19th-century mansion that was formerly a fancy weekend residence. Polished parquet floors, lofty ceilings, and eclectic, tasteful decor combined with welcoming staff and lavish regional breakfasts make you feel as if you're a privileged guest in a home. Make sure you get a room in the house itself and not the new annex. Standard rooms on the ground floor are nice enough (although without private bathrooms), but the real treasure is the suite decked out with an antique four-poster bed, veranda, and Jacuzzi. There is also a terrace pool.

Set amidst the leafy gardens of a former sugarcane plantation, **Hotel 7 Colinas** (Ladeira de São Francisco 307, tel. 81/3493-7766, www.hotel7colinas.com.br, R$202–338 d) offers a tranquil refuge after a day of steep hills and busy cobblestoned streets. Dispersed among low-slung buildings, the pleasant rooms are comfortable, with good spring mattresses and air-conditioning, and verandas that open onto the garden. The leisure areas are the real draw. Surrounded by tropical foliage is a beautiful pool, and the restaurant and bar areas are very attractive. There's nowhere better to immerse yourself in the spirit of colonial Olinda than at the **Pousada do Amparo** (Rua do Amparo 199, tel. 81/3439-1749, www.pousadadoamparo.com.br, R$240–460 d). The 11 apartments—of various sizes, some with balconies—are distributed between two adjoining 200-year-old buildings. All are heavy on charm, and some are outright lavish. Exposed brick, wooden beams, and dark wood antiques (including a few four poster beds) are rampant, and views from the back—overlooking a secluded garden pool and, beyond, a sea of palms—are enchanting. The romantic Restaurante Flor de Coco serves delicious food, and there is a lovely bar as well.

Food

Olinda has a serious gastronomic scene, enhanced by the fact that many of its eateries occupy centuries-old colonial houses (many with palmy gardens). On the weekend, it is a favorite dining destination for Recifenses. Located in a fetching historic house, **Patuá** (Estrada do Bonsucesso 399, Bonsucesso, tel. 81/3055-0833, 7 A.M.–midnight Mon.–Thurs., noon–4 P.M. and 7 P.M.–1 A.M. Sat.–Sun., R$16–26), is a case in point. The menu features regional fare—fish, seafood, and *carne-de-sol*—with some unusual contemporary twists. Caramelized banana chips with shrimp in a Vietnamese sauce make a great starter before segueing into *surubim* fish in a shiitake cream, served with crab risotto and flambéed banana. Mouthwatering desserts include a fresh coconut milk pudding with crystalized rose petals.

Sitting on a steep and quiet little street, **Oficina do Sabor** (Rua do Amparo 335, tel. 81/3429-3331, www.oficinadosabor.com, noon–4 P.M. and 6 P.M.–midnight Tues.–Fri., noon–1 A.M. Sat., noon–5 P.M. Sun., R$25–35) is an enticing place, its walls awash in colorful folk art. It is renowned for the preparation of Pernambucano culinary specialties with uncommon flair. *Carne-de-sol, macaxeira,* seafood, coconut milk, and fresh *feijão* are all flawlessly combined with local fruits and spices. Try the classic filet of *carne-de-sol pernambucana* served with pureed manioc and *jerimum* (a local pumpkin) or the more innovative *jacamarão,* shrimp bathed in an aromatic jackfruit sauce. For dessert, indulge in fresh mint sorbet topped with clove and cinnamon liqueur. If you can, grab a veranda table with spectacular panoramic views.

⬛ Maison do Bonfim (Rua do Bonfim 115, Carmo, tel. 81/3429-1674, www.maisondobonfim.com.br, 6 P.M.–1 A.M. Mon., noon–4 P.M. and 6 P.M.–1 A.M. Wed.–Sat., noon–9 P.M. Sun., R$24–34) is a charming little restaurant that serves traditional French recipes. Passed down from the chef's family, they are often livened up with startling fusions of tropical fruits. Fish and seafood are especially tasty— the "bucket" of *moules marinières* (marinated mussels) is one of the best you'll taste this side of the Equator—and, *bien sûr,* the wine list is good. Delicious Italian food can be found at **Don Francesco** (Rua Prudente de Morais 358, tel. 81/3429-3852, noon–3 P.M. and 6:30–11:30 P.M. Mon.–Fri., 6:30 P.M.–midnight Sat., R$15–22), an intimate place with a terrace looking onto a back garden that supplies the fresh herbs and vegetables for the kitchen. The Italian chef's homemade pastas, topped with the likes of organic pesto made with sheep ricotta, basil, and crushed brazil nuts, are his forte. The tiramisu is pretty sublime.

For a light bite, **Creperia** (Praça Conselheiro João Alfredo 168, Carmo, tel. 81/3429-2935, 11 A.M.–11 P.M., R$10–16) is a cozy option with works by local artists on the walls and a breezy outdoor terrace. Aside from a vast array of tasty crêpes, both savory and sweet (try the *Olinda,* filled with chocolate, bananas, ice cream, raisins, and rum), the menu features salads and crunchy, thin-crust pizzas. For a more local version of a crêpe, head to Alto da Sé, where, everyday from morning to midnight,

30 *tapioqueiras* prepare *tapiocas,* made with crunchy manioc flour. The queen of them all is Tia Lu, who has been preparing this favorite snack for over 40 years. The classic *tapioca* filling is freshly grated coconut and melted cheese. But alternative (and more filling) variations abound, such as cheese mixed with *carne-de-sol,* shrimp, and even guava jelly.

Information and Services

The **tourist office** (Rua do Bonsucesso 183, tel. 81/3439-9434, 9 A.M.–6 P.M. daily) is near the Largo do Amparo. You'll also find a small information booth at Praça do Carmo, where buses from Recife arrive. There are no banks in Olinda's historic center. The closest ATM is at the **Banco do Brasil** (Av. Getúlio Vargas 1470, Bairro Novo). For Internet access, head to **Olind@.com** (Praça João Pesoa 15, Carmo, tel. 81/3429-4365, 9 A.M.–10 P.M. daily), a cyber café where you can also get coffee and snacks.

Getting There

Olinda is basically a neighborhood of Recife. As such, municipal bus service is very regular and quite fast (30 minutes from the center of Recife). The final stop is the terminal at Praça do Carmo, from where you can begin your ascent to the town's various colonial treasures. Buses depart from both bus stops in Boa Viagem (on Av. Engenheiro Domingos Ferreira) and Santo Antônio (on Av. Dantas Barreto)—from either, take any bus marked "Rio Doce" or "Casa Caiada." You can also spring for a taxi (essential at night).

INLAND FROM RECIFE

The major inland destination from Recife is the town of Caruaru (135 kilometers/84 miles from Recife). Lying on the edge of the Sertão, it contains the biggest open air market in the Northeast, where you can find locally produced *artesanato.* As you head west from the palmy coastal region, the countryside begins to change. A series of undulating hills blanketed in jade green sugarcane offers a visual reminder of the crop that made Pernambuco so rich. Gradually, the lushness of the hills fades into sepia tones, giving way to a harsher landscape of ruddy brown earth populated by herds of cattle and fields of thorny palma, a type of cactus that serves as sustenance for both cattle and humans during the frequent droughts that plague the Sertão. In actual fact, this region, known as the *agreste,* gives you a foretaste of the Sertão itself, which begins after Caruaru, and is much starker and more desert-like.

Caruaru

Famous throughout Brazil for its massive outdoor market, its animated Festa de São João, and its rich cultural and artistic traditions that reflect the vivid culture of the Sertão, Caruaru is definitely worth at least a day trip from Recife. If you hop an early bus from Recife, you have ample time to wander through the market, dawdle over lunch, and check out the ceramicists' ateliers at Alto do Moura.

SIGHTS

The highlight and raison d'être of a visit to otherwise ramshackle Caruaru is the traditional **Feira de Caruaru** (Parque 18 de Maio, Centro, 6 A.M.–5 P.M. daily). Seeming to engulf the entire town, this daily market lures buyers from all over the Northeast, who arrive to purchase everything from cheap clothing and made-in-China electronics to great creamy blocks of *coalho* cheese, bottles of herb-infused *cachaça,* and popular folk remedies to cure every ailment under the sun. The market is divided into sections, some of which are quite unusual. At the bird market, multicolored warblers (some of them illegal to sell) preen from hand-built wooden cages, while at the *troca-troca* market (*trocar* means to swap or exchange), you'll encounter people bartering donkeys for bicycles and CDs for cooking gas. Tuesday is an especially big day due to the cattle market and Feira da Sulanca, a clothing bazaar that lures thousands of bargain hounds eager to swipe up articles for as little as R$1. Friday and Saturday are also packed. For tourists, the most interesting part is the Feira de Artesanato, where you'll find a vast array of regional handicrafts made of everything from cotton and leather to polished coconut shells. The most sought-after articles are the brightly painted ceramic figures (made famous by Mestre Vitalino) of Sertanejo "types" ranging from *cangaçeiros* to *forró* musicians. The ones found here are more expensive and of inferior quality than those you'll encounter in Vitalino's nearby hometown of Alto do Moura.

Although you can't purchase them, you'll definitely be impressed by the ceramic figures on display at the **Museu do Barro** (Praça Colonel José de Vasconcellos 100, Pátio de Eventos, tel. 81/3701-1533, 8 A.M.–7 P.M. Tues.–Sat., R$1), many of which are by Mestre Vitalino. Along with other examples of traditional ceramic work and pottery from all over the Sertão, this museum constitutes one of the finest collections of folk art in Brazil.

FESTIVALS AND EVENTS

The interior's equivalent of Carnaval, **Festa de São João** takes place all over the Northeast, but the biggest and most legendary celebration takes place in Caruaru (although the town of Campina Grande, in neighboring Paraíba, begs to differ). Every night, square dances, known as *quadrilhas* (a descendant of the ballroom quadrilles popular in 19th-century France) bring together thousands who stomp and twirl and then refresh themselves at *barracas* serving typical food commemorating the harvest. Most delicacies are made with corn, including *pamonha,* a dense corn pudding, and *canjica,* a creamy dessert made with white corn. Streets are decorated with colorful paper banners and balloons, and residents dress up in country-style gear with lots of plaids, ginghams, and straw hats. Caruaru's Festa de São João is particularly famed for its *bandas de pífanos*—marching bands led by a fife (*pífano*) player, whose members don Napoleonic-style leather hats typical of the *cangaçeiro*).

Although the official Festa de São João festivities take place between June 23 and 24, in Caruaru the whole month of June is one big São João celebration with *forró* balls and feasting that lead up to the main event. If you plan to stay in town during this time, be warned you'll need to book far in advance.

FESTAS JUNINHAS

June is an important month in the northeastern states due to a trio of popular *festas* devoted to a three beloved saints (Antônio, Pedro, and João) and known collectively as the Festas Juninhas. In honor of this powerful triumvirate, fruit liqueurs flow, corn and peanuts are roasted over open fires, fireworks explode, and everyone swings to the strains of *forró*. São Pedro, patron saint of rain, is especially important in the parched Sertão, and Santo Antônio, patron saint of marriage, is assiduously courted by singles of both sexes on the prowl for a mate. However, the one who inspires the most hoopla is São João, whose feast day falls on June 24, the winter solstice in South America.

ACCOMMODATIONS AND FOOD

Although Caruaru is a very colorful place, the town itself is not very attractive. Most people visit it as a very full day trip from Recife. Nonetheless, if you want to soak up a little atmosphere and catch some nightly *forró*, consider checking into the **Hotel Central** (Rua Vigário Freire, Centro, tel. 81/3721-5880, www.hotelcentralcaruaru.com.br, R$69–81 d), which, as its name implies, has the advantage of being quite central (other hotels are closer to the bus station). Rooms are fairly basic, but sizable, and some have nice old-style parquet floors. Breakfasts feature lots of regional goodies. During São João, prices multiply fivefold.

To sample regional cuisine, try **Bar da Perua** (Rua Aliança 105, Cohab, tel. 81/3722-3266, 11 A.M.–4 P.M. daily, R$12–20), where you can stuff yourself on roasted *bode*, *carne-de-sol*, and *galinha ao molho pardo* (chicken cooked in its own blood). For a drink or a snack, the Feira de Caruaru has a whole section of *barracas* where you can sample local fare ranging from *carne-de-sol* with *macaxeira* (pureed manioc) to sweeter options such as *pamonha* and *arroz doce* (rice pudding). This is a lively place to hang out and have a beer or *cachaça* while listening to local *forró* musicians jamming. You'll often here *repentistas* as well—northeastern troubadours who make their living singing verses of poetry, which they wittily improvise on the spot.

INFORMATION AND SERVICES

In Caruaru, the **tourist office** (Praça Colonel José de Vasconcelos 100, tel. 81/3722-2021, 7:30 A.M.–1 P.M. Mon.–Fri.) is centrally located. Online, log on to www.caruaru.com.br for information in Portuguese. Good English info can be found on www.recifeguide.com/pernambuco/caruaru.

GETTING THERE

Although the *rodoviária* (tel. 81/3721-3869) is on the outskirts of town, all buses make stops in the center. From Recife, **Caruaruense** (tel. 81/3452-2500) and **Progresso** (tel. 81/2121-9000) offer bus service to Caruaru with departures every 30–60 minutes. The ride takes two hours and includes a stop in Bezerros. If you're driving, follow the BR-232.

Another option is to take an organized day trip from Recife. **Luck Viagens** (tel. 81/3464-4800, www.luckviagens.com.br) runs trips to Caruaru for R$70 per person that includes a visit to the market and the ateliers in Alto do Moura, with time-out for an atmospheric lunch in Nova Jerusalém.

Around Caruaru
ALTO DO MOURA

Only 6 kilometers (4 miles) away from Caruaru is the village of Alto do Moura, whose claim to fame is being the hometown of Mestre Vitalino (1909–1963). The main street is named after him, and the first house on the left, the **Casa de Mestre Vitalino** (Rua Mestre Vitalino, tel. 81/3722-0397, 8 A.M.–noon and 2–5 P.M. Mon.–Sat., 8 A.M.–noon Sun.) has been converted into a small museum where you can view the artist's home with his personal objects and *figurinhas de barro* (clay figures). Many of the humble houses along Rua Mestre Vitalino are also ceramics studios, some of which are

PERNAMBUCO AND ALAGOAS

operated by Mestre Vitalino's talented children and grandchildren (his granddaughter Marliete makes miraculously tiny miniature figures).

The other big name in terms of *figurinhas* is a former colleague of Mestre Vitalino's named Zé Caboclo, whose clay figures are larger and more expressive. You'll find his work at the **Casa de Arte Zé Caboclo** (63 Rua Mestre Vitalino, tel. 81/3722-2379), along with figures made by some of his offspring. Although simply wandering around and checking out the artists at work is fascinating, if you are inspired to buy (and you will be), this is the best place to do so.

If you want to have a meal in Alto do Moura, *bode* is the undisputed specialty at **Bode Assado do Luciano** (Rua Mestre Vitalino 511, tel. 81/3722-0413, 10 A.M.–5 P.M. Tues.–Sun., R$10–18).

To get here from Caruaru, take a taxi or hop the "Alto do Moura" bus that passes down Rua 13 de Maio at two-hour intervals.

BEZERROS

The other major type of *artesanato* that is synonymous with the Pernambucano Sertão is woodcuts. An ancient Chinese tradition, this art arrived in the Northeast in the 19th century as a means to illustrate the little booklets of stories known as *literatura de cordel*. Famous for its woodcut traditions is the small town of Bezerros (www.bezerrosonline.com), located 25 kilometers (16 miles) from Caruaru along the BR-232, which leads to Recife. Renowned throughout Brazil, the town's most famous printer is J. Borges, whose bold, expressive illustrations constitute mini portraits of Sertanejo life. You can view (and purchase—for ridiculously low prices) his works printed on paper, ceramic tiles, and even T-shirts at his atelier, the **Memorial J. Borges** (Av. Major Aprígio da Fonseca 420, tel. 81/3728-0364), a whole section of which is devoted to *literatura de cordel*.

For a terrific overview of popular art from all over the state, visit the **Centro de Artesanato de Pernambuco** (BR-232 Km 107, tel. 81/3728-2094, www.artesanato.pe.gov.br,

9 A.M.–6 P.M. Tues.–Sat., 9 A.M.–1 P.M. Sun., R$1), which contains a boutique. Among the many objects on view are the colorful papier-mâché Carnaval masks that are also a specialty of Bezerros's traditional artists. You can see even more of them at the **Casa de Cultura Popular Lula Vassoureiro** (Rua Otávia Bezerra Vila Nova 64, tel. 81/9102-0665, 8 A.M.–5 P.M. daily), a museum and atelier operated by Lula Vassoureiro, who has been making masks since he was 8 years old.

NOVA JERUSALÉM

One of the more surreal presences in the Sertão is that of the world's largest outdoor theater, designed as a granite replica of the ancient city of Jerusalem. It's located in the small town of Fazenda Nova, 50 kilometers (31 miles) northwest of Caruaru, and every Holy Week, the 3-meter (10-foot) ramparts and 70 towers provide the backdrop for the world's biggest reenactment of the Passion of Christ play. Aside from a cast of a few hundred local citizens, star wattage is provided by Globais (stars from Globo television network's nightly soaps) in the roles of Jesus, Mary, and Joseph. Even if you're not religious, you might consider checking out the sheer Cecil B. DeMille spectacularity of it all. During Easter, you can get to Fazenda Nova directly by bus or book an excursion from Recife. During other times of the year, you can catch a bus from Caruaru.

SOUTH OF RECIFE

The beautiful coral-lined beaches south of Recife are some of the finest in the Northeast. Stretching from Cabo de Santo Agostinho to Tamandaré, 113 kilometers (70 miles) from the capital, this coastline, nicknamed the Costa dos Arrecifes (Coast of Reefs), can be explored in day trips from Recife or by checking into a rustic beachfront *pousada* or more comfortable Porto de Galinhas resort.

Cabo de Santo Agostinho

Only (33 kilometers/21 miles) from Recife, Cabo de Santo Agostinho consists of three main seaside villages. **Gaibu** is a popular resort

reefs and pools at Porto de Galinhas

with lots of palms and sand and tons of mellow beach bars framed by rocky hills. While the rough waves—great for surfing—are dangerous, there is a calmer area that's more propitious for bathing. For a seafood lunch, **Opará** (Av. Beira-Mar 79, tel. 81/3512-0954, 11 A.M.–10 P.M. daily) is highly recommended. Much prettier and more deserted is the small crescent-shaped bay of **Praia de Calhetas.** Framed by a dramatic backdrop of primitive boulders sprouting lush vegetation, it is 3 kilometers (2 miles) from Gaibu. The beach hot spot is **Bar do Artur** (Rua dos Carneiros 17, tel. 81/3522-6382, 10 A.M.–6 P.M.), where you can feast on *peixada* and *lagosta na telha* (lobster grilled on a ceramic tile). For more information on Cabo de Santo Agostinho and photos, log on to www.cabo.pe.gov.br.

GETTING THERE
To get to Gaibu by bus from Recife, take a **Cruzeiro** (tel. 81/2101-9000) bus to the town of Cabo de Santo Agostinho, and then grab a local bus to the village. By car, follow the BR-101 and then the PE-060. From Recife, many hotels and travel agencies offers day trips to Gaibu and Calhetas.

Porto de Galinhas
Porto de Galinhas's beaches are so beautiful that it's no wonder the place has turned into such a hot destination, renowned throughout Brazil for its soft white sands and warm natural pools that you could easily float in for a week. Although dangerously popular and increasingly developed, this former fishing village is lovely in off-season (at least during the week—on weekends, it is justifiably mobbed by Recifenses). Coral reefs off the coast are ideal for snorkeling and diving. Within close proximity of Porto are the beaches of Maracaipe (famed for its surfing), Serrambi, Cupe, and Muro Alto, all of which can vie for title of idyllic tropical getaway.

Incidentally, the village's odd name "Port of Chickens" has a sinister source that has no relation to the carved wood chickens you'll see all over town. In centuries past, Porto provided a safe harbor for ships that trafficked illegally in African slaves (a practice that continued even after abolition). Following the inhumane practices of the times, the slaves were packed together so tightly that they were referred to as "chickens."

SPORTS AND RECREATION

The obvious thing to do in Porto de Galinhas is simply float in the warm, bath-like water. If you want to get out close to the reef, you can easily hire one of the picturesque *jangadas* to take you out (in busiest times, you'll often have to line up to do so). A one-hour trip costs R$8. Most *pousadas* and hotels can organize trips by *jangada* and dune buggy to nearby beaches such as Praia de Serrambi and Praia de Muro Alto (a three-hour trip costs around R$100).

Snorkeling outings are popular. Aside from Porto de Galinhas, there are plenty of underwater attractions off the more tranquil reefs of Maracaípi and those surrounding **Ilha de Santo Aleixo,** an island with fabulous deserted beaches than can be reached by *jangada,* boat, or catamaran. Other outings include guided hikes or horseback rides through the lush forest. You can also take a *jangada* trip through the mangroves around **Pontal de Maracaipe,** with a stop at **Projeto Hipocampo,** a reserve dedicated to the protection of extremely rare Brazilian seahorses that are native to the region. **Pé no Mangue** (Rua da Esperança 101, tel. 81/3552-1935, www.penomangue.com.br) offers a wide range of nicely priced (around R$20–40 pp), guided half-day excursions for small groups. Popular excursions include kayak trips up the Rio de Maracaípe, hikes through the native Atlantic forest, and even moonlit snorkeling outings with flashlights.

ACCOMMODATIONS

As recently as the early '90s, Porto de Galinhas was little more than a palm-shaded fishing village. Today, it boasts more than 150 hotel options, from a spate of new five-star, all-inclusive mega resorts (most of them to the north on Praia do Cupe and Praia de Muro Alto) to more basic *pousadas*. Prices rise significantly during high season, sometimes up to 50 percent.

If you want to be stationed right in the middle of Porto itself, a fetching budget option is **Pousada Porto Verde** (Praça 1, Porto de Galinhas, tel. 81/3552-1410, www.pousada-portoverde.com.br, R$85–115). The clean, basic rooms feature air-conditioning and views that overlook a tropical garden with a pool. A friendly, homey atmosphere reigns. Slightly removed from the village, but right on a fabulous stretch of beach, **Pousada Canto do Porto** (Av. Beira Mar, Praia de Porto de Galinhas, tel. 81/3552-2165, www.pousada-cantodoporto.com.br, R$150–200 d) offers a variety of attractive accommodations. The best are the deluxe beach bungalows with wraparound verandas, where the ocean itself is a major part of the decor. Though considerably smaller, the "economic" apartments aren't bad, though they have neither verandas nor nice views. Amenities include a restaurant and Internet access.

Around 6 kilometers (4 miles) north of Porto along the PE-009, the ◖ **Pousada Tabapitanga** (Praia do Cupe, tel. 81/3552-1037, www.tabapitanga.com.br, R$240–410 d) is an extremely enticing option that sets itself apart from the more aggressively Club Med-style resorts on this beach. Tabatinga's service is personalized, and its vast and beautifully furnished private bungalows are decked out quite luxuriously with king-sized beds, flatscreen TVs, and verandas with hammocks. Breakfasts (featuring lots of regional goodies) are outrageously lavish. Lunch and dinner are also available, as are *caipifrutas,* served on the beach or around the gorgeous pool.

Only 2 kilometers (1 mile) south of Porto de Galinhas, access by a dirt road has ensured Praia de Maracaípe's semi-seclusion, although there are a handful of attractive bars and restaurants. The **Pousada dos Coqueiros** (Rua Projetada 7, Praia de Maracaípe, tel. 81/3552-1294, www.pousadadoscoqueiros.com.br, R$140–200) plays up the getaway factor, in style. The large rooms are soothingly cool and modern with palms poking in through the windows and private verandas. Other relaxing options include flaking out by the lovely pool and lounging in the *redário,* a palm thatched structure where various *redes* (hammocks) are suspended.

FOOD

Considered one of the finest restaurants in the region, ◖ **Beijupirá** (Rua Beijupira, Porto de Galinha, tel. 81/3552-2354, www.beijupira.com.br, noon–midnight daily, R$30–45)—named after a delicious local fish—is also one of the most romantic, especially after dusk when lanterns glow and hundreds of candles are lit. Don't be alarmed if you can't find the items listed on the menu in your pocket dictionary. The hybrid names—such as *lagostanga*, a fusion of *lagosta* (lobster) with *manga* (mango)—are as creative as the dishes themselves, which mix fish, seafood, and meat with tropical fruits.

For a meal with a view, head to **Peixe na Telha** (Av. Beira-Mar, Praia de Porto de Galinhas, tel. 81/3552-1877, 11 A.M.–10 P.M. daily, R$20–30), whose patio faces right onto the beach. While admiring the bright sails of the *jangadas*, you can down a beer or dig into copious fish and shrimp *moquecas*. The house specialty, *peixe na telha*, consists of fish grilled on a red roof tile. Portions are monstrous, serving two or even three. Should you want to sink your teeth into some red meat, head to **Tio Dadá** (Rua da Esperança 167, Porto de Galinhas, tel. 81/3552-1319, 11:30 A.M.–midnight daily, R$15–25), a local *churrascaria* (also with great beach views) that serves sizzling hunks of beef and lamb as well as chicken and fish, accompanied by grilled vegetables and rice.

INFORMATION AND SERVICES

The **tourist office** (Rua da Esperança 188, tel. 81/3553-1480, 9 A.M.–5 P.M. Mon.–Fri., 9 A.M.–3 P.M. Sat.–Sun.) is easy to find. You can also log on to www.portodegalinhas.com.br, an informative site (in Portuguese) with enticing photos. You'll find ATMs at the Banco do Brasil (Via Porto de Galinhas) and the Banco 24 Horas inside the Petrobras gas station on Rua da Esperança.

GETTING THERE AND AROUND

Porto de Galinhas is 70 kilometers (43 miles) south of Recife. During the day and early evening, **Cruzeiro** (tel. 81/2101-9000) buses leave hourly from Recife's *rodoviária,* via Boa Viagem and the airport. The trip takes two hours. You can cut your time in half if you take a taxi from the airport or downtown (you should be able to bargain a price of around R$100 for up to four people—paying by the meter will cost far more). If you rent a car, follow the BR-101, the PE-60, and then the PE-38 to Porto de Galinhas (on weekends, traffic can be heavy).

Visiting surrounding beaches from Porto de Galinhas is easy. Minivans leave from the Petrobras gas station for Praia do Cupe at 30-minute intervals. Stops are made at *pousadas* along the way. You can also grab a dune buggy taxi from the village heading to Cupe or Maracaípi for R$15–20.

Tamandaré

The colonial fishing village of Tamandaré is far more secluded and undeveloped than Porto de Galinhas, 60 kilometers (37 miles) to the north. Set amidst an ecological reserve of tropical forest, mangroves, and coral reefs, its 16 kilometers (10 miles) of unspoiled beaches are breathtakingly beautiful. The crème-de-la-crème is the mirage-like 5-kilometer (3-mile) **Praia dos Carneiros** (with private access via buggy taxis from Tamandaré), where you can choose between the warm bath-like waters of turquoise sea pools and equally lulling green waters of the Rio Formoso. If you're looking for utter respite, this is the place to visit.

ACCOMMODATIONS AND FOOD

The little colonial fishing village of Tamandaré has a lazy, sun-bleached charm. With its summer houses and beach bars, it is the closest thing to urban around these parts. In and around Tamandaré, accommodations are fairly rustic and, surprisingly, not that cheap. There are, however, many bungalow-with-kitchen options. Located right on the beach, the **Pousada Baía dos Corais** (Rua Miramar, tel. 81/3465-4090, www.baiadoscorais.com.br, R$120) is a pleasant enough place, sunny and breezy, with large clean rooms and a pool. For food, head to **O Pescador** (Rua Raul de Pompeia, tel.

Fernando de Noronha

81/3676-1345, 11 A.M.–10 P.M. daily, R$15–25) which serves up fresh fish and seafood local style. Try the *sinfonia maritima,* an irresistible seafood stew flavored with coconut milk, and the fish with shrimp sauce.

If you want to be right on the stunning Praia dos Carneiros, one of the nicest options is (**Sítio da Prainha** (Praia dos Carneiros, tel. 81/3441-1718, www.sitiodaprainha.com.br, R$250 d). Accommodations are in eight private, sprawling bungalows, which sleep up to four. Equipped with air-conditioning, TVs and DVDs, they have a breezy, beach house vibe, enhanced by their idyllic location amidst a coconut plantation overlooking the beach. The best feature is the cotton hammocks, strung from the palms, which catch the tradewinds. Dinner at the beachside restaurant (open to the public) is included in the rate.

INFORMATION AND SERVICES
Log on to www.guiatamandare.com.br, a Portuguese site with highly seductive photos of Tamandaré's beaches. The Banco do Brasil has an ATM that accepts international cards.

GETTING THERE
Cruzeiro (tel. 81/2101-9000) offers bus service from Recife (100 kilometers/62 miles away) to Tamandaré. If you're driving, follow the BR-101 and the PE-060.

(FERNANDO DE NORONHA
Ever fantasized about being cast away on a deserted island? Fernando de Noronha is an archipelago of 21 islands, 550 kilometers (342 miles) from Recife, that easily lives up to the wildest dreams of both escapists and ecotourists. You'll find primitive beaches, mountains shrouded in tropical vegetation, and a fantastic array of exotic flora and fauna, ranging from pelicans and sea turtles to (friendly) sharks and great schools of dolphins. Aside from offering great hiking, surfing, and snorkeling, Fernando de Noronha is also considered one of the foremost diving spots on the planet due to spectacularly clear waters with visibility of up to 50 meters (164 feet).

Founded by the Portuguese in the early 1500s, Fernando de Noronha traded colonial hands various times before the Portuguese took definitive control of the archipelago in the late 1600s. For the next three centuries, the main island of Fernando de Noronha functioned as the world's most gorgeous political prison (which led to the disappearance of a considerable chunks of native vegetation—brush was used by escaped prisoners to build hide-outs and getaway vessels), and as both an American and Brazilian military base. Today, the main island is the only one that is inhabited. Relying largely on tourism for its livelihood, the local population of 3,000 mostly resides in the village of Vila dos Remédios, situated on the northern tip.

In 1988, Fernando de Noronha was transformed into Brazil's first ecological marine reserve, with more than 70 percent of its territory administered by IBAMA, the Brazilian environmental agency. IBAMA takes its mission seriously: All visitors to the island must pay an environmental tax, and there are limits on where you can go and when. Development is tightly controlled. For a long time, visiting Fernando de Noronha meant roughing it Robinson Crusoe-style in rustic accommodations with few creature comforts beyond a hammock and the seabreeze. The ecological rules still prevail (on some beaches even polluting sunscreen is a no-no), but since the island caught on as the ultimate honeymoon destination for Brazilian celebs, there has been an influx of eco-chic *pousadas* decked out with the requisite Japanese hot tubs, plasma TVs, and wireless access. Given its distance from the mainland, the island was never a cheap getaway; imported food and drink, as well as gas, were always much costlier than their continental counterparts. However, spurred on by Fernando de Noronha's *it* spot status, even the most modest bungalow accommodations charge upwards of R$200 for the privilege of bunking down in paradise. Once you've factored in the airfare, the idyll becomes quite a costly one—although if you can afford it, you won't be disappointed.

Planning in advance for your trip is recommended. In Recife and Natal, many travel agencies sell all-inclusive packages—including airfare, accommodations, and tours. Although there are package tours for 2–3 days, if you're going to travel so far (and pay so much), not to mention be confronted with so much natural beauty, it's worth staying closer to a week. In terms of weather, the best time to visit is the drier period between August and November (when the offshore waters are at their clearest).

Sights

The main town of Vila dos Remédios comprises the island's "historical" center. Colonial vestiges consist of the **Igreja Nossa Senhora dos Remédios,** a pretty baroque hilltop church; **Palácio São Miguel,** which houses the island's administrative offices; and the atmospheric ruins of the **Forte dos Remédios,** an 18th-century Portuguese fortress littered with cannons. At the foot of the church, the tiny **Museu Histórico** (8 A.M.–4 P.M. daily) traces the island's history.

Beaches

Fernando de Noronha's main draw is its spectacular beaches. If you have a weakness for the color blue, you will be brought to your knees by the various shimmering hues of turquoise, aquamarine, cobalt, and azure that color the ocean. The west coast of the island, known as Mar de Dentro (Inside Sea) has calmer waters. The more turbulent east coast waters are referred to as the Mar de Fora (Outside Sea). The island has some 20 beaches, all of them stunners. Some of them boast soft white sand derived from pulverized coral, while others have darker sand that betrays volcanic origins. The three unanimous disputees for title of most beautiful beach in Brazil (according to Brazilian travel writers and tourist polls) are Baía do Sancho and Baía dos Porcos (Mar do Dentro), and Praia do Leão (Mar de Fora).

The approach to **Baía do Sancho** is fittingly dramatic. A steep metal staircase descending a rugged cliffside requires you to squeeze through a hole carved out of rock in order to reach the soft sands. The ruddy red cliffs overgrown with primitive jungle provide a hypnotic backdrop from the beach. It's equally hard to take your eyes off the jade waters blossoming with coral that make Sancho one of the best snorkeling sites on the island. From the top of the cliffs, where the view is equally fantastic, a trail leads to the ruins of the Dois Irmãos fortress. If you continue along the rocky trail, you'll arrive at **Baía dos Porcos,** an incandescently blue bay framed by sculpted volcanic rocks whose beach vanishes during high tide. At low tide, rocks form natural pools where you can sit amidst glittering fish and gaze at the twin cones of the Ilha dos Dois Irmãos rising out of the water. The largest beach of all, **Praia do Leão,** is mysteriously (and mercifully) the least visited. Untamed and windswept, its sweeping white sands are the favorite hatching grounds for numerous birds and sea tortoises. During mating season, access is controlled by IBAMA.

On the Mar de Dentro side, other standout beaches include **Praia do Boldró** and **Praia Cacimba do Padre.** Between the months of November and April, waves of up to 5 meters (16.5 feet) transform these beaches into a surfers' delight. Otherwise, at low tide, sheltered pools appear that are ideal for snorkeling. Overlooking the beach, the ruins of Forte São Pedro do Boldró are a popular spot for watching the sunset. Boldró is also the only beach that lays claim to having a restaurant right on the sand. More "urban" due to their proximity to Vila dos Remédios are **Praia do Cachorro, Praia do Meio,** and **Praia da Conceição.** Locals hang out at the sprinkling of *barracas* set against imposing backdrop of Morro do Pico.

On the Mar de Fora side, **Praia da Atalaia** is a snorkeler's dream. At low tide, pools form amidst the coral, creating aquariums chockfull with colorful sponges, fish, lobsters, octopuses, turtles, and even harmless barracuda and sharks. IBAMA allows only 100 people on the beach a day (four groups of 25—each of which is allowed a frustratingly brief 30 minutes in the water). Lineups form at the adjacent beach of **Baía do Sueste,** where you can rent

masks and snorkels (R$10 a day) and cool your heels in the tranquil waters while waiting for your turn at Atalaia.

Sports and Recreation
DIVING
Fernando de Noronha is arguably one of the best diving spots on the planet. The average water temperature is a balmy 28°C (82°F), visibility extends to a depth of 50 meters (164 feet), and the profusion of brightly colored sea fauna will give you the impression of swimming through an award-winning National Geographic documentary. The only drawback is the price: a 30-minute monitored "baptismal" plunge goes for R$250. Diving companies that offer lessons and outings include **Atlantis** (tel. 81/3619-1225, www.atlantisnoronha.com.br), with friendly, English-speaking staff, and **Águas Claras** (Alameda do Boldró, tel. 81/3619-1225, www.aguasclaras-fn.com.br). Diving on your own is prohibited by IBAMA.

SNORKELING AND PLANASUB
Snorkeling can be done during low tide at many of the beaches around the island, with honorable mention going to Baía do Sancho, Baía dos Porcos, Praia do Boldró, and Praia de Atalaia. If you don't bring your own mask, snorkel, and fins, you can rent them for around R$15 at **Santuário** (tel. 81/3619-1247), a tour operator in Porto de Santo Antônio that also runs snorkeling outings. An inspired *noronhense* riff on snorkeling is *planasub:* After gearing up, you grip an acrylic flutterboard attached by rope to a boat, which then takes you offshore where you can see fish swimming around coral banks and wrecked ships. Being towed instead of having to kick and paddle is a wonderfully liberating sensation. From Porto de Santo Antônio, **Abatur** (tel. 81/3619-1365) offers *planasub* trips for small groups at the cost of R$80 for 45 minutes.

SURFING
The Mar de Dentro beaches of Praia de Conceição, Boldró, Cacimba do Padre, and do Meio offer some of the best surfing in Brazil—at least between the months of

November and March (the rest of the year, you'll be disappointed) when terrific barrels and breaks form, measuring up to 5 meters (17 feet). Make sure to bring your own boards and gear since there are no surf shops.

BOAT EXCURSIONS

Boat excursions depart from the harbor of Porto de Santo Antônio, near Vila dos Remédios. Aside from trips to various beaches, the most popular destination is the **Baía dos Golfinhos,** at the southern tip of the island, where you can see large schools of *golfinhos* (dolphins) come to feed and frolic in the calm bay waters. Both **Abatur** and **Santuário** offer three-hour excursions for R$80 with stops for snorkeling at Baía do Sancho. You can also view the dolphins from the **Mirante dos Golfinhos,** a lookout point above the bay (the beach itself is off limits). The best time is in the early morning, when they are cavorting around and leaping in and out of the water. A 2-km (1.2-mile) trail leads to the Mirante from the parking lot above the Baía do Sancho.

Accommodations

Accommodations range from spartan simplicity to eco-chic luxury. The one thing you can count on is extremely inflated prices (although discounts are available outside of high season). Most basic "budget" *pousadas* are modest affairs operated out of local residences, with small rooms, a modicum of decorative flair (aside from ubiquitous kitschy dolphins), and friendly, but sometimes improvised service. You'll find most options split between Vila da Trinta and Floresta Nova, which are both suburban areas close to Vila dos Remédios's historic center. **Pousada Monsieur Rocha** (Rua Dona Juquinha 139, Vila da Trinta, tel. 81/3619-1227 www.pousadamrocha.com, R$195–230 d) is a basic but well-run choice. The bright whitewashed rooms have air-conditioning and Internet access is available. Only a three-minute walk from Vila dos Remédios, it's also across the street from the local bus stop.

In Floresta Nova, **Pousada Maratlântico** (Quadra M, Lote 6, tel. 81/3619-1915, www.pousadamaratlantico.com.br, R$210–280 d) is also simple, but more atmospheric—a pleasantly faux rustic lodge with lots of dark wood paneling and furniture, set amidst a pretty garden. The hotel serves afternoon tea (a weird feature in these parts) and rents snorkeling equipment. The very pretty **Pousada Beco de Noronha** (Rua das Acácias, Floresta Nova, tel. 81/3619-1568, www.becodenoronha.com.br, R$320–500 d) also goes for the rustic lodge look, although the trappings are more polished and refined. The four sizable rooms are seductively furnished with earthy colors, organic fibers, and regional artisanal elements. Ecologically sound, the *pousada* runs on solar energy and all garbage is recycled. Buggies can be rented on-site. Seeing as a trip to Fernando de Noronha is already busting your budget, you might want to go all out and (at least for one romantic night) check into the aptly named ◖ **Pousada Maravilha** (BR-363, Praia de Sueste, tel. 81/3619-0028, www.pousadamaravilha.com.br, R$1,420–1,720 d). This luxurious *pousada* is as unforgettable as the island itself; a secluded oasis perched above the Praia de Sueste where everything is exquisitely designed to harmonize with the sublime natural environs. The rooms—either in private bungalows or the main lodge—are soothing refuges decked out in white and natural woods. Creature comforts range from home theaters and iPods (in the bungalows) to king-sized beds with fine linens. Terraces and decks are outfitted with hammocks and futons. A sauna and the "infinity" pool that seems to be falling into the bay below only add to the sense of hedonism. The restaurant is considered one of the best on the island, and service is top of the line. Children under 10 aren't permitted.

Food

Since everything is imported, food tends to be more expensive on Noronha. Indeed, some of the dishes that show up on fancier menus wouldn't be out of place in Rio or São Paulo. For exotic food lovers, one of the main island staples is *tubarão* (shark). Rest assured that you won't be sinking your teeth into any of the friendly (and protected) ones you swim up against during the day—the edible sharks come from Natal. The island's favorite *petisco* is *bolinhos de tubalhau,* crunchy fried fish balls in which shark fills in for the more traditional *bacalhau* (cod). It is also a presence in *tubalhoada,* in which slivers of shark meat, doused in olive oil, are baked along with tomatoes, peppers, potatoes, and olives. You can sample such concoctions—along with kid-pleasing shark burgers—at the terrace snack bar/restaurant of the **Museu do Tubarão** (Porto Santo Antônio, tel. 81/3619-1365, 9:30 A.M.– 6:30 P.M. Mon.–Sat. and 11:30 A.M.–6:30 P.M. Sun., R$12–22), which pays homage to the 11 species that reside in the island's waters. On display are lots of jaws (naturally), along with interesting info such as the impressive fact that the average shark generates 30,000 teeth during its lifetime.

For lunch on the sand, head to 🄲 **Meu Paraíso** (Praia do Boldró, tel. 81/3619-1635, 10 A.M.–7 P.M. daily, R$20–30), a restaurant/ bar with a delicious natural setting. If you linger long enough over your fish or seafood, you can catch the sunset. Another classic gathering place for a seafood snack and a sunset is **Bar Duda Rei,** located on the island's most "urban" beach, Praia da Conceição. In town, **Cacimba Bistrô** (Praça Presidente Eurico Dutra, Vila dos Remédios, tel. 81/3619-1200, noon–3 P.M. and 6:30–10:30 P.M., R$30–40) is a lovely intimate place with charming decor whose varied menu features healthy fare such as (whole wheat) penne with seafood and tofu lasagna.

Although it's a bit out of the way (behind the airport) and extremely simple, 🄲 **Ecologiku's** (Estrada Velha do Sueste, tel. 81/3619-1807, 7–10:30 P.M., R$20–35) serves some of the best cooking on the island. The menu is limited to fish and seafood dishes inspired by the daily catch. The *moquecas* are very good. Also popular is the house specialty, an aromatic concoction of shrimp, lobster, and octopus known as the *sinfônia ecologiku.* The view of Morro do Pico from the plastic tables is quite mesmerizing.

Information and Services

Although there's a small **tourist office** in Vila

dos Remédios in the Palácio São Miguel (tel. 81/3619-1352) open (in theory) during office hours, you're better off consulting two excellent bilingual websites: www.noronha.pe.gov.br and www.noronha.com.br. Listings and information are extensive and up-to-date and there are lots of seductive photos as well as handy maps.

No banks in Fernando de Noronha accept international cards or exchange currency, so make sure you bring a healthy wad of *reais* from the mainland (chances of being robbed are very slim). Although *pousadas* and diving operators accept credit cards, most other places do not. Likewise, since everything on the island is imported, come equipped with sunscreen, mosquito repellent, flip-flops and other sundries to avoid paying heavily inflated prices.

For Internet access, head to **Cia da Lua** (Bosque dos Flamboyants, tel. 81/3619-1631, www.ciadalua.com.br, 9 A.M.–11 P.M. Mon.– Sat., 5–11 P.M. Sun.) in Vila dos Remédios, a charming cyber café that serves *tapiocas,* sandwiches, and juices. There is a second location at the airport.

Getting There

There are flights to Fernando de Noronha from both Recife and Natal. During high season (Jan.–Feb. and July), these are often booked far in advance. From Recife both **Trip** (tel. 0300/789-8747, www.voetrip.com.br) and **Varig (Nordeste)** (tel. 0300/788-3000, www.varig.com.br) offer daily flights. A round-trip usually costs upwards of R$900. In Recife, you can purchase tickets or complete packages at **Dolphin Travel** (Av. Engenheiro Domingos Ferreira 4267, Boa Viagem, tel. 81/3465-7224, www.dolphintravel.com.br) or **Karitas Turismo** (Rua Agenor Lopes 292, Boa Viagem, tel. 81/3466-4300, www.karitas.com.br). The **Aeroporto Fernando de Noronha** (tel. 81/3619-1311) is located in the center of the island. A taxi ride to Vila dos Remédios (or most other places) is around R$20.

Note: All visitors to Fernando de Noronha must pay an environmental tax before arriving. Save yourself a big lineup at the airport and pay over the Internet by logging on to www.noronha.pe.gov.br. If you're staying for a week or less, the tax is around R$33 per day.

Getting Around

Measuring 17 square kilometers (6.5 square miles), Fernando de Noronha is quite manageable to get around. Its one paved road, the 7-km (4.5-mile) BR-363 might be Brazil's shortest federal highway, but it links Vila dos Remédios, the port, the airport, most of the beaches and *pousadas*.

The main way of getting around the island is by buggy. Renting one gives you the freedom to visit all the beaches you want when you want. Just remember that gas is imported and much more expensive than on the mainland. The two main companies are **LocBuggy** (tel. 81/3619-1490, www.locbuggy.com.br) and **Locadora Morro do Farol** (tel. 81/3619-1392, www.locadoramorrodofarol.com.br), both of which also rent out Jeeps, motorbikes, and motorboats. Daily rental fees for buggies are around R$120. You can also easily take advantage of the island's many buggy-taxis, which are quite easy to hail. A more economic option is take the microbus that runs up and down the BR-363, from Porto Santo Antônio

to Baía Sueste. It circulates at 30-minute intervals between 5 A.M. and 10 P.M., and only costs R$2.50.

You can rent mountain bikes at **Pousada Solimar** (tel. 081/3619-1965), in Vila dos Remédios, for R$25 a day—or else, quite simply, walk. Distances between Vila dos Remédios and many of the surrounding beaches are quite close. Moreover, numerous hiking trails weave through areas protected by IBAMA. Two of the easiest and most popular walks are those linking the Mirante dos Golfinhos with Baía do Sancho and Praia do Boldró with Praia do Cachorro (best undertaken when the tide is out). For more extensive hiking with a guide, contact the local eco-guide association, located in the building shared by **IBAMA** (tel. 81/3619-1128) and the **TAMAR** project (Av. do Boldró, tel. 81/3619-1171, 8 A.M.–10:30 P.M. daily), which is dedicated to the preservation of Brazil's sea turtles. Aside from nightly nature talks (in Portuguese), TAMAR has a small café and boutique selling turtle paraphernalia. During hatching season, when baby turtles emerge from their eggs and migrate en masse into the ocean, you can accompany biologists who track and study them.

Alagoas

Alagoas is one of the smallest and poorest states in the Northeast. It is also one of the most enchanting, largely due to its absolutely stunning white-sand beaches, which rank among the most beautiful and unspoiled in Brazil. The presence of coral reefs along much of the coastline ensure that the captivating blue-green waters are ideal for bathing as well as snorkeling and diving. The laid-back capital of Maceió has its share of terrific beaches and makes a good base for exploring the coasts both north and south. Although Maceió has preserved relatively few vestiges of its past, the colonial towns of Marechal Deodoro and Penedo, on the banks of the Rio São Francisco, are well worth visiting for a

taste of regional traditions and a glimpse into Alagoas's past.

MACEIÓ

Like Pernambuco, Alagoas began colonial life as a major producer of sugarcane. Maceió grew up around an 18th-century sugarcane plantation that was strategically situated between the open sea and the Lagoa Mundau, an immense inland lagoon that provided a sheltered natural harbor for the shipping of sugar, and later tobacco, coconut, and spices. In 1839, Maceió became the state capital, but it wasn't until the latter part of the 20th century that Maceió shook off its small town languor. In the last few decades, the city has gone on a building spree,

PERNAMBUCO AND ALAGOAS

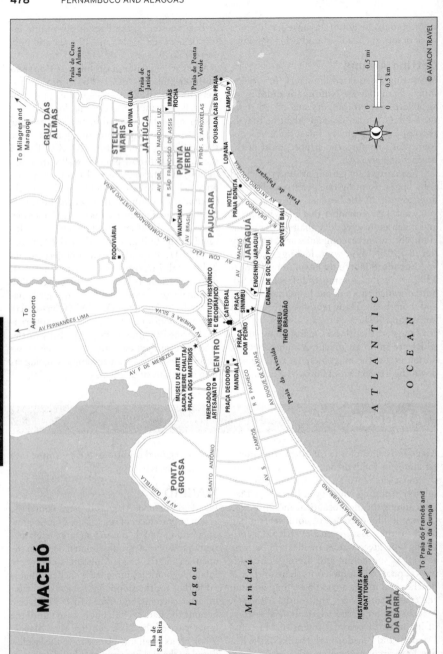

MACEIÓ

Lagoa Mundaú

Lagoa

Mundaú

Ilha de Santa Rita

To Milagres and Maragogi

Praia de Cruz das Almas

Praia de Jatiúca

Praia de Ponta Verde

CRUZ DAS ALMAS

STELLA MARIS

JATIÚCA

DIVINA GULA

IRMÃS ROCHA

PONTA VERDE

AV. DR. JÚLIO MARQUES LUZ

R. SÃO FRANCISCO DE ASSIS

R. PROF. S. ARROXELAS

POUSADA CAIS DA PRAIA

LAMPIÃO

LOPANA

AV. ANTÔNIO GOUVEIA

Praia de Pajuçara

HOTEL PRAIA BONITA

SORVETE BALI

AV. GRANDO TENÓRIO

AV. BRASIL

WANCHAKO

PAJUÇARA

AV. COMENDADOR GUSTAVO PAIVA

RODOVIÁRIA

To Aeroporto

AV. FERNANDES LIMA

AV. MARRIA E SILVA

AV. COM. LEÃO

AV. MACEIÓ

JARAGUÁ

ENGENHO JARAGUÁ

CARNE DE SOL DO PICUÍ

CAIS DE SOL DO PICUÍ

INSTITUTO HISTÓRICO E GEOGRÁFICO

CATEDRAL

PRAÇA SINIMBU

PRAÇA DOM PEDRO

MUSEU THÉO BRANDÃO

CENTRO

MUSEU DE ARTE SACRA PIERRE CHALITA/ PRAÇA DOS MARTÍRIOS

MERCADO DO ARTESANATO

PRAÇA DEODORO

MANDALA

AV. F. DE MENEZES

R. S. PACHECO

AV. DUQUE DE CAXIAS

Praia da Avenida

ATLANTIC OCEAN

PONTA GROSSA

R. SANTO ANTÔNIO

AV. F.B. QUINTELLA

CAMPOS

AV. S.

To Praia do Francês and Praia da Gunga

AV. ASSIS CHATEAUBRIAND

RESTAURANTS AND BOAT TOURS

PONTAL DA BARRA

© AVALON TRAVEL

0   0.5 mi

0   0.5 km

disfiguring parts of its pretty colonial center with generic modern edifices, and developing its coastline, which in recent years has experienced a tourist boom. Although Maceió is a pleasant enough town, what really lures visitors are the surreally turquoise waters and white-sand beaches located right within the city, and north and south along the coast.

Sights

Maceió is pretty much a beach town with little in the way of historic or cultural sights. However, in the compact Centro, behind Praia da Avenida, a smattering of handsome neoclassical government palaces, colonial churches, and monumental *praças* hint at an elegant architectural past. The **Praça dos Martírios** (also known as Praça Marechal Floriano Peixoto) is an attractive square flanked by the creamy white Palácio do Governo and the Igreja Bom Jesus dos Martírios, an eclectically styled church with a resplendent blue-and-white Portuguese *azulejo* facade. Adjacent to Centro, the *bairro* of **Jaraguá,** sheltering the city's 19th-century port, is one of the Maceió's oldest neighborhoods. Over the last 10 years, many of its century-old mansions and warehouses have undergone restoration, receiving brightly painted makeovers and being converted into bars and cultural venues.

As you're strolling around Centro, you might as well take a peek at several modest museums. Occupying an imposing onion-domed palace, the **Museu Théo Brandão** (Av. da Paz 1490, Centro, tel. 82/3221-2651, 9 A.M.–noon and 2–5 P.M. Tues.–Fri., 2–5 P.M. Sat.–Sun., R$2) provides an interesting insight into local culture via its engaging collection of folk art and crafts, most of it from Alagoas. Thursday nights at 7 P.M., folkloric groups perform music from throughout the state.

The pale pink **Instituto Histórico e Geográfico** (Rua do Sol 382, Centro, 8 A.M.–noon and 2–5 P.M. Mon.–Fri.) has a rather musty collection of documents and artifacts associated with Alagoan history. However, it's worth stopping in to check out the personal effects of the infamous local bandit, Lampião (see

the sidebar *The Bonnie and Clyde of Brazil*), accompanied by mesmerizing photos of him and his not so merry band of outlaws. Included is the iconic image of the severed heads of the famous *cangaçeiro* and his crew, taken after the police finally gunned them down in 1938. The photo was circulated throughout the Northeast—along with the heads themselves (preserved in formaldehyde)—in order to prove that the greatly feared (and equally revered) bandits were indeed out of commission.

The **Museu de Arte Sacra Pierre Chalita** (Praça Marechal Floriano Peixoto 44, Centro, 8 A.M.–noon and 2–5:30 P.M., tel. 82/3223-4298) has a modest collection of religious art and colonial furnishings culled from around the Northeast.

Beaches

Maceió is famed for having some of the most splendid urban beaches in Brazil. Impressive as they are, they don't compare with the more pristine and undeveloped versions located north and south of the city. Nonetheless, since most of Maceioenses' urban life revolves around the *orla* (coast), if you want to get a taste of the local lifestyle, the city beaches are definitely worth checking out (be prepared for major crowds on weekends and in the summer).

Only 2 kilometers (1.2 miles) east of Centro, crescent-shaped **Praia de Pajuçara** is Maceió's most urbanized beach, lined with high-rises, hotels, bars, and *barracas* hawking *água de coco* (coconut water) and *caipirinhas.* It's hard to believe that a century ago it was still a little fishing village. The beach is wide with calm emerald waters that are good for swimming. When the tide is low, for R$15 an hour, you can hire a *jangada* to take you out to the *piscinas* (swimming pools) offshore. In these warm pools, you can wallow around to your heart's content and sip on cocktails served from floating bars.

Continuing east is the more trendy and upscale **Praia de Ponta Verde,** where the most luxurious hotels and restaurants are located. Until the 1950s, this pretty beach, framed by dense foliage and coconut palms, was so untamed that its vegetation served as camouflage

THE BONNIE AND CLYDE OF BRAZIL

The Bonnie and Clyde of the Brazilian Northeast were a couple of equally alluring Depression-era bandits called Lampião and Maria Bonita, who were the scourge of the Sertão as well as charismatic (and very funkily dressed) folk heroes. Lampião was the nickname of Virgulino Ferreira da Silva, born in 1895 into a peasant family living in the arid Sertão of Pernambuco. Until the age of 21, Virgulino worked as a leathercraft artisan. He also possessed an uncommon (for the time and place) literary bent. However, after his father – who was involved in a deadly feud with other local families – was killed by police, in true Wild West spirit, Lampião then swore to wreak vengeance. His nickname supposedly comes from the fact that he customized a shotgun to shoot so fast that the resulting flash resembled the sudden flare of a gas lantern, or *lampião*.

For the next 20 years, together with his wife, Maria Déa (nicknamed Maria Bonita, or "Pretty Mary"), and a band of loyal but ruthless outlaws known as *cangaçeiros*, Lampião went on a violent rampage, brazenly stealing police weapons and using them to attack, terrorize, and steal from wealthy landowners and small towns throughout the Northeast. To protect themselves from the merciless sun and sharp thorns of the Caatinga's thorn trees, the *cangaçeiros* decked themselves out from head to toe in leather, which they embellished (most of them being practiced at leatherwork) with intricate and colorful embroidery, coins, and metal scraps resembling chunks of medieval armor. These desert dandies also had a weakness for French perfume – Lampião, in particular, stole great quantities of it from the wealthy homes he broke into. Both vain and charismatic, Lampião and Maria Bonita were early media darlings – they courted their fame, inviting reporters to photograph them in their stylish leather finery, with their ammunition belts casually slung across their hips and dark glasses filtering out the blinding rays of the sun.

Their cunning ability to elude capture for so long, coupled with their outrageous crimes, turned Lampião and his band into Public Enemy Number One and front page material. Wealthy landowners lived in fear and entreated upon the federal government to send a special force of soldiers – the *cangaçeiros* referred to them as *macacos* (monkeys) due to their mud-brown uniforms and obedience to the law – to hunt them down. They did so to no avail – until 1938 when Lampião was ambushed by the police with machine guns. After a shootout, Lampião, Maria Bonita, and their gang of nine were killed and their heads were cut off.

Although brutal Lampião was certainly no saint – he and his band stole, killed, raped, and pillaged – his defiant rebel stance against the establishment and the wealthy landowners who treated the Sertão's peasants as feudal serfs turned him into a Robin Hood-esque legend during his lifetime. Following his death, he became a national folk hero, the subject of poems, stories, songs, TV miniseries, films, comic books, and thousands of the mimeographed stories illustrated with woodcuts, known as *literatura de cordel,* which to this day are popular throughout the Northeast interior.

for modest society youths to come and bathe in private, a practice that earned it the name of Praia das Acanhadas (Shy People Beach). There is still a profusion of palms, as well as sophisticated *barracas* where you can kick back with a *chopp* and listen to live music.

Further along, the beaches of **Jatiúca** and **Cruz das Almas** are sought after by Maceió's *surfista* crowd, but are still fairly urban. If you're seeking less crowded sands, continue north along the *orla* (there are plenty of buses that leave from Centro), stopping at any stretch of sugary white sand that takes your fancy. **Jacarecica, Guaxuma, Garça Torta,** and **Riacho Doce** are all seductive. The last beach on the municipal bus line is **Praia de Pratagi**, a wide expanse of fluffy sand with natural pools 15 kilometers (9 miles) from Centro. The mermaid statue erected on one of the coral reefs honors the Candomblé *orixá* Iemanjá, whose title is "Queen of the Seas." For this reason, this beach is often referred to as **Praia do Mirante da Sereia** (*sereia* is Portuguese for mermaid).

Sports and Recreation

Aside from its beaches, Maceió is known for the **Lagoa de Mundaú,** a freshwater lagoon fed by the Rio Mundaú. Surrounded by mangrove swamps and coconut palms, and dotted with fishing communities that live off the abundance of crabs, shrimp, and *sururu* (a local shellfish), the *lagoa* is a lovely place for a drink and a portion of fresh crab or shrimp while watching the sun set. During the day, boat excursions sail around the lagoon and its handful of islands. For information about departures, visit the *barracas* at Pontal da Barra, where the traditional lace-makers make and display their wares.

Entertainment and Events
NIGHTLIFE

Most of Maceió's nightlife takes place in the upscale beach neighborhoods of Pajuçara, Ponta Negra, and Jatiúca as well as the restored old *bairro* of Jaraguá, which has a somewhat more bohemian edge.

One of the nicest ways to kick back in

Maceió is take advantage of nature's bounty—both in terms of the setting and the seafood. Aside from a late afternoon beer at the rustic waterfront *barracas* surrounding Lagoa de Mundau, all beaches have *barracas* where you can sip on *caipirinhas* and feast away on crab, oysters, and *sururu.* Among the most sophisticated beach bars in town is **Lopana** (Av. Sílvio Carlos Viana, Ponto Verde, tel. 82/3231-7484, 8 A.M.–midnight Tues.–Sun.). Straddling Pajucara and Ponta Verde beaches, this *barraca* has it all—air-conditioning, wireless Internet, waiters that take your order with Palm Pilots, and even catamaran excursions up and down the coast. The menu has tasty fare such as spicy buffalo sausage and crunchy shrimp as well as lots of healthy juices, salads, and sandwiches. If you crave something sweet, go for the tropical fruit salad topped with *mangaba* ice cream.

For listening or dancing to *forró,* the classic, if slightly touristy address is **Lampião** (Av. Álvaro Otacílio, Jatiúca, tel. 82/3325-4376, 8 P.M.–close Tues.–Sun.), which has the advantage of overlooking the beach. A few blocks inland, **Divina Gula** (Rua Engenheiro Paulo Brandão Nogueira 85, Jatiúca, tel. 82/3235-4400, www.divinagula.com.br, 11:30 A.M.–1 A.M. Tues.–Sun.) is an immensely popular restaurant/bar. Some of the most appetizing food in the city is served up by the Mineiro owners, who daringly mix hearty Minas classics with Alagoan produce such as *carne-de-sol,* shrimp, and manioc. Try *desfiada confiada;* manioc puree topped with layers of grated zucchini, shredded *carne-de-sol,* cured Mineiro cheese, and sautéed *banana da terra* (plantain). The rustic ranch-style interior is very welcoming, but at night, the tables on the sidewalk are the coveted place to kick back with a beer or *cachaça* and feast on delicious appetizers.

As the weekend approaches Jaraguá heats up, particularly the streets surrounding Rua Sá de Albuquerque. Occupying a renovated old house, **Engenho Jaraguá** (Rua Silvério Jorge 285, tel. 82/9978-0989, 8 P.M.–close daily) is a mellow *boteco* conducive to late night conversations. *Cachaça* infused with herbs and

PERNAMBUCO AND ALAGOAS

barracas along Maceió's oceanfront

spices goes nicely with regional *petiscos* such as roasted quail, grilled *coalho* cheese, and *carne-de-sol*. From Thursday to Saturday, live MPB is performed. Nearby, **Mandala** (Rua Barão de Maceió, Centro, tel. 82/3223-7863, 11–6 P.M. Mon.–Wed., 11 A.M.–close Thurs.–Fri., 8 P.M.–close Sat.) is a cool gallery/bar with lofty ceilings and a warm atmosphere that's haunted by the city's arty crowd. This is a good place to check out the local cultural scene: The walls showcase works by Maceioense artists while indie bands take to the small stage on Friday and Saturday nights from 8 P.M.–close. During the week, this is an excellent place for a nicely priced self-service buffet lunch.

FESTIVALS AND EVENTS

In the third week of November, the city gets its ya-yas out during **Maceió Fest,** an out-of-season Carnaval that is a watered down version of Salvador's with plenty of *trio elétricos* blasting ear-splitting *axé* music.

Shopping

Alagoas is rich in artisanal traditions, and Maceió is a great place to pick up well-made local crafts. The city is especially famous for its *rendas,* or lacework, and specifically for *filé,* a style that bears a resemblance to fish netting (*filé* means net) and that is similar to crochet. Often dyed in tropical colors, *filé* items range from towels and tablecloths to blouses and skirts that possess a definite hippie-chicness. You can view a traditional community of *rendeiras* at work at the **Núcleo Artesanal do Pontal da Barra,** on the shores of the Lagoa (8 A.M.–6 P.M. daily). Over 200 shops and ateliers sell well-made wares at very good prices.

Other places to check for regional handicrafts are the **Armazém do Sebrae** (Av. da Paz 878, Jaraguá, tel. 82/3223-8200, 9 A.M.–6 P.M. Mon.–Fri., 9 A.M.–2 P.M. Sat.) and the **Mercado do Artesenato da Pajuçara** (Rua Melo Morais 617, Levada, 8 A.M.–6 P.M. Mon.–Sat., 8 A.M.–noon Sun.), both of which have a wider sampling of *artesanato* from all over the state. Enticing finds include wood carvings, ceramics, and unusual brightly colored baskets, woven from coconut fibers, which are dyed and decorated with intricate geometric patterns. The main mall in town is **Shopping Iguatemi** (Av. Gustavo Paiva 2990, Mangabeiras, tel. 82/2126-1010, www.iguatemimaceio.com.br, 10 A.M.–10 P.M. Mon.–Sat., 3–9 P.M. Sun.), behind Jatiúca.

Accommodations

There's not really any compelling reason to stay in Centro, which has only a few budget hotels. You'll find a considerable array of both standard and luxury options in the beach neighborhoods of Pajuçara, Ponta Verde, and Jatiúca.

R$50-100

The cheapest beds to be had in Maceió's chicest hood of Ponta Verde can be found at the **Albergue da Juventude Algamar** (Rua Prefeito Abdon Arroxelas 327, Ponta Verde, tel. 82/3231-2246, alag@superig.com.br, R$48–55 d). Occupying a fetching house on a quiet little street only two blocks from the beach, this friendly hostel's small, pastel-painted dorm rooms are a backpacker's bargain at only R$25–36 per person. Prices for double rooms increase by 50 percent between December and February. Modern conveniences include a laundry room and communal kitchen.

It's only a 20-minute bus ride up north along the *orla* to ◖ **Pousada Cavalo Marinho** (Rua da Praia 55, Riacho Doce, tel. 82/3355-1247, www.pousadacavalomarinho.com, R$45–110 d), where you'll feel hours away from civilization. Facing onto pretty Riacho Doce beach, where major traffic consists of fisherfolk unloading their catch, this rustic *pousada* gives off a summery beach-house vibe that is very conducive to relaxation. Within the vicinity are simple bars and restaurants with good local cuisine.

R$100-200

The only decent budget *pousada* in town that has the privilege of being right on the beach is **Pousada Cais da Praia** (Av. Álvaro Otacílio 4353, Jatiúca, tel. 82/2121-3636, www.caisdapraia.com.br, R$95–145 d). From the outside, the brick boxlike exterior seems out of place on a tropical beach, but the bright rooms, all of which have sea views, are clean and modern, with air-conditioning and free

wireless Internet connection. Outside, beneath swaying palms is a cool blue pool surrounded by shrubbery.

Housed inside a square, pistachio-colored, two-story building, **Pousada Pérolas do Mar** (Rua Cônego Antônio Firmino Vasconcelos 68, Jatiúca, tel. 82/3235-2220, www.pousadaperolasdomar.com.br, R$99–120 d) scores points for the mod design of its 18 simple, comfortable rooms (with and without sea views) and cool little café in tones of ebony and avocado. **Hotel Praia Bonita** (Av. Dr. Antônio Gouveia 943, Pajuçara, tel. 82/2121-3700, www.praiabonita.com.br, R$179–199 d) is a refreshingly styling place with a handsome exterior, a glossy marble lobby, and large bright rooms with blond wood fixtures that conjure up an Ikea showroom. Rooms with sea views are more expensive.

OVER R$300

After undergoing a major facelift in 2007, **San Marino Suite** (Rua Dr. Noel Nutels 437, Ponta Verde, tel. 82/2121-9000, www.sanmarinosuite.com.br, R$290–340 d) is looking good and feeling quite comfortable. The sizable rooms have been repainted in soothing colors, and lighting is subtle. Flatscreen TVs, air-conditioning, and gorgeous designer bathrooms contrast nicely with the regional pottery and vases of tropical flowers that add a welcome dose of personality.

Inaugurated in 2007, ◖ **Hotel Brisa Tower** (Av. Álvaro Otacílio 4201, Jatiúca, tel. 82/2122-4000, www.hotelbrisatower.com.br, R$454–495 d) is Maceió's first designer hotel, and it is quite a stunner. The exterior is an angled mass of mirrored towers that wouldn't be out of place in midtown Manhattan. Inside, everything is sleek and minimalist without being cold or cliché. The sleek **La Pasta Gialla** restaurant serves up the finest Italian food in town. Designed by local decorators, the rooms—all with gorgeous sea views—are exceptionally stylish.

Food

Maceió is the meeting point of two major culinary influences—the sea and the Sertão. A legacy of the fishing communities that line the coast is the abundance of lobster, shrimp and crabs (both fresh and saltwater) along with fish such as *dourado, cavala,* and *beijupira,* traditionally served with rice and *pirão* (a puree made with manioc flour). Meanwhile, a source of revenue for many families is *sururu,* a little mollusk harvested from the mud surrounding freshwater lagoons such as Lagoa de Mundaú. You'll find *sururu* everywhere (it is believed to be an aphrodisiac) in forms ranging from the chowder-like *caldo de sururu* served in bars to entrées such as *sururu de capote,* in which it's cooked in its shell along with tomatoes, peppers, and garlic (not unlike French mussels). From the hot and barren Sertão comes a predilection for *carne-de-sol,* prepared in a variety of manners, usually with fried or pureed manioc. Finally, don't leave town without trying the local version of a crêpe. Made from crunchy white manioc flour (not tapioca) mixed with grated coconut, *tapiocas* are cooked on hot plates and stuffed with a variety of fillings, both sweet and savory. Popular fillings include *carne-de-sol, coalho* cheese, and guava jelly. You'll find *tapioqueiras* (the women who make them) along the beaches of Pajuçara, Ponto Verde, and Jatiúca.

CAFÉS AND SNACKS

For a sweet heat antidote, head to **Sorvete Bali** (Av. Dr. Antônio de Gouveia 481, Pajuçara, tel. 82/3231-8833, www.sorvetesbali.com.br), with locations on the beaches of Ponta Verde as well as Pajuçara. The 70 flavors include fruits from the Northeast and North, such as *bacuri, murici, graviola, jaca,* and *sapoti* as well as exotica such as *caipirinha, milho verde* (corn), papaya with cassis, and honey with pollen (made from regional honey).

BRAZILIAN

Some of the best *carne-de-sol* in town can be savored at **Carne de Sol do Picuí** (Av. da Paz 1140, Jaraguá, tel. 82/3223-5313, www.picui.com.br, 11 A.M.–11 P.M. Mon.–Sat., 11 A.M.–9 P.M. Sun., R$20–30), where the chef is constantly searching for ways to make the meat as tender as possible (one trick is to cure it in the early morning rays of the sun). Seven types of *carne-de-sol* are served here, from the classic filet mignon and *picanha* (rump steak) to more unorthodox buffalo and ostrich. Traditional accompaniments include *feijão tropeiro* and grilled *coalho* cheese. The *sorvete de rapadura,* made with caramelized sugarcane, provides the perfect ending to any meal.

■ **Irmãs Rocha** (Rua Comandante José Pontes Magalhães 222, Jatiúca, tel. 82/3325-9080, 11:30 A.M.–11:30 P.M. Tues.–Sun., R$22–32) is named after the four Rocha sisters who, between them, know pretty much everything about Alagoan cuisine. For a best-of sampling, start off with the *combinado de petiscos,* which offers tastes of the ocean, the lagoon's mangroves, and the Sertão. The interior, decked out like a typical *casa do Sertão,* comes equipped with swinging hammocks that are ideal for a post-meal siesta. For fish and seafood, try the simple, but welcoming **O Peixarão** (Av. Dr. Júlio Marques Luz 50, Jatiúca, tel. 82/3325-7011, www.opeixarao.com.br, 11 A.M.–11 P.M. daily, R$18–28), which serves up very tasty fresh fish and seafood accompanied by rice and *pirão*. The original O Peixarão is on the shores of the Lagoa Mundaú (Av. Alípio Barbosa da Silva 532, Pontal da Barra, tel. 82/3351-9090, 11 A.M.–5 P.M. Sun.–Thurs., 11 A.M.–11 P.M. Tues.–Sun.). The house specialty, *peixarão,* is a an aromatic stew of fish cooked in a sauce of shrimp and coconut milk.

INTERNATIONAL

While Alagoan cuisine is hardly humdrum, even more exotic is the Japanese-tinged Peruvian fare served at ■ **Wanchako** (Rua São Francisco de Assis 93, Jatiúca, tel. 82/3377-6024, www.wanchako.com.br, noon–4 P.M., and 7–11:30 P.M. Mon.–Sat., R$30–40). Despite being neighbors, Peruvian fare is hard to come by in Brazil. This soothingly attractive restaurant corrects this culinary lapse with a tantalizing menu that takes advantage of the local abundance of fresh fish and seafood. There are ceviches galore—the lime-marinated seafood is ideally refreshing in the hot climate—as well as crunchy coconut shrimp with tangerine salsa, and grilled fish with green risotto and *aguaymanto* (an Andean fruit) jelly. For dessert, the chilled *graviola* torte is irresistible. An equally refined dining experience can be had at **Lua Cheia** (Rua General França Albuquerque 250, Garça Torta, tel. 82/3355-1186, 6–11 P.M. Wed.–Fri., noon–midnight Sat., noon–5 P.M. Sun., R$20–35). The tables at this charming French restaurant are dispersed among the terrace of a house overlooking the pretty Praia da Garça Torta; the ideal setting to savor dishes such as whiskey-flambéed shrimp in saffron sauce.

Information and Services

There are **tourist offices** on Praia de Pajuçara (Av. Dr. Antônio Gouveia, 8 A.M.–2 P.M. Mon.–Fri., tel. 82/3315-5700) as well as at the *rodoviária* (8 A.M.–11 P.M. daily) and the airport (8 A.M.–11 P.M. daily). SETUR (Rua Boa Vista 453, Centro, tel. 82/3315-5703) is the state tourist office for Alagoas. You can also log on to www.maceiotur.com.br (in Portuguese), and www.maceioturismo.com.br and www.turismo.al.gov.br, both with awkwardly translated English pages.

In Centro, you can withdraw cash at the ATMs of Banco do Brasil and HSBC, both located near the Instituto Histórico on Rua do Livramento. You'll also find ATMs at Shopping Iguatemi. The main post office is also in Centro (Rua João Pessoa 57). For Internet access, try **Monkey** (Ponta Verde Center, Av. Engenheiro Mário Gusmão 513, Ponta Verde, tel. 82/3357-8041, 9 A.M.–midnight Mon.–Thurs., 9 A.M.–3 A.M. Fri.–Sat., noon–3 A.M. Sun.) and Shopping Iguatemi.

CITY TOURS

Both **Maceió Turismo** (Rua Firmínio de Vasconcelos 685, Pajuçara, tel. 82/3231-0843, www.maceioturismo.com.br) and **Jaraguá Turismo** (Rua Jangadeiros Alagoanos 999, Pajuçara, tel. 82/3337-2780, www.jaraguaturismo.com.br) offers city tours as well as excursions to surrounding beaches north and south of the city.

Getting There and Around

Maceió is connected by air to most major Brazilian cities, including São Paulo, Salvador, and Recife. The **Aeroporto Zumbi dos Palmares** (BR-104 Km 91, tel. 82/3214-4000) is on the outskirts of town. A taxi into the Centro will cost around R$50–60. Much closer is the *rodoviária* (Av. Leste-Oueste, Feitosa, tel. 82/3221-4615), where you can catch buses for points up and down the coast as well as to Recife (4 hours) and Salvador (8 hours). From the *rodoviária* there is also no shortage of municipal buses to Centro and the beaches of Pajuçara, Ponto Verde, Jatiúca, and others further north. The Estação Ferroviária (train station) in Centro is the departure point for local buses going south to Praia do Francês and Marechal Deodoro.

Maceió and the surrounding coastline are very well served by bus. However, if you want to do some beach-hopping without being a slave to bus schedules, you can rent a car at **Avis** (Rua José Pontes Magalhães 211, Jatiúca, tel. 82/3355-2235, www.avis.com.br) or **Hertz** (Aeroporto Zumbi dos Palmares, tel. 82/3342-0033, www.hertz.com.br). Try to stay clear of Centro with a car, since it gets clogged up with traffic.

SOUTH OF MACEIÓ

The beaches south of Maceió along the AL-101 are close enough to be almost suburban, as is the case of the famous Praia do Francês, the most famous beach resort in Alagoas. However, only a few extra kilometers brings you to more deserted sands. For a dose of colonial charm, visit the languorous and deliciously untouristy town of Marechal Deodoro, the first capital of Alagoas.

Praia do Francês

Around 22 kilometers (14 miles) south of Maceió, Praia do Francês gained nationwide fame in the '80s for its white sands, hypnotic blue-green seas, and Tahiti-worthy coconut palms. A major tourist mecca, Praia do Francês gets crowded in the summer and on weekends, when its beachside bars and restaurants are stuffed to the gills with day-tripping Maceioenses (many whom have vacation houses in the vicinity) and sun worshippers from all over Brazil. While the rough waves at the southern end are the fiefdom of surfers (and the site of international competitions), the calm waters protected by coral reefs are popular with families and enthusiasts of water sports such as sailing, jet-skiing, and banana boating.

ACCOMMODATIONS AND FOOD

Although you can easily commute to Praia do Francês in a day trip from Maceió, there are a fair number of reasonably priced hotel options should you want to stick around for a couple of days. **Capitães de Areia** (Rio Vermelho 13, tel. 82/3260-1477, www.capitaesdeareia.com.br, R$80–140 d) is a cheery *pousada* operated by a couple of recent transplants from São Paulo who were so seduced by Praia do Francês that they decided to move here. The clean, simple rooms are livened up by bursts of color, and have small verandas overlooking a swimming pool. For housekeeping accommodations, the modern but very pleasant condo-like **Residenza Casa Del Sole** (Rua São Pedro 699, tel. 82/3260-1870, www.residenzacasadelsole.com, R$130–140 d) is ideal. The pretty one- and two-bedroom apartments, featuring kitchens and living rooms, are nicely decorated with local art. Bright tropical colors reign, as do natural fibers and bamboo. There is a large pool and an attractive reception and breakfast area.

Aside from beach *barracas,* a good place for fish and seafood is the simple, but welcoming **Parada de Taipas** (Av. Caravelas, tel. 82/3260-1609, 11 A.M.–10 P.M. daily, R$15–25). The owner claims to be the inventor of a dish that's become synonymous with Praia do Francês—*chiclete de camarão* (which translates into "shrimp bubblegum"), in which shrimp is sautéed with garlic, green peppers, and tomato sauce, and then mixed with melted mozzarella and a sour cream (this is the gummy part). A bit more *soigné* is **Chez Patrick** (Rua Marisia 15, tel. 82/3260-1377, noon–10 P.M. Tues.–Sat., noon–5 P.M. Sun., open Mon. Dec.–Feb.,

R$20–32), an intimate little restaurant whose walls are hung with paintings by local artists. The menu takes advantage of the abundance of fresh fish and seafood to create bistro dishes with French flair.

GETTING THERE

Getting here from Maceió is easy—hourly municipal buses, and even more frequent minibuses and vans, leave from the *rodoviária* and stop in front of Maceió's old train station, behind the harbor.

Marechal Deodoro

Alagoas's first capital, this atmospheric colonial town, 28 kilometers (17 miles) south of Maceió, is immaculately preserved (in 2006 it was declared a National Heritage Site) and definitely worth a day trip. Originally named Vila Madalena de Sumaúna, the town was founded in 1611, on the shores of the Lagoa Manguaba, as a defensive outpost to safeguard the colony's lucrative *pau brasil* (brazilwood) trade from marauding pirates and bandits. Its current name came about in 1939, in honor of homegrown son Marechal Manuel Deodoro da Fonseca (1827–1892). A trained soldier, Deodoro not only staged Brazil's first military coup—supplanting Emperor Dom Pedro II and officially proclaiming Brazil a republic—but also became the nation's first president in 1889. His disastrous tenure proved an inauspicious start to Brazil's republican era; after unsuccessfully dissolving Congress, and declaring a state of siege, Deodoro resigned after only two years in power.

SIGHTS

Marechal Deodoro is quite small, but you can easily spend a couple of hours ambling around its lazy, cobblestoned streets and ogling its pretty pastel houses and colonial churches. You'll find the most splendid architecture on the elegant Praça Comendador Firmo Lopes, where you'll see the **Igreja de Santa Maria Magdalena,** an imposing, mid-18th-century church, which sits adjacent to the late-17th-century **Convento de São Francisco.** Part of the convent's deliciously tranquil interior houses the **Museu de Arte Sacra** (tel. 82/3263-1623, 8 A.M.–5 P.M. daily, R$2), featuring religious objects and icons along with a rich collection of expressively carved, exquisitely painted wooden saints. The other museum in town is the **Casa do Marechal Deodoro** (Rua Marechal Deodoro, tel. 82/3263-2608, 8 A.M.–5 P.M. daily). Located in the house in which Brazil's first president grew up, the personal knickknacks and period furniture on display are worth a quick glance.

SHOPPING
Marechal Deodoro is renowned for its *rendeiras* (lace-makers), whose delicate wares are on display (and sale) at the **Espaço Cultural Santa Maria Madalena da Lagoa do Sul** (Rua Marechal Deodoro, 8 A.M.–5 P.M. Mon.–Sat.).

GETTING THERE
You can easily combine Marechal Deodoro with a visit to Praia do Francês, only 6 kilometers (3.5 miles) away (municipal buses from Maceió pass through Praia do Francês on their way to Deodoro).

◖ Barra de São Miguel
Located 38 kilometers (24 miles) south of Maceio, Barra de São Miguel is another favorite Maceioense beach getaway. Aside from the more urbanized **Praia de Barra de São Miguel** (closest to the small town of Barra), there are a handful of more remote reef-sheltered alternatives within close proximity. During low tide, you can take a boat or kayak out to the reefs for some snorkeling. Stunning as these beaches are, they pale in comparison with **Praia do Gunga.** Often included in the top ranking of Brazil's most enchanting beaches, Gunga is around 5 kilometers (3 miles) from Barra's village. It's most easily accessible by a 20-minute boat or schooner trip from the village quay or from Praia de Barra (though you can also get there by buggy). The beach consists of an impossibly white stretch of sand shaded by whispering palms (the land behind it consists of a vast coconut farm) that is bathed on one side by a warm turquoise sea, and on the other, by

the equally bath-like waters of the freshwater Lagoa do Roteiro. Gunga's fame means it gets packed with excursions from Maceió, particularly during holidays. However, if you walk a little, you'll be able to find a private chunk of paradise for yourself.

ACCOMMODATIONS AND FOOD
Strangely enough, many Alagoan beach resorts exhibit a fondness for brick as a construction material in *pousadas.* Located on a quiet little street, **Pousada Barra Sol** (Rua Con. Osman de Carvalho, www.pousadabarrasol.com, R$120–150 d) is no exception. However, natural woods, plants, and colorful accents add a softening effect. Tidy rooms are kept cool due to stone floors. The decorative scheme includes bamboo furniture and sherbet-toned walls. Another brick affair just off the beach is **Lua Pousada** (Av. Moema Cavalcante 385, tel. 82/3272-1359, www.luapousada.com.br, R$75–140 d). If anything, the beige-colored bricks are even more omnipresent. However, there is also plenty of shrubbery and a nice attempt to decorate by integrating local objects such as woven baskets and ceramic bowls. Here too, rooms are basic, but spotless, and there is a pool.

Aside from *lanchonetes* and *barracas,* there aren't an overwhelming number of eating options in Barra de São Miguel, particularly in off-season. With outdoor tables overlooking the sea, **Bar e Restaurante do Tio** (Praça São Pedro, tel. 82/3272-1152, 9 A.M.–5 P.M. daily, closed on Mon. off-season, R$15–25), is a relaxing place to indulge in local fish and seafood supplied by local fisherfolk. Aside from the more obvious shrimp and fish, try the *massunim* (a smaller version of mussel) and the *sururu* omelette.

INFORMATION
For information about Barra, you can check out the municipal website (www.barradesaomiguel-al.com.br), which, though only in Portuguese, has complete restaurant and hotel listings. For cash, the Banco do Brasil in the village center accepts international ATM cards.

GETTING THERE

Numerous buses run hourly up and down the coast from Maceió's *rodoviária* to Barra de São Miguel, passing through Praia do Francês.

◖ Penedo

One of the most picturesque and interesting colonial towns of the Northeast, Penedo, situated 170 kilometers (106 miles) south of Maceió, sits dramatically atop a cliff overlooking Brazil's longest national river, the Rio São Francisco. The river, a source of livelihoods and legends—not to mention transportation—colors Penedo's rich culture, and taking jaunts up and down its deep blue waters makes for a wonderful outing. The town itself, which is overlooked by most tourists, is an architectural jewel with a handful of majestic baroque churches and colonial buildings in faded shades of rose, blue, and saffron. But Penedo is far from being a living museum. Despite its languid pace, it can get busy around the market, a daily affair whose transactions are fascinating to watch as you down a shot of herb-infused *cachaça* at a bar.

Penedo was founded in the mid-1500s as a defensive outpost on the Rio São Francisco. The Portuguese weren't happy with French traders' use of the river to transport valuable *pau brasil* wood, nor were they pleased with the local Caeté Indians who had killed (and supposedly eaten) Brazil's first bishop, who bore the appetizing name of Sardinha (sardine). In 1637, the town was conquered by invading Dutch troops as part of a plan to stake out a colony in the Brazilian Northeast. The Dutch erected an imposing fortress before being expelled in 1645. In 1660, the first Franciscan monks arrived in Penedo and kicked off a baroque building frenzy of ornate churches, convents, and chapels along with an educational tradition that left its mark on the town's social and cultural traditions for centuries to come.

SIGHTS

Penedo possesses an rich collection of colonial architecture, including a handful of magnificent baroque churches. Construction of the **Igreja de Nossa Senhora da Corrente** (Praça 12 de Abril, 8 A.M.–5 P.M. Tues.–Sat., 8 A.M.–4 P.M. Sun.) began in 1764, but wasn't completed until the late 19th century. It's considered a masterpiece of Brazilian rococo; there are some strikingly beautiful blue-and-white *azulejo* panels, but most impressive is the main altar, a sumptuous feast of burnished gold that contrasts with pale blue and pink marble trompe l'oeil. Next to it is an alcove where slaves were hidden before escaping to freedom via a secret passageway (Penedo was an abolitionist hothouse).

Older still is the impressive complex consisting of the **Igreja de Nossa Senhora dos Anjos** and the **Convento de São Francisco** (Praça Rui Barbosa, tel. 82/3551-2279, 8–11:30 A.M. and 2–5 P.M. Tues.–Fri., 8–11 A.M. Sat.–Sun.), built between the 17th and 18th centuries on the site of the Dutch Forte Nassau, and inhabited by Penedo's Franciscans. The austere facade hardly prepares you for the interior's baroque exuberance, which features gold leaf galore and lots of delicious trompe l'oeil as well as a palmy cloister. A small museum with antique furnishings traces the history of the Franciscan order. Built in 1758, the recently restored **Igreja de São Gonçalo Garcia dos Homens Pardos** is striking for its neo-gothic belltowers and its limestone facade.

A couple of small museums are worth taking a look at. The **Casa de Penedo** (Rua João Pessoa 126, tel. 82/3551-2008, 8 A.M.–noon and 2–6 P.M. Tues.–Sun., R$2) traces the history of the town via an interesting collection of photographs and artifacts, many belonging to Penedo's most illustrious families. The **Museu do Paço Imperial** (Praça 12 de Abril 9, tel. 82/3551-2498, 11 A.M.–5 P.M. Tues.–Sat., 8 A.M.–noon Sun., R$3) is located in an 18th-century mansion that earned its name, the Paço Imperial, when Dom Pedro II stayed here during an 1859 visit. Today it houses a collection of 17th- and 18th-century religious art as well as furniture and decorative objects.

ENTERTAINMENT AND EVENTS

Held on the second Sunday in January, the **Festa do Bom Jesus dos Navegantes** is a splendid fluvial procession in which over 100 decorated

THE RIO SÃO FRANCISCO

Affectionately known as "Velho (Old) Chico" – Chico is the diminutive of Francisco – the São Francisco is to the Brazilian Northeast what the Mississippi is to the American South. At 2,800 kilometers (1,740 miles), it is Brazil's largest national river, flowing through five states: Alagoas, Sergipe, Pernambuco, Bahia, and Minas Gerais (where its source is). It is also somewhat of a geographical miracle – responsible for sustaining lives and livelihoods in what is otherwise one of the most brutally parched regions on the planet. In fact, due to recent irrigation projects, the Vale do São Francisco region is now Brazil's major pro-

ducer of tropical fruits as well as a fledging region of vineyards.

Although the paddlewheel steamboats that once navigated up and down the river have disappeared, you can still see dugout canoes whose bows are adorned with monstrous figureheads. Known as *carrancas*, the role of these fiercely gruesome wooden effigies is to provide safe passage by scaring off the river creatures believed to inhabit the river's depths. Although authentic *carrancas* are hard to come across, you can pick up reproductions in Penedo to help keep evil spirits at bay in your home.

boats take to the river accompanying a sculpted effigy of Bom Jesus. The event is the highlight of several days of merrymaking that includes performances of traditional dance and music.

SPORTS AND RECREATION

To get a feel for the mighty Rio São Francisco, hop a boat to the towns of **Neópolis** or **Santo do São Francisco** on the Sergipe side of the river. Although there isn't anything much to see, you can have a drink, check out the local pottery made from riverbank clay, and take panoramic pictures of Penedo. For more of an adventure, head by bus or car, down to the little fishing village of **Piaçabuçu** (22 kilometers/14 miles away), located near the mouth of the river. From Piaçabuçu, by boat or dune buggy, you can reach the mouth of the river and the surrounding wild dune beaches of **Pontal do Peba. Delta 1** (Praça Prof. Ronulfo Victor de Araújo, tel. 82/3552-1226) runs three-hour excursions for around R$30 per person. If you want to go solo, you can also easily find boats for hire at Piaçabuçu's riverside dock.

ACCOMMODATIONS AND FOOD

The small and familial **Pousada Colonial** (Praça 12 de Abril 21, tel. 82/3551-2355, R$80 d) is a simple, but atmospheric guest house occupying a whitewashed colonial building. Rooms

sport dark wood floors and antique furnishings. Although they are smaller, request a room whose wooden shutters open to offer lovely views of the river framed by flamboyant trees. An unsightly modern blemish on the town's otherwise colonial skyline, the **Hotel São Francisco** (Av. Floriano Peixoto 237, tel. 82/3551-2273, www.hotelsaofrancisco.tur.br, R$108–180 d) is an early '60s attempt at luxury that is ugly from the outside, but quite spacious and comfortable on the inside. Rooms are well-appointed, air-conditioned, and offer fantastic views. There is a pool with lots of jazzy fountains and cascades, and a vast dining area where the daily breakfast spreads are very lavish.

Apart from being the most scenic eatery in town, **Forte da Rocheira** (Rua da Rocheira 2, tel. 82/3551-3273, 11 A.M.–4 P.M. Sun.–Thurs., 11 A.M.–4 P.M. and 6–10 P.M. Fri.–Sat., R$18–28)—built right into rocky cliffside overlooking the Rio São Francisco—is a fine place to stuff yourself on river fare such as tilapia in white wine sauce and the more exotic *jacaré* (caiman) cooked in palm oil, lime juice, and grated coconut. For dessert, try the homemade caramel-flavored *doce de leite*.

INFORMATION AND SERVICES

The **tourist office** (Praça Barão de Penedo, tel. 82/3551-2727, 8–11 A.M. and 2–5 P.M.

Mon.–Fri.) has maps of the town with all attractions. Banks with ATMs are located behind the riverfront.

GETTING THERE

To get to Penedo from Maceió, follow the coastal AL-101 south and then west from Piaçabuçu. **Real Alagoas** (tel. 82/3356-1027 in Maceió) operates several daily buses that will leave you right in the center of town.

NORTH OF MACEIÓ

The northern coast of Alagoas, much of it still undeveloped by tourism, dishes up some of Brazil's most paradisiacal beaches. Protected by coral reefs that are a snorkelers' delight, a large stretch of the coastline is actually a series of natural pools whose Caribbean blue waters are as placid as a lagoon's and as warm as a lulling bath. The blindingly white sands are as soft as sugar and are idyllically framed by a sea of coconut palms. Although settlements such as Barra de Santo Antônio and Maragogi have blossomed into small tourist resorts, for the most part, human encroachment upon nature rarely extends beyond simple little fishing villages. The string of beaches start right in Maceió itself, extending up the coast from Praia do Mirante da Sereia all the way to Alagoas's frontier with Pernambuco. Although frequent buses and collective minivans from Maceió journey up the coast, for the freedom of beach-hopping and exploring more remote spots off the beaten track, you might want to consider renting a car.

Barra de Santo Antônio

Around 40 kilometers (25 miles) north of Maceió, Barra de Santo Antônio is a pretty little fishing village. Founded by the Dutch in the 17th century, it has a smattering of colonial buildings and is also reputed for its lively Carnaval. However, its greatest lures are its natural attractions. Bisected by the Rio Santo Antônio, Barra is surrounded by stunning beaches and natural ocean pools. A five-minute ride to the other side of the river, by fishing boat or ferry (if you have a car), brings you to the Ilha da Croa, which is actually a narrow sandy peninsula dotted with natural pools. You can loll around in the warm clear blue water or take a boat to the nearby **Praia do Carro Quebrado**, a truly wild and gorgeous beach backed by sandy cliffs painted in shades that run from pale tan to deep ocher, whose name (Broken Car Beach) is a testament to the difficulty of getting here by car (although you can take a dune buggy). Also close to Barra de Santo Antônio (and accessible by boat) is the **Praia de Tabuba,** known for its exceptionally crystalline waters.

ACCOMMODATIONS AND FOOD

Among the few accommodations around, the best place to stay is the Swiss-run **Pousada Arco-Íris** (Loteamento Tabuba, tel. 82/3291-1250, www.tabuba.tk, R$75–150 d), a sprawling, breezy, very well-kept guesthouse nestled in a shock of greenery, right off Praia de Tabuba. The attractive rooms are cool and comfortable, and the restaurant serves up tasty local and international fare. Kayaks, mountain bikes, and Windsurfers are all available for rent.

Other eating options consist of basic seafood restaurants and beach *barracas*. In town, **Estrela Azul** (tel. 82/3291-1599) is a good choice that is particularly reputed for its shrimp dishes. During the day both Praia do Carro Quebrado and Ilha da Croa have rustic *barracas* that serve icy and beer along with the fresh catch of the day (be forewarned that none have bathrooms). Particularly friendly is *Bar do Piú* on Ilha da Croa, where you can feast on a plate of fresh butter fried shrimp sauteed in onions for a mere R$15.

GETTING THERE

By bus, both **Transporte Tropical** (tel. 82/3221-1694) and **Real Alagoas** (tel. 82/3326-7332) operate buses to Barra de Santo Antônio from Maceió. By car, follow the AL-101 north.

C São Miguel dos Milagres

This tranquil little fishing village, 110 kilometers (68 miles) north of Maceió, is one of

ZUMBI DO PALMARES AND *QUILOMBOS*

During the long period of slavery in Brazil, tales abound of the many slaves who succeeded in escaping into remote regions of the unexplored interior, where they formed their own autonomous and self-sufficient communities known as *quilombos*. The most famous of these *quilombos* was Palmares, founded around 1600, in the hills 70 kilometers north of Maceió. It was here that Zumbi was born in 1655. The grandson of a Congolese princess who was sold into slavery, Zumbi was kidnapped by Portuguese soldiers as a young boy. "Given" to a Jesuit missionary who baptized him Francisco, Zumbi studied Portuguese and Latin before escaping and returning to Palmares at the age of 15. By then, Palmares, together with surrounding *quilombos*, had formed a loose union known as the Republic of Palmares, which extended from the banks of the Rio São Francisco into Pernambuco. Boasting a total population of 30,000, this unofficial kingdom had became a shining symbol of slave resistance throughout Brazil. It had also become a dangerous symbol of subversion to the Portuguese colonial government and the plantation owners of the Northeast whose livelihood depended on slaves. They launched attacks on the *quilombos* – which were fortified like medieval cities featuring defenses constructed from palm thatch and thorn trees instead of stones –

but to little avail, especially with Zumbi on the scene.

Brave and intelligent, by his early 20s, Zumbi had earned a reputation as an invincible warrior, leading brilliant counteroffensives that drove back Portuguese forces on numerous occasions. By 1680, he had became leader of the Republic of Palmares and was viewed by colonial settlers as invincible. Even when, after 94 years of successful resistance, Palmares finally succumbed to Portuguese forces in 1694, a wounded Zumbi fled and went into hiding. He was captured the following year only after a former companion ratted him out to the authorities, who promptly arrested him. Decapitated, his head was sent to Recife and exhibited on a stake in a public square as proof that Zumbi wasn't immortal. The plan backfired – Zumbi became a poster child for abolitionists and a source of black pride.

Long after the end of slavery, *quilombos* continued to exist in isolation, consequently preserving centuries-old African traditions. Today, there are close to 1,000 communities throughout Brazil. Meanwhile, Zumbi has become a national hero for Afro-Brazilians and a symbol of black freedom in a country where racism is still a serious issue. The day of his death (November 20) is commemorated as a national holiday known as **Dia da Consciência Negra** (Black Consciousness Day).

Alagoas's oldest settlements, with a whitewashed colonial church and a charming cluster of historic houses in faded pastel hues, completely surrounded by thick palm forests. In fact, this whole stretch of coastline is rife with coconut plantations (a bonus is that sweet, refreshing *água de coco* is cheaper and more plentiful than water). Aside from its utterly relaxing vibe, the beaches in the vicinity of São Miguel—among them Toque, Porto da Rua, Tatuamnunha, Patacho, Lages, and Porto de Pedras—are stunners, and their reef-protected waters (the reefs themselves can be reached by boat) are flooded with a carnival of colorful fish. While São Miguel remains deliciously

untrampled by tourism, a number of extremely charming and quite sophisticated *pousadas* have opened up on remote beaches, making this an ideal destination for a getaway with style.

ACCOMMODATIONS AND FOOD

São Miguel's accommodation offerings are truly some of the most attractive on the whole Northeast coast (with fine restaurants to boot). In most cases, to get to these *pousadas*—located amidst tiny fishing villages or on secluded beaches—you'll need a car, although if you call ahead, staff will pick you up in São Miguel or even in Maceió.

The most luxurious option on this coast is

PERNAMBUCO AND ALAGOAS

© LUÍS EDUARDO VAZ/EMBRATUR

São Miguel dos Milagres

the gorgeously secluded **Pousada do Toque** (Rua Felisberto de Ataíde, Praia do Toque, tel. 82/3295-1127, www.pousadadotoque.com.br, R$400–960 d), located on the Praia do Toque, only 2 kilometers (1.2 miles) from São Miguel. Set amidst an Edenic garden right off the deserted beach, the hotel features solar-energized cabanas, in various degrees of eco-chic, outfitted with fine Italian linens, DVD players, and even Jacuzzis. The philosophy is to make guests feel utterly relaxed, and at home, by offering them privacy as well as the run of the sprawling estate, which features swimming pools, a tennis court, a wine cellar, bar, and plenty of decks and verandas for lounging. The gourmet restaurant (dinner is included in the rate) serves up divine creations with fresh produce harvested from the sea as well as the on-site organic garden.

Another 2 kilometers (1.2 miles) up the coast, near the pretty little fishing village of Porto da Rua, **Pousada Côté Sud** (Praia do Porta da Rua, tel. 82/3295-1283, www.pousadacotesud.com.br, R$175–295 d) is owned by a Belgian couple (former shoemakers), who

brought their refined sense of craftsmanship to the design of this beautiful beachside guesthouse. Accommodations are in cool bungalows, finished and decorated by local artisans, and awash in natural fibers and earthy tones. The lush grounds include an elevated pool with a stunning view of the beach and a romantic gourmet restaurant that traffics in both French and local cuisine (dinner is included in the rate). Service is highly attentive. The owners can arrange a variety of outings, ranging from horseback riding and snorkeling to shrimp and crab fishing (after which you can have your catch cooked for you). To keep the peace, children under 13 aren't allowed.

Around 8 kilometers (5 miles) from Barra de São Miguel, on the deserted sands of Praia do Lage, **Pousada Aldeia Beijupirá** (Praia do Lage, tel. 82/3298-6549, www.aldeiabeijupira.com.br, R$285–480 d) couldn't be more removed from civilization if it tried. In fact, the back-to-nature *pousada* is modeled after a local indigenous village. Guests inhabit palm-thatched chalets (known as *malocas*) whose cool bleached interiors are soothingly minimalist.

Accoutrements range from light fixtures made from shrimp nets to decorative sea shells in the beautiful bathrooms (a little less aboriginal are the home theaters and Jacuzzis). The romance factor is upped by the hotel's no-kids-under-16 policy. Simpler and more affordable, the small, family-run **Pousada Costa das Pedras** (Rua Dr. Fernando Lima 28, Porto de Pedras, tel. 82/3298-1176, www.costadaspedras.com.br, R$70–130 d) is a very pretty and welcoming guesthouse in the colonial fishing village of Porto de Pedras, 15 kilometers (9 miles) north of São Miguel. The cozy rooms—three doubles, a triple, and a quadruple—are furnished with locally embroidered lace and brightly woven bedspreads and carpets. The upstairs apartment for two is larger and more posh. The flavorful home-cooked fare served in the restaurant is easily the best food in town. Located on the banks of the Rio Manguaba, Porto de Pedras offers the possibility of trips upriver for freshwater swimming and exploration of the mangroves as well as bathing and snorkeling on the beach. The town's hilltop lighthouse offers wonderful views of the surrounding coast.

INFORMATION
For information about São Miguel and surrounding beaches, log on to the bilingual site www.saomigueldosmilagres.net, which has extensive listings and mesmerizing photos.

GETTING THERE
By bus, both **Transporte Tropical** (tel. 82/3221-1694) and **Real Alagoas** (tel. 82/3356-1324) operate buses from Maceió. By car, follow the AL-101 north to Usina Santo Antônio and then turn off onto the AL-435.

Maragogi
Halfway between Maceió and Recife (130 kilometers/81 miles from both), Maragogi is the most popular beach destination in Alagoas (excluding the capital). The village sits between the banks of the Rio Maragogi and an unbelievably turquoise sea. The beach is a pretty lively place, crammed with hotels, restaurants, bars, and boutiques selling local handicrafts, but those in search of peace and tranquility need merely venture a few kilometers to the more deserted beaches of São Bento, Japaratinga, and Bitingui, to the south, or Barra Grande, Ponta de Manga, and Peroba to the north. Although they are accessible by car, bus, and collective minivans, you can also get to them by boat, dune buggy, on horseback, or even mountain bikes (the sand along these beaches is notoriously hard packed—which makes it a delight to stroll, ride, or pedal upon).

Part of the Costa dos Corais (Coral Coast), this coastal stretch is renowned for its immense ocean pools, framed by coral reefs, which can be reached by boat. In many places, during low-tide you can walk out far out towards the reefs. The most famous and fabulous of all the natural pools along Alagoas's coast are known as the Galés and are located off Maragogi. The entire coastal region is part of an environmentally protected area of reefs that extends for 135 kilometers (84 miles).

SPORTS AND RECREATION
Most of the regular excursions to the Galés last two hours and cost R$30 (R$70 if you plan to dive), but you can also hire your own private boat. The majority of outings are organized by beachfront restaurants such as **Ponto de Embarque** (Av. Beira Mar 327, tel. 82/3296-1400). **Explorer Diving and Adventure** (Miramar Maragogi Resort, tel. 82/9361-6449) offers diving lessons, rents equipment, and operates excursions. It also rents kayaks, banana boats, and Windsurfers.

ACCOMMODATIONS AND FOOD
In Maragogi itself, **Pousada Portal do Maragogi** (Praia do Maragogi, tel. 82/3296-2045, www.portaldomaragogi.com.br, R$140–190 d) is a fairly nice beachfront option. The *pousada* itself faces right onto the sand and has a cluster of palm thatched parasols beneath which you can swing away the day (at least part of it) in a hammock by the sea. Double, triple, and quadruple rooms are comfortable and modern, with large beds and air-conditioning. For more seclusion, a great choice

is the **Bitingui Praia Hotel** (Praia de Bitingui, tel. 82/3297-1000, R$188–218d), which sits upon the largely deserted Praia de Bitingui (12 kilometers/7.5 miles) south of Maragogi), one of the loveliest beaches in the area. Nestled amidst a coconut grove, this attractively appointed, medium-sized beach hotel has comfortable apartments and individual chalets, as well as a large pool. The hotel organizes a host of activities from buggy, horseback, and kayak outings to diving trips. Rates include dinner.

To sink your teeth into fish and seafood, one of the better places in town is the laid-back restaurant **Gaivotas** (Av. Senador Rui Palmeira 800, Praia de Maragogi, tel. 82/3296-1195, 9 A.M.–5 P.M. Mon., 9 A.M.–11:30 P.M.

Tues.–Sun., R$20–32), whose owner (somewhat ironically) hails from the landlocked state of Minas Gerais.

INFORMATION

For information about Maragogi and the surrounding beaches log on to the bilingual site www.maragogi.tur.br or www.maragogionline.com (with an English page), both of which have listings, maps, and enticing photos.

GETTING THERE

By bus, both **Transporte Tropical** (tel. 82/3221-1694) and **Real Alagoas** (tel. 82/3356-1324) operate buses from Maceió. The trip takes 2.5 hours. By car, follow the AL-101 north.

THE NORTHEAST COAST

The 1,300-kilometer (800-mile) coastline that rises north from Pernambuco to the small state of Rio Grande do Norte, before sloping west like a sultry shoulder through the state of Ceará and continuing into the state of Maranhão, is practically one long, non-stop, utterly spectacular beach. However, one cannot confuse its endlessness with monotony. Beaches along this stretch of Northeast coast range from fine, white sands backed by rugged red cliffs to vast Saharan-like dunes where dune buggies (and dromedaries) reign supreme. An abundance of coral reefs mean that waves are often too puny for serious surfing. However, thrill seekers can navigate gigantic dunes on sandboards while snorkelers explore the clear blue pools that appear during low tide. Many beaches, such as the famously secluded Jericoacoara, are quite remote, and can only be reached after hours of four-wheeling through the dunes. Others, such as Pipa and Canoa Quebrada, have developed into charmingly sophisticated resorts, but without losing that palmy, hippie, flip-flop vibe. There are plenty of dunes to go around, but the biggest of all are located in the Parque Nacional dos Lençóis Maranhenses, a vast lunar landscape of stupendous 50-meter (165-foot) dunes dotted with thousands of tiny green oasis-like lakes. All in all, it's impossible not to unwind. Nonetheless, should you require a dose of city life, the modern capitals of Natal and Fortaleza offer (aside from impressive beaches), an appealing mixture of urban energy and laid-back northeastern hospitality, plenty of seafood, and infectious *forró* music.

HIGHLIGHTS

Dune Buggying in Natal: Natal is famed for its coastline of quasi Saharan sand dunes, and the best way to navigate them is by dune buggy (page 504).

Praia da Pipa: Charming hotels, gourmet restaurants, and chic boutiques haven't spoiled the laid-back vibe or idyllic beauty of one of the most famous dolphin-studded beaches on Brazil's northeastern coast (page 511).

Canoa Quebrada: This hip beach town combines a mellow atmosphere with the high drama of crumbling red cliffs, immense white dunes, and luminous blue waters (page 527).

Jericoacoara: Remote and unspoiled Jericoacoara is more than just one of the planet's most revered and worshipped beaches – it's an otherworldly experience (page 529).

Projeto Reviver (Praia Grande) in São Luís: Crammed with pastel-colored palaces and pulsing with reggae and pounding drums, São Luís's historic center is one of the most atmospheric colonial ensembles in Brazil (page 535).

Lençóis Maranhenses: One of Brazil's most spectacular national parks features immense snow-white dunes with valleys that contain jade-green lagoons (page 543).

LOOK FOR ◖◗ TO FIND RECOMMENDED SIGHTS, ACTIVITIES, DINING, AND LODGING.

A transition state between the sun-baked aridness of the Northeast and the rainy, lushness of the Amazon rainforest, Maranhão's island capital of São Luís is one of Brazil's oldest and most fascinating cities. Often overlooked by tourists, São Luís possesses a striking colonial center awash in mansions and palaces whose facades are covered in ornately patterned Portuguese *azulejos* (ceramic tiles). The local culture, with its renowned reggae scene and *tambor de crioula* drumming and dances, was greatly influenced by the African slaves who came to work in the region's colonial sugar plantations. African elements are also visible in the fantastically colorful Bumba-Meu-Boi festivities that take place in June. Across the bay of São Marcos from São Luís, Maranhão's first capital, Alcântara, is a wonderfully atmospheric place. As you wander among its grand colonial mansions, in various states of decay, you'll be struck by how the town is being invaded by the dense tropical forest that surrounds it.

THE NORTHEAST COAST

PLANNING YOUR TIME

With the exception of São Luís, the main draw of the Northeast coast is its beaches. So how you plan your time really depends on whether you're restless and want to beach hop, or would rather just choose one or two idyllic getaways where you can veg out. Rio Grande do Norte is a small state. By basing yourself in Natal, you can very easily spend 5–7 days exploring the coastline north and south of the city, while stopping for a couple of days at Praia da Pipa. Sprawling Ceará deserves a little more time. If you avoid the tourist traps, Fortaleza, while not beautiful, is an interesting and vibrant city that warrants a day or two, and more if you want to do some day trips. You'll be disappointed if you don't stay over in Canoa Quebrada, and plan at least 4–5 days for Jericoacoara (it takes close to a day just to get there). Some people end up staying in "Jeri" for weeks. As for São Luís, three days is the minimum you'd want to stay. Having come so far, it would be a crime not to add another three days to explore the dunes and lagoons of the Lençóis Maranhenses. Traveling between Natal and Fortaleza is easy, and all of Ceará's beaches are quite accessible by bus and car (some of Rio Grande do Norte's are more difficult to access without wheels). São Luís is quite isolated. Bus service from other cities takes forever and plane fare is fairly steep. Adventurous souls with time on their hands (a week or two) can travel by Jeep (and, in parts, by dune buggy) up the entire coastline, from Natal to São Luís.

Due to its proximity to the Equator, you'll find the Northeast coast hot year-round. Rio Grande do Norte and Ceará are notoriously sunny. Even during the so-called "rainy season," which generally occurs March–May—you're treated to quick downpours more than days of drizzle. Under the sway of the Amazon's climate, Maranhão is considerably wetter, particularly between January and May. If you want the beaches to yourself, avoid peak seasons of January, February, and July when both Rio Grande do Norte and Ceará are mobbed by Brazilian and international tourists.

HISTORY

Like Bahia and Pernambuco, this entire stretch of the Northeast coast was hotly contested by colonial powers in the 1500s, with the Portuguese battling the Dutch and French for control over the major colonial outposts of Natal, Fortaleza, and São Luís. The only Brazilian city that was actually founded by the French, São Luís was named in honor of French king Louis XIII. For their part, the Dutch succeeded in taking control of Natal and Fortaleza in the 1630s and São Luís briefly in the 1640s. Ultimately, however, the Portuguese persevered. Aside from São Luís, which prospered as the result of its important maritime port and vast sugar and cotton plantation, until well into the 19th century, these remote administrative capitals—and the isolated countryside surrounding them—remained sleepy and remote. Main economic activities revolved around fishing and limited agriculture, most notably sugar, cotton, and cashews. The parched Sertanejo interior of Rio Grande do Norte and Ceará proved propitious for little more than cattle raising. To this day, the region is one of the poorest and most affected by drought in Brazil. Years go by with little or no rainfall. In recent years, regional industries have made headway in Ceará and Maranhão. However, tourism has been the biggest source of the development boom that has transformed Natal and Fortaleza as sun worshippers from southern Brazil and western Europe flock to the region's incomparable beaches. While infrastructure and services have improved, the downside of development has been a flood of ugly high-rises in both cities and a problematic increase in child prostitution.

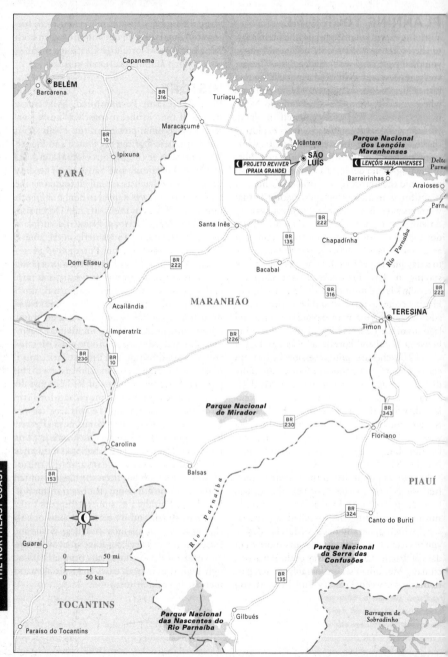

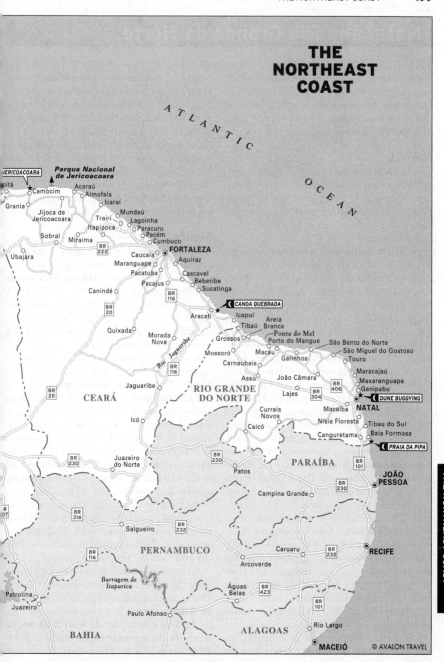

THE NORTHEAST COAST

ATLANTIC OCEAN

JERICOACOARA

Parque Nacional de Jericoacoara

pitá
Camocim
Acaraú
Almofala
Grania
Jijoca de Jericoacoara
Icaraí
Mundaú
Trairi
Lagoinha
Itapipoca
Paracuru
Sobral
Miraima
Pecém
Cumbuco
Ubajara
BR 222
FORTALEZA
Caucaia
Aquiraz
Maranguape
Pacatuba
Cascavel
Beberibe
Canindé
Pacajus
Sucatinga
BR 20
BR 116
CANOA QUEBRADA
Aracati
Icapuí
Areia Branca
Tibaú
Ponta do Mel
Quixada
Grossos
Porto do Mangue
São Bento do Norte
Morada Nova
Macau
São Miguel do Gostoso
Rio Jaguaribe
Mossoró
Galinhos
Touro
BR 116
Carnaubais
Maracajaú
Jaguaribe
Assú
João Câmara
Maxaranguape
RIO GRANDE DO NORTE
Lajes
BR 304
BR 406
Genipabu
CEARÁ
NATAL
DUNE BUGGYING
Icó
Currais Novos
Macaíba
Caicó
Nísia Floresta
Tibau do Sul
Baía Formosa
Canguretama
PRAIA DA PIPA
BR 20
BR 230
BR 230
Juazeiro do Norte
Patos
PARAÍBA
BR 101
JOÃO PESSOA
BR 230
BR 316
Campina Grande
Salgueiro
BR 232
PERNAMBUCO
Caruaru
BR 232
RECIFE
BR 116
Arcoverde
Águas Belas
BR 423
Barragem de Itaparica
BR 101
Petrolina
Paulo Afonso
ALAGOAS
Rio Largo
Juazeiro
BAHIA
MACEIÓ
© AVALON TRAVEL

Natal and Rio Grande do Norte

The tiny state of Rio Grande do Norte is known foremost for its vast sand dune beaches (and the dune buggies required to navigate them). In fact, it was only when the buggy came along that tourists came along as well to enjoy some of Brazil's wildest and unspoiled beaches.

NATAL

The main reason for visiting the small capital of Rio Grande do Norte is to take advantage of its endless amounts of sun and sand. In truth, Natal's beaches never stop. They just keep going for hundreds of kilometers in either direction.

In 1501, Portuguese navigator Amerigo Vespucci landed 32 kilometers (20 miles) north of Natal at the northeastern tip of South America (and the closest point to Europe from Brazil), a spot he christened Cabo São Roque. Despite this new discovery, for decades Portugal showed little interest in the sweeping coastline inhabited by the Potiguar tribe. But in 1597, annoyed by the growing *pau brasil* (brazilwood) trade between French pirates and the Potiguar, the Portuguese decided to get territorial. They proceeded to build the Forte dos Reis Magos, an imposing fortress that guarded the entrance to the Rio Potengi from the sea. Officially established on December 25, 1599, the village that rose up around the fort became known as Natal (Christmas). Once the French were expelled, subsequent Dutch invaders were defeated, and the aggressive Potiguar subdued, Natal settled down into its role as a small outpost. The presence of great sand dunes kept Rio Grande do Norte from enjoying the heady sugarcane riches of other northeastern colonial towns. Despite its coastline, for centuries the state's main source of revenue came from the cattle that were raised in the interior, but traded and shipped from Natal.

During World War II, Natal's strategic proximity to Western Europe and Africa led to the establishment of an American air base that became the Allies' military base for operations into North Africa. As a result, thousands of American pilots and soldiers flooded Natal's dunes, and Natalenses became the first Brazilians to be introduced to ketchup, bubble gum, and blue jeans. However, it wasn't until the latter 20th century that the growth of the salt and petroleum industries—Rio Grande do Norte is the largest salt producer in Brazil and has the biggest inland oil reserves in Brazil—coupled with nascent tourism, caused the city to grow in leaps and bounds, acquiring a modern skyline of high-rise condos and hotels.

Sights

What few historical sights Natal possesses are located in the *bairros* of Ribeira and Cidade Alta, which fan out from the **Forte dos Reis Magos** (Av. Presidente Café Filho, tel. 84/3502-1099, 8 A.M.–4:30 P.M. daily, R$3). The most impressive of the all too few vestiges of the past is the star-shaped fort itself. Poised majestically along a reef, it is separated from the tip of the city by a sandbar. Construction on the fort began on January 6, 1598—the feast day of the Reis Magos (Three Kings). Inside, the most important historical artifact on display is the Marco de Touros, a limestone cross engraved with the herald of the Portuguese king. The cross, originally planted in the village of São Miguel do Gostoso in 1501, symbolizes the first claim to Portuguese territory in Brazil. In 1962, it was transferred to the fort because villagers—who had come to view it as a miraculous object—had taken to chipping pieces off to make curative teas for ailing family members. The fort itself was built using a mixture of stone, sand, whale oil, and oyster shells. From its ramparts, the views of the city and coastline are quite stupendous.

A couple of leisurely hours is enough to explore the rest of what's left of historic Centro. The heart of the colonial city is **Praça André de Albuquerque.** It is flanked on one side by the 17th-century **Igreja Matriz de Nossa Senhora da Apresentação** (tel. 84/3615-2808, 4–6:30 P.M. Mon.–Sat., 6–10 A.M.

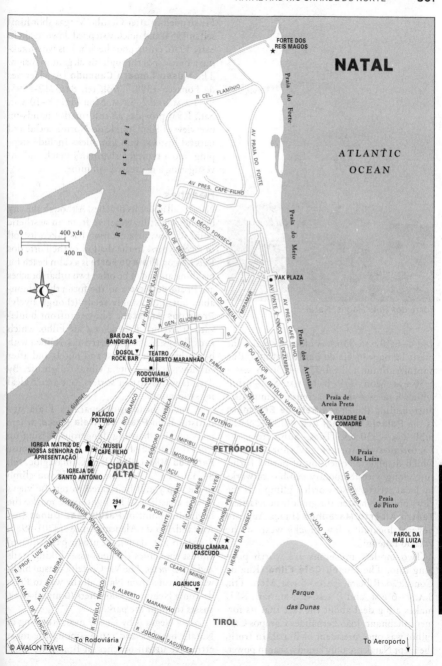

NATAL

FORTE DOS REIS MAGOS

ATLANTIC OCEAN

Rio Potengi

Praia do Forte

Praia do Meio

Praia dos Artistas

YAK PLAZA

R CEL. FLAMÍNIO

AV PRAIA DO FORTE

AV PRES. CAFÉ FILHO

R DECIO FONSECA

R SÃO JOÃO DE DEUS

AV DUQUE DE CAXIAS

R DO AREIAL

MIRIMAR

AV VINTE E CINCO DE DEZEMBRO

AV PRES. CAFÉ FILHO

R GEN. GLICÉRIO

R GEN.

R DO MOTOR

BAR DAS BANDEIRAS

DOSOL ROCK BAR

TEATRO ALBERTO MARANHÃO

RODOVIÁRIA CENTRAL

FARIAS

AV GETÚLIO VARGAS

Praia de Areia Preta

PEIXADRE DA COMADRE

PALÁCIO POTENGI

AV RIO BRANCO

AV DEODORO DA FONSECA

R CEL. J MANOEL

R POTENGI

Praia Mãe Luiza

IGREJA MATRIZ DE NOSSA SENHORA DA APRESENTAÇÃO

MUSEU CAFÉ FILHO

CIDADE ALTA

IGREJA DE SANTO ANTÔNIO

R MIPIBU

R MOSSORÓ

R AÇU

PETRÓPOLIS

VIA COSTEIRA

Praia do Pinto

294

AV MONSENHOR VALFREDO GURGEL

AV MON. W GURGEL

R APODI

AV PRUDENTE DE MORAIS

AV CAMPOS SALES

AV RODRIGUES ALVES

AV AFONSO PENA

AV HERMES DA FONSECA

R JOÃO XXIII

FAROL DA MÃE LUIZA

MUSEU CÂMARA CASCUDO

R CEARÁ MIRIM

AGARICUS

R PROF. LUIZ SOARES

AV ALM. A. DE ALENCAR

AV OLINTO MEIRA

R REGULO TINOCO

R ALBERTO

MARANHÃO

R JOAQUIM FAGUNDES

TIROL

Parque das Dunas

To Rodoviária

To Aeroporto

0   400 yds
0   400 m

© AVALON TRAVEL

Forte dos Reis Magos, Natal

and 4–6:30 P.M. Sun.). A block away lies the pretty baroque **Igreja de Santo Antônio** (Rua Santo Antônio, tel. 84/3211-4236, 6 A.M.– 5:30 P.M. Mon.–Fri., 8–11 A.M. Sat.–Sun.), which houses a small sacred arts museum. Surrounding the **Praça Sete de Setembro** is the **Palácio Potengi** (tel. 84/3232-9727, 8:30 A.M.–5:30 P.M. Tues.–Sun., free), the Victorian-style former governor's palace, which displays a collection of period furniture along with temporary exhibits of works by local artists. Also worth a glimpse is the city's premier theater, the grandly neoclassical **Teatro Alberto Maranhão** (Praça Augusto Severo) located a few blocks west of the Palácio Potengi.

Two modest museums are worth popping into. The **Museu Café Filho** (Rua da Conceição, Ribeira, 8 A.M.–5 P.M. Mon.–Fri., 8 A.M.–6 P.M. and 8 A.M.–2 P.M. Sat., R$1) makes a big deal about the fact that its former inhabitant, João Fernandes Campos Café Filho, was once president of Brazil. In truth, the inept Natalense only lasted a year in power.

He stepped in after Getúlio Vargas shot himself in 1954, and quickly stepped down again in early 1956, citing poor health. It is worth taking a quick spin through his elegant mansion. The **Museu Câmara Cascudo** (Av. Hermes da Fonseca 1398, Tirol, tel. 84/3212-2795, 8–11 A.M. and 2–5 P.M. Mon.–Fri., 8–10 A.M. Sat., R$3) provides an informative hands-on overview of Rio Grande do Norte's social and natural history. Fun gimmicks include stepping into a typical fisherman's shack and investigating a re-created salt mine.

Beaches

Natal is all about its beaches. Although the city beaches are still attractive from an aesthetic point of view, urbanization has taken its toll in recent years. In the shadow of the Forte dos Reis Magos, **Praia do Forte** is a calm beach for paddling around. The other two urban beaches are **Praia do Meio** and the formerly fashionable, but increasingly seedy (though lively) **Praia dos Artistas.** The oceanfront boulevard of Avenida Presidente Café Filho, which runs alongside Praia dos Artistas, is lined with beach bars, restaurants, and hotels and after sundown it has quite a vibrant nightlife. By day, its waves attract surfers, but aren't ideal for swimming.

A rocky headland separates Praia dos Artistas from **Praia de Areia Preta,** where reefs making bathing dangerous. Rising up from the far end of the beach is the lighthouse **Farol da Mãe Luiza** (Rua Camaragibe, tel. 84/3201-0477, 2–5 P.M. Sun.). If you climb to the top you'll be treated to terrific views of the coastline. The lighthouse marks the beginning point of **Parque das Dunas** (Av. Alexandrino de Alencar, tel. 84/3201-3985, 8 A.M.–6 P.M. daily), an urban park situated amidst the dunes that possesses hiking trails and *lanchonetes*. The Via Costeira coastal highway that runs from Natal all the way to Praia de Ponta Negra, 10 kilometers (6 miles) away, passes through the park.

Ponta Negra is by far the most stunning of Natal's beaches and ranks among the most attractive urban beaches in Brazil. Its most unique feature is the gigantic sand dune at the southern tip. Known as **Morro da Careca** (Bald Man's Hill), its nickname accurately evokes the dune's resemblance to a bald head (although the lush foliage surrounding the strip of white sand makes it look more like an inverted mohawk). Over the last few years, all the action that used to be take place in Natal's more central beaches has migrated to Ponta Negra. However, although the beach is still undeniably gorgeous—featuring both calm and wavy waters—it's also become quite touristy. There are an amazing number of European sun worshippers, and sadly, a number of young (often underage) prostitutes ready to service them. The southern strip of the beach is particularly full of hotels, trendy restaurants, and bars, along with a colorfully diverse mix of locals, foreigners and *ambulantes* (vendors) hawking their wares along the sands. At night, Ponta Negra is the most happening place in the city. For more peace and tranquility, head to the more sedate and upscale northern tip. Ultimately, Ponta Negra is like a small city unto itself and you can easily spend all your days and nights here.

Nightlife

Most of Natal's nightlife takes place in the lively beach neighborhoods of Praia dos Artistas (in Centro) and Alto da Ponta Negra (above the beach in Ponta Negra). The old riverside *bairro* of Ribeira, adjacent to Cidade Alta, lures a young and alternative crowd. Since parts of Centro—Ribeira and Praia dos Artistas, in particular, can be a little louche, especially at night—taxis are recommended.

CENTRO

The three airy, plant-festooned salons that compose **294** (Av. Deodoro da Fonseca 294, Cidade Alta, tel. 84/3211-1783, 11 A.M.–11 P.M. Tues.–Fri., 11 A.M.–10 P.M. Sat.–Sun.) make this laid-back bar a favorite happy-hour option. The seafood *petiscos*, such as crab with coconut and the organic oysters, are highly reputed, and you can easily make a meal out of the shrimp and vegetables cooked in coconut milk and

served with toasted bread. Natal's boho bar par excellence is **Bar das Bandeiras** (Largo do Chile, no phone, 11 A.M.–11 P.M. Tues.–Fri., 11 A.M.–10 P.M. Sat.–Sun.), whose name comes from ships' flags (*bandeiras*) that serve as decoration. For years, this historic bar has attracted a mix of sailors and students, poets and prostitutes, who gather to chat, listen to jukebox tunes, and nibble on simple home-cooking. This is a great place to soak up some authentic local atmosphere.

Nearby, the bars around Praça Pôr do Sol are ideal for watching the sunset over the Rio Potengi, while Rua Chile has alternative clubs and performance spaces such as the **Dosol Rock Bar** (Rua Chile 40, Ribeira, tel. 84/3642-1520, www.dosol.com.br, 5–10 P.M. and 11 P.M.–close Sat.–Sun., cover R$7–10), a renovated warehouse where you can rock out to local underground bands.

PONTA NEGRA

Located within the cozy "dungeon" of the castle-like Lua Cheia Hostel, the **Taverna Pub Medieval** (Rua Dr. Manoel Augusto Bezerra de Araújo 500, tel. 84/3236-3696, www.tavernapub.com.br, 10:30 P.M.–close Mon.–Sat., cover R$10–20) has long worn the crown of the most happening dance spot in town. Ever since he was a kid, the Paulistano owner has had a fondness for things medieval, which explains the mildly kitschy decorative scheme of shields, banners, and armor. However, the music (which leans towards pop, rock, and MPB), is definitely contemporary, as are the imaginative themes of the *festas* that occur nightly. On the same street, the **Samsara Lounge** (Rua Dr. Augusto Bezerra Araújo 141, tel. 84/3291-3136, 7 P.M.–close Mon.–Sat.) lives up to its Buddhist inspired name by offering a mellow haven for a more grown-up set to kick back with a cocktail in the subtly lit lounge or on the terrace. On weekends from 11 P.M. on, there are live performances of jazz, blues and bossa nova.

For something a little more rowdy, nearby is **Sgt. Pepper's Rock Bar** (Rua Dr. Augusto Bezerra Araújo 130, tel. 84/9133-6377,

THE NORTHEAST COAST

www.sgtpeppers.com.br, 7 P.M.–2 A.M. daily), with amped up rock, tattooed waiters, and a mixed crowd (including—surprisingly for Ponta Negra—a fair number of locals) that spills out onto the sidewalk. The *petisco* menu is quite varied. Try mini hamburgers topped with bacon and blue cheese, or the roasted onions stuffed with *carne-de-sol*. If you want to catch some *forró*, head to **Rastapé** (Rua Aristides Porpino Filho 2198, Alto de Ponta Negra, tel. 84/3219-3164, www.rastapenatal.com.br, 10 P.M.–4 A.M. Wed. and Fri.–Sat.), a relaxed and rustic place where you can sip *cachaça* and watch couples whirl each other round.

Entertainment and Events
PERFORMING ARTS
Natal's premier theater is the opulent neoclassical **Teatro Alberto Maranhão** (Praça Augusto Severo, Ribeira, tel. 84/3222-3669 www.teatroalbertomaranhao.rn.gov.br), which hosts dance, theater, and musical events. Occupying a beautifully restored old mansion, **Centro Cultural Casa da Ribeira** (Rua Frei Miguelinho 52, Ribeira, tel. 84/3211-7710, www.casadaribeira.com.br) provides a charming and essential escape valve for local artists. Alternative theatrical, dance, and musical performances are held here, along with film screenings and art exhibits. There is also an attractive café.

FESTIVALS AND EVENTS
Carnatal (www.carnatal.com.br) is the name of Natal's out-of-season Carnaval. For four days in late November/early December, the streets surrounding the Machadão stadium in the *bairro* of Lagoa Nova go crazy as the stars of Salvador's mega Carnaval whip the crowds into a frenzy with throbbing *axé* music sung from the tops of *trio elétricos* (massive stages on wheels).

Sports and Recreation
Although Natal's surf, sand, and sunshine lend themselves to many activities, you really can't leave town without taking a spin through the sand dunes in a buggy.

◖ DUNE BUGGYING
In Rio Grande do Norte, beaches and buggies are an inseparable pair. Young buggy drivers, known as *bugueiros,* are rampant in Natal. Before setting off, however, a *bugueiro* will considerately inquire whether you want the jaunt to be *com emoção* or *sem emoção* (i.e., with or without emotional thrills). Respond at your own risk.

Some people take to buggy riding, while others aren't so crazy about (literally) getting sand in their face. However, racing madly through the dunes (with or without stunts) is an unforgettable experience. From Natal, you can take half-day and full-day trips along the north and south coastlines. This is an ideal way of getting an overview of the region's beautiful beaches, many of which you can't get to by bus. You can book buggy excursions through hotels and tour agencies, as well as directly with the *bugueiros* themselves. (Before taking off, ask to see the official SETUR certification of the *bugueiro*). You'll find lots along Praia dos Artistas and Ponta Negra.

Patrícia Turismo (Rua Praia Pititinga, Ponta Negra, tel. 84/3236-4217) offers a popular full-day trip that follows the coastline north of Natal to Genipabu, with stops at various beaches and the freshwater lagoons of Pitangui and Jacumã. The trip costs R$240 for up to four people (although a quartet can get kind of cramped). Meanwhile, if you try buggying and *really* like it, you can travel all the way to Fortaleza—a four-day trip! **Buggy & Cia.** (Rua Guilherme Tinoco 1274, Tirol, tel. 84/9416-2222, www.buggyecia.com.br) offers such an excursion, along with more placid day trips south to Praia da Pipa and north to Genipabu. **Aventura Turismo** (tel. 84/3206-4949, www.aventuraturismo.com.br) offers the journey (in a more comfortable Jeep instead of buggy) for R$1,250 per person, which includes transportation, lodging, breakfast, and guides.

Shopping
In Centro, a former 19th-century orphanage and prison now houses the **Centro de Turismo**

(Rua Aderbal de Figueiredo, Petrópolis 980, tel. 84/3211-6149, 8 A.M.–7 P.M. Mon.–Sat.). Each cell is occupied by a vendor selling regional handicrafts such as lace, pottery, wood carvings, and blue-and-white painted *azulejos* (ceramic tiles), a tradition handed down from the Portuguese. There is a tourist office here as well as a dance hall where, every Thursday night, live *forró* attracts both gringos and locals. In Ponta Negra, you'll find a wide array of handicrafts at the **Shopping do Artesanato Potiguar** (Av. Engenheiro Roberto Freire 8000, Ponta Negra, tel. 84/3215-9781, 10 A.M.–10 P.M. Mon.–Sat., 3–9 P.M. Sun.). For more contemporary items, head to the mall at **Praia Shopping** (Av. Engenheiro Roberto Freire 8790, Ponta Negra, www.praiashopping.com.br, 10 A.M.–10 P.M. Mon.–Sat., 3–9 P.M. Sun.).

Accommodations

Although Natal has lots of hotels in the city, the beach at Ponta Negra is much nicer and you'll find scads of options. If you want more tranquility, consider staying in the nearby coastal beaches of Redinha or Genipabu (to the north).

CENTRO

The sole advantage to staying in Centro is that prices are (slightly) more affordable. Recently purchased by the American Best Western hotel chain, the only thing odd about **Yak Plaza** (Av. Presidente Café Filho, Praia do Meio, tel. 84/3202-4224, www.yakplaza.com.br, R$130 d) is its name. Otherwise it's a very comfortable, if blandly standard, beach hotel that is well located close to Praia dos Artistas and Cidade Alta and with easy access to Ponta Negra. Rooms are large and air-conditioned and there are two pools, one on a pleasant deck overlooking the sea.

PONTA NEGRA

The **Albergue da Juventude Lua Cheia** (Rua Dr. Manoel Augusto Bezerra de Araújo 500, Ponta Negra, tel. 84/3236-3696, www.luacheia.com.br, R$80–90 d) is definitely not what you'd expect a youth hostel in a beach resort to look like. The exterior is built to resemble a medieval castle, complete with towers and a drawbridge. Inside the Middle Ages theme continues with bunks (R$33–43 pp) located in cellar-like dorm rooms that sleep six. Although the excess brick is a little heavy, the place has a weird charm and the staff is friendly. The larger dining area and courtyard garden are quite atmospheric and the bonus is that one of Natal's hottest nightspots is located in the "dungeon" (see *Nightlife*).

Offering great value, the American-owned **Hotel Belo Horizonte** (Rua Francisco Gurgel 8852, Ponta Negra, tel. 84/3219-4188, www.belohorizonte.com.br, R$82–129 d) has spotless bright and spacious double and triple rooms decorated in neutral tones. Although it's located three minutes from the beach, you can view the ocean from the outdoor pool and bar. The staff can help organize buggy tours and trips to surrounding beaches. Differentiating itself from most of the modern resorts and apart-hotels along Ponta Negra is the intimate and organic **◖ Pousada Manga Rosa** (Av. Erivan França 240, Ponta Negra, tel. 84/3219-0508, www.mangarosanatal.com.br, R$160–190 d), a stylishly rustic hotel built around a mango tree. Located right on the beach, its multiple balconies and verandas gaze right upon Morro de Careca. Rooms, while fairly standard, have nice decorative flourishes such as artisanal lamps. The overall relaxing atmosphere is complemented by the attentive service.

The most romantic and sophisticated hotel on the entire coast is without a doubt the **◖ Manary Praia Hotel** (Rua Francisco Gurgel 9067, Ponta Negra, tel. 84/3204-2900, www.manary.com.br, R$480–770 d). "Manary" is a Potiguar term for "well-being," which is something of an understatement considering the exquisite complex of neocolonial villas that are set amidst exuberant gardens. Aside from a prime beach location, there are two cool blue swimming pools along with waterfalls and fish ponds. The lofty rooms are luxurious with fine linens, carefully chosen art, and wide balconies. The tastefully furnished common areas are simultaneously refined and relaxing. Serving polished contemporary versions of regional cuisine, the restaurant is a gastronomic high point.

Food

Natal is a great place to indulge in regional (*potiguar*) specialties. Choose between hearty Sertanejo fare, such as sun-dried beef and roasted goat, and fresh fish and seafood dishes (lobster and shrimp are particularly abundant) from the coast.

CENTRO

A local institution, **Peixada da Comadre** (Rua Doutor José Augusto Bezerra de Medeiros 4, Praia dos Artistas, tel. 84/3202-3411, 11:30 A.M.–3:30 P.M. and 6:30–10 P.M. Wed.–Sat., 11:30 A.M.–5 P.M. Sun., R$18–26) has been serving up local fish and seafood specialties for almost 80 years. In her eighth decade, owner Dona Francisca presides over the kitchen, where the fresh catch of the day is transformed into traditional dishes such as the house *peixada,* chunks of fish swimming in a vegetable stew accompanied by rice and *pirão.* More recently, a second outlet opened in Ponta Negra (Av. Praia de Ponta Negra, tel. 84/3219-3016).

When migrants from Rio Grande do Norte's interior get homesick, they head to 🄲 **Mangai** (Av. Amintas Barros 3300, Lagoa Nova, tel. 84/3206-3344, www.mangai.com.br, 11 A.M.–10 P.M. daily, R$14–20). A ranch-style decor coupled with waiters sporting straw hats and leather sandals conspire to conjure up a slightly hokey version of a typical Sertanejo farm. However, what really satiates customers' nostalgia is the banquet of regional specialties served at the vast buffet. Among the delicacies you'll encounter are *carne-de-sol na nata* (sun-dried beef in cream), *sovaco de cobra* (shredded *carne-de-sol* cooked with corn and manioc flour), and gororoba (*carne-de-sol* with manioc and cheese). If it sounds as if there's a lot of *carne-de-sol,* rest assured that there is also a large choice of salads as well. There are also mouthwatering *doces* such as creamy *cocada* (a sweet coconut dessert) and *cartola oba-oba*

(fried banana topped with Sertanejo cheese, caramelized sugar, cinnamon, and chocolate). Although it's slightly off the beaten track, this restaurant is highly recommended as an appetizing introduction to the culinary traditions of the northeastern interior. It's also worth skipping out on your hotel breakfast to indulge in the fabulous Sertanejo spreads served from 7 A.M. Tuesday–Sunday.

Agaricus (Av. Afonso Pena 529, Petrópolis, tel. 84/3211-4796, noon–3 P.M. and 6–11 P.M. Mon.–Fri., 9 P.M.–1 A.M. Sat., noon–4:30 P.M. Sun.) is the Latin term for a common mushroom (the Portuguese word is *cogumelo*). Those seeking an alternative to seafood and sun-dried beef won't find a more unusual alternative than the contemporary dishes featuring fresh organic shiitakes and *champignons* (imported weekly from a farm in Rio Grande do Sul) served a this attractive restaurant. Start off with a mushroom carpaccio followed by a shrimp, fresh mushroom, and passion fruit risotto. Rest assured that there are plenty of non-mushroom items on the menu, among them desserts such as mango, passion fruit, and rum cheesecake.

PONTA NEGRA

Occupying a sprawling and stylishly modern adobe house with a privileged view of the sea, 🄲 **Camarões Potiguar** (Rua Pedro da Fonseca Filho 8887, Ponta Negra, tel. 84/3209-2425, www.camaroes.com.br, 11:30 A.M.–3:30 P.M. and 6:30 P.M.–midnight daily, R$20–25) specializes in *camarões* (shrimp) cultivated at the restaurant's own aquatic farms. Influences are both regional (*camarão cajueiro* stars shrimp topped with crushed cashews in a passion fruit sauce, accompanied by manioc gratinéed with *coalho* cheese) and international (*camarão au gratin* features shrimp cooked in a stew of white wine, Dijon mustard, hearts of palm and béchamel sauce with a gratin of gruyère). Both locals and foreigners flock here (which explains the translated menu). Leave room for dessert: The *profiteroles pirangi* (featuring a filling of cashew sorbet) are pretty sublime.

The succulent *carne-de-sol* served at **Tábua de Carne** (Av. Engenheiro Roberto Freire 3241,

Ponta Negra, tel. 84/3642-11138, www.tabua-decarne.com.br, 11:30 A.M.–11:30 P.M. daily, R$20–30) hails from Picuí, a town in the neighboring state of Paraíba that is as famous for its sun-dried beef as Bordeaux is for fine wines. At this carnivore's heaven, the *carne-de-sol* is made from filet mignon and comes accompanied with such fixings as green *feijão*, fried manioc, and pumpkin puree. A la carte portions serve three, but you can also choose the R$22 *rodízio* option, which includes various meats along with a buffet of regional dishes.

Piazzale Italia (Av. Deputado Antônio Florêncio de Queiroz 12, Rota do Sol, Ponta Negra, tel. 84/3236-2697, noon–3 P.M. and 6 P.M.–midnight daily, R$20–30) is considered the finest Italian restaurant in town by both Brazilian gourmets and visiting Italians in-the-know. The latter swear by the homemade *grano duro* pasta as well as imported ingredients such as skinless tomatoes, pine nuts, and porcini mushrooms. The thin-crust pizzas topped with everything from classic prosciutto to local fresh lobster are also highly appreciated. Located in a large house, the restaurant boasts various ambiances, but the most popular by far is the outdoor terrace with its scenic views.

Casa de Taipa (Rua Doutor Manoel Augusto Bezerra de Araújo 130-A, Alto de Ponta Negra, tel. 84/3219-5798, daily, R$5–12) is a delightfully laid-back hangout with a palm thatched roof, sandy floors, and adobe walls decorated with local art (for sale). The city's premier *tapiocaria* serves up a delicious array of this Northeast version of a crêpe made with crunchy manioc flour. Classic versions are filled with melted *coalho* cheese or coconut milk, but there are more unorthodox fillings as well, such as fresh crab with basil, cheese, and sun-dried tomato. Coffee and drinks are also served, as is homemade ice cream to accompany the sweet *tapiocas*.

Information and Services

The main tourist office is in the **Centro de Turismo** (Rua Aderbal de Figueiredo 980, Petrópolis, tel. 84/3211-6149, 7 A.M.–11 P.M. Mon.–Fri.). You'll also find branches at the airport (tel. 84/3643-1811, 9 A.M.–5 P.M. daily) and the *rodoviária* (tel. 84/3205-1000, 7 A.M.–11 P.M. daily). In Ponta Negra, there's an office inside the **Praia Shopping** (Av. Engenheiro Roberto Freire, Ponta Negra, tel. 84/3232-7248, www.praiashopping.com.br, 10 A.M.–10 P.M. Tues.–Fri., 10 A.M.–6 P.M. Sat.), where you'll also find branches of Banco do Brasil and Banco 24 Horas with ATMs and access to the Internet.

In the event of an emergency, dial **193** for an ambulance or the fire department **190** for the police. There is a special tourist police (Av. Engenheiro Roberto Freire 8790, tel. 84/3232-7404) unit in Ponta Negra. For medical treatment, try the **Hospital Monsenhor Walfredo Gurgel** (Av. Hermes Fonseca 817, Tirol, tel. 84/3232-7536, www.walfredogurgel.gov.br).

CITY TOURS

Eco Travel (Av. Jaguararí 4990, Green Mall, Loja 26, Candelária, tel. 84/3234-4068, www.ecotravel.com.br) offers a variety of Jeep tours and expeditions up and down the coast as far as Jericoacoara in Ceará. Trips can be customized for groups as small as two people and include various forms of accommodation as well as bilingual guides. **Cariri Ecotours** (Av. Prudente de Morais 4262, Loja 3-B, Tirol, tel. 84/3234-4068, www.caririecotours.com.br) has a really interesting assortment of guided tours by Jeep, van, and small buses throughout Rio Grande do Norte and the neighboring states of Ceará, Paraíba, and Piauí (including many into the Sertão) that mix natural and cultural attractions. Lasting from one day to one week, trips are customized for small groups and are led by multilingual guides. Aside from many buggy excursions up and down the coast, **Buggy & Cia.** (Rua Guilherme Tinoco 1274, Tirol, tel. 84/9416-2222, www.buggyecia.com.br) offers a fantastic 12-day adventure to the Parque Nacional dos Lençóis Maranhenses, which combines hiking with transportation by truck and boat.

Getting There

Flights from all over Brazil arrive at the **Aeroporto Augusto Severino** (Rua Eduardo

Gomes, tel. 84/3643-1000), which lies 15 kilometers (9.5 miles) from the center of town and 12 kilometers (7.5 miles) from Praia Ponta Negra. A taxi costs R$35–40 (downtown) and R$25–30 to Ponta Negra. You can also take a municipal bus marked "Via Costeira," which passes through Ponta Negra and the Via Costeira coastal highway on its way to Centro.

Long-distance buses arrive at the **rodoviária** (Av. Capitão Mor Gouveia 1237, Cidade Esperança, tel. 84/3205-4377), which is 5 kilometers (3 miles) away from both downtown and Ponta Negra.

Getting Around

Natal is quite small and it is easy to get around Centro on foot. Getting to and from Centro and Ponta Negra is quick and simple by bus. From Centro to Ponta Negra, take any bus marked "Via Costeira" or "Ponta Negra"—from Ponta Negra, hop any bus bound for "Centro" or "Cidade Alta" (buses will take the coastal highway or inland avenues). Taxis are affordable and easy to hail. You can also call **Disk Taxi Natal** (tel. 084/3223-7388) or **CoopTax** (tel. 0800/84-2255). Fare from Centro to Ponta Negra is R$25–30.

If you want to rent a car, driving is fairly non-stressful. Streets are wide and traffic is generally calm. A car is a great plus if you want to explore less accessible beaches north and south of Natal that aren't served by bus. **Localiza** (tel. 84/3206-5296, www.localiza.com) and **Avis** (www.avis.com.br) both have offices at the airport (tel. 84/3087-1403). Much more fun is to heed the "when in Rome . . ." adage and rent a buggy so you can really take to the sands. To reserve a buggy (with or without a driver) contract **Buggy & Cia** (Rua Guilherme Tinoco 1274, Tirol, tel. 84/9982-3162, www.buggyecia.com.br) and **Buggy Tour** (tel. 84/3236-3280).

BEACHES SOUTH OF NATAL

The coastline south of Natal is a seductive mixture of dunes and lagoons, coconut groves and dramatic red cliffs. Limpid ocean pools are protected by coral reefs. Aside from snorkeling,

you can indulge in some dolphin watching. The relative remoteness of many of the beaches has kept most from becoming overly developed. Although a few can be reached by buses leaving from the local *rodoviária,* others require a car, or hopping a ride in a van, buggy, or Jeep. Most *bugueiros* and travel agents in Natal offer half and full-day trips that go as far as the legendary Praia do Pipa. Along the way, you'll get a taste of numerous beaches such as Cotovelo, Pirangi, Búzios, Tabatinga, and Tibau do Sul.

Pirangi

Separated by the Rio Pirangi, the twin beaches of Pirangi do Norte and Pirangi do Sul are only 10 kilometers (6 miles) south of Ponta Negra along the RN-063 (Rota de Sol). The calm waters are ideal for swimming and windsurfing, and its palm-fringed white sands are dotted with friendly little *barracas* as well as beach homes belonging to wealthy Natalenses. Boats can take you to the reefs 1 kilometer (0.6 mile) offshore where you will encounter excellent snorkeling. Pirangi do Norte has achieved *Guinness Book of World Record fame* for sheltering the world's most immense **cashew tree** (Av. Deputado Márcio Marinhos, tel. 84/3238-2684, 7:30 A.M.–5:30 daily, R$2). Nearby, **Inhepoan** (Rua do Cajueiro 100, tel. 84/3238-2958, 7 A.M.–6 P.M. daily) is an atelier where you can pick up locally made handicrafts along with a bottle of cashew *licor,* a heady local delicacy made from the tree's fruit.

Búzios to Tibau do Sul

Búzios is another favorite getaway of upscale Natalenses. The northern stretch of the beach has limpid waters while the southern end's wild waves lure surfers. Búzios segues into **Barra de Tabatinga,** another lovely beach framed by rugged reddish cliffs. From the summit's Mirante dos Golfinhos, you're treated to a spectacular view of the coastline, and of the dolphins that appear during low tide (usually between 1–3 P.M.). Since this period coincides with lunchtime, take advantage of the scattered bars and restaurants that offer fish and seafood dishes along with glorious views. From Natal,

THE WORLD'S OLDEST CASHEW TREE

The world's oldest cashew tree is alive and well and growing in Pirangi do Norte. Already more than a century old, it still has a long life ahead since the life span of its species is around 400 years, give or take a decade. The entire tree currently covers an area of approximately 7,500 square meters (81,000 square feet), and all of its branches – which curve down to the ground due to their weight – are still growing, except for one locals refer to as "salário mínimo" (minimum wage). If you arrive during harvest season, after paying R$2 (which goes towards its upkeep), you can feast firsthand on a few of the 80,000 delicious fruits the tree bears each year. A local fisherman named Luiz Inácio de Oliveira was responsible for planting the tree, in 1888. When he passed away at the age of 93, Oliveira was found lying in the shade of the tree's branches.

buses with a final destination of Tabatinga travel to both of these beaches.

To get to **Tibau do Sul** is somewhat trickier. You'll need to take a buggy, Jeep, or boat along the coast or, if you're driving from Natal, take the BR-101 and then the RN-003 from Goianinhas. It's only 6 kilometers (3.5 miles) north of Praia da Pipa (and easily reached by van), but most travelers bypass its series of small, empty, cliff-protected beaches en route to its more famous neighbor to the south. However Tibau do Sul's beaches are strikingly unique. Their natural beauty is enhanced by the proximity of the **Lagoa Guaraira,** a freshwater lagoon ideal for swimming, boating, or kayaking as well as watching a picture-perfect sunset.

Should you want to stay awhile, the **Rio Mar Pousada** (Av. Gauraíras 56, tel. 84/3246-4103, www.pousadariomar.com.br, R$150–200 d) offers a half dozen spacious and quite appealing chalets with living rooms and verandas featuring splendid views of the Lagoa and its surrounding lushness. The attractive grounds include a pool and lots of greenery.

Even if you don't stay overnight, you can easily spend a whole day pampering yourself at **Ponta do Pirambu** (Rua Sem Pescoço 252, Praia de Ponta do Pirambu, tel. 84/3246-4333, www.pontadopirambu.com, 9 A.M.–5 P.M. daily), a fantastic leisure complex set amidst an idyllic patch of nature. An ingenious complex made of palm fronds and recycled wood shelters a massage and therapy center, a lounge full of hammocks, and a gourmet restaurant. Wooden walkways lead to a swimming pool. If you're feeling a little too lazy to walk to the beach, you can always take the bamboo panoramic elevator. Entrance to the complex (including a drink) is R$40 (children under 7 are free). Tibau do Sul is easily accessed by buggy or boat from neighboring Pipa.

BEACHES NORTH OF NATAL

Heading north from Natal—by bus or buggy—the beaches get increasingly wild and the dunes more impressive. Half- and full-day buggy tours from Natal give you a "best of" the closest series of beaches stretching from Redinha, across the Rio Potangi, to Mariú, 50 kilometers (31 miles) north. Although some of the beaches are lined with summer houses, most are tranquil little fishing villages with a few basic *barracas* and restaurants serving fried fish and simple seafood dishes. The most famous draws are Genipabu with its shifting dunes and dromedaries, and Pitangui and Jacumã, with their alluring freshwater lagoons. Praia de Maracajaú is renowned for the ideal snorkeling around its vast offshore reefs.

Redinha

The first beach north of Natal, Redinha, is only a 10-minute ferry ride across the Rio Potengi. A small fishing village with reef-protected waters and pleasant *barracas* serving fried fish and icy beer, it also offers a great

fishing nets in Rio Grande do Norte

© EMBRATUR

view of Natal and is a very easy day trip, although it can get crowded on weekends. The *balsa* (ferry) runs daily 6:10 A.M.–9:50 P.M. and costs R$1 for foot passengers and R$5 for cars. Alternatively, you can take a bus from the local *rodoviária* that crosses the newly completed Ponte Newton Navarro.

Genipabu

Another fishing village is Genipabu, 25 kilometers (16 miles) from Natal, whose fine sand dunes are even more spectacular. The quintessential postcard images of Natal's dunes are usually taken here. Genipabu is the primary destination of Natal's *bugueiros* since the constantly shifting dunes practically cry out to be buggied over (if you come here on your own, there are also many local *bugueiros* who can take you for a spin). Equally fun is trying to run up and down the dunes, or traveling across them by mule or dromedary. Yes, dromedaries were long ago imported here from the Sahara and they hardly look out of place at all. Although you're definitely paying for the gimmick, it's hard to resist a ride even if costs R$40

for a half hour. Another very fun way to get sand up your nose is to indulge in *esquibunda,* in which you place your posterior on a wooden board and go tobogganing down the dunes.

You can also take advantage of the waters of the mesmerizingly blue Lagoa de Genipabu, a freshwater lagoon fringed by lush plants and cashew trees. For lunch amidst the dunes (getting there involves a 10-minute trek through the sand), head to **Bar 21** (tel. 84/3224-2484, 10 A.M.–6 P.M. Tues.–Sun.), for delicious fish and seafood. Should you be enticed to spend the night, the **Pousada Soleil** (Av. da Praia 91, tel. 84/3225-2064, www.pousadasoleil.com.br, R$90–180 d) is a simple little beachfront place with clean, basic rooms and a cheery atmosphere. Buses to Genipabu leave at 45-minute intervals from Natal's *rodoviária.*

Pitangui, Jacumã, and Mariú

Located 45 kilometers (28 miles) north of Natal, Pitangui is a little fishing village with an enticing palm-fringed beach. Aside from swimming in the ocean you can also float, kayak, and pedal around the Lagoa Pitangui.

Set amidst snow-white dunes, the lagoon is also a great place to try *aerobunda*—which involves attaching yourself to a cable and swinging (butt-first) across the sand and into the water. The same fun can be had at the adjacent beach of **Jacumã**. Each *aerobunda* descent costs R$5.

For snorkeling, **Muriú**, 50 kilometers (30 miles) from Natal, is a wonderful destination. From the beach, boats take you 1 kilometer (0.6 mile) offshore to reef-protected pools where you can get an eyeful of colorful fish. Since the region is known for its shrimp farms and lobster fishing, this is the place to stuff yourself on crustaceans.

Maracajaú

Maracajaú, which lies 60 kilometers (37 miles) north of Natal, offers some of the best snorkeling in Rio Grande do Norte. When the tide recedes, the extensive coral reefs located 6 kilometers (3.5 miles) offshore form vast natural pools known as *parrachos,* whose warm and particularly limpid waters (reached by boat) are transformed into fantastic open-air aquariums. Depending on the tides, depths range 2–6 meters (7–20 feet). The shallower regions are equipped with floating bars. **Maracajaú Diver** (Praia da Maracajaú, tel. 84/3261-6200, www.maracajau.com.br) offers two-hour snorkeling excursions out to the reefs for R$60, along with "baptismal" diving excursions for R$160. Check out the website for info about Maracajaú. Although there are no buses to Maracajaú, you can easily hire a taxi or buggy to bring you here from Natal.

◖ PRAIA DA PIPA

One of the most justifiably famous beaches on the Northeast coast is Praia da Pipa, which rivals Jericoacoara for the title of hippest tropical beach getaway. It is certainly the most happening. Surfers discovered the tiny fishing village, 65 kilometers (40 miles) south of Natal, back in the 1970s. Since then, an endless trail of both native and foreign paradise junkies have been seduced by the tiny town. Yet despite the onslaught of charming eco-*pousadas,* gourmet

JANGADAS

Both an icon and way of life along the Northeast coast, *jangadas* are rough-hewn and picturesque rafts with billowing sails that are an angler's best friend. Of indigenous origin, *jangadas* are ideally constructed to glide over rough surf and are light enough to be hauled over dry land. A major means of transportation, they are everywhere. For travelers, nothing could be more idyllic.

restaurants, and chic boutiques, not to mention hordes of getaway artists and revelers that descend upon it come summertime, Pipa hasn't lost its laid-back allure (or its dirt roads). And its beaches remain astonishingly beautiful with sugary white sand offset by spectacular red cliffs. Whether you're into snorkeling or surfing, dolphin watching or simply sprawling in the sun, you'll be hard pressed to find a more relaxing or ravishing beach destination. For this reason, although you can easily visit Pipa on a day trip from Natal, you'd be doing yourself a disservice if you didn't stick around for at least two or three days.

Beaches

Praia da Pipa itself is very attractive, but pretty urbanized due to numerous *barracas,* fishing boats, and bronzing bodies flaunting the latest in bikini wear. It gets very packed in the summer, but is quite tranquil during off-season. The water is a mesmerizing blue-green and when the tide goes out, natural pools form amidst the coral reefs. Within walking distance are more unspoiled and enticing beaches. Most are only accessible on foot during low tide—otherwise you'll need to take a van, buggy, or boat. Heading north, a 30-minute walk will bring you to **Praia do Curral,** followed by **Praia do Madeiro.** Both are splendid white-sand beaches set against towering red cliffs, whose emerald waters are known as the Enseada dos Golfinhos (Bay of Dolphins) due to these mammals' fondness for feeding here. Although Curral is completely secluded (so bring water and snacks), you'll find *barracas* on Madeiro's beach, which is also popular with bodyboarders.

South from Pipa is the beautiful **Praia do Amor,** which can be reached along the beach at low tide as well as from the a road leading down from the scenic clifftops above, known as Chapadão. While Amor's heart-shaped beach is popular with sunbathers, its waves are revered by surfers and bodyboarders. The *surfista* scene is at its fever pitch and the beachside *barracas* are filled with ripped dudes and their lovely ladies. In contrast, neighboring **Praia das Minas** is wide, long, and empty. Excellent for walking, it's also a hatching spot for the region's sea turtles. Also tranquil is **Praia de Sibaúma,** a tiny fishing village that was originally a *quilombo* community formed by runaway slaves. On the other side of the Rio Catu from Sibaúma, **Barra do Cunhau** also has a fine beach and lots of great local fish and seafood restaurants.

Nightlife

At night, Pipa literally lights up as visitors step into their finest flip-flops and take to the bars and clubs on and around Avenida Baía dos Golfinhos. Start the night off at **Tribus Bar** (Av. Baía dos Golfinhos, Galeria das Cores, 7 P.M.–close daily), whose deep jewel-toned hues of green and red have earned it the unofficial name of the *"bar da melância"* (watermelon bar). This is where young blood of all stripes warm up for the night ahead to hiphop and reggae. Less urban is **Garagem Barco Bar** (Rua da Cruzeiro, tel. 84/3246-2154, 10:30 A.M.–1 A.M. daily), which occupies a boat situated on the beach. When the tide is high, waves crash against the sides, giving you the sensation of being stranded at sea. Although the bar is open during the day, at night it's very romantic. Special *festas* take place whenever there's a full moon. Otherwise, you can mellow out to live MPB, jazz, and bossa nova while sipping on *caipifrutas* made with mango and *graviola*.

For all-night partying, the classic address is

Calangos (Av. Baía dos Golfinhos 1050, tel. 84/3246-2396, Thurs.–Sun., cover R$10), a rowdy nightclub that only starts buzzing after midnight. Thursday features live *forró* while other nights are devoted to reggae, rock, and electronica.

Sports and Recreation
HIKING

Before colonial settlers began clearing the land to plant *feijão* and manioc, the southern coast of Rio Grande do Norte was covered with native Atlantic forest. Although only small patches have survived, a considerable swath has been preserved in the **Santuário Ecológico de Pipa** (tel. 84/3211-6070, 8 A.M.–5 P.M. daily, R$5), 2 kilometers (1.2 miles) north of town between Praia do Curral and Praia do Madeiro (in fact you can access the park from the Madeiro beach). Although maps are available at the entrance, the easy hiking trails that lead through the forest are very well marked.

BUGGY AND JEEP TRIPS

Buggy excursions are a big deal in Pipa. However, unlike the beaches north of Natal where you actually careen around in sand dunes, Pipa's lack of dunes mean that buggies zoom along flat beaches, up and down hills, and over rivers. The most adventurous jaunt is a full-day outing (R$270 for four people) that goes south to the primitive Praia do Sagi, on the frontier of Paraíba, with stops at lagoons and beaches along the way. Half-day trips are also available to Sibaúma, Barra do Cunhaú, and Baía Formosa, 25 kilometers (16 miles) south, Insiders are already predicting that this stretch of gorgeous unspoiled beaches is going to be the next Pipa. For more information contact **Pipatour** (Av. Baía dos Golfinhos 673, Loja 2, tel. 84/3246-2234, www.pipatour.com.br).

A crowd pleaser for adrenaline junkies and adventure sports enthusiasts is the full-day Jeep adventure tour run by **Pau de Arara** (tel. 84/3246-2377, www.paudeararapipa .spaces.live.com). *Pau de arara* is a Portuguese expression that refers to the open flatbed trucks in which poor northeastern migrants fled the

© EDITORA PEIXES/EMBRATUR

dunes at Praia da Pipa, Rio Grande do Norte

drought and poverty of the Sertão and traveled south to Rio and São Paulo in search of a better life. With room for 13 eager adventure tourists, these modified Jeeps take you on a full-day adventure (R$85 pp) that includes stops for swimming in the natural pools of Praia de Sibaúma, sailing and kayaking at Barra do Cunháu, sandboard and *esquibunda* ("bum skiing") fun in the dunes of Tibau do Sul, and a final rest stop at the nearby Lagoa de Guaraíras where you munch on crêpes and watch the sunset.

BOAT EXCURSIONS

From Praia do Curral's beach, you can often see dolphins. However, to see them at close range, take a 90-minute boat trip (R$25) into their midst where (after donning a life jacket) you can swim among them as they perform their marine acrobatics. **Pipatour** (see *Buggy and Jeep Trips*) organizes several daily outings. If you have a whole day to kill, ask to go out in Galego's boat. Aside from being a sailor, Galego is a chef. After you mingle with the dolphins, he'll take you to Tibau do Sul, where you can hang out around the Lagoa Guaraíras

while he prepares a splendid seafood banquet that includes fresh oysters and grilled shrimp (the excursion, including lunch costs R$75.).

Accommodations

Radiating an all-natural vibe, **Pousada Alto da Pipa** (Rua da Gameleira 555, tel. 84/3246-2281, www.pousadaaltodapipa.com.br, R$90–130 d) is a tranquil and charmingly hippie trippie place awash in bright colors and natural fibers. Rooms are simple yet pretty. A ramshackle tropical garden, decked out with fish ponds and a small pool, is inhabited by tortoises, tiny *mico* monkeys, and hummingbirds.

The **Pousada Lounge** (Rua Beijupirá 230, tel. 84/3246-2718, www.pousadalounge.com.br, R$120–160 d) is a lounge in the purest sense of the word in that the interiors and exteriors alike are utterly conducive to sprawling around and mellowing out. The soothing whitewashed rooms are creatively furnished with patchwork quilts, throw pillows, local pottery, and dried starfish. Simple but full of character, they lead onto gardens where cool music will lull you to sleep as you relax in

THE NORTHEAST COAST

a hammock or lounge chairs shaded by a cluster of passion fruit vines.

Perched upon a hill with sweeping views of Praia da Pipa, the **Pousada Mirante de Pipa** (Rua do Mirante 1, tel. 84/3246-2251, www.mirantedepipa.com.br, R$160–200 d) is the eco-dream of a couple of Carioca fugitives who replanted the property with native woods and fruit trees, and then built 10 distinctive "eco-chalets" using only natural wood and stone. Completely integrated into the surroundings, each bungalow is rustic, spacious and extremely restful. The owners can organize buggy and boating tours of the region.

Although Pipa has no shortage of charming hotels, the most tropically luxe is **(Toca da Coruja Pousada** (Av. Baía dos Golfinhos 464, tel. 84/3246-2226, www.tocadacoruja.com.br, R$406–890 d), an eco-chic oasis nestled amidst a jungly estate. In keeping with Pipa's green vibe, organic forms and materials reign, but in harmony with creature comforts such as swimming pools, an outdoor fitness room, and a romantic restaurant that serves fusion cuisine. All rooms are beautifully appointed with fine linens and gorgeous bathrooms. The recently constructed deluxe luxury bungalows with four-poster king-sized beds, CD and DVD players, and a private solarium containing a Jacuzzi are definitely worth splurging for.

Food

Among the many travelers who visit Pipa, there is a considerable number who decide they can't bear to leave. Instead, they open restaurants—which accounts for the great state of the town's gastronomic scene.

Artist Rita Gava came to Pipa on vacation from the state of Espírito Santo and never went home. Instead, inspired by her mother's great cooking, she opened **(Panela de Barro** (Rua do Cruzeiro 56, tel. 84/3246-2611, 12:30–11 p.m. daily, R$25–35), located on a hillside overlooking the beach. The house specialties are the tasty shrimp and fish *moquecas* served in the typical *panelas de barro* (clay casseroles) of her home state. But Gava likes to innovate as well, which accounts

for the presence of inventions such as lobster "stroganoff" and grated coconut merengue torte with lime rind.

When world travelers Lucas and Nicole Kondo first arrived in Pipa, they only had R$100 between them. To earn money, they started making and selling organic sandwiches. The sandwiches proved so popular that, instead of continuing their travels, the couple stayed put and opened **Tapas** (Rua dos Bem-Te-Vis 8, tel. 84/9414-4675, 6:30–11:30 p.m. daily, closed May–June, R$15–25), a relaxing little restaurant that serves up tapa-sized portions of dishes inspired by their globe trotting. Aside from the quintessential Spanish *tortilla,* you'll also find Thai red curry, ceviche, and filet mignon in a sauce of peppers, anchovies, and sherry.

Housed inside a cozy yellow *casa* shaded by palms, **Cruzeiro do Pescador's** (Rua dos Concris 1, Chapadão, tel. 84/3246-2026, www.cruzeirodopescador.com.br, 11:30 a.m.–3 p.m. and 7–11 p.m. daily, closed Mon. offseason, R$28–40) laid-back ambiance belies the fact that its Paulistano proprietor takes his cooking seriously. Fish and seafood are the menu's stars and they are accessorized with unusual flair. Start off with oysters in coconut milk. Then consider shrimp in a gratinée of four cheeses served in an *abacaxi* (pineapple), or charcoal grilled *pescado* fish sprinkled with garlic and lemon tea.

Nostalgic Americans can get a gastronomic shot of home at **Pacífico** (Rua dos Bem-te-Vis 6, tel. 84/9982-8981, 6:30 p.m.–midnight daily, closed Tues. off-season, R$20–30), where Cordon Bleu–trained Californian chef James Halper, brings Stateside culinary influences to this intimate bistro. Specialties include fish tacos and Pacific tuna lightly grilled with sweet and sour soy sauce. For dessert, try the ice-cream cookie sandwich.

For a light and inexpensive meal, head to **Aruman** (Av. Baía dos Golfinhos 734, tel. 84/3246-2398, 2 p.m.–midnight daily). Amidst the *movimento* of Pipa's main drag, you can chill out at the sidewalk tables and feast on a crêpe (or two). An inspired savory filling blends shrimp and sun-dried tomatoes with pureed manioc and tangy *coalho* cheese. For dessert, the banana-chocolate crêpe with cashews is pretty irresistible. For a more local version of a crêpe, Benvinda of **Benvinda Tapiocaria** (Rua da Gameleira 17, tel. 84/3246-2341, 1–11 P.M. daily) is revered for her delicious *tapiocas* filled with ingredients such as cheese, shrimp, and *carne-de-sol*.

Information
Although there is no tourist office in Pipa, an excellent bilingual site, www.pipa.com.br, is loaded with information. Many places accept credit cards, but it's wise to stash up on cash since, to date, the local Banco do Brasil's ATM doesn't accept international cards.

Getting There and Around
Pipa is 80 kilometers (50 miles) south of Natal. The town is easily reached by bus from Natal's long-distance *rodoviária*. **Oceano** (tel. 84/3205-3656) offers service, with departures every 1–2 hours throughout the day. The trip takes about an hour. By car, follow the BR-101 from Natal to Goianinha, then take the RN-003. If you're coming by buggy, you can go along the coast. You can also take a taxi directly from Natal's airport, which will cost around R$120.

For getting around, there are buggies as well as scads of vans and microbuses that shuttle between Pipa and surrounding beach towns such as Tibau do Sul to the north and Barra do Cunháu to the south.

Fortaleza and Ceará

One of the largest, poorest, and most arid of the northeastern states, Ceará has a distinctive identity of its own. Fortaleza, its vibrant, bustling, modern capital, is a major tourist hub. Yet, while Fortaleza's beaches are attractive, the coastline stretching north and south from the city offers some of the most fabulous beaches in all of Brazil, not to mention the most distinctive. The truth is that the tropical beaches in other parts of Brazil are likely to have look-alikes in the Caribbean, Thailand, or Polynesia. However, with the exception of eastern Rio Grande do Norte, nowhere else will you encounter the striking blend of crumbling red cliffs, gleaming white sand, and intensely blue waters that are particular to Ceará. Moreover, much of the coastline is framed by gigantic dunes that are ideal for buggying, skiing, or tobogganing. Once you've spent a day or two exploring Fortaleza, hit the road and surrender yourself to Nature's intoxicating cocktail of sand, sun, and surf.

FORTALEZA
After Salvador and Recife, Fortaleza is the largest and most important of the Northeast

capitals. However, unlike the other two metropolises, practically nothing remains of Fortaleza's colonial past. In fact, the city's signature skyline is crammed with multistoried office and apartment buildings, not to mention mega tourist hotels. While distinctly lacking in charm, these high-rises lend the city an aura of modernity and dynamism that is unique in this part of the Northeast, and which spills over into the vibrant cultural scene and intense nightlife.

Fortaleza's saving graces—and modus operandi—are the photogenic urban beaches around which much of its social life revolves. The city's are both idyllic and urbane, especially Praia do Futuro, which mingles sweeping white sands and clean blue waters with a string of sophisticated *superbarracas* where you can surf the web (or the waves), get a massage or a manicure, and feast on fresh lobster.

Fortaleza itself was founded in 1600 by the Portuguese, who showed little interest in the area until the Dutch arrived on the scene in 1637 and constructed a formidable five-pointed fortress overlooking the sea. For a few years, the Dutch managed to stave off the Portuguese. However, they were no match for the fierce

THE NORTHEAST COAST

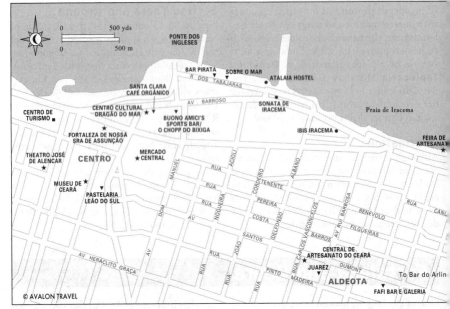

Tabajara Indians who repeatedly attacked them. By 1654, the Portuguese had retaken the fortress. They rechristened it Fortaleza Nossa Senhora de Assunção, which became the name of the small village that grew up around it. For a long time, Fortaleza's geographic isolation, coupled with frequent droughts and Indian attacks, kept it from developing into anything more than a colonial outpost. It was only in the 1820s, when Brazilian ports opened up to international commerce, that Fortaleza became a major shipping center from which Ceará's cotton and beef were transported to Europe. In particular, wealth from the cotton trade led to the creation of an enlightened elite with progressive ideas.

Inspired by Baron Haussman's Paris, in the mid-late 1800s Fortaleza underwent a major overhaul, gaining wide avenues, grand palaces, public gardens and cafés (only a few of which remain). In 1884, the state government passed legislation abolishing slavery—four years before the rest of Brazil—and, around the same time, Cearenses were at also at the forefront of the battle for a republican Brazil.

More recently, following the end of the military regime in 1985, Fortaleza was the first municipal government in Brazil to elect a woman as mayor (and a leftist one—from the Workers' Party—at that).

During much of the 20th century, Ceará struggled with misery, primarily due to the harsh conditions in the drought-ridden Sertão. Waves of poor migrants from the interior flooded Fortaleza. Often unable to find work in the capital, many continued on to Rio and São Paulo. Meanwhile, in recent years, the city and coastal areas have flourished as a result of new industries and a thriving tourist trade, coupled with enlightened state governments who have made significant headway in diminishing poverty through efficient education and health programs.

Sights

While Fortaleza has retained little of its history, the small heart of the city, Centro, is teeming with life. Despite the heavy traffic and numerous sidewalk vendors, it is an interesting place to explore. Its small size and grid-plan layout

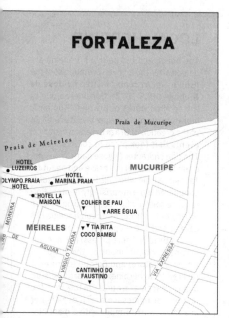

make it easy to walk around. The area is safe during the day, but keep your eye on your belongings in case of pickpockets.

A perfect starting point for exploring Centro is at the waterfront, where you can gaze upon the **Fortaleza de Nossa Senhora de Assunção** (Av. Alberto Nepomuceno, Centro, tel. 85/3255-1600, 8 A.M.–4 P.M. daily). This massive bleached fortress (now occupied by the army) is not the original 17th-century edifice built by the Dutch, but a reconstruction dating back to 1812. Opposite the fortress are the rather gloomy neo-gothic cathedral and the **Mercado Central** (Av. Alberto Nepomuceno 199, Centro, tel. 85/3454-8586, 7:30 A.M.–6:30 P.M. Mon.–Fri., 8 A.M.–4 P.M. Sat., 8 A.M.–noon Sun.). Despite its bland, modern exterior, the market is a fascinating place to wander around and check out the local merchandise.

Fortaleza's most interesting museum is the **Museu do Ceará** (Rua São Paulo 51, Centro, tel. 85/3101-2611, 9 A.M.–5 P.M. Tues.–Sun., R$2). Housed in an impressive neoclassical building, the collection relies on diverse artifacts—including furniture, clothing, fossils

and *literatura de cordel* (traditional northeastern folk tales that are illustrated with woodcuts and printed on cheap folio paper)—to evoke Ceará's rich history and culture. Particularly moving is the display dedicated to four fishermen who, in 1941, sailed by *jangada* from Fortaleza to Rio de Janeiro with the mission of bringing Ceará's poverty to the attention of Getúlio Vargas's government. Their epic journey was captured beautifully on celluloid by Orson Welles, who filmed it as part of his 1942 must-see documentary, *It's All True*.

Rua São Paulo also leads onto the highly animated **Praça José de Alencar,** which is dominated by what is easily the city's most stunning edifice. Named in honor of Ceará's most renowned poet and novelist, the early 20th-century **Theatro José de Alencar** (Praça José Alencar, Centro, tel. 85/3101-2583, 8 A.M.–5 P.M. Mon.–Fri., 8–11:30 A.M. Sat., R$4) mixes a delicate neoclassical cast iron structure (shipped over piece by piece from Scotland) with art nouveau stained-glass windows in rich jewel tones. Tropical embellishment is provided by the surrounding gardens designed by Burle Marx. Every 17th day of the month, the theater commemorates its inauguration with free performances. If you can't take in a performance, it's worthwhile taking the guided tour.

A few blocks north towards the sea, the **Centro do Turismo** (Rua Senador Pompeu 350, Centro, tel. 85/3101-5508, 8 A.M.–6 P.M. Mon.–Sat., 8 A.M.–noon Sun.) is a former prison whose former cells are now occupied by vendors selling Cearense art and handicrafts. Before inspecting the wares, check out the really fine collection of traditional *artesanato* on display at the small **Museu de Arte e Cultura Popular** (8 A.M.–5 P.M. Mon.–Sat., 8 A.M.–11 P.M. Sun.). Also on exhibit are modern pieces by local artists who have drawn on the region's rich artistic traditions for inspiration, often in strikingly unusual ways. The prisoners' former exercise yard now houses a pleasantly shady café.

Two blocks east of the market, in the neighborhood of Iracema, is the **Centro Dragão do**

Mar de Arte e Cultura (Rua Dragão do Mar 81, Iracema, tel. 85/3488-8600, www.dragaodomar.org.br, museums open 2–9 P.M. Tues.–Sun., R$2), a striking contemporary complex of steel and glass that harmonizes nicely with the restored historic buildings surrounding it. "Dragão do Mar" (Dragon of the Sea) was the nickname of Francisco José do Nascimento, a courageous sailor who became an abolitionist hero in the 1880s when he refused to transport slaves in his *jangada*. The cultural center named in his honor is a wonderful oasis and a major gathering point for Fortalezenses. Day and night, there is always something going on here, and the more laid-back, untouristy scene provides a welcome contrast to the hype of Iracema. Aside from gallery spaces, you'll find cinemas, a theater, a bookshop, a handicrafts boutique, a planetarium, and a scenic café that serves the best organic espresso in town. The Centro Dragão do Mar also houses two museums. The **Museu de Arte Contemporânea do Ceará** exhibits contemporary works by Brazilian and international artists while the **Memorial da Cultura Cearense** displays regional folk art.

Beaches

Fortaleza's beaches are the be all and end all of the Cearense capital. Life without them would be unimaginable. Too bad that most of their brilliant blue waters are too polluted for swimming. However, that doesn't seem to stop locals and tourists alike from mobbing them night and day.

Adjacent to Centro is **Praia de Iracema,** the most legendary and urbanized of the city's long string of beaches. Although its boardwalk is nice to walk along, Iracema is actually less of a beach than a perpetual seaside party zone. Come late afternoon, its many bars—particularly those on Ponte dos Ingleses, a pier that's become a classic sunset-watching point—start filling up with the happy-hour crowd. After sundown, its numerous restaurants and nightclubs follow suit.

More attractive and upscale is **Praia de Meireles,** which lies east of Iracema. Although

LOCAL HEROINE

The beach and the *bairro* of Iracema are named after the beloved protagonist of the 1865 novel *Iracema,* written by **José de Alencar** (1829–1877). Considered one of the seminal works of Brazilian Romantic literature, *Iracema* is a passionate retelling of the creation of Brazil based on historical events that took place in colonial Ceará. The title character (whose name is an anagram for America) is a brave and beautiful Tabajara virgin who falls in love with (or is conquered by) a surprisingly genteel Portuguese soldier who happens to be a sworn enemy of her tribe. Although Iracema has a tragic end, the couple's son, Moacir, symbolizes Brazil's (more or less) harmonious origins, brought about by the fusion of America (nature) and Europe (culture). A revered local heroine, there are five statues of Iracema around Fortaleza – the one on her namesake beach depicts her in a feisty warrior mode with a giant bow arched in the direction of the sea.

its waters aren't recommended for swimming, Meireles's beach is wider and more pleasant to hang out on. The glittery high-rise hotels lining the main ocean boulevard of Avenida Beira Mar are reminiscent of Copacabana, as is the shady boardwalk that attracts joggers, walkers, and bikers. Just as nice as strolling is kicking back with a cool coconut water at one of the many *barracas* on the sand. Every evening from 6 P.M.–close, a popular *feira de artesanato* takes place along the waterfront featuring a hit-and-miss array of handicrafts.

Praia de Meireles segues into the less busy, but equally posh and built-up **Praia de Mucuripe.** A picturesque aspect of this beach is the presence of traditional fishing *jangadas,* their faded sails flapping in the wind. The southern stretch of the beach is where the fisherfolk haul their daily catch up to the **Mercado de Peixe** (fresh fish market). If the glistening shrimp and fish prove excessively appetizing, buy some and take them over to Edileison's bar

(16-D). While you enjoy a cool beer, Edileison will fry the catch up right in front of you.

From Mucuripe, the coast bends south and leads to **Praia do Futuro,** the only beach in Fortaleza where the water is truly clean enough for swimming. Unlike at the other beaches, the open sea has strong waves that attract surfers. Praia do Futuro is famed for its super-*barracas* offering food, drinks, bathrooms, and showers, as well as also super-sophisticated extras ranging from kiddie water parks and Jacuzzis to stages where live bands perform for hundreds of revelers. You should stick to these *barracas* or their more humble brethren if you come here on a weekday. During off-season, in particular, the beach can get empty, and there have been reports of holdups. If you hang around until evening, make sure to take a taxi back to the center of town. Otherwise, from downtown, take any bus marked "P. Futuro" or "Caça e Pesca."

Nightlife

Fortaleza is famous for its pulsating nightlife. You'll find tons of bars in the beach neighborhoods of Iracema (particularly around Rua das Tabajaras) and Meireles. There are also scads of places where you can listen and dance to live music, especially *forró,* which Cearenses claim is more popular here than anywhere else in the Northeast (no mean feat).

PRAIA DE IRACEMA

Back in the '50s, when Fortaleza's original port was located at Iracema, this neighborhood was boho central for local journalists, artists, and literati. A few of their old-time haunts still survive, but many more have become rather tacky beer halls, pack-'em-in restaurants, and mega clubs. Viewed the number of tourists here, Iracema is also the notorious walking grounds for Fortaleza's working girl population (many of whom are underage). Lively and colorful, but also somewhat seedy and overblown, Iracema's nightlife is at least worth checking out (even if you then decide to go elsewhere).

Begin the evening by watching the sunset at one of the *barracas* along the Ponte de Inglês, accompanied by cold beer and fried shrimp. Then stroll along lively **Rua Tabajaras,** home of the famous **Bar Pirata** (Rua da Tabajaras 325, Iracema, tel. 85/4100-6161, www.pirata.com.br, 8 P.M.–3 A.M. Mon., cover R$30), whose vertiginous Monday *forró* nights have been luring visiting gringos ever since *The New York Times* called them the wildest Monday nights on the planet.

The Centro Cultural Dragão do Mar, and immediate vicinity, has a bustling happy-hour scene that continues late into the night. **Buoni Amici's Sport Bar** (Rua Dragão do Mar 80, Iracema, tel. 85/3219-5454, www.buoniamicis.com.br, 4 P.M.–close daily, cover R$5–15) is an always happening spot. Housed in a restored early 20th-century warehouse, it boasts soaring ceilings and lots of soccer paraphernalia. During the week, *futebol* fans gather to watch games and scarf down pizza and beer. From Friday onwards, the bar hosts lively dance parties commanded by DJs who play an intoxicating mix of samba, MPB, and *carimbó,* a local musical style that mixes indigenous and African elements. Check for topnotch shows of Brazilian music as well. **O Chopp do Bixiga** (Rua Dragão do Mar 108, Iracema, tel. 85/3219-7690, www.choppdobixiga.com.br, 4 P.M.–close daily) is another favorite gathering point. Live music is performed nightly and, on weekends, the second floor of this converted mansion becomes a sizzling disco. Aside from classic *chope de cerveja,* Bixiga's gimmick is *chope de vinho* (wine on draft), which is truly an acquired taste for gringos. Easier to succumb to are the gargantuan sandwiches such as the *Trem de 11* (11:00 Train), which consists of filet mignon, bacon, ham, peas, matchstick potatoes, and mayo, all piled on top of a baguette.

PRAIA DE MEIRELES

Compared to Iracema, upscale Meireles and the adjacent *bairros* of Aldeota, Dioníso Torres, and Varjota offer quieter nightlife options. **Fafi Bar e Galeria** (Rua Norvinda Pires 55, Aldeota, tel. 85/3261-3049, 6 P.M.–close Wed.–Sat., cover R$3–4) is an arty little bar/gallery space with funky decor and subtle lighting. A great musical selection, ranging from blues and jazz to samba and indie-rock, accounts for the diversity of the clientele that often spills out on onto the sidewalk.

Bar do Arlindo (Rua Joaquim Nabuco 2186, Dionísio Torres, tel. 85/3286-1436, 3 P.M.–close Mon.–Sat.) is a great place to soak up some authentic Fortalezense atmosphere. This classic *boteco*, decked out with plastic tables and chairs, is a favorite hangout for locals intent on enjoying frosty beer (or fiery *cachaça*) and chatting up a storm. After last call, die-hard regulars always punch out at the time clock that's part of the bar's decor. Tuesday nights are reserved for live *chorinho* and Saturdays are for samba. To nibble on, there are lots of homestyle *petiscos* such as *feijão verde*.

For a taste of Ceará's Interior, head to **Arre Égua** (R. Delmiro Gouveia 420, Varjota, tel. 85/3267-2325, www.arreegua.com.br, 8 P.M.–close Tues.–Fri.), a cultural space whose architecture replicates the typical structures and materials of the Sertão. At the bar, you can feast on Sertanejo delicacies such as shredded *carne-de-sol* with gratinéed cheese and lamb rice (a dish that feeds four). The house cocktail is a potent mixture of *cachaça* and cointreau, which is served on fire. The real fun begins at 9 P.M. when Dona Zefa's band breaks into traditional *forró*.

Entertainment and Events
PERFORMING ARTS

There is always something happening at the **Centro Dragão do Mar de Arte e Cultura** (Rua Dragão do Mar 81, Iracema, tel. 85/3488-8600, www.dragaodomar.org.br), which has a theater and cinema. It's also worthwhile checking to see what musical and dance events are being performed at the opulent **Theatro José de Alencar** (Praça José Alencar, Centro, tel. 85/3101-2583, 8 A.M.–5 P.M. Mon.–Fri., 8–11:30 A.M. Sat., R$4). The **Centro Cultural SESC Luís Severiano Ribeiro** (Praça Ferreira, Centro, tel. 85/3253-3332) is a cultural center housed inside what was formerly Fortaleza's most glamorous movie palace, the vaguely art deco Cine São Luís. Crystal chandeliers and marble floors make this a grand place to take in a film.

FESTIVALS AND EVENTS

Although Fortaleza has a Carnaval in the summer, it is nothing compared to the out-of-season "winter" Carnaval known as **Fortal.** Held during the last weekend of July, the festivities erupt along Praia de Meireles's Avenida Beira Mar. The event draws hundreds of thousands of skimpily clad and inebriated souls bent on dancing the days and nights away to the ear-shattering pulse of Bahia's biggest *axé* music stars.

Sports and Recreation

Although they aren't the best for swimming, Fortaleza's urban beaches are good for water sports such as surfing, windsurfing, and kitesurfing. **Bioboard Travel** (Av. Senador Virgilio Távora Mar 261, Meireles, tel. 85/3242-1642, www.bioboard.com.br) offers lessons and equipment, as well as surfing, windsurfing, and kitesurfing outings around Fortaleza and to nearby beaches such as Cumbuca. **Brothers Wind School** (Av. Beira Mar, Mucuripe 4260, tel. 85/9984-1967) offers lessons and rents Windsurfers, sailboats, and kayaks.

For a wilder beach experience, the **Cooperativa de Buggy de Fortaleza** (Via Local 31, Apt. 16, Porto das Dunas, tel. 85/9108-1504) organizes full-day dune buggy outings to beaches east of Fortaleza for around R$300 (for three people). **Trip da Areia** (Rua do Dragão do Mar, Canoa Quebrada, tel. 88/3421-7041, www.tripdaareia.com.br) is a highly reputed outfit that runs a terrific array of multiday beach expeditions by Jeep and buggy. Trips go up and down the coastline of Ceará as far south as the dunes of Natal, and as far north as the Parque Nacional dos Lençóis Maranhenses. Also recommended is **Dunnas Expedições** (Rua Leonardo Mota 1394, Loja 5, Aldeota, tel. 85/3264-2514, www.dunna.com.br), which specializes in eco-Jeep trips that go way off the beaten path, both along the coast and into the interior.

Shopping

Ceará is renowned for the variety and quality of its traditional *artesanato*, and Fortaleza is a good place to stock up on pieces to add to your

© SETURCE/EMBRATUR

windsurfing in Fortaleza

burgeoning folk art collection. You'll find lots of wood carvings, ceramics, and leather goods, but two artisanal traditions that really stand out are woven hammocks and lacework.

No matter what Brazilian beach you happen to be on, if you ask the vendors hawking hammocks where their wares come from, the inevitable response will be "Ceará." The region's cotton cultivation, together with its weaving traditions, make this the best place in Brazil to pick up a *rede*. Some are very intricate, and they make excellent gifts for layabout friends back home. Meanwhile, you'll find ample proof of Cearenses' needle skills in the exquisite embroidery, lace, and crochet used to make everything from pillows and tablecloths to blouses and skirts.

The best places for *artesanato* include the **Mercado Central** (particularly good for hammocks) and the **Centro de Turismo** (see *Sights*). **Ceart** (Av. Santos Dumont 1589, Centro, tel. 85/3101-1644), which also has a boutique in the Centro Cultural Dragão do Mar (tel. 85/3226-6917), sells pricier, but very good quality *artesanato*. You can also peruse the stands at the nightly **Feira Noturna** held on Avenida Beira Mar, although you'll have to search hard amidst the profusion of souvenirs and tourist trinkets.

For contemporary fashion and beachwear head to a couple of small malls in the chic hood of Aldeota (inland from Meireles): **Shopping Buganvilia** (Av. Dom Luís 1113) and **Aldeota Open Mall** (Av. Desembargador Moreira 1011, tel. 85/3433-2300). Dirt cheap clothing, shoes, and jewelry of the R$1.99 variety can be found by plunging into the bazaar-like commercial area surrounding Praça José Alencar, poetically known as the **Beco da Poeira** (Dust Alley).

Accommodations

Fortaleza is a major tourist destination with plenty of hotels to choose from. Centro has some good bargains. However, while the area bustles during the day, it is pretty dead at night. Most people tend to stay in the beach neighborhoods where all the action takes place. For proximity to the city's restaurants and nightlife, Iracema and Meireles are good choices. Upscale Mucuripe tends to be a bit more tranquil. While

THE NORTHEAST COAST

Praia do Futuro is great for swimming during the day, it is far from the center and dangerous at night. For the most part, hotels are rather innocuous, modern high-rises that are strong on amenities (you'll want air-conditioning or a good fan to fight the heat), but light on character. Be aware that in summer months and July, prices can often double.

CENTRO

Centro's character and lack of tourists can be refreshing, although you won't have beach access. A nice antidote to the usual high-rise hotels, **Pousada Toscana** (Rua Rufino de Alcecar 272, tel. 85/3088-4011, www.pousada toscana.com.br, R$42 d) is an impossible-to-beat budget option. Not far from Praia de Iracema, it's located in a faded villa close to the Mercado Central. The 10 rooms are airy and spotless, but very spare. Basic amenities such as air-conditioning, breakfast, and a TV all cost extra.

PRAIA DE IRACEMA

Located in a fetching villa, the **Atalaia Hostel** (Av. Beira Mar 814, Iracema, tel. 85/3219-0755, www.atalaiahostel.com.br, R$70 d) is a pleasant and well-maintained hostel with a coveted beachfront location. Aside from dormitories (R$32 pp), private rooms range from doubles to quadruples. The staff is very helpful. Extras include Internet, a communal kitchen, and laundry services. Like all hotels in the Ibis chain, **Ibis Iracema** (Rua Dr. Atualpa Barbosa Lima 660, Iracema, tel. 85/3052-2450, www.accorhotels.com.br, R$89 d) offers comfortable, no-nonsense, modern rooms with little character, but unbeatable prices. Amenities include a restaurant and a nice pool. Breakfast is extra. More upscale, but still good value is the beachfront **Sonata de Iracema** (Av. Beira-Mar 848, Iracema, tel. 85/4006-1600, www.sonatadeiracema.com.br, R$170–200), whose large, bright, if bland rooms all have sea views. There is an attractive pool area with a bar, as well as a restaurant, fitness room, and Internet access.

PRAIA DE MEIRELES

The French-owned ◖ **Hotel La Maison** (Av. Desembarador Moreira 201, Meireles, tel. 85/3242-7017, www.hotellamaison.com.br, R$77–110 d) is a favorite of French backpackers in search of low frills with flair. This pretty budget hostel is located in a renovated house only a few blocks from the beach. Basic air-conditioned rooms are enlivened with colorful accents and hanging art, and there is a small, charming courtyard garden. Internet is available and the owner, Francis, is very helpful. **Hotel Marina Praia** (Rua Paula Barros 44, Meireles, tel. 85/3242-7734, www.hotelmarinapraia.com.br, R$95–120) is another small-scale cozy hotel located in a residential building and surrounded by a pretty little garden. The simple air-conditioned rooms have polished hardwood floors, good lighting, and brightly painted walls. The staff is extremely friendly and there is Internet access.

More luxe is the **Olympo Praia Hotel** (Av. Beira Mar 2380, Meireles, tel. 85/3266-7200, www.olympopraia.com.br, R$240–295 d), a low-slung resort on a tranquil stretch of Meireles. It is sleek and tasteful, if a little lacking in warmth. The sizable air-conditioned rooms are awash in neutral tones with natural wood accessories. Bathrooms are swish and gleaming. The bar, restaurant, and pool areas are also pretty styling. **Hotel Luzeiros** (Av. Beira-Mar 2600, Meireles, tel. 85/4006-8585, www.hotelluzeiros.com.br, R$260–320 d) is Fortaleza's attempt at an international-style design hotel. It succeeds very nicely in the lobby, two restaurants, and bars, all of which are achingly minimalist. As for the rooms, the suites are quite posh and lovely. However, the standard rooms, while quite comfortable, are disappointingly basic. All rooms have at least partial sea views, and there is a nice pool and fitness room, as well as a business center with Internet access.

Food

Fortaleza is Brazil's lobster capital. This crustacean is cheaper and more abundant here

BEACH *BARRACAS*

Throughout the Northeast, beach-going would be unimaginable without the ever-present *barracas*, seaside restaurant/bars where friends and family settle in for a long day of chatting, drinking beer, and nibbling on portions of fried fish and seafood, interrupted by the occasional foray into the ocean to cool off (although many *barraca* devotees actually never set foot in the water). The classic *barraca* is no more than a basic shelter made from boards and palm thatch furnished with a smattering of tables and chairs. However, over the years, the *barraca* has evolved, perhaps nowhere more so than along Fortaleza's Praia do Futuro, which is renowned for its series of sophisticated *super-barracas*. Bathroom and shower facilities and abundant food and drink are but bare essentials at these private beach clubs, which are outfitted with mega restaurants and amenities ranging from personal lockers to playgrounds and aquatic parks for the kids. Open daily, *barracas* really fill up on the weekends as well as Thursday nights, when legendary *carangueijadas* take place, along with shows of live rock, MPB, and *forró*.

Most *barracas* tend to cater to a specific clientele. Among the most popular are:

· **Atlantidz** (Av. Zezé Diego 5581, tel. 85/3249-4606) – the most Las Vegas due to its kitschy decor inspired by the lost city of Atlantis

· **Cabumba** (Av. Zezé Diego 3911, tel.

85/3262-4187) – unofficial gay and lesbian headquarters

· **Chico do Carangueijo** (Av. Zezé Diego 4930, tel. 85/3262-0108) – where fresh crab is king

· **Coco Beach** (Av. Zezé Diego 6421, tel. 85/3249-9879) – loved by families because of the water slide and weekend buffets (*feijoada* on Saturday and seafood on Sunday)

· **Crocobeach** (Av. Zezé Diego 3125, tel. 85/3234-0370) – takes the mega concept to the max with a convenience store, Internet café, beauty salon, ice cream parlor, and surfing school

· **Lounge Beach** (Av. Zezé Diego 5053, tel. 85/3262-6760) – an Ibiza wannabe with sprawling sofas, sushi platters, and oh-so-mellow music

· **Vila Galé** (Av. Zezé Diego 3125, tel. 85/3486-4400) – the most tony and tranquil (owned by the hotel of the same name)

· **Vira-Verão** (Av. Zezé Diego, tel. 85/3262-6227) – headquarters of the bronzed and buff kitesurfing and windsurfing set

Should you prefer to mingle with locals more than gringos and the upper classes, rest assured that there are plenty of more rustic (and cheaper) *barracas* to be found.

than in any other part of Brazil. But Ceará's coastline yields all sorts of fish and seafood. Try the classic fisherman's dish *peixada cearense,* which combines fresh fish such as *robalo, cavala,* and *beijupirá* with cabbage, carrots, potatoes, onions, and hard-boiled eggs. The ensemble is baked in an oven before receiving a last-minute drizzle of fresh coconut milk. Beach *barracas*—particularly those at Praia do Futuro—are a great place for fresh seafood snacks such as crab, fresh oysters, and grilled snapper sprinkled with sea salt.

CENTRO

In Centro, two popular Fortalezense pit stops are ideal for a snack or light meal. Over the decades, it's become a long-standing tradition to pull up a stool at **Pastelaria Leão do Sul** (Praça Ferreira, Centro, tel. 85/3231-0306, 9 a.m.–6:30 p.m. Mon.–Fri., 9 a.m.–1:30 p.m. Sat., R\$2–4). It's a cramped but atmospheric little place decorated with old photos of Fortaleza, and locals swear by the crisp, deep-fried *pasteis* (turnovers) stuffed with chicken, beef, and cheese. The classic accompaniment is a glass of *caldo de cana* (sugarcane juice).

Equally popular, although much newer is the **Santa Clara Café Orgânico** (Rua Dragão do Mar 81, Iracema, tel. 85/3219-6900, www.santaclara.com.br, 3–10 P.M. Tues.–Sun., R$3–7), located in the tower of the Centro Cultural Dragão do Mar. Apart from getting a java jolt from the organic coffees, espressos, and iced cappuccinos (you can buy the beans to go as well), you can tuck into a mouthwatering array of sweet and savory pastries, sandwiches, crêpes, and *tapiocas.* For a cheap local lunch with plenty of atmosphere, consider the various food stalls and per kilo restaurants at the **Mercado Central** (see *Sights*).

PRAIA DE IRACEMA
Sobre O Mar d'Iracema (Rua dos Tremembés 2, Iracema, tel. 85/3219-7999, 11 A.M.–1 A.M. daily, R$20–30) is a classic address for seafood specialties such as *peixada cearense* and *lagosta sobre o mar,* in which fresh lobster is grilled in its shell and served with vegetables. On Friday and Saturday, dining is accompanied by live music.

PRAIA DE MEIRELES
Meireles and the adjacent neighborhoods of Aldeota and Varjota make up Fortaleza's gastronomic zone. **Coco Bambu** (Rua Canuto de Aguiar 1317, Meireles, tel. 85/3242-7557, R$15–25) boasts sandy floors and a jungly decor that includes Technicolor toucans and parrots. The restaurant began life as a fun place to enjoy a mouthwatering selection of crêpes, *tapiocas,* and pizzas (made with wheat and corn flour). Recently, it added a more intimate dining room with exposed brick and chandeliers, where diners can enjoy sushi and Asian fusion cuisine. The per kilo buffet of regional dishes has won over the lunch crowd. And on Friday nights, DJs transform the place into funky town.

Removed from the buzz of Meireles's beach scene, **(Cantinho do Faustino** (Rua Delmiro Gouveia 1520, Varjota, tel. 85/3267-5348, noon–3 P.M. and 7 P.M.–midnight Mon.–Fri., noon–1 A.M. Sat., noon–4 P.M. Sun., R$20–30) is located in the charming home of chef José Faustino Paiva. Paiva makes creative use of local produce (including herbs and vegetables culled from his rooftop garden) in contemporary dishes such as lobster in a sauce of *mororó* (a type of wild cashew), roasted kid with broccoli rice, and shrimp and lobster *moqueca.* For dessert, try the *sorvetes* made from unlikely ingredients such as olives and buriti (the rich orange fruit of a native palm).

(Colher de Pau (Rua Frederico Borges 206, Varjota, 11 A.M.–midnight Sun.–Thurs., 11 A.M.–1 A.M. Fri.–Sat., Varjota, tel. 85/3219-3773, www.restaurantecolherdepau.com.br, 6 P.M.–12:30 A.M. daily, R$15–20) is a classic address for regional home-cooked dishes such as *arroz-de-carneiro* (a local version of a lamb risotto) and *peixada.* You'll also find the tenderest *carne-de-sol* in town, served with *baião-de-dois* (the *dois* in question are beans and rice, bound together with melted *coalho* cheese). For dessert, sample the *doces* made with guava or *caju.* The restaurant's cozy interior is reminiscent of a Cearense country house. Outdoor tables shaded by leafy trees are also very pleasant. Live MPB and samba are performed nightly.

You'll need at least two companions to devour the overly generous and amazingly cheap portions of home-cooked fish and seafood served at **Tia Rita** (Rua Frederico Borges 336, Varjota, tel. 85/3267-5879, 10 A.M.–midnight, R$10–15). The pargo with shrimp sauce is made using 1.5 kilos (3.3 pounds) of fish, while the *mariscada* is a seafood stew overflowing with crab, octopus, mussels, shrimp, fish, and fish eggs. For simple home-cooking in a no-frills setting, you won't do any better.

Beat Fortaleza's heat with a scoop or two of *sorvete* from **Juarez** (Av. Barão de Studard 2023, Aldeota, tel. 85/3244-3848, 6 A.M.–10:30 P.M. daily). Every day owner João José Juarez heads to the market at 4 A.M. to buy the fresh *sapotis, graviolas, cajás* and other fruity flavors that have tempted locals for over 40 years.

PRAIA DO FUTURO
Fortalezenses rarely go a week without treating themselves to a banquet of fresh *carangueijo* (crab), a feast lustily referred to as a *carangueijada.* Thursday is the traditional day for *caranguejada,* and you'll find the city's beach

barracas full of locals expertly whacking away at crabs with wooden mallets. The sight (and sound) is something to behold. *Carangueijada* central is Praia do Futuro, where *barracas,* both mega and modest, stay open late into the night. The most renowned crab temple of all is **Chico do Carangueijo** (Av. Zezé Diogo 4930, tel. 85/3262-0108, 8 A.M.–6 P.M. Fri.–Wed., 8 A.M.–2 A.M. Thurs.), where the *carangueijada* tradition reputedly began. Live *forró* accompanies the proceedings.

Information

The main Ceará **tourist office** is the **Centro de Turismo** (Rua Senador Pompeu 350, Centro, tel. 85/3488-7411, 8 A.M.–6 P.M. Mon.–Sat., 8 A.M.–noon Sun.), where you can get a free city map. The staff can help you plan trips up and down the coast of Ceará, which can be tricky if you're trying to get to remote beaches without direct bus service. There is also a branch at the airport (tel. 85/3477-1667, 6 A.M.–11 P.M. daily). On the Internet, there are lots of useful sites including the state's bilingual site, www.setur.com.gov.br, and two good English-language sites: www.visitfortaleza.com and www.fortalezabeaches.com.

Services

You'll find lots of banks in Centro and Meireles. There are branches of Banco do Brasil with ATMs in Centro (Av. Barão do Rio Branco 1515) and in Meireles (Av. Aboliçao 2308). The main post office is at Rua Senador 38 in Centro.

For Internet service, try **Cyber Net** (Av. da Abolição 2655, Meireles, tel. 85/3242-5422, 9 A.M.–9 P.M. Mon.–Fri., noon–8 P.M. Sat.–Sun.) or the **Evolution Vídeo Cyber Café** (Av. da Abolição 3230, Meireles, tel. 85/3242-9833, 8 A.M.–9 P.M. Mon.–Sat., 8:30 A.M.–6:30 P.M. Sun.).

In the event of an emergency, dial **193** for an ambulance or the fire department, and **190** for the police. There is a special **tourist police** unit (Av. Almirante Barroso 805, Iracema, tel. 81/3101-2488) at Praia de Iracema. For medical treatment, try the **Hospital Batista**

Memorial (Av. Padre Antônio Tomas 2058, Aldeota, tel. 85/3224-5417).

Getting There

The airport and *rodoviária* are both in the southern suburb of Fátima. Transportation to Centro or the beaches is easy. Flights from most major Brazilian cities arrive at **Aeroporto Internacional Pinto Martins** (Av. Senador Carlos Jereissati 3000, tel. 85/3477-1200), Long-distance buses arrive at the **Rodoviária João Tomé** (Av. Borges de Melo 1630, Fátima, tel. 85/3256-2100). There are numerous daily buses to Natal (8 hours) and Recife (12 hours), and one a day to Salvador (22 hours), Rio (48 hours), and São Paulo (52 hours). Taxis from either the airport or *rodoviária* will cost R$25–35 to downtown. You can also flag down an *executivo* bus that follows a circuitous route from the airport, via the *rodoviária,* through Centro and the beaches of Iracema and Meireles.

Getting Around

A modern, grid-planned city, Fortaleza itself is easy to navigate and offers good bus service. Buses that circulate between Centro and the closer urban beaches include those marked "Grande Circular" and "Mucuripe." Taxis are cheap, easy to find, and recommended for getting around at night. To reserve one in advance, call **Disque Taxi** (tel. 85/3287-7222) or **Chame Taxi** (tel. 85/3491-1133). Although driving within Fortaleza is a hassle due to traffic, renting a car is useful to get to far-flung beaches. Try **Avis** (tel. 85/3392-1369, www.avis.com.br) or **Localiza** (tel. 85/3308-8350, www.localiza.com.br). Both have offices at the airport. Should you want to rent a dune buggy, try **Locabuggy e Automóveis** (Av. Abolição 2950, Loja 1, Meireles, tel. 85/3242-7212, www.locabuggy.com.br).

CITY TOURS

Various tour companies offer half-day city tours and full-day excursions to surrounding beach destinations east and west of the city. Destinations range from the nearby Beach Park (R$30) to beaches such as Cumbuco, Caponga,

Morro Branco, and Canoa Quebrada (east of Fortaleza) and Lagoinha and Mundau (west of the city). Trips cost R$30–40 per person. **Ernanitur** (Av. Senador Vigílio Távoa, 2nd floor, Sala A, Meireles, tel. 85/3533-5333, www.ernanitur.com.br) and **Nettour** (Av. Rui Barbosa 780, Aldeota, tel. 85/3268-3099, www.nettour.com.br) are two good options (their city tours cost between R$20–25). Both also organize overnight packages to Jericoacoara.

EAST OF FORTALEZA

Fortaleza's urban beaches look good—and are certainly fun to stroll, loll, or snooze upon. However, when it comes to actually going swimming, it's better to head beyond the urban sprawl. The coastline running east of Fortaleza—from the town of Aquiraz to Ceará's frontier with Rio Grande do Norte—is known as the Costa do Sol Nascente (Coast of the Rising Sun). Its beachscapes are composed of white dunes, red cliffs, and fishing *jangadas* that set off long before sunrise to bring in the daily catch. If you're looking for peace and tranquility, with only an occasional dose of urban excitement, consider basing yourself at one of the beaches along this coast.

Linked to Fortaleza by the well-paved CE-040 coastal highway, these beaches can be easily visited in a day trip by car or organized excursion. Buses operated by São Benedito depart regularly from the central *rodoviária*.

Aquiraz

The Costa do Sol Nascente begins with the unspoiled beaches of **Porto das Dunas** and **Prainha,** located in the pretty historic town of Aquiraz (www.aquiraz.ce.gov.br). Founded in the early 1700s by Jesuit priests, Aquiraz served as Ceará's first capital.

SIGHTS

Sights here include a lovely old church and an intriguing 19th-century meat market. The town is particularly reputed for the intricately detailed embroidery and lacework made by local *rendeiras*. Porto das Dunas is the famous home of **Beach Park** (Rua Porto das Dunas 2734, tel. 85/4012-3000, www.beachpark.com.br, 9:30 A.M.–5 P.M. daily in the summer, Thurs.–Mon. during off-season, R$80). This much hyped Disneyesque theme park will thrill kids. Included among the 18 water rides are giant slides to "river" pools with simulated currents, and "ocean" pools with simulated waves. If they don't want to join in the fun, adults can veg out at the mega-*barraca* on the beach, which serves succulent crab.

GETTING THERE

From Fortaleza, take the coastal bus marked "Beach Park" that leaves from a stop on the corner of Avenida Domingos Olympio and Avenida Aquanambi.

Beberibe

The town of Beberibe (www.beberibe.com.br), 85 kilometers (53 miles) from Fortaleza, is known for the spectacular **Praia de Morro Branco.** Aside from its great beach, Morro Branco is famed for the **Labirinto das Falésias,** a series of "labyrinths" formed by fissures in the dune-shaped cliffs behind the beach. For a R$5 contribution, local guides will lead you through the maze. You'll be duly astonished by the colored sands that range from creamy whites and fleshy pinks to oranges, yellows, russets, and purples. The wide array of tonalities inspires the local production of glass bottles containing scenes "painted" with colored sand. These can be kitschy, but quite fascinating as well. While Morro Branco is a sophisticated hub, replete with bars and restaurants, the nearby beach of **Praia das Fontes,** is much more tranquil. The *"fontes"* in its name refer to the fresh water springs that bubble up from the red rock cliffs on the beach. Popular activities on both beaches include dune buggy rides, *jangada* trips, and kitesurfing.

ACCOMMODATIONS AND FOOD

For lunch, tuck into grilled lobster, *peixada cearense,* or *carne-de-sol* at the restaurant belonging to the **Hotel das Falésias** (Av. Assis Moreira 314, Praia das Fontes, tel. 85/3327-3052, www.hotelfalesias.com.br, R$18–24).

© SETUR-CE/EMBRATUR

Canoa Quebrada, one of Ceará's popular beach getaways

Perched on the edge of a cliff, it offers stunning views. Should you want to spend the night, the spacious though fairly basic double rooms cost R$120.

GETTING THERE
Buses operated by **São Benedito** (tel. 85/3272-1232, www.saobenedito-ce.com.br) depart at regular intervals from Fortaleza's central *rodoviária*. By car, follow the CE-040 coastal highway.

◖ Canoa Quebrada
Two hours east of Fortaleza (160 kilometers/99 miles), the poetically named Canoa Quebrada (Broken Canoe) is one of Ceará's most popular beach getaways. A former fishing village that became a 1970s hippie haven and is now merely hip, Canoa Quebrada possesses a youthful yet distinctly cosmopolitan vibe that draws an international crew of sun and sand worshippers. By day, all the action takes place on the pinkish dunes, where buggies zoom around like roller coasters, and on the turquoise waters, which are dotted with kitesurfers and triangle-sailed

jangadas. But at night, the bars on Broadway (yes, Canoa has a great white way) start pulsing with tanned bodies intent on dancing until the sun comes up. You can visit Canoa Quebrada in a day trip from Fortaleza. However, to really take advantage of its laid-back ambiance, you need to give yourself some time to unwind. If you favor tranquility over a party scene, try to come during the week.

BEACHES
The main beach of **Praia da Canoa Quebrada** is quite dramatic with its rusty cliffs, soft white-sand beach, and warm, reef-protected waters. However, it is also quite busy. On foot, you can (and should) go east towards the more tranquil beaches of **Majorlândia, Quixaba,** and **Lagoa da Mata.** You can go even further by buggy. The most popular trip is a three-hour journey that takes you to the splendid **Praia da Ponta Grossa,** 54 kilometers (34 miles) away, with stops at other beaches along the way. This half-day outing costs around R$180. It's best undertaken in the afternoon, when it's less hot and you can stop to watch the sunset from the

THE NORTHEAST COAST

dunes of Ponta Grossa. Although you'll be approached by buggy drivers on the beach, for safety's sake, book a licensed *bugueiro* through a hotel. You can also contact the **Associação dos Buqueiros de Canoa Quebrada** (Rua Dragão do Mar, tel. 88/3421-7175).

NIGHTLIFE

Canoa Quebrada's nightlife sizzles on a stretch of Rua Dragão do Mar known as **Broadway.** If you're looking for action, you'll find it at places such as **Bar do Reggae,** which reels in the Bob Marley groupies, and **Bar Meu Xodó,** which attracts aficionados of *forró.* Dancing fiends can whip themselves into a frenzy at **No Name,** the newest disco in town, which plays a variety of tunes. Meanwhile, those in search of more sedate surroundings can hide away at **Cafeteria Espresso Brasil.** During the height of the summer, the festivities take to the beach where various *barracas* sponsor *luaus* (sans roasted pig and leis) in the sand.

ACCOMMODATIONS AND FOOD

Canoa's *pousadas* are all fairly basic and quite affordable (eco-chic has yet to arrive). If you come during off-season, you can easily find a room for under R$100. **Pousada Lua Estrela** (Rua Nascer do Sol 106, tel. 88/3421-7030, www.luaestrela.com.br, R$80–95 d) is an appealingly rustic, family-run *pousada.* Although only some rooms have air-conditioning, there is a small pool for cooling off, and the panoramic views of red tiled roofs, palms, and the beach beyond are splendid. **Pousada Aruanã** (Rua dos Bugueiros, tel. 88/3421-7154, www.pousadaaruana.com.br R$120–180 d) is a newish and very attractive place featuring two-story bungalows set amidst a palmy garden with a pool. Both standard and superior rooms (with air-conditioning) are tastefully furnished with lots of wood, organic fibers and soft lighting. All have verandas, most of which look out over the sea. **Pousada La Dolce Vita** (Rua Descida da Praia, tel. 88/3421-7213, www.canoa-quebrada.it, R$130–160 d) is a relaxing place with friendly staff, attractive grounds, and a great pool. The chalet accommodations, each named

after a Fellini film, are warm and nicely decorated (with vintage film posters of course). The restaurant serves tasty Italian fare.

Like its hotels, Canoa's restaurants are laid-back and light on one's pocketbook. For lunch, you're best off digging into a plate of shrimp, lobster, or fresh fish served at the beach *barracas.* Avoid the *megabarracas* closest to town: the more atmospherically primitive ones further east such as **Freedom Bar, Lazy Days,** and **Caffé Della Praia** all have good nibbles. For dinner, **Natural Bistrô** (Rua Dragão do Mar 52, tel. 88/3421-7162, 6:30 P.M.–midnight daily, R$15–25) is one of the prettiest of Canoa's restaurants with rustic decor and soft, amber lighting. The menu offers an assortment of healthy seafood dishes such as fresh fish prepared with yogurt, and shrimp with *chuchu* (a native vegetable) in orange sauce. Also recommended is the attractive Spanish-run **Costa Brava** (Rua Dragão do Mar, tel. 88/3421-7088, 6 P.M.–midnight Mon.–Sat., R$18–28), where you can feast on paella or the more unusual *fideoa,* a Catalonian version of paella with angel hair spaghetti substituting for rice. Carnivores can dig into an Argentinean *picanha* (rump steak).

INFORMATION

For tourist information, check out www.canoa-quebrada.com, in Portuguese, and the bilingual site www.canoa-quebrada.es.

GETTING THERE

Nordeste (tel. 85/3205-4199, www.viacaonordeste.com.br), **Guanabara** (tel. 85/3235-2467, www.expressoguanabara.com.br), and **São Benedito** (tel. 85/3272-1232, www.saobenedito-ce.com.br) offer frequent bus service from Fortaleza's *rodoviária* to the nearby town of Aracati, 9 kilometers (6 miles) inland from Canoa Quebrada. From here, you can catch a municipal bus to Canoa or take a taxi (around R$20). If you're driving, follow the CE-040 to Aracati and follow the turnoff to Canoa.

WEST OF FORTALEZA

The coastline running west of Fortaleza towards Maranhão is known as the Costa do Sol

Poente (Coast of the Setting Sun). Its beaches tend to be more deserted, but no less spectacular than those to the east. The star attraction is Jericoacoara, a primitive paradise set amidst magnificent dunes that is routinely celebrated by international travelistas as one of the planet's most perfect beaches. Linked to Fortaleza by the well-paved CE-085 coastal highway, most beaches, with the exception of Jericoacoara, can be easily visited in a day trip by car, organized excursion, or bus.

Cumbuco

Popular Cumbuco offers endless activities on a palm-fringed beach. You can ride dune buggies, quadricycles, or horses through the sands, enjoy freshwater bathing in various lagoons, or take to the calm but murky ocean waters for kitesurfing, windsurfing, and *jangada* trips. If you're feeling active, you'll love the place. However, if it's seclusion you're after, the crowds and insistent vendors coaxing you to rent a boat, bike, or buggy will become tiresome.

GETTING THERE
Cumbuco is only 35 kilometers (22 miles) west of Fortaleza. It is easily reached by van or by taking a bus operated by **Vitória** (tel. 85/3342-1148), which stops on Avenida Abolição in Meireles and Avenida Imperador in Centro.

Lagoinha

One of the most beautiful beaches along the Sunset Coast, Lagoinha is 100 kilometers (62 miles) west of Fortaleza. A pirate hideout turned fishing village, its palm-shaded beaches are backed by dunes that range in hue from creamy white to orangey-pink. You can explore them by quadricycle or buggy. The most popular excursion leads to the Lagoa das Alméceges, where you can bathe in crystalline waters and snack on seafood at the *barracas* along the shore. Like Cumbuco, Lagoinha can get unbearably crowded on the weekends.

ACCOMMODATIONS AND FOOD
Should you want to spend the night, **Pousada Mar à Vista** (Av. Francisco Henrique Azevedo 170, tel. 85/3363-5038, www.pousada-maravista.com. R$70–90 d), perched on a cliff above the beach, is a decent, basic option with small, but clean, air-conditioned rooms. The patio restaurant is a good place to savor seafood with a view, or to watch the sunset while downing a cool *caipirinha*.

GETTING THERE
Viação Pegasus (tel. 85/3256-5100) offers bus service from Fortaleza's *rodoviária*. The journey takes two hours.

Flexeiras and Mundaú

If you're longing for more remote beaches, your wish will be fulfilled by traveling to the tiny fishing villages of Flexeiras and Mundaú, around 130 kilometers (81 miles) from Fortaleza (near the town of Trairi). Along this stretch of coastline, tourism is still in its nascent stages. Flexeiras boasts sweeping white sands and reef protected waters that are ideal for swimming. Mundaú offers more of the same, with the addition of the freshwater pleasures of the Rio Mundaú, whose banks are lined with tangled mangroves.

ACCOMMODATIONS
Both towns possess friendly little restaurants and modest *pousadas*. For simple, clean accommodations right on the beach, try **Pousada Cabôco Sonhadô** (Rua das Malvinas, Mundaú, www.caboco.com.br, tel. 85/3351-9047, R$60–80 d), where you'll be lulled to sleep by the sound of the breeze in the surrounding palms.

GETTING THERE
Viação Paraipaba (tel. 85/3256-5100) has bus service from the *rodoviária* to Trairi and Mundaú.

◖ JERICOACOARA

For some time now, international travel writers have been raving about Jericoacoara. Hence, you'll understand the presence of so many global beach worshippers, despite the remoteness (320 kilometers/200 miles) west of Fortaleza) of this rustic little fishing village.

Of course, when you finally get to "Jeri," you'll also understand that it deserves such worship. However, the biggest mistake these travel writers make is calling Jeri a "beach." It's actually much more.

Jericoacoara is what you get when a desertscape of constantly shifting dunes—some of them over 30 meters (100 feet) high—collides with the majesty of the open sea. Wandering or buggying through these dunes is mesmerizing. Depending on the hour of the day, the sun tints them burnished gold, searing yellow, deep orange, and purply pink. Moreover, you can never be quite sure if the ocean is swallowing up the desert or vice versa. Aside from all this natural drama, there is also an idyllic tropical beach involved. A 30-minute Jeep ride away from the village of Jeri is the Lagoa de Jijoca, a turquoise lagoon surrounded by creamy white sand that adheres perfectly to the ideal of the classic tropical beach championed by travel writers.

Jericoacoara is a popular package tour destination. However, its distance—a seven-hour bus trip from Fortaleza to the village of Jijoca, followed by an hour truck or buggy ride (23 kilometers/14 miles) through the dunes—has left it happily free of the tourist hordes that descend upon Ceará's other beaches. Trappings of civilization—such as electricity, Internet, and sushi—have arrived. So have many foreigners who, unable to face going back to civilization, have remained and opened up charming yet simple *pousadas* and restaurants. Happily, these new transplants are respectful of the unspoiled nature that reigns. Moreover, the Brazilian government's designation of Jeri as an environmentally protected zone has strictly regulated development and enforced recycling. Nonetheless, Jeri does get booked up in the summer. Should you want to experience the full effect of its seclusion, you'd be advised to visit during the off-season (Aug.–Nov. and Mar.–June).

Beaches

Near the village, the **Praia de Jericoacoara** is a stunning sight with its massive half-mooned shaped dune facing out onto the water. At the end of the day, tourists gather along the crest to watch the sun set (the dune's unofficial name is Duna do Pôr-do-Sol, or "Sunset Dune"). The moment is always accompanied by whistles and applause. The beach's shallow waters make swimming difficult but are ideal for windsurfing. To the right, a 10-minute walk leads to **Praia da Malhada,** which is much better for bathing. At low tide, you can continue on, past Praia do Pontal, to **Pedra Furada,** a striking rock formation with a hole in the middle. Around 10 kilometers (6 miles) farther east, **Praia do Preá** has wind conditions that make it a mecca of kitesurfers. Meanwhile, if you want to travel back in time to Jeri of 20 years ago, take a buggy 30 kilometers (19 miles) west up the coast to the tiny fishing village of **Tatajuba,** whose beach is utterly primitive.

While Jeri's ocean is ideal for water sports, for sunning and splashing around many prefer the sugary sands and crystalline jade waters of the **Lagoa de Jijoca.** This freshwater lagoon consists of pure rainwater. So much of it evaporates during the dry season that it separates into two smaller lagoons. Closer to the town of Jijoca, the **Lagoa do Paraíso** is dotted with rustic *pousadas* and restaurants. A couple of palm-thatched bars are the only sign of civilization at **Lagoa Azul.** When winds are strong, windsurfing, kitesurfing, and *jangada* outings are popular on both lagoons. Buggies and *jardineiras* (open-back trucks that serves as taxis) go back and forth from Jeri to Jijoca. The ride takes 30 minutes.

Nightlife

Believe it or not, Jeri does have a nightlife, especially during the summer. Tuesdays, Thursdays, and Sundays everybody heads to the dimly lit **Mamá África** (Rua das Dunas) for mellow reggae and MPB. Wednesdays and Saturdays are dedicated to *forró* at the *tradicionalíssimo* **Casa do Forró** (Rua do Forró), where locals are as plentiful as tourists. Tunes of all sorts can be heard at **Planeta Jeri** (Rua Principal), which is where most revelers begin and often end the night.

Sports and Recreation

Although Jeri feels as if it's at the end of the world, there is lots to keep you occupied apart from sprawling in a dune with a book. Sand activities range from yoga and *capoeira* classes to navigating the dunes by buggy, sandboard, or on horseback. A five-hour buggy outing to Tatajuba (with a stop for a fresh lobster lunch on the shores of Lagoa da Torta) costs R$160 for up to 4 people. Contact the **Associação dos Bugueiros** (tel. 88/3669-2284) or **Agência By Boogie** (tel. 88/3669-2277). Horses can be rented from the **Associação dos Cavaleiros,** on Praia de Jericoacoara for R$25 an hour.

Meanwhile, Jeri's ideal wind conditions make it a fine place to indulge in surfing, windsurfing and, especially kitesurfing. **Club dos Ventos** (tel. 88/3669-2288, www.club-ventos.com.br) provides lessons for beginners and rents equipment to fans of both kitesurfing (R$150 for four hours) and windsurfing (R$100 a day). The best season for both sports is between June and December when wind conditions blow at an average of 25 knots.

Accommodations

In keeping with the primitive environs, Jeri's *pousadas* are all appropriately rustic, although many proprietors have ingeniously taken advantage of organic materials and regional artistic traditions to create ambiances that are quite seductive. In the tiny village of Jeri itself, **Pousada Ibirapuera** (Rua da Dunas 6, tel. 88/3669-2012, www.pousadaibirapuera.com.br, R$120–150 d) is one of Jeri's original *pousadas* and offers good value. The air-conditioned rooms consist of small lofts with a bedroom upstairs and living room downstairs. The brick buildings are softened by a lush garden festooned with hammocks, shady cashew trees, and a curvy blue pool. Windsurfing boards are available for rent. Just a few steps from the beach, **Pousada Calanda** (Rua das Dunas, tel. 88/3669-2285, www.pousadacalanda.com, R$70–130 d) is a very friendly and mellow option with a lovely rambling garden filled with fruit trees, hammocks, and colorful throw pillows. Rooms are pretty basic, but cheery. The home-cooked meals are downright delicious. Amenities include a small pool, 24-hour bar, and Internet.

It's close to impossible to get more primitive chic than **Vila Kalango** (Rua das Dunas, tel. 88/3669-2289, www.vilakalango.com.br, R$250–350 d). Tarzan and Jane never had it this good. Nestled right on the beach, accommodations are divided between rustic brick bungalows and wooden huts suspended on stilts, all of which are creatively and beautifully decorated with natural fibers and ingeniously recycled objects. This is one place where you're actually encouraged to track around sand—in fact, a wonderful lounge of hammocks, pillows, and futons is located in a soft patch. Moreover, the beauty of the pool, restaurant, and palmy grounds—all of which overlook the Duna do Pôr-de-Sol—will have you pounding your chest in delight.

Food

Given its community of expats and nature lovers, Jeri boasts a large selection of eating options, with a definite emphasis on healthy cooking. During the day, you might want to partake of the *barraca* fare served on the beach. **Bar Alexandre** is Praia de Jericoacoara's official beach bar, with wooden tables beneath fruit trees and a nearby natural well where you can wash off salt water before digging into delicious fish and seafood dishes. On the shores of the Lagoa do Paraíso, **Chez Loran** (tel. 88/3669-1195) is an equally enticing place for lunch that serves somewhat more elaborate dishes such as curried fish and snapper sautéed with garlic. The pizzas that emerge from the wood-burning oven at **Nômade** (Rua da Farmácia, tel. 88/3669-2103, 6 P.M.–midnight daily, closed Sun. in off-season, R$10–20) are considered the best in town, with unusual toppings such as leeks, zucchini, smoked ham, and chutney. The laid-back ambiance makes them all the more enjoyable.

Chocolate (Rua do Forró 214, tel. 88/3669-2190, noon–midnight daily, 4 P.M.–midnight April and June, closed May, R$15–25) is an

© EMBRATUR

fishing on Praia de Jericoacoara

intimate, romantic eatery. From the terrace you can gaze at the beach while feasting on an imaginative menu of salads, risottos and pasta dishes (one ambitious sauce combines arugula, anchovies, and cinnamon). The chocolate desserts are wickedly good.

The rustic setting (with a lovely back garden) at **(Carcará** (Rua do Forró 530, tel. 88/3669-2013, noon–11:30 P.M. Mon.–Sat., closed in May, R$14–28) belies its sophisticated menu. Dishes run the gamut from ceviche and sashimi to regional specialties such as *carne-de-sol com arroz de leite* (sun-dried beef accompanied by rice bathed in melted *coalho* cheese) and *lagosta tropical* (grilled lobster with fresh tropical fruits). For a healthy, light meal or snack, **Café Brasil** (Beco do Buaxelo 65, tel. 88/3669-2272, open daily) serves thick sandwiches on homemade wheat bread stuffed with unusual fillings such as chicken, cashews, and pineapple. Also on the menu are sweet and savory *tapiocas* and fresh fruit juices. Meanwhile, those who wake up (or go to bed) at the crack of dawn swear by the fresh-baked coconut, cheese, and banana buns that emerge early from the ovens of charming little **Padaria Santo Antônio** (Rua São Francisco, 2–7 A.M. daily).

Information and Services

Although Jeri doesn't have a tourist office, you'll find tons of sites on the Internet, including the following: www.jericoacoarasite.com.br, www.jeri-brazil.org, and www.portaljericoacoara.com, all of which are bilingual. There are no banks in town, so make sure you bring plenty of cash (in small denominations), although some restaurants and hotels accept credit cards.

Getting There

There are two main options for getting to Jeri. The easiest, cheapest, and most common way is to take a bus from Fortaleza's *rodoviária*. **Redenção** (tel. 85/3256-2728, www.redencaoonline.com) has two daily buses that will take you all the way to Jijoca (a six-hour ride). The bus picks up passengers at both the central and long-distance *rodoviárias* as well as Avenida Beira Mar. Known as Jeri's parking lot, Jijoca is where people stash their cars before boarding the *jardineiras* that run back and forth across the dunes between Jijoca and Jeri (a breathtaking but bumpy 40-minute ride). You can also drive to Jeri via the CE-085, but you'll have to leave your car in Jijoca. A longer, more expensive, but unforgettably scenic alternative is to travel up the coast by Jeep, hitting all the beaches between Fortaleza and Jeri, which could take a day or even more. Adventure tour operators (see *Sports and Recreation* in the *Fortaleza* section) such as **Trip da Areia** (tel. 88/3421-7041, www.tripdaareia.com.br) and **Dunnas Expedições** (tel. 85/3264-2514, www.dunna.com.br) specialize in such trips.

Maranhão

Although Maranhão is considered to be a Northeast state, its wet climate, relatively lush vegetation, and significant indigenous influences announce your arrival into the threshold of the Amazon. Instead of parched Sertão, Maranhão's interior is marked by rivers and the omnipresent *babaçu* palm, which provides Maranhenses with everything from soap and cooking oil to charcoal and timber. Along the coast, particularly in the alluring, if somewhat dilapidated colonial cities of São Luís and Alcântara, European and, especially, African influences, are more palpable, creating an intoxicating local culture. Despite its relative poverty, the state capital of São Luís is easily one of Brazil's most beguiling and beautiful historic cities. There are enough historic and cultural attractions to keep you well occupied for at least three days—more if you come during June when the city plays host to the sumptuous Bumba-Meu-Boi festivities. If you can squeeze in an extra few days, it's worth taking a long, but unforgettable side trip from São Luís to the Parque Nacional dos Lençóis Maranhenses, where you'll be treated to a surreal landscape of endless white sand dunes dotted with thousands of tiny lakes. In terms of weather, Maranhão's rainy season lasts from January to June, but you can count on at least some rapid downpours all year-round.

SÃO LUÍS

Somewhat crumbling, but terribly charismatic, Maranhão's island capital has a flavor quite unlike any other of Brazil's northeastern cities. Its very origins are unique in that São Luís was the only Brazilian city to be founded by the French.

While the Portuguese were busy taking care of business further east in Olinda, Recife, and Salvador, in 1612, French commander Daniel de la Touche sailed into the Bay of São Marcos with 500 men. After erecting a fortress and forging an alliance with the local Tupinambá Indians, the French began building a city, which they named in honor of King Louis XIII. France's foothold in Brazil was short-lived. It wasn't long before the Portuguese got wind of the new colony, and by 1615, the French had been sent packing, the Tupinambá had been punished, and Portuguese settlers claimed the city as their own.

By the 18th century, São Luís was thriving as a result of cotton, sugar, and rice plantations whose great output was assured by Indian labor and vast numbers of slaves imported from Africa. The city boasted one of the Northeast's busiest ports, and wealthy aristocrats and shipping magnates poured their riches into building magnificent palaces overlooking the Baía de São Marcos. To deflect the hot sun, protect against dampness, and simply to impress their neighbors, the upper classes plastered the facades of buildings with gleaming *azulejos* (ceramic tiles) imported from Portugal. The most traditional were embossed with intricate motifs in hues of yellow and blue.

Although its palaces and *azulejos* survived—albeit often in a dilapidated state—São Luís itself never fully recovered from the decline that followed the abolition of slavery and the demise of its plantation economy. Only recently have the city's fortunes began to improve somewhat. The mining of iron ore in the interior coupled with an important aluminum industry and a

THE NORTHEAST COAST

new deepwater port have given a small jump-start to the economy. Meanwhile, in the later 1990s, the beginnings of tourism—combined with the recognition of São Luís's colonial center as a UNESCO World Heritage Site—were instrumental in launching Projeto Reviver, a project that has been responsible for slowly recuperating São Luís's architectural treasures and bringing its historic heart back to life.

Aside from cobblestoned *praças* and restored *palácios,* the city is bursting with cultural riches, a legacy of slavery that transformed São

Luís—along with Rio and Salvador—into one of the Brazilian cities where African religion, culture, music, and cuisine are still strong. This influence is apparent in the city's many popular *festas* as well as the music that regularly fills the streets, be it the powerful drumming of *tambores de crioula* or the slower, more mellow rhythms of reggae.

Sights

São Luís is a sprawling city spread out along an island peninsula. However, the oldest and most interesting parts are concentrated on the island's tip, at the point where the Rio Anil flows into the Baía de São Marcos. Within the old city center, known as Centro, lies the neighborhood of Praia Grande. This colonial ensemble of cobblestoned streets and restored (and still crumbling) palaces falls under the jurisdiction of the Projeto Reviver (which is why you'll often hear the *bairro* referred to as "Reviver"). Almost all of São Luís's sights, and most of its action, are concentrated in this dense, fascinating, and easy-to-wander-around area. The only confusing aspect is that many streets have more than one name.

◖ PROJETO REVIVER (PRAIA GRANDE)

The neighborhood known as Reviver or Praia Grande is a long area bordered by Rua Afonso Pena to the east and Avenida Beira Mar to the west. A good place to begin exploring is at its northernmost edge, where you'll find two magnificent squares. **Praça Benedito Leite** is an elegant, green park dominated by the **Igreja da Sé** (Praça Dom Pedro II, tel. 98/3222-7380, 8 A.M.–noon and 2:30–5:30 P.M. daily). The city's main cathedral, it was built in 1690 by Jesuits in honor of Nossa Senhora da Vitória, who had supposedly helped the Portuguese oust the French from São Luís. Inside, the main baroque altar is awash in gold, and you can detect some local *babaçu* palms depicted in the painted ceiling frescoes.

Adjacent to Praça Benedito Leite is the much grander **Praça Dom Pedro II,** whose far end gazes out over the Baía de São Marcos. Two particularly majestic palaces line the square. The **Palácio dos Leões** (Av. Dom Pedro II, tel. 98/2108-9000, 2–5 P.M. Mon., Wed., and Fri.) was constructed in 1766 as the state governor's residence, on the site of the original Fortaleza de São Luís erected by the French. Guided visits (in Portuguese) allow you to view the elegant salons filled with 18th- and 19th-century paintings and furniture. Next door, the stately **Palácio La Ravardière,** built in 1689, is one of São Luís's oldest edifices. Still exercising its original function as City Hall, its name (and the statue on its threshold) pays

homage to São Luís's dashing French founder, Daniel de La Touche, also known as Sieur de la Ravardière.

On the opposite side of the *praça* from the palaces, a flight of steep limestone steps leads down the picturesque, bar-lined street known as **Beco Catarina Mina.** Near the end of the stairs is the mansion of Catarina Rosa Ferreira de Jesus, an African slave of great beauty who, after purchasing her freedom, became a wealthy and successful merchant by supplying manioc flour to the Portuguese. The staircase marks your descent into the heart of colonial Praia Grande, where block after block of *azulejo*-encrusted mansions alternate with peeling buildings in blistered and faded pinks, blues, jades, and saffrons. Running parallel to each other are three main streets that cut lengthwise through the *bairro* and are home to most of its treasures: **Rua da Palma, Rua do Giz,** and **Rua da Estrela.**

Beco Catarina Mina ends on **Rua Portugal,** a street whose buildings showcase a dazzling array of colorful tile work. Close by, the arches of the early 19th-century **Casa das Tulhas** (Rua da Estrela, Praia Grande, 6 A.M.–8 P.M. Mon.–Fri., 6 A.M.–6 P.M. Sat., 6 A.M.–1 P.M. Sun.) give way to the Mercado Praia Grande, a traditional and very charming market hidden away behind the Casa's colonial facade. It's worth wandering past the stands selling dried shrimp, medicinal herbs, exotic fruit, cotton hammocks, and Indian basketry. Make sure to stop for a drink in order to take in the surrounding activity while you quench your thirst.

Compared to other historical cities in Brazil, São Luís is bereft of splendid colonial churches. Apart from the cathedral, the most interesting one is the striking early-18th-century **Igreja do Desterro** (Largo do Desterro), whose onion-like Byzantine domes are a strange, but beautiful, surprise. The **Convento das Mercês** (Rua da Palma, 502) was founded in 1654 by celebrated Jesuit preacher Antônio Vieira, whose sermons are highly regarded as Brazil's early literary writings. The hibiscus-colored exterior is quite arresting. However, you can skip the museum inside—a worshipful collection of memorabilia honoring a former Brazilian president (1985–1990) and all-powerful governor of Maranhão, José Sarney. On the edge of Praia Grande, the **Igreja do Carmo** (Praça João Lisboa) dates back to 1627. It has suffered various modifications over time, including the 1866 addition of the white-and-yellow Portuguese *azulejos* covering its facade.

São Luís has an impressive number of small, but interesting, museums. Most are located in Praia Grande's historic mansions and palaces. Many of the visits are guided (often only in Portuguese).

The **Casa do Maranhão** (Rua do Trapiche, Praia Grande, tel. 98/3218-9955, www.culturapopular.ma.gov.br/casadomaranhao.php, 9 A.M.–7 P.M. Tues.–Sun., free) is a must-see museum if you want some excellent insight into Maranhão's spectacular Bumba-Meu-Boi festivities. Housed in a 19th-century customs building on the waterfront, the museum traces the history of this *festa* from pagan times and early Christianity up to the rich syncretic makeover it received in northeastern Brazil, where it was influenced by African and indigenous cultures. Even if your knowledge of Portuguese is nil, musical instruments, videos, and sumptuous costumes and accessories will whet your appetite to see the real thing. The **Centro de Cultura Popular** (Rua do Giz 221, Praia Grande, tel. 98/3218-9924, www.culturapopular.ma.gov.br/centrodecultura.php, 9 A.M.–7 P.M. Tues.–Sun., free) goes one step beyond the Casa do Maranhão. Also known as the Casa da Festa, it boasts four floors of colorful displays that provide a wonderful overview of rich cultural traditions from around the state. Aside from a refresher in Bumba-Meu-Boi, captivating photographs and regalia provide you with an indelible impression of festivals such as Carnaval, the Festa do Divino, and rituals linked to Tambor de Mina, Maranhão's important Afro-Brazilian religion (similar to Candomblé).

Lodged inside a splendid *azulejo*-covered house, the **Casa de Nhôzinho** (Rua Portugal 185, Praia Grande, tel. 98/3218-9951, www.culturapopular.ma.gov.br/casadenhozinho.php, 9 A.M.–7 P.M. Tues.–Sun., free) showcases Maranhão's typical *artesanato* with a beguiling array of objects from daily life, including pottery, fishing implements, wonderful toys made from scrap materials, and artifacts from numerous indigenous groups. A special gallery is devoted to the works of Mestre Nhozinho (1904–1974), a Maranhense artisan renowned for the wood carvings he sculpted out of buriti palm. The toys he made and gave to poor children are quite ingenious.

The **Museu de Artes Visuais** (Rua Portugal 273, Praia Grande, tel. 98/3218-9938, 9 A.M.–7 P.M. Tues.–Fri., 9 A.M.–6 P.M. Sat.–Sun., free) serves up an artistic mishmash culled from private collections that mixes centuries (17th to 20th) and genres (baroque religious art, Brazilian modernism, works by contemporary Maranhense artists). The most interesting part of this museum is its overview of *azulejo* manufacturing, illustrated by some fine samples of glazed tiles from Portugal, Spain, Germany, and France.

The **Cafua das Mercês** (Rua Jacinto Maia 43, Desterro, 9 A.M.–6 P.M. Mon.–Fri., free) consists of a small house and courtyard (with a replica of a whipping post) that was formerly São Luís's slave market. The haunting, claustrophobic atmosphere and handful of chains and torture instruments leave more of an impact than the sprinkling of West African artifacts that aspire to constitute a Museu do Negro.

CENTRO

Beyond Praia Grande's frontiers lie a couple of other interesting museums. Occupying a gracious early-19th-century mansion, the **Museu Artístico e Histórico do Maranhão** (Rua do Sol 302, Centro, tel. 098/3218-9920, 9 A.M.–7 P.M. Tues.–Fri., 9 A.M.–6 P.M. Sat.–Sun., R$1) conjures up the lifestyles of the rich and powerful in São Luís's economic heyday. Furnished as if people were still living in them, rooms are replete with lots of dark, gleaming wooden furniture, crystal chandeliers, and delicate English and French porcelain, most of which was donated by descendants of the former proprietors. Just around the corner, another grand mansion houses the **Museu de Arte Sacra** (Rua 13 de Maio 500, Centro, tel. 98/3218-4537, 9 A.M.–6 P.M. Tues.–Fri., 2–6 P.M. Sat.–Sun., free), which possesses an excellent collection of 17th- to 19th-century religious art rescued from churches throughout Maranhão.

On the same street as the Museu Artístico e Histórico, you can't help but notice the coral-colored neoclassical facade of the **Teatro Arthur Azevedo** (Rua do Sol 180, Centro, tel. 98/3218-9900, Visits at 3 P.M. and 5 P.M. Tues.–Fri., R\$3). Built in the early 19th century with money from local cotton barons, the second biggest theater in Brazil is a grand imitation of European theaters of the time. Recently restored and reopened, it's worthwhile taking a guided tour to observe the opulence of its interior.

During the 17th and 18th centuries, São Luís had many public fountains that supplied water to the populace. Two that are still in existence are the **Fonte das Pedras** (Rua São João) and **Fonte do Ribeirão** (Largo do Ribeiro). The latter is truly splendid, with water pouring out of bronze spigots that are set into the mouths of a quintet of fierce-looking heads. The heads are set into a bright blue wall, behind which a series of subterranean tunnels lead to underwater wells. According to local legend, these tunnels are inhabited by a giant serpent that, one day, will rise up with its tail and smash the city, causing it to sink to the bottom of the sea.

Beaches

Unlike in other northeastern cities, beaches are not a main attraction in São Luís. Although clean, sweeping and wide, the sands are an uninspiring beige and the water is murky. Due to the city's proximity to the Equator, the tides are enormous. As a result, when the tide goes out, you have to walk for ages just to feel the ocean lapping against your knees. When the tide is high, rough waves and currents make swimming dangerous. Nonetheless, the beaches do offer a relaxing break. Crowded on weekends, they're almost deserted during the week.

It's easy to get to the beaches by bus or car from Centro. All you need to do is cross the Ponte José Sarney that spans the Rio Anil, on the other side of which is the modern, commercial district of São Francisco. From here, Avenida Ana Jansen leads past the Lagoa de Jansen to **Ponta d'Areia,** the first of many tony, but completely characterless beach neighborhoods, which serve as residences and playgrounds for São Luís's middle class and elite. The main drag, Avenida Litorânea, then follows the ocean past the long beaches of **São Marcos, Calhau,** and **Olho d'Agua.** São Marcos has a pleasant boardwalk lined with animated bars that are popular with surfers. Equally nice is Calhau with its many *barracas* where you can take refuge from the sun (or rain). Vendors sell various snacks, including fresh oysters, which they will open right in front of you and douse with lime juice. You can easily feast on dozens.

Nightlife
BARS

São Luís is a pretty quiet city. Although there are some options across the bridge in the beach *bairros* of Ponte d'Areia and Calhau, the most lively and interesting nightlife takes place in Praia Grande's bars, specifically in the streets surrounding the Casa das Tulhas. Between Thursday and Saturday, live music draws large crowds. A favorite spot to check out the action is **O Armazém da Estrela** (Rua da Estrela 401, tel. 98/3254-1274, Praia Grande, 11 A.M.–midnight Mon.–Sat.). Apart from serving good food and cocktails, this restaurant/bar has an attractive gallery/café where you can check your email and purchase CDs by local musicians. Somewhat more bustling, **Antigamente** (Rua da Estrela 220, Praia Grande, tel. 98/3232-3964, 10 A.M.–3 A.M. Mon.–Sat.) lures crowds with live MPB performances while the more funky and alternative **Chez Moi** (Rua do Giz 17, Praia Grande, tel. 98/3221-5877, 8 P.M.–close) features different types of music every night of the week. The bars on Beco Caterina Mina are quite picturesque and fill up during happy hour.

In Centro, **Ambulatório Santos** (Rua

© MICHAEL SOMMERS

Projeto Reviver (Praia Grande) neighborhood in São Luís

Humberto Campos 205, tel. 98/3232-7521) is a pharmacy that offers cures for all ailments. Aside from giving vaccines, the friendly owner, Seu Tonico, prescribes homemade liqueurs infused with medicinal fruits and herbs. One of the most popular brews is Bom Que Doi ("So Good It Hurts"), a brew of *cachaça,* lime, honey, cinnamon, anise, and cloves that leaves imbibers feeling *alegre.* As a side note, Seu Tonico is father of homegrown talent, Zeca Baleiro, one of Brazil's most prolific and interesting contemporary musicians.

LIVE MUSIC

São Luís is associated with two very distinctive types of music with strong African roots: *tambor de crioula* and reggae.

Tambor de crioula is a traditional form of dance and music that dates back to the early colonial days of slavery. While men pound out frenzied rhythms of long drums (played horizontally), women dance in a circle, dressed in bright, billowing hoop skirts and lace blouses. Associated with the cult of São Benedito (a black

saint), *tambor de crioula* groups perform during Carnaval as well in the streets of Praia Grande.

Few foreigners are aware that São Luís is South America's reggae capital. Back in the '70s, the city's proximity to Jamaica allowed tunes by Bob Marley, Peter Tosh, and others to be picked up by shortwave radio, which were then adapted into Portuguese. In São Luís, reggae—live or played by DJs—is blasted through a massive wall of multiple speakers known as *radiolas.* Dancing is done in a romantic cheek-to-cheek style. The most authentic reggae *festas* are held in the poor suburbs, but a few take place in Praia Grande and the beach areas, which are safer for gringos. *Festas* usually occur between Thursday and Saturday, beginning at around 8 P.M. In Praia Grande, try **Bar do Porto** (Rua Trapiche 49, tel. 98/3232-6418) and **Roots Bar** (Rua da Palma 85, tel. 98/3221-7580). **Bar do Nelson** (Av. Litorânea 135, Calhau, 9 P.M.–close Fri.–Sat.) is a classic bar with a cult following.

Entertainment and Events
PERFORMING ARTS

Located in an attractively renovated old warehouse near the waterfront, the **Centro de Criatividade Odylo Costa Filho** (Rampa do Comércio 200, Praia Grande, tel. 98/3248-9934) is a worthwhile place to check out the local arts scene. Aside from a gallery space and a theater that hosts plays and dance performances, there is a small art house cinema that screens interesting films. Also check for concerts at the ornate **Teatro Arthur Azevedo** (Rua do Sol 180, Centro, tel. 98/3218-9900).

FESTIVALS AND EVENTS

São Luís is a hothouse for popular and religious celebrations. While nobody ever talks about its **Carnaval,** in recent years, traditional *blocos* (groups) and *bandas* have been resurrected. The resulting festivities give you a real taste of Brazilian Carnavals of yore. Brass bands play *marchinhas* (marches) and traditional Afro *blocos* pound out *tambor-de-crioula* rhythms while lithe dancers whirl like dervishes. Residents of all ages take to the streets of the *centro histórico*

BUMBA-MEU-BOI

São Luís isn't the only place in Brazil that hosts Bumba-Meu-Boi, but it is the definitive place to observe one of the country's most captivating spectacles, combining music, art, and pageantry. Drawing on indigenous, African, and Portuguese folk elements, Bumba-Meu-Boi consists of a series of theatrical dances performed over several nights in mid-late June. Visually stunning, the festivities feature troupes of well-known folk characters in brilliant costumes. They are accompanied by musicians playing brass instruments and drums, the most unique of which is the deep, throbbing *bumba*.

The *festa* revolves around the magical tale of a plantation owner who leaves a slave to take care of his prize bull (*boi*), which dies and then comes back to life with the help of forest spirits. Bumba-Meu-Boi troupes are like samba schools. There are many groups within the city and rivalries exist as to who can put on the most dazzling spectacle featuring the story's characters. The *bois* are exceptionally resplendent – their costumes are festooned in ribbons, sequins, and embroidery fanciful enough to make a Parisian couturier's jaw drop. It's impossible to resist joining in the dancing and singing that invades the streets of Praia Grande and Centro. If you miss the main celebration, you can catch Bumba-Meu-Boi troupes performing throughout the month of July at the Convento das Mercês.

and Praia Grande in masks and sequins. The atmosphere is heavy on *alegria* and light on mayhem. Even bigger and more spectacular than Carnaval the not-to-be-missed **Bumba-Meu-Boi** festivities, which take place in June. One of Brazil's most spectacular and moving popular celebrations, the *festa* combines African, Indian, and European melodies and rhythms and lots of pageantry.

Shopping

São Luís is a rich source of folk and indigenous art and *artesanato*. Located in a vast warehouse on the edge of Praia Grande, the state-run **Centro de Artesanato** (Rua São Pantaleão 1332, Madre de Deus, 9 A.M.–7 P.M. Mon.–Sat., 10 A.M.–2 P.M. Sun.) reunites souvenir-style handicrafts from around Maranhão including hand-painted *azulejos,* miniature Bumba-Meu-Boi bulls with embroidered costumes, lacework, and ceramics. You'll also find *doces* and liqueurs made from local fruits such as buriti, *bacuri,* and *cupuaçu*. In Praia Grande, there are lots of interesting little shops. Check out the market stalls at the **Casa das Tulhas** (see *Sights*). **Arte Indígena** (Rua do Giz 66, tel. 98/3221-2940, Praia Grande, 9 A.M.–9 P.M. Mon.–Sat., noon–7 P.M. Sun.)

features basketry, jewelry, and other objects made by Maranhense indigenous groups.

Accommodations

Although there are plenty of modern hotels in the beach neighborhoods of Ponta d'Areia and Calhau, the beaches aren't that fantastic. Moreover, the hotels, which range from bland to hideous, are overpriced for what you get. São Luís's real interest lies in its history, culture, and architecture, which makes Praia Grande and Centro the best places to stay.

An insanely inexpensive option is the **Albergue Juventude Solar das Pedras** (Rua da Palma 127, tel. 98/3232-6694, www.ajsolardaspedras.com.br, R$40–50 d), a youth hostel located in an old building right in the middle of the historical center. Although the rich blue facade gives off cheery vibes, the rooms, while clean and functional, are a little spare and sad. However, where else can you get a dorm room for R$15–20 per night with breakfast (and access to Internet, kitchen and laundry facilities)? More atmospheric are the common spaces, where exposed stone walls and wooden floors reveal the building's former character. A little more money gets you more privacy and personality.

The once grand **Lord Hotel** (Rua de Nazaré

258, Centro, tel. 98/3221-4674, R$65–80 d) is a little faded and threadbare, but if you're a sucker for retro ambiance, you'll be charmed by the high ceilings along with the '40s fixtures and furnishings. Make sure you get a room with a view overlooking the Praça Benedito Leite. While not right in Praia Grande, the **Pousada Colonial** (Rua Afonso Pena 112, Centro, tel. 98/3232-2843, www.clickcolonial.com.br, R$110 d) is close enough. This colonial building plastered in white, blue, and lemon *azulejos* has been carefully renovated. Both the comfortable, if somewhat small, air-conditioned rooms and the common spaces are bright, spacious, and well cared for. The best rooms are those overlooking the street.

For palatial surroundings, check into one of the immense rooms at the **C Pousada Portas da Amazônia** (Rua do Giz 129, Praia Grande, tel. 98/3222-9937, www.portasdaamazonia.com.br, R$89–159 d), a handsomely restored mansion dating back to 1839. The decor mingles antiques with local *artesanato* and organic materials such as bamboo, wicker, and stone. Rooms boast thick wooden floorboards and cathedral ceilings. Large windows either overlook a sea of colonial rooftops (a little noisy) or a tropical courtyard garden (more tranquil) where breakfast is served. Although this hotel isn't luxurious, the spaciousness and palpable flavor of the past make it seem that way. There is a cyber café on-site as well as a pizzeria that opens in the evening.

The **Hotel Grand São Luís** (Av. Pedro II 299, Centro, tel. 98/2109-3500, www.grand-saoluis.com.br, R$185–205 d) is the only hotel in the historical district that offers three-star comfort. It recently reopened after undergoing major renovations of the original, not-so-swinging '70s-era hotel. If you're seeking convenience and modern comforts, such as a trio of swimming pools and a tiny fitness room, you'll appreciate this hotel, but if you're looking for warmth and/or charm you won't find it here.

Food

São Luís is a seafood lover's paradise. Both the ocean and the region's many rivers yield abundant fish, oysters, crab, and jumbo-sized shrimp. Maranhão's most characteristic specialty is *arroz-de-cuxá*. This rice-based dish is made with the mildly pungent leaves of a local plant called *vinagreira*, to which dried shrimp, toasted sesame, and manioc flour are added. Also try the *torta de camarão*, a type of frittata stuffed with dry or fresh shrimp, a recipe that was originally invented by slaves. Maranhão's proximity to the Amazon explains the presence of a couple of the most ambrosial fruits you'll ever taste: *cupuaçu* (whose popularity has spread throughout Brazil) and the much rarer *bacuri*. Savor them as thick juices or for dessert as mousse-like *cremes*.

Instead of Coca Cola or Guaraná, Maranhenses swear by Jesus. The name of this bright pink soft drink has no connection to the son of God. Instead, it pays homage to local pharmacist Jesus Norberto Gomes, who invented it back in 1920. Jesus' ingredients include cinnamon, cloves, and the jolting presence of *guaraná*. In markets and bars, you'll also see plenty of bottles of a distilled substance that ranges in color from pale lilac to ultraviolet. Known as *tiquira*, this popular Maranhense version of *cachaça* is made from fermented manioc and it packs quite a wallop.

With its tables spread out across a patio overlooking the Baía de São Marcos, **C Base de Lenoca** (Av. Dom Pedro II, Centro, tel. 98/3231-0599, 11 A.M.–midnight daily, R$15–25) offers a picturesque setting where you can savor delicious Maranhense fare. Specialties include *caldeirada maranhense,* a stew of jumbo shrimp swimming in coconut milk, and *casquinhas de carangueijo,* in which crab meat sautéed with garlic, tomato, and lime juice is served in its shell. Located on the second floor of a colonial building, the lavish spreads at the **Restaurante SENAC** (Rua de Nazaré 242, Centro, tel. 98/3222-6377, noon–3 P.M. Mon.–Fri., 8 P.M.–midnight Fri., R$15–25) are prepared and ceremoniously served by local students of the SENAC restaurant school. The lunch buffets change daily. The best is the Maranhense banquet, which allows you to sample regional cooking until you're ready to burst.

Housed in a colonial *palacete,* **Antigamente** (Rua da Estrela 220, Praia Grande, tel. 98/3232-3964, 10 A.M.–3 A.M. Mon.–Sat., R$15–30) has a varied menu of adequate fare ranging from meat and fish to pasta dishes. Although usually loaded with tourists, its sidewalk tables in the heart of the colonial center are a terrific spot to while away a few hours in the company of beer and the famous *caldeirada de frutos de mar,* a hearty seafood gumbo with cilantro and lime. At night, live music is often performed. The classiest joint in Praia Grande is **O Armazém da Estrela** (Rua da Estrela 401, tel. 98/3254-1274, Praia Grande, 11 A.M.–midnight Mon.–Sat., R$28–38), whose sophisticated upstairs dining room seduces local socialites with its tiled floors and exposed stone walls along with its refined menu featuring dishes such as beef medallion cooked in red wine and snapper fillets bathed in *cajá* sauce.

For a swanky meal along the beach, head to **Porto Maracangalha** (Av. Litorânea 2, Quadro 9, Calhau, www.portomaracangalha.com.br, 11:30 A.M.–midnight daily, R$25–35), a charming eatery whose walls are decorated with colorful works by local artists including the restaurant's chef, Melquíades Dantas. Dantas is the inventor of an addictive *geleia de pimenta* (pepper jelly) that accompanies the beef *pastéis,* which is a great starter. Entrées feature seafood dishes such as anchovy fillets topped with shrimp with *arroz-de-cuxá* and a celebrated *caldeirada maranhense.* The breezy veranda overlooking the beach is a wonderful place to sample the extensive menu of cocktails and *cachaças.*

Information

You'll find **tourist offices** at Praça Benedito Leite (Rua da Palma 53, Centro, tel. 98/3212-6211, 9 A.M.–6 P.M. daily) and Praia Grande (Rua do Portugal 165, tel. 98/3231-0822, 9 A.M.–6 P.M. daily) as well as at the airport (tel. 98/3244-4500) and the *rodoviária* (tel. 98/3249-4500). On the Internet, the state government has a good bilingual website (www.turismo.ma.gov.br). The municipal website (www.saoluis.ma.gov.br) is in Portuguese only. **Lotus Turismo e Aventura** (Rua Marcelino Almeida 25, Praia Grande, tel. 98/3221-0942, www.lotusturismo.com.br) offers tours of the coastline around São Luís, as well as trips to Alcântara and the Parque Nacional dos Lençóis Maranhenses.

Services

For banking, you'll find Banco do Brasil branches in the *centro histórico* (Av. Dom Pedro II, tel. 7898/3215-4992), in front of the Palácio dos Leões, and in Praia Grande (Travessa Boa Ventura 26-B, tel. 98/3232-5060). There is an HSBC on Rua João Lisboa, near Praça João Lisboa, on the edge of Praia Grande. The main post office is also on Praça João Lisboa.

Livraria Poem-Se is a bookstore that also sells magazines and CDs and has Internet access. It has a location in the *centro histórico* (Rua do Sol 451, tel. 98/3221-1869, 8 A.M.–6 P.M. Mon.–Fri., 8 A.M.–1 P.M. Sat.) and in Praia Grande (Rua Joao Valberto 52, tel. 98/3232-4068, 8 A.M.–6 P.M. Mon.–Fri., 8 A.M.–1 P.M. Sat.).

In an emergency, dial **193** for the fire department, **192** for an ambulance, and **190** for the police. The special **tourist police** headquarters is in Praia Grande (Rua da Estrela 427, tel. 98/3232-4324). For medical assistance in the Centro Histórico, try the **Santa Casa de Misericórdia** (Rua do Norte 233, tel. 98/3221-5447).

Getting There

Air fare to São Luís is not that cheap, but the alternative is long hours spent on buses. There are few direct flights from major Brazilian cities. You'll often need to make a connection in Fortaleza or Brasília. The **Aeroporto Marechal Cunha Machado** (Av. dos Libaneses, Tirirical, tel. 98/3245-4500), is 13 kilometers (8 miles) from the *centro histórico.* A taxi to the center costs R$35–40.

Long-distance buses to São Luís are much cheaper, but take forever. There is no direct service along the coast from Fortaleza— instead you have to go via Piaui and change in

Parnaíba or Teresina (ultimately, you'll spend 15 hours on the road). Coming from Recife, Salvador, or Brasília also usually entails a connection in Teresina. The long-distance *rodoviária* (Av. dos Franceses, Santo Antônio, tel. 98/3249-2488) is 10 kilometers (6 miles) from the *centro histórico*. A cab will cost between R$25–30. You can also take a municipal bus to the **Terminal de Integração,** the local bus station located along the waterfront at Praia Grande.

Getting Around

In terms of buses, the only ones you'll really need to take are those that shuttle between the Terminal de Integração (marked "Praia Grande") and the beaches (marked "Ponta d'Areia" or "Calhau"). Bus fare is R$1.60. For other destinations, and after sundown, you should resort to taxis, which are easy to hail. You can also reserve one by calling **Cocoma** (tel. 98/3231-1010). Renting a car is not really necessary, unless you want to drive to the Lençóis Maranhenses. If so, **Avis** (www.avis.com.br) has an office at the airport (tel. 98/3245-5957) and at Calhau (Av. dos Holandeses 5, tel. 98/3226-6675), and **Localiza** (www.localiza.com) is at the airport (tel. 98/3245-1566).

ALCÂNTARA

Across the Baía de São Marcos from São Luís—about an hour and a half by boat—lies the hauntingly beautiful colonial town of Alcântara. Founded in 1648, its picturesque hilltop was the favored dwelling place of Maranhão's wealthy sugar and cotton plantation owners. During its 18th- and 19th-century heyday, it was one of Brazil's most sumptuous colonial towns. The abolition of slavery resulted in the end of the high life. The ruined plantation owners decamped to São Luís, leaving their freed slaves in the abandoned town. Subsequently, like a city out of a Gabriel García Márquez novel, Alcântara slipped into oblivion. The road leading to São Luís (an eight-hour drive) became overgrown as did the town itself. Indeed, its dilapidated baroque treasures—many now in ruins—seem to be slowly on the verge of being swallowed up by steamy tropical jungle. What Alcântara lacks in lost grandeur, it more than makes up for in atmosphere. It is truly an alluring place to while away a day.

Sights

Approaching Alcântara by boat is an experience in itself as you view its church domes, red tile roofs, and lithe imperial palms slowly emerge from a swathe of emerald jungle. Despite the many ruins, there are over 300 17th- and 18th-century mansions spread around the hilltop in various states of disrepair. The main square of Praça da Matriz is truly impressive. Lined on three sides by once grand palaces, and with a splendid view overlooking the bay, the heart of the square is dominated by the rust brick ruins of the **Igreja Matriz de São Mathias.** In the center stands the *pelourinho* (whipping post used for slaves) tattooed with the Portuguese crown's coat-of-arms. On one side of the *praça* sits the **Museu Histórico** (9 A.M.–2 P.M. daily, R$1). Occupying an *azulejo*-covered mansion that belonged to of one of Alcântara's aristocratic families, the museum displays a small collection of engravings, furnishings, and objects that evoke the city's days of glory. Included is the iron bed specially made for the visit of Emperor Dom Pedro II.

On **Rua da Amargura** (Street of Bitterness), you can see the ruins of the Palácio Negro, which served as the slave market, and of the Casa do Imperador. Alcântara's leading families fought tooth and nail over who would have the privilege of building the house that would lodge Dom Pedro II during an official visit. To the townspeople's eternal disappointment, despite the lavish welcome they had prepared for him, the emperor never made it to Alcântara (rumor has it he was waylaid by a seductive Indian maiden). Rua Grande is also full of treasures, including the 17th-century **Igreja do Carmo** (8 A.M.–1 P.M. and 2–5 P.M. Mon.–Fri., 9 A.M.–2 P.M. Sat.–Sun.), whose original baroque splendor has been restored to its former glory.

A short walk from the town brings you to the fairly primitive **Praia da Baronesa.** Framed by jungle, the beach is a nice place to sit at a *barraca* and feast on fresh fish and icy beer while watching for *guarás*. A diet of pink shrimp explains the lipstick-red plumage of these birds (known in English as scarlet ibises). Their appearance against the canopy of green foliage presents a shocking contrast. Also in the vicinity of Alcântara is Brazil's satellite-launching center, home of the Brazilian space program (visitors aren't allowed).

Festivals and Events

One of Maranhão's most legendary popular celebrations, the **Festa do Divino** mobilizes Alcântâra's entire population during two weeks in May. A colorful fusion of African and Catholic elements, the *festa* also provides a resolution to the no-show of Dom Pedro II with celebrations revolving around the figures of a sumptuously attired emperor and empress (two local children) who are paraded through town to much fanfare. Commemorations include fireworks, music, and dancing to the pounding drums played by matriarchs of Tambor de Mina *terreiros*. Moist coconut tarts shaped like tiny tortoises, known as *doce-de-especies*, are distributed to all the children.

Accommodations and Food

Most people visit Alcântara as a day trip. Should you be very struck by the place, there are several *pousadas* where you can spend the night, including the **Pousada dos Guarás** (Praia da Baronesa, tel. 98/3337-1339, R$60–85 d). Located right on the beach, these palm-thatched bungalows are simple but utterly tranquil. A seaside restaurant/bar serves up delicious fresh fish. For food in town, **Restaurante da Josefa** (Rua Direita 33, tel. 98/3337-1109, 6:30 A.M.–10:30 P.M. daily) is a cozy homestyle eatery presided over by Dona Josefa, whose tasty home-cooking includes generous portions of fish, seafood, and chicken dishes with myriad fixings.

Getting There

Ferries to Alcântara depart from São Luís's **Terminal Hidroviário** (tel. 98/3232-6929) on Praia Grande's main waterfront. Departure times can be affected by the tides. In fact, during low tide, you may need to depart or return via the Yacht Club in Ponto d'Areia (check first at the terminal). Tickets cost R$10. Be aware that sometimes the crossing can be a little choppy. Alternatives are to take a faster but more expensive motorboat or a slower but more scenic catamaran. All boat and information schedules are available at the terminal.

◖ LENÇÓIS MARANHENSES

One of Brazil's most spectacular natural attractions, the Lençóis Maranhenses—250 kilometers (155 miles) east of São Luís—is a fantastic desert of immense white sand dunes that bear a striking resemblance to billowing *lençóis*, or sheets. Some of the dunes are 50 meters (164 feet) high. Every year when the rains come (from December to May), their valleys fill with water, forming a series of jade lagoons whose mirror-like surfaces reflect the piercing blue sky filled with drifting clouds and gliding egrets. The majesty of the landscape is impossible to express. But the sense of timelessness is impressive; particularly when trekking through the sand, you turn around to see that the wind has wiped out the only sign of civilization—the footprints you made only five minutes earlier.

Parque Nacional dos Lençóis Maranhenses

The Lençóis Maranhenses are within the Parque Nacional dos Lençóis Maranhenses, a protected area that is around the size of Rhode Island. No cars are allowed in the park (although Jeeps can take you within close proximity). To explore the dunes on foot, you'll need to hire a guide or go as part of an excursion. The closest town is nearby Barreirinhas, a six-hour bus ride from São Luís, where there are plenty of hotels and restaurants as well as guides and tour operators. The best time to visit are the sunny days between June and September when the lagoons are still full enough to bathe in (by December, they've often completely evaporated). You can explore the park from Barreirinhas by Jeep or boat.

© AYRSON HERÁCLITO

Parque Nacional dos Lençóis Maranhenses

BY JEEP

The closest and easiest way to explore the dunes is by taking the half-day Jeep trips that visit nearby lagoons, including the particularly gorgeous **Lagoa Bonita** and **Lagoa Azul.** Try to go in the afternoon (when it's cooler and the light is more golden), since you'll be able to watch the sun set over the dunes. A full-day Jeep outing to the village of **Santo Amaro do Maranhão** allows you to visit the enchanted **Lagoa da Gaivota,** one of the largest and deepest of all the park's lagoons, whose colors change like a 1970s mood ring. **Tropical Adventure** (tel. 98/3349-1987, www.tropical-adventure-expedicoes.com), **Ecotrilha** (tel. 98/3349-0372, www.ecotrilha.com), and **Ecodunas** (tel. 98/3349-0545, www.ecodunas.com.br) all operate Jeep trips, which start at around R$50 per person for a half-day trip.

BY BOAT

The **Rio Preguiças** is a river that passes close to Barreiras. It winds through a landscape of buriti palm forests, mangrove swamps, and sand dunes, passing tiny palm thatched villages, until it finally flows into the ocean. With a guide, you can descend the river by launch or by a small motorboat known as a *voadeira.* Excursions include stops for swimming and lunch in the fishing village of **Caburé,** which lies on a sandbar between the river and the sea. You'll also stop in the village of **Mandacaru** to climb up the **Farol Preguiças,** a picturesque lighthouse that offers fantastic 360-degree views of the dunes. Another option is to hire a boat to take you downriver to **Atins,** an idyllic village ensconced in the dunes, which is surrounded by some stunning lagoons such as the Lagoa Tropical. Although you can visit Atins in a day trip, it's worthwhile staying overnight so you can explore the surrounding dunes and lagoons on foot (and soak up the relaxing vibes).

Tropical Adventure and **Ecodunas** can organize these boat trips for you. A full-day excursion for up to four people costs around R$50 per person (not including lunch). You can also negotiate directly with a boat operator and guide (a boat trip to Atins should cost around R$80).

Sports and Recreation

An utterly relaxing way of taking in the dune-scapes is to float by them in a rubber inner tube known as *boia cross*. Half-day trips feature 90 minutes of floating down Rio Cardosa, an emerald colored river that's a 45-minute Jeep ride from Barreirinhas. For a more panoramic view, splurge for the 30-minute flight that will give you an unforgettable bird's-eye view over the dunes (for the best light, reserve the morning or late afternoon). **Ecodunas** can organize both trips for you. *Boia-cross* costs around R$50 per person while a flight is R$150 per person.

Shopping

Barreirinhas is buriti country. Locals use the fibers from this palm to make everything from roofing thatch to baskets, hats, and handbags that are the epitome of organic chic. You'll find a wide array of items at the **Casa das Sementes** (Av. Brasília 12, tel. 98/3349-0576) and the **Centro de Artesanato** (Praça do Trabalhador).

Accommodations and Food

Barreirinhas is a pleasant little town with sandy beaches carved out by the Rio Preguiças. There are plenty of *pousadas* to choose from, although some are a little on the tacky side.

Despite its newness, the **Hotel Rio Preguiças** (Av. Brasília 80, tel. 98/3349-0925, www.riopreguicashotel.com.br, R$150–165 d) has the retro feel (if not charm) of a small town Brazilian hotel of the '60s or '70s. Centrally located on the main square of Praça do Matriz, the standard air-conditioned rooms are spotless and innocuous. Balconies with hammocks overlook the leafy *praça*. A more attractive budget option is the **Pousada Encantes do Nordeste** (Av. Boa Vista, tel. 98/3349-0288, www.encantesdonordeste.com.br, R$130–150 d). Its rustic chalets are nestled in a lush garden close to the Rio Preguiças (where you can swim). The air-conditioned rooms are simple but homey and the staff is friendly. Although it's 4 kilometers (2.5 miles) from the center of town, most excursions will pick you up at the *pousada*. At

night, you can easily take a cab or *moto-taxi* to the center, or stay in and watch DVDs.

For more luxury, consider the **Porto Preguiças Resort** (Carnaubal Velho, tel. 98/3349-1800, www.portopreguicas.com.br, R$290–350 d), located 2 kilometers (1.2 miles) from town near the river. Although not quite luxurious (especially for the price), the pseudo rustic and slightly spartan chalet accommodations are spacious and comfortable with fancy linen sheets and thick cotton towels. The sprawling grounds' enticing features include a sand-bottom swimming pool, a private river beach with a floating bar, and pergolas where you can flake out in a hammock. The resort's very attractive **Restaurante Sgte. Peppers** (noon–10 P.M. daily, R$20–30), decorated with local ceramics and overlooking the pool, is reputed for its sophisticated regional and international fare. It is also a seductive spot for pre-dinner cocktail.

For food, there are various restaurants along Avenida Beira-Mar, all of which take advantage of the pretty river views. **Marina Tropical** (Av. Beira-Rio, tel. 98/3349-1143, 11 A.M.–11 P.M. daily, closed Sun. during off-season, R$12–20) specializes in seafood dishes such as shrimp *moqueca* bathed in coconut milk, but also serves meat and pasta as well as a very decent and nicely priced per kilo buffet at lunch. **Restaurante do Carlão** (Rua Coronel Godinho, tel. 98/3349-0016, 11 A.M.–10 A.M. daily, R$15–22) wins kudos for having the most interesting menu in town: fresh fish and seafood are all imaginatively prepared using exotic local fruits such as *murici, caju*, and *açai* to make sauces and garnishes that look and taste quite out of the ordinary. Don't leave town without sampling some of the sweets made from the glossy amber fruit of the buriti palm.

At **Tá Delícia** (Travessa Vereador Zé Diniz, tel. 98/3349-0576), you can sample homemade *sorvete de buriti* while **Doces Dagente** (Av. Brasília) sells buriti candies, preserves, and brick-like *doce de buriti* packed in wooden boxes to go.

Should you desire a more primitive setting, consider shacking up in the tiny fishing town of **Atins** (which is less touristy than nearby Caburé). Set amidst a cluster of palms, **Pousada Rancho dos Lençóis** (tel. 98/3349-5005, www.ranchopousada.com, R$90 d) offers rustic chalets that house up to four people. An inviting restaurant serves fish and seafood dishes accompanied by organic garden-grown vegetables and *doces* made from local fruits. Reservations are necessary. An hour walk through the dunes will bring you to the simple shack that houses **Restaurante da Luzia** (Canto de Atins, tel. 98/9132-3187, 10 A.M.–midnight daily). Your physical efforts will be amply rewarded by a massive portion of fresh shrimp barbecued over hot coals.

Information and Services

There is no tourist office in Barreirinhas, but local tour agencies have lots of information about the park, as does the local branch of **IBAMA** (tel. 98/3231-3010), which administers the park. On the web, you can check out www.barreirinhas.ma.gov.br. The **Banco do Brasil** (Av. Joaquim Soeiro de Carvalho) has a 24-hour ATM.

Getting There

There are various ways of getting to Barreirinhas from São Luís. **Cisne Branco** (tel. 98/3243-2847) operates several daily buses that depart from the *rodoviária*. The trip takes around five hours. Should you want more comfort (i.e., air-conditioning), contact **VanExpress** (tel. 098/3256-4027), a minivan service that picks you up at your São Luís hotel. Fewer stops speed up the journey significantly to 3–4 hours. Departures, however, depend upon demand.

The fastest and most scenic, but also most expensive, mode of transportation is flying. **Litorânea Aero Taxi** (tel. 98/3217-6181, www.litoraneataxiaereo.com.br) offers several daily flights that take 40 minutes and cost R$230. A definite bonus is the overhead view of the dunes.

Although it's not that practical—a car is useless in the dunes—should you want to drive, the BR-135 and MA-402 highways that lead to Barreirinhas are in relatively good condition.

From São Luís, various tour agencies can organize your trip to the Lençóis Maranhenses—whether it's simply reserving transportation or customizing an entire package that includes Jeep and boat outings. **Giltur** (Rua do Giz 46, Praia Grande, tel. 98/3232-6041, www.giltur.com.br) is recommended, as is **Ecodunas** (tel. 98/3349-0545, www.ecodunas.com.br), which organizes a variety of adventure excursions that depart from São Luís.

THE AMAZON

More than just the planet's largest rainforest and its greatest river system (with over 1,000 tributaries), the Amazon is a mythical entity capable of evoking extremes. On one hand, there is the primeval earthly paradise, replete with virgin forests and Indians who have managed the staggering feat of never having had contact with Western "civilization." On the other, there is the deadly "green hell," an unbearably hot and humid no-man's land in whose tangled green landscape one could easily lose one's bearings and end up as a meal for jaguars, anacondas, or piranhas.

Myths aside, the reality of the Amazon is equally inspiring. Occupying close to 60 percent of Brazil's landmass, the Earth's most ecologically diverse and—despite ongoing devastation—most unspoiled virgin rainforest is a sight most people can't resist conjuring up when they think of Brazil. Dense, green, wet, and full of the promise of adventure, the rainforest provides an unforgettable experience for those who venture the distance to get there. In most cases, you won't encounter the pristine jungle teeming with wildlife that BBC nature documentaries might have led you to believe exists. Deforestation, urbanization, and less eco-friendly forms of tourism have definitely taken their toll, and aside from birds and some reptiles, you're likely to see more large creatures in the region's zoos than in the actual forest. However, if you adjust your expectations and take pains to get yourself off the beaten path (i.e., away from urban centers), you will discover a truly rich and unique part of the world with singular landscapes, cultures, and people.

© ROALD ANDRETTA/LOBA DO MAR/EMBRATUR

HIGHLIGHTS

▌ Mercado Ver-o-Peso: For 300 years, Belém's fascinating riverside market has served as an essential and exotic link between this colonial capital and the jungle beyond (page 558).

▌ Ilha de Marajó: Deserted beaches, exuberant vegetation, a centuries-old ceramics tradition, and thousands of water buffalo make this Switzerland-sized island an idyllic and intriguing retreat (page 571).

▌ Alter do Chão: In the middle of the Amazon, Alter do Chão is a mini beach resort with sugary white sands and clear green waters (page 579).

▌ Teatro Amazonas in Manaus: This sumptuous opera house in the middle of the jungle is a testament to the heyday of the Amazon's rubber boom (page 586).

▌ Jungle Lodges (Hotéis de Selva): There's no better way to get a feel for the rainforest than by shacking up in its squawking, chirping, ribbeting depths (pages 592 and 601).

▌ Reserva de Desenvolvimento Sustentável de Mamirauá: This sustainable eco-reserve is the hottest eco-spot along the Rio Solimões. Canoeing through the flooded forests in search of the red-faced uakari monkey is only one of the amazing activities available here (page 599).

▌ Arquipélago de Anavilhanas: The largest freshwater archipelago in the world boasts more than 400 deserted islands, virgin rainforest, and the possibility of swimming with pink dolphins (page 599).

▌ Riverboat Trips: Set sail upon the Rio Negro and Rio Solimões on a riverboat. Riverboat trips allow you to cover the most territory in the Amazon, while enjoying the comforts of its rustic or luxury accommodations, depending on your budget (page 602).

LOOK FOR ▌ TO FIND RECOMMENDED SIGHTS, ACTIVITIES, DINING, AND LODGING.

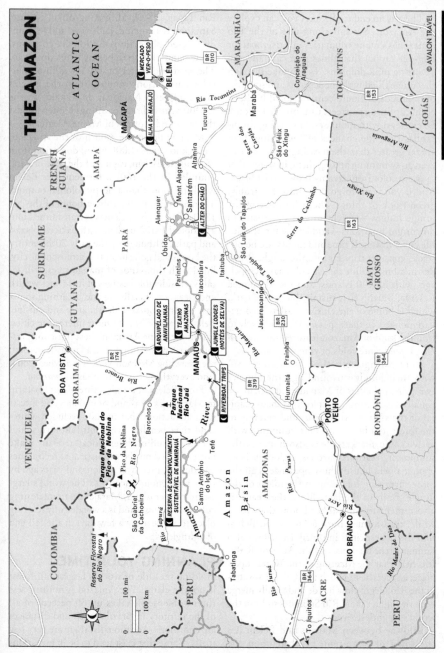

THE AMAZON

© AVALON TRAVEL

There is no end to the ways you can explore the Amazon. Set sail along one of the Rio Amazonas's many tributaries in a riverboat (or dug-out canoe) that glides past caimans and cavorting pink dolphins. Take a hike through the jungle filled with the screams and squawks of hundreds of fluorescently colored birds, or climb up into the trees' canopy where you'll be eye-level with monkeys. Go fishing for piranhas (yes, the chances of you eating them are far greater than them eating you). You can even go swimming among them, in waters that range in color from creamy brown to jet black. And if you want to go deep into the steamy, green thick of things, check into one of the jungle lodges—which range from rustic to downright luxurious—and let the forest wildlife come to you. If time and money are no obstacle, consider trips far into the jungle. Prime destinations include the Anavilhanas archipelago, with its 400 islands, and the Mamirauá Reserve, Brazil's first sustainable jungle park, which is home of the elusive scarlet-faced uakari monkey. In these spots, you're still likely to find the kind of Amazon featured in *National Geographic* centerfolds of yore.

Contrasting (sometimes shockingly so) with their jungly surroundings, the region's two principal cities of Manaus and Belém are equally fascinating to explore. Manaus, capital of the state of Amazonas, and gateway to the forest, is a busy river port humming with activity and markets. It is also home to the sumptuous Teatro Amazonas, a glorious belle epoque opera house whose opulence is all the more surprising for being in the midst of the jungle. Built in the late 1800s, the Teatro is a testament to the rubber boom that, for a while, transformed both Manaus and Belém into the richest cities in Brazil. Manaus is also famous as the birthplace of the Amazon River. It is here that the Meeting of the Waters takes place, a spectacle in which the dark clear waters of the Rio Negro flow beside and finally merge with the lighter hued Rio Solimões to form the world's mightiest river.

Midway between Manaus and Belém lies the town of Santarém, perched upon the Rio Tapajós. Steeped in Amazonian culture, Santarém is a languid, laid-back, and very undiscovered place blessed with the gorgeous, white-sand river beaches of Alter do Chão. The surrounding region has a wealth of marvelous attractions ranging from the jungles of the Floresta Nacional do Tapajós to the 12,000-year-old rock paintings hidden amidst the caves and grottoes of Monte Alegre.

Meanwhile, at the mouth of the Amazon, 1,600 kilometers (1,000 miles) downriver from Manaus sits Belém, capital of the state of Pará. Founded in the 1600s, for centuries Belém was little more than a sleepy colonial outpost. Then along came the rubber boom of the late 1800s. Overnight, Belém was transformed into a "tropical Paris" packed with palaces, plazas, and parks. Although by the early 20th century the boom had gone bust, this atmospheric city, lined with thousands of mango trees, still retains considerable vestiges of its former wealth and elegance. As a living and breathing showcase of Amazonian culture, arts, and cuisine, Belém is one of Brazil's most interesting cities. It is home to the Amazon's best museums, restaurants, and nightlife, and a fantastic market, the sprawling Mercado Ver-o-Peso, where you'll find everything from piranhas to *guaraná*.

From Belém, it is only a three-hour boat trip to Marajó, a vast island of marshes and forests with attractions that include secluded white-sand river beaches, water buffalo farms, and ceramics studios where local artisans make pottery based on the sophisticated techniques and designs used over a thousand years ago by their indigenous ancestors. The world's largest freshwater island, Marajó has an interesting culture all its own and is a wonderfully relaxing place to while away a few days at the tail end of a jungle trip.

PLANNING YOUR TIME

Holding the title of world's largest rainforest is no idle claim. The Amazon is nothing less than immense (it takes up 60 percent of all of the territory in Brazil alone!) and distances are enormous. Additionally, there are very few roads. Those that exist tend to be in precarious shape, which leaves you dependent on riverboats or airplanes for most of your transportation. Unless you're a jungle junkie or a river rat, the best and most efficient way to explore the Amazon is to base yourself in either Manaus or Belém—or else to split your time between the two. Three days in each city is a minimum since each is a fascinating destination in its own right (although Belém offers more historical and cultural attractions than Manaus, which is more modern and less attractive). From both you can venture forth into the surrounding area, in accordance with how much time you have at your disposal. From Belém, set aside 3–4 days for a trip to Ilha de Marajó, or to the beaches on Ilha de Mosqueiro or Ilha de Algodoal. From Manaus, you can spend a day or two in nearby Presidente Figueiredo, with its dozens of waterfalls, or 2–3 days in jungle lodges within a short distance of the city. To really get a feel for the jungle, you should definitely set aside a minimum of 4–5 days, which could be spent on an organized excursion up the Rio Negro or Rio Solimões or at a far-flung jungle lodge in an area such as the Mamirauá Reserve or the Anavilhanas archipelago.

If neither time nor comfort is a major issue, the classic Amazonian trip is a boat ride from Manaus to Belém, or vice-versa, which will set you back 5–6 days, the price of a hammock (or a cabin), and a lot of bug repellent. On the way, you can stop at Santarém, whose surrounding attractions (most notably the beaches of Alter do Chão) deserve at least three days. If you're pressed for time and don't want to miss Santarém, you can easily fly there from both Belém and Manaus. In general, despite the cost, flying between far-flung Amazonian destinations saves you an awful lot of time that could be spent on more varied and diverting activities than sitting on a crowded boat in the middle of the river.

The Amazon is always fairly wet, humid, and hot, as in temperatures of 35–40°C (95–104°F) and humidity levels of 80 percent. Belém is one of the rainiest cities on the planet. December to June is considered the wet season, and July to November is considered slightly less wet. The good thing about Belém's rains is that they are torrential, but they pass. Belenenses have dealing with the daily downpours down to a fine art. They're able to predict when a storm is coming—and blowing over—quite well. Manaus and the Amazonian Basin possess a more pronounced dry season, which lasts roughly from July to November and sees somewhat cooler temperatures (23–30°C, 73–86°F). If you plan on traveling into the jungle, the season you choose will have a significant impact on your trip due to the vast flooding of the Amazon and its tributaries. During the dry season, the water recedes, leaving beaches exposed and forest floors dry and hikable. Fishing is also better at this time. However, the wet season's high waters give you access (by boat) to temporarily flooded forests known as *igapós,* where you'll see more wildlife. Although it's always hot during the day, nights in the forest can be cooler, so it's always a good idea to have long pants and a light jacket or sweater. A light blanket is recommended if you're going to be on a riverboat. As for Santarém, it receives less rain than either Belém or Manaus—the better with which to soak up sun on its lovely beaches.

Regardless of when you visit, a vaccine for yellow fever is necessary (proof is required). You can get these shots for free at public health clinics throughout Brazil, but you'll need to have the injection 10 days prior to entering the Amazon. Some tropical disease experts also recommend taking antimalarial pills, even though they're not always effective and can have strong side effects. As a precaution, bring lots of mosquito repellent and wear long sleeves, especially around the sunrise and sunset hours when mosquitos are on the prowl. Most accommodations offer mosquito netting.

HISTORY

The Amazon region boasts some of the oldest traces of pre-Colombian civilization in the Americas. Advanced indigenous cultures were fishing, growing corn, and making highly decorative ceramic vessels thousands of years before the arrival of any Europeans. The first white man to arrive on the scene was

THE AMAZON

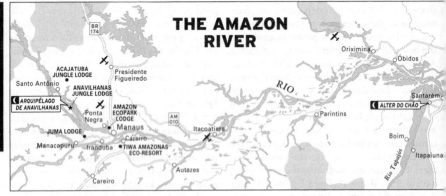

Spanish navigator Vicente Yañez Pinzón, in 1501. Pinzón was searching for the mythical land of gold and plenty known as Eldorado. Upon observing the great muddy Amazon River streaming out into the blue Atlantic, he was so impressed that he mistakenly referred to the river as the "Mar Dulce," or Sweet Sea (i.e., not salty). Evidently though, Pinzón wasn't impressed enough to actually sail up the Amazon. That privilege would belong to Portuguese explorer Pedro Teixeira who, in 1639, not only entered the Amazon, but sailed 3,200 kilometers (2,000 miles) upstream. In doing so, he claimed all of the territory east of Ecuador for the Portuguese crown. Although in 1616, a fortified outpost had been built at the river's mouth—giving birth to the town of Belém—most of the Amazon remained wild and remote for decades. The first Europeans to take interest in settling the region were Catholic missionaries who sailed up the river and established missions in Indian villages. In return for "seeing the light," the Indians were expected to work as unpaid labor. They also unwittingly introduced the white men to the secret riches of the forest: precious woods, vanilla beans, cinnamon, pepper, and Brazil nuts. As word got out, Portuguese traders and merchants looking to make a buck settled along the river and enslaved Indians to help them gather, cultivate, and ship these coveted items off to Europe. Indians who weren't amenable to such working conditions were slaughtered or

forced to retreat farther into the forest (where some remain to this day).

When Brazil became independent in 1822, the Amazon was still very isolated from the rest of the country and quite undeveloped. Cultural and economic ties to Europe, and even America, were stronger than those to Rio de Janeiro. In truth, Belém and Manaus were much closer in travel distance to Lisbon and New York than they were to the Brazilian capital. Interestingly, it was an American innovation that completely transformed the region in the 19th century. In the 1840s, Charles Goodyear invented vulcanization, a process by which natural rubber could withstand incredibly high and low temperatures, and hence be used to manufacture rubber tires, boots, rainwear, and electrical insulation. At the time, sources of natural rubber were scarce. Yet unbeknownst to the rest of the world, Amazonian Indians had been using the milky sap of the *hevea brasilienses* (a.k.a. rubber tree) to make natural rubber for centuries. Once the white man got ahold of this Amazonian secret, all hell broke loose.

Fortune seekers from all around the globe descended upon the Amazon, the only known source of the rubber tree. Conquering vast swathes of forests, they built complexes for processing rubber, and lodgings for the masses of *seringueiros* (rubber tappers) who swarmed to the area in search of work. Aside from *caboclos* (local riverside dwellers of mixed Indian

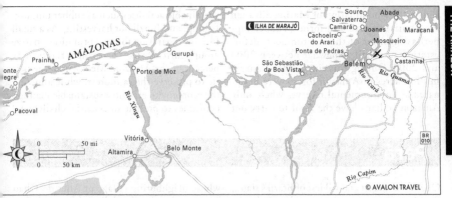

and European ancestry), there were many poor immigrants who traveled from Brazil's Northeast. For the most part, these workers were treated like slaves. Conditions were so brutal that many succumbed to numerous diseases and died. As for the fortune-seeking "rubber barons" (as they were called), many struck it rich. The steamships that sailed down the Amazon and across the Atlantic, carrying cargoes of precious rubber, made the return journey stocked with fine English porcelain, the latest French fashions, Italian wines, and other finery that allowed the barons to live it up in the middle of the jungle as if they were in London or Paris. Imported materials were also used to build and furnish both public and private palaces that sprang up amidst the elegant new avenue and squares of Belém and Manaus. By the dawn of the 20th century, both cities were fabulously wealthy and their ruling elites had ambitions of them surpassing even Rio de Janeiro as the most glamorous and progressive capitals in Brazil. The heady atmosphere was such that there were tales of rubber barons who lit their cigars with large denomination bills and sent off their dirty laundry to be washed and ironed in Europe. Steel magnate Andrew Carnegie supposedly stated (wistfully): "I should have chosen rubber."

However, a decade later, practically overnight, the boom went bust. After *hevea brasilienses* seeds were smuggled out of the Amazon by a crafty Englishman, new plantations in British colonies of Malaysia and Ceylon supplanted Brazil as a cheaper and more efficient source of rubber. The industry experienced a brief revival during World War II, when the Japanese interfered with East Asian rubber production. However, the subsequent popularization of synthetic rubber in the 1940s and '50s brought the rubber era to a definitive end.

After the demise of rubber, the Amazon fell into a spectacular decline from which it never fully recuperated. Over the last few decades, there have been various mini-booms linked to the excavation of gold and minerals as well as cattle ranching and, most recently, the lucrative cultivation of soybeans. While spawning economic growth and attracting landless migrants from the poor Northeast to the region, these activities have also led to the continued devastation of the precious rainforest. In the 1980s, deforestation of the Amazon reached a peak, causing vocal environmentalists (including rock star Sting) to alert the world to the threats facing the world's largest source of oxygen and freshwater. Equally threatened are over 13,000 plant species (the majority still unidentified) whose potential uses as food, medicine, and cosmetics are seemingly unlimited. Since the late 1990s, with the help of multi-agency police operations and high-tech satellite monitoring, the Brazilian government has increasingly cracked down on illegal forest clearing and logging. Moreover, following President

Lula's 2003 nomination of Marina Silva (an Amazonian native and former rubber tapper) as minister of the environment, deforestation rates fell somewhat between 2003 and 2007. During this time, more than 49 million acres of Amazon forest were designated as environmental reserves where only Amazon Indians have the right to carry out sustainable activities such as rubber tapping, fishing, and Brazil nut harvesting. As a small form of reparation for past brutalities, native groups currently have permanent rights to 21 percent of the Amazon. Meanwhile, the battle to preserve the rainforest, while allowing the economy to grow in a sustainable manner, continues to present an essential challenge.

Pará

One of the largest and wildest of Brazil's states, Pará is a vast region of savannahs, wetlands, and lush rainforest through which the Rio Amazonas makes its journey downstream to the Atlantic. At its mouth, the river spans a vast 330 kilometers (207 miles) in width. In fact, the Indians who lived along its estuary referred to it as *pa'ra,* meaning "great ocean."

To this day, Pará has somewhat of a feudal reputation. Rich landowners with immense holdings (both legal and illegal) are constantly in conflict with poor workers, who toil as indentured laborers, as well as members of the *movimento sem terra* (landless movement) who occupy their lands. Conflicts are often resolved with guns. Both landowners and migrants have wreaked havoc on Pará's forests (particularly in the east), burning great swaths for the purposes of farming and raising cattle. Further devastation is the result of mineral excavation, hydroelectric projects (Pará's Tucurui dam is the world's largest hydroelectric plant), and soybean cultivation, activities that have brought significant prosperity to the region in recent years.

Perched at the mouth of the Amazon, in eastern Pará, the colonial capital of Belém is a fascinating city with a rich local culture. Apart from its considerable charms, it makes a good base from which to visit Ilha de Marajó, renowned for its beaches and buffalo ranches. Western Pará—reached by sailing upriver from Belém—is considerably less developed. The most interesting region is the area surrounding the city of Santarém, a languorous port city along the disarmingly blue Rio Tapajós, whose neighboring village of Alter do Chão boasts unexpectedly idyllic white-sand river beaches. Here you'll find large patches of unspoiled jungle as well as a typical *caboclo* villages where Amazonian river culture remains very much alive.

BELÉM

Pará's river capital is an intoxicating mélange of faded elegance, dilapidation, and revitalization. One of Brazil's most interesting capitals (and the only "historic" city in the Amazon), Belém was settled by the Portuguese, who were worried about colonial rivals having access to the possible riches that lay up the Amazon. After constructing a formidable-looking fort that defended their claim to the territory by guarding the Amazon's estuary, the Portuguese set about exploiting the forest's treasures—timber and spices—while exploiting the local Indians as labor. In the area surrounding Belém, forest was cleared to make way for sugar and rice plantations similar to those in neighboring northeastern states. Thought to be hardier than local Indians (who easily fell victim to European diseases), African slaves were imported to work the plantations. Despite the creation of a small elite, Pará's colonial economy never took off like that of neighboring Maranhão. In fact, by the late 1700s, the population had stagnated to the extent that the Portuguese crown was actually offering incentives for Portuguese settlers to marry and procreate with Indian women (the result of this miscegenation is Pará's significant *caboclo* population).

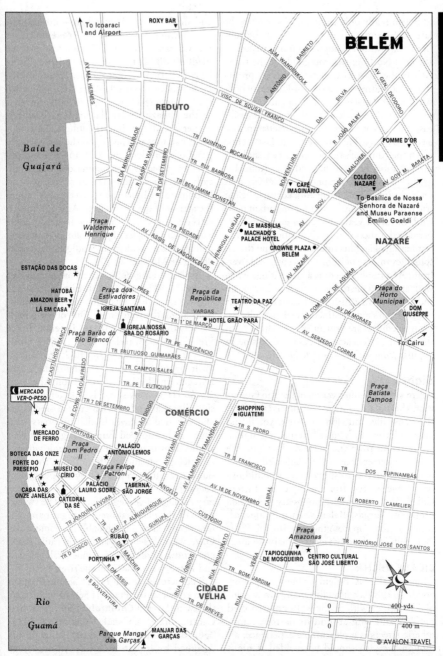

To Icoaraci and Airport

ROXY BAR

BELÉM

ALM. WANDENKOLK

BARRETO

R. ANTÔNIO

AV. GEN. DEODORO

VISC. DE SOUSA FRANCO

SILVA

DA

REDUTO

R. JOÃO BALBY

POMME D'OR

Baía de Guajará

AV. MAL HERMES

TR. QUINTINO BOCAIÚVA

JOSÉ MALCHER

R. DA MUNICIPALIDADE

R. GASPAR VIANA

R. 28 DE SETEMBRO

TR. RÚI BARBOSA

TR. BENJAMIM CONSTAN

BOAVENTURA

GOV.

CAFÉ IMAGINÁRIO

COLÉGIO NAZARÉ

AV. GOV. M. BARATA

To Basílica de Nossa Senhora de Nazaré and Museu Paraense Emílio Goeldi

Praça Waldemar Henrique

AV. ASSIS DE VASCONCELOS

TR. PIEDADE

R. HENRIQUE GURJÃO

AV.

LE MASSILIA

MACHADO'S PALACE HOTEL

CROWNE PLAZA BELÉM

NAZARÉ

ESTAÇÃO DAS DOCAS ★

AV. PRES.

Praça dos Estivadores

AV. NAZARÉ

Praça do Horto Municipal

DOM GIUSEPPE

HATOBÁ ▼
AMAZON BEER ▼
LÁ EM CASA ▼

IGREJA SANTANA ♦

Praça da República

TEATRO DA PAZ ★

AV. COM. BRAZ DE AGUIAR

AV. DR. MORAES

Praça Barão do Rio Branco

IGREJA NOSSA SRA DO ROSÁRIO ♦

VARGAS

TR. 1° DE MARÇO

HOTEL GRÃO PARÁ ●

AV. SERZEDO CORRÊA

To Cairu

AV. CASTILHOS FRANCA

R. CONS. JOÃO ALFREDO

TR. FRUTUOSO GUIMARÃES

TR. PE. PRUDÊNCIO

TR. CAMPOS SALES

Praça Batista Campos

[MERCADO VER-O-PESO

TR. 7 DE SETEMBRO

TR. PE. EUTIQUIO

★

AV. PORTUGAL

COMÉRCIO

SHOPPING ■ IGUATEMI

TR. S. PEDRO

MERCADO DE FERRO ★

R. JOÃO DIOGO

TR. AVERTANO ROCHA

TR. S. FRANCISCO

BOTECA DAS ONZE ▼

Praça Dom Pedro II

PALÁCIO ANTÔNIO LEMOS ★

AV. ALMIRANTE TAMANDARÉ

TR. DOS TUPINAMBÁS

FORTE DO PRESÉPIO ★

MUSEU DO CÍRIO ♦

Praça Felipe Patroni

RUA

AV. 16 DE NOVEMBRO

AV. ROBERTO CAMELIER

CASA DAS ONZE JANELAS ♦

PALÁCIO LAURO SODRE ★

TABERNA SÃO JORGE ▼

ÂNGELO

CABRAL

CATEDRAL DA SÉ ♦

TR. JOAQUIM TÁVORA

TR. CAP. P. ALBUQUERQUE

GURUPÁ

CUSTÓDIO

RUBÃO ▼

TR. DR. MALCHER

Praça Amazonas

TR. HONÓRIO JOSÉ DOS SANTOS

TR. D. BOSCO

PORTINHA ▼

R. DE ÓBIDOS

RUA TRIUNVIRATO

VEIGA

TAPIOQUINHA DE MOSQUEIRO ▼

CENTRO CULTURAL SÃO JOSÉ LIBERTO

R. DE ASSIS

R. S. BOAVENTURA

RUA DE BREVES

CIDADE VELHA

RUA

TR. BOM JARDIM

Rio Guamá

Parque Mangal das Garças

MANJAR DAS GARÇAS ▼

0   400 yds

0   400 m

© AVALON TRAVEL

Belém really only came into its own in the late 19th century with the onset of the rubber boom, which brought fabulous wealth to the city. Nothing was too good for the filthy rich rubber barons who poured their profits into making their city a best-of-Europe hybrid, with grand Parisian-style avenues and squares, splendid Italian-influenced theaters and basilicas, and state-of-the-art English streetlamps and electric trolleys. The city went into fast decline when the Amazon's rubber industry went belly up, but most of the ornate edifices from this grand era survived. Despite the decadence that set in during the mid–late 20th century, Belém still remains the Amazon's most important port. And, in recent years, the city's downtown experienced a successful revitalization, with the restoration of architectural treasures and the inspired revamping of its historic center and riverfront. As a result, Belém is a fascinating city to walk around. Due to the mixture of European, Indian, and African influences, it also boasts one of Brazil's most distinctive regional cultures, whose elements are present in everything from the flavorful delicacies of Paraense cuisine to popular *festas* such as Círio de Nazaré.

Sights

Belém sits at the intersection of the Rio Guamá with the Baía de Guajará. The river defines Belenense life, and along its banks you'll find many of the city's most interesting sights. Fanning out from the Forte do Presépio, the historic quarter known as Cidade Velha is rife with a wonderful mishmash of old buildings that range in style from baroque to art deco. Cidade Velha's northern boundary is Avenida President Vargas, Belém's main boulevard, which stretches up from the waterfront to Praça da República, the city's elegant main square.

CIDADE VELHA

Cidade Velha is Belém's oldest neighborhood. To this day, it retains many lovely colonial buildings with adobe walls and red-tiled roofs. Wandering around its narrow, atmospheric streets is a pleasurable experience, although the area should be avoided at night

and on Sundays. It was here—around the early-17th-century **Forte do Presépio** (Praça Frei Caetano Brandão 117, Cidade Velha, tel. 91/4009-8828, 10 A.M.–6 P.M. Tues.–Sun., R\$2, free Tues.)—that the city sprang to life. From this fortress overlooking the Rio Guamá, the Portuguese jealously guarded the entrance to the Amazon while launching conquests deeper and deeper into the jungle. The enormous cannons perched upon the ramparts are proof of their defensive zeal. Inside the fort a small but interesting museum (somewhat ironically) pays homage to the local Tapajós and Marajoara Indians that thrived here before the arrival of the Portuguese. Among the artifacts unearthed in archaeological sites are some wonderful examples of pre-Colombian pottery, notably vessels made by the indigenous peoples of Ilha de Marajó.

It wasn't long before the Portuguese had settled in. With the wealth earned from the sugar trade, aristocrats built sumptuous mansions along the waterfront. One of the grandest was the **Casa das Onze Janelas** (Praça Frei Caetano Brandão, tel. 91/4009-8821, 10 A.M.–6 P.M. Tues.–Sun., R\$2, free Tues.), built by sugar baron Domingos da Costa Barcelar in the late 1600s. From the *onze janelas* (11 windows) of his pale yellow mansion, Barcelar and his rich cronies sipped tea and watched as slaves loaded up boats with sugar and unloaded European goodies that would allow them to live in the jungle without sacrificing style and comfort. Today, the mansion is a cultural center that juggles a permanent collection of Brazilian modernists with temporary exhibits of contemporary art. The sweeping balcony once haunted by sugar barons is now occupied by a fashionable bar, Boteco das Onze, where Belenenses and tourists alike snack on *coxinhas de carangueijo* (tender crab pastries) and watch the sun set over the river.

The picturesque Praça Frei Caetano Brandão (also known as the Praça da Sé) is anchored by the twin-towered **Catedral da Sé** (Praça Frei Caetano Brandão, Cidade Velha, tel. 91/3223-2362, 8 A.M.–noon and 2–6 P.M. daily). It was designed by Italian architect Antônio José

© CHRISTIAN KNEPPER/EMBRATUR

Parque Mangal das Garças in Belém's Cidade Velha

Landi, who had numerous commissions in Belém. The interior is an unremarkable mishmash of baroque and neoclassical styles with a lot of glossy marble imported from Italy. Also on the *praça* is the early baroque **Igreja de Santo Alexandre.** Built by local Indians, it features some delicate woodwork. The church, along with its annex, the former archbishop's palace, houses the **Museu de Arte Sacra** (Praça Frei Caetano Brandão, Cidade Velha, tel. 91/4009-8802, 10 A.M.–6 P.M. Tues.–Sun., R$4, free Tues.), which exhibits a collection of religious paintings and carved wooden saints.

Just around the corner, on a pretty little street, the **Museu do Círio** (Rua Padre Champagnat, Cidade Velha, tel. 91/4009-8846, 10 A.M.–6 P.M. Tues.–Sun., R$2) conjures up the pageantry and frenzy (both sacred and profane) of Círio de Nazaré, Belém's most important popular and religious festival (see *Festivals and Events*). Aside from gazing at photographs of the processions, you can also admire the artistry of emblematic objects such as embroidered banners, images of Nossa Senhora de Nazaré, and feather-light toys made of

miriti, an Amazonian palm, made especially for the *festa* by *caboclo* artisans from a tiny town in the Paraense interior.

Nearby, on Praça Dom Pedro II you'll see two magnificent palaces that conjure up Belém's late-19th-century days of rubber glory. Once the city hall, the **Palácio Antônio Lemos** is an elegant neoclassical construction with a striking powder blue and white facade. After being abandoned, it later underwent restoration. It currently houses municipal government offices along with the **Museu de Arte do Belém** (Praça Dom Pedro II, Cidade Velha, tel. 91/3283-4687, 10 A.M.–6 P.M. Tues.–Fri., 9 A.M.–1 P.M. Sat.–Sun., R$1), whose permanent collection of paintings is less impressive than the palace itself. The interior is a Versailles-worthy series of courtyards and grand salons decked out in crystal chandeliers, bronze and marble statues, and beautiful belle epoque furniture. Slippers are provided so you won't scratch the gorgeous parquet floors.

Next door, the gleaming white **Palácio Lauro Sodré** is another edifice that was designed by Antônio Landi in the 1770s. The former residence of Pará's governors, it now lodges the **Museu do Estado do Pará** (Praça Dom Pedro II, Cidade Velha, tel. 91/4009-8838, 1–6 P.M. Tues.–Fri., 9 A.M.–1 P.M. Sat.–Sun., R$4, free Tues.). Once again, aside from some exquisite furniture, the rather musty historical artifacts are less interesting than the palace interior. The ground floor reception salons overlooking the *praça* (where good temporary exhibits are often held) are particularly opulent, as is the grand marble staircase leading upstairs to older and more sedate rooms where you'll find the permanent collection.

◖ MERCADO VER-O-PESO

Synonymous with Belém itself is the sprawling Mercado Ver-o-Peso (Blvd. Castilhos França, 6 A.M.–2 P.M. daily), which stretches out along the river. Just as Belém is the gateway to the Amazon rainforest, the market serves an essential link between the city and the jungle. For over 300 years, boats have sailed down the river from the depths of the Amazon to unload their wares at the Mercado, whose name, Ver-o-Peso (See the Weight) is derived from the Portuguese habit of weighing all merchandise in order to calculate tributes to the crown. The main building, with its twin neo-gothic towers and cast-iron structure imported from Scotland in the late 1800s, was originally known as the Mercado de Ferro (Iron Market). Today, it is only one section of the immense bazaar, which also includes hundreds of *barracas* as well as a tented area containing bars and restaurants where you can sample Paraense specialties such as fried fish, *maniçoba*, and *açaí*.

The market is somewhat ramshackle and chaotic (keep an eye on your belongings at all times due to pickpockets). Yet the colorful jumble adds to the adventure of wandering through the labyrinth of stalls where you'll encounter exotica ranging from cobra teeth and pirarucu tongues (used by Indians as a kitchen grater) to herbal potions guaranteed to make you filthy rich or lucky in love. The initial assault on your senses is a little overwhelming. The liquid gold of bottled *tucupi* clashes with the deep green of ground manioc leaves, the

soft rose blush of a *jambu* fruit, and the rich purple of *açaí*. There are also the smells: the sweet perfume of *bacuri* and *graviola* mingling with the pungent saltiness of cured beef and fresh fish. And the noises: the snip of scissors separating seeds from the pearly flesh of a *cupuaçu*, the crack of Brazil nuts being removed from their shells, the singsongy cries of merchants touting their wares. Aside from the gorgeous jumble of fruits, fish, spices, *doces*, and ceramics, one of the most interesting sections is the area devoted to indigenous herbal remedies that will cure whatever ails you—physically or spiritually. The women who hawk these potions, known as *mandingueiras*, swear by the miraculous recipes that have been passed down through generations. They range from powdered vulture's liver (great for a hangover) to the bottled genitalia of a *boto*, or pink river dolphin, which is purported to be a foolproof love potion. Although it has no curative properties, a Ver-o-Peso best-seller is extract of *pau-rosa*, an Amazonian tree whose bark is one of the main ingredients in Chanel No. 5 perfume.

ESTAÇÃO DAS DOCAS

In 2001, an inspired renovation transformed the 19th-century steel cargo warehouses that lined Belém's seedy riverside port area into an airy and modern complex known as the Estação das Docas (Blvd. Castilhos França, tel. 91/3215-5525, 10 A.M.–1 A.M. Tues.–Fri., 9 A.M.–3 A.M., Fri.–Sun.). Aside from a cultural center with a theater, cinema, and galleries, the three warehouses contain boutiques and bookstores as well as a bar, a café, the famous Cairu *sorveteria*, and a cluster of gourmet restaurants. Featuring large glass walls overlooking the docks and the river, the Estação das Docas has become one of Belém's hippest hangouts. By day, it's a lovely place to walk around (there is a scenic view of the bay from the boardwalk), quaff microbrewery beer, nibble on buffalo kebabs, and watch the sun set. At night, live music shows are often performed on a movable stage that has been fashioned out of a former loading trolley. Tourist excursions along the river depart from the dock's small *hidroviária*.

AÇAÍ

Rich, purple, and ultra-healthy *açaí* has become all the rage throughout Brazil, especially in body-conscious Rio de Janeiro where Zona Sul juice and *açaí* bars are as common as gyms. More often than not, this Amazonian wonder fruit is served as a sweet energy booster, its nutritional value amped up by honey, *guaraná* powder, banana slices, and granola.

Savoring *açaí* on its home turf is a whole other story. In the Amazon, *açaí* is consumed by everyone, not just health food enthusiasts. Cheap, bountiful, and an excellent source of calcium, minerals, and vitamins B1 and B2, it can easily serve as a meal on its own. In fact, in many Amazonian river communities it does. *Açaí* is also a main source of livelihood for many families. The fruit comes from a palm species known as an *açaizeiro*. At a young age, many *caboclos* and Indians learn how to shimmy up the tree, a knife between their teeth, to cut down the dark berry-sized fruit.

In Belém, *açaí* consumption is three times higher than that of milk. Many mothers prefer to give babies pacifiers filled with *açaí*. Unlike in the rest of Brazil, *açaí* is not eaten with sugar. Instead, as an accompaniment to fish, *açaí* is thickened with manioc flour and used as a substitute for *feijão*, which is the main staple in the rest of the country. This is the way you'll see it served at Belém's Mercado-Ver-o-Peso, one whole section of which is reserved for *açaí*. Aside from the market, there are *açaí* stores all over the city. Using machines, the pulp is stripped from the seeds and then sold in plastic pouches. Belenenses all have their favorite suppliers. Quality and price depend on the thickness of the pulp (the more diluted, the cheaper) and its origin (the crème de la crème comes from the Ilha das Onças, or Island of Jaguars). The fruit's popularity can be observed every time a Paraense sticks out his or her tongue – more often than not it will be (temporarily) stained dark purple.

PRAÇA DA REPÚBLICA AND TEATRO DA PAZ

Belém's main square is the leafy Praça da República, an elegant green park with a small amphitheater that offers respite to Belenenses of all ages. On one side of the *praça* sits the Teatro da Paz (Praça da República, tel. 91/4009-8750, 9 A.M.–5 P.M. Tues.–Fri., 9 A.M.–1 P.M. Sat., R$4), a deep rose colored, white pillared, neoclassical theater inaugurated in 1878. Inspired by Milan's Teatro Scala, Belém's rubber barons financed the splendid building, whose interior is decked out in precious woods, gilt mirrors, crystal chandeliers, and glossy Italian marble. In the auditorium, note the ceiling mural of Apollo on his chariot, being pulled through the Amazon. The guided tours are recommended.

NAZARÉ

From Praça da República, Avenida Nazaré cuts through the upscale neighborhood of the same name. Belém is renowned for its centuries-old mango trees and Nazaré's streets are lined with a dark-green leafy canopy. Keep a lookout for the bright yellow pulp on the sidewalks (much more slippery than a banana peel) and for the possibility of mangoes falling on your head (particularly October–December). Aside from mangos, Nazaré possesses many pastel-colored, historic buildings, some of which house chic boutiques and restaurants.

On the corner of Avenida Nazaré and Avenida Generalíssimo Deodoro lies Belém's most famous church, the **Basílica de Nossa Senhora de Nazaré** (Praça Justo Chermont, Nazaré, tel. 91/4009-8400, 6 A.M.–7:30 P.M. Mon.–Fri., 6 A.M.–noon and 3–9 P.M. Sat.–Sun.). Completed in 1908, it was modeled after Rome's St. Peter's Basilica. Aside from its spiritual importance (this is where the image of Nossa Senhora de Nazaré, the patron saint of Pará, is housed), this majestic white church is a stunner. The exterior is impressive for its majestic simplicity offset by the giant *samauma* tree in front. More awe-inspiring is the splendid marble interior, which is accessorized with beautiful stained-glass windows, ornate wooden ceiling carvings, and intricate, colored tile mosaics reminiscent of Moorish architecture. Every October, the church and the statue of the saint are the focal point for Círio de Nazaré (see *Festivals and Events*), one of Brazil's most lavish religious and popular festivals.

After the basilica, Avenida Nazaré turns into Avenida Magalhães Barata. Two blocks further is the not-to-be-missed **Museu Paraense Emílio Goeldi** (Rua Magalhães Barata 376, Nazaré, tel. 91/3219-3369, www.museu-goeldi.br, 9 A.M.–5 P.M. Tues.–Sun., R$3). Founded in 1895, the museum was the world's first research center devoted to the flora, fauna, and cultures of the Amazon. To date, it is also considered one of the best. Located on a vast estate, the museum has an impressive collection of Indian artifacts, including a great display of the distinctive and delicate pre-Colombian ceramic vessels made by the indigenous groups that once inhabited the Ilha de Marajó. Better yet is the introduction it provides to the jungle itself. Simply strolling around amidst towering mahogany and rubber trees, past lagoons strewn with giant *Victoria amazonica* water lilies, will get you in a jungly frame of mind. The art nouveau-style aquarium is chock-full of electric eels, flying fish, *matamata* turtles, and black piranhas. And you can familiarize yourself with mammals you may never see in the actual jungle, such as spider monkeys, tapirs, anteaters, and ultra-rare spotted jaguars as well as more common, but surreally Day-Glo toucans and macaws.

Two blocks from the museum, the **Parque da Residência** (Av. Magalhães Barata 830, Nazaré, tel. 91/4009-8721, 9 A.M.–9 P.M. Tues.–Sun.) is a small, but very pretty park surrounding the former governor's residence. This handsome mansion is now headquarters to the Secretary of Culture. It functions as a cultural center with a gallery space, theater, and the excellent Restô do Parque (see *Food*). Reward yourself for walking in the heat with a refreshing ice cream at the 100-year-old train wagon that has been converted into a *sorveteria*.

CENTRO CULTURAL SÃO JOSÉ LIBERTO

A short cab ride from Cidade Velha, the Centro Cultural São José Liberto (Praça Amazonas, tel. 91/3344-3500, 10 A.M.–8 P.M. Tues.–Sat., 3–8 P.M. Sun., R$4) occupies an early-18th-century Franciscan monastery on Praça Amazonas. Back in the day, the square was a former execution ground and the neighboring monks routinely accompanied criminals to their hangings. In the 18th century, the monastery was converted into a prison, which was abandoned before a major overhaul in the 1990s gave it a happier reincarnation as a cultural complex. Most of the Centro's exhibits and activities revolve around Pará's abundance of precious and semiprecious stones (for this reason it is also known as the Pólo Joalheiro, or Jewelry Zone). The colonial part of the complex houses the **Museu das Gemas do Estado,** which boasts a dazzling collection of Amazonian rocks and minerals (in rough and polished states). Having whetted your appetite for jewels, check out the **Casa do Artesão,** a series of ateliers where you can watch local artisans hard at work cutting, polishing, and creating intricate and original jewelry from the stones you saw in the museum. If you're struck by the buysies, the final products can be purchased in on-site boutiques. In an adjacent modern annex, you'll find a café and a Cairu *sorveteria* outlet as well as exhibition areas and some stands selling handicrafts, including some very attractive ceramics in the tradition of Marajoara pottery.

PARKS

Belém has a number of parks that conspire to give you a foretaste of what's in store if and when you embark upon a trip into the depths of the Amazonian rainforest. The most central of these, **Parque Mangal das Garças** (Passagem Carneiro da Rocha, Cidade Velha, tel. 91/3242-5052, www.mangal.com.br, 10 A.M.–6 P.M. Tues.–Sun., R$6 for a passport to all attractions), is located along the edge of Cidade Velha, on the banks of the Rio Gaumá. Inaugurated in 2005, the park is yet another example of the inspired renewal projects that have taken hold of

© CHRISTIAN KNEPPER/EMBRATUR

samples of Marajoara pottery for sale in the Centro Cultural São José Liberto's adjacent annex

Belém over the last decade. Strolling around the park is very pleasant. The landscaping mixes plants and trees from different Amazonian ecosystems as well as lagoons dotted with bright white herons and scarlet ibises. Birders will have a field day at the **Aviário das Aningas.** At the entrance to the aviary, you're given an illustrated guide to all the feathered creatures that live here. The fun part is walking around the jungly atmosphere, while keeping score of who can catch sight of a giant stork or bright red *guará* first. Once you've checked off all 150 birds, go for a rematch at the **Borboletário Márcio Ayres.** Upon entering this pavilion, you'll once again be furnished with an illustrated guide—only this time, your eyes will be peeled for the resplendent Amazonian *borboletas* (butterflies) and jewel-like *beija-flores* (hummingbirds) that flap and dart amidst the misty environment. The park's main complex, an indigenous structure of *ipê* wood and palm fibers, houses the Mangal das Garças restaurant and the **Museu Amazônico de Navegação,** a small museum that traces the Amazon's tradition of boat-building as well as the history of river transportation in Pará. For a terrific view of the river looking towards the Cidade Velha, walk along the wooden walkways that lead out to a viewing platform suspended above the muddy banks. For even better views, take the elevator to the top of the Farol de Belém, the rather odd-looking, modern lighthouse located in the middle of the park. On your way out, stop by the **Armazém do Tempo,** a renovated shipbuilding warehouse converted into a gallery where you can purchase books and CDs by local musicians. You'll also find a good mix of local *artesenato* ranging from indigenous jewelry, made from the seeds of fruit such as *açai* and *pupunha,* to delicate toys made from miriti palm fibers.

More untamed Amazonian foliage can be found at the **Bosque Rodrigues Alves** (Av. Almirante Barroso 2305, Bairro do Marco, tel. 91/3276-2308, 8 A.M.–5 P.M. Tues.–Sun., R$1), an untamed 19th-century botanical garden filled with 2,500 regional species, most of which are typical of virgin rainforest.

THE AMAZON

Meandering trails lead past a lagoon brimming with fish and turtles to an orchidarium and a small aquarium. Among the rare and very weird mammals you can glimpse up-close are the *jupará*—which resembles a cross between a cat, a bear, and a monkey—and the Amazonian manatee, whose Portuguese name, *peixe boi* ("fish-cow"), says it all. Although this sausage-like creature could never win any beauty contests, in the water, it moves with all the grace of Esther Williams.

Entertainment and Events
NIGHTLIFE

Much of Belém's nightlife is centered on the Estação das Docas as well as the area near Avenida Souza Franco, confusingly known as "Docas." For live music, check out the *bairro* of Condor, on the banks of the Rio Guamá (accessible by taxi).

For years, Belém's bohemians have been congregating at **Rubão** (Travessa Gurupá 312, Cidade Velha, tel. 91/9122-4232, 7 P.M.–close daily), a classic *boteco* with cheap, icy beer, simple, tasty snacks (the crab is excellent), and a warm unpretentious atmosphere presided over by owner and local institution, Rubão. The tables out in the street are great for people-watching. Beer connoisseurs who have grown weary of Brahma and Antarctica will appreciate **Amazon Beer** (Estação das Docas, Boulevard Castilho França, Campina, tel. 91/3212-5401, 5 P.M.–midnight Mon.–Wed., 5 P.M.–3 A.M. Thurs.–Fri., 11 A.M.–close Sat., 11 A.M.–midnight Sun.), which brews its own beer without the use of additives. Among the five varieties are "forest," a traditional pilsen, "black," an aromatic dark malt beer, and the exotic "bacuri," flavored with subtle hints of this delicious local fruit. An ideal accompaniment is a portion of *bolinhos de pato* (crunchy balls stuffed with shredded duck, *jambu,* and *tucupi*). The bar really fills up Monday–Wednesday during happy hour, when a fixed price gets you all-you-can-drink beer along with a buffet of appetizers. Saturday's *feijoada* is accompanied by *chorinho.* The rest of the week, you're likely to hear MPB or jazz.

The **Roxy Bar** (Av. Senador Lemos 231, Umarizal, tel. 91/3224-4514, 7:30 P.M.–1 A.M. Tues.–Thurs., 7:30 P.M.–close Fri.–Sat.) is a favorite haunt for those in search of a more quiet, intimate scene that continues into the wee hours. The walls are decorated with images of classic Hollywood stars. Famous names inspire the varied menu offerings, such as the Charlton Heston (beef filet in an creamy herb sauce with matchstick potatoes) and the Saddam Hussein (steak topped with ham and cheese served with french-fried potatoes).

One of the most seductive and popular bars in town, **Boteco das Onze** (Praça Frei Caetano Brandão, Cidade Velha, tel. 91/3224-8559, 4 P.M.–close Mon., noon onwards Tues.–Sun., cover R$6–8) occupies the historic Casa das Onze Janelas. Outside, a wide terrace gazes out over the Baía de Guajará. The terrace is popular during happy hour when Belenenses gather to drink *chope* or killer *tangirsoscas* (vodka and fresh tangerine juice), and nibble on *petiscos* such as *casquinha de caranguejo com jambu* (a fresh crab salad seasoned with *jambu*). For a full-fledged meal, head inside where stone walls, wooden beams, and candles create a romantic atmosphere enhanced by jazz, pop, and MPB standards.

Located in a handsome old mansion with enormous windows, **Café Imaginário** (Travessa Quintino Bocaiúva 1086, Reduto, tel. 91/3230-5235, 6 P.M.–3 A.M. Tues.–Sun., cover R$3) is a mixture of bar and mini cultural center that attracts local artists and musicians. This is one of the best places to hear live performances of jazz, blues, and MPB, held nightly from 11 P.M.–close. Another major draw is the legendary *jambu* pizza, whose main ingredient comes from an organic *jambu* plantation. Before indulging, knock back a *caipirinha* made with regional fruits such as *cupuaçu, graviola,* and *taperabá.*

Taberna São Jorge (Travessa Joaquim Távora 438, Cidade Velha, tel. 91/8146-4546, 11 A.M.–3 P.M. Mon., 11 A.M.–midnight Tues.–Fri., 4 P.M.–midnight Sat., cover R$3) is a cozy corner bar (also open for lunch) that is known for its tomato red walls, plastered with images of São Jorge, as well as its original *petiscos,* most of which are based upon the classic Brazilian duo of rice and beans. Try the *bolinho de feijão,* crisp balls of manioc flour filled with black bean puree. On Tuesday nights, live *chorinho* is performed.

PERFORMING ARTS

It's always worth taking a look to see what's on at the beautiful **Teatro da Paz** (Praça da República, tel. 91/4009-8750). If you're in the mood for a film, check out the schedule at the **Cinema Olympia** (Av. Presidente Vargas 918, tel. 91/3223-1883). Built in 1912, Belém's (and Brazil's) oldest movie theater still in operation received a recent and timely overhaul, and now screens independent and art films.

FESTIVALS AND EVENTS

One of the biggest and most spectacular religious and popular festivals in Brazil is **Círio de Nazaré** (www.ciriodenazare.com.br). It's held during the second Sunday of October, and millions of Paraenses throng the streets of Belém to join in the procession carrying the statue of Nossa Senhora de Nazaré from the Catedral da Sé to the Basílica de Nazaré.

Considered the patron saint of all Paraenses and protectress of Belém, the cult of Nossa Senhora de Nazaré dates back to 1700 when a *caboclo* named Plácido found a statue of the Virgin lying in a creek located in the present-day *bairro* of Nazaré. Plácido took the statue home with him. But when he woke up the next morning, he was astonished to discover that it had returned to its original spot. After taking the statue home once again, it reappeared at the creek. The amazed *caboclo* built a small chapel (later replaced by the Basílica de Nazaré) to house the Virgin. Word of the miracle got around and pilgrims and supplicants from all over Pará came seeking Nossa Senhora's blessing and divine intervention.

By the end of the 1700s, her popularity had become so great that a public *festa,* the Círio de Nazaré, was organized so that the entire city could pay homage to the Virgin. The first procession took place in 1793. The image of Nossa Senhora de Nazaré, splendidly arrayed and covered in flowers, was carried in a chariot through the muddy streets by bulls. By the 20th century, Belém's streets had become paved and bulls were no longer necessary. Instead, the thick rope attached to the carriage—measuring 350 meters (1,150 feet)—was now pulled by penitents who, to this day, jostle ferociously for the chance to grip their hands around the rough sisal and literally bleed (by the procession's end there is blood in the streets) for the honor of transporting the Virgin.

Although the Sunday procession constitutes the most important event, the *festa* actually kicks off on Friday afternoon with Nossa Senhora de Nazaré's departure from the Basílica to a church in the nearby town of Ananindeua. As the Virgin glides by in an open car, Belenenses hovering in decorated windows and spilling into the streets toss rose petals and confetti. The following dawn, the Virgin once again takes to the road, this time in an open truck, surrounded by a cavalcade of cars and motorcycles, en route to the town of Icoaraci. Here, the image is loaded onto a spectacularly decorated boat. Since Nossa Senhora de Nazaré is also the patron saint of river navigators, the Virgin's crossing of the Rio Guamá to Belém is accompanied by a fleet of hundreds of festively adorned wooden boats. This river spectacle is best viewed from the ramparts of the Forte do Presépio. The Virgin's arrival in Belém is greeted with a fireworks display. Much merrymaking then ensues throughout the Cidade Velha, lasting all night until the climactic procession that takes place on Sunday morning. The Virgin's return to the Basílica is usually completed by midday. Afterwards people get together with family and friends and feast upon favorite dishes such as *pato no tucupi* and *maniçoba.* If you want to be in town for Círio, make sure to book a hotel far in advance.

Shopping

Belém is a great source for Amazonian artifacts ranging from beautiful indigenous art to more practical items such as energy-boosting *guaraná* powder and woven hammocks (essential for any boat trip or back yard porch). You'll find a wide sampling of the best the Amazon has to offer at the **Mercado Ver-o-Peso** (see *Sights*). The best hours for both browsing and buying are the between 6 A.M. and 9 A.M. when wares are at their most abundant and the sun isn't too strong.

In Cidade Velha, charming Rua Gaspar Viana is home to lots of interesting little stores where you can find hammocks for that boat trip up the Amazon. **Artíndia** (Av. Presidente Vargas 762, tel. 91/3223-6248) has a fine selection of authentic Indian art and objects (they have a smaller boutique at the Estação das Docas as well). For local crafts, books, and CDs, stop by the **Armazém do Tempo** (Passagem Carneiro da Rocha, Cidade Velha, tel. 91/3242-5052, www.mangal.com.br, 10 A.M.–10 P.M. Tues.–Sun.), located in the Parque Mangal das Garças. For beautiful jewelry crafted from precious and semiprecious Amazonian rocks by local artisans, head to the Museu das Gemas located inside the **Centro Cultural São José Liberto** (Praça Amazonas, 10 A.M.–8 P.M. Tues.–Sat., 3–8 P.M. Sun., tel. 91/3344-3500).

For more contemporary items, try the city's most fashionable mall, **Shopping Iguatemi** (Travessa Padre Eutíquio 1078, Batista Campos, tel. 91/3250-5353, www.iguatemi-belem.com.br, 10 A.M.–10 P.M. Mon.–Sat., 3–9 P.M. Sun.). Aside from national boutiques, you'll also find fast food joints, cinemas, and cyber cafés.

Accommodations

Surprisingly, viewing the city's recent sprucing up of the city for tourists, Belém doesn't have many decent hotels. Many of the more centrally located options are pretty down-and-out, and even standard mid- and upper-range options are disappointing. Fortunately, there are a few exceptions.

Apart from its ideal location on Praça da República, **Hotel Grão Pará** (Av. Presidente Vargas 718, tel. 91/3321-2121, www.hotel-graopara.com.br, R$90 d) is a spotless and recently renovated mid-'60s era hotel that offers excellent value. The sizable air-conditioned rooms are rather bland, but well-maintained and the staff is helpful.

Another terrific deal is **Le Massilia** (Rua Henrique Gurjão 236, Reduto, tel. 91/3222-2834, www.massilia.com.br, R$90–110 d). One of Belém's only intimate hotels, the standard but comfortable air-conditioned rooms are housed in low-slung brick villas with cool tile floors and polished wooden fixtures. Aside from a refreshing pool and courtyard, there is a very decent French restaurant (the hotel's owner is French) serving excellent *steak au poivre* and *escargots*. The hotel also organizes city tours and fishing and boating excursions. On the same street is a new modern hotel, the **Machado's Plaza Hotel** (Rua Henrique Gurjão 2000, Reduto, tel. 91/4008-9817, www.machadosplazahotel.com.br, R$220 d). The spotless, attractive furnished rooms lack views, but have welcome splashes of color, nice lighting, and wireless Internet access. There is a also small pool and a fitness room.

If you want to constantly be reminded that you are indeed in the Amazon, **Beira Rio Hotel** (Av. Bernardo Sayão 4804, Guamá, tel. 91/4008-9000, www.beirariohotel.com.br, R$140–180 d) is a good choice. The basic but cheery rooms all look out over the Rio Guamá, and the reputed bungalow-style restaurant is suspended above its waters. The hotel's only drawback is its isolated location. The close proximity of several *favelas* mean that you'll need to rely on buses (by day) or taxis to get around.

When it opened in 2006, the **Crowne Plaza Belém** (Av. Nazaré 375, Nazaré, tel. 91/3202-2000, www.crownebelem.com.br, R$330–450 d) usurped the title of Belém's swishest hotel from the long-reigning (but tired) Belém Hilton. With easy access to Centro and surrounded by lots of restaurants, this gleaming if somewhat stark new behemoth boasts massive rooms outfitted with comfy beds, large-screen plasma TVs, and large bathrooms. Geared more towards execs than leisure travelers, the hotel is efficient and friendly, although the decor lacks personality. Amenities include a small pool, sauna, fitness center, and Internet access.

TACACÁ AND OTHER AMAZONIAN SPECIALTIES

For those who seek to challenge their palates, the Amazon provides an unforgettable feast. The region's rivers and rainforests provide an endless supply of exotic ingredients, and nowhere else in Brazil will you encounter so much indigenous influence. Belém is the Amazon's culinary capital, and the city's signature dish, **tacacá**, is an intoxicating fusion of key ingredients that provides an excellent initiation to the region's cuisine. To some, *tacacá* is a broth, to others it is a drink, or even a stew. Regardless, it mixes shrimp with **tucupi**, a thick yellow liquid extracted from the roots of the manioc plant, and *jambu*, a creeping plant whose leaves cause a pleasant tingling and numbness of your lips. Served piping hot in *cuias* (hollowed-out gourds), *tacacá* gets an extra kick from the addition of *pimenta de cheiro*, a yellow pepper whose aroma is pungent and piquant, and *alfavaca*, a wild Amazonian version of basil.

Tucupi (which is cooked for some 12 hours in order to remove poisonous acids) shows up in other specialties, such as the iconic **pato no tucupi**, an aromatic duck stew, and **maniçoba**, the Paraense equivalent of *feijoada* in which different portions of pork and sausage are cooked together along with dark green leaves from the manioc plant (which require a week's cooking to remove their toxins). Such dishes are often accompanied by **arroz de jambu** (rice flavored with *jambu* leaves) and **farinha d'água**, manioc flour that, having been left to soak in the river, has a soft, fluffy consistency.

Among the many fish you'll come across, two of the most prevalent are **filhote** and **pirarucu**. *Filhote* appears in myriad recipes, often as the main ingredient in **peixada**, a stew that includes potatoes, tomatoes, garlic, and cilantro. Known as the Amazonian *bacalhau* (cod), pirarucu is Brazil's largest fish (measuring up to 2.5 meters/8 feet and weighing up to 80 kilograms/176 pounds). It is usually dried and salted before being grilled on a hot tile or cooked in coconut milk, and then served with *farinha* and light, buttery **feijão manteguinha**, a type of bean from the region of Santarém.

For snacks, **caranguejo** (crab) is very popular. Whole crabs cooked with lemon and garlic are known as **caranguejo toc-toc**, due to the "toc toc" noise that comes from hammering their shells with tiny wooden mallets. Meanwhile, **unhas de caranguejo** (crab claws), which are less work to eat, have extremely tender meat. Another mainstay is **casquinha de caranguejo**, in which shredded crab meat is sautéed with cilantro, alfavaca, and lime and served in its shell.

The region best lives up to its reputation as a paradise of earthly delights when it comes to its fruits. The names in themselves are seductive: **cupuaçu, bacuri, murici, uxi, taperabá, tucumã, bacaba,** and **pupunha.** But wait until you smell and taste them, which you can do in forms that include juices, compotes, *doces*, jellies, *cremes*, puddings, liqueurs, and *sorvetes*. The most highly addictive are *cupuaçu* and *bacuri*, both of whose pearly flesh is an ambrosial mixture of sweetness and tanginess. But the most famous of all is **açaí**, a dark purple and pungent fruit, which is consumed in a variety of manners including as juice, ice cream, or, more popularly, as an accompaniment to fish. Finally, if you're a fan of large, oily and irresistibly rich Brazil nuts, you'll find them all over in Pará, where they're known as **castanhas-do-Pará**, and are sold plain, salted, or caramelized – by vendors on the streets of Belém.

Food

Seductive for its exotic colors and flavors, Paraense cuisine is gaining fame throughout Brazil. However, the best place to savor the region's cuisine is in Belém—either at an atmospheric restaurant (many of which are located in tourist attractions) or at the one of the street *barracas* where local women sell local delicacies such as the famous *tacacá*.

CAFÉS AND SNACKS

To savor the most typically Belenense of Pará's many delicacies, you'll have to head to a simple *barraca* across the street from the **Colégio Nazaré** (Av. Nazaré, Nazaré, tel. 91/3274-4874, 3–8 P.M. daily). From this spot, for the last 37 years, Maria do Carmo has been serving up what many consider to be the most perfect *tacacá* in town. Maria do Carmo attributes the success of her fragrant broth to quality ingredients such as the giant shrimp imported from Maranhão and *jambu* purchased daily from the Ver-o-Peso market.

Another equally beloved snack is the *tapiocas* (crunchy crêpes made from manioc flour) that Andreia Dias Gonçalves has been making since she was a young girl in Pará's interior. Locals flock to her stand, **Tapioquinha de Mosqueiro** (Complexo São José Liberato, Cidade Velha, 9 A.M.–7 P.M. Tues.–Sun.) for their early morning and late afternoon *tapioca* fix. In terms of fillings, there are more than 60 sweet and savory possibilities. However, the most popular is *molhada,* in which the *tapioca,* filled with freshly grated coconut, is dipped in coconut milk and then wrapped in a banana leaf.

Tucked away amidst the old mansions of Cidade Velha, **Portinha** (Rua Doutor Malcher 463, Cidade Velha, tel. 91/3223-0922, 5–10 P.M. Tues. and Thurs.–Sun.) is easily identifiable by the locals who line up in front of this tiny *lanchonete* to feast on homemade pastries, all of which have an Amazonian twist. For example, instead of ground beef, the Lebanese *esfihas* are stuffed with duck, *jambu,* and *tucupi.* There are also turnovers filled with smoked sausage and pupunha, and rolls stuffed with sun-dried tomatoes, buffalo mozzarella,

and Brazil nuts. If you want a meal, regional dishes such as *maniçoba* and *tacacá* are prepared daily.

Perhaps the most famous ice cream parlor in the country, (**Cairu** (Travessa 14 de Março 1570, Nazaré, tel. 91/3212-5595, noon–midnight Mon.–Thurs., noon–2 A.M. Fri.–Sun.) has been churning out its lip-smacking *sorvetes* for close to 50 years. Purists can indulge in Amazonian flavors made from local fruits such as *bacuri, murici, sapoti, graviola,* and *açaí,* while novelty-seekers can try the *"mestiços"* (mixed breeds) such as *carimbó* (*cupuaçu* and Brazil nut) and *maria isabel* (*bacuri,* shortbread, and coconut). The ice creams are so delectable that five-star restaurants in Rio and São Paulo proudly feature them on their dessert menus. There are 11 locations around Belém, including one at the Estação das Docas.

REGIONAL

Paulo Martins, the proprietor of (**Lá em Casa** (Blvd. Castilhos França, Estação das Docas, tel. 91/3212-5588, www.laemcasa.com, noon–midnight daily, R\$20–30) is considered an ambassador of Paraense cuisine. Having learned everything he knows about local cooking from his mother, Martins travels throughout Brazil and the world introducing foodies to the aromas and flavors of the Amazon. In Belém, he serves up classic recipes such as *pato no tucupi* and grilled pirarucu along with the new concoctions he is always creating in his kitchen laboratory. Recent inventions include shrimp with *bacuri,* black *maniçoba* pasta with Paraense haddock in a curry sauce, and diced *tambaqui* served with *jambu* rice and fried bananas. Desserts will blow your mind, especially the *doce de cupuaçu* gratinéed with creamy buffalo cheese from the Ilha de Marajó. Aside from the airy riverside Docas restaurant (which features a lunch buffet), a second restaurant, festooned with jungle fronds, recently opened in Umarizal (Travessa Dom Pedro 1546, tel. 91/3223-1212).

Strangely enough, restaurants specializing in Amazonian fish (as opposed to meat or seafood) are hard to come by in Belém. A glorious exception to this rule is (**Remanso de Peixe**

(Travessa Barão do Triunfo 2950, Casa 46, Marco, tel. 91/3228-2477, 11:30 A.M.–3 P.M. and 7–10 P.M. Tues.–Sat., 11 A.M.–3 P.M. Sun., R\$20–30). Despite this restaurant's off-the-beaten-path location—hidden away in a pleasant villa in the residential *bairro* of Marco—both locals and tourists have no problem seeking it out in order to savor dishes made from fresh fish purchased daily at the Mercado Ver-o-Peso. By far the most popular dish is the *moqueca paraense,* a bubbling stew of local filhote, crab legs, and shrimp, cooked in a broth of *tucupi, jambu,* tomatoes, and herbs, and served piping hot in an cast iron pot. Its success is such that the owners patented the recipe. Leave room for desserts such as cappuccino pudding with preserved *bacuri.*

INTERNATIONAL

The finest Italian food in town can be found at **Dom Giuseppe** (Av. Conselheiro Furtado 1420, Batista Campos, tel. 91/4008-0001, www.domgiuseppe.com.br, 6 P.M.–midnight daily, noon–3 P.M. Sun., R\$20–30), a charming house with wooden floors and white and red accents. Although recipes are devoutly Italian, the tastes are sharply enhanced by the use of ingredients supplied by local producers. For instance, the smooth, creamy, mozzarella comes from regional buffalo herds while the semolina used in the polenta is from a local manioc farm. Even the chocolate that is the mainstay of rich desserts such as the brownie topped with cream *sorvete* and cashews comes from cocoa grown in the interior of Pará. The wine list is quite impressive.

   Hatobá (Blvd. Castilhos França, Estação das Docas, tel. 91/3212-3143, noon–midnight Sun.–Thurs., noon–2 A.M. Fri.–Sat., R\$20–35) specializes in quite decent sushi and sashimi, but you can also find a wide selection of other fare ranging from salads, chicken, beef, and fish dishes to pastas and regional specialties. Lunch functions as a self-service buffet. The riverside location also makes Hatobá a favorite happy-hour haunt, particularly Sunday–Thursday 5–9 P.M., when sushi and appetizers are half-price.

VARIED

For Belém's workers, the next best thing to going home for a tasty lunch is heading to **Pomme d'Or** (Av. Generalíssimo Deodoro 1513, Nazaré, tel. 91/3202-9800, 11:30 A.M.–3:30 P.M. daily, R\$10–18). The ranch-style house with high ceilings and wooden beams serves up a daily banquet of 50 dishes including hearty beef stews, shrimp with *pupunha* and roquefort, salads and even sushi. Saturday is devoted to *feijoada,* while Sunday is the day to sample regional specialties such as *pato no tucupi* and *maniçoba.* The same owners operate the more refined **Restô do Parque** (Av. Magalhães Barata 830, São Bráz, tel. 91/3229-8000, noon–3:30 P.M. Tues.–Sun., R\$10–28). At the entrance to the Parque da Residência, this pretty wooden house with glass windows is a favorite lunch spot for both executives and tourists who appreciate the small buffet featuring dishes such as beef filet in *cupuaçu* sauce and *bacalhau* with pesto.

   An even more enticing setting is that proffered by **❰ Manjar da Garças** (Mangal das Garças, Cidade Velha, tel. 91/3242-1056, noon–4 P.M. Tues.–Sun., 8 P.M.–midnight Tues.–Thurs., 8 P.M.–2 A.M. Fri.–Sat., R\$20–30). Located within the Parque Ambiental Mangal das Garças, the restaurant consists of a vast Swiss Family Robinson-style bungalow on stilts with a palm thatched roof and stunning views of the Rio Guamá. The jungly ambiance enhances the appreciation of sophisticated dishes that take advantage of local ingredients. Examples include crunchy almond-crusted filhote served with *jambu* risotto and shrimp with leeks bathed in a sauce of apples and Brazil nuts. For dessert, the *bacuri* profiteroles swimming in melted chocolate are pretty sublime. Lunch features a buffet of hot and cold dishes while the dinner menu is à la carte. Live music adds to the mood.

Information

In the center of town, you'll find the municipal tourist office **Belémtur** (Rua Dr. Malcher 592, Nazaré, tel. 091/3283-4850, www.belemtur.com.br, 8 A.M.–noon and 1–6 P.M. Mon.–Fri.) and the state tourist office **Paratur** (Praça

Maestro Waldemar Henrique, Reduto, tel. 91/3212-0669, www.paratur.pa.gov.br). Both supply good free city maps. Staff rarely speak English, but are friendly. Each also has an information booth at the airport.

Services
You'll find lots of banks on Avenida Presidente Vargas, including Banco do Brasil (no. 248), HSBC (no. 670), and Bradesco (no. 998), all of which have ATMs that accept international cards. The main **post office** is also on Avenida Presidente Vargas (no. 498).

For Internet access, the business center at the **Hilton Hotel** (Av. Presidente Vargas 882, tel. 91/3225-0028, 7:30 A.M.–10:30 P.M. Mon.–Fri., 7:30 A.M.–6:30 P.M. Sat.–Sun.) is convenient. Less expensive is the **Empório Cyber Café** (Rua Ângelo Custódio 85, Cidade Velha, tel. 91/3212-7646).

In the event of an emergency, dial **192** for an ambulance or the fire department, **190** for the police. For medical treatment try the **Hospital da Ordem Terceira** (Travessa Frei Gil de Vila Nova 59, Centro, tel. 91/3216-2777). **Farmácia Big Ben** (Av. Serzedelo Correa 15, Nazaré, tel. 91/3241-8642, 8 A.M.–10 P.M. Mon.–Fri., 8 A.M.–4 P.M. Sat.) is a conveniently located pharmacy, close to Praça da República, with late hours.

Getting There
Most visitors coming from southern Brazil choose to fly to Belém. There are many flights (although few are direct) from major cities; however, airfare is quite costly. If you're traveling along the Northeast coast, you can easily hop a bus, which is comfortable and far more affordable. And if you have time (and patience) to spare, you can indulge in the classic river journey—a 4–5-day voyage down the mighty Amazon—from Manaus.

BY AIR
Flights from cities around Brazil (including Manaus and Santarém) arrive at the **Aeroporto Internacional de Val-de-Cães** (Av. Júlio César, tel. 91/3210-6039), which is around 15 kilometers (9 miles) from the center of town. A taxi

to downtown costs between R$35–40. You can also take a municipal bus. Buses marked "Pres. Vargas" head to Praça da República, while those marked "Ver-O-Peso" head to Cidade Velha.

BY BUS
Long distance buses arrive at the **Rodoviária São Brás** (Av. Almirante Barroso, São Brás, tel. 91/3246-7442), just east of Nazaré. Taking a bus to Belém inevitably involves a long haul. The closest Brazilian capital, São Luís, is a 12-hour ride. **Boa Esperança** (tel. 91/3266-0033) provides service to cities along the Northeast coast such as São Luís, Fortaleza, Natal, and Recife while **Itapemirim** (tel. 91/3226-3458, www.itapemirim.com.br) operates buses to southern cities such as Salvador, Rio, and São Paulo.

BY BOAT
Taking a boat up the Amazon to Manaus is on many people's journey-of-a-lifetime lists (although sailing *down* the Amazon is actually faster). The reality is certainly not quite as romantic as you might have envisioned. Boats keep to the middle of the river, which makes seeing wildlife or even vegetation up close an exceptional occurrence. However, if you don't mind crowds, lots of basic rice-and-beans-style cooking, and a landscape that after five days can grow a little monotonous even to the most botanically inclined, you should definitely consider this trip. If you treat it less like a sightseeing excursion and more as an authentic insight into life along one of the world's great waterways—complete with swinging hammocks, blaring music, idle conversations, and lots of loading and unloading of exotic wares—you will certainly be in for an adventure. Riverboats generally charge around R$500 for a private cabin. Outfitted with bunks that sleep 2–4 people, cabins offer privacy, security, and the luxury of your own bathroom, but can be cramped and stuffy. A cheaper alternative is to buy a hammock and string it up among those of the other passengers on the ship's deck. An upper deck hammock space (with more breeze and less motor noise) costs around R$300. Try

to purchase your ticket in advance (you can often negotiate a discount) and arrive on board early to stake out hammock space.

For information about departures and tickets, visit the **Terminal Fluvial** (Av. Marechal Hermes, Centro, tel. 91/3224-6885). Located 1 kilometer (0.6 mile) downstream from the Estação das Docas, this is where all the riverboat companies have their offices. Boats also depart from here. Although the terminal is safe by day, be careful at night and always take taxis. Different companies operate boats that travel upstream on different days of the week. **Macamazon** (tel. 91/3222-5604) and **Amazon Star** (tel. 91/3241-8624, www.amazonstar.com.br) operate riverboats (including some more comfortable, air-conditioned vessels) to various destinations up the Amazon, including Santarém (2.5 days away) and Manaus.

Getting Around

Most of Belém's principal attractions are in the Cidade Velha or Nazaré and can easily be walked to. For further-flung destinations there are plenty of buses—major hubs include Avenida Presidente Vargas, Praça da República and the Mercado Ver-o-Peso. Taxis are also easy to hail and quite inexpensive. It's recommended you take them for getting around at night. To reserve one, call **Coopertaxi** (tel. 91/3257-1720).

Driving in Belém is pretty easy, although there are a lot of one-way streets. Should you want to rent a car to get around the city or head to some nearby beaches such as Ilha da Mosqueira, or even to Ilha de Marajó, there is an **Avis** at the airport (tel. 91/3257-2277) and at the Hilton (Praça da Républica, tel. 91/3225-1699).

CITY TOURS

For tours of Belém and the surrounding region, there are two well-reputed tour operators that have lots of experience with foreign tourists. Their outings and excursions are all interesting and nicely priced, and many of the staff and guides speak English. Aside from the day outings listed below, they offer trips and packages to destinations such as Ilha de Marajó and Santarém.

Amazon Star Turismo (Rua Henrique Gurjão 236, Reduto, tel. 91/3241-8624, www.amazonstar.com.br) offers a terrific variety of tours including half-day walking tours (R$25) to the city's major historic attractions. Also popular are the full-day hiking tours that take you across the Rio Guamá to a patch of rainforest. Aside from spotting wildlife, you get to visit a traditional *caboclo* village and a stop for a refreshing dip in the river. The trip, including a guide and lunch, costs R$120. For bird-lovers who can deal with getting up at the crack of dawn, Amazon Star offers a unique excursion (R$55) to Ilha do Papagaio (Parrot Island), an island off the shore of Belém that is the roosting spot for hundreds of brightly colored parrots. After a hotel pickup, you sail to the island to watch the birds awaken and fly away, their bright plumage merging with the gaudy colors of the sunrise.

Valverde Turismo (Estação das Docas, tel. 91/3212-3388, www.valverdeturismo.com.br) is another reputed tour operator. Aside from a similar half-day city walking tour, Valverde offers half-day tours to the beach town of Icoaraci (R$60). Romantics should definitely take the two-hour "sunset" boat tour (R$25) that departs nightly from the Estação das Docas and navigates the river as the sun sinks below the horizon and the city lights come twinkling on.

Around Belém

By bus (or car) and by boat, there are several interesting side trips you can make within the vicinity of Belém. The most popular destinations are the beaches along the banks of the region's rivers. Avoid the dirty and crowded ones closest to the city itself as well as weekends, when most beaches are swarmed by day-tripping Belenenses.

ICOARAÇI

Only 25 kilometers (16 miles) north of the city (local buses marked "Icoaraçi" pass along Av. Presidente Vargas), Icoaraçi (www.icoaraci .com.br) is a pleasant river town renowned for its ceramic workshops. Dozens of potters have kept alive the techniques and forms of the distinctive pottery made by Marajoara Indians. Aside from replicas of the creamy white and red vessels adorned with geometric and primitive motifs, there are also some strikingly original designs. Although the pieces are fragile, the potters are as good at packing as they are at sculpting. Also not to be missed is a meal at ◖ **Na Telha** (Rua Siqueira Mendes 363, tel. 91/2227-0853, www.restaurantenatelha.com.br, 11 A.M.–midnight daily, R$15–20). This local restaurant is famed for its delectable fresh fish dishes—such as *filhote* bathed in a sauce of shrimp—cooked on a piping hot *telha* (red ceramic roofing tile). For starters, order the delicious *bolinhos de pirarucu.*

ILHA DO MOSQUEIRO

For a beach trip you can do in a day, your best bet is Ilha do Mosqueiro (www.mosqueiro.com.br), 70 kilometers (44 miles) east of Belém, which has some attractive sandy beaches, particularly once you get away from the little town of Vila Mosqueiro. From the town's main square, you can catch local buses to beaches such as Praia Morubira and Praia Marahú. The most unspoiled of all is Praia do Paraíso, where you'll encounter white sands fringed by green vegetation and clean, emerald waters for bathing.

Should you want to spend the night, the ◖ **Hotel Farol** (Praça Princesa Isabel 3295, tel. 91/3771-2095, www.hotelfarol.com.br, R$70–120 d) is a once grand early-20th-century hotel that was a favorite retreat of Belém's rubber barons. Facing the attractive Praia do Farol, the simple, but spotless rooms are divided between the original building and a more modern annex. Opt for the former with its curving walls, sweeping hallways, polished marquetry, and bay windows overlooking a tropical garden and the beach. An atmospheric restaurant with columns and wonderful tiled floors serves simple home cooked dishes such as shrimp frittata. For access to lovely Praia do Paraíso, check into the **Hotel Fazenda Paraíso** (Av. Beira Mar, tel. 91/3204-4666, www.hotelpousadafazenda.com.br, R$150

d), a sprawling attractive beachfront hotel with comfortable, modern rooms and pleasant grounds that include the odd presence of a clover-shaped swimming pool. The cheery wood-and-brick chalets are ideal for families or groups of three to five. Booking ahead is recommended if you're coming on a weekend.

Getting to Mosqueiro (connected by a bridge to the mainland) is easy from Belém. Frequent buses leave daily from the *rodoviária*. By car, you need merely follow the well-paved BR-316.

ILHA DE ALGODOAL

The finest beaches within reach of Belém are the primitive windswept dunes that ring the idyllic Ilha de Algodoal (www.algodoal.com). Due to its distance from Belém (a five-hour trip), visiting Algodoal involves staying at least one night. Though once you arrive, you likely won't be in a hurry to leave. The island's name is inspired by the abundance of a native plant known as *algodão de seda* (silk cotton). Its pods release fluffy white down that often wafts around the island like stray snow flakes. Fishing communities only settled here in the early 20th century, and to this day, the island's quartet of tiny fishing towns (the largest of which is Algodoal) are terribly bucolic and laid-back. Water is pumped from natural wells, electricity only arrived in 2005, and transportation is by bike, boat, or horse (there are no motorized vehicles—or banks either for that matter, so stock up on cash before coming). There are, however, abundant idyllic beaches, freshwater lagoons, lily-pad covered marshes, and unspoiled native vegetation. The islanders are hospitable and the only interruption to the tranquility that reigns is the infectious rhythm of *carimbó,* a local dance set to pounding log-like drums that originated with the African slaves that came to coastal Pará in the 17th century.

Various rustic *pousadas* and camping grounds have sprung up to meet the demands of young backpackers and savvy eco-tourists (during holiday periods, you should reserve accommodations in advance). Most *pousadas* are located in and around the village of Algodoal itself, which is close to the island's most beautiful

POROROCA

One of the most intriguing of the Amazon River's many unusual phenomena is the *pororoca*, which in the Tupi language means a "great crashing." *Pororocas* occur when high ocean tides sweep up-river, creating long, giant waves. In March and April, when the difference between high and low tides is most pronounced, the waves can reach 4 meters (13 feet) in height. For this reason, certain riverside towns have become meccas for freshwater surfers. In fact, since 1999, the town of São Domingos de Capim, 30 kilometers (19 miles) from Belém, hosts an annual surfing competition known as the Campeonato Nacional de Surfe na Pororoca.

beaches—Praia do Farol and Praia da Princesa. The loveliest place to stay on the island is the aptly named **Jardim do Eden** (tel. 91/9997-0467, www.chez.com/algodoal, R$90 d), which is immersed in the untamed natural landscape of Praia do Farol. Atmospheric lodgings are in bungalows made from old bricks and volcanic rock. All possess small kitchens and sleeping room for up to five people. The restaurant serves delicious breakfasts as well as very good fish and seafood dishes. The owners, a hospitable and multilingual Brazilian-French couple, can organize all sorts of outings: from fishing and canoeing trips to nature walks where you can spot monkeys, tortoises, and wild orchids in bloom.

Ilha de Algodoal is 163 kilometers (101 miles) northeast of Belém. From the *rodoviária*, **Rápido Excelsior** (tel. 91/3249-6365) operates five daily buses to the town of Marudá, where you can catch a boat to the island. Boats depart at 8:30 A.M., 10:30 A.M., 12:30 P.M., and 5 P.M. daily (extra boats at 9:30 A.M. and 2:30 P.M. Fri.–Sun.). Fare is R$5 and the crossing takes 40 minutes. Driving from Belém, take the well-paved BR-316, PA-136, and PA-318 to Marudá, where you can leave your car in a parking lot for R$5 a day.

◖ ILHA DE MARAJÓ

These days, there's nowhere else on Earth that the lyrics "Oh give me a home, where the buffalo roam . . ." apply to better than Ilha de Marajó. Bathed by waters of the Rio Amazonas, Rio Tocantins, and the Atlantic Ocean, this Switzerland-sized island some 90 kilometers (56 miles) northwest of Belém boasts lovely beaches, mangrove swamps teeming with exotic cranes, herons, ibises, and thousands and thousands of water buffalo. On the largest river island in the world, buffalo are a major source of food (succulent steaks and creamy cheese) and transportation; they are far better than horses or cars at wading through muddy wetlands—for this reason, buffalo tow the municipal garbage trucks. They are also a major source of livelihood—aside from food, their hides supply the local leather industry. In fact, they outnumber the human population by a ratio of 3:1. Although at first glance, they might appear a little ornery, the buffalo are actually very docile. Moreover, those that serve as transportation vehicles receive special training to deal with tourists.

There are various stories surrounding the water buffalo's arrival on Marajó. One version credits their introduction to 18th-century Franciscan monks, while another claims they were survivors of a capsized boat that was transporting buffalo from India to French Guyana. Buffalo aside, Ilha de Marajó is a fascinating place. Despite its relative accessibility, Ilha de Marajó is also somewhat of a secluded world unto itself. Geographically, its vegetation is split between the flat wetlands of the eastern coast, which conjure up the Pantanal of Mato Grosso (particularly during the floods that occur between February and May) and the tangled forests of the remote western coast. Historically, the island possesses a rich heritage. Between 1000 B.C. and A.D. 1300, it was inhabited by a group of Indians that was believed to have had a very sophisticated culture. Evidence of this lost civilization came to light in the 19th century when, after the annual floods, local farmers began to find shards of finely-wrought pottery and funeral urns stuck in the thick matting of their buffalos. The pottery, which came to be known as *cerámica marajoara,* consisted of highly original vessels made of local white clay mixed with substances such as ground tree bark and tortoise shells. Color was added via charcoal (black) and *urucum* (an ocher colored powder used in cooking to this day). Before being baked and varnished, the pottery was decorated with intricate designs illustrating scenes from life such as marriage and hunting ceremonies. To this day, the island has maintained this ceramics tradition, with local artists continuing to create exquisite pieces inspired by the ancient Marajoara techniques and motifs.

Visitors to Ilha de Marajó stay on the island's eastern coast (closest to Belém). If you're traveling independently and without a car, your best bet is to base yourself in one of the picturesque villages of Soure, Salvaterra, or Joanes. It is difficult to get around the island on public transport (although you can easily rent a bike). If you want to see more than beaches, it's best to arrange a tour out of Belém that includes a stay at a working buffalo *fazenda,* a number of which operate as ecotourist *pousadas.*

Sights

The two main towns on Ilha de Marajó are Soure and Salvaterra. **Soure** (www.soure.tur.br) is the largest and most lively of the two. Founded in the 17th century on the mouth of the Rio Paracauari, it is an enticing place with pastel-painted houses shaded by palms and mango trees. Most of the island's hotels, restaurants, and services (including the island's Banco do Brasil with an ATM that should accept international cards) can be found here as well as the closest semblance to a nightlife. During the second weekend of November, Soure hosts its own small, but enchanting Círio de Nazaré.

Surrounding the town are some wonderful beaches. A 3-kilometer (2-mile) walk (or bike ride) north brings you to **Praia Barra Velha,** and a little further on, across the Rio Araruna, is the even more striking **Praia de Arauna. Praia do Pesqueiro** is a more popular beach, 9 kilometers (6 miles) from Soure (accessible by bus). Its blue-green waters are dotted with fishing boats. Their catch of the day is served at the palm-thatched beach *barracas.*

On the other side of the Rio Paracauari, facing the Baía de Marajó, equally pretty **Salvaterra** (www.salvaterra.tur.br) has a more languid air and boasts proximity to **Praia Grande,** a sweeping ocean beach backed by palms. Around 16 kilometers (10 miles) south of Salvaterra is **Joanes.** This tiny village is known for its pretty golden sand beach and the atmospheric ruins of a 17th-century church built by Jesuits who were the first Europeans to settle the island. A historic source of contention between Spain and Portugal revolves around the fact that, in 1500, Spanish navigator Vicente Yañez Pinzón landed on Joanes's beach—two months before Pedro Alvarez de Cabral "discovered" Brazil and claimed it as Portuguese territory.

Although you can see examples of *cerámica marajoara* in Belém's Museu Emílio Goeldi and the Forte do Presépio, the largest and most splendid collection of these unique thousand year-old pieces is housed in the **Museu do Marajó** (Av. do Museu 1983, tel. 91/3578-1102, www.museudemarajo.com.br, 8 A.M.–6 P.M. daily, R$2), along with other vestiges of Marajoara culture. Located in the pretty town of **Cachoeira do Arari,** 70 kilometers (43 miles) from Salvaterra, the museum can be reached by boat or car or van along a bumpy dirt road.

Buffalo Farms

On Marajó, numerous buffalo *fazendas,* or farms, are open to visitors. Aside from a chance to get firsthand insight into the daily lives of Marajoanos and a behind-the-scenes look at a working buffalo farm (you can often ride the buffalos), many of these farms are located on plains and wetland areas that are rife with wildlife. Among the creatures you're likely to see are monkeys, capybaras, *jacarés* (caimans) and the flamboyantly pink and scarlet ibises, known as *guarás.* In all cases, advance reservations are necessary.

Located 12 kilometers (7.5 miles) from

a typical beachscape, Ilha de Marajó

Soure, **Fazenda Bom Jesus** (4a Rua Km 8, tel. 91/3741-1243) is owned by Eva Abufaiad, a veterinarian and agricultural engineer who really knows her buffalo as well as birds such as blue storks, parrots, and *guarás,* all of which can be easily spotted here. During the day, three-hour visits cost R$20 and include a home-cooked Marajoara snack. Only 2 kilometers (1.2 miles) from Soure, **Fazenda Araruna** (tel. 91/3741-1474) has its own lovely river beach that is popular with *guarás* and can be reached by a two-hour ride on the back of a buffalo. Those who are buffalo-shy can explore the area by horseback or canoe. Outings cost R$20–30.

Some *fazendas* offer accommodations as well. Although no longer a working farm, **Fazenda São Jerônimo** (Rodovia Soure-Pesqueiro Km 3, tel. 91/3741-2093, R$110–130 d) is a picturesque estate (close to Soure) with lots of creeks and a private beach where you can swim. You can take a guided hike through groves of coconut palms and native fruit trees, or a canoe trip through mangrove swamps. Each two-hour activity costs R$25–30 per person.

Accommodations in a low-slung ranch house are simple but appealing, with regional furnishings and air-conditioning. The restaurant (reservations required), serves delicious home-cooked food (including buffalo) for both lunch and dinner.

A 45-minute boat trip and buffalo-cart ride away from Soure, the **Fazenda Sanjo** (tel. 91/9145-4475, tel. 91/3242-1380, www.sanjo.tur.br, R$350 for a two-day package) is an authentic family-run ranch where you'll be made to feel so at home that before you know it, you'll be rustling up the buffalos on horseback. Once you've finished helping out with milking and making cheese, you can savor some delicious dishes made from the farm's herds. Lodgings in the main farm house are simple, but cozy and comfortable.

More secluded is the **Fazenda Nossa Senhora de Carmo** (tel. 91/3212-6244, amazonstar@amazonstar.com.br, R$800 for a three-day package including transportation from Belém), which is reached by taking a boat inland down the Rio de Camará. Accommodations are in the rather grand-looking whitewashed, tile-roofed ranch house. Although lacking in luxury (no air-conditioning or private bathrooms), the rooms are comfortable and quite atmospheric. The common areas are charmingly decorated with antiques. Rates include all meals (prepared with fresh farm produce) as well as diverse nature activities such as kayak and canoe trips, horseback and buffalo riding, fishing, birding, and wildlife safaris led by English-speaking guides. While you can make reservations directly with these *fazendas* (often cheaper), several agencies in Belém sell packages to them, including **Amazon Star** (tel. 91/3241-8624, www.amazonstar.com.br) and **Valverde** (tel. 91/3212-3388, www.valverdeturismo.com.br).

Shopping

In Soure, various local artists create beautiful pottery modeled after traditional *cerâmica marajoara*. One of the island's most reputed ceramicists is Carlos Amaral. A descendant of the Aruá Indians who inhabited the island before the arrival of the Portuguese, Carlos learned traditional pottery techniques from his grandmother and has spent his life studying the graphic symbols used by his Marajoara ancestors. You can view and purchase his work at his atelier, **M'Barayo Cerâmica** (Travessa 20, tel. 91/3741-1719, 8 A.M.–7 P.M. Mon.–Sat., 8 A.M.–noon Sun.). Another good place to find Marajoara replicas along with woven items and other local *artesenato* is the **Sociedade Marajoara das Artes** (3a Rua, 8 A.M.–7 P.M. Mon.–Sat., 8 A.M.–noon Sun.).

Accommodations

For the most part, accommodations on Marajó are fairly relaxed and rustic. Make sure to reserve in advance during holidays or long weekends when Belenenses vacation here. Apart from *fazenda* lodges, most accommodations are divided between Soure and Salvaterra.

In Soure, a very pretty budget option is **Pousada O Canto do Francês** (6a Rua, São Pedro, tel. 91/3741-1298, thcarliez@ig.com.br, R$70–80d). Set amidst lush green gardens, rooms are soothing with bleached walls and

polished wooden furniture. Common rooms are tastefully decorated with antiques and local artifacts. English is spoken and the French owner, Thierry, can organize excursions. You can also rent a bike to tool around to nearby beaches.

Staying in Salvaterra gives you the advantage of being right on the lovely sands of Praia Grande. **Pousada Boto** (Rodovia Alcindo Cancela, tel. 91/3765-1539, www.pousadaboto.com.br, R$70–90 d) is an amazing deal. The cheery bungalow accommodations are smallish and basic, but the leafy gardens, friendly staff, and three-minutes-from-the-beach location more than compensate. The food is quite decent and you can rent bikes and motorcycles to explore the island. Fancier, but still incredibly affordable is **Pousada dos Guarás** (Av. Beira-Mar, tel. 91/3765-1149, www.pousadadosguaras.com.br, R$130–150 d). Scattered amidst a sprawling palm-studded estate overlooking the beach, the private bungalow accommodations are quite fetching. Local art hangs upon brightly colored walls and curtains and bedspreads are stamped with oversized tropical flowers. There is a sizable pool and a scenic restaurant with an extensive menu of both regional and international dishes. When booking, you can request an all-inclusive package that includes numerous activities and guided excursions to natural attractions, buffalo *fazendas,* and Soure. Aside from the hotel restaurants, various *barracas* sell simple, delicious fish and seafood specialties right on the beach.

If you're in the mood for total tranquility, consider staying in the charming little fishing village of Joanes. Owned by a Brazilian-Belgian couple, the ⟨ **Pousada Ventânia** (tel. 91/3646-2067, www.pousadaventania.com, R$80–90 d) is a friendly and delightfully rustic *pousada* perched upon a cliff overlooking a secluded beach. Its lofty position ensures constant breezes (and very few mosquitos). The basic, pleasant rooms have views of the Baía de Marajó and sleep up to four. Aside from renting out bikes and canoes, the owners can organize inexpensive guided outings.

Food

Abundant fresh fish and seafood aside, Marajó is renowned for two very distinctive culinary specialties. The first, of course, is water buffalo, which comes in many guises. More tender and flavorful than beef, buffalo meat is also lower in cholesterol. As a main course, two of the most popular buffalo recipes are *filé marajoara,* in which a prime cut of succulent meat is topped with creamy melted buffalo cheese (which resembles a fine mozzarella), and *frito de vaqueiro* ("cowboy fried"), in which less noble parts are cut into cubes, sautéed, and eaten with *pirão de leite* (a puree of milk and manioc flour). You'll also fined more refined inventions such as buffalo steak in *cupuaçu* sauce. Meanwhile, buffalo milk shows up in everything from butter and cheese to desserts such as the classic *doce de leite,* a rich caramel pudding. The second Marajoano delicacy is more rarefied, and also more likely to repulse squeamish gringos. It consists of a type of mollusk, known as *turu,* that can be found living inside dead trees located around the island's mangrove swamp. Milky white in color and gelatinous in consistency, *turu* is treated like an oyster. Locals are prone to eat them raw with a spray of lime. In bars and restaurants, however, you'll come across *caldo de turu,* in which the mollusk is added to a broth of coconut milk, lime juice, garlic, and cilantro.

One of the best places to sample local fare in Soure is at **C Paraíso Verde** (Travessa 17 2135, Umarizal, tel. 91/3741-1581, 10 A.M.–10 P.M., R$10–20), an aptly named restaurant set amidst ferns and native fruit trees, where the *filé marajoara* is pretty divine. On the road leading from Soure to Praia de Pesqueiro, **Delícias da Nalva** (4a Rua 1051, tel. 91/9188-3764, 10 A.M.–10 P.M. daily, R$10–20) also has a lovely garden setting. Recommended for local dishes, it is a particularly good place to try *caldo de turu.* In Salvaterra, **Bosque dos Aruãs** (2a Rua, tel. 91/3765-1115, 11 A.M.–3 P.M. and 6–10 P.M.), located within the *pousada* of the same name, serves nicely prepared fish, meat, and chicken dishes along with regional dishes.

Getting There and Around

Getting to Ilha de Marajó from Belém is quite easy. **Araparí Navegação** (tel. 91/3212-2492) operates daily ferry service (6:30 A.M. and 2:30 P.M. Mon.–Sat., 10 A.M. Sun., R$14) from Belém to Salvaterra. Departing from Portão 15 at the Docas do Pará (right near the Estação das Docas), the journey takes three hours. Another alternative is the car ferry that leaves from the nearby town of Icoaraci. Operated by **Henvil** (tel. 91/3249-3400), boats leave at 6:30 A.M. and 7:30 A.M. daily. Tickets (R$70 per car) can be purchased in advance at the Henvil kiosk at Belém's *rodoviária.*

On Marajó, all ferries dock at the Porto de Camará. From here you can easily get a bus or van to take you to Joanes and Salvaterra, 30 minutes away. From Salvaterra, a five-minute boat takes you across the river to Soure. If you confirm your arrival in advance, most *pousadas* or *fazendas* will agree to have someone pick you up at the docks.

Since public transport is sketchy, if you're without a car, the best way to get around is the island by taxi or *moto-taxi* (available in Soure and Salvaterra). You can also rent a bike (a service offered by many *pousadas*).

In Belém, specialized travel agencies offer complete packages that include all accommodations, meals, and excursions on Marajó, as well as transportation to and from the island from Belém. More information about these, check with **Amazon Star Turismo** (Rua Henrique Gurjão 236, Reduto, tel. 91/3241-8624, www.amazonstar.com.br).

SANTARÉM

The second largest city in Pará, Santarém is a drowsy, yet quite interesting river port town. By boat, it is around 50 hours upstream from Belém. It makes a great stopping place if you're riding up or down the Amazon between Belém and Manaus. Aside from offering a first-hand glimpse into Amazonian culture, the surrounding region boasts natural treasures of great beauty that can easily transform any "stopover" into a week's stay. The most popular destination are the unexpectedly white-sand beaches of nearby Alter do Chão, which are famously (and not unjustly) hyped by the state tourist office as the "Amazonian Caribbean." Although Santarém receives less rain than either Belém or Manaus, the surrounding countryside, much of it quite unspoiled, is a scenic mixture of wetlands and jungle. Take one of various trips up and down the Rio Tapajós (a tributary of the Amazon) or to the nearby Floresta Nacional do Tapajós, a national park, to get a taste of virgin rainforest.

Santarém is located at the confluence of the Rio Tapajós and the Rio Amazonas and the "meeting" of the blue-green waters of the Tapajós with the milky brown-colored Rio Amazonas is a sight that rivals the more celebrated merging of the Rio Negro with the Rio Solimões in Manaus. During the dry season (June–Dec.) the Tapajós recedes by several meters, exposing a seductive string of white-sand river beaches backed by lush green vegetation.

As a source of life and livelihoods, the Rio Tapajós has a long history that dates back to the earliest civilizations in the Americas. Archaeological evidence reveals the presence of prehistoric Indian groups who fished along the riverbanks and planted corn in the fertile hills surrounding Santarém. In the cliffs surrounding the town of Monte Alegre, they left splendid paintings in caves and on rocks that date back 12,000 years. Other excavations have unearthed shards of pottery that have proved far older than anything other vestiges encountered in the Americas.

Indian culture was still thriving when the first Europeans arrived at the beginning of the 16th century. Santarém itself was founded in the 1660s as a Jesuit missionary outpost. Tapajós Indians that weren't converted to Christianity were subsequently enslaved, slaughtered, driven into the jungle, or wiped out by infectious diseases. Apart from trade involving spices such as pepper, cloves, and vanilla, the little town remained an isolated jungle outpost until well into the 19th century, when it suddenly exploded into a prosperous trading center as a result of the Amazonian rubber boom. Ironically, it was in Santarém that the seeds were sown for Amazon rubber's dramatic demise. The culprit was an Englishman by the name of Henry Wickham who moved here in 1874, and soon after began smuggling precious rubber seeds back to London's Kew Gardens. From England, saplings were sent to plantations in the British colonies of Ceylon and Malaysia. By the end of the century, the Asian plantations were producing rubber in greater quantities and far more cheaply than those in the middle of the Brazilian jungle. As a result, the once-thriving Amazonian industry boom went bust.

Today, rubber still contributes to the local economy, along with timber, minerals, jute, fish, and Brazil nuts. However, in recent years, the greatest impact on Santarém and the surrounding region has been the introduction of soybean cultivation and processing. While the lucrative crop has brought new wealth to the area, it has also led to the rampant clearing of swaths of forest stretching all the way south to Mato Grosso do Sul. In the early 1970s, the construction of the highway leading from Cuiabá to Santarém was expected to open up the area and bring great development to the area. At the time, such ambitions proved premature—by the '80s, the jungle had once again reclaimed the asphalt, much of which has become impassable. However, spurred on by the soybean boom, the federal government is committed to reopening this crucial route, which could spell major changes for Santarém in years to come.

Sights

Santarém has very few actual attractions. The town's only museum is the **Centro Cultural João Fona** (Praça Barão de Santarém, 8 A.M.–5 P.M. Sun.–Fri.). Housed in a handsome canary yellow 19th-century mansion, the small, but very interesting collection provides an insightful look at Santarém's history and culture. Apart from some beautiful pieces of Tapajoara pottery dating back 5,000 years, there are recent examples of indigenous art as well as paintings that portray the town and river during colonial times. Otherwise, the most compelling thing you can do in Santarém is simply wander around soaking up the atmosphere of an Amazonian port town. The constant bustle of boats coming and going and passengers boarding and disembarking is quite a fascinating spectacle.

For a pleasant stroll along the river, start at the Praça Matriz, site of the town's oldest church, the 18th-century **Igreja Matriz da Nossa Senhora da Conceição.** From here, head west along the main waterfront drag, **Avenida Tapajós,** towards the gigantic eyesore that houses U.S.-based Cargill's soybean processing plant. Along the way, stop to check out the action and produce at the Mercado Municipal, where you'll see a dazzling array of fish as well as a local delicacy, the very tiny local shrimp called *aviu*. For an excellent view of the meeting of the Rio Tapajós and the Rio Amazonas (which run together side by side for several kilometers) climb the hill that rises up from the waterfront to the **Mirante do Tapajós.**

Sports and Recreation

Flaking out on beaches, boating down the river past traditional *caboclo* communities, exploring thick forests—there are plenty of ways of enjoying Santarém's natural attributes. For information about the surrounding area as well as guided ecotours, check in with **Amazon Tours** (Travessa Turiano Meira 1084, tel. 93/3522-1928, www.amazonriver.com.), a tour agency operated by an American expat named Steven Alexander, who has lived in Santarém with his wife since 1979. A passionate defender of the Amazon's rich biosphere (and an equally fervent critic of politicians and businesses bent on destroying it), Alexander runs guided city tours as well as river boat trips, excursions to Alter do Chão, and visits to his own private nature reserve, **Bosque Santa Lúcia,** a patch of rainforest on the outskirts of town where you can hike amidst native trees, birds, and monkeys. He can also put you in touch with guides to take you to farther flung attractions. **Santarém Tur** (Rua Adriano Pimentel 44, tel. 93/3522-4847, www.santaremtur.com.br) also

has a friendly staff that runs city tours and trips over land or by boat to natural attractions.

Shopping

Santarém is a great place to pick up inexpensive and well-made local and indigenous *artesanato*. **Loja Muiraquitã** (Rua Senador Lameira Bittencourt 131, tel. 93/3522-7164) has a diverse array of intriguing objects ranging from wood carvings to musical instruments. At **Cerámica Tapajoara** (Rua Ururara 318, Santana, tel. 93/3524-5189), you'll find replicas of traditional pottery made thousands of years ago by Tapajó Indians. Not to be missed are the wonderfully original clothing and accessories made by **Dica Frazão** (Rua Floriano Peixoto 281, tel. 93/3522-1026) out of her home that doubles as an atelier and museum. In her 80s, Dica is a local legend, a stylist whose remarkable items made out of natural fibers such as buriti palm, canarana straw, and tree bark, and accessorized with colorful seeds and feathers, are notable for their refined tailoring that can easily be called Amazon chic.

Accommodations

Occupying a pretty pale blue house built in 1910, the family-run **Brisa Hotel** (Rua Senador Lameira Bittencourt 5, tel. 93/3522-1018, R$70–80 d) is one of a series of historic houses on Santarém's oldest street. High-ceilinged rooms are very plain, but clean, and a friendly atmosphere reigns. Facing the Mercado Modelo, the **Hotel Rio Dourado** (Rua Floriano Peixoto 799, tel. 93/3522-4021, R$90–115 d) is a cheery, modern place jazzed up with lots of tropically hued decorative accents. The colorful air-conditioned rooms—with white tiled or hardwood floors—are quite comfortable, although some of the furniture is sort of cheap looking. Internet access is available. Fans of '70s tropical architecture will be thrilled by the **Amazon Park Hotel** (Av. Mendonça Furtado 4120, tel. 93/3522-3361, www.amazonparkhotel.com.br, R$115–130 d). Located 4 kilometers (2.5 miles) from downtown, this big boxy concrete complex was built in 1971, anticipating that the construction of the Transamazônica BR-163

TAPAJOARA POTTERY

Excavations in the Santarém region have uncovered evidence that prehistoric peoples were making pottery 10,000 years ago, However, 2,000 years ago the fierce and talented group known as the Tapajós Indians really hit their stride. By combining clay with *cauxixi*, a type of river sponge, the Tapajós created a unique mixture that was both resistant and light as porcelain. With it, they formed exuberantly shaped vessels, which they decorated with sophisticated designs featuring native fauna such as caimans and spotted jaguars. Many of these receptacles were used for religious rituals and celebrations. Some were used by priests to imbibe mind-tripping potions made from hallucinogenic plants such as ayahuasca. Others were used for ceremonies in which the Indians literally drank their recently departed loved ones by mixing their cremated ashes with brews made from fermented corn or wild rice.

The Tapajós also made *muiraquitãs*, which were carved out of a green stone. These frog-shaped amulets were used to ward off disease and promote fertility. Today, original Tapajoara pottery commands fortunes on the international art market, where its quality is considered on par with prehistoric pieces created by Andean peoples. For far smaller sums, replicas of both Tapajoara pottery and good luck *muiraquitãs* can be found in *artesanato* shops in Santarém and Belém.

highway from Cuiabá to Santarém would turn the city into a big boom town. The highway quickly deteriorated and so did the hotel. A recent renovation has spruced the place up considerably. The large rooms have been attractively refurbished and, defying the Fascist-style exterior, are quite homey. The common rooms—including a bar, lounge, and restaurant—have a swank '70s modernist grandeur. The verdant grounds feature a circular pool and lots of shady mango trees. The views out over the river are quite splendid.

Food

Housed in a lovely old mansion, the down-to-earth, **❰** **Peixaria Piracatú** (Av. Mendonça Furtado 174, Prainha, tel. 93/3523-5110, 11 A.M.–1 A.M. daily, R$12–22) is one of the best places in town to savor Amazonian fish. Whet your appetite with a portion of crunchy *bolinhos de piracuí* or a kebab of smoked pirarucu before feasting upon specialties such as *caldeirada de tambaqui* or *surubim* cooked with fresh corn. The most popular dish is *pirarucu à Juarez Simões,* in which the river's largest fish is gratinéed with cheese and banana and served with mashed potatoes. For a happy ending to your meal, choose between the equally irresistible *cremes* made from *cupuaçu* and *graviola.* **O Mascote** (Praça do Pescador 10, tel. 93/3523-2827, 10 A.M.–2:30 P.M. and 5 P.M.–midnight daily, R$10–20) combines a scenic waterfront location with reasonably priced and expertly prepared local dishes. At lunch, you can stuff yourself on an all-you-can-eat buffet, while dinner features specialties such as *tucunaré* in shrimp sauce and *caldeirada de peixe,* a stew featuring the daily catch. At night, O Mascote is a popular gathering spot, particularly on weekends when live music is performed. Surprisingly, one of Santarém's best loved restaurants doesn't serve fish at all. The specialty at **Mutunuy 2** (Travessa Muriano Meira, 1680-B, tel. 93/3522-7909, R$7–15) is buttery, charcoal-roasted chicken served with rice, manioc flour, and potato salad. Simple, but lip-smackingly delicious.

Information and Services

Santarém's tourist office, **Santur** (Rua Floriano Peixoto 777, tel. 93/3523-2434) has information about the town and surrounding area. You can also log on to www.santarem.pa.gov.br, which has good information in Portuguese. Also check with **Amazon Tours** and **Santarém Tur** (see *Sports and Recreation*).

© EMBRATUR

boating along the river

The latter sells plane tickets to Belém and Manaus. For money matters, on Avenida Rui Barbosa, you'll find a Banco do Brasil, as well as an HSBC and Bradesco, all with ATMs that accept international cards.

Getting There and Around

Santarém lies roughly halfway between Belém and Manaus. You can get here by plane (speedy and expensive) or boat (cheap and slow) from both cities. The state of the roads means that getting here by bus or car is out of the question.

BY AIR

Both national and (cheaper) regional carriers offer service to Santarém from Belém and Manaus. The small **Aeroporto Maria José** (Rodovia Fernando Guilhon, Praça Eduardo Gomes, tel. 93/3523-1990) is 14 kilometers (9 miles) from the center by bus or taxi.

BY BOAT

Boats going up and down the Amazon from Belém and Manaus arrive and depart daily from the busy **Docas do Pará** port, 2 kilometers

(1.2 miles) west of the center of town. **Marquês Pinto Navegação** (Rua do Imperador 746, tel. 93/3523-2828) and **Antônio Rocha** (Rua 24 de Outubro 1047, tel. 93/3522-7947) are two companies that have boat service to both cities, but your best bet is to go to the docks and check out for yourself which boat is leaving and when. A trip to Belém usually takes 2–2.5 days while Manaus is usually 3–4 days. Sometimes you can even negotiate the price. To visit smaller towns in the region such as Monte Alegre, head to the smaller port at Praça Tiradentes. Minibuses marked "Orla Fluvial" circulate at regular intervals between the Docas do Pará and the center of town, passing by the Praça Tiradentes port.

Although you can get around town easily by foot, if you find the heat is making you lazy, you can easily hail a taxi or *moto-taxi*.

AROUND SANTARÉM
◖ Alter do Chão

Around 35 kilometers (22 miles) from Santarém lies Alter do Chão, a beach resort that is one of the most stunning natural sites in the Amazon region. Its claim to fame is gleamingly white river beaches. Easily accessible from Santarém by bus (on one of the region's very few paved roads), the beach fills up on weekends. If you want to stay awhile (and you will), there are several *pousadas*. The best time to come is during the dry season (June to December) when the river recedes—by up to 10 meters (33 feet)—and leaves the beaches more exposed.

BEACHES

The village of Alter do Chão is blessed with soft white-sand beaches bathed by the blue waters of the Rio Tapajós to the west and the green waters of Lago Verde to the east. The main river beach facing the town is actually a large sand bar. During the rainy season, it becomes an island, known as Ilha de Amor (Island of Love), that can be reached by canoe-taxi. Throughout the year, its rustic *barracas* serving beer and fried fish make it an utterly relaxing place to while away the day (although it can get pretty packed on weekends and holidays). You can also rent canoes and kayaks to explore the **Lago Verde.** By car or boat, you can get to farther flung, but equally seductive beaches along the Tapajós such as **Pindobal, Cabutuba,** and **Aramanai.** One thing to watch out for is stingrays. Since they aren't fond of waves, make sure you splash around a lot before making your way into unknown waters.

SPORTS AND RECREATION

Should you feel like venturing forth along the Rio Tapajós, there are countless destinations that you can explore by boat. **Amazon Planet** (Travessa Copacabana 150, tel. 93/3527-1172, www.amazonplanetadventur.com.br) and **Mãe Natureza** (Praça Sete de Setembro, tel. 93/3527-1264) are two well-run ecotour outfits owned by expats (Italian and Argentinean, respectively) that operate numerous outings throughout the region. Among the trips they offer are boat tours, snorkeling and fishing excursions, and forest hikes, as well as multiday expeditions to secluded points up and down the river. A full-day outing usually costs around R$60 per person. Both operators can

also hook you up with houses for rent in Alter do Chão—an inexpensive option should you decide to stay for a while.

FESTIVALS AND EVENTS

If you're around during the second week in September, don't miss the **Festa do Cairé.** One of the most important traditional festivals in Pará, the *festa* dates back to the earliest contact between Jesuit missionaries and local Indians. Both indigenous and Catholic elements commingle in the ornate religious pageantry that, in true Brazilian style, is tempered with singing, dancing, and merrymaking.

SHOPPING

Araibá (Travessa Antônio A. Lobato) has a wonderful selection of high-quality and very reasonably priced *artesanato* by local Indians including colorful necklaces, wood carvings, and masks.

ACCOMMODATIONS AND FOOD

Cozy and rustic, **Pousada Tupaiulandai** (Rua Pedro Teixeira 300, tel. 93/3527-1157, R$60–70 d) is a good budget option. Rooms are quite large and comfortable, although somewhat lacking in decor. Breakfasts are good and the owners are very hospitable. Just off the main *praça* and close to the beach, the **Pousada Agualinda** (Rua Dom Macedo Costa, tel. 93/3527-1314, www.agualinda.com.br, R$80–90) is a newish hotel with cool tile floors, lots of attractive woodwork, and a fondness for pale pink. Air-conditioned rooms are basic, but tidy and pleasant, and accommodate up to four. Internet access is available.

By far the best hotel is the **Hotel Beloalter** (Rua Pedro Teixeira, tel. 93/3527-1230, www.beloalter.com.br, R$175–205 d), located on the shore of Lago Verde, a turquoise lake fringed by lovely beaches, which is only a short walk or canoe ride from the village. Lodgings are spread through an immense tropical garden that includes a pool and a placid lagoon. The air-conditioned rooms are spacious and very comfortable, if a little spartan. Although they cost a bit more, much more attractive and jungly are the two "ecological" rooms decked out entirely in native woods and fibers. Even better is the treehouse. The on-site restaurant is pleasantly rustic and serves well prepared regional cooking for lunch and dinner.

In town, the scenic beachfront restaurant in the **Pousada Alter do Chão** (Rua Lauro Sodré 74, tel. 93/3527-1215, 9 A.M.–5 P.M. Mon.–Fri., 9 A.M.–11 P.M. Sat.–Sun., extended to 9 A.M.–11 P.M. daily in Feb., July, and Nov., R$10–18) is a good spot for inexpensive and very tasty fish dishes. Equally recommended is the laid-back and friendly **Tribal** (Travessa Antônio A. Lobato, 11 A.M.–3 P.M. and 6–11 P.M., R$10–15), where you can dig into generous portions of fish as well as grilled chicken and beef.

INFORMATION AND SERVICES

To date there are no ATMs in Alter de Chão, so make sure you bring plenty of cash from Santarém. For tourist information, check with the operators listed in *Sports and Recreation.*

GETTING THERE

There is frequent bus service from Santarém to Alter do Chão, especially on weekends, when buses leave almost hourly from Praça Tiradentes. The trip takes around an hour.

Floresta Nacional do Tapajós

One of the Amazon's few national parks within easy reach of an urban center, the Floresta Nacional do Tapajós offers 30,000 hectares of unspoiled rainforest full of hiking trails. Although lacking the *National Geographic*-worthy wilderness of the jungles further up-river, the landscapes is nonetheless impressive, particularly when you find yourself dwarfed by the gigantic *sumaúna* tree, which make a baobab look like a bonsai. Aside from hiking through the forest, you can explore its streams and flooded wetlands by canoe. Within the park's boundaries are several very small river communities whose inhabitants still make a living from rubber tapping.

GETTING THERE

Visiting the park (which is only 40 kilometers/25 miles from Santarém) can be easily done in a day trip as part of packaged tour from Santarém or Alter do Chão.

Belterra and Fordlândia

By the beginning of the 20th century, the Amazon's rubber industry had long been overtaken by Asian plantations, However, in the 1920s, American automobile scion Henry Ford got a bee in his bonnet that Santarém was the ideal place for him to build a plantation that would supply rubber for his Model T's tires. Ford purchased a vast tract of land, 100 kilometers (62 miles) southwest of Santarém, and then began shipping all the materials necessary for the construction of a rubber plantation town in the midst of the jungle. The spitting image of a quintessential Midwestern town circa 1925, **Fordlândia** possessed cute little row houses with front gardens, a hospital, school, church, and even a cinema (aside from a rubber processing plant). Unfortunately, poor soil conditions, fungi that attacked the rubber trees, and the outbreak of diseases such as malaria doomed the project. Never one to give up, in 1934, Ford purchased another tract of land, only 30 kilometers (90 miles) from Santarém (on the eastern bank of the Tapajós), called **Belterra,** where he installed yet another Made-in-America community. Although Belterra fared somewhat better than Fordlândia, the outbreak of World War II hampered transportation of supplies and equipment, and the introduction of synthetic rubber knocked the bottom out of natural rubber prices. By the end of the war, Ford had had enough. Having squandered over 25 million dollars, he gratefully sold both areas to the Brazilian government for $200,000. Today, both of these utopian cities are eerily intact (Fordlândia's rubber plant is still in operation), their retro Americana jarringly out of place in the midst of the Amazon jungle.

GETTING THERE

Fordlândia is quite far from Santarém—an 8–10-hour boat ride south along the Rio Tapajós. However, Belterra can easily be visited in a day trip as part of a tour. For more information contact **Amazon Tours** or **Santarém Tur** in Santarém.

Monte Alegre

Pretty far off the beaten track, the small riverside town of Monte Alegre is one of the most fascinating detours you can make in this part of the Amazon. Perched on the northern bank of the Rio Amazonas, 120 kilometers (75 miles) downstream from Santarém, Monte Alegre is spread out upon a steep hillside. From the loftier heights, you're treated to mesmerizing panoramic views of the river weaving through a landscape of undulating green wetlands and freshwater lagoons, which stretches as far as the eye can see. At sunset, the vision is quite magnificent—not only is the entire scene bathed in luminous colors, but the skies are filled with the silhouettes of egrets, storks, and herons who come to settle down for the night in trees close to the town.

SIGHTS

In Monte Alegre, natural attractions certainly aren't lacking. Aside from boat trips up and down the river, only 10 kilometers (6 miles) from town is the Estância das Águas Sulfurosas. These Jacuzzi-like sulfur hot springs are said to cure whatever ails you. You can get to them easily by taxi. For cooler waters, head to the idyllic Cachoeira do Paraíso, a waterfall that's also close by.

However, Monte Alegre's most fascinating attraction is the wealth of prehistoric rock and cave paintings hidden in the surrounding hills. Rendered in disarmingly bright oranges and scarlet pigments, the forms range from abstract figures to human and animal representations that are very expressive. Even more striking are the hand-prints tattooed onto the stone. They are so palpably human that seeing them will send a couple of shivers down your spine. The

paintings were initially discovered in the 1850s, by Alfred Russel Wallace, a British naturalist and archrival of Charles Darwin, and then were completely forgotten until the 1980s when American archaeologist Anna Roosevelt (great-granddaughter of Teddy Roosevelt) rediscovered the area. Subsequent excavations unearthed prehistoric tools, which like the paintings, were shown to date back over 12,000 years—making Monte Alegre the oldest site of prehistoric civilization in the Americas. To see the paintings, you'll need a guide and four-wheel-drive transportation. The town expert of the paintings, **Nelsi Sadeck** (Rua do Jaquara 320, tel. 93/3533-1430), offers guided visits to the caverns that usually take a whole day and cost around R$200. He can also organize boat trips up and down the river. Also check with ecotour operators in Santarém and Alter do Chão, which offer excursions to Monte Alegre.

ACCOMMODATIONS AND FOOD

Although Monte Alegre receives few tourists, there are a few basic, but quite adequate *pousadas*. Those in the Cidade Alta have the benefit of incredible views. Try the **Pousada Panorama II** (Praça Engenheiro Fernando Guilhon 500, tel. 93/3533-1716, R$75 d), a comfortable if not especially attractive hotel at the top of the hill, which is one of the better hotels in town. The same owners operate the simpler **Panorama I** (Travessa Oriental 100, tel. 93/3533-1716, R$75 d). Accommodations are in four simple, tidy bungalows. The restaurant, with a great view, is considered one of the best for home-cooked fish dishes.

GETTING THERE

It's easy to get to Monte Alegre by boat (a 5–6-hour journey) from Santarém. There are daily departures from the Praça Tiradentes docks. Moreover, many larger boats going from Belém to Santarém also stop here.

Amazonas

Sharing borders with Peru and Colombia, Amazonas is the major state of the western Amazon: It is also the largest, and most geographically remote, of all Brazil's states. It is here that you'll find the largest patches of intact rainforests and the greatest number of Brazilian Indians, some of whom still manage to maintain traditional lifestyles. It is also where the mighty Amazon river is born, 6 kilometers (4 miles) from Manaus, at the spectacular confluence of the Rio Solimões and the Rio Negro, known as the Meeting of the Waters. In Amazonas, the river and its tributaries dominate daily life. Almost all transportation is by boat—riverboats, speedboats, or dug-out canoes—that are constantly shuttling people and goods up and down the rivers and their tributaries. And the very rhythms of the river—its seasonal floods and rare, but occasional droughts—regulate the lives of the magnificent array of flora and fauna as well as human inhabitants.

The sole "center of civilization" amidst the seemingly endless green wilderness is Amazonas's capital city of Manaus, which is home to two million people, or half the population of the entire state. Although it has a unique flavor and boasts some interesting sights, this ramshackle frontier town on the fringe of the jungle functions first and foremost as a gateway to exploring the natural treasures of the Western Amazon.

MANAUS

Bustling, booming, and somewhat chaotic, the capital of Amazonas is a commercial hub and river port that is a feast for the senses. Aside from serving as the point of departure for all forays up and down the Amazon and into the rainforest, Manaus has a rough-edged, colorful vibrancy and culture all its own. While much of the city is modern, numerous architectural landmarks, including its magnificent opera house, attest to its importance as the Amazon's 19th-century rubber capital.

Unlike Belém, Manaus has a much more recent history. The city's origins can be traced back to an early 17th-century mission settlement along the banks of the Rio Negro. Over time it blossomed into a small trading center. However, it wasn't until 1856 that the town of Manaus—named after the Manaós Indians—officially come into being. Shortly after, the Amazonian rubber boom hit and Manaus's fortunes soared. Speculators from all over the world descended upon the Amazon, hoping to strike it rich. Many did, due to the fact that as the world demand for Brazilian rubber rose, so did prices. Meanwhile, exports were booming. The shrewd governor of Amazonas, Eduardo Gonçalvez Ribeiro, slapped a 25 percent export tax on rubber and then proceeded to spend the vast sums collected on transforming the backwater town into a glittering city. The grandeur of the sweeping boulevards, monumental squares, and palatial public buildings was matched by the rubber barons' splendid mansions. Manaus was one of the first cities in the world to have electric street lights and boasted the first electric trolley system in South America. Ribeiro also hired architects, artists, and master builders from all over Europe to build a sumptuous new opera house with imported materials such as marble, crystal, and wrought iron. When some rubber barons voiced discontent that the main cupola was being covered with glazed tiles instead of gold, the extravagant governor assured them that in time, as rubber profits increased, he would tear the theater down and build an even grander one.

Unfortunately, by 1915, the bottom had fallen out of the Brazilian rubber industry. A devastated Ribeiro committed suicide, rubber barons put their mansions up for sale, and Manaus fell into a stagnant torpor from which it wouldn't emerge until the 1960s. In 1966, in order to stimulate the region's almost nonexistent economy, the military government transformed Manaus into a *zona franca*, or free trade zone. Electronics assembly plants mushroomed

CONSERVATION VS. COLONIALISM

If you're surprised to discover that Brazil is currently the world's fourth biggest producer of greenhouse gases, you may be even more astonished to know that the main culprit is the world's most potent green symbol: the Amazon forest. Of course, it isn't the forest's existence, but its rapid and ongoing devastation (to date more than a fifth of the forest has been lost and an area equivalent to six soccer fields is destroyed on a daily basis) that is responsible for this destruction. Indeed, an estimated 70 percent of greenhouse gases emitted by Brazil are due to deforestation endorsed by powerful business and political groups who want to integrate the vast region into the booming Brazilian economy by implanting highways, ports, dams, mining, logging, and agricultural projects.

For this reason, international – and particularly American – attempts to develop conservation projects within the Amazon have been met with suspicion. In truth, a surprisingly large portion of the Brazilian population views the actions of environmental groups and NGOs (non-governmental organizations) as a veiled form of colonialism. A 2005 nationwide survey carried out by Ibope, the nation's leading polling organization, discovered that 75 percent of Brazilians thought the nation's natural riches could provoke a foreign invasion. Close to 60 percent admitted to distrusting environmental organizations, which are perceived as smokescreens for foreign economic and financial interests that covet the Amazon's valuable natural resources. Among the many documents that support such conspiracy theories is a widely reproduced map, supposedly published in American public school geography books, which labels the forest as an "international reserve" and refers to Brazilians as "monkeys" unable to manage it. With the U.S. invasion of Iraq, Brazilians became even more wary of American military designs on their forest, pointing out that, in his 2000 presidential campaign, George W. Bush had referred to a plan for taking control of the Amazon.

throughout the city and the population multiplied exponentially with the influx of workers seeking jobs in the booming electronics industries. It used to be that all TVs, radios, sound systems, telephones, blenders, and other electronics equipment bought in Brazil were "Made in Manaus." Although the opening of Brazil's markets to imports beginning in the 1990s ended Manaus's retail monopoly, the electronics industry is still going strong and it's not uncommon to see Brazilians at Manaus's airport laden down with computers, DVD players, and digital cameras.

Sights

Most of Manaus's sights are located around the port and the oldest part of Centro that spreads up from the Rio Negro to the area surrounding the Teatro Amazonas. It is easy to get around Manaus's somewhat grungy center by day. However, at night, the neighborhood around Praça da Matriz is pretty dodgy, and the riverfront and dock area is downright dangerous. A maximum of two full days is really all you need to see most of Manaus's major attractions before heading out into to the depths of the jungle.

PORTO FLUTUANTE (FLOATING PORT)

If you arrive in Manaus by boat, you'll disembark at the famous Porto Flutuante (Floating Port), a concrete pier that was designed to rise and fall along with the Rio Negro (which, depending on the season, can vary as much as 14 meters/46 feet). Built in 1902 by a British company, Manaos Harbour Limited, this is where all large ships dock, and the bustle of passengers boarding and disembarking is quite a sight. For this reason, even if you don't arrive via water, Manaus's rambunctious, busy port is a fitting place to take your bearings and begin a tour of the city. Although the very well-organized but rather sterile modern Estação Hidroviária is quite new, it is no coincidence that the customs house across the street, known as the **Alfândega** (Rua Marquês de Santa Cruz), is evocative of Victorian London. Inaugurated in

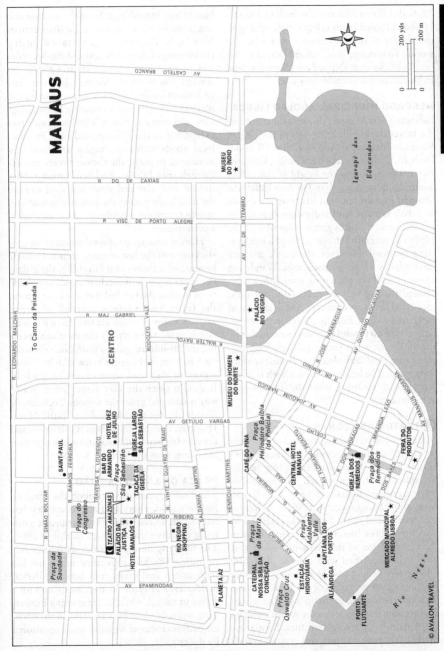

MANAUS

To Canto da Peixada →

CENTRO

AV CASTELO BRANCO

R DQ DE CAXIAS

R VISC DE PORTO ALEGRE

AV 7 DE SETEMBRO

R MAJ GABRIEL

R LEONARDO MALCHER

R SIMÃO BOLIVAR

R RAMOS FERREIRA

TRAVESSA E. LOURENÇO

R RODOLFO VALE

R WALTER RAYOL

★ MUSEU DO INDIO

★ PALACIO RIO NEGRO

★ MUSEU DO HOMEN DO NORTE

Igarapé dos Educandos

AV GETULIO VARGAS

• SAINT-PAUL

BAR DO ARMANDO ▲

HOTEL DEZ DE JULHO ▲

IGREJA LARGO SÃO SEBASTIÃO

Praça São Sebastião

★ TACACA DA GISELA

▢ TEATRO AMAZONAS ★

PALÁCIO DA JUSTIÇA ★

HOTEL MANAUS •

RIO NEGRO SHOPPING ■

Praça do Congresso

Praça da Saudade

AV EDUARDO RIBEIRO

R VINTE E QUATRO DE MAIO

R SALDANHA

HENRIQUE MARTINS

MARTINS

▼ PLANETA A2

AV EPAMINODAS

CAFÉ DO PINA ■

Praça Heliodoro Balbia (da Policia) •

CENTRAL HOTEL MANAUS •

R MOREIRA

R M DIAS

R JOAQUIM NABUCO

AV EDUARDO RIBEIRO

AV JOAQUIM NABUCO

R COELHO

R DR AIMINIO

R JOSE PARANAGUA

AV QUINTINO BUCAIUVA

AV MARTINS MOREMA

AV EFIGENIO SALES

AV FLORIANO PEIXOTO

IGREJA DOS REMEDIOS ■

Praça dos Remédios

R DOS ANDRADAS

R DOS BARES

R MIRANDA LEÃO

FEIRA DO PRODUTOR ★

MERCADO MUNICIPAL ALFREDO LISBOA ★

CATEDRAL NOSSA SRA DA CONCEIÇÃO ♦

Praça da Matriz

AV RIBEIRO

Praça Adalberto Valle

CAPITANIA DOS PORTOS ■

ESTAÇÃO HIDROVIARIA ★

ALFANDEGA ★

Praça Oswaldo Cruz

PORTO FLUTUANTE ■

Rio Negro

© AVALON TRAVEL

200 yds
200 m
0   0

1906, this fine edifice was also built by Manaos Harbor Limited in an eclectic style that mingles medieval and Renaissance elements. The world's first example of a prefabricated building, its bricks were shipped over from England in blocks, and reassembled on site.

MERCADO MUNICIPAL ADOLFO LISBOA

Following Rua Marquês de Santa Cruz towards the newer docks will bring you to the elegant Mercado Municipal Adolfo Lisboa (Rua dos Barés 46, Centro, 8 A.M.–6 P.M. daily). Designed in the 1880s, during the height of the rubber boom, by none other than Gustave Eiffel, the wrought iron art nouveau structure is a replica of Paris's famous (and sadly demolished) Les Halles market. For hygienic purposes, in the 1990s the market's interior received a modernizing overhaul. However, the exotic produce on display is a feast for the senses. Wandering around you'll see glistening river fish, multicolored fruit of varying shapes and textures, medicinal herbs and potions, and *artesenato* of indigenous origin. Equally interesting is the adjacent **Feira do Produtor,** a wholesale market by the waterfront where you can observe haggling, purchasing, and the unloading of exotic produce from boats. The best time to visit both markets is in the early morning, when the atmosphere is at its most vibrant.

◀ TEATRO AMAZONAS

Without a doubt, nothing conjures up the sheer lavishness of the Amazonian rubber boom's heyday like the Teatro Amazonas (Av. Sete de Setembro 1540, Centro, tel. 93/3232-4450, www.teatroamazonas.com.br, 9 A.M.–5 P.M. Mon.–Fri.). Inaugurated in 1896, this sumptuous neoclassical opera house was financed by the city's rubber barons. They went all out in the construction of this none-too-subtle rose pink palace crowned with a dome of 36,000 vivid green, yellow, and blue mosaic tiles that pay homage to the colors of the Brazilian flag. To adorn the interior, the finest ingredients from Europe were shipped across the Atlantic and up the Amazon: Alsatian glazed tiles, Portuguese marble, Venetian mirrors and crystal, French bronze and furnishings, Scottish cast iron columns and banisters, and electrical fixtures from New York. The main stage curtain depicting the meeting of the Rio Negro and Rio Solimões was painted by Brazilian artist Crispim do Amaral (but in Paris!). Meanwhile, Italian artist Domenico de Angelis is responsible for the opulent ceiling frescoes featuring Indians, jaguars, and even a capybara. There were only two exceptions to the all-imported rule. Precious local woods such as mahogany and jacaranda were used to make the theater's seats and exquisitely inlaid floors. And homegrown rubber (mixed with clay and sand) was used to pave the road leading up to the entrance so that late-arriving carriages wouldn't create noise during a performance.

Having undergone several restorations over the course of the last century, required mostly because of termites and humidity, these days the opera house is in excellent condition. Aside from hosting the Festival Amazonas de Ópera, the Teatro has an intense schedule of performances, many of which are free. Even if you do decide to see a concert, it's also worthwhile taking the 30-minute guided tour. Note the sidewalk in front of the opera house with its "wave" mosaic of black and white stones. Ring a bell? It should since the very same "wave" walkway is stamped upon the famous Copacabana boardwalk designed by Roberto Burle Marx. However, the original pattern is this one—and the curving bands of black and white represent the Meeting of the Waters.

PRAÇA DE SÃO SEBASTIÃO

The Teatro Amazonas sits upon the Praça de São Sebastião, a very pleasant square that has once again become a favorite Manauense gathering spot after undergoing a facelift in 2004. The formerly decrepit historic buildings surrounding the *praça* received much-needed renovations and many now house galleries, boutiques, and cafés. By day, locals stop for a coffee or *tacacá,* while in the evening hipsters hang out at outdoor bars and take in the open-air performances of regional music sponsored by the city.

On the *praça*, you'll also find the **Igreja Largo São Sebastião** (5–9 A.M. and 3–7 P.M. daily). From the outside, this late 19th-century church sports a very untropically solemn gray facade. However, the interior is adorned with gleaming Italian marble, pretty stained glass windows, and luminous ceiling frescoes imported from Italy. Close to the church, the **Palácio de Justiça** (Av. Eduardo Ribeiro, Centro, tel. 92/3248-1844, 9 A.M.–5 P.M. Tues.–Sat., 4–9 P.M. Sun.) is very palatial indeed. Built in 1900, its stately facade mingles elements of French Second Empire style with English neoclassicism. The building housed the Amazonas state court until 2006, when it was converted into a cultural center. All the original furnishings are intact, and you can literally sit in the place of a judge, juror, or culprit during a guided tour. You can also take in an art exhibit or a catch a film.

AVENIDA SETE DE SETEMBRO
Following Avenida Eduardo Ribeiro south towards the waterfront, you'll soon reach the Centro's main artery, Avenida Sete de Setembro. To the left, dominating the leafy Praça da Matriz is the **Catedral de Nossa Senhora da Conceição** (tel. 92/3234-7821, 9 A.M.–5 P.M. Mon.–Sat.). Also known as the Igreja Matriz, this spare but handsome neoclassical cathedral was built in 1878 after the original 17th-century wooden church (Manaus's first) burnt down.

Walking in the other direction (east) along Avenida Sete, you'll pass the pretty triangular Praça da Polícia (also known as Praça Heliodora Balbi) before arriving at the **Museu do Homem do Norte** (Rua Quintino Bocaiuva 626, Centro, tel. 92/3633-1074, 9 A.M.–5 P.M. Mon.–Fri., free). This ethnographic museum offers insight into the lives of the men (and women) of Brazil's North with displays devoted to prehistoric peoples, Indians, and *caboclos*. Particularly interesting is the collection of artifacts related to traditional activities (extraction of rubber, Brazil nuts, *guaraná*), popular *festas,* and life on the Mighty Amazon. The museum possesses a small boutique selling regional crafts and a tourist information office.

Further on along Avenida Sete, the ornate **Palácio Rio Negro** (Av. Sete de Setembro 1546, Centro, 9 A.M.–6 P.M. Mon.–Fri., free) is a magnificent example of nouveau riche rubber baron ostentation. This saffron-colored mini-palace was built in 1903 by a wealthy German rubber merchant named Waldemar Scholtz, who was notorious for his extravagant garden parties and his pet lion. With the rubber boom went bust, Scholtz had to sell off his prize palace. It subsequently fell into the hands of the state and became the governor's palace. Today, the building functions as a cultural center. Amidst the lavish period fixtures and furnishings, there are usually some interesting temporary art exhibits. After taking a guided tour of the palace, you can also check out the trio of small on-site museums. Worth wandering through are the Museu de Numismática, featuring a collection of coins and bills from around the world, and the Pinacoteca do Estado, which exhibits an intriguing collection of paintings by 19th and 20th-century Manauense artists. Less interesting is the Museu da Imagem e Som, although it sometimes screens engaging films and documentaries. Before leaving the complex, take a peek in the backyard to see life-sized replicas of a typical Indian village, a *caboclo* house, and a demonstration of rubber processing.

A few blocks further east, the **Museu do Índio** (Rua Duque de Caxias 356, Praça 14, tel. 92/3635-1922, 8:30–11:30 A.M. and 2–4:30 P.M. Mon.–Fri., 8:30–11:30 A.M. Sat., R$5) provides an excellent overview of the history, culture, and day-to-day life of the upper Amazon's indigenous peoples. The more than 3,000 objects and artifacts—varying from bows, arrows, and blow darts to pottery, masks, and drums used for long-distance communication—are artfully displayed and accompanied by descriptions in English as well as Portuguese. The museum is run by the Irmãs Salesianas, an order of nuns who have various missions along the Amazon. Adjacent to the museum is **Koonoly** (Rua Bernardo Ramos 60, tel. 92/8167-1972, 11:30 A.M.–3 P.M. Mon.–Fri.), a combination restaurant and crafts shop that is operated by a cooperative of Indian villages. Edible offerings include fish dishes such as *quinhapira,* a stew of *tucunaré* cooked in *tucupi* and spiked with fiery peppers, and *popeca,* fish rolled up in banana leaves.

If you have some extra time, you might want to venture out to the **Museu de Ciências Naturais da Amazônia** (tel. 92/3644-2799, 9 A.M.–noon and 2–5 P.M. Mon.–Sat., R$12). Tucked away in a predominantly Japanese-Brazilian suburb, this museum will help you bone up on your Amazonian beasts. On display, you'll find preserved reptiles and gigantic spiders (creepy) as well as beetles and butterflies (gorgeous). Among the live species gliding around in a smallish aquarium is the pirarucu, the Amazon's largest (and one of its most delicious) fish. Getting here is a bit tricky. You'll need to take the 519 bus from Praça da Matriz and then walk for 15 minutes.

MUSEU DO SERINGAL VILA PARAÍSO

In 2001, the Portuguese-Brazilian production team of a film entitled *A Selva (The Jungle)* built an entire rubber plantation in the midst of the jungle, an hour from Manaus. When filming was completed, the replica of a late-19th-century *seringal* (rubber plantation) was converted into the Museu do Seringal Vila Paraíso (Igarapé São João, tel. 92/3658-6159, 8 A.M.–4 P.M. Wed.–Sun., R$5). A visit to this open-air museum will take you on an evocative journey into the late-19th-century world of rubber tapping, where you can observe actual rubber trees along with displays depicting the harrowing living and working conditions of the *seringueiros* (tappers). Canoe taxis leave from the Marina David in Ponta Negra and sail up the Rio Negro to the museum. The trip usually costs around R$12 and takes 25 minutes.

ENCONTRO DE ÁGUAS (MEETING OF THE WATERS)

Visiting the Encontro de Águas, or Meeting of the Waters—the point at which the muddy Rio Solimões hooks up with the bluish-black Rio Negro to form the Rio Amazonas—is like climbing to the top of the Empire State Building in New York. It's something you have

to do, which is why this natural phenomenon is usually swarming with bobbing boats stuffed with camera-brandishing tourists. However, not even the theme park flavor (and traffic jams) can put a damper on the strange spectacle of the two rivers, which flow side by side for several kilometers before finally merging at a point some 10 kilometers (6 miles) from Manaus. On one side, you have the Rio Negro, whose darkness is a result of decomposing jungle vegetation that creates high acid levels. On the other is the Rio Solimões, whose light brown color betrays the presence of run-off soil from the Andes. And the differences don't end there. While the Rio Negro meanders along sluggishly at 3 kilometers (2 miles) per hour, the Solimões rushes by at 7 kilometers (4.5 miles) per hour. If you trail your finger in the water, you'll also notice that the Rio Negro is considerably warmer than the Solimões.

You can check out the Meeting of the Waters on your own, by taking the 713 bus from the Praça da Matriz to the CEASA port, where there are always plenty of boats for hire as well as a municipal ferry that crosses the river. Most people, however, tend to visit the Meeting of the Waters as part of a guided trip (it is a classic attraction featured on many excursions). Usually offered as day trips, boats leave at 9 A.M. and return at 4 P.M. The standard R$110 fee includes lunch on a floating restaurant. Tours inevitably include a stop at the **Reserva Ecológico do Lago de Janauari,** a ecological reserve located on a tributary of the Rio Negro whose *igarapés* (narrow creeks) and *igapós* (temporarily flooded forests) you can explore by canoe (or on foot, during the dry season). The park's most fascinating feature is the gigantic *Victoria amazonica,* lily pads whose platter-shaped leaves, the size of coffee tables, dot the many lagoons. The gorgeous lilies themselves have a three-day life span: When they blossom, they are milky white (day 1), they then turn a blushing pink (day 2), and deepen to scarlet before withering up and dying (day 3). Although these excursions have become classic to the point of hokey, they are enjoyable in a Disneyland kind of way, and will certainly encourage you to wander off the beaten path and further into the jungle.

Recreation

Fittingly for a city that is essentially plunged into the middle of the jungle, there are numerous natural attractions in and around Manaus ranging from patches of rainforest to river beaches.

PARKS

For a preview of the rainforest, it's worth exploring Manaus's tropical parks. The **Bosque da Ciência** (Rua Otávio Cabral, Petrópolis, tel. 92/3643-3293, 9 A.M.–noon and 2–5 P.M. Tues.–Sun., R$2) is a surviving chunk of jungle maintained by the Instituto Nacional da Pesquisa da Amazônia (INPA), a research center where you can inspect Amazonian flora and fauna ranging from rare orchids and caimans to giant otters and the extremely rare and odd-looking *peixe-bois* (manatees). Aside from walking paths, there is a suspended tree trekking trail that allows you to inspect the forest canopy up close. To get here, take the 519 bus from Praça da Matriz, which stops right in front of the entrance.

Operated by CIGS, a jungle survival unit of the Brazilian army, the **Parque Zoológico do CIGS** (Estrada da Ponta Negra, São Jorge, tel. 92/3625-1966, www.cigs.com.br, 9 A.M.–4:30 P.M. Tues.–Fri., 9 A.M.–6 P.M. Sat.–Sun., R$3) houses a diverse array of Amazonian animals rescued by military men during their training exercises in the forest. Beyond the more common caimans, monkeys, and macaws, you'll also run into black and spotted jaguars and a snake pit full of anacondas. It's hard not to feel torn by the animals' living conditions, which (mirroring Brazilian realities) range from spacious and well-equipped outdoor environments to prison-like cages. To get here, take the 120 bus from Praça da Matriz.

Parque do Mindú (Av. Perimetral, tel. 92/3236-7702, 8 A.M.–5 P.M. Tues.–Sun.) is Manaus's largest patch of greenery. It contains four native ecosystems laced with walking trails and suspended tree-trekking walkways.

PIRANHAS

When it comes to the famous flesh-eating piranhas, forget about all those Hollywood horror flicks in which bad guys thrown into vats of saber-toothed piranhas are instantly devoured. In the Amazon, piranhas are everywhere – on restaurant menus (piranha soup is delicious) and, of course, in the water. Which doesn't mean you're a goner if you fall overboard or decide to go for a dip in the river. In truth, piranhas prefer still water to currents and they never attack en masse. In fact, there are no stories on record of anyone ever being seriously injured, let alone being nibbled or gobbled to death. Nonetheless, they can inflict painful bites and are indeed attracted to blood. If in doubt about what's lurking beneath the surface of a river, ask locals, who usually know the preferred hangouts of these fanged fish.

The park's most famous inhabitant is the almost extinct *sauím-de-manaus,* a micro monkey known for its two-toned pelt (white and caramel), large pointy ears, and rapid shimmying up and down trees that has earned it the nickname *macaquinho elevador* (elevator monkey). To get here, take the 423 or 433 bus from Praça da Matriz.

BEACHES

Optimistically nicknamed "the Amazon's Copacabana," **Praia da Ponta Negra** is a far cry from Rio's famous beach. Although the presence of the Hotel Tropical and a boardwalk stuffed with restaurants, bars, sports facilities, and an amphitheater has turned the area into a major tourist and recreational center, raw and ugly high-rises have given it an unseemly urban edge. It's pleasant enough to walk around Ponta Negra, or to have a drink overlooking the river while watching the sunset. Due to river flooding, the beach only appears during the dry season (August to January). Nonetheless, if you want to beat the tropical heat, there's nothing like refreshing swim in the Rio Negro. Ponta

Negra is located 18 kilometers (11 miles) from the center of Manaus. To get here take the 120 bus from Praça da Matriz.

For more tranquil and idyllic surroundings, head to the wilder beaches a little further out of town. **Praia da Lua** and the even more lovely **Praia do Tupé** (20–25 kilometers/12–16 miles away from Manaus) offer white sands backed by green foliage. Access to both beaches is by boat from the Estação Hidroviária. The trip down the Rio Negro takes about an hour. Like Ponta Negra, these beaches disappear during the rainy season.

AMAZON ECOPARK

Only a 30-minute boat trip up the Rio Negro, Amazon Ecopark is a jungle-lodge set amidst a private nature reserve. Even if you don't stay at the hotel, you're free to come and explore the surroundings, which include the Amazon Monkeys Jungle, a sanctuary devoted to the care (and subsequent release into the forest) of illegally captured monkeys. Many ecotour companies offer half-day and full-day trips here that include transportation, hiking, and canoe trips through the jungle, and visits to the monkey sanctuary.

Entertainment and Events
NIGHTLIFE

Manaus isn't famous for its nightlife, but its size guarantees that you certainly won't be bored. In Centro, you'll find lots of lively bars around the Mercado Municipal and Avenida Joaquim Nabuco as well as in the vicinity of the Teatro Amazonas. Otherwise, the most happening area is the beach neighborhood of Ponta Negra, which buzzes throughout the day and far into the night.

The most lively of Ponta Negra's waterfront bars is **Laranjinha** (Calçadão da Ponta Negra, Ponta Negra, tel. 92/3658-6666, 5 P.M.–close Mon.–Sat., 3 P.M.–close Sun.). The breezes coming off the river as well as frequent performances by sometimes tacky folkloric groups attract plenty of tourists as well as locals. Among the culinary treats are *caldeiradas,* thick chowders made from local river fish. Close by,

Avenida do Turismo is full of bars and dance halls playing everything from local boleros and *forró* to classic rock.

One of the best places to hear great live music is **Ton Biz** (Av. do Turismo 4004, tel. 92/3239-0202, 5 P.M.–close Mon.–Fri., noon onwards Sat.–Sun., cover R$7), where a small stage hosts *forró* (Thurs.) and MPB and Brazilian rock (Fri.–Sat.). Os Tucumanus, a popular homegrown band, frequently appears to play tunes with a definite indigenous edge. Complementing the music is the eco-Amazonian bar itself: a bungalow with a thatched roof, bamboo walls, and furniture built from beautiful local woods such as *ipê* and *maçaranduba.* The garlic grilled pirarucu with shrimp and vegetables easily feeds four.

In the center of town, **Planeta A2** (Rua Saldanha Marinho 780, Centro, tel. 92/3234-7373, 11 P.M.–6 A.M. Thurs.–Sat., R$10) is a funky gay and lesbian club that's equally popular with heteros. Occupying a three-story house, there is a bar on each floor, as well as lounges, dance floors, and a jungly backyard. Resident DJs heat up the night with doses of electronica, pop and disco. Go-go boys and drag queens add the requisite shot of camp. Near the Teatro de Amazonas, **Bar do Armando** (Rua 10 de Julho 593, Centro, tel. 92/3232-1195, 2 P.M.–3 A.M. Mon.–Sat.) started out as a 1950s corner grocery store. When big supermarket chains arrived in Manaus in the '70s, owner Armando converted his store into a friendly neighborhood bar that hasn't lost any of its retro mom-and-pop flavor. Clients are welcome to choose background music from Armando's record collection before relaxing at red plastic tables with a cool beer and a thick *pernil* (pork) sandwich. Another relaxing place for a beer is at the *tradicionalíssimo* **Café do Pina** (Praça Heliodoro Balbi 3, Centro, tel. 92/9185-6333, 6:30 A.M.–11 P.M. Mon.–Sat.). Shaded by hundred-year-old trees, the sidewalk tables scattered around the square popularly known as the Praça da Polícia provide a favorite gathering place for Manauenses who stop off for coffee or an ice cold beer throughout the day and into the night. This is a terrific spot for people-watching.

PERFORMING ARTS

Taking in a concert or dance performance at the landmark **Teatro Amazonas** (Praça São Sebastião, Centro, tel. 92/3622-1880, www.teatroamazonas.com.br) is an unforgettable experience. It's worth the price of a ticket merely to soak up the sumptuous ambiance. However, Manaus's opera house draws an impressive roster of talents from all over Brazil and the world. Monday night performances are free. Also worth checking out is the **Centro Cultural Usina Chaminé** (Av. Lourenço da Silva Braga, Centro, tel. 92/3633-3026), an artfully renovated sewage plant with a beautiful interior that hosts art exhibits as well as music and dance performances.

FESTIVALS AND EVENTS

Every year, from late April through May, the **Festival Amazonas de Ópera,** attracts a lineup of big-name national and international soloists who perform a mixture of classical operas and Brazilian compositions in the magnificent Teatro Amazonas. The schedule of performances and tickets are available at the *teatro* several weeks in advance (see *Sights*).

Shopping

Everyone who comes to Manaus inevitably wants to purchase traditional arts and handicrafts made by Amazonas's indigenous groups. There is no shortage of places to find interesting items such as elaborately woven baskets, unusual seed jewelry, and ceramic pottery. Aside from the **Mercado Adolpho Lisboa** (see *Sights*), you can also check out the wares for sale at the **Feira de Artesanato** (Praça Tenreiro Aranha, 8 A.M.–6 P.M. Mon.–Sat.). On the *praça,* you'll also find **Artíndia** (Praça Tenreiro Aranha, Centro, tel. 92/3232-4890, 7:30 A.M.–noon and 2–5:30 P.M. Mon.–Fri.), which is operated by FUNAI, the Brazilian ministry of Indian affairs. The **Museu do Índio** (see *Sights*) has a fine selection of *artesanato* as does adjacent **Koonoly** (Rua Bernardo Ramos 60, Centro, tel. 92/8167-

1972, 8:30 A.M.–5:30 P.M. Mon.–Fri.). A quick cab ride away, the **Central de Artesanato Branco e Silva** (Rua Recife 1999, Parque Dez, tel. 92/3236-1241, 9 A.M.–6 P.M. Mon.–Fri., 9 A.M.–4 P.M. Sat.) reunites two dozen regional artisans who create some very fine and original works of art using all native, organic materials including palm fibers, tree bark, and brightly colored bird feathers.

The streets behind the Mercado Adolpho Lisboa, particularly Rua dos Barés, have stores where you can pick up a cheap and well-made hammock. For more fashionable fare, check out the dozens of boutiques at **Shopping Amazonas** (Av. Djalma Batista 482, Parque 10, tel. 92/3303-9000, www.amazonasshopping.com.br, 10 A.M.–10 P.M. Mon.–Sat., 3–9 P.M. Sun.). Easily reached by bus from Praça da Matriz, Manaus's biggest *shopping* also has the usual cinemas, fast food eateries, ATMs, and cyber cafés.

Accommodations

Be prepared for the fact that Manaus doesn't have a lot of great accommodation options. Budget hotels in Centro are pretty basic, and will cost more than what they would in other Brazilian cities. Meanwhile, if you choose a so-called three-star downtown, you'll be sorely disappointed by inferior quality, shabby furnishings, and rates that will leave you feeling ripped off.

Located not too far from the Teatro Amazonas, **Hotel Dez de Julho** (Rua Dez de Julho 679, Centro, tel. 92/3232-6280, www.hoteldezdejulho.com, R$65–80) is the safest, cleanest, and cheapest hotel you'll find in Manaus. The fair-sized air-conditioned rooms are comfortable enough, though quite spartan and a little noisy. The staff is friendly and breakfasts are quite decent. Also good value is the **Central Hotel Manaus** (Rua Dr. Moreira 202, Centro, tel. 92/3622-2600, www.hotelcentralmanaus.com.br, R$130 d). The air-conditioned rooms won't win any style awards, but high ceilings, cool tile floors, and solid wood furnishings are pleasant. There is a decent on-site restaurant with

24-hour room service. Right across from the Teatro Amazonas, **Hotel Manaós** (Av. Eduardo Ribeiro 881, Centro, tel. 92/3633-5744, www.hotelmanaos.com.br, R$150–180 d) is a modern and efficiently run hotel. Air-conditioned rooms are standard and smallish, but quite comfortable and nicely finished. The best ones are those on the second and third floors that have terrific views of the Teatro Amazonas. Although the price is more than what it's worth, this hotel is one of Manaus's best values.

An alternative to Manaus's desultory upscale hotels is playing house at the **Saint-Paul** (Rua Ramos Ferreira 1115, Centro, tel. 92/2101-3800, www.manaushoteis.bur.br, R$220–270d), a centrally located *apart-hotel* complex that's a favorite with business execs on extended trips. The spacious and spotless one and two-bedroom suites have living areas and small "American kitchens." They are quite comfortable, even if the only thing alleviating the sterile atmosphere is large blown-up photos of Amazonian flora. Conveniences include a pool, sauna, fitness center, and restaurant.

Ever since it first opened in the mid-1970s, the legendary **Tropical Manaus Eco Resort Experience** (Av. Coronel Teixeira 1320, Ponta Negra, tel. 92/2123-5000, www.tropicalhotel.com.br, R$330–475 d) has been whetting appetites of travelers whose dreams of "roughing it" in the Amazon include living it up in high style. Set amidst a patch of jungle, spanning the banks of Rio Negro, this sprawling and very scenic resort is neither luxurious nor stylish, but it has managed to retain some grandeur. Rooms are very comfortable, if somewhat dated—those in the "colonial" wing, outfitted with hardwood floors and dark wood furnishings, have more personality. Bathrooms, however, are gleamingly modern. The amenities are endless, and include various bars, shops, restaurants, swimming pools, and a spa as well as tennis courts, a playground, an archery range, an orchid hothouse, and a (rather sad) zoo housing Amazonian animals. There is even a jungle survival course. While you're 20 kilometers (12 miles) from downtown Manaus,

you're only a quick walk from Ponta Negra's river beaches and nightlife. This is an ideal choice if you're traveling as a family.

JUNGLE LODGES (*HOTÉIS DE SELVA*)

One of the best ways to get to a sense of the rainforest is to actually stay in its midst. While primitive options exist for hard-core environmentalists, there are an increasing number of high-priced, high-style choices. Whether across the river from Manaus or hundreds of kilometers away, there are plenty of unforgettable eco-options to choose from. All of them organize guided forest and river tours in the rate. If you're pressed for time (or money), some offer a "day-use" option.

In truth, the concept of a jungle lodge within the vicinity of Manaus itself is somewhat of a fallacy. As the city has grown and the surrounding forest has been cleared for ranching and agriculture, original rainforest and all the wildlife it supports have become

Macaco-pregos (capuchin monkeys) are a common sight in the rainforest.

increasingly scant. If you crave a bona-fide jungle experience, you'll need to distance yourself considerably from the city. However, if you find yourself with little time and a hankering for a greener experience than you can get by staying in downtown Manaus and taking day trips, there are a couple of good choices. Listed are the jungle lodges within easy reach of Manaus itself.

First of all, although they receive a lot of hype, you'll definitely want to avoid the Ariaú Jungle Towers and the Jungle Othon Palace, both of which are overpriced, extremely touristy mega hotels with lots of glitz. They will satisfy visitors who come to the Amazon in search of gyms, spas, and posh jewelry boutiques, but otherwise they have little charm and no authenticity. Instead, try the **Tiwa Amazonas Ecoresort** (tel. 92/9995-7892, www.tiwa.com.br, R$550–800 d). Perhaps the most "urban" jungle lodge in the Amazon, it is only a 20-minute motorboat ride across the Rio Negro from the Tropical Manaus. Although the Tiwa tries hard—accommodations are in pseudo-rustic log cabins on stilts facing a small lagoon—the "jungle" surroundings are replanted forest and if you walk far enough, you'll hit asphalt. However, the lodgings themselves are very pleasant and there is a lovely pool and a beach. Packages include treetop trekking and spotting caimans along with excursions to the Meeting of the Waters.

Further afield, but still close to Manaus is the ◖ **Amazon Ecopark Jungle Lodge** (Igarapé do Tarumã-Açu, tel. 92/3622-2612, www.amazonecopark.com.br, R$830–1,400 for two-day package). A 45-minute boat ride from town, the lodge is nestled amidst a lush private reserve on the banks of the Rio Tarumá. Canoe outings take you along the river and into *igarapés* where you'll see lots of birds. You'll also visit a local Indian village for a more or less unfiltered glimpse of traditional indigenous life and culture. All tours are led by excellent English-speaking guides. For leisure, there are beautiful white-sand beaches where you can swim as well as freshwater pools for those who can't rid their subconscious of all those piranha movies. Kids,

in particular, will adore the monkey sanctuary, where they can interact with primates saved from the clutches of wildlife smugglers. Accommodations are quite comfortable with fine bedding, air-conditioning, nice lighting, and attractive decorative touches such as hand-woven carpets and indigenous art. The restaurant serves creative food that takes advantage of local fish and fruits.

Food

Manaus is a delight for fish lovers. Although the region's river boasts more than 2,000 species, four in particular are likely to make an appearance on your plate. The meat of the gigantic pirarucu is used to make everything from crunchy *bolinhos* and soups to stews such as *pirarucu de casaca,* in which it is dressed in a "coat" (*casaco*) of potatoes, olives, onions, tomatoes and boiled eggs. *Tambaqui* is delicious when roasted in its skin over hot charcoal. *Tucunaré* is a popular ingredient in *caldeiradas,* thick chowders that are seasoned with *tucupi* and *jambu* leaves. And of course, you've heard of piranha, which (when defanged) makes a delicious soup that is considered to be an aphrodisiac.

Also irresistible are the endless variety of Amazonian fruits. Botanists have uncovered 200 types (and are still counting). Indians believe the forest's fruits are divine gifts. You'll find it easy to concur when you savor fruits such as *maracujá-de-mato* (a type of wild passion fruit), *biribá, sapucaia, bajurá, piquiá,* as well as the more popular *cupuaçu, bacuri,* and *açaí,* all of which are used to make fresh juices, ice creams, and myriad desserts. Although not quite as big as the ones Carmen Miranda wore on her head, giant *pacova* bananas grow to lengths of 50 centimeters (20 inches). In the center of town, you'll find *barracas* where you can purchase fried *pacova* chips or *pacova* cubes that are drizzled in condensed milk. Also don't skip town without biting into a *sanduíche caboclinho,* a vegetarian offering made with a baguette and slices of a yellow Amazonian fruit known as *tucumã.* Since the fruit is pretty strong, you might want to dilute it by ordering

GUARANÁ

Although Coca-Cola has made inroads in Brazil, as both a refreshing soft drink and a pick-me-up, it has never usurped the place of Guaraná. Moreover, Coke has none of the health (nor reputed aphrodisiac) benefits that the Indians of central Amazonas first discovered centuries ago, when they began harvesting the tiny red *guaraná* berry, whose visible black seed resembles a tiny eye. Aside from its antioxidant and antibacterial properties, *guaraná* contains around four times as much caffeine as coffee beans. Since the 1920s, *guaraná* has been a key ingredient in the eponymous soft drink (in diluted form, so the kids won't get a buzz). While major brands of bottled Guaraná, such as Antarctica and Kuat, are rampant throughout Brazil, smaller labels such as Baré, Real, and Tuchauá can only be found in Manaus. However, Indians and purists prefer imbibing the real thing, which involves mixing dried *guaraná* powder (which is quite chalky and bitter) with sweetened *guaraná* syrup and any number of local fruits. In Manaus, **Guaraná Saterê** (Rua Marcília Diaz 237, Centro, tel. 92/3233-8113, 7 A.M.-7 P.M. Mon.-Fri., 7 A.M.-5 P.M. Sat.) is a traditional *casa* that specializes in *guaraná*. Aside from getting an instant jolt on the spot, you can also purchase the fruit in dried and powdered form.

a *x-caboclinho*, in which the *tucumã* is attenuated with melted *coalho* cheese ("x").

CAFÉS AND SNACKS

Right in front of the Teatro Amazonas, **Tacacá da Gisela** (Largo São Sebastião, Centro, tel. 92/8803-4901, 4–10 P.M. daily) has become a tourist attraction in its own right. The thick broth featuring *tucupi, jambu* leaves and shrimp prepared by *tacaqueira* Rosa Maria is considered the best in town. Chairs set up on the sidewalk make this a relaxing place to hang out, especially on Wednesday afternoons when local musicians get together to jam. **Casa da Pamonha** (Rua Barroso 375, Centro tel. 92/3233-1028, 7 A.M.–7 P.M. Mon.–Sat.) is a simple little place where locals stop by throughout the day for baked goods and coffee as well as the beloved *caboclinho* sandwiches. During lunch, there is a nicely priced vegetarian per kilo self-service buffet.

For a simple dinner, join locals who head to **Casa da Sopa** (Av. Constelação 22, Conjunto Morada do Sol, Aleixo, tel. 92/3648-8667, www.casadasopamanaus.com, 7 P.M.–midnight Tues.–Sun., R$10), where you can eat soup to your heart's content for a fixed price. The *casa* makes over 80 varieties of steaming broth, ranging from chicken noodle to Amazonian inventions such as pirarucu with banana and heart of palm. On any given night, there are 14 varieties to choose from. Modeled after an indigenous dwelling, the restaurant is outfitted with local woods and palm fibers, imbuing it with a mellow vibe.

Nothing staves off Manaus's heat better than an ice cream. With nine locations to choose from, **Glacial** (Av. Getúlio Vargas 188, Centro Comercial Amazônia, Centro, tel. 92/3233-7940, www.glacial.com.br, 10 A.M.–11:30 P.M. daily) serves up some of the best in town by mixing Italian gelato-making techniques with Amazonian ingredients such as Brazil nuts, *tucumã, taperabá,* and *pupunha*.

CONTEMPORARY

Paraense Sofia Bendelak studied biology and worked in fashion before deciding to become a chef. Fascinated with the Amazon's edible bounty, she moved to Manaus and opened **◖ Bistrô Ananã** (Travessa Padre Ghisland 132, Centro tel. 92/3234-0056, 7:30 P.M.– 12:30 A.M. Fri.–Sat., R$22–35), where she has taken regional cuisine to new contemporary heights. Constant experimentation yields inspired creations such as gazpacho made with green *açaí*, crunchy *tapiocas* filled with pâté of smoked pirarucu, and duck cannelloni in a *taperaba* sauce. The carefully presented dishes are complemented by a modern decor featuring lots of warm natural woods and soft lighting, and soothing strands of bossa nova in the background.

REGIONAL

The best place in town to savor typical Amazonian cuisine is **[C Choupana** (Rua Recife 790, Adrianópolis, tel. 92/3635-3878, www.restaurantechoupana.com.br, 11 A.M.–3 P.M. and 6:30–11:30 P.M. Tues.–Sat., 11 A.M.–4 P.M. Sun., R$25–35). The setting— a palm thatched bungalow supported by tree trunk pillars and chairs woven with organic fibers—will get you in the mood to savor specialties such as *pato no tucupi,* served with *jambu.* The real forte here is Amazonian river fish such as grilled *tambaqui* accompanied with sautéed vegetables and fried *pacova* bananas. For dessert, the *cupuaçu*-chocolate torte gets you very close to heaven. **Turiyá Amazônia** (Rua Riu Purus 260, Adrianópolis, tel. 92/3633-3033, 10 A.M.–1 A.M. Tues.–Sat., 4–11 P.M. Sun.–Mon., R$8–15) is a laid-back corner restaurant/*lanchonete* that serves delicious snacks and meals that are often surprisingly exotic (even by Amazonian standards). You'll find basics such as healthy *açaí* (topped with banana, condensed milk, and/or granola) as well as *caboclinho* sandwiches featuring *tucumã* mixed with fillings such as banana or *coalho* cheese. The pizza topped with *jambu* is a big happy-hour hit as are the *tapiocas,* filled with combinations such as dried pirarucu with banana or chocolate and *cupuaçu* jelly. If you're feeling really adventurous, dig into the *pirarucu encantando,* in which the shredded fish is topped with layers of fried banana, melted *coalho* cheese, and *tucumã* puree, or the truly unusual *picadinho de tartaruga,* featuring sautéed turtle meat.

Canto da Peixada (Rua Emílio Moreira 1677, Praça 14, tel. 92/3234-3021, 11:30 A.M.–3:30 P.M. and 6:30–11:30 P.M. Mon.–Sat., R$30–40) is Manaus's oldest and most venerated *peixaria,* specializing in expertly prepared Amazonian fish. Whet your appetite with the crisp, turnover-like *pastéis de pirarucu* before digging into a *caldeirada* (stew) featuring *tucunaré* or a perfectly grilled tambaqui. Cleanse your palate with *cupuaçu* or passion fruit mousse. Although the decor is nothing special, the service is very attentive.

INTERNATIONAL

For a change from Amazonian fare, nothing beats a good, old-fashioned pizza. **Tavola Redonda** (Av. André Araújo 1603, Aleixo, tel. 92/3611-4433, 5–11 P.M. Tues.–Sun., R$15–20) serves up delicious thin-crust versions with a variety of traditional toppings (i.e., no piranha) as well as some pasta dishes. The atmosphere is nicely mellow with wood furnishings and big glass windows overlooking the street. Most of the fish you'll taste at **Shin Suzuran** (Av. Djalma Batista 3694, Parque Dez, tel. 92/3236-5333, 11:30 A.M.–3 P.M. and 6:30–11 P.M. daily, R$40–50)—tuna, salmon, robalo—is flown in directly from São Paulo before being sliced and diced into melt-in-your-mouth sushi and sashimi by owner/sushiman Hiroyo Takano. Although Takano emphasizes traditional Japanese cooking, he is occasionally inspired enough by local fare to create dishes such as sushi with seaweed, ginger, and grilled *tucunaré.*

Information

The main state tourist office, **Amazonastur** (Rua Saldanha Marinho 321, Centro, tel. 92/2123-3800, www.amazonastur.am.gov.br, 9 A.M.–6 P.M. Mon.–Fri.), is located near the Teatro Amazonas. It has several tourist kiosks known as **Central de Atendimento ao Turista,** with branches in Centro (Av. Eduardo Ribeiro 666, Centro, tel. 92/3622-0767, 9 A.M.–6 P.M. Mon.–Fri., 9 A.M.–2 P.M. Sat.) as well as at the airport (tel. 92/3652-1120, 7 A.M.–11 P.M. daily) and the *hidroviária* (tel. 92/3233-8698, 8 A.M.–5 P.M. Mon.–Fri.). Aside from city maps, the helpful staff can provide you with information regarding tour operators (i.e., which ones are legit). For extensive information and listings, in Portuguese only, check www.manausonline.com.

Services

For exchanging money or withdrawing cash from an ATM, there's a **Banco do Brasil** (Rua Guilherme Moreira 315, Centro) downtown.

You'll also find banks on Avenida Eduardo Ribeiro, including a Bradesco on the corner of Rua Saldanha Marinho. The **main post office** (Rua Marechal Deodoro, 117) is just off Praça da Matriz.

For Internet access, try **Powernet Cyber Café** (Rua 24 de Maio 94, Centro, tel. 92/3233-3927, 8 A.M.–8 P.M. Mon.–Sat.) and **Discover Internet** (Rua Marcílio Diaz 320, Loja 7, Centro, tel. 92/3233-0211, 8:30 A.M.–7 P.M. Mon.–Fri., 8:30 A.M.–5 P.M. Sat.).

In the event of an emergency, dial **192** for an ambulance **193** for the fire department, and **190** for the police. For medical treatment try the **Hospital 28 de Agosto** (Rua Recife 1581, Adrianópolis, tel. 92/3642-4272). The **Hospital de Doenças Tropicais** (Av. Pedro Teixeira 25, Dom Pedro, tel. 92/3238-1711) specializes in tropical diseases and also gives free yellow fever vaccines.

Getting There

Considering its distance from everywhere else, most people arrive in Manaus by air (there are even direct flights from Miami). Due to the precarious state of the roads throughout Amazonas, bus travel is minimal. The most prevalent means of regional travel is boat.

Flights arrive at the **Aeroporto Eduardo Gomes** (Av. Santos Dumont, Tarumã, tel. 92/3652-1212), which is 17 kilometers (10 miles) from the center of town. A taxi downtown costs around R$40–45. You can also take municipal bus 306. If you're going to Ponta Negra, there is a Fontur minibus that takes passengers to the Tropical Manaus for R$15, with stops in Centro.

Long-distance buses arrive at the *rodoviária* (Rua Recife 2784, Flores, tel. 92/3642-5805), 10 kilometers (6 miles) north of Centro. To get downtown, take the 306 bus or a taxi (R$35–40).

If you arrive by boat from Belém or Santarém, you'll disembark at the **Estação Hidroviária** (Rua Marquês de Santa Cruz 25, Centro, tel. 92/3621-4359) on the Porto Flutuante, which is in the heart of the city. If you don't have too much luggage you can walk to hotels in Centro.

Getting Around

Most of Centro can be easily explored by foot. To get to Ponta Negra, take the 120 bus or a taxi (R$40–45). Praça da Matriz is the main transportation hub—from here you can hop a municipal bus to just about anywhere. Alternatively, taxis are cheap and plentiful (and recommended at night). Aside from hailing one in the street, you can call **Amazonas Rádio Taxi** (tel. 92/3233-1625). As for renting a car, there is really not much point. You can easily walk to most city sights, while everything outside Manaus is basically jungle. The only place you can really drive to is Presidente Figueiredo. Should you want to rent a car to get there, try **Interlocadora** (Rua Duque de Caxias 750, Centro, tel. 92/3232-1558).

CITY TOURS

Visiting Manaus and the surrounding area can be done by bus, boat, or even plane. **Viverde** (Rua das Guariúbas 47, Parque Acariquara, 26, tel. 92/3248-9988, www.viverde.com.br) is a highly recommend tour operator, as is the slightly more expensive **Fontur,** located inside the Hotel Tropical (Estrada da Ponta Negra, tel. 92/3658-3052, www.fontur.com.br). Both offer half-day city tours of Manaus's major attractions for around R$75. Most guides speak English and the buses are blessedly air-conditioned. Both operators also offer full-day river boat tours to the Meeting of the Waters and the Reserva Ecológica do Lago de Janauari. For a bird's-eye view of the Amazon, Viverde will also take you up in a hydroplane that departs from the river, in front of the Hotel Tropical Manaus. A 30-minute flight over the fabulous patchwork of city, forest and Meeting of the Waters costs a whopping R$450 per person, but the view from above is truly unforgettable.

FROM MANAUS INTO THE AMAZON JUNGLE

Most people's ultimate destination is not Manaus itself, but the Amazon jungle. Staying in Manaus for a couple of days allows you to get a taste of the jungle with side excursions and day trips. But if you want to get away from civilization (and the distance it takes to "get away" is constantly increasing), experience "virgin" forest, and see some wildlife, the best way to do so is by taking a longer tour or excursion into the rainforest, with the option of sleeping on a boat or in the jungle itself at a camp or jungle lodge, known as a *hotel de selva*. Depending upon your interests as well as time and money constraints, there are several options available.

One way is to book an excursion with a specialized ecotourist agency based in Manaus. An average tour lasts 2–6 days and usually includes typical outings such as hiking in the jungle and canoeing through *igarapés* (narrow creeks) and *igapós* (temporarily flooded forests) in search of wildlife. Guaranteed sightings include flocks of birds and frolicking schools of pink dolphins. Less frequent are monkeys and sloths. Almost impossible are jaguars. The famous piranha is omnipresent and piranha fishing with a bamboo pole and a chunk of beef as bait is a classic activity few tourists can resist. The best times for viewing animals are around sunrise and sunset. However, as you can tell by the symphonic screeches, squawks, grunts, shuffles, and ribbets, nighttime is when the forest really comes to life. A popular (and somewhat spooky) nocturnal pastime is looking for caimans with a flashlight. They are quite easy to identify by their glow-in-the-dark eyes. As proof that these reptiles have a softer side, your guide will inevitably grab a baby caiman by the neck and invite you to caress its spiny carapace.

Many tours also include visits to the homes of local *caboclos* (mixed descendants of Indians and Portuguese) who live in stilt houses along the river. Many are quite poor and have little contact with the rest of Brazil. These visits can be interesting—watching milky latex being heated over a fire to become rubber and manioc being pounded into *farinha* (flour) that is a main food staple—and sometimes a little exploitative.

Accommodations on tours may vary greatly. They can range from basic bunks on a boat, and hammocks or tents in the jungle, to a night at an exclusive jungle lodge with air-conditioning and gourmet meals. Make sure you know what you're getting for your money. Consider how much roughing it in the wilds you're prepared for. You'll want to make sure of your guides' qualifications (most guides work as freelancers, and it's nice if they not only speak English, but also know something about the Amazon's flora and fauna instead of improvising as they go along). It's also worth confirming the type of transportation that will be used to explore smaller waterways—noiseless motors or old-fashioned paddle canoes are better than noisy and polluting motorboats that scare off wildlife.

Another way of exploring the forest is to book yourself into one of the many jungle lodges that have increasingly sprung up along banks of the Rio Negro and Rio Solimões. Similar to excursions, jungle lodges sell packages (usually 2–6 days) that include similar jungle and river activities along with (often very good) meals, and sometimes, transportation from Manaus. Lodges range from basic rustic to eco-chic, and are generally fairly pricy. Keep in mind that your exposure to locals will be minimal. Aside from the jungle lodges' owners and guides, most of your companions will be other environmentally minded gringos.

Finally, given that boats are the main means of transportation in the Amazon, you can very easily hop one and go wherever you want. Regardless of whether you splurge for a luxury riverboat for well-heeled ecotourists, or string up your freshly purchased hammock alongside those of Amazonenses traveling downriver in the direction of Belém, adventure is guaranteed.

Presidente Figueiredo

Located 107 kilometers (64 miles) north of Manaus on the road to Venezuela, Presidente Figueiredo is a small town that has recently become a favorite ecotourist getaway. Although the surrounding region is replete with rainforest, creeks and rivers, and caves containing prehistoric paintings, the main attraction is 100 waterfalls that have won the town the nickname of Terra das Cachoeiras (Land of Waterfalls). These aren't just any waterfalls

FESTIVAL FOLCLÓRICO DE PARINTINS

For Amazonenses, the last week in June is as eagerly awaited as Carnaval in Rio de Janeiro due to the most famous *festa* popular in all of the Brazilian North: the Festival Folclórico de Parintins. Parintins itself is an otherwise uneventful river town around halfway between Santarém (20 hours by boat) and Manaus (26 hours by boat). Although it's hardly the most accessible place to visit (if you don't have the time or inclination for a boat trip, you can fly to Parintins, but make sure to book accommodations and purchase tickets months in advance), the population multiplies exponentially when the "Boi Bumba" (as the festival is popularly known) comes to town. The unusual and very colorful celebrations, resembling Carnaval with pronounced indigenous elements, take place in a massive bull-shaped arena called the Bumbadromo, with seating capacity for 35,000 people. Here, two rival groups, Boi Caprichoso and Boi Garantido, compete in the reenactment of a version of the Bumba-Meu-Boi story imported from Maranhão, in which a plantation owner's bull is killed and then brought back to life in order to save the slave who was assigned to take care of it in his master's absence. The intense rivalry between the two groups is emphasized by their contrasting colors – Caprichoso members and supporters of Caprichoso wear blood red while those of Garantido sport bright blue – and by a strange rule: While one group performs its elaborate two-hour-long pageant in the arena, supporters of the other school must remain completely silent. The roles are reversed when it's the other group's turn to strut their stuff. Consequently, while you can hear a pin drop in one half of the stadium, in the other half the crowds are going wild.

either. Tributaries of the Rio Negro, the water of these numerous falls is a striking jet black color. Diving into the pools and opening your eyes underwater is an intense experience. So is splashing around and getting a pummeling massage amidst a setting of rocks, ferns, and tropical forest that is downright Edenic. Among the best falls closest to town are Suframa (11 kilometers, 7 miles), Iracema (12 kilometers, 7.5 miles) and Santuário (16 kilometers, 10 miles). If you don't have a car, you can easily hire a taxi or *moto-taxi* to reach them.

ACCOMMODATIONS AND FOOD

Although Presidente Figueiredo can be enjoyed in a day, if you want to relax and soak up the falls in a more leisurely fashion, it's worthwhile spending the night at one of the half dozen simple *pousadas* in and around town. **Pousada Cuca Legal** (Rua Manaus 1895, tel. 92/3324-1138, www.pousadacucalegal.com.br, R$85–95 d) is a nice choice right in the center of town. Rooms are a bit small, but bright and tidy. The grounds are nicely landscaped with a pool, and the restaurant serves good food. The *pousada* staff can organize outings to falls and caves as well as forest hikes.

GETTING THERE

Getting to Presidente Figueiredo is easy via the BR-174, basically the only paved road heading out of Manaus. If you want to rent a car, the trip is a very scenic one. Several bus companies (including Sempre Viva and Transgil) offer daily service from Manaus's *rodoviária*. The journey takes two hours, and you'll find a tourist information kiosk at the bus station upon your arrival. Tour operators also offer day trips here (leaving quite early in the morning).

Up the Rio Solimões

The muddy river that stretches west from Manaus all the way to Brazil's border with Peru and Colombia is known as the Rio Solimões. Although it is actually more of a café-au-lait color, the Rio Solimões is known as a "white" river due to the fact that its waters are laden with a high concentration of rich soil. As a result, during the wet season when the river floods the surrounding land, it leaves highly fertile silt deposits that encourage plant, animal, and insect life. The ramifications for ecotourists are twofold: While you'll tend to see more wildlife along the Rio Solimões than along the Rio Negro, you'll also have to fend off more mosquitos.

Traveling upstream by boat along the Rio Solimões, there are several areas that offer stunning expanses of prime rainforest with the possibility of viewing wildlife. Only a half-day journey from Manaus is the area surrounding **Lago Mamori,** where you can glimpse lots of birds, caimans and pink river dolphins and the piranha fishing is great. Further along, and more remote, is the **Lago Juma.**

◖ RESERVA DE DESENVOLVIMENTO SUSTENTÁVEL DE MAMIRAUÁ

By far, the hottest eco-spot along the Rio Solimões is the Reserva de Desenvolvimento Sustentável de Mamirauá (Mamirauá Sustainable Development Reserve, tel. 92/3233-9025, www.mamiraua.com.br). The largest protected area of *varzéa* (Amazonian forest that is seasonally flooded with "white" river water) within Brazil, the reserve is monitored by the Instituto de Desenvolvimento Sustentável de Mamirauá, whose mission is to combine conservation and scientific research with the creation of sustainable employment and lifestyles for local inhabitants. Apart from traditional fishing and agriculture, an increasing percentage of the local *caboclo* population work as guides and forest patrollers. Their efforts have not been in vain: The forest is in pristine condition and exploring its jungles, rivers, and lagoons will give you the sensation of having returned to a primordial Eden. As a result, Mamirauá is one of the best places to see wildlife. Aside from caimans, pink dolphins, sloths, and myriad birds and monkeys, if you're lucky you might even get to see the very rare scarlet-faced uakari monkey. Located at the confluence of the Solimões with the Rio Japurá, the reserve is close to the town of **Tefé,** which also happens to be the last outpost of civilization along the Solimões. To visit the reserve on your own involves a two-day boat trip to Tefé (or a far speedier and more expensive one-hour direct flight from Manaus).

Up the Rio Negro

The dark river that flows into Manaus from the remote reaches of northwestern Amazonas is known as the Rio Negro. Its somber hue is actually more dark reddish-brown than black, yet it is known as a "black" river due to the fact that its waters are filled with rotting vegetation from low-lying forests. The abundance of decaying organic matter results in a high level of acidity. As a result, its waters don't have the same fertilizing properties as "white" rivers such as the Solimões. A bonus is that the high acidity kills insect larvae, which results in a low instance of mosquito attacks.

◖ ARQUIPÉLAGO DE ANAVILHANAS

The most fascinating, easily accessible destination along the Rio Negro is the Arquipélago de Anavilhanas. The second-largest freshwater archipelago in the world, it boasts upwards of 400 islands. During the dry season, many of them are fringed with beautiful white sands beaches. If you don't mind sharing with flocks of wild birds, you'll have them completely to yourself. Should you want to go swimming, you'll very likely share the warm waters with schools of friendly pink dolphins. Getting here on your own is fairly easy. A boat ride to the town of Novo Airão (located in the middle of the archipelago) is about a day's journey (eight hours) from Manaus. You can also take a bus (six hours) from the *rodoviária.*

Ecotours and Excursions

There are scores of tour operators who will offer to take you up the Rio Solimões, the Rio Negro, and its tributaries. Some will even take you on both. Most people go on excursions that last 2–4 days, but it's possible to find 1–2 week excursions that journey into very remote areas. Long before you get to Manaus, it's best to do some research and check out tour companies' websites in advance. Take a look at the boats and accommodations available and make sure guides speak English and have some knowledge of the

PINK RIVER DOLPHINS

Of the five species of freshwater dolphins in the world, the most legendary – and supposedly the most brainy – are the pink dolphins of the Amazon. Nicknamed *botos* by Brazilians, these friendly, sensitive mammals boast a brain capacity that is 40 percent larger than that of humans. Perhaps this helps explain the fact that they have lived in harmony with the Amazon's indigenous groups for centuries. It also may explain why recent human-devised (and brainless) devastation of the Amazonian environment has put their very existence at risk. Although to date, there is no ready explanation for its characteristic pink flush, possible factors include iron content in the river water and capillaries near the surface of the skin.

Among the region's indigenous peoples, dolphin lore abounds. Popular narratives run the gamut from magical myths, in which they appear as unpredictable beasts with semi-divine powers, to headline-worthy true tales of dolphins who saved capsized fishermen by pushing them safely to shore.

jungle. If in doubt, also check the company's credentials with Amazonastur, the state tourist bureau. Ecotourism has become a big business, and the minute you get to Manaus you'll be accosted at the airport, *rodoviária,* and/or ports by locals offering excursions. Just give them a firm, but polite *"Não, obrigado/a."* Even if they flash a brochure from a reputed agency (such as those listed here) refuse—there have been reports of scammers impersonating legitimate operators. Before you fork out any money, get in writing everything that's included in the price of your excursion. Usually a decent budget excursion will cost R$150–200 per day while a more specialized excursion with more upscale accommodations will set you back R$250–400 a day.

Amazon Gero's Tours (Rua Dez de Julho 679, Sala 2, Centro, tel. 92/9983-6273, www .amazongerotours.com) is run by experienced and friendly English-speaking guide Geraldo ("Gero") Mesquita. Gero customizes reasonably priced tours throughout the region, especially along Rio Solimões around the areas of Lago Mamori and Lago Juma (Gero owns his own jungle lodge, the Ararinha Jungle Hotel, in the region). Accommodations can be on boats, in jungle lodges, in hammocks, or even with local families in villages.

Also highly recommended is **Swallows and Amazons** (Rua Quintino Bocaiúva 189, Centro, Sala 13, tel. 92/3622-1246, www.swallowsandamaazontours.com), a small company owned by American Mark Aitchison and his Brazilian wife, Tania, that custom designs topnotch riverboat, jungle lodge, and adventure tours for small groups that usually last for a week or more. Swallows and Amazons organizes trips along the still wild and unspoiled upper Rio Negro, including the Arquipélago Anavilhanas (close to which lies its own floating jungle lodge, the Araras Lodge). The all-inclusive excursions cater to various interests and can include activities such as diving, bird-watching, fishing, as canoeing as well as stays with *caboclo* families.

For completely off-the-beaten-track and into-the-*Heart of Darkness* jungle tours you've always fantasized about, **Amazon Mystery Tours** (Rua Brasil 27, Redenção, tel. 92/3228-3733, www.amazon-outdoor.com) specializes in trips to remote tributaries and private reserves to which it has exclusive access. Those who want a back-to-nature experience can stay in tents, while others seeking creature comforts can bunk aboard a posh yacht. Among the activities Amazon Mystery offers are kayaking and tree climbing into the lofty heights of the rainforest's upper canopy—a truly amazing experience.

For budget travelers, **Amazonas Indian Turismo** (Rua dos Andradas 311, Centro, tel. 92/3622-0204) is a long-standing operator that offers good basic tours led by Amazonian Indians (most of whom speak English). Groups are small and, as such, can be personalized. For longer getaways into the depths of the jungle, the company has its own very rustic camp with hammocks and outhouses on the Rio Urubú, 200 kilometers (124 miles) from Manaus.

(Jungle Lodges (Hotéis de Selva)

Staying in a jungle lodge is one of the preferred ways of experiencing the Amazon. Spending a few days in a lodge is a wonderful way to experience the jungle because you'll be living in it. Perched ideally (and idyllically) right on a river (often on stilts), many are situated amidst primary rainforest. Lodges vary significantly in terms of size, price, and comfort level. As a general rule, farther away (from Manaus) and smaller (intimate and personalized vs. noisy and touristy) is better. While you want enough creature comforts (fans and mosquito netting are helpful) to keep you from being miserable, since the whole idea is to get in touch with nature, you don't really need cable TV or a spa.

ALONG THE RIO SOLIMÕES

Located 100 kilometers (62 miles) south of Manaus, the **Juma Lodge** (Lago do Juma, tel. 92/3245-1177, www.jumalodge.com.br, R$1,100–1,800 pp for a three-day package) is a three-hour boat ride from Manaus along the Rio Solimões. Completely integrated into the preserved jungle, this intimate and totally secluded lodge is an exercise in camouflage. Wooden structures on stilts, connected by suspended walkways, are designed according to indigenous techniques. The cabins feel like tree houses. All of them feature verandas that gaze onto either bird-filled branches or the river, where it is not uncommon to see dolphins cavorting. For exploring on your own, the lodge has dugout canoes you can paddle around in.

The most radically eco of all the Amazon's lodges, the (**Pousada Uacari** (tel. 97/3343-4160, www.uakarilodge.com.br, R$1,100–2,000 pp for a three-day package) boasts an unbeatable location in the midst of the Reserva Mamirauá. Getting here requires flying or sailing up the Rio Solimões to Tefé, and then taking a 90-minute speedboat ride (provided by the *pousada*). The rustic accommodations are in floating wood cabins that are simple but attractive. All water comes from the river itself and is heated by solar energy. Recycling is a mantra. As part of the reserve's commitment to sustainable development, local communities are involved in the operation of the *pousada* as well as leading jungle tours. Scientists who work at the Mamirauá Sustainable Research Institute are frequently present. Not only do they conduct nature talks to guests, but you can often accompany them into the field.

ALONG THE RIO NEGRO

One of the more affordable jungle lodges, the **Acajatuba Jungle Lodge** (Lago Acajatuba, tel. 92/3642-0358, www.acajatuba.com.br, R$380–780 pp for a two-day package) is located on a tranquil lake formed by the Rio Acajatuba, a tributary of the Rio Negro. While accommodations are rustic—no hot water or electricity—they are charmingly located in suspended *malocas* (traditional circular-shaped Indian dwellings made of wood and palm thatch) that offer terrific views of the lake and encroaching jungle. Hammocks are strategically placed throughout the property and abundant wild macaws and toucans provide a continuous soundtrack.

The recently inaugurated (**Anavilhanas Jungle Lodge** (Novo Airão, tel. 92/3622-8996, www.anavilhanaslodge.com, R$1,110–1,900 pp for a four-day package) is probably the most elegant *hotel de selva*. The entire structure is an enchanting lesson in jungle minimalism. Its 16 air-conditioned rooms, paneled in tropical woods and decorated with Amazonian *artesanato*, are complemented by an open-air lounge area with lots of books and DVDs. There is also a gorgeous pool and a pretty restaurant that serves gourmet fare such as *dourado* fish in ginger sauce and coconut flan. For adventure, you have the 400 plus islands of the Arquipélago Anavilhanas at your disposal. All guides are knowledgeable locals who know the *igarapés* and *igapós* like the back of their hands.

ALONG THE RIO AMAZONAS

One of the few Amazonian jungle lodges that is actually on the Amazon, the **Amazon**

Riverside Hotel (Rio Amazonas, tel. 92/3622-2789, www.mainan.com.br, R$850–1,250 pp for a two-day package) is a very attractive option only one hour downriver from Manaus. Owned by the Manauense-Japanese Tsuji family, the lodge receives a number of Japanese tourists who are obviously seduced by the soothing and immaculate wooden rooms and the creative fusion menu that results in dishes such as tambaqui sashimi and tempura made with native veg such as okra and pumpkin. The kitchen will also cook up any piranha you might catch (the piranha fishing is excellent here). A nature trail leading through the forest leads to a hilltop lookout with stunning views.

◖ Riverboat Trips

An alternative to staying put in a jungle lodge is to choose a riverboat as your headquarters, which will allow you to cover far more territory. Many ecotourist agencies operate or can book you onto a riverboat that will cruise up and down the Rio Solimões and/or Rio Negro. Accommodations range from basic cabins with wooden bunks to cruise-worthy luxury with fine dining. To venture into the forest itself you'll be transferred into smaller vessels that will allow you to penetrate more secluded and wildlife-rich *igapós* and *igarapés*. **Viverde** (Rua das Guariúbas 47, Parque Acariquara, tel. 92/3248-9888, www.viverde.com.br) can reserve trips on riverboats and charter boats for private groups. You can also directly contract **Amazon Clipper Cruises,** based at the Hotel Tropical in Ponta Negra (tel. 92/3656-1246, www.amazonas-travel.com.br/amazon_clipper_i.html), which runs 3–4-day excursions along both the Rio Negro and Rio Solimões, for R$900–1,200. The **Iberostar Grand Amazon** (Amazon Jungle Cruise, Hidroviária do Amazonas, tel. 92/2126-9900, www.iberostar.com) runs similar tours, with the added bonus of accommodations on a luxury cruise ship with smashing cabins featuring king-sized beds, plasma TVs, and private verandas as well as multiple pools, restaurants, and bars. However, amidst all the champagne and pampering, the Iberostar's crew takes its eco-activities seriously. Aside from offering excellent guided tours in small launches and nightly wildlife lectures, the library is stuffed with books about every aspect of the Amazon's climate, culture, history, flora, and fauna. Daily rates hover around R$700. While the price is steep, it includes absolutely everything (including the champagne).

If you really want to rough it, and have a much more authentic (not to mention way cheaper) adventure, you can always hop aboard one of the local wooden passenger boats that ferry people (and cargo) throughout the Amazon. For major routes—along the Amazon to Santarém and Belém; along the Rio Solimões to Tefé; up the Rio Negro to Novo Airão—there is more or less regular service (on large and small boats) from Manaus. Since these boats are for transport and not for tourism, don't expect to see much, if any, wildlife, since the boats generally stick to the middle of the main rivers, far from either shore. Also don't expect a lot of comfort. If you opt for one of the few private, but cramped, stuffy, and basic cabins (which usually sleep 2–4 people), you'll have privacy, security, and your own bathroom (a big luxury), and that's about it. If you're on a serious budget and want to hang with the locals, than you can buy a hammock and string it up on deck. There are usually first-class and second-class hammock areas—the advantage of first-class hammock space is that you'll be on a higher deck with exposure to more breezes (and farther away from the noisy engine). The experience is often sardine-like, not to mention noisy (between music playing, babies crying, and all-night gossip sessions). However, this is a good way to hang out with locals in a non-touristy setting. All meals—lots of edible, but very basic rice, beans, and fish as well as filtered water—are included, although you should bring some mineral water and safe snacks such as bananas or energy bars as a reserve. The term "shared bathrooms" is somewhat of an understatement. You'll also want to keep a constant eye on your belongings. Keep in mind that delays are frequent and that traveling downriver is always quicker than upriver. It's best to purchase tickets a day or two in advance and to stake out hammock space at least an hour before the boat leaves.

The quintessential boat trip is the 4–5-day journey down to the mouth of the Amazon in Belém. A cabin usually costs R$700–800, while a first-class hammock space goes for R$240. Departures are usually on Wednesday and Saturday. Most boats to Belém also stop off at Parintins, Santarém, and Monte Alegre. The two-day journey to Santarém costs R$300 for a cabin and R$100 for first-class hammock space with departures on Tuesday and Thursday. Boats depart from the **Hidroviária do Amazonas** (Rua Marquês de Santa Cruz 25, Centro, tel. 92/3621-4359), where you can get schedules for all boats and buy tickets. Purchase tickets from the kiosks and not from the vendors on the street. **AJATO** (Rua Barés 3, Centro, tel. 92/3622-6047) runs speedboats down to Santarém (R$200, 13–15 hours) and up to Tefé (R$180, 11–13 hours), which significantly reduce the journey time. Prices include two daily meals and boats leave from the **Porto Moderna** behind the Mercado Municipal. Boats traveling up the Rio Negro depart from the somewhat louche **Porto São Raimundo,** 1.5 kilometers (1 mile) northwest of the Porto Flutuante (take a cab).

BACKGROUND

The Land

Considering the country's immensity, it's hardly surprising that Brazil's geography is so incredibly varied. The fifth-largest country in the world after Canada, China, Russia, and the United States, Brazil is the largest country in South America (occupying roughly half the continent). It shares borders with every South American country except Chile and Ecuador.

GEOGRAPHY

The Instituto Brasileiro do Meio Ambiente (IBAMA) is the federal agency in charge of studying and monitoring Brazil's natural environment. IBAMA's researchers have recognized seven distinct ecosystems within Brazil: the Amazonian rainforest, the Caatinga, the Atlantic rainforest, the coastal region, the Cerrado, the Pantanal wetlands, and the southern plains.

Amazonian Rainforest

The world's largest tropical rainforest, the Amazon is also one of the world's richest sources of biological diversity. It's home to 40,000 plant species, 2,000 birds and mammals, 3,000 fish, and 2.5 million insect species—and these are merely the species that have been identified. Despite human encroachment upon the forest, the majority of it is uninhabited. Furthermore, with the Amazon River

itself boasting thousands of tributaries, there are still many areas that remain remote and completely unknown to humans.

Rainforests exist in regions that receive at least 2 meters (6.5 feet) of annual rainfall. In the Amazon, this accounts for humidity levels that are usually higher than 80 percent. Flooding of the Amazon itself and its tributaries can cause water levels to rise by as much as 15 meters (49 feet), transforming forest floors into lakes and driving most wildlife—butterflies, birds, sloths, and monkeys—up into the highest tree canopies. Some parts of the forest, known as *igapó*, are permanently flooded, whereas others, known as *várzea* are only flooded seasonally.

The Amazon Basin holds about 17 percent of the world's fresh water. With a length of 6,400 kilometers (4,000 miles), the mighty Rio Amazonas is the largest river in Brazil—and the greatest river in the world because it carries 119,000 cubic meters (4.2 million cubic feet) of water into the sea every *second*. Beginning in Peru, the river flows eastward until it empties into the Atlantic Ocean near the city of Belém. All in all, its more than 1,000 tributaries add up to more than 7,047,000 square kilometers (2,722,000 square miles) of water. The Amazon is also home to Brazil's highest mountain, Pico Neblina. Located near the Venezuelan border, it rises to a height of 3,014 meters (9,888 feet).

Caatinga

A marked contrast to the lushness of the Amazon is the parched dryness of the scrubby Caatinga vegetation that characterizes much of the interior of northeastern Brazil, an area known as the Sertão. Caatinga covers approximately 11 percent of Brazilian territory. Although the Sertão's legendary droughts and tales of hardship have led many Brazilians to conjure up images of an inhospitable moonscape where only cacti grow, the semi-arid Caatinga actually possesses a wet season as well as a dry season. During the latter, rivers dry up, leaves disappear, and cracks appear in the sun-baked earth. However, when the torrential

© EMBRATUR

Parque Nacional de Aparados da Serra, Rio Grande do Sul

rains do come (in the summer months), the low scrub and thorn trees suddenly burst into green.

Atlantic Rainforest

When the first Portuguese arrived in Brazil, a dense Atlantic forest, the Mata Atlântica, blanketed the entire coastline from Rio Grande do Norte in the north to Rio Grande do Sul in the south. Stretching west by an average of 200 kilometers (124 miles) into the interior, this ancient rainforest (far older than the Amazon) measured 1 million square kilometers (621,000 square miles). However, five centuries of brazilwood extraction, sugar and coffee cultivation, farming, logging, urbanization, and industrialization have taken their toll. Today, only 7 percent of Mata Atlântica remains in patches (notably in southern Bahia, Rio de Janeiro, São Paulo, and Paraná). However, the surviving forest is surprisingly lush and rife with unique forms of flora and fauna unknown anywhere else in Brazil or the world. Rare mammals include the lion tamarin and woolly spider monkey (the largest primate in the Americas), while plant life includes rare bromeliads, orchids, ferns, and surviving specimens of *pau brasil,* the wood that lent Brazil its name. Thankfully, much of the remaining forest is now carefully preserved (at least in theory) as nature reserves and national parks.

Coastal Region

Brazil boasts an enormous coastline that stretches 8,000 km (5,000 miles) and includes a vast array of interesting formations including rocky cliffs, enormous dunes, boulders, sandy coves, coastal plains, forests, and *manguezais,* or mangroves. Mangroves are unique systems that appear wherever a river flows into a bay or estuary. They extend along the coast as far north as Pará and as far south as Santa Catarina. Soil rich with river sediment and organic matter nourishes the dense mangrove vegetation, which in turn attracts fish, storks and ibises, and shrimps, crabs, and mussels. Traditionally, some local populations viewed mangroves as muddy, humid, unhygienic swamps. They tried to drain them or use them as garbage dumps. Only recently has their important role in maintaining the delicate equilibrium of marine life been recognized. As a result, many have become protected environments.

Southern Plains

Southern Brazil, extending from Santa Catarina into Rio Grande do Sul, is covered with a vast plain where low vegetation, mosses, and lichens thrive along with cacti and bromeliads. South- and westward, the plain gradually transforms into the grassy Pampas, a rolling green carpet studded with occasional cork and fig trees.

Cerrado

The vast highland plains of the Central-West region (known as the Planalto) that surround Brasília and stretch west through Goiás into Mato Grosso and Mato Grosso do Sul are covered with a distinctive type of vegetation known as Cerrado. Resembling the dry, scrubby, savannah-like landscapes

of eastern Africa, Cerrado is a surprisingly rich and unique ecosystem, over 40 percent of whose roughly 10,000 plant species don't exist anywhere else on Earth. Aside from straw-colored grasses and scrubby bushes, characteristic vegetation ranges from thick-barked trees and primitive-looking buriti palms to blossoming *ipê,* jacaranda, and the ubiquitous *pequi* tree, whose spiky orange fruit is used in local cooking. Due to widespread clearing of the land for farming, more than half of this precious ecosystem has been destroyed. While efforts have been taken in recent years to preserve considerable chunks of the Amazon and Atlantic rainforests, conservation strategies in the relatively unknown Cerrado are virtually nonexistent aside from a few existing nature reserves.

The Pantanal

The world's greatest inland wetlands, the Pantanal is a vast plain that is constantly flooded with waters from the Andes, the Planalto, and the Rio Paraguai Basin. Extending from the Central-West states of Mato Grosso and Mato Grosso do Sul to Bolivia and Paraguay, the region measures 250,000 square kilometers (96,500 square miles) and covers an area larger than the United Kingdom. The Pantanal is actually a complex system fed by more than 100 rivers. Depending on the season, the entire region is drastically transformed. The wet season, which lasts from November to March, is marked by rains and rising rivers, which turn the area into a vast aquarium dotted with islands. During this period, wildlife moves to higher ground and transportation is by boat only. The "dry season," which extends from April to October, is characterized by the slow draining of floodplains. Receding water leaves rich sediment behind where pasture sprouts. As a result, the area is ideal for cattle raising (the bovine population far outnumbers humans). Instead of a distinctive flora and fauna of its own, the Pantanal has a lot of everything else—including plants and animals that are typical of the Amazon forest, the Cerrado, and even the Caatinga. Due to its relative seclusion, you'll find wildlife in much greater numbers in the Pantanal than in the Amazon, making the region a not-to-be-missed mecca for wildlife enthusiasts as well as fresh-water fishing aficionados.

CLIMATE

Due to the country's immense size, Brazil's climate is extremely varied. The Equator runs through the northern part of the country while the Tropic of Capricorn crosses through the south (running parallel to São Paulo). As you head from north to south, the temperature, humidity, and precipitation levels change greatly. Brazil boasts four distinctive climactic zones: subtropical, equatorial, tropical, and semi-arid. Ninety percent of the country is situated in the tropical zone, where there is very little seasonal variation. Rain is frequent and temperatures range 25–35°C (77–95°F). However, as you head south, seasonal variations become more distinct, resembling those of the continental United States and Europe, with hot, steamy summers and cool winters. In the southern states of Santa Catarina and Rio Grande do Sul, temperatures can plunge low enough to produce frost and even snow.

With the exception of the Sertão, which receives very little rainfall, the rest of the country receives a lot of rain. Although rains are common throughout the year, coastal regions have distinctive rainy seasons where downpours are daily occurrences and can even last for several days. In the Southeast, violent downpours flood the streets of Rio and São Paulo in the summer months between December and March. In the Northeast, along the coast between Bahia and Pernambuco, rainy season generally coincides with the winter months between June and August. Rain is much less frequent in the permanently sunny states of Rio Grande do Norte and Ceará, where temperatures remain constant year-round. Close to the Equator, Maranhão, and especially the Amazonian state of Pará, receive the most rain throughout the year, with annual averages of 3,500 mm (138 inches) in some parts. The rest of the Amazon, along with the Pantanal, receives a lot of rain as well, but both regions also have a more pronounced dry season that lasts from March to October.

ENVIRONMENTAL ISSUES
Amazon Deforestation

The number one environmental issue that comes to mind when one thinks about Brazil is the destruction of the Amazon jungle. To date, an estimated 18 percent of the world's largest and most diverse rainforest has suffered deforestation, and an equal portion has suffered from degradation (mostly caused by logging). The worst damage to the forest took place during the 1970s and '80s. During these years, the military government was eager to open up the hitherto inaccessible region to development and invested in Transamazonian highways that cut through the jungle from north and south and east to west. The asphalting of the Amazon (parts of which subsequently fell into disrepair and were reclaimed by jungle) created links between the region's major cities. It also paved the way for large-scale logging, agriculture, and cattle ranching, most of which took place with complete disregard to the welfare of the forest and its indigenous peoples. Further damage resulted from the installation of vast hydroelectric dams; the disruption of natural river cycles had a serious impact on the environment.

Over the last 10 years, various factors—ranging from increased global and national environmental consciousness to more enlightened political and business policies that have recognized the value of sustainable development—have led to some positive results. Other factors have contributed to reducing devastation. The flood of poor immigrants that, in former decades, swamped the Amazon in search of jobs and cheap land has dried up. At present, contrary to popular belief, most of the farming, cattle raising, and logging are carried out on the 20 percent of Amazonian territory that has already been cleared. Moreover, strict new international laws governing the origins of Amazonian timber means that wood is harvested in accordance with rigid environmental regulations. However, the biggest culprits of deforestation continue to be cattle-raising and large-scale production of soybeans. Soya not only serves as cattle feed, but is also a lucrative cash crop that is in great demand on world markets (Brazil is currently the world's largest producer of soybeans).

Historically, economic expansion been at odds with the preservation of natural ecosystems, as evidenced by the destruction of Brazil's Mata Atlântica and ongoing threats to the Pantanal and the Cerrado. After President Lula appointed Marina da Silva—a former rubber tapper from the state of Acre—as minister of the environment, the government began to crack down more seriously on illegal deforestation and make attempts to preserve large swathes of virgin forest as national parks. Moreover, to date, more than 20 percent of Amazonian territory has been transformed into Indian reserves where indigenous people carry out sustainable activities ranging from small-scale fishing, agriculture, and rubber tapping to harvesting nuts and collecting leaves and roots that are crucial ingredients in medicines and cosmetics. As a result of these and other policies, the rate of deforestation has actually decreased in the last few years. Nonetheless, many obstacles remain. Part of the problem lies with local and state governments (with the notable exceptions of Amazonas and Acre), along with wealthy landowners, whose greed, cronyism, and oligarchic values privilege short-term riches at the expense of long-term sustainable development.

Pollution

Both air and water pollution are a big problem in Brazil. Pollution from industry and vehicle exhaust fumes is a problem in Rio and Belo Horizonte, but is notorious in São Paulo, where skies can become thick with smog. To diminish pollution, Sampa's municipal government implemented a rotation system, whereby cars whose license plates end in odd numbers alternate days on the road with those whose plates end in even numbers. However, with more people purchasing cars, this solution falls short of addressing the problem. Water pollution is an issue throughout the country. In urban areas, lack of water and sewage treatment in some poor neighborhoods—particularly in *favelas* (slums)—is a hazard. In rural areas, pesticides, industrial waste, and the degradation of aquatic ecosystems due to the installation of hydroelectric plants are responsible for the pollution of lakes and rivers. Meanwhile, oceans are at the mercy of accidents because of heavy shipping activities and offshore oil drilling.

In recent years, progress has been made in addressing some of these problems. As Brazil has increasingly become a global economic player, to compete in world markets Brazilian manufacturers have had to adopt stringent environmental regulations, which include the recycling of waste and alternative forms of energy production. City governments such as Rio's have taken small steps to integrate—instead of ignore—*favelas* by attempting to provide basic services to which all citizens are entitled. Meanwhile, growing tourism, particularly ecotourism, has provided a cash incentive for government, businesses, and local populations to preserve the environment and look for sustainable means of development. Although most Brazilians are hardly enlightened in terms of littering, the country does boast one of the highest rates of recycling of any nation.

Flora and Fauna

TREES AND PLANT LIFE

More than a quarter of the world's known plant species can be found in Brazil. As the world's largest tropical rainforest, the Amazon boasts an astonishing range of trees (many festooned with Tarzan-worthy vines and creepers). Among the most legendary species are wild rubber trees and Brazil nut trees (capable of producing 455 kilograms/1,000 pounds of nuts in a year), along with rosewood and mahogany trees, whose beautiful hardwood is always much in demand for fine furniture. The extremely fertile Atlantic forest is also famous for other native woods, including jacaranda and *ipê*, with its bright purple and yellow blossoms.

Other Brazilian trees are more sought after for their fruits than for their wood. Throughout the tropical zones of the coast and the interior, Brazilians depend on diverse varieties of local palms. The Amazon is renowned for many fruit-bearing species, particularly those that yield *pupunha* and the energy-packed *açaí*. In Ceará and Maranhão, livelihoods depend upon the *carnaúba* and *babaçu* palms whose all-purpose fruits and fibers are used to make products ranging from wax, cooking oil, and soap to rope, timber, and thatch. Alagoas and northern Bahia are lined with swaying plantations of coconut palms, while southern Bahia is where you'll find the *dendê* palm, whose bright orange oil is used in Bahian cuisine. In the Cerrado, the fruit of the *buriti* palm is also made into various delicacies.

Fruit trees are everywhere you go, even in cities. In the Amazon, you can feast on *cupuaçu*, *bacuri*, and *muriti*, while the Northeast is rife with mango, papaya, *cajú* (cashew), *jaca* (jackfruit), *graviola*, *mangaba*, and guava trees. The Cerrado boasts exotic species such as *pequi*, *araticum*, and *cagaíta*. Bananas are ubiquitous and there are many types, ranging from the tiny *banana nanica* (dwarf banana) to the immense *banana pacova*, which

© MICHAEL SOMMERS

wild heliconia

can measure up to 50 centimeters (20 inches). In southern Brazil, you can still glimpse the umbrella-shaped *araucárias*, a variety of pine tree whose nuts were much appreciated by local indigenous groups back in the days when these trees were rampant.

Although you'll rarely find them in florists' shops (when buying flowers, Brazilians weirdly prefer to go with decidedly nontropical roses, carnations, and chrysanthemums), in the wild you'll be treated to more than 200 species of delicate and brightly colored orchids as well as bright red heliconia, birds of paradise, and glossy anthuriums. In the Amazon, the giant lilies that emerge from the platter-sized pads of the *Victoria amazonica* are captivating because of their size and because they change color during each day of their three-day life-span. Aside from the beauty of many Brazilian plants, their leaves and roots are used extensively for medicinal and cosmetic purposes.

MAMMALS

Brazil has an intriguing variety of exotic mammals. While smaller than wildlife you'll encounter in Africa, Brazilian animals are equally strange and fascinating. The largest creatures you might see—although they're extremely elusive—are cats such as jaguars and panthers. The *onça pintada* (spotted jaguar) inhabits the Amazon and the Pantanal and may be sometimes be spotted in the Cerrado. These cats prefer night to day, as does the all-black *onça preta*, also a native of the Amazon. A more commonly seen beast is the furry, ring-tailed *coati*, which uses its snout to root around for food on the ground or in the trees. A distant relative is the *guaxarim*, or crab-eating raccoon, which sports a black eye mask just like its North American cousins and lives near rivers in the Amazon and Pantanal. Another common sight in the Pantanal is the *capivara* (capybara), the world's biggest rodent. More like a giant guinea pig than a rat, *capivaras* are at home on land and in water. They can grow to lengths of 1 meter (3.3 feet) and weigh up to 70 kilograms (155 pounds).

Lontras (otters) are common in rivers of the South and Southeast, while the more rare *ariranha* (giant otter), which can measure up to 2 meters (6.5 feet), inhabits the lakes and rivers of the Pantanal and the Amazon. The Pantanal is a good place to spot wild deer such as the antlered *cervo-de-pantanal*. *Antas* (tapirs) are long-snouted foraging creatures that can grow to the size of a pony. Although fairly common in forested areas, they are very shy. Also common in forests are *caititus* (peccaries), wild boars that can grow up to 1 meter (3.3 feet) in length and often travel in trampling herds of up to 50. *Tamanduas* (anteaters) are surreal-looking creatures with long snouts and even longer furry tails. They spend much of their days sucking up tens of thousands of ants with their sticky tongues. The largest variety, the *tamandua bandeira*, grows to lengths of 2 meters (6.5 feet) and is a native of the Cerrado. *Tatus* (armadillos) are nocturnal and hard to see. Some species of *tamandúas* and *tatus* are endangered because their meat is considered a delicacy in rural areas. Another really odd-looking beast is the *preguiça* (sloth), who lives up to its name by doing little more than dozing in trees. When a *preguiça* does decide to make a move, it does so very slowly.

Primates

Of the world's 250 primate species, over 70 are found in Brazil. Many of these are actually unique to Brazil. In whatever part of the country you happen to visit, *macacos* or *micos* (monkeys) are a common sight, even in major cities. You'll spot many different types in the Amazon forest, including the tiny, pale-faced *mico-de-cheiro* (squirrel monkey) and the much larger *macaco preto* (spider monkey), whose long, spindly limbs and tail account for it measuring up to 1.5 meters (5 feet). *Guaribas* (howler monkeys) are also common, although since they inhabit tree canopies, you're much more likely to hear them than see them. Red howlers inhabit the Amazon, black howlers dwell in the Pantanal, and brown howlers can be spotted in the Mata Atlântica. Beware: If they feel threatened, howlers will shower you with their excrement. Cute, tuft-headed *macaco-pregos* (capuchin monkeys) are ubiquitous throughout Brazil, including in Rio's Floresta da Tijuca.

Among the most rare and physically striking monkeys in Brazil are the uakari and the *mico-leão* (lion tamarin). Uakaris are endangered but can be glimpsed at the Amazon's Marirauá Reserve. The fuzzy red uakari bears the nickname *macaco-inglês* (English monkey) due to its bald pink head and blushing red complexion. With faces that are framed by shaggy manes, *mico-leãos* really do resemble tiny lions (*leãos*). The rarest and most splendid of the species is the *mico-leão-dourado*, whose pelt and mane are a brilliant tawny-gold. A native of the Mata Atlântica of Rio de Janeiro, this striking squirrel-sized monkey was saved from extinction by the Associação Mico-Leão-Dourado (www.micoleao.org.br).

Aquatic Mammals

Of all the fascinating forms of wildlife in the Amazon, one of the easiest to observe is the legendary *boto* (pink river dolphin), an almost blind but very friendly creature whose skin is a startling shade of pink. At Novo Airão, in Amazonas, you can actually swim among these gentle animals. The more conservatively colored *tucuxi* (grey dolphin) can also be seen in Amazonian waters as well as up and down the Atlantic coastline. Much rarer and infinitely weirder looking is another native of the Amazon, the *peixe-boi* (manatee), a vast sausage-like beast that actually does, as its name implies, resemble a cross between a fish (*peixe*) and a bull (*boi*).

In terms of sea mammals, Brazil's Atlantic coast is home to seven species of whales. Following centuries of brutal slaughter, schools of frolicking *baleias francas do sul* (southern right whales) are back in circulation and can be easily spotted (between June and October) at the protected marine sanctuary off the coast of Praia do Rosa, in Santa Catarina. If you're in Bahia during the same time (in Praia do Forte or the Parque Nacional Marinho de Abrolhos), you can view the equally rare *baleias jubarte* (humpback whales) breeding. Meanwhile, one of the best places in the world for viewing vast schools of dolphins is on the island of Fernando de Noronha, whose sheltered coves are a favorite feeding spot for large schools of *golfinhos rotadores* (spinning dolphins).

REPTILES

Of course, the first thing that comes to mind when one hears the words Brazil and reptiles together in the same sentence is anacondas. Hero of trashy Amazonian terror movies, the anaconda does indeed live up to its fearful reputation. Adults can grow to well over 10 meters (33 feet) in length, and many live to be more than 20 years old. When it comes time to mate, a bunch of males wind themselves around a female for several weeks, after which the female shows her appreciation by eating one or two of her partners. Due to their size, anacondas have no predators (aside from humans in search of snakeskin), but they aren't shy about wrapping themselves around large prey and squeezing them to death before swallowing them whole (this includes people, although very rarely).

At home on dry land and in water, anacondas are common in the Amazon and the Pantanal. Other constrictors (known as *jibóias*) are considerably smaller (3–5 meters, 10–16 feet) and limit their crushing and feasting to small animals. While it's rare to come across poisonous *cobras* (snakes), which usually only attack when threatened, there are quite a few of such varieties including *víboras* (vipers), *cascavéis* (rattlesnakes), and *cobras coral* (coral snakes).

Brazil possesses several species of *jacarés* (the term used for both alligators and caimans). In the Pantanal, you'll encounter *jacarés-do-Pantanal* (Paraguayan caiman) everywhere (and probably even eat a couple as well—if you're up to it, the meat is surprisingly tender). The Amazon's tributaries are also overflowing with reptiles. The largest, but quite rare, is the *jacaré açu*, or black caiman, which grows to lengths of 6 meters (20 feet). Much more common is the smaller *jacaré tinga* (spectacled caiman).

Along the Atlantic coast, five species of formerly endangered *tartarugas marinhas* (sea turtles) are now thriving thanks to the creation of Projeto Tamar, a national project aimed at saving the turtles from humans who once hunted them for their shells and eggs. Today, in many seaside communities, locals help scientists monitor the reptiles (some of whom live to be over 100 years of age) at research stations situated all along the coast from Ceará to São Paulo.

FISH

Whether you want to catch them, eat them, or merely admire them, Brazil's waters are filled with eye-catching and mouthwatering fish. Along the Atlantic coast, sunken galleons and kilometer-long protective reefs offer ideal opportunities for snorkeling and diving amid gaudily hued schools. Inland, the Amazon and the Pantanal together boast close to 3,000 species living in their rivers, lakes, and tributaries.

The Amazon is home to some particularly exotic specimens. On the small end of the scale are the dozens of species of infamous fanged piranhas. Then there is the regally red- and silver-scaled pirarucu, the king of freshwater fish, which can grow to lengths of 3 meters (10 feet) and weigh up to 200 kilograms (440 pounds). The pirarucu is a favorite Amazonian delicacy, as are the much smaller but common *pirapitinga* and *tambaqui*, both of which are from the piranha family. The *tambaqui* usually uses its sharp teeth to crack open seeds and nuts, but if none are available, it will easily resort to carnivorism. Many varieties of catfish are also common; they make use of their "whiskers" to help them find food on river bottoms. Among the most common are the *piraiba*, which can grow to lengths of 3 meters (10 feet), and the golden-scaled *dourado* (dorado), which is enjoyed at tables throughout Brazil.

Freshwater inhabitants you'll want to steer clear of are *arraias* (stingrays), who live in still riverbeds. Their sting draws blood and can really hurt. *Poraquês* (electric eels) are also no laughing matter. They grow to over 2 meters (6.5 feet) in length, and a zap from one will send a 600-volt charge through your body.

BIRDS

Both hard-core and amateur birders will literally have a field day in Brazil. Not only is Brazil home to a fantastic diversity of winged creatures, but the riotous colors of their plumages are as spectacular as a Carnaval *desfile* (parade). In the Amazon and Atlantic rainforests and, in particular, the Pantanal you'll have plenty of opportunities to be awestruck by the Technicolor hues of *ararás* (macaws) and *papagaios* (parrots). Measuring around 90 centimeters (35 inches), macaws are the largest and most exhibitionistic of these birds. They can often be found in pairs, usually making quite a ruckus. The *arará vermelha* (scarlet macaw) is perhaps the most magnificent of all, its deep crimson face offset by brilliant blue and green wings. In addition to the Amazon and the Pantanal, it inhabits the Cerrado, as does the no-less-impressive *arará-canindé* (blue-and-yellow macaw), whose bright turquoise head and back contrast with a golden chest. Unfortunately, their beauty makes them a hot commodity on the illegal animal-trafficking circuit. In fact, poaching is responsible for the near extinction of the *arará-azul* (hyacinth macaw), which at 1 meter (3.3 feet) is the largest parrot on the planet. Once endemic throughout the Pantanal, today there are less than 3,000 of these birds. Their rich indigo feathers and yellow ringed eyes are astonishingly beautiful. Fortunately, the Projeto Arara Azul (www.projetoararaazul.org.br), whose headquarters is also in the Pantanal, is committed to the study and protection of these birds.

Other striking avian species are *tucanos* (toucans), who can be found in various forest habitats throughout Brazil. Residing in treetops where they can easily feast on fruit, these cartoon-like creatures are easily recognizable by their enormous, brightly colored bills (which are often as large as their bodies). Although the bills appear as if they would weigh the birds down, they consist of a spongy substance that is lighter than Styrofoam.

Wherever you travel in Brazil, you're bound to see plenty of *garças* (herons), *cegonhas* (storks), and other large, elegantly long-legged water birds. Two particularly unforgettable specimens are the bright red *guará* (scarlet ibis) and the *tuiuiú*, a tall stork. The bright crimson finery of the *guará* is often on display on Ilha de Marajó, Pará, and in Alcântara, in Maranhão. Meanwhile, the *tuiuiú* is the Pantanal's unofficial mascot, measuring 1.5 meters (5 feet), with an ebony head and a slender pink neck.

Among the various species of birds of prey, which include falcons, hawks, and eagles, the fiercest and most regal is the *águia real* (harpy eagle), an Amazonian bird that feasts on monkeys and other small prey.

In terms of size, Brazil can claim to possess both the largest and smallest birds in the Americas. The *ema* (rhea) is an ostrich-like flightless bird that can grow to the height of 1.5 meters (5 feet) and weigh 35 kilograms (77 pounds). In a metrosexual twist, male *emas* are not only responsible for building nests and incubating the giant eggs, but for raising the young chicks as well. Meanwhile, along with Ecuador, Brazil has the world's largest variety of tiny *beija-flores* (hummingbirds)—the

Portuguese name means "flower kisser." These tiny iridescent birds, which can measure as little as 6 centimeters (2.3 inches) and weigh only 2 grams (0.07 ounce), can be seen fluttering their aerodynamic wings throughout the country, including in cities where people often put out feeders for them. They drink up to five times their weight in nectar each day.

History

With alternating degrees of hope and cynicism, Brazilians have long referred to their country as the *"país do futuro"* ("country of the future"). However, Brazil's complex identity has been shaped by a fascinating past unlike that of any other nation in the Americas.

PREHISTORY

The verdict is still out as to when and from where the first indigenous populations arrived in South America. Dates vary from 10,000 to 30,000 years ago, and origins range from Asia (via a land bridge over the Bering Sea) to Africa (via canoe). Regardless of these conflicting theories, Brazilian Indians never developed the sophisticated cultures of their Andean neighbors, the Incas. As such, to date, very few pre-Colombian traces have been uncovered aside from the richly decorative glazed ceramic pots fashioned by the Marajó and Tapajó Indians of the Amazon and the expressive rock paintings found in the isolated caves of Gruta da Lapinha (Minas Gerais), the Parque Nacional da Serra da Capivara (Piauí), and the Amazonian town of Monte Alegre (Pará). However, the identities of the peoples who created these works are shrouded in mystery.

When the first Portuguese explorers arrived in 1500, an estimated 3–4 million Indians lived in Brazil. Scattered in small groups, and speaking well over 100 languages, most lived in villages, where they survived by hunting, fishing, and gathering as well as cultivating crops such as corn and manioc. One of the main groups was the Tupi-Guarani, a seminomadic people who originally spread out from the Amazon Basin, migrating south and east to the coast. It was the fierce Tupi that greeted the first Portuguese navigators and their crew. The

Europeans were quite enthralled with these "noble savages," and quickly began chronicling their lifestyles in manners both factual and fictional. When German mercenary Hans Staden was captured by a Tupi group in 1552, he was ritually fattened up and prepared for the feast—Tupi tradition involved eating one's enemies, with the aim of imbibing their courage. When Staden was ready to become stew, his very un-warrior-like display of tears so disgusted the Tupi that they released him. Although wimpy in the eyes of his captors, Staden wrote a tell-all memoir of his adventures, which became a major bestseller back in Europe and considerably raised curiosity about the vast new land across the ocean.

PORTUGUESE CONQUEST

In 1500, Portuguese explorer Pedro Alvares Cabral had set sail from Portugal in search of a western trade route to India. On April 22, his fleet of 13 ships arrived on the southern coast of Bahia (where Porto Seguro lies). Clambering ashore, the Portuguese planted a cross and held a mass at the spot they baptized Terra da Vera Cruz (Land of the True Cross). They spent the next 10 days exchanging trinkets with the local Tupi and evaluating the prospects of this palmy new land, which the Indians referred to as Pindorama (Land of Palms). The only potential spoil that sparked their interest was a native tree with a rich, glossy hard wood that yielded a deep red dye. When the expedition returned to Portugal, word got out about this exotic timber, known as *pau brasil*—*pau* means wood and *brasil* is said to be a derivation of *brasa*, a red, hot coal. Although the Portuguese were still much more interested in the spices and ivory of their African and Asian colonies, over the next few decades, ambitious traders sailed across the Atlantic to the land of the *brasil* wood, which soon became shortened to "Brazil." In return for metal tools and hardware, they had the Tupi cut down and harvest great quantities of brazilwood, whose crimson dye was highly coveted by European weaving factories.

Portugal only officially became interested in Brazil when French and Spanish merchants began showing a little too much interest in the new territory. Consequently, in 1532, in an attempt to stake claim to Brazil without actually have to take it on as a colony, King João III divided the Brazilian coast into 15 vast parcels, known as *capitânias,* which he distributed to various aristocratic cronies with the agreement that they would defend the territories, and hopefully find some more riches with which to further fill the crown's coffers. With the exception of Pernambuco, Bahia, and São Vicente (São Paulo), the *capitânia* concept proved a great failure. Without the presence of trained soldiers, Indians burned down fragile settlements and massacred their inhabitants. King João decided he would have to go the colonial route after all. In 1549, he abolished the *capitânias* and named Tomé de Sousa as the new governor general of Brazil. Accompanied by a force of soldiers, Jesuit priests, ex-convicts, and bureaucrats, Sousa arrived in Salvador da Bahia that same year and claimed the city as the capital of the Brazilian colony.

SUGAR AND SLAVERY

By the mid-1500s, *pau brasil* supplies were already drying up. However, in Pernambuco and Bahia, sugarcane had been successfully introduced to the rolling coastal hills. Tomé de Sousa incentivized the cultivation of sugar, which at the time was an exorbitantly expensive rarity in Europe. As Indians, who wouldn't become allies, were systematically wiped out, their lands were occupied by vast plantations that sprang up throughout the Northeast. Although attempts were made to enslave Indians to work the plantations, those who were domesticated often fell prey to European diseases to which they had no immunity. The alternative was to take advantage of the thriving African slave trade that was already making fortunes for European investors, including Portugal.

Beginning in the 1550s, Portugal began importing vast quantities of slaves from its African colonies of Mozambique and Angola, as well as West Africa and Congo. Transported like sardines in the holds of ships, those that survived the suffocating voyage were herded into slave markets such as Salvador's Mercado Modelo and then sold to plantation owners. They were forced to work grueling 16–17-hour days in scalding heat only to be herded at night into *senzalas,* dark and filthy quarters, in which they were often piled on top of one another so that their body heat could warm their masters on cool nights. Aside from horrible working and living conditions, slaves received cruel and unusual treatment for misbehaving or trying to escape. Punishments would range from being publicly flogged at pillories in main town squares (Salvador's Largo do Pelourinho, or Square of the Pillory, was the site of one such whipping post) to being subject to extreme forms of torture ranging from balls and chains to waterboarding.

The production of sugar became the number one source of profits for the Portuguese crown. It also created a wealthy colonial elite who poured their wealth into building extravagant churches and ornate mansions to adorn the thriving capitals of Salvador and Olinda. Sugar would also lay the foundations for the organization of Brazil's economy—as an exporter of monocultures (sugar, coffee, rubber, etc.), each of which would experience a boom-and-bust cycle—as well as its society. Plantation life—with the slaves in the *senzala* and the white aristocrats in their ornate mansions, known as *casa grandes*—would come to permeate Brazilian society. And its extreme legacy of a dual society that pits rich vs. poor and black vs. white exists to this day. While on one hand, plantation owners were cruel and racist towards slaves, they had no compunction about fornicating with them. Masters who didn't have a black mistress or legions of illegitimate *mulato* offspring were the exception, not the rule.

The consequence of this confusing behavior (aside from lots of slave women succumbing to syphilis) was the extreme miscegenation of Brazil's population. In modern times, this has given rise to the myth of Brazil's racial harmony, but it also set the standard for a hidden but deeply rooted racism and glaring inequality that still pervades Brazilian society and manifests itself in subtle but shocking ways.

EUROPEAN THREATS AND INVASIONS

Portugal's thriving colony incited the envy of its European neighbors. In the early 1500s, the robust *pau brasil* commerce had lured French interests. In 1550, a French expedition sailed into the Baía de Guanabara and staked claim to the area, with the intent of creating a southern colony baptized French Antarctica. The Portuguese were not at all pleased with this plan. In 1565, they founded the city of São Sebastião do Rio de Janeiro, and a few years later, they had successfully expulsed the French from the region. When the determined French tried to get a foothold in the Northeast by founding a city of their own, called Saint-Louis, in 1594, the Portuguese succeeded in giving them the boot in 1615, and changing the city's name to the more patriotic sounding São Luís.

Even more serious was the threat of the Dutch, who, with lucrative but tiny sugar-producing colonies in the Caribbean, were salivating at the chance of adding the vast Northeast to their possessions. Their initial foray into Brazil—an attack upon and occupation of Salvador in 1624—was short-lived when they were driven back by Portuguese troops. However, the persistent Dutch, sponsored by the expansive Dutch West Indian Company, then set their sights on Pernambuco, which at the time was the world's largest producer of sugar. After burning the capital of Olinda to the ground in 1637, the Protestant Dutch established their own colonial headquarters. To govern the new colony, along came Mauritz van Nassau, an enlightened university-educated count, who not only increased the output of sugar, but also placated the Portuguese Catholic sugar barons by installing a policy of religious tolerance and creating strategic alliances with remaining Indian groups. By 1640, the capital of Mauritzstaad (later renamed Recife) was a booming port city, and Pernambuco was more stable and richer than it had ever been. Moreover, much to Portuguese chagrin, the Dutch had successfully extended their foothold from Maranhão in the north to Alagoas in the South. Brazilians might have been speaking Dutch today if Mauritz van Nassau hadn't resigned, in 1644, disgusted with the greed and narrow-mindedness of the Dutch West Indian Company administrators. With popular Nassau's departure, the Portuguese settlers rose up throughout the Northeast. Throughout the next decade, the Dutch were massacred and their plantations razed. Finally, only Recife was left in Dutch hands, and after two decisive battles in 1648 and 1649, they surrendered in 1654, leaving all of Brazil definitively in Portuguese hands.

JESUITS AND *BANDEIRANTES*

Of course, Portugal's major rival for control of South America had always been Spain. Back in 1494, when both nations were the undisputed colonial powers of the world, the Treaty of Tordesilhas had preemptively sought to settle future territorial disputes by carving the New World into two large pieces. An imaginary line that stretched from the mouth of the Amazon River to the south of Santa Catarina effectively sliced the South American continent in half. Although according to the rules, everything west of the line belonged to Spain, and everything east belonged to Portugal, in reality, the imaginary frontier—much of which stretched through impenetrable rainforest of the Amazon and Pantanal wetlands of Mato Grosso—was difficult to monitor.

Jesuit missionaries, who had tight connections with the Portuguese crown, were the first to work their way deep into the unknown Brazilian interior. The first missionaries arrived in Salvador in 1549 and set to work building the second-largest Jesuit college after Rome. Intent on converting (and subjugating) the local Indian population, they headed west into the Amazon and south towards the Pampas bordering Brazil, Argentina, and Uruguay, and founded missions into which Indians were herded. Throughout the 1600s, Jesuit influence in Brazil grew enormously. While some Jesuits exploited Indians, using them as unpaid labor, and exposed them to fatal diseases, others protected them from Portuguese settlers intent on enslaving the "savages." The most famous of these humanitarian missionaries was Antônio Vieira, a former adviser to the king, who was based in São Luís. Vieira's sermons preaching tolerance and criticizing inhumane treatment of Indians were so eloquent that they were published in Europe, and so controversial that they led furious settlers to expel him from Brazil in 1661. Meanwhile, the Jesuits in Rio Grande do Sul were so protective of the Guarani Indians that, in 1752, when the Treaty of Madrid divided up the region containing a dozen missions between Spanish and Portuguese settlers, the missionaries stood by the Guarani in refusing to leave. The noble resistance proved futile. Both Jesuits and Indians were massacred by Spanish and Portuguese troops. Moreover, the missionaries' role was a major factor in the order's definitive expulsion from Brazil in 1760.

The other people responsible for the exploration and opening up of Brazil's vast interior were the *bandeirantes*. Rough and ready bands of explorers in search of riches and Indians to enslave, *bandeirantes* took their name from the *bandeiras* (flags) that accompanied their roving expeditions. The first *bandeirante* expeditions began in the early 17th century. The main point of departure was São Paulo, due to its strategic location on the banks of the Rio Tietê, one of the few major rivers that flowed west into the interior. Many *bandeirantes* were *mestiços*, the progeny of Portuguese fathers and Indian mothers. Their Indian heritage gave them knowledge of navigating the dangers of the wilderness, but didn't stop them from unceremoniously wiping out any indigenous groups that happened to cross their path with arms and (more commonly) diseases. The distances covered by these ruthless but intrepid explorers were immense, and their discoveries filled in the contours of the Brazilian map. Many towns throughout the western regions of Goiás, Mato Grosso, and even the lower Amazon were founded by *bandeirantes*, whose expeditions often lasted for years.

Although in the early decades, the *bandeirantes* certainly found many Indians, the riches eluded them until the late 1600s. In 1695, a small group of *bandeirantes* happened upon some glittering nuggets in a river, at the spot that is now Sabará, in Minas Gerais. The find kicked off the biggest gold rush in the New World. Although deposits were found as far west as Goiás and Mato Grosso, most of the glitter was concentrated in the central mountainous region that came to be known as Minas Gerais (General Mines). During the boom years, which lasted 1700–1750, hundreds of thousands of fortune hunters descended upon the region. Many died poor, of hunger and disease; others grew filthy rich. Overnight, precarious miners' outposts blossomed into towns such as Ouro Preto, Mariana, São João del Rei, and Tiradentes, where wealthy merchants poured their money into grandiose mansions, posh restaurants and hotels, and sumptuous baroque churches whose interiors were awash in gold leaf. Vast numbers of slaves were imported (some directly from Africa, others from Bahia) to work the mines, where conditions proved worse than in the sugarcane fields.

Naturally, Portugal (which was increasingly in debt) was thrilled with the discovery of gold. Built by slaves, roads constructed out of thick stone led through the mountains of Minas and down to the ports of Rio de Janeiro and Paraty, from where the gold was shipped off to Lisbon. In fact, it was Rio's newfound importance as a strategic maritime port that elevated the humid and filthy backwater town on the shores of Guanabara Bay to capital of Brazil (a title it usurped from Salvador in 1763). The move signaled the beginning of the end of the northeastern Brazil's economic and political supremacy in favor of the southeastern "triangle" formed by Minas Gerais, Rio de Janeiro, and São Paulo.

INDEPENDENCE

The gold boom was explosive, but fleeting. By the mid-1700s, the precious metal was increasingly hard to find. But the Portuguese crown still insisted on taxing and appropriating every last nugget. Gradually Brazilian settlers' anger rose and, fanned by revolutionary ideas imported from France, culminated in the revolt known as the Inconfidência Mineira. Led by an Ouro Preto dentist known as Tiradentes ("Toothpuller"), a dozen outraged Mineiro citizens conspired to rise up against the Portuguese. After their plans were discovered, all plotters were exiled to Mozambique and Angola, with the exception of Tiradentes. The Toothpuller was hung in public in Rio before having his severed body parts paraded around Ouro Preto as a warning to future rebels. The horrific measures only succeeded in transforming Tiradentes into a national hero and fanning the flames of independence. Indeed, the Inconfidência Mineira was only one of many popular revolts that erupted throughout the 18th century as settlers who increasingly considered themselves native Brazilians chafed under the authority of Portugal and its colonial administrators.

While citizens of all other South American nations waged battles against their colonial oppressors to achieve independence, Brazil's road to independence took a surprising and unlikely turn. In 1807, having already conquered most of Europe, Napoleon had his eyes set on Portugal. As the French emperor's troops descended upon Lisbon, King João VI of Portugal and his entire court jumped aboard a fleet of ships and fled across the ocean to Brazil. In 1808, the king and his royal retinue of 15,000 disembarked in Rio de Janeiro, which immediately became the new capital of the Portuguese empire. The court's presence quickly transformed Rio from a muddy, mosquito-infested, rough colonial town to a thriving and increasingly elegant capital with grand avenues, parks, and palaces. It also became incredibly cosmopolitan as the king opened the ports to European traders (primarily its English allies) and invited artists, scientists, and scholars from all over Europe to take up residence in Rio. João himself was so taken with his tropical court that he was loath to relinquish it, even after the English defeated Napoleon. When he finally returned to Portugal in 1621 to quell a popular uprising, he left his son Pedro in charge as Prince Regent of Brazil.

Young Pedro was impetuous and impatient. Just like his new Brazilian subjects, he quickly grew fed up with having to comply with rules set down by Portugal, whose interests were increasingly at odds with those of its thriving colony. This rebellious stance came to a head in 1822. On September 7, Pedro was getting ready to ride his horse on the shores of the Ipiranga River, near São Paulo, when a messenger arrived with a handful of letters from Lisbon. The demands of the Portuguese court so angered him that he uttered the famous cry "Independence or death!" thus declaring Brazil independent. With crises enough of their own at home, Portugal put up little resistance aside from some last-chance battles in Salvador, Fortaleza, and Belém between Brazilians and loyal Portuguese. On December 1, Pedro crowned himself Dom Pedro I, and became the first and only New World emperor.

EMPIRE

Due to his headstrong and autocratic nature (coupled with numerous sex scandals), Pedro I's imperial reign was short-lived. In 1824, he presided over the creation of Brazil's first constitution and, in theory, accepted his status as constitutional monarch. In practice, just as he had refused to cooperate with Portugal's government, he wouldn't share power with Brazilian members of parliament. When increasingly pressed to do so, he once again lost his temper and abdicated. In 1831, he returned to Portugal, leaving Brazil in the hands of his 5-year-old son, Pedro II. Without a strong leader in charge, over the next decade revolts broke out throughout the country, from Pará and Maranhão in the north to Rio Grande do Sul. Brazilians fought against

Portuguese loyalists, slaves rebelled against their masters, the poor rose up against the privileges of wealthy landowners.

Faced with the risk of the country being torn apart, Pedro II was quickly crowned emperor in 1840. Although only 14, Dom Pedro II was a highly intelligent, progressive, and judicious leader who was admired by both the conservative elite and the more liberal republicans. His authority quickly quelled the regional uprisings, and under his long reign Brazil enjoyed growth and stability. During this time, the Southeast definitively eclipsed the Northeast in importance, spurred on by Rio's political and cultural importance and the beginning of the lucrative coffee boom, which brought a flood of European immigrants to the fertile hills of Rio de Janeiro, São Paulo, and Paraná as well as to the cities of the South.

ABOLITION OF SLAVERY

A main reason for the demise of the Northeast was slavery, or rather its end. Since Brazil's earliest days as a colony, an estimated 10 million slaves had been shipped across the Atlantic from Africa—roughly 10 times the number transported to the United States. Despite the cruel punishments they faced, many slaves revolted. Countless others escaped. Throughout Brazil, but particularly in the Northeast, the fugitives established isolated communities known as *quilombos*. Although they lived a subsistence existence, many were able to preserve the religious and cultural traditions of their African ancestors, some of which survive to this day. The most biggest and most famous *quilombo* of Palmares, located in northern Alagoas, functioned as a veritable republic. Led by the fierce warrior Zumbi, the *quilombo* was able to defend itself from white settlers and government troops for years. Although Zumbi was finally betrayed and killed, he became a national symbol of black resistance.

However, there was no way Brazilian plantation owners were going to give up their lifestyle and wealth by voluntarily liberating slaves, as dictated to them by their English trading partners, who abolished slavery in 1807. Although they paid lip service to the British by pretending to embark upon reforms, in reality their efforts were *para inglês ver* ("for the English to see")—an expression that is still used today to express the act of pretending to do something (but not really doing it). The English weren't fooled. During the 1830s and '40s, they sent navy vessels to the Brazilian coast to capture slave ships and confiscate their human cargo. As a result, Brazil abolished the slave trade in 1854, but slavery was still legal in Brazil. As a growing abolitionist movement spread across more enlightened regions of the country, Dom Pedro II reluctantly signed laws freeing the children of female slaves (1871) and (the very few) slaves over the age of 65 (1885). Finally, on May 13, 1888, his daughter, Princesa Isabel, signed the Lei Áurea, giving Brazil the dubious distinction of being the last of the New World nations to ban slavery.

The end of slavery had several major repercussions. It brought about the demise of the northeastern sugar and cotton plantation economies and caused the region (and its landowning elite) to enter a long period of decadence that would take a century to recuperate from. It also created a vast population of free but poor and uneducated black Brazilians, who had to fend for themselves and find work (a phenomenon that often sadly led to a life of "paid" slavery).

Politically, abolition was the final straw that broke the Brazilian empire. For some time, fueled by Europe's republican tendencies, Brazil's growing urban intellectual classes had been clamoring for the end of the monarchy. Increasingly, Pedro II's staunchest defenders had been the conservative land-owning elite. But when he had the gall to end slavery, they too turned their backs on him. The final nail in the emperor's coffin was the ill-fated Paraguay War (1865–1870), in which Brazil, Argentina, and Uruguay ganged up on their puny, but fierce, neighbor Paraguay. Although they practically eliminated the male population of Paraguay, the powerful allies didn't emerge unscathed from battle. Brazil lost 100,000 men and racked up serious debts, and Pedro II lost the support of the military. In 1889, a group of army officers, led by Marechal (Marshall) Manuel Deodoro da Fonseca, staged a bloodless coup d'état. Dom Pedro returned to Europe, where he died two years later in Paris.

REPUBLIC

Although the idea had been to install a liberal republic, Deodoro preferred to become the nation's first of many military dictators. Within weeks, however, he proved so incompetent that not even the military would back him, and he was forced to step down. His deputy, Marechal Floriano Peixoto, was even worse. After he too was forced to resign, Brazil finally received its first democratically elected president in the person of Prudente de Morais.

The first Brazilian republic (1890–1930) coincided with a period of economic boom spurred on by two major cash crops: coffee and rubber. By 1890, coffee represented two-thirds of Brazil's exports and was responsible for propelling the small town of São Paulo into a thriving city that gradually became the economic hub of Brazil. Coffee barons built lavish mansions along the country lane that would gradually morph into Avenida Paulista. They also wisely invested in industry (initially textiles), foreseeing the day that Brazil's coffee boom might go bust. The rubber barons of the Amazon were not nearly so shrewd. In the mid-19th century, Charles Goodyear's invention of vulcanization coincided with the (re)discovery of the latex produced by an Amazonian tree known as *hevea brasiliensis* (the region's Indians had been making rubber for centuries). Floods of fortune seekers from all over the world descended upon the primitive rainforest to tap for this rare commodity coveted by budding First World industries. The fabulous fortunes made were spent on transforming the cities of Belém and Manaus into tropical versions of Paris, with grand boulevards, theaters, and pretensions (such as wearing fur coats to go to the opera). But when rubber seeds were secretly smuggled out of the forest by an Englishman to British colonies in Asia whose plantations were much more efficient, the rubber boom went bust, and the barons went

bankrupt. The Amazon returned to its former slumber, from which it would only awaken in the late 20th century.

Like São Paulo, Minas Gerais boasted a large population and thriving economy. Although coffee grew in Minas's lush hills, the richest and most powerful interests were the landowners who raised dairy cows. Together with São Paulo's coffee barons, they formed a powerful elite and became so influential in national government that Brazilian politics came to be defined as the system of *café com leite* (coffee with milk), an allusion to the fact that not only did these local interests dominate all policies, but that all presidencies during this period alternated between cronies from São Paulo and Minas. Thanks to the privileges enjoyed and the corruption that ensued, it wasn't long before popular revolts began to take place, particularly among the growing number of working-class Brazilians.

GETÚLIO VARGAS AND THE ESTADO NOVO

The increasing dissatisfaction with *café com leite* politics came to a head in 1930. The Great Depression knocked the bottom out of the coffee market. To save the coffee elite from ruin, the government spent millions buying coffee at a fixed rate, only to burn the harvest for lack of foreign buyers. Workers and leaders from other parts of the country were outraged. Violent revolts broke out in the Northeast, Rio, and Rio Grande do Sul, home of a charismatic and populist politician named Getúlio Vargas. When a military coup deposed the government, Vargas became Brazil's new president—for the next 15 years. An astute politician, fervent nationalist, and flamboyant populist (along the lines of his colleague in neighboring Argentina, Juan Perón), Vargas ushered in a new era. He jump-started Brazilian industry by nationalizing the burgeoning oil, steel, and electrical sectors. He endeared himself to the masses by creating a health and social welfare system. He implemented a minimum wage and labor laws and extended the right to vote to women. The way he carried out these radical reforms was by declaring himself dictator and establishing a regime known as the Estado Novo (New State), which went into effect in 1937. Opposition parties were prohibited, the press was censored, and dissidence was punished with jail sentences. While democracy went into hiding, his centralized government broke the hold of the regional elite, and agriculture and industry thrived.

When World War II broke out, Brazil remained neutral although Vargas flirted with both the Axis and the Allies. Coaxed by promises of generous American financial aid in return for the right to establish U.S. military bases along the Northeast coast, Vargas finally chose the Allied side in 1942, sending Brazilian soldiers to participate in the invasion of Italy. However, the contradiction between fighting for freedom abroad while running a fascist dictatorship at home proved difficult to justify. At the end of the war, military pressure convinced Vargas to relinquish his powers in 1945. However, Vargas always remained largely popular with the Brazilian people, who returned him to power in 1950—this time as a democratically elected president. However, without his fascist powers to protect him, his tenure was marred by public accusations of corruption. The fiercest attacks were spearheaded by a Carioca journalist with political ambitions of his own, named Carlos Lacerda. When an attack on Lacerda's life was traced to one of Vargas's bodyguards, the ensuing scandal was so great that Vargas was asked to resign. Instead, on the night of August 4, 1954, he went into his bedroom at the Palácio do Catete, in Rio, and shot himself through the heart after leaving a love letter/suicide note to the Brazilian people. Popular grief was so great that Lacerda was forced to leave the country.

JK AND BRASÍLIA

Juscelino Kubitschek (popularly known as "JK") won the 1956 presidential elections with the aid of the snappy campaign slogan "Fifty years in five" (i.e., he would accomplish in five years what most leaders could only accomplish in 50). The visionary and determined Kubitschek—who had cut his political teeth as mayor of Belo Horizonte and governor of Minas Gerais—promised Brazilians a future of great growth and change. He set about making good on his promise by immediately hiring a team of highly talented modernist architects to build a utopian new Brazilian capital in the geographical heart of the nation. Although the spot for Brasília's construction was literally located in the middle of nowhere, Kubitschek's ambitious goal was to open up Brazil's vast and deserted interior to settlement and development. Many critics thought he was insane—particularly Rio's political elite, who were loath to forsake the Cidade Maravilhosa for the dry and dusty Planalto Central—but the *"bossa nova presidente"* proved them wrong. With a team led by brilliant architect Oscar Niemeyer, construction of the space-age capital advanced at rapid speed.

In the end, Kubitschek fulfilled his promise to the people. Before his term was over, he presided over the April 21, 1960, inauguration of the new capital, an event that was celebrated with much pomp. The only problem was the massive bill. Despite the fact that Kubitschek had presided over a period of strong economic growth, the costs of building Brasília left the nation in serious debt, which would later play a factor in the astronomic rates of inflation that gripped Brazil in the 1970s.

MILITARY RULE (1964-1985)

JK was succeeded by much lesser men. Neither Jânio Quadros (who lasted only six months in power) nor his vice president and successor, João Goulart, possessed the skill necessary to deal with rising inflation or resolve the growing social conflicts that pitted urban workers against factory owners and rural peasants against rich landowners. Moreover, with a Cold War fear of communism in the air, Goulart's leftist leanings terrified the Brazilian right (including the military), particularly when the new president decided to explicitly support the trade unions and peasant organizations. On March 31, 1964, with implicit backing of the U.S. government, led by a small group of right-wing generals, military troops carried out a quick and nonviolent coup. While Goulart was deposed and went into exile in Uruguay, the generals set to work transforming Brazil into a military dictatorship. Humberto Castelo Branco became president—the first in a series of generals to lead the country by iron rule over the next quarter of a century. Congress was dissolved, political parties were banned, unions were outlawed, and the media was censored. The situation grew even more drastic when General Emílio Garrastazú Medici took over in 1969. The next five years proved to be the most brutal of Brazil's military regime. Thousands of people were arrested, jailed, tortured, and even killed for even the most indirect criticism, "subversive" political beliefs, or the expression of ideas deemed unsuitable by the regime. Many leading artists and intellectuals (among them leading musicians such as Chico Buarque and Gilberto Gil, along with professor and later president Fernando Henrique Cardoso) went into exile during these years. While Brazil's dictatorship was less hard-line than those of its neighbors, Chile and Argentina—where hundreds of thousands were made to "disappear"—there was widespread hatred of the military leaders, who were not only cruel, but corrupt as well.

During the first decade of military rule, Brazil experienced phenomenal rates of economic growth that surpassed 10 percent a year. This period became known as the "Economic Miracle." Industry boomed and an exodus of workers from the poor Northeast migrated en masse to the manufacturing hub of São Paulo, which grew to become Latin America's financial and economic powerhouse. While many found factory jobs and other low-wage employment, others clustered in shacks on the growing city outskirts. Indeed, while some Brazilians grew rich, far more remained miserable as these slums, known as *favelas,* began to mushroom in major cities.

To further stimulate development, the government drummed up foreign investors to finance immense (and controversially dubious) mega projects such as the Itaipu Dam, near Iguaçu Falls, and the Transamazônica highway (which opened up access through the impenetrable forest, all the way to the Peruvian border). The problem came when the oil crisis of 1974 punctured the Economic Miracle. By the beginning of the '80s, as inflation soared and Brazilian currency took a nosedive, foreign investors started clamoring for Brazil to pay up its enormous and constantly multiplying debts.

PERIOD OF *ABERTURA* (1979-1985)

Increasingly fed up with censorship, corruption scandals, and a crippled economy, Brazil's middle classes and workers began to express widespread opposition to the military dictatorship. In São Paulo, a series of workers' strikes spread like wildfire. A leader for the illegal unions was a young worker from Pernambuco who had lost a finger in a factory accident. Luís Inácio da Silva (who went by the nickname Lula) was a fierce and charismatic leader. When the government sent troops to repress the striking workers, Lula and his colleagues stood their ground. The government was forced not only to back down, but to legalize unions as well. Fearing mass revolts, President João Figueiredo also began to implement certain reforms, part of a gradual *"abertura"* (opening) process that would pave the way for Brazil's return to democratic rule. Censorship rules were relaxed and political dissidents were allowed to return from exile. In 1982, the first democratic municipal and state elections were held.

Federal elections were called for 1985. The military government had allowed several official opposition parties to be formed. Among them was the Partido dos Trabalhadores (PT), or Workers' Party, one of whose founders was Lula. However, loath to completely relinquish power, the generals also decided that the new president would be elected by an electoral college made up of members with strong military sympathies. The opposition parties' furor erupted in a campaign for *"direitas já"* (direct elections now), which propelled millions of outraged citizens to the streets. Despite the overwhelming support of the public and opposition parties, the military-friendly Senate managed to defeat the *direitas já* amendment. However, they couldn't defeat Tancredo Neves, a highly respected Mineiro politician who had been Getúlio Vargas's minister of justice. As the opposition candidate running against yet another general, Neves not only seduced electoral college voters from all the opposition parties, but swayed many disenchanted military stalwarts as well. As a result, in January of 1985, Neves won a resounding majority. Throughout Brazil, elated citizens took to the streets to celebrate the end of military dictatorship and the beginning of a Nova República (New Republic).

RETURN OF DEMOCRACY

Brazilians anxiously waited for the first civilian president in two decades to be sworn in as president. Tragically, the night before his inauguration ceremony, Tancredo Neves was rushed to the hospital with a bleeding stomach tumor. Although the tumor wasn't fatal, the hospital was. Neves caught septicemia, a bacterial infection that led to his death. After millions mourned him, they watched the televised swearing in of his vice president, José Sarney, an old-school and uninspiring former state governor from Maranhão. As Brazil's first new democratic president, Sarney quickly dashed Brazilians' hopes of a better future. Due to the ballooning foreign debt, inflation was so high that currencies were adopted and discarded with regularity. Meanwhile, an uncensored press was free to report the endless string of financial scandals that sullied the government's reputation and filled struggling Brazilians with disgust.

Things only got worse with the election of Sarney's successor: a pretty-boy millionaire and karate champ named Fernando Collor de Melo. A dashing figure who wouldn't have been out of place on a nightly *novela* (soap opera), Collor had been governor of the small northeastern state of Alagoas and was a member of one of its oldest and richest families. After narrowly defeating Lula da Silva of the PT in 1990, he presided over a government whose disasters reached epic proportions. Collor's solution to controlling hyper inflation was to freeze Brazilians' bank accounts, a measure that quickly incited the wrath of the middle classes (poor Brazilians don't have bank accounts and, at the time, rich Brazilians had their money stashed overseas). Feelings of outrage spread throughout the populace when it came to light (via Collor's own brother, Pedro) that Collor and his cronies had been siphoning billions of dollars in public money into private accounts. The scandal was so great that Congress began impeachment proceedings, spurred on by hundreds of thousands of Brazilians who took to the streets demanding justice. Forced to step down in September of 1992, Collor was banned from political office for eight years. Much of this time, he spent in Miami, working on his tan and plotting his comeback, which—in keeping with Brazilian political norms—took place when he was re-elected in 2006 for an eight-year term as a senator for his home state of Alagoas.

Collor was replaced by his vice president, Itamar Franco, a weak figure who nonetheless had the inspired decision to select as his finance minister a clever politician and savvy economist named Fernando Henrique Cardoso. Known popularly as "FHC," Cardoso was a widely respected São Paulo sociologist with leftist leanings who went into exile during the military dictatorship. By the time he joined Franco's government, his politics had migrated to the center-right, as had his economics, which were influenced by years spent teaching and studying in the United States. FHC took on Brazil's floundering economy by implementing the "Plano Real" in 1994. By creating a new currency, the *real,* and tying its value to the U.S. dollar, Cardoso finally brought runaway inflation to a grinding halt for the first time in decades. When elections were held the following year, he easily defeated his rival, Lula.

With FHC as president for the next eight years (1994–2002), the New Republic finally had its first serious and competent leader. Inflation remained low and the economy began to grow in leaps and bounds, spurred on by rampant privatization of corrupt and inefficient public companies, the opening up of the Brazil's frontiers to foreign capital and interests, and the relaxation of importation barriers. Although initially, inefficiently run companies that had survived due to lack of foreign competition sank, many others were forced to get competitive in a hurry, and they did so, reaching international levels of quality, efficiency, and innovation. Massive economic reforms were accompanied by the beginnings of much-needed political and social reforms with particular focus upon the critical areas of health and education. However, the eternally gaping distance between Brazil's haves and have-nots was hardly bridged at all. Moreover, during FHC's second presidential term a series of large-scale corruption scandals once again revealed the fundamentally rotten state of Brazil's political and justice systems.

THE PARTIDO DOS TRABALHADORES AND PRESIDENT LUÍS INÁCIO DA SILVA

After competing (and being narrowly defeated) in every presidential election since 1990, in 2001 the charismatic leader of the Partido dos Trabalhadores (PT), Luís Inácio ("Lula") da Silva, finally triumphed on his fourth attempt. Lula's victory was truly a watershed moment in Brazil's turbulent, and often tragic, political history. In a country that for 500 years had been ruled by members of the wealthy elite, it was nothing short of miraculous that a poor boy from the drought-ridden Sertão of Pernambuco, without a university education, should rise to the nation's most powerful position. As a boy, Lula had escaped poverty by traveling to São Paulo crammed into the back of a truck. Arriving in the big city, he rose from a shoeshine boy to factory worker to union leader and champion of workers' rights to leader of the PT. But nobody ever thought he'd wind up president.

Excluding conservatives made nervous by his Marxist rants of the past, Brazil's masses, along with its intellectual and artistic classes, went wild over Lula's triumph. In the heady early months of his mandate, the popular and populist soccer-playing and *churrasco*-eating president was greeted as something of a messiah. However, his common touch aside, the apprehensive rich and right-wingers needn't have worried. Over the years, Lula had toned down his firebrand rhetoric substantially (becoming known as "Lula Light"). Aside from awarding top government ministries to radical leftist dissidents of the dictatorship years and making no secret of his friendships with Cuba's Fidel Castro and Venezuela's Hugo Chavez, Lula (much to the dismay of more hard-core members of the PT) stayed the central course mapped out by his predecessor, FHC.

Economically, he continued to steer Brazil on the road to increasing globalization, which has resulted in a booming Brazilian economy. More importantly, his government has made headway in addressing some of the glaring social disparities that have always led Brazil to being compared to an uneasy fusion of Belgium and Bangladesh. Increasing numbers of children are attending school (with the aid of subsidies paid to parents). And for the first time in history, the standard of living of Brazil's poor is finally on the upswing as minimum salaries rise, interest rates fall, and credit has become easily available to people who want to buy homes or start small businesses. The situation has improved the most in the Northeast and North, which were traditionally the most neglected of Brazil's regions.

On the downside, while the PT was revered for its socialist ideals and integrity during its 20-year role as the main opposition party to successive governments, once the party came to power, it wasn't long before the "power corrupts" adage kicked in. By 2005, scams and scandals began to erupt on a massive scale, and many idealists and die-hard supporters of the Workers' Party felt incredibly betrayed that the PT of all parties should prove as immoral as all the rest. Amid flying accusations, rather than face interminable investigations that would bring government reforms to a standstill, many of Lula's scandal-tainted ministers chose to resign. Through it all, Lula claimed to know nothing about anything. While the PT's reputation was severely tarnished, Lula himself emerged unscathed (with the nickname the "Teflon president" since nothing bad "stuck" to him). Despite the damage done to the party, Lula was elected to a second presidential term in November 2006.

To date, Brazil has come a long way towards becoming a mature and stable democracy with a robust economy. Within Latin America, Brazil has emerged as a regional leader and an inspiration to other nations. Meanwhile, its self-sufficiency in oil, its vanguard position in terms of biodiesels, and its increasingly important role as a supplier of raw and finished products have propelled Brazil onto the world stage, where it is routinely compared with other emerging powers such as China and India. At home, major problems still exist, particularly in terms of public safety, quality of public health and education, corruption, and poverty. Despite some improvements, much-needed reforms to the justice and political systems are needed to end the culture of impunity that reigns at all levels, and which prevents Brazil from living up to its potential and evolving into a truly significant global player. However, obstacles aside, it can safely be said that at no other time in history have the reality of Brazil's present and the promise of this *país do futuro* appeared so closely aligned.

Government

The Federal Republic of Brazil is a democratic system of government that resembles the federal United States of America. The elected president is both the head of state and the head of the federal government. Brazil's current Constitution dates from 1988.

ORGANIZATION

Brazil's national government consists of three branches: the executive, the legislative, and the judiciary. The head of the executive branch is the President of the Republic, who is elected to office by universal suffrage. Voting is done by an extremely high-tech, computerized ballot system. Error or fraud is almost impossible. Voters who can't read can choose the candidate of their choice by selecting a head shot. To this day, Brazilians are amazed by the infamous system of chads in the United States. Voting is mandatory for all literate citizens between 18 and 70 years of age. Brazilians who don't vote must present an official justification or pay a (small) fine.

The president chooses a running mate who will be the vice president. Should anything happen to the president, the vice president assumes his or her position for the rest of the four-year term. Once elected to office, the president may appoint his/her own ministers, which he or she can also dismiss at any time. According to the Brazilian Constitution, if there is just cause, Congress can vote to have the president be removed from office through impeachment.

Brazil's legislative power is concentrated in the hands of the National Congress (Congresso), which consists of two houses: The Chamber of Deputies (Câmara dos Deputados) is the lower house, and the Senate (Senado) is the upper house. The Chamber of Deputies seats 513 deputies representing each of the Brazilian states in numbers proportional to their population. Deputies are elected by popular vote for terms of four years. The Senate seats 81 senators—three for each of Brazil's 26 states and three for the Federal District of Brasília. Senators are elected for terms of eight years. Both deputies and senators can run for reelection as many times as they want.

The judiciary is headed by the Federal Supreme Court, which is the highest court in the land. Its main headquarters are in Brasília, but the court's jurisdiction extends throughout the country. Its 11 judges are appointed for life by the president upon approval from a Senate majority; judges in state courts are also appointed for life.

POLITICAL PARTIES

Brazil's party system is fairly chaotic to an outsider. Parties are created and disappear all the time, and candidates easily and opportunistically switch from one to another without any compunction (recently passed reforms have tried to limit this habit). Most often this party switching occurs a few months prior to an election. Both the party names and more commonly used acronyms are confusing to keep track of, even for Brazilians. Many have no ideological affiliation whatsoever. There are, however, a few main parties whose delegates usually compete for major positions. Presently, after being the country's main opposition party, the traditionally left-wing Partido dos Trabalhadores (Workers' Party), or PT, wields power in the federal government. Other major parties that hover around the center and center-right include the Partido do Movimento Democrático Brasileiro (Brazilian Democratic Movement Party), or PMDB; the Partido da Social Democrácia Brasileira (Brazilian Social Democracy Party), or PSDB; and the Democratas (Democrats) or DEM, which recently changed its name from the Partido Frente Liberal (Liberal Front Party), or PFL. Currently, governing Brazil is all about making strategic alliances with members of other parties in order to pass (or defeat) legislation. In general, reaching a consensus involves enormous amounts of time and energy (not to mention bribes—in the form of favors or money).

Ironically, in spite of the many scandals and cover-ups, in some ways, the operation of Brazilian Congress is extremely transparent. In theory, any Brazilian (or visiting tourist) can sit in on the daily sessions in the Chamber of Deputies or Senate (you will often be amazed at the low attendance, particularly on a Friday). Moreover, Senate debates are broadcast live on a television station known as TV Senado. During major government scandals, this can make for quite dramatic viewing.

JUDICIAL AND PENAL SYSTEMS

Brazilian law is derived from Portuguese civil law. The principal legal document is the National Constitution of 1988, which divides power between federal and state judicial branches. State-level courts preside over all civil and criminal cases (with appeals taken to regional federal courts). The Supreme Court (Supremo Tribunal Federal) makes final, binding decisions on legal matters and is also in charge of interpreting the Constitution. Justice, when it is delivered in Brazil, is famously slow. Loopholes are seemingly endless and lawsuits can be delayed by numerous appeals. Often a final ruling can be delayed for years, if not decades.

Justice is definitely not blind in Brazil. The rich, white, and powerful often literally get away with murder while the poorer you are and the darker your skin tone, the greater your chances of being beaten up, tossed in a crowded cell, and locked away. Crime is a big problem throughout all of Brazil, but the shamelessness with which white collar crime is committed is staggering. Through fraud, embezzlement, kick-backs, and bribes, billions of dollars in public funds are routinely siphoned away from the people who need it most. Then as the have-nots resort to ever more violent holdups, kidnappings, and break-ins, Brazil's elite largely wall themselves up in closed condominium complexes with electric fences, cameras, and bodyguards. It's a very vicious, not to mention tragic, cycle and one of Brazil's greatest challenges. In recent years, some small instances of justice have shaken the complete impunity with which the rich and powerful operate. However, in most cases, change is difficult because it's in the interest of many of those in the upper echelons that the status quo remain the same.

Similarly, by law, penal conditions for criminals who have committed the same crime vary depending on the perp's degree of education. Those without a high school diploma get thrown in overcrowded cells that are reputed for their squalor and violence. Meanwhile, a doctoral degree earns you the privilege of a cleaner, solitary cell or at least one that is shared with two or three other diploma-bearing criminals.

Economy

In terms of natural resources, Brazil has always been incredibly wealthy. Until the 20th century, the economy was based on a series of cycles that exploited a single export commodity: brazilwood in the 16th century, sugarcane in the 16th and 17th centuries, gold, silver, and gemstones in the 18th century, and finally coffee and rubber in the 19th century. Apart from these boom and bust cycles, agriculture and cattle-raising were constant activities, but both were mainly limited to local consumption. Industrialization began in the early 20th century but didn't really kick in until the 1950s, which coincided with the beginnings of Brazil's major automobile, petrochemical, and steel industries.

After a difficult sink-or-swim period that accompanied the opening up of the economy to the world in the mid-1980s, Brazil has enjoyed healthy growth rates of 4–5 percent a year. The country now ranks as the world's 10th largest economy in terms of GDP (according to IMF and World Bank calculations), just behind Canada. Brazil's economy is larger than that of all other South American countries and increasingly competitive, high-quality, and innovative Brazilian goods are steadily making their presence felt in international markets. As a result of its newfound clout, Brazil is able to go head-to-head with the United States and Europe during global trade talks. Moreover, Brazil has been largely unaffected by the recent recessionary tendencies affecting the United States and Europe. Rich in natural resources and capable of supplying most of its own needs in terms of food, primary resources, energy, and manufactured products, Brazil is extremely self-sufficient. Well prepared to withstand rising imported fuel and food costs that are proving devastating for other countries, the country also boasts a domestic market of 185 million people that have more disposable income to burn than ever before.

AGRICULTURE

Brazil's moderate climate coupled with its fertile soil and its immense territory makes it an ideal place for the cultivation of many crops. Brazil is a leading world producer of coffee, soybeans, rice, corn, sugarcane, cocoa, and citrus fruits such as limes and oranges (Brazil supplies 80 percent of the world's orange juice). It is also the planet's largest exporter of both chicken and beef (Brazil currently has the largest herd of cattle in the world). Brazilian land is some of the cheapest on the planet. In recent years, feeling crowded on their small plots, an increasing number of European farmers have invested in vast farms in the Central-West and North, where they are amazed at how fast crops grow. Indeed, over the last two decades "agri-business" has become increasingly high-tech. As a result, today Brazil boasts one of the world's most productive agricultural sectors.

INDUSTRY AND FINANCE

Brazilian industry, which is extremely diversified and well-developed, currently accounts for around one-third of the country's GDP. Although traditionally, major industrial activities have been concentrated in the Southeast (particularly São Paulo and Minas) and the South, in the last few years, significant investments have been made in the Northeast and the North. Among Brazil's leading manufacturing industries are the automobile, aircraft, steel, mining, petrochemical, computer, and durable consumer goods sectors. Additionally, the country has a diverse and sophisticated service industry. Financial services are particularly well-developed. São Paulo is Latin America's largest financial center, and its stock exchange, Bovespa, is the second-largest equity option exchange in the world.

ENERGY

Brazil used to import 70 percent of its energy from overseas. However, since 2006, the nation has been capable of meeting all its own energy needs. Brazil is the world's leading supplier of hydroelectricity. To date, more than 90 percent of the country's electricity needs are supplied

BRAZIL'S ECONOMY IS IMPROVING

Although it seemed to take forever, at long last there is proof that Brazil's riches – both natural and man-made – are finally beginning to be shared by all Brazilians.

Under President Lula's sound economic stewardship, public debt has plummeted, interest rates have decreased, and credit and loans have become much more accessible for working Brazilians. The creation of new jobs, higher real salaries, and more disposable income for all Brazilians is finally diminishing the gaping abyss that only recently earned Brazil the dubious distinction of having one of the world's biggest discrepancies between rich and poor. Between 2001 and 2006 (according to figures released by Rio's prestigious Getúlio Vargas Foundation), while the top 10 percent of Brazilian wage earners saw their income rise by 7 percent, the earnings of the bottom 10 percent soared by 58 percent. Between 2003 and 2007, minimum wage increased by 36 percent. Moreover, more than 40 million poor Brazilians have benefited from increased social spending via programs such as Bolsa Familia, which provides subsidies to families who incentivize their children to attend school. As a result, a record number of poor and working-class Brazilians are now creeping up into the swelling middle classes.

With their newfound disposable income, Brazilians are buying like never before, spurred on by an increasingly strong *real*, falling prices of locally made and imported goods, and the ability to buy almost everything from groceries and plasma-screen TVs to air tickets, cars, and homes in *prestações sem juros* – no-interest payments that can be parceled out over months or even years.

by enormous hydroelectric dams such as Itaipu in Paraná and Tucuruí in Pará. Brazil has also flirted with nuclear energy with the building of Angra I, Angra II, and the soon-to-be inaugurated Angra III reactors, all of which are located in an otherwise idyllic spot of coastline in the state of Rio de Janeiro.

In late 2007, as rising oil prices sent the planet into panic, Brazil became the envy of the many countries when the national oil giant Petrobras discovered a vast deepwater reserve off the coast of Rio de Janeiro. The so-called Tupi reserve is estimated to hold up to 8 billion barrels of oil and could lead to Brazil becoming the newest member of OPEC. However, it's not as if Brazil is beholden to the increasingly coveted fossil fuel. Following the first oil crisis of 1974, the government's visionary solution was to begin converting sugarcane into ethanol as a cheaper and nonpolluting fuel for all vehicles. Today, Brazil is the world's number one producer of sugarcane alcohol; all Brazilian vehicles are flex fuel models that run on gas, alcohol, and a mixture of both.

TOURISM

In the last decade, Brazilian tourism has developed enormously. Traditionally, aside from Argentineans who used to invade the southern coast before their currency took a nosedive, international visitors rarely ventured beyond Rio de Janeiro. Since 2000, there has been a major spike in tourists from North America and especially Europe. The increase is largely due to the proliferation of domestic charters and air routes as well as a more sophisticated tourism infrastructure in unspoiled destinations far off-the-beaten path. In 2007, Brazil was the fourth-largest tourist destination in the Americas and the second largest in Latin America, after Mexico. However, much greater than the growth of international tourism has been the rise in the number of Brazilian themselves who are increasingly able to travel. Because of its endless natural attractions, Brazil's major tourism niche is ecotourism, which has the advantage of providing sustainable development. Particularly in the North and Northeast, tourism is playing a pivotal role in the development of local economies. At the moment, the still-growing sector accounts for 4 percent of GDP and, directly and indirectly, accounts for 7 percent of all jobs. Ranked in terms of number of tourists, Brazil's most visited cities are Rio de Janeiro, Salvador, São Paulo, Florianópolis, and Foz do Iguaçu.

People and Culture

DEMOGRAPHICS

According to recent statistics released in May 2008 by the Brazilian statistics bureau, IBGE, Brazil has a population of more than 186 million people, making it the sixth most populous country in the world. Until the mid-20th century, Brazil was a largely rural place. However, today more than 70 percent of the people live in major cities, most of which line the coast. In contrast, the vast Amazonian region is practically deserted. The most populous Brazilian city is São Paulo with 11 million people (according to 2007 IBGE figures), followed by Rio de Janeiro with 6.1 million, and then Salvador with 2.9 million. Indeed, the vast majority of the population is concentrated in the Southeast states of Rio de Janeiro, Minas Gerais, and São Paulo.

Life expectancy among Brazilians has improved greatly in recent decades. In 2008, the average life-span of Brazilian women was 76.4 years, while for men it was 68.8 years. Meanwhile, the days of big families are a thing of the past. The average Brazilian woman today bears 1.86 children. Although the official literacy rate of Brazilians over the age of 15 is 89 percent, the concept of "literacy" should be taken with a grain of salt. Included among so-called "literate" Brazilians are many people who can do little more than write numbers and their names, and recognize a few dozen simple words.

ETHNICITY AND RACE

Five centuries of commingling has resulted in a population that is extremely diverse, which explains the endless array of physical types as well as an impressive openness towards biological, cultural, and religious differences.

Indigenous Groups

When the Portuguese first arrived in Brazil in 1500, an estimated 5 million indigenous people, most belonging to the Tupi and Guarani groups, were inhabiting this vast territory. Today, only about 700,000 (representing 0.4 percent of the total population) of their descendants remain. Although indigenous groups live throughout Brazil, the majority reside in the least populated areas of the Central-West and the Amazon. The degree to which they have succeeded in preserving the traditions and lifestyles of their ancestors varies enormously. However, there are indeed small communities deep within the Amazon

© MICHAEL SOMMERS

The vast majority of Brazilians are descended from a mixture of indigenous peoples, Africans, and Europeans.

RACISM IN BRAZIL

In the early 20th century, noted Brazilian anthropologist Gilberto Freyre gave rise to the official myth of Brazil as a paragon of racial harmony, whose spontaneous mixture of indigenous peoples, Africans, and Europeans stood as a utopic counterpoint to the polarized conflicts that characterized race relations in the United States. To this day, many Brazilians still believe in the myth. Foreigners are inevitably impressed by the easy mingling of people, regardless of color, and of the fact that so many African elements – samba, *capoeira*, Carnaval – have become icons of Brazilianness, espoused by all Brazilians.

However, dig deep enough and the myth begins to crack. Precisely what makes racism in Brazil so insidious is that, unlike racism in the United States, it isn't in your face – it's thus easier to deny it exists and maintain a status quo in which the whiter you are, the more money, education, and opportunities you have. As you travel around in Brazil, take note of the politicians, the business leaders, the models and TV stars, the domestic tourists, the kids in private school uniforms, and the people walking around in swanky neighborhoods, eating in upscale restaurants, staying in hotels, and flying on airplanes with you. The vast majority are white. Few tourists will come into contact with Brazilians who live in *favelas* (slums). However, you will notice that the majority of those living on the streets, performing menial jobs or selling wares on the sidewalk, lining

up for buses, or working as doormen, cleaning women, or nannies, are inevitably black. If you're a white man in Brazil and you walk around with a black Brazilian female friend, the immediate conclusion is that you're a john and your friend is a prostitute (or else that she's a gold-digger and you're rich husband material). A dark-skinned mother with a lighter-skinned child will often be assumed to be the child's nanny (and treated as such).

The result of this type of racism isn't hate crimes or white supremacy groups. But the fact is that white Brazilians overwhelmingly dominate government, business, and the media. (Two notable exceptions are soccer and music, where black Brazilians are revered.) Fortunately, in recent years, change has finally begun to take root. In 2002, the Brazilian government made it mandatory to teach African and Afro-Brazilian history and culture as part of the universal school curriculum. Federal and state universities recently began implementing quotas in an attempt to redress the fact that only 3 percent of black Brazilians have university degrees. As president, Lula da Silva made two notable appointments of Afro-Brazilians. President Lula also nominated another Afro-Brazilian, Edson Santos, to head the newly created Ministry of Racial Equality. Before stepping down to resume his music career in 2008, Gilberto Gil, the Bahian composer and musician (and former city councillor of Salvador) spent six years as a highly effective minister of culture.

(protected by FUNAI, the federal agency of Indian affairs) that have never had contact with "civilization." Meanwhile, according to the results of a recent mitochondrial DNA survey, an estimated 60 million Brazilians can lay claim to at least one ancestor from an indigenous tribe. Brazilians who are descended from both indigenous tribes and Europeans are known as *caboclos*.

Africans

Between the early days of colonial Brazil and the abolition of slavery in 1888, it's estimated

that more than 4 million slaves were brought to Brazil from Africa. The majority of them were Bantu peoples from Portugal's African colonies, such as Mozambique and Angola, as well as Yoruba from the western coast nations of Benin and Nigeria. Although you'll find Brazilians of African descent throughout the country, the largest black communities are in Rio and the coastal areas of the Northeast, particularly Salvador da Bahia, where 85 percent of the population boasts some African ancestry.

Overall, only 7 percent of Brazilians (roughly 13 million) consider themselves to be "black." However, according to the 2006 IBGE census, more than 92 million Brazilians can claim to possess some African ancestry. They are often referred to by the traditional appellate *"pardo,"* meaning colored (*pardo* is actually a beige-caramel color). Due to a tradition of miscegenation (Portuguese had no compunction about having extraconjugal relationships with their slaves), most Brazilians are of mixed race, or *mulato* (Brazilians descended from a mixture of Africans and Indians are known as *cafuzos*). However, the varying shades of skin color and the way in which they are perceived and projected among different social milieus is extremely complex and nuanced.

The official designation these days is *afro-descendente* or *afro-brasileiro*. Applicable to anyone with African origins, these terms are based more on cultural identity than skin color. In terms of skin color, Brazilians have come up with hundreds of (often extremely creative) terms to designate themselves (and confound racial categorization). These range from *preto retinto* (repainted black) and *jabuticaba* (a dark purple berry-like fruit), both of which refer to darker skin tones, to *jegue quando foge* (donkey when it runs away) and *formiga* (ant), on a somewhat lighter scale. Many of these euphemistic designations have their origin in a subtle yet deeply rooted racism that is still very much alive in Brazil. As a result, darker skinned Brazilians sometimes try (often subconsciously) to *embranquecer* (to become more white) by choosing a non-black identity for themselves. This phenomenon explains why only 7 percent of Afro-Brazilians refer to themselves as *"negro."* Instead, many mixed-race Brazilians refer to themselves as *"mulatos,"* or even *"mulatos claros"* (light-skinned *mulatos*).

Europeans

The first Europeans to set foot in Brazil were the Portuguese who claimed the territory as their own. The next five centuries saw various waves of immigration; as a result the vast majority of Brazilians can lay claim to some Portuguese ancestry. It wasn't until the mid- to late 19th century that other Europeans began to arrive en masse in Brazil. Lured by the promise of vast tracts of fertile land, growing cities, and the beginnings of industry, large numbers of Italians, Germans, and Spaniards, followed by Poles and Ukrainians, flocked to the sparsely populated states of the South and to São Paulo. To this day, the South has a distinctly European character, and blond hair and blue eyes are quite common. São Paulo, in particular, has been a magnet for immigrants from all over the world. Aside from Europeans, the city boasts the largest population of Japanese outside of Japan and of Lebanese outside of Lebanon.

REGIONALISM

While Brazil easily absorbs different peoples into its national melting pot, at the same time, historical and geographical specificities have led to the creation of some very distinctive regional cultures. Indeed, despite the shared language, national references, and a strong national identity as "Brazilians," it's not uncommon for a Paulistano or Catarinense visiting Bahia or Maranhão, for example, to suffer from some degree of "culture shock" when confronted with differences in lifestyle, mentality, language, and cuisine. The reverse is equally true. While some of these regional stereotypes are somewhat clichéed—and Brazilians themselves have great fun in conflating and exaggerating them for their own mirth—as with any stereotype there often exists an underlying kernel of truth. As such, you will find that Bahians live up to their fame for being ultra laid-back, Paulistanos really are efficient workaholics, Cariocas have hedonism down to an art form, Mineiros are taciturn and reserved, Gaúchos exhibit a fierce pride, and inhabitants of the northeastern Sertão possess a tough and rough-edged temperament that reflects their surroundings.

RELIGION

Officially, Brazil is the world's largest Catholic country in terms of population. In reality, however, Brazil's great talent for syncretism and diversity has resulted in a country with an amazing number of religions, sects, and communities.

Deus (Universal Kingdom of God's Church), and numerous tangents thereof, have taken root, offering succor and solutions to Brazil's poor (often for a price).

Afro-Brazilian Religions

African slaves who were brought to Brazil arrived bereft of everything except their faith. Although the Portuguese strictly banned all such forms of "demon worship," slaves were particularly adept at camouflaging the worship of their deities under the guise of pretending to worship Catholic saints. The consequences of this mingling of religious symbols can be seen today in many religious rituals and celebrations that fuse Catholicism with African and even indigenous religious elements.

The end of slavery did not bring about immediate tolerance for Afro-Brazilians to openly practice purer forms of their faith. Candomblé, Brazil's largest Afro-Brazilian cult, was banned well into the 20th century, even in Salvador and parts of Bahia where *terreiros* (traditional houses of worship) are widespread. Today, less than one percent of Brazilians adhere to Candomblé and other popular Afro-Brazilian cults, such as Umbanda (which mixes Candomblé practices with spiritualist and indigenous elements). However, in places such as Salvador, Rio, and São Luís, Afro-Brazilian religious elements have entered into mainstream culture. Notable examples include the popularization of Yoruba terms (all Candomblé ceremonies are conducted in the Yoruba language) and of ritual dances and sacred foods (such as Bahia's famous *acarajés*). Wide segments of the population participate in *festas* honoring *orixás* (deities) in which *presentes* (gifts) are often offered. In Rio and Salvador, you will often find the beaches littered with flowers washed ashore after being offered to the immensely popular *orixá* Iemanjá, goddess of the seas.

Other Faiths

There are numerous spiritualist and esoteric cults practiced throughout Brazil. One of the most popular forms of spiritualism is

Igreja e Convento de São Francisco, Salvador, Bahia

© MICHAEL SOMMERS

Catholicism

According to the latest IBGE census, around 75 percent of Brazilians identify themselves as Roman Catholic. Despite the strong presence of churches, endless references to Deus (God), various incarnations of Nossa Senhor (the Virgin), and prayers, promises, and processions offered up to saints, the majority of Brazilians aren't practicing Catholics. While Catholicism is a strong presence in the collective culture, the Catholic church in Brazil has a much less rigid reputation than in other Latin American countries.

Protestantism

Only around 16 percent of Brazilians adhere to some form of Protestantism. However, in the last two decades, an endless number of evangelical and pentecostal churches have been sprouting like wildfire, particularly in poor rural and suburban neighborhoods where churches such as the immensely popular Igreja Assembleia de Deus (Assembly of God Church) and Igreja Universal do Reino de

THE LONGING THAT IS *SAUDADE*

Saudade is the Portuguese word that has most defied translation. Its origins stem from the Latin term *solitatem*, which means "loneliness" or "solitude." Yet as years have gone by, *saudade* has acquired rich layers of meaning that mingle nostalgia, longing, melancholy, and missing (someone or something). Trying to define the sentiment back in 1912, the English writer A. F. G. Bell wrote: "The famous *saudade* of the Portuguese is a vague and constant desire for something that does not and probably cannot exist, for something other than the present, a turning towards the past or towards the future; not an active discontent or poignant sadness but an indolent dreaming wistfulness." Bell was referring to Portugal, where the term was coined. But of course *saudade* migrated to the New World, where it fit right in with Brazilians' emotionally open natures. Brazilians liberally – and very sincerely – sprinkle their conversations with *"Estava com saudades"* ("I was really missing you") or *"Da uma saudade!"* ("I really miss this/that"). Unsurprisingly, *saudades* also turn up with great frequency in Brazilian music. In fact, the first bossa nova song ever written was Tom Jobim's *"Chega de Saudade."* If you listen to the song in Portuguese, you'll get some idea of what *saudade* can mean; the most frequently translated English version of "No More Blue" doesn't even come close.

Kardecism, which was named after 19th-century spiritualist Allan Kardec. Its followers believe in multiple reincarnations and in the idea that the spirits of the dead—who can be communicated with during séances—are present among the living. Spiritualism is so popular that it often works its way into the Globo television network's nightly *novelas.*

Other popular cults draw inspiration from Brazil's indigenous cultures. This is the case with **Santo Daime** and **União da Vegetal,** both of which revolve around imbibing a hallucinogenic potion, ayahuasca, which Amazonian indigenous people have used for centuries as a way of achieving transcendental insights. The small but faithful following includes a significant number of middle-class, urban dwellers of São Paulo, Brasília, and the South.

LANGUAGE

Brazilians speak Portuguese (not Spanish!) and are responsible for the fact that Portuguese is the 6th most spoken language in the world. Since it crossed the Atlantic from Portugal, Brazilian Portuguese has undergone various modifications. The differences between the Portuguese written and spoken in Portugal and that of Brazil are similar to the differences between American and British English. Brazilian Portuguese is a constantly evolving, dynamic, and very melodic language. Like the country itself, it is a colorful hybrid that has absorbed words and expressions from all the major groups that make up Brazilian society. Early on, Portuguese settlers were quick to incorporate indigenous terms from Tupi and Guarani languages, in particular, terms used to designate the vast compendium of exotica for which no Portuguese words existed. To this day, most names of places (Ipanema, Ibirapuera, Paraná, Caruaru) are Tupi-Guarani, as are names of many foods (*pipoca* is popcorn, *mandioca* is manioc, *abacaxi* is a pineapple), animals (*tatu* is an armadillo, a *jacaré* is a cayman, *tucano* is a toucan), and trees (*ipê,* jacaranda). A legacy of slavery was the inclusion of words from African languages (primarily Bantu, and to a lesser extent Yoruba, which is spoken in the region of Benin and Nigeria and used in Candomblé rituals), ranging from specific terms such as *samba* and *capoeira* to colloquial expressions such as *cafuné* (a caress on the head) and *caçula* (the youngest born). Later on, the arrival of European immigrants in the 19th and 20th century introduced new expressions, especially in French—*chaise longue,* Réveillon (New Year's Eve), the expression *bom apetite*— and English: *trem* (train), *outdoor* (billboard), *jeans,* and *email.*

Written Portuguese tends to be more formal (although less so than in Portugal), but spoken Portuguese is extremely casual with a fabulous array of slang and idiomatic expressions that vary wildly depending on regions and even city neighborhoods (and which you'll be hard-pressed to understand). There is some difference in terms of regional accents, but as a foreigner you'll find it difficult to pick up on most of them. The most detectable of regional accents include those of the city of Rio de Janeiro (exaggerated and slightly nasal), the interior of São Paulo (flat with Anglo-Saxon retroflex *r*'s), Rio Grande do Sul's (with a very strong Spanish influence), and Bahia's (which is slow and melodic).

Art and Architecture

With so much diversity, beauty, and extremities packed into its immense territory, it's no wonder that artistry and creativity run rampant in Brazil. Culture, both "high" and "low," but especially *cultura popular,* is seemingly everywhere—in the masterful elaboration of a tall tale at a bar table, the intricate embroidery of a tablecloth, the expressive sculpting of a clay *figurinha,* not to mention the 45-minute choreographed spectacle of enormous floats, dazzling costumes, and thousands of samba-ing singers and dancers vying for the yearly championship title during Rio's famous Carnaval. With endless sources of inspiration, there are no limits to Brazilians' creativity.

MUSIC

Of the various forms of artistic expression, the one that is most particular and reflects the very essence and soul of Brazil is its music. In terms of sheer genius and variety, it's hard to overexaggerate the impact of Brazilian music. Between samba, bossa nova, *forró,* and MPB (Música Popular Brasileira), Brazil's contribution to the world music scene is immeasurable. Meanwhile, within Brazil itself, music is inseparable from daily life. It plays a starring role in all types of celebrations, both sacred and profane. There is music in the beach vendor's cries of shrimp for sale as well as in the samba rhythms teenage boys pound against the metal siding of an urban bus. And it is tattooed into the collective consciousness in such a way that you'll immediately feel as if your education is very lacking. (Brazilians inevitably know *all* the words to *all* the songs, and are not at all timid about singing them for you).

Music in Brazil is also inextricably linked to dance. Many music styles—samba, *forró, frevo, carimbó, bumba-meu-boi*—are accompanied by dance steps, and it's close to impossible for most Brazilians to stay inert once the music heats up. Needless to say, the effortlessness, grace, flair, and controlled abandon with which the vast majority of Brazilians cut a rug is beyond compare.

Influences

The uniqueness and diversity of Brazilian music is yet another consequence of the country's distinctive mélange of indigenous, African, and European influences. In early colonial days, Jesuit missionaries were already cleverly adapting religious hymns to indigenous tribal music with Tupi lyrics in order to up their chances of converting Brazilian Indians.

With the arrival of slaves came percussion instruments—drums, *cuias,* rattles, and marimbas—that were played during communal jams. Although the Portuguese elite tried to resist these African rhythms on grounds that they incited libidinous dances that were quite immoral, their objections were in vain. These rhythms made their way out of the slaves' quarters and into plantation homes and, from there, spread throughout the country, creeping

© MICHAEL SOMMERS

berimbaus, traditional one-string instruments brought to Brazil by African slaves

into popular 19th-century musical styles such as *maxixe* and *frevo* (both of which also drew heavily on Polish polkas).

Samba

However, it was in early-20th-century Rio, amid the working class neighborhoods of liberated black slaves who had migrated to the city from Bahia, that modern samba was born. Officially, samba made its presence known for the first time during Rio's Carnaval of 1917, which featured a ditty called *Pelo Telefone,* composed by Donga, a talented young Carioca composer and musician. The rhythm was so contagious that even Rio's white upper classes were hooked. By the 1930s the launch of Brazil's phonographic industry combined with the spread of national radio allowed samba hits to be broadcast throughout the country and quickly soak into the collective consciousness.

The 1930s and '40s were the "Golden Age" of samba, with composers such as Noel Rosa, Ary Barroso, Lamartine Babo, Cartola, and Ismael Silva penning a string of classics that were popularized by the likes of Carmen

Miranda (who, pre-Hollywood, was one of Brazil's preeminent musical stars). There are many different varieties of samba. The classic samba from the '30s and '40s is known as *samba-canção,* in which a slow-tempo samba is belted out by a singer backed by a small band. The more frenetic *samba de enredo* was custom-made for Rio's Carnaval. It involves one or two singers accompanied by a deafening chorus of hundreds of drummers and back-up singers (which, together, constitute a samba school). More recently, in the 1990s, in dance halls and corner bars, swinging *samba pagode* took the genre back to its roots, led by performers such as the immensely popular and down-to-earth Zeca Pagodinho. Other major samba performers that have marked the genre since the 1970s include Beth Carvalho, Alcione, Clara Nunes, Paulinho da Viola, Martinho da Vila, and Martinho's daughter, Mart'nália, whose career has taken off in the last few years.

Bahia is also known for its samba. *Samba de roda* (in which musicians and dancers form a circle) is prevalent throughout the Bahian interior, while Salvador is the birthplace of

CARMEN MIRANDA

Forget about Hepburn, Hayworth, and Grable. In the mid-1940s, Carmen Miranda was the most highly paid female star in Hollywood. As the "Brazilian Bombshell," this tiny Carioca, who tottered upon foot-high platforms and beneath towering turbans piled high with juicy tropical fruits, proved herself to be much larger than life in a string of Technicolor musical comedies produced by 20th Century Fox. With her rolling eyes, gyrating hips, and deliriously nonsensical songs, such as "Tico Tico Na Fuba" and "Boom Chica Boom," Carmen took America by storm. She also became the strangest – and perhaps most successful – good will ambassador that ever existed between the United States and Brazil. Never before, and never again, would Hollywood – and the world – see a spectacle quite as spectacular as the "Lady in the Tutti Frutti Hat."

popularity due to the masterful compositions by Pixinguinha, a Carioca. The classic *choro* trio consists of a flute, *cavaquinho* (a small four-string guitar that resembles a ukelele), and percussion instrument all played together in a loose manner reminiscent of jazz. After falling out of favor for decades, traditional *choro* has made a comeback in the bars of Rio and São Paulo.

Northeastern Music

The northeastern Sertão gave birth to a wealth of distinctive musical styles that gradually spread throughout Brazil as the 20th century wore on. In the 1940s, armed with a deep voice and an accordion, Pernambucano musician Luíz Gonzaga was crowned the king of the *baião*, a plaintive bluesy style of music whose lyrics sang of the harsh life of Brazil's poorest and most arid region. *Baião* proved popular at local dance halls and paved the way for the more sophisticated *forró*, which to this today has become immensely popular throughout all of Brazil. *Forró's* jaunty two-step is played by an accordion-led trio featuring a triangle and a *zabumba* (bass drum).

Tackling plaintive themes of lost love and betrayal, *música sertaneja* is a more contemporary, commercial (and often more schmaltzy) version of traditional *música caipira* (American-style country music), which is typical of the Brazilian interior. Popularized by cowboy duos with names such as Chitãozinho and Xororó and Leonardo and Leandro, *música sertaneja* is popular not only in the Northeast, but even more so in the Central-West and rural areas of Minas, São Paulo, and Paraná.

Bossa Nova

Although poor rural and urban areas alike have proved fertile for the germination of many of Brazil's musical styles, one of the genres most famously associated with Brazil was the product of an inspired mixture of samba and imported American jazz that grew out of jam sessions held at the swank Zona Sul apartments of Rio's artists and intellectuals during the 1950s. Bossa nova was the name given to the cool, urban, modernist style that was

samba-reggae, a Jamaica-tinged form promoted by local groups such as Olodum and Didá. *Samba-reggae* is only one tangent of the genre known as *axé* music, a frenetic and infectious dance music that emerged during Salvador's Carnaval in the 1980s, at the moment when a generation of rising stars were taking to the streets atop massive *trio-elétricos* (stages on wheels). For years, the biggest *axé* stars have been Daniela Mercury, Ivete Sangalo, and Margarete Menezes. The trio has served as the genre's ambassadors, performing these infectious hits throughout Brazil and overseas.

Choro

Choro (which means "crying") is another musical style (little known outside Brazil) that also developed in Rio at the dawn of the 20th century. Delicate and slightly melancholy, *choro* music is influenced by Argentinean tangos as well as European polkas, mazurkas, and waltzes. During the 1930s, *choro* enjoyed great essentially a slowing down and breaking up of a classic samba rhythm. The godfather of bossa nova was an eccentric and insanely talented Bahian composer/musician by the name of João Gilberto. Two equally talented men (and famous bon vivants)—the classically trained pianist Antônio Carlos Jobim and poet/diplomat Vinícius de Morais—set about writing bossa's most famous hits, including "A Garota de Ipanema" ("The Girl from Ipanema"), whose most unforgettable international version was crooned by Astrud Gilberto, João Gilberto's wife at the time. Ironically, Astrud is quite unknown in Brazil, but Gilberto's daughter, Bebel Gilberto, has picked up where her father left off and made an international career of doing slick lounge versions of bossa tunes for the iPod set. Meanwhile, bossa's fresh jazziness allowed it to cross over into an immediate jazz standard, which was covered by American artists ranging from Stan Getz and Frank Sinatra to Ella Fitzgerald and Miles Davis. Bossa put Brazilian music on the international map for the first time. Because it was so overplayed, with the years bossa gained an elevator music aura abroad. However, in Brazil, the repertory of classics such as "Corcovado," "Chega de Saudade," and "Desafinado" have been, and continue to be, reverently covered by Brazil's top singers, among them Nara Leão, Elis Regina (both tragically dead), and Gal Costa.

MPB and Tropicália

MPB stands for Música Popular Brasileira (Popular Brazilian Music) and is a rather generic and all-encompassing term that refers to all forms of Brazilian "popular" urban music—folk, pop, rock—created from the '60s to contemporary times. MPB generally features original songwriting but can also include revisited classics (including *samba-canções*) from the 1930s, '40s, and '50s. Most often, songs are interpreted by the composer or by a singer/interpreter, and frequently accompanied by piano or guitar, along with other instruments.

The term MPB was coined during the early '60s as Brazil sought new and modern ways of revisiting its identity amid the growing oppressiveness of the military dictatorship. Brazilian television, at the time a very new medium, began to broadcast Festivais de Música Popular Brasileira. These live competitions featured up-and-coming singers, who performed songs by young composers in the hopes of landing recording contracts. Winners became overnight sensations. The first of these festivals, held in 1965, was won by a tiny yet feisty 20-year singer from Rio Grande do Sul by the name of Elis Regina. Elis set the standard for MPB. Her rich voice and unbridled emotion tackled songs by a generation of talented young composers—including Chico Buarque, Milton Nascimento, Edu Lobo, Ivan Lins, and João Bosco—up until her untimely death, by a drug overdose, in 1982.

Although there have been plenty of male MPB composers who also perform their songs (quite beautifully in the case of Milton Nascimento, Chico Buarque, Jorge Ben Jor, and Roberto Carlos), the most famous interpreters of MPB have always been women. Aside from Elis, major figures of the last 30 years include Maysa, Nana Caymmi, Joyce, Simone, Zizi Possi, Angela Rô Rô, Marina Lima, Adriana Calcanhoto, Marisa Monte, and Ana Carolina (some of whom also compose their own music). Two female interpreters who deserve special attention are Gal Costa and Maria Betânia, both from Bahia. Over the years, Gal has morphed from a sensual Janis Joplin into a technically impeccable diva, while low-voiced and ever-passionate Betânia has lately put out some provocative self-produced CDs featuring repertoires of little-known gems from musical eras of the past.

At the height of the military dictatorship of the late 1960s and early '70s, Gal became the muse of a movement that became known as Tropicália. Revolving around the creative energies of young singer/composers extraordinaire Caetano Veloso, Gilberto Gil, and Tom Zé (all of whom also hail from Bahia), Tropicália fused folksy flower-power with electric guitars and international influences such as the Beatles with regional styles such as *baião* and samba. Aside from being master wordsmiths, Caetano and Gil were charismatic figures—so charismatic in fact, that both were arrested by the military government and then forced into exile in Europe (along with Chico Buarque). Back in Brazil since the mid-'70s, both have continued to evolve, traveling in new musical directions and creating a prolific body of work. Elected minister of culture (2002–2006), Gilberto Gil passed legislation that recognized samba (in all its forms) as a National Artistic Patrimony.

Brazilian Rock and Rap

Tropicália's more psychedelic tangent was represented by a way-out trio known as Os Mutantes (who insisted on singing many of their songs in English). Os Mutantes's lead singer was a red-headed Paulistana (descended from American confederates) by the name of Rita Lee, who went on to have an original career as the always humorous and provocative "Queen of Brazilian Rock." Brazilian rock's heyday, however, was during the 1980s. This decade was marked by the emergence of seminal bands such as Barão Vermelho, Legião Urbana, and Os Titãs, along with icons such as Cazuza, Renato Russo, and Cássia Eller (all of whom met with untimely deaths). Since then, Brazilian rock—which generally appeals to a young, white, middle-class urban crowd—has faded into the musical background, although most big cities have at least a small indie scene.

The 1990s also saw the emergence of Brazilian rap. Like its American counterparts, Brazilian rap was born in the *favelas* of Rio and São Paulo and featured young black Brazilians who tackled themes of social injustice and violence. A Carioca take on rap is funk, which attracts massive audiences and features lyrics that are so sexually explicit that you don't know whether to be shocked or laugh yourself silly. Among the biggest names in rap are Gabriel O Pensador, MV Bill, Marcelo D2, and the Racionais MC.

Brazilian Music Today

In recent years, there has been a revived interest in traditional and regional forms of Brazilian music and their preservation. However, on the MPB front, no seminal creative figures have emerged that can rival the cultural and musical impact of the original talents forged during the 1960s and '70s (many of whom—now in their 60s—still continue to produce eagerly anticipated new works). This isn't to say there are no interesting individuals who are carving out their own distinctive paths. Artists such as Zeca Baleiro and Lenine, both of whom merge pop with traditional musical styles from their native states of Maranhão and Pernambuco (respectively) produce challenging and provocative work. The contemporary takes on samba by Seu Jorge, who was raised in a Rio *favela,* have earned him international accolades, while in São Paulo, Fernanda Porta has been successful at deftly mixing samba with electronica and drum 'n' bass. Ultimately, what characterizes MPB today is a continued willingness towards musical *mestizagem;* the seamless blending of contemporary and international with traditional and local sounds to create hybrids that end up being distinctly Brazilian.

FINE ARTS AND ARCHITECTURE

Earliest known examples of "Brazilian" art were actually paintings of Edenic landscapes done by European artists who were fascinated by the new colony's profusion of exotica. When the Dutch occupied Pernambuco in the mid-1600s, artists Frans Post and Albert Eckout were assigned to dutifully register the native flora and fauna as well as indigenous inhabitants. Widely reproduced in Europe, their portraits constituted the first images of the American continent painted by artists of some renown.

For the next three centuries, artists in Brazil devoured styles that were in vogue in Europe. Although some did so mimetically, others "tropicalized" these styles, giving them a unique "Brazilianness." The most remarkable instance of this tendency occurred with the rise of Barroco Mineiro that developed in 18th-century Minas Gerais during its massive gold boom. Magnificent churches were built using local materials and decorated in a baroque style whose details, colors, and excessive

CANNIBALISM IN BRAZILIAN MODERN ART

During the Semana de Arte de São Paulo of 1922, Oswald de Andrade, a leading modernist intellectual and playwright, introduced the metaphor of *antropofagia* (cannibalism) that would become a guiding concept in all modern Brazilian art. Andrade's notion was derived from a traditional indigenous practice of cannibalism. Contrary to popular belief, Brazil's indigenous groups didn't eat people to satisfy their hunger pangs. Instead, they recognized that even their staunchest foes possessed gifts they didn't share. The ritual of eating the enemies they captured in skirmishes was a way of absorbing some of their more admirable qualities (bravery, cleverness, etc.). Andrade proposed that Brazilian artists become cannibals as well: devouring aspects of the European vanguard as well as traditional African and Indian arts and, after digesting them, making use of them to produce a uniquely Brazilian art that would reflect Brazil itself, with its bright colors, exuberant nature, and diverse population.

flourishes were unique in reflecting their tropical surroundings. The two major figures of Barroco Mineiro were master builder and sculptor Aleijadinho and the painter Athayde, whose works are spread throughout the *cidades históricas* of Ouro Preto, Mariana, Tiradentes, and São João del Rei.

In the mid-19th century, Brazil's independence coincided with the flourishing of a romantic style of painting that saw artists such as Victor Meireles and Pedro Américo portraying national heroes and historic events in epic style. In terms of architecture, the sobriety and elegance of French neoclassicism held sway in the capital of Rio de Janeiro, where grand monuments such as the Teatro Municipal, the Biblioteca Nacional, and the Museu Nacional de Belas Artes aspired to conjure up a tropical version of Baron Haussman's Paris. In the early 20th century, a flirtation with Art Nouveau gave way to art deco in the '30s and '40s. You'll see some glorious examples of art deco in Rio (particularly in Copacabana) as well as most other large cities.

It wasn't until the 1920s that Brazilian artists consciously broke with European traditions in the pursuit of art that was typically Brazilian. Led by Oswald and Mário de Andrade, in 1920, the Semana de Arte Moderna de São Paulo created an artistic manifesto and shocked the conservative elite by severing ties with academic, European schools. Brazilian modernists such as Anita Malfatti, Emiliano di Cavalcanti, Tarsila do Amaral, Victor Brecheret, and Lasar Segall were the leading painters and sculptors that emerged from the Semana de Arte Moderna. Espousing a philosophy of national art and culture that revolved around the notion of *antropofagia* (or cannibalism), they created works that, while fed by what was going on in Europe, were also nourished by themes, forms, and subject matter that were distinctly Brazilian. The generation of artists that followed them (painters Alberto de Veiga Guignard, Cândido Portinari, Flávio de Carvalho, and Cícero Dias and sculptors Maria Martins, Bruno Giorgi, and Alfredo Ceschiatti) continued to explore the notion of Brazilian Modernism.

While each artist followed his or her own individual path, many contributed their talents to adorning public buildings, particularly the government buildings of the new capital of Brasília, today considered the greatest modernist ensemble in the world. Designed by leading architects Lúcio Costa and Oscar Niemeyer, Brasília was modeled after Le Corbusier's ideals of functional, pared-down structures with glossy surfaces and plenty of windows that emphasized natural lighting. Niemeyer, however, softened the rigid, box-like linearity of the style by adding sweeping curves that reflected the sensuality and natural forms so characteristic of Brazil. Other important contributors to Brazilian modernist architecture include Afonso Eduardo Reidy (who designed Rio's Museu de Arte Moderna), Lina Bo Bardi (creator of São Paulo's iconic MASP), and renowned landscape architect Roberto Burle Marx, who was responsible for countless public gardens throughout the country.

In 1951, the first Bienal de Artes Plásticas de São Paulo was held in the newly built Pavilhão de Artes in Parque do Ibirapuera. Over time, the event has grown into one of the most important biennials in the art world. The '50s coincided with major experiments in abstract and concrete art carried out by leading figures such as Lygia Pape, Amilcar de Castro, Iberê Camargo, and Lygia Clark. In the '60s, Clark, along with provocative and crazily talented Hélio Oiticica, began creating vanguard art installations that focused on relationships between objects and the space around them. The iconic example of this period was Oiticica's famous *parangolé*, a cape-like work of "wearable art" made famous by the fact that musician and writer Caetano Veloso wore one during the height of Tropicália.

Keeping up with trends in other parts of the world, contemporary Brazilian art has been marked by the successive rise of Pop, installation, performance, video, and digital art. Today, names such as Cildo Meireles, Adriana Varejão, Vic Muniz, Sérgio Camargo, Jac Leirner, and Beatriz Milhazes are internationally renowned figures, and their works are included in leading museums and galleries. Although characterized by hits and misses, contemporary architecture—some of the best examples of which can be seen in São Paulo—has also stayed true to the precepts of "cannibalism," with names such as Isay Weinfeid, Ruy Ohtake, Márcio Kogan, and Marcelo Ferraz creating works that bridge cutting-edge universal technology and tendencies with a valorization of local aesthetics and materials.

CINEMA

Cinema has always been very popular in Brazil. By the 1930s, even the smallest towns in the northeastern interior had their own modest movie palaces screening Hollywood flickers. In Rio, Praça Floriano became known as Cinelândia after the elegant downtown square was lined with sumptuous art deco movie palaces. Rio was also the birthplace of the Brazilian film industry. In 1930, Cinédia studios began churning out a series of popular romances and burlesque musical comedies known as *chanchadas,* some of which satirized Hollywood fare. A few of these films featured a very young Carmen Miranda, then at the height of her fame as a recording star. In the 1940s, both Atlantida and Vera Cruz also appeared on the scene to produce popular melodramas along with *chanchadas.* During the 1950s, Vera Cruz attempted to attract viewers by emulating Hollywood's tradition of commercial genre films. A massive soundstage was built where the studio could churn out highly popular detective stories and westerns. Production values were high, but young independent directors chafed at the degree of commercialization and Americanization of the final product.

Dreaming of a *cinema novo* (new cinema), and inspired by Italian Neo-Realism, directors such as Nelson Pereira dos Santos, Ruy Guerra, and Anselmo Duarte took to making low-budget films, many shot on location in the arid Sertão, that highlighted the stark realities of the Brazilian Northeast in expressive black and white imagery. If not wildly popular at home, these films were a hit with international critics. Lima Barreto's *O Cangaceiro* (1953) brought to the screen the story of the legendary Sertanejo bandit, Lampião. In 1962, Duarte's *O Pagador de Promessas* scooped up a Palme d'Or award for best film at the 1962 Cannes Festival. One of the most daring and experimental figures of the movement dubbed Cinema Novo was a brilliant Bahian director by the name of Glauber Rocha. In groundbreaking films such as *Terra em Transe* and *Deus e o Diabo na Terra do Sol,* "Glauber" drew on French New Wave influences to tackle pressing sociopolitical issues such as hunger, violence, and poverty, once again using the Northeast as a metaphorically charged setting. Combining wonderful mise-en-scene with an absence of conventional narrative, Glauber's films were adored by intellectuals, but difficult for the public to watch.

In 1964, the beginning of the military dictatorship caused Cinema Novo to experience a sudden demise. Government hardliners censored any criticism of Brazil and forced many directors into exile. Instead, in 1969, the government created Embrafilme, a state-run production company whose goal was to develop Brazilian filmmaking. Although censorship, bureaucracy, and favoritism severely limited artistic expression, Embrafilme did provide enough capital to maintain a small industry that funded the production of important films by major directors such as Bruno Barreto's *Dona Flor e Seus Dois Maridos* (*Dona Flor and Her Two Husbands*, 1976), Cacá Diegues's *Bye Bye Brasil* (1979), Hector Babenco's *Pixote* (1981), and Nelson Pereira dos Santos's *Memórias do Cárcere* (*Memories of Prison*, 1984).

The end of Brazil's military dictatorship also meant the end of Embrafilme and a state-subsidized film industry. By the early '90s, only three or four Brazilian films a year were being released. Fortunately, things improved under the government of Fernando Henrique Cardoso, with the introduction of new incentive laws whereby private companies that invested in film productions would receive tax breaks. In 1993, Carla Camurati's whimsical historical comedy *Carlota Joaquina* (about the Portuguese royal family's picaresque adventures in 19th-century Brazil) was a big hit and signaled the beginning of Brazilian cinema's resurrection. Eager to see their lives depicted onscreen, Brazilians flocked to the cinema in record numbers, despite the fact that, since the 1970s, more than two-thirds of movie theaters had been closed down (and often converted into evangelical churches)-the result of the popularization of television and the increased price of movie tickets. Not only did the number of films produced gradually grow, but the quality was on par with the best of world cinema, and was recognized as such by foreign critics, who showered awards on productions such as Bruno Barreto's *O Que É Isso Companheiro?*

(Four Days in September, 1998), an Oscar-nominated film that told the gripping true story of the kidnapping of the U.S. ambassador to Brazil by left-leaning guerillas.

Walter Salles, one of Brazil's most important new directors, succeeded in taking home the Oscar for Best Foreign Film the following year for *Central do Brasil* (*Central Station*), the story of a curmudgeonly elderly woman (played by Oscar-nominated Fernanda Montenegro) who makes a living writing letters for illiterate migrants in Rio's Central Station and ends up accompanying a young homeless boy on a search throughout the Northeast to find his father. His follow-up film, *Abril Despedeçado* (*Behind the Sun*, 2001), was a dark, brooding tale of vengeance among rival families in the Northeast, starring acclaimed young actor Rodrigo Santoro. Another big hit set in the Sertão was Andrucha Waddington's 2000 comedy *Eu, Tu, Eles* (*Me, You, Them*), based on the true story of a woman with three husbands, whose lively soundtrack by Gilberto Gil did much to popularize traditional *forró* music. Waddington's more recent *Casa de Areia* (*House of Sand*) (2005) is a hauntingly poetic film about a mother and daughter (played by Fernanda Montenegro and her real-life actress daughter, Fernanda Torres) sent to live for years in the middle of the isolated desert of the Lençóis Maranhenses.

Aside from being entertaining, many of these films are loyal to Cinema Novo's mandate of offering critiques of Brazil's many social problems. While many films have chosen the Brazilian Northeast as a backdrop to portray the trials and tribulations of contemporary Brazil, others have taken to the urban jungles of Rio and São Paulo to offer glimpses of the violence and poverty. One of the most accomplished new directors to tackle such themes is Fernando Meirelles. With a background in advertising, Meirelles started his cinematic career with *Domésticas* (*Maids*, 2001), which offered a humorous yet realistic glimpse into the lives of the many women who work as maids for wealthy and middle-class families. His follow-up film *Cidade de Deus* (*City of God,* 2002) took both Brazil and the world by storm in with its brilliantly acted story of survival amid the gang warfare typical of a Carioca *favela.* The fragmented editing, hurtling pace, and use of *favela* dwellers as actors was inspired and brought Meirelles (who then went on to direct the English-language film *The Constant Gardener*) an Oscar nomination for best director.

In 2007, José Padilha—director of the harrowing documentary *Ônibus 174* (*Bus 174,* 2002), which was based on the 2000 hijacking of a municipal Rio de Janeiro bus in broad daylight and the police's bungling of the rescue of passengers—created another uproar with his controversial fictional feature debut. The film, entitled *Tropa da Elite* (*Elite Squad*), provided a shocking glimpse at the armed warfare between drug lords and a special squad of Rio's military police created to "protect" *favela* residents. Buzz about the film (based on very true events) was so great that when a prior cut was released via the Internet, an estimated 12 million Brazilians purchased pirated copies in the street, making the film (which later took home the Golden Bear award for best film at the Berlin International Film Festival) one of the most widely watched Brazilian films of all time.

Brazil's burgeoning feature film industry has been accompanied by a renaissance in the production of documentary films. Many delve into social themes, such as Eduardo Coutinho's excellent *Edifício Master* (2002), which offers an intimate glimpse into the lives of 37 families that inhabit a crowded 12-story Copacabana apartment building. An extraordinary number of documentaries pay homage to Brazil's musical legends, among them Carmen Miranda, in Helena Solberg's *Bananas Is My Business* (1994); Vinícius de Morais, in Miguel Faria Jr.'s *Vinicius* (2005); and Lírio de Ferreira and Hilton Lacerda's *Cartola* (2006).

BRAZILIAN LITERATURE

Jorge Amado was one of Brazil's most beloved 20th-century writers. His picaresque and colorful novels are inevitably set in his home state of Bahia, and are populated by a charismatic (if somewhat caricatural) cast of sensual *mulatas,* fishermen, charming tricksters, and Candomblé priestesses. There is usually a shot of magical realism involved in these highly readable tales. Among his most enduring novels are *Gabriela, Clove, and Cinnamon* and *Dona Flor and Her Two Husbands.*

Mário de Andrade was one of the leading figures of Brazil's modernist movement, and his novel, *Macunaíma* (1928), is a Brazilian classic. The title character is a mutant figure from the jungle who begins life as an Indian and then morphs into a black man and a white man. While changing identities, he stars in a variety of comical adventures that integrate all sorts of popular Brazilian myths, folklore, and cultural elements into a highly enjoyable narrative patchwork that is utterly Brazilian.

Machado de Assis is not widely known outside of Brazil, but among international literati he has earned a place among the all-time greats. This 19th-century author was extremely vanguard, bringing a modernist sensibility and style, not to mention a rapier wit, to bear upon the lifestyles of the rich and corrupt in fin-de-siècle Rio. His two most famous novels, *Posthumous Memoirs of Brás Cubas* and *Quincas Borba,* are both wonderfully imaginative and mordantly funny. His short stories are also quite brilliant. Try *The Psychiatrist and Other Stories.*

Paulo Lins, a well-known photojournalist, grew up in Rio's poor and dangerous Cidade de Deus *favela,* infamous for its violent gangs and brutal drug traffickers. His background supplied the fodder for the gripping novel *City of God,* which was subsequently made into the highly acclaimed, eponymous film by Fernando Meirelles.

Clarice Lispector was one Brazil's most intelligent and elegantly witty 20th-century writers. Her depth, human insight, and sense of word play are impressively displayed in her numerous short stories, which are meticulously crafted but don't make for light reading. Her most famous and most accessible novel, *The*

Hour of the Star, is a compact and searing tale of a miserable and homely northeastern migrant girl's day-to-day trials and tribulations in Rio de Janeiro.

Graciliano Ramos was a novelist from Alagoas who was largely responsible for introducing social realism and regionalism into Brazilian literature in the early 20th century. Written in pared-down prose, his most famous work, *Barren Lives,* portrays the bleak lives of families trying to survive in the hard, arid Sertão of the Northeast.

Moacyr Scliar is one of Brazil's most distinguished contemporary authors. A Jewish doctor from Rio Grande do Sul, he expertly crafts short stories and novels that often touch on the issue of Jewish identity (specifically in Brazil). Apart from his short stories, his best-known novels include *The Centaur and the Garden* and *Max and the Cats.*

ESSENTIALS

Getting There

AIR

Most international travelers enter Brazil by plane. The two main gateways are Rio de Janeiro and, increasingly, São Paulo. Most major airlines service both Rio's Tom Jobim airport and São Paulo's Guarulhos airport. From the United States, **American Airlines** (U.S. tel. 800/433-7300, www.aa.com), **Continental** (U.S. tel. 800/231-0856, www.continental.com), **Delta** (U.S. tel. 800/241-4141, www.delta.com), and **United** (U.S. tel. 800/241-6522, www.ual.com) all offer daily flights from major cities including New York, Washington, D.C., Miami, Atlanta, Chicago, Houston, and Los Angeles. **Air Canada** (Canada tel. 888/247-2262, www.aircanada.ca) has direct daily flights from Toronto, and **British Airways** (U.K. tel. 0845/702-0212, www.britishairways.com) operates direct flights from London.

Currently, one Brazilian carrier offers international service. **TAM** (U.S./Canada tel. 888/235-9826, www.tam.com.br) provides flights to the rest of Latin America, Europe, and major cities in the United States and Canada, including Miami, New York City, and Toronto.

From Europe, Portugal's national airline,

© MICHAEL SOMMERS

TAP (www.flytap.com), offers flights to northeastern capitals such as Salvador, Recife, Natal, and Fortaleza (with connections in Lisbon). If you're going to Manaus, TAM and United operate direct flights from Miami that are much more convenient than flying all the way to São Paulo for a connecting flight. American Airlines currently offers direct flights to Salvador and Recife via Miami.

If you're planning to travel around to far-flung regions of Brazil, it may make sense for you to buy a **Brazil Airpass,** which can only be purchased abroad (much to the chagrin of Brazilians) along with your international ticket. Currently, TAM offers a pass that allows you four domestic flights to any destination TAM flies to (which is basically everywhere). The pass costs US$529 (if you travel to Brazil on TAM). Otherwise it costs US$699, with an additional US$180 per flight. Various restrictions apply, such as no refunds once you've made your first domestic flight. Rebooking costs US$100.

Due to the rising price of fuel and increased airport taxes, flights are more expensive than they used to be. A round-trip flight (without taxes) for $1,000 from New York to Rio or São Paulo is considered a very good deal these days. To shop around for cheap fares, consult www.expedia.com, www.travelocity.com, and www.cheaptickets.com. In the United States, a very good travel agency (run by friendly English speaking Brazilians) is the Houston-based **Globotur** (U.S. tel. 800/998-5521, www.globotur.com). It consistently comes up with great fares for travelers in the United States and Canada. Also recommended is **Brazil Nuts** (tel. 800/553-9959 or 914/593-0266, www.brazilnuts.com). Based in Naples, Florida, it has a highly informed staff and can book flights and hotels as well as customize tours to both major and off-the-beaten path destinations.

BOAT

Many international cruise ships to South America make stops along Brazil's Atlantic coast. The biggest port of call is Rio de Janeiro (www.portosrio.gov.br). Other popular stops include the perpetually sunny northeastern beach capitals of Fortaleza (www.docasdoceara.com.br), Recife (www.portodorecife.pe.gov.br), and Salvador (www.codeba.com.br). Although an entire cruise can be quite pricy, sometimes portions can be purchased at substantial discounts. In terms of river travel, those who have lots of time to burn and aren't averse to roughing it can sail down the Amazon River from Iquitos in Peru or enter the Pantanal by Rio Paraguai from Asunción, Paraguay.

BUS

Although it's possible to drive or travel by bus to Brazil from all neighboring countries, in most cases distances are quite enormous. Apart from Santa Elena de Uairén in Venezuela, the most accessible and common entry points are from Brazil's neighbors to the south, including Argentina and Paraguay at Foz do Iguaêu and Uruguay at Jaguarão.

There is frequent bus service between Rio, São Paulo, and the capitals of the south from Montevideo (Uruguay), Buenos Aires (Argentina), Asunción (Paraguay), and even Santiago (Chile). Roads are generally quite good. International bus companies include **Pluma** (tel. 0800/646-0300 throughout Brazil, www.pluma.com.br) and **Crucero del Norte** (tel. 11/5258-5000 in Buenos Aires, www.crucerodelnorte.com.ar).

TRAIN

If you're coming from Bolivia, a favorite route of backpackers is to hop aboard the Trem da Morte (Train of Death)—whose name comes from the dangerous of habit of riding along the train's roof—that runs between Santa Cruz and Quijarro (near Corumbá), a town at the southwestern edge of the Pantanal, in the state of Mato Grosso do Sul. For more information, contact the **Ferroviaria Oriental** (www.ferroviariaoriental.com), whose main office is in Santa Cruz.

Getting Around

AIR

Because of Brazil's vast distances, flying is an ideal way to get from one region to another in record time. After two years of chaos (2006–2007) in which a combination of traffic controller strikes, a significant rise in travelers, and congested airports resulted in enormous delays, canceled flights, and furious passengers running onto the tarmac, the situation has improved significantly, thanks to the rerouting of flights and expansion of runways in major airports. Brazil's airports are modern and very well equipped, often cleaner and more polished and pleasant than counterparts in the Northern Hemisphere (of course, they are mainly frequented by those who can afford to fly). They are inevitably equipped with cafés, restaurants, bookstores, boutiques, banks, and Internet cafés. So should your flight be delayed, you will not suffer by having to wait around for a couple of hours.

There are numerous daily flights available to and from Rio and São Paulo and all the state capitals. Prices between destinations in the Southeast, South, Brasília, and the Northeast are quite reasonable (although they are rising due to increasing fuel costs). Flights to cities in the Amazon, such as Manaus and Belém, cost quite a bit more. Due to lack of passable roads, the Amazon is a region where flying is a must (unless you want to spend days on a boat). Although there are many regional *aerotaxis*, it's safest to stick to the main domestic operators.

In recent years, numerous domestic airlines have started up, while others have gone out of business. Currently, the major players are **TAM** (tel. 888/235-9826, www.tam .com.br) and **GOL** (tel. 0300/115-2121, www .voegol.com.br). To date, **Varig** (tel. 800/468-2744, www.varig.com), which recently went bankrupt and then was repurchased (by GOL) has fewer domestic routes than previously. Two recent upstarts include **Web Jet** (tel. 0300/21-01234, www.webjet.com.br) and **Azul** (www .voeazul.com.br).

The airlines now offer various fares depending on when you fly and how far in advance you book. Great promotions (such as paying full fare one way and receiving your return ticket for R$1 for certain routes) are often advertised online. Even if you don't purchase online (with a credit card), you can comparison shop and then take your findings to any local travel agent, who can then purchase the ticket for you. For the best fares, it's worthwhile booking as far in advance as possible. Budget airlines pop up from time to time and it is worth checking with travel agents for alternatives. Depending on the conditions of your ticket, you can usually change your flight or get a refund (within 24 hours), although you might need to pay a fee. Confirm with the airline or travel agency beforehand.

Barring delays, flying within Brazil is usually a much less stressful experience than flying in Europe or North America. You can check in an hour before the flight's departure (although make sure you factor in traffic delays), and security checks are refreshingly hassle-free and nonhumiliating. The carriers themselves are top of the line: clean, comfortable, with gracious cabin staff and (miracle of miracles!) free food and drink.

BUS

With the exception of the Amazon, you can get absolutely anywhere you want to go by bus. Brazil has an excellent bus system covering the entire country. Service between capital and major cities within the states and along the coasts is usually very efficient and will cost less than half the plane fare. Long-distance buses leave punctually (don't be late), and the comfortable vehicles themselves (often Mercedes-Benz buses) are equipped with plush, fold-back seats, air-conditioning, bathrooms, TVs, and coolers with free mineral water. Although bathrooms start out clean, by the end of the trip they are usually less so. When you buy your ticket, you can reserve your seat—choose one at the front or the middle of the bus (the bathroom is at the back). Also beware that air-conditioning can be very heavy duty. Make sure you have a sweater and long pants (or a towel or light blanket), or you will freeze to death. On overnight buses between major cities, you can opt for a deluxe *leito* bus. *Leito* means bed, and the large, fully reclining seats, which come with sheets and pillows, will lull you to sleep. *Leitos* usually cost 2–3 times as much as a regular bus but are cheaper than flying.

Buses are operated by hundreds of private companies (national, regional, and local), but prices are compatible between rivals. More and more companies have websites (listed throughout this guide) where you can check schedules and prices and even purchase tickets in advance. For shorter trips, advance purchase isn't necessary, but for interstate travel, especially during high-season or holiday periods, it's recommended you purchase your ticket in advance. Although major companies sell tickets via travel agents, often your best (and only) option is to purchase them at the *rodoviária*, or bus terminal, where all companies have kiosks with schedules. When purchasing a ticket, specify you want it *sem seguro* (without insurance), an added fee that bequeaths a small sum of money to your loved ones should you be involved in a fatal bus crash (not likely).

Traveling by bus in Brazil is safe, but do keep an eye on your belongings at all times. Luggage stowed beneath the bus is quite secure (it can only be retrieved with a baggage claim). Otherwise, keep valuables close by, particularly at night, and take them with you at rest stops, Except for *leitos*, most long-distance buses make stops every 2–3 hours. This gives you a chance to stretch your legs, grab some food or a drink, and use a clean bathroom. It's nonetheless advisable to bring some mineral water and a snack, such as biscuits (cookies), fruit, or nuts.

DRIVING

Driving in Brazil is not for the faint of heart. Brazilians have a love affair with speeding and are hardly sticklers for following the rules of the road. As the economy has improved in recent years, more and more people have purchased cars (on five-year installment plans), which means traffic in major cities is increasingly congested, and not just in Rio and São Paulo, whose traffic jams are nightmarish. In the Northeast and the North, the state of the roads can be dismal once you get out of the major cities, although main coastal highways are kept in good shape. Until recently, drunk driving was a major problem. However, in July 2008, Brazil's lamentable record for having one of the highest vehicle accident death tolls caused the government to enact the law of Zero Tolerance. This has resulted in police-organized blitzes around the country. Drivers are stopped arbitrarily and must take a Breathalyzer test. If even the slightest amount of alcohol is detected, you're looking at a R$955 fine and a suspension from driving for one year. Whether this law will actually be enforced universally over the long run remains to be seen, but it's always best to be on your guard when driving back from a long day at the beach (where it's a Brazilian tradition to knock back more than a few).

Despite the pitfalls, there are some places where renting a car is a definite plus. For visiting natural attractions around big cities, having a car gives you much more freedom to hit off-the-beaten track places where buses don't go (if they do, it's likely they'll make 200 local stops, or that the one daily departure is at 5 A.M.). Also, for beach hopping cars can come in very handy since you can hit secluded coves not accessible by bus. If you do rent a car, try to avoid traveling on big holiday weekends, when traffic is guaranteed to be atrocious. Also avoid driving at night. Outside of major cities, roads are poorly lit and bumps and potholes are common. In more isolated regions, you could be a victim of a highway robbery. In cities, stick to main streets, especially at night. When parking, whether you need help or not, you'll usually be guided into a space by an informal parking attendant. Aside from helping you back out, he'll promise to watch over your car as well. Whether he does or not, it's customary to tip him R$1–2 since he makes his living this way. Nonetheless, don't leave any valuables in the car, even in the trunk.

An international driver's license is more widely recognized than a foreign license, but the latter is valid for up to six months. Major international car rental chains such as Avis, Budget, Hertz, and Localiza can usually be found throughout all major cities and airports (numbers are listed throughout the guide). Rates for unlimited mileage range R$100–150 a day. Prices don't necessarily include insurance, so check beforehand.

TAXIS

Taxis are an efficient way of getting around cities—or to close-by beaches—and are considerably cheaper than in North America or Europe. You can flag one down anywhere. City cabs are metered and have two rates, or *bandeiras*. Bandeira 2, which is more expensive than Bandeira 1, is in effect after 8 P.M. and on Sundays and holidays, and sometimes during the "holiday" month of December. Sometimes, cab drivers will refer to a rate sheet—this happens when fares are raised but haven't yet been factored into the meter. If you hit it off with a cab driver, ask for his/her card. Often he/she will give you special rates for trips to airports or other long journeys. In small towns and for longer trips in cities, you can often propose a set price instead of paying the metered fare. Many airports have taxi kiosks where you prepay your fare according to distance. Although the fare is more expensive, these cabs are generally more comfortable, and you won't have to worry about getting scammed.

VANS

In rural areas, along beaches, and increasingly in major cities such as Rio and Salvador, VW vans, also known as *kombis* or *lotações,* are an alternate and unofficial source of public transportation. The term *lotação* is the most apt of all—*lotar* means to fill up, and that's precisely what these vans tend to do, stuffing as many people as possible inside. Although fares are similar to those you'll pay on a bus, vans have the advantage of careening along at high speeds that will get you to your destination more quickly. In beach areas, particularly along the northeastern coasts, vans are much more frequent than local bus lines. Even if you don't understand Portuguese, riding in a van can be a fun, if cramped, experience.

Visas and Officialdom

VISAS

In terms of foreigners entering the country, Brazil practices a policy of reciprocity. This means that if your country requires Brazilians to have travel visas, you will have to get a visa from the nearest Brazilian consulate before entering Brazil. To date, citizens of Canada, the United States, and Australia require visas. Citizens of the United Kingdom (and other European Union countries) and New Zealand don't need visas, but do need a passport that is valid for six months and a return ticket. Upon arrival, you'll be given a 90-day tourist visa.

Various types of visas are available. What differs is the cost, processing time, and documentation necessary. Currently, a single-entry tourist visa that has a validity of 90 days costs US$100 for Americans, CDN$90 for Canadians, and A$90 for Australians. Count on 1–2 weeks for processing. You'll need to submit a passport photo, show proof of a return ticket, and can often only pay with a money order.

All visitors who arrive in Brazil and go through customs will receive an entry form, which you should *not* lose. You'll need to hand it back to the Polícia Federal when leaving the country. Should you want to extend your stay, you can renew your visa, 15 days before it expires, at the visa section of the Polícia Federal headquarters in any major city. The fee for renewal is the equivalent of US$10. If you overextend the 180-day limit, you won't be deported, but you will pay a fine. The federal police headquarters is also where you should head if your passport is lost or stolen. You'll need to make a report in order to get a temporary travel document from your consulate. Then you'll need to return once again to the Polícia Federal to receive an official stamp.

Artists and/or academics who are coming to Brazil for a short time are better off traveling on a tourist visa. Those with a long-term research or study project will need to apply for a *visto temporário,* which can be issued for six months, one year, or even two years. To get one, you must be sponsored by a recognized Brazilian educational institution confirming your project. Processing can take several months.

Before coming to Brazil, make copies of your passport. Also bring a second photo ID with you. By law, in Brazil you are always required to have a picture ID. In many circumstances— from renting headphones in a museum to entering an office building—you will need to show or even leave your ID.

CUSTOMS

At Brazilian customs (*alfândega*), officials are generally more interested in Brazilians who went on major shopping sprees abroad than foreign visitors. However, since checks are random, you might find your luggage being inspected. Visitors can bring in objects for their own personal use, including cameras and laptop. If they are new, you may be asked to register the item to make sure you take it with you when you leave. (It's a good idea to bring receipts for new items.) If you're bringing things for Brazilian friends, keep them to a minimum (i.e., don't show up with four digital cameras, five iPods, and two laptops). Should you be discovered, you will end up paying duty on them. Gifts purchased overseas that are worth more than US$500 should be declared.

Before heading to customs, you might want to start shopping at the airport duty-free shops (yes, you can purchase duty-free upon arrival as well as prior to departure), where you can indulge in up to US$500 of purchases. Prices are quite competitive, particularly items such as alcohol and perfume. Should you be visiting with any Brazilians on your trip, the gift of a fine bottle of imported whiskey will earn you their undying gratitude.

BRAZILIAN EMBASSIES AND CONSULATES

The Brazilian Embassy in the **United States** is in Washington, D.C. (tel. 202/238-2700, www.brasilemb.org). You'll also find main consulates in New York (tel. 917/777-7777, www.brazilny.org), Miami (tel. 305/285-6200, www.brazilmiami.org), and Los Angeles (tel. 323/651-2664, www.brazilianconsulate.org). In **Canada,** the Brazilian Embassy is in Ottawa (tel. 613/237-1090, www.brasembottawa.com) and the main consulate is in Toronto (tel. 416/922-2503, www.consbrastoronto.org). In **Britain,** the embassy is in London (tel. 020/7499-0877, www.brazil.org.uk). In **Australia,** it is in Canberra (tel. 02/6273-2372, www.brazil.org.au).

FOREIGN CONSULATES AND EMBASSIES IN BRAZIL

Foreign embassies are all located in Brasília, while major consulates are found in both Rio de Janeiro and São Paulo. Smaller consulates can be found in state capitals such as Porto Alegre, Recife, Salvador, and Manaus. For specific numbers and listings, check the main embassy web pages: **Australian Embassy** (tel. 61/3248-5569, www.brazil.embassy.gov.au), **British Embassy** (tel. 61/3325-2710, www.ukinbrazil .fco.gov.uk), **Canadian Embassy** (tel. 61/3321-2171, www.canada.org.br), **United States Embassy** (tel. 61/3321-7272, www.embaixada-americana.org.br).

Consulates in Rio de Janeiro: Australia (Av. Presidente Wilson 231, Suite 23, Centro, tel. 21/3824-4624), Canada (Av. Atlântica 1130, 5th floor, Copacabana, tel. 21/2543-3004); United Kingdom (Praia do Flamengo 284, Flamengo, tel. 21/2555-9600), United States (Av. Presidente Wilson 147, Centro, tel. 21/3823-2000).

Consulates in São Paulo: Australia (Alameda Ministro Rocha Azevedo 456, Jardim Paulista, tel. 11/3085-6247), Canada (Av. das Nações Unidas 12901, 16th floor, tel. 11/5509-4321) United Kingdom (Rua Ferreira de Araujo 741, tel. 11/3094-2700), United States (Rua Henri Dunant 500, Chácara Santo Antônio, tel. 11/5186-7000).

Sports and Recreation

With its endless coastline, warm sea waters, and lush mountains, not to mention outstanding climate and magnificent landscapes, Brazil offers plentiful opportunities for nature buffs and sports aficionados of all types.

HIKING AND TREKKING

There is no end to places to hike in Brazil. There are trails in natural reserves and state and national parks in almost every state, but hiking trails are the best in the rugged, lush, and mountainous national parks of the Central-West interior and along the coastlines of Rio, São Paulo, and the South. Top areas include the Chapada Diamantina, in the interior of Bahia; the Serra do Cipó in Minas Gerais; the Chapada dos Veadeiros, in Goiás; the Chapada dos Guimarães, in Mato Grosso; the Serra dos Órgãos and Itatiaia in Rio as well as the Serra da Bocaina spanning Rio and São Paulo; and the Serra Gaúcha in Rio Grande do Sul. In general, hiking is most comfortable April–November (although temperatures can be quite cool in the South). During the summer, scalding sun and soaring temperatures can prove uncomfortable and exhausting.

CLIMBING

Brazil has lots of climbing challenges for climbers of every level. Many scaleable mountains have the advantage of being right on a tropical beach, which means coming down to a refreshing ocean dip. Rio has lots of great climbing opportunities, within the city itself and in the surrounding Serra dos Órgãos and Parque Nacional de Itatiaia. For more information see *Sports and Recreation* in the *Rio de Janeiro* chapter. Like hiking, climbing is best between the months of April and November.

HANG GLIDING AND PARAGLIDING

Those with Icarus fixations will enjoy gliding through Brazilian skies. One of the most famous gliding spots on the planet is without a doubt Rio de Janeiro, where you can take off from the jungly heights of the Parque Nacional da Tijuca and merge with the glorious vista of mountains, beaches, and the Baía da Guanabara before landing on the beach.

DUNE BUGGYING

The Northeast coast—from Rio Grande do Norte through Ceará to the Parque Nacional dos Lençóis Maranhenses, in Maranhão—is one long strip of glorious, often deserted beach, with long smooth stretches alternating with snow-white Saharan dunes. There are countless great day trips from Natal or Fortaleza. Those who don't mind sand in their faces can even consider tackling a longer journey.

SURFING

With its laid-back vibe, balmy weather, and endless coastline, it's little wonder that Brazil has a notorious *surfista* scene. The breaks and rollers on the southern coast are particularly enticing. The state of Santa Catarina, particularly the east coast beaches of Floripa and Garopaba, is a big surfer haven, as is São Paulo's northern coast around Maresias and on Ilhabela. Rio rocks when it comes to surf. Búzios and Niterói are surfer meccas, but the city itself is a great place to catch a wave (and to get lessons at many surfing academies). Urbanites show off their mettle at Arpoador, while serious surfers head farther south to Prainha. The Northeast coast generally has calmer waters, but you can find some good waves in Itacaré, Bahia, and in

Porto de Galinhas, Pernambuco, as well as the paradisiacal island of Fernando de Noronha. In general, surf is best in the winter months between June and September.

WINDSURFING

Windsurfing has become a popular sport all along Brazil's coastline. On the coasts of Rio and São Paulo, particularly in Búzios and Ilhabela, there is a pretty solid windsurfing scene. However, the Northeast coast, particularly in the state of Ceará, is where true fanatics should head due to the combination of warm waters and ideal wind conditions (particularly from July to December). Urbanites can rent equipment along Fortaleza's downtown beaches, while back-to-nature buffs should head to the beautifully secluded Jericoacoara.

SNORKELING AND DIVING

If you bring a mask and snorkel to Brazil, there are always calm coves worth poking around. The warm waters of the Northeast have the best snorkeling. The Coral Coast, which extends from northern Alagaos into southern Pernambuco, offers a 135-kilometer (84-mile) stretch of protected reefs that are ideal for snorkeling. The beaches surrounding São Miguel dos Milagres and Maragogi, in Alagoas, and Tamandaré and Porto de Galinhas, in Pernambuco, are all terrific snorkeling destinations. In Rio Grande do Norte, you can snorkel at beaches both north and south of Natal, with special mention going to the offshore reefs of Maracajaú (which can also get very crowded). Meanwhile, the area surrounding Bonito, in Mato Grosso do Sul, is famous for *flutuação*, during which, outfitted with snorkel, mask, and life jacket, you'll go floating down the region's astonishingly crystalline rivers alongside myriad colored fish.

As for diving (*mergulho*), there are a few really standout spots, including the Reserva Biológica do Avoredo, off the coast of Porto Belo, in Santa Catarina; Arraial do Cabo, north of Rio; off Ilhabela, in São Paulo; the Parque Nacional Marinho dos Abrolhos, off the coast of Caravelas, in southern Bahia; and the phenomenally crystalline and rigidly protected waters surrounding the island of Fernando de Noronha. Waters tend to have best visibility in the summer months (between November and February). All of these destinations have diving operators that offer excursions, rental equipment, and lessons for beginners.

FISHING

Despite the immensity of its Atlantic coast, it's Brazil's rivers that offer some of the best freshwater sportfishing in the world. Fed by various rivers including the Rio Paraguai, the Pantanal is a favorite destination for those serious about sportfishing. There are many fishing lodges (*hotéis de pesca*) along rivers, as well as "botels"; floating hotels specifically geared towards anglers. Top spots include the area surrounding Cáceres (on the Rio Cuiabá), in Mato Grosso, and the areas surrounding the towns of Aquidauana, Miranda, and Corumbá, in Mato Grosso do Sul. Fishing season is between March and October. The other great fishing destination is, unsurprisingly, the Amazon, where you can go after the enormous pirarucu or the much smaller but infamously fanged piranha—both of which are considered delicacies. Various tour companies run excursions out of Belém and Manaus.

WILDLIFE-WATCHING

Hands down, the best place for communing with Brazil's unusual fauna is the Pantanal. From *fazenda* lodges located deep within the wetlands (and often only accessible by boat or plane), you can hike, boat, and ride horses in search of animals as strange and wonderful as capybaras, giant otters and anteaters, *jacarés* (caimans), and even elusive jaguars, not to mention a fabulous array of squawking, screeching, and colorful birds including the beautiful and rare *arará azul* (hyacinth macaw). In fact, bird-watchers will be enthralled in the Pantanal, as well as in the Amazon rainforest. Overall, it's much harder to see larger mammals in the Amazon—your best bet is to stay in a jungle lodge in the middle of the forest itself where, you can explore the river's tributaries by boat—but aside from birds, you're guaranteed to view plenty of caimans and pink river dolphins.

Along the coast, whale-watching is possible along the southern coast of Santa Catarina, particularly around the Ilha do Campeche, on the east coast of Floripa, and Praia do Rosa, south of the city. In Bahia, you can also take offshore trips to see whales frolicking, particularly in Praia do Forte and Caravelas. Whale-watching is best between July and November, when whales swim north from Antarctica for the hatching and nursing of their young. Fans of dolphins can see—and often swim among—these intelligent creatures, in the Amazon basin around Manaus (particularly Novo Airão) and in the warm waters around Praia da Pipa, in Rio Grande do Norte, and, most impressively, those surrounding the island of Fernando de Noronha.

SOCCER

It's hardly a secret that soccer (known in Portuguese as *futebol*) is not just Brazil's national sport, but a passion that borders on the fervently religious. It was introduced by a Brazilian-born man by the name of Charles Miller, who in 1894 returned from higher studies in England toting a soccer ball and equipment. The first soccer games played in São Paulo proved enormously popular, and *futebol* rapidly swept through the country like wildfire.

Today, Brazil is the only country in the world to have won five World Cups (1958, 1962, 1970, 1994, and 2002), and during World Cup games, the entire country shuts down to cheer on the Selecão Brasileira (or to scream advice to the coach or players). While Brazilians are ferocious in their support of their teams, they are equally fierce at criticizing any botched play

or strategy; consequently the range of emotions witnessed in any stadium or around any TV set is impressive. You're as likely to witness big macho guys hugging and kissing each other for joy after a victory as you are to see them sobbing tragically following a defeat. In Brazil, *jogadores de futebol* rank as the country's reigning celebrities, despite the fact that many of them spend most of the year overseas, playing for top European teams.

Aside from watching *futebol* (a year-round pastime since there is no "season") everywhere you go, you'll see Brazilians (mostly males) playing *futebol*. Whether it's on the floodlit sands of Copacabana, the dilapidated streets of an urban *favela*, or a cleared makeshift field in the midst of the Amazon forest, soccer is ubiquitous. Often, players are barefoot and goal posts are rolled-up T-shirts; however, the passion is always the same.

VOLLEYBALL

In Brazil, volleyball is equally popular with men and women. Like soccer, *vôlei* is often played on the beach (barefoot). The possibility of a soft landing allows players to go all out in trying to dive for the ball (although you do risk getting sand up your nose). A variation of volleyball is *futevôlei*, in which no hands are allowed. Instead players use a combination of fancy footwork and hard-headedness.

FRESCOBALL

Frescoball is a popular Brazilian beach sport in which two players lob a rubber ball back and forth using two paddle-like rackets. Invented in 1946 on Copacabana beach by a local resident named Lian Pontes de Carvalho, frescoball's popularity quickly spread to beaches throughout Brazil, and more recently, to other countries as well.

Accommodations

Brazil has accommodations for every inclination and budget—from hostels crammed with backpackers and rented rooms in simple homes to Amazonian jungle lodges and chic boutique hotels lost in paradise. As international tourism has increased, and Brazilians themselves—encouraged by a booming economy and relatively cheaper air fares—have begun to travel more, tourist infrastructure has become quite sophisticated, even in spots deemed to be in the middle of nowhere.

Outside of big cities, in most places, R$100 per night, for a couple, will get you some comfortable digs. In big cities, the same level of comfort can be had for R$150 per night, per couple.

Rates are almost always based on double occupancy, but single travelers can always try bargaining for a lower rate. In fact, everyone should bargain. No self-respecting Brazilian ever pays the rates listed at the reception—known as *balcão* (counter) rates. Outside of high season (Christmas–Carnaval and July)—when advance reservations are recommended—many hotels offer significant discounts of up to 50 percent. São Paulo and Brasília—in which everybody clears out during high season—offer their deep discounts during holidays and long weekends. You can also ask for a *desconto* if you stay in one hotel over several nights. In this guide, most rates for larger hotels do not factor in special Internet or holiday promotions or those obtained via travel agents or websites. Don't let high prices dissuade you. It's possible to live it up in a fantastic luxury hotel for considerably less than it would cost you in North America or Europe.

Advance reservations are recommended throughout high season, and are essential if some major *festa* (Reveillon, Carnaval, São João, Bumba-Meu-Boi) is going to be erupting during your visit. For confirmation, some hotels may ask for a deposit of 50 percent (for one night) or that you pay one night (if you're staying for several) up front.

No matter what the price, rates always include *café de manhã,* or breakfast. This can range from a cup of coffee, a roll, and a piece of fruit to a lavish spread. In the Northeast and Minas Gerais, in particular, even in simple places, breakfast is a lavish affair with freshly baked breads and cakes, cheeses, fruit jellies, and freshly squeezed juice.

CAMPING

Camping is a possibility in and around major beach resorts up and down the coast, where lots of Brazilian youths regularly flock in the summer. Aside from specific campsites, some beachfront *pousadas* allow people to pitch tents and share facilities. The problem with camping (aside from mosquitos and rain) is security. At a campsite or *pousada,* you'll definitely have to watch over your valuables. And if you foolishly decide to pitch a tent in the wilderness, you'll be putting not only your belongings at risk, but yourself. For information about sites, consult with the **Camping Clube do Brasil** (tel. 21/2532-0203, www.campingclube.com.br). With headquarters in Rio, it operates close to 50 sites throughout Brazil.

HOSTELS

The best accommodations deals to be had in Brazil are in simple *pousadas* (guesthouses) or *albergues de juventude* (youth hostels). There are some very well-equipped versions of the latter. Although standard dorms are a steal at R$30–40 a person, couples and families can often snag private rooms that work out to be the same price. Contrary to stereotype, many of Brazil's hostels are cheery and friendly places (many in restored houses) with gardens, lounges, and room to swing in a hammock and meet up with fellow travelers. An International Youth Hostel Association card isn't necessary, but it gets you discounts of around R$5–10 a night. If you're traveling during summer or school vacations, be forewarned that beds fill quickly, so it's wise to reserve in advance. For a list of more than

80 hostels, consult the **Federação Brasileira dos Albergues de Juventude** (tel. 21/2531-1085, www.hostel.org.br), whose headquarters are in Rio.

POUSADAS

A *pousada* is generally a guesthouse or bed-and-breakfast, but the definition is as elastic as *pousadas* themselves are varied. Some *pousadas* are really basic hotels with four walls, a sheet-covered mattress, a window, and that's it. Others are welcoming, intimate, family-owned lodges where you'll be made to feel as if you've just moved in. Still others qualify as refined and luxurious boutique hotels with creature comforts and amenities galore. Ultimately, a *pousada* distinguishes itself from a hotel by its size (small—many are often located in houses or bungalows as opposed to high-rise hotels) and B&B-style. *Pousadas* are rare in big cities, particularly Rio, São Paulo, and Brasília, but you'll find them everywhere else, particularly in beach areas.

Some of Brazil's most captivating *pousadas*—many of which are included in this guide—are members of an association called Roteiros de Charme. These *pousadas* all offer great comfort, outstanding service, and exquisite furnishings. Often, they are located in historic homes or in idyllic locations. For more information, contact the **Roteiros de Charme** headquarters in Rio de Janeiro (tel. 21/2287-1592, www.roteiros-decharme.com.br).

HOTELS

Like *pousadas*, Brazilian hotels are quite varied. Although they receive star ratings (from one to five), these ratings are more impressionistic than accurate, and not all hotels have stars. In general, hotels are confined to big cities and are located within multistory high-rises, although you'll come across some older, cheaper, and shabbier ones as well. A *quarto* usually refers to a room without a bathroom, which is what you'll get if you check into an *apartamento*, along with basic amenities such as a *ventilador* (fan) or air-conditioning, a TV, a stocked mini-fridge, and a phone. Usually apartments are

ranked as standard, superior, and *luxo* (luxury). Depending on the hotel, the luxury can be a mild upgrade from the standard or can include pampering on a rock star-and-royalty scale. In beach towns, rooms with sea views are highly coveted and usually cost more. Be aware that some hotels add a local service tax onto the rate, which may add another 15 percent onto your tab. In Rio, for example, there is a 5 percent service tax.

APART-HOTELS

In big cities, especially Rio and São Paulo, you'll find apart-hotels, also known as flats. Located in modern high-rises, they are usually frequented by business travelers who want a sense of a home-away-from-home. Cheaper than hotels of the same caliber, apart-hotels usually have a living room and kitchen where you can make your own meals; however, they also have hotel amenities such as security, and sometimes a pool and/or fitness room, restaurant, and even room service.

MOTELS

Motels in Brazil are nothing like the friendly family variety North Americans are accustomed to. In Brazil, motels are where couples go for encounters of an amorous/sexual nature. Many rendezvous are illicit, but often they provide getaways for harried middle-class couples in search of a quickie or teens or twenty-somethings who get no privacy at home. Viewed that their primary purpose is to set the stage for an hour or night of passion, motels usually feature kitsch-erotic decor and accessories and staff that are extremely discreet. Depending on the location and/or the price, motels can be sleazy and dangerous or quite posh with heart-shaped beds and whirlpools, mirrored ceilings, TVs and wet bars, and so on. Aside from undeniably atmospheric, they are usually pretty inexpensive (rates are by the hour and the night).

JUNGLE LODGES AND FAZENDA LODGES

If you dream of visiting the unspoiled Amazon rainforest, the best (and most comfortable) way of doing so is to check into one of the many jungle lodges that can be reached by boat from Manaus (and are actually in the rainforest). Usually located on a suspended complex of stilts overlooking a river, jungle lodges vary from rustic to (overly) luxurious; who needs the trappings of a five-star hotel in the middle of the world's largest rainforest? Most of them, however, are quite comfortable and ecologically correct, relying on natural materials to blend into their surroundings.

Similarly, if your heart is set upon visiting the Pantanal, you should definitely consider staying at a *fazenda* lodge. Similar to jungle lodges, *fazenda* lodges are located deep within the Pantanal's wetlands, providing you with a unique and privileged location from which to view the region's teeming wildlife. A *fazenda* is a ranch, and most of these lodges are actually

working cattle farms (the Pantanal is cattle country); guests can also participate in, or at least witness, life on the farm. Although there are a few basic options, the majority of *fazenda* lodges, while rustic, are fairly comfortable. A few feature accommodations in historic ranch houses with original antique furnishings. You'll also find *fazenda* lodges on the Ilha de Marajó, at the mouth of the Amazon River. The *fazendas* here are devoted to vast herds of water buffalo that are raised on the island.

Despite the fact that meals and all (or most) guided excursions and nature activities (and sometimes transfers) are included in the rates, both jungle lodges and *fazenda* lodges are fairly pricy (usually a 2–3-night minimum stay is required). However, in both cases, they offer the best way of experiencing both of these two unique ecosystems.

Food

If invited to free associate about "Brazilian cuisine," most foreigners would be hard-pressed to conjure up anything beyond *feijoada,* the ubiquitous national stew of beans, salted beef, pork, and sausage, and *caipirinha,* the hipster cocktail du jour in which *cachaça* (Brazilian version of rum) is shaken up with crushed ice, lime, and sugar. Often, Brazilian restaurants abroad tend to traffic in watered-down versions of Bahian cooking, which entices with its strong flavors and exotic African influences. There are also Brazilian *churrascarias* that delight meat lovers by serving up prime cuts of barbecued beef, even though *churrasco,* a hallmark of the Gaúcho culture of the Pampas, is as popular in Argentina and Uruguay as it is in southern Brazil.

When you travel to Brazil, you won't encounter a uniform Brazilian cuisine. Of course, certain basic staples compose the foundations of the Brazilian diet—most famously, the classic duo of *arroz e feijão* (rice and beans), which can be found all over Latin America, but which Brazilians love as they do

their mothers. I know Brazilians who return from journeys to Paris, London, and Rome, and the first thing they do to *matar as saudades* ("kill" their homesickness) is cook up a pot of *feijão* or *feijoada* (and invite 20 people over). However, the most fascinating discovery you'll make about Brazilian cuisine is that there isn't one—rather, there are many. Ultimately, Brazilian cooking is the sum of its regions, which means that the food you'll encounter is as diverse, surprising, and unforgettable as the country itself. Brazilians love food, and every social occasion, from a birthday party to an afternoon on the beach or a night at a bar, comes replete with some sort of wonderful *petisco* or *tira-gosto* (appetizer) to nibble on. In general, cooking is simple but honest. What makes a Brazilian dish seem elaborate is the sheer abundance of ingredients, all of them natural (it's very easy to avoid chemical additives in Brazil), and the savoir faire with which they are combined. Whether following traditional family recipes or creating daring new dishes that merge imported techniques with

feijoada and a *caipirinha*

authentic homegrown cuisine easily goes to Minas Gerais. Reflecting its mountainous landscapes, Mineiro cooking is quite robust. Most popular are dishes featuring pork or chicken. *Frango com quiabo* (chicken with okra) is a classic, as is *frango ao molho pardo* (chicken stewed in its own blood, which, far from gruesome, is downright delicious). *Tutu ao mineiro,* a thick puree, and *feijão tropeiro* are two bean dishes that are served as accompaniments. Other common side dishes are vegetables such as jade green chuchu, sweet pumpkin, and shredded *couve* (kale), sautéed in garlic. Brazil's leading dairy producer, Minas is renowned for a white creamy cheese known as *queijo de Minas.* It turns up most famously in *pães de queijo,* light and addictive cheese balls that go down well with a shot of espresso, and as a consort of guava jelly in the popular pairing known as *Romeu e Julieta.*

South

As Brazil's most recently settled region, the cooking of the South is largely influenced by the 19th-century European immigrants—Italians, Germans, and Poles—who populated its cities and the small farms of its countryside. You'll easily find polenta, sauerkraut, and even *varenikes* throughout the South. There are, however, a few distinctive specialties. Paraná is renowned for *barreado,* a heavy but flavorful stew of beef, bacon, potatoes, and spices sealed with a covering of manioc flour, and then stewed for hours in a clay casserole. Florianópolis is a great place to stuff yourself on raw oysters as well as white and pink shrimp. And while Rio Grande do Sul's considerable Italian population explains the presence of Brazil's primary wine growing region, a much more distinctive legacy is that of the Gaúcho cowboys whose traditional meal of Pampas-fed beef, rubbed in salt and slowly charred over hot coals, can be savored in numerous *churrascarias.*

Central-West

The vast plains of the Central-West are dominated by the scrubby vegetation of the Cerrado,

local fare, Brazilians generally put a lot of effort and care into the food they prepare, and you're sure to appreciate the results.

Throughout this guide, considerable attention has been devoted to both local and regional cuisines. Nonetheless, the following overview will give you an appetizing overview of the specialties of each geographic region.

REGIONAL CUISINE
Southeast

Neither Rio de Janeiro nor São Paulo has a true cuisine of its own. Because Rio housed the Portuguese royal court in the 19th century, a certain Portuguese influence can still be detected in there; hence the popularity of *bacalhau* (salted cod) and certain egg-based desserts, such as the custardy *quindim.* São Paulo was built by immigrants, but the people who left the biggest imprint on its culinary scene were Italians, thus explaining the popularity of pasta and, especially, pizza. However, aside from the classic Saturday afternoon *feijoada* that is a tradition in both capitals, the award for most distinctive and which yields some unique and exotic fruits. Among the most distinctive is the *pequi,* a heavily perfumed orange fruit that flavors everything from rice and chicken dishes to liqueurs. In Goiás, a specialty is *empadão,* a large torte-like version of an *empada* (empanada) stuffed with fillings such as chicken, pork, sausage, cheese, and hearts of palm. Farther west, the untamed frontier regions of Mato Grosso and Mato Grosso do Sul are cattle country. However, the river-fed wetlands of the Pantanal ensure an abundance of exotic freshwater fish, such as *pacu, pintado,* and *piraputanga,* as well as plenty of caiman steaks.

Northeast

The Northeast has several distinctive culinary traditions within its vast expanse. The most famous dishes are those hailing from Bahia's capital of Salvador and the surrounding coastal region known as the Recôncavo, where African influence is extremely pronounced. Ingredients such as dried shrimp, coconut milk, *pimenta malagueta* (hot pepper), and the pungently scented, amber oil of the *dendê* palm flavor dishes such as *moqueca* (a stew of fish and/or seafood) and *bobó de camarão,* in which shrimp is combined with pureed manioc. Many dishes are traditionally used in Afro-Brazilian Candomblé rituals. Such is the case with *acarajé,* the crunchy bean fritter prepared by Bahianas on *praças* and street corners.

Fish and seafood are abundant along the entire coast, stretching from Alagoas all the way up to Maranhão. *Peixada* is a popular fish stew. You'll also find shrimps, crabs, and (in Fortaleza) lobsters galore. North of Bahia, the dry, arid interior known as the Sertão leaves a strong imprint on the culture of the coast. In terms of food, this translates into *carne-de-sol* (sun-dried meat), *queijo coalho* (a rubbery white cheese that's delicious when grilled and drizzled with molasses), and *feijão.*

Native manioc (*mandioca*) was a major staple of the Tupi-Guarani Indians that caught on with the arrival of colonial settlers. Also known as *macaxeira* and *aipim,* manioc shows up on the menu in various guises throughout Brazil. However, with the exception of the Amazon, nowhere else is it as popular as in the Northeast, where you'll find it boiled, fried (manioc french fries are the best), and pureed. Manioc flour, *farinha de mandioca,* is an essential companion at all meals, as is *farofa,* in which *farinha* is sautéed with butter, onions, garlic, and even bananas. When added to broth, *farinha* become a thick mush known as *pirão.* It is also used to make crunchy crêpe-like *tapiocas,* a favorite snack throughout the Northeast.

North

Northern Brazil is dominated by the Amazon River and surrounding rainforest, and its abundance of fish and fruits provide the main ingredients for local fare. Among the many fish you're likely to bite into are *filhote* and the mighty pirarucu, which is usually dried and salted before being grilled on a hot tile or cooked in coconut milk. Two of the most common and delectable fruits you'll come across (and never forget) are *cupuaçu* and *bacuri,* which can be savored in the form of juice and ice cream as well as frothy creams and mousses. The dark purple *açai,* whose thick pulp is chock-full of nutrients, is a major source of sustenance, while the fruit of the *guaraná* plant provides a natural pick-me up. The influence of the indigenous culture that predominates throughout the Amazon is also apparent in the region's most popular dishes. *Tacacá* is a shrimp-filled broth, thickened with *tucupi,* a thick yellow liquid extracted from manioc, and flavored with *jambu* leaves that will leave your mouth tingling and slightly numb. *Tucupi* is also the main ingredient in *pato no tucupi,* a duck stew that, along with piranha soup, has become an edible trademark of the Amazon.

MEALS

In general, meals in Brazil—both in private homes and in restaurants—are relaxed and casual affairs. That said, Brazilians usually have good table manners. One thing they don't do in restaurants is eat with their hands. For example, pizza is always eaten with a knife and fork.

If you're out eating or drinking with Brazilian

friends, when the bill comes it's customary to divide up the total evenly, no matter who ate or drank what. Sitting around and calculating who ate what and who owes what is considered petty. Since most restaurants and bars add a 10 percent (optional) service charge onto the bill, tipping isn't usual, although it's customary to round up the bill, and even add a couple of *reais*, if you feel service was exceptional.

Breakfast

The classic Brazilian breakfast, or *café de manhã* is pretty simple. At its most basic, it involves strong coffee, freshly baked bread, with butter, cheese, and sometimes ham, and fruit and/or fruit juice (either fresh or from frozen pulp). In more rural areas, breakfasts can be much more copious, with homemade cakes, breads, and biscuits, porridges made from corn, rice, or tapioca, scrambled eggs, and, in the Northeast, *carne-de-sol*. In better hotels, they are likely to take on a banquet-like appearance. If you need to fend for yourself, you have many options. You can head to a *bar de suco*, or juice bar, for a thick *vitamina* made with oats, milk, and pulverized fruit, where you'll also find healthy *salgados* (savory pastries filled with everything from shrimp to hearts of palm). Some *padarias* (bakeries) as well as *lanchonetes* (snack bars) serve breakfast fare for Brazilians on the run. Popular items are grilled rolls with butter (*pão grelhado com manteiga*). The addition of cheese makes it a *queijo quente;* with ham and cheese it becomes a *mixto quente*.

Lunch

Lunch, or *almoço*, is the major meal of the day. In big cities and small towns alike, the classic version of a working person's lunch is a portion of meat (usually beef or chicken) accompanied by rice, beans, and some form of a small salad or boiled vegetable. All sorts of restaurants serve up such items as daily specials. And depending on what region you're in, you'll also have options that reflect the local cuisine. If you're lunching solo, ask for a "PF" or *prato feito*. You'll be served all of the above on one plate for an economical price of around R$5–6.

If there are two of you, or even three, you can opt for the *prato comercial,* in which the same meal is brought to you on a tray, with each item served in its own dish. This could cost between R$10–15. Although the food prepared in such places is simple, non-fussy fare, in smaller restaurants it is often home-cooked (*caseira*) and very tasty, particularly in smaller towns.

Of course, there is also great variety of restaurants where you can order, à la carte, both Brazilian and international specialties. In general, most portions are enough to serve two people, and sometimes three. Usually only more expensive restaurants serve *pratos individuais*. If you're worried about the quantity of food, you can ask for a *meia-porção* (half portion).

Dinner

In most Brazilian homes, dinner is a light affair. Often people have *café com leite* along with a simple sandwich or buttered rolls. *Sopas* (soups) are also very popular. Of course, when company is involved, things get more elaborate. And if they're going out for a night on the town, there is a vast array of dining options to choose from, particularly in the bigger cities.

DRINKS
Coffee

All those clichés you've heard about Brazil as the land of coffee are true. *Café* is seemingly everywhere, and Brazilians always seem to be drinking it, for the most part with vast amounts of sugar or sweetener (*adocante*). Sometimes, it's served pre-sweetened, so if you want your coffee black, ask for it *sem açúcar*. Instead of the big mugs of silty, watered down stuff popular with the Starbucks generation, Brazilians like their *café* small and potent. In fact, served in espresso or little plastic cups (if you're drinking one from the vendors who sell thermoses of the stuff in the streets), it is popularly known as *cafezinho* (little coffee). *Cafezinhos* can be enjoyed all day long, and they usually are, often in accompaniment with some sort of sweet or savory pastry. And no meal is complete without one, although if you order a *cafezinho* with your dessert (as opposed to after), people will look at

CACHAÇA

What rum is to Cuba, tequila to Mexico, and vodka to Russia, *cachaça* is to Brazil. Distilled from fermented sugarcane juice, to which sugar is then added, *cachaça* packs a wallop – its alcohol content is between 38 and 48 percent. Whether it's drunk pure or as the base of the world-famous and highly addictive national cocktail known as the *caipirinha* (*cachaça*, sugar, crushed ice, and lime), Brazilians swear by their *cachaça*. In fact, the average Brazilian imbibes about 3 gallons (or 12 liters) of the stuff in a given year, which explains current production level of 1.3 billion liters.

Caipirinhas and other cocktails are usually made with the clear, industrially manufactured varieties – such as Pitú and 51 – that you can buy in any supermarket. Dirt cheap, these are pretty foul-tasting on their own, and if you want to savor *cachaças* on par with the world's finer aged whiskies, you're better off choosing from one of the thousands of artisanal varieties, produced at small mills throughout the country (most famously in Minas Gerais). These are more often golden in hue, with a variety of fragrances and tastes, often depending on the wooden barrels they are aged in, many of which are made from native trees such as almond, brazilwood, and the exotically named *ipê, jequitibá, tibiriça,* and *jatobá*. These *cachaças* are usually sold directly to bars, restaurants, supermarkets, and discerning consumers.

Cachaça began life as a drink imbibed by African slaves who worked on sugarcane plantations, and then was a poor man's poison. However, over the past decade, the fabrication of artisanal and even organic *cachaças* has led to a major boost in *cachaça*'s rep, with aficionados sipping it pure. Recently, the government and producer associations succeeded in trademarking the *cachaça* name with the goal of marketing it – at home and abroad – as a fine alcohol. Nonetheless *cachaça* is nothing if not democratic, and it shows up around the nation under a variety of names, including *pinga* (as in drop), *cana* (cane), *aguardente* (burning water), *mardita* (from *maldita* meaning "the damned one"), *água-que-passarinho-não-bebe* ("water that birds don't drink"), and *aquela-que-matou-o-guarda* ("that which killed the cop"). Aside from *caipirinhas*, other popular (and potent) *cachaça* potions include:

- **batida** – *Cachaça*, milk, and the pulp of fresh fruit; it's like a sweet milkshake with a kick. It tends to give hangovers. Popular flavors include passion fruit, coconut, and pineapple.

- **bombeirinho** – The Brazilian version of a Kir Royal is *cachaça* and gooseberry (*groselha*) syrup.

- **capeta** ("demon") – This is a truly diabolical mix of *cachaça* along with cinnamon, red-hued fruit juice (cherry, strawberry, or grape), red wine, vodka, and sugar. It is served in large portions, with dry ice added to enhance fumes.

- **leite de onça** ("jaguar's milk") – This favorite during the Festas Juninas mixes *cachaça* with milk, condensed milk, and cinnamon.

- **quentão** ("hot stuff") – Similar to a sangria, this hot mixture of cheap (sweet) wine and *cachaça*, spiked with ginger, cinnamon, and cloves, is also a popular favorite during the Festas Juninas.

- **rabo-de-galo** ("rooster's tail") – *Cachaça* is mixed with red vermouth.

you funny. In the morning and in the evening, *leite* (milk) is sometimes added. Until recently, the best of Brazil's coffee was exported, but in the last few years, a gourmet coffee scene has begun to emerge. Rio and São Paulo have seen the birth of gourmet coffee shops; aside from savoring organic and exclusive blends from all over Brazil (although the best beans are from Minas), you can purchase beans to take home with you.

Juices

Travelers to Brazil are usually blown away by the diversity of fresh fruit juices available throughout the country. You can get juice all over Brazil, in *lanchonetes, bars,* and especially in *bares de suco* (juice bars), which are usually festooned with cornucopias of fresh fruit waiting to be pulverized in front of your eyes. Juice bars are most plentiful in urban beach neighborhoods where they are staples of health-obsessed, body-baring Brazilians. In Rio's Zona Sul neighborhoods of Copacabana, Ipanema, and Leblon, they are omnipresent. Aside from run-of-the-mill tropical fruits such as papaya, mango, guava, and abacaxi (pineapple), you'll often find exotic fruits of the Northeast (*siriguela, umbu,* and *cajá*) and the Amazon (*bacuri, cupuaçu,* and the super-healthy *açaí*). Even vitamin-packed vegetables such as *cenoura* (carrot) and *beterraba* (beet) are blender worthy.

Freshly squeezed orange juice (*suco de laranja*), which you'll find everywhere (Brazil is the world's number one producer and exporter of OJ), is the only juice served pure and unadulterated. Other fruits are mixed with water (filtered), milk (becoming a *vitamina*), or orange juice. Sugar (*açúcar*) is added, as is ice (*gelo*). If you want your juice *sem gelo* and *sem açúcar*, ask for it *natural*. You can often mix one or more fruits and, in fact, hard-core juice bars offer a menu of juice cocktails for whatever ails you. Energizers usually feature *guaraná* powder or syrup and *açaí;* anti-stress drinks add *suco de maracujá,* a natural sedative (which Brazilians give to hyperactive children).

Should you have an upset stomach or a hangover, a foolproof cure is to drink an *água-de-coco,* the fresh water from a green coconut. It's sold at kiosks along many beach areas and at beach *barracas* and fruit stands; the vendor will hack open a hole in the coconut with a machete and give you a straw to slurp on the refreshing tonic. After, with the same machete, he or she will hack open the coconut, so you can scoop out the custardy white meat. Another popular drink sold in the streets is *caldo de cana,* or sugarcane juice. Usually the cane is pulverized right before your eyes and the subsequent juice can be drunk straight up or with the addition of lime.

Soft Drinks

Brazilians have a fondness for soft drinks (*refrigerantes*), especially at the end of a heavy meal as a sort of appetite cleanser. The two most popular soft drinks are Coca Cola and the even more popular Guaraná, a champagne cola flavored with the Amazonian *guaraná* berry (in doses small enough so that its caffeine content doesn't kick in). There are many national brands of Guaraná, and some regional ones as well, such as Jesus, a shocking pink version made in Maranhão. To cut the sweetness, ask for *limão* (a slice of lime) with your Coke and *laranja* (a slice of orange) with your Guaraná.

Beer

As refreshing as *sucos* and *refrigerantes* may be, nothing beats the heat like a *cerveja estupidamente gelada,* otherwise known as a "stupidly cold" beer. It's hard to overexaggerate Brazilians' love of beer. *Cerveja* is a day-to-day companion enjoyed not just at the corner bar, but at a meal, on a beach, in the street, at a *festa.* A lot of foreigners used to dark malts and microbrewery ales with nuanced flavors scoff at pale Brazilian beer with its low alcohol content and supposedly weak, watery taste. However, if you're going to be drinking all day (or night) in 40°C (104°F) heat, you'll come to appreciate the lightness of Brazilian beer. Just make sure it is always *bem gelada* (nicely chilled). The idyllic beer is the *véu de noiva,* in which the bottle arrives at your table cloaked in a thin layer of frost that resembles "a bride's veil."

Most bars sell beer in 600 milliliter bottles, but fancier places sell so-called "long necks," similar to those you'll find in North America and Europe. At supermarkets, on beaches, and in the streets, beer is often sold in *latas* (cans). There are various rival national brands (Brahma, Antarctica, Skol, Nova Schin) and some very good regional ones (particularly in São Paulo and the South), such as Bohemia (from Rio de Janeiro) and Serramalte (from Rio Grande do Sul). *Chope* is a pale draft—both Brahma and Antarctica have their own versions—with a nice foam that is particularly popular in Rio and São Paulo. Essential bar vocab includes *"mais uma"* ("another beer, please") and *"a saideira"* ("last call").

Wine

Unlike its neighbors, Chile and Argentina, Brazil is not a big wine country, although in recent years there has been an increased interest in drinking fine wines. You'll find decent wines in most large city supermarkets and very good ones in fine restaurants, although few are actually from Brazil itself. The main wine-growing region is the Vale dos Vinhedos in Rio Grande do Sul (close to Argentina) where descendants of Italian immigrants from Veneto cultivate *vinhos* that can be quite good (try a bottle of Miolo, one of the top and most traditional wineries). Overall, Brazil's tropical climate isn't really conducive to wine drinking (in the Northeast people often serve even red wine chilled). The exceptions are São Paulo and the South, where cool winters and the strong Italian influence have resulted in more of a wine culture.

PLACES TO EAT

Aside from your classic sit-down restaurant serving à la carte fare, you have a wide variety of eating venues in Brazil.

Comida por Quilo

Highly popular and very affordable are restaurants serving *comida por quilo*, where you help yourself to a self-service buffet and then pay for your food by weight. You'll find kilo restaurants all over Brazil. They range from very basic (and sometimes unappetizing) to banquet-like extravaganzas featuring fine cuisine. Many places—such as Bahia and Minas Gerais—offer per kilo buffets of regional specialties, which (if you choose well) allow you to sample a wide variety of local specialties. Natural food restaurants serving health food also usually operate on a per kilo system. There are also dessert options. Complimentary coffee and tea are usually offered at the end of the meal. The best thing about per kilo restaurants is that you can choose exactly what and how much you want to eat. This is particularly useful for individual travelers. Unfortunately, most kilo restaurants are only open for lunch. An average meal in a kilo restaurant will set you back R$8–20, depending on the sophistication of the food and your appetite.

Rodízio

Rodízio (which means rotation) refers to a type of restaurant in which you pay a set price and then choose from a rotating display of food proffered by waiters who circle endlessly between the kitchen and the dining room. Since you can feast until you're full, it's recommended that you go on an empty stomach. Most often, you'll find *rodízio* in *churrascarias,* where an endless parade of freshly grilled meat will make the rounds. All it takes is the slightest signal to a waiter, and that appetizing piece of meat that was on a skewer will be on your plate. Other popular forms of *rodízio* include pizza, pasta, and sushi.

Bars

For many Brazilians, the local bars act as a home away from home. More than just a place to knock back a few cold beers or a shot of *cachaça,* bars are where you watch the end of a *novela* or a nail-biting *futebol* match, and converse with friends (or strangers) late into the night. In Brazil, there's no such thing as a quick drink. Rather, people spend hours at a bar. It isn't surprising that most traditional bars, or *botecos,* often serve (very tasty) food to their loyal clientele. For the happy-hour or late-night crowd, it is common to nibble on snacks known as *petiscos* or *tira-gostos*. Options vary tremendously according to the region and the sophistication of the bar, but universal classics include *bolinhos de bacalhau* (crunchy codfish balls) and *caldo de feijão* (a thick bean soup often accompanied by cilantro and pork rinds). One or several *porções* of these snacks can easily serve as a meal, and in fact, tablesful of Brazilians often communally share one or more dishes in lieu of dinner. However, lots of bars do also serve full meals, which run the gamut from home-cooked *pratos fixtos* to innovative and sophisticated fare on par with some of Brazil's finest restaurants.

Throughout this guide, *Bars* and *Restaurants* have separate listings, but there is often enormous overlap between the two. Many bars are an excellent option for a meal (especially at night). They are often more laid-back, convivial and affordable than your classic restaurant, and they often feature live music.

On the Beach

For Brazilians who live along the coast (which is the majority of the population), the beach, like bars, is like a second home. Most Brazilians don't have backyards and they don't have a culture of picnicking in parks. In fact, they don't have a culture of picnicking, period. Who needs to picnic when every type of food you might desire is sold on the beach itself? If you're spread out on a towel on an urban beach, should hunger hit you need only stop one of the endless parade of vendors hawking everything from *picolés* (popsicles) to grilled skewers of shrimp. Meanwhile, in cities, small beach towns, and even seemingly deserted stretches of sand, you'll always encounter at least one *barraca,* or rustic beach bar, that will serve up freshly grilled fish or shrimp, and often lots more. In the Northeast, in particular, beach *barracas* are everywhere. Aside from shade, cool drinks, showers, and bathrooms, they often provide delicious and affordable lunch and snacks that you can enjoy without having to change out of your bathing suit.

On the Street

Throughout Brazil you'll find an enormous array of cheap and delicious snacks. In general, they serve as a *lanche* (snack), but they can also substitute a light meal. Some of the best cooking you'll taste—*tacacá* in Belém, *acarajé* in Salvador, *tapiocas* in Maceió, *pastéis* in São Paulo—is made and prepared on the street. Although many people are leery of purchasing food on the street, in general, hygienic conditions are fairly strict. Keep in mind that those who prepare and sell food in public places sell to locals, and if word gets around that something was off, bad, or rotten, their business will suffer. That said, use your judgment and stick to places in main areas where you see a lot of people lining up and/or eating.

SPECIAL CONCERNS

Depending on where they go, **vegetarians** will have either an easy or challenging time in Brazil. In major cities as well as popular ecotourist destinations (even in the middle of nowhere), you'll always find a *restaurante natural,* serving *comida vegetariana.* In cities such as Rio and São Paulo, some of these are extremely good. Another good option for vegetarians is *comida por quilo* restaurants, where there are always some salads and cooked veggies as well as beans and usually at least one fish dish. Other good options are juice bars, which often serve healthy vegetarian sandwiches. Along the coast, of course, you'll never lack for fish or seafood. And in the Pantanal and Amazon, there are plenty of freshwater fish. (If you don't eat fish, however, you'll have a difficult time.) Problems can arise once you get inland and away from big cities into meat-eating territory where vegetables serve as sparse garnish. At least, no matter where you go, there's always plenty of fresh fruit.

Brazilians in general adore **children** and they are very welcome in restaurants (as long as they're fairly well-behaved). If your child is a conservative eater, once again, *comida por quilo* restaurants can be a great option due to the amount of choice involved. Also a good bet are the (increasingly sophisticated) food courts found in shopping centers in major cities throughout the country.

Conduct and Customs

Overall, Brazil is a very relaxed and casual place, although sometimes appearances can be deceiving. Underneath the freewheeling, sensual vibe, you'll sometimes find a conservative core. Brazil has the largest Catholic population on the planet, and though the practice of Catholicism in Brazil is considered to be much less rigid and conservative than in other Latin American countries, a great many people do take it seriously. If you're entering a place of worship—Christian or otherwise—take care to dress and behave with a certain degree of modesty. In some official buildings, among them the government buildings as well as municipal theaters and even libraries and archives, similar forms of decorum apply: women should not wear shorts or micro skirts, men should wear long pants, and flip-flops should be avoided.

GREETINGS

Brazilians are extremely warm and friendly, and this is apparent in the way they greet each other. If you're meeting a woman—whether a long-lost friend or a stranger—you'll greet her with two kisses (*beijos*), one on each cheek. Women kiss men as well, while men greeting men shake hands. However, among younger men as well as male friends and family members, back slapping, hugging (*abraços*), and other forms of friendly physical contact are quite common. When taking leave of each other, the same hugging and kissing rituals apply. If anything, they are much warmer on account of intimacies (and alcohols) shared.

PUBLIC DISPLAYS OF AFFECTION

Brazilians are naturally very affectionate, which can sometimes cause confusion for foreigners. A lot of friendly hugging and kissing goes on in public, and the sense of privacy and personal space is quite different than in North America. Brazilians not only love to be together (Garbo's "I want to be alone" is a very foreign concept), but when they're together, they sit close and touch one another a great deal. In general, such behavior merely demonstrates a natural playfulness and lack of hang-ups about expressing affection, and you shouldn't treat it as sexual. When they want to be, Brazilians can be great and thoroughly effective flirts, and the expression *jogar o charme* (cast your charm) is often recommended (both seriously and tongue-in-cheek) as a way of getting something (a discount, a restaurant table, a favor).

Another thing about Brazilians is that they tend to be far less hung up about their bodies (and revealing them in public) and about sex matters in general than North Americans. However, it's a serious mistake to confuse sensuality with licentiousness or with an "anything goes" attitude. And looking sexy should not be equated with someone wanting to have sex.

JEITO BRASILEIRO (THE BRAZILIAN WAY)

Dar um jeito or *um jeitinho* is a common Brazilian expression that sums up a quintessentially Brazilian philosophy as well as an art form and a way of life. Literally (and inadequately) translated, it means "give a way," which doesn't begin to do justice to the rich and subtle inferences the expression embraces. *Dar um jeito* is a Brazilian's typical recourse when confronted with the many *pepinos* ("cucumbers"; i.e., problems) that daily life throws their way. When faced with an awkward situation or a difficult problem, Brazilians rarely confront it head on—usually a futile tactic since the *pepino* is often the result of inflexible and sometimes absurd rules or government bureaucracy. Instead, they rely on a wide range of indirect *jeitos* or strategies, among them diplomacy, craftiness, flexibility, and charm, to get around an obstacle or extricate oneself from a predicament. The whole point is to not lose your cool and make a big scene, which Brazilians, a nonconfrontational people, only resort to *in extremis*. When they do, it's known as *um escândalo* and involves an impressive display of melodrama.

CHORAR: THE BRAZILIAN ART OF BARGAINING

In Brazil, bargaining is more than just haggling for a good price. It is a lively social ritual, and once you get the hang of it, you will likely enjoy yourself so much that subsequent trips to the impersonal aisles of supermarkets and department stores will seem downright dull. The best way to bargain with someone is to *chorar* or "cry." This doesn't mean you have to literally burst into tears (although this technique actually works wonders), but you do have to haggle down the cost of an object based on some operatic tale of woe that will convince the seller that you have suffered immensely and are thus deserving of a discount. For instance, when you arrive at an airport and are confronted with the inflated prices a cab driver is charging for a ride into town, you do the following: complain about how many delays you faced, lament that your luggage was lost, curse the fact that security tore through your bags, etc. Based on your acting chops, you'll be able to knock 5-10 percent off the fare. While a greater command of Portuguese makes for highly effective *chorando*, exaggerated facial gestures, hand-wringing, and sign language can do wonders. Although the person you're bargaining with will do his or her share of "crying," too, once you get your discount, you'll find that you're actually both satisfied – due to the sheer satisfaction of having had a good "cry."

Tips for Travelers

TRAVELERS WITH DISABILITIES

For the most part, Brazil is very poorly equipped to deal with travelers with disabilities. Although in Rio and São Paulo, the number of hotels, restaurants, public buildings, and tourist attractions with wheelchair access and ramps is growing, they are the minority. Moreover, getting to them is very difficult. Sidewalks and streets are often uneven, traffic is chaotic, and there are almost no ramps. Very few buses, and no taxis, are equipped to deal with wheelchairs. For more information about traveling overseas with a disability, contact **Access-able** (U.S. tel. 303/232-2979, www.access-able.com), based in Wheat Ridge, Colorado.

TRAVELING WITH CHILDREN

If a trip is well-planned, kids usually love Brazil. And, indeed, Brazilians really love kids. In fact, in Brazil, families are often more welcome in many places than in North America. Meanwhile, on beaches and in small towns, it's easy for your kids to meet and play with Brazilian kids, who, like their parents, are usually outgoing and friendly. Often kids playing together breaks the ice for parents to get to know each other as well.

In terms of traveling throughout Brazil with kids, since distances are so great, it's really best to stick to one or two regions and then take small day trips. Flying long distances can be tiring and may sometimes involve delays. Buses take even longer, and kids can get bored and fidgety. Children pay full fare on buses, but on planes, they pay half price between the ages of 2 and 12. If you plan on renting a car, and you have an infant, consider bringing a baby seat. Rental companies don't have them, and they are expensive in Brazil.

In hotels, children under 6 can usually stay for free in their parents' room—an extra bed is often provided. Older children often only pay supplements. In and around popular vacation areas, such as beach resorts, there are many hotels geared towards families, which are equipped with playgrounds, games rooms, TV lounges, and swimming pools as well as gardens for running around. Of course, there is always the beach. Make sure you choose a

WHAT TO TAKE

Brazil is a famously casual place in terms of **clothing.** To blend in and minimize hassles from insistent vendors or thieves, it helps to dress down. You won't find many baggy cargo shorts or oversized T-shirts, though. The jeans worn by men and women alike are fitted and stylish. Aside from in São Paulo, colors rule—black is far less popular than in North America and Europe, and during the day dark colors soak up heat.

Brazilians take great pride in their **beachwear.** You won't find men wearing Speedos or surfing shorts (aside from surfers) or women wearing one-piece bathing suits. Consider purchasing swimwear in Brazil so as not to stand out too much. If you plan to do some snorkeling, it's a good idea to bring your own **snorkeling gear.**

Even during the summer, bring a long-sleeved shirt or light jacket to keep you warm in intensely air-conditioned environments. A sweater and heavier jacket are necessary for mountain regions and the South and Southeast during winter months.

A **money belt** is a must in Brazil. You never want to carry cash or cards in easy-to-pick pockets.

place with calm waters and access to shade. Perhaps the biggest enemy of children is the sun. Make sure you bring plenty of sunscreen from home since it's outrageously expensive in Brazil. For disposable diapers, you'll find Pampers and other brands in most supermarkets and pharmacies.

With the great variety of food in Brazil, even picky young eaters should have no problem if you don't venture too far off the beaten track. If all else fails, there's *comida a quilo* and the food courts at the local *shoppings*. Most restaurants have high chairs. If not they can improvise. Although few restaurants have children's menus or portions, regular portions are often so large that kids can share.

WOMEN TRAVELERS

Machismo has a strong hold in Brazil; however, it's generally a more tepid version than in other Latin American countries. Although Brazilians respect women, North American notions of political correctness have never caught on here. And the definition of what constitutes sexual harassment is far more lax in Brazil (although an increasing number of cities have a *delegacia de mulheres,* where an all-female staff specializes in crimes against women). Flirting is a way of life and is usually harmless. As a *gringa,* traveling alone or with other women,

you'll definitely incite curiosity and inevitably receive some intense stares and/or come ons, particularly in the North and the Northeast, where fair-skinned foreigners stand out more. For the most part, these are all harmless. The problem is that you might feel targeted if every time you go out for a drink (a woman by herself in a bar is a rarity) or to the beach, you're being bothered. If that's the case, try to join a group, or at least stick close to one (on the beach, for example). If saying a firm *"não"* and walking away isn't dissuading an insistent suitor, head immediately to a safe place (a hotel or restaurant). Avoid deserted areas by day, and always take taxis at night.

SENIOR TRAVELERS

Brazil is known for having a strong youth culture, and as a result many activities and venues tend to be geared towards a younger public. It's rather uncommon to see groups of elderly Brazilians traveling the way you would in North America and Europe. In fact, in most major cities elderly Brazilians are not very visible, the exception being Rio de Janeiro, especially Copacabana. The hassle and discomfort of public transportation and long-distance traveling, coupled with messy traffic, poor road conditions, and uneven and crowded sidewalks, make traveling throughout Brazil

snorkeling in Maragogi, Alagoas

or even getting around most cities a sometimes daunting experience. The overbearing heat and strong sun often exacerbate matters. That said, Brazilians are generally sensitive to the needs of seniors. Although discounts for seniors on public transportation and at museums and movies are generally accorded based on showing Brazilian ID, if you have proof of age (60 or 65) you can receive *um desconto para idosos*.

GAY AND LESBIAN TRAVELERS

A lot of gay and lesbian foreigners associate Brazil with images of transvestites, Carnaval drag queens, and the muscle boys of Ipanema and allow themselves to think that Brazil is a very gay-friendly place. In reality, it is and it isn't. Brazil is more gay and lesbian tolerant than many other Latin American countries. You'll see both gay and lesbian romances played out on nightly *novelas,* and there are openly gay and lesbian celebrities (although they are hardly activists). Both Rio and São Paulo have intense gay scenes (though almost

nonexistent lesbian scenes), with a wide range of bars, clubs, and even small neighborhood enclaves. Other major cities, such as Salvador, Recife, and Florianópolis, also have gay venues and gay beaches (or portions of beaches). As with heterosexuals, gays and lesbians are also much more open about flirting in public. However, overall, the scene in Brazil is much more GLS (*gay, lesbica, e simpatisante;* that is, gay, lesbian, and "sympathetic") than exclusively gay and lesbian. Gay men, lesbians, and straight people mix much more, and the result is a less overt and politicized gay and lesbian presence than in North America or Europe.

Ultimately, many Brazilians don't mind if you're gay or lesbian, but they don't want to be reminded of it; i.e., they can deal with the fact of a same-sex romance in theory, but don't want to see signs of it (public kissing or hand-holding) or hear you referring explicitly to your homosexuality. Two men or women living together, traveling together, or sharing a hotel room is not a problem, but the implicit agreement is that you're two friends (even if deep down, people may suspect you're not). Although the drag queen and flamboyant queen are very much an accepted part of the culture (during Carnaval, even in small rural towns, the most macho of men don wigs, miniskirts, and lipstick), there is a difference between spectacle and humor, and the reality of day-to-day life. Brazil is ultimately a macho culture, and explicit signs of homosexuality can incite insults and even violence. Even in supposedly cosmopolitan cities such as Rio and São Paulo, violence against gays is not unheard of. In the more conservative Northeast and rural areas, it is even more common. For more information about the gay and lesbian scene in Brazil, in Portuguese, check out www.guiagaybrasil.com.br, which has GLS listings for cities all over Brazil. If you're traveling to Rio, check out the English-language Rio Gay Guide at www.riogayguide.com.

Health and Safety

BEFORE YOU GO

Before your trip, it's always good idea to check with your country's travel health recommendations for Brazil. You'll find lots of up-to-date information and travel advisories on the following websites: **Australia** (www.dfat.gov.au/travel/), **Canada** (www.phac-aspc.gc.ca/tmp-pmv/pub-eng.php), **United Kingdom** (www.direct.gov.uk/en/TravelAndTransport/TravellingAbroad/index.htm), **United States** (www.cdc.gov/travel/). Another good source is the **MD Travel Health** website (www.mdtravelhealth.com), which has complete travel health information, updated daily for both physicians and travelers.

Vaccinations

It's a good idea to check the validity of your vaccinations some weeks (or even months) prior to departure. The one vaccination that is required for Brazil is **yellow fever.** This is absolutely essential for visiting the Amazon region, but there have been isolated but recent occurrences in the Pantanal, Brasília, and even Minas Gerais and Bahia. Be sure to bring an international certificate of vaccination since Brazilian authorities will sometimes ask for proof of vaccination for travelers going to and from the Amazon. If you've been in any other South American country (with the exception of Chile and Argentina) 90 days prior to coming to Brazil (as well as some African ones) you will also need proof of yellow fever vaccination. Since it takes 10 days for the vaccine to take effect, you can either have it at home or, if you're going to spend time in a big city or the coast before heading to the Amazon, you can easily get the vaccine in Brazil at any public *posto de saúde* (health clinic)—ask at any pharmacy for the nearest location—where it will be administered free of charge. Other recommended vaccines include **hepatitis A, hepatitis B, typhoid,** and **rabies shots** (many domestic animals in Brazil aren't always vaccinated against rabies).

What to Bring

Bring any prescription medication that you're taking in its original packaging. Just in case, ask your pharmacist or doctor to give you the generic names for any medication. You will usually be able to purchase the same drug at any Brazilian pharmacy (although the brand name will be different). Not only can you get many prescription drugs over the counter in Brazil, but they're often a lot cheaper than in North America or Europe. Do, however, bring plenty of mosquito repellent, sunscreen, and aspirin or Tylenol (which are more expensive in Brazil). Aloe vera or other relief for sunburn is also a good idea, as is calamine lotion or witch hazel to take the irritating itch out of any mosquito bites.

Insurance

If you have medical coverage, check and see if it covers you for expenses incurred overseas. If not, you might want to consider buying travel insurance. In either case, find out if the insurer will make payments directly or reimburse you afterwards. Most insurers do the latter. Regardless, most of the best Brazilian clinics and hospitals (which are private) will make you pay for service up front.

HEALTH PRECAUTIONS

Tropical heat and humidity favor the growth of bacteria and cause food and organic matter in general to spoil and rot very quickly. As a result, hygiene standards in Brazil are quite high. Nevertheless, it's wise to take certain precautions so as not to spend your trip with an upset stomach or diarrhea.

In terms of food, be attentive to the conditions of any food you purchase on the street. Fruit with peels (bananas, mangos, papaya) is safer than fruit without (which should be carefully washed). Similarly, boiled vegetables are safer than raw ones (unless you know they've been well washed) or veg that have been sitting around in mayonnaise. You should also be careful with seafood (such as shrimp). If something looks poorly cooked, or smells or tastes slightly off, spit it out and discontinue eating.

Brazilian tap water is supposedly safe to drink in large cities, although few people actually do (in part due to the heavy chlorine taste). Most Brazilians drink filtered water or mineral water, either *natural* or *com gas* (carbonated), and you should too (although brushing your teeth or rinsing fruit with tap water is perfectly fine). Mineral water is inexpensive and available everywhere: at restaurants, bars, bus stations, gas stations, supermarkets, and pharmacies. And you should really stick to it, or soft drinks. Ice is usually made from filtered water. However, if you're in an out-of-the-way place that seems a bit dodgy, you might want to order your drink without it (*sem gelo*). Also make a habit out of drinking from cans with a straw (which will invariably be offered to you). If drinking beer from a can, make sure you wipe the top off with a napkin or even your shirt.

PHARMACIES

Pharmacies are everywhere in Brazil. Most are open until 10 P.M. In most central neighborhoods, you'll always find one that stays open 24 hours and on Sunday. All *farmácias* have at least one licensed pharmacist trained to deal with minor medical problems and emergencies, which could save you a trip to a clinic or hospital (the only problem is it's very unlikely that the pharmacist will speak any English). You'll be able to find good medicine for whatever ails you (upset stomach, diarrhea, headache, rashes, a cold or cough), even though you probably won't recognize the names.

CLINICS AND HOSPITALS

Brazil has a very good health system—as long as you can pay for it. All Brazilians have access to public hospitals for free. In theory, this is fantastic. In practice, the state of many public hospitals is truly frightening. There is a saying among Brazilians that a sick person who goes into a public hospital usually gets worse instead of cured. While doctors and nurses are often qualified, lack of funds often makes public hospitals precarious. Moreover, the sight of sick and suffering people lining up on the sidewalk as early as 2 A.M. and then waiting for hours, in the hot sun, to get medical attention is truly tragic. For all these reasons, if you require medical attention head to a private clinic, unless you have a real emergency. Middle class and wealthy Brazilians usually pay high health insurance premiums that give them access to state-of-the-art First World clinics, particularly in major cities. You can have access to them as well, but it will cost you. Consulates can recommend good hospitals, clinics, or specialists, although English-speaking doctors are rare.

TRAVELER'S DIARRHEA

To avoid diarrhea be careful about the source of the water you drink and the food you eat. Even so, you might get diarrhea simply as a result of being exposed to different types of bacteria. In the event you do get sick, aside from taking medication (it's a good idea to pack Imodium), drink lots of fluids. Particularly

IVO PITANGUY

If Brazil is the plastic surgery capital of the world, then Ivo Pitanguy is the celebrity surgeon who put it on the map. Pitanguy, whose father was a surgeon, began his pioneering techniques in reconstructive surgery by working on wounded World War II soldiers and, later on, burn victims. When he opened his own private clinic in Rio de Janeiro, he set the stage for what would be one of Brazil's most renowned industries. With cutting-edge technology and rock-bottom prices – not to mention an idyllic location for recuperation – Rio, always a city where appearances mattered enormously, became a mecca for celebrities from around Brazil and the world in search of a little nip or tuck. Recently, the city has become a prime destination for "cosmetic vacationers" – a new breed of tourists who combine going under the scalpel with post-operative trips to beaches and mountain retreats.

good for diarrhea and upset stomachs are *água de coco* (fresh coconut water) and *suco de lima,* a juice made from a citrus fruit that is a cross between an orange and a lime. If your diarrhea is serious after 2–3 days, you should go to a pharmacy and ask for an antibiotic and an antidiarrheal drug. If you see blood and have a fever, chills, or strong abdominal pains seek medical treatment.

DENGUE

Dengue fever is a viral infection that, like many tropical diseases—including malaria and yellow fever—is transmitted by mosquitos. Dengue isn't caused by just any old mosquito, but by a species known as *aedes* that breed in stagnant water, usually in densely populated urban areas with improper drainage. Plant containers and abandoned rubber tires are particularly common breeding grounds. Dengue mosquitos usually attack during the daytime and are most common during hot, humid rainy periods. In recent years, Rio de Janeiro has had large dengue epidemics during its rainy summer months. Although rarely fatal, dengue is like having a really debilitating case of flu. Symptoms include fever, aching muscles, headaches, nausea, weakness, vomiting, and a rash. In general, the worst symptoms last 5–7 days, but full recuperation can take longer. Diagnosis is via a blood test. There is no vaccine for dengue, nor is there treatment aside from rest, plenty of liquids, and acetaminophen (Tylenol). Do not take aspirin. Only severe cases require hospitalization. The best thing you can do to avoid infection is to take precautions to avoid getting bitten in the first place (see *Mosquitos*).

AIDS AND STDS

Brazil has one of the highest numbers of people living with HIV infections. According to statistics, more than 20 percent of infected people are women. Although Brazil has one of the world's most highly respected and effective AIDS policies—aside from creating low-cost generic drugs, the Brazilian government's fight against AIDS involves free medication and medical follow-up for all patients for life—it doesn't prevent people from getting HIV in the first place. Condoms—known as *camisinhas* ("little shirts")—are widespread (you'll find them in all pharmacies and many supermarkets) and there is not so much a stigma as a resistance to using them. As a result, you really have to be careful about HIV and STDs. Whether you're with a man or a woman, always insist upon using a condom.

SUN EXPOSURE

When you arrive at a Brazilian beach from the cold and gray Northern Hemisphere, your first instinct will to be to sprawl in the sand for a day, but try to exercise some self-control and expose yourself to the sun gradually. The tropical sun, particularly during the summer months, can cause a lot of damage. Brazilians have the highest rate of skin cancer in the world; many don't use sunscreen because of its exorbitant cost. Using a strong sunscreen (bring it from home) that filters out UVA and UVB rays is essential. SPF 30 is the minimum you should use. Even so, if you're foolish enough to stay in the sun between the deadliest hours of 11 A.M.–2 P.M., you will still get burned. On many beaches, you can rent a parasol or head to a thatched *barraca* for shade come high noon. Children and those with fair, sensitive skin should use a much higher SPF. A hat is always essential, whether you're on the beach or practicing any outdoor sport, and you'll be practically blinded without a pair of sunglasses with a protective filter. Remember to drink lots of liquids all the time, even if you're not thirsty. Beer and *caipirinhas* might be refreshing, but alcohol actually dehydrates. An ideal replenishing drink is *água de coco*.

MOSQUITOS

Mosquitos can be very irritating. They can also be carriers of diseases such as yellow fever, dengue fever, and malaria. They are especially a problem in urban areas during hot rainy seasons (in which dengue can be a problem) and in chronically wet regions such as the Amazon and the Pantanal. Aside from getting necessary vaccines, the best way to prevent mosquito bites is to wear effective repellent (containing DEET) as well as long pants, long sleeves, and closed shoes. Be careful not to get repellent close to your eyes or mouth. Sleep with mosquito netting, and if your windows don't have screens, make sure you close them. Mosquitos don't like wind, so if you have a fan in your room keep it on. Burning mosquito coils helps, but you might still hear a bit of buzzing, and the odor can be somewhat overwhelming.

SAFETY

The subject of crime and security in Brazil is an extremely important and complex one. Violent crime, holdups, robberies, and drug warfare in major cities dominate the Brazilian news media (often in a sensationalist manner) and have a major social impact. An increasing number of middle-class Brazilians are moving to closed condominium complexes with electric fences and 24-hour security. Wealthy Brazilians are the leading buyers of security

systems and of bulletproof cars in the world. Meanwhile, poorer Brazilians who reside in peripheral neighborhoods or *favelas* live in fear of bus holdups, stray bullets, or drug traffickers. If you come into contact with Brazilians, read the papers, or watch TV, you will definitely hear such stories, and while the tone may be alarmist or melodramatic, the occurrences themselves are true. There's no need for paranoia, but don't let yourself be complacent.

Having lived in Brazil for 10 years, I don't know *anybody* who has never been robbed. I myself have been robbed on various occasions. Aside from having my house broken into (someone climbed up my building and in through the window), on the other occasions, I have to admit that I was in the wrong place at the wrong time: a deserted, if central street at night (7 P.M.), and in the midst of a multitude of drunk and celebrating people (upon the occasion of a popular street festival), during which someone succeeded in sliding a hand into my pocket and making off with the contents.

Safety Tips

These experiences are typical of instances in which traveling foreigners might find themselves at risk. However, such situations are easy to avoid. Unless you're on a very busy or major street in a good neighborhood, don't walk around at night in a city you don't know. While downtown business areas of major cities such as Rio, São Paulo, Salvador, and Recife may hum with energy by day, at night and on weekends (especially Sunday) they turn into ghost towns and should be avoided. If you're going to be amid a crowd (an outdoor performance, a parade, Carnaval) leave all valuables and original documents at home. Carry a small change purse around your neck or a money belt.

While public transportation is safe enough during the day, at night (when holdups are more likely), always take a taxi, even if it's just a few blocks to your destination. If you've rented a car, be careful where you park. Particularly at night, you don't want to be on a dark or isolated side street. If you're at a stoplight, you should keep your windows rolled up, since if you're stuck in traffic, you can easily be held up. In fact, at night, in many major cities, drivers slow down at stoplights, but don't actually stop their cars (a practice sanctioned by law).

You should never be walking around (night or day) with a lot of cash in a purse or pocket. Do, however, keep a few small bills that you can easily access. Fumbling around for money in public (on a bus or at a market) leaves you exposed to robbery. Similarly, when you go to the beach, don't bring any valuables with you. Bring enough cash for drinks or snacks and that's it. Keep all your possessions with you (in a neat pile or a cheap, preferably local beach bag) within your line of vision; there are tales of tourists dozing in the sun and waking up to find their possessions gone. If you're on your own and want to go swimming, ask someone to watch your stuff. This is very common on Brazilian beaches.

If you're going to be taking money out at an ATM, make sure nobody is watching you. Even though ATMs are open until 10 P.M., the best time to take out money is during the day, in a busy area (preferably in an airport or shopping mall). Be careful on Sunday, when commercial areas are very quiet. Once again, if you're withdrawing a lot of cash, put it in a money belt.

Major cities are the most problematic in terms of crime, although in major tourist destinations such as Rio and Salvador there has been a major effort to have police on patrol, which has increased safety in the most touristic areas. Nonetheless, always have your wits about you. In smaller towns, rural areas, and beach destinations, you will definitely feel more relaxed. Crime is much lower, and you can let your guard down somewhat (although don't be lulled into complete carelessness).

While in the South and Southeast, it's easier to blend in physically with the local population; in the North and Northeast, if you are of fair European stock you will often stand out simply because of your physical type. Gringos are uniformly considered easy targets, not only because they are all thought to be rich, but because they are often careless. One thing to do

is try to camouflage yourself: get a bit of a tan, don't talk loudly in a foreign language, and try to dress like the locals (casually, but smartly, no flashy jewelry, expensive footwear, or fashionable designer duds). Also be careful about where you flash your camera, particularly if it has a big zoom lens. The smaller and more compact your camera, the better. Don't unfold big maps in public or look like lost or unsure of where you're going. Without being neurotic, try to always be aware of where you are and what's going on around you. Trust your instincts. If a bar, street, or neighborhood feels dodgy, make a fast exit. If you feel someone is watching you or following you, speed up your pace, cross the street, or enter a shop or public building. Be aware of possible scams such as being approached by so-called officials at airports who want you to go with them (after you've come out of the arrivals section). Another notorious *golpe* (scam) is "Boa Noite Cinderela" ("Good Night Cinderella"), in which someone slips a drug into your drink and, while you're knocked out, robs you blind. This trick usually befalls unsuspecting romantics who hook up with a potential conquest in a bar. If you find yourself in this situation, don't leave your drink unguarded (such as by going to the bathroom).

Police

The North American or European association of police as (for the most part) a symbol of law and order doesn't hold true in Brazil. When trouble occurs, most Brazilians avoid the police. Because police officers are grossly underpaid and subject to corruption and violence, it is sometimes difficult to distinguish them from the bandits and drug traffickers they are supposedly battling. This is, of course, a generalization, and there are exceptions to the rule.

In Brazil, there are various types of police. The most efficient (and well-paid, and thus less corrupt) of the bunch are the **Polícia Federal,** who deal with all matters concerning passports, visas, and immigration. They have offices at all international airports as well as at frontier posts and in state capitals, and are generally helpful. The **Polícia Militar** are a hangover from the era of military dictatorship. They dress in soldier-like khaki uniforms accessorized with tough lace-up boots and berets (even in the tropical heat). You'll often see them supposedly keeping the peace on street corners. Although they can be rough with Brazilian indolents, they leave foreigners alone. The plainclothes **Polícia Civil** deal with solving crimes. If you're robbed and you want to report the crime, in many places you'll need to go to the nearest *delegacia,* or station. Be prepared if you want an official report: You'll need to wait in line, and nobody will speak English. Unless you really need a report for insurance purposes, you might want to just let it go. In a major city, such as Rio or Salvador, you'll have better luck with a **delegacia de turismo.** This special police force specializes in crimes against foreign tourists, and some of their agents speak rudimentary English.

Theft

Most crime in Brazil takes place in poorer neighborhoods that you'll probably never see.

If you take all the precautions discussed, it's not that likely that you'll be robbed. Even if you are, in most cases it will consist of a *furto* (small theft) in which your pockets are picked or someone grabs your bag and takes off. However, *assaltos* (holdups) do occur. In the event that you are held up by someone, do not resist. Although outside of *favelas* controlled by drug traffickers in major cities armed robbery is somewhat rare, you could find yourself being threatened with a knife or a broken bottle. Quickly and calmly hand over whatever the thief wants. It is a no-brainer between your money, watch, jewelry, or documents and your life. Accidents happen when people get very upset or try to resist, making the robber nervous and prone to act impulsively. If you need to make a report to the police, try the special tourist police, *delegacia de turismo,* which you'll find in major cities. Otherwise, you'll have to deal with the overly worked and not always sympathetic Polícia Civil. Even if you do report a robbery, it's extremely unlikely you'll get your possessions back.

Information and Services

MONEY

Brazil's currency is the *real* (pronounced "ray-ALL"; the plural, *reais,* is pronounced "ray-EYES"). One *real* (R$1) can be divided into 100 *centavos.* You'll come across bills in denominations of 1, 2, 5, 10, 20, 50, and 100 *reais* (although R$1 bills are rare, having been replaced by a two-toned R$1 coin). Bills are easy to distinguish since each is a different color. Coins are trickier, since some have several versions, but you'll find coins worth 5, 10, 25, and 50 *centavos.* Because they were virtually worthless, there are no longer any 1-*centavo* coins. If you're purchasing something, the total will be rounded up or down (if the total comes to R$4.37 the cashier will expect R$4.35; if it comes to R$1.38, you'll get change for R$1.40).

Exchanging Money

Although you might want to bring some U.S. dollars for an emergency (in the event you can't get cash from an ATM or if your card gets lost or stolen), you'll usually lose money exchanging dollars at either a bank or a *casa de câmbio* (exchange house). Major hotels will also exchange dollars, as will airport banks (open seven days a week). Regular banking hours are 10 A.M.–4 P.M. Monday–Friday. Since the Brazilians *real* has stabilized in recent years, U.S. dollars (which were hoarded by all Brazilians in the face of rampant inflation) have become less coveted. In fact, since 2006, the U.S. dollar has declined considerably against the increasingly robust *real.* Dollars are not accepted in many places these days, and once-attractive black market exchange rates are a thing of the past. Likewise, don't bother with travelers checks, which very few places will exchange.

ATMs

The best way to deal with money concerns in Brazil is to bring an international Visa or MasterCard (or both to give you more options) and withdraw cash from bank machines. Not only is this the most secure method, but you'll get the best exchange rate. Most major branches of Banco do Brasil and Bradesco have at least one ATM that accepts Visa/PLUS cards, while Bradesco, HSBC, and Citibank accept MasterCard/Cirrus. Meanwhile, red Banco 24 Horas ATMs accept all cards, all of the time. In all cases, you need to have a four-digit PIN number. All ATMs have an option in English. More and more ATMs in all major and reasonably sized cities accept international cards. If you're going to a small town or somewhere off the beaten track, it's best to stock up on cash beforehand, although credit cards will be accepted by most hotels and larger restaurants.

For city ATMs, your best bets are banks in downtown commercial areas, areas with lots of tourist activity, airports, bus terminals, and shopping centers. For security reasons, bank ATMs are open 6 A.M.–10 P.M. daily. Most have a withdrawal limit of R$1,000 (although Bradesco's is R$600). To check out locations online in advance, consult the sites for Visa/PLUS (www.visa.com) and MasterCard/Cirrus (www.mastercard.com). During big holidays, such as New Year's, Carnaval, and any long weekend, it's wise to stock up on cash in advance since sometimes the machines run dry.

Credit Cards

Most Brazilian hotels, restaurants, and stores accept international credit cards. Using a card not only alleviates carrying around big wads of cash, but also offers the most advantageous exchange rate. The only thing it won't get you is the discounts (usually of 10 percent) that you can ask for (and usually get) if you pay for accommodations or shopping items in cash (*em dinheiro*). Visa and MasterCard are the most widely accepted cards (once again,

bring both to increase your payment possibilities), although many places will take American Express and Diners Club.

Money Wires

Should you have an emergency and require a money wire, Banco do Brasil has a partnership with Western Union. A person can send you money from North America via Western Union (www.westernunion.com), to any Banco do Brasil branch. Once you've specified the city you're in, all you need to do (aside from standing in a long line) is show up with your passport and the wire transaction code and get your cash.

MAPS AND TOURIST INFORMATION
Tourist Information

Before traveling to Brazil, it's helpful to check out some of the books and Internet resources (which include the Embratur website operated by the Brazilian Ministry of Tourism) listed in the *Resources* chapter. Once you're in Brazil, you will find municipal, regional, and state tourist information offices and kiosks throughout Brazil. In general, you can get free maps and some brochures as well as help with accommodations, renting cars, acquiring guides, or organizing excursions or sporting activities. Often, they will have transportation schedules for local buses and boats. In smaller towns, you can often get information about renting a room in a private home.

Apart from major cities, it is rare to find tourist offices where people speak anything other than Portuguese. Sometimes you'll encounter staff that are not actually that knowledgeable, a fact compensated for by general friendliness and a willingness to help. In smaller towns, tourist office opening and closing hours are often not strictly adhered to, particularly in the off-season.

Maps

The maps in this guidebook are for the most part limited to central areas of major Brazilian cities and important regional destinations such as coastlines and national parks. For more detailed city and local maps, you can almost always get your hands on something at the local tourist office in the city or town you're visiting. Sometimes, better maps will cost you around R$5. In major cities, *bancas de revista* (newsstands) and bookstores usually sell city and state maps. Otherwise, the best maps are produced by Quatro Rodas, which sells regional maps for all of Brazil as well as a detailed foldout map of Brazil that comes for free with its annually published **Guia Quatro Rodas** (a Brazilian equivalent of France's Michelin). The *Guia Quatro Rodas* is a guide that is biblical in size and content. Updated yearly, this 1,000-page tome (a bargain at only R$40) has listings (in Portuguese) for basically every tourist destination in Brazil, along with lots of maps (its strengths are big cities and close-ups on specific regions). Quatro Rodas also puts out a similar guide that deals exclusively with Brazilian beaches. For highway maps, purchase the *Guia Quatro Rodas Estrada* map for around R$20. You can also purchase a CD-ROM version with a digitized version of all maps. All you need to do is type in your destination, where you want to stop, how much you want to spend on gas, and Quatro Rodas will calculate the best route, how much time you'll spend, and how much gas you'll need. It will indicate hotels, restaurants, and monuments as well as gas stations, car mechanic shops, and banks. You can purchase all Quatro Rodas maps and guides, including the CD-ROM version, in major *bancas de revista* and bookstores throughout the country.

The Quatro Rodas website (www.viajeaqui.abril.com.br/g4r)—which is only in Portuguese, but quite easy to navigate—has an option by which you type in a street name and number and you can pinpoint an exact address on a map that also permits zooming in and out. For long-distance travel, there is an option that allows you to type in the city of origin and the destination city, and you'll be shown a map indicating possible routes. Easier for English speakers is **Google Maps** (www.maps.google.com). Type in your city destination (such as Rio de Janeiro) and then keep clicking on the area you're interested in to zoom in for more detail. If you're looking for a specific address, click on the "Get Directions" option and then type in the street name, followed by the number, and the neighborhood (for example: Rua Barão da Torre, 116, Ipanema).

COMMUNICATIONS AND MEDIA
Postal Service
It's easy to identify post offices (*correios*) by their bright yellow-and-blue marquees. Every main city has a rather grandiose main Correios building as well as dozens of small post offices. Aside from commercial centers, airports and major shopping centers usually have postal kiosks. With the introduction of Internet, the once interminable lines are now gone. When sending a letter or parcel, you can send it *simples* (regular mail) or *registrada* (registered). Sedex is the Correios's version of Fedex and is quite efficient. The Correios sells cardboard boxes of various sizes as well as postcards and very beautiful aerograms. For envelopes, you'll often have to go to a *papelaria* (stationery store). There are no adhesive envelopes in Brazil, but the Correios will always have a pot of glue and a brush and you can proceed to make a big mess. Postage within Brazil is very inexpensive, but sending letters or packages abroad can be expensive depending on weight. On the bright side, intensely colorful Brazilian postage stamps (*selos*) are quite stunning.

Telephones
Brazilian phone service is quite efficient, if not exactly cheap. Local calls are charged by the minute. Calls within Brazil have become somewhat cheaper in recent years with the privatization of the phone industry; however, international calls are pretty astronomical, and unless it's essential, you're better off emailing or Skype-ing with loved ones at home. If you make an international call from a hotel, it will be even more exorbitant (it will be much cheaper if you ask people back home to call you).

Throughout Brazil, you will see dome-shaped

phone booths known as *orelhões* ("big ears"), where you can make local calls and long-distance calls throughout Brazil. There used to be considerable lineups at *orelhões,* but with the popularity of cell phones, you'll now find them abandoned (and often not working). To use an *orelhão,* you'll need to purchase a phone card, *cartão telefônica,* sold at any news kiosk or often by vendors in busy streets. They usually come in 40 and 60 units (*unidades*). A quick local call will use up 1 or 2 units. A short long-distance call will quickly use up an entire card.

Brazil has several telephone companies, or *operadoras,* and whenever you make a long-distance call outside of your area code (known as a DDD), you'll have to precede the phone number with a two-digit number belonging to one of them. Embratur (21) is the biggest one, with national and international coverage. Other *operadoras* are Intelig (23) and Oi (31). When calling a number in Brazil, dial 0 followed by the *operadora* code, followed by the DDD, followed by the number. An example of a call to Rio (whose area code is 21) would be: 0/21-21-3333-3333. An example of an international call to Canada or the United States (whose country code is 1) would be: 00/21-1-416-921-7777). It is also possible to make a collect call (*uma chamada a cobrar*) from Brazil via the Embratel operator. To do so, call 0800/703-2111.

Cell phones are immensely popular throughout Brazil. In fact, many poorer Brazilians prefer a cell phone to more expensive home phones that entail hefty monthly rates. Calling to or from a cell phone, however, is more expensive than calling from a fixed phone. If you're calling long distance, charges are extremely steep. You'll find cell phone coverage in most places throughout Brazil. Your own cell phone should work in Brazil if it is compatible with international GSM standards. Contact your cell phone provider before your trip to confirm. However, since roaming charges will be really high, you're much better off buying a Brazilian SIM chip with TIM (www.tim.com.br), the only provider that provides nationwide service. Alternatively, you can rent a cell phone at airports with a company such as **PressCell** (tel.

21/3322-2692 in Rio, tel. 11/3253-0077 in São Paulo, www.presscell.com.br).

Internet

Internet service is spreading like wildfire through Brazil. Although only around 10 percent of the people have Internet at home, cyber cafés in bookstores, bars, and shopping malls are ubiquitous, as are LAN houses, dark (but air-conditioned) dens where adolescents while away the day playing games and blogging (Brazilians are the second biggest population of bloggers in the world after Americans). It's hard not to find somewhere to check your email. Even small towns, isolated beach resorts, and the Amazon forest (via satellite) will generally have a computer or two where you can connect. Prices vary R$3–10 an hour, depending on location (tourists areas are usually more expensive), but service (via broadband) is uniformly quite rapid. Headphones and microphones often allow you to Skype. More and more places (cafés and shopping malls) also have free wireless access in the event you have a laptop or cell phone with Internet. Moreover, most hotels, *pousadas,* and even youth hostels throughout Brazil have invested in Internet, not only for themselves, but for their guests (although sometimes you'll have to pay an exorbitant hourly rate). As a result, no matter where you are, you'll have no trouble checking your emails or downloading digital photos.

Newspapers and Magazines

Brazil's most reputed newspaper is the São Paulo–based *Folha de São Paulo,* a mildly left-leaning paper popular with liberals and intellectuals. Sort of a Brazilian equivalent of *The New York Times,* it has its devotees as well as its detractors, but it is definitely an important journalistic reference. For foreigners, it is a good source of arts and culture listings for São Paulo. Also good is the slightly more conservative, Rio-based *Jornal do Brasil.* You'll find both papers sold throughout the country. In Rio, *O Globo,* owned by the Globo media giant that also owns radio stations, a record company, and the famous Globo television network, also puts out a popular daily paper that has good arts listings for the city of Rio. Otherwise, major cities throughout the country publish their own newspapers, although they are more provincial in character.

Brazil has magazines galore. The three weekly news magazines along the lines of *Time* and *Newsweek* are *Istoé, Época* (owned by Globo), and *Veja.* None of them are quite as hard-hitting and high-quality as they used to be in the pre-Internet age. If you buy *Veja* in Rio and São Paulo, you'll receive a free *Time Out*-style city guide with the upcoming week's cultural and arts listings and events along with shopping news and restaurant reviews. *Veja Rio* (www.vejario.abril.com.br) and *Veja São Paulo* (www.vejasaopaulo.abril.com.br) can be found online, as can *Veja* guides to other cities, such as Brasília, Salvador, and Recife, all with reviews and listings (in Portuguese). If you're interested in Brazilian food and restaurants, *Gula* is a great magazine (similar to *Gourmet*). *Bravo* is an intelligent and attractive magazine devoted to the Brazilian and international art world. *Trip* and *TPM* are two funky magazines aimed at hipster twenty-something females. Brazilian *Vogue* is fun for visiting fashionistas. Meanwhile, curious travelers might want to check out *Viagem e Turismo,* a gorgeously photographed monthly travel mag that always puts out interesting special editions on different Brazilian regions (it is published by Abril, which also publishes the *Quatro Rodas* maps and guides).

You can get your hands on major English-language papers, particularly *The International Herald Tribune,* and all sorts of international magazines (sometimes they are a month or two old) at airport bookstores and major *bancas de revistas* (newsstands) in Rio and São Paulo. Rio and São Paulo's many bookstores also carry a wide selection of English-language press and books, including guidebooks. These are harder to find in other cities, but the spread of mega bookstores such as Siciliano and Saraíva means you can usually find English-language magazines and books in these *livrarias,* most of which are located in glitzier shopping malls. Because these items are imported, they will cost a lot more than you would pay for them back home.

NOVELAS

Brazilian *novelas* are much more than soap operas. They are one of the country's biggest forms of popular entertainment and a major cultural touchstone. No matter where you are in Brazil – whether a shack in the middle of the Sertão or a luxury condo in Leblon or Jardins – between 6 P.M. and 10 P.M., you can rest assured that tens of millions are Brazilians are tuned into the same sagas night after night. And if they aren't within range of a TV, it is a given that sooner or later the topic of who slapped whom or slept with whom will come up in conversation.

Television

Wherever you wander in Brazil, even in the most modest and isolated outpost in the middle of nowhere, there will inevitably be a shack with a lit-up TV and someone watching it. Brazilian TV is a great unifier, and no matter how much the landscape, temperature, or accent changes, you'll see people watching the same soccer games, *novelas,* newscasts, reality shows, and live audience shows. For the most part, Brazilian TV is also pretty terrible.

The major networks beamed across the nation are SBT, Record, Bandeirantes, MTV (a Brazilian version of the American music network), Globo, and TV Educadora, a state-owned educational network that has a mix of high-brow round tables, films, and very good cultural programming (including great live music performances).

The all-powerful Globo is the leading network. Its nightly *novelas* (which air at 7 P.M., 8 P.M., and 9 P.M. Mon.–Sat.) are the most watched of all nightly programs. These soap operas go all out in terms of sets, costumes, lighting, and production and star a roster of gorgeous (and usually pretty talented) actors, actresses, and models, all of whom are part of a permanent stable of stars, known as Globais, that hearkens back to the Hollywood studio system. When these Globais aren't participating in a *novela,* miniseries, or other Globo production, they make commercials and give the paparazzi and gossip columnists endless fodder. If you don't speak Portuguese, you will find *novelas* cheesy and melodramatic. If you do understand the language, you will still find them cheesy and melodramatic, but you'll easily get drawn into them, and perhaps become addicted.

You don't need to understand much Portuguese to watch the broadcast of a live *jogo de futebol*. The machine-gun fire of words rattled off by Brazilian sports commentators with jacked-up fervor and excitement will have you alternately biting your nails and cheering for joy, even if you've never been much of a soccer fan.

In basic Brazilian hotels, you'll usually receive these basic Brazilian channels (sometimes only Globo, depending on your location). However, in moderate to luxury lodgings, you'll be treated to cable with BBC, CNN, some superior Brazilian cable channels, and lots of American cable series.

WEIGHTS AND MEASURES

Brazil uses the metric system. Throughout this book, measurements are given in both standard and metric. However, you'll also find a conversion chart at the back of this guide.

Depending on where in the country you're located, the electric current varies from 100 to 240 volts, although most common is 110 volts, meaning you won't have problems with electronic devices from North America. Most laptops and battery rechargers come equipped with adaptors and power units that convert automatically to changes in voltage. Most outlets have two flat prongs. Should you need a cheap adaptor, you'll find one easily at any hardware store or larger supermarket.

Until June 2008, Brazil had four different time zones. Now it only has three. The main time zone includes São Paulo, Rio, and the entire coastline going inland as far as Brasília. Westward, the states of Mato Grosso and Mato Grosso do Sul (containing the Pantanal) and the entire Amazon region (excluding Pará) are one hour behind Rio time. Meanwhile, the island of Fernando de Nornonha, off the coast of Pernambuco, is one hour ahead of Rio time. During the Brazilian summer (North American winter) most of the country (with the exception of the Northeast) goes on daylight saving time (which makes the days longer). During this time, Rio, São Paulo, Minas, and the South spring forward, meaning that they are two hours ahead of New York City. Otherwise, the time difference between New York and Rio is only one hour (when it's noon in New York, it's 1 P.M. in Rio).

RESOURCES

Glossary

açaí a high-energy deep purple Amazonian fruit

acarajé a crunchy bean fritter cooked in palm oil and filled with dried shrimp, pepper, *vatapá*, and *caruru* that is a favorite snack in Bahia

água de coco milk from a green coconut (great for a hangover)

aldeia a small village

alegria joy, happiness, mirth

artesanato popular art and handicrafts

axé a type of fast-paced commercial pop associated with Carnaval in Salvador

azulejo Portuguese glazed ceramic tile

baía bay

Bahian person or thing from Bahia

Bahiana person or thing from Bahia; it also refers to Afro-Brazilian women (usually wearing traditional white turbans and lace petticoats) who sell typical Brazilian food

bairro neighborhood

bandeirantes early colonial explorers who set off from São Paulo to explore and settle Brazil's vast unknown interior from São Paulo

barraca small rustic kiosk or beach bar

bloco large Carnaval group

botequim/boteco laid-back, traditional, neighborhood-style bar, mostly associated with Rio

caboclinho folkloric dance with indigenous origins that is popular in the northeast, particularly Pernambuco; it is also the name of a sandwich made with the *tucumã* fruit, a favorite snack in Manaus

caboclo person of mixed race (Indian and European), often used to describe residents of the Amazon region

cachaça distilled sugarcane, the Brazilian equivalent of rum

cachoeira waterfall

cafezinho an espresso-sized coffee drink

caipirinha classic Brazilian cocktail made with *cachaça*, crushed ice, lime, and sugar

caipiroska *caipirinha* in which vodka replaces *cachaça*

camarão shrimp

Candango native of Brasília

Candomblé Afro-Brazilian religion whose practice is particularly strong in Bahia

cangaçeiro early 20th-century bandits from the Northeast interior, the most famous of which was Lampião

capoeira Afro-Brazilian mixture of martial art and dance

Carioca person or thing from Rio de Janeiro

Carnaval Carnival

carne-de-sol sun-dried meat

caruru a traditional Afro-Bahian dish of diced okra flavored with *dendê* and dried shrimp

Cerrado dry vegetation of scrubland and palms found in the Central-West.

chope draft beer

choro/chorinho type of instrumental music from the Northeast

comida por quilo popular self-service buffet restaurant where you pay for food by weight (per kilo)

costa coast

cupuaçu deliciously sweet, milky white Amazonian fruit

dendê palm oil used in Bahian cooking

doce sweet; often *doce* refers to candies or preserved fruit, such as *doce de goiaba* (preserved guava)

doce de leite creamy fudge-like pudding

empada empanada

farinha flour (generally manioc flour, which is dusted over meals)

farofa manioc flour toasted with butter and other seasonings as an accompaniment to meals in the Northeast

favela urban slum

fazenda ranch, farm, country estate

feijão beans

feijoada classic Brazilian stew of beans and salted pork and beef

feira open-air market

ferroviária train station

festa celebration, party

forró country-style type of music and dance from the Northeast

fortaleza fortress

frescoball popular Brazilian beach sport

frevo frenzied style of music and dance from Recife, popular during Carnaval

furto small theft

Gaúcho person or thing from Rio Grande do Sul

Globo Brazil's biggest television and media conglomerate. Its glamorous soap stars are known as "Globais."

GLS a Brazilian slang term for *gay, lesbica, e simpatisante;* i.e., gay friendly

golpe scam

gringo foreigner

guaraná Amazonian berry used as a pick-me-up. In small doses it flavors Brazil's national cola.

IBAMA Instituto Brasileiro do Meio Ambiente; government environmental organization in charge of all national parks and reserves and the protection of endangered flora and fauna

Iemanjá popular Afro-Brazilian goddess of the seas

igapó seasonally flooded patch of Amazonian rainforest

igarapé narrow river or creek that flows through the Amazon forest

igreja church

ilha island

jacaré caiman

jangada rustic sailboat used by fishermen of the Northeast

lanchonete snack bar, food stand

largo small square or plaza

literatura de cordel printed folios, illustrated with block prints, that recount popular tales of the Northeast

litoral coastline

loja store or shop

mangue mangrove swamp

maracatu a traditional group of dancers linked to Afro-Brazilian culture and religion (a famous fixture of Recife's Carnaval); also a percussive musical style that has become a popular genre in Pernambuco

Mata Atlântica native Atlantic rainforest, whose remaining patches can still be found along the Brazilian coast, mostly in Bahia and the Southeast

mercado market

Metrô subway

Mineiro a person or thing from Minas Gerais

moqueca typical Bahian stew of fish and or seafood cooked with tomatoes and green peppers in palm oil and coconut milk

morro hill, small mountain

mosteiro monastery

MPB Música Popular Brasileiro; i.e., classic Brazilian pop

mulato person of mixed African and European heritage

nordeste the Northeast of Brazil

novelas popular nightly television soap operas

orixá a Candomblé divinity

orla oceanfront

pastel a deep-fried pastry stuffed with a variety of fillings (especially popular in São Paulo)

pau brasil brazilwood tree, coveted by early colonial explorers, which inspired Brazil's name

Paulistano/Paulista a person or thing from the state of São Paulo

petiscos nibbles or appetizers (usually served in bars)

Planalto the high central plains regions fanning out from Brasília

pousada an inn, guesthouse, or bed-and-breakfast

praça square or plaza

praia beach

rodízio a type of restaurant service in which you pay a fixed price and then can choose from a rotating selection of items (usually *churrasco* or pizza)

rodovia highway

rodoviária bus terminal

rua street

salgado any savory type of pastry

samba a rhythmically fast, drum-based Brazilian style of music with strong African influences

serra mountain range

Sertanejo resident of the northeastern Sertão, as well as a popular style of country music

Sertão the poor, desert-like, and often drought-ridden interior of the Northeast

shopping shopping mall

sorveteria ice cream parlor

tapioca type of crêpe made from crunchy manioc flour and served with fillings

terreiro house and surrounding area where Candomblé rituals are performed

tira-gosto appetizer

trio elétrico vast stage on wheels upon which singers and musicians perform during Carnaval in Bahia

tucupi liquid distilled from manioc that is used in Amazonian cooking, most famously in a duck dish known as *pato no tucupi*

Tupi Indigenous people and language that thrived along coastal Brazil before the arrival of European explorers

tutu mineiro thick bean puree that is a classic side dish in Minas Gerais

vatapá a traditional Afro-Bahian dish in which cashews, dried shrimp, palm oil, and coconut milk are combined into a thick purée

Portuguese Phrasebook

Although most Brazilians are taught English at school, the quality of the teaching is so poor that it's hard to get more out of them than "Hi... How are you?...The book is on the table." Outside of Rio de Janeiro, São Paulo, and more sophisticated tourist areas, where at least a little English may be spoken, you will have two linguistic alternatives. The first is to try speaking Spanish, which is similar in many ways to Portuguese (although while Brazilians might understand you, you'll have a more difficult time understanding their replies). The second is to learn a few basic expressions in Portuguese. Although pronunciation can be tricky, Brazilians will love the fact that you are making an effort and will usually be very encouraging. Brazilian Portuguese is quite different from the Portuguese spoken in Portugal. In terms of speaking and comprehension, Brazilian Portuguese is easier since Brazilians pronounce words as they are written while Portuguese tend to distort certain sounds. Depending on the region you are in, accents and expressions will be different. A wonderfully innovative language, Brazilian Portuguese is full of colorful expressions and sayings as well as borrowed words from diverse idioms.

PRONUNCIATION

Portuguese is spoken as it is written. However, things take a turn for the complex when confronted with the challenging vowel sounds.

Vowels

So-called non-nasal vowels are fairly straightforward:

a is pronounced "ah," as in "father" in words like *garota* (girl).

e is pronounced "eh," as in "hey" in words like *fé* (faith). At the end of a word, such as *fome* (hunger), it is pronounced "ee," as in "free."

i is pronounced "ee," as in "free," in words such as *polícia* (police).

o is pronounced "aw" as in "dog," in words such as *loja* (shop). At the end of a word,

such as *minuto* (minute), it veers from "oh," as in "go," to "oo" as in "too."

Much more complicated are the nasal vowels. Nasal vowels are signaled by a tilde accent (~) as in *não* (no), or by the presence of the letters **m** or **n** following the vowel, such as *bem* (good) or *ponte* (bridge). When pronouncing them, it helps to exaggerate the sound, focus on your nose and not your mouth, and pretend there is an hidden "ng" on the end.

Consonants

Portuguese consonant sounds are a breeze compared with the nasal vowels. There are, however, a few exceptions to be aware of.

c is pronounced "k," as in "catch," in words like *casa* (house). However, when followed by the vowel **e** or **i,** or when sporting a cedilha accent (̦), as in *caçar* (to hunt) it is pronounced "s," as in "soft," in words like *cidade* (city).

ch is pronounced "sh," as in "shy," in words like *chá* (tea).

d is usually pronounced as in English. The exception is when it is followed by the vowel **e** or **i** – in words such as *parede* (wall) – it acquires a "j" sound similar to "jump."

g is pronounced "g," as in "go," in words like *gado* (cattle). However, when followed by the vowel **e** or **i,** it is pronounced like the "s" in "vision" in words like *gigante* (giant).

h is always silent. Words like *horário* (schedule) are pronouned like "hour" in English.

j is pronounced like the "s" in "vision," in words like *jogo* (game).

n is usually pronounced as in English. The exception is when it is followed by **h** – in words such as *banho* (bath) – when it acquires a "ny" sound similar to "new."

r can be pretty complicated. At the beginning of a word, such as Rio de Janeiro, or when found in twos, such as *carro* (car), it is pronounced as a very guttural "h" as in "home."

t is usually pronounced as in English. The exception is when it is followed by the vowel **e** or **i** – in words such as *morte* (death) – when it acquires a "ch" sound similar to "chalk."

x is pronounced like "sh," as in "shy," when found at the beginning of words such as *xadres* (chess). Otherwise, it is pronounced "z" as in "zoo," in words such as *exercício* (exercise).

Stress

Most Portuguese words carry stress on the second-to-last syllable. *Janeiro* (January), for example, is pronounced "ja-NEI-ro." There are, however, some exceptions. The stress falls on the last syllable with words that end in r – *falar* (to talk) is pronounced "fa-LAR" – as well as words ending in nasal vowels – *mamão* (papaya) is pronounced "ma-MAO." Vowels with accents over them – ~, ´, `, ^ – indicate that the stress falls on the syllable containing the vowel. As such, *inglês* (English) is pronounced "ing-LES" and *cardápio* (menu) is pronounced "car-DA-pi-o."

PLURAL NOUNS AND ADJECTIVES

In Portuguese, the general rule for making a noun or adjective plural is to simply add a "s." For example, the plural of *casa branca* (white house) is *casas brancas*. However, there are various exceptions. For instance, words that end in nasal consonants such as "m" and "l" change to "ns" and "is," respectively. The plural of *botequim* (bar) is *botequins*, while the plural of *hotel* (hotel) is *hotéis*. Words that end in nasal vowels also undergo changes. "Ão" becomes "ãos," "ães," or "ões," as in the case of *mão* (hand) which becomes *mãos* and *pão* (bread) which becomes *pães*.

GENDER

Like French, Spanish, and Italian, all Portuguese words have masculine and feminine forms of nouns and adjectives. In general, nouns ending in **o** or consonants, such as *cavalo* (horse) and *sol* (sun) are masculine, while those ending in **a**, such as *terra* (earth) are feminine. Many words have both masculine and feminine versions determined by their *o/a* ending, such as *menino* (boy) and *menina* (girl). Nouns are always preceded by articles – *o* and *a* (definite) and *um* and *uma* (indefinite) that announce their gender. For example, *o menino* means "the boy" while *a menina* means "the girl." *Um menino* is "a boy," while *uma menina* is "a girl."

DIMINUTIVES

Brazilians have a great fondness for using the *diminutivo* (diminutive), which accounts for the flood of *"inhos"* and *"zinhos"* attached to most words. Although the diminutive's true function is to indicate smallness in size – a *cafezinho* is an espresso-sized coffee, a *casinha* refers to a modest house – in Brazil, the diminutive is first and foremost used as a sign of affection between friends and family members. Since Brazilians are very affectionate, these are used more often than are standard names. Men named Luiz are inevitably called Luizinho and women named Ana become Aninha. A *filho* (son) is a *filhinho*, a *mãe* (mother) is *mãezinha*, a *namorado* (boyfriend) is a *namoradinho*, and even a beloved *cachorro* (dog) is often a *cachorrinho*. Moreover, Brazilians possess a great talent for recounting everything from *historinhas* (stories) to *fofoquinhas* (gossip), and in the recounting the diminutive is often used for emphasis. It can also be used to downplay an event – a *joguinho* is a *jogo* (game) without importance – or to placate someone (asking a client to wait just a *minutinho* for service is somehow less onerous than having to wait an entire *minuto*). There are, however, some instances in which a diminutive might refer to something quite different. A *camishinha* is not a small *camisa* (shirt), but a condom. An *abóbora* is a pumpkin, while an *abobrinha* is a zucchini.

BASIC AND COURTEOUS EXPRESSIONS

Hello *Olá*
Hi *Oi*
Good morning *Bom dia*
Good afternoon/evening *Boa tarde*
Good night *Boa noite*
See you later *Até mais tarde, até breve*

Goodbye *Tschau*
How are you? *Como vai?/Tudo bem?*
Fine, and you? *Tudo bem, e você?*
So so *Mais ou menos*
Not so good *Meio ruim*
Nice to meet you. *Um prazer.*
You're very kind. *Você é muito(a) simpático(a)*
Yes *Sim*
No *Não*
I don't know. *Não sei.*
Please *Por favor*
Thank you *Obrigado (if you're male),*
Obrigada (if you're female)
You're welcome. *De nada.*
Excuse me. *Com licença.*
Sorry *Desculpa*
What's your name? *Como se chama?/Qual é*
seu nome?
My name is... *Meu nome é . . .*
Where are you from? *De onde vem?*
I'm from... *Sou de . . .*
Do you speak English? *Fala inglês?*
I don't speak Portuguese. *Não falo*
Portuguese.
I only speak a little bit. *Só falo um*
pouquinho.
I don't understand. *Não entendo*
Can you please repeat that? *Por favor,*
pode repetir?
What's it called? *Como se chama?*
What time is it? *Que horas são?*
Would you like . . . ? *Gostaria de . . . ?*

TERMS OF ADDRESS

I *eu*
you *você*
he/him *ele*
she/her *ela*
we/us *nós*
you (plural) *vocês*
they/them *eles/elas*
Mr./Sir *Senhor*
Mrs./Madame *Senhora or Dona*
young man *moço or rapaz*
young woman *moça*
guy/fellow *rapaz, cara*
boy/girl *garoto/garota*
child *criança*

brother/sister *irmão/irmã*
father/mother *pai/mãe*
son/daughter *filho/filha*
husband/wife *marido/mulher*
uncle/aunt *tio/tia*
grandfather/grandmother *avô, avó*
friend *amigo/amiga*
colleague *colega*
boyfriend/girlfriend *namorado/namorada*
single *solteiro/a*
divorced *divorciado/a*

TRANSPORTATION

Where is . . . ? *Onde é/Onde fica . . . ?*
How far away is . . . ? *Qual é a distância*
até . . . ?
Which is the quickest way? *Qual é o*
caminho mais rápido?
How can I get to . . . ? *Como eu posso*
chegar . . . ?
Is it far? *É longe?*
Is it close? *É perto?*
bus *ônibus*
the bus station *a rodoviária*
the bus stop *a parada de ônibus*
How much does a ticket cost? *Quanto*
custa uma passagem?
What is the schedule? *Qual é o horário?*
When is the next departure? *Quando é a*
próxima saida?
What time do we leave? *Á que horas vamos*
sair?
What time do we arrive? *Á que horas vamos*
chegar?
first *primeiro*
last *último*
next *próximo*
Are there many stops? *Tem muitas*
paradas?
plane *avião*
Is the flight on time? *O vôo está na hora?*
Is it late? *Está atrasado?*
I'd like a round-trip ticket. *Quero uma*
passagem ida e volta.
I have a lot of luggage. *Tenho muita*
bagagem.
Is there a baggage check? *Tem guarda*
volumes?

boat *barco*
ship *návio*
ferry boat *ferry, balsa*
port *porto*
Is the sea calm or rough? *O mar está calmo ou turbulento?*
Are there many waves? *Tem muitas ondas?*
I want to rent a car. *Quero alugar um carro.*
Is it safe to drive here? *É seguro dirigir aqui?*
gas station *posto de gasolina*
Can you fill up the gas tank? *Pode encher o tanque?*
To drive fast/slowly *dirigir rapidamente/ devagar*
parking lot *estacionamento*
stoplight *o sinal*
toll *pedágio*
at the corner *na esquina*
sidewalk *a calçada*
dead-end street *rua sem saida*
one-way *mão unica*
The car broke down. *O carro quebrou.*
I need a mechanic. *Preciso dum mecânico.*
Can you fix it? *Pode consertar?*
The tire burst. *O pneu furou.*
Where can I get a taxi? *Onde posso achar um taxi?*
Is this taxi free? *Está livre?*
Can you take me to this address? *Pode me levar para este endereço?*
Can you stop here, please? *Pode parar aqui, por favor?*
north *norte*
south *sul*
east *este*
west *oueste*
left/right *esquerda/direita*
straight ahead *tudo direito*

ACCOMMODATIONS

To stay in a hotel *Ficar num hotel*
Is there a guesthouse nearby? *Tem pousada perto daqui?*
Are there any rooms available? *Tem quartos disponivéis?*
For today? *Para hoje?*
I'd like to make a reservation. *Queria fazer uma reserva.*

I want a single room. *Quero um quarto simples.*
Is there a double room? *Tem quarto duplo?*
With a double bed or two singles? *Com cama de casal ou duas camas solteiras?*
With a fan or air-conditioned? *Com ventilador ou ar condicionado?*
Is there a view? *Tem vista?*
private bathroom *banheiro privado*
shower *chuveiro*
key *chave*
Is breakfast included? *O café de manhã é incluido?*
How much does it cost? *Quanto custa?*
Can you give me a discount? *É possivel ter um desconto?*
It's too expensive. *É muito caro.*
Is there something cheaper? *Tem algo mais barato?*
for just one night *para uma noite só*
for three days *para três dias.*
Can I see it first? *Posso dar uma olhada primeiro?*
quiet/noisy *tranquilo/barulhento*
comfortable *confortável*
change the sheets/towels *trocar os lençóis/toalhas*
soap *sabão*
toilet tissue *papel higiênico*
Could you please wake me up? *Por favor, pode me acordar?*

FOOD

to eat *comer*
to drink *beber*
I'm hungry. *Estou com fome.*
I'm thirsty. *Estou com sede.*
breakfast *café de manhã*
lunch *almoço*
dinner *jantar*
a snack *um lanche*
a light meal *uma comida leve*
I just want to nibble. *Só quero beliscar.*
Are the portions large? *As porções são grandes?*
Is it enough for two? *Dá para duas pessoas?*
Can I order a half portion? *Posso pedir uma meia-porção?*

Can I see the menu? *Pode dar uma olhada no cardápio?*
Is it all-you-can-eat? *Pode comer a vontade?*
Can you call the waiter over? *Pode chamar o garçom?*
Is there a free table? *Tem mesa livre?*
I'd like a cold beer. *Quero uma cerveja gelada.*
Another, please. *Mais uma, por favor.*
Do you have wine? *Tem vinho?*
Red or white? *Tinto ou branco?*
I'd like more ice please. *Quero mais gelo, por favor.*
This glass is dirty. *Este copo está sujo.*
Can you bring me another? *Pode me trazer outro?*
Do you have juice? *Tem suco?*
I'd like it without sugar. *Quero sem açúcar.*
Do you have sweetener? *Tem adocante?*
carbonated mineral water *água mineral com gaz*
I'm a vegetarian. *Sou vegetariano.*
I'm ready to order. *Estou pronto para pedir.*
Can I have some more time? *Pode me dar mais um tempinho?*
well done *bem passado*
medium *ao ponto*
rare *mal passado*
hot *quente*
cold *frio*
sweet *doce*
salty *salgado*
sour *azedo*
flatware *talheres*
fork *garfo*
knife *faca*
soup spoon *colher de sopa*
tea spoon *colher de chá*
dessert *sobremesa*
Can you bring coffee please? *Pode trazer um cafezinho?*
with milk *com leite*
Can you bring the bill please? *Pode trazer a conta por favor.*
It was delicious. *Foi deliciosa.*

Meat
red meat *carne*
chicken *frango, galinha*
pork *porco, leitão*
ham *presunto*
turkey *peru*
sausage *salsicha*

Fish and Seafood
fish *peixe*
seafood *frutas do mar, mariscos*
freshwater *água doce*
tuna *atum*
shrimp *camarão*
crab *carangueijo, siri*
squid *lula*
octopus *polvo*
lobster *lagosta*

Eggs and Dairy
eggs *ovos*
hard-boiled egg *ovo cozido*
scrambled eggs *ovos mexidos*
whole milk *leite integrado*
skim milk *leite desnatado*
powdered milk *leite em pó*
cream *creme de leite*
butter *manteiga*
cheese *queijo*
yogurt *iogurte*
ice cream *sorvete*

Vegetables
vegetables *verduras/legumes*
salad *salada*
lettuce *alface*
carrot *cenoura*
tomato *tomate*
potato *batata*
cucumber *pepino*
zucchini *abobrinha*
couve *kale*
cabbage *repolho*

Fruits
mango *manga*
papaya *mamão*
passion fruit *maracujá*

apple *macã*
orange *laranja*
lime *limão*
pineapple *abacaxi*
grape *uva*
strawberry *morango*
watermelon *melância*
guava *goiaba*
jackfruit *jaca*
cashew fruit *cajú*

Seasoning and Spices

salt *sal*
black pepper *pimenta do reino*
hot pepper *pimenta*
cilantro *coentro*
parsley *salsa*
ginger *gengibre*
mint *hortelã*
basil *manjeiricão*
onion *cebola*
green onion *cebolinha*
garlic *alho*
cooking oil *óleo*
olive oil *azeite*
vinegar *vinagre*
brown sugar *açúcar mascavo*
cinnamon *canela*
clove *cravo*
nutmeg *noz moscada*
vanilla *baunilha*

Baked Goods

bread *pão*
whole wheat bread *pão integral*
cookies *biscoitos*
cake *bolo, torta*
flour *farinha*

Cooking

roasted, baked *assado*
boiled *cozido*
steamed *a vapor*
grilled *grelhado*
barbecue *churrasco*
fried *frito*
breaded *à milanesa*

Drinks

water *água*
milk *leite*
soft drink *refrigerante*
juice *suco*
ice *gelo*
beer *cerveja*
wine *vinho*

MONEY AND SHOPPING

to buy *comprar*
to spend a lot of money *gastar muito dinheiro*
to shop *fazer compras*
for sale *à venda*
Until what time does the bank stay open? *Até que horas o banco fica aberto?*
I'm out of money. *Estou sem dinheiro.*
I don't have change. *Estou sem troco.*
ATM *caixa automática*
Do you accept credit cards? *Aceita cartão de crédito?*
Can I exchange money? *Posso trocar dinheiro?*
money exchange *câmbio*
Is there a discount if I pay in cash? *Tem desconto se pagar em dinheiro?*
That's too expensive. *É caro demais.*
That's very cheap. *É muito barato.*
more *mais*
less *menos*
a good price *Um preço bom.*
Let's bargain. *Vamos negociar.*
Is it on sale? *Está em promoção?*
It's a good deal. *É um bom negócio.*
What time does the store close? *A que horas fecha a loja?*
salesperson *vendedor/a*
Can I try it on? *Posso provar?*
It doesn't fit. *Não cabe bem.*
too tight *muito apertado*
too big *grande demais*
Can I exchange it? *Posso trocar?*

HEALTH

Can you help me? *Pode me ajudar?*
I don't feel well. *Não me sinto bem.*
I'm nauseous. *Estou com nausea.*

I've got a headache. *Estou com dor de cabeça.*

I've got a stomachache. *Estou com dor de barriga.*

fever *um febre*

pain *uma dor*

infection *uma infeção*

cut *um corte*

burn *uma queimadura*

vomiting *vomitando*

I can't breathe. *Não posso respirar.*

I'm sick. *Estou doente.*

Is there a pharmacy close by? *Tem uma farmácia perto daqui?*

Can you call a doctor? *Pode ligar para um médico?*

I need to go to a hospital. *Preciso ir para o hospital.*

pill *pílula*

medicine *remédio/medicamento*

antibiotic *antibiótico*

ointment *pomada/creme*

cotton *algodão*

toothpaste *pasta de dentes*

toothbrush *escova de dentes*

condom *preservativo/camisinha*

SAFETY

Is this neighborhood safe? *Este bairro é seguro?*

dangerous *perigoso*

roubo *robbery*

thief *ladrão*

mugging *assalto*

mugger *assaltante*

Call the police! *Chame a polícia!*

Help! *Socorro!*

COMMUNICATIONS

to talk, speak *falar*

to say *dizer*

to hear *ouvir*

to listen *escutar*

to shout *gritar*

to make a phone call *fazer um telefonema/ligar*

What's your phone number? *Qual é seu numero de telefone?*

the wrong number *o numero errado*

collect call *uma chamada a cobrar*

international call *uma chamada internacional*

Do you have Internet here? *Tem Internet aqui?*

I want to send an email. *Quero mandar um email.*

What's your email address? *Qual é seu endereço de email?*

post office *os correios*

letter *carta*

postcard *postal*

package *um pacote*

box *uma caixa*

to send *enviar*

to deliver *entregar*

stamp *selo*

weight *peso*

NUMBERS

1 *um, uma*

2 *dois, duas*

3 *três*

4 *quatro*

5 *cinco*

6 *seis*

7 *sete*

8 *oito*

9 *novo*

10 *dez*

11 *onze*

12 *doze*

13 *treze*

14 *quatorze*

15 *quinze*

16 *dezesseis*

17 *dezessete*

18 *dezoito*

19 *dezenove*

20 *vinte*

21 *vinte e um*

30 *trinta*

40 *quarenta*

50 *cinquenta*

60 *sessenta*

70 *setenta*

80 *oitenta*

90 *noventa*
100 *cem*
101 *cento e um*
200 *duzentos*
500 *quinhentos*
1,000 *mil*
2,000 *dois mil*

TIME

What time is it? *Que horas são?*
It's 3 o'clock. *São três horas.*
It's 3:15. *São três e quinze.*
It's 3:30. *São três e meia.*
It's 3:45. *São três e quarenta-cinco.*
In two hours. *Daqui a duas horas.*
Sorry for being late. *Desculpe o atraso.*
Did I arrive early? *Cheguei cedo?*
before *antes*
after *depois*

DAYS AND MONTHS

day *dia*
morning *manhã*
afternoon *tarde*
night *noite*
today *hoje*
yesterday *ontém*
tomorrow *amanhã*
week *semana*
month *mês*
year *ano*
century *século*
Monday *segunda-feira*
Tuesday *terça-feira*
Wednesday *quarta-feira*
Thursday *quinta-feira*

Friday *sexta-feira*
Saturday *sábado*
Sunday *domingo*
January *janeiro*
February *fevereiro*
March *março*
April *abril*
May *maio*
June *junho*
July *julho*
August *agosto*
September *setembro*
October *outubro*
November *novembro*
December *dezembro*

SEASONS AND WEATHER

season *estação*
spring *primavera*
summer *verão*
autumn *outuno*
winter *inverno*
weather *o tempo*
sun *sol*
It's sunny. *Está fazendo sol.*
rain *chuva*
Is it going to rain? *Vai chover?*
clouds *nuvens*
cloudy *nublado*
It's hot. *Faz calor.*
It's cold. *Faz frio.*
a cool breeze *uma brisa fresca*
a strong wind *um vento forte*
dry air *ar seco*
wet *molhado*

Suggested Reading

TRAVEL LITERATURE

Bishop, Elizabeth. *One Art*. New York: Farrar, Strauss and Giroux, 1995. America's poet laureate, Elizabeth Bishop was also a steadfast and elegant letter writer. On a South American cruise, Bishop stopped off in Rio de Janeiro, fell ill after eating a cashew fruit, and was nursed back to health by Lota Macedo Soares, a wealthy and very clever Carioca with whom she fell in love. The subsequent years she spent in Brazil are chronicled with sharpness and affection in the letters published in this tome.

Haddad, Annette, and Scott Doggett (eds). *Travelers' Tales Brazil: True Stories*. New York: Travelers' Tales Guides, 2004. This great collection of travel essays—penned by a variety of writers and excerpted from books and magazines—offers a multifaceted view of Brazil through many lenses.

Lévi-Strauss, Claude. *Tristes Tropiques*. New York: Penguin, 1992. The famous French anthropologist supposedly hated traveling and explorers, but quickly changed his mind when he traveled to Brazil in the 1930s and found himself face to face with the fascinating Indian groups of the Amazon Basin. Lévi-Strauss's prose offers an engaging mixture of ethnographic description and autobiographical impressions.

Page, P. K. *Brazilian Journal*. Toronto: L. & O. Dennys, 1987. In the 1950s, Canadian poet P. K. Page found herself in Rio when her husband became Canada's ambassador to Brazil. Despite bouts of cultural shock, Page fell in love with Brazil. Her descriptions of Rio's glamorous last days as the nation's capital are simple, lyrical, and ultimately moving.

Wallace, Alfred Russel. *A Narrative of Travels on the Amazon and the Rio Negro*. Whitefish, MT: Kessinger Publishing, 2006. Naturalist Alfred Russel Wallace was both a colleague and rival of Charles Darwin. Both men visited Brazil in the mid-19th century, but Wallace chose to slash (and shoot) his way through the Amazon Basin, taking minute and highly evocative notes of all the exotica that crossed his path.

HISTORY AND SOCIETY

De Jesus, Carolina Maria. *Child of the Dark*. New York: Signet, 2003. Written between 1955 and 1960, these intimate journal entries by Carolina de Jesus offer a rare first-hand glimpse of the life of a single, black mother of three who lived in a São Paulo *favela* and earned a living picking garbage. Through a chance encounter with a journalist, her diary was published in 1960 and de Jesus became something of a celebrity.

Fausto, Boris. *A Concise History of Brazil*. Cambridge, MA: Cambridge University, 1999. One of Brazil's leading historians and a professor at the University of São Paulo, Fausto does an admirable job of condensing five centuries of events and outsized personalities into one comprehensive and highly readable narrative.

Hemming, John. *Tree of Rivers: The Story of the Amazon*. New York: Thames and Hudson, 2008. This former director of the Royal Geographic Society is author of *Red Gold: The Conquest of the Brazilian Indians*, which is considered the definitive history of Brazil's indigenous peoples. In his most recent book, Hemming gives a fascinating account of life along the mythic river. His characters range from classic (Indians, explorers, missionaries, and rubber barons) to contemporary (hardcore environmentalists, ecotourists, and soya and cattle agro-millionaires).

Levine, Robert M., and John Crocitti, eds. *The Brazil Reader: History, Culture, Politics*. New York: Duke University Press, 1999. An intelligently edited volume of essays on myriad and often subtle aspects of Brazilian history, society, and daily life. The texts range from academic to alternative, but all are thought-provoking and do a fine job of tackling Brazil's overwhelming diversity and complexity.

Mattoso, Katia M. de Queiroz. *To Be a Slave in Brazil, 1550–1888.* New York: Rutgers, 1987. Mattoso provides Balzacian details that movingly bring to life the harrowing existence of slaves in colonial Brazil as seen through the eyes of both slaves and their masters.

Morley, Helena. *Diary of Helena Morley.* London: Virago, 2008. Alice Dayrell Caldeira Brant was a bright, rebellious, and imaginative girl of English ancestry. She grew up in Diamantina, Minas Gerais, in the late 19th century, when its once-glittering diamond mines were already in decline. In the 1940s, aged 62, Brant published her teenage diaries under the pseudonym Helena Morley. Immensely popular, the book became widely regarded as a fascinating record of life in a provincial mining town. The English version was translated by American poet Elizabeth Bishop.

Page, Joseph A. *The Brazilians.* New York: Da Capo Press, 1996. In an attempt to explain "Brazilianness," this highly readable cultural history of Brazil draws on politics, economics, sports, literature, pop culture, religion, and historical events and figures.

CULTURE AND MUSIC

Bellos, Alex. *Futebol: The Brazilian Way of Life.* London: Bloomsbury, 2002. A compelling look at Brazil's national pastime (some would say religion) that traces the fascinating history of soccer from its humble beginnings to its overblown present. Bellos is an accomplished journalist, and he mixes insightful reporting with highly entertaining anecdotes.

Castro, Ruy. *Bossa Nova—The Story of the Brazilian Music that Seduced the World.* Chicago: Chicago Review Press, 2003. One of Brazil's most prolific journalists, Castro conjures up the heady days of Ipanema in the late '50s and early '60s when fascinating characters such as João Gilberto and Tom Jobim pioneered the cool syncopated sound that took the world by storm. Aside from detailing the history of bossa nova, the book offers a slice of Carioca life from that time.

Guillermoprieto, Alma. *Samba.* New York: Vintage, 1991. A former dancer and contributor to *The New Yorker,* Guillermoprieto spent a year in Rio de Janeiro's Zona Norte neighborhood with Mangueira, one of the city's most traditional samba schools, as its 5,000 members prepared for Carnaval. This result is a vibrant, passionate, and beautifully written backstage narrative.

McGowan, Chris, and Ricard Pessanha. *The Brazilian Sound: Samba, Bossa Nova, and the Popular Music of Brazil.* Philadelphia: Temple University Press, 1998. A thorough and well-written compendium of popular Brazilian music styles and major performing artists, this book serves as a useful introduction to Brazil's rich musical world. The text is accompanied by photos and a vast discography.

Peterson, Joan, and David Peterson. *Eat Smart in Brazil: How to Decipher the Menu, Know the Market Foods & Embark on a Tasting Adventure.* Corte Madera, CA: Gingko Press, 2006. Illustrated with mouthwatering photos, this highly readable book acts as a culinary companion, introducing you to the ingredients, recipes, and diverse regional cooking traditions of Brazil.

Sullivan, Edward J. (ed.), *Brazil Body and Soul.* New York: Guggenheim Museum, 2003. Published to coincide with Brazil's 500-year anniversary and the subsequent "Best of" survey exhibited by the Guggenheim Museum, this massive catalog provides a mesmerizing overview of Brazilian art. Included are early explorers' depictions of "paradise," Aleijadinho's baroque marvels, Modernism, folk art from throughout the Northeast, and interesting sections on indigenous and Afro-Brazilian art. The thoughtful essays are illustrated with stunning, high-quality photos.

Veloso, Caetano. *Tropical Truth: A Story of Music and Revolution in Brazil.* New York: Da Capo Press, 2003. Brilliant, charming, and sometimes aggravating Bahian singer/composer Caetano Veloso is one of MPB's most creative figures. In this colorful memoir, he provides an insider's look at the generation-defining musical movement of the late '60 and '70s, which became known as Tropicália.

Internet Resources

Brasil Sabor
www.brasilsabor.com.br
This site takes you on a detailed and mouthwatering journey throughout Brazil with itineraries whose focus is food in all its forms. Organized by region, everything from native ingredients and local markets to hidden-away restaurants, street *barracas,* and vanguard chefs is described in vivid prose, accompanied by sumptuous photographs. While much of the Portuguese section is complete, the English section is in its beginning stages.

Brazil.com
www.brazil.com
This practical site is a decent general guide with information on major destinations as well as samples of airfares and hotel rates (with links). It also offers Brazil basics and tips for planning your trip.

Brazzil Magazine
www.brazzil.com
Brazzil Magazine features informative and concise articles, essays, and news pieces about various elements of Brazilian political, economic, social, and cultural life, largely written by English-speaking Brazilian specialists and savvy gringos living in Brazil. The site features some useful links and classified ads.

BrazilMax
www.brazilmax.com
Billing itself as the "hip guide to Brazil," BrazilMax is operated by award-winning American journalist Bill Hinchberger, who has lived and worked in Brazil for over 20 years.

Hinchberger and a stable of other talented expats pen the succinct travel articles and travel-related features that are regularly updated. Brazilmax is a great source for critical reviews and helpful hints. It also offers a range of services from music downloads to customized itineraries and personal ads.

Brazil Travel Blog
www.braziltravelblog.com
This engagingly written and highly informative blog is written by Tony Galvez, a Spanish expatriate living in São Paulo. Published in English and Spanish, his discriminating traveler's tips and information are spot-on and his many journeys, illustrated with captivating photographs make for enticing reading.

Embratur
www.braziltour.com
The official site of Embratur, the Brazilian ministry of tourism, has a very well-organized multilingual site that allows you to browse potential journeys according to region, itinerary, or interest (ecotourism, beaches, culture, sports, business travel). It also has up-to-date tips and resources for travelers concerning travel logistics (visas, vaccinations, airports, etc.).

Gay Travel Brazil
www.gaytravelbrazil.com
This small but informative site focuses on gay travel in Brazil. It concentrates mainly on Rio and São Paulo (with gay-friendly hotel recommendations), but also provides general info and gay tips to all the major cities. Apart from booking flights, Gay Travel Brazil works with

gay-friendly tour operators and guides in Brazil who can organize customized excursions.

Made in Brazil
www.madeinbrazil.typepad.com

Made in Brazil is a freewheeling blog that riffs on Brazilian fashion, celebrity gossip, and travel (with an emphasis on hipster clubs, restaurants, and bars). It has some good travel info and interesting pop culture tidbits.

Maria-Brazil
www.maria-brazil.org

Maria-Brazil is a welcoming travel site for lovers of Brazil and all things Brazilian that is operated by an American expat who divides her time between Rio and Miami. Aside from a "little black book" of great "insider" Rio listings, "Maria" shares her favorite places from all over Brazil as well as Brazilian recipes and information on music and festivals.

Index

A

Abismo Anhumas: 438
Academia de Cozinha e Outros Prazeres: 116
açai fruit: 559
acarajes: 21, 340
accessibility: 663
accommodations: general discussion 652-654; Brasília 404; Rio de Janeiro 72-78; Salvador 332-337; São Paulo 149-152; useful phrases 683; see also specific place
Aeroporto Augusto Severino: 507-508
Aeroporto Coronel Horácio de Matos: 359
Aeroporto Deputado Luís Eduardo Magalhães (Dois de Julho): 344
Aeroporto Eduardo Gomes: 596
Aeroporto Fernando de Noronha 476
Aeroporto Internacional (Campo Grande): 431
Aeroporto Internacional (Corumbá): 436
Aeroporto Internacional Afonso Pena: 198
Aeroporto Internacional de Brasília-Presidente Juscelino Kubitschek: 407
Aeroporto Internacional de Val-de-Cães: 568
Aeroporto Internacional dos Guararapes: 458
Aeroporto Internacional Foz do Iguaçu: 210
Aeroporto Internacional Pinto Martins: 525
Aeroporto Internacional Salgado Filho: 238
Aeroporto Internacional Tom Jobim: 88
Aeroporto Jorge Amado: 371
Aeroporto Marechal Cunha Machado: 541
Aeroporto Marechal Rondon: 422-423
Aeroporto Maria José: 579
Aeroporto Santos Dumont: 88
Aeroporto Zumbi dos Palmares: 485
Afro-Brazilians: 629-630, 631; Dia da Consciência Negra 491; Museu Afro Brasil 135; Museu Afro-Brasiliero 310-311
agriculture: 626
águia real (harpy eagle): 612
Agulhas Negras: 100
AIDS: 668
air pollution: 608
air travel: general discussion 12, 643-644, 645; Belém 568; Belo Horizonte 262; Brasília 407; Campo Grande 431; Corumbá 436; Cuiabá 422-423; Curitiba 198; Fernando de Noronha 476; Florianópolis 225; Fortaleza 525; Iguaçu Falls 210; Ilhéus 371; Lençóis 359; Maceió 485; Manaus 596; Natal 507-508; Porto Alegre 238; Porto Seguro 376; Recife 458; Rio de Janeiro 88; Salvador 344; San Luís 541; Santarém 579; São Paulo 161-162
Alagoas: 10, 441-445, 477-494; highlights 442; history 444-445; Maceió 477-485; map 443; planning your time 444
Alcântara: 542-543
Aleijadinho: 270, 272, 273, 280, 281, 283
Alfandêga: 585-586
Algodoal Island: see Ilha de Algodoal
alligators: 611
Alter do Chão: 14, 23, 24, 579-581
Alto da Sé: 459
Alto do Moura: 467-468
Alto Paraíso de Goiás: 413-414
Amado, Jorge: 312, 369, 641
Amazonas: 10, 17, 583-603
Amazon Basin: 605
Amazon Ecopark: 590
Amazon region: 10, 23-24, 547-603, 604-605, 607-608, 609, 656; Amazonas 583-603; deforestation 607-608; flora 609; food 656; highlights 548; history 551-554; maps 549, 552-553; Pará 554-582; planning your time 550-551
Amazon River: 547-550, 601, 605; map 552-553; see also Amazon region
Americel Hall: 402
anacondas: 417, 611
Andaraí: 355, 361
Andersen, Alfredo: 192
Andrade, Mário de: 641
Andrade, Oswald de: 638
Angra dos Reis: 20, 108-111
animals: see fauna
Anima Mundi: 144
antas (tapirs): 610
anteaters: 610
antiques: 68-69, 148; see also shopping
Antonina: 201-202
Apaga-Fogo: 377
apart-hotels: 653; see also accommodations
Aquário Municipal: 421
Aquário Natural: 438
Aquidauana: 432
Aquiraz: 526
Araçaipe: 377
Aramanai: 580
ararás (macaws): 612
architecture: see art and architecture
Arco do Teles: 31

Arcos da Lapa: 37
Arembepe: 345-346
ariranha (giant otter): 610
Armação: 217
armadillos: 610
Armazém do Tempo: 561
Arquipélago de Anavilhanas: 599
Arraial d'Ajuda: 377-379
Arraial d'Ajuda Eco Parque: 377
Arraial do Cabo: 102-103
arraias (stingrays): 612
art, architecture, and culture: 392, 633-642,
    637-639; suggested reading 689-690; *see
    also* crafts
art centers: *see specific place*
Arte em Toda Parte: 463
Aruba: 321
As Cavalhadas: 17, 410
Assis, Machado de: 641
Atins: 544
Atlantic rainforest: 605-606; flora 609
ATMs: 672
Auditório Ibirapuera: 134, 142-143
Australian Embassy: 648
Avenida Paulista: 8, 19; accommodations 150-
    151; food 155-157; map 131; nightlife 139-140;
    sights 130-132
Avenida Rio Branco: 35
Aviário das Aningas: 561
Azeda/Azedinha: 104
azulejo tiles: 311, 536

B

Babilônia Feira Hype: 69
Back Door: 370
backpacking: *see hiking*
Bahia: 9-10, 15, 21, 300-385; Chapada
    Diamantina 355-362; food 21; highlights 301;
    history 304-305; map 302; planning your
    time 303-304; Recôncavo 351-355; Salvador
    305-345; southern coast 362-385
Bahia, Hansen: 353
Baía de Camamu: 365-366
Baía de Guanabara: *see Guanabara Bay*
Baía de Todos os Santos: 322-324
Baía do Sancho: 473-474
Baía dos Golfinhos: 475
Baía dos Porcos: 474
Baía do Sueste: 474
baião music: 635
Bairro do Recife: 447-448
Baixio: 350
Balé da Cidade: 142

Balé Folclórico da Bahia: 328
baleias francas do sul (southern right whales):
    611
baleias jubarte (humpback whales): 611
Ballet Stagium: 143
Bananal: 19-20, 172-174
bananas: 609
bandeirantes: 248, 391, 616-617
banks: general discussion 671-672; Belém 568;
    Belo Horizonte 262; Brasília 407; Campo
    Grande 431; Cuiabá 422; Fortaleza 525;
    Florianópolis 224; Foz do Iguaçu 210; Maceió
    485; Manaus 595-596; Olinda 465; Ouro
    Preto 277; Penedo 490; Porto Alegre 235;
    Recife 458; Rio de Janeiro 87; Salvador 343;
    San Luís 541; São Paulo 161
Bardobeco: 15
bargaining: 663
Barra: accommodations 336-337; food 341-
    342; map 320-321; sights 319-321
barracas: 523
Barra da Lagoa: 216
Barra da Tijuca: 53
Barra de Itariri: 350
Barra de Santo Antônio: 490
Barra de São Miguel: 487-488
Barra de Tabatinga: 508-509
Barra de Una: 175
Barra do Cai: 383
Barra do Cunhau: 512
Barra Grande: 16, 365
Barra Velha: 374, 382
Barreirinhas: 543, 545-546
bars: 660-661; *see also* nightlife
Basílica de Nossa Senhora de Nazaré: 24,
    559-560
Basílica e Convento de Nossa Senhora do
    Carmo: 449
Basílica e Santuário do Bom Jesus de
    Matosinhos: 280
Basílica Menor de São Pedro dos Clérigos: 278
bathing suits: 46
batida cocktail: 658
Batuba: 370
beaches: 14, 46; Amazon 589-590; Arraial
    d'Ajuda 377; Arraial do Cabo 102-103;
    Barra 320-321; Búzios 104-105; Cabo Frio
    102; Caraíva 382-383; Caravelas 384;
    Copacabana 45-48; dos and don'ts 46;
    Fernando de Noronha 473-474; Fortaleza
    518-519; Garopaba 227-228; Ilha de
    Catarina 216-218; Ilhabela 178-180; Ilha do
    Mel 203; Ilhéus 370; Ipanema 50-51; Itacaré

367; Leblon 50-51; Maceió 479-481; Morro
de São Paulo 362-363; Natal 502-503;
Niterói 91-93; Paraty 113; Porto Belo 225-
226; Porto Seguro 373-374; Rio de Janeiro
45-48, 50-51; São Sebastião 175-176;
Trancoso 380; Ubatuba 183-184; see also
specific beach (praia); specific place
Beach Park: 526
beach vendors: 523, 661
Beberibe: 526-527
beer: 659-660
beija-flores (hummingbirds): 612-613
Bela Vista: 153
Belém: 10, 23, 24, 550, 554-569; map 555
Belo Horizonte: 9, 15, 249-264;
accommodations 258-259; entertainment/
events 254-257; food 259-262; information/
services 262; map 250-251; sights 249-254;
sports/recreation 257-258; transportation
262-263
Belterra: 581-582
Bembé do Mercado: 351
beverages: 236, 594, 657-660
Bezerros: 468
Biblioteca Nacional: 36, 390, 397
Biblioteca Pública: 252
Bico do Pagagaio: 110
bicycling: Campos do Jordão 167; Fernando de
Noronha 477; Lençóis 359; Rio de Janeiro
70; Trancoso 380; see also specific place
Bienal do Recôncavo: 353
biodiversity: 604
birds/bird-watching: general discussion
612-613; Aviário das Aningas 561; Buraco
das Araras 437; Lagoa Timeantube 347;
Pantanal 417; Parque das Aves 207-208; see
also specific place
Biribiri: 298-299
Bixiga: 153
Boa Viagem: 449, 452-453, 456-457
Boa Viagem Beach: 317
Boa Vista: 448-449, 451-452, 456
boating: general discussion 644; Alter do Chão
580; Amazon 569, 579, 602-603; Angra dos
Reis 109; Arraial do Cabo 103; Búzios 106;
Fernando de Noronha 475; Ilha de Santa
Catarina 219; Ilha do Mel 203; Ilha Grande
109; Morro de São Paulo 363; Paraty 113;
544; Praia do Pipa 513; Rio de Janeiro 71;
Salvador 332; Santarém 577; São Sebastião
176
Boca da Barra: 364
Boca do Rio: 321

Boiçucanga: 176
Boipeba Island: see Ilha de Boipeba
Bombas: 226
bombeirinho cocktail: 658
Bombinhas: 226
Bonaparte, Napoleon: 28
Bonfim: 316-317
Bonito: 436-440
books/bookstores: Festa Literária
Internacional 114; Rio de Janeiro 68; São
Paulo 147; suggested reading 688-690
Borboletário Márcio Ayres: 561
border crossings: 210
Bosque Alemão: 193
Bosque da Ciência: 589
Bosque Papa João Paulo: 193
Bosque Rodrigues Alves: 561-562
Bosque Santa Lúcia: 577
bossa nova: 635-636
Botafogo: accommodations 74; food 80-81;
nightlife 62-63; sights 42-43
botequins (bars): 59; see also nightlife
boto (pink river dolphin): 600, 611
Brasília: 9, 15, 386-408, 620; accommodations
404; addresses 396; entertainment/events
401-402; food 404-407; history 390-391;
information/services 407; maps 388-389,
394-395; orientation 396; planning your
time 389-390; shopping 402; sights 387,
393-401; sports/recreation 402-403;
transportation 407-408
Brava: 113
Brava da Almada: 184
brazilwood: 613-614
breakfast: 657
Brique de Redenção: 235
British Embassy: 648
buffalo: 571-574
buggies, dune: see dune buggying
Bumba-Meu-Boi: 17, 539
Buraco das Araras: 437
bus travel: general discussion 12, 644,
645-646; Belo Horizonte 262; Brasília 407,
408; Curitiba 198; Rio de Janeiro 88, 89;
Salvador 344; São Paulo 162, 163; see also
specific place
butterflies: 561
Búzios (Natal): 508-509
Búzios (Rio de Janeiro): 14, 104-108

C
Caatinga region: 604
Cabo de Santo Agostinho: 468-469

Cabo Frio: 101-102
Cabral, Pedro Alvares: 304, 613
Caburé: 544
Cabutuba: 580
Cáceres: 427
cachaça: 21, 114, 173, 257, 654, 658
Cachoeira: 351-355
Cachoeira da Fumaça: 355, 357-358
Cachoeira da Laje: 180
Cachoeira da Primavera: 356
Cachoeira da Saia Velha: 403
Cachoeira das Andorinhas: 415
Cachoeira da Sentinela: 299
Cachoeira da Toca: 180
Cachoeira da Usina: 173
Cachoeira de Ramalho: 361
Cachoeira do Arari: 572
Cachoeira do Bracui: 173
Cachoeira do Lageado: 169
Cachoeira do Roncador: 361
Cachoeira dos Cristais: 299
Cachoeira do Sossego: 357
Cachoeira Grande: 415
Cachoeiras de Bonsucesso: 410-411
Cachoeiras do Rio do Peixe: 437
Cachoeira Véu da Noiva: 424
Cachoeirinha: 356
Cafua das Mercês: 536
caimans: 417, 611
caipirinha cocktail: 658
caititus (peccaries): 610
Caixa d'Aço: 225
Cajaíba: 113
Calhau: 537
Camburi: 23, 175-176, 184
Camburizinho: 23, 175-176
Caminho de Escravos: 298
Caminho de Ouro: 113
camping: 652
Campo Grande (Mato Grosso do Sul): 15, 428-432; map 429
Campo Grande (Salvador): 318
Campos do Jordão: 166-169
Canadian Embassy: 648
Canasvieiras: 216
Candomblé: 328-329, 631
Canecão: 55
Canela: 241-243
Cânion da Fortaleza: 243
Cânion de Itaimbezinho: 239, 243
Canoa Quebrada: 14, 527-528
canoeing: 367; *see also* boating
Canto da Lagoa: 216

Canto Grande: 226
Capela de Nossa Senhora da Conceição: 347
Capela do Padre Faria: 273
Capela Dourada: 448
Capela Imperial do Amparo: 294
capeta cocktail: 658
capivara: 417, 610
capoeira: 333
capuchin monkeys: 610
capybara: 417, 610
car travel: general discussion 12, 646-647; Brasília 407, 408; Rio de Janeiro 89-90; Salvador 344-345; São Paulo 163; *see also specific place*
Caraíva: 14, 382-383
Caravelas: 383-385
Cardoso, Fernando Henrique: 622-623
Carnatal: 504
Carnaval: 11, 17; Florianópolis 220; Olinda 462-463; Ouro Preto 274; Porto Seguro 375; Recife 453-454; Rio de Janeiro 56-58; Salvador 330-331; San Luís 538-539; São Luís do Paraitinga 171; São Paulo 144
Caruaru: 465-467
Casa da Alfândega: 214
Casa da Câmara e Cadeia: 353
Casa da Chica da Silva: 294
Casa da Cultura (Recife): 449
Casa das Onze Janelas: 556
Casa das Rosas: 132
Casa das Tulhas: 535
Casa da Xilogravura: 167
Casa de Anita: 230
Casa de Benin: 313
Casa de Câmara e Cadeia: 373
Casa de Cora Coralina: 415
Casa de Cultura (Paraty): 112
Casa de Cultura Jorge Amado: 369
Casa de Cultura Mario Quintana: 235
Casa de Cultura Popular Lula Vassoureiro: 469
Casa de Juscelino Kubitschek: 294-295
Casa de Mestre Vitalino: 467
Casa de Nhôzinho: 536
Casa de Penedo: 488
Casa de Petrópolis: 95
Casa de Santos Dumont: 94
Casa do Artesão: 560
Casa do Baile: 254
Casa do Barão de Mauá: 95
Casa do Maranhão: 536
Casa do Marechal Deodoro: 487
Casa dos Contos: 271
Casa-França-Brasil: 32

Casa Romário Martins: 192
Cascata do Caracol: 241-242
cascavéis (rattlesnakes): 611
cashew tree, world's oldest: 508, 509
Castelo Gárcia d'Ávila: 346-347
Cataratas do Iguaçu: *see* Iguaçu Falls
Catedral Basílica: 310
Catedral Basílica de Nossa Senhora de
    Assunção: 278
Catedral Basílica de Nossa Senhora do Pilar:
    283
Catedral Basílica Menor: 192
Catedral da Sé (Belém): 556-557
Catedral da Sé (Olinda): 459
Catedral da Sé (São Paulo): 123
Catedral de Nossa Senhora da Conceição: 587
Catedral de Santo Antônio: 294
Catedral de São Pedro de Alcântara: 94
Catedral de São Pedro dos Clérigos: 448
Catedral de São Sebastião: 369
Catedral Metropolitana: 37
Catedral Metropolitana de Nossa Senhora da
    Aparecida: 397-398
Catedral Metropolitana Nossa Senhora Madre
    de Deus: 234
Catedral Municipal: 214
Catete: accommodations 73-74; food 80; map
    39; sights 38-40
catfish: 612
Catholicism: 630-631
cave paintings: 263, 582
Caverna Aroe Jari: 424
caves: 183, 203, 263, 264, 357, 424, 437
Ceará: 10, 515-533
cegonhas (storks): 612
Central-West region: 606, 655-656
Centro (Belo Horizonte): 249-252
Centro (Rio de Janeiro): 13, 20;
    accommodations 72; food 78-79; map
    32-33; nightlife 59-61; sights 29-36
Centro (Salvador): accommodations 336; food
    340-341; sights 317-318
Centro (São Luís): 536-537
Centro (São Paulo): 19; accommodations
    149-150; food 153-154; map 124; nightlife
    137; sights 123-126
Centro Cívico (Curitiba): 193
Centro Cultural Banco do Brasil (Brasília): 402
Centro Cultural Banco do Brasil (Rio de
    Janeiro): 13, 20, 32, 54
Centro Cultural Banco do Brasil (São Paulo):
    125
Centro Cultural Casa da Ribeira: 504

Centro Cultural Dannemann: 353
Centro Cultural dos Correios: 31-32
Centro Cultural FIESP: 143
Centro Cultural João Fona: 576-577
Centro Cultural São José Liberto: 560
Centro Cultural SESC Luís Severiano Ribeiro:
    520
Centro Cultural Usina Chaminé: 591
Centro da Lagoa: 216
Centro de Arte Hélio Oiticica: 35
Centro de Artesanato de Pernambuco: 468
Centro de Artesanato Mineiro: 257
Centro de Criatividade Odylo Costa Filho: 538
Centro de Cultura Popular: 536
Centro de Interpretación de la Natureza: 207
Centro Dragão do Mar de Arte e Cultura:
    517-518, 520
Centro Referencial da Cultura Terena: 432
Cepilho: 113
ceramics: 467-468; *see also* crafts; pottery
Cerrado: 9, 403, 606
cervo-de-pantanal: 610
Chácara Santa Inêz: 173-174
Chafariz de São José: 287
Chapada Diamantina: 10, 355-362; map 356
Chapada dos Guimarães: 423-425
Chapada do Veadeiros: 412-417
children, traveling with: 661, 663-664
chimarão: 21
chorar (bargaining): 663
choro music: 635
churches/places of worship: *see specific
    church* (basílica, capela, catedral, igreja)
churrasco: 21, 654
Churriado Canyon: 243
Cidade Baixa: 314-316, 339-340
Cidade del Este: 204
Cidade de Pedra: 424
cidades históricas (historical cities): *see*
    Congonhas; Diamantina; Mariana; Ouro
    Preto; Sabará; São João del Rei; Tiradentes
Cidade Velha: 24, 556-558
Cimitério Bizantino: 360
Cinelândia: 13, 20, 35
cinema: general discussion 639-641; Anima
    Mundi 144; Brasília 402; E Tudo Verdade
    144; Festival de Brasília de Cinema Brasileiro
    402; Festival de Cinema 240; Festival
    Internacional de Cinema 402; Festival
    Internacional de Cinema Ambiental 416;
    Mostra de Cinema 288; Mostra Internacional
    de Cinema de São Paulo 144; Rio de Janeiro
    55; São Paulo 143

Circo Voador: 55
Circuito das Cachoeiras: 424
Círio de Nazaré: 17, 563
Cisne Negro: 143
Citibank Hall: 55, 143
climate: general discussion 11, 607, 687;
    Alagoas 444; Amazon 551; Bahia 304;
    Brasília 390; Northeast 497; Pantanal 390,
    419; Pernambuco; Rio de Janeiro 27; South
    region 189
climbing: general discussion 649; Bonito
    438; Iguaçu Falls 207; Itacaré 367; Parque
    Nacional do Itatiaia 100; 167; see also hiking
clothing: 664; see also fashion
coastal region: 606
coati: 610
cobras coral (coral snakes): 611
cocoa cultivation: 368-369
coffee/coffee industry: 120, 172-173, 619,
    657-659
Collor de Melo, Fernando: 622
Comida di Buteco: 256
comida per quilo buffets: 660
communications: 673-676; useful phrases 686
conduct and customs: 46, 662-663
Confeitaria Colombo: 13
Congonhas: 279-281
Congonhas Airport: 161-162
Congresso Nacional: 399
Conjunto Nacional: 130
conservation: 584
consulates/embassies: 648-649
Convento das Mercês: 535-536
Convento de Santo Antônio: 34
Convento de São Francisco (Marechal
    Deodoro): 486-487
Convento de São Francisco (Olinda): 459, 461
Convento de São Francisco (Penedo): 488
Convento dos Humildes: 351
Convento Franciscano: 448
Copacabana: 8, 13, 14, 20, 45-48;
    accommodations 75-76; food 81-82; map 47;
    nightlife 63-64; sights 45-48
Coralina, Cora: 415
coral snakes: 611
Corcovado: 8, 13, 20, 40-41
Coroa Vermelha: 374, 384
Corredor da Vitória: 318-319
Corumbá: 434-436
cosmetic surgery: 668
Cosme Velho: 13, 20, 40-41
Costa do Sol: 101-108
Costa do Sol Nascente: 526

Costa, Lúcio: 392
Costa Verde: 20, 108-117
crafts, shopping for: Alto do Moura 467-468;
    Belém 563-564; Belo Horizonte 257;
    Bezerros 468; Campo Grande 430;
    Corumbá 435; Cuiabá 421; Curitiba 194-195;
    Diamantina 296; Embu 164; Florianópolis
    220; Fortaleza 520-521; Ilha de Marajó 574;
    Maceió 482-483; Manaus 591; Miranda 432;
    Natal 504-505; Olinda 463; Recife 454;
    Rio de Janeiro 69; San Luís 539; Santarém
    577; São Paulo 148; Tiradentes 290; see also
    specific craft
Credicard Hall: 143
credit cards: 672
crime: 669-671
Cristo Redentor: 40-41
cruises: 644
Cruz das Almas: 481
Cruz do Pascoal: 314
Cuiabá: 15, 420-423
Cumbuco: 529
Curitiba: 190-199; map 191
currency: see money
Curuípe: 373
customs, cultural: see conduct and customs
customs regulations: 648
cycling: see bicycling

D

dance: Balé Folclórico da Bahia 328; capoeira
    333; see also music; nightlife
Daniela: 216
da Silva, Luís Inácio: see Lula
Daslu: 147
Daspu: 147
daylight saving time: 676
deer: 610
deforestation: 584, 607-608
demographics: 628
dendê palm: 609
dengue fever: 668
Deodoro da Fonseca, Manuel: 486, 619
Dia da Consciência Negra: 491
Diamantina: 9, 293-299
diamond mining: 293, 299; Museu do Diamante
    294
diarrhea: 667-668
Di Cavalcanti, Alfredo: 398
dinner: 657
Diogo: 16, 350
Dique de Tororó: 332
disabled travelers, tips for: 663

diving: general discussion 650; Angra dos Reis 109; Arraial do Cabo 103; Barra da Una 175; Búzios 105; Fernando de Noronha 474; Galés 493; Ilhabela 180; Ilha de Santa Catarina 218-219; Ilha Grande 109; Morro de São Paulo 363; Paraty 113; Reserva Biológica Marinha da Ilha do Arvoredo 226; Rio Formoso 438; Salvador 332; Ubatuba 184; *see also flutuação; specific place*
Do Costa: 367
dolphins: 475, 600, 611
Domingas Dias: 22-23, 183
dorado: 612
drinks: 236, 594, 657-660
driving: *see car travel*
dune buggying: 504, 508, 512-513, 520, 527-528, 531, 649

E

Eco-Museu Univali: 226
economy: 626-628
Ecoparque do Una: 371
ecosystems: 604-607
ecotourism: 599-601 *see also tours*
Edifício Copan: 126
Edifício Itália: 126
Edifício Martinelli: 125
Edifício Niemeyer: 252
Edifício Sé: 123
Eixo Monumental: 392-397
Eixo Rodoviário: 393
electrical current: 676
electric eels: 612
Elevador Lacerda: 308
ema (rhea): 417, 612
embassies/consulates: 648-649
Embu: 164-166
emergencies: Belém 568; Belo Horizonte 262; Brasília 407; Curitiba 198; Florianópolis 224-225; Fortaleza 525; Manaus 596; Maranhão 541; Natal 507; Porto Alegre 238; Recife 458; Rio de Janeiro 87-88; Salvador 344; San Luís 541; São Paulo 161
Encantadas: 203
Encontro de Águas: 588-589
energy: 626-627
entertainment: Belo Horizonte 254-256; Brasília 401-402; Ouro Preto 273-274; Recife 453-454; Rio de Janeiro 54-58; Salvador 324-331; São Paulo 142-144; *see also festivals/events; nightlife*
entry forms: 12, 647
environmental issues: 584, 607-608

Ermida Dom Bosco: 403
erva maté beverage: 236
Escorregadeira: 356-357
Espaço Cultural da Marinha: 34
Espaço Cultural Goiandira do Couto: 416
Espaço Cultural Santa Maria Madalena da Lagoa do Sul: 487
Espaço Lúcio Costa: 399
Espíritu Santo: 10
Esplanada dos Ministérios: 397-400
Estação Carioca: 38
Estação Cosme Velho: 41
Estação da Luz: 19, 127
Estação das Docas: 558
Estaçao de Estrada de Ferro: 172
Estação Natureza Pantanal: 435
Estação Pinacoteca: 127-128
Estaleiro: 225
Estância Mimosa: 437
Estrada do Coco: 345-348
Estrada Graciosa: 200
Estrada Parque do Pantanal: 434
Estrada Real: 295
ethnicity: 628-630
E Tudo Verdade: 144
events: *see festivals/events*

F

Farol da Barra: 319-320
Farol da Mãe Luiza: 502
Farol das Conchas: 203
Farol Preguiças: 544
Farol Santa Marta: 230
fashion: Belo Horizonte 257; Rio de Janeiro 66-67; Salvador 331; São Paulo 145-146
fauna: general discussion 609-613; Jardim Zoológico 149; Pantanal 417; Parque Zoológico do CIGS 589; *see also specific place*
favelas (slums): 50-51
Fazenda do Coqueiros: 20
Fazenda do Resgate: 173
Fazenda dos Coqueiros: 172
fazenda lodges: 15, 419, 426, 432, 433-434, 653-654; *see also jungle lodges*
Fazenda Primavera: 370
Fazenda Yrerê: 369-370
feijoada: 21, 654
Feira Central: 430
Feira da Liberdade: 128
Feira de Aniguïdades: 69
Feira de Arte e Artesanato: 257
Feira de Artesanato: 195

Feira de Caruaru: 466
Feira de São Cristovão: 44-45
Feira de São Joaquim: 315
Feira do Largo de Coimbra: 274
Feira do Produtor: 586
Feira Hippie: 69
Feiticeira: 179
Fernando de Noronha: 14, 444, 472-477
Festa da Boa Morte: 351
Festa da Santa Bárbara: 329
Festa de Iemenjá: 330
Festa de Nossa Senhora da Ajuda: 353-354
Festa de Nossa Senhora da Boa Morte: 353, 354
Festa de São Benedito: 375
Festa de São João (Caruaru): 466
Festa de São João (Lençóis): 358
Festa de São João (Mucugê): 360
Festa de São Sebastião: 380
Festa do Bom Jesus dos Navegantes: 488-489
Festa do Bonfim: 17
Festa do Cairé: 580
Festa do Divino (Maranhão): 543
Festa do Divino (Rio de Janeiro): 114
Festa do Divino Espírito Santo (Pirenópolis): 410
Festa do Dívino Espírito Santo (São Luís): 171
Festa do Glorioso Divino Espírito Santo: 364
Festa Dois de Julho: 328
Festa Literária Internacional: 114
Festas dos Reis: 351
Festa Senhor dos Navegantes: 329
Festas Juninas: 17, 358, 467
Festival Amazonas de Ópera: 591
Festival da Jabuticaba: 266
Festival da Pinga: 114
Festival de Arte Negra: 256
Festival de Brasília de Cinema Brasileiro: 402
Festival de Cinema: 240
Festival de Inverno (Campos do Jordão): 167
Festival de Inverno (Chapada dos Guimarães): 424
Festival de Inverno (Ouro Preto): 274
Festival de Inverno de Lençóis: 358
Festival de São Roque: 91
Festival Folclórico de Parintins: 598
Festival Internacional de Cinema: 402
Festival Internacional de Cinema Ambiental: 416
Festival Internacional de Cultura Alternativa: 345
Festival Internacional de Cultura e Gastronomia: 288

Festival Internacional de Dança: 256
Festival Internacional de Pesca: 427
Festival Internacional de Teatro: 256
Festival Ora-Pró-Nobis: 266
festivals/events: 17; Belém 563; Belo Horizonte 256; Caruaru 466; Florianópolis 220; Goiás Velho 416; Gramado 240; Manaus 591; Olinda 462-463; Ouro Preto 274; Paraty 114; Pirenópolis 410; Porto Alegre 235; Recife 453-454; Rio de Janeiro 55-58; Salvador 328-331; São Paulo 144 *see also specific festival*
film/cinema: *see* cinema
finance: 626
fish/fishing: general discussion 422, 565, 611-612, 650; Alter do Chão 580; Festival Internacional de Pesca 427; Pantanal 419; Parque Nacional Marinho dos Abrolhos 384; piranhas 589
Flamengo (Bahia): 322
Flamengo (Rio de Janeiro): accommodations 74; food 80-81; map 39; nightlife 62-63; sights 42-43
Flexeiras: 529
flora: 609; *see also* gardens
Floresta da Tijuca: 70
Floresta do Nacional Tapajós: 24
Floresta Nacional do Tapajós: 581
Florianópolis: 213-225, 655; map 215
Floripa: *see* Florianópolis
flowers: 609
flutuação (floatation): 438
flying: *see* air travel
Fonte das Pedras: 537
Fonte de Ceu: 363
Fonte do Ribeirão: 537
food: general discussion 21, 654-661; Academia de Cozinha e Outros Prazeres 116; Amazonian cuisine 565; Bahian cuisine 338; Belo Horizonte 259-262; Brasília 404-407; Comida di Buteco 256; Festival Internacional de Cultura e Gastronomia 288; Mineiro cuisine 260; Ouro Preto 276-277; Pantanal cuisine 422; Paranaense cuisine 196; Rio de Janeiro 78-86; safety 667; Salvador 337-343; São Paulo 152-160; useful phrases 683-685; *see also specific place*
Fordlândia: 581-582
forró music: 451, 635
Fortal: 520
Fortaleza: 10, 515-526; map 516-517
Fortaleza de Nossa Senhora de Assunção: 517
Fortaleza de Santa Cruz: 91

Fortaleza de Santo Antônio de Ratones: 219
Fortaleza Nossa Senhora dos Prazeres: 203
Forte das Cinco Pontas: 449
Forte de Copacabana: 48
Forte Defensor Perpétuo: 112
Forte de Monte Serrat: 317
Forte de Santa Cruz do Anhatorim: 219
Forte de Santo Antônio Além do Carmo: 314
Forte do Presépio: 556
Forte dos Reis Magos: 500, 502
Forte dos Remédios: 473
Forte São Marcelo: 315-316
Forte São Mateus: 102
Foz do Iguaçu: 204-210; map 205
frescoball: 651
fruit: 565, 609, 659
Fundação Casa de Jorge Amado: 312
Fundação Cultural Ema Gordon Klabin: 132-133
Fundação Maria Luiza e Oscar Americano: 136

G

Gabinete Português de Leitura: 318
Gaibu: 469-470
Galeria Arte & Memória: 361-362
Galeria Fundação Pierre Verger: 309
Galés: 493
galleries: see specific gallery
Gamboa: 363
garças (herons): 612
Garça Torta: 481
gardens: Bosque Rodrigues Alves 561-562;
    Jardim Botânico (Brasília) 403; Jardim
    Botânico (Curitiba) 193, 194; Jardim
    Botânico (Rio de Janeiro) 52; Jardim dos
    Pinhais 169; São Paulo 148-149
Garibaldi, Anita: 230
Garimpo Real: 299
Garopaba: 227-228
Gaúchos: 231
Gávea: 52-53, 65-66
gay/lesbian travelers, tips for: 60, 138, 343,
    665-666
Genipabu: 510
geography: 604-607
Gil, Gilberto: 636-637
Gilberto, João: 636
Giorgi, Bruno: 400
Gipóia Island: see Ilha Gipóia
Giramundo: 256
"Girl from Ipanema, The": 48, 636
Glória: accommodations 73-74; food 80; map
    39; sights 38-40
glossary: 677-679

Goiás: 9, 409-417, 656
Goiás Velho: 414-417
gold rush: 248, 265, 267-268, 272, 278,
    390-391, 409
golf: 380
golfinhos rotadores (spinning dolphins): 611
Goulart, João: 620-621
government: 624-625
Gramado: 239-241
Grande da Deserta: 113
Grande Island: see Ilha Grande
greetings: 662
Grumari: 53
Grupo Corpo: 256
Grupo Galão: 256
Gruta Azul: 357
Gruta da Lapinha: 263
Gruta da Pratinha: 357
Gruta das Encantadas: 203
Gruta da Torrinha: 357
Gruta do Centenário: 264
Gruta do Lago Azul: 437
Gruta do Lapão: 357
Gruta do Maquiné: 263
Gruta que Chora: 183
Gruta Rei do Mato: 263
Guaiú: 377
Guanabara Bay: 13
guará (scarlet ibis): 612
guaraná berry: 594
guaribas (howler monkeys): 610
Guarujá: 175
Guarulhos International Airport: 161
guaxarim: 610
Guaxuma: 481
Guerra dos Farrapos: 231

H

handicrafts: see crafts
hang gliding: 71, 169, 649
harpy eagle: 612
health/safety: 666-671; useful phrases
    685-686
herons: 612
high season: 11
Higienópolis: accommodations 152; food 154-
    155; sights 129-130
hiking: general discussion 649; Alter do Chão
    580; Bonita 437; Canela 242; Cerrado
    403; Chapada Diamantina 356-358, 361;
    Ecoparque do Una 371; Fernando de Noronha
    477; Horto Florestal 167; Iguaçu Falls 207; Ilha
    Grande 109-110; Nova Friburgo 99; Paraty

113; Parque Estadual da Serra do Mar 170, 184; Parque Estadual de Ilhabela 180; Parque Estadual do Caracol 241–242; Parque Estadual do Marumbi 200; Parque Nacional da Chapada dos Guimarães 423–424; Parque Nacional da Chapada dos Veadeiros 412–413; Parque Nacional da Serra da Bocaina 173; Parque Nacional da Serra dos Órgãos 97; Parque Nacional da Tijuca 70; Parque Nacional de Aparados da Serra 243; Parque Nacional de Brasília 403; Pedra do Baú 167; Porto Belo 226; Rio de Janeiro 71; Santuário de Vida Silvestre Vagafogo 411; Santuário Ecológico de Pipa 512; Serra Gaúcha 240; Tiradentes 290; Vale da Lua 414; see also specific place
history: 613–624; suggested reading 688–689; see also specific place
horse racing: 52
Horto Florestal: 167
hospitals: see medical care
hostels: 652–653; see also accommodations
hotels: 653; see also accommodations
howler monkeys: 610
hummingbirds: 612–613
humpback whales: 611
hyacinth macaw: 417, 612
hydroelectricity: 626–627
hygiene: 667

I

Iate Tênis Clube: 254
IBAMA (Instituto Brasiliero do Meio Ambiente): 604
Icoaraçi: 569–570
Igatu: 361–362
Igreja da Ordem de Nossa Senhora do Carmo: 266
Igreja da Ordem Terceira de São Domingos de Gusmão: 310
Igreja da Ordem Terceira de São Francisco (Curitiba): 192
Igreja da Ordem Terceira de São Francisco (Recife): 448
Igreja da Ordem Terceira de São Francisco (Salvador): 311
Igreja da Ordem Terceira de São Francisco da Penitência: 13, 34
Igreja da Ordem Terceira do Carmo e Convento do Carmo: 313
Igreja da Ordem Terceira e Convento do Carmo: 353
Igreja das Chagas do Seráphico Pai São Francisco: 125–126
Igreja da Sé: 535
Igreja de Matriz: 172
Igreja de Nossa Senhora da Ajuda: 353
Igreja de Nossa Senhora da Conceição da Praia: 316
Igreja de Nossa Senhora da Corrente: 488
Igreja de Nossa Senhora da Misericórdia (Olinda): 461
Igreja de Nossa Senhora da Misericórdia (Porto Seguro): 373
Igreja de Nossa Senhora da Penha: 373
Igreja de Nossa Senhora das Mercês: 288
Igreja de Nossa Senhora de Carmo: 278
Igreja de Nossa Senhora de Monte Serrat: 317
Igreja de Nossa Senhora de Santana Sacramento: 424
Igreja de Nossa Senhora do Amparo: 461
Igreja de Nossa Senhora do Carmo (Olinda): 461
Igreja de Nossa Senhora do Carmo (Ouro Preto): 270
Igreja de Nossa Senhora do Carmo (São João del Rei): 283
Igreja de Nossa Senhora do Monte: 461
Igreja de Nossa Senhora do Rosário (Florianópolis): 214
Igreja de Nossa Senhora do Rosário (São João del Rei): 283–284
Igreja de Nossa Senhora do Rosário dos Pretos (Ouro Preto): 271
Igreja de Nossa Senhora do Rosário dos Pretos (Sabará): 265
Igreja de Nossa Senhora do Rosário dos Pretos (Tiradentes): 288
Igreja de Nossa Senhora dos Anjos: 488
Igreja de Nosso Senhor do Bonfim (Pirenópolis): 410
Igreja de Nosso Senhor do Bonfim (Salvador): 316–317
Igreja de Santa Isable: 360
Igreja de Santa Maria Magdalena: 486
Igreja de Santa Rita dos Pardos Libertos: 112
Igreja de Santíssima Trindade: 288
Igreja de Santo Alexandre: 557
Igreja de Santo Antônio: 502
Igreja de Santo Antônio Além do Carmo: 314
Igreja de São Benedito: 202
Igreja de São Francisco de Assis (Belo Horizonte): 253–254
Igreja de São Francisco de Assis (Mariana): 278
Igreja de São Francisco de Assis (Ouro Preto): 15, 271–272

Igreja de São Francisco de Assis (São João del Rei): 13, 281-283
Igreja de São Francisco de Assis (São Paulo): 126
Igreja de São Francisco de Paula (Tiradentes): 288
Igreja de São Francisco de Paula (Goiás Velho): 415
Igreja de São Gonçalo Garcia dos Homens Pardos: 488
Igreja de São João Batista: 380
Igreja de São Jorge: 369
Igreja do Carmo (Alcântara): 542
Igreja do Carmo (São Luís): 536
Igreja do Desterro: 535
Igreja do Mosteiro de São Bento: 20, 34
Igreja do Nossa Senhora da Santa Efigênia do Pretos: 272-273
Igreja e Convento de São Francisco: 16, 311
Igreja e Mosteiro de São Bento: 459-461
Igreja Largo São Sebastião: 587
Igreja Madre de Deus: 448
Igreja Matriz de Nossa Senhora da Apresentação: 500-502
Igreja Matriz de Nossa Senhora da Conceição: 577
Igreja Matriz de Nossa Senhora da Conceição de Antônio Dias: 272
Igreja Matriz de Nossa Senhora da Purificação: 351
Igreja Matriz de Nossa Senhora de Ajuda: 377
Igreja Matriz de Nossa Senhora de Conceição: 266
Igreja Matriz de Nossa Senhora de Remédios: 112
Igreja Matriz de Nossa Senhora do Pilar: 271
Igreja Matriz de Nossa Senhora do Rosário: 410
Igreja Matriz de Santo Antônio (Recife): 449
Igreja Matriz de Santo Antônio (Tiradentes): 15, 287
Igreja Matriz de São Mathias: 542
Igreja Matriz do Nossa Senhora do Pilar: 15
Igreja Nossa Senhora da Candelária: 32-34
Igreja Nossa Senhora da Conceição dos Militares: 449
Igreja Nossa Senhora da Glória do Outeiro: 38-40
Igreja Nossa Senhora da Piedade: 318
Igreja Nossa Senhora das Dores: 112
Igreja Nossa Senhora de Carmo da Antiga Sé: 31
Igreja Nossa Senhora do Boqueirão: 314
Igreja Nossa Senhora do Carmo: 294

Igreja Nossa Senhora do Ó: 265-266
Igreja Nossa Senhora do Rosário (Diamantina): 294
Igreja Nossa Senhora do Rosário (Embu): 164
Igreja Nossa Senhora do Rosário (Lençóis): 356
Igreja Nossa Senhora do Rosário (Paranaguá): 202
Igreja Nossa Senhora do Rosário (Paraty): 112
Igreja Nossa Senhora do Rosário dos Pretos: 312-313
Igreja Nossa Senhora dos Remédios: 473
Igreja Santo Antônio dos Anjos: 230
Igreja São Benedito: 373
Igreja São Francisco de Assis: 294
Igreja São Pedro dos Clérigo: 310
Iguaçu Falls: 9, 204-210
Ilha Anchieta: 184
Ilhabela: 14, 178-182; map 179
Ilha de Algodoal: 570-571
Ilha de Anhatorim: 219
Ilha de Boipeba: 14, 16, 364-365
Ilha de Itaparica: 323-324
Ilha de Marajó: 10, 11, 14, 24, 571-575
Ilha de Maré: 324
Ilha de Paquetá: 91
Ilha de Porto Belo: 225-226
Ilha de Ratones Grande: 219
Ilha de Santa Catarina: 8, 211-225, map 212
Ilha de Santo Aleixo: 470
Ilha do Campeche: 217
Ilha do Mel: 202-204
Ilha do Mosqueiro: 570
Ilha do Papagaio: 24
Ilha do Prumirim: 184
Ilha Fiscal: 34
Ilha Gipóia: 111
Ilha Grande: 14, 109-111
Ilhéus: 368-371
Imbassaí: 16, 348-350
Inconfidência Mineira: 268, 270
independence: 617
indigenous people: general discussion 613, 628-629; Amazon region 551-552; Memorial da Cultura Indígena 428-430; Memorial dos Povos Indígenas 397; Museu do Índio (Manaus) 587-588; Museu do Índio (Rio de Janeiro) 43; Pataxó 374; Tamoio 27
industry: 626
information and services: 671-676; *see also specific place*
Instituto Baleia Jubarte (Caravelas): 384
Instituto Baleia Jubarte (Praia do Forte): 346

Instituto Brasiliero do Meio Ambiente (IBAMA): 604
Instituto Butantan: 136
Instituto Histórico e Geográfico: 479
Instituto Itaú Cultural: 143
Instituto Moreira Salles: 52-53
Instituto Ricardo Brennand: 450
Instituto Tomie Ohtake: 133
insurance, medical: 666-667
Internet access: general discussion 674; Belém 568; Belo Horizonte 262; Fernando de Noronha 476; Fortaleza 525; Manaus 596; Olinda 465; Ouro Preto 277; Rio de Janeiro 87; Salvador 343-344; San Luís 541; São Paulo 161; see also specific place
Internet resources: 690-691
Ipanema: 8, 13, 14, 20; accommodations 76-78; food 82-86; map 49; nightlife 64-65; sights 48-51
Irmandade da Boa Morte: 353, 354
Isabel, Princesa: 94
Itacaré: 366-368
Itacarezinho: 367
Itacimirim: 373
Itacoatiara: 91-93
Itaim Bibi: 133
Itaipu Dam: 208
Itamambuca: 183
Itapuã: 321-322
Itatiaia: 100
itineraries, suggested: 13-24

J

Jabaquara: 180
Jacarecica: 481
jacarés (alligators/caimans): 611
Jacumã: 510-511
Jaguaribe: 321
jaguars: 610
jangada rafts: 511
Jaraguá: 479
Jardim Botânico (Brasília): 403
Jardim Botânico (Curitiba): 193, 194
Jardim Botânico (Rio de Janeiro): 20, 52, 65, 86
Jardim Botânico (São Paulo): 148-149
Jardim dos Pinhais: 169
Jardim Zoológico: 149
Jardins: 19; accommodations 151-152; food 157-159; map 131; nightlife 140-142; sights 132-133
Jatiúca: 481
Jericoacoara: 10, 14, 529-533

Jesuit missionaries: 615-617
jewelry: 67-68, 296, 560
jiboias (constrictors): 611
JK: see Kubitschek, Juscelino
Joanes: 572
João Fernandes: 104
João Fernandinho: 104-105
João VI: 617
Joquei Clube: 52
Judaism: 447
juices: 659
jungle lodges: 23-24, 592-593, 597, 601-602, 653-654
Juqueí: 175
Juréia: 175

KL

Kardecism: 631
kayaking: 175, 176; see also boating
kitesurfing: Búzios 105-106; Fortaleza 520; Ilha de Santa Catarina 218; Jericoacoara 531; see also specific beach
kombis (van taxis): 647
Kubitschek, Juscelino: 253, 294-295, 386, 390, 392, 393, 620
Labirinto das Falesias: 526
lace-making: 487; see also crafts
Lacerda, Carlos: 620
Lagoa Azul (Chapada dos Guimarães): 424
Lagoa Azul (Jericoacoara): 530
Lagoa Azul (Lençóis Maranhenses): 544
Lagoa Bonita: 544
Lagoa da Conceição: 216, 221, 223
Lagoa da Gaivota: 544
Lagoa da Mata: 527
Lagoa de Cassange: 366
Lagoa de Jijoca: 530
Lagoa de Mundáu: 481
Lagoa do Paraíso: 530
Lagoa Guaraira: 509
Lagoa Rodrigo de Freitas: 51-52, 65, 86
Lagoa Timeantube: 347
Lagoinha (Ceará): 529
Lagoinha (Porto Belo): 226
Lagoinha do Leste (Santa Catarina): 14, 217
Lagoinha do Norte (Florianópolis): 216
Lago Juma: 599
Lago Mamori: 599
Lago Negro: 240
Lago Paranoá: 403
Lago Verde: 580
Laguna: 229-230
Lampião: 479, 380

land: 604-608
language: 632-633, 677-687
Lapa: 13, 18, 20; accommodations 72-73; map 32-33; nightlife 61-62; sights 36-37
Lapa Doce: 357
Largo da Carioca: 34
Largo da Ordem: 192
Largo das Forras: 287
Largo das Guimarães: 38
Largo de Boticário: 41
Largo de Santo Antônio: 314
Largo de São Francisco: 125-126
Largo do Pelourinho: 312-313
laundry services: 88; see also specific place
Lavagem do Bonfim: 329-330
Leblon: accommodations 76-78; food 82-86; map 49; nightlife 64-65; sights 48-51
leite de onça cocktail: 658
Leme: accommodations 75-76; food 81-82; nightlife 63-64
Lemos, Gaspar de: 27
Lençóis: 355-360
Lençóis Maranhenses: 14, 543-546
Lerner, Jaime: 190, 192
Liberdade: food 154; sights 128-129
Linha Verde: 348-351
Lins, Paulo: 641
lion tamarins: 610
Lisboa, Antônio Francisco: see Aleijadinho
Lispector, Clarice: 641-642
literature: 641-642; see also books/bookstores
Litoral Norte: 8, 175-185
lontras (otters): 610
lotaçóes (van taxis): 647
Lula: 621-622, 623-624
lunch: 657
Luz: 126-128

M
macacos (monkeys): 610
macaws: 417, 612
Maceió: 10, 444, 477-485; map 478
Maceió Fest: 482
magazines: 674-675
mail: see postal services
Majorlândia: 527
Malacara Canyon: 243
malls: 66; see also specific place
MAM: see Museu de Arte Moderna
mammals: 610-611
manatees: 611
Manaus: 10, 17, 23, 550, 583-596; map 585
Mandacaru: 544

Mangal das Garças: 24
mangroves: 606
Mangue Seco: 350-351
maps: 672-673; see also specific place
Maradajaú: 511
Maragogi: 493-494
Marajoara pottery: 569-570, 574
Marajó Island: see Ilha de Marajó
Marajó people: 613
Maranhão: 10, 533-546
Marco da Posse: 373
Marco Zero: 447
Marechal Deodoro: 486-487
Maresias: 14, 176
Mar Grande: 323
Maria Fumaça train: 275, 279, 286
Mariana: 9, 275, 277-279
Marimbus: 361
Mariscal: 226
Mariú: 510-511
markets: Belém 558; Belo Horizonte 257; Campo Grande 430; Caruaru 466; Curitiba 195; Diamantina 295; Florianópolis 214; Fortaleza 517; Manaus 586; Porto Alegre 233; Recife 448-449; Rio de Janeiro 44-45, 69; Salvador 314-315; São Paulo 126, 128
Marx, Roberte Burle: 54
Massarandupió: 350
Mata Atlântica: 605-606
Mato Grosso: 9, 15, 419-427
Mato Grosso do Sul: 9, 15, 427-436
meals: 656-657
measurements: 676
media: 674-676
medical care: general discussion 667; Belém 568; Belo Horizonte 262; Brasília 407; Fortaleza 525; Manaus 596; Recife 458; Rio de Janeiro 87-88; Salvador 344; San Luís 541; São Paulo 161; useful phrases 685-686; see also specific place
medications: 666
Meeting of the Waters: 17, 23, 588-589
Meirelles, Fernando: 640-641
Memorial da América Látina: 136-137
Memorial da Cultura Cearense: 518
Memorial da Cultura Indígena: 428-430
Memorial do Imigrante: 129
Memorial do Rio Grande do Sul: 233
Memorial dos Povos Indígenas: 397
Memorial JK: 393
Mercado Central (Belo Horizonte): 257
Mercado Central (Fortaleza): 517
Mercado de Peixe: 518-519

Mercado Modelo: 314
Mercado Municipal (Diamantina): 295
Mercado Municipal (São Paulo): 126
Mercado Municipal Adolfo Lisboa: 586
Mercado Público (Florianópolis): 214
Mercado Público (Porto Alegre): 233
Mercado São José: 448
Mercado Ver-o-Paso: 24, 558
metric system: 676
Metrô (Rio de Janeiro): 89
Metrô (São Paulo): 162-163
micos (monkeys): 610
Mina Brejo-Verruga: 362
Mina de Ouro da Passagem: 278
Mina do Chico Rei: 272
Minas Gerais: 9, 13, 21, 245-299, 655; Belo
    Horizonte 249-264; Congonhas 279-281;
    Diamantina 293-299; food 21, 655;
    highlights 246; history 248; map 247;
    Mariana 277-279; Ouro Preto 267-276;
    planning your time 246-248; Sabará 265-
    267; São João del Rei 281-286; Tiradentes
    287-293
Minerão: 258
Miranda: 432-434
Miranda, Carmen: 42-43, 635
Mirante da Geodésia: 424
Mirante dos Golfinhos: 475
Mirante do Tapajós: 577
missionaries: 189, 615-617
Mojiquiçaba: 377
money: 671-672; *see also* banks
money belts: 664
monkeys: 610
Monte Alegre: 582
Monte Olimpo: 200
Monumento ao Dois de Julho: 318
Monumento ás Bandeirantes: 134
moqueca: 21
Morais, Vinícius de: 636
Morretes: 200-201
Morro da Careca: 503
Morro da Cruz: 99
Morro de Elefante: 166
Morro de São Jerónimo: 424
Morro de São Paulo: 14, 16, 362-364
Morro de Urca: 44
Morro do Farol de Taipu: 365-366
Morro do Pai Inácio: 357
Mosqueiro Island: *see* Ilha do Mosqueiro
mosquitos: 669
Mosteiro de São Bento (São Paulo): 125
Mosteiro de São Bento (Salvador): 318

Mostra de Cinema: 288
Mostra Internacional de Cinema de São Paulo:
    144
motels: 653; *see also* accommodations
MPB: *see* Música Popular Brasileira
Mucugê: 355, 360-361
Mundaí: 373
Mundaú: 529
Museu Abelardo Rodrigues: 312
Museu Afro Brasil: 135
Museu Afro-Brasileiro: 16, 310-311
Museu Alfredo Andersen: 192
Museu Amazônico de Navegação: 561
Museu Arquidiocesano: 278
Museu Artístico e Histórico do Maranhão: 536
Museu Café Filho: 502
Museu Câmara Cascudo: 502
Museu Carlos Costa Pinto: 319
Museu Carmen Miranda: 42-43
Museu Casa do Pontal: 54
Museu Casa Guignard: 271
Museu Chácara do Céu: 13, 20, 38
Museu da Casa Brasileira: 133
Museu da Cidade (Recife): 449
Museu da Cidade (Salvador): 312
Museu da Imagem e do Som (MIS): 132
Museu da Imigração Japonesa: 129
Museu da Imperial Irmandade de Nossa
    Senhora da Glória: 40
Museu da Incondfidência: 270
Museu da Língua Portuguesa: 19, 127
Museu da República: 40
Museu das Bandeiras: 415
Museu das Cavalhadas: 410
Museu das Gemas do Estado: 560
Museu de Aleijadinho: 272
Museu de Arqueologia e Etnologia
    (Paranaguá): 202
Museu de Arqueologia e Etnologia (Salvador):
    310
Museu de Arte Contemporánea (Niterói): 91, 93
Museu de Arte Contemporánea (São Paulo):
    134
Museu de Arte Contemporânea do Ceará: 518
Museu de Arte da Bahia: 318
Museu de Arte de Pampulha: 254
Museu de Arte de São Paulo: 19, 131-132
Museu de Arte do Belém: 557
Museu de Arte do Rio Grande do Sul: 233-234
Museu de Arte e Cultura Popular: 517
Museu de Arte Moderna (Recife): 449
Museu de Arte Moderna (Rio de Janeiro): 20, 42
Museu de Arte Moderna (Salvador): 16, 316

Museu de Arte Moderna (São Paulo): 19, 134-135
Museu de Arte Sacra (Belém): 557
Museu de Arte Sacra (Curitiba): 192
Museu de Arte Sacra (Marechal Deodoro): 486-487
Museu de Arte Sacra (Porto Seguro): 373
Museu de Arte Sacra (São Luís): 537
Museu de Arte Sacra (São Paulo): 128
Museu de Arte Sacra da Bahia: 318
Museu de Arte Sacra da Boa Morte: 415
Museu de Arte Sacra de Pernambuco: 461-462
Museu de Arte Sacra do Recôncavo: 353
Museu de Arte Sacra Pierre Chalita: 479
Museu de Artes e Ofícios: 249-252
Museu de Artes Visuais: 536
Museu de Ciência e Técnica da Escola de Minas: 270-271
Museu de Ciências Naturais da Amazônia: 588
Museu de Estanho: 284
Museu de Folclore Edison Carneiro: 40
Museu de História Natural e Antropologia: 421
Museu de Pedras Ramis Bucair: 421
Museu de Porto Seguro: 373
Museu de Valores: 397
Museu do Açude: 70
Museu do Barro: 466
Museu do Ceará: 517
Museu do Círio: 557
Museu do Diamante: 294
Museu do Estado de Pernambuco: 450
Museu do Estado do Pará: 558
Museu do Homem do Norte: 587
Museu do Homen do Nordeste: 450
Museu do Índio (Manaus): 587-588
Museu do Índio (Rio de Janeiro): 43
Museu do Ipiranga: 136
Museu do Mamulengo: 462
Museu do Marajó: 572
Museu Dom Bosco: 428
Museu do Oratório: 15, 270
Museu do Ouro: 265
Museu do Paço Imperial: 488
Museu do Pantanal: 435
Museu do Rio Cuiabá: 421
Museu do Seringal Vila Paraíso: 588
Museu dos Ex-Votos do Senhor do Bonfim: 317
Museu Hansen Bahia: 353
Museu Histórico (Alcântara): 542
Museu Histórico Abílio Barreto: 252-253
Museu Histórico de Exército: 48
Museu Histórico de Santa Catarina: 215
Museu Histórico Nacional: 36

Museu Imperial: 94
Museu Internacional de Arte Naïf do Brasil: 13, 20, 41
Museu Júlio de Castilhos: 234
Museu Lasar Segall: 135-136
Museu Nacional (Brasília): 390, 397
Museu Nacional (Rio de Janeiro): 44
Museu Nacional de Belas Artes: 13, 20, 36
Museu Naútico da Bahia: 320
Museu Oscar Niemeyer: 193
Museu Padre Anchieta: 123
Museu Padre Toledo: 287
Museu Paraense Emílio Goeldi: 24, 560
Museu Paranaense: 192
Museu Regional (Cachoeira): 353
Museu Regional (São João del Rei): 284
Museu Regional de Olinda: 462
Museu Tempostal: 312
Museu Théo Brandão: 479
Museu Udo Knoff de Azulejaria e Cermâmica: 311
museums: see specific museum
music: 451, 633-637, 538; shopping for 68, 147; suggested reading 689-690; see also entertainment/events; nightlife
Música Popular Brasileira (MPB): 636-637
música sertaneja: 635
Mutá: 373

N

Nassau, Mauritz van: 615
Natal: 10, 500-508; map 501
national parks: Aparados da Serra 243-244; Brasília 403; Chapada Diamantina 355; Chapada dos Guimarães 423-424; Chapada dos Veadeiros 412-413; Iguaçu 206-207; Itatiaia 100-101; Marinho dos Abrolhos 384; Monte Pascoal 382; Serra da Bocaina 173; Serra do Cipó 263-264; Serra dos Órgãos 97-98; Serra Geral 243; Superagüi 203; Tijuca 70
Nazaré: 559-560
Neópolis: 489
Neves, Tancredo: 622
newspapers: 674-675
Niemeyer, Oscar: 91, 134, 135, 136, 142-143, 193, 252, 253, 254, 386, 390, 392, 393, 397, 398, 399, 400, 638-639
nightlife: Belém 562-563; Belo Horizonte 254-256; Brasília 401-402; Búzios 106; Florianópolis 219-220; Maceió 481-482; Manaus 590-591; Natal 503-504; Ouro Preto 273-274; Paraty 113-114; Porto Seguro

374-375; Praia da Pipa 512; Recife 450-453; Rio de Janeiro 59-66; Salvador 324-327; São Luís 537-538; São Paulo 137-142; *see also specific place*

Niterói: 91-93

North Coast: *see* Litoral Norte

Northeast region: 10, 495-546; Ceará 515-533; food 656; highlights 496; history 497; Maranhão 533-546; map 498-499; planning your time 497; Rio Grande do Norte 500-515

Nova Brasília: 203

Nova Friburgo: 99-100

Nova Jerusalém: 469

novelas (soap operas): 675

numbers: 686-687

O

Oficina de Cerâmica Francisco Brennand: 450

Ohtake, Ruy: 133

oil reserves: 627

Oiticica, Hélio: 35

Olho d'Agua: 537

Olinda: 10, 441, 444-445, 459-465; map 460

Olivença: 370

onça pintada (spotted jaguar): 610

onça preta (black jaguar): 610

Ópera de Arame: 194

orchids: 609

Orquestra Sinfônica do Estado de São Paulo: 142

Orquestra Sinfônica Municipal: 142

O Sul: *see* South region

otters: 610

Ouro Preto: 9, 15, 267-277; map 269

P

packing: 664, 666

Paço Imperial: 13, 20, 31

Padilha, José: 641

Palácio Anghangabaú: 125

Palácio Antônio Lemos: 557

Palácio Boa Vista: 166

Palácio Conde d'Arcos: 415

Palácio da Alvorada: 400

Palácio da Justiça: 399

Palácio das Artes: 252

Palácio de Cristal: 94

Palácio de Justiça (Manaus): 587

Palácio do Catete: 20, 40

Palácio do Governo: 252

Palácio do Planalto: 400

Palácio do Rio Branco: 308

Palácio dos Leões: 535

Palácio Itamaraty: 398-399

Palácio La Ravardière: 535

Palácio Lauro Sodré: 557-558

Palácio Piratini: 234

Palácio Potengi: 502

Palácio Princesa Isabel: 95

Palácio Quitandinha: 94-95

Palácio Rio Negro (Manaus): 587

Palácio Rio Negro (Petrópolis): 95

Palácio São Miguel: 473

Palmares: 491

palm trees: 609

Pampas: 606

Pampulha: 253-254

Pampulha Airport: 262

Pantanal: 9, 15, 386-391, 417-440, 606-607, 656; maps 388-389, 418

Pântano do Sul: 217

Panteão da Pátria: 399, 400

panthers: 610

Pão de Açúcar: 8, 43-44

papagaios (parrots): 612

Paquetá Island: *see* Ilha de Paquetá

Pará: 10, 21, 554-583

Parada Gay: 17

paragliding: 169, 218, 649; *see also specific beach*

Paraná: 190-210, 655

Paranaguá: 202

Paraty: 18, 22, 111-117

Paraty-Mirim: 22, 113

Parintins: 598

Parque Barigüi: 193

Parque da Cidade: 403

Parque da Ferradura: 242

Parque da Luz: 128

Parque da Pedreira: 193-194

Parque da Residência: 560

Parque das Aves: 207-208

Parque das Cachoeiras: 437

Parque das Dunas: 502

Parque das Esculturas: 447

Parque das Mangabeira: 253

Parque das Ruínas: 38

Parque do Catete: 20, 40

Parque do Estado: 148

Parque do Flamengo: 42

Parque do Ibirapuera: 8, 19, 133-134

Parque do Mindú: 589

Parque do Pinheiro Grosso: 242

Parque Estadual da Serra do Mar: 170

Parque Estadual de Ilhabela: 180

Parque Estadual de Vila Velha: 199
Parque Estadual do Caracol: 241-242
Parque Estadual do Marumbi: 200
Parque Estadual do Pico do Itacolomi: 274-275
Parque Farroupilha: 235
Parque Knorr: 239-240
Parque Lage: 52
Parque Mangal das Garças: 560-561
Parque Municipal (Belo Horizonte): 252
Parque Municipal do Mucugê: 360
Parque Nacional da Chapada Diamantina: 355
Parque Nacional da Chapada dos Guimarães: 423-424
Parque Nacional da Chapada dos Veadeiros: 412-413
Parque Nacional da Serra da Bocaina: 173
Parque Nacional da Serra do Cipó: 263-264
Parque Nacional da Serra dos Órgãos: 97-98
Parque Nacional da Serra Geral: 243
Parque Nacional da Tijuca: 70
Parque Nacional de Aparados da Serra: 243-244
Parque Nacional de Brasília: 403
Parque Nacional do Iguaçu: 206-207
Parque Nacional do Itatiaia: 100-101
Parque Nacional do Superagüi: 203
Parque Nacional dos Lençóis Maranhenses: 543-544
Parque Nacional Iguazú (Argentina): 207
Parque Nacional Marinho dos Abrolhos: 384
Parque Nacional Monte Pascoal: 382
Parque Natural do Caraça: 264
Parque Tanguá: 193
Parque Tingüi: 193
Parque Trianon: 130-131
Parque Zoológico do CIGS: 589
parrots: 612
Partido dos Trabalhadores: 623-624
Passadiço da Glória: 295
Passeio Público (Curitiba): 192
Passeio Público (Rio de Janeiro): 36
passports: 11-12
Pataxó people: 374
Pátio de São Pedro: 448
Pátio do Colégio: 123
pato no tucupi: 21
pau brasil: see brazilwood
Pavilhão da Bienal de Arte: 134
peccaries: 610
Pedra do Baú: 167
Pedra do Sal: 322
Pedra Furada: 530
Pedro I: 93, 94, 617-618

Pedro II: 93, 94, 617-619
peixe-boi (manatee): 611
Peixoto, Floriano: 619
Pelourinho (Pelô): 16; accommodations 332-336; food 338-339; map 306-307; sights 305-313
Penedo (Alagoas): 488-490
Penedo (Parque Nacional do Itatiaia): 100
Península de Maraú: 365-366
people: 628-633; *see also* indigenous people
Perequê: 225
performing arts: see theater
Pernambuco: 10, 441-477; Fernando de Noronha 472-477; highlights 442; history 444-445; map 443; Olinda 459-465; planning your time 444; Recife 445-459
Petrópolis: 93-97; map 95
pewter: 284
Pharmácia Popular: 172
pharmacies: 667; *see also* medical care
Piaçabuçu: 489
Piatã: 321
Picinguaba: 184
Pico Agudo: 169
Pico da Caledônia: 99
Pico dos Barbados: 355
Pico Neblina: 605
Pina: 452, 456
Pinacoteca do Estado: 19, 127-128
Pindobal: 580
Pinheiros: 133, 159-160
pink river dolphins: 600, 611
Pinzón, Vicente Yañez: 552
piraiba (catfish): 612
Pirangi: 508
piranhas: 589, 611-612
pirarucu: 612
Pirenópolis: 409-412
Pitangui: 510-511
Pitanguy, Ivo: 668
Planalto: 606
Plano Inclinado Gonçalves: 309
plants: 609
plastic surgery: 668
Poço Azul: 403
Poço do Brejo: 362
Poço do Diabo: 357
Poço Encantado: 361
Poconé: 425-427
Poço Serrano: 356
police: 670-671; *see also* specific place
political parties: 625
pollution: 608

Pólo Joalheiro: 24
Ponta d'Areia: 537
Ponta das Canas: 178
Ponta de Humaitá: 317
Ponta do Corumbau: 383
Ponta dos Castelhanos: 364
Ponta Grande: 373
Pontal de Maracaipe: 470
Pontal do Peba: 489
Ponta Negra: 14, 18, 23, 502
Ponta Verde: 14, 479-481
Ponte Hercílio Luz: 213-214
Ponto das Canas: 216
population: 628
poraquês (electric eels): 612
pororoca: 571
Portas Abertas: 38
Porto Alegre: 231-238; map 232
Porto Belo: 225-227
Porto da Barra: 14, 16, 319
Porto das Dunas: 526
Porto de Galinhas: 469-471
Porto do Frade: 178
Porto Flutante: 584-586
Porto Jofre: 425-427
Porto Seguro: 371-377; map 372
Porto Verão Alegre: 235
Portuguese conquest and colonization: 613-617
Portuguese language: 632-633; glossary
    677-679; Museu da Língua Portuguesa 127;
    phrasebook 680-687
postal services: general discussion 673;
    Belém 568; Recife 458; Rio de Janeiro
    87; Salvador 343; São Paulo 161; *see also
    specific place*
pottery: 569-570, 574, 577, 578; *see also*
    crafts
pousadas (guesthouses): 653; *see also*
    accommodations
poverty: 50-51
Praça André de Albuquerque: 500
Praça Barão de Guaicui: 295
Praça Benedito Leite: 535
Praça Castro Alves: 317-318
Praça Conselheiro Mota: 294
Praça da Aclamação: 352-353
Praça da Ajuda: 353
Praça da Alfândega: 233-234
Praça da Independência: 435
Praça da Liberdade (Belo Horizonte): 252
Praça da Piedade: 318
Praça da Purificação: 351
Praça da República (Belém): 559

Praça da República (Cuiabá): 421
Praça da República (Recife): 448
Praça da República (São Paulo): 126
Praça da Savassi: 252
Praça da Sé (Salvador): 309
Praça da Sé (São Paulo): 123
Praça de São Sebastião: 586-587
Praça do Cruzeiro: 393
Praça Dom Pedro II: 535
Praça dos Martírios: 479
Praça dos Três Poderes: 393, 399
Praça Doutor Aristides Milton: 352
Praça Floriano: 35
Praça Garibaldi: 192
Praça José de Alencar: 517
Praça Marechal Deodoro: 234
Praça Minas Gerais: 277
Praça Municipal (Salvador): 308
Praça Pedro Ramos: 172
Praça Santa Rita: 265
Praça Tiradentes: 270
Praça Vidal Ramos: 230
Praça Villaboim: 130
Praça XV: 31
Praça XV de Novembro: 214
Praia Barra da Lagoa: 216
Praia Barra Velha: 572
Praia Brava (Búzios): 105
Praia Brava (Cabo Frio): 102
Praia Brava (Florianópolis): 216
Praia Cachadaço: 18, 22, 113
Praia Cacimba do Padre: 474
Praia da Armação (Búzios): 104
Praia da Armação (Santa Catarina): 217
Praia da Atalaia: 474
Praia da Baronesa: 542-543
Praia da Barra do Sai: 175
Praia da Canoa Quebrada: 527
Praia da Caraíva: 382
Praia da Conceição: 474
Praia da Concha: 367
Praia da Fazenda: 184
Praia da Ferradura: 105
Praia da Ferradurinha: 105
Praia da Ferrugem: 227
Praia da Fortaleza (Ilha do Mel): 203
Praia da Fortaleza (Ubatuba): 183
Praia da Galheta: 217
Praia da Joaquina: 14, 217, 218, 219
Praia da Justa: 183
Praia da Lagoinha do Leste: 217
Praia da Lua: 590
Praia da Malhada: 530

Praia da Parnaioca: 110
Praia da Pipa: 14, 511–515
Praia da Pitinga: 377
Praia da Ponta Grossa: 527–528
Praia da Ponta Negra: 589–590
Praia das Caravelas: 105
Praia das Conchas: 102
Praia das Minas: 512
Praia da Sununga: 183
Praia das Virgens: 104
Praia da Tainha: 226
Praia de Arauna: 572
Praia de Areia Preta: 502
Praia de Barra de São Miguel: 487
Praia de Calhetas (Cabo de Santo Agostinho): 469
Praia de Calhetas (São Sebastião): 176
Praia de Castelhanos: 179
Praia de Cueira: 364
Praia de Curuípe: 383
Praia de Cururupe: 370
Praia de Engenhoca: 367
Praia de Espelho: 383
Praia de Fora: 203
Praia de Fora das Encantadas: 203
Praia de Geribá: 105
Praia de Iracema: 518, 519, 522, 524,
Praia de Jericoacoara: 530
Praia de Jurerê: 216
Praia de Manguinhos: 104
Praia de Meireles: 518, 519–520, 522, 524
Praia de Morro Branco: 526
Praia de Mucuripe: 518
Praia de Pajuçara: 479
Praia de Pepino: 53
Praia de Ponta Verde: 479–481
Praia de Pratagi: 481
Praia de Puruba: 22, 183
Praia de Satu: 383
Praia de Sibaúma: 512
Praia de Solidão: 217
Praia de Tabuba: 490
Praia de Taipe: 377
Praia de Taipu de Fora: 365
Praia do Amor: 512
Praia do Antigo: 18, 113
Praia do Boldró: 474
Praia do Bonete: 179
Praia do Cachorro: 474
Praia do Campeche: 217
Praia do Canto: 104
Praia do Carro Quebrado: 14, 490
Praia do Cedro: 183

Praia do Curral (Ilhabela): 179
Praia do Curral (Praia da Pipa): 511–512
Praia do Dentista: 111
Praia do Félix: 183
Praia do Fome: 179
Praia do Forno: 103, 105
Praia do Forte (Cabo Frio): 102
Praia do Forte (Florianópolis): 216
Praia do Forte (Natal): 502
Praia do Forte (Paraty): 113
Praia do Forte town: 16, 346–348
Praia do Francês: 485–486
Praia do Farol: 203
Praia do Futuro: 14, 519, 524–525
Praia do Grauça: 384
Praia do Gunga: 487
Praia do Jabaquara: 113
Praia do Julião: 179
Praia do Lázaro: 22, 183
Praia do Leão: 474
Praia do Leme: 48
Praia do Madeiro: 511–512
Praia do Mar Grossa: 230
Praia do Matadeiro: 217
Praia do Meio (Fernando de Noronhas): 474
Praia do Meio (Natal): 502
Praia do Meio (Paraty): 113
Praia do Miguel: 203
Praia do Milionários: 370
Praia do Mirante da Sereia: 481
Praia do Moçambique: 216
Praia do Mucugê: 377
Praia do Papa-Gente: 347
Praia do Parracho: 377
Praia do Pepê: 53
Praia do Peró: 102
Praia do Pesqueiro: 572
Praia do Pontal: 113
Praia do Preá: 530
Praia do Prumirim: 22, 183
Praia do Rio Verde: 380
Praia do Rosa: 14, 229
Praia dos Amores: 104
Praia dos Anjos: 103
Praia dos Santinho: 216
Praia dos Artistas: 502
Praia dos Carneiros: 471
Praia dos Coqueiros: 380
Praia dos Fontes: 526
Praia do Silveira: 227
Praia dos Ingleses: 216
Praia dos Naufragados: 218
Praia do Sono: 18, 113

Praia dos Ossos: 104
Praia dos Tucuns: 105
Praia do Sul: 370
Praia do Tupé: 590
Praia do Viana: 179
Praia Grande (Arraial do Cabo): 103
Praia Grande (Ilha de Marajó): 572
Praia Grande (Ilha do Mel): 203
Praia Havaizinho: 367
Praia Iemanjá: 384
Praia Jeribucaçu: 367
Praia José Gonçalves: 105
Praia Lopes Mendes: 22
Praia Mole: 217
Praia Olho de Boi: 105
Praia Rasa: 104
Praia São José: 367
Praias dos Nativos: 380
Praia Siriú: 227
Praia Toque-Toque: 23
Prainha (Aquiraz): 526
Prainha (Arraial do Cabo): 103
Prainha (Itacaré): 367
Prainha (Rio de Janeiro): 53
Prainha (Santa Catarina): 217
Prateleira: 100
precipitation: see climate
Prédio do Banespa: 125
preguiça (sloth): 610
prehistory: 582, 613
prescriptions: 666
Presidente Figueiredo: 597-598
primates: 610
Primeira Praia: 362
Procissão de Fogaréu: 416
Projeto Hipocampo: 470
Projeto Reviver: 535-536
Projeto Tamar: 183, 346, 611
pronunciation: 680-681
Protestantism: 631
Puerto Iguazú: 204

QR

Quadrado: 379-380
Quarta Praia: 362-363
Quatro Ilhas: 226
quentão cocktail: 658
Quinta da Boa Vista: 44
Quixaba: 527
rabo-de-gail cocktail: 658
racism: 614-615, 629
rafting: Parque Estadual da Serra do Mar 170; Rio de Contas 367; Rio Formoso 438; Rio

Iguaçu 207; Serra Gaúcha 240; see also specific place
rail travel: see train travel
rainfall: see climate
rainforest: 547-554, 584, 596-603, 604-606; see also Amazon region
Ramos, Graciliano: 642
rap music: 637
rappelling: see climbing
rattlesnakes: 611
Real Gabinete Português de Leitura: 34-35
Recanto da Cachoeira: 20, 173
Recife: 10, 441, 445-459; map 446
Recife Antigo: 447-448, 451, 455-456
Recôncavo: 351-355, 656
recreation: see sports/recreation; specific sport/recreation
Recreio dos Bandeirantes: 53-54
Redinha: 509-510
Refúgio Família Sperry: 240
reggae: 538
regionalism: 630
religion: 328-329, 630-632
rental cars: see car travel
reptiles: 136, 611
República: 321
Resende: 367
Reserva Biológica Marinha da Ilha do Arvoredo: 226
Reserva de Desenvolvimento Sustentável de Mamirauá: 599
Reserva de Preservação Ambiental Sapiranga: 347
Reserva Ecológico do Lago de Janauari: 588
Reserva Indígena de Jaqueira: 374
Reserva Mamirauá: 18
Reserva Marinha da Ilha das Cabras: 180
restaurants: see food
Reveillon: 17, 55
rhea: 417, 612
Riacho Doce: 481
Ribeirão da Ilha: 218
Rio Amazonas: see Amazon River
Rio Baía Bonita: 438
Rio da Prata: 438
Rio de Janeiro: 8, 13, 18, 19, 20, 21, 25-90, 655; accommodations 72-78; entertainment/events 54-58; food 21, 78-86, 655; history 27-28; information/services 86-88; maps 30, 32-33, 39, 47, 49; nightlife 59-66; planning your time 27; shopping 66-69; sights 26, 29-54; sports/recreation 69-72; transportation 88-90

Rio Formosa: 438
Rio Grande do Norte: 10
Rio Grande do Sul: 9, 21, 231-244, 655
Rio Guamá: 24
Rio Iguaçu: 205
Rio Negro: 588, 599-601
Rio Preguiças: 544
Rio São Francisco: 489
Rio Solimões: 588, 598-599, 601
Rio Sucuri: 438
Rio Tapajós: 24, 576, 580
Rio Vermelho: 321-322, 337, 342-343
riverboats: see boating
Rocha, Glauber: 639-640
Rocinha: 53
rock music: 637
rodízio restaurants: 660
Rodoviária de Brasília: 393
Rodovia Transpantaneira: 425-427
Rua das Flores: 192-193
rubber industry: 552-553, 556, 583, 588, 619

S

Sabará: 265-267
Saco do Céu: 22
Saco do Mamanguá: 113
safety: see health/safety
sailing: Barra da Una 175; Búzios 105-106;
   Ilhabela 180; Rio de Janeiro 71; Semana
   Internacional da Vela 180; see also boating;
   specific place
Sala Cecília Meireles: 54
Salão de Areias Coloridas: 356
Sala São Paulo: 128, 142
Salles, Walter: 640
Salto de Itiquira: 403
Salvador: 9, 15-16, 305-345, 656;
   accommodations 332-337; entertainment/
   events 324-331; food 337-343, 656;
   information/services 343-344; maps 306-
   307, 320-321; shopping 331-332; sights 305-
   324; sports/recreation 332; transportation
   344-345
Salvaterra: 24, 572
samba: 58, 144, 634-635; see also Carnaval
Sambaqui: 218
Sambódromo (Rio de Janeiro): 56-57
Sambódromo (São Paulo): 144
Sampa: see São Paulo
sandboarding: 218
Santa Bárbara: 264
Santa Casa de Misericórdia (Cachoeira): 352
Santa Casa da Misericórdia (Salvador): 309

Santa Catarina: 8
Santa Catarina island: see Ilha de Santa
   Catarina
Santa Catarina state: 211-230
Santander Cultural: 233
Santarém: 10, 23, 575-579
Santa Teresa: 13, 20; accommodations 73; food
   79-80; nightlife 62; sights 37-38
Santiago: 176
Santo Amaro: 351
Santo Amaro do Maranhão: 544
Santo André: 376
Santo Antônio (Recife): 448-449, 451-452,
   456
Santo Antônio (Salvador): 313-314, 332-336,
   338-339
Santo Antônio de Lisboa: 218
Santo Antônio do Pinhal: 169-170
Santo Daime: 631
Santo do São Francisco: 489
Santos: 175
Santuário de Vida Silvestre Vagafogo: 411
Santuário do Caraça: 264
Santuário Dom Bosco: 401
Santuário Ecológico de Pipa: 512
São Conrado: 53
São Félix: 353
São João del Rei: 9, 13, 281-286; map 282
São Jorge: 414
São José: 448-449, 451-452, 456
São José do Barreiro: 19-20, 173
São Luís: 10, 533-542; map 534
São Luís do Paraitinga: 170-172
São Marcos: 537
São Miguel dos Milagres: 14, 490-493
São Paulo: 8, 19, 21, 118-164, 655;
   accommodations 149-152; entertainment/
   events 142-144; food 21, 152-160, 655;
   history 120-121, 129; information/services
   160-161; maps 122, 124, 131, 165; nightlife
   137-142; planning your time 119-120;
   shopping 144-148; sights 119, 121-137; sports/
   recreation 148-149; transportation 161-164
São Paulo Bienal de Arte: 134
São Sebastião: 175-178
Sarney, José: 622
saudade: 632
scarlet ibis: 612
Scliar, Moacyr: 642
scuba diving: see diving
seasons: 11
sea turtles: 183, 346, 611
Secretária de Estado: 252

Segall, Lasar: 135-136
Segunda Praia: 362
Semana Farroupilha: 235
Semana Internacional da Vela: 180
Semana Santa (Diamantina): 296
Semana Santa (Ouro Preto): 274
senior travelers, tips for: 664-665
Sepultura: 226
Sergipe: 10
Serra da Mantiqueira: 166-170
Serra do Mar: 170-174
Serra Gaúcha: 8, 238-243
Serra Verde Express: 199-200
Sertão: 10, 441, 605
Serviço Social do Comércio: 142
SESC: 142
sexually transmitted diseases: 668
shopping: bargaining 663; Belém 563-564;
    Belo Horizonte 256-257; Brasília 402;
    Curitiba 194-195; Embu 164; Maceió 482-
    483; Manaus 591; Ouro Preto 274; Paraty
    114; Recife 454; Rio de Janeiro 66-69;
    Salvador 331-332; São Paulo 144-148; useful
    phrases 685; see also crafts; markets
Sinagoga Kahal Zur Israel: 447
Siribinha: 350
Sítio do Conde: 350
Sítio Roberto Burle Marx: 54
size: 604
slavery: 491, 614-615, 618-619, 629
sloths: 610
slums: 50-51
snakes: 611
snorkeling: general discussion 650, 664;
    Fernando de Noronha 474; Ilha Grande 109;
    Ilhabela 180; Morro de São Paulo 363; Porto
    de Galinhas 470; Praia do Forte 347; see
    also specific place
soap operas: 675
soccer: general discussion 651; Belo Horizonte
    257-258; Rio de Janeiro 71-72; São Paulo
    149
soft drinks: 594, 659
Solar da Marquesa dos Santos: 123
Solar do Unhão-Museu de Arte Moderna: 316
Soure: 24, 572
southern plains: 606
southern right whales: 611
South region: 809, 186-244; food 655;
    highlights 187; history 189-190; map 188;
    Paraná 190-210; planning your time 189;
    Rio Grande do Sul 231-244; Santa Catarina
    211-230

spider monkeys: 610
spinning dolphins: 611
sports/recreation: 649-651; Rio de Janeiro
    69-72; São Paulo 148-149; see also specific
    place
squirrel monkeys: 610
STDs: 668
Stella Maris: 322
stingrays: 612
storks: 417, 612
street vendors: 661
Subconsulado Francês: 356
sugarcane cultivation: 444-445, 614-615
sunscreen: 668-669
Supremo Tribunal Federal: 399
surfing: general discussion 649-650;
    Fernando de Noronha 474-475; Fortaleza
    520; freshwater 571; Ilha de Santa Catarina
    218; Jericoacoara 531; Paraty 113; Rio de
    Janeiro 71; Ubatuba 183; see also specific
    beach
swimwear: 46

T

tacaça: 21, 565
Tamandaré: 471-472
tamanduas (anteaters): 610
tambaqui (piranha): 612
tambor de crioula music: 538
Tamoio people: 27
Tancredo Neves International Airport: 262
Tapajoara pottery: 578
Tapajó people: 613
Taperapuã: 373
tapirs: 610
tartarugas marinhas (sea turtles): 611
Tassimirim: 364
Tatajuba: 530
tatus (armadillos): 610
taxis: general discussion 647; Belo Horizonte
    263; Brasília 408; Recife 458; Rio de
    Janeiro 89; Salvador 344; São Paulo 163;
    see also specific place
Teatro Alberto Maranhão: 502, 504
Teatro Alfa: 143
Teatro Amazonas: 17, 23, 586, 591
Teatro Apolo: 448
Teatro Arthur Azevedo: 537, 538
Teatro Castro Alves: 318, 327-328
Teatro Cultura Artística: 143
Teatro da Paz: 559, 563
Teatro Guaíra: 194
Teatro Imperial: 265

Teatro João Caetano: 54
Teatro Municipal (Ilhéus): 369
Teatro Municipal (Ouro Preto): 271
Teatro Municipal (São Paulo): 125, 142
Teatro Nacional Cláudio Santoro: 397, 402
Teatro Oficina: 143
Teatro Princesa Isabel: 453
Tefé: 599
telephone services: 87, 673-674; see also
    specific place
television: 675-676
Templo da Voa Vontade: 401
Terceira Praia: 362
Teresópolis: 98-99
Terra das Cachoeiras: 597-598
Terreiro de Jesus: 309-310
theater: Belo Horizonte 256; Curitiba 194;
    Porto Alegre 234; Recife 453; Rio de
    Janeiro 54; Salvador 327-328; São Paulo
    142-143
Theatro José de Alencar: 517, 520
Theatro Municipal (Rio de Janeiro): 35, 54
Theatro São Pedro: 234
theft: 669-671
Tibau do Sul: 509
time: 687
time zones: 676
Tiradentes (person): 268, 617
Tiradentes (town): 8, 13, 287-293; map 289
Tiririca: 367
Toque-Toque Grande: 176
Toque-Toque Pequeno: 176
Torre de Televisão: 15, 397
toucans: 612
tourism: 627-628
tourist offices: general discussion 672; Belém
    567-568; Belo Horizonte 262; Brasília 407;
    Fortaleza 525; Maceió 485; Manaus 595;
    Ouro Preto 277; Rio de Janeiro 86-87;
    Salvador 343; San Luís 541; São Paulo 160;
    see also specific place
tours: Amazon 569, 596-597, 599-601; Belém
    568; Bonito 440; Brasília 408; Cuiabá 423;
    Fernando de Noronha 475, 477; Fortaleza
    525-526; Iguaçu Falls 206-207; Maceió 485;
    Manaus 596; Natal 507; Pantanal 431-432;
    Parque Nacional Marinho dos Abrolhos
    384; Porto Alegre 238; Recife 458-459;
    Rio de Janeiro 90; Salvador 345; São Paulo
    163-164; see also boating
train travel: 169, 199-200, 275, 279, 644
Trancoso: 14, 379-382
Transpantaneira: 425-427

transportation: general discussion 12,
    643-647; Rio de Janeiro 88-90; Salvador
    344-345; São Paulo 161-164; useful phrases
    682-683; see also specific place
trees: 609
trekking: see hiking
Trindade: 18, 22, 113
Tropicália: 636-637
tucanos (toucans): 612
tucuxi (grey dolphin): 611
tuiuiú stork: 612
Tupi-Guarani people: 613
turtles: 183, 346, 611
tuta à mineiro: 21

UV

uakari monkeys: 610
Uakti: 256
Ubatuba: 22, 182-185
Ubatumirim: 183
União da Vegetal: 631
United States Embassy: 648
Urca: 43-44, 63, 74-75
Usina do Gasômetro: 235
vaccinations: 12, 666
Vaila do Abraão: 109
Vale da Lua: 414
Vale do Capão: 358
Vale do Paty: 361
vans: 647
Vargas, Getúlio: 40, 619-620
vegetarian options: 661
Vermelha do Sul: 183
Vespucci, Amerigo: 500
Viaduto do Chá: 125
viboras (vipers): 611
Víeira, Antônio: 616
Vila Abraão: 20, 22
Vila dos Remédios: 473
Vila Ilhabela: 178
Vila Madalena: 19, 133, 159-160
vipers: 611
visas: 11-12, 647-648
volleyball: 651

WXYZ

water, drinking: 667
water pollution: 608
weather: see climate
websites: 690-691
whales/whale-watching: 227, 346, 611; Instituto
    Baleia Jubarte 384; Parque Nacional
    Marinho dos Abrolhos 384

wheelchair access: 663
wildlife: see fauna
windsurfing: general discussion 650; Búzios
    105–106; Fortaleza 520; Ilha de Santa
    Catarina 218; Jericoacoara 531; see also
    specific beach
wine: 660
wire transfers: 672

women travelers, tips for: 664
woodcuts: 468; see also crafts
World War II: 500
yellow fever vaccinations: 12, 666
youth hostels: see hostels
Zona Norte: 29, 44–45
Zona Sul: 13, 20, 29
Zumbi do Palmares: 491

List of Maps

Front color map
Brazil: 2-3

Discover Brazil
chapter divisions map: 9
The 21-Day Best of Brazil: 13
Two Weeks Along the Amazon: 23

Rio de Janeiro
Rio de Janeiro City: 30
Centro and Lapa: 32-33
Glória, Catete, and Flamengo: 39
Copacabana and Leme: 47
Ipanema and Leblon: 49
Rio de Janeiro State: 92
Petrópolis: 95

São Paulo
São Paulo City: 122
Centro: 124
Avenida Paulista and Jardins: 131
São Paulo State: 165
Ilhabela: 179
Ubatuba: 182-183

The South
The South: 188
Curitiba: 191
Foz do Iguaçu and Vicinity: 205
Ilha de Santa Catarina: 212
Florianópolis (Centro): 215
Porto Alegre: 232

Minas Gerais
Minas Gerais: 247
Belo Horizonte: 250-251
Ouro Preto: 269
São João del Rei: 282
Tiradentes: 289

Bahia
Bahia: 302
Pelourinho: 306-307
Barra and Vicinity: 320-321
Chapada Diamantina: 356
Porto Seguro: 372

Brasília and the Pantanal
Brasília, Goiás, and the Pantanal: 388-389
Brasília: 394-395
The Pantanal: 418
Campo Grande: 429

Pernambuco and Alagoas
Pernambuco and Alagoas: 443
Recife: 446
Olinda: 460
Maceió: 478

The Northeast Coast
The Northeast Coast: 498-499
Natal: 501
Fortaleza: 516-517
São Luís: 534

The Amazon
The Amazon: 549
The Amazon River: 552-553
Belém: 555
Manaus: 585

Acknowledgments

As I've discovered over the last year, writing a guidebook (particularly one this hefty), like any long journey, can be at times daunting, addictive, exhausting, and exhilarating. Although much of the work involved was necessarily solo, along the way there were (happily) many people who joined in and made contributions—both small and enormous. I would like to thank some of them below.

I don't know if there is such thing as a travel gene, but the ease, passion, and second-nature-ness of travel was instilled in me almost from the start by Monty and Helen, who not only made it seem as effortless and fundamental as breathing, but injected an essential mixture of curiosity, intelligence, humor, and sensitivity into the proceedings—for this I can't thank you enough. Thank you also to Monty for expert "practical" advice and to Helen for telling me to "go to the beach" when the going got tough.

Thank you to Heids E. (who gave me my first assignment writing *"Quoi de Neufs?"* in Paris) for convincing me that everyone should write at least one travel guide in his/her life.

At Avalon Travel, thank you to Kevin Anglin and Mike Morgenfeld for help with maps and Tabitha Lahr for always-timely input and feedback regarding images. Thanks to Grace Fujimoto for early help and guidance and to publisher Bill Newlin for providing support and appreciating the nature of such a large undertaking. Most of all, thanks to my editor, Erin Raber, for her flexibility, understanding, and going to bat for me on several key occasions.

More than anyone else above the Equator, this book could not have been produced without the absolutely vital input and collaboration of Annie Leah Sommers, my invaluable and beloved "Editor Anne," whose sensitivity, smarts, attention to detail, and total dedication were in keeping with all my expectations—and yet she still managed to surpass them all the same. Annie, I'm sorry for the "rustics," but it was nonetheless a big, fat joy (as always) to work with you, and your contributions (editorial and emotional) have been enormous.

Over the years, I've developed a profound admiration and affection for Brazil, but to me Brazil is much more than landscapes—it's about people. That I got there at all, decided (and was able) to stay, and have never been able to leave has much to do with certain *brasileiros/as* to whom I want to express in Portuguese deep-felt *obrigados*.

A Tinny que estava presente no início, que encheu a minha cabeça com histórias, e que me trouxe para cá—isso foi um presente tão enorme (tu ne sais pas). A Zé Carlos que me levou até o Bonfim e nunca me largou e que me ensinou, mais do que ninguém, sobre a importância de alegrias e saideiras. A Mel Maraux, melhor "ex-mulher" de todos os tempos, pelas afinidades instantâneas e os multiplos apoios, risos, e momentos de companheirismo. Existem pessoas que têm a sorte de ter um Heráclito na vida—eu tenho dois (que moram no meu coração e não pagam aluguel): Little Bet, sem você, as voltas pelo Dique e o suco de maracujá, nao sei se teria ficado, e tudo que eu entendo e não entendo do homen sertanejo, comida da gente, de ir para a feira e tantas outras brasilianidades aprendi com você. Little Fo, obrigado pelas eternas Fo-focas (fotográficas e outras), rsssss, e fugas fundamentais—dos antigos tempos no Alfitos até a era da Rota praia/shopping/café/acarajé. Aos meus eternos Josés (Myroka, Edi, e Little Alice), reelmente não sei o que dizer porque a viagem até agora tem sido tão longa, cheia, e gostosa—mas nas melhores famílias é assim, né? Bom, "last, but not least," obrigado ao meu Lui, cujo entusiasmo, solidariedade, compreensão, e ajuda (e os melhores mapas do mundo!) foram maravilhosos e absolutamente fundamentais—por isso, e tudo, te amo "grande."

Apesar de todas as horas de pesquisa exigidas na redação deste guia, se eu entender um pouco sobre o Brasil hoje em dia é por causa da convivência com vocês. Acho que fragmentos de todos são presentes neste trabalho, dando um tempero caprichado, essencial e bem brasileiro— por isso, estou orgulhoso e grato.

Meus agradecimentos à Embratur, pelo apoio *e pela ajuda, em particular ao Romualdo Sousa Neto e à Renata Braga de Faria.*

A special thanks to Tony Galvez, who generously contributed many of this book's terrific photographs.

www.moon.com

DESTINATIONS | ACTIVITIES | BLOGS | MAPS | BOOKS

MOON.COM is all new, and ready to help plan your next trip! Filled with fresh trip ideas and strategies, author interviews, informative blogs, a detailed map library, and descriptions of all the Moon guidebooks, Moon.com is all you need to get out and explore the world—or even places in your own backyard. As always, when you travel with Moon, expect an experience that is uncommon and truly unique.